G
B
1991
GUIDE

THE PUB-LOVER'S ESSENTIAL REFERENCE BOOK

Edited by Jeff Evans

CAMRA

CAMPAIGN FOR REAL ALE

34 Alma Road, St Albans,
Herts, AL1 3BW

CONTENTS

Editor: Jeff Evans. **Deputy Editor:** Jill Adam. **Additional Research and Assistance:** Steve Cox, Iain Loe, Iain Dobson, Roger Protz, Brian Glover, Malcolm Harding, Jo Bates, Jenny Mellors, Carol Couch, Su Tilley, Clare Stevens, Jenny Hopkins. Thanks to Brian Glover for Fringe Benefits. **Maps:** David Perrott. **Cover and Design:** Neville Andrews/PIA Communications, Newbury, Berks. **Illustrations:** Phil Evans. **Published by:** Campaign for Real Ale Ltd., 34 Alma Road, St Albans, Herts, AL1 3BW. Tel. (0727) 867201 **Typeset and Printed:** Cambridge University Press. Special thanks to Philip Lunn and Richard Jacobs.
ISBN 1 85249 003 9 © Campaign for Real Ale 1990/91

This book could not have been produced without the help and dedication of thousands of CAMRA members nationwide. Many thanks.

INTRODUCTION

This promised to be an eventful year.

With the top off 1989's MMC Report into the brewing industry, we awaited with dry throats the promise held within. Of course, we were aware that this was to be no vintage product, knowing that the recipe had been tempered to meet the palates of the national brewers. But, as with all brews which continue to ferment, we expected something tasty at the end.

And tasty it has been, if somewhat cloudy. We enjoyed the flavour of the new guest beer law, despite the underlying bitterness surrounding its introduction, and savoured the cheerful effervescence of the smaller brewers which has ensued. However, the sediment of big brewers' evasiveness has soured the taste and left us wondering just how the next mouthful will prove.

Yes, it's been a confusing year. A lot of good has come out of it – not least a handful of exciting new breweries and the news that Tolly Cobbold beers are to be returned to their Ipswich home (a bold, imaginative and praiseworthy management buy-out). But, at the same time, a Pandora's box of uncertainties and troubles has been thrown open. Whitbread, in its usual contemptuous manner, has disposed of two breweries, and, as the *Guide* goes to press, the Elders/Grand Metropolitan pubs-for-breweries nightmare has yet to be resolved.

Another concern is the future of the pub. Across the land, country gems, town centre locals and roadside inns are being raped and pillaged. There's one near you. Not even the Rover's Return was safe. It needed grand old Cec Newton to spring from retirement to preserve this 'heritage' pub from conversion to an American-style bar. How about bringing back the handpumps as well, Cec?

More encouraging news is that CAMRA membership continues to grow – and rapidly. We say this not through self-gratification but because it clearly signifies that more and more people are truly interested in the beer that they drink and will not let themselves be pushed around by those caring little for the consumer who has made them rich.

This guide is a celebration of Britain's great beers: *real ales*, beers with flavour, brewed from traditional ingredients, by traditional methods and served by traditional means of dispense – far removed from the insipid, cold, gassy, convenience keg beers once foisted upon us by the big brewers. Visit these excellent pubs, drink the wonderful beer and enjoy yourselves. I hope that when we take the opener to the 1992 edition we can drink long and satisfyingly, with none of the sourness of the last twelve months.

Good Health!

Jeff Evans: Editor

HOME THOUGHTS AND ABROAD

Steve Cox *considers the upheaval taking place in the brewing world and its consequences for Good Beer.*

WELCOME GUESTS? The first of May might make you think of dancing round the maypole, or Bank Holiday traffic jams. But, for many beer lovers, 1 May 1990 heralded the introduction of the long-awaited guest beer law. Following the 1989 Monopolies and Mergers Commission Report, all tenants of national brewers are now entitled to stock a brand of real ale of their choice, bought from the supplier of their choice. (And it must be a *real* ale: a cask-conditioned beer, not a keg beer or lager.)

CAMRA has been campaigning for this since the mid seventies. The guest beer should widen consumer choice and offer genuine opportunities for the independent brewers to prosper. A poll conducted by the MMC found that two-thirds of tenants would like to stock an extra beer, the main thing stopping them being their brewery. And there's little doubt that the public want it.

The arrival of the guest beer law has produced a spurt of energy from the brewers. Nationals have returned to advertising real ale, encouraged also by a perceptible growth in real ale sales in a stagnant beer market. Regional and local independents have geared up their promotions and some have even introduced guest beers in their own pubs. The small independent brewers have launched regional cooperatives, helping each other in wholesaling, offering a wider range with less wasted time for the brewers. This development in particular might be the beginning of even greater strength in the small brewery movement. We hope to see hundreds more breweries bloom up and down the country, using the guest beer market to the full.

So what's the problem? The national brewers are keen to control what guests, if any, appear in their pubs. After all, if tenants genuinely shop around, the public might come to know and love genuine local beers… with a dreadful effect on their established national bilge. So the national brewers' dirty tricks departments have been working overtime to keep their tenants cowed and cooperative. Letters to these tenants make interesting reading.

Rent rises and rent reviews are being used to put pressure on tenants, and threaten penalties for those who step out of line (although the legislation does make discrimination in rents or prices illegal). The brewers are being difficult about means of dispense, threatening to stop tenants using existing equipment or having new equipment installed. Tenants are told they must inform their management exactly whose beers they are selling and when. The brewers are also extending their own ranges, by adding a few 'guest beers' supplied by themselves. Their hope is that, faced with enormous hassle if they buy outside the price list, most tenants will opt for the brewery-approved deal. Some of these brewery-supplied guest beers are reasonable real ales, but they are the well-known brands, and would do well anyway. Furthermore, the national brewers are restricting their range of guest beers depot by depot, so that drinkers in one region will not become acquainted with other beers over the border, resulting in the same limited choice locally. The original intention of the guest beer, a hassle-free choice by tenants from all possible suppliers, is being gradually subverted, so that tenants will meekly stock from a short-list of three provided by their brewery.

What's CAMRA doing? To disperse the clouds of doubt and confusion overhanging tenants, we have circulated 40,000 copies of our leaflet outlining guest beer rights. We are running local and national promotions with the independent brewers. We are using our hundreds of events and beer festivals a year as show-pieces for the 450 genuine independent real ales of the UK. We are ever vigilant on abuses by the brewers, and we will continue to lobby to make sure the guest beer works – as with any of the Monopolies and Mergers Commission changes. It is too important an opportunity to miss. We are going to be quick to complain when the guest beers are served in less than excellent condition. After all, it is in no-one's interests for there to be a wider range of drab mouthwash on offer.

But ultimately, the important thing we are doing is just to be ordinary consumers, and asking for what we want. (Let's be adventurous; we can drink Brand X anywhere.) If consumers are clear what they want and loud enough about it, the big companies will find they cannot ignore us. So everyone reading this should go into their local pubs and ask for a guest beer. Ask for something different: a beer from a small brewery. Support pubs which show imagination. And if the publican is being hassled by the brewery, then complain. After all, the big brewers thought they had the consumer cowed when they tried to get rid of real ale in the first place. And look what hit them!

THE NERVOUS NINETIES

It doesn't take much brain to predict enormous change in the brewing industry in the nineties. The shake-up created by the Monopolies and Mergers Commission Report will occur alongside the fundamental changes threatened by 1992 and the European single market. The industry might go in one of two ways: into a more concentrated and less diverse market, dominated by a handful of Eurobrew cartels and ghastly retailers; or into a market where traditional beer and traditional pubs can thrive. Where we go depends in part on whether our representatives in Westminster and Brussels/Strasbourg put the consumer's interest first.

The hope (what CAMRA is fighting for) is that changes, such as the guest beer, will safeguard the diversity of the beer market for future generations to enjoy. The fear is that death by takeover, death by closure of breweries, death by rationalisation, will continue to destroy that diversity at an ever increasing rate. These are exciting, but also dangerous times to be beer lovers who care about their choice.

One key indicator as to where we are going will be the fate of the proposed Grand Metropolitan/Elders merger. After fast and furious lobbying by CAMRA, this complex deal was referred to the Monopolies and Mergers Commission for investigation; they report just before publication of this guide. If, when you are reading this, the deal has been allowed to go ahead, it will act as a green light for a massive carve up of the brewing industry. Giant companies will leap into bed with each other, and the industry will pass into the tight control of no more than three monster groups.

Failure to block the merger will mean that competition policy has been scrapped and the consumer will now be left to suffer a dramatic reduction in choice.

The turmoil operates at every level. The decision by Boddingtons to sell its breweries and become a pure pub owner may well be followed by other brewers who have lost their pride. At the other end of the market, hosts of new, small pub-owning companies are springing up, the long-awaited renaissance of the pub chain being triggered by the sale, in job-lots, of low barrellage pubs from the Big Six. All sorts of people are buying pubs – wholesalers, a taxi firm, a football club – and starting a pub chain will be the retirement home for ex-brewery directors in the 1990s. Some of these chains treat their tenants well, have a wide range of beers, look after their pubs and are clearly 'A Good Thing'. Other pub chains cannot find their bottoms with both hands. Worst of all are those chains which appear to be in the pocket of the original owner, a clever trick so ownership changes but nothing else does.

1992 means that the European brewing market will become a battleground. Rationalisation, takeover and merger will parallel the creation of the Big Six in Britain, only on a European scale. The worst case is that a handful of companies will come to control the world brewing industry, leaving us in a brave new world of ghastly, global brands. In that future, we will be told we are lucky to have real ale left at all. If we do.

CAMRA realises the threat this poses. We are already talking to our allies, sister consumer groups in Europe and further afield. We are making this conceptual leap to working at an international level because, increasingly, that is where decisions are being made. A Europe of beer lovers, where traditional beers pass freely from country to country and traditional producers enjoy a prosperous future, is worth fighting for.

There are plenty of people who wish CAMRA would shut up shop. They tell us our work has been done. On the contrary, if we are going to raise a pint to celebrate the 21st century, it is more important than ever that CAMRA is here. Otherwise that pint will be chill and tasteless, and manufactured in a bleak factory on a motorway, owned by Global Fizz.

Steve Cox is CAMRA's Campaigns and Communications Manager.

THE FUTURE OF THE BRITISH PUB

Ted Bruning

On holiday in the country, I came across the perfect village pub. This particular perfect pub – and there are many – was a long, low, white-painted stone building divided into three. At either end was a stone-floored bar, separated by a central section which was the village shop. All three sections shared a single servery, so the landlady could dole out baked beans and Mars bars with one hand while reaching for the optic with the other. The end which served as the public bar, even at midday in winter, in a tiny village, was already well-filled with locals deep in conversation, so we tried the saloon – distinguished as such by being wallpapered rather than just painted – to wash down brown breadcakes, overloaded with home-cured ham, with beautifully-kept XB. Even that bar soon filled up: business was clearly very good.

Returning to work, I was confronted with three almost identical stories of village pubs – by all accounts fairly similar to the one I had so much enjoyed – which were in danger of being closed down and converted into housing. The only difference I could discern was that the one I had visited was in the North York Moors, while the other three were in the Cotswolds. Even though the businesses appeared to be perfectly viable, they were still worth more on the market as weekend homes for the rich.

SOCIAL DEVELOPMENTS

This comparison, perhaps rather too neatly, expresses how the economic, social and demographic changes which affect every one of us also affect the places where we like to drink. If these changes render country villages less practical as self-contained economic and social units, then their pubs will close. If heavy industry is destroyed, then the ten-pints-a-night manual labourers will disappear from urban pubs. If acres of London's Victorian terraces are gentrified, their street-corner pubs will be transformed into wine-bars.

Neither do the rising costs which make home-owning or running a business desperate for many of us pass the publican by. Prolonged high interest rates, the poll tax, reformed business rates and the new fashion among brewers for setting 'market' rents threaten to overwhelm 5,000 or more pubs which are at present only marginally profitable. And there are new forms of competition, too. Fifty years ago the only other mass-entertainment venues which troubled the publican were the workingmen's club, the cinema and the dog-track. Now they have to attract customers away from the TV, the video, the restaurant and the disco, too.

"It's the man about our hop-pole tax!"

Changes like these affect everything, but there are some institutions which are flexible and fundamental enough to survive, if not unscathed, at least recognisably, over centuries. The pub is one of them. You'll never meet a publican who doesn't moan about business, much as you'll never meet a farmer who will confess to being rich. But the Home Office tells us that there are more full on-licences every year; industry statistics show pubs raking in more cash, in real terms, than ever; and, while the residential property market has gone from boom to bust, pub prices have continued to rise and are only now beginning to stabilise.

MEETING THE CHANGE

It may seem heretical to say so here, but the underlying cause of the pub trade's ability to flourish through recent difficulties has been the brewing industry's ability to meet change and exploit it. The retail revolution of recent years was not created by the brewing industry. But the brewers have shown the resourcefulness – and for that matter the resources – to adapt their massive estates to meet it. In fact the way they have done this has influenced their whole outlook to the extent that it looks like becoming the single most significant factor in the future pattern of the licensed trade.

Two or three generations ago, brewers saw their estates merely as vehicles for their manufactured output. Most brewers had interests in minerals and wines and spirits, as well as in beer, and their pubs were tied on virtually everything. Rents were low and the major profit came from manufacturing. Less and less is this the case. Pub tenancies are now free on everything but beers, with the MMC Report making in-roads here, too; and publicans have developed profitable food businesses. As a result, brewers have come to see pubs as pure retailing ventures, with the profit lying not between brewer and publican but between publican and customer.

This emphasis on retailing has brought about great changes in the nature of individual pubs, as their owners pump in money to adapt them to public tastes. We have seen the ghastlier manifestation of the 'theme' pub come and largely go. Other developments, such as the family room, the food counter, the smokeless bar and low-alcohol beer, look more permanent. With the recent travails of Sock

Shop and Storehouse, it may be that the heat of the retail revolution is behind us. But the most significant effect on the brewing industry, the shift in perception of profit-centre, is likely to be permanent. If the emphasis has shifted supply as the major factor to supply as an almost incidental area of concern, there is no longer any imperative in the pub operator owning the means of production. In the past small brewers such as Heavitree, Beards and Grays abandoned their breweries in favour of their pubs; now Boddingtons has followed it, and Grand Metropolitan was toying with the idea for months if not years before the pubs-for-breweries swap with Elders came to light.

In fact there have already been faltering steps in the retailing direction from most of the major brewers. Grand Met has set up its own chain of quasi-free houses in Clifton Inns, as has Allied with Nicholson Inns, Devenish with Inn Leisure, Vaux with Vaux Free Inns, and Camerons with Tap & Spile. Whitbread has imported Marston's Pedigree and Brakspear's Bitter to beef up its cask portfolio, and Taylor Walker has done the same with Young's.

The report of the Monopolies and Mergers Commission seems only to confirm this trend: rather than bucking the industry, as it seemed to do at first, it is really only reinforcing ideas which were already present. At the time of writing, the MMC has yet to approve the Elders/Grand Met deal; if it does, the trend of separation of retailer from manufacturer will be demonstrated in its most dramatic possible form. A huge retail empire with massive buying-power will be served by an equally awesome manufacturing empire with highly efficient production and distribution and strong brands already firmly in place.

PUB CHAINS

Scottish & Newcastle's move to comply with the MMC rules point ultimately in the same direction. With only a touch over 2,000 pubs in its estate, S&N had only to sell a few to escape the MMC's provisions. This it quickly did – but it made it clear from the outset that it would not be selling these pubs to their incumbents. Instead, a string of medium-size free trade companies sprang up – and most of them promptly signed supply deals with S&N.

Of course, at this stage it is too early to predict exactly how the remaining three of the Big Six will comply. In theory they will have

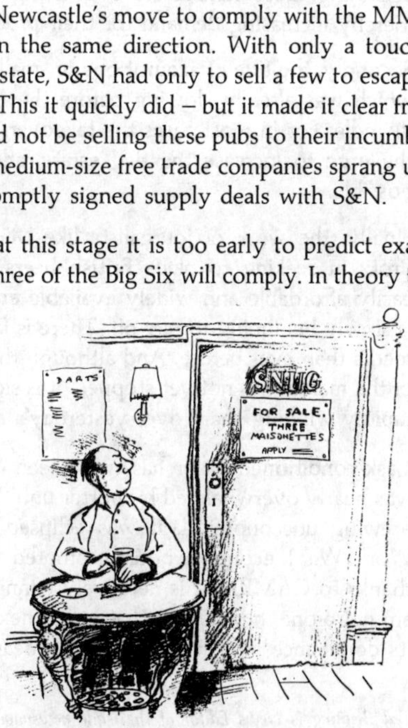

to create between them 8,000 entirely free houses, either sold off or leased out 'at arm's length'. My guess would be that they would choose to sell or lease their surplus pubs, as S&N has done, to small chains of around 20–50 each. However they choose to play it, it is certain that over the course of years the vertical integration of the industry will be significantly weakened. The controllers of these small chains will at first undoubtedly buy their beers from the same breweries they bought their pubs from, as has happened with the S&N sell-off. But how long this state of affairs will last is anyone's guess. My own feeling is that the fragmentation of ownership, however marginal cynics may see it as, must inevitably lead to a fragmentation of supply. The multiplication of pub chains that we are beginning to see represents a multiplication of buying decisions. Some buyers will be influenced only by pricing considerations. Some will be looking to sell strong national brands, others for quirky local brews. Some will be heavily influenced by back-up services; others will fall prey to the charms of individual sales reps.

THE EFFECT ON ALE

These questions of ownership and control must seem abstruse, even irrelevant, to the public. How can they affect the product this book exists to praise? Simply, this fragmentation is a source of long-term hopes for the regional and micro-brewers of the country and, indeed, for the beer-lover on the pleasure side of the bar. And when placed in the context of other contemporary trends, there is even better cause for long-term hope. For a start, there is the guest beer market, also created by the MMC Report. Wise heads in the regional breweries have seen this as more promising than the Report's main provision, for while the guest market will not add much to their volume of sales, it does offer them a chance of becoming more familiar to a growing number of drinkers and thereby increasing demand for their products in other outlets.

Secondly, the tide of acquisitions of small breweries by large ones, which was already slowing before the MMC Report, must now dwindle. For in most cases the takeovers have been prompted by the urge to increase the tied estate, and this will no longer be possible.

Finally, the work of journalists like Michael Jackson and Roger Protz in seeking to place British beers where they belong – as easily affordable and widely available everyday gourmet treats – is slowly beginning to pay off. There is far more about beer in the media than ever before. And although the growth of lager's share of the market has not yet stopped, it is slowing, while cask ales are rapidly winning share over yesterday's enemy, keg.

Cask-conditioned bitter has twice seen off strong competitors. It was nearly overwhelmed by porter until World War I made porter brewing uneconomical. It was eclipsed by mild until the post-World War II economic boom prompted drinkers to trade up. Now, thanks to CAMRA, it is decisively winning the war against keg. I am not alone in believing that in the next 20 years it will reassert its dominance over lager – but that, dear reader, is up to you.

*Ted Bruning is News Editor of the trade newspaper, the **Morning Advertiser**.*

HUNTING BEER ON THE BOX

Writer/presenter **Michael Jackson** *explains the background to Channel 4's* ***The Beer Hunter****, the series which broke new ground for the grain.*

Whining about wine is an occupational hazard for those of us who earn our livings by writing about beer. Not that we dislike the drink itself – some of us rather enjoy it – but we are jealous of the space and time it wins in the media. Newspapers and general interest magazines carry columns on wine every week, but respond with puzzlement to the notion that they might do the same for beer. (There are honourable exceptions. In Britain, *The Guardian* ran a beer column weekly for a couple of years in the 1970s, and that gesture is still remembered with gratitude.)

Publishers love works on the grape but cannot really believe they make money from books on the grain. Television in Britain justifiably ogles Jancis Robinson, and on both sides of the Atlantic doffs a hat to Hugh Johnson. For years, it seemed to turn a blind eye to beer. Hugh Johnson's book *The World Atlas of Wine* was, I am happy to acknowledge, the inspiration for my original *World Guide to Beer*, published in 1977, but that was a long time ago. There are now shelves full of books, by a variety of authors, unfolding the mysteries and delights of fine beer to the consumer. If the true appreciation of beer is to reach a wider audience, it needs television.

From the moment my first book on beer was published, I began to receive phone calls from independent producers with an eye to a documentary film or a series. None of these projects ever came to maturity, though I was always eager that they should. One day when my thoughts were far from this question, an acquaintance in the film industry asked why I never did anything in his medium. I should, he said, be making the running myself. This I did and was put in touch with a commissioning editor at Channel 4, Gwynn Pritchard. To my great satisfaction, Gwynn was engaged by the idea, but there then followed a couple of years of meetings, and, as budget and co-production possibilities were juggled, we never seemed to be making real progress. My hopes would rise and fall, and eventually I put the notion out of my mind. This is always a good ruse. No sooner had I forgotten about it than Gwynn phoned. There were funds available, but we had to snap them up. Could I start filming the next month?

I was in the midst of working on a book about single malt Scotches, and was some way from finishing it, but somehow I managed to give the necessary attention to the series. Channel 4 commissions series to independent production companies, and, after meetings with three of them, we went with the third into the frame, Hawkshead. Hawkshead had made, among other excellent

Michael Jackson sinks a pint of XXXB at the Bateman brewery, for the benefit of cameraman Chris O'Dell.

films, a series on cooking, featuring the Roux brothers, and I got along well with Executive Producer Carol Haslam from the moment she revealed a liking for single malts.

From the start, Channel 4 had stipulated that the series would comprise six films. Series are usually made up of six, seven or 13 parts. This is because the year is divided into units each of 13 weeks – or one quarter. It was decided that the six films would be shared between two directors: John Carlaw and Bob Bee.

I already had ideas about the theme and storyline of each film, and – as far as could be established from my short synopses – these thoughts seemed workable to Gwynn, Carol and the directors. Because I was already acquainted with the management of most of the breweries I wished to film, and had ideas as to whom I wished to interview, a good week was saved in preliminary research. This still left me with a further week of phoning and setting up, and then a week of location scouting, after which John and I would collaborate on a shooting script. The shooting script sets out exactly what is to be filmed, in what order this is then envisaged as appearing in the finished film, and how it will be linked by the presenter's pieces-to-camera. A week's filming would follow.

Back in London I would look at the rushes with John, wincing over fluffs and other infelicities until they had all hit the famous floor of the cutting room, then a rough assembly of the film would be made. In the month or six weeks while John and the film editor turned this rough assembly into a fine-cut, I would go out with Bob on the next film. When we returned, I would add the commentary to the fine-cut.

By overlapping John and Bob's films, we were able to make the whole series in about eight months, between March and October of 1989. Eight months may seem plenty enough for six half-hour films, but with only one director the series would have taken a year.

A week's shooting might also sound lavish, though we shot three or four hours' film for every 30 minutes of running time. Sometimes a week was easily adequate, but in other films it barely sufficed. In Czechoslovakia, there are so few motorways that it took us every moment of our week to cover the locations: taverns in Prague, breweries in Pilsen and Budweis, a maltings in another city, a glassworks in yet a further town, a wedding somewhere else... I had written into my synopsis background scenes like the wedding and glassworks, and I am glad I did; I felt the Czech film worked very well. In other cases, I perhaps tried to cram too much into my stories. On reflection, I felt that about the German film.

There was little difficulty in deciding which countries to feature. Czechoslovakia, Germany, Belgium, Britain and the United States were obvious choices. This left one slot: should it be The Netherlands, Denmark or Ireland? In the end, I chose The Netherlands because I feared that a film on Denmark or Ireland might seem too much like a commercial for Carlsberg or Guinness. Now that the series has (I hope) established its credibility and integrity, I'd like to make further films in those two countries. Channel 4 has indicated that it is willing to talk about a further series, though there is not yet a firm commitment.

As far as the actual filming was concerned, I had experience of talking to a camera in a studio, with autocue, but I had never done it on location, without the magic prompter. 'Be natural!', the director would command. It is not natural to walk across a room while pouring a beer. Nor is it natural to pour a beer while looking elsewhere – at a camera. It is even less natural to do all of this while chattering away – trying all the while to remember the script. It would be natural to talk spontaneously, but that does not work. Spontaneous comments in pieces-to-camera leave the director with elements that will not cut together logically.

We had been filming all day at a beer festival when the director became impatient with me: 'You are not being natural! You are acting!'.

'No, I'm not.'

'Yes, you are. You're acting drunk!'

'I am not acting drunk. I *am* drunk...'

That was just another occupational hazard. Then there was the pub scene where the local drunkard kept engaging me in conversation in the middle of a piece-to-camera. When the landlady gently threw him out, he simply hammered on the door for the benefit of our sound recordist. Then there was the windmill that refused to turn in Amsterdam, the power failure that severely limited coverage of the Great British Beer Festival...

It was all worthwhile when the series finally aired and I was stopped by a stranger in the street. He turned out to be a truck-driver with no previous knowledge of beer. 'I had to drive to Prague the other week', he told me. 'Have you ever tried that Pražanka beer...?'

THE LOST BEERS

Roger Protz

It's the milds I miss most. London and the surrounding areas are now as barren as the Arctic wastes if you fancy a glass of dark ale. Mild hangs on to the mash tun by the tips of its scrabbling fingers in East Anglia and the Thames Valley. But in London, apart from a few ales imported from out of town, it's a case of Bitter, Bitter Everywhere, Nor Any Mild to Drink.

It wasn't always the case, London was awash with mild when I was a young drinker. My first local, the Old King Lud at the bottom of Fleet Street, had mild brewed in old Sam Whitbread's Chiswell Street brewery. It was my lunchtime tipple. Bitter was, quite simply, too bitter for my youthful tastebuds. It's not just mass advertising that suborns youngsters into drinking lager. Mild was a marvellous bridge to bitter when you put down the pop bottle and tentatively picked up your first beer glass.

The taste of Whitbread's mild has left no lasting impression. Fuller's Hock has. I recall a day of blazing sun in 1976 when CAMRA launched a guide called *Real Ale on the Waterways* by taking a press party on a boat along the Regent's Canal. The guide, in publishers' parlance, was a turkey. Sadly but suitably, it sank without trace. But the floating launch was a splendid occasion, made memorable for me by the cask of Fuller's dark mild we had on board. I left the other topers to empty the container of London Pride. I stayed with the Hock for the duration of the voyage. In spite of the name, it had nothing in common with a German wine and I marvelled at its nutty, malty and chocolatey aroma and taste.

Hock became the beer I drank in Fuller's pubs and it sent me on a voyage of mild discovery. Even in the late seventies, there was much to enjoy in the London area. I pulled, at random, the 1978 edition of the *Good Beer Guide* from the shelf and was astonished by the choice of tasty, low gravity ales available then.

London's other independent, Young's of Wandsworth, had a Best Malt Ale. But the big brewers also added some dark delights. Charrington had closed its Mile End brewery but it still supplied its pubs with a pleasant mild, produced by Mitchells and Butlers in Birmingham. Courage, from its quaintly castellated plant, cheek-by-jowl with Tower Bridge, brewed a nicely balanced dark mild along with bitter and Directors. And from the London–Essex border, Ind Coope produced a coppery mild to accompany its lightly-hopped bitter. Every one of those distinctive milds, part of Britain's rich and idiosyncratic contribution to the world of beer, has gone. In the case of both Charrington and Courage, the breweries have gone, too, and I include in the list of lost ales such beers as Charrington IPA and Courage Best, brewed several hundred miles from their birthplace and lacking the tart, tangy bite of a true Cockney bitter.

In Plymouth I discovered a mild that was wondrous to behold. Plymouth Heavy, like Hock, was a curious name for a mild. It must have caused wandering Scots to blink when they came across a jet black ale that bore no resemblance to the equivalent of a bitter across the border. Courage's Heavy had got its name, it seemed, in order to cash in on the popularity of another Devonian mild called Tivvy. Heavy looked for all the world like Guinness, lurking darkly in the glass beneath a white collar of foam. But the taste was nothing like the Irish stout. It was light, delicate and quenching, with hints of chocolate, nut and coffee. The Plymouth brewery was a delight, too, with its cool, tiled rooms and traditional tuns and coppers. But Courage closed it and Heavy heaved its last.

In East Anglia neither Paine's nor Tolly Cobbold beers were highly rated by connoisseurs, save for their milds. Paine's mild was roastily delicious while Tolly's Ipswich mild had a fine rounded palate despite a modest gravity that at 1030° scarcely troubled the hydrometer. In the curious way of the brewing world, Tolly bought Paine's and closed the brewery and then Brent-Walker bought Tolly ... and closed the brewery. The Tolly beers, when brewed by Camerons of Hartlepool, for me counted as lost ales. The resurrection of the Ipswich brewery is good news.

Even when breweries were not being closed, their owners axed mild after mild on the grounds of falling demand. If they had used a fraction of the cash they devote to lager to promote their milds, and had served them from sensibly small casks, then several would still be around to give refreshment and pleasure, especially to those on low incomes who are increasingly priced out of the modern South East pub.

In the West of England there was a splendid tradition of light bitters with humble gravities yet packed with delicious malt-and-hop character. They were known, dismissively, as 'boy's bitters'. They were wonderfully refreshing and slid easily and effortlessly down the throat. They were yet another brilliant example of the brewer's art. Those beers, with gravities of 1030° or 1032° at the most, were not, in brewer's parlance, 'fully attenuated'. Fermentation was stopped with some malt sugars left in the brew. With a generous seasoning of hops, they had a surprisingly rounded balance in the mouth. Best of the boy's brews was Hall & Woodhouse's Badger Bitter. It went, and the Dorset brewery, questing for a share of the 'premium' market, has added a strong bitter with a silly name of Tanglefoot that suggests instant insobriety.

The Midlands had an excellent light ale, too, in Ruddles Bitter, known as 'Blue' and weighing in at 1032°. Splendidly spicy and quenching, it was the ideal session bitter. But long before Ruddles sold its birthright and became a Watney's subsidiary, the brewery had a rush of blood and increased the gravity to 1037°. It is now just another, very ordinary 'ordinary' bitter.

The Breweries Section of that long-ago 1978 guide promised 'new real ales' from several Watney breweries. Those were the days when Grand Metropolitan's brewing division was attempting to repair the damage of its ludicrous and lamentable failure with Red keg bitter. The combine admitted in public that it had misread the beer market and promised local beers to meet local tastes. Most of the new ales did not last long, such as the cask beer for London named Fined Bitter, so called, said CAMRA wags, because it had so few outlets that it was hard to find.

But Truman did produce a fine cask beer called Tap Bitter, light, quaffable and well-hopped in the Brick Lane tradition. When it was phased out Truman replaced it with a veritable galaxy of new cask beers – a mild, two bitters and a genuine strong ale called Sampson: one pint and you could kill a lion. One by one, by that terrible attrition that big brewers bring to their wares, they were axed, until only the best bitter remained. And then – you've guessed – the Truman brewery was closed and the bitter was sent packing to Ushers in Wiltshire. And now Ushers is likely to go, too.

The most depressing aspect of the Breweries Section of the 1978 *GBG* is the listing for Whitbread. Hard to believe, but the combine, among the Big Six national groups, was comparatively popular in CAMRA circles for the range of its beers and the number of plants producing them. It had breweries in Blackburn, Cardiff, Castle Eden, Cheltenham, Faversham, Leeds, Liverpool, Luton, Marlow, Portsmouth, Rhymney, Romsey, Salford, Samlesbury, Sheffield, Tiverton and Wateringbury in Kent. Today only Castle Eden, Cheltenham, Samlesbury (keg only) and Sheffield remain.

'Boddingtons' has been added, with singular duplicity, in Manchester. Not only has Whitbread closed its own Liverpool brewery but it has acquired and now butchered Higsons. Proud Merseyside lacks a brewery and Higsons' wonderfully tart and fruity ales are now manufactured in Sheffield and, with crass insensitivity, trunked across the Pennines for 'Higsons' pubs.

Higsons' beers are lost beers even though the name remains. They are an insult to Liverpudlians with their fierce, insular pride. Other names survive, too. But Wethered and Fremlins and Flowers and Strong's brewed at Cheltenham, and Chester's, ex-Salford, brewed at Sheffield, are bowdlerised beers, a giant, marketing-led conglomerate's way of holding two fingers up to the consumer.

There have been gains as well as losses. Back in 1978 John Smith's brewed no real ale. It has come back into the fold with two good-tasting beers. The explosion of micro brewers has brought a plentitude of new and often beautifully-crafted beers.

But there is sadness in looking back and seeing again those long-dead beers that once gave so much pleasure. With planning and foresight, many of them could have survived if brewers had put the consumer ahead of the balance sheet. And many of the breweries need not have closed if national combines had ignored the weasel advice of the marketing experts to go down the route of centralised mega-keggeries churning out lacklustre apologies for European beers.

If breweries occasionally listened to the people in their pubs they wouldn't make so many mistakes. And I could even now be enjoying a cool, fragrant, malty glass of Fuller's Hock.

Roger Protz is a former Editor of the ***Good Beer Guide****, Associate Editor of the CAMRA newspaper,* ***What's Brewing****, and a freelance journalist and broadcaster.*

ALL THE BEST PUBS HAVE REAL COAL FIRES – OFFICIAL!

Colin Carr

The evidence is truly overwhelming. Most pub-going adults in Britain today agree that there's nothing quite like a real coal fire. From the South East to the North West, Greater London to Scotland, a new independent survey of 1,000 adults indicates that real ale is just part of a pub's attraction.

Any landlord or brewery out there thinking of watering down the appeal of their pubs by blocking up the chimneys and installing imitation fires in their lounges and bars should STOP – and just consider the following. According to the new survey, undertaken by one of the UK's leading market research companies, Research Surveys of Great Britain, an amazing 91 per cent of regular pub-goers agree that: 'A real coal fire creates a more welcoming atmosphere than an imitation coal effect fire in a traditional pub'.

That's not a half-hearted opinion! Support for real fires came from all areas of the country covered by the survey, but was especially strong in Greater London itself, the North of England and Scotland. *Meanwhile, 80 per cent of the UK's regular pub-goers believe that a real coal fire is an important part of the great British pub.* The most enthusiastic real coal fire supporters who agreed with this statement were aged between 35 and 44, although real fires in pubs proved generally very popular with all age and social groups.

If that evidence of the attractions of a genuine coal fire is not enough, then an even stronger case is made by the fact that: *70 per cent of regular pub-goers agree that a real coal fire is preferable to* **any** *other focal point in a traditional pub*. This is especially the case among regular pub-goers in the East Midlands (where 80 per cent agreed), the North (75 per cent), South West and Yorkshire & Humberside (both 71 per cent).

Abandon the original oak beams, chuck out the Toby jugs and forget the feature fireplace if there is nothing burning in the grate. A spokesman for British Coal explained: 'Pub-goers want the real thing, and this survey proves it. Imitation gas fires in pubs are as dead as keg beer and we're heading back to the traditional comforts of a living fire'.

Fortunately, more than a thousand pubs in this guide are already listed as solid fuel users. Their landlords don't need a survey to remind them of something they've known for years.

Ideal for pubs this year, and new to the market, is the arrival of a remote control open fire, the Charnwood Fireflow. The Fireflow is an open fire which actually feeds itself with solid fuel, can be controlled from afar at the touch of a button and even takes away its own ashes – automatically. All you need to install this up-market real coal fire is an open fire and a chimney on an outside wall.

But there is something more to consider. Like real ale, real bread and real fires, home-produced Real British Coal has certain qualities that distinguish it from the rest. Unlike many imported coals and smokeless fuels, British coal (the product) has been carefully graded and quality controlled, but with imported coals you don't know what it is you are actually paying for in addition to solid fuel. Imagine wasting your money trying to burn bits of metal, rock and coal dust in your fire. What is more, there are over 100 different varieties of housecoal produced in the UK, and many of them are recommended for specific uses, whether on open fires, roomheaters, boilers or solid fuel cookers.

UK solid fuel users, in pubs or at home, know they can buy Real British Coal whenever they want from their local Approved Coal Merchant. And further information on solid fuel is freely available at the end of a phone, simply dial 100 and ask for Freefone Real Fires.

New independent research shows that a real coal fire is unbeatable as an added attraction for traditional pubs.

PUBS FOR FAMILIES

Jill Adam

Is the old adage that children should be seen and not heard finally to be buried? Will the 1990s at last see the British public taking a positive attitude to children by encouraging a more 'child-friendly society'? However much Mrs Thatcher favours Victorian values, we are next year to become officially part of a Europe whose citizens would be horrified at the way British children are so often excluded from social gatherings. Children have been regarded as second-class citizens for far too long and nowhere is their exclusion more evident than in that most social of meeting places, the British pub.

The law regarding children entering pubs is partly to blame and should have been changed years ago. At present it is confusing to say the least and publicans who are reluctant to admit children can easily use it as an excuse not to do so. George Orwell, writing as long ago as 1946, understood the problem and lamented in the *Evening Standard* (in a piece about a fictitious pub): '... though, strictly speaking, they are only allowed in the garden, the children tend to seep into the pub and even to fetch drinks for their parents. This I believe is against the law, but it is a law that deserves to be broken, for it is the puritanical nonsense of excluding children – and therefore to some extent, women – from pubs that has turned these places into mere boozing-shops instead of the family gathering-places that they ought to be.'

Help may be at hand. *The Publican* magazine, a trade journal, carried out a poll in 1990 among its readers to find out attitudes of licensees to children in pubs. 83% said that they wished to see the law changed so that children should be given greater access to pubs. As the law now stands, only children over the age of 14 are admitted into a public bar. Families with younger children are restricted to the pub garden, or a family room which does not have a bar. *The Publican* launched a campaign in April 1990 to get the law changed so that any licensee may apply for a children's certificate. This would mean that, after fulfilling certain criteria, the pub would be granted a certificate to allow children to be admitted to the public bar until 8pm.

This change could be achieved, says *The Publican*, by a simple amendment to the present law. It would allow many more pubs to admit children which currently are unable to do so because of lack of suitable facilities, for instance those with just a single room. It would also appease those who go down to the pub to get away from their families by imposing a time limit of 8pm.

Obviously, opposition from the hardened drinking brigade will be strong. There are plenty of people who ardently believe that a pub is not a suitable place for youngsters to go. I believe just as strongly that the opposite is true. We grow up with the idea that pubs are mysterious, forbidden places, so that when we reach our majority we cannot wait to discover what lies in store for us in these dens of iniquity. No wonder we are breeding a nation of lager louts! If we are brought up with the idea that a pub is a social meeting place where people gather to converse, play games and be entertained, and where alcohol is consumed in moderation, then surely that would be an improvement.

Allowing more children into more pubs is likely to encourage licensees and publicans to provide better facilities all round. Okay, some will prefer to keep to the absolute basic, sawdust-on-the-floor-type atmosphere to provide for their regular clientele no greater service than simply somewhere to drink. However, there is a growth nowadays in good pub food, a service which allows families far greater choice when going out for a meal. Pub food is generally more affordable than in a restaurant (which also, incidentally, are generally anti-children), and more palatable than the ubiquitous burger bars where so many parents with children tend to end up in a strange town, simply because there is nowhere else to go.

More enlightened licensees will go one step further. By creating an enjoyable and pleasant atmosphere for the whole family, the local pub can become a regular venue, not just for Dad out for a night with the lads (although he may use the same pub). It takes a certain investment to install decent garden equipment, but the resulting profit from soft drink sales must prove worthwhile. By the same token, a little effort taken to make a family room comfortable and welcoming, providing some simple amusements (even just board games, scrap paper and crayons) will pay off in terms of additional custom.

In the spring of 1990 CAMRA launched the new Alma guide *The Best Pubs for Families* at the *Schweppes/Publican* Family Pub of the Year at Brackley in Northants. This pub is an obvious winner, with terrific facilities for families: an acre of garden with slides, swings, a bouncy castle and an outdoor (reasonably-priced) burger bar. Inside, children are given the run of a long lounge and conservatory which is attached to the main bar. The landlord puts on free entertainment on Sundays for children – magicians, puppet shows and the like. I am not suggesting that every pub should follow suit. Indeed, it was not even that which impressed me most about the pub on my first visit. What *really* impressed me was the attitude of the staff. I had gone to the pub to meet a reporter from a woman's magazine. As we were sitting chatting, a young woman entered the pub with a toddler on one hand and a baby on her hip. She looked around her a little nervously, and was immediately taken by a member of staff to a table, provided with highchairs and extremely efficient, courteous service.

How many pubs do you know where that situation would be repeated? The likely answer is none at all. Am I being too optimistic in hoping that by the end of the decade it may be the norm?

Jill Adam is Editor of ***The Best Pubs for Families****, published by Alma Books, and has been Deputy Editor of the* ***Good Beer Guide*** *for 5 years.*

YOUR ROUND, I THINK, SERGEANT?

Creator **Colin Dexter** *reveals more about Inspector Morse, the beer drinker's detective*

The real point is this: what does Lewis order at the bar for his curmudgeonly chief? For tightfisted Morse quite certainly *is*; and the hapless Lewis (on half the salary) appears ever fated to fork out for a man who never expresses a single word of gratitude to boot. So why so mean, Inspector *Morose*?

It is often said (probably correctly) that every first book of fiction is likely to be semi-autobiographical; and Morse certainly shares a good many of my own interests – and weaknesses: from his first appearance in *Last Bus to Woodstock* he devotes ever-loving attention to Wagnerian opera, cryptic crosswords, attractive women, and (why not?) good beer. Yet deliberately, too, I sought to make him significantly different from myself, and I gave him one or two quite contemptible qualities: thus, for example, he is too readily irascible; he is reprehensibly cruel in ticking off subordinates in the presence of others; *and* he is most reluctant to pay his round in a pub – surely, this last, the most unforgivable of the social sins, especially since Morse has persuaded himself that he is all the more likely to crack any case with the aid of a gallon of ale. You see, Morse has always pretended that alcohol clears his brain wondrously ('pretended'?) and that any hours spent at the bar with a pint (and with Lewis) are a positive plus in his hounding down of the Devil – in the guise of the murderer.

Now such a claim cannot be wholly disregarded, although at the very least it may be argued that booze would seem positively to impair rather than to improve some of our faculties. There are perhaps two types of men and women: those who after drinking rather too liberally find their speech slurring towards incoherence, whilst at the same time their legs retain a sort of dogged sobriety; and, on the other hand, those whose speech maintains every semblance of coherent clarity, but whose feet, on setting forth, appear determined to depart in opposite directions. Morse, as usual, tends to disprove any theory: walking and talking (especially after a touch of the malt) – talking and walking – it is all the same: bad! But – he knows it – he can always *think* in such circumstances.

As a bachelor, he's got through the guilt barrier of drinking. He knows, at last, that there is little point in pretending to anyone else – although he is happy to continue pretending to himself. It was a questionnaire in one of the staidest Sundays (or was it the *News of the World*? – Morse takes both) that alerted him to the perils of drink, with the first four questions reading as follows:

(a) Do you ever feel tempted to drink alone?

(b) Have you ever found yourself waiting impatiently for opening-time?

(c) Have you ever woken up in the morning and vowed never to touch alcohol again?
(d) Would you feel desperate on a North Welsh Sunday if you found all the pubs shut?

Now (a) was surely a sick joke, *wasn't it*? And (b) was little healthier, since Morse had only filled in the questionnaire as something to do in the five minutes remaining before opening-time. But he knew all about (c); almost every morning for the past 30 years he did decide to abandon alcohol. As for (d), he could give no definite answer, though he made a mental note never to find himself anywhere near Snowdonia on a Sunday. Looking at the interpretation of readers' 'scores', Morse read with sinking spirits that just five 'yes's (he had ten of them) quite certainly spelt medium- and long-term hazards for bladder, kidneys, and liver alike, as well as posing big problems with business efficiency, social acceptability, psychological adjustments, and sexual prowess. It had been an unfortunate little incident, and Morse vowed that in future he would avoid all similar questionnaires like the plague – or like Snowdonian Sundays.

But why beer? The answer is that, like me, Morse is a *quantity* man – a man who finds nothing quite so incomprehensible as the sight of a delicate lady sipping indefinitely at a thinly fluted glass of sherry. This does not mean, of course, that quality is out: just that a quart is twice a pint is twice a half. Certainly there is something immensely satisfying about a solid swig of beer.

My own taste for beer developed very early on. My father was much addicted to it; and most evenings he would do the rounds of the three locals, drinking mild. At about 9pm he would return with seven or eight half-pint bottles of Ind Coope Pale Ale sticking out of his various pockets, and my brother and I (this was in the mid 1940s) would be given one apiece as we worked our way through Greek and Latin grammars. A few years later, at Cambridge, my

taste turned to Greene King, and I spent perhaps too many hours in that beautiful city savouring their brews. Now a diabetic (seek not the cause!), I am earnestly exhorted to exercise an Aristotelian moderation in all things.

I myself know little or nothing about the glorious processes involved in the brewing of good beer, and was rightly, if gently, castigated by *What's Brewing* for not knowing casks from kegs in the Morse story filmed at Brakspear's and McMullen's. But I do know enough about what a good pint tastes like; and that brings me back to the nature of Sergeant Lewis's order with which I began. Well, the simple truth is that Morse would far prefer a nondescript beer in good nick to a superbly brewed specimen that's kept poorly. How not? No brewers (presumably) are anything but proud of the beer that flows from their tuns; but sometimes, alas, things do seem to go wrong in the middle somewhere, and those same brewers would doubtless be appalled at the 'beer' on sale in some of their outlets.

A lot of beer has been drunk in the *Inspector Morse* programmes; and with a fifth (and final) series scheduled for early 1991, we shall doubtless find Lewis continuing to buy a few more pints still. But Chief Inspector Morse is adamant: 'When I drink, I think. And when I have to think, I have to drink,' he says. So there's no point in arguing. Certainly not with me, because I know exactly what Morse means. There is a malaise affecting authors called 'writer's block': when it strikes a little stimulus may be required.

I was once invited to address Oxford's BMA group. In the questions that followed my talk, one doctor asked how I got my ideas. In answer, I said that I could not always afford to wait for the Muse, but preferred to force the issue somewhat by stimulating the imagination with a dram or two of alcohol. The next day the secretary of the BMA called round with two bottles of Glenfiddich – or rather, as he put it – 'two bottles of imagination'.

Let me sign off with a story from the *Inspector Morse* series. I wrote a plot, set in the Randolph Hotel in Oxford, in which Morse is waiting (see above!) for the bar to open one lunchtime. He is already tired, cross, and thirsty; he walks into the Chapters Bar at 10.30am; he orders (*via* Lewis, naturally) a glass of bitter, and proceeds to down his pint at a single draught. The shooting was scheduled for 7.30am (!) and I was myself seated – an extra – in the bar, beside an antique grandfather-clock. John Thaw duly managed his swallowing act with practised aplomb; but, as always, the director wondered about a second take – and a second take there was, John once again managing (just!) to play the scene as directed. Fine! Fine! The crew was about to dismantle the camera-rails when someone noticed that the grandfather-clock... yes, oh dear! The clock was giving the time as 8.45. So there was nothing for it but... Well let me just say that I then began to appreciate what a professional actor is occasionally called upon to perform in his vision of higher things.

THE HERITAGE BREWERY MUSEUM

Brian Glover

If the word 'museum' still conjures up images of dark, forbidding buildings, endless corridors and dusty exhibit cases, you have not been to Burton upon Trent recently. There, instead of the usual dry displays, is a living drop of our past, still steaming away to whet the appetite – and wet the throat – of thirsters after knowledge of our national drink.

Visitors to the Heritage Brewery Museum, which opened its doors to the public in 1989, not only discover a typical Victorian brewery, complete with steam engine, but can also 'see, sniff and sample' the magic art of brewing, with a free glass of beer poured in for those over 18.

Originally built in 'the capital of brewing' for Thomas Sykes of Liverpool in 1881, the square tower brewhouse in Anglesey Road was taken over by Everards of Leicester in 1898. When Everards built their own new brewery in Leicester in 1985, it looked as if the old Tiger Brewery had roared its last, and was about to follow much of the town's brewing history down the bulldozed path to demolition. Instead, East Staffordshire Council, backed by organisations like CAMRA, the Victorian Society and SAVE Britain's Heritage, stepped in to rescue one of Burton's last links with its past from becoming another heap of rubble. Everards agreed to continue brewing their Tiger Bitter and Burton Mild at the old plant, under a five-year agreement, and now new contracts are being made with other brewers to produce their beers at the site. The Heritage Brewery, as it became known, also brews its own Heritage Bitter and corked bottles of powerful Thomas Sykes Old Ale, a vintage port-like brew.

Under director Michael Knights, work has also begun on the slow and costly process of restoring the brewery buildings to their original glory. Pride of place goes to the Buxton-Thornley steam engine, which was scrapped in 1970, but then the pieces tracked down, put back together and returned to their former home.

Besides the gleaming copper and repainted mash tun room, a function room has been built in the kegging shed, and the new reception offices house an introductory video. Visitors can also see special collections of bottled beers and old pub glasses. Future plans include restoring the brewery's own railway sidings and cottages, plus the old cooper's shop and blacksmiths. They also hope, at a later date, to add the distinctive Clarence Street

Maltings, behind the brewery, to their attractions. Both the brewery and maltings are part of a conservation area.

'We are now entering a new phase of expansion. Visitors are up 20 per cent on last year,' said director Michael Knights, who, with his beard and welcoming smile, looks just the part of a Victorian brewer. He is aptly pictured, sampling malt, on the museum's publicity leaflets. One of the guides, Joanna Stevenson, says they receive all sorts of visitors, from CAMRA members and 'folk from the old days of brewing taking a trip down memory lane' to families on a day out on one of the museum's special summer show days: 'People are genuinely interested – and flabbergasted by the intricacies of making beer. Even non beer drinkers are fascinated.'

The charitable venture is supported by the Friends of the Heritage Brewery Museum. Chairman Andrew Cunningham explains why their work is so vital: 'The historical brewing heritage of this country is dwindling all the time, as old plants close and buildings are demolished or converted. It is in this context that the Heritage Brewery Museum becomes even more important. Not only is it an excellent example of a Victorian brewery, but it is also still brewing on its fine old equipment, and an operational unit is much more valuable than a static display. To this can be added a wholly appropriate location in Burton upon Trent, a town whose very name is synonymous with beer throughout the world, plus the opportunity to complement the excellent displays of the nearby Bass Museum of Brewing.'

* *The Heritage Brewery Museum, Anglesey Road, is open Tuesday to Saturday, 10am–2pm, October to Easter, and Monday to Saturday, 10am–4pm, Easter to September. Price: adults £2.50, OAPs £2, children £1, family ticket £5.50. Tel. (0283) 69226*

* *Those wishing to join the Friends of the Heritage Brewery Museum should send a cheque for £10, payable to the Friends, to M. Field, 16 Moorlands Avenue West, Dewsbury, West Yorkshire, WF13 2LB. Members receive a quarterly magazine, keeping them informed of progress at the museum.*

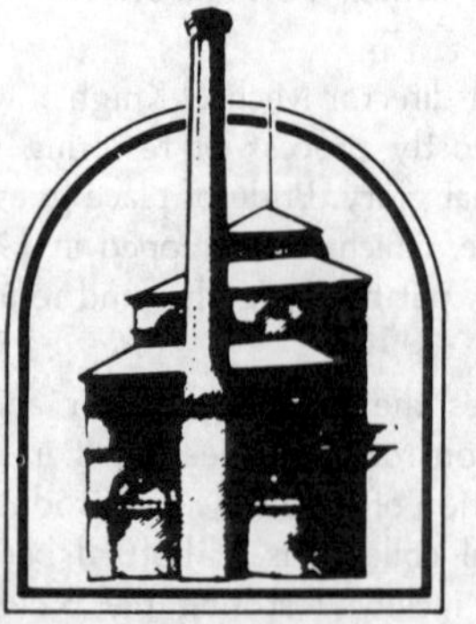

*Brian Glover is a former editor of the CAMRA newspaper, **What's Brewing**, and author of several specialist beer publications.*

PURSUING A PINT IN PARLIAMENT

Joe Ashton MP

You would think that the Mother of Parliaments, which appears on virtually every postcard sent abroad, would be proud to have the finest examples of traditional English ale in the realm. Not a bit of it. English wines, yes. Real ale, never.

That's why, for over two years now, I have been conducting a campaign to get some decent beer in the House. For a hundred years the place has hummed on Budget Day to the old music hall song of 'I am the man, the very fat man, who watered the workers' beer' (especially when Nigel Lawson was Chancellor), but the fact is that the Services Committee, which runs the catering department, does the job for him. It consists solely of wine buffs who have hijacked the cellars to keep their fine wines under lock and key and now refuse to give them up.

There must have been some real beer there thirty years ago, because all ale was real then. The problem in Parliament was that they didn't sell much from Thursday night to Monday lunchtime, and, in the hot weather, it went off.

So, in a sleight of hand con trick, back in the late 1960s, the upper-crust wine drinking MPs let the beer drinkers of Geordieland think they had accomplished a coup, by hauling a weekly supply of keg Federation Bitter all the way from Durham. They installed it in a new bar called 'Annie's', where MPs and the press could get together (the press pay more often than not) and leak and plot until midnight, without worrying about strangers sticking their opinions in.

At the time, it made a nice change from the other two bars: one called the 'Smoke Room', with deep leather armchairs and white-coated waiters, as in the Reform Club (but no draught beer); and the 'Strangers Bar', commonly known then as 'Little Kremlin' on account of the spit and sawdust on its floor and its sticky counter dating from 1888.

The Westminster staff also have a bar – and it has real ale, though not very well-kept. There is nothing to stop MPs calling in, but the bobbies and doorkeepers don't want to be trotting out the 'yessirs' when off-duty any more than corporals in their mess do. So we rarely go in. All of which means that it is ten times easier to get a free lunch at the Savoy than to get a pint of Arkell's or Sam Smith's or Tetley in Parliament.

The despairing part of it is that all the Labour MP beer drinkers come from the North East, Scotland, South Yorkshire and Wales, which tend to be real ale deserts, and not rural areas of good beer like the West Country and East Anglia. Furthermore, London MPs go home for tea, as they don't get a lodging allowance, meaning that, apart from a handful of Members like Greg Knight, the Tory MP for Derby (who worked as a drummer in workingmen's clubs), Nicholas Winterton and myself, there are very few supporters of this cause.

The Workingmen's Club and Institute Union has an enormous all-party lobby in the Commons and the Lords, and appears to have no trouble at all in getting an amendment onto the statute book to let clubs open for an extra hour on Sundays. But fight for real ale? It's a nuisance. Next thing you know club members will be wanting it with their bingo. And what next? Harvey Wallbangers? The brewers' interests, too, are all-powerful, as was shown recently by the way in which they induced the Government to water down (pun intended) the Monopolies and Mergers Commission proposals on free houses and guest beers.

Add to this the perennial invitations to free lunches (always with wine and not ale), sent to MPs by PR companies, and how can we win? In fairness, though, in this health-conscious age and in the mortal fear of by-elections, there are very few Members who take up such invitations. How can you get through a regular day of 10am to midnight after a Beaujolais lunch? All the same, it didn't stop a PR company ringing me once to say I had won a 'bucket of rocks' for the juiciest quote of the week when I refused to accept

a free taxi. The 'rocks' turned out to be a six pack of 'Rolling Rock' American lager.

Why oh why can't Allied Breweries lobby like this for a pint of Taylor Walker? They did send their real ale expert to meet us and demonstrate how to lay on real ale without a cellar, but it turned out that the only other storeroom had also been nicked. Would you believe by the banqueting department as a cool place to store its table flowers?

There is a legend that the staff in Parliament were given the right to booze on the premises not just because the water wasn't fit to drink, but because, in 1849, just a few years after the magnificent, wedding cake building was finished, two nightwatchmen (ex-jailbirds) stoked up the primitive central heating system with wooden tally sticks one Sunday night, went off to the pub across the road and caused the biggest fire of the century. It kept the poor of London warm for weeks. Nobody was killed but two fell off Westminster Bridge because of the enormous crowd gathering on it, all crying 'Burn, damn you, burn!', and praying the MPs were in it.

But for the twenty-odd years I have been in Parliament, it has meant a nightly trek down Whitehall to the Red Lion, opposite the Cenotaph, or, in the opposite direction, to the Westminster Arms on Storey's Gate, which proudly advertises itself as the only bar in London from where you can see Big Ben (thanks to one of Hitler's bombs) — except that the multi-storey Queen Elizabeth Centre has now been built in front.

It is a very sad tale, like my other two campaigns – to get the Minister of Trade to compel pubs to put original gravity on the pump (they do it on petrol, don't they?), and to compel pubs to have no-smoking areas (approved by 99 votes to 90, but put on the back burner by Mrs Edwina Currie when she was a minister). We are no nearer a parliamentary handpump now than we were twenty years ago.

As a gesture, and only because I provided free samples and earned it some embarrassing publicity, the toffee-nosed Services Committee has now agreed to stock bottles of Grolsch and Pilsner Urquell (in my opinion the best lager in Europe). Even then there was a strict warning from the wine gang that, if they didn't sell, they would be withdrawn.

So now I have to empty the pint-and-a-third bottles of Urquell instead of strolling down to the Red Lion for an Ind Coope Burton Ale. It costs more, fills me up more quickly, and I don't get the exercise. Serves them right if it all ends up in a by-election.

Joe Ashton is Labour MP for Bassetlaw, a mining area centred around Worksop, Nottinghamshire. He has been a member of CAMRA since its inception.

HOW TO USE THIS GUIDE

The following pages are the result of the untiring efforts of CAMRA members throughout the country. Their enthusiasm and dedication to the cause of good beer results in this annual feast of great pubs – nearly 5,000 of them.

Each pub has been chosen for a number of reasons, but, most importantly, for the quality of its beer. As our surveyors come from a broad range of backgrounds, have varied interests and span an age group from 18 to 80 (any advances?), naturally the pubs selected are not all the same. You will find bustling town-centre boozers, idyllic country hostelries, young people's haunts, and pubs with those quiet, cosy corners where conversation is the only required entertainment. In short, there is something for everyone; above all, these are places where the beer is the best in the area.

The pubs are listed county by county, from A to Z. The three counties of Yorkshire you will find under Y; similarly East and West Sussex fall under S. Greater London and Greater Manchester appear under L and M respectively; West Midlands is among the Ws. English counties are listed first, followed by the Welsh and Scottish, then the British islands and the province of Northern Ireland.

Within each county, towns and villages are featured alphabetically, and pubs within those towns and villages are included in the same way. The map at the front of each county section concentrates only on that county. Bear in mind that it is worthwhile checking the neighbouring counties if you are in the vicinity of the county border. The key map on the inside back cover will offer a guideline. The county maps also feature independent breweries which brew in the county.

The inside front cover provides a ready reference on how to read the pub entries, including an explanation of what the symbols stand for, but it is worth noting how opening hours are displayed. We give the lunchtime session followed by the evening, with any variation from day to day, or from season to season, given in brackets. Sunday hours are not listed, unless they differ from the norm (12–3; 7–10.30).

Most importantly, the beers are printed in alphabetical order of brewery, and then increasing gravity order within each brewery. Winter ales are quoted for pubs that are known to sell them, but are clearly only available at that time of year. The Breweries Section clarifies which beers are seasonal and so this information is not repeated in the pub entries.

Finally, no payment is accepted for the inclusion of any pub or brewery. We would, however, like to express our thanks once again to British Coal for its continued sponsorship and support.

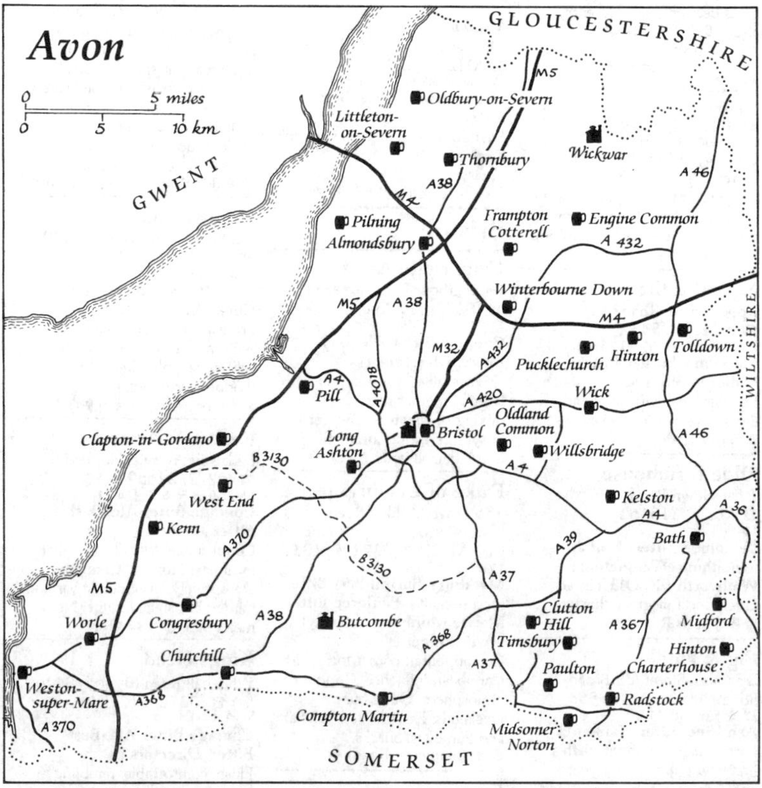

Butcombe, *Butcombe*; ***Ross***, *Bishopston, Bristol*; ***Smiles***, *Bristol*; ***Wickwar***, *Wickwar*

Almondsbury

Bowl Inn
16 Church Road, Lower Almondsbury (off A38)
☎ (0454) 612757
11–3; 6–11
Courage Bitter Ale, Best Bitter, Directors; John Smith's Bitter H
Very popular and attractive 17th-century, one-bar pub, supposedly haunted by the 'Grey Lady'. Good food, reasonably priced. Separate restaurant and function room. Accommodation in small country cottage next door. ⛫ ❀ ⛰ ◖◗ ♣ P

Bath

Belvedere Wine Vaults
25 Belvedere, Lansdown Road
☎ (0225) 330264
11–3; 5.30–11
Draught Bass; Charrington IPA H
Welcoming, unpretentious local with quiet lounge bar. Q ⊞ ♣

Coeur de Lion
17 Northumberland Place
☎ (0225) 465371
11–11
Cornish JD Dry Hop Bitter, Original, Draught Steam Bitter, Royal Wessex Bitter H
Generally reckoned to be the smallest pub in Bath, sited in a picturesque city-centre passageway. Fine stained glass window. ≋ (Spa)

Devonshire Arms
139 Wellsway (A367)
☎ (0225) 428837
11–2.30 (3 Sat); 6–11
Draught Bass; Wadworth 6X H
Recently-refurbished, with occasional live music. Car park tiny. ◖ ⊞ ♣ P

Fairfield Arms
1 Fairfield Park Road
☎ (0225) 310594
11–2.30 (3 Sat); 6–11
Courage Best Bitter; John Smith's Bitter H
Welcoming local on north-eastern outskirts of city. ❀ ⊞ ♣

Hatchetts
6–7 Queen Street
☎ (0225) 425045
11–11
Miners Arms Own Ale, Guvnor's Special Brew H
Good food at lunchtime in pleasant surroundings. Lively in the evening; upstairs bar popular with the younger set. Two guest beers usually available. ◖ ⊞ ≋ (Spa)

King William
36 Thomas Street (A4)
☎ (0225) 428096
11–11
Archers Village Bitter, Best Bitter, ASB H
Lively street-corner boozer. Guest beer. ⊞ ♣

Larkhall Inn
St Saviours Road, Larkhall (200 yds NW of jct A4/A46)
☎ (0225) 425710
11–2 (2.30 Sat); 6–10.30 (11 Fri & Sat)
Courage Best Bitter, Directors H
Distinctive pub with unusual

brass beer engines. No entry after 10.30pm Fri/Sat.
⛫ Q ❀ ⊞ ♣

Midland
14 James Street West
☎ (0225) 425029
11–3; 5.30–11 (11–11 Sat)
Courage Bitter Ale, Best Bitter, Directors [H]
Large central pub opposite the old Green Park station – now a Sainsbury supermarket. No food Sun. ◐ ⊞ ≠ (Spa) ♣ P

New Westhall
Upper Bristol Road (A4)
☎ (0225) 425432
11–2.30; 5.30–11 (11–11 Sat)
Marston's Border Bitter, Pedigree Bitter [H]
Popular local with pool and darts. Live music weekends.
⛫ ❀ ◐ ◑ ⊞ ♣ P

Olde Farmhouse
1 Lansdown Road
☎ (0225) 316162
12–11
Butcombe Bitter; Hall & Woodhouse Tanglefoot; Wadworth 6X, Old Timer [H]
Lively local of great character.
⛫ ❀ ◐ ⊞ ♣ P

Pig & Fiddle
2 Saracen Street (off Broad Street) ☎ (0225) 460868
12–3; 5 (6 Sat)–11
Ash Vine Bitter, Tanker [H]
Former fish restaurant, Bath's first new pub in many years' and Ash Vine's only pub, apart from its brew pub, the White Hart at Trudoxhill, Somerset. Two guest beers and Thatcher's cider. No food Sun. ❀ ◐ ≠ ⌽

Rose & Crown
6 Brougham Place, St Saviours Road, (400 yds NW of A4/A46 jct)
☎ (0225) 425700
11–2.30; 5–11 (11–11 Sat)
Butcombe Bitter; Marston's Pedigree Bitter [H]
Friendly, out-of-town local, worth seeking out. Guest beer.
⊞ ♣ ⌽

Smith Brothers
11–12 Westgate Buildings
☎ (0225) 330470
11–3; 5.30–11 (11–11 summer)
Thomas Hardy Country Bitter, Royal Oak [H]
Spacious, one-bar, central pub with public bar section. Guest beer. Q ◐ ≠ (Spa) ♣ P

Star
23 The Vineyards (A4)
☎ (0225) 425072
11–2.30; 5.30–11
Draught Bass [G]**; Charrington IPA; Wadworth 6X, Old Timer** [H]
Atmospheric, classic town pub. Bass served from the jug. Q ⊞ ♣

Victoria
Millmead Road, Oldfield Park
☎ (0225) 425903
11–3.30; 5.30–11 (11–11 Sat)
Courage Bitter Ale, Best Bitter [H]
Friendly three-bar workingman's local in south-western suburb of city.
◐ ⊞ ♿ ≠ (Oldfield Park) ♣

Bristol

Cambridge Arms
Coldharbour Road, Redland
☎ (0272) 735754
11–11
Courage Bitter Ale, Best Bitter, Directors [H]
Comfortable, well-run pub with large garden at rear. Good mixing of clientele. Can get busy. Interesting meals (till 7 only). Bar billiards. ❀ ◐ ◑ ♣ P

Duke of Cambridge
158 Lower Ashley Road, Easton (B4051, 50 yds E of jct 3 M32) ☎ (0272) 511031
11–11
Marston's Burton Best Bitter (occasionally), **Pedigree Bitter, Merrie Monk** (occasionally), **Owd Rodger** [H]
Cosmopolitan corner local with Caribbean influence. Good atmosphere. Quite busy weekends. Discos Wed, Fri, Sat and Sun eves. Snacks.
❀ ≠ (Stapleton Road) ♣

Farm
Hopetown Road, St Werburgh's
☎ (0272) 243622
11.30–2.30; 6 (5.30 summer)–11
Ruddles County; Ushers Best Bitter [H]
Popular pub by St Werburgh's city farm, well worth seeking out. Rural atmosphere created by local allotments and city farm animal noises. Landlord recently won Ushers cellarmanship 1st prize. Pleasant garden. No food at weekends. Q ❀ ◐ ♣

Greyhound
32 Princess Victoria Street, Clifton ☎ (0272) 734187
11–11
Courage Best Bitter, Directors; John Smith's Bitter [H]
Small pub: two bars, side entrance and corridor. Busy, narrow front bar; food-oriented back bar with wide choice of meals. Popular with business community in historic Clifton 'village'. Fine old facade. ◐

Highbury Vaults
164 St Michael's Hill (off B4051) ☎ (0272) 733203
11–11
Brains SA; Smiles Brewery Bitter, Best Bitter, Exhibition [H]
Wonderful evocation of a pre-war pub, deservedly popular. Atmospheric, small front bar; large rear bar split into small, snug-type areas. Enclosed sunny courtyard at rear. Children welcome till 8.30pm. Home-cooked food includes veg dishes. Two guest beers.
Q ❀ ◐ ◑ ⊞ ≠ (Clifton Down) ♣

Highwayman
Hill Street, Kingswood (A420)
☎ (0272) 671613
11.30–2.30; 5.30–11
Halls Harvest Bitter; Ind Coope Burton Ale [H]
Pre-war, traditional building with modern interior. Single central bar; pleasing 'olde worlde' surroundings. English and foreign menu. ❀ ◐ ◑ ♿ P

Kellaway Arms
Kellaway Avenue, Horfield
☎ (0272) 246694
11–2.30 (3 Fri & Sat); 6–11
Courage Bitter Ale, Best Bitter [H]
Comfortable, friendly, two-bar local near Horfield Common. Deceptively large public bar and garden but small lounge. No meals Sun. Q ❀ ⇔ ⊞ ♣

Kings Head
Whitehall Road (B4465/B4469 jct) ☎ (0272) 517174
11–3; 6–11
Courage Bitter Ale, Best Bitter, Directors [H]
Plush, comfortable, rambling local, deservedly popular. Skittle alley incorporated in public bar. ⛫ ❀ ◐ ⊞ ♣ P

Kings Head
60 Victoria Street (B4053, 250 yds NW of A4)
☎ (0272) 277860
11 (12 Sat)–3; 5.30 (7 Sat)–11
Courage Bitter Ale, Best Bitter [H]
Small Victorian gem, restored but unspoilt. Next to church with leaning tower. Full of original features and character. No food weekends. Four-pint jug discount beer at off-peak times Mon–Fri. Lovely snug.
Q ◐ ≠ (Temple Meads)

Knowle Hotel
Leighton Road, Knowle
☎ (0272) 777019
11–2.30 (3 Sat); 5.30 (6 Sat)–11
Ind Coope Burton Ale; Smiles Best Bitter; Tetley Bitter [H]
Large friendly pub. Quiz night Wed. ❀ ◐ ⊞ ♣

Old Castle Green
Gloucester Lane, Old Market (off A420 300 yds from A4044 jct) ☎ (0272) 550925
11–11 (may vary Sat)
Marston's Burton Best Bitter, Pedigree Bitter, Owd Roger [H]
Small and successful, with a cosmopolitan clientele and an

old public bar atmosphere to suit all tastes. Good quality food with veg option. ▦ ◖ ◗ ♣

Old Duke
45 King Street
☎ (0272) 277137
12–2; 7–11
Courage Best Bitter, Directors [H]
Bristol's world-renowned jazz centre. A must for all lovers of trad jazz (admission charged on jazz nights). Lunchtime meals, but rolls only Sat. ▦ ◖

Old England
43 Bath Buildings, Montpelier (off A38) ☎ (0272) 247870
12–2.30; 6–11 (12–11 Sat)
Halls Harvest Bitter; Ind Coope Burton Ale [H]
Old, 'no-frills', split-level public house serving local cosmopolitan and predominantly young community. WG Grace cricketing connections, as well as ghost in redundant skittle alley. Separate pool room.
▦ ◖ ⇌ (Montpelier) ♣

Park House
154 St John's Lane, Bedminster
☎ (0272) 663905
11–3; 6.30–11
Courage Bitter Ale, Best Bitter [H]
Small, regulars' pub. Lunchtime snacks. ⊟ ♣

Phoenix
15 Wellington Road
☎ (0272) 558327
11.30–11
Draught Bass; Smiles Brewery Bitter [H]; **Wadworth 6X** [G]
Unspoilt corner local close to Broadmead shopping centre. Popular with locals of all ages. Friendly atmosphere. Up to three guest beers.
▦ ⇌ (Temple Meads)

Plough & Windmill
194 West Street, Bedminster
☎ (0272) 663460
11–2.30 (3 Sat); 5.30 (7 Sat) – 11
Courage Best Bitter [H]
Several traditional rooms with sporting themes. Snack bar food only. ▦ ⇌ (Parson Street) ♣ ⌽

Portwall Tavern
Portwall Lane, Redcliffe
☎ (0272) 273998
11–11 (11–2.30; 7–11 Sat)
Courage Best Bitter; John Smith's Bitter [H]
Solid looking, one-bar pub with brass in profusion.
◖ ◗ ♿ ⇌ (Temple Meads) ♣

Pride of the Forest
18 Unity Street, St Phillips
☎ (0272) 298109
11.30–11 (11.30–3; 7–11 Sat)
Wadworth IPA, 6X, Old Timer [H]
Small town pub with food and lots of bar games in aid of charity. A friendly pub worth a visit. No food Sun.
◖ ◗ ⇌ (Temple Meads) ♣

Prince of Wales
Stoke Lane, Westbury-on-Trym
☎ (0272) 623715
11–3; 7–11 (11–11 Sat)
Courage Bitter Ale, Best Bitter, Directors [H]
Friendly pub in residential area with good-size single bar. Guest beer. ♘ ▦ ◖ ♣

Sportsmans Arms
20 Wade Street, St Judes (off B4050) ☎ (0272) 559323
11–3; 6.15–11
Courage Bitter Ale, Best Bitter; John Smith's Bitter [H]
Homely, L-shaped and open-plan local with a pleasing tiled front. Snack-type, with-chips meals (not Sun). Whist played.
▦ ◖ ♣

Star
4–6 North Street, Bedminster
☎ (0272) 663588
11–2.30; 5.30–11
Ind Coope Burton Ale; Smiles Best Bitter [H]
Popular, large, one-bar pub. Two dartboards. Food includes vegetarian dishes. ▦ ◖ ♿ ♣

Victoria
20 Chock Lane, Westbury-on-Trym (off Eastfield Road)
☎ (0272) 500441
11.30–2.30; 5–11
Draught Bass; Hall & Woodhouse Tanglefoot; Wadworth 6X, Old Timer [H]
Popular, warm and friendly pub, comfortably furnished. Out-of-the-way, down a quiet lane. Live music first Sun lunchtime each month. Can get quite crowded. ▦ ◖ ♣

Try also: Swan, Midland Road

Churchill

Crown Inn
Skinners Lane (off A38)
OS447598 ☎ (0934) 852995
11–3; 6–11
Butcombe Bitter; Cornish Vallence's Bitter; Cotleigh Harrier SPA; Exmoor Ale [G]
Cottage-style stone-built pub in quiet lane. Best range of beers in area. Busy. Keg cider from one of the handpumps. Guest beers.
⌂ Q ▦ ◖ ⊟

Try also: Stag & Hounds (Banks's)

Clapton-in-Gordano

Black Horse
OS474741 ☎ (0272) 842105
11–3; 6–11
Courage Bitter Ale, Best Bitter [G]
300 year-old stone built pub, a very friendly centre of village life. History of pub and village in photos on walls.
⌂ Q ♘ ▦ ◖ ♿ ♣ ⌽ P

Clutton Hill

Hunters Rest
King Lane (off A37)
OS633601 ☎ (0761) 52303
11.30–3; 6.30–11
Butcombe Bitter; Draught Bass; Courage Best Bitter; Wadworth 6X [H]
Renovated 16th-century local with figure-of-eight miniature railway in garden.
⌂ ♘ ▦ ◖ ◗ ♿ Λ ♣ P

Compton Martin

Ring O' Bells
☎ (0761) 221284
11.30–2.30; 7–11
Butcombe Bitter; Wadworth 6X [H]
Perfect pub in every way: regulars' bar with pub games; cosy lounge with real log fire; true family room; large garden with children's amenities. Guest beers.
⌂ Q ♘ ▦ ◖ ◗ ⊟ ♿ Λ ♣ P

Try also: New Inn, Blagdon (Wadworth)

Congresbury

White Hart
Wrington Road (A370)
☎ (0934) 833303
11.30–3; 6–11
Butcombe Bitter; Hall & Woodhouse Badger Best Bitter, Tanglefoot; Wadworth 6X [H]
Suburban pub. Table skittles played. ⌂ ♘ ▦ ◖ ◗ ⊟ ♿ ♣ P

Try also: Old Inn (Free)

Engine Common

Cross Keys
North Road (off A482)
☎ (045 422) 314
12–2.30; 6–11
Courage Bitter Ale, Best Bitter, Directors; John Smith's Bitter [H]
17th-century two-bar pub with stone-floored bar. Comfortable village local with lively clientele. Charitable events during year. ⌂ Q ◖ ⊟ ⇌ ♣ P

Frampton Cotterell

Rising Sun
43 Ryecroft Road (off B4058/A432)
☎ (0454) 772330
11.30–3; 7–11
Hall & Woodhouse Tanglefoot; Marston's Pedigree Bitter; Smiles Best Bitter; Wadworth 6X [H]
Small, single-bar pub, a real free house, with a new central

porched entrance. Separate restaurant area. Guest beers. Well worth seeking out. Eve meals Fri/Sat only.
Q ❀ ◖ ◗ ⊟ ♣ P

Try also: Golden Lion (Courage)

Hinton

Bull
(off A46, 1 mile SW of M4 jct 18) ☎ (027 582) 2332
11.30–2.30; 7 (6 summer)–11
Hall & Woodhouse Tanglefoot (summer); **Wadworth IPA, 6X, Old Timer** [H]
Country local with splendid garden for children. Full meals (including veg option) served in lounge. ⌂ Q ♞ ❀ ◖ ◗ ⊟ ⛺ ♣ P

Hinton Charterhouse

Rose & Crown
High Street (B3110)
☎ (022 122) 722153
11.30 (11 Sat)–3; 6–11
Draught Bass; Charrington IPA; Marston's Pedigree Bitter; Wadworth 6X, Old Timer [G]
Comfortable, wood-panelled lounge bar and separate restaurant. Skittles, darts and dominoes. ⌂ ❀ ◖ ◗ ♿ ♣ P

Kelston

Old Crown
On A431 ☎ (0225) 42032
11–2.30 (12–2 Sun); 6.30–11
Draught Bass; Butcombe Bitter; Smiles Best Bitter; Wadworth 6X, Old Timer [H]
Traditional 18th-century coaching inn with flagstoned floor and unusual handpumps. Separate restaurant. Large garden. No lunch Sun.
⌂ Q ❀ ◖ ◗ ♣ P

Kenn

Drum & Monkey
Kenn Street (B3133)
☎ (0272) 873433
11–2.30 (12–2.30 Sun); 6–11
Courage Best Bitter [H]
Pleasant, country two-bar pub near Clevedon. Recent winner of Courage Bristol South Beer and Cellar Award.
Q ❀ ◖ ◗ ⊟ ♣ ○ P

Littleton-on-Severn

White Hart
OS596901 ☎ (0454) 412275
11–2.30; 6–11 (11–11 Sat)
Smiles Brewery Bitter, Best Bitter, Exhibition; Wadworth 6X [H]
16th-century country pub, recently enlarged but maintaining original character. Live jazz Wed eves. Range of traditional games includes boules and table football. Regular guest beer.
⌂ Q ♞ ❀ ◖ ◗ ♣ P

Long Ashton

Angel
172 Long Ashton Road (A370)
☎ (0272) 392244
11–2.30 (3 Sat); 5.30 (6 Sat)–11
Courage Best Bitter, Directors; John Smith's Bitter [H]
Lovely, old, unspoilt village pub with courtyard seating area in summer and blazing log fire in winter. Cosy bar, snug and dining room (children allowed if eating). No meals Sun/Mon eves. ⌂ ❀ ◖ ◗ ⊟

Bird in Hand
17 Weston Road
☎ (0272) 392329
11–2.30 (3 Sat); 6.30–11
Draught Bass; Charrington IPA [H]
Main road, two-bar regulars' pub. Friendly. ❀ ◖ ⊟ ♣ P

Try also: Miners Arms (Courage)

Midford

Hope & Anchor
(B3110) ☎ (0225) 832296
11.30–2.30; 6.30–11
Draught Bass; Butcombe Bitter; Marston's Pedigree Bitter; Wadworth 6X [H]
Nestling between the old Somerset and Dorset railway line and the disused Somerset Coal Canal, a 300 year-old pub with restaurant and small family room. ⌂ ♞ ❀ ◖ ◗ P

Midsomer Norton

White Hart
The Island (off B3355)
☎ (0761) 412957
11–3; 5.30–11
Draught Bass; Charrington IPA [G]
Victorian establishment with many rooms. Old mining relics and local photographs adorn the walls. A minor classic. Taunton cider on gravity dispense. No Sun lunch. ♞ ◖ ⊟ ♿ ♣ ○

Oldbury-on-Severn

Anchor Inn
Church Road
☎ (0454) 413331
11.30–2.30 (3 Sat); 6.30 (6 Sat)–11
Draught Bass [G]; **Butcombe Bitter; Hook Norton Best Bitter; Marston's Pedigree Bitter; Theakston Best Bitter** [H], **Old Peculier** [G]
Excellent two-bar village pub in pleasant surroundings. Interesting and varied meals with local flavour. Beer is among the cheapest in Avon but no compromise on quality. Traditional pub games played.
⌂ Q ❀ ◖ ◗ ⊟ ♿ ♣ P

Oldland Common

Crown & Horseshoe
North Street (off A4175)
OS672718 ☎ (0272) 323165
11–2.30; 6.30–11
Courage Bitter Ale, Best Bitter [H]
'Olde-worlde', cottage-style pub at the back of village. Brass in abundance. Q ❀ ⊟ ♿ ♣ P

Paulton

Red Lion
High Street (B3355)
☎ (0761) 412157
11–3; 6–11
Ind Coope Burton Ale; Tetley Bitter; Wadworth 6X [H]
A friendly, spacious pub with large games area. Serves Taunton cider. No food Sun.
◖ ◗ ⊟ ♣ ○ P

Pill

Star Inn
Bank Place ☎ (027 581) 4926
11–2.30; 6 (7 Sat)–11
Butcombe Bitter; Smiles Best Bitter, Exhibition; Tetley Bitter [H]
One-room village pub with a relaxed and friendly atmosphere. Wood panelling and stone interior. Live folk and blues groups Wed eves. Guest beers. ⌂ ◖ ♣

Pilning

Plough Inn
Pilning Street (off B4055)
☎ (045 45) 2556
11–2.30; 6.30–11
Draught Bass; Wadworth IPA, 6X [H], **Farmer's Glory, Old Timer** [G]
Large two-roomed pub with children's room. Out-of-town mixture of new and old decor. Friendly atmosphere.
⌂ ♞ ❀ ◖ ◗ ⊟ ♣ P

Pucklechurch

Rose & Crown
Parkfield Road (off B4465)
☎ (027 582) 2351
11–3; 6 (7 Sat)–11
Draught Bass; Hall & Woodhouse Tanglefoot; Wadworth IPA, 6X [H], **Old Timer** [G]
Two-bar 'olde-worlde' pub with a side hatch in front lounge. Attractive village local, decorated with horse brasses and popular in evenings. Separate restaurant. Large car park. ⌂ ❀ ◖ ◗ ⊟ ♣ ○ P

Radstock

Waldegrave Arms
Market Place (A367)
☎ (0761) 34359
11–2.30 (3.30 Fri & Sat); 6–11
Courage Best Bitter; John Smith's Bitter Ⓗ
Spacious, main-road hotel with two very different bars. No eve meals on Sun. Q ⛼ ◐ ◑ ⊞ ♣ P

Thornbury

Knot of Rope
High Street ☎ (0454) 412147
11–11
Banks's Mild, Bitter; Hanson's Bitter Ⓔ
Well-appointed pub, reputedly haunted and complete with secret tunnels. Large public bar. Full menu, bar meals and an eating area. Very cheap beer for the area. ⌂ ◐ ⊞ P

Timsbury

Seven Stars
North Road (B3115)
☎ (0761) 70398
11.30–2.30; 7–11
Courage Best Bitter Ⓗ & Ⓖ
Pleasant split-level village local. Separate pool room.
⌂ ✿ ⊞ ♣ ⚘ P

Tolldown

Crown
On A46, ½ mile from M4 jct 18
☎ (0225) 891231
11–2.30; 6–11 (11–11 summer)
Wadworth IPA, 6X, Old Timer Ⓗ
16th-century, Cotswold-stone roadside inn, handy for visiting nearby Durham House and deer park. No eve meals Sun/Mon.
⌂ ✿ ◐ ◑ ⊞ ♣ P

West End

Blue Flame
Off A38 near Nailsea
OS690449 ☎ (0272) 856910
11–3; 6–11 (11–11 Sat)
Draught Bass; Smiles Best Bitter, Exhibition Ⓗ
An unpretentious early 19th-century building set slightly back from the lane. A small public bar with very basic furniture and decoration and an open fire. Small separate room. Genuine rural pub, often busy with local farmers.
⌂ Q ♨ ✿ ♿ ⛺ ♣ ⚘ P

Weston-Super-Mare

Major from Glengarry
10–14 Upper Church Road
☎ (0934) 629594
11.30–3; 6–11 (11–11 Sat in summer)
Draught Bass; Butcombe Bitter; Wadworth 6X, Farmer's Glory, Old Timer Ⓗ
Large open-plan inn with well defined eating and play areas. Friendly licensees. Traditional pub games played. Quizzes. Guest beers. ♨ ◐ ◑ ♣

Wick

Rose & Crown
High Street (A420)
☎ (027582) 2198
11.30–2.30; 5.30–11
Courage Best Bitter, Directors; John Smith's Bitter; Wadworth 6X Ⓗ
Comfortable and spacious old inn (circa 1640). Old photographs and bric-a-brac of the area depict a bygone era. Splendid period restaurant with varied, sensibly-priced menu.
⌂ Q ✿ ◐ ◑ ⊞ ♿ P

Willsbridge

Queens Head
Willsbridge Hill, Bath Road, (A431, 150 yds NW of A4175 jct) ☎ (0272) 322233
11–2.30; 6.30–11
Courage Bitter Ale, Best Bitter Ⓗ
Delightfully unspoilt, multi-roomed, wood-panelled 17th-century local near Bitton Steam Railway and Willsbridge Mill. Snacks only. Car park 25 yds down road. Q ♨ ⊞ ♣ P

Winterbourne Down

Golden Heart
Down Road ☎ (0454) 773152
11–3; 5–11 (11–11 Sat)
Courage Best Bitter, Directors Ⓗ
Recently renovated, 400 year-old coaching inn. Separate restaurant. ⌂ Q ✿ ◐ ◑ ♿ P

Worle

Nut Tree
Ebdon Road (1 mile from M5 jct 21) ☎ (0934) 510900
11–3; 5.30–11 (11–11 Fri & Sat)
Brains SA; Theakston Best Bitter; Wadworth 6X; Younger Scotch Ⓗ
Large, converted stone farmhouse with spacious open-plan interior and friendly atmosphere. Very varied menu, including home-made ice cream.
⌂ Q ♨ ✿ ◐ ◑ ⊞ ♿ ♣ P

OPENING HOURS

The law regarding opening hours was relaxed, not before time, in 1988. Now pubs in England and Wales may open at any time during the permitted hours of 11am to 11pm (earlier opening is allowed by some local licensing districts). Sunday hours are standard: 12–3 and 7–10.30. The opening hours given for each pub description are correct at the time of going to press. However, publicans are at liberty to take advantage of the new flexibility and may stay open longer than hours shown, or indeed close during the afternoons without prior notice. Where Sunday hours differ from those given above, this is noted. The Scottish licensing laws are more generous as far as opening is concerned and pubs may stay open longer.

Bedfordshire

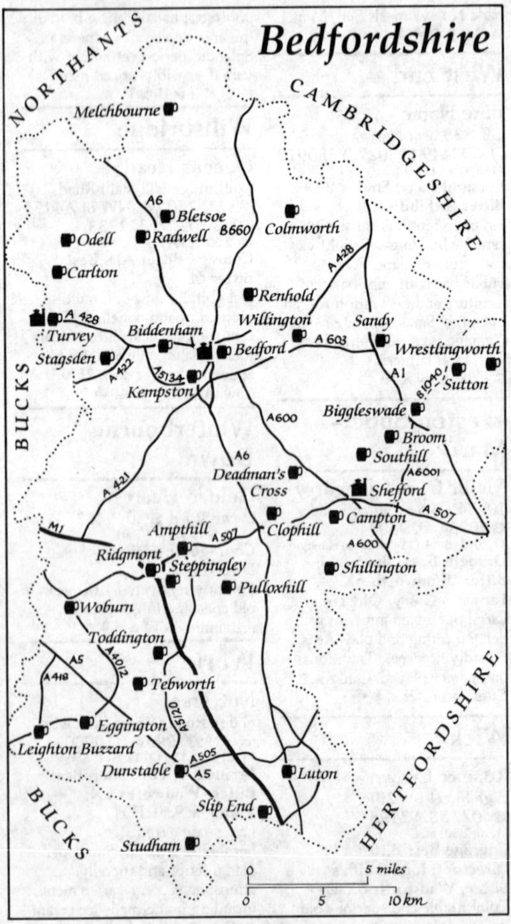

Banks & Taylor, *Shefford*; **Nix Wincott**, *Turvey*; **Charles Wells**, *Bedford*

Ampthill

Old Sun

87 Dunstable Street (A5120)
☎ (0525) 403101
11–2.30 (2 Mon); 6–11
Banks & Taylor SOS; Marston's Pedigree Bitter; Whitbread Wethered Bitter, Flowers Original H
Two small, attractive bars and separate games room. Neat, pretty garden to rear. Mainly used by younger customers, the pub has strong sporting connections (Ampthill rugby club drinks here). No food weekends. Whitbread guest beer. P

Bedford

Clarence

13 St John's Street (A6)
☎ (0234) 52781
11–3; 5.30–11 (11–11 Sat)
Benskins Best Bitter H
Large town pub with quiet lounge and games-oriented public bar. Good value bar meals (Mon-Sat). Open all day if busy. ≠ (St John's) P

Fleur de Lis

12 Mill Street (off A6)
☎ (0234) 211004
10.30–2.30 (3 Sat); 5.30 (7 Sat)–11
Charles Wells Eagle Bitter H
Well-run town pub with excellent social mix. Parking difficult lunchtimes. No food Sun.

Flowerpot

25 Tavistock Street (A6/A428 jct) ☎ (0234) 56565
11–11
Greene King IPA, Abbot Ale H
Oldest pub in Bedford (1595), featuring original ship's beam. Coaching stables at rear and award-winning garden. Good bar food available, except Sun lunch and Fri–Sun eve.

Biddenham

Three Tuns

Main Road (village loop S of A428) OS022499
☎ (0234) 54847
11.30–2.30; 6–11
Greene King IPA, Abbot Ale H
Delightful village inn with excellent range of home-cooked food. Children permitted in dining area. Large garden with play area. Skittles played. No food on Sun. P

Biggleswade

White Hart

Market Square
☎ (0767) 314219
11–2.30 (3.30 Thu-Fri, 4.30 Sat); 5.30 (7 Sat)–11
Greene King IPA, Abbot Ale H
Old, oak-beamed, low-roofed pub in corner of market square.
Q ≠ P

Bletsoe

Falcon

Rushden Road (A6)
☎ (0234) 781222
11–2.30; 5.30–11
Charles Wells Eagle Bitter, Bombardier H
17th-century coaching inn with large riverside garden and play area. Families welcome. Landlord flies the flag outside and hates plastic!
Q P

Broom

Cock

High Street (100 yds N of B658) ☎ (0767) 314411
12–2.30 (incl. Sun); 6–11
Greene King IPA, Abbot Ale G
Multi-roomed village local with beer served direct from cellar. Separate skittles room. No food Sun eve. P

Campton

White Hart

Mill Lane (off A507)
☎ (0462) 812657
11.30–3; 7–11 (11–11 Sat)
Charles Wells Eagle Bitter, Bombardier H
Popular one-bar village pub with comfortable sitting-room-style lounge end. Public end has flagstone floor and huge

fireplace. Petanque played in summer. Varied menu; no food Sun lunchtime. Regular guest beers. ⌂ ❀ ◖ ◗ ♿ ♣ P

Carlton

Fox
High Street (3 miles N of A428 at Turvey) OS953553
☎ (0234) 720235
10.30–2.30; 6–11
Adnams Broadside; Charles Wells Eagle Bitter 🄷
18th-century, friendly, thatched village inn with excellent restaurant and bar food. Near Harrold Country Wildlife Park. No food Sun eve or Mon.
Q ❀ ◖ ◗ P

Try also: Royal Oak (Banks & Taylor)

Clophill

Stone Jug
Back Street (2nd right N of A6/A507 roundabout)
☎ (0525) 60526
11–3; 6–11
Banks & Taylor Shefford Bitter; Courage Directors; John Smith's Bitter 🄷
Deservedly popular free house with amiable atmosphere and competitive prices. No food on Sun. Guest beers always available. ⌂ ⛼ ❀ ◖ ♣ P

Colmworth

Wheatsheaf
Wilden Road (off B660) OS101574 ☎ (023062) 370
11–2.30; 6–11
Adnams Bitter; Draught Bass; Marston's Pedigree Bitter 🄷
17th-century country pub to south of village. Separate restaurant and bar menu includes exotic sausages. Children's play area in garden. Very low beams in bar – mind your head! Guest beers.
⌂ Q ❀ ◖ ◗ ⊟ ♣ P

Deadman's Cross

White Horse
Deadman's Cross (A600)
☎ (023066) 634
12–3 (2.30 winter); 5.30 (7 Sat & winter)–11 (12–3; 7.30–10.30 Sun)
Banks & Taylor Shefford Bitter, SOS 🄷
Friendly roadside pub with excellent food in bar and restaurant. Book-lined bar with inglenook fireplace. Disabled access is via front door. No meals Mon eve.
⌂ Q ⛼ ❀ ◖ ◗ ♿ P

Dunstable

Bull
115 High Street North (A5)
☎ (0582) 663443
11–11
Courage Best Bitter, Directors 🄷
Cosy one-bar pub with darts, dominoes and crib. Live music on Tue eve. Home of Rocky, the dart-fetching dog. No meals at weekend. ❀ ◖ ♣ P

Highwayman Hotel
London Road (A5)
☎ (0582) 61999
11–2.30; 6–11
Charles Wells Eagle Bitter, Bombardier 🄷
Spacious, comfortable lounge bar attached to hotel. Locals' public bar. Separate restaurant.
❀ ⛹ ◖ ◗ ⊟ ♿ ♣ P

Try also: Star & Garter (Courage)

Eggington

Horseshoes
Off A4012 OS956252
☎ (0525) 210282
11.30–2 (3 Sat); 6–11
Benskins Best Bitter 🄷
Basic public and cosy saloon adorned with transport paraphernalia and much brass. Small snug reached by flight of stairs. Has electric organ. No Sun lunch. ⌂ Q ⛼ ❀ ◖ ⊟ ♣ P

Kempston

Wellington
16 Bedford Road (B531)
☎ (0234) 50975
12–3; 6 (7 Sat)–11
Adnams Broadside; Charles Wells Eagle Bitter 🄷
Traditional corner local on main road, with variety of good food. No meals Sun eve. ❀ ◖ ◗ ⊟

Leighton Buzzard

Ashwell Arms
Ashwell Street (off A418)
☎ (0525) 372080
11–2.30; 5.30–11 (11–11 Sat)
Adnams Broadside; Charles Wells Eagle Bitter 🄷
Recent modest refurbishment suits pub well. Comfortable and cosy public bar with games annexe. Very quiet saloon bar.
⌂ Q ⊟ ♣

Golden Bell
Church Square
☎ (0525) 373330
11–3; 5–11
ABC Best Bitter; Wadworth 6X 🄷
Old town-centre pub decked out in Laura Ashley and illuminated in 30s style. Popular with all ages and never too crowded. ◖ ≹

Star
Heath Road (A418)
☎ (0525) 377294
11–2.30; 6–11
ABC Best Bitter; Draught Bass; Wadworth 6X 🄷
Very comfortable pub, crowded lunchtimes by the business community; quieter but still busy in evenings. Interesting sewing machine tables and cricket bats. Very small car park. A pub to take your Mum and Dad to! Q ❀ ◖ ◗ ♣ P

Try also: Sun (Courage)

Luton

Gardeners Call
151 Hightown Road
☎ (0582) 29037
11–3; 5.30–11
Greene King XX Dark, IPA, Abbot Ale 🄷
Two-bar town pub with contrasting saloon and public bars and a strong local following. Meals Mon-Fri.
❀ ◖ ⊟ ≹ ♣ P

George II
70 Bute Street
☎ (0582) 28916
11–11
Greene King IPA, Abbot Ale 🄷
Busy town-centre pub, handy for bus and rail travellers and Arndale shoppers. Quiz night Mon; live music most Sun eves. No meals Sun lunch. ◖ ≹ ♣

Two Brewers
43 Dumfries Street
☎ (0582) 23777
11.30–2.30 (3 Fri, 4 Sat); 5.30 (7 Sat)–11
Banks & Taylor Shefford Bitter, SOS, SOD 🄷
Lively locals' pub just off town centre; popular with builders, bikers and bank managers! Back yard for outside drinking.
❀ ◖ ♿ ♣

Try also: Bricklayers Arms (B&T); **Mother Redcap** (Greene King)

Melchbourne

St John's Arms
Knotting Road (off A6) OS030663 ☎ (0234) 708238
11–4; 6–11
Greene King IPA, Abbot Ale 🄷
Former gamekeeper's lodge with fine collection of jugs and a warm welcome. Flexible about afternoon closure – knock if pub seems closed. Separate pool room in converted barn; occasional garden barbecues in summer. ⌂ ⛼ ❀ ◖ ◗ ⛺ ♣ P

Odell

Mad Dog
Little Odell OS955575

Bedfordshire

☎ (0234) 720221
11–2.30; 6–11
Greene King IPA, Abbot Ale [H]
Thatched pub near Harrold-Odell Country Park. Reputed ghost near inglenook and children's roundabout in garden. Home-cooked food includes veg dishes. ♛ Q ❀ ◖ ◗ P

Try also: Bell (Greene King)

Pulloxhill

Cross Keys
High Street ☎ (0525) 712442
11–2.30; 6–11
Adnams Broadside; Charles Wells Eagle Bitter [H]
15th-century pub with small traditional bar at front and large restaurant of rather more recent construction at rear. Popular for good value food. Jazz evening on Sun. Large grounds entertain such unusual activities as archery and ballooning.
♛ Q ❀ ◖ ◗ ♿ ▲ P

Radwell

Swan
Felmersham Road OS004575
☎ (0234) 781351
12–2.30; 6.30–11 (closed Sun eve)
Charles Wells Eagle Bitter, Bombardier [H]
17th-century thatched country inn with restaurant and quiet bar. High quality food includes veg choice. ♛ Q ❀ ◖ ◗ P

Renhold

Three Horseshoes
42 Top End (1 mile N of A428)
☎ (0234) 870218
10.30–2.30; 6–11 (11–11 Sat)
Greene King XX Dark, IPA, Abbot Ale [H]
Friendly village pub with children's play area in garden. No meals Tue eve or Sun.
♛ Q ❀ ◖ ◗ ⊟ ♣ P

Ridgmont

Rose & Crown
89 High Street (A418, near M1 jct 13) ☎ (052528) 245
10–3; 5.30 (6 winter)–11
Adnams Broadside; Mansfield Riding Traditional Bitter; Charles Wells Eagle Bitter [H]
Popular, friendly pub and restaurant, with separate games area. Set in large grounds, with barbecues in summer. Lounge is famous for its Rupert Bear theme. Booking advised for restaurant. ♛ ❀ ≍ ◖ ◗ ⊟ ▲ ♣ P

Sandy

Bell
Station Road (50 yds S of B1042) ☎ (0767) 80267
11–2.30 (3 Fri & Sat); 5.30–11
Greene King IPA, Abbot Ale [H]
Friendly one-bar local opposite station. Handy for RSPB HQ at Sandy Lodge. No meals Sun.
♛ ❀ ◖ ◗ ⇌ ♣ P

Try also: Lord Nelson (Whitbread)

Shillington

Musgrave Arms
Apsley End Road
☎ (0462) 711286
11–3; 6–11
Greene King IPA, Abbot Ale [G]
Two tiny bars, each with a huge fireplace. The lounge has low beams; public has clay tile floors and scrubbed tables. Restaurant open Thu–Sat eves – good value 'specials' Tue and Wed. No meals Mon eve or Sun.
♛ Q ❀ ◖ ◗ ⊟ ♿ ♣ P

Try also: Crown (Whitbread)

Slip End

Frog & Rhubarb
Church Road
☎ (0582) 452722
12–3; 5.30–11
Adnams Bitter; Greene King IPA, Abbot Ale [H]
Large split-level pub. Live music on Sat eves. ❀ ◖ ◗ ♣ P

Southill

White Horse
High Road (1 mile W of B658)
☎ (0462) 813364
11–3; 6–11
Whitbread Flowers IPA, Wethered Bitter [H]
Large country inn with restaurant. Miniature railway in garden. Two function rooms include a banqueting suite. Children welcome in restaurant. Brief walk from Southill Park cricket ground. Shove-ha'penny played. No meals Sun eve.
♛ ❀ ◖ ◗ ⊟ ♣ P

Stagsden

Royal George
High Street (A422) OS982490
☎ (02302) 2801
11–2.30; 6 (7 Sat & winter)–11
Adnams Broadside; Charles Wells Eagle Bitter [H]
Friendly village pub with large garden (including livestock), near well-known bird gardens. Ale brought to lounge from public bar. Menu caters for vegetarians. Lunchtime meals, except Mon: eve meals Thu and Fri only. ♛ ❀ ◖ ◗ ⊟ ▲ P

Steppingley

French Horn
5 Church Road
☎ (0525) 712051
12–3; 7 (6.30 Sat)–11
ABC Best Bitter; Draught Bass; Tetley Bitter; Wadworth 6X [H]
Old inn (parts date from 14th century) with public bar somewhat dominated by pool table. Larger, L-shaped lounge bar and separate restaurant (booking advised). Restaurant closed Sun eve and Mon; no bar meals weekend eves. Food highly recommended. Guest beer occasionally.
♛ Q ❀ ◖ ◗ ⊟ ♣ P

Studham

Red Lion
Church Road
☎ (0582) 872530
11–3; 6–11 (11–11 Sat)
Adnams Bitter; Courage Directors; Hook Norton Old Hookey; Ruddles Best Bitter, County; Theakston Best Bitter [H]
Comfortable and friendly one-bar pub overlooking the common. Bar billiards. Monthly quiz eve. Good range of home-cooked, good value food.
♛ Q ❀ ◖ ◗ ♣ P

Sutton

John O'Gaunt
High Street OS222474
☎ (0767) 260377
12–2.30; 7–11 (may vary)
Greene King IPA [H]
Attractive country village pub near golf course, with good range of bar food (not Sun). Boules court in garden.
Q ❀ ◖ ◗ ⊟ ♣ P

Tebworth

Queens Head
The Lane ☎ (05255) 4101
11–3 (3.30 Sat); 6 (7 Sat)–11
Adnams Broadside [G]; **Charles Wells Eagle Bitter** [H], **Bombardier** [G]
Two small bars, popular with locals and visitors alike. Very hospitable and entertaining. Weekly sing-songs. Broadside and Bombardier alternate. No meals Sun. ♛ ❀ ◖ ⊟ ♣ P

Try also: Plough, Wingfield (Free)

Toddington

Bedford Arms
64 High Street (A5120)
☎ (05255) 2401
11–3; 6–11
Charles Wells Eagle Bitter [H]
Attractive pub both outside and in, with magnificent rambling garden to the rear. Two warm and comfortable lounge bars.

Can be crowded at weekends.
♜ ❀ ◖ P

Oddfellows Arms
Conger Lane (village green)
☎ (05255) 2021
11–3; 6–11
Benskins Best Bitter; Ind Coope Burton Ale; Tetley Bitter ⊞
Attractive 15th-century pub with hanging baskets. Three bars, ranging from the two-tabled public to the immaculate Croft Bar, with its gallery and huge open fire. Pavement tables for summer drinking.
♜ ❀ ◖ ⊟ ♣

Sow & Pigs
19 Church Square (A5120)
☎ (05255) 3089
11–11
Greene King XX Dark, IPA, Abbot Ale ⊞
Village institution, rich in atmosphere and full of colourful characters. Appealingly chaotic interior is somewhat haphazardly furnished; features include piano and harmonium. Pigs (even flying ones) everywhere! 'Pig Snout' game played. No food Sun. Car park via Park Road and St George's Close. ♜ Q ❀ ◖ ♣ P

Try also: Angel (Whitbread)

Turvey

Three Fyshes
Bridge Street (A428)
☎ (023064) 264
11.30–3; 5.30–11
Marston's Pedigree Bitter, Owd Rodger; Nix Wincott Two Henrys, Old Nix ⊞
17th-century beamed and flagstoned, riverside free house. Brewery on site brews for pub and local free trade. Wide range of food; easy-going atmosphere with many house pets in evidence (visiting hounds also welcome). Hood skittles played.
♜ ❀ ◖ ◗ ⊟ ♣ ⊖ P

Willington

Crown
17 Station Road (off A603)
☎ (0234) 838308
12–2.30; 6.30–11
Greene King IPA, Abbot Ale ⊞
Warm, welcoming one-bar village pub near National Trust dovecote and lock on River Ouse. Aviary in garden. No meals Mon eve. ♜ ❀ ◖ ◗ ♣ P

Woburn

Magpie
Bedford Street (A418)
☎ (0525) 290219
12–2.30 (3 Sat); 6–11
Ruddles Best Bitter, County; Webster's Yorkshire Bitter ⊞
Old coaching inn with basic but comfortable public and tiny lounge bar. Restaurant with excellent food. Entry to car park not recommended for large cars! Guest beer. Q ❀ ⛟ ◖ ◗ ⊟ P

Royal Oak
George Street
☎ (0525) 290610
11–3; 5.30–11 (11–11 Sat)
Greene King IPA, Abbot Ale ⊞
Multi-roomed pub with low rafters. Usually packed. Emphasis on food. Q ❀ ◖ ◗ ♣

Try also: Black Horse (Free)

Wrestlingworth

Chequers
High Street (B1042)
☎ (076723) 256
11–2.30; 6–11
Greene King IPA, Abbot Ale ⊞
Brass-bedecked old village pub with large open fire. Dining area with home-cooked food; large garden with aviary and children's log cabin. No meals Sun eve. ♜ Q ❀ ◖ ◗ ♿ P

DISPENSE METHODS

Air pressure: means of forcing beer to the bar using an air compressor. Popular in Scotland.

Beer Engine another name for the handpump.

Economiser: a beer serving device in which any beer which spills over the glass during serving is returned to the cask and recycled. Familiar amongst Tetley drinkers in the North; unpopular with Health and Safety officials. Also known as the Autovac.

Electric Pump: means of drawing beer to the bar without manual effort. Often serves half a pint for each push of the button. Seen mostly in the North, the Midlands and throughout the club scene.

Gravity: means of serving beer by allowing it to pour directly from the cask into the glass.

Handpump: a manual device for drawing beer from the cask. A distinctive and characterful sight on the British pub bar.

Sparkler: a device which is fitted to the beer tap to produce a tight foaming head. Mostly seen in northern outlets.

Top Pressure: means of forcing beer to the point of sale with carbon dioxide.

Berkshire

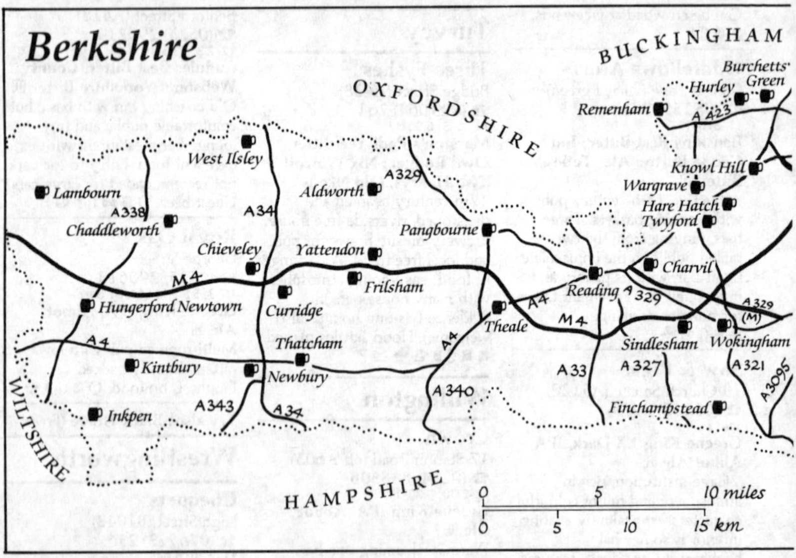

Aldworth

Bell
Off B4009 OS557797
☎ (0635) 578272
11–3; 6–11 (not Mon)
Arkell's 3B Best Bitter, Kingsdown Ale; Hall & Woodhouse Badger Best Bitter; Morrells Dark ⊞
Dates from 1340 in parts. Has been in the same family for 250 years. Old-fashioned, untouched hatch bar and original tap room with one-handed clock. Popular with walkers starting nearby Ridgeway walk. Try the filled hot rolls. Families welcome in tap room. ⛫ Q ◉ ⊟ ♣ P

Try also: Four Points (Free)

Bracknell

Royal Oak
Bay Road, Bullbrook (A329)
☎ (0344) 483865
11–3 (4 Sat); 5.30 (7 Sat)–11
Courage Best Bitter, Directors ⊞
Clean, one-bar town pub, with low ceiling and piped music. Limited menu eves. ◉ ◗ ♣ P

Burchetts Green

Red Lion
Applehouse Hill (A423)
☎ (062882) 4433
11–11
Brakspear Bitter, Special, Old Ale ⊞
Two-bar country pub with a friendly, intimate atmosphere. Has been a public house since 1750. Plenty of seating on front terrace for warm summer eves. Undergoing major internal changes in 1990. ⛫ Q ◉ ◖ ◗ P

Chaddleworth

Ibex
3 miles off A338
☎ (048 82) 311
11–2.30; 6.30–11
Courage Best Bitter, Directors ⊞
Lovely, cosy, unspoiled country pub with three small bars. Landlord is an ex-National Hunt jockey, consequently many customers are from the racing world. Reasonable, varied food. Large car park. Pretty walled garden. ⛫ Q ◉ ◖ ◗ ⊟ ♣ P

Charvil

Lands End
Lands End Lane (1 mile along Park Lane, off A3032)
OS781748 ☎ (0734) 340700
10–2.30 (4 Sat); 6–11
Brakspear Bitter, Special, Old Ale ⊞
Excellent pre-war pub surrounded by narrow lanes. Large garden with play equipment leads down to river. Small family room. No meals Sun. ⛴ ◉ ◖ ⊟ ♣ P

Chieveley

Wheatsheaf
High Street (½ mile from M4 jct 13) ☎ (0635) 248378
11.30–2.30; 6.30 (7 Sat) –11
Morland Original Bitter, Old Masters ⊞
Jovial village pub frequented by sporting fraternity. One bar split into two sections. Opening hours often extended by popular demand! Wholesome food at reasonable prices. Bar billiards. ⛫ ◉ ◖ ⛺ ♣ P

Cookham

Railway Tavern
Lower Road, Cookham Rise (next to station, 400 yds off B4447) ☎ (06285) 29519
10.30–2.30 (3 Sat & Sun); 5.30 (6 Sat)–11
Marston's Pedigree Bitter; Whitbread Wethered Bitter, Wethered Winter Royal ⊞
Two-bar local. The saloon bar and dining area are adorned with steam loco pictures. No meals Sun. Bar skittles played. ◉ ◖ ◗ ⊟ ♿ ⇌ ♣ P

Try also: Crown (Courage)

Curridge

Bunk
400 yds off B4009
☎ (0635) 200400
11–2.30; 6–11
Adnams Bitter; Arkell's 3B Best Bitter; Morland Original Bitter; Theakston XB ⊞
Cosy, open-plan pub with separate restaurant. Close to M4 jct 13. Good home-cooked food and a relaxing atmosphere. No meals Sun eves. ⛫ Q ◉ ◖ ◗ P

Eton

Crown & Cushion
High Street ☎ (0753) 861531
11–3; 5.30–11 (11–11 Sat, & Fri in summer)
Courage Best Bitter, Directors; John Smith's Bitter ⊞
500 year-old original building. The cosy saloon has an intimate

snug bar at the rear. Popular at lunchtime when food is good value (home-made dishes; meals till 8pm; no meals Sun). Quieter eves. Wonderful coal fire. ⌂ Q ❀ ⌸ ◐ ◑ ⊟ ♿ ⇌ (Windsor) ♣ P

Watermans Arms
Brocas Street (behind College boat house, 50 yds from bridge)
☎ (0753) 861001
10.30–3; 5.30–11 (11–11 Fri & Sat)
Courage Best Bitter, Directors; John Smith's Bitter [H]
Single-bar pub with low, beamed ceiling and many rowing pictures. Conservatory (suitable for children) looks out onto courtyard patio area where barbecues are held in summer. Good value food.
⌂ ⛀ ❀ ◐ ◑ ♿ ⇌ (Windsor) ♣

Eton Wick

Pickwick
32 Eton Wick Road (B3026)
☎ (0753) 861713
11–2.30; 5.30–11
Young's Bitter, Special, Winter Warmer [H]
The most westerly of the Young's houses, this comfortable village local lies at the Eton end of the village. Devil-Among-the-Tailors game played. Meals Wed eve.
❀ ◐ ♣ P

Finchampstead

Queens Oak
Church Lane (Off B3016)
OS793639 ☎ (0734) 734855
11–2.30 (3 summer); 6–11 (varies Sat)
Brakspear Bitter, Special, Old Ale [H]
Old pub on Devil's Highway. Interesting collection of old bills and photos of early times of the pub in small no-smoking snug. Large lounge with TV. Pizzas are a speciality. No food Sun.
⌂ ❀ ◐ ◑ ▲ P

Frilsham

Pot Kiln
On Yattendon to Bucklebury Road ☎ (0635) 201366
12–2.30; 6.30–11
Arkell's 3B Best Bitter; Morland Original Bitter; Ringwood Fortyniner [H]
Remote country pub with excellent views. Built on site of old brick kilns which were closed after the war. Popular with walkers. Live folk music Sun eve. No meals Mon eve or Sun. Hot rolls available at all times. ⌂ Q ⛀ ❀ ◐ ◑ ⊟ P

Hare Hatch

Queen Victoria
Blakes Lane (just off A4 towards Upper Wargrave) OS809783
☎ (0734) 402477
12–3; 5.30–11
Brakspear XXX Mild, Bitter, Special, Old Ale [H]
Convivial, low-ceilinged 17th-century country pub. Always busy but saved from closure some years ago by local CAMRA action. Imaginative home-cooked food always available. ⌂ Q ❀ ◐ ◑ ♣ P

Holyport

Belgian Arms
Holyport Street
☎ (0628) 34468
11–2.30; 5.30–11
Brakspear Bitter, Special, Old Ale [H]
Ancient wisteria-clad village local tucked away just off the green. Formerly known as the 'Eagle' or 'Prussian Eagle', it was renamed during WWI to avoid suggestion of Prussian support. Superior garden overlooking the pond houses children's play equipment. No meals Sun eve.
⌂ Q ❀ ◐ ◑ ♿ P

Rising Sun
Forest Green Row
☎ (0628) 23639
11–2.30 (3 Fri & Sat); 5–11
Morland Original Bitter, Old Masters [H]
Deservedly popular country local, converted from two gamekeepers' cottages. Two bars: traditional public and comfy, cosy lounge. Hearty weekday lunches and friendly service. Excellent value for the area. ⌂ Q ❀ ◐ ⊟ ♣ P

Try also: Red Lion, Oakley Green (Benskins)

Hungerford Newtown

Tally Ho
Wantage Road (A338 ½ mile S M4 jct 14) ☎ (0488) 682312
11–2.30; 6–11
Wadworth IPA, 6X [H], **Old Timer** [G]
Comfortable, friendly pub of late Victorian period. Frequented by locals and passers-by. ⌂ Q ❀ ◐ ◑ P

Hurley

Black Boy
Henley Road (A423)
☎ (062882) 4212
11–2.30 (3 Sat); 6–11
Brakspear Bitter, Old Ale [H]
16th-century pub with single bar which has a beamed ceiling, small bar counter and a large stove to one end. Emphasis on home-cooked food. Pub name relates to Charles II.
⌂ Q ❀ ⌸ ◐ ◑ ▲ P

Inkpen

Swan
Craven Road, Lower Inkpen OS359643 ☎ (04884) 326
11.30–2.30; 6.30–11 (not Mon)
Brakspear Bitter; Bunces Old Smokey; Hook Norton Best Bitter; Whitbread Flowers Original [H]
Large 16th-century inn near famous Combe Gibbet. Excellent menu features English and Singaporean dishes (not Sun). Three open fires. Guest beers. ⌂ Q ❀ ◐ ◑ ♣ P

Kintbury

Blue Ball
High Street (off A4)
☎ (0488) 58515
11–2.30; 6–11 (11–11 Sat)
Courage Best Bitter; John Smith's Bitter [H]
Beams, brick, wood panels, a warm welcome and a fire to match in this typical, busy village pub. Dogs permitted on lead, but no children inside. Small car park.
⌂ Q ❀ ◐ ⊟ ♿ ⇌ ♣ P

Try also: Dundas Arms (Free)

Knowl Hill

Seven Stars
Bath Road (A4)
☎ (062882) 2967
11–3; 5.30–11
Brakspear XXX Mild, Bitter, Special, Old Ale [H]
Large 16th-century coaching inn with skittle alley. Good for wedding receptions. Always a

warm welcome. Family room till 9pm. No meals Mon eve.
▲ Q ♞ ✿ ⇔ ◖ ◗ ♣ P

Lambourn

George Hotel
High Street ☎ (0488) 71889
10.30–3; 6–11
Arkell's 3B Best Bitter, Kingsdown Ale (winter) [H]
Smart, friendly pub with three drinking areas in famous racing village. Opens at 8.30am for breakfasts. Excellent plain food. Collection of copper measures, from ½ gill to one gallon. Eve meals by arrangement.
✿ ⇔ ◖ ♣ P

Try also: Wheelwrights Arms (Morland)

Langley

Harrow
High Street ☎ (0753) 43700
11–3; 5 (6.30 Sat)–11
Courage Best Bitter, Directors [H]
300 year-old former coaching inn in village. A genuine two-bar local. Welcoming licensee and friendly staff serve a boisterous public and a cosy, intimate lounge. Don't trust the clock in the lounge!
✿ ◖ ◗ ⊞ ♿ ⇄ ♣ P

Maidenhead

North Star
Westborough Road (off A4 at W end of town)
☎ (0628) 22711
11–2.30; 6–11
Courage Best Bitter [H]
Small, two-bar pub much used by local community. Note old Nickolson price list in the public bar. The pub's name recalls the first loco to reach Maidenhead (1835). Q ⊞ ♣

Try also: Albion (Courage)

Newbury

Bacon Arms Hotel
10 Oxford Street (100 yds from clock tower)
☎ (0635) 31822
11–2.30; 5.30 (6.30 Sat)–11
Courage Best Bitter, Directors [H]
A well-run pub and hotel with a quiet and relaxing atmosphere. A popular lunchtime venue for business people. ▲ ✿ ⇔ ◖ ◗ P

Red House
12 Hampton Road (go to St John's roundabout on the Andover Road and then ask!)
☎ (0635) 30584
12–3; 7–11
Archers Best Bitter; Marston's Pedigree Bitter [H]
Hard-to-find rambling pub in converted house between Baptist chapel and undertakers. Much-loved by its regulars. NB Do not confuse with pub of same name just west of town. Occasional live music. ⇄ ♣

Try also: Catherine Wheel (Courage)

Old Windsor

Oxford Blue
Crimp Hill (off A308)
☎ (0753) 861954
11–11
Friary Meux Best Bitter; Ind Coope Burton Ale; Tetley Bitter [H]
Building over 300 years-old with a back bar full of airline memorabilia. Has been local CAMRA Pub of the Year. Good value, home-cooked food. Pub's name has military connections.
Q ✿ ⇔ ◖ ◗ P

Pangbourne

Cross Keys
Church Road (30 yds from A329 towards M4)
☎ (0734) 843268
11–3; 6–11
Courage Best Bitter, Directors [H]
Comfortable two-bar pub with riverside patio and collection of caged birds. Summer barbecues.
▲ Q ♞ ✿ ⇔ ◖ ◗ ⊞ ⇄ ♣

Try also: Star

Reading

Eldon Arms
19 Eldon Terrace (off Kings Road) ☎ (0734) 573857
10.30–3; 5.30 (6 Sat)–11
Hall & Woodhouse Tanglefoot; Wadworth IPA, 6X, Old Timer [H]
All a good boozer should be, but parking difficult. Popular back-street pub with bustling public and quieter lounge. No meals Sun. ◖ ⊞ ♣

Horn
St Marys Butts
☎ (0734) 574794
11–3; 5.30–10.30 (11–10.30 Wed & Thu, 11–11 Fri & Sat)
Courage Best Bitter, Directors [H]
Sit and watch the world go by from this traditional town-centre pub which is popular with shoppers, traders and business people. No meals Sun. ✿ ◖

Sun
16 Castle Street (near civic centre) ☎ (0734) 575106
11–3 (4 Sat); 5 (7 Sat)–11
Courage Best Bitter, Directors; John Smith's Bitter [H]
Historic town pub – parts date from the 16th century. Comfortable, split-level bar with friendly, efficient service. Once housed elephants in the cellar! No food Sun. ✿ ◖ P

Wallingford Arms
2 Caroline Street/Charles Street (off ring road near swimming pool) ☎ (0734) 575272
11–3; 5.30–11 (11–11 Sat)
Morland Original Bitter, Old Masters [H]
Good, solid local with comfortable bars and a convivial atmosphere. Not easy to find but worth the effort. No meals Sun. Bar billiards. ▲ ✿ ◖ ⊞ ♣ P

Try also: Sweeney & Todd, Castle Street (Free)

Remenham

Two Brewers
Wargrave Road (just before Henley Bridge, A321/A432 jct) ☎ (0491) 574375
11–3; 6–11
Brakspear Bitter, Special [H], **Old Ale** [G]
Comfortable, oak-panelled pub near to river in Henley. Run by young couple, new to pub trade. You can see Brakspear's brewery just across the river.
▲ Q ♞ ✿ ⇔ ◖ ◗ ⊞ ⇄ (Henley) ♣ P

Sindlesham

Walter Arms
Bearwood Lane (off B3030/A329) ☎ (0734) 780260
11–2.30; 5 (5.30 Sat)–11
Courage Best Bitter, Directors [H]
Striking country pub, just out of suburbia. Always popular, efficient and friendly. Well-known for its food; imaginative menu. Quality accommodation.
▲ Q ✿ ⇔ ◖ ◗ P

Slough

Alpha Arms
Alpha Street (off High Street)
☎ (0753) 22727
11–3 (12–2.30 Sun); 5.30–11
Courage Best Bitter, Directors; John Smith's Bitter [H]
Small side-street local with friendly atmosphere. Former local CAMRA Pub of the Year. Traditional and still unspoilt. Parking can be difficult.
Q ✿ ◖ ♿ ⇄ ♣

Try also: Herchel Arms (Courage)

Thatcham

Kings Head
59 Broadway ☎ (0635) 62145
11–3; 5.30–11
Courage Best Bitter [H]
Historic old coaching inn on the

Bath Road. Due for major refit. Landlord also runs nearby White Hart. ♜ ❀ ⊨ ◐ ⊟ ⇌ ♣ P

Theale

Falcon
31 High Street (near M4 jct 12)
☎ (0734) 302523
10.30–11
Courage Best Bitter, Directors 🄷
17th-century coaching inn busy at lunchtime with office trade. No meals weekends.
❀ ◐ ⊟ ⇌ ♣ P

Lamb at Theale
22 Church Street (old A4)
☎ (0734) 302216
10–2.30; 5.30–11 (11–3; 6–11 Sat)
Courage Best Bitter, Directors 🄶
True village local, largely unmodernised. Separate function room with skittles. No meals Sun. ♜ Q ⚇ ❀ ◐ ⊟ ⇌ ♣ P

Red Lion
Church Street (old A4)
☎ (0734) 302394
11–2.30; 5.30–11
Halls Harvest Bitter; Ind Coope Burton Ale 🄷
Atmospheric, cosy bar with comfortable nooks for customers who seek privacy. Eve meals Sat only (snacks through the week). No meals Sun. Skittle alley. ❀ ◐ ⇌ ♣ P

Twyford

Duke of Wellington
High Street ☎ (0734) 340456
11–2.30 (3 Sat); 5 (6 Sat)–11
Brakspear XXX Mild, Bitter, Special, Old Ale 🄷
Friendly 16th-century village pub. Popular public bar and quieter lounge, with occasional visitations by a ghostly highwayman. Sheltered garden, no food at weekends.
❀ ◐ ⊟ ⇌ ♣ P

Kings Arms
12 Wargrave Road (A321)
☎ (0734) 340014
11–3; 6–11 (11–11 Sat)
Brakspear XXX Mild, Bitter, Special, Old Ale 🄷
Friendly pub of mid-60s design. Unpretentious bar and separate room with bar billiards, pool and jukebox. Good value, home-cooked meals (not Sun lunch). ◐ ◑ ⇌ ♣ P

Wargrave

Bull
High Street ☎ (0734) 403120
11–3; 6–11
Brakspear Bitter, Special 🄷
Outstanding 17th-century village pub with exposed beams and huge log fire. Great reputation for home-cooked food (children can eat weekends). No meals Sun eve.
♜ Q ❀ ⊨ ◐ ◑ ⇌

Greyhound
High Street ☎ (0734) 402556
11–2.30; 5.30–11
Courage Best Bitter, Directors 🄷
A real pub, well-run, with busy public bar, comfortable family room and cosy snug. Family room sometimes not available eves. Last of a dying breed.
♜ Q ⚇ ❀ ◐ ⊟ ⇌ ♣ P

West Ilsley

Harrow
Off A34 at W end of village OS471826 ☎ (063 528) 260
11–2.30 (3 Sat); 6–11
Morland Original Bitter, Old Masters 🄷
Superb two-bar village pub opposite cricket ground in downland village where Morland started brewing. Close to ancient Ridgeway. Excellent food: try the home-made rabbit pie. (Warning – due for brewery's one-bar treatment in 1990.) ♜ ❀ ◐ ◑ ⊟ ⛺ ♣ P

White Waltham

Beehive
☎ (062 882) 2877
11–2.30; 6–11
Marston's Pedigree Bitter; Whitbread Wethered Bitter, Castle Eden Ale 🄷**, Flowers Original** 🄶
Very pleasant and solidly traditional village pub opposite the cricket pitch. Friendly regulars. Fresh fish comes direct from Billingsgate. No meals Sun eve. Petanque pitch.
♜ Q ❀ ◐ ◑ ⊟ ♣ P

Windsor

Carpenters Arms
4 Market Street
☎ (0753) 863695
11–3; 6–11 (11–11 Fri, Sat & summer)
Draught Bass; Charrington IPA 🄷
Two-level pub, with a fine exterior, in tourist area, opposite the castle. Floor tiling reveals former ownership by Ashby's of Staines. Several drinking areas overlook the cobbled streets which surround the pub. No meals Sun. Bar billiards. ◐ ⇌ ♣

Prince Christian
King's Road ☎ (0753) 860980
11–3; 5–11
Brakspear Bitter; Fuller's London Pride; Ruddles Best Bitter 🄷
Windsor's only free house, with modest prices for the area. An easy walk from tourist Windsor and the famous castle. No food weekends. ◐ ♿ ⇌

Wokingham

Crooked Billet
Honey Hill (off B3430 2 miles SE of town) OS826667
☎ (0734) 789256
11–11
Brakspear Bitter, Special, Old Ale 🄷
Excellent, extended country pub. Features many chiming clocks. Wide food range ensures busy lunchtime trade. Ramp access for wheelchair to bar.
♜ Q ❀ ◐ ◑ ♣ P

Metropolitan
Rose Street ☎ (0734) 781171
11–3; 5.30–11 (11–11 Sat)
Morland Original Bitter, Old Masters 🄷
Homely pub set in the preservation area of the town centre. Cosy lounge and separate public bar. Landlady has collection of pottery faces in lounge. No meals Sun. ◐ ⊟ ♣ P

Queens Head
23 The Terrace (top of Station Road) ☎ (0734) 781221
11–3; 5.30–11
Morland Original Bitter, Old Masters 🄷
Charming single-bar pub retaining much old-world character. Popular with local and business people. Garden at rear through pub. Aunt Sally. No meals Sun. ❀ ◐ ⇌ ♣

Try also: Ship (Fuller's)

Wraysbury

Green Man
28 Station Road (off B376)
☎ (0784) 812404
11–2.30 (3 Sat); 6–11
Friary Meux Best Bitter; Ind Coope Burton Ale 🄷
Two-bar pub near station. Lounge predominantly used by diners; boisterous public has the remains of a Ring the Bull pitch, last used in the late 1940s.
❀ ◐ ◑ ⊟ ⇌ ♣ P

Yattendon

Royal Oak
The Square ☎ (0635) 201325
11.30–3; 5.30–11
Adnams Bitter; Hall & Woodhouse Tanglefoot; Wadworth 6X 🄷
Picturesque, high-class hotel in splendid village setting, with excellent cuisine and friendly atmosphere. Expensive restaurant.
♜ Q ❀ ⊨ ◐ ◑ P

Join CAMRA — see page 504!

Buckinghamshire

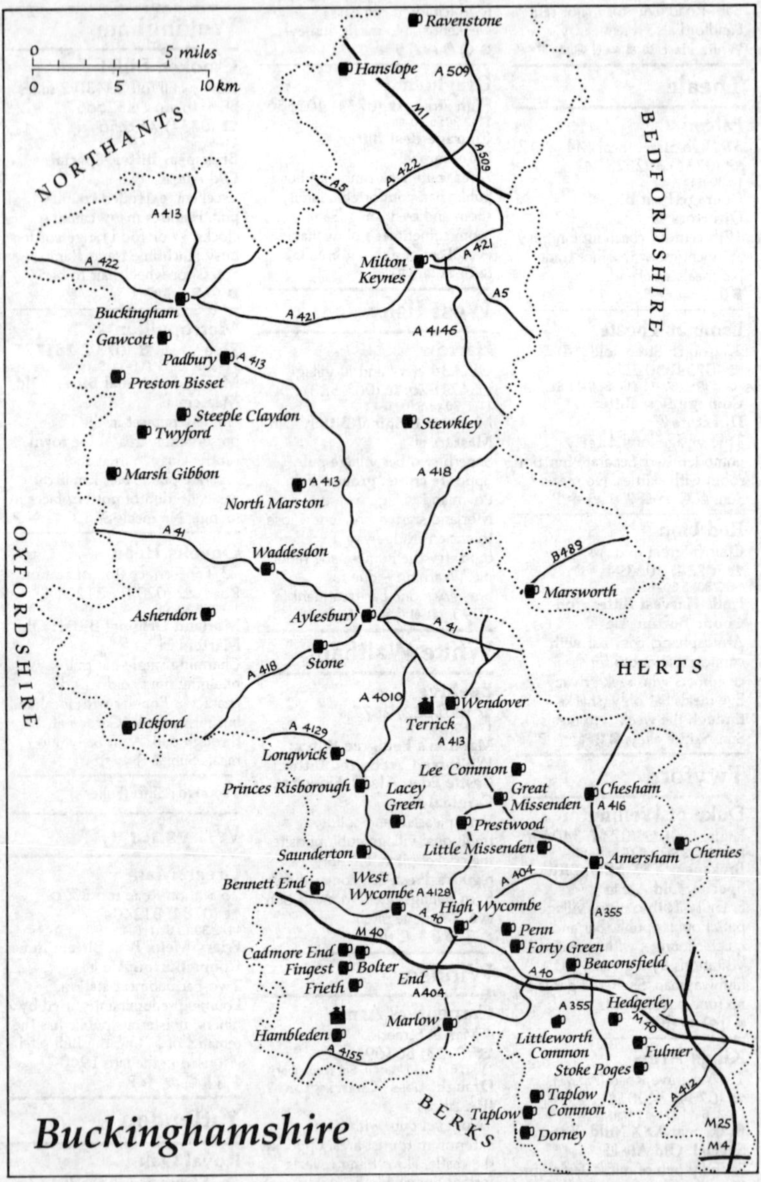

Chiltern, *Terrick*; **Old Luxters**, *Hambleden*

Amersham

Kings Arms
30 High Street (A413)
☎ (0494) 726333
11–11
Benskins Best Bitter Ⓗ; **Ind Coope Burton Ale** Ⓖ
Attractive 15th-century inn. Restaurant (closed Sun eve and Mon) has won many awards. Quiz eves. Guest beer.
Q P

Queens Head
Whielden Gate (A404 1 mile S of town) OS941957
☎ (0494) 725240
11–2.30; 6–11
Benskins Best Bitter; Ind Coope Burton Ale Ⓗ
Well-run and popular country pub below road level. Pub games and occasional live music. P

Try also: Eagle (Allied)

Ashendon

Red Lion
Lower End (cul-de-sac beside

church) OS704143
☎ (0296) 651296
12–2.30; 7–11 (closed Sun eve)
Adnams Bitter; Hall & Woodhouse Badger Best Bitter; Wadworth IPA, 6X Ⓗ, **Old Timer** Ⓖ
A free house since 1989, bought from ABC. Spacious L-shaped bars to lounge standard. Hilltop position in village overlooks northern Vale of Aylesbury. ⌂ ❀ ◖ ◗ ♣ P

Aylesbury

Aristocrat
1 Wendover Road (A413)
☎ (0296) 415366
11–3; 5–11
Fuller's Chiswick Bitter, London Pride, ESB Ⓗ
Lively pub with plenty of character. Interesting pictures of English aristocrats displayed around the walls. The only Fuller's pub in Aylesbury. No meals Sun. ❀ ◖ ◗ ♿ ⇌ ♣

County Arms
124 Cambridge Street
☎ (0296) 23552
10.30–2.30; 5.30 (6.30 Sat)–11
Benskins Best Bitter; Tetley Bitter Ⓗ
One of Aylesbury's few remaining traditional boozers, serving good value food and beer. ❀ ◖ ⊟ ♣ P

Old Plough & Harrow
22 Stoke Road
☎ (0296) 23306
11–3; 5 (6 Sat)–11
Courage Best Bitter, Directors Ⓗ
Popular pub on notorious gyratory road system. Has thriving darts, crib, quiz and football teams. ⌂ ❀ ♣ ⇌ P

Beaconsfield

Old Hare
41 Aylesbury End (near A40)
OS944901 ☎ (0494) 673380
11–2.30; 5.30–11
Benskins Best Bitter; Ind Coope Burton Ale; Tetley Bitter Ⓗ
Highly recommended, cosy pub with low beams, stained glass windows and a striking exterior. No food Sun eve. ⌂ Q ❀ ◖ ◗

Try also: Prince of Wales (Free)

Bennett End

Three Horseshoes
Horseshoe Road (off A40)
OS783973 ☎ (0494) 483273
12–2.30; 7–11
Brakspear Bitter Ⓗ
Unspoilt 18th-century inn with view to match. Not easy to find but well worth the effort. Eve meals Tue–Sat. Accommodation on offer includes a water bed.
⌂ Q ❀ ⛌ ◖ ◗ ⊟ ♣ P

Bolter End

Peacock
On B482 ☎ (0494) 881417
11–2.30; 6–11
ABC Best Bitter; Draught Bass Ⓗ
Popular country pub with emphasis on good-value food. Eve meals Mon–Sat.
⌂ Q ❀ ◖ ◗ ♿ P

Buckingham

New Inn
Bridge Street
☎ (0280) 815713
10–11
ABC Best Bitter; Draught Bass; Wadworth 6X Ⓗ
Outstanding small pub with a big welcome. Sri Lankan cuisine a speciality. Full family facilities in cellar bar. ⌂ ⚘ ❀ ◖ ◗

Try also: Grand Junction (ABC)

Cadmore End

Blue Flag
On B482 (2 miles S of M40 jct 5) ☎ (0494) 881183
11–2.30; 6–11
Adnams Bitter; Morland Original Bitter; Theakston XB; Wadworth 6X; Webster's Yorkshire Bitter Ⓗ
Impeccable service and a warm welcome in this well-appointed pub. No-smoking area. Strong emphasis on food, including fish specialities. Q ⛌ ◖ ◗ ♿ P

Try also: Ship (Brakspear)

Chenies

Red Lion
Off A404 OS022980
☎ (09278) 2722
11–3; 5.30–11
Benskins Best Bitter; Ind Coope Burton Ale; Tetley Bitter Ⓗ
Comfortable village pub recently refurbished to form one L-shaped bar, with a separate eating area to the rear. Diners can often outnumber drinkers. Mind the step! Guest beer.
Q ⚘ ◖ ◗ P

Chesham

Black Horse
The Vale (2 miles N of centre on Cholesbury Road)
OS964046 ☎ (0494) 784656
11–2.30; 6–11
Benskins Best Bitter; Friary Meux Best Bitter; Ind Coope Burton Ale; Young's Special Ⓗ
Pleasant and popular country pub with low beams. Huge garden. Meals available every session. ❀ ◖ ◗ P

White Horse
Amersham Road
☎ (0494) 771991
11–2.30; 5.30–11
Benskins Best Bitter Ⓗ
Small one-bar town pub. Beer occasionally served direct from the cask. ◖ ⊖ ♣ P

Dorney

Pineapple
Lake End Road
☎ (0628) 662353
11–3; 5–11
Friary Meux Best Bitter; Ind Coope Burton Ale Ⓗ
Building dates from 1743 and was originally two cottages. The saloon bar is the original pub and the public bar is in the second cottage. Very cosy atmosphere. No food Sun.
⌂ Q ❀ ◖ ⊟ ♣ P

Fingest

Chequers
$1\frac{1}{2}$ miles from B482 turning, $\frac{1}{2}$ mile W of Lane End OS778991
☎ (049 163) 335
11–3; 6–11
Brakspear Bitter, Special, Old Ale Ⓗ
Smart, comfortable pub with separate areas, including no-smoking. Outstanding food includes veg. Picturesque and expansive garden. Norman church opposite, with a distinctive floodlit twin-gabled Saxon tower. No food Sun eve.
⌂ Q ❀ ◖ ◗ P

Forty Green

Royal Standard of England
Off B474 at Knotty Green Garage OS923919
☎ (0494) 673382
11–3; 5.30–11
Eldridge Pope Royal Oak; Marston's Pedigree Bitter, Owd Rodger; Webster's Yorkshire Bitter Ⓗ
Ancient and historic free house. Very popular at all times, despite being difficult to find! Good food bar; Royal Standard house bitter on handpump.
⌂ Q ⚘ ❀ ◖ ◗ ♿ P

Frieth

Prince Albert
Moor End OS798906
☎ (0494) 881683
11–2.30 (3 Sat); 5.30–11
Brakspear XXX Mild, Bitter, Special, Old Ale Ⓗ
Exceptional beer, service, dog and atmosphere (no smell of chips!). ⌂ Q ❀ ◖ ♿ ♣ P

Buckinghamshire

Fulmer

Black Horse
Windmill Road
☎ (028 16) 3183
11–2.30; 6–11
Courage Best Bitter, Directors [H]
One of the few three-bar pubs in the area. Dates from the 17th century when, prior to becoming a pub, it lodged the workmen who built the church next door. Central bar has a flagstone floor. No meals at weekends. ⌂ Q ◖ ◗ ⊟ ♣ P

Gawcott

Cuckoo's Nest
New Inn Lane
☎ (0280) 812092
10.30–3 (not Mon); 6–11
Hook Norton Best Bitter; Marston's Pedigree Bitter [H]
Welcoming village local with a small traditional public bar and a well-appointed lounge. Live music each Sun lunch. Guest beer in summer. ⌂ ❀ ⊟ ♿ ♣

Great Missenden

White Lion
57 High Street
☎ (024 06) 2114
11–2.30; 5.30–11 (11–11 Sat)
Benskins Best Bitter [H]
Solid Victorian pub with strong accent on games. Pub has five darts teams, and crib, dominoes and pool teams. Aviary next to car park. No food Sun.
❀ ◖ ♿ ⛺ ⇌ ♣ P

Try also: Cross Keys (Allied)

Hambleden

Stag & Huntsman
1 mile N of A4155
☎ (0491) 571227
11–2.30; 6–11
Brakspear Bitter, Special; Old Luxters Barn Ale; Wadworth 6X, Farmer's Glory [H]
Unspoilt three-bar pub in picturesque, brick and flint National Trust village. Extensive menu (not Sun eve), with seafood a speciality. Guest beers. ⌂ ❀ ⛿ ◖ ◗ ⊟ ♿

Hanslope

Globe
Hartwell Road (½ mile N of village) ☎ (0908) 510336
11–3; 6–11
Banks's Bitter [E]
Large, roadside village pub. Traditional lounge and small public bar, with separate pool room. Children's play area in garden, and small menagerie. No food Mon eve. ❀ ◖ ◗ ⊟ ♿ P

Hedgerley

White Horse
Village Lane (1 mile E of A355)
☎ (0753) 643225
11–2.30 (3 Sat); 5.30 (6 Sat)–11
Marston's Pedigree Bitter; Whitbread Wethered Bitter, Castle Eden Ale, Wethered SPA, Flowers Original [G]
300 year-old village local featuring a magnificent, traditional public bar with flagged floor and roaring log fire. Unchanged in centuries, save for electric lighting. Price list in public bar dates from 1956! Well worth seeking out. Beer range may vary. No food Sun. ⌂ Q ❀ ◖ ⊟ ♣ P

High Wycombe

Bell
Frogmore (A4128, 100 yds from A40) ☎ (0494) 21317
11–3; 5.30–11
Fuller's Chiswick Bitter, London Pride, Mr Harry, ESB [H]
Outstanding pub in the centre of town. No food Fri, Sat or Sun eve. ◖ ◗ ♿ ⇌

General Havelock
114 Kingsmead Road
☎ (0494) 20391
11–2.30 (3 Fri); 5.30 (5 Fri)–11
Fuller's Chiswick Bitter, London Pride, Mr Harry, ESB [H]
A large, beamed pub with a mixed clientele. Notable fireplace; pictures of Guide Dogs for the Blind connected with pub. No food Sun.
⌂ ❀ ◖ ◗ ♣ P

Wendover Arms
180a Desborough Avenue
☎ (0494) 26476
11–2.30 (3 Sat); 5 (6 Sat)–11
Brakspear XXX Mild, Bitter, Special, Old Ale [H]
Sensibly renovated 1930s pub in prominent location. Successful combination of locals', societies', and businesspersons' gathering place. Only mild in Wycombe. No food Mon eve. ❀ ◖ ◗ P

Try also: Queen (Fuller's)

Ickford

Royal Oak
2 Bridge Road ☎ (084 47) 633
11.30–3.30; 6–11 (11–11 summer)
Morrells Light, Dark, Bitter [H]
Genuine one-bar village local with good atmosphere and friendly welcome. Games include Aunt Sally. No food Sun. ❀ ◖ ♣ P

Lacey Green

Pink & Lily
Pink Road, Parslow's Hillock
OS826018 ☎ (024 028) 308
11.45 (11 Sat)–3; 6–11
Brakspear Bitter, Special; Glenny Hobgoblin; Ruddles County; Wadworth 6X [H]
Spacious and popular, with large garden at rear. Brooke bar is an original snug dedicated to a minor poet. Games include Ringing the Bull. Main meals and excellent bar food (not Sun eve). ⌂ Q ❀ ◖ ◗ ♣ P

Lee Common

Bugle
Off A413 OS906043
7–11 (11–2.30; 7–11 Sat, 12–2.30; 7–10.30 Sun)
Brakspear Bitter [H], **Special** [G]
Quiet country local with large games room. Opening hours can vary! Q P

Little Missenden

Crown
Off A413 ☎ (024 06) 2571
11–2.30 (12–2.30 Sun); 6–11
Hook Norton Best Bitter; Marston's Pedigree Bitter; Morrells Varsity [H]
Totally unspoilt old village inn which can get very busy. Has been in the same family since 1923. Games include shove-ha'penny and bar skittles. Snacks available lunchtimes (not Sun). ⌂ Q ❀ ◖ ♿ ♣ ⌀ P

Red Lion
Off A413 ☎ (024 06) 2876
11–2.30 (12–2 Sun); 5.30–11
Benskins Best Bitter [H]; **Ind Coope Burton Ale** [G]
Excellent unspoilt village pub offering all home-cooked food. Small river garden. Plans for large car park at rear of pub. Upstairs room available for private dinners or meetings. Piano sing-along on Fri and Sat eves. Shut the Box played. Guest beer.
⌂ Q ⛿ ❀ ◖ ◗ ♿ ♣ P

Littleworth Common

Blackwood Arms
Common Lane (E of Burnham to Beaconsfield Road)
OS936863 ☎ (028 14) 2169
11–2.30; 5.30–11
Arkell's 3B Best Bitter; Ballard's Wassail; Burts BB; Chiltern Three Hundred Old Ale; Mitchell's Best Bitter; Pitfield Black Knight Stout [H]
Country pub on one side of common which is very popular with walkers in summer. Varying beer range; extensive

menu with many home-cooked dishes. Eve meals till 8.30pm. ⌂ Q ✿ ◐ ◗ P

Longwick

Red Lion
Thame Road (A4129)
☎ (08444) 4980
12–2.30; 6–11
ABC Best Bitter; Fuller's London Pride; Hook Norton Best Bitter Ⓗ
Substantial roadside inn. Spacious and comfortable, with attractive dining area. No meals Sun eve. Q 🛏 ◐ ◗ ♣ P

Marlow

Chequers
High Street ☎ (06284) 2053
11–11
Brakspear Bitter, Special Ⓗ
16th-century inn with two bars and a restaurant, opposite former Wethered's brewery. Over 21s only in the bars.
⌂ Q ✿ 🛏 ◐ ◗ ≢

Clayton Arms
Quoiting Square, Oxford Road (off West Street)
☎ (06284) 3037
10.30–2.30; 6–11
Brakspear XXX Mild, Bitter, Old Ale Ⓗ
Town-centre gem with two small bars. Landlord has lived here for over 60 years. A genuine local, one of 18 pubs in town selling real ale.
⌂ Q ⊟ ♿ ≢ ♣

Try also: Coach & Horses (Courage)

Marsh Gibbon

Plough
Church Street ☎ (08697) 305
11–2.30 (3.30 Sat); 6–11
Morrells Dark, Bitter Ⓗ
Pleasant, two-bar, 16th-century pub which caters for all ages. Separate dining room with extensive menu. Live music on alternate Sats.
⌂ Q ✿ ◐ ◗ ⊟ ▲ ♣ ⌓ P

Marsworth

Red Lion
Vicarage Road (off B489 near canal bridge) OS919147
☎ (0296) 668366
11–2.30; 6–11
ABC Best Bitter; Draught Bass; Wadworth 6X Ⓗ
Splendid village pub with contrasting bars on two levels. The large public bar contains a noticeboard for local information. Games include shove-ha'penny and bar billiards. Home-made curries available (no meals Sun). Guest beer. ⌂ Q ✿ ◐ ◗ ⊟ ♣ ⌓ P

Milton Keynes

Bull Hotel (Vaults Bar)
High Street, Stony Stratford
☎ (0908) 567104
10.30–11
ABC Best Bitter; Draught Bass; Eldridge Pope Royal Oak; Fuller's London Pride; Gale's HSB; Wadworth 6X Ⓗ
Small Victorian bar adjoining historic coaching house. Folk club meets Sun lunch. Guest beers. ✿ 🛏 ◐ ◗ ♿ ♣ P

Cricketers
Oldbrook Boulevard, Oldbrook
☎ (0908) 678844
11–3; 4.30–11 (11–11 Sat)
Greene King XX Dark, IPA, Abbot Ale Ⓗ
Splendid estate pub replete with cricketing memorabilia; the autographed bats should keep any buff busy! Views over cricket green. No meals Sun eve.
✿ ◐ ◗ ♿ ≢ P

Cross Keys
34 Newport Road, Great Woolstone (1 mile from M1 jct 14) ☎ (0908) 679404
11–2.30; 5.30–11 (11–11 Sat)
Charles Wells Eagle Bitter, Bombardier Ⓗ
Old country thatch now enveloped by city but still retaining authentic village atmosphere. Cheap beer, pleasant garden and good food. A haven for quiz nuts!
Q ✿ ◐ ◗ ⊟ P

Foresters Arms
Wolverton Road, New Bradwell
☎ (0908) 312348
11–11 (11–4; 6–11 Sat)
Charles Wells Eagle Bitter Ⓗ
No-frills, two-bar local.
✿ ⊟ ≢ (Wolverton) P

Grebe
Kensington Drive, Great Holm
☎ (0908) 260320
11–2.30 (3 Sat); 5.30 (6 Sat)–11
Greene King IPA, Abbot Ale Ⓗ
Modern estate pub with smart 'designer' interior. Single lounge bar with separate no-smoking area. No food on Sun.
🚭 ✿ ◐ ♿ ♣ P

New Inn
2 Bradwell Road, New Bradwell
☎ (0908) 312094
11–11 (11–4; 6–11 Sat)
Adnams Broadside; Charles Wells Eagle Bitter, Bombardier Ⓗ
Lively canalside pub. Good-value bar food with separate dining room upstairs.
✿ ◐ ◗ ⊟ ≢ (Wolverton) P

Prince Albert
17 Vicarage Road, Bradwell Village ☎ (0908) 312080
11–2.30 (5 Sat); 5.30 (7 Sat)–11
Adnams Broadside; Mansfield Riding Traditional Bitter; Charles Wells Eagle Bitter, Bombardier Ⓗ
Recently-enlarged village local, with single comfortable lounge bar. Children's play area in garden. No meals Sun/Mon eves. ⌂ ✿ ◐ ◗ ♣ P

Royal Engineer
Stratford Road, Wolverton
11–2.30; 6–11
Charles Wells Eagle Bitter Ⓗ
Friendly Victorian street-corner local, with large public bar and tiny lounge, opposite BR works.
◐ ⊟ ≢ (Wolverton) P

North Marston

Bell
25 High Street
☎ (029667) 635
11–3; 6–11
ABC Best Bitter; Draught Bass; Wadworth 6X Ⓗ
Friendly and comfortable, with original fireplace and much timber. Split-level bar with good food available. No meals Sun eve. ⌂ ✿ ◐ ◗ ♣ P

Padbury

New Inn [and Filling Station]
Aylesbury Road (A413)
☎ (0280) 813173
10–2.30; 5.30–11
ABC Best Bitter Ⓗ
Traditional roadside pub in little village. The small bars of much charm are a step back in time.
⌂ Q ✿ ⊟ ♣ P

Penn

Horse & Jockey
Church Road, Tylers Green
☎ (049481) 5963
10.30–2.30; 5.30–11
Benskins Best Bitter; Ind Coope Burton Ale Ⓗ
Spacious and comfortable pub with food available at all times. Guest beers. ✿ ◐ ◗ ♿ ♣ P

Preston Bisset

Old Hat
Main Street ☎ (02804) 355
11–2.30; 7 (6 Sat)–11
Hook Norton Best Bitter Ⓗ
Unspoilt village local of much character. Small cosy bar with splendid wooden settle. ⌂ Q ♣

Prestwood

Kings Head
Wycombe Road (A4128)
☎ (02406) 2392
11–11
Brakspear XXX Mild, Bitter, Special, Old Ale; Greene King Abbot Ale; Marston's Pedigree Bitter Ⓖ

Buckinghamshire

A regular beer festival with up to 11 ales on gravity dispense, from independent brewers.
⌂ Q ⊞ P

Princes Risborough

Whiteleaf Cross
Market Square
☎ (084 44) 6834
10–2.30 (3 Sat); 5.30 (6 Sat)–11
Morland Original Bitter, Old Masters Ⓗ
Immaculate town tavern with good-value bar meals. No food on Sun. ❀ ◐ ◑ ⇌ ♣

Try also: George & Dragon (Benskins)

Ravenstone

Wheatsheaf
☎ (0908) 55555
6.30–11 (12–11 Sat)
Fuller's ESB; Greene King IPA; Hook Norton Best Bitter; Marston's Pedigree Bitter Ⓗ
Small homely pub in picturesque village. Parts of the building date from the 12th century, and it stands on the site of an old priory. Regular guest beers. No food Tue eve. ⌂ ❀ ◑ ♣ P

Saunderton

Golden Cross
Wycombe Road (A4010)
☎ (024 024) 2293
12–2.30; 5.30 (6.30 Sat)–11
ABC Best Bitter; Ind Coope Burton Ale Ⓗ
Comfortable roadside pub with secluded garden. Imaginative bar food. No meals Sun/Mon eves. Games include petanque.
Q ❀ ◐ ◑ ⊞ ⇌ ♣ ○ P

Steeple Claydon

Old Sportsman
North End, off Main Road
OS696271 ☎ (029673) 8242
6–11 (11–2.30; 6–11 Sat)
Hook Norton Best Bitter Ⓗ, **Old Hookey** Ⓖ
Unspoilt village pub with a character of its own. Hard to find so ask for directions. Tiny lounge and separate pool room.
⌂ Q ❀ ⊞ P

Stewkley

Swan
High Street North
☎ (0525) 240285
11–3; 6 (5.30 summer)–11
Courage Best Bitter, Directors Ⓗ
Excellent Georgian pub in centre of village. Always a good atmosphere. Separate restaurant (no food Sun). ♨ ❀ ◐ ◑ ♣ P

Stoke Poges

Plough
Wexham Street
☎ (028 16) 2633
11–3 (12–2.30 Sun); 5–11
Benskins Best Bitter; Ind Coope Burton Ale; Tetley Bitter Ⓗ
Traditional wayside village inn. very much a locals' pub, with strangers made welcome. Low, beamed ceiling; log fire; good food; pub dogs. Awayday trips to rugby matches are regularly arranged. Bar skittles played.
⌂ Q ❀ ◐ ♿ ♣ P

Try also: Stag (Courage)

Stone

Waggon & Horses
39 Oxford Road (A418)
☎ (0296) 748740
11–2.30 (10.30–3 Sat); 6–11
ABC Best Bitter; Ind Coope Burton Ale Ⓗ
Pleasant roadside pub with two separate bars. Cellarmanship award for excellent Burton Ale. Good-value food at all times.
Q ◐ ◑ ⊞ ♣ P

Taplow

Old Station Inn
Bath Road ☎ (0628) 22922
11–11
Benskins Best Bitter; Ind Coope Burton Ale Ⓗ
Present building is circa 1931, but its origins go back to 1838 when the railway terminated at Maidenhead, on the embankment above the pub. Single bar divided into three separate areas. Garden very suitable for children who are also catered for on the menu.
⌂ ❀ ◐ ◑ ⇌ ♣ P

Taplow Common

Feathers
Taplow Common Road (opp. Cliveden House)
☎ (0628) 664646
12–2.30 (3 Sat); 5.30–11
Benskins Best Bitter; Ind Coope Burton Ale; Tetley Bitter Ⓗ
Large single bar with two open fires. The games room was the original kitchen and still has the old range. Ask behind the bar for Devil Amongst the Tailors, Bagatelle, shove-ha'penny, Nine Men's Morris and other games. Bar billiards. ⌂ Q ❀ ◐ ♣ P

Twyford

Red Lion
Church End ☎ (0296) 730339
11.30 (11 Sat)–2; 6–11
ABC Best Bitter; Ind Coope Burton Ale Ⓗ
Tiny, unspoilt, 17th-century pub across a long front garden. Wonderful, cosy atmosphere.
⌂ Q ❀ P

Waddesdon

Five Arrows
High Street (A41, next to Waddesdon Manor)
☎ (0296) 651727
10–11 (10–3; 7–11 Sat)
Bateman XB, XXXB; Hook Norton Best Bitter Ⓗ
Ornate, grandiose Rothschild building, with unpretentious lounge bar. Home of Owlswick morris men. Selection of real ales changes. ❀ 🛏 ◐ ◑ P

Wendover

Red Lion
High Street (A413)
☎ (0296) 622266
11–11
Fuller's London Pride; Greene King Abbot Ale; Marston's Pedigree Bitter; Morland Original Bitter; Charles Wells Eagle Bitter Ⓗ
Rambling 16th-century coaching inn, very popular as a historical community centre for the village. Table service every day in every bar. ⌂ 🛏 ◐ ◑ ⇌ P

West Wycombe

George & Dragon Hotel
High Street (A40)
☎ (0494) 464414
11–2.30; 5.30–11 (11–11 Sat)
Courage Best Bitter, Directors Ⓗ
19th-century coaching inn with original timbered bar and splendid garden. No meals Sun eve. ⌂ Q ♨ ❀ 🛏 ◐ ◑ P

All the pubs listed in the *Good Beer Guide* are selected and inspected by volunteer CAMRA members. You can have your say, too. Suggestions for pubs to be included in (or excluded from) future editions are very welcome and will be passed on to the local CAMRA branch. Use the form on page 502.

THE GBG QUIZ

Set by Roy Bailey

Perhaps it is the influence of so many television quiz shows, but whenever two or three people are gathered together in a hostelry these days, sooner or later someone will suggest that they start a pub quiz team. This is presumably inspired by the thought that it would make a nice change to use the cerebral cortex as well as the right arm.

Pub quizzery is certainly becoming more and more popular all over the country, with leagues being organised to help while away not just the long winter evenings, but also the long summer afternoons. I recently learned of some local quiz teams whose activities take place between spring and autumn, enabling them to come up with an excellent excuse to spend hours of sunlit pleasure sitting in country pub gardens – assuming that one needs such an excuse!

I cannot help feeling, however, that a pub quiz, like football, is really a pastime for the winter. I have spent many happy evenings sitting around a roaring fire, a pint of ale in my hand and my mind grappling with such problems as the name by which Agnes Gouxha Bojaxhiu is better known. Yes, I was amazed, too, to learn that it is Mother Theresa.

Some breweries, such as Courage and Thwaites, run quiz leagues which promote interest in their pubs and beer. Other competitions are community based, helping to raise funds for worthy causes. One in a West Berkshire village, held in a different local pub every six months and attracting 15 teams, started as a way of re-roofing the village hall. Whatever their motivation, such quizzes are a sociable and enjoyable aspect of the pub scene, be it a large urban tavern or a small country inn.

Our quiz (divided into five rounds, increasing in difficulty and spread throughout the book) is not really designed as an aid to help you mount the Shrieking Turnip Trivial Pursuit or the Masons' Arms Mastermind, although some of the questions may come in useful. It is really just a bit of fun to test your knowledge of pubs, brewing and beer (not forgetting cider). Armed with this year's *GBG*, you may be able to impress the regulars at your local and convince them that you should be Chairman of CAMRA. On the other hand, you could easily become Megabore '91. But remember that answering questions in any quiz is like working in a well-known Cardiff brewery. You have to rack your Brains!

*An ex-CAMRA branch chairman, Roy Bailey is a film and video producer and freelance writer. He was a finalist in BBC TV's **Mastermind** in 1988. Quiz answers can be found on pages* 494/495.

Cambridgeshire

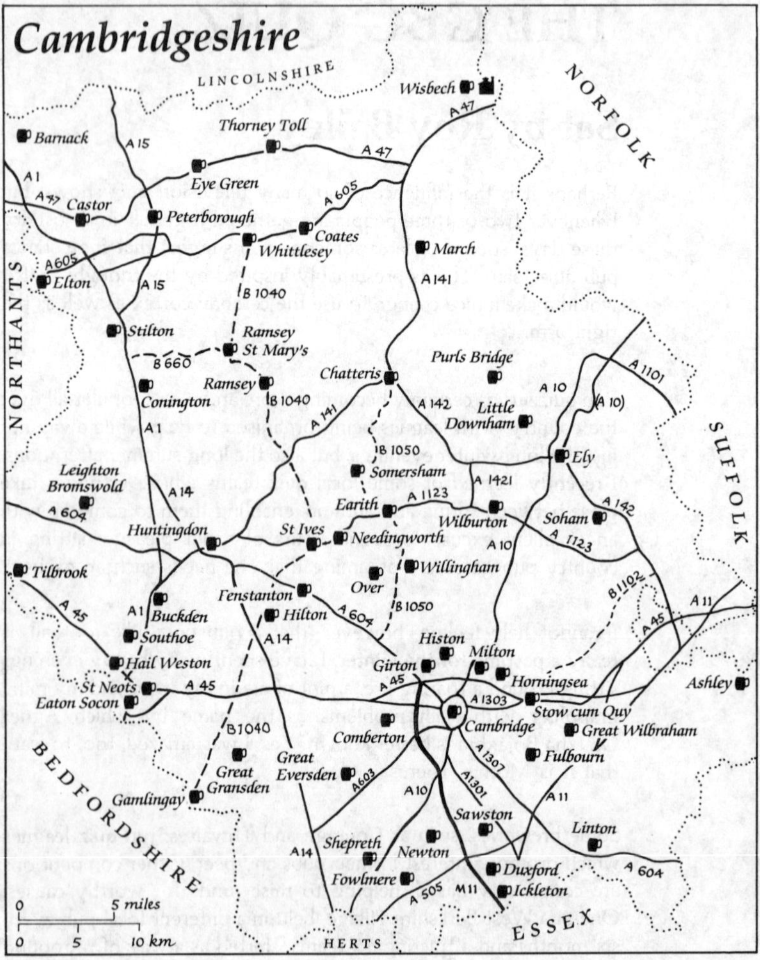

Elgood's, *Wisbech*

Ashley

Crown
24 Newmarket Road
☎ (0638) 730737
11.30–2.30; 6–11 (11.30–11 Sat)
Greene King IPA, Rayments BBA, Abbot Ale ⊞
Thriving village local. Play tree for children in garden. Bar snacks and meals include daily special, vegetarian and fondue.
♣ P

Try also: Red Lion, Cheveley (Greene King)

Barnack

Millstone
Millstone Lane
☎ (0780) 740296
11–3; 6–11
Adnams Bitter; Everards Tiger Best Bitter, Old Original ⊞
Stone-built village local, close to 'Hills and Holes' – former stone quarry for many churches. Guest beers. Good value menu caters for children and vegetarians (no eve meals Sun/Mon). ♿ P

Try also: White Hart, Ufford

Buckden

Falcon
Mill Road ☎ (0480) 811612
11–2.30; 6.30–11
Charles Wells Eagle Bitter ⊞
Situated just outside main village on road to Offords. Single lounge bar with separate games room at rear. Traditional pub games include Northamptonshire skittles, now sadly rare this far east. Two gardens: one enclosed with patio and barbecue for summer.
♣ P

Cambridge

Ancient Druids
Napier Street
☎ (0223) 324514
11–2.30 (4 Sat); 5.30 (5 Sat)–11
Adnams Broadside; Ancient Druids Kite Bitter, Druid's Special, Merlin; Charles Wells Eagle Bitter, Bombardier ⊞
A modern pub with its own micro-brewery. Excellent food (not Sun eve), curries especially recommended. Adjoins Grafton

Shopping Centre and car park
▦ ◖ ◗

Bird in Hand
73 Newmarket Road
☎ (0223) 60622
11–11
Greene King IPA, Abbot Ale Ⓗ
Pub with a warm, truly traditional atmosphere, next door to the Cambridge Evening News offices. Meals and snacks available. Public car park opposite. ⌂ ▦ ◖ ◗

Cambridge Blue
85 Gwydir Street
☎ (0223) 61382
11–2.30; 6–11
Banks & Taylor Shefford Bitter, SPA, SOS, SOD Ⓗ
Busy, friendly little pub, with no-smoking bar and snug. Surprisingly large garden with a petanque pitch. Excellent, home-made food. Three guest beers.
⌂ Q ▦ ◖

Cow & Calf
St Peters Street
☎ (0223) 311919
12–3; 5.30 (6.30 Sat)–11
Courage Directors; Elgood's Bitter; Greenalls Shipstone's Bitter; John Smith's Bitter; Nethergate Bitter Ⓗ
Smashing little pub near the Folk Museum and Shire Hall. Home-cooked lunches – try the hot salt beef sandwiches. Use Shire Hall car park in the evening. ⌂ ◖ ♣ ◌

Free Press
Prospect Row
☎ (0223) 68337
12–3; 6–11
Greene King IPA, Abbot Ale Ⓗ
Hearty little pub. Good food at lunchtime with vegetarians well catered for. ⌂ Q ▦ ◖

Panton Arms
Panton Street
☎ (0223) 355733
11–2.30; 6–11 (11–11 Fri & Sat)
Greene King XX Dark, IPA, Abbot Ale Ⓗ
Excellent pub, once the brewery tap of the now-demolished Panton Brewery. Eve meals until 8pm (not Sun). ▦ ◖ ◗ ⊟ ♣

Tap & Spile (The Mill)
13–14 Mill Lane
☎ (0223) 357026
11–11
Camerons Strongarm; Tolly Cobbold Bitter Ⓗ
Old pub refurbished in traditional style, providing an ever-changing range of ales from independent brewers. Uncomplicated lunchtime food. Six guest beers. ◖

Tram Depot
5 Dover Street (off East Road, opp. AHEC) ☎ (0223) 324553
11–3; 5–11 (11.30–11 Sat)
Earl Soham Gannet Mild, Victoria Bitter, Albert Ale Ⓗ
Once the stables of the Cambridge Street Tramway Co., now superbly converted into a warm, traditional pub. Home-cooked food (vegetarians well catered for). Public car park behind pub. Q ▦ ◖ ◗

White Hart
2 Sturton Street
☎ (0223) 66536
11.30–2.30; 6–11
Adnams Bitter; Ind Coope Burton Ale; Tetley Bitter Ⓗ
Traditional street-corner local. The landlord has won several cellarmanship awards, as reflected in the quality of the beer. Cheap, wholesome lunches. ⌂ ◖ ⊟ ♣

White Swan
109 Mill Road
11–3.30; 5.30–11
Greene King XX Dark, IPA, Abbot Ale Ⓗ
Very friendly local pub. One bar with public bar and lounge areas. Lunchtime and evening meals planned. Public car park in Gwydir Street. ▦ ⇌

Try also: Portland Arms (Greene King)

Castor

Royal Oak
Peterborough Road (A47)
☎ (0733) 380217
11–2.30 (3 Sat); 6–11
Ind Coope Burton Ale; Tetley Bitter Ⓗ
Listed building with thatched roof and considerable charm. Cosy atmosphere; low-beamed ceiling. Stroke the cat at your peril! ⌂ Q ▦ ♣ P

Chatteris

Cock
41 London Road
☎ (035 43) 2026
11–3; 6–11
Webster's Yorkshire Bitter Ⓗ
Large converted house with ornate ceilings. Popular with all ages. Petanque. ▦ ◖ ◗ ♣ P

Coates

Vine
4 South Green
☎ (073 120) 343
10.30–2.30 (4 Sat); 6–11
Charles Wells Eagle Bitter, Bombardier Ⓗ
1950s-style lounge with open fire. Large, enclosed garden is ideal for children, with swings and climbing frame. No food at weekend. ⌂ Q ▦ ◖ ⊟ ♿ ♣ P

Comberton

Grapevine
5 Green-End ☎ (0223) 263059
11–3; 6–11 (11–11 Sat)
Adnams Bitter; Greene King IPA; Ruddles Best Bitter Ⓗ
Comfortable pub whose garden and children's play area overlook the village pond.
⌂ ▦ ♣ P

Conington

Huntsman
Great North Road (beside A1, 1 mile S of Stilton)
☎ (0487) 832407
11–3; 6–11
Draught Bass Ⓗ
Well-restored roadside inn (formerly the Crown & Woolpack). A welcome change from the usual trunk road keg food outlets. Guest beers.
Q ⛟ ◖ ◗ P

Duxford

Wheatsheaf
4 St Peters Street
☎ (0223) 832284
11–2.30 (12–2.30 Sun); 6–11
Greene King IPA, Abbot Ale Ⓗ
Comfortable village pub with large garden. No food at weekend. ⌂ ▦ ◖ ⊟ ♣ P

Earith

Riverview Inn
High Street ☎ (0487) 841405
11–2.30; 5–11
Marston's Burton Best Bitter, Pedigree Bitter Ⓗ
Popular, 17th-century riverside inn with wood-panelled lounge bar and restaurant. Very varied food menu. Guest beers.
⌂ ▦ ⛟ ◖ ◗ P

Eaton Socon

Crown
Great North Road (A45, St Neots bypass)
☎ (0480) 212232
11–2.30; 5.30–11
Samuel Smith OBB; Tetley Bitter Ⓗ
Small ivy-clad free house – often crowded. Small restaurant. Guest beers. Camping nearby at Wyboston Lakes. ▦ ◖ ◗ ▲ P

Millers Arms
Ackerman Street
☎ (0480) 74197
11–2.30; 6–11
Greene King XX Dark, IPA, Abbot Ale Ⓗ
Small 'village' pub on the green. The only pub in Eaton Socon not on the former Great North Road. Garden being extended to include paddock.
⌂ ⛟ ▦ ◖

Elton

Cambridgeshire

Crown
8 Duck Street (off A605)
☎ (0832) 280232
11.30–2.30; 6–11
Greene King IPA; Marston's Pedigree Bitter 🄷
Grade II listed building on village green. Rebuilt in 1985 after a major fire. Large, comfortable bar and new restaurant (veg option). Games include shove-ha'penny and 'Pope Joan'. Guest beers.
⌂ ❀ ◖ ◗ ♣ P

Ely

Angel
Station Road
☎ (0353) 662462
11–2.30; 6–11
Camerons Strongarm; John Smith's Magnet 🄷
Straightforward, no-frills pub, popular with dominoes players. Plain, cheap bar meals and snacks at lunchtime.
⌂ Q ❀ ⊟ ◖ ⇌ ♣

Eye Green

Greyhound
41 Crowland Road (A1073, ½ mile from A47)
☎ (0733) 222487
11–2.30 (3 Sat); 7–11
Charles Wells Eagle Bitter, Bombardier 🄷
Basic, popular village local with lounge and public bar.
⌂ Q ❀ ⊞ ♣ P

Fenstanton

King William IV
High Street (off A604)
☎ (0480) 62467
11–2.30; 6.30–11
Greene King XX Dark, IPA, Abbot Ale 🄷
Village pub separated into eating and drinking areas by beams and settles. Pleasantly situated on the village green, which has a clock tower and pond. Recently acquired by Greene King from Tolly Cobbold. ❀ ◖ ◗

Fowlmere

Queens Head
Long Lane ☎ (076382) 288
12–3 (4 Sat); 6 (7 Sat)–11
Greene King IPA, Abbot Ale 🄷
Excellent village local. Darts, dominoes and Shut the Box played in the comfortable public. Cosy lounge displays landlord's collection of bottled beers. A cheese lover's paradise at lunchtimes. ⌂ Q ❀ ◖ ⊞ ♣

Fulbourn

Bakers Arms
Hinton Road
☎ (0223) 880606
Greene King XX Dark, IPA, Abbot Ale 🄷
Popular village local with a large garden to enjoy in summer. ❀ ◖ ♣ P

Gamlingay

Cock
Church Street
☎ (0767) 502255
11–2.30; 6–11
Greene King IPA, Abbot Ale 🄷
Timber-framed pub of some character. Wood-panelled interior gives a well-worn feeling. Large inglenook fireplace in lounge bar. Garden and car park at rear of pub.
⌂ ❀ ◖ ◗ P

Hardwicke Arms
The Cross ☎ (0767) 50727
12–2.30; 7–11
Charrington IPA; Marston's Pedigree Bitter; Tetley Bitter 🄷
Excellent, unchanged pub on village crossroads. Lounge bar features an impressive inglenook. Guest beers always available. ⌂ ◖ ◗ P

Girton

George
7 High Street
☎ (0223) 276069
11–3; 6–11
Courage Best Bitter; John Smith's Bitter; Tolly Cobbold Mild 🄷
Very popular village local with quiet lounge. Full restaurant menu offers a lunchtime special and veg option. Booking recommended for Sun lunch. No eve meals Sun/Mon.
Q ❀ ◖ ◗ ⊞ ♣ P

Try also: Black Horse, Dry Drayton

Great Eversden

Hoops
High Street ☎ (0223) 262185
12–2.30 (may vary in summer); 7–11
Mansfield Riding Traditional Bitter; Charles Wells Eagle Bitter, Bombardier 🄷
Thriving village local, welcoming to visitors. Large garden has lots of room for children. No food Mon.
⌂ ❀ ⊟ ◖ ◗ ♣ P

Great Gransden

Crown & Cushion
☎ (07677) 214
12–11 (12–2.30; 6–11 Mon)
Adnams Broadside; Charles Wells Eagle Bitter 🄷, **Bombardier** 🄶
Split-level pub with single bar. Good, home-cooked food. Outdoor pool table in garden; small menagerie. Regular live music sessions. ⌂ ❀ ◖ ◗ P

Great Wilbraham

Carpenters Arms
10 High Street
☎ (0223) 880202
11–2.30; 7–11
Greene King XX Dark, IPA, Abbot Ale 🄷
Idyllic village local in 17th-century listed building. Home-made bar meals. The malt whisky collection isn't the only spirit in the place – something 'walks' along the upstairs corridor! Early eve meals Wed–Sat. ⌂ ❀ ◖ ◗ ⊞ ♣ P

Try also: Bell, Bottisham

Hail Weston

Royal Oak
High Street (off A45)
☎ (0480) 72527
11–2.30 (3 Sat); 6–11
Adnams Broadside; Mansfield Riding Traditional Bitter; Charles Wells Eagle Bitter, Bombardier 🄷
Picturesque, thatched village pub which has a large children's playground and pleasant family room with games. No eve meals Sun/Mon. ⌂ ⊳ ❀ ◖ ◗ ♣ P

Hilton

Prince of Wales
High Street (B1040)
☎ (0480) 830257
11–2.30; 6–11 (11–11 Sat, closed Mon in winter)
Adnams Bitter; Draught Bass; Marston's Pedigree Bitter 🄷
Friendly village free house with small public bar and larger well-furnished lounge. Guest beers.
⌂ ❀ ◖ ◗ ⊞ P

Histon

King William IV
8 Church Street
☎ (0223) 233930
11–2.30 (12–2.30 Sun); 5 (6 Sat)–11
Adnams Bitter; Greene King IPA; Hook Norton Best Bitter; Wadworth 6X; Webster's Yorkshire Bitter 🄷
Sociable village pub. Bar snacks (not Sun). ⌂ ❀ ⊞ ♣ P

Try also: Red Lion (Free)

Horningsea

Plough & Fleece
High Street ☎ (0223) 860795
11.30–2.30; 7–11
Greene King IPA, Abbot Ale 🄷
Unspoilt village pub. Nice old garden with playthings for children. Excellent reputation for

food, concentrating on old English recipes; try the chocolate pudding. Eve meals Tue–Sat. ⌂ Q ❀ ◖ ◗ ⊟

Huntingdon

Victoria
Ouse Walk ☎ (0480) 53899
11–2.30; 6–11
Camerons Traditional Bitter, Strongarm Premium; Tolly Cobbold Old Strong Ⓗ
Hard-to-find, back-street pub, but well worth the effort. One long bar divided into distinct areas. Good choice of food.
⌂ ❀ ◖ ◗ ♣ ⌓

Ickleton

New Inn
10 Brookhampton Street
☎ (0799) 30946
12 (11 Sat)–2; 7–11
Greene King XX Dark, IPA, Abbot Ale Ⓖ
Tiny, two-bar pub with fine brick and flint exterior. Limited food menu, but definitely no chips. ⌂ Q ❀ ◖ ◗ ⊟ ♣ P

Leighton Bromswold

Green Man
☎ (0480) 890238
12–2.30 (not Mon); 7–11 (closed Tue)
Fuller's London Pride; Hook Norton Best Bitter; Theakston Old Peculier Ⓗ
Comfortable rural free house with collection of brewery mirrors. Winner of 'Best-Kept Village in Huntingdonshire' award. Reasonable prices. Guest beers. Hood skittles played.
Q ♞ ❀ ◖ ◗ ♣

Linton

Crown
11 High Street
☎ (0223) 891759
12–2.30; 6–11
Bateman XB; Marston's Pedigree Bitter; Nethergate Bitter Ⓗ
Long, narrow, attractively-appointed pub, with separate restaurant, situated in one of the finest streets in the county. Guest beers. ⌂ ❀ ◖ ◗ P

Little Downham

Anchor
25 Main Street
☎ (0353) 699494
11–3; 6.30–11
Greene King IPA; John Smith's Bitter Ⓗ
Popular and welcoming village local that also serves good food (not Sun). The varied menu caters for vegetarians. Well worth finding. ⌂ Q ❀ ◖ ◗ P

March

Ship
11 Nene Parade
☎ (0354) 56999
11–3 (10.30–3.30 Wed); 6–11 (11–11 Sat)
Greene King XX Dark, IPA, Abbot Ale Ⓗ, **Winter Ale** Ⓖ
17th-century, thatched riverside pub with unusual carved ceiling beams. Convivial atmosphere appreciated by all. Good home-cooked food with veg option (not Mon). 🛏 ◖ ◗ ♣

Milton

Jolly Brewers
5 Fen Road ☎ (0223) 860585
11.30–2.30; 6 (7 Sat)–11
Tolly Cobbold Bitter, Original Ⓗ
An old pub that once had its own brewery. Eve meals Tue–Sun. ⌂ ❀ ◖ ◗ ⊟ ♣ P

Waggon & Horses
39 High Street
☎ (0223) 860313
12–2.30; 5 (7 Sat)–11
Bateman XB; Nethergate Bitter Ⓗ
A large, comfortable pub with a varied range of guest beers.
⌂ ❀ ◖ ⌓ P

Needingworth

Chestnuts
85 High Street
☎ (0480) 63456
11–3; 5.30–11
Draught Bass; Greene King IPA, Abbot Ale Ⓗ
Unusually-configured, lounge-bar pub. Once a wine bar, but now has more of a pub feel. Separate dining room. Guest beers. ⌂ ❀ ◖ ◗ P

Newton

Queens Head
Fowlmere Road
☎ (0223) 870436
11.30–2.30; 6–11
Adnams Bitter, Old, Broadside (summer), **Tally-Ho** Ⓖ
Wonderfully-unspoilt village pub. Belinda the Goose guards the car park and also appears on the inn sign (with Anne of Cleves!). Freshly-made sandwiches, home-made soup and real baked potatoes (no microwave here) complement the beer. ⌂ Q ❀ ◖ ◗ ⊟ ♣ ⌓ P

Over

Exhibition
2 King Street ☎ (0954) 30790
11–2.30; 7–11
Camerons Strongarm; Marston's Pedigree Bitter; Tolly Cobbold Bitter Ⓗ
Former beer house now extended and renovated. Good value food (lunchtimes and Tue and Thu–Sat eves). ⌂ ❀ ◖ ◗ P

Peterborough

Bogart's Bar
17 North Street
☎ (0733) 49995
11–3 (4 Sat); 5.30 (7 Sat)–11 (closed Sun)
Adnams Broadside; Hook Norton Best Bitter; Marston's Pedigree Bitter; Taylor Landlord Ⓗ
Once the Ostrich public house, then a home-brew shop. Now an oasis in the real ale desert of Peterborough city centre. Currently has six handpumps; three guest beers. ◖ ⇄

Boy's Head
Oundle Road (A605)
☎ (0733) 65021
11.30–11
Courage Directors; John Smith's Bitter Ⓗ
Lively pub built on Saxon graveyard. Large, well-used public bar. Live music in lounge at weekends. Good value food – chips with everything.
🛏 ◖ ◗ ⊟ ♣ P

Crab & Winkle
Loxley Centre, Davids Lane, Werrington (50 yds E of A15)
☎ (0733) 322377
11–2.30; 5.30–11 (11–11 Sat)
Greene King XX Dark, IPA, Abbot Ale Ⓗ
Friendly, new estate pub at northern extremity of city. Live music at weekends. Named after nearby disused railway line to the coast. Bar snacks both sessions. Q ♿ ♣ P

Crown
749 Lincoln Road, New England
☎ (0733) 41366
11–3; 5–11 (11–11 Fri & Sat)
Adnams Bitter; Draught Bass; Charrington IPA Ⓗ
Excellent locals' pub serving a lively cross-section of the community. Street-corner building with mock Tudor facade. Good value food (children's menu). Diverse entertainment.
⌂ ❀ ◖ ◗ ⊟ ♣ ⌓ P

Hand & Heart
12 Highbury Street
☎ (0733) 69463
10.30–2.30 (3.30 Fri & Sat); 6–11
John Smith's Magnet Ⓗ
Typical back-street, locals' pub. Still has original Warwick's Brewery windows. Well-known locally as a giant in darts and dominoes. ⌂ Q ⊟ ♣

Swiss Cottage
2 Grove Street
☎ (0733) 68734

10.30–11
John Smith's Bitter [H]
Back-street local; roughly in the style of an alpine chalet!
▦ ◖ ⊟ ⇌ ♣

Woolpack
29 North Street, Stanground
☎ (0733) 54417
11–3; 7–11
Brakspear Special; Marston's Pedigree Bitter; Whitbread Wethered Bitter, Castle Eden Ale [H]
Refurbished village pub, five minutes' ride from city centre. Stone fireplace; collection of militaria. Garden leads to old course of River Nene – boat moorings available. Guest beer.
▦ ♣

Try also: Gladstone Arms (Free)

Purls Bridge

Ship Inn
☎ (035 478) 578
11.30–2.30; 7–11 (closed Mon)
Greene King IPA [H]
Isolated Fenland pub, two miles down dead-end road from the village of Manea. Consists of one refurbished lounge bar with dining area. ▲ Q ▦ ◖ ◗

Ramsey

Jolly Sailor
Great Whyte
☎ (0487) 813388
11–2.30; 6.30–11
Camerons Traditional Bitter, Strongarm; Courage Directors [H]
Town-centre pub with a timeless feel. In same family for many years though passed from Watney to Brent-Walker in 1989. Interesting local photographs on walls. Q ▦ ⊟

Three Horseshoes
Little Whyte
☎ (0487) 812452
11–2.30; 6–11
John Smith's Bitter, Magnet [H]
Busy back-street pub with distinct northern flavour. Back bar converted to a restaurant.
⇿ ◖ ◗ ⊟

Ramsey St Mary's

White Lion
Hern Road (B1040)
☎ (073 129) 386
12–3; 7–11
Adnams Broadside; Charles Wells Eagle Bitter, Bombardier [H]
Isolated pub in long Fenland village. Greatly improved since Charles Wells took it over from Watney Mann. Good value varied menu caters for children and vegetarians.
▲ Q ▦ ◖ ◗ ⊟ ♣ P

St Ives

Oliver Cromwell
Wellington Street
☎ (0480) 65601
10.30–2.30; 6–11
Adnams Broadside; Greene King IPA [H]
Busy lounge-bar pub largely unchanged in recent years. Close to riverside quay and historic bridge. Note the unusually ornate pub sign. Pub clock keeps to GMT. Q ▦

St Neots

Wheatsheaf
Church Street ☎ (0480) 77435
11–2.30; 7 (6 Fri)–11
Greene King XX Dark, IPA, Abbot Ale [H], **Winter Ale** [G]
Cheerful locals' pub, ten years in the *Good Beer Guide*. Excellent XX Dark, which is becoming hard to find in the area. ▲ ▦ ♣

Sawston

University Arms
84 London Road
☎ (0223) 832165
12–2.30; 6–11
Beer range varies
Friendly free house with an ever-changing range of beers, three or four usually available at any one time. ♘ ▦ ◖ ◗ ♣ ◡ P

Shepreth

Plough
12 High Street, Frog End
☎ (0763) 60923
12–2.30; 7–11 (11–3; 6.30–11 Sat)
Courage Best Bitter, Directors; Charles Wells Eagle Bitter [H]
First-rate, one-bar pub with separate restaurant open in the evening. Guest beer.
▲ ♘ ▦ ◖ ◗ ⇌ ♣ P

Soham

Carpenters Arms
27 Brook Street (from Fordham Road go down Staples Lane, turn right) ☎ (0353) 720869
11–11
Adnams Bitter; Greene King IPA; Marston's Pedigree Bitter [H]
Lively local, somewhat hidden away but well worth finding. Snacks and meals available 12–10.30pm. ▦ ◖ ◗ ♣ P

Somersham

Windmill
☎ (0487) 840328
11–2.30; 6.30–11
Greene King IPA [H], **Abbot Ale** [G]
Cottage-style pub, one mile west of Somersham. Two contrasting bars. ♘ ▦ ◖ ◗ ⊟ ♣ P

Southoe

Bell
On A1 (Northbound)
☎ (0480) 810981
11–2.30; 6–11
Charles Wells Eagle Bitter, Bombardier [H]
Comfortable, food-oriented lounge bar and restaurant, right on A1. Access is difficult for southbound traffic. ▦ ◖ ◗ P

Stilton

Bell
Old Great North Road
☎ (0733) 242626
11–2.30; 6–11
Courage Directors; Ind Coope Burton Ale; Marston's Pedigree Bitter; Tetley Bitter [H]
17th-century, stone-built coaching inn. Recent restoration work has returned this inn to its former glory. James I, Cromwell and Dick Turpin have all been guests here. Good, but expensive food (veg option).
▲ Q ▦ ⇿ ◖ ◗ P

Stow cum Quy

Prince Albert
Newmarket Road
☎ (0223) 811294
11.30–3; 5–11
Bateman Dark Mild; Greene King IPA [H]
Lively pub with a broad selection of guest beers.
▲ ▦ ◖ ◗ ♣ P

Try also: Kings, Reach (Free)

Thorney Toll

Black Horse
Wisbech Road (A47)
☎ (073 128) 218
11–2.30; 6 (7 winter)–11
Elgood's Bitter, Winter Warmer [H]
Two-roomed pub with pool in one and collection of miniatures in the other. Popular stop for East Coast traffic. Coaches welcome. May be open summer afternoons. ▲ ♘ ▦ ◖ ◗ ⊟ ♣ P

Tilbrook

White Horse
High Street (A45)
☎ (0480) 860764
11–2.30; 6–11
Charles Wells Eagle Bitter, Bombardier [H]
Ex-Watney pub on the edge of village, now completely rebuilt but retaining good public bar. Note the former Three Shuttles pub sign. Large garden with children's play equipment. Hood skittles. ▦ ◖ ◗ ⊟ ♣ P

Whittlesey

Boat
2 Ramsey Road (B1040)
☎ (0733) 202488
11–2.30 (5 Sat); 7 (6.30 Fri & Sat)–11
Elgood's Bitter, GSB Ⓗ
Traditional, small town pub with lively crowd in two bars. Excellent beer, food and accommodation. Popular with visiting anglers.
⌂ Q ❀ ⛟ ◐ ◑ ⊟ ≋ ♣ P

Bricklayers Arms
9 Station Road
☎ (0733) 202593
11–3; 6–11
Ruddles Best Bitter; Webster's Yorkshire Bitter Ⓗ
Popular town local with large, basic bar and modernised lounge. Eve meals Sat only. Bar skittles. ⌂ ❀ ◑ ⊟ ♿ ≋ ♣ P

Wilburton

Kings Head
High Street ☎ (0353) 741029
12–2.30; 6.30–11
Adnams Bitter; Greene King IPA, Abbot Ale; Wadworth 6X Ⓗ
Excellent, two-bar pub with patio-style restaurant.
⌂ ❀ ◐ ◑ ⊟ ♣ P

Willingham

Three Tuns
Church Street ☎ (0954) 60437
11–2.30 (12–2.30 Sun); 6–11
Greene King XX Dark, IPA, Abbot Ale Ⓗ
A traditional village pub – if only they were all like this. Lunchtime snacks. ❀ ⊟ ♣

Wisbech

King's Head
13 Old Market
☎ (0945) 65402
11–3; 6–11
Elgood's Bitter, GSB Ⓗ
Good town pub consisting of a public bar decorated with enamel signs, a lounge bar, and a patio overlooking the River Nene. Selection of malt whiskies. ❀ ⛟ ◐ ◑ ⊟ ♿ ♣

Red Lion
32 North Brink
☎ (0945) 582022
11.30–2.30; 6 (7 Sat)–11
Elgood's Bitter, Winter Warmer Ⓗ
Popular pub close to Elgood's brewery, set amongst classical Georgian buildings, overlooking tidal River Nene. Smart lounge bar and separate restaurant (no meals Mon eve). ❀ ◐ ◑ P

Wisbech Arms
Exchange Square
☎ (0945) 584387
10.30–2.30; 5.30–11 (10.30–11 Sat)
Courage Directors; John Smith's Bitter Ⓗ
Excellent, one-roomed locals' pub with no food. Opposite fruit and vegetable auction rooms. ⊟ ♿ ♣ P

THE GBG QUIZ

Round One: Basics

1. How many pints in a kilderkin?
2. Which brewery's beer is sold at the following TV pubs:
   Rover's Return (*Coronation Street*)?
   The Woolpack (*Emmerdale*)?
   The Drover's Arms (*All Creatures Great and Small*)?
   The Queen Victoria (*EastEnders*)?
3. Which is the highest pub in England?
4. Why was porter so called?
5. Give the christian names of the founders of the following breweries:
   Courage
   Hansons
   Wadworth
   Whitbread
   Truman
6. What does the word 'lager' mean?
7. Which is Britain's largest brewing company?
8. What does IPA stand for?
9. What is perry?
10. What does the abbreviation NABLAB stand for?
11. What is a sleeve?
12. Which beer from the British Isles is brewed under licence in many other countries?
13. Which Queen preferred London bitter to champagne?
14. What is Keg Buster's favourite beer?
15. Who started a chain of pub breweries with a type of beer cask in each name?

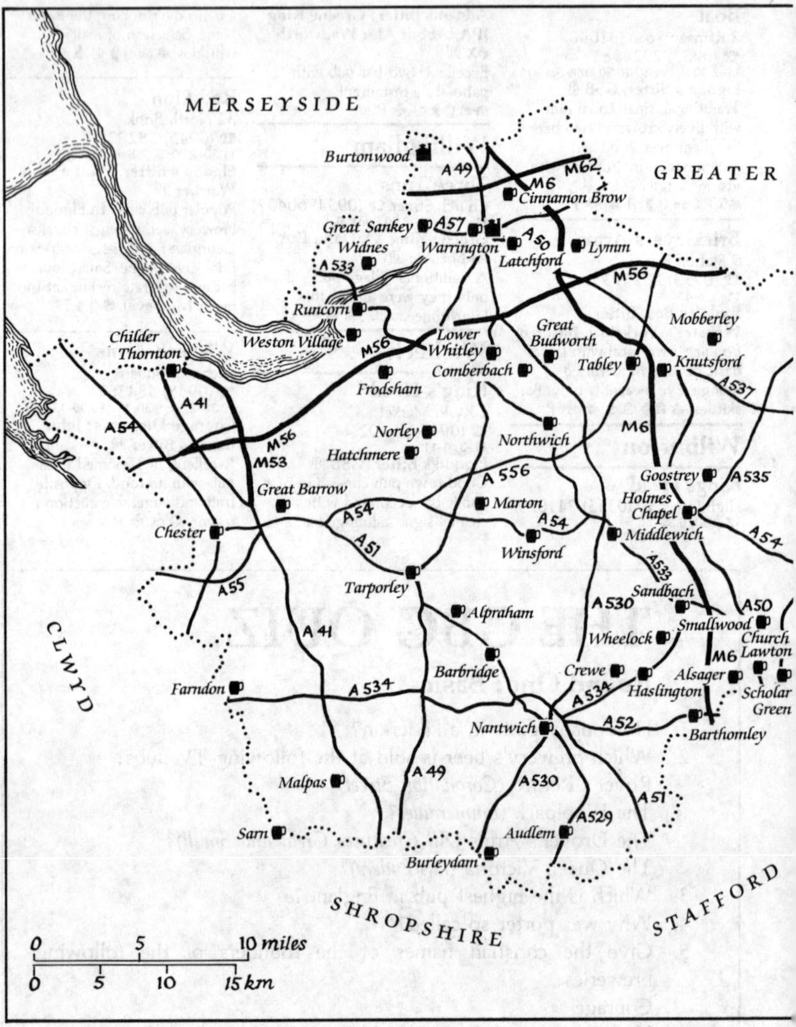

Burtonwood, *Burtonwood*; **Greenalls**, *Warrington*

Alpraham

Travellers Rest
Chester Road
6–11 (12–3; 6–11 Sat)
McEwan 70/-; Tetley Mild, Bitter H
Award-winning locals' pub. Quiet and friendly, although prone to occasional sing-songs. Bowling green. Q P

Alsager

Mere Inn
Crewe Road (B5077)
☎ (0270) 882019
11–3.30; 5.30 (6.30 Sat)–11
Greenalls Bitter H
Small pub opposite Alsager Mere. Lunches Tue–Sat only.
P

Audlem

Bridge
Shropshire Street (A525)
11–3; 7–11
Marston's Burton Best Bitter, Pedigree Bitter, Merrie Monk H
Locals' and boaters' pub; a refreshment stop before tackling the Audlem Flight. Occasionally has other Marston's beers. Piano played some eves. Table skittles.
P

Barbridge

Barbridge Inn
Chester Road (off A51)
☎ (0270) 73266
12–3; 6.30 (5.30 Fri & Sat)–11
(11.30–3; 5.30–11 summer)
Whitbread Boddingtons Mild, Boddingtons Bitter H
Popular stopping point for canal users. Near junction of Shropshire Union Canal and Middlewich branch. Canal theme in main bar; sports theme in public bar. Summer barbecues in garden. Occasional live jazz.
P

Barthomley

White Lion
Audley Road
11–3; 6–11
Burtonwood Best Bitter [H]
Beautifully thatched and half-timbered pub, dated 1640 and little altered since. Landlord of 41 years standing.
⌂ Q ❀ ⊞ ♣ P

Bollington

Lord Clyde
36 Clarke Lane
☎ (0625) 573202
11–3; 5.30–11
Greenalls Bitter, Thomas Greenall's Original Bitter [H]
Recently-modernised, small, one-room pub near Macclesfield Canal, named after Colin Campbell who was put in charge at the outbreak of the Indian mutiny. ⌂ Q ❀ ♣ P

Meridian
Palmerston Street
☎ (0625) 573883
11–3; 5.30–11
Whitbread Boddingtons Mild, Boddingtons Bitter [H]
Multi-roomed pub, popular with all age groups. Bar skittles played. ⌂ Q ⊞ ♣

Vale
Adlington Road
☎ (0625) 575147
11.30–3; 7–11
Taylor Landlord; Thwaites Best Mild, Bitter [H]
Once three terraced houses, now a comfortable one-room pub. No food Mon. ⌂ Q ◖ P

All Bollington pubs sell real ale.

Bosley

Queens Arms
Leek Road ☎ (0260) 223267
11.30–3; 5.30–11
Whitbread Boddingtons Bitter [H]
Large detached 17th-century inn, set in beautiful surroundings with pleasant garden to rear. Clean and attractive open bar area with small room off main room for families. No food Mon eves.
⌂ ≿ ❀ ◖ ◗ P

Buglawton

Church House
Buxton Road
☎ (0260) 272466
11–3; 6–11
Robinson's Best Mild, Best Bitter [E]
Roomy pub with excellent bar meals (not Sat eve) and restaurant. Unusual pub sign combined with pigeon cote.
⌂ ≿ ❀ ◖ ◗ ♿

Try also: Robin Hood (Marston's)

Burleydam

Combermere Arms
A525, ½ mile from A530 jct
11.30–3; 7–11
Draught Bass; Marston's Pedigree Bitter; Younger Scotch [H]
17th-century pub, reputedly haunted. Guest beer.
⌂ Q ≿ ❀ ◖ ◗ ♿ ♣ P

Chester

Albion
Park Street ☎ (0244) 340345
11–3; 5.30–11
Greenalls Mild, Bitter, Thomas Greenall's Original Bitter [H]
Excellent, unspoilt street-corner pub, close to the city walls. Decorated with WW1 memorabilia (and unusual wallpaper!). Good lunches with no fry-ups. No eve food Fri–Sat.
⌂ Q ◖ ◗ ⊞ ♣

Boathouse
The Groves
11.30–4; 6–11 (11–11 summer)
McEwan 70/-; Theakston Best Bitter; Younger IPA [H]
Riverside pub comprising two smart lounge bars, one with family facilities. Extensive range of foreign bottle-conditioned beers. Draught beers may vary (within S & N range).
≿ ❀ ◖ ◗ ♿ P

Cherry Orchard
5 Chapel Lane, Boughton
☎ (0244) 324013
11–11
Courage Directors; John Smith's Bitter [H]
Rambling one-room pub partitioned off into several areas. A roadhouse with a local's feel. ◖ ◗ ♣ P

Clavertons
Lower Bridge Street
☎ (0244) 312320
11–11
Lees Bitter, Moonraker [H]
Basement wine bar-type pub, popular with young people. Often crowded at weekends with restricted access. ❀ ◖ ◗

Faulkner Arms
Faulkner Street, Hoole (off A56)
☎ (0244) 324941
11–11
Greenalls Mild, Bitter, Thomas Greenall's Original Bitter [H]
Deservedly popular street-corner local close to Hoole shopping area. Q ❀ ◖ ◗ ⊞ ♣

Little Oak
99 Boughton (A41)
☎ (0244) 318682
12–3; 6–11
Greenalls Bitter, Thomas Greenall's Original Bitter [H]
Lovely terraced pub frontage masks a modernised interior which retains some character. Popular with local law college students. ❀ ◖ ♣

Olde Custom House
Watergate Street
11–3; 5.30–11
Marston's Border Mild, Border Exhibition, Border Bitter, Pedigree Bitter [H], **Owd Rodger** [G]
Historic pub, a meeting place for many clubs and societies. Public bar, two lounges and no jukebox. Q ◖ ⊞ ♣

Cheshire

Childer Thornton

Halfway House
New Chester Road (A41)
☎ (051) 339 2202
1 (12 Fri, 11 Sat)–11
John Smith's Bitter Ⓗ
Friendly traditional pub atmosphere in several rooms of an old coaching inn, halfway between Birkenhead and Chester. 🚸 ❀ ⊟ ♣ P

White Lion
New Road (200 yds off A41)
☎ (051) 339 3402
11.30–3; 5–11.30 (11.30–11 Fri & Sat)
Thwaites Best Mild, Bitter Ⓗ
Small, busy, two-room old country local with friendly atmosphere. Attracts customers from near and far; second room used by families at lunchtime only, but gets crowded. No food Sun. ♨ Q 🚸 ❀ ◐ P

Church Lawton

Lawton Arms
Knutsford Road (A50)
11–3; 5.30–11
Robinson's Best Mild, Best Bitter Ⓔ
A locals' pub; mainly a lounge with separate snug and games room. ♨ Q ⊟ ♣ P

Cinnamon Brow

Millhouse
Ballater Drive (off A574)
☎ (0925) 811405
11–4; 6.30–11
Holt Mild, Bitter Ⓗ
Large, modern pub built in late 1980s to cater for new residential areas. Spacious, basic bar; plush lounge. Quiz night every Mon. ❀ ◐ ⊟ ♣ P

Comberbach

Drum & Monkey
The Avenue (off A599)
☎ (0606) 891417
11.30–3 (4 Sat); 7–11
Tetley Mild, Bitter Ⓗ
Close to Marbury Country Park. An open-plan pub with a brass monkey taking pride of place. Snacks available at lunchtime. ♣ P

Congleton

Grapes
18 Willow Street
☎ (0260) 274863
11.30–3; 5.30–11 (11–11 Fri & Sat)
Tetley Bitter Ⓗ
Traditional terraced local featuring many relics of the past, including a North Cheshire Breweries glass door and a Victorian cooking range.
♨ Q ❀ ◐ ⊟ ♣

Wharf
121 Canal Road
☎ (0260) 272809
11–3; 5.30–11 (may vary)
Greenalls Mild, Bitter Ⓗ
One of the few traditional places left in an area of modern housing development. Popular with locals and travellers along the Macclesfield Canal. Car park used by local pigeon fanciers for racing. Q ❀ ⊟ ⇌ ♣ P

Try also: Waggon & Horses (Marston's)

Crewe

British Lion
Nantwich Road (A534)
12–4 (3 Tue & Wed); 7–11
Ind Coope Burton Ale; Tetley Dark Mild, Bitter Ⓗ
Small, very busy town pub, mainly used by locals. Known as the 'Pig'. ♨ ♿ ⇌

Horseshoe
North Street (B5078)
☎ (0270) 584265
12–4; 7–11
Robinson's Best Mild, Best Bitter Ⓗ, **Old Tom** (winter) Ⓖ
Old pub, divided into several rooms. ♨ ⊟ ♣ P

Kings Arms
Earle Street
11–4; 7–11 (11.30–3; 5.30–11 Tue–Thu, 11.30–4; 5.30–11 Fri)
Whitbread Chester's Best Mild, Chester's Best Bitter, Boddingtons Bitter, Trophy Ⓗ
Town-centre pub (near banger racing track) with four rooms, each with its own character and regulars. Mild is the most popular pint here.
♨ ⊟ ♣

Try also: Crown (Robinson's)

Disley

Crescent
45 Buxton Road (A6)
☎ (0663) 62638
11.30–3; 5.30–11 (11.30–11 Fri & Sat)
Robinson's Best Mild, Best Bitter, Old Tom Ⓗ
Thriving terraced local, whose reputation for good food has extended beyond its devoted village regulars.
♨ ❀ ◐ ◗ ⇌ ♣ P

Try also; White Lion (Wilson's)

Eaton

Plough
Macclesfield Road (A536, 2 miles from Congleton)
☎ (0260) 280207
12–3; 7–11
Banks's Mild, Bitter Ⓗ
Village centre pub, revitalised in recent years by ex-brewer Clive Winkle. Much emphasis on food and can get busy as a consequence. This does not detract from the welcoming atmosphere. ♨ ◐ ◗ P

Farndon

Greyhound
High Street (B5130)
☎ (0829) 270244
12–3; 5.30–11 (7–11 Sat)
Greenalls Mild, Bitter, Thomas Greenall's Original Bitter Ⓗ
Pleasant homely hotel by River Dee and 14th-century bridge. Residents include donkeys Henry and Guinness.
♨ Q ❀ 🛏 ⊟ ♣ P

Frodsham

Golden Lion
High Street (A56)
☎ (0928) 32179
11–3; 6–11 (may vary)
Samuel Smith OBB Ⓗ
Over 100 years old and known as the Corner House. Large single bar services a lounge and two tiny snugs. Part of old Frodsham which has so far escaped the attention of the modern architect's imagination.
♨ ◐ ⇌ ♣

Goostrey

Crown
111 Main Road
☎ (0477) 32128
11–3; 5.30–11
Marston's Burton Best Bitter, Pedigree Bitter Ⓗ
Imposing 16th-century pub in sought-after dormitory village. Homely lounge and traditional tap room. Wide range of food (not Sun eve or Mon). Nearest pub to Jodrell Bank Radio Telescope.
♨ Q 🚸 ❀ 🛏 ◐ ◗ ⊟ ⇌ ♣ P

Great Barrow

White Horse
Main Road (B5132, off A51)
12–3; 6–11 (12–11 Sat)
Banks's Mild, Bitter Ⓔ
Attractive village pub whose location is reflected in its country flavour. Compact lounge bar area; varied pub activities. No food Mon.
♨ ❀ ◐ ◗ ♣ P

Great Budworth

George & Dragon
High Street ☎ (0606) 891317
12–3; 7–11
Ind Coope Burton Ale; Tetley Dark Mild, Bitter Ⓗ
Popular local in the centre of attractive and prestigious village. Warm, welcoming lounge faces the impressive church; busy public bar to the rear. Upstairs restaurant.

Interesting carved wooden horse rails near the solid oak front door. P

Great Sankey

Manor House

362 Liverpool Road (A57, 600 yds from A562 jct)
☎ (0925) 722890
12–3; 6–11
Ind Coope Burton Ale; Jennings Bitter; Tetley Bitter [H]
Large old black and white roadside pub in residential area. Open-plan and split-level, with wood panelling and partitions. Stained glass around long bar. Food includes veg meals. Formerly a nunnery.
(Sankey) P

Haslington

Hawk

137 Crewe Road (A534)
11–11
Robinson's Best Mild, Best Bitter [E]
15th-century roadside inn with separate restaurant. An exposed panel inside reveals the original wattle wallings. P

Hatchmere

Carriers

Delamere Road (B5152) OS554722
11–3; 5.30–11
Burtonwood Dark Mild, Best Bitter [H]
Open-plan and spacious split-level lounge has french windows opening out to garden and mere; unusual public bar. Regular live music. On the edge of Delamere Forest, a magnet for walkers and picnickers. Hatchmere also attracts fishermen. Eve meals at weekends. ♣ P

Henbury

Cock Inn

Chelford Road (A537)
☎ (0625) 23186
12–3; 5.30–11
Robinson's Best Mild, Best Bitter, Old Tom [H]
Comfortable main road pub just outside Macclesfield, with both local and passing trade. Children welcome in restaurant.
Q P

Holmes Chapel

Swan

29 Station Road
☎ (0477) 32259
11–2.30; 4.30–11 (11–11 Fri & Sat)
Samuel Smith OBB [H]
Former coaching inn with good food. Interesting old black stove on display.
♣ P

Knutsford

Builders Arms

Mobberley Road (off A537)
☎ (0565) 4528
11.30–3; 5.30–11
Marston's Mercian Mild, Burton Best Bitter, Pedigree Bitter [H]
Small and busy local with keen games emphasis. Q ♣

White Lion

94 King Street ☎ (0565) 2018
11–3 (3.30 Sat in winter); 5.30–11 (11–11 Sat in summer)
Hydes' Anvil Bitter; Tetley Bitter [H]
Tasteful pub with extensive range of cheese and pâté lunches — doggie bags provided! No food Sun.
Q ♣

Latchford

Penny Ferry

Thelwall Lane (off A50)
☎ (0925) 38487
11–5; 6.30–11
Burtonwood Dark Mild, Best Bitter [H]
Near to Latchford Locks and the famous Manchester Ship Canal ferry service, this modern pub has an unusual sunken games area, and nautical photos adorn the walls. ♣ P

Lower Whitley

Chetwode Arms

Street Lane (off A49)
☎ (0925) 73203
11–3; 5.30–11 (11–11 Sat)
Greenalls Mild, Bitter [E]
A popular and welcoming country local which appeals to most tastes. Distinctive character in each of the six rooms, ranging from a stone-floored public bar to a plush dining area overlooking the bowling green. Active bowling, pool, darts, golf and chess societies. ♣ P

Lymm

Spread Eagle

Eagle Brow (A6144)
☎ (092575) 3139
11.30–11
Lees GB Mild, Bitter [H], **Moonraker** [E]
Ornate old pub near Lymm village cross and 200 yds from canal moorings. Three separate rooms: basic bar, small cosy snug and large plush lounge on two levels. Snug popular with locals, particularly early evening. Ballroom upstairs.

Wheatsheaf

Agden Brow (A56)
☎ (092575) 2567
11–3; 5.30–11 (11–11 Sat & summer)
Hydes' Anvil Mild, Bitter [H]
Roadside pub dating back well over 200 years. Recently-extended but still has a strong following in the public bar.
♣ P

Macclesfield

Baths Hotel

Green Street (behind station)
11–3 (not Mon–Fri); 5.30–11
Whitbread Boddingtons Mild, Boddingtons Bitter [H]
Thriving pub named after now defunct public baths. Basic and friendly. ♣

Bridgewater Arms

174 Buxton Road (A537)
☎ (0625) 22660
11–4; 5.30–11
Wilson's Original Mild, Wilson's Original Bitter, Webster's Yorkshire Bitter [H]
Friendly pub named after the Duke of Bridgewater and situated next to the canal he built. ♣

British Flag

Coare Street ☎ (0625) 25500
11–3 (12–2 Sun); 5.30–11
Robinson's Best Bitter [H]
Comfortable locals' pub with a sizeable games room. Boasted 'ginger beer manufacturing' in the 1860s. ♣

Castle

Church Street ☎ (0625) 27866
11–3 (3.30 Sat); 7.30–11
Tetley Mild, Bitter [H]
One of the oldest pubs in Macclesfield, in a quaint cobbled street. The key to Macclesfield Castle, which once stood nearby, is still kept at the pub. No food Sun. Q ♣

Evening Star

87–89 James Street (400 yds from A536/A523 jct)
☎ (0625) 24093
11–3 (12–2 Sun); 5.30–11
Marston's Mild, Burton Best Bitter, Pedigree Bitter [E]
A friendly little local tucked away in the back streets. Difficult to find by car: a maze of blocked streets. Quiet at lunchtimes but busier evenings and weekends. Q ♣

George & Dragon

23 Sunderland Street
☎ (0625) 21898
11–4 (3 Tue & Wed); 5.30 (7 Sat)–11
Robinson's Best Mild, Best Bitter [E]
Locals' pub with pool table, darts and skittles. Next to bus and railway stations. Eve meals 5.30–7pm. ♣

Try also: Puss in Boots

Malpas

Cheshire

Red Lion
1 Old Hall Street (B5395)
☎ (0948) 860368
11–11
Draught Bass; Hanby Drawwell Bitter [H]
Well-kept old village inn with its own sauna and solarium. Try the landlord's own whisky. Restored adjacent cottage due to be opened in summer 1990 for extra accommodation. Beers may vary.
⌂ Q ☋ ✿ ⊨ ◖ ◗ ♣ ○ P

Marton

Plough
Beauty Bank (off Whitegate Road, 1½ miles from A54 jct) OS623683 ☎ (0606) 889455
11–2.30; 5.30–11 (11–11 Sat)
Robinson's Best Mild, Best Bitter [H], **Old Tom** [G]
Tiny village alehouse now vastly altered and extended, with emphasis on bar food (eve meals Tue–Sat). One of the very few remaining tap rooms locally. Handy for Whitegate Way footpath; near reputed centre of Cheshire and site of Vale Royal Abbey.
✿ ◖ ◗ ⊟ ♣ P

Middlewich

Boars Head
Kinderton Street (A54)
☎ (0606) 843191
12–3.30; 5.30–11
Robinson's Best Mild, Best Bitter [E]
Large, multi-roomed pub on outskirts of town, next to canal. Spacious lounge, small tap room, games room and TV lounge. Brass lines mean handpumps are for show only.
Q ☋ ⊨ ◖ ⊟ ♣ P

Mobberley

Bird in Hand
Knolls Green
☎ (0565) 873149
11.30–3; 5.30–11
Samuel Smith OBB, Museum Ale [H]
Pleasant, multi-roomed roadside pub serving good food – lunches Mon–Sat; eve meals Tue–Sat. ⌂ Q ☋ ✿ ◖ ◗ ♿ P

Try also: Chapel House

Nantwich

Bowling Green
The Gullet (behind parish church) ☎ (0270) 626001
11–11
Ruddles Best Bitter, County; Webster's Yorkshire Bitter, Choice [H]
Split-level pub, popular with young people with a good atmosphere. Recently-added restaurant. No eve meals Mon.
Q ☋ ✿ ◖ ◗ ♿ ⇌ ♣ P

Vine
42 Hospital Street
☎ (0270) 624172
12–3; 7–11
Burtonwood Best Bitter [H]
Traditional two-roomed, 16th-century town-centre pub. Local CAMRA 'Pub Of The Year 1990'. ⌂ Q ⊨ ⊟ ⇌ ♣

Try also: Rifleman (Robinson's)

Newbold

Horseshoe
Fence Lane (off A34 at Astbury church) OS863602
☎ (0260) 272205
11–3; 6–11
Robinson's Best Mild, Best Bitter [E]
Isolated country pub, formerly part of a farmhouse. Difficult to find but worth the effort. Children welcome in side room till 8.30. Small car park.
⌂ ☋ ✿ ◖ ♣ P

Try also: Egerton (Robinson's)

Norley

Tigers Head
Pythchleys Hollow (School Bank) OS572727
☎ (0928) 88309
11.30–3; 4.45–11 (11–11 Thu–Sat)
Burtonwood Dark Mild, Best Bitter [E]
Popular, welcoming 17th-century village local with a split-level lounge area and a basic tap room. ⌂ ✿ ◖ ◗ ⊟ P

Northwich

Freemasons
Castle Street (A559)
☎ (0606) 79310
11–11
Ruddles Best Bitter; Wilson's Original Mild, Wilson's Original Bitter, Webster's Yorkshire Bitter [H]
Small, cosy friendly pub at top of Castle Hill. When busy, it can be very cramped in the tiny locals' bar. ⊟ ♣

Poynton

Boars Head
Shrigley Road (1½ miles E of Poynton on A523)
11–3; 5.30–11.30 (11–11 Sat)
Whitbread Boddingtons Mild, Boddingtons Bitter [E]
Unpretentious pub, convenient for outdoor activities; close to Macclesfield Canal, west entrance to Lyme Park and adjacent to the Middlewood Way. ⌂ ✿ ⊟ ♣ P

Try also: Bulls Head

Rainow

Highwayman
(A5002, N of Rainow)
☎ (0625) 573245
11.30–3; 7–11
Thwaites Bitter [H]
400 year-old country pub with magnificent views.
⌂ ☋ ✿ ◖ ◗ ⊟ ♣ P

Runcorn

Barley Mow
56 Church Street (Old Town)
☎ (0928) 75235
11–3; 5 (7 Sat)–11
Walker Mild, Bitter [H]
Typical town-centre pub; comfortable but quiet lounge and more boisterous tap room, popular with locals. Restored in recent years but retains its gritty northern charm. Near to incongruous Runcorn-Widnes Bridge. ⌂ ✿ ◖ ⊟ ♿ ⇌ ♣

Windmill
Windmill Hill (off A533, 1 mile from A56 jct)
11–3; 6–11
Hydes' Anvil Light, Bitter [E]
Ultra-modern, but pleasant and relaxing interior. Lounge is split-level, with several pieces of antique furniture; bar populated by locals. Octagonal pub boasting a pyramid-style roof with a light at the top.
✿ ◖ ⊟ ♣ P

Sandbach

Iron Grey
49 Middlewich Road
11–3.30; 5.30–11
Robinson's Best Mild, Best Bitter [H]
A recent refurbishment has destroyed much of the character that this small town terrace pub once had. In spite of this, the locals have remained loyal. Bar snacks only. ⌂ ✿ ♿ ♣

Swan & Chequers
16 Hightown
11–3 (4 Thu–Sat); 5.30 (7 Sat)–11
Robinson's Best Mild, Best Bitter [E]
Large town-centre pub.
✿ ◖ ♿ ♣ P

Sarn

Queens Head
Off B5069 OS440447
☎ (094 881) 244
11.30–3; 5–11
Marston's Border Mild, Burton Best Bitter [H]
Small pub alongside old mill brook in hunting country. Home-cooked meals in separate cosy bistro.
⌂ Q ✿ ⊨ ◖ ◗ ⊟ ♣ P

Scholar Green

Globe
Drumber Lane (off A34)
12–3 (Mon, Fri, & Sat); 7–11
Marston's Pedigree Bitter 🄷
Pub with three small rooms: central bar, lounge and darts room. Parking difficult.
Q ♨ ⊞ ♣ P

Smallwood

Bluebell
Spen Green (1 mile W of village, on lane to A34) OS821607
12–3; 6–11
Greenalls Bitter 🄷
300 year-old rural pub, once part of a farm. Low beams, stone floors and antique benches. ⌂ Q ❀ ⊞ ♣ P

Sutton

Lamb
Hollins Lane (3 miles off main London road) OS932713
11.30–3; 7–11
Tetley Bitter 🄷
Pleasant village pub set back slightly from the road. Built in 1938 with local stone, to replace former pub of same name. Good place to start or finish a ramble in the nearby hills. No separate public bar but good basic tap/games area. Eve meals Thu–Sun only.
⌂ ❀ ◐ ◗ ♣ P

Tabley

Windmill
Chester Road (A556, 50 yds from M6 jct 19)
☎ (0565) 2670
12–3; 7–11
Robinson's Best Mild, Best Bitter, Old Tom 🄷
Multi-roomed old roadside pub, just off motorway. Cosy atmosphere with comfortable furniture and subtle lighting. Popular and friendly, a taxidermists' delight. Tends to be busy with office workers early evening. Coaches by appointment only. Eve meals Thu–Sun only in winter.
⌂ ❀ ⛿ ◐ ◗ ⊞ P

Tarporley

Rising Sun
High Street (A49, near A51 jct) ☎ (0829) 732423
11–2.30; 5.30–11
Robinson's Best Mild, Best Bitter 🄷
Authentic old inn of quality and character. Several rooms with antique furniture and old Worthington mirrors. Can be very busy during mealtimes, but also a village meeting place early evenings. Children allowed in dining room. No food Sun eve. ◐ ◗ P

Timbersbrook

Coach & Horses
Dane in Shaw Bank (1 mile N of Congleton on Rushton-Spencer road) OS890619
☎ (0260) 273019
11–3; 6–11
Robinson's Best Mild, Best Bitter 🄴
Pleasant hostelry situated north of Congleton. Through lounge with small tap room behind fireplace. Popular with locals. Occasional live entertainment plus regular unusual events. Play area in garden. No eve meals Mon. ⌂ ❀ ◐ ◗ Ʌ P

Warrington

Lord Rodney Hotel
Winwick Road
☎ (0925) 30037
11.30–3; 6 (7 Sat)–11
Tetley Mild, Bitter 🄷
Large corner pub close to Tetley Walker brewery. Stained glass windows with a nautical theme. Large basic bar with pool and TV; smaller lounge. The plusher rear lounge continues sea-faring decor. ⛿ ◐ ◗ ⇌ (Central) ♣

Lower Angel
27 Buttermarket Street
☎ (0925) 33299
11–4 (4.30 Fri & Sat); 6.30–11
Ind Coope Burton Ale; Walker Mild, Bitter, Best Bitter, Winter Warmer 🄷
Small, friendly two-roomed town-centre pub with fine Walker tiled frontage. Comfortable lounge and basic bar. A haven in a town where real ale and good pubs are thin on the ground. Resident ghost, Dick Peabody, inhabits lounge! Guest beers. ⊞ ⇌ (Central) ♣

Weston Village

Royal Oak
Heath Road South
☎ (0928) 565839
12–3; 7–11 (11–11 Fri)
Marston's Burton Best Bitter, Pedigree Bitter 🄷
Friendly village pub overlooking the Mersey estuary. Small cosy lounge; quiet back room. Meeting room available upstairs. Very busy lunchtimes, with staff from nearby ICI works. Quiz nights Tue. ❀ ◐ ◗ ⊞ ♣

Wheelock

Commercial
Crewe Road (A354)
8–11 (closed lunchtime, except Sun 12–2)
Marston's Burton Best Bitter, Pedigree Bitter; Whitbread Boddingtons Bitter 🄷
Georgian house with old-fashioned and airy atmosphere, enhanced by wicker seats. Interesting Birkenhead Brewery notice in gents. By canal bridge 154. ⌂ Q ⊞ ⏀

Widnes

Victoria
20 Ann Street West
☎ (051) 495 1495
11.30–11
Tetley Mild, Bitter 🄷
Traditional three-roomed pub with large lounge. Live entertainment most Fri, Sat, and Suns. ⌂ ❀ ◐ ⊞ ♣

Wilmslow

Farmers Arms
Chapel Lane
☎ (0625) 532443
11–11
Whitbread Boddingtons Mild, Boddingtons Bitter 🄷
Traditional and thriving town local, with excellent bar lunches and busy tap room. No food Sun. ⌂ Q ♨ ❀ ◐ ♣ P

Horse & Jockey
144 Gravel Lane (off B5085)
☎ (0625) 582158
12–3.30; 5.30–11 (11.30–11 Sat)
Greenalls Mild, Bitter 🄷
Large locals' pub close to Mobberley Road. Big public bar with pool table and darts.
❀ ⊞ ♣ P

Try also: Riflemans

Wincle

Wild Boar
On A54, halfway between Congleton and Buxton
☎ (02607) 219
11–3; 7–11
Robinson's Best Mild, Best Bitter 🄷
Traditional, welcoming, stone-built pub high on the moors. Warming open fires in cold weather. Fortnightly clay-pigeon shoots can make Sunday lunchtimes very busy. A popular venue for local sledging and skiing during snowy weather. ⌂ ♨ ❀ ◐ ◗ P

Winsford

Brighton Belle
On A54, next to railway station
☎ (0606) 593292
12–3; 5.30–11 (11–11 Fri)
Burtonwood Best Bitter 🄷
Large plush lounge, smaller locals' bar. Restaurant is a Pullman carriage which ran on the London-Brighton line in the 1930s. Country and western night every Fri.
Q ❀ ◐ ◗ ⊞ ⇌ ♣ P

FRINGE BENEFITS: Tegestology

When you next lift your pint, glance underneath – at the beermat left lying on the table, always assuming it has not already been idly flipped on the floor.

Often, it has been scribbled on, as impoverished drinkers attempt to work out if they can afford another round. Sometimes, it has been torn as nervous fingers worry they have missed last orders. But for some, this tatty piece of beer-soaked cardboard is worth much more than the expensive liquid swilling around in their glass. Keen collectors might pay hundreds of pounds for a pre-war beermat from an obsolete brewery.

So look again. If the mat is thick and pitted and advertises SOS Old Strong at 4½d a nip bottle, you might have stumbled across an early mat from Southams of Shrewsbury, which the landlord has just rooted out from the darkest corner of his cellar. The odds are probably a million to one, but you can strike lucky.

But don't despair. Modern mats are just as valuable – as a pictorial record of present-day breweries and their beers. And those from small local breweries quickly become quite rare.

Remember, always ask the landlord if it is all right to take a couple. It is not just a matter of courtesy; it is in your own interest, for often he will find others for you from behind the bar. But the quickest way to build a collection is by joining the British Beermat Collectors Society, which holds regular meetings around the country where new issues can be obtained and older mats swapped with other collectors or bid for in auction.

The Society was founded in 1960 when Chris Walsh decided to discover if there were other mad matters by advertising in *Exchange & Mart*. The enthusiastic response led to the Society's formation. The first presidents were comedians Morecambe and Wise. I suspect Eric and Ernie had something to do with creating the official term for a mat collector – a tegestologist. This mouthful is supposed to be easier to say while chewing six mats.

If you wish to join, send £7 (payable to the BBCS) to the secretary, Brian West, 10 Coombe Hill Crescent, Thame, Oxfordshire OX9 2EH. Members receive a monthly magazine giving details of new beermats and meetings.

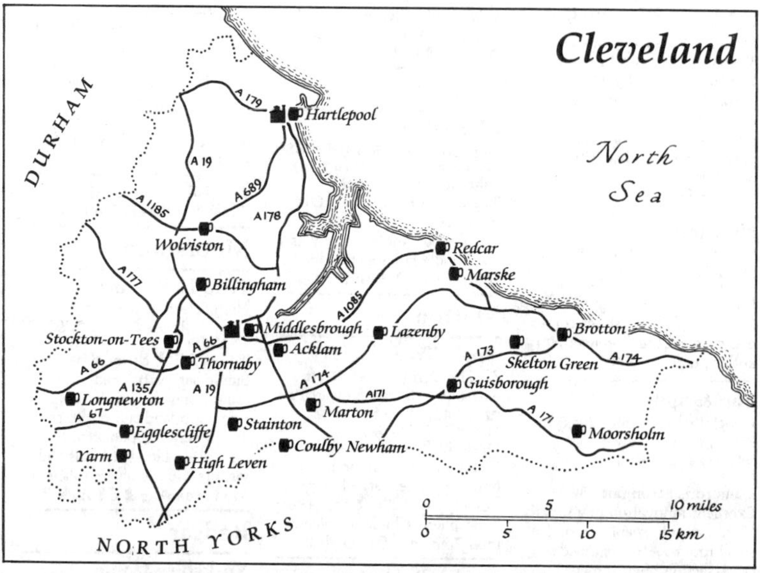

Brent-Walker (Camerons), *Hartlepool;* ***North Yorkshire,*** *Middlesbrough*

Acklam

Master Cooper
291 Acklam Road
☎ (0642) 819429
11–11
Samuel Smith OBB, Museum Ale Ⓗ
Listed building, former restaurant and fish and chip shop. Single L-shaped room. Plans to reveal original beams and ceilings. ⌂ ❀ ☾ P

Billingham

Black Horse
The Green ☎ (0642) 553869
11–11
Vaux Double Maxim; Wards Sheffield Best Bitter Ⓗ
Recently renovated, traditionally decorated public bar and separate open-plan lounge with food servery at one end. ☾ ◗ ⊟ P

Brotton

Green Tree
90 High Street ☎ (0287) 76377
12–4; 7.30–11
Camerons Strongarm Ⓗ
On site of former manor house, parts dating back to 1300s; has been an inn for over 400 years. Cosy and warm village pub with unusual pub games. 5p off a pint for all pensioners. Two family rooms – one ideal for toddlers. Bar snacks both sessions. ⌂ Q ♉ ⊟ ♿ ♣

Coulby Newham

Coulby Hotel
Stokesley Road (off B1365)
OS498144 ☎ (0642) 590757
11–11
Courage Directors Ⓗ
Old farmhouse imaginatively converted for family use, and including an over 21s room. Previous leisure centre now converted to function rooms. 150-seater restaurant – book for Sun lunch. Overnight accommodation designed to cater for disabled.
♉ ❀ ⊨ ☾ ◗ ♿ P

Egglescliffe

Pot & Glass
Church Road ☎ (0642) 780145
11–3; 5.30–11
Draught Bass Ⓗ
Two-roomed rural gem. Ornate bar fronts were made from furniture by former licensee, now buried opposite in churchyard. Long and fascinating history. Resident ghost! Good value, home-cooked food. Eve meals on request. Q ♉ ❀ ☾ ⊟ ♣ P

Guisborough

Huntsman
Enfield Chase, Hunters Hill (Hunters Hill Estate. Enquire locally!) ☎ (0287) 38618
12–3 (4 Fri, 11.30–4.30 Sat); 6.30–11
Ruddles Best Bitter Ⓗ
Large single-roomed modern estate pub, nicely set out. Popular with the young. Disco and quiz on Mon and Thu. Occasional live entertainment on Sat. Lunchtime snacks.
♿ ♣ P

Ship
145 Westgate ☎ (0287) 32233
11.30–11
Draught Bass Ⓗ
Terraced town-centre local; basic but cosy, decorated with maritime relics. Regular clientele. Large enclosed rear garden. Limited overnight accommodation and camping nearby. ⌂ ❀ ⊨ ⅄ ♣

Voyager
The Avenue (left at 2nd traffic lights from centre towards Middlesbrough)
☎ (0287) 34774
11–3; 6–11
Camerons Traditional Bitter, Strongarm; Everards Old Original Ⓗ
Modern one-roomed estate pub, well-laid-out with bar areas and restaurant on different levels. Good value meals. Plenty of garden play apparatus for children. ❀ ☾ ◗ ♿ ♣ P

Try also: Abbey (Samuel Smith); **Globe** (Camerons)

Hartlepool

Jacksons Arms
Tower Street ☎ (0429) 862413

Cleveland

12–4; 7–11 (11–3; 5–11 Wed, 11–11 Thu–Sat)
Draught Bass; Taylor Landlord; Theakston XB, Old Peculier; Whitbread Trophy 🄷
A traditional style has been maintained for this renovated old building: a comfortable, plush lounge and bar with bare board floor. Two guest beers.
⊞ ♿ ≹ ♣

New Inn
Durham Street (off Northgate)
☎ (0429) 267797
11–4 (11–11 Fri & Sat)
Camerons Strongarm 🄷
Clean and friendly street-corner pub on headland. Frequent entry in this guide. Q ⊞ ♣

Tap & Spile
Elwick Road, Stranton (next to the Camerons Brewery)
☎ (0429) 273954
11–11
Camerons Strongarm 🄷
Excellent renovation of a superb Victorian pub, keeping separate small rooms. Attracts a wide cross-section of customers. Strong commitment to charity fundraising and traditional music and dance (folk club Sun). Garden planned. Guest beers
Q ☋ ◖ ⊞ ≹ ♣

Try also: Gillen Arms

High Leven

Fox Covert
Low Lane (between Yarm and Thornaby on A1044)
☎ (0642) 760033
11–3; 5–11
Vaux Samson, Double Maxim 🄷
Distinctive cluster of whitewashed former farm buildings. Warm and comfortable open-plan interior. Alterations in progress to provide more space and better facilities whilst retaining the pub's character. Imaginative menu. ⌂ ❀ ◖ ◗ ♣ P

Lazenby

Nag's Head
High Street ☎ (0642) 440149
11.30–4.30; 7–11
Draught Bass 🄷
Cosy, spacious and well-decorated pub with rural scenes on walls. Weekday lunches are popular with the business community. ◖ ♣

Longnewton

Vane Arms
Darlington Road (off A66)
☎ (0642) 580404
11.30–3; 7–11
Draught Bass; Stones Best Bitter 🄷
Nicely renovated two-roomed village pub, offering a varied menu of home-cooked meals.
⌂ Q ❀ ◖ ◗ ⊞ ♣ P

Marske

Clarendon
High Street ☎ (0642) 490889
11.30–3; 5.30–11 (11–11 Fri & Sat)
John Smith's Magnet; Theakston Best Bitter, Old Peculier 🄷
Popular pub known locally as the Middle House. Friendly atmosphere. Q ♿ ≹ P

Marton

Apple Tree
32 The Derby (in estate off Marton Road opp. Stewart Park)
☎ (0642) 310564
11–4; 6–11 (11–11 Sat)
Draught Bass 🄷
Classy modern pub on private housing estate. Large lounge cleverly divided to create a cosy atmosphere. Children welcome until 7pm. ☋ ❀ ◖ ⊞ ♿ ♣ P

Try also: Rudd's Arms (Whitbread)

Middlesbrough

Empire Hotel
Linthorpe Road
☎ (0642) 242589
11–11
Marston's Pedigree Bitter; Whitbread Trophy, Castle Eden Ale 🄷
Recently decorated. Music can be loud at times. Tasty, inexpensive meals practically all day. ❀ 🛏 ◖ ◗ ⊞ ♿ ≹ ♣

Star & Garter
Southfield Road
☎ (0642) 245307
11–3; 5.30–11 (11–11 Fri & Sat)
Draught Bass; Stones Best Bitter; Taylor Landlord; Theakston Old Peculier 🄷
Award-winning conversion from old workingmen's club. Fine Victorian-styled rooms use features from old pubs. Discreet games area; large L-shaped lounge with quieter corners. Guest beers. ❀ ◖ ◗ ⊞ ≹ ♣ P

Tap 'n' Barrel
86 Newport Road (next to bus station) ☎ (0642) 219995
11–11
North Yorkshire IPA, Flying Herbert 🄷
Cosy pub, refurbished from former shop and bar. Ever-changing array of guest beers. Victorian-style decor downstairs; eating/function room upstairs, where children are welcome. Chess played.
☋ ◖ ♿ ≹ ♣ ♁

Westminster Hotel
Parliament Road
☎ (0642) 424171
11.30–3.30 (11–4.30 Fri & Sat); 7–11
John Smith's Magnet 🄷
Local pub built in 1938 and virtually unchanged. Three rooms, including snug with feature fireplace. Children admitted to snug lunchtimes.
⌂ Q ☋ 🛏 ⊞ ♣ P

Try also: Princess Alice (Bass); **Southfield Hotel**

Moorsholm

Toad Hall Arms
High Street (2 miles off A171, Whitby Road) ☎ (0287) 60155
12–2.30; 7–11
Tetley Mild, Bitter 🄷
Single bar, partitioned into lounge and snug with views over moorland and out to sea. This family-run pub attracts an interesting blend of locals and visitors. Good value meals (not Mon eve). ⌂ Q ❀ ◖ ◗ ⛺ ♣ P

Redcar

Yorkshire Coble
West Dyke Road (S end of racecourse) ☎ (0642) 482071
11–3 (4 Fri & Sat); 6–11
Samuel Smith OBB 🄷
Large, typical Sam Smith's estate pub with strong regular clientele. Comfortable lounge with large bar and games room.
❀ ◖ ◗ ♣ P

Skelton Green

Green Inn
Boosbeck Road
☎ (0287) 50475
11–3; 7–11
Camerons Strongarm 🄷
Unspoilt terraced local in old ironstone mining area. Several rooms; often busy. Bar snacks.
⌂ Q ❀ ⊞ ♣

Stainton

Stainton Inn
☎ (0642) 599902
11.30–3; 6–11
Camerons Strongarm; Everards Old Original 🄷
Imposing red brick Victorian pub in village centre. Extended in 1987 into cottages next door. Strong emphasis on food. Rare outlet for Everards. ❀ ◖ ◗ ♿ ♣ P

Stockton-on-Tees

Board Inn
38 Bishopton Lane
☎ (0642) 673130
11–11
Courage Directors; John Smith's Bitter, Magnet 🄷
Refurbished town-centre pub. Bar snacks (not Sun). ⊞ ≹ ♣

Elm Tree
Elm Tree Avenue

☎ (0642) 677942
11.30–3 (3.30 Thu, 4 Fri, 4.30 Sat); 6–11
Courage Directors; John Smith's Bitter [H]
Modern estate pub built in 1985 and converted to real ale in 1986. Several separate rooms in Art Deco style. Children welcome in conservatory until 8pm. Menu includes daily home-cooked special.
◐ ◑ ♿ ♣ P

Parkwood Hotel
64–66 Darlington Road, Hartburn ☎ (0642) 580800
11–3 (4 Sat); 5–11
Vaux Lorimers Best Scotch, Double Maxim; Wards Sheffield Best Bitter [H]
Comfortable old hotel in leafy suburb. Converted in 1964 from a large house, former home of shipbuilding Ropner family. One of the listed beers is always available (range changes). Excellent garden play area for children. ◐ ◑ ♣ P

Stockton Arms
Darlington Road
☎ (0642) 580104
11–11
Draught Bass [H]
Imposing corner pub in smart tree-lined suburb. Warm, friendly and welcoming interior. Licensee takes great pride in his cask beer. Traditional pub catering for all tastes. Imaginative menu. Children welcome in restaurant and pool room. ◐ ◑ ♣ P

Sun Inn
Knowles Street (off High Street)
☎ (0642) 615676
11–4; 5–11 (11–11 Wed & Sat)
Draught Bass [H]
Totally unspoilt workingmen's pub. One of country's great drinking establishments. Claims to sell more Draught Bass than any other pub in the country.
≹ ♣

Try also: Dovecot Arts Centre

Thornaby

Cleveland Hotel
Bridge Street (near station)
☎ (0642) 676917
12–11 (12–5; 7–11 Sat)
Theakston XB; Younger No. 3 [H]
Cosy little pub where there's always a good welcome from the landlord. ◐ ≹ ♣

Wolviston

Wellington
31–33 High Street
☎ (0642) 644439
11–3.30; 5.30–11
Draught Bass [H]
Friendly traditional village pub with a welcoming atmosphere. Good quality food (not Sun).
Q ◐ P

Yarm

Harvester
Davenport Road, Layfield Farm
☎ (0642) 785841
11.45–3; 6–11
Webster's Choice *or* **Ruddles Best Bitter, County** [H]
Smart modern estate pub with separate games area. Part of lounge is partitioned for children. Eve meals Thu–Sat only. ◐ ◑ ♿ ♣ P

Ketton Ox
100 High Street
☎ (0642) 788311
11–2.30; 5.30–11 (11–11 Sat & summer)
Vaux Samson, Double Maxim [H]
Impressive former coaching inn in village conservation area. Oval windows blocked in on facade betray site of former cock-fighting room. Long and interesting history. Warm, open-plan interior. Booking advised for meals, served Thu–Sun. ◐ ◑ ♣

Complaining about a bad pint

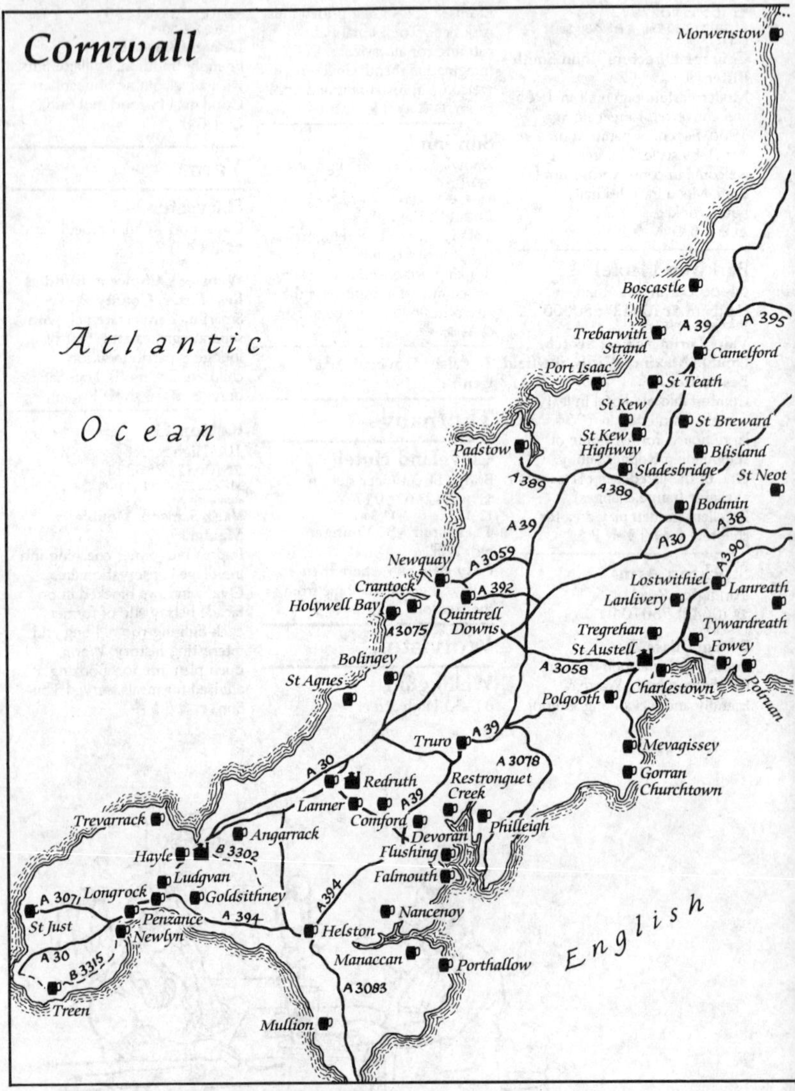

Cornish, *Redruth*; **Paradise**, *Hayle*; **St Austell**, *St Austell*

Altarnun

Rising Sun Inn

Off A30, on Camelford Road, 1 mile N of village OS825215

☎ (0566) 86636

11–3; 5.30–11

Bateman XB; Butcombe Bitter; Cotleigh Tawny Bitter; Exmoor Ale; Hook Norton Best Bitter; Whitbread Flowers Original H

A lively 16th-century country pub, popular with both locals and visitors. Unspoilt rural setting on the fringe of Bodmin Moor. Ever-changing range of guest beers.

♣ P

Angarrack

Angarrack Inn

Off A30 ☎ (0736) 752380

11–2.30; 6–11

St Austell Bosun's Bitter, HSD H

Very comfortable and welcoming village pub. Extensive, good-value menu of home-cooked food (veg option).

P

Blisland

Royal Oak

Churchtown

☎ (0208) 850739

11.30–3; 6–11

Draught Bass H

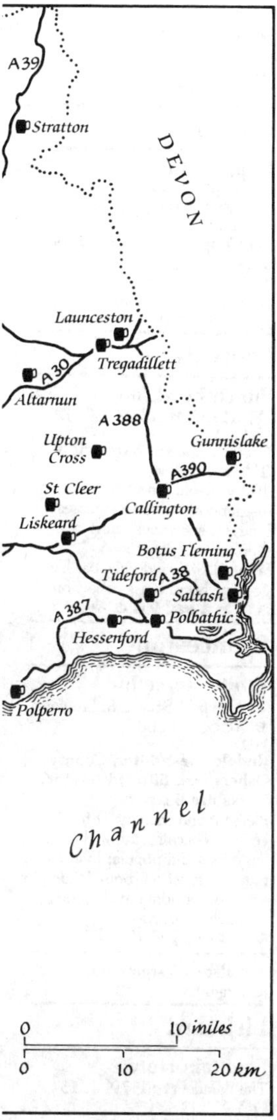

Friendly inn situated close to Bodmin Moor in the only Cornish village with a green. Patio and pond; family room. Church worth a visit. No food Sun eves. Guest beers (two in summer, one in winter) and cider (summer only).
♜ Q ♞ ❀ ◐ ◑ ⊞ ⛺ ♣ ◌ P

Bodmin

Masons Arms
Higher Bore Street
☎ (0208) 72607
11–3; 5–11
Ushers Best Bitter Ⓗ
Warm and friendly local, reputed to have the oldest continuous licence in Cornwall. Guest beers.
Q ♞ ❀ ⛿ ◐ ◑ ⊞ ♣ P

Bolingey

Bolingey Inn
Penwartha Road (near B3284)
☎ (0872) 572794
11–3; 6.30–11
Cornish JD Dry Hop Bitter, Draught Steam Bitter, Royal Wessex Bitter Ⓗ
Delightfully secluded country inn, a short distance from the tourist beaches of Perranporth. As yet unspoilt by brewery 'improvements'.
♜ ♞ ❀ ◐ ◑ ⊞ ⛺ ◌ P

Boscastle

Cobweb
☎ (08405) 278
11–2.30; 6–11 (11–11 summer)
Draught Bass; St Austell XXXX Mild, Tinners, HSD; Wadworth 6X Ⓗ
This large, four-storey building, dating from 18th century, was once a warehouse. A popular watering hole, set in an attractive harbour village, with many old artefacts hanging from beams in the public bar. Guest beers. ♜ Q ♞ ❀ ◐ ◑ ♣ P

Botus Fleming

Rising Sun Inn
Off A388 ☎ (0752) 842792
12–3; 6–11 (may vary)
Ruddles County; Ushers Best Bitter Ⓗ
Unspoilt and unpretentious country pub with 12th-century origins, tucked away in a quiet village on the outskirts of Saltash. A happy, friendly pub now in third generation of family ownership. Village-brewed cider when in season.
♜ ❀ ⊞ ♣ ◌ P

Try also: Coryton Arms (St Mellion)

Callington

Bulls Head
Fore Street ☎ (0579) 83387
11–3; 6.30–11 (11–11 Sat)
St Austell HSD Ⓗ
15th-century town pub with old stone fireplaces and oak beams. A passage once connected the inn to the nearby church. Sat eve piano sing-alongs in the lounge. A comfortable free house in the same ownership for over 40 years. Q ◐ ⊞ ♣ P

Try also: Coachmakers (Bass)

Camelford

Masons Arms
Market Place
☎ (0840) 213309
11–3; 6–11 (11–11 summer)
St Austell Tinners, HSD Ⓗ
A busy 300 year-old town pub, set in a long, low building, which was once flooded up to four feet during the 1940s.
♜ ❀ ⛿ ◐ ◑ ⊞ ♣

Charlestown

Rashleigh Arms
Near the harbour
☎ (0726) 73635
11–11
Draught Bass; Cornish Royal Wessex Bitter; Ruddles County; Wadworth 6X Ⓗ
Large Georgian pub and hotel set in this much filmed, picturesque port. Good food. Three bars, including snug; new restaurant and family room. Guest beer.
♞ ❀ ⛿ ◐ ◑ ⊞ ♿ ♣ P

Comford

Fox & Hounds
On A393, Falmouth-Redruth road ☎ (0209) 820251
11–3; 6–11
Draught Bass; St Austell Bosun's Bitter, HSD Ⓖ
Comfortable country pub with restaurant. Prize-winner in flower and garden competition.
♜ ❀ ◐ ◑ ⊞ ⛺ ♣ P

Crantock

Old Albion
Langurroc Road
☎ (0637) 830243
11–3; 6–11 (11–11 Fri, Sat & summer)
Courage Best Bitter, Directors Ⓗ
Look for the thatched cockerel on the roof of this much photographed village pub. The interior is homely, though often busy in summer. Food during summer only. ♜ ♞ ❀ ◐ ◑ ⛺ P

Devoran

Old Quay Inn
St Johns Terrace
☎ (0872) 863142
11–3; 6–11
Cornish Original, Draught Steam Bitter, Royal Wessex Bitter Ⓗ
Friendly, welcoming pub with fine views overlooking Devoran Quay and Devoran Creek.
♜ ❀ ⛿ ◐ ◑ ♣ P

Falmouth

Four Winds
Grenville Road
☎ (0326) 311369
11–3; 6.30–11
St Austell Bosun's Bitter, XXXX Mild Ⓗ
Pleasant two-bar estate pub with additional sun lounge and children's play area. A rare outlet for Mild, and worth the

trip for that alone.
♞ ❀ ◐ ◑ ⊞ ♿ P

Seven Stars
The Moor ☎ (0326) 312111
11–3; 6–11
Draught Bass; Courage Directors; St Austell HSD Ⓖ
Unchanged for centuries, with the same family in charge for at least five generations. Tobacconists next door forms part of the pub. Guest beer.
Q ❀ ⊞

Flushing

Royal Standard
Off A393 ☎ (0326) 74250
11–2.30; 6.30–11
Draught Bass; Cornish JD Dry Hop Bitter; Whitbread Flowers IPA Ⓗ
Pub at entrance to the village: beware of swans nearby in road.
⌂ ❀ ◐ ◑ ♣

Fowey

Ship Inn
3 Trafalgar Square
☎ (0726) 833751
11–3; 6–11 (11–11 summer)
St Austell Tinners, HSD Ⓗ
Comfortable and friendly 16th-century inn which has historical connections with the Rashleigh Family and Sir Francis Drake.
⌂ ♞ ⊨ ◐ ◑ ⛺ ♣

Goldsithney

Crown
Fore Street (B3280)
☎ (0736) 710494
11–3; 6–11
St Austell Bosun's Bitter, XXXX Mild, HSD Ⓗ
Attractive and comfortable village pub with warm atmosphere. Very popular restaurant (bookings advisable). Also excellent, home-cooked bar meals. ⌂ Q ❀ ◐ ◑ ♿ ⛺

Gorran Churchtown

Barley Sheaf
Village centre
☎ (0726) 843330
12–2.30; 7–11 (11–3; 6–11 summer)
Draught Bass; St Austell Tinners; Wadworth 6X Ⓗ
Lively village local which is reputed to be haunted. Barbecues and live entertainment in summer. Three guest beers and local farm cider available in summer.
⌂ Q ♞ ❀ ⊨ ◐ ◑ ⊞ ⛺ ⍥

Gunnislake

Queen's Head
Albaston ☎ (0822) 832482
11–2.30 (3 Sat); 6–11
Courage Best Bitter, Directors Ⓗ
Excellent village local on edge of spectacular Tamar Valley. An unspoilt pub which has had the same well-respected landlord for many years. Good value bar snacks. Taunton draught cider.
⌂ Q ❀ ⊞ ⛺ ⇌ ♣ ⍥

Try also: Rising Sun (Free)

Hayle

Bird in Hand
Trelissick Road (off B3302)
☎ (0736) 753365
12–3; 6–11 (11–11 summer)
Paradise Bitter, Artists Ale Ⓗ
Brew pub in former coach house, set in grounds of bird park. Guest beers. Unfortunately future of the brewery is in doubt. ♞ ❀ ◐ ◑ ⛺ ⇌ ♣ P

Helston

Blue Anchor
50 Coinagehall Street
☎ (0326) 562821
11–4; 6–11
Blue Anchor Medium, BB, Special, Extra Special Ⓗ
Superb 15th-century thatched pub, once a monks' resting place and later a tin-miners' pay office. Beer (splendidly strong) brewed in old brewhouse in yard. Skittle alley at rear has bar with mural of regular customers. Jazz Wed eves. Simple bar snacks.
⌂ Q ♞ ♿ ⛺

Hessenford

Copley Arms
On A387 ☎ (05034) 209
11–11
St Austell Tinners, HSD Ⓗ
14th-century country pub in picturesque riverside setting with oak beams and real fires. Good home-made food makes for a busy trade so jostle for table space in the summer or enjoy *al fresco* eating outside.
⌂ Q ♞ ❀ ◐ ◑ ⊞ ♿ ⛺ ♣ P

Holywell Bay

Treguth Inn
Off A3075 ☎ (0637) 830248
11.30–2.30; 7–11 (11–11 summer)
Courage Best Bitter, Directors Ⓗ
Thatched roof and interior beams add to the atmosphere of this pub, which becomes busier as the holiday season progresses. Good sandy beach and leisure park within close walking distance.
⌂ ♞ ❀ ◐ ◑ ⊞ ♿ ⛺ P

Lanlivery

Crown Inn
Off A390 OS080590
☎ (0208) 872707
11–3; 6–11 (flexible)
Draught Bass; Welsh Brewers Worthington BB; Butcombe Bitter Ⓗ
Comfortable 12th-century inn with inglenook and exposed beams. Home-cooked food.
⌂ Q ❀ ⊨ ◐ ◑ ⊞ ♿ ⛺ ♣ P

Lanner

Coppice Inn
On A393, Falmouth-Redruth road ☎ (0209) 216668
11–3; 6–11
Ind Coope Burton Ale; Tetley Bitter Ⓗ
Pleasant pub with spacious grounds and excellent food.
⌂ ♞ ❀ ◐ ◑ ⛺ P

Lanreath

Punch Bowl Inn
Off B3359 ☎ (0503) 20218
11–3; 6–11
Draught Bass; Charrington IPA (summer) Ⓗ
400 year-old inn with magnificent velveteen chaises longues, enormous lounge fireplace and flagstoned farmer's kitchen. Public bar has a genuine horse brass collection.
⌂ Q ♞ ❀ ⊨ ◐ ◑ ⊞ ♿ ♣ P

Launceston

White Horse Inn
14 Newport Square, St Stephens
☎ (0566) 772084
11–11
Ruddles Best Bitter, County; Ushers Best Bitter; Webster's Yorkshire Bitter Ⓗ
Pleasant and friendly 18th-century coaching inn with two large bars and popular live music in function room. Wide selection of home-made food available all day.
⌂ Q ❀ ⊨ ◐ ◑ ♣ ⍥ P

Try also: Westgate Inn (Courage)

Liskeard

Fountain Hotel
The Parade ☎ (0579) 42154
11–3; 5.30–11
Courage Best Bitter Ⓗ
Comfortable town-centre hotel built in 1730 as a coaching inn. Still worth a stop. Quiet lounge has separate dining area.
♞ ❀ ⊨ ◐ ◑ ⊞ ♣ P

Try also: Barley Sheaf (St Austell); **Tavern an Carow** (Courage)

Longrock

Mexico Inn
On old A30
☎ (0736) 710625
12–2.30; 5.30–11
Draught Bass; Courage Best Bitter, Directors Ⓗ
Originally the offices of the Mexico Mine, now an outstanding free house with

varied home-made food to suit all tastes. P

Lostwithiel

Royal Oak
Duke Street (just off A390) ☎ (0208) 872552
11–3; 5.30–11
Draught Bass; Fuller's London Pride; Marston's Pedigree Bitter; Whitbread Flowers IPA, Flowers Original [H]
Busy, friendly 13th-century inn with a good restaurant and accommodation. One of the largest selections of beers in Cornwall, with at least two guest beers.
Q P

Try also: Globe; Talbot

Ludgvan

White Hart
On B3309 ☎ (0736) 740574
11.30 (11 summer)–3; 6–11
Cornish JD Dry Hop Bitter, Original [G]
14th-century pub next to church, in attractive setting and with interesting interior.
Q P

Manaccan

New Inn
☎ (032623) 323
11–2.30; 6–11 (may vary summer)
Cornish JD Dry Hop Bitter, Original [H]
Very traditional thatched pub in village centre. Prides itself on good home-cooked food. No jukebox or fruit machines.
Q P

Mevagissey

Ship Inn
Fore Street ☎ (0726) 843324
11–3; 5.30–11 (11–11 summer)
St Austell Bosun's Bitter, Tinners, HSD [H]
An Elizabethan house recently refurbished to a high standard, maintaining its nautical theme. Bar is often flooded at high spring tides. Menu caters for children and vegetarians; locally-caught fish a speciality.

Try also: Fountain; Kings Arms

Morwenstow

Bush Inn
Crosstown OS208151
☎ (028883) 242
12–2.30; 7–11
St Austell Tinners, HSD [H]
An out-of-the-way pub in Rev Hawker country. Comfortable bar with slate floor and simple wooden furniture. Guest beers.
Q P

Mullion

Old Inn
☎ (0326) 240240
11–2.30; 6–11
Cornish JD Dry Hop Bitter, Original [H]
Centrally-situated historic, partly-thatched inn dating from 16th century. Accommodation includes a self-catering cottage.
P

Nancenoy

Trengilly Wartha
On B3291 OS731282
☎ (0326) 40332
11–2.30; 6–11 (may vary)
Courage Directors [G]
A delightful remote country pub with beer-loving owners who ring the changes for our interest and delight. Always three guest beers. Super grub.
Q P

Newlyn

Fishermans Arms
Fore Street ☎ (0736) 63399
10.30–2.30; 5.30–11
St Austell Tinners, HSD [H]
Popular local with superb views over the harbour and Mounts Bay. Magnificent inglenook.
Q

Newquay

Buccaneer
29 Mount Wise
☎ (0637) 874470
11.30–3 (summer only); 7–11
Marston's Pedigree Bitter; Whitbread Pompey Royal [H]
Hotel-attached bar which has greatly increased its local trade since its introduction of real ale. Superb beaches and surf within short walking distance. At least two guest beers. P

Padstow

Golden Lion
Lanadwell Street
☎ (0841) 532797
10.30–2.30; 5.30–11
Cornish Original [H]
Padstow's oldest pub. Intimate bar with low ceilings, home of the (original) 'obby 'oss used in the May Day celebrations.

Try also: London (St Austell)

Penzance

Mount's Bay Inn
Werrytown ☎ (0736) 63027
11–2.30; 5.30–11
Draught Bass [H]
Warm and welcoming genuine free house, attractively refurbished and with good food. Guest beers. Q

Turks Head
Chapel Street ☎ (0736) 63093
11–3; 5.30–11 (11–11 summer)
Cornish Original, Draught Steam Bitter, Royal Wessex Bitter [H]
Very popular pub dating back to 1233, with very attractive interior and excellent varied menu. Q

Philleigh

Roseland Inn
Off A3078 OS870394
☎ (087258) 254
11.30–2.30; 7–11 (11–2.30; 6–11 Sat)
Cornish JD Dry Hop Bitter, Original [H]
A superb example of a 17th-century village pub, well cared-for and untouched by the developers. Low beams, cob walls and hunting prints; open fire; plenty of fresh flowers and a warm welcome. Frequented by farmers, fishermen and the local rugby team. Eve meals summer only. Q P

Try also: Plume of Feathers, Portscatho (St Austell)

Polbathic

Halfway House
On A387
11–3; 6–11 (may vary summer)
Courage Best Bitter, Directors [H]
Large roadhouse with a collection of bars boasting rosettes for equestrian events. Comprehensive menu and accommodation available.
Q P

Polgooth

Polgooth Inn
Off A390/B3273
☎ (0726) 74689
11–3; 6–11
St Austell Bosun's Bitter, Tinners, HSD [H]
A nicely-appointed local, with emphasis on food.
Q P

Polperro

Three Pilchards
Lansallos Street
☎ (0503) 72233
11–3; 6–11 (11–11 summer)
Courage Best Bitter, Directors [H]
Friendly fishing pub, popular with ramblers. Interesting menu.

Try also: Blue Peter (Free); **Millhouse Hotel** (St Austell)

Polruan

Lugger
The Quay ☎ (072687) 364

Cornwall

11–3; 6–11 (11–11 summer)
St Austell Tinners, HSD ⊞
Squiffy-roofed pub with split-level bar — beware of the over-friendly cat. A welcome port of call when catching the foot ferry off Fowey. ⌂ ◐ ◗ ⊟ ♣

Try also: Russell (St Austell)

Porthallow

Five Pilchards
☎ (0326) 280256
11–2.30 (or later); 6–11
Cornish Original; Greene King Abbot Ale ⊞
Quiet winter pub situated on beach, with lovely views to Falmouth. Superb collection of brass ships' lamps, model ships and wreck histories. Very popular in summer when guest beers available.
⌂ Q ⚘ ⊨ ◐ ◗ ♿ ♁

Port Isaac

Golden Lion
13 Fore Street
☎ (0208) 880336
11–3; 6–11 (11–11 summer)
St Austell Bosun's Bitter, Tinners, HSD ⊞
Small pub overlooking the harbour, once the haunt of smugglers. The Bloody Bones bar under the pub (open summer only) once housed the brewery. Eve meals summer only. ⌂ ♞ ⚘ ◗ ⊟ ♣

Quintrell Downs

Two Clomes
East Road ☎ (0637) 874427
12–2.30; 7–11
Beer range varies ⊞
Thick stone walls and clome ovens by the fireplace give rise to the name. Chalet accommodation for holidays. Range of beers like a mini-beer festival. ⌂ Q ♞ ⚘ ◐ ◗ ♿ ▲ ⥱ P

Redruth

Tricky Dickies
Tolgus Mount (off A30)
OS684482 ☎ (0209) 219292
11–11
Greene King Abbot Ale; Marston's Pedigree Bitter ⊞
Tastefully renovated old tin-mine smithies; several artefacts on display. Good food; jazz Tue; squash/exercise facilities for the energetic. Children welcome. ⚘ ◐ ◗ ♿ ▲ P

Try also: Basset Arms, Portreath

Restronguet Creek

Pandora Inn
Off A39 OS814371
☎ (0326) 72678
11–2.30; 6.30–11 (11–11 summer)
Draught Bass; St Austell Tinners, HSD ⊞
13th-century thatched pub at waterside, accessible from both road and water. Snacks in bar; restaurant upstairs (*à la carte*). A classic pub. ⌂ Q ♞ ⚘ ◐ ◗ ▲ P

St Agnes

Railway Inn
10 Vicarage Road
☎ (0872) 552310
11–3; 7 (5 Fri)–11 (11–11 summer)
Cornish JD Dry Hop Bitter, Original ⊞
Endless brass polishing is required in this pub that is overflowing with collectables. As yet unspoilt by the brewery. Eve meals summer only.
Q ♞ ⚘ ◐ ◗ ⊟ ♿ ▲ P

Try also: Driftwood Spars (Free)

St Breward

Old Inn
OS098773 ☎ (0208) 850711
11.30–3; 6–11
Ruddles County; Ushers Best Bitter ⊞
Claimed to be the highest pub in Cornwall, a nice solid granite building, next to church. The stone bar fronts were once part of a pigsty. ⌂ ♞ ⚘ ◐ ◗ ⊟ ♣ P

St Cleer

Stag Inn
Fore Street (2 miles N of Liskeard) ☎ (0579) 42305
11–3; 7–11
Draught Bass; Marston's Pedigree Bitter; St Austell XXXX Mild, HSD; Whitbread Flowers Original ⊞
Friendly traditional village inn with warm cosy atmosphere. Popular with both locals and tourists. Close to many features of historic interest on this fringe of Bodmin Moor. Excellent good-value food. Occasional guest beers. ⚘ ◐ ◗ ⊟ ♿ ♣ P

Try also: Market Inn (Courage)

St Just

Star Inn
1 Fore Street
☎ (0736) 788767
11–11
St Austell Tinners, HSD ⊡
Very welcoming 18th-century, typical Cornish village pub, just off town square.
⌂ Q ♞ ⚘ ⊨ ◐ ◗ ♿ ♣ ♁

St Kew

St Kew Inn
☎ (020 884) 259
11–3; 6–11 (11–11 summer)
St Austell Tinners, HSD ⊞
A traditional old pub with the public bar situated in old kitchen. Large fireplace and ancient slate floor. Strong local following. Steaks a speciality.
⌂ Q ⚘ ◐ ◗ ⊟ ♁ P

St Kew Highway

Red Lion
☎ (020 884) 271
11–2.30; 6–11
Draught Bass ⊞
17th-century pub with small cosy front bar and spacious back bar/games room.
⌂ ⚘ ⊨ ◐ ◗ ⊟ ♣ ♁ P

St Neot

London Inn
Off A38, W of Dobwalls
☎ (0579) 20263
11–3; 6–11
Ruddles County; Ushers Best Bitter ⊞
16th-century inn in small village on the edge of Bodmin Moor. Skittle alley available. Church next door is famous for its stained glass windows. No food Sun eves.
⌂ ⚘ ◐ ◗ ⊟ ▲ ♣ P

St Teath

White Hart Hotel
☎ (0208) 850281
11–3; 6–11
Ruddles County; Ushers Best Bitter ⊞
Large bustling 400 year-old pub with three busy bars. Captain Bligh of the 'Bounty' was born locally in 1753.
⌂ ♞ ⚘ ⊨ ◐ ◗ ⊟ ♣ P

Saltash

Two Bridges
13 Albert Road
☎ (0752) 848952
1–11 (11–11 Sat)
Courage Best Bitter, Directors ⊞
Cosy country cottage-style interior; live pianist some nights; regular feature menus and 'beer drinkers' club nights.
⌂ ⚘ ◐ ◗ ⥱

Sladesbridge

Slades House Country Inn
☎ (020 881) 2729
11–3; 6–11
Draught Bass; St Austell Tinners, HSD ⊞
A much-renovated roadside pub dating from 1588. Once had its own brewhouse to serve the bargees working the nearby River Allen. Always popular with passing trade.
⌂ Q ⚘ ⊨ ◐ ◗ ⊟ ♣ P

Stratton

Tree Inn

Fore Street ☎ (0288) 352038
11–11
Draught Bass; St Austell Tinners [H]
Historic 13th-century manor house of the Grenville family. A fine coaching inn with four bars and restaurant set around a courtyard. Live folk music Fri. Skittle alley.
♨ ♞ ⛓ ⛺ ◖ ◗ ⊞ ♣ P

Tideford

Rod & Line
Church Road
11–3; 6–11
Courage Best Bitter [G]
Basic village pub which is popular with farmers and commuters. Always a warm welcome from the cheeky, cheery host. Food every day except Sun lunch.
♨ Q ♞ ⛓ ◖ ◗ P

Trebarwith Strand

Port William
OS488864 ☎ (0840) 770230
11–11
St Austell Tinners, HSD [H]
Comfortable 200 year-old building overlooking beach, recently extended to include new stone bar. Interesting self-cooling cellar. Regular live music and guest beers.
♨ ♞ ⛓ ◖ ◗ ♣ ⊖ P

Treen

Logan Rock Inn
Off B3315 ☎ (0736) 810495
11–3; 6–11
St Austell Tinners, HSD [H]
Outstanding small country pub near beautiful coastal scenery and Minack Open Air Theatre at Porthcurno. The pub is National Trust property.
♨ Q ♞ ⛓ ◖ ◗ ⊞ ♿ ♣ P

Tregadillett

Eliot Arms
☎ (0566) 772051
11–2.30; 6–11
Cornish Original, Royal Wessex Bitter [H]
A pleasing pub now bypassed by the A30. Comfortable surroundings with good food. Clocks and curiosities hang on every wall and ceiling. Selection of pub games. South-West winner of the Bulmers Innkeeper award 1990. ♨ ♞ ⛓ ◖ ◗ ⊞ ♣ P

Tregrehan

Britannia Inn
On A390 ☎ (0726) 812889
11–11
Draught Bass; Courage Best Bitter; St Austell Tinners [H]
Roadside 16th-century inn, three miles east of St Austell. Well known for food (available all day). It has restaurants and a large safe garden with playground for children.
♨ Q ♞ ⛓ ◖ ◗ ⊞ P

Trevarrack

Tyringham Arms
Off A3074 ☎ (0736) 740434
11–3; 6–11 (1 am Fri, Sat & summer)
Draught Bass [H]
Comfortable free house in converted school. Good value meals; caravan site and chalet accommodation nearby. Guest beer in holiday season.
♨ ♞ ⛓ ◖ ◗ ⛺ P

Truro

City Inn
Pydar Street ☎ (0872) 72623
11–11
Courage Best Bitter, Directors [H]
Only proper pub in the town, nicely refurbished. Excellent collection of jugs on display. Family garden with an aviary.
Q ⛓ ◖ ◗ ⇌ ♣ ⊖ P

Try also: Globe Inn (Cornish); **Daniel Arms** (Bass)

Tywardreath

New Inn
Fore Street ☎ (072681) 3901
11–3; 6–11
Draught Bass [G]; **St Austell Tinners** [H]
Popular village local near Par. Darts and jukebox in separate room. Secluded garden off lounge. No food Sun.
Q ♞ ⛓ ⛺ ◖ ⊞ ⛺ ⇌ (Par) ♣ P

Try also: Wych Way (Free)

Upton Cross

Caradon Inn
On B3254 ☎ (0579) 62391
11–3; 5.30–11
St Austell HSD; Wadworth 6X; Whitbread Flowers Original [H]
Delightful and welcoming 17th-century country inn, popular with both locals and holiday-makers. Pool and bar billiards room. Occasional guest beers. ♨ ⛓ ◖ ◗ ♿ ♣ P

Try also: Manorhouse Inn, Rillamill

Cumbria

Dent, *Dent*; **Hartleys**, *Ulverston*; **Hesket Newmarket**, *Hesket Newmarket*; **Jennings**, *Cockermouth*; **Yates**, *Westnewton*

Alston

Angel Inn
Front Street (100 yds from town centre towards Penrith
☎ (0434) 381363
11–4; 7–11
McEwan 70/-; Tetley Bitter [H]
A cosy, friendly atmosphere in a 15th-century inn. A fine high-grated fireplace makes an interesting focal point in the one-bar drinking area. Good value home-cooked bar meals (not Tue eve). Alston is handy for those walking the Pennine Way. ⛪ ❀ ⛟ ◐ ◗ ⛺ ♣

Blue Bell
Town Foot (downhill from town centre)
☎ (0434) 381566
11–2.30; 6–11 (11–11 Sat)
McEwan 70/-; Theakston Best Bitter [H]
Cosy, stone-built pub in England's highest market town. An impressive fire ensures a warm welcome all year round. May carry an extra beer in summer. ⛪ Q ❀ ⛟ ◐ ◗ ⛺ ♣ P

Ambleside

Golden Rule
Smithy Brow (off A591 towards Kirkstone Pass)
☎ (05394) 32257
11–11
Hartleys Mild, Bitter, XB [H]
Deservedly-famous, unspoilt, no-nonsense drinkers' pub. Three rooms; one bar; no music. Popular with locals, students, climbers, walkers and tourists. Golden (brass) Rule

hangs above the bar. Meals May–Oct only. ⌂ Q ❀ ☾ ◗ ♣ P

Waterhead Hotel (Stringers Bar)
Lake Road (opp. Steamer Pier at A591/A5075 jct)
☎ (053 94) 32566
11–3; 6–11 (11–11 summer)
Marston's Pedigree Bitter; Theakston Best Bitter, Old Peculier [H]
Spacious lounge bar with real fire and fine views across the lake to Langdale Pikes. Up to six beers usually available. Wide selection of bar snacks, including local specialities.
⌂ ❀ ⟗ ☾ ◗ ♣ P

Try also: Churchill Hotel

Arnside

Fighting Cocks
Promenade ☎ (0524) 761203
11–3 (4 Sat); 6 (7 winter)–11
Thwaites Mild, Bitter [E]
Large, bright, cheerful, open lounge with magnificent views over the river towards South Lakeland. Vault at the rear is separated by three glazed arches. Restaurant open weekends only in winter.
Q ❀ ☾ ⊞ ≷ ♣ P

Aspatria

Grapes Hotel
Market Square (A596)
☎ (0965) 20292
11–3; 6–11
Yates Bitter [H]
17th-century coaching inn with cosy lounge and lively young-persons' bar. Nearest outlet to the Yates brewery (1½ miles).
⌂ ❀ ⟗ ☾ ⊞ ≷ P

Barngates

Drunken Duck Inn
(Off B5286) OS351012
☎ (096 66) 347
11–3; 6–11
Jennings Bitter; Tetley Bitter; Theakston XB, Old Peculier; Yates Bitter [H]
One of the more famous pubs in the South Lakes. The building (formerly the Barngates Inn) is reputed to be 400 years old. The amusing legend about the pub's name can be read inside. Pub has fishing rights for nearby Tarn. ⌂ Q ☋ ❀ ⟗ ☾ ◗ ▲ P

Barrow-in-Furness

Blue Lamp Hotel
Crellin Street (300 yds off A590) ☎ (0229) 24124
11–11
Thwaites Best Mild, Bitter [H]
One plush room (L-shaped), with luxurious seating; the bar is resplendent in hand-carved oak panelling. Friendly welcome; excellent bar snacks and meals. ⟗ ☾ ≷ ♣

Wheatsheaf Hotel
Anson Street (off A590 near rugby ground)
☎ (0229) 37515
11–3; 7–11
John Smith's Bitter [H]
Popular pub with a strong Navy following, as well as locals of all ages. Historic listed building with comfortable surroundings and a homely atmosphere. Games-oriented.
Q ❀ ⟗ ☾ ⊞ ♿ ♣

Blackbeck

Blackbeck Bridge Hotel
On A595, 1 mile N of Calderbridge ☎ (094 684) 661
11–3; 6.30–11
Theakston XB; Younger Scotch [H]
Large hotel with a restaurant off the bar. Q ⟗ ☾ ◗

Blencow

Clickham Inn
On B5288, 3 miles W of Penrith ☎ (085 33) 406
11–3; 6–11
Marston's Burton Best Bitter, Pedigree Bitter, Merrie Monk [H]
Attractive roadside inn on old main road to Keswick. Regular live music (mainly Sat nights), usually of a C&W/folk feel. Good bar food, specialising in local dishes. Extensive veg menu. Pool room.
⌂ ❀ ☾ ◗ ▲ ♣ P

Boot

Woolpack Inn
OS190010 ☎ (094 03) 230
11–3; 6–11
Theakston Best Bitter; Younger IPA [H]
Last watering hole before Hardknott Pass.
⌂ Q ❀ ⟗ ☾ ◗ ⊞ ♿ ▲ ♣ P

Bouth

White Hart
½ mile off A590
☎ (0229) 861229
11–3; 6–11 (11–11 summer)
Ind Coope Burton Ale; Jennings Bitter; Mitchell's Bitter; Tetley Bitter; Younger Scotch [H]
Only pub in a village voted the best in Lakeland and rightly so. Two real fires in the bar; peaceful countryside all around. Bar football in a separate room at the rear. Well recommended.
⌂ Q ☋ ❀ ☾ ◗ ▲ ♣ P

Bowmanstead

Ship Inn
☎ (053 94) 41224
11–3; 5.30–11 (11–11 summer)
Hartleys XB [H]
Comfortable, small pub, sign-posted on the road to Coniston. Families are welcome here. No special room is designated for them, but there is a snug adjoining the main room.
⌂ Q ❀ ⟗ ☾ ◗ ▲ ♣ P

Bowness-on-Windermere

Hole in't Wall (New Hall Inn)
Lowside (behind St Martins church) ☎ (096 62) 3488
11–11
Hartleys XB [H]
Olde-worlde, renovated smithy which hasn't lost its character.
⌂ ❀ ☾

Brampton

Nags Head
Market Place ☎ (069 77) 2284
11–3; 5.30–11
Hartleys XB; Marston's Pedigree Bitter [H]
Beautifully-renovated, split-level town pub with original low ceilings and wooden beams. Busy on market days. Friendly and family-run. Good value food. ☋ ❀ ⟗ ☾ ◗ ♣

Scotch Arms
Main Street ☎ (069 77) 2397
11–4; 7–11
Theakston Best Bitter [H]
A lively locals' pub where a friendly service is assured. A basic menu is nearly always available. Car park at rear.
☾ ◗ ⊞ ♿ ♣ ↺ P

Broughton in Furness

Manor Arms
The Square ☎ (0229) 716286
3–11 (12–11 Fri & Sat)
Matthew Brown Mild; Theakston Best Bitter [H]
Friendly village inn with two real fires. Two regular guest beers and a 'Guest Beer of the Month'. Be careful with the steps to the toilets! Soup, coffee and toasties served all day. Parking in The Square. ⌂ Q ❀

Try also: Black Cock

Burgh by Sands

Greyhound
Off B5307, 6 miles W of Carlisle ☎ (022 876) 76579
11–11
Thomas Greenall's Original Bitter [H]
18th-century house converted into a pub by State Management in 1936.

Cumbria

Extensive renovations have created an open-plan layout. Excellent children's play area in garden. ❀ ◖ ◗ ⛺ ♣ P

Buttermere

Bridge Hotel
On B5289 OS175170
☎ (059685) 266/252
11–3; 6–11 (may vary summer)
Theakston Best Bitter, XB, Old Peculier 🄷
Originally a cornmill, first licensed 1735. Has had various names, including 'the Victoria', after the Queen who stayed here. Interesting memorabilia all round bar area.
Q ❀ 🛏 ◖ ◗ ⊟ ⛺ P

Cark in Cartmel

Engine Inn
Station Road
☎ (05395) 58341
11–3; 6.30–11
Draught Bass; Stones Best Bitter 🄷
Homely country inn with unusual match sculptures behind the bar. Traditional oak beams adorn the ceilings. Pub usually quiet apart from folk eves and the horse race traffic two weekends a year.
⛫ Q ❀ 🛏 ◖ ◗ ⇌ ♣ P

Carlisle

Beehive
Warwick Road
☎ (0228) 32923
11–3; 7–11
Theakston Best Bitter 🄷
Comfortable two-roomed pub with a good landlord. Handy for the football ground. ❀ ⊟ P

Caledonian
Botchergate (near station)
☎ (0228) 28468
11–11
Whitbread Flowers IPA, Boddingtons Bitter, Castle Eden Ale 🄷
Large one-roomed city-centre pub, decorated in typical Whitbread fashion. Popular with the younger generation, (particularly at weekends) and, consequently, it has an excellent choice of music on the jukebox. Good value bar meals.
◖ ♿ ⇌ ♣

Coach & Horses
Kingstown Road (A7, 600 yds S of M6 jct 44)
☎ (0228) 25535
11.30–3; 5.30–11
Theakston Best Bitter, XB 🄷
Excellent roadside inn of typical State Management Scheme design. Small, well-furnished public bar and a larger, very comfortable lounge. Regular allcomers quiz night every Thu.
❀ ◖ ◗ ⊟ ♿ ♣ P

Crown Inn
Scotland Road, Stanwix (old A7 1 mile N of town)
☎ (0228) 512894
11–11
Matthew Brown Mild; Younger Scotch, IPA 🄷
Recently renovated but not spoilt roadside inn, retaining existing wood panels. Pub games in bar. ◖ ⊟ ♿ ♣

Howard Arms
Lowther Street (next to Lanes shopping centre)
☎ (0228) 32926
11–3; 5.30–11 (11–11 Fri & Sat)
Theakston Best Bitter, XB 🄷
Very busy multi-roomed city-centre pub with splendid tiled frontage. Interesting collection of State Management memorabilia. ⛫ ❀ ◖

Woolpack Inn
Milbourne Street
☎ (0228) 32459
11–3; 5.30–11 (may extend, 11–11 Thu–Sat)
Jennings Mild, Bitter 🄷
Large local with an extraordinary welcome. Large lounge, snug bar and games room. Mural depicts Carlisle's history. After a short time you'll feel you've been a regular for years! Large selection of whiskies. ❀ 🛏 ◖ ◗ ⇌ ♣ P

Cartmel

Cavendish Arms
Through the arches off the Square ☎ (05395) 36240
11.30–3; 5.30–11
Draught Bass 🄷
Deservedly the busiest of the pubs in Cartmel, specialising in Aberdeen Angus grillsteaks. The traditional oak-beamed bar is adorned with copper and brass. Crowded on race days.
⛫ Q ❀ 🛏 ◖ ◗ ♿ ⛺ P

Try also: Pig & Whistle

Cartmel Fell

Masons Arms
Strawberry Bank OS413895
☎ (04488) 486
11.30–3; 6–11
Bateman XB; Thwaites Bitter; Yates Bitter 🄷
Very beautiful inn, set in breathtaking scenery. Very busy for food at all times (excellent range includes veg meals). Large selection of foreign bottled beers, as well as a home-brew on draught. Guest beer.
⛫ Q 🐈 ❀ 🛏 ◖ ◗ ⟳ P

Clifton

George & Dragon
On A6, 3 miles S of Penrith
☎ (0768) 65381
11–3; 7–11 (may extend in summer)
Tetley Bitter 🄷
Excellent example of a traditional Cumbrian inn, stone-built and set back from the main road in the middle of a cottage terrace. Modernization – including the addition of a pool room – hasn't detracted from its 'cosy-cottage' feel.
⛫ Q ❀ 🛏 ◖ ◗ ♿ ⛺ ♣

Cockermouth

Swan Inn
Kirkgate (follow signs to Lorton from main street) OS124306
☎ (0900) 822425
11–3; 7–11
Jennings Mild, Bitter 🄷
Cosy regulars' pub in select historic area of Cockermouth. Close to All Saints Church and the site of the school attended by Wordsworth and Fletcher Christian. Hard to find but worth it. Q ⊟ ♣

Coniston

Crown Inn
Tiberthwaite Avenue
☎ (05394) 341243
11–11
Hartleys Mild (summer), **XB** 🄷 & 🄴
Large pub with separate dining and family rooms, a comfortable lounge area and basic public bar. Some snacks served all day. Large car park and outdoor area cater for the tourist season, though this is one of the less busy pubs. Relaxing atmosphere.
⛫ Q 🐈 ❀ 🛏 ◖ ◗ ⊟ ⛺ ♣ P

Cummersdale

Spinners Arms
☎ (0228) 32928
11–3; 5.30–11
Matthew Brown Mild; Theakston Best Bitter 🄷
Small village pub designed, like other State Management pubs, by Harry Redfern.
❀ ◖ ◗ ⛺ ♣

Dalton-in-Furness

Brown Cow
10 The Green
☎ (0229) 62553
11–3; 6–11 (all day Sun for food)
Matthew Brown Bitter; Theakston Best Bitter, XB; Younger Scotch 🄷
Friendly bar, popular with diners for its large menu including veg meals. Large dining room upstairs, leaving space in the bar for quiet drinking. Don't be put off by the number of cars outside.
⛫ Q ❀ ◖ ◗ ⇌ P

Dent

Sun Inn
Main Street (near the church)
☎ (05875) 208
11–3; 6–11 (11–11 summer if busy)
Theakston XB, Old Peculier; Younger Scotch [H]
17th-century inn at the top of the cobbled Main Street, with original beams and a no-smoking room. The 'old' doms table is played on every night. Popular with fellwalkers, cyclists and hikers (people using the Settle–Carlisle line have a most enjoyable walk to the pub).
⛫ Q ❀ ⛟ ◖ ◗ ♿ ⛺ ♣ P

Try also: George & Dragon

Dovenby

Ship Inn
On A594, 3 miles NW of Cockermouth
☎ (0900) 822522
11–2.45; 6–11
Jennings Mild, Bitter [H]
Modernised traditional country pub with warm welcome. Swings in garden for children.
⛫ ❀ ⛟ ◖ ◗ ⊟ ♿ ♣ P

Eaglesfield

Black Cock
Off A5086, 2 miles SW of Cockermouth
☎ (0900) 822989
11–3; 6–11
Jennings Bitter [H]
Only pub in village, but attracts discerning drinkers from near and far. ⛫ Q ❀ ♣ P

Eamont Bridge

Beehive Inn
$1\frac{1}{2}$ miles S of Penrith on A6
☎ (0768) 62081
12–3; 6–11
Hartleys XB [H]
Busy roadside inn, with a noteworthy sign, on the edge of the Lake District; popular with tourists and locals. Good, wholesome food. Pool room. Guest beer. ⛫ ❀ ◖ ◗ ⛺ ♣ P

Egremont

Blue Bell
Main Street (A595)
☎ (0946) 820581
11–3; 6–11
Hartleys XB; Robinson's Best Bitter [H]
Tastefully-modernised, well-kept popular pub with quiz nights. ⛫ ❀ ♣

Elterwater

Britannia
Off B5343 ☎ (09667) 210
11–11
Hartleys XB; Jennings Mild, Bitter [H]
Welcoming pub with a large area for diners and a very small, snug bar round the side. The large outdoor area and the village green serve as overflows for the pub in summer, offering an opportunity to take in the good views and peaceful surroundings.
⛫ Q ❀ ⛟ ◖ ◗ ⊟ ⛺ ⌽ P

Embleton

Wheatsheaf
Keswick end of Embleton Main Road, parallel to A66
☎ (059681) 408
11–3; 6 (5.30 Fri & Sat)–11
Jennings Bitter [H]
Warm, clean and friendly, with food at fair prices. Separate games room. ⛫ Q ❀ ◖ ◗ ⛺ ♣ P

Goose Green

String of Horses
B5299/B5305 jct 10 miles S of Carlisle ☎ (06996) 358
12–3; 7–11 (may vary summer, 11–11 Sat)
Marston's Burton Best Bitter, Pedigree Bitter [H]
Two-roomed, warm and cosy pub at gateway to Caldbeck Fells on the old geese drovers' route from Whitehaven to Carlisle. Very friendly and family-run. ⛫ Q ❀ ◖ ◗ ⊟ ♣ P

Gosforth

Globe
The Square (off A595)
☎ (09405) 235
11–3; 6.30–11
Theakston Best Bitter, XB [H], **Old Peculier** [E]
Lively and friendly village pub with separate games room.
⛫ ❀ ⛟ ◖ ◗ ♣

Try also: Wheatsheaf Inn (Bass)

Grange-over-Sands

Hard Cragg Hall Hotel
Grange Fell Road (near B5277)
☎ (04484) 3353
11–11
John Smith's Bitter, Magnet [H]
Welcoming public bar in a large hotel in a non-commercialised seaside town. Good food served in the oak-panelled bar and dining rooms, all possessing large open fireplaces.
⛫ Q ⛮ ❀ ⛟ ◖ ◗ ⇌ ♣ P

Grasmere

Dale Lodge Hotel (Tweedies Bar)
Langdale Road ☎ (09665) 300
12–3 (not Mon-Fri); 7–11 (11.30–11 summer)
Ruddles County; Whitbread Boddingtons Bitter [H]
Popular centre-of-village bar in former tweed shop. Separate bistro dining area and separate family room which doubles as pool room in winter. Regular guest beers. ⛮ ❀ ◖ ◗ ♣

Try also: Travellers Rest (Free)

Great Broughton

Punchbowl Inn
Main Street (1 mile off A66)
☎ (0900) 824708
11–3; 6.30–11 (11–11 Fri & Sat)
Jennings Bitter [H]
Small, friendly village pub with cosy atmosphere. Parking limited to five cars.
⛫ Q ⊟ ♿ ♣ P

Great Langdale

Old Dungeon Ghyll Hotel
100 yds off B5343 at head of valley OS285061
☎ (09667) 272
11–11
Hartleys Mild; Theakston Best Bitter, XB, Old Peculier; Yates Bitter [H]
Traditional walkers' and climbers' bar at the head of one of Lakeland's most popular valleys. Winner of the CAMRA regional Pub of the Year award in 1990. Open all day Sun for coffees. ⛫ Q ❀ ⛟ ◖ ◗ ⊟ ⛺ ⌽ P

Grizebeck

Greyhound
On A595 ☎ (0229) 89224
12–3; 6–11
John Smith's Bitter [H]
200 year-old roadside inn, set at the foot of Kirkby Fell near one of the largest slate quarries in the country. A comfortable pub with warped bar, several fires and, of course, a local slate floor. Imaginative range of meals for all tastes. ⛫ Q ⛮ ❀ ⛟ ◖ ◗ ⊟ ♿ ⛺ ⇌ (Kirkby) P

Harrington

Galloping Horse
Main Road (B5296)
☎ (0946) 830083
11–3; 6–11
Jennings Bitter [H]
Spacious and welcoming pub in residential area of village. Children welcomed. Quizzes; chess played. ❀ ◖ ⊟ ⇌ ♣ P

Hawkshead

Kings Arms
The Square ☎ (09666) 372
11–11
Matthew Brown Mild; Tetley Bitter; Theakston Best Bitter, Old Peculier [H]
The best of four good real ale

pubs in this attractive village. A small, lively local, popular with the many tourists that visit the village. Separate restaurant and good value accommodation (or there are three campsites close by). ⌂ Q ❀ 🛏 ◖ ◗ ⛺ ♣

Hayton

Stone Inn
☎ (0228) 70498
11–3; 5.30–11
Hartleys XB; Ind Coope Burton Ale; Tennent's 80/-; Tetley Bitter; Theakston Best Bitter [H]
Attractive and cosy village local with a comfortable atmosphere. Serves a range of unusual toasties. Friendly landlord.
⌂ Q ♘ P

Helton

Helton Inn
6 miles S of Penrith on Haweswater road
☎ (093 12) 232
12–3 (not winter); 6 (8 winter)–11 (not Mon in winter)
Theakston XB [H]
Splendid end-of-terrace inn with simple decoration and a relaxed atmosphere. Excellent outdoor drinking area with fine views over the Lowther Valley. Good, well-presented home-cooked bar meals (weekends only in winter). Self-catering cottage attached to pub. ⌂ Q ❀ 🛏 ◖ ◗ ♣ P

Try also: Gate Inn, Yanwath (Free)

Hensingham

Sun Inn
100–101 Main Street (A595)
☎ (0946) 695149
11–4; 6.30–11
Jennings Bitter [H]
Busy, unpretentious local pub, popular with all ages. ♣

Try also: Richmond (S&N)

Hesket Newmarket

Old Crown
☎ (069 98) 288
11.30–3; 5.30–11
Hesket Newmarket Wrynose Light Bitter, Blencathra Bitter, Doris's 90th Birthday Ale, Old Carrock Strong Ale; Thwaites Bitter [H]
Very friendly fellside village local with good home-cooking and its own brewery at the back. Shelves full of books and a large assortment of games.
♘ ◖ ◗ ⊟ ♣

Heversham

Blue Bell
Princes Way (A6, 2 miles N of Milnthorpe) ☎ (053 95) 62018
11–3; 6–11
Samuel Smith OBB, Museum Ale [H]
A 16th/17th-century traditional, large, country roadside hotel. Extensive range of meals.
⌂ Q ♘ ❀ 🛏 ◖ ◗ ⊟ ⛺ ♣ P

Holme

Smithy
Milnthorpe Road
☎ (0524) 781302
11.45–2.30; 6 (7 Fri & Sat)–11
Thwaites Best Mild, Bitter [E]
Despite having a large main bar, can still be crowded summer weekends. Outdoor play area.
❀ ◖ ◗ ⊟ ♿ ♣ P

Try also: Royal, Burton-in-Kendal (Mitchell's)

Kendal

Castle Inn
Castle Street (near St George's church) ☎ (0539) 729983
11–11
Jennings Bitter; Tetley Bitter [H]
A pleasant two-roomed local off the tourist routes. Fish tank in lounge. Original Duttons window set in a wooden frame adorns a wall in the public bar.
◖ ⊟ ≢ ♣

Duke of Cumberland
Shap Road ☎ (0539) 724054
11–11
Vaux Bitter, Samson [H]
Popular, friendly pub near station. Reputed to have last bottle of Kendal Auld Ale produced by Whitwell Marks before its closure. ◖ ≢ P

Sawyers Arms
Stricklandgate (100 yds from A6/A591 jct in NW part of town) ☎ (0539) 729737
10.30–3; 6–11
Hartleys XB; Robinson's Best Bitter [H]
Interesting pub with a collection of old cigarette packets and matchboxes. Advice on all aspects of angling freely given! An engraved Hartleys window next to entrance. Live music on various eves: folk, rock, etc.
🛏 ≢ ♣

Try also: Ring-O-Bells (Vaux)

Keswick

Dog & Gun
Lake Road ☎ (076 87) 73463
11–3; 6–11 (11–11 summer)
Theakston Best Bitter, XB, Old Peculier [H]
Large town-centre pub, very popular for its food. ◖ ◗ ⊟

George Hotel
St John's Street
☎ (076 87) 72076
11–11
Theakston Best Bitter; Yates Bitter [H]
Old coaching inn, now a smart hotel in the middle of town. Popular with climbers. Limited car parking. Eve meals till 8.30pm. ⌂ Q 🛏 ◖ ◗ ⊟ ♣ P

Try also: Twa Dogs (Jennings)

Kirkbampton

Rose & Crown
Main Street ☎ (022 876) 492
12–(varied closing; closed winter); 7–11
Webster's Yorkshire Bitter [H]
Unspoilt, busy two-roomed local, offering darts, pool and ringboard. Very much a dominoes pub. Ruddles County available at times.
⌂ Q ❀ ◖ ◗ ⊟ ⛺ ♣

Kirkby Lonsdale

Royal
Main Street ☎ (052 42) 71217
11–3 (3.30 Thu); 6–11
Tetley Bitter; Theakston XB; Younger Scotch [H]
Large, rambling hotel, serving real ale in two contrasting bars. Eve meals in the 'Ostler's' Thu–Sun. Guest beer.
⌂ Q ♘ ❀ 🛏 ◖ ◗ ⊟ ♿ ♣ P

Try also: Snooty Fox (Hartleys)

Lanercost

Blacksmiths Bar (Abbey Bridge Inn)
(Off A69 near Brampton)
☎ (069 77) 2224
12–3; 7–11
Ruddles Best Bitter (summer); **Yates Bitter** [H]
Beautifully-converted 17th-century smithy. Attractive low-ceilinged bar leads to a raised lounge area, and the lovely spiral staircase climbs to a restaurant above the bar. Bar meals available most of the time. ⌂ Q ❀ 🛏 ◖ ◗ ♣ P

Levens

Hare & Hounds
400 yds off A590
☎ (0448) 60408
11–3; 6–11
Vaux Lorimers Best Scotch [E], **Samson** [H]; **Wards Sheffield Best Bitter** [E]
Historic pub circa 1714, with low ceiling, original beams and cosy settles. Dedicated landlord. No meals midweek lunchtimes in winter. ❀ ◖ ◗ ⊟ ⛺ ♣ P

Try also: Lyth Valley Hotel

Lindal in Furness

Railway Inn
London Road (off A590)

☎ (0229) 62889
11–3; 7–11
Theakston Best Bitter [H]
Cheerful village local owned by a beer connoisseur. Pleasant children's play area at the rear. Regular guest beer always available. ♨ ❀ ♣

Lindale

Lindale Inn
On B5277, off A590
☎ (053 95) 32416
11–11
Younger Scotch [H]
Old coaching inn with a friendly, efficient welcome. Stone jugs and copper artefacts adorn the walls in this large pub with exposed oak beams. Quite food-oriented: serves Sun lunches and a children's menu.
Q ❀ 🛏 ◖ ◗ ⊞ P

Low Hesket

Rose & Crown
On old A6, Carlisle–Penrith road ☎ (069 74) 73346
11–3; 6–11
Marston's Mercian Mild, Burton Best Bitter, Pedigree Bitter [H]
Traditional two-roomed roadside pub with timber beams. Well worth a detour off the motorway. Camping 1½ miles away. ♨ ❀ ◖ ◗ ⊞ ⛺ ♣ P

Melmerby

Shepherds Inn
Village Green (off A686, Penrith–Alston road)
☎ (076 881) 217
11–3; 6–11 (may extend)
Marston's Burton Best Bitter, Merrie Monk, Pedigree Bitter, Owd Rodger [H]
Extremely popular fellside inn, nestling under the Pennines in an attractive setting by the village green. Excellent bar meals – winner of numerous awards. Good range of malt whiskies. Games area.
♨ Q ◖ ◗ ⛺ ♣ P

Milnthorpe

Coach & Horses
☎ (044 82) 3210
11–3; 6–11
Mitchell's Dark Mild, Best Bitter [H]
Open-plan lounge with an adjoining public bar area. Locals and tourists make it a popular pub. ♨ ❀ ◖ ♣ P

Monkhill

Drovers Rest
400 yds W of Kirkandrews on Eden OS343587
☎ (0228) 76591
12–3; 5.30–11
Jennings Mild, Bitter [H]
Traditional, welcoming and popular pub in tiny village. Skilfully enlarged and refurbished to retain its character. Haaf-netting connections. Food limited to (substantial) snacks. Family room lunchtimes only.
♨ 🚼 ♿ ♣ P

Moota

Laal Moota
On A595 opp. Bothe brick quarry ☎ (0965) 20414
11–3 (not Mon–Fri in winter); 5.30–11 (11–11 summer)
Ruddles Best Bitter; Webster's Yorkshire Bitter, Wilson's Original Bitter [H]
Meals available only in newly-opened lounge. Small cosy bar.
♨ Q ❀ ◖ ◗ ⊞ ♿ ⛺ ♣ P

Near Sawrey

Tower Bank Arms
On B5285 ☎ (096 66) 334
11–3; 6–11 (11–11 summer)
Matthew Brown Mild; Theakston Best Bitter, XB; Younger Scotch [H]
Popular with diners and drinkers alike. Situated next to Beatrix Potter's home and recognizable from one of her books. Stone-flagged floors contribute to the Lake District atmosphere that the pub generates so well.
♨ Q ❀ 🛏 ◖ ◗ ⛺ ♣ P

Try also: Sawrey Hotel, Far Sawrey (Free)

Nether Wasdale

Strands
On main road OS125041
☎ (094 06) 237
11.30–2.30; 6–11
Hartleys XB; Robinson's Best Bitter [H]
Comfortable pub and restaurant in lovely remote area of western lakes. Wastwater, Scafell and quieter tourist areas nearby.
♨ Q 🚼 ❀ 🛏 ◖ ◗ ⛺ P

Try also: Screes (Free)

Penrith

Agricultural Hotel
Castlegate (200 yds from railway station towards town centre) ☎ (0768) 62622
11–3; 5–11 (11–11 Tue & Wed)
Marston's Burton Best Bitter, Merrie Monk, Pedigree Bitter [H]
No jukebox or fruit machines. Live jazz alternate Thu eves. Good home-cooked food. A classic town pub.
♨ Q ❀ 🛏 ◖ ◗ ⇌ ♣ P

Lowther Arms
3 Queen Street (400 yds N of clock tower) ☎ (0768) 62792
11–3; 7–11 (may extend in summer)
Theakston Best Bitter, XB [H]
Excellent refurbishment of a former basic, keg-only pub. The use of traditional materials has created a cosy 'country-style' pub in the town centre. Bookings preferred for eve meals. ♨ ◖ ◗ ⇌ ♣

Rosthwaite

Scafell Hotel (Riverside Bar)
☎ (059684) 208
11–11
Theakston Best Bitter, XB, Old Peculier [H]
Cafeteria-style bar serving snacks and meals to fell-walkers (boots allowed). At the rear of a large, upmarket, country house hotel (which does not sell real ale in its bar). ♨ 🛏 ◖ ◗ ⊞ ⛺ P

Rowrah

Stork Hotel
Rowrah Road (A5086)
☎ (0946) 861213
11–3; 5.30–11
Jennings Mild, Bitter [H]
Quiet, family-run pub, with hunting and hound-trailing mementos. Nearest pub to the International Rowrah Karting Track (go-karts) and handy for Ennerdale. ♨ 🚼 ❀ 🛏 ⊞ ♿ ♣ P

St Bees

Manor House
Main Street (B5345)
☎ (0946) 822425
11–4; 5.30–11
Theakston Best Bitter [H]
Friendly coaching inn with a cosy bar and a plush lounge. Regular guest beer.
♨ Q ❀ 🛏 ◖ ◗ ⊞ ⛺ ⇌ ♣ P

Scales

White Horse Inn
Set back from A66
☎ (059683) 241
11.30–2.30; 6.30–11 (11–3; 6–11 summer)
Jennings Bitter [H]
Low, whitewashed building tucked neatly under the foot of Blencathra. The pub boasts a real fire at either end of the narrow, low-ceilinged lounge bar. A warm informal atmosphere prevails. Good well-presented bar food (eve meals all week summer; Fri–Sun winter). ♨ Q ◖ ◗ ⛺ ♣ P

Sedbergh

Dalesman
Main Street ☎ (053 96) 21183
11–3; 6–11 (11–11 summer)
Ind Coope Burton Ale; Tetley Mild, Bitter [H]
Pub dating back to 16th–17th-century, close to the Dales Walk route. Dalesman Bitter specially

brewed for the pub. A small restaurant, known as the Buttery, is attached to the bar area. ⌂ ❀ ⊨ ◐ ◑ ⛺ ♣ P

Try also: Red Lion (Marston's)

Swinside

Swinside Inn

OS242218 ☎ (059682) 253
12–3; 6 (7 winter) –11
Jennings Bitter Ⓗ
Olde-worlde bar open all year; second bar open in summer. Walkers welcomed (centre for walking in the Newlands Valley area of the National Park). Separate restaurant.
⌂ Q ❀ ⊨ ◐ ◑ ⊟ ♿ ⛺ ♣ P

Ulverston

Devonshire Arms

Victoria Road (left at Coronation Hall)
☎ (0229) 52537
11–3; 6–11 (11–11 Thu)
Thwaites Mild, Bitter Ⓗ
A two-roomed local with a comfortable lounge. Numerous pictures reflect the landlord's interest in aviation.
Q ◐ ⊟ ⇌ ♣ P

Kings Head

☎ (0229) 52892
11–11 (11–3; 6–11 Tue)
Theakston Best Bitter Ⓗ
Small, oak-beamed old pub in an attractive village. Popular with old and young alike. Very good value bar snacks. Crown green bowling at the back. Guest beer.
⌂ Q ❀ ⊨ ◐ ⇌

Warwick on Eden

Queens Arms Inn and Motel

☎ (0228) 60699
11–3; 7–10.30
Marston's Pedigree Bitter; Whitbread Trophy, Castle Eden Ale Ⓗ
Excellent free house with separate restaurant. Good choice of meals.
⌂ Q ❀ ⊨ ◐ ◑ ♣ ⊙ P

Whitehaven

Central

104 Duke Street
☎ (0946) 692796
11–4; 6.30–11 (11–11 Fri & Sat)
Matthew Brown Mild; Theakston Best Bitter, XB; Younger IPA, No.3 Ⓗ
Popular front lounge with quieter back bar. By far the best range of cask-conditioned beers in town. ◐ ⊟ ⇌ (Bransty) ♣

Wigton

Victoria

King Street ☎ (06973) 42672
11–11
Jennings Mild, Bitter Ⓗ
Friendly and smart, two-roomed, town-centre pub, almost opposite bus station.
♿ ⇌ ♣

Windermere

Greywalls Hotel (Greys Inn)

Elleray Road (300 yds from railway station)
☎ (09662) 3741
11–11
Theakston Best Bitter, XB, Old Peculier Ⓗ
Busy, loud town pub well-supported by locals.
⌂ ☺ ❀ ⊨ ◐ ◑ ♿ ⇌ P

Try also: Brookside (S&N)

Workington

Commercial Inn

4 Market Place
☎ (0900) 603981
11–4; 6–11
Jennings Bitter Ⓗ
Quiet, friendly pub just out of town centre. Next to the covered market. ♣

George IV

29 Stanley Street (over railway viaduct, just off quay)
11–11
Jennings Bitter Ⓗ
Cosy, back-street local on one of the oldest streets in town. Long-serving landlady. ⌂ ⇌ ♣

Special Cask Bitter, from the days when Whitbread were proud to present a beer "Brewed on Merseyside"

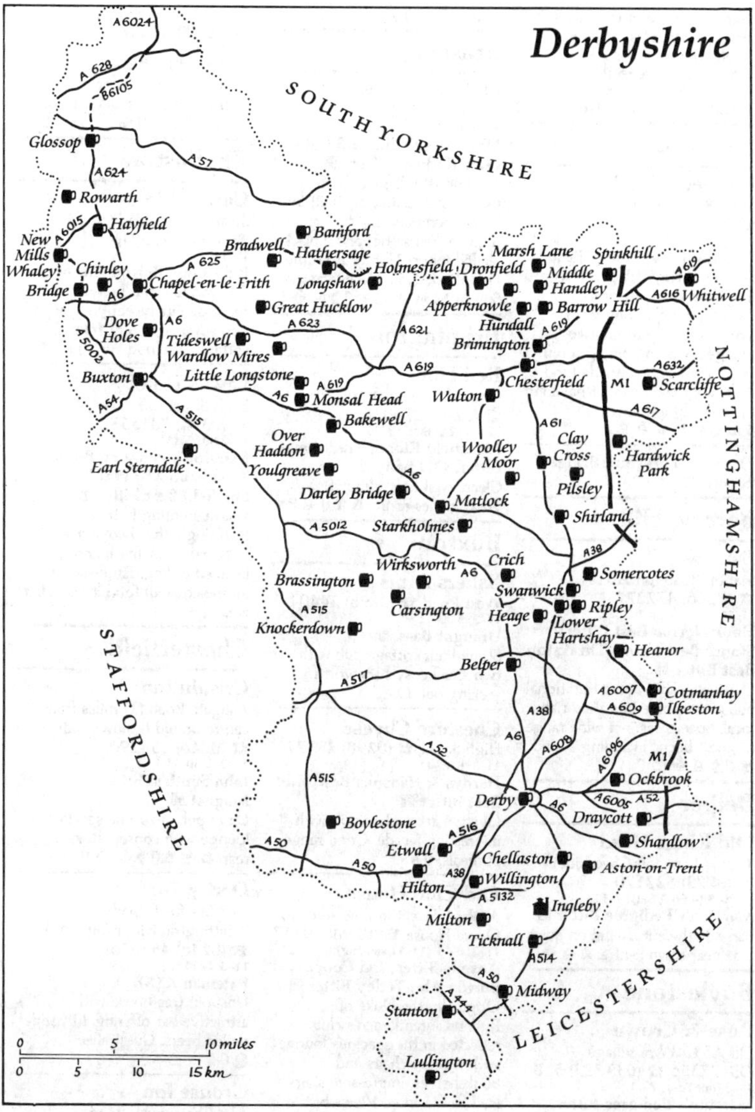

Lloyds, *Ingleby*

Apperknowle

Yellow Lion
45 High Street
☎ (0246) 413181
12–2 (3 Sat); 5–11
Alloa Arrol's 80/-; Stones Best Bitter; Tetley Bitter H
Busy stone-built village free house with comfortable lounge and separate restaurant. Extensive menu includes veg dishes. Good range of bar snacks. Winner of several CAMRA awards. Guest beers.
Q ❀ ◑ ◗ ♿ ♣ P

Try also: Barrack (John Smith's)

Aston-on-Trent

White Hart
Derby Road ☎ (0332) 792264
11–11
Marston's Pedigree Bitter H; **Owd Rodger** (winter) G
Welcoming village local. Bar and lounge are both cosy and inviting. ⛫ ❀ ⊟ ♿ ♣ P

Try also: Malt Shovel (Allied)

Bakewell

Manners
Haddon Road (A6 S side of town) ☎ (0629) 812756
11–11
Robinson's Best Bitter H
Friendly local, a short distance

Derbyshire

from the centre of this busy market town. Has just been extensively refurbished. P

Try also: Red Lion (Free)

Bamford

Derwent Hotel
Main Road (A6013)
☎ (0433) 51395
11–11
Draught Bass; Stones Best Bitter; Tetley Bitter; Wards Sheffield Best Bitter [H]
Country hotel dating from 1890, with tap room, two lounge areas and dining room. Well-priced, home-made food. A friendly and unspoilt haven in the heart of a tourist area. P

Try also: Yorkshire Bridge (Stones)

Barrow Hill

Barrow
Station Road (off A619)
☎ (0246) 472277
11–11
Hook Norton Best Bitter; Stones Best Bitter; Theakston Best Bitter [H]
Unusual graffiti and a traditional pub atmosphere in a Victorian local. Specialises in a wide range of guest beers, including a mild. P

Belper

Old Kings Head
1 Days Lane (off Cheapside)
☎ (0773) 822170
11.30–3 (4 Fri & Sat); 7–11
Marston's Pedigree Bitter [E]
Early 15th-century inn on quiet lane near town centre.

Boylestone

Rose & Crown
Off A515 W of village
OS177356 ☎ (033 523) 518
11–3 (not Tue); 7–11
Marston's Pedigree Bitter, Owd Rodger (winter) [H]
Whitewashed pub in pleasant pastoral setting. Two small low-ceilinged rooms. Q P

Bradwell

Valley Lodge
Church Street (B6049)
☎ (0433) 20427
11–4; 7–11
Draught Bass; Stones Best Bitter; Wards Sheffield Best Bitter; Younger IPA [H]
A warm welcome in a lively village pub, set in the Peak National Park. Three large, well-appointed rooms cater for all age groups. Home-cooked menu includes large range of veg dishes. P

Brassington

Olde Gate Inne
☎ (062985) 448
12–3; 6–11
Marston's Pedigree Bitter [H], **Owd Rodger** (winter) [G]
Traditional village pub of exceptional character; built in 1616. Scrubbed-top tables, high-backed settles and a black-leaded range. Not far from the High Peak Trail. No eve meals Sun or Mon. Q P

Brimington

Red Lion
Church Street (A619)
☎ (0246) 273628
12–4 (12–2 Sun); 7–11
Mansfield Riding Traditional Bitter, Old Baily [H]
Clean, well-kept pub with a good games room. P

Buxton

Bakers Arms
West Road ☎ (0298) 24404
11–3; 5.30–11
Draught Bass [E]
Stone-built cottage pub with two small cosy bars worth seeking out. Q

Cheshire Cheese
High Street ☎ (0298) 25371
11–3; 5.30–11
Hardys & Hansons Best Mild, Best Bitter [H]
Lively market place pub with interesting facade. Good range of meals.

Old Club House
3 Water Street (follow signs to Opera House ☎ (0298) 70117
11–3; 6–11 (11–11 summer)
Ansells Bitter; Ind Coope Burton Ale; Tetley Bitter [H]
Originally the Duke of Rutland's gentlemen's club, as reflected in the spacious lounge with its easy chairs and bookshelves. Impressive stairs lead to the snug. Views of the elegant Opera House. Water Street is closed during Buxton Festival, when the area assumes a continental air.

Carsington

Miners Arms
☎ (062985) 207
11–3; 6–11
Draught Bass [G]
A one-roomed, comfortable country local. Friendly atmosphere with live music and occasional sing-alongs.
P

Chapel-en-le-Frith

Roebuck
Market Place (off A6)
☎ (0298) 812274
11–3; 5.30–11
Tetley Mild, Bitter [H]
A pub of great character; overlooking the market place, by the stocks.

Chellaston

Corner Pin
Swarkestone Road (A514)
☎ (0332) 705715
11–11
Ind Coope Burton Ale [H]
Comfortable and popular roadside inn, recently expanded into adjoining cruck-framed cottage. No food Sun. P

Lawns Hotel
High Street (off A514)
☎ (0332) 701553
11–2.30; 5–11
Marston's Pedigree Bitter; Theakston XB; Wards Sheffield Best Bitter [H]
Warm, inviting hotel bar featuring a thatched surround over bar, brick finish and beamed ceiling. Emphasis on (home-cooked) food in main bar area. P

Chesterfield

Crispin Inn
Ashgate Road ($1\frac{1}{2}$ miles from centre on old Baslow road)
☎ (0246) 234290
11–3; 5.30–11
John Smith's Bitter, Magnet [H]
Large pub, now one spacious lounge with conservatory at rear. P

Derby Tup
327 Sheffield Road, Whittington Moor (off A61)
☎ (0246) 454316
11–3; 5–11
Bateman XXXB [H]
Unspoilt free house with attractive bar offering 11 hand-pulled beers. Guest ales.
Q

Grouse Inn
136 Chatsworth Road, Brampton (A619)
☎ (0246) 279632
12–3; 6.30–11
Draught Bass; Stones Best Bitter [H]
Popular local on route to Peak District.

Portland Hotel
West Bars ☎ (0246) 234502
11–3; 5.30–11
Courage Directors; John Smith's Bitter, Magnet [H]
Mock-Tudor hotel with fine wood-panelled interior, facing imaginatively-restored, traditional market place. Three of the bars are warmed by a real fire. Separate restaurant.
P

Royal Oake
The Shambles
☎ (0246) 205508
11–3; 7–11
Stones Best Bitter [H]
One of the oldest buildings in town; this remarkable 13th-century, half-timbered inn has an interesting bar entered by the higher door. ⊕ ⇌ ♣

Steelmelters Arms
68 St Johns Road, Newbold Moor ☎ (0246) 450856
11–3.30; 7–11
Vaux Samson; Wards Sheffield Best Bitter [H]
Friendly local, recently-refurbished, but retaining an original and unusual high bar.
♣

Welbeck Inn
Soresby Street
☎ (0246) 271643
11–3; 5.30–11
Hardys & Hansons Best Bitter [E]
Two-roomed town pub, just off north side of market place.
❀ ◐ ◑ ⊕ ⇌ ♣

Chinley

Squirrels
1 Green Lane (B6062)
☎ (0663) 50001
11–11
Ind Coope Burton Ale; Lloyds Derby Bitter; Tetley Mild, Bitter [H]
Impressive three-storey, stone-built pub. Imposing at first glance but a warm welcome awaits inside. Good selection of malt whiskies. Two guest beers.
❀ ⊨ ◐ ◑ ⇌ ♣

Clay Cross

Cannon
4 Thanet Street (off A61)
☎ (0246) 250078
11–3; 7–11
Courage Directors [H]
Mock-Tudor pub and restaurant taken over as a family concern in 1988 and tastefully refurbished under the supervision of the landlord, a former master builder. Live music some nights, with quiz night every Tue. ❀ ◐ ◑ P

Try also: New Inn (Tetley)

Cotmanhay

Bridge Inn
Bridge Street (off A6007)
☎ (0602) 322589
11–11
Hardys & Hansons Best Mild, Best Bitter [E]
Traditional village local adjacent to Erewash Canal, serving the cheapest beer in the area. Landlord a real character who permits no swearing in the bar 'where eagles dare'. A rare find.
Q ❀ ⊕ ♿ ♣ P

Try also: Trumpet (Shipstone's)

Crich

Cliff Inn
Cromford Road (NW of village)
☎ (077385) 2444
11–3; 6–11
Hardys & Hansons Best Mild, Best Bitter [H]
Popular, stone-built local with two small rooms. Not far from National Tramway Museum.
❀ ◐ ◑ ⊕ P

Darley Bridge

Square & Compass
Main Road ☎ (0629) 733255
11.30–3; 6–11 (11–11 Sat)
Robinson's Best Mild, Best Bitter [E]; **Old Tom** (Xmas) [G]
Warm and welcoming 18th-century pub, popular with all ages. A centre for keen players of darts, dominoes, cribbage and pool. Fishing available on River Derwent. ♜ ❀ ⊨ ◐ ◑ ♿ ⛺ ♣ P

Derby

Alexandra Hotel
Siddals Road
☎ (0332) 293993
11–3; 4.30–11
Bateman Dark Mild, XB, XXXB, Victory Ale; Marston's Pedigree Bitter [H]
Very pleasing decor and atmosphere; wooden floors and subtle wall coverings. Display of bottled beers in the bar. Guest beers a speciality. Good home-cooked food (not Sun).
⊨ ◐ ◑ ⇌ ♣ P

Brunswick Inn
11 Railway Terrace
☎ (0332) 290677
11–11
Bateman Dark Mild; Burton Bridge Bridge Bitter [H]; **Hook Norton Old Hookey** [G]; **Marston's Pedigree Bitter; Taylor Landlord; Wards Kirby Strong** [H]
The oldest (1842) purpose-built railway pub in the world. Retains its stone-flagged floor. No-smoking room always open. East Midlands CAMRA Pub of the Year 1989. Various guest beers and draught scrumpy always available.
Q ♉ ◐ ⊕ ♿ ⇌ ♣ ⌒ P

Crompton Tavern
Crompton Street
☎ (0332) 292259
11–3; 5–11
Vaux Samson; Wards Thorne Best Bitter, Sheffield Best Bitter; Taylor Landlord [H]
U-shaped room catering for young people. More beers planned. Regular live music and entertainment. ◐ ♣

Dolphin Inn
Queen Street
☎ (0332) 49115
11–11
Draught Bass; M&B Mild, Highgate Mild, Springfield Bitter; Stones Best Bitter; Worthington BB [H]
Derby's oldest surviving and most picturesque pub, built same year (1530) as the cathedral tower in whose shadow it stands. One of the four rooms is devoted to the memorabilia of a former local brewery. Good food.
Q ❀ ◐ ◑ ⊕ ♣ P

Furnace
Duke Street ☎ (0332) 31563
11–3 (12–2.30 Sun); 6–11
Hardys & Hansons Best Mild, Best Bitter [H]
Popular beerhouse with open-plan interior featuring photographs of bygone Derby. Close to St Mary's Bridge and the historic Bridge Chapel. ❀ ♣

New Flower Pot
25 King Street
☎ (0332) 44449
11.30–3; 6–11 (11–11 Sat)
Draught Bass; M&B Highgate Mild [H]
Small and very basic pub. Guest beer. ♣

Station Inn
Midland Road
☎ (0332) 360114
11–3; 7–11
Draught Bass [G]
Narrow pub used mostly by postal workers. ⇌ ♣

Strutts
73 London Road (A6)
☎ (0332) 44421
11–11
Mansfield Riding Dark Mild, Riding Traditional Bitter, Old Baily [H]
One large lounge with 1920s decor, catering for younger people. ❀ ◐ ⇌ P

Vine Inn
37 Whitaker Street (off Normanton Road, via Rose Hill Street) ☎ (0332) 41473
11–3 (4 Fri); 7–11
Draught Bass; M&B Mild [H]
Long-established, back-street local in redeveloped area. Popular with all sections of a mixed community. Offiler's Brewery started here in 1886.
⊕ ♣

Try also: Great Northern (Allied)

Dove Holes

Railway

Derbyshire

Buxton Road
☎ (0298) 812265
11–3; 6–11
Hardys & Hansons Best Mild, Best Bitter [H]
Weatherbeaten roadside pub in exposed moorland. Comfortable, with a cosy lounge. P

Draycott

Travellers Rest
Derby Road (A6005)
☎ (033 171) 2332
11–2.30; 6–11
Marston's Mercian Mild, Pedigree Bitter [H]
Modernised, double-fronted Victorian local with separate games room and skittle alley.
P

Dronfield

Old Sidings
91 Chesterfield Road (B6057)
☎ (0246) 410023
12–11
Vaux Samson, Double Maxim; Wards Thorne Best Bitter, Sheffield Best Bitter, Kirby Strong [H]
Lively pub with L-shaped lounge on two levels; comfortably-furnished, with a railway theme. Restaurant in basement (eve meals Wed–Sat). Quiz Wed night. P

Earl Sterndale

Quiet Woman
On B5053 ☎ (029 883) 211
11–3; 5.30–11
Marston's Mercian Mild, Burton Best Bitter [H]
Superb example of a village local. Situated on the White Peak Way. P

Etwall

Hawke & Buckle
Main Street (A516)
☎ (028 373) 3471
11.30–2.30; 7–11
Marston's Pedigree Bitter [H]
Smartly-modernised village local with a comfortable lounge and smaller bar with games area.
P

Glossop

Bulls Head
Church Street, Old Glossop (off A57) ☎ (045 74) 3291
12–3; 7–11 (12–2.30; 7.30–10.30 Sun)
Bass Mild XXXX, Light 5 Star, Draught Bass; Stones Best Bitter [H]
Pleasant three-roomed local, well off the beaten track. A warm welcome assured. Good value food. Q P

Crown
Victoria Street (towards Hayfield on A624)
11–3; 5.30–11
Samuel Smith OBB [H]
A true local; comfortable and friendly with an accent on pub games.

Prince of Wales
Milltown (off A57)
11–3; 5.30–11
Marston's Mercian Mild, Burton Best Bitter, Pedigree Bitter [H]
Cosy and characterful, stone-built, end-of-terrace pub. Keeps out the worst of the Glossop winters.

Great Hucklow

Queen Anne
Off B6049 ☎ (0298) 871246
12–3 (not Mon–Fri in winter); 7–11
Tetley Mild, Bitter [H]
Warm, friendly village local with tiny tap room. Lounge doubles as a dining room (lunches Sat/Sun only).
Q P

Hardwick Park

Hardwick Inn
1 mile S of M1 jct 29
☎ (0246) 850245
11.30–3; 6.30–11
Theakston XB; Younger Scotch [H]
17th-century inn, owned by the National Trust, at gates to historic Hardwick Hall. Restaurant is closed Mon; no eve meals Sun. P

Hathersage

Plough
Leadmill Bridge (B6001, 1 mile from village) ☎ (0433) 50319
11.30–3; 7–11 (11.30–11 Sat & bank hols)
Stones Best Bitter [E]
Comfortable pub, converted from a farmhouse on banks of River Derwent. Strong local trade, but visitors always welcome. Spacious split-level lounge and small intimate tap room.
Q P

Hayfield

George Inn
Church Street
11–3; 5.30–11
Burtonwood Best Bitter [H]
Historic stone pub with stained glass windows and photographs of old Hayfield. An ideal start or finish for walks on Kinder Scout.
P

Sportsman
Kinder Road (follow signs to campsite) ☎ (0663) 42118
6–11 (may extend Sat & summer)
Thwaites Bitter [H]
White-painted, stone-built pub on narrow road winding up to Kinder Scout. A long bar in lounge serves separate arch-linked rooms, for diners, darts and pool. Plans to sell mild. Upstairs children's room.
P

Heage

White Hart
2 Church Street (off B6374)
☎ (077 385) 2302
11.30–3.30; 6–11
Draught Bass [E]
Large, attractive, multi-roomed pub, of early 17th-century origin. P

Heanor

Crown Inn
Church Street
☎ (0773) 712006
11–3; 7–11
Hardys & Hansons Best Mild, Best Bitter [H]
Popular, friendly, games-oriented bar; lounge is cosy and relaxing.

New Inn
107 Derby Road (A608)
☎ (0773) 719609
11–4; 7–11
Home Mild, Bitter [E]
Popular, friendly and compact local at top of Tag Hill.
P

Hilton

Old Talbot
Main Street ☎ (028 373) 3728
12–2.30; 7–11 (may vary)
Draught Bass [E]
Friendly village local with two rooms. Q P

Holmesfield

Travellers Rest
20 Main Road
☎ (0742) 890446
12–4; 7–11 (may extend afternoons)
Home Bitter; Younger No. 3 [H]
Pleasant two-room pub with pool in tap room and comfortable, if somewhat spartan, lounge.
Q P

Hundall

Miners Arms
Hundall Lane
☎ (0246) 413183
11.30–4.30; 7–11
Wards Sheffield Best Bitter; Younger No. 3 [H]
Cosy pub, comfortably-furnished, with an unusual carved bar. Barbecues Sun lunchtime in summer.
P

Ilkeston

Durham Ox
Durham Street (off A6007/B6096)
☎ (0602) 324570
11–4; 6–11 (11–11 Sat)
Wards Mild, Thorne Best Bitter, Sheffield Best Bitter Ⓔ
Busy, popular back-street pub with open-plan interior and separate pool area. Cheap B&B; real ale beef casserole always available. Sun night quiz. Has been in every edition of this guide. Knock on side window if not open on time. 🏠 ❀ 🛏 ◖ ♣ P

Flowerpot
Chapel Street (off A6007/B6096)
☎ (0602) 320484
11–11
Greenalls Shipstone's Mild, Shipstone's Bitter Ⓔ
Well-established, old street-corner pub; one of a dying breed worshipped by Shipstone's lovers. Convenient for shoppers at Albion centre. Separate pool room. Excellent lunches; home-made pizzas always available. ❀ ◖ ⊟ ♿ ♣ P

Rutland Cottage
Heanor Road (A6007)
☎ (0602) 304875
11–3; 6–11 (11–11 Fri & Sat)
Greenalls Shipstone's Mild, Shipstone's Bitter Ⓔ&Ⓗ
Well-appointed roadside pub of considerable character, just on edge of town. If handpumped beer is required, please specify. Excellent lunches.
🏠 ⚒ ❀ ◖ ⊟ ♿ ♣ P

Try also: Needlemakers (Shipstone's)

Knockerdown

Knockerdown Inn
On B5035, between Brassington and Bradbourne turns ☎ (062 985) 209
11–3; 5.30–11
Marston's Pedigree Bitter Ⓖ
Isolated, modern roadhouse; popular and comfortable.
🏠 ◖ P

Little Longstone

Packhorse
Off B6465, near Monsal Head
☎ (062 987) 471
11–3; 5–11 (11–11 Sat)
Marston's Burton Best Bitter, Pedigree Bitter Ⓗ
Ancient unspoilt village local which has been a pub since 1787. Small comfortable lounge; the tap room is popular with ramblers. 🏠 Q ❀ ◖ ⊟ ⛺ ♣

Longshaw

Grouse
On B6054, 2 miles N of Calver
☎ (0433) 30423
12–3; 7–11
Vaux Lorimers Best Scotch; Wards Sheffield Best Bitter, Kirby Strong Ⓗ
Originally built as a farmhouse in 1804; the hayloft, barn doors and stone trough survive. Comfortable lounge at front leads to conservatory, overhung with vines, and adjoining tap room. No food Mon or Tue.
🏠 Q ❀ ◖ ◗ ♣ P

Lower Hartshay

George Inn
Main Road (off A610)
☎ (0773) 742597
12–4; 7–11
Hardys & Hansons Best Mild, Best Bitter Ⓗ
One of the few Hardys & Hansons pubs with handpumps in the area. A basic village local with a friendly atmosphere. Games include skittles.
❀ ◖ ◗ ⊟ ♣ P

Lullington

Colville Arms
Coton Road ☎ (082 786) 212
11–3 (not Mon–Fri); 7–11
Draught Bass; Marston's Pedigree Bitter Ⓗ
18th-century village pub, the most southerly in the county. Basic, wood-panelled bar, smart lounge and separate games/meeting room. Bowling green in garden. 🏠 ❀ ⊟ ♣ P

Marsh Lane

Fox & Hounds
Main Road (B6056)
☎ (0246) 432974
12–3; 7–11
Burtonwood Best Bitter Ⓗ
Comfortable lounge and traditional tap room. Large beer garden and play area alongside a good-sized car park. Meals Thu–Mon. 🏠 ❀ ◖ ◗ ⊟ ♣ P

Matlock

Sycamore Inn
9 Sycamore Road (up hill from Crown Square, left by county offices, 400 yds)
☎ (0629) 57585
11–3.30; 6–11
Draught Bass Ⓗ
Comfortable, traditional pub away from the bustle of the town. Q ❀ ◖ ⊟ ♿ P

Thorn Tree
48 Jackson Road (on hill behind county offices)
☎ (0629) 582923
11.30–3 (not Tue); 7–11
Draught Bass; Mansfield Old Baily Ⓗ
Small, unspoilt local, popular with darts players and office workers. Fine atmosphere and a friendly welcome. Worth searching out. Q ❀ ⊟ ♣

Middle Handley

Devonshire Arms
Westfield Lane (off B6052)
☎ (0246) 432189
11–3; 7–11
Stones Best Bitter Ⓗ
Friendly and popular village local with central bar.
Q ❀ ♿ ♣ P

Midway

Wheel Inn
597 Burton Road (A50)
☎ (0283) 221759
11.30–3; 7–11
Draught Bass Ⓗ
Busy, main road pub, internally-modernised. Bar and open-plan lounge both have coal fires.
🏠 ❀ ◖ ⊟ ♣ P

Try also: Crown Inn, Newhall (Bass)

Milton

Swan Inn
Main Street ☎ (0283) 703188
11–2.30 (3.30 Sat); 7–11
Marston's Pedigree Bitter Ⓗ
Popular village pub with smart lounge and locals' bar. No food Mon or Sun eve. ❀ ◖ ◗ ⊟ ♣ P

Monsal Head

Monsal Head Hotel
☎ (062 987) 250
11–11
John Smith's Bitter; Theakston Best Bitter, Old Peculier Ⓗ
150 year-old country hotel with elegant, genteel lounge in main building. Most of the real ales are in the rear bar which was once stables for the long-gone Bulls Head. It now features a large inglenook, stall seating and manger. House beer from Lloyds. Guest beers.
🏠 Q ⚒ ❀ 🛏 ◖ ◗ ⊟ ⛺ ♣ ⍉ P

New Mills

Crescent
Market Street
☎ (0663) 43889
11–3; 5.30–11
Tetley Mild, Bitter Ⓗ
Attractive stone-fronted pub in crescent-shaped terrace.
◖ ◗ ⊟ ⇌ (Central) ♣

Fox Inn
Brookbottom Hamlet (up St Mary's Road)
11–3; 5.30–11
Robinson's Best Mild, Best Bitter Ⓗ
Old, whitewashed pub in small hamlet which can be reached on foot via the woodland cart-track from Strines station. Low-ceilinged lounge and separate

pool room.
✿ ◐ ◑ ≈ (Strines) ♣ P

Masons Arms
High Street ☎ (0663) 44292
11.30–4.30; 7–11
Robinson's Best Mild, Best Bitter [E]
Cosy, welcoming, stone pub in narrow street. Two low-ceilinged rooms have access to the small bar. Separate pool room. ⌂ ♣ P

Ockbrook

Royal Oak
Green Lane (between A52 and A6096) ☎ (0332) 662373
11–3; 6–11
Draught Bass [H]
Characterful village meeting place with four small rooms. No food Sun. ⌂ Q ✿ ◐ ⊟ ♿ ♣ P

Over Haddon

Lathkill Hotel
½ mile SW of B5055
☎ (0629) 812501
11.30–3; 6–11
Wards Mild, Thorne Best Bitter, Sheffield Best Bitter [H]
Free house in an idyllic setting, overlooking one of the Peak's most picturesque dales. Fine oak-panelled bar with traditional-style leather and wood furnishings. Excellent food. Children welcome only at lunchtime.
⌂ ☺ ✿ ⊭ ◐ ◑ ⊟ ▲ ♣ P

Pilsley

Gladstone Arms
Morton Road
☎ (0773) 872285
11–3; 7–11
Home Bitter [H]
Lively, stone-built local in centre of old pit village. Entertainment at weekends.
⌂ ✿ ⊟ ♣

Ripley

George Inn
Lowes Hill (off A61)
☎ (0773) 748719
12–5; 7–11 (11–11 Fri & Sat)
Bateman Mild, XB, XXXB [H]
Modernised, open-plan pub with rare brews for the area. Lunchtime snacks. ✿ ♣ P

Hollybush
51 Brook Lane, Marehay (off A61 S of town)
☎ (0773) 42558
11–3; 6–11
Greenalls Shipstone's Bitter [H]
Spacious pub overlooking cricket ground. ✿ ◑ ⊟ ♣ P

Try also: Three Horseshoes (Wards)

Rowarth

Little Mill
☎ (0663) 43178
11–3; 5.30–11
Hartleys Bitter; Robinson's Best Mild, Best Bitter; Ruddles County [H]
Restaurant-style pub set in a lovely location in a wooded valley. Outdoor drinking area has swings for children. Belgian bottled beers and guest ales available. ☺ ✿ ◐ ◑ P

Scarcliffe

Horse & Groom
On B6417 ☎ (0246) 823152
11–4; 7–11
Home Bitter [H]
Beamed coaching inn with children's play area to rear.
⌂ Q ✿ ◐ ⊟ ♣ P

Shardlow

Canal Tavern
London Road (A6)
☎ (0332) 792844
11.30–3; 5.30–11
Hoskins Beaumanor Bitter, Penn's Ale, Premium [H]
1780, Grade II listed, canalside warehouse in lovely setting, excellently-converted into a single-bar pub with original beams and brick floor. Adjoining restaurant is open lunch and evening every day. Guest beers. ✿ ◐ ⌒ P

Try also: Malt Shovel (Marston's)

Shirland

Duke of Wellington
Main Road (A61)
☎ (0773) 833256
11–3; 6–11
Home Bitter [E]
Busy roadside pub with cosy lounge and large tap room.
⌂ ✿ ⊟ ♣ P

Try also: Woolpack (John Smith's)

Somercotes

Horse & Jockey
Leabrooks Road (B6016)
☎ (0773) 602179
11–3; 7–11
Home Mild, Bitter [H]
Deservedly-popular, unspoilt local with several rooms.
⌂ Q ✿ ⊟ ♣

Spinkhill

Angel Hotel
26 College Road (off A616 2 miles from M1 jct 30)
☎ (0246) 432315
12–3; 7 (6 summer)–11
Ind Coope Burton Ale; Tetley Bitter [H]
Large, rambling village local and country inn. Comfortable L-shaped lounge with separate restaurant/function room. Games room with snooker table in basement. Guest beers.
⌂ Q ✿ ⊭ ◐ ◑ ♣ P

Stanton

Gate Inn
Woodlands Road (A444)
☎ (0283) 216818
11–3; 6–11
Marston's Pedigree Bitter [H]
A popular pub despite a low local population. Plain bar and smart lounge form an L-shape, with a dining area off the bar. Highly-regarded locally for good pub food (not Sun).
✿ ◐ ◑ ⊟ ♣ P

Try also: Plough Inn, Rosliston (Marston's)

Starkholmes

White Lion
Starkholmes Road (old Matlock Green–Cromford coach road)
☎ (0629) 582511
11–3; 6–11
Home Bitter [H]
Unspoilt village local in beautiful location overlooking Derwent Valley. Good range of food until 8.30pm.
Q ✿ ◐ ◑ ♿ ♣ P

Swanwick

Gate Inn
The Delves (E of A61 via the Green) ☎ (0773) 602039
11.30–3; 7–11
Courage Best Bitter, Directors; John Smith's Bitter [H]
Smart, open-plan pub with bar, lounge and restaurant areas. No food Sun or Mon eve.
✿ ◐ ◑ ♣ P

Ticknall

Staff of Life
7 High Street
☎ (0332) 862479
11.30–2.30; 6–11
Draught Bass; Burton Bridge Bridge Bitter; Everards Old Original; Hook Norton Old Hookey; Marston's Pedigree Bitter; Taylor Landlord [H]
A food house with a bar. A good choice of beers with up to 14 available at all times. Menu caters for children and vegetarians. ✿ ◐ ◑ P

Wheel Inn
50 Main Street (A514)
☎ (0332) 862966
11.30–3; 7–11
Draught Bass [H]
Lively, atmospheric local with tiny smoke room and larger bar.

Handy for Calke Abbey. No food Sun. ♨ Q ❀ ◐ ⊟ P

Tideswell

Anchor Inn
Four Lane Ends (A623/B6049)
☎ (0298) 871371
11–3; 6–11
Hartleys XB; Robinson's Best Mild, Best Bitter, Old Tom Ⓗ
500 year-old pub on cross-roads. Traditional tap room with dartboard; spacious oak-panelled lounge with dining room at rear.
♨ ❀ ◐ ◗ ⊟ ♿ ⛺ ♣ P

George Hotel
Commercial Road (B6049)
☎ (0298) 871382
11–3; 7–11
Hardys & Hansons Best Mild, Best Bitter Ⓗ
Stone-built country hotel in centre of village. Comfortable lounge with dining room off, and small snug leading to tap room, which has dartboard and pool table.
♨ Q ❀ 🛏 ◐ ◗ ⊟ ⛺ ♣ P

Try also: Horse & Jockey (Tetley)

Walton

White Hart Inn
Matlock Road (1½ miles W of A617) ☎ (0246) 566392
11–3; 5–11
Courage Directors; John Smith's Bitter Ⓗ
Pleasantly-situated roadside inn with vast outdoor drinking and children's play area. Ideal for summer eves. Noted for its food (eve meals Thu–Sat only).
♨ ❀ ◐ ◗ ♿ P

Wardlow Mires

Three Stags Heads
A623/B6465 jct
☎ (0298) 872268
11 (7 Mon)–11
Matthew Brown Mild Ⓖ**; Theakston Old Peculier; Younger Scotch Bitter, No. 3** Ⓗ
Carefully-restored, 17th-century farmhouse pub. Bar heated by an ancient cooking range, still used for meals. Two rooms with a third soon to be added for diners. Live music Wed/Sat eve; popular with hikers. Dogs welcome. Meals served 12–10.30pm.
♨ Q ❀ ◐ ◗ ⛺ ♣ P

Whaley Bridge

Navigation
Wharf Street (off A6)
☎ (06633) 2308
11–3; 5.30–11
Whitbread Boddingtons Bitter Ⓗ
Comfortable, stone-built pub, tucked away but close to the terminus of Peak Forest Canal and station. ◐ ⊟ ⇌ ♣ P

Shepherds Arms
Old Road (off A6)
☎ (06633) 2384
11–3; 5.30–11
Marston's Mercian Mild, Burton Best Bitter, Pedigree Bitter Ⓗ
Excellent, ageless local with stone-flagged vault, cosy lounge and small pleasant garden.
❀ ◐ ⊟ ⇌ ♣ P

Whitwell

Jug & Glass
Portland Street (off A619)
☎ (0909) 720289
12–3; 7–11
John Smith's Bitter, Magnet Ⓗ
Compact pub in centre of village. ♨ ❀ ⊟ ♣ P

Willington

Green Dragon
The Green (A5132 by railway bridge) ☎ (0283) 702327
11–2.30; 7–11
Ansells Bitter; Ind Coope Burton Ale Ⓗ
L-shaped single room, retaining low beams. Formerly part of railway cottages. No food Sat/Sun eve. ♨ ❀ ◐ ◗ P

Try also: Rising Sun (Marston's)

Wirksworth

Hope & Anchor
Market Place (B5032/B5035)
☎ (062982) 4620
11–4; 7–11 (11–11 summer)
Home Bitter Ⓔ
Old, stone-built pub of great historical interest, with large bar and small lounge dominated by a 17th-century chimney.
♨ Q ❀ 🛏 ◐ ◗ ⊟ ♣ P

Try also: Red Lion (Allied)

Woolley Moor

White Horse Inn
White Horse Lane (off B6014)
☎ (0246) 590319
11.30–2.30 (3 Sat); 6.30–11
Draught Bass Ⓗ
Almost legendary for fine ale and food. Set in excellent walking country; the less active can enjoy the beautiful view of the rolling Derbyshire hills. Ogston Bird Sanctuary is nearby. Regular guest beer. Inventive menu (not Sun eve). Not to be missed.
Q ❀ ◐ ◗ ⊟ ♿ ⛺ ♣ P

Try also: Miners Arms (Mansfield)

Youlgreave

George Inn
Church Street (off A6)
☎ (0629) 636292
11–3; 6–11
Home Mild, Bitter Ⓗ
Large, lively local across from village church. Popular with hikers who are asked to use the public bar. Haddon Hall and Arbor Low are nearby.
⛆ ❀ ◐ ◗ ⊟ ⛺ ♣ P

Try also: Bulls Head (Marston's)

THE SYMBOLS

- ♨ real fire
- Q quiet pub – in at least one bar
- ⛆ indoor room for children
- ❀ garden or other outdoor drinking area
- 🛏 accommodation
- ◐ lunchtime meals
- ◗ evening meals
- ⊟ public bar
- ♿ easy disabled access
- ⛺ camping facilities at the pub or nearby
- ⇌ near British Rail station
- ⊖ near Underground station
- ♣ pub games
- ⌽ real cider
- P pub car park

Devon

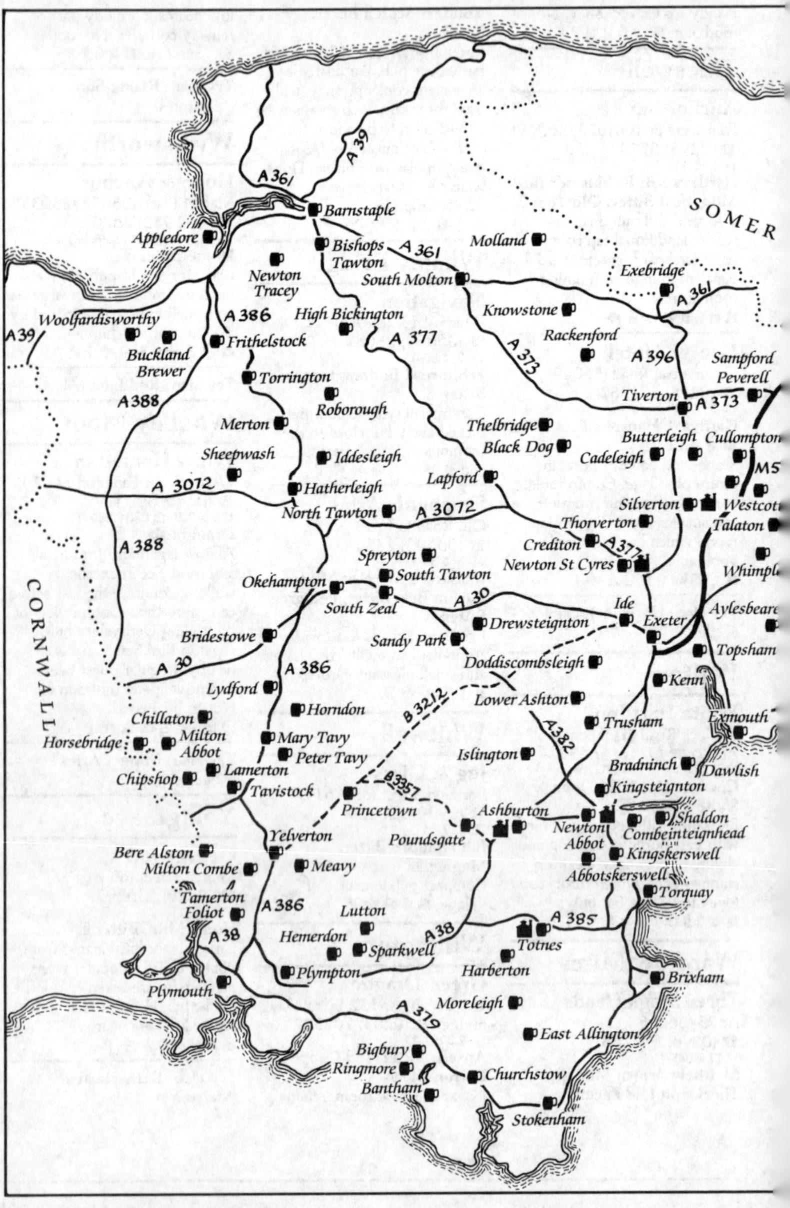

Barron, *Silverton*; **Beer Engine**, *Newton St Cyres*; **Blackawton**, *Totnes*; **Mill**, *Newton Abbot*; **Thompson's**, *Ashburton*

Abbotskerswell

Two Mile Oak

Totnes Road (A381)
☎ (0803) 812411
11–2.30; 6–11
Draught Bass; Eldridge Pope Royal Oak Ⓖ; **Whitbread Flowers IPA** Ⓗ
15th-century coaching house. Food-dominated lounge but the public bar retains an old-fashioned atmosphere.
⛫ ❀ ◖ ◗ ⊕ P

Appledore

Coach & Horses

5 Market Street
11.30–2.30; 6.30–11 (11–11 Fri & Sat)
Ushers Best Bitter Ⓗ
Very popular locals' pub

offering well-presented home-made food. Pub games include euchre, darts and skittles.
⌂ Q ◖◗ ♣

Seagate Hotel
The Key
11–3; 6–11 (11–11 summer)
Ind Coope Burton Ale; Tetley Bitter (summer) Ⓗ
Waterfront hotel popular with locals and tourists. Tetley is on cask-breather. Landlord friendly. One bar has jukebox.
♞ ❀ ⛟ ◖◗ ♿ ♣ P

Ashburton

London Inn
11 West Street
☎ (0364) 52478
11–3; 5–11
Thompson's Mild, Best Bitter, IPA Ⓗ
Comfortable coaching house with enormous, meandering lounge. Home of Thompson's Brewery. ⌂ ◖◗

Axminster

Axminster Inn
Silver Street (behind the church)
☎ (0297) 34947
11–11
Palmers BB, IPA Ⓗ
Originally a farmers' local, part of the pub was once a fishmonger's and later an insurance agency. Much of the original character has been retained. Was owned by the Stuart family for over 100 years, prior to 1985. Skittle alley. ⌂ ♞ ❀ ⛟ ⊟ ≹ ♣ ☌

Millwey
Chard Road (A358, on the edge of town) ☎ (0297) 32774
11–2.30; 6.30–11
Palmers BB, IPA Ⓗ
A modern estate-type pub. Meals most evenings and each lunchtime. ❀ ◖◗ ⊟ ♣ P

Try also: Cavalier (Free)

Axmouth

Ship Inn
B3172 (1 mile S of Boshill Cross) ☎ (0297) 21838
10.30 (11 Sat)–2.30 (12–2.30 Sun); 5.30 (6 Sat)–11 (11–2; 6–11 winter)
Cornish Original, Royal Wessex Bitter Ⓗ
Village inn with good food, a collection of dolls and several owls. ⌂ Q ❀ ◖◗ ⊟ ♿ ⛺ ♣ ☌

Aylesbeare

Halfway Inn
Sidmouth Road (A3052)
☎ (0395) 32273
11–2.30; 5.30–11
Cornish Royal Wessex Bitter Ⓗ
Two-bar country pub and restaurant. Scotch corner always stocks over 100 different whiskies. No eve meals served Sun/Mon from Jan to April.
❀ ◖◗ ⊟ ♿ ⛺ ♣ P

Bantham

Sloop Inn
☎ (0548) 560215
11–3; 6–11
Draught Bass; Ushers Best Bitter; Whitbread Flowers IPA Ⓗ
Large pub with restaurant. Very busy in summer. Bar skittles played. ⌂ Q ❀ ⛟ ◖◗ ♣ ☌ P

Barnstaple

Corner House
108 Boutport Street
☎ (0271) 43528
11–3; 5–11 (11–11 Fri & Sat)
Draught Bass Ⓗ
Atmospheric, wood-lined town bar with long-established reputation. Nice collection of toby jugs and stone bottles. The last proper town pub in North Devon. Regular guest beers.
Q ♣

Beer

Anchor Hotel
Fore Street ☎ (0297) 20386
11–2.30; 6–10.30 (11 Sat)
Charrington IPA; Hall & Woodhouse Badger Best Bitter Ⓗ
Warm, friendly pub with nice staff. Large bar areas and excellent restaurant (booking advisable in summer months and weekends). Fresh fish dishes and varied cuisine. Guest beers. Cider available in summer.
⌂ ❀ ⛟ ◖◗ ⊟ ⛺ ♣ ☌

Try also: Beer Social Club (Free)

Bere Alston

Edgcumbe Hotel
On main street
☎ (0822) 840252
11.30–2.30 (3 Sat); 6.30–11
Courage Best Bitter, Directors Ⓗ
Basic village pub. ≹

Bigbury

Royal Oak Inn
On main street
☎ (0548) 810313
11.30–3; 5.30–12
Draught Bass; Palmers IPA Ⓗ
Village local with foody lounge. No eve meals Mon during winter. Q ❀ ⛟ ◖◗ ⊟ ⛺ P

Bishops Tawton

Three Pigeons
☎ (0271) 72269
11–3.30; 6–11
Whitbread Flowers IPA Ⓗ
Good, basic, friendly local. Shove-ha'penny and skittles played. Q ♞ ❀ ◖◗ ⊟ ♣ P

Black Dog

Black Dog Inn
Village centre (2 miles S of B3042) ☎ (0884) 860336
11–2.30; 6.30–11
Draught Bass; Wadworth 6X; Whitbread Flowers IPA Ⓗ
Rural inn located at crossroads. Good value-for-money food in

separate restaurant. Skittle alley.
♜ ♉ ❀ ◖ ◗ ♿ ⛺ ♣ P

Bradninch

Castle Inn
Fore Street ☎ (0392) 881378
11.30–2.30; 6–11
Ind Coope Burton Ale Ⓗ
Old coaching house recently renovated to a high standard. Warm, friendly atmosphere and comfortable surroundings. Good home-cooked meals. Mr Collins has recently been awarded membership of Guild of Master Cellarmen. Castle Ale house beer supplied by Allied.
❀ ◖ ◗ ♣ P

Bridestowe

Fox & Hounds
A386 (on B3278 jct)
☎ (082 282) 206
11–3; 6–11
Whitbread Flowers IPA, Flowers Original Ⓗ
Large pub on Dartmoor, near Lydford Gorge. Skittle alley available for hire.
♜ Q ♉ ⛟ ◖ ◗ ⛺ P

Brixham

Burton
32 Burton Street (off the Dartmouth road)
☎ (080 45) 2805
11–3; 5.30–11
Courage Best Bitter Ⓗ**, Directors** Ⓖ
Small but busy back-street pub. An unusual wood-panelled boozer with a strong local following. ♜ ◖ ⊕ P

Buckland Brewer

Coach & Horses
High Street OS421206
☎ (023 75) 395
11–2.30; 5.30–11
Whitbread Flowers IPA, Flowers Original Ⓗ
Old coaching inn in middle of village. Low ceiling – watch your head! Real fire in both bars. Quiet bar to left has games room at back. Friendly and popular with locals.
♜ Q ❀ ◖ ◗ ⊕ P

Burlescombe

Ayshford Arms
Off B3181, 2 miles NE of M5 jct 27 ☎ (0823) 672429
12–3 (not Mon); 7–11
Draught Bass; Cotleigh Tawny Bitter; Theakston Best Bitter Ⓗ
Spacious, lively pub serving good food, including a choice of veg dishes. Separate restaurant, guest beers. ♜ Q ❀ ◖ ◗ ⊕ ♿ P

Butterleigh

Butterleigh Inn
☎ (088 45) 407
12–3; 6 (5 Fri & Sat)–11
Cotleigh Harrier SPA, Tawny Bitter, Old Buzzard Ⓗ
Friendly village inn with stained glass porch. Popular for food and top-rate ales.
♜ Q ❀ ⛟ ◖ ◗ ⊕ ♿ ♣ ⌀ P

Cadeleigh

Cadeleigh Arms
☎ (088 45) 238
11–2.30; 6–11
Draught Bass; Cotleigh Tawny Bitter; Fuller's London Pride Ⓗ
Homely, traditional country pub. Live music at least one Fri eve a month. Regular guest beers. ♉ ❀ ◖ ◗ ♣ P

Chillaton

Chichester Arms
6 miles NW of Tavistock
OS432818 ☎ (082 286) 283
11–3; 6–11 (11–11 Sat, 12–2.30; 7–11 winter)
Courage Best Bitter, Directors Ⓗ
White-walled, one-bar pub set on roadside by village junction.
♜ ⛟ ◖ ◗ P

Chipshop

Chipshop Inn
2½ miles off A384, W of Tavistock ☎ (0822) 832322
12–2.30; 7 (6.30 Fri & Sat)–11
Exmoor Ale; Fuller's London Pride; Marston's Pedigree Bitter Ⓗ
One-bar country pub on remote crossroads. Large collection of mirrors; skittle alley for hire. Guest beers. ♜ ❀ ◖ ◗ ⛺ ♣ P

Churchstow

Church House Inn
☎ (0548) 852237
11–2.30; 6–11
Draught Bass; Ruddles County; Ushers Best Bitter Ⓗ
Pub very popular for food, especially carvery. Large lounge area and car park. ♜ ❀ ⛟ ◖ ◗ P

Clayhidon

Half Moon Inn
4½ miles S of Wellington
☎ (0823) 680291
12–3; 7–11
Draught Bass; Cotleigh Tawny Bitter, Old Buzzard Ⓗ
Old, but well cared for, village local. Nice views across Culm Valley. Games include darts and skittles.
♜ Q ♉ ❀ ◖ ◗ ♿ ⛺ ♣ ⌀ P

Combeinteignhead

Wild Goose
☎ (0626) 872241
11–2.30; 6–11
Exmoor Ale; Mill Janner's Ale; Wadworth 6X Ⓗ
17th-century farmhouse full of character. Traditional jazz on Mon nights. Guest beer; good range of food. Altogether mildly (but pleasantly) eccentric.
♜ ◖ ◗ P

Crediton

Crediton Inn
Mill Street ☎ (036 32) 2882
11–11
Barron Exe Valley Bitter Ⓗ
Lively town-centre local, built in 1852/3. Inn sign depicts St Boniface. Skittles. ◖ ◗ ⇌ P

Exchange
113 High Street
☎ (036 32) 5853
11–3; 5–11 (11–11 Sat & summer)
Courage Best Bitter, Directors Ⓗ
Comfortable, open-plan lounge area with steak and wine bar function room. Award-winning garden and toilets.
Q ♉ ❀ ◖ ◗ ⇌

Cullompton

Manor House Hotel
2–4 Fore Street
☎ (0884) 32281
11–11
Draught Bass; Whitbread Flowers Original Ⓗ
16th-century town-centre hotel. Good value food. Regular guest beer. ♉ ❀ ⛟ ◖ ◗ ♿ ♣

Dawlish

Prince Albert
28 The Strand (parallel to High Street) ☎ (0626) 862132
11–2.30; 5–11
Draught Bass; Whitbread Flowers IPA Ⓗ
Cosy and convivial house. Also known as the 'Hole in the Wall'. Q ◖ ⇌

Doddiscombsleigh

Nobody Inn
Off B3193
12–2.30 (incl. Sun); 6–11
Draught Bass; Whitbread Flowers IPA Ⓗ
Ancient pub/restaurant on eastern edge of Dartmoor. Large range of wines and malt whiskies. Nobody's Bitter house beer. ♜ Q ⛟ ◖ ◗ ⌀ P

Drewsteignton

Drewe Arms
The Square (off A30/A382)
10.30–2.30; 6–11
Whitbread Flowers IPA Ⓖ
Original, old, unspoilt Devon village pub with oldest and longest serving landlady in country. Bulmer cider available.
♜ Q ♣ ⌀

East Allington

Fortescue Arms
Off A381 ☎ (054 852) 215
12–2; 6.30–11
Palmers IPA [H]
Village local with bar and food areas split. ♨ Q ❀ 🛏 ◖ ◗ ⊟ ⚲ P

Exebridge

Anchor Inn
On B3222 ☎ (0398) 23433
11–2.30; 6–11
Ruddles County; Ushers Best Bitter; Webster's Yorkshire Bitter [H]
Pleasant inn beside the Exe, with children's garden and good food. Mentioned in Blackmore's *Lorna Doone*; Webster's is sold as 'Doone Ale'. Draught cider available in summer.
♨ Q ☋ ❀ 🛏 ◖ ◗ ⊟ ♿ ⛺ ♣ ⚲ P

Exeter

Chaucers
High Street ☎ (0392) 422365
11–11 (closed Sun)
Draught Bass; Halls Harvest Bitter [H]
Newly-opened basement bar under C&A. Plans for guest beer. Harvest is sold as 'Chaucers Bitter'. Very food-oriented lunchtime.
Q ◖ ⇶ (Central)

Cowley Bridge Inn
Cowley Bridge Road
A377/A396 jct)
☎ (0392) 74268
11–2.30; 6–11
Eldridge Pope Royal Oak; Marston's Pedigree Bitter; Whitbread Flowers IPA, Flowers Original [H]
Comfortable, friendly, non-glitter pub, popular with students and train spotters. Impressive collection of woodsaws adorns the walls. The Addlestones cider is not traditional. ♨ Q ◖ ◗ ⊟ ♣ P

Double Locks
Canal Banks, Marsh Barton (on towpath) OS933301
☎ (0392) 56947
11–11
Eldridge Pope Royal Oak; Everards Old Original; Exmoor Ale; Marston's Pedigree Bitter, Owd Rodger; Wadworth 6X [H]
Highly-successful, slightly eccentric canalside pub with huge outside area (volleyball!). Two rooms suitable for families, plus atmospheric old bar. Good value food – barbecues in summer. Frequent live music and always something going on. Possibility of mild on beer menu. Four ciders and regular guest beers.
♨ ☋ ❀ ◖ ◗ ⊟ ⛺ ♣ ⚲ P

Great Western Hotel
Station Approach, St Davids
☎ (0392) 74039
11–3; 5–11
Draught Bass; Charrington IPA [H]
Busy railway hotel with two comfortable lounge bars. Popular with thirsty travellers. Good value food.
Q 🛏 ◖ ◗ ♿ ⇶ (St Davids) P

Mill on the Exe
Bonhay Road
11–11
Furgusons Dartmoor Best Bitter, Dartmoor Strong; Ind Coope Burton Ale; Tetley Bitter [H]
Converted mill beside a weir. Two large bars plus function room. Nice waterside beer garden – but watch the children.
❀ ◖ ◗ ⇶ (St Davids) P

Ship Inn
St Martin's Lane
☎ (0392) 472040
11–2.30 (12–2 Sun); 5–11
Draught Bass; Whitbread Flowers IPA, Flowers Original [H]
Old, friendly pub between the cathedral and high street shops, with an Armada/Sir Francis Drake theme. Busy at lunchtimes with the office fraternity. Serves good value snacks/meals in pub, and in the separate restaurant upstairs. Whitbread guest beers.
◖ ◗ ⇶ (Central) ⚲

Victoria Inn
36 Victoria Street
☎ (0392) 54176
11–2.30; 5.30–11 (11–11 Fri & Sat)
Cornish Draught Steam Bitter, Royal Wessex Bitter; Greene King Abbot Ale; Ruddles Best Bitter [H]
Converted, large one-bar pub near university, with green tiled exterior. ◖ ◗ ♿

Well House
Cathedral Close
☎ (0392) 58464
11–2.30; 6–11 (11–11 summer)
Barron Exe Valley Bitter; Draught Bass [H]
Oasis of independent beer next to cathedral green. Ancient cellar inhabited by Black Death victim. Good value food. At least two interesting guest beers. 🛏 ◖ ⇶ (Central)

Exmouth

Grove
The Esplanade (W end of the sea front) ☎ (0395) 272101
11–3; 5.30–11 (11–11 summer)
Beer range varies
Very warm and friendly, 1989-opened seafront pub. Traditional bar and timber decor/furniture. Good home-cooked food, including locally-caught seafood and steak and kidney pie in real ale. Stages occasional mini beer festivals. Always five ales from all over the country available.
☋ ❀ ◖ ◗ ♿ ⇶ P

Feniton

Nog Inn
Ottery Road (opp. station)
☎ (0404) 850210
11–3; 6–11
Cotleigh Tawny Bitter [H]
Cheerful pub with squash court and possessive cat. Stages own beer festival and offers regular guest beers (at least four always on). ♨ Q 🛏 ⊟ ⇶ ♣ ⚲ P

Frithelstock

Clinton Arms
Off Bideford Road (2 miles from Torrington) OS464195
☎ (0805) 23279
11.30–2.30; 6–11
Draught Bass [G]
Comfortable family pub with very jovial and entertaining landlord. Two separate restaurants and conservatory. Landlord doesn't like term public bar – has had recent royal patronage. Crib, draughts and backgammon.
♨ Q ❀ 🛏 ◖ ◗ ♿ ♣ P

Harberton

Church House
☎ (0803) 863707
11–2.30; 6–11
Courage Best Bitter; Marston's Pedigree Bitter [H]
Enormous, heavily-beamed lounge and well-equipped family room. Some real antique furnishings and lots of real food.
♨ Q ☋ ◖ ◗ ⚲

Hatherleigh

Tally Ho
14 Market Street
☎ (0837) 810306
11–2.30; 6–11
Butcombe Bitter; Eldridge Pope Royal Oak; Tally Ho Potboiler's Brew [G]
Ancient market town pub with accent on Italian home-cooking. Brand new brewery on premises. ♨ Q ❀ 🛏 ◖ ◗ ⚲ P

Hemerdon

Miners Arms
Off A38 at Plympton
☎ (0752) 343252
11–3; 5.30–11
Draught Bass [H]&[G]; Furgusons Dartmoor Best Bitter [H]; Marston's Pedigree Bitter [G]; Ruddles County; Ushers Best Bitter [H]

Split-level, former tin miners pub set on the edge of Plympton suburbia. Many exposed beams support a low ceiling; large granite fireplace. Spacious car park. ⌂ ⊛ ◖ ◗ ⊟ P

High Bickington

Old George Inn
Poplar Terrace
☎ (0769) 60513
11–3; 6–11
Butcombe Bitter [G]; Ind Coope Burton Ale; Wadworth 6X [H]
16th-century village inn. No food Tue/Wed eve.
⌂ ⚭ ◖ ◗ ♣ P

Holcombe Rogus

Prince of Wales
☎ (0823) 672070
12–2.30; 7–11
Draught Bass; Cotleigh Harrier SPA, Tawny Bitter, Old Buzzard [H]
Pleasant country pub, the first to be owned by Cotleigh Brewery. Has interesting handpumps resembling a cash register. The Old Buzzard steak pie is recommended. Regular guest beers.
⌂ Q ⚭ ⊛ ◖ ◗ ♣ ⊖ P

Honiton

Railway
Queen Street (off New Road)
☎ (0404) 43686
11.30–2.30; 5.30–11
Courage Best Bitter, Directors [H]
A pleasant locals' pub, overlooking the station. Owes its existence to the entrepreneurial first landlord. Opened in 1860 and became a free house when sold by Heavitree in 1976.
⚭ ⊛ ◖ ◗ ⊟ ⇌ ♣ P

White Lion
194 High Street
☎ (0404) 42066
11–2.30; 5–11
Archers Village Bitter; Cornish Draught Steam Bitter; Marston's Pedigree Bitter; Wadworth 6X [H]
The original White Lion was across the road, where it burned down twice. Moved to its present site around the turn of the century. A comfortable, one-bar local with live music Thu eves. No eve meals Sun.
⚭ ⊛ ⊠ ◖ ◗ P

Try also: Heathfield; Volunteer (Free)

Horndon

Elephant's Nest
Off A386, $1\frac{1}{2}$ miles E of Mary Tavy ☎ (082 281) 281
11–3; 6.30–11
Palmers IPA; St Austell Tinners, HSD; Wadworth 6X [H]
Splendid moorland pub named after a former landlord's beard! A very large garden. ⌂ Q ◖ ◗

Horsebridge

Royal Inn
6 miles W of Tavistock on River Tamar OS400749
☎ (082 287) 214
12–2.30; 7–11
Draught Bass; Greene King Abbot Ale; Marston's Pedigree Bitter; Royal Inn Tamar, Horsebridge Best, Right Royal, Heller [H]
This 15th-century pub was once a nunnery. No children admitted. Excellent and unusual food (not Sun eve).
⌂ ⊛ ◖ ◗ ⊟ ♣ P

Iddesleigh

Duke of York
On B3217 ☎ (0837) 810253
11.30–3; 6.30–11
Cotleigh Tawny Bitter; Wadworth 6X [G]
14th-century, thatched village pub. Super inglenook fireplace, genuine beams and old stillage behind bar. Definitely nothing modern. All food prepared on the premises (no food Mon eve). Children welcome in room next to main bar. Guest beers.
⌂ Q ⚭ ⊛ ⊠ ◖ ◗ ▲ ♣ ⊖

Ide

Huntsman
2 High Street ☎ (0392) 72779
11–3; 5.30–11
Cornish JD Dry Hop Bitter, Draught Steam Bitter, Royal Wessex Bitter [H]
Thatched village inn beside a ford. Boasts the longest pub sign in Britain. No food Sun. Bar billiards. ⌂ Q ⊛ ◖ ◗ ♣ ⊖ P

Ilsington

Carpenter Arms
☎ (03646) 215
11–2.30; 6–11
Whitbread Flowers IPA [G]
Timeless, one-bar village local with serious darts players. Run by an experienced and friendly couple. ⌂ ⊛ ♣ ⊖

Kenn

Ley Arms
Off A38 at Kennford
☎ (0392) 832341
11–2.30; 6–11
Draught Bass; Exmoor Ale; Greene King Abbot Ale; Wadworth 6X; Whitbread Flowers IPA [H]
Thatched village pub with excellent carvery.
⌂ ⚭ ⊛ ◖ ◗ ▲ P

Kilmington

New Inn
The Hill (100 yds off A35)
☎ (0297) 33376
11–2.30; 7 (6.30 summer)–11
Palmers BB, IPA [G]
Cheerful village pub with large garden and play area. No food Mon. ⌂ Q ⚭ ⊛ ◖ ◗ ⊟ ♣ P

Kingskerswell

Bickley Mill
Stoney Combe (1 mile W of town) ☎ (080 47) 3201
11–2.30; 6.30–11
Draught Bass; Eldridge Pope Royal Oak; Wadworth 6X [H]
Large, 13th-century, converted mill. Terraced garden has roaming peacocks. Good food; live music Sat nights. Modernised in lounge style throughout. ⌂ ⚭ ⊛ ⊠ ◖ ◗ ▲ P

Kingsteignton

Old Rydon
Rydon Lane ☎ (0626) 54626
11–2.30; 6–11
Draught Bass; Wadworth 6X [H]
Substantial old pub/restaurant at the back of a housing estate, well worth finding. 'Old Rydon house beer is brewed by Mill.
⌂ Q ⊛ ◖ ◗ P

Knowstone

Masons Arms
☎ (03984) 231
11–3; 7 (5.30 summer)–11
Cotleigh Tawny Bitter; Hall & Woodhouse Badger Best Bitter; Hook Norton Best Bitter [G]
Delightful, thatched village inn. Public bar with large open fire; cosy small lounge. Quiet calm prevails out of season. Occasional guest beers.
⌂ Q ⚭ ⊛ ⊠ ◖ ◗ ▲

Lamerton

Blacksmiths Arms
On A384 (4 miles from Tavistock) ☎ (0822) 612962
11.30–2.30; 6.45–11
Draught Bass [H]
Medium-sized, one-room pub, dominated by a U-shaped bar. Emphasis on food. ⌂ ⊛ ◖ ◗ ▲ P

Lapford

Old Maltscoop Inn
☎ (0363) 83330
11.30–2.30; 6–11
Adnams Broadside [G]; Draught Bass [H]; Eldridge Pope Royal Oak [G]; Wadworth 6X [H]

Real village inn with wooden stillage behind bar serving cask beers by gravity. Old inglenook fireplace. Regular guest beers.
⌂ Q ♞ ❀ 🛏 ◐ ◑ ▲

Lower Ashton

Manor Inn
Near Christow
☎ (0647) 52304
11.30–2.30; 5.30–11 (closed Mon in winter)
Cotleigh Tawny Bitter; Eldridge Pope Royal Oak; Wadworth 6X [H]
Small village pub in quiet, pretty Teign Valley. Spoof, shove-ha'penny and darts played. ⌂ Q ❀ ◐ ◑ ⊟ ▲ ♣ P

Lutton

Mountain Inn
3 miles N of A38
☎ (075 537) 247
11–3; 6 (7 Mon–Wed in winter)–11
Butcombe Bitter; Exmoor Ale; Furgusons Dartmoor Best Bitter; Ind Coope Burton Ale [H]
Cottage-style bar and furnishings, with exposed cob walls and large granite fireplace. Set in sleepy village. Car parking requires good manners!
⌂ ❀ ♁ P

Lydford

Castle Inn
On B3278 OS509848
☎ (082 282) 242
11–3; 6–11
Courage Best Bitter; Ushers Best Bitter [H]
Stone-flagged, 16th-century free house by castle.
⌂ Q ♞ ❀ 🛏 ◐ ◑ ♿ ▲

Manor Inn
Off A386, near Lydford Gorge entrance OS503832
☎ (082 282) 208
11–3; 6–11
St Austell Tinners, HSD [H]
Stone-walled inn by gorge and stream.
⌂ Q ♞ ❀ 🛏 ◐ ◑ ♿ ▲ ♣

Mary Tavy

Mary Tavy Inn
On A386 ☎ (082 281) 326
11–3; 7.30–11
St Austell Tinners; Ushers Best Bitter [H]
Large roadside inn on edge of the moor. Extensive clock collection. ⌂ Q ♞ ❀ 🛏 ◐ ◑ ▲

Meavy

Royal Oak
Off A386 ☎ (0822) 852944
11–3; 6–11
Blackawton Bitter; Courage Best Bitter; Furgusons Dartmoor Strong [H]
Classic country pub near village green, next to church. Popular with walkers, ramblers and city folk. Inches cider.
⌂ Q ❀ ◐ ◑ ⊟ ▲ ♣ ♁

Merton

Malt Scoop
☎ (080 53) 260
12 (11 Summer)–2; 7–11
Butcombe Bitter [H]
Pub which has been in same family since 1906. ♿ P

Milton Abbot

Edgcumbe Arms
On A384 ☎ (082 287) 229
11.30–2.30; 6.30–10.30 (11 Fri & Sat, 11–3; 6–11 summer)
Draught Bass; Wadworth 6X; Whitbread Best Bitter [H]
19th-century pub with large stone fireplace. Friendly, cosy and convenient. Guest beers.
⌂ ◐ ◑ ⊟ P

Milton Combe

Who'd Have Thought It
Off A386 ☎ (0822) 853313
11–3; 6.30–11
Eldridge Pope Royal Oak; Exmoor Ale; Palmers IPA; Wadworth 6X [H]
Lovely, 16th-century, slate flag-stoned pub, set in a steeply-wooded valley near to Lopwell Dam. Extensive range of bar snacks and main meals available.
Q ❀ ◐ ◑ ♿ ♁ P

Molland

London Inn
☎ (076 97) 269/719
10.30–2.30; 6–11
Cornish Vallence's Bitter [H]
Traditional Devon inn on the lower reaches of Exmoor. One of a dying breed of pubs. Menagerie in the front entrance area. ⌂ Q ♞ ❀ ◐ ◑ ⊟ ▲ ♣ P

Try also: Black Cock

Moreleigh

New Inn
On B3207 ☎ (054 882) 326
12–2; 6.30–11
Palmers IPA [G]
Excellent traditional village pub, off the track. Not fancy; not modernised; not spoilt. Has reputation for good steaks. Highly-recommended.
⌂ Q ◐ ◑ ♣ ♁ P

Newton Abbot

Wolborough Inn
Wolborough Street
☎ (0626) 61667
11–2; 6 (7 Sat)–11
Tetley Bitter [H]
Very small, sports-oriented local; darts, pool and euchre played. 🛏 ◐ ♣

Newton St Cyres

Beer Engine
☎ (0392) 851282
11–2.30; 6–11 (12 Fri, 11.30–12 Sat)
Beer Engine Rail Ale, Piston Bitter, Sleeper Heavy [H]
Basic, but mildly eccentric, village boozer that brews its own (crystal-clear) ales downstairs. Strong railway connections. Live music Fri and Sat nights, with licensed extensions. ⌂ ♞ ❀ ◐ ◑ ≉ ♣ P

Newton Tracey

Hunters Inn
On B3232 ☎ (027 185) 339
11.30–2; 6–11 (11–11 summer)
Marston's Pedigree Bitter; Whitbread Flowers IPA, Flowers Original [H]
The old part of this pub is very cosy and it has two bars, one quiet. Skittle alley and restaurant are modern. Large car park; patio beer garden. Euchre and skittles played.
⌂ ♞ ❀ ◐ ◑ ⊟ ♿ ♣ P

North Tawton

Green Dragon
12–3; 7–11
Robinson's Best Mild, Bitter; Whitbread Boddingtons Bitter [H]
Comfortable, two-roomed pub.
⌂ ⊟ ♣ P

Okehampton

Plume of Feathers
38 Fore Street ☎ (0837) 52815
10.30–11 (may vary)
Courage Best Bitter, Directors [H]
Pleasant town-centre pub, busy at lunchtimes. Good value B&B.
Q 🛏 ◐ ⊟ ♿ ♣ ♁ P

Ottery St Mary

London Inn
Gold Street ☎ (0404) 814763
12–2; 7–11
Draught Bass; Hall & Woodhouse Badger Best Bitter; Marston's Owd Rodger; Mitchell's ESB; Wadworth Old Timer; Young's Special [H]
18th-century coaching house with genuine oak beams, horse brass, etc. 'Olde-worlde' restaurant; two function rooms; skittle alley and pool room. Guest beers. Two real ciders.
⌂ Q ❀ 🛏 ◐ ◑ ⊟ ♿ ♣ ♁ P

Try also: Kings Arms (Courage)

Peter Tavy

Devon

Peter Tavy
Off A386, N of Tavistock
☎ (082 281) 348
11–3; 6.30–11
Butcombe Bitter; Courage Best Bitter, Directors; Eldridge Pope Royal Oak; Exmoor Ale H
Ancient moorland pub with low ceilings, flagstones and settles. Excellent veg food, though expensive.

Plymouth

Archer Inn
11 Archer Terrace (off B3241)
☎ (0752) 667654
11–3; 6–11 (11–11 Thu–Sat)
Draught Bass H
Small, darts-dominated local close to city centre. Public car park opposite is free after 4pm. Over footbridge from railway station along North Road West.

Brown Bear
20 Chapel Street, Devonport (A374) ☎ (0752) 564663
11–3; 5.30–11
Courage Best Bitter, Directors G
Main road local which has moved slightly upmarket. Restaurant extension complements existing bar. Eve meals Wed–Sat only. P

Complex
Keyham Road (opp. dockyard's Albert Gate)
11–3; 6–11 (11–11 Wed–Fri)
Adnams Bitter; Cornish Draught Steam Bitter; Eldridge Pope Royal Oak; Marston's Pedigree Bitter; St Austell HSD; Whitbread Boddingtons Bitter H
Sizeable two-bar pub often frequented by dockyard and Navy personnel. Beers may vary.
(Devonport/Dockyard)

Dolphin Hotel
14 The Barbican
☎ (0752) 660876
11–11
Draught Bass G
Spartan dockside hostelry frequented by fishermen. Opposite disused GWR quayside station, alongside which fishing vessels moor.

Ferry House
888 Wolseley Road, St Budeaux ☎ (0752) 361659
11–3; 6–11
Courage Best Bitter H
Pub with splendid view over Tamar Estuary. Q

Pym Arms
16 Pym Street, Devonport
☎ (0752) 561823
11–3; 6–11
Draught Bass; Eldridge Pope Royal Oak; Fuller's London Pride G**; St Austell XXXX Mild** H**, HSD; Wadworth 6X** G
A beer drinker's den, fitted out with 'genuine' fake beams that defy the normal constraints of construction. Heavily-populated with students in term-time. Only real mild for miles. Guest ales. (Devonport)

Stopford Arms
172 Devonport Road (A3041)
☎ (0752) 562915
11–2.30 (3 Sat); 6–11
Courage Best Bitter, Directors H
Clean and tidy, small city local.
(Devonport)

Swan Inn
Cornwall Beach, Devonport
☎ (0752) 568761
12–3; 7–12
Ruddles Best Bitter, County; St Austell HSD; Ushers Best Bitter; Wadworth 6X; Webster's Yorkshire Bitter H
Stone-walled within, split-level drinking house with emphasis on music. Situated by the Tamar with good views of sunsets. 10p off at lunchtime, before 9pm, and all day Sun. Additional beers available.

Thistle Park Tavern
1 Sutton Road, Coxside (off A374) ☎ (0752) 667677
12–3; 7–11
Eldridge Pope Royal Oak; Greene King Abbot Ale; Marston's Owd Rodger; Ruddles County; St Austell HSD; Wiltshire Old Grumble H
Basic boozer with pool table and strong range of real ales. Old Grumble is sold as 'Weedkiller'.

Three Crowns
The Parade, The Barbican
☎ (0752) 229324
11–11 (11–2.30; 6–11 Mon)
Courage Best Bitter, Directors H
Comfortable, one-bar pub. Public bar is now a children's room, vending appropriate goods. Car park adjacent.

Plympton

Lyneham Inn
Off A38, at Deep Lane Plympton turn off
☎ (0752) 336955
11–3; 6–11
Courage Best Bitter H

Poundsgate

Tavistock Inn
On A384, between Ashburton and the moor. ☎ (036 43) 251
11–2.30; 6–11
Courage Best Bitter H
Traditional granite pub in an isolated hamlet. Cosy, slightly rugged front bar; side room and plenty of outside seating. All day breakfasts. Good atmosphere.

Princetown

Plume of Feathers
Plymouth Hill (B3212/B3357 jct)
11–11
Draught Bass; St Austell Tinners, HSD H
Large, two-bar pub in village centre. The oldest building in Princetown and a coach house since 1785. Popular with walkers and Army.
P

Rackenford

Stag
Off B3221 ☎ (088 488) 369
12–2.30; 6–11
Cotleigh Tawny Bitter H
Reputedly Devon's oldest inn (1237). Genuine beams and stone flags. Function room available. P

Ringmore

Journey's End Inn
Off A379, near Kingsbridge
☎ (0548) 810205
11.30–2.30; 6.30–11
Butcombe Bitter; Exmoor Ale; Fuller's ESB; Wadworth 6X H
Old, wood-panelled, thatched bar; modern, wicker-filled extension, and a parrot called Scrumpy. St Ancombe cider.
Q P

Roborough

Olde Inn
OS855817 ☎ (080 53) 247
11–3; 6–11 (11–11 Sat)
Adnams Mild H
Traditional, thatched North Devon pub with at least six guest beers always available. Probably the best value-for-money beer in the South West and certainly in North Devon. A 500 year-old pub with folk music on Tue and jazz on Thu. Definitely no children. Bar menu only. Q

Sampford Peverell

Globe Inn
16 Lower Town
☎ (0884) 821214
11–11
Whitbread Flowers IPA, Flowers Original E
Large pub with excellent children's play area. Backs on to the Grand Western Canal.

Regular guest beers.
🏠 🐎 ❀ ◖ ◗ ⊞ ⇌ ♣ P

Sandy Park

Sandy Park Inn

On A382 Whiddon Down–Moreton Hampstead road ☎ (064 73) 433538
11.30–11
Barron Exe Valley Bitter; Eldridge Pope Royal Oak; Marston's Pedigree Bitter; Palmers IPA G&H
Classic crossroads inn near Dartmoor, with stone floor and rustic furniture. Dining room (recently-extended) serves good home-cooked food (book in advance). 🏠 Q 🛏 ◖ ◗ ♿ ♁

Seaton

Sleeper

Marine Place (50 yds from seafront) ☎ (0297) 24386
11–2.30; 6–11 (11–11 Sat & summer)
Beer Engine Rail Ale, Piston Bitter, Sleeper Heavy H
Friendly, lively, seaside pub run by the licensee of the Beer Engine. 🐎 ◖ ◗ ⊞ ⅄ ♣

Shaldon

Shipwrights Arms

Ringmore Road
☎ (0626) 873237
11–3; 5–11
Courage Best Bitter, Directors H
Two-tier public bar with nautical flavour and view over the estuary. 🐎 ❀ ◖ ◗ ⊞ ♣

Sheepwash

Half Moon Inn

The Square ☎ (040923) 376
10.30–2.30; 6–11
Draught Bass; Courage Best Bitter H
Stone-floored fishing hotel in the village square. 🏠 Q 🛏 ◖ ◗ P

Sidford

Blue Ball Inn

On A3052, outskirts of village
☎ (0395) 514062
11–2.30; 5.30–11
Cornish JD Dry Hop Bitter, Draught Steam Bitter, Royal Wessex Bitter H
Three-bar, whitewashed, cob and thatch pub. Large inglenook fireplace in public bar; comfy lounge. Pretty garden with outdoor food service area, but watch small children as gates open directly onto main road.
🏠 🐎 ❀ 🛏 ◖ ◗ ⊞ ♣ ♁ P

Sidmouth

Old Ship

Old Fore Street
☎ (0395) 512127
11–2.30; 6–11
Cornish Draught Steam Bitter; Marston's Pedigree Bitter; Whitbread Boddingtons Bitter H
Panelled and beamed old pub with smuggling associations. Very busy in summer. Separate upstairs restaurant with skeleton of wattle and daub wall. Daily specials (good fish) on excellent menu. 🏠 Q ◖ ◗

Try also: Swan (Devenish)

Silverton

Three Tuns

14 Exeter Road
☎ (0392) 860352
11.45–2.30 (3 Sat); 5.45–11
Courage Best Bitter, Directors; Fuller's London Pride; John Smith's Bitter H
Well-managed pub in a former brewery. 🏠 🐎 ❀ 🛏 ◖ ◗ ♿ P

South Molton

Town Arms

East Street ☎ (07695) 2531
11–2.30; 6.30–11 (11–11 Sat)
Gibbs Mew Premium Bitter, Salisbury Best H
Small town-centre local.
🏠 🛏 ◖ ◗ P

South Tawton

Seven Stars

Off A30 at Whiddon Down
☎ (0837) 840292
11–3; 6–11 (may vary)
Eldridge Pope Royal Oak; Palmers IPA H
Stone-built village pub with one bar and a restaurant. One guest beer always available.
🏠 ❀ 🛏 ◖ ◗

South Zeal

Oxenham Arms

Off A30 ☎ (0837) 840244
11–2.30; 6–11
Draught Bass; St Austell Tinners G
Granite-built village inn with a genuine 'olde-worlde' feel. Strongly-recommended; excellent accommodation. Draught cider available in summer. 🏠 Q 🐎 ❀ 🛏 ◖ ◗ ⅄ ♁

Sparkwell

Treby Arms

☎ (075 537) 363
11.30–3; 6.30–11
Draught Bass; Ind Coope Burton Ale H
Compact and cosy village local with interesting bottle collection. No eve meals Mon.
🏠 ❀ ◖ ◗ ♁ P

Spreyton

Tom Cobley

On B3219 ☎ (064723) 314
12–3; 6–11
Cotleigh Tawny Bitter; Marston's Pedigree Bitter H
Quiet village local with fine function room and indoor barbecue. Home-made food (not Tue). Guest beers. Very welcoming.
🏠 Q 🐎 ❀ 🛏 ◖ ◗ ⅄ ♣ P

Stokenham

Tradesman's Arms

On A379
12–2.30; 7–11
Adnams Bitter; Draught Bass; Ushers Best Bitter H
Quiet village pub on busy A379. Luscombe cider.
🏠 ❀ ◖ ◗ ⊞ ♁ P

Talaton

Talaton Inn

On B3176 ☎ (0404) 82214
12–3; 7–11
Draught Bass; Cornish Royal Wessex Bitter H
Popular, friendly village pub with separate restaurant serving good-quality, home-cooked food. Darts and skittles played: euchre on Sun eve.
Q 🐎 ❀ ◖ ◗ ♣ P

Tamerton Foliot

Seven Stars Inn

Seven Stars Lane (B3373)
☎ (0752) 772901
11–3; 6–11
Courage Best Bitter H
Small village pub overtaken by suburbia. New conservatory restaurant at the rear (children here only). 🐎 ❀ ◖ ◗ ⊞

Tavistock

Bedford Inn

Plymouth Road (A386)
☎ (0822) 613221
11.30–2.30; 6.30–11
Draught Bass; Courage Best Bitter; Ruddles County H
Lively bar with mixed clientele, attached to three-star hotel.
🏠 ❀ 🛏 ♣

Thelbridge

Thelbridge Cross Inn

On B3042 OS790120
☎ (0884) 860316
11.30–3; 6.30–11
Draught Bass; Wadworth 6X H
Splendid, isolated, but busy, crossroads pub. Good food. Regular guest beers.
🏠 🐎 ❀ 🛏 ◖ ◗ ⊞ ♿ ⅄ ♣ ♁ P

Thorverton

Exeter Inn

☎ (0392) 860206
11–3; 6–11
Courage Best Bitter,

Directors; John Smith's Bitter 🄷
Old coaching inn with superb collection of farm implements and its own well. Skittle alley and function room available. Monthly folk club (last Fri each month). ⛫ ⛂ ⛃ ◖ ◗ ♿ ♣ ⌓ P

Tiverton

Four in Hand
23 Fore Street
☎ (0884) 252765
11–3 (11–11 Sat)
Draught Bass 🄷
Busy town bar near cinema and bus station. Q ◖ ♿ ♣

Racehorse
Wellbrook Street (W of the river) ☎ (0884) 252606
11–11
Ruddles County; Ushers Best Bitter; Webster's Yorkshire Bitter 🄷
Popular local with large function room at rear. Meals all day. ⛫ ⛃ ◖ ◗ ♣ P

White Horse
12 Gold Street
☎ (0884) 252022
11–11
Draught Bass; Cotleigh Tawny Bitter 🄷
Small but friendly town-centre local with own football team. Good value food (no eve meals at weekends). ⛃ ⛟ ◖ ◗ ♿

Topsham

Bridge Inn
Bridge Hill ☎ (039 287) 3862
12–2 (incl. Sun); 6–10.30 (11 Fri & Sat)
Exmoor Ale; Marston's Owd Rodger; Theakston Old Peculier; Wadworth 6X, Farmer's Glory; Wiltshire Old Devil 🄶
Excellent family-run free house on bank of River Clyst. Pink exterior and totally unspoilt interior, dating back many centuries. Don't be fooled by the Whitbread Tankard sign outside. 14 beers usually available, all from the cask. Well worth a visit. ⛫ Q ⛂ ⛃ ≹ P

Torquay

Crown & Sceptre
2 Petitor Road
☎ (0803) 38290
11–3; 6–11
Courage Best Bitter, Directors; John Smith's Bitter 🄷
200 year-old village pub, now engulfed by the Torbay conurbation. Regular folk music. Much local character.
⛫ ⛂ ⛃ ◖ ◗ ⛋ ⌓

Torrington

Hunters Inn
Well Street ☎ (0805) 23832
11–11
Whitbread Flowers IPA, Flowers Original 🄷
Deservedly-popular town pub with friendly locals and bar staff. ⛫ ⛂ ⛟ ◖ ◗ ♣ P

Puffing Billy
Old Station House (A386, bottom of Station Hill)
☎ (0805) 23050
11–3; 6 (5.30 summer)–11
Wadworth 6X 🄷
Old railway station converted to pub, with emphasis on food. Guest beer. ⛫ ⛂ ⛃ ◖ ◗ ⛺ ♣ P

Totnes

Albert Inn
32 Bridgetown (over river on Paignton road)
☎ (0803) 863214
11–11
Courage Best Bitter; Wadworth 6X 🄷
Lively traditional pub with two bars. ⛫ ⛃ ◖ ◗ ⛋

Trusham

Cridford Inn
☎ (0626) 853694
11.30–2.30; 7–11 (11–3; 6–11 summer)
Draught Bass; Cotleigh Old Buzzard 🄶**; Exmoor Ale** 🄷
Enterprising village pub, converted from 14th-century farmhouses. Ancient main bar with stone floor; newer public bar. B&B in adjoining buildings. Families welcome. Euchre and shuttle box played. Local farm cider.
⛫ Q ⛃ ⛟ ◖ ◗ ⛋ ⛺ ♣ ⌓ P

Westcott

Merry Harriers
On B3181, 2 miles S of Cullompton ☎ (0392) 881254
12–2.30 (12–2 Sun); 7–11
Draught Bass 🄷
Friendly roadside pub with restaurant. Reputation for good food. ⛫ ⛃ ◖ ◗ ♿ ♣ P

Whimple

Paddock Inn
On A30, Honiton side of village ☎ (0404) 822356
11–2.30; 6–11
Beer Engine Piston Bitter; Courage Directors 🄷
Large roadside inn with restaurant bar/dining area and bar in regency red velvet. The family area/games room is comfortably furnished, too. Restaurant has reputation for good value, home-cooked food. Specialises in imported beers from all over the world. Bromells cider (take-away only). Paddock 'Pedigree' house beer.
Q ⛂ ⛃ ◖ ◗ ⛺ ≹ ♣ ⌓ P

Try also: New Inn, Broadclyst (Whitbread)

Woolfardisworthy

Farmers Arms
☎ (023 73) 467
11–2.30; 6–11
Whitbread Flowers IPA 🄷
Popular local in rapidly-growing village. Beer mat collection on bar ceiling. Whitbread guest beer in summer. ⛫ ⛃ ◖ ◗ ⛋ ♣

Yelverton

Rock Hotel
200 yds from A386/B3212 jct ☎ (0822) 852022
11–3; 6–11
Draught Bass; Charrington IPA; St Austell HSD; Whitbread Flowers Original 🄷
Yelverton's oldest building, popular with families. Good family room with videos for the children – the only family room for miles. Q ⛂ ⛃ ◖ ◗ ⛋

Try also: Fox Hunter (Courage)

All the pubs listed in the *Good Beer Guide* are selected and inspected by volunteer CAMRA members. You can have your say, too. Suggestions for pubs to be included in (or excluded from) future editions are very welcome and will be passed on to the local CAMRA branch. Use the form on page 502.

FRINGE BENEFITS: Labology

Beer labels, like mats, provide a smiling stagger down memory lane: reminders of good pubs, grand beers, great breweries and happy nights. The difference is in their length of liquid history.

Labels roam much further back down memory lane than mats, beyond even the limited horizon of this century. Mats only dripped into our pub culture in the 1930s, but labels have been stuck on beer bottles and our great grandfathers' memory since the 1840s, today providing colourful evidence of breweries and beers no one alive has ever tasted.

Like stamps, they are simple to keep, being easily fixed into albums. Mats, and particularly bottles, can soon take over half a house. They are also, with their many fine designs, extremely attractive. So it is a surprise to learn that labology – label collecting – was originally started as an organised hobby by a brewery as a public relations exercise.

Guinness Exports floated the idea in 1958, publicising the pastime widely and even setting up an office in London, before their enthusiasm waned and the Labologists Society was taken over as an independent body run by collectors.

The old-fashioned method of obtaining beer labels was to soak them off bottles brought back from the pub or off-licence – after, of course, draining the contents. The problem with this basic approach is that many glues are extremely stubborn, resulting in a torn specimen and a tearful collector. Soaking also wrinkles the paper and labels that have passed through brewery crates and pub shelves are often damaged before the bottle is even opened.

To find mint labels it is better to write direct to the breweries, enclosing an SAE. To obtain older samples it is best to join the Labologists Society. Like the mat collectors, they produce a regular newsletter and arrange meetings. To join send £5 (payable to the Labologists Society) to Graham Tubb, 66 High Street, Puckeridge, Ware, Herts, SG11 1RX.

Dorset

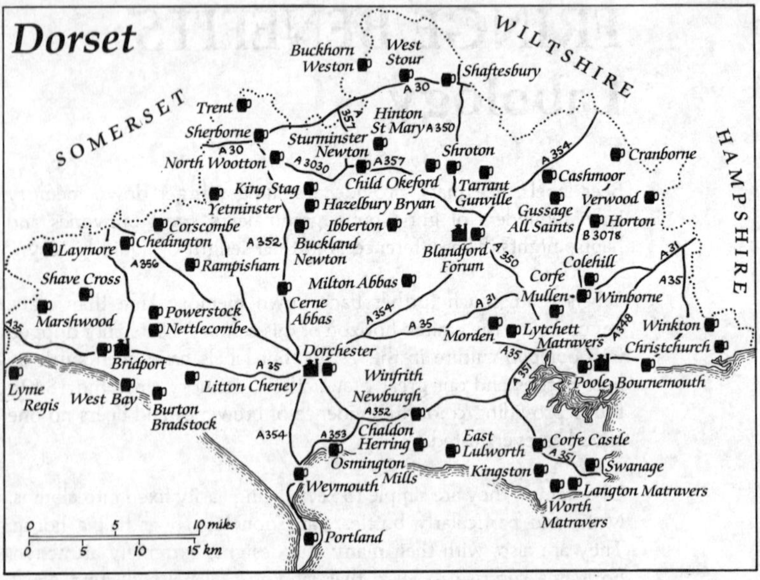

Eldridge Pope, Goldfinch, *Dorchester*; **Hall & Woodhouse**, *Blandford Forum*; **Palmers**, *Bridport*; **Poole**, *Poole*

Blandford Forum

Half Moon
Whitecliff Mill Street
☎ (0258) 452318
11–11
Hall & Woodhouse Badger Best Bitter Ⓗ
Basic locals' town pub, with a friendly atmosphere. Separate games room. Q ◐ ♣ ⌂ P

Bournemouth

Brunswick Hotel
199 Malmesbury Park Road, Charminster (S of B3063)
☎ (0202) 290197
10.30–2.30; 5.30–11 (10.30–11 Mon, Fri & Sat)
Marston's Pedigree Bitter; Whitbread Strong Country Bitter, Flowers Original Ⓗ
Pub of the Year for East Dorset CAMRA. Friendly back-street local with a folk club on Fri eve. Guest beers. ♨ ♘ ❀ ◐ ⊞ ♣

Criterion
41–43 Old Christchurch Road (off The Square)
☎ (0202) 290070
11–11
Draught Bass; Charrington IPA Ⓗ
Busy, Victorian town-centre bar with adjoining wine bar. Large lounge upstairs. Occasional eve bouncers. Sun lunch summer only. ◐ ♣

Grange Hotel
57 Southbourne Overcliff Drive
☎ (0202) 433093
10.30–3; 4.30–11
Draught Bass; Courage Directors; Marston's Pedigree Bitter; Ringwood Fortyniner Ⓗ
Cliff-top bars, catering for all, in beer desert. Live entertainment Wed and Fri, pianist Sun lunchtimes. Wide range of home-cooked fare includes veg option. ♘ ❀ ⛟ ◐ ◑ ♿ P

Old Thumper
113 Poole Road, Westbourne
☎ (0202) 768586
11–3; 5–11
Ringwood Best Bitter, XXXX Porter, Fortyniner, Old Thumper; Wadworth 6X Ⓗ
Recently-improved and enlarged bar among shops, with friendly staff.
◐ ◑ ≠ (Branksome)

Bridport

Oddfellows Arms
172 North Allington (B3162)
☎ (0308) 22665
11–3; 5.45–11
Palmers BB, IPA Ⓗ
Popular local. Untouched, friendly bar. ❀ ⛟ ♣ ⌂

Ropemakers
West Street ☎ (0308) 421255
11–3; 6–11 (11–11 Fri & Sat)
Palmers BB, IPA, Tally Ho Ⓗ
Large well-modernised bar, with lots of wood. Near centre of busy small town. No food Sun eve. ❀ ◐ ◑ ♿ P

Buckhorn Weston

Stapleton Arms
2 miles N of A30
☎ (0963) 70396
11.30–2.30; 6.30–11
Exmoor Ale; Greene King Abbot Ale Ⓗ
Spacious village pub. Lounge bar with dining area and large public bar. Comfortable overnight stop. Two guest beers and Lazy Daisy cider.
♨ Q ❀ ⛟ ◐ ◑ ⊞ ♿ ⛺ ♣ ⌂ P

Buckland Newton

Gaggle of Geese
Off B3143 OS687050
☎ (03005) 249
12–3; 6.30–11
Hall & Woodhouse Badger Best Bitter; Wadworth 6X; Whitbread Boddingtons Bitter Ⓗ
Friendly village local with games room and skittle alley. Guest beers.
♨ Q ♘ ❀ ◐ ◑ ♿ ⛺ ♣ P

Burton Bradstock

Three Horseshoes
On B3157 ☎ (0308) 897259
11–2.30; 6–11

Palmers BB, IPA, Tally Ho [H]
Large village pub, popular with locals and crowded with holiday-makers in summer. Menu offers veg and children's options. ⌂ Q ⚯ ⊛ ⊟ ◖ ◗ ♿ ▲ P

Cashmoor

Cashmoor Inn
On A354, 7 miles NE of Blandford ☎ (0725) 52230
11–3; 6–11
Hall & Woodhouse Badger Best Bitter, Tanglefoot [H]
Coaching inn dating from 1667 with wishing well in lounge. Occasional live entertainment. Restaurant bar offers veg meals.
⌂ Q ⊛ ⊟ ◖ ◗ ▲ ♣ ⌽ P

Cerne Abbas

Red Lion
Long Street ☎ (03003) 441
11.30–2.30; 6.30–11
Wadworth IPA, 6X [H]
Pub exterior rather overdone in pretty village, but inside is a large attractive bar. Food good and served amiably and promptly. ⌂ ⊛ ◖ ◗ ♿ ▲ ♣

Chaldon Herring

Sailors Return
1 mile off A352 OS791834
☎ (0305) 853847
11–2.30; 7–11
Eldridge Pope Best Bitter; Wadworth 6X; Whitbread Strong Country Bitter [H]
Thatched country pub with two bars and a separate restaurant. Good value bar food. Guest beer. Q ⊛ ◖ ◗ ♿ ♣ ⌽ P

Chedington

Winyards Gap Inn
On A356 ☎ (093 589) 244
11–3; 7 (6 Fri, Sat & summer)–11
Draught Bass; Eldridge Pope Dorchester Bitter; Exmoor Ale [H]
Large comfortable pub at foot of National Trust hillside. Wide range of food including vegetarian. Self-contained accommodation available. Good views. Guest beer.
⌂ Q ⚯ ⊛ ⊟ ◖ ◗ P

Child Okeford

Saxon Inn
Gold Hill OS830133
☎ (0258) 860310
11.30–2.30; 7–11
Draught Bass; Charrington IPA [H]
Small, intimate pub hidden up a narrow lane. Name derives from nearby Hambledon Hillfort. Menu offers veg and children's meals. ⌂ ⚯ ⊛ ◖ ◗ ♿ ♣

Christchurch

Castle Tavern
7 Church Street
☎ (0202) 485199
10.30–3; 6–11
Draught Bass; Ringwood Best Bitter, Fortyniner, Old Thumper [H]
Haunted town-centre pub with 300 year-old frontage; caters for the younger crowd; live entertainment. Dogs accepted; children only in summer.
⚯ ◖ ◗ ⇆ ♣

Kings Arms Hotel
Castle Street
☎ (0202) 484117
11–2.30; 5.30–11 (11–11 summer)
Draught Bass [H]
Large bar opposite the castle. Carvery and restaurant in comfortable hotel.
⚯ ⊛ ⊟ ◖ ◗ ♿ ⇆ P

Colehill

Barley Mow
Long Lane OS032023
☎ (0202) 882140
11–2.30; 5.30–11
Hall & Woodhouse Badger Best Bitter, Tanglefoot [H]
Fine country pub hidden in the quiet lanes of Colehill. Two cosy bars, one with an attractive inglenook and original beams. Large secluded beer garden at the rear. Good family room and children's meals.
⌂ Q ⚯ ⊛ ◖ ◗ ♿ ▲ ♣ P

Corfe Castle

Fox
West Street (off A351)
☎ (0929) 480449
11–2.30; 7 (6 summer)–11
Whitbread Fremlins Bitter, Pompey Royal [G]
Unspoilt 16th-century inn. Large garden has fine views of the castle and surroundings.
⌂ Q ⊛ ◖ ⊞ ▲

Corfe Mullen

Lambs Green Inn
Lambs Green Lane (200 yds from Wimborne bypass, A31)
☎ (0202) 880099
11–2.30; 6–11
Draught Bass; Charrington IPA [H]
Modern pub, built onto old-fashioned restaurant. Large garden, scenic view. Summer barbecues. ⊛ ◖ ◗ ♿ ▲ P

Corscombe

Fox
Off A356 OS526053
☎ (093 589) 330
12–2.30; 7–11
Butcombe Bitter; Exmoor Ale [G]
Traditional village pub with stone-flagged floor and slate bars. Food includes veg option. Draught cider summer only.
⌂ Q ⚯ ⊛ ◖ ◗ ⊞ ▲ ♣ ⌽ P

Cranbourne

Fleur de Lys
5 Wimborne Street (B3078)
☎ (07254) 282
11–2.30; 6–11
Hall & Woodhouse Badger Best Bitter, Tanglefoot [H]
Subject of a Rupert Brooke poem, this pleasant 16th-century coaching inn serves excellent food.
⌂ Q ⊛ ⊟ ◖ ◗ ⊞ ♿ ⌽ P

Dorchester

Old Ship
High West Street
☎ (0305) 264455
10.30–11 (10.30–2.30; 4.30–11 winter)
Eldridge Pope Dorchester Bitter, Thomas Hardy Country Bitter, Royal Oak [E]
Typical town pub on the main street. Often crowded. Eve meals summer only. Guest beer.
⚯ ⊛ ◖ ◗ ♿ ⇆ ♣

Tom Brown's
47 High East Street
☎ (0305) 264020
12–2.30 (2 Sun); 7–11
Goldfinch Tom Brown's Best Bitter, Flashman's Clout Strong Ale [H]
Home-brew free house, taking its inspiration from *Tom Brown's Schooldays*. One down-to-earth bar with bare boards. Good jukebox.
⌂ ⊟ ⇆ ♣

White Hart
53 High East Street
☎ (0305) 263545
11–3; 6.30–11
Adnams Bitter; Hall & Woodhouse Badger Best Bitter, Tanglefoot [H]
Popular, friendly pub with opera-singing landlord. Plenty of diversions, including crib, pool, skittles, mah jong and quizzes. Good value bar food. Enjoy a sing-along when the skittles teams are playing.
⌂ Q ⊛ ⊟ ◖ ◗ ♿ ⇆ ♣ P

East Lulworth

Weld Arms
On B3070 ☎ (092941) 211
11–2.30; 6.30–11
Cornish JD Dry Hop Bitter, Royal Wessex Bitter [H]
Picturesque pub, about three miles from Lulworth Cove. Two small snug bars, often filled with locals, and a large comfortable lounge for diners; excellent food. ⌂ ⚯ ⊛ ⊟ ◖ ◗ ⊞ ♿ ▲ P

Gussage All Saints

Drover's Inn

2 miles NW of Horton
OS003106 ☎ (0258) 840084
11–2.30; 6–11 (11–11 summer)
Butcombe Bitter; Courage Directors; Marston's Pedigree Bitter; John Smith's Bitter; Wadworth 6X; Whitbread Flowers Original Ⓗ
200 year-old village pub, with two large brick fireplaces, old beams and a dining area. Largest range of real ales in Dorset. Good food: home-made specials include fresh fish.
⛫ Q ❁ ◖ ◗ ♣ ⌀ P

Hazelbury Bryan

Antelope
Pidney (off B3143) OS745091
☎ (0258) 817295
10.30–2.30; 6–11
Hall & Woodhouse Badger Best Bitter Ⓖ
Remote country pub with real local character. Probably the cheapest prices in Dorset. Walking into the bar is like stepping back in time.
Q ❁ ♣ ⌀

Hinton St Mary

White Horse
300 yds E of B3092
OS786163 ☎ (0258) 72723
11–2.30; 6.30–11
Wadworth 6X Ⓗ
Easily-missed village pub. Proper public bar with tiled floor and wood-panelled walls. Guest beer. Book for Sun lunch; no food Sun eve.
⛫ Q ♘ ❁ ◖ ◗ ♣ P

Horton

Horton Inn
On B3078, 7 miles N of Wimborne ☎ (0258) 840252
10–2.30; 6–11
Courage Directors; Ringwood Best Bitter; Wadworth 6X Ⓗ
18th-century coaching inn with high quality food and accommodation. Lounge attracts smarter set; 'no motorcyclists' sign. ⛫ Q ❁ ⛀ ◖ ◗ ⛺ P

Ibberton

Crown
4 miles SW of A357, from Shillingstone OS788077
☎ (0258) 817448
11–2.30; 6–11
Draught Bass; Charrington IPA Ⓗ
Idyllic local, off the beaten track, nestling under Bulbarrow Hill.
⛫ Q ♘ ❁ ◖ ◗ ♿ ♣ ⌀

King Stag

Green Man
On B3143 ☎ (0258) 817338
11–3; 7–11
Exmoor Ale; Wadworth 6X Ⓗ
Picturesque pub with roomy, comfortable interior and skittle alley. Veg and children's dishes available. ⛫ Q ❁ ◖ ◗ ⛺ P

Kingston

Scott Arms
8 West Street (B3069)
☎ (0929) 480270
11–2.30; 6.30–11
Cornish Royal Wessex Bitter Ⓗ
Dates from 1650, with a lady ghost who closes doors. Breathtaking views of Corfe's famous ruin and a photographic record of cinema and TV films made locally. No eve meals Tue or Sun. ⛫ ♘ ❁ ⛀ ◖ ◗ ⊕ P

Langton Matravers

Kings Arms
On B3069, 2 miles W of Swanage ☎ (0929) 422979
11–2.30; 6.30–11
Whitbread Strong Country Bitter, Flowers Original Ⓗ
Traditional Purbeck pub with many small rooms and flagstone floors. ⛫ Q ♘ ❁ ⊕ ⛺ ⌀

Laymore

Squirrel
On B3162 ☎ (0460) 30298
11.30–2.30; 6–11
Cotleigh Harrier SPA; Courage Directors; Wadworth 6X Ⓗ
Large red brick building in middle of nowhere. Plain bar, popular with locals, with small family annexe. Guest beer and local cider.
⛫ ♘ ❁ ⛀ ◖ ◗ ♿ ⛺ ♣ ⌀

Litton Cheney

White Horse Inn
OS549900 ☎ (03083) 539
11.30–2.30; 6.30–11
Palmers BB, IPA, Tally Ho Ⓗ
Very local pub in winter, but popular with tourists who can find it in summer. Eve meals summer only.
⛫ ❁ ◖ ◗ ♿ ⛺ ♣ ⌀ P

Lyme Regis

Angel Inn
Mill Green ☎ (02974) 3267
11–2.30; 6–11
Palmers BB, IPA Ⓗ
Northern 1950s-type locals' pub; plain but very friendly. Barrels ranged behind bar. Collection of over 600 bottled beers. Old lepers' well nearby.
⛫ Q ♘ ⛀ ⊕ ⛺ ♣ P

Royal Standard
Marine Parade (off Cobb)
☎ (02974) 2637
10–2.30; 7–11 (11–11 summer)
Palmers BB, IPA, Tally Ho Ⓗ
Very old pub on the beach. Now candlelit on Thu to aid the darts players! Popular with the young. ⛫ ❁ ◖ ◗ ♿ ♣ ⌀

Lytchett Matravers

Chequers Inn
High Street (off A350, 3 miles NW of Upton) OS941956
☎ (0202) 622215
11–2.30; 6–11 (11–11 summer)
Draught Bass; Cornish Royal Wessex Bitter; Ringwood XXXX Porter Ⓗ
Modernised pub offering 18 country wines, bar snacks and restaurant. Very welcoming staff. Children's play area with animals. ⛫ ♘ ❁ ♿ ⛺ ♣ P

Marshwood

Bottle
On B3165 ☎ (02977) 254
11–3; 6–11
Exmoor Ale; Wadworth 6X Ⓗ
Authentic, traditional pub with two small bars. In heart of good walking country. Skittle alley. Cider summer only.
⛫ Q ♘ ❁ ⛀ ◖ ◗ ♿ ⛺ ♣ ⌀

Milton Abbas

Hambro Arms
3 miles N of A354 from Winterborne Whitchurch
OS810020 ☎ (0258) 880233
11–2.30; 7 (6.30 summer)–11
Cornish JD Dry Hop Bitter, Royal Wessex Bitter Ⓗ
A fine, thatched, whitewashed inn dating from 1760 and situated in one of Dorset's most picturesque villages. Noted for food. ⛫ Q ❁ ⛀ ◖ ◗ ⊕ ♿ ♣ P

Morden

Cock & Bottle
On B3075, ½ mile N of A35
☎ (092945) 238
11–2.30; 7–11
Hall & Woodhouse Badger Best Bitter, Tanglefoot Ⓗ
Unspoilt village pub in rural setting, with a friendly welcome for all. ⛫ Q ❁ ♣ P

Nettlecombe

Marquis of Lorne
Off A35, 4 miles NE of Bridport OS518956
☎ (030885) 236
11–2.30; 6–11
Palmers BB, IPA Ⓗ
Panelled bar, more like a living room. Popular in summer, despite being hard to find. Has reputation for good food.
⛫ Q ❁ ⛀ ◖ ◗ ♣ P

North Wootton

Three Elms
On A3030 ☎ (0935) 812881

11–2.30; 6.30 (6 Fri & Sat)–11
Ash Vine Bitter; Fuller's London Pride; Greene King Abbot Ale; Smiles Best Bitter; Wadworth 6X; Whitbread Boddingtons Bitter Ⓗ
Modern comfortable pub with extensive food trade, catering for vegetarians too. Matchbox car collection. Beer range may vary. ⛃ ⛘ ◐ ◑ ♿ ♣ ⌂ P

Osmington Mills

Smugglers Inn
1½ miles from A353
☎ (0305) 833125
11–2.30; 6–11 (11–11 summer)
Courage Best Bitter, Directors; Ringwood XXXX Porter, Old Thumper (summer) Ⓗ
Popular family pub near the sea, decorated with old beams from Mudeford Quay, as well as plastic ones! Good food; pricey. Cider in summer. Guest beer.
♨ ⛵ ⛃ ⛘ ◐ ◑ Å ♣ ⌂ P

Poole

Bermuda Triangle
10 Parr Street, Parkstone (off A35) ☎ (0202) 748087
11.30–2.30; 5.30–11
Adnams Broadside; Fuller's ESB; Hook Norton Best Bitter Ⓗ
Modernised, small traditional pub featuring navigational aids. High prices; beers may vary. Guest beers. ◐ ◑ ⇌ (Parkstone)

Bricklayers Arms
41 Parr Street, Lower Parkstone
☎ (0202) 740304
11–2.30; 6–11
Eldridge Pope Dorchester Bitter, Thomas Hardy Country Bitter, Royal Oak Ⓗ
Small pub with friendly, though smokey, atmosphere. Live music eves (not Thu) in music bar at the back. ♨ ⛃ ◐ ⇌ (Parkstone)

Dorset Knob
164 Alder Road, Parkstone (A3040) ☎ (0202) 748427
11–3; 6–11 (11–11 Fri & Sat)
Hall & Woodhouse Badger Best Bitter, Tanglefoot Ⓗ
Regulars' pub with various sporting activities, and a fortnightly quiz. Patio with pergola. Rumoured haunt of the ghost of a girl murdered in the 19th century. No food Sun.
♨ ⛵ ⛃ ◐ ⊞ ♿ ♣ P

Grasshopper
141 Bournemouth Road, Lower Parkstone (A35)
☎ (0202) 741463
11–2.30; 6–11
Hall & Woodhouse Badger Best Bitter, Tanglefoot Ⓗ
Former 19th-century farmhouse, extensively upgraded. Restaurant caters for children and vegetarians; daily special.
⛃ ◐ ◑ ♿ P

Inn in the Park
26 Pinewood Road, Branksome Park ☎ (0202) 761318
11–2.30 (3 Sat); 5.30 (6 Sat)–11
Ringwood Best Bitter; Wadworth IPA, 6X Ⓗ
Plush pub near the sea, with dining area. Framed cigarette cards on walls. Children welcome at lunchtime.
♨ ⛵ ⛃ ⛘ ◐ ◑ P

Lord Nelson
The Quay (opp. Poole Pottery)
☎ (0202) 673774
11–3; 5–11
Gale's BBB; Hall & Woodhouse Badger Best Bitter, Tanglefoot Ⓗ
Busy, noisy quayside pub with numerous nautical artefacts and flagstone floors. Regular evening bands and loud music. Shower facilities for visiting yachtsmen. ⛵ ⛃ ◐ ♿

Portland

Clifton Hotel
50 Grove Road
☎ (0305) 820473
10.30–3; 7–11
Cornish JD Dry Hop Bitter, Royal Wessex Bitter Ⓗ
Busy local off the main road to Portland Bill. Large, rather characterless bar. Skittle alley.
♨ Q ⛵ ⛃ ◐ ◑ ♿ P

Powerstock

Three Horseshoes
3 miles NE of Bridport OS516962 ☎ (030885) 328
11–3; 6–11
Palmers BB, IPA Ⓗ
Remote country pub in picturesque setting beneath Eggardon Hill. Deservedly popular for food (especially fish). Families always welcome.
♨ Q ⛃ ⛘ ◐ ◑ ⊞ Å ♣ ⌂ P

Rampisham

Tigers Head
1 mile off A356 OS561023
☎ (0935) 83244
11–2.30; 6.30–11
Butcombe Bitter Ⓖ**; Greene King Abbot Ale** Ⓗ**; Wadworth 6X** Ⓖ
Small, flinty pub in a rambling village in the depths of the countryside. Popular with locals and visitors. Good food includes rabbit pie. ♨ Q ⛵ ⛃ ⛘ ◐ ◑ ♣ P

Shaftesbury

Old Two Brewers
St James Street
☎ (0747) 52210
11–3; 5.30–11
Courage Best Bitter; Wadworth 6X; Young's Special Ⓗ
Excellent free house local with old world charm. Various nooks and crannies for intimate drinking. Three main areas, one for games. Guest beers.
♨ Q ⛃ P

Shave Cross

Shave Cross Inn
Off B3162 OS415980
☎ (0308) 68358
12–2.30; 7–11 (may close Feb)
Draught Bass (summer)**; Eldridge Pope Royal Oak; Hall & Woodhouse Badger Best Bitter** Ⓗ
Enlarged old pub with several connecting rooms. Popular for food. Busy in summer but hard to find. ♨ Q ⛃ ◐ ◑ Å ♣ P

Sherborne

Britannia
Westbury ☎ (0935) 813300
10.30–2.30; 6–11 (10.30–11 Sat)
Beer range varies Ⓗ
Plain public and smart lounge bar with occasional organ music. Constantly changing choice of two beers, competitively priced.
⛘ ◐ ◑ ⇌ ♣ ⌂ P

Digby Tap
Cooks Lane ☎ (0935) 813148
11–2.30; 5.30–11
Beer range varies Ⓗ
Splendid side-street tavern with stone-flagged floors, between station and abbey. Constantly changing range of four beers. No food Sun. ◐ ⇌ ♣ ⌂

Skippers
Horsecastle (A352)
☎ (0935) 812753
11.30–2.30; 5.30 (6.30 Sat)–11
Draught Bass; Butcombe Bitter Ⓗ
True drinkers' pub with good eating facilities (veg option). Bottle collection includes some rarities. Three or more guest beers. Cider in summer.
⛃ ◐ ◑ ⌂ P

Shroton

Cricketers
½ mile W of A350 OS859127
☎ (0258) 860421
11–3; 6.30–11
Hall & Woodhouse Badger Best Bitter; Oakhill Bitter Ⓗ
Friendly local with a good restaurant, popular with walkers on the Wessex Ridgeway and visitors to Hambledon Hill with its fine views of the Blackmore Vale. Guest beer.
♨ Q ⛃ ◐ ◑ ♿ ♣ P

Sturminster Newton

Dorset

Bull
On A357 ☎ (0258) 72435
11–2.30; 6–11
Hall & Woodhouse Badger Best Bitter; Charles Wells Eagle Bitter [H]
16th-century inn: thatched, low-beamed and full of character. Warm welcome from marathon-running landlord. Skittle alley. Fish meals a speciality. ♨ Q ♞ ❀ ◖ ◗ ♣ P

Swanage

Red Lion
High Street ☎ (0929) 423533
10.30–3; 6–11
Whitbread Strong Country Bitter, Flowers Original, Wethered Winter Royal [G]
Friendly locals' pub which attracts summer tourists. Collections of keys, tools, etc.
♨ ♞ ❀ ◖ ⊞ ♣ 🍎 P

Tarrant Gunville

Bugle Horn
2 miles N of Tarrant Hinton at A354 OS925128
☎ (0258) 89300
11.30–3; 6–11 (11.30–11 Sat)
Ringwood Best Bitter; Wadworth 6X [H]
Friendly free house on a road which is reputedly haunted by a phantom coach and horses.
♨ Q ♞ ❀ ◖ ◗ ♣ P

Trent

Rose & Crown
Off B3148 ☎ (0935) 850776
12–2.30; 7–11
Oakhill Bitter, Yeoman Ale [H]
Cosy, friendly pub in small village. Inventive cuisine has made it very popular. Guest beer. ♨ Q ♞ ❀ ◖ ◗ ♿ ▲ 🍎 P

Verwood

Albion Inn
Station Road (B3081)
☎ (0202) 825267
11–2.30; 5 (6 Sat)–11
Gibbs Mew Salisbury Best [H]
Friendly locals' pub by former station, with railway photos in lounge. Wesley, a former landlord, is said to haunt the pub. ❀ ◖ ◗ ♣ P

West Bay

Bridport Arms Hotel
☎ (0308) 22994
11–2.30; 6.30–11 (11–11 summer)
Palmers BB, IPA, Tally Ho [H]
Fine seaside hotel by harbour, close to beach. Menu caters for children and vegetarians.
Q ♞ ❀ 🛏 ◖ ◗ ⊞ ▲ P

West Stour

Ship
On A30 ☎ (0747) 85640
11–2.30; 6.30–11
Eldridge Pope Thomas Hardy Country Bitter, Royal Oak (winter); **Marston's Pedigree Bitter** (summer); **Wadworth 6X** [H]
Stone-built inn on main road. Traditional bar with flagged floor leads through to lounge and separate restaurant (open Tue–Sat eve, Sun lunch). Beer prices rather high. Guest beer in summer. ♨ Q ❀ 🛏 ◖ ◗ ⊞ P

Weymouth

Kings Arms
15 Trinity Road
☎ (0305) 770055
10–11
Cornish Royal Wessex Bitter; Marston's Pedigree Bitter [H]
Quayside pub with traditional bar, decorated with boating artefacts. Plusher lounge with comfy armchairs. Q ◖ ⊞ ♿ ♣

Ship Inn
Custom House Quay
☎ (0305) 773879
10–3; 6–11 (11–11 summer)
Hall & Woodhouse Badger Best Bitter, Tanglefoot [H]
Large quayside steakhouse with first-floor lounge and restaurant overlooking the harbour. Downstairs bar popular with young people. Very lively at weekends. ♞ ◖ ◗ ⊞

Waterloo
1 Grange Road
☎ (0305) 784488
11–2 (3 Sat); 6.30–11
Gibbs Mew Local Line, Salisbury Best [H]
Corner pub just off Esplanade. Single bar with dartboard. Small town garden available in summer. ❀ ◖ ◗ ♿ ≢ ♣

Weatherbury Hotel
7 Carlton Road, North (off A354) ☎ (0305) 786040
11–2.30; 5.30–11 (11–11 Sat)
Draught Bass; Charrington IPA [H]
Lively out-of-town local with the largest selection of real ales in the area. Live music. Guest beers. Home-cooked fare.
❀ 🛏 ◖ ◗ ≢ ♣ P

Wimborne

Vine
Vine Hill, Pamphill (off B3082)
☎ (0202) 882259
11–2.30; 7–11
Whitbread Strong Country Bitter [H]
Smallest pub in East Dorset. Children's swing in large garden. Dogs accepted. Footpaths nearby.
Q ❀ ⊞ ♣ 🍎 P

Winfrith Newburgh

Red Lion
On A352 ☎ (0305) 852814
10–2.30; 6.30–11
Hall & Woodhouse Badger Best Bitter, Tanglefoot [H]
Large, ivy-clad roadside inn with two contrasting bars. Good view of nuclear power station!
♨ Q ♞ ❀ 🛏 ◖ ◗ ⊞ ♿ ▲ ♣ P

Winkton

Fisherman's Haunt
Salisbury Road (B3347)
☎ (0202) 484071
10.30–2.30; 6–11
Draught Bass; Courage Directors; Ringwood Fortyniner, XXXX Porter [H]
Popular two-star, 17th-century house overlooking River Avon. Restaurant. ♨ ♞ ❀ 🛏 ◖ ◗ ♿ P

Lamb Inn
Burley Road ☎ (0425) 72427
11–2.30; 5.30–11 (11–11 Sat)
Gale's HSB; Marston's Pedigree Bitter; Ringwood Best Bitter, XXXX Porter, Old Thumper; Wadworth 6X [H]
Comfortable and friendly free house in green field setting. Restaurant bar offers veg option. ♨ ❀ ◖ ◗ ⊞ ♣ P

Worth Matravers

Square & Compass
Off B3069 OS977777
☎ (0929) 43229
11–3; 6–11
Marston's Pedigree Bitter; Whitbread Strong Country Bitter, Pompey Royal [G]
Splendid Purbeck monument of the 14th century, with stone floors and roof. Magnificent views. CAMRA Regional Pub of the Year 1989. ♨ Q ❀ ▲ 🍎

Yetminster

White Hart
Off A37 ☎ (0935) 872388
11.30–2.30; 7–11
Draught Bass; Oakhill Bitter [H]
Popular free house situated in village centre. Two bars, including a comfortable lounge.
♨ Q ♞ ❀ ◖ ◗ ⊞ ♿ ≢ ♣ P

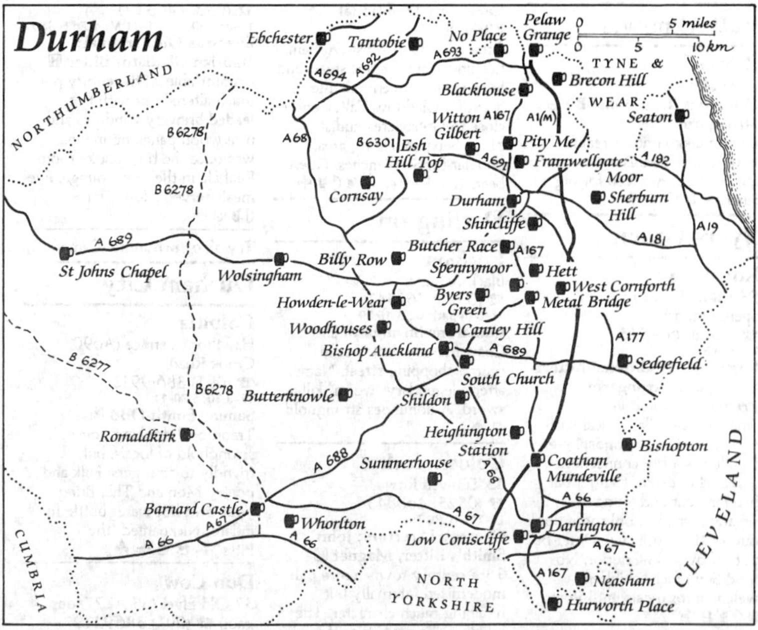

Barnard Castle

Kings Head
Market Place
☎ (0833) 690333
11–3; 6–11 (11–11 summer)
Courage Directors; John Smith's Bitter Ⓗ
Former coaching hotel, now split into nursing home and separate bars. Dickens stayed here whilst researching *Nicholas Nickleby*. ❀ ◖◗ ⊟ ♿ ▲ P

Three Horse Shoes
Galgate ☎ (0833) 38774
11–4; 7–11 (11–11 Wed)
Draught Bass Ⓗ
Lively town-centre pub with a good traditional feel. Fine collection of old railway photos.
⛫ Q ❀ ◖◗ ⊟ ▲ ♣

Try also: Beaconsfield (Vaux); **Golden Lion** (Bass)

Billy Row

Dun Cow
Old White Lea (off A689)
OS149372
7–11; 12–3 (Sun only)
Vaux Samson; Wards Sheffield Best Bitter Ⓗ
Isolated pub in rural setting. Tiny bar with display of pint tankards; larger lounge complete with range. A step back in history ⛫ Q ❀ ⊟ ♣ P

Bishop Auckland

Henknowle Manor
Off St Andrew's Road (in housing estate near fire station, 1 mile S of centre)
☎ (0388) 661721
11–3; 6.30–11 (12–11 Fri, 11–11 Sat)
Vaux Samson, Double Maxim Ⓗ
Large, many-roomed pub in old farmhouse. Pool, darts, dominoes and quoits; Also concert room with live music, etc. Good prices. Caters for everyone. ❀ ⊟ ♿ ≷ ♣ P

Sportsman
Market Place
☎ (0388) 607376
11–4; 6–11 (11–11 Mon & Tue)
Marston's Pedigree Bitter; Whitbread Trophy, Castle Eden Ale Ⓗ
Spacious town pub with quiet lunchtimes and busy evenings; popular with younger clientele. Recently-enlarged bar area is quickly filled with eager tipplers. Everyone made welcome; resident ghost. ⛫ ◖ ≷ ♣

Bishopton

Talbot
The Green ☎ (0740) 30371
11–11 (may close afternoons)
Camerons Traditional Bitter, Strongarm; Everards Old Original Ⓗ
Pleasant, popular old local in leafy village. Long L-shaped lounge; tiny snug with dartboard; carvery (no food Sun). Small sheltered garden.
⛫ Q ❀ ◖◗ ♣ P

Blackhouse

Charlaw Inn
Wheatley Green, Edmondsley (B6532) ☎ (0207) 232085
11–3; 6–11
McEwan 80/-; Theakston XB; Younger No. 3 Ⓗ
Busy country pub with large lounge and conservatory; lively bar. ⛟ ❀ ◖◗ ⊟ ♣ P

Brecon Hill

Smiths Arms
Castle Dene (from Chester-le-Street, past golf course, first left)
☎ (091) 385 6915
1–4 (Sat only); 7–11
Stones Best Bitter Ⓗ
Neat three-roomed pub in isolated spot near A1(M) motorway. Small bar decorated with rural items; larger, comfortable lounge has wall pictures of movie stars; pool room. All rooms have coal fires. Shove-ha'penny played.
⛫ Q ❀ ⊟ ♣ P

Butcher Race

Coach & Horses
On A167 (Croxdale-Thinford road) ☎ (0388) 814484
11–11
Vaux Bitter, Samson Ⓗ
Large, welcoming, roadside pub with pleasant decor and friendly landlord. A good stop for hungry or thirsty travellers.
⛫ ❀ ◖◗ P

Durham

Butterknowle

Royal Oak
Front Street
Camerons Traditional Bitter, Strongarm [H]
Good village pub. A real fire in both rooms creates a welcoming atmosphere. A haven for pigeon fanciers. ⌂ Q ⊟ ♣

Byers Green

Royal Oak
93 High Street (off A688 near Spennymoor)
☎ (0388) 609518
11–3 (5 Sat); 7–11
Camerons Traditional Bitter, Strongarm, Strongarm Premium (winter) [H]
Small, lively village local with excellent friendly atmosphere. Landlord's army connections revealed in decor. Central bar between bar and lounge; separate 'small' pool room (look out for tiny pool cue). Don't be put off by plain exterior. No food Sun lunch; children welcome for meals until 9pm.
❀ ◖ ◗ ⊟ ♣

Try also: Queens Head, Newfield (Tetley)

Canney Hill

Sportsman
1 mile N of town, now by-passed by new A689
☎ (0388) 603847
11–3; 6.30–11
Camerons Traditional Bitter, Strongarm; Everards Old Original [H]
Popular, out-of-town pub. Open-plan bar and lounge; separate snug. Former racing links reflected in decor. Summer barbecues in large garden. Guest beers. ⌂ ❀ ◖ ⊟ ♣ P

Coatham Mundeville

Foresters Arms
On A167, near A1(M) jct
☎ (0325) 320565
11.30–3 (4 Sat); 6–11
John Smith's Bitter, Magnet [H]
Solid, old stone-built local with two comfortable rooms and traditional character: bric-a-brac, old photos, jugs and plates a-plenty. ⌂ Q ❀ ◖ ⊟ ♣ P

Try also: Stables (Free)

Cornsay

Blackhorse Inn
Main Street, Cornsay village (2 miles W of B6301)
☎ (091) 373 4211
12–3 (Sun only); 7–11
Camerons Traditional Bitter [H]
Situated in rural West Durham, this underrated pub is smart and hospitable. It overlooks the beautiful Gladdow Valley and is close to Greenacres nudist camp. Separate eating area, popular for Sun lunches. Guest beers (weekends). Q ❀ ◖ ◗ ♣ P

Darlington

Falchion
Blackwellgate
☎ (0325) 462541
11–3 (4 Sat); 6.30–10.30
Camerons Strongarm [H]
Cosy, friendly, little bar in central shopping street. Named after a legendary 'worm'-killing sword. A dominoes stronghold!
⊟ ♣

Golden Cock
13 Tubwell Row
☎ (0325) 468843
11–11 (10.30 Tue)
Courage Directors; John Smith's Bitter, Magnet [H]
18th-century town-centre pub – modernised internally but retaining much character. The building site next door should become a shopping centre by 1992! Bar billiards played – the only tables in town. ♣

Pennyweight
Bakehouse Hill, Market Place
☎ (0325) 464244
11–11
Vaux Lorimers Best Scotch, Double Maxim; Wards Sheffield Best Bitter [H]
Busy, one-room market place pub; modern layout but with a traditional 'feel'. Good value plain lunches. Guest beers. ◖

Tap & Spile
99 Bondgate
☎ (0325) 463955
11–3; 7–11 (11–11 Fri & Sat)
Camerons Traditional Bitter, Strongarm [H]
Re-creation of a Victorian alehouse, with exposed brickwork, bare floorboards and stained glass. Five or more regularly-changing guest beers. Cosy and popular. ◖ ♣

Traveller's Rest
West Auckland Road, Cockerton (A68, 1 mile W of centre) ☎ (0325) 463430
11–3 (4 Fri & Sat); 6–11
John Smith's Bitter, Magnet [H]
Attractive, two-roomed local in a now-urbanised village. Large, comfortable lounge and a small plain bar. The entrance is decorated with old local photos.
Q ⊟ ♣

Turk's Head
22 Bondgate
☎ (0325) 463191
11–3; 5.30–11 (11–11 Mon, Fri & Sat)
Everards Old Original; Hadrian Gladiator Bitter [H]
Comfortable 17th-century pub, much altered but with fine leaded brewery windows and nice wood panelling in what was once the tiny smoke room. Real ale in the front lounge. Eve meals served Mon–Thu.
◖ ◗ ⊟ ♣

Try also: Britannia (Camerons)

Durham City

Colpitts
Hawthorn Terrace (A690, Crook Road)
☎ (091) 386 9913
12–3.30; 5.30–11
Samuel Smith OBB [H]
Traditional drinking house; a stronghold of locals, but friendly to strangers. Folk and poetry Mon and Thu. Bring your own hot water bottle to inflate! Nicknamed 'the Pitts'. ⌂ ♨ ⊟ ≢ ♣

Dun Cow
37 Old Elvet (off A177, opp. gaol) ☎ (091) 386 9219
11–11
Whitbread Castle Eden Ale [H]
Unspoilt city pub; small friendly bar, larger comfortable lounge. Popular with prison and university staff. Snacks of pie and peas, and sandwiches recommended. Guest beers.
Q ⊟ ♿ ≢

Elm Tree
12 Crossgate
☎ (091) 386 4621
12–2.30; 6–10.30 (11–11 Sat)
Vaux Samson, Double Maxim; Wards Sheffield Best Bitter [H]
Very popular city pub at top of steep hill, but worth the climb. Traditional bar and comfortable lounge. ⊟ ≢ ♣

Half Moon
New Elvet ☎ (091) 386 4528
11–11
Draught Bass [H]
Well-run, virtually unspoilt city-centre pub. Good range of sandwiches. ≢

Queens Head Hotel
2 Sherburn Road, Gilesgate (A181/Sunderland road jct)
☎ (091) 386 5649
11–3; 7–11 (11–11 Fri & Sat)
Belhaven 80/-; Camerons Traditional Bitter; Marston's Pedigree Bitter; Yates Bitter [H]
Busy pub at fork junction. Basic bar with pool table and neat lounge with side room serve a varied clientele. Contemporary decor. Live music Thu and Sun. Guest beers. Popular for B&B.
❀ 🛏 ◖ ≢ ♣ P

Shakespeare
Saddler Street
☎ (091) 386 9709
11–11
McEwan 80/-; Theakston Best Bitter, XB; Younger No. 3 [H]
Very popular, three-room pub, with an interesting facade and internal layout. Friendly staff and locals. Best refreshment halt to and from the cathedral.
Q ▥ ⇋

Victoria Hotel
86 Hallgarth Street (on A177 near Dunelm House)
☎ (091) 386 5269
11–3; 6–11
McEwan 80/-; Theakston Best Bitter [H]
A listed building, popular with locals and students. The three rooms are old but cosy. Large selection of whiskies.
⌂ Q ⊷ ▥ ♿ ⇋

Woodman Inn
23 Gilesgate
☎ (091) 386 7500
11–11
McEwan 80/-; Theakston XB [H]
Lively pub, just out of city centre, renowned for its sandwiches. Landlady has won awards for services to charity.
♿ ♣

Try also: New Inn (Bass); **Rose Tree** (Vaux)

Ebchester

Chelmsford
Front Street ☎ (0207) 560213
11–11
Vaux Samson [H]
Popular village pub with busy bar and quiet lounge. Enthusiastic darts and dominoes teams. Children's menu.
⌂ ♞ ❀ ◖ ◗ ♣ P

Esh Hill Top

Board Inn
Off A691 OS285327
☎ (091) 373 1237
12–11
McEwan 80/-; Theakston Best Bitter [H]
Many-roomed pub, with warm homely atmosphere. Superb panoramic view. Main room littered with knick-knacks. Meals represent good quality and value. ⌂ Q ♞ ◖ ◗ ▥ ♣ P

Framwellgate Moor

Tap & Spile
27 Front Street (old Great North Road)
☎ (091) 386 5451
11–3; 6–11
Camerons Traditional Bitter, Strongarm Premium [H]
Traditional-style pub with stone walls and wooden floor. Four rooms, including family room. Up to six guest beers and regular beer festivals. No food Sat. Bar skittles.
⌂ ♞ ◖ ▥ ♿ ♣ ◌

Try also: Marquis of Granby (Samuel Smith)

Heighington Station

Locomotion One
Heighington Lane, Newton Aycliffe (1 mile W of Aycliffe village) ☎ (0325) 320132
11–3; 5.30–11 (11–11 Sat)
Courage Directors; McEwan 80/-; John Smith's Magnet; Taylor Landlord; Theakston Best Bitter [H]
Historic 1860s railway station converted into a pub of character. George Stephenson placed his engine 'Locomotion' on the lines of the Stockton and Darlington Railway here in Sept 1825. Trains still run to the door (Bishop Auckland branch). Guest beers. ⌂ ❀ ◖ ◗ ⇋ P

Hett

Hett Village Inn
1 mile off A167, N of Ferryhill
☎ (0388) 815036
12–2 (Sat only); 7–11
S&N beers vary [H]
Tasteful, open-plan inn in pleasant village. Quiz night Tue. Enterprising menu offers generous portions. Guest beers.
♞ ❀ ◖ ◗ ♿ ▲ P

Howden-le-Wear

Australian
Church Road (off A689)
☎ (0388) 762666
11–3; 6–11
Camerons Traditional Bitter, Strongarm [H]
Long, narrow bar with darts room off; separate lounge. A busy, no-frills village local.
⌂ ▥ ♣

Hurworth Place

Comet
16 Tees View (A167)
☎ (0325) 721268
11–3; 5.30–11 (11–11 Sat)
Courage Directors; John Smith's Bitter, Magnet [H]
Dignified old pub overlooking the River Tees and the 15th-century Croft bridge. Named after a famous local bull which fetched 1,000 guineas in 1810. Food-oriented lounge; workmanlike bar. No meals Mon eve. ◖ ◗ ▥ ♣ P

Low Coniscliffe

Baydale Beck
On A67 ☎ (0325) 469637
11–3; 5–11 (11–11 Fri & Sat)
Courage Directors; John Smith's Bitter [H]
On the very edge of Darlington, and catering for the needs of the mostly 'dry' west side of town. Two busy rooms and a conservatory, popular with families. Near Tees Cottage – an historic pumping station, now a working museum. Eve meals Thu–Sat.
⌂ Q ♞ ❀ ◖ ◗ ▥ ♿ ♣ P

Metal Bridge

Wild Boar
☎ (0740) 654268
11.30–2.30; 6–11
Draught Bass [H]
Pleasant family pub. Emphasis on meals but consistently excellent ale. Q ◖ ◗ P

Neasham

Fox & Hounds
24 Teesway
☎ (0325) 720350
11–3 (4 Sat); 6.30–11
Vaux Samson; Wards Sheffield Best Bitter [H]
Good village pub near scenic stretch of River Tees. Busy, friendly bar, enlarged lounge for meals, and a new family conservatory (no-smoking). Children's play equipment outside. Q ♞ ❀ ◖ ◗ ▥ ♿ ♣ P

No Place

Beamish Mary Inn
Off A693 OS215532
☎ (091) 370 0237
11–3; 6–11 (11–11 Sat)
McEwan 80/-; Theakston Best Bitter, XB [H]
Victorian bar with a lot of character. Main bar is filled with memorabilia, including an Aga cooker. Plans for music club; live music twice a week. Limited parking. Restored Victorian bedrooms feature old working wirelesses. ⌂ ❀ ⊷ ▥ ▲ ♣ P

Try also: Sun Inn, Beamish Museum (S&N)

Pelaw Grange

Wheatsheaf
On Chester-le-Street–Birtley road ☎ (091) 388 3104
11–11
Stones Best Bitter [H]
Lively bar with good atmosphere; large, comfortable lounge with conservatory. Good value food; popular with families. ♞ ❀ ◖ ◗ ▥ ♿ ♣

Pity Me

Lambton Hounds
62 Front Street (off A167)

☎ (091) 386 4742
11–3; 5.30–11 (11–11 Fri & Sat)
Vaux Lorimers Best Scotch Ⓗ
A real locals' pub, with a pleasant lounge and intimate dining room. Bar remains unchanged after refurbishment. Regular social events; quoits played. Traditional home-cooked food (veg and children's dishes).
⌂ Q ☕ ❀ ⛯ ◖ ◗ ⊕ ♣ P

Try also: Newton Grange (Camerons)

Romaldkirk

Kirk Inn
☎ (0833) 50260
11–3; 6–11
Whitbread Castle Eden Ale Ⓗ
Welcoming, single-bar pub on the village green next to the 'Cathedral of the Dales'. Acts as village post office before morning opening. Guest beers. Limited but adventurous menu.
⌂ ❀ ◖ ◗ ⛺ ♣ ⊖ P

St Johns Chapel

Kings Arms
Market Place (B6293)
☎ (0388) 537268
11–3; 7–11
Stones Best Bitter Ⓗ
Good old-fashioned Dales hotel; comfortable interior. Large garden offers spectacular Fellside views. Q ❀ ⛯ ◖ ◗ ♣

Seaton

Seaton Lane Inn
On B1404, ¾ mile W of Seaham
☎ (091) 581 2038
12–3; 6.30–11
Theakston Best Bitter Ⓗ
Recently-extended and refurbished oasis in eastern Durham beer desert. Bar snacks served both sessions. Q ❀ P

Sedgefield

Golden Lion Inn
1 East End (near town centre) ☎ (0740) 20371
11–11
Theakston Old Peculier Ⓗ
Traditional village pub offering very friendly service. Excellent rapport between landlord, staff and customers. ⌂ ◖ ⊕ ♣ P

Try also: Nags Head (Bass)

Sherburn Hill

Moor Edge
Front Street (A181, 4 miles from Durham city centre)
☎ (091) 372 1618
12–3; 7–11 (11–4; 6.30–11 Fri & Sat)
Vaux Lorimers Best Scotch, Samson Ⓗ
Typical village pub; bar and lounge with coal fires. Its character gradually being restored. Ask for cask beer. Quoits played. ⌂ Q ⊕ ♣ P

Shildon

Timothy Hackworth
107 Main Street
☎ (0388) 772525
11–3; 6.30–11
Camerons Traditional Bitter, Strongarm Ⓗ
Small, tidy town pub with one open-plan room and a lively atmosphere. Opposite one of the country's first railway stations. ◖ ⇌ ♣ P

Try also: King William (Camerons)

Shincliffe

Rose Tree Inn
Low Road West (A177 Stockton road)
☎ (091) 386 8512
11.30–3; 5–11 (11–11 summer)
Vaux Double Maxim; Wards Sheffield Best Bitter Ⓗ
Pleasant village pub in picturesque area, albeit near main road. Popular with families in summer and students at all times. Modern lounge and tidy bar. Cask beer prices above average. ❀ ◖ ◗ ⊕ ♣ P

Seven Stars
On A177, 2 miles from Durham city centre
☎ (091) 384 8454
11–3.30; 6.30–11
Vaux Lorimers Best Scotch; Wards Sheffield Best Bitter Ⓗ
A smart village pub in a salubrious part of Durham. Neat, small bar and very comfortable lounge. Separate dining area. Very quiet.
Q ❀ ⛯ ◖ ◗

Try also: Avenue (Vaux)

South Church

Red Alligator
Crown Street (1 mile S of centre on Shildon Road)
☎ (0388) 605664
11–3; 6–11
Wards Sheffield Best Bitter Ⓗ
Open-plan, comfortable lounge-style pub with central bar. Grand National winner of same name was trained nearby. Stands in the shadow of England's largest parish church.
Q ❀ ◖ ◗ ♿ ♣ P

Spennymoor

Ash Tree
Carr Lane (on Greenways Estate) ☎ (0388) 814490
12–2 (4 Sat); 7–11
Tetley Bitter Ⓗ
Opened in 1980, this one-roomed estate pub has always served real ale in an area awash with keg beers. The hub of the community. ❀ ◖ ◗ P

Summerhouse

Raby Hunt
On B6279 ☎ (032 574) 604
11.30–3; 6.30–11
Marston's Burton Best Bitter, Pedigree Bitter Ⓗ
Neat, welcoming, old stone free house in a pretty whitewashed hamlet. Homely lounge; bustling, two-part locals' bar. Magnificent Raby Castle is five miles up the road. Excellent home-cooked lunches (not Sun). Occasional guest beers.
⌂ Q ❀ ◖ ⊕ ♿ ♣ P

Tantobie

Bird Inn
White-le-Head (B6311, off A692) ☎ (0207) 232416
11–3; 7–11
Belhaven 80/-; Marston's Pedigree Bitter Ⓗ
Popular village pub with lively bar and quiet lounge. Regular well-chosen guest beers.
❀ ◖ ⊕ ♿ ♣ P

West Cornforth

Square & Compass
7 The Green (old part of village, off B6291) ☎ (0740) 654606
11–3; 7–11
Bass Light 5 Star, Draught Bass; Stones Best Bitter Ⓗ
Popular and friendly village pub in beautiful setting. Well-kept ale and reasonably-priced food (veg and children's options). Pictures of Old Cornforth enliven the walls. Shove-ha'penny played. ❀ ◖ ◗ ♣ P

Whorlton

Bridge Inn
☎ (0833) 27341
11–4 (not Wed); 7–11
John Smith's Bitter Ⓗ
Cosy village pub with two bars (one for restaurant use), situated on village green. Close to Whorlton Lido and the old suspension bridge over a spectacular stretch of the Tees.
⌂ Q ❀ ◖ ◗ ⛺ ♣ P

Try also: Four Alls, Ovington (Free)

Witton Gilbert

Glendenning Arms
Durham Road (A691, Lanchester road)
☎ (091) 371 0316
11–4; 7–11
Vaux Samson Ⓗ
Consistent *Good Beer Guide* entry, unchanged since its early days. Two rooms in traditional style with horse racing and

hunting mementoes. Welcoming landlord; very popular with locals. ♜ Q ⊟ ♣ P

Travellers Rest
Durham Road (A691, Lanchester road)
☎ (091) 3710458
11.30–3; 6–11
McEwan 70/-, 80/-; Theakston Best Bitter, XB, Old Peculier; Younger No. 3 Ⓗ
Excellent example of a contemporary village pub with no-smoking area and conservatory; ideal for children. Restaurant offers a good variety of food. Draws visitors from wide area. Boules played.
♜ Q ⚘ ❀ ◖◗ ♣ P

Try also: Centurion (Vaux)

Wolsingham

Bay Horse Hotel
Upper Town (B6296, Tow Law road) ☎ (0388) 527220
11–3; 6–11
Tetley Bitter Ⓗ
Tidy, two-roomed inn on edge of town. Warm welcome (children included) and a good reputation for meals.
⚘ ❀ ⛟ ◖◗ ⊟ P

Try also: Black Lion

Woodhouses

Bay Horse
☎ (0388) 603422
11–3 (12–2 Sun); 7–11
Camerons Traditional Bitter, Strongarm; Tolly Cobbold Bitter Ⓗ
In tiny hamlet, becoming surrounded by semi-detached suburbia. A pleasant, open-plan pub with original bar area preserved. Huge open fire; walls adorned with original paintings of old Auckland. Occasional live music. ♜ Q ❀ ◖◗ ♣

Your Round, I Think, Sergeant? (see page 22)

Essex

***Crouch Vale**, South Woodham Ferrers; **Ridleys**, Hartford End*

Abridge

White Hart
Ongar Road (A113)
☎ (037 881) 3104
10–3; 6–11
Draught Bass; Charrington IPA Ⓗ
Friendly country pub adjacent to river, with separate dining area serving good meals at reasonable prices (not Sat or after 9pm). Nice interior decor. Live music Sun–Wed eves.
⌂ ◐ ◗ P

Arkesden

Axe & Compasses
2 miles N of B1038
OS483344 ☎ (079985) 272
11–2.30; 6–11
Greene King IPA, Abbot Ale Ⓗ
Comfortable and welcoming; a superb 17th-century local in a picturesque village. Restaurant, bar meals (not Mon eve) and outside barbecue (summer weekends) cater for 'foodies'. Well worth seeking out.
⌂ Q ❀ ◐ ◗ ⊞ ♣ P

Aveley

Sir Henry Gurnett
Romford Road
☎ (0708) 864042
11–3; 6–11
Courage Directors; Greene King Abbot Ale; Marston's Pedigree Bitter; Whitbread Flowers IPA, Best Bitter, Castle Eden Ale Ⓗ
Country pub in a converted barn which was once Sir Henry's house. Playground for children and a natural duck pond. Upstairs restaurant is open all day Sun. New 33-room hotel in grounds. Camping at Stubbers (1 mile).
⌂ ❀ ⛺ ◐ ◗ Ⓐ P

Basildon

Towngate Theatre
Pagel Mead (next to town hall)
☎ (0268) 531343
11–3; 5 (6 Sat)–11 (11–11 Fri)
Greene King IPA, Rayments BBA, Abbot Ale Ⓔ, **Winter Ale** Ⓖ
Two bars attached to the theatre; downstairs bar is more like a pub. Beer dispensed through hand-pulled electric pumps. Live jazz Sun lunchtimes. Eve meals finish at 8pm. Veg curries available Fri/Sat eves. Car park free eves/Sun. Q ❀ ◐ ◗ ♿ ⇌ P

Baythorne End

Swan
On A604 (don't miss it, it's hard to turn round to go back!)
☎ (044085) 306
11–3; 6–11
Greene King IPA Ⓗ, **Abbot Ale** Ⓖ
Pleasantly restored old roadside inn with live music Sun eve. Varied choice of food available, from bar snacks to *à la carte* menu in restaurant. No eve meals on Sun
⌂ Q ❀ ◐ ◗ ⊞ ♣ P

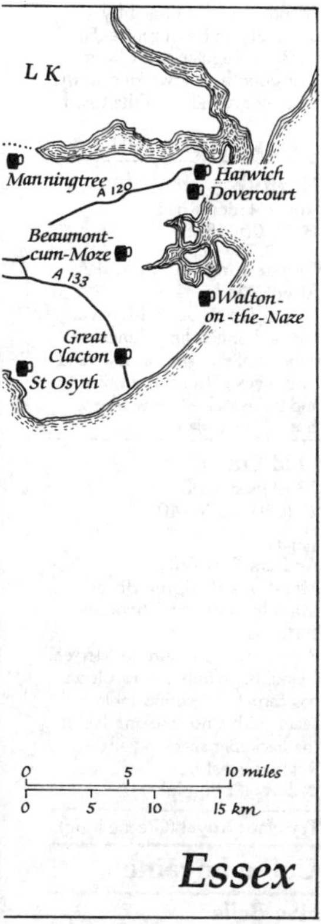

Beaumont-cum-Moze

Swan Inn
Chapel Road (between B1035/B1414)
☎ (0255) 861359
10.30–2.30; 6–11
Adnams Bitter [H]
As isolated as Essex can be: always quiet; a pub where conversation comes first. Handpumps fitted recently, so beer quality now better than ever. Attractive area for drinking outside. ▲ Q ❁ ◐ ◑ ▣ P

Billericay

Chequers
44 High Street (B1007)
☎ (0277) 651804
10–3; 5.30 (7 Sat)–11
Benskins Best Bitter; Ind Coope Burton Ale; Tetley Bitter [H]
Charming 16th-century pub located in centre of historic town. Licensee is justifiably proud of his cellarman awards. Guest beer. ◐ ▣ ⇌ ♣ P

Coach & Horses
36 Chapel Street (behind church in High Street)
☎ (0277) 622873
10–3; 5.30–11 (10–11 Fri & Sat)
Greene King IPA, Abbot Ale [H]
Pleasant, friendly locals' pub with a fine collection of china and copper jugs. No food Sun.
▲ ❁ ◐ ⇌ ♣ P

Birdbrook

Plough
The Street (1 mile off A604)
OS706411 ☎ (044085) 336
11–2.30; 5.30–11
Adnams Bitter; Greene King IPA, Abbot Ale [H]
Charming village local with excellent bar snacks and meals; restaurant open Wed–Sat. Limited parking.
▲ Q ❁ ◐ ◑ ▣ ♣ P

Boreham

Queens Head
Church Road
☎ (0245) 467298
10.30–2.30; 6–11
Greene King IPA, Abbot Ale [H]
Excellent, friendly and traditional 17th-century village pub, in same family for over 50 years. A true local. Good value in every way. No food Sun.
Q ❁ ◐ ▣ ♿ ♣ P

Braintree

Boar's Head
High Street ☎ (0376) 20119
10.30–3; 7–11
Ridleys IPA [H]
Comfortable, two-bar town-centre pub, reputedly haunted. Car park is off access road to rear. ▲ ◐ ⇌ ♣ P

Brightlingsea

Sun Inn
128 New Street
☎ (020630) 2179
11–2.30; 6.30 (5.30 summer)–11
Tolly Cobbold Bitter, Original [H]
Traditional weatherboarded Essex local. Separate parking area. Pricey! ▲ ❁ ◐ ◑ ▣ ♿ ♣ P

Broad Green

Kings Arms
On A120 ☎ (0376) 61581
11–3.30; 5.30–11 (10.30–11 Sat)
Greene King IPA, Abbot Ale [H]
Small friendly roadside pub, popular with locals. Good selection of food at reasonable prices. ▲ Q ❁ ◐ ◑ ♿ ♣ P

Broads Green

Walnut Tree
Off A130 OS694125
☎ (0245) 360222
11–2.30; 6.30 (6 summer)–11
Ridleys IPA [G] & [H]
Clean, pleasant three-bar country pub. Includes well-furnished lounge and basic public, with real fire and trophy cabinet. Entrance to both through cosy middle snug. Hot and cold lunchtime snacks.
▲ Q ❁ ▣ ♣

Bulmer Tye

Fox
On A131 (S of Sudbury)
☎ (0787) 77505
11.30–2.30 (3 occasionally); 6.30–11
Greene King IPA, Abbot Ale [H]
Cosy, friendly roadside inn offering traditional home-cooked food (snacks only eves). Collection of plates and maps decorate the walls. Tables in pretty garden make it a good summer venue.
▲ Q ❁ ⟗ ◐ ▣ ⛺ ♣ P

Bures Hamlet

Swan Inn
1 Station Hill
☎ (0787) 228121
12–11
Greene King XX Dark, IPA, Abbot Ale [H]
Basic public bar with wooden benches lining the walls, stools at bar and tiled floor. Lounge and restaurant are more plush, with carpets. Many genuine beams throughout and an open fire in each bar.
▲ Q ❁ ◐ ◑ ▣ ♿ ⇌ ♣ P

Burnham-on-Crouch

New Welcome Sailor
74 Station Road
☎ (0621) 784778
10.30–3; 6–11 (10.30–11 Sat)
Greene King IPA, Abbot Ale [H]
Real community pub in the best tradition. Pub games from darts to chess played. ♿ ⇌ ♣ P

Olde White Harte
The Quay ☎ (0621) 782106
11–3; 6–11
Adnams Mild, Bitter; Tolly Cobbold Bitter [H]
Charming old riverside pub. Sit on private jetty for superb views of river. Only Mild in Burnham. ▲ Q ❁ ⟗ ◐ ◑ P

Burton End

Ash
1 mile from Stansted Airport
OS533238 ☎ (0279) 814841
11.30–3; 5.30–11
Greene King Rayments BBA, Abbot Ale [H]
Busy, small, former Rayments thatched, timber-framed pub near pretty hamlet by Stansted

Airport. Popular with airport staff lunchtimes. Surprisingly, aircraft noise is not a problem. Good simple food at reasonable prices. (No eve meals Tue, and Sun only during cricket season.) Disabled access to lounge only. Petanque played.
⌂ Q ❀ ◐ ◑ ⊞ ♿ ♣ P

Butcher's Pasture (Little Easton)

Stag
1 mile off B184 (old A130)
OS608241 ☎ (037 184) 214
11–2.30; 6.30–11
Ridleys IPA [G]
Unspoilt village pub with plain wooden benches and tables in public bar. Near wartime USAAF airfield. Lovely view over Chelmer Valley from large garden. Licensee and his wife took over pub in 1952. Cold food only. ⌂ Q ❀ ⊞ ♣ P

Canewdon

Chequers Inn
High Street ☎ (0702) 258251
11–3; 7–11
Charrington IPA; Fuller's ESB; Greene King IPA, Abbot Ale; Marston's Pedigree Bitter [H]
Ex-Ind Coope local, saved from demolition and now totally refurbished with many beams and horse brasses. Split-level with separate dining area in former beer cellar (no food Mon eve/Sun). Range of beers liable to change. ♨ ❀ ◐ ◑ ♿ P

Castle Hedingham

Bell Inn
10 St James Street (B1058)
☎ (0787) 60350
11.30–3; 6.30–11
Greene King IPA, Abbot Ale [G]
Excellent genuine timbered pub near castle and not far from Colne Valley Steam Railway. Families always welcome. No eve meals Mon.
⌂ Q ♨ ❀ ⊨ ◐ ◑ ⊞ ♣ P

Chatham Green

Windmill
Off A131 ☎ (0245) 361357
10–3; 6–11
Ridleys IPA [G]
Simple quiet country pub with darts and pool. Garden contains remains of windmill and splendid outside toilets!
⌂ Q ❀ ♣ P

Chelmsford

Endeavour
351 Springfield Road
☎ (0245) 257717
11–11 (closes 2 Sun lunch)
Greene King IPA, Abbot Ale [H], Winter Ale [G]
Comfortable, quiet and traditional, three-roomed pub. Food (no lunch Sun) includes veg option. ⌂ Q ◐ ◑ ⊞ ♣

Partners
Lower Anchor Street
☎ (0245) 265181
11–2.30 (3 occasionally); 5.30–11 (11–11 Sat)
Adnams Bitter, Old; Greene King IPA, Abbot Ale; Marston's Pedigree Bitter [H]
Friendly street-corner local with games/family room and small patio. No food weekends. Guest beers. ♨ ❀ ◐ ♣ P

Red Lion
147 London Road
☎ (0245) 354902
1.30–3; 6–11 (11–11 Fri & Sat)
Adnams Extra; Ridleys Traditional Mild, IPA [H]
Basic public bar with pool table; comfortable saloon; long public bar. ◐ ⊞ ♣

Coggeshall

Porto-Bello Inn
25 Bridge Street (B1024)
☎ (0376) 561062
11–3 (Sat only, 12–2 Sun); 6–11
Nethergate Bitter, Old Growler [H]
Friendly local; small bar area with separate games room. Pool and petanque played. Car park opposite, by small river. Guest beers. ⌂ ❀ ♣ P

Try also: Fleece

Colchester

Artilleryman
54–56 Artillery Street
☎ (0206) 576024
10.30–2.30; 4.30–11 (10.30–11 Sat)
Greene King XX Dark, IPA, Abbot Ale [H]
Friendly basic town pub, noted for generous charity support. The best pint of Dark for miles. Difficult parking. No food Sun.
Q ❀ ◐ ⊞ ≷ (Hythe/St Botolphs) ♣

British Grenadier
67 Military Road
☎ (0206) 579654
11–2.30 (3 Fri & Sat); 6–11
Adnams Bitter [H], Old [G]; Ridleys IPA [H]
Street-corner pub in new part of town. Traditional pub games available on request. Pool table in back bar; darts in the public bar. Happy hour 6–7.
⊞ ≷ (St Botolphs) ♣

Dragoon
82 Butt Road
☎ (0206) 573464
11–3; 5–11 (11–11 Fri & Sat)
Adnams Bitter [H], Old [G]; Ridleys IPA; Wadworth 6X [H]
Friendly pub unspoiled by proximity to town centre. Food till 7pm. Regular guest beers. Last good beer if walking to the football ground from the town centre!
⌂ ❀ ◐ ◑ ⊞ ≷ (St Botolphs) ♣

Norfolk
North Station Road
☎ (0206) 45257
11–2.30; 5.30–11
Greene King XX Dark, IPA, Abbot Ale [H]
Friendly town pub with naval theme. Popular lunchtimes (when hot snacks available) and early eves with nearby office and industrial estate workers.
❀ ≷ (North) ♣ P

Odd One Out
28 Mersea Road
☎ (0206) 578140
11–2.30 (Fri & Sat only); 5.30 (6 Sat)–11
Archers Best Bitter; Marston's Pedigree Bitter; Mauldons Bitter; Thwaites Bitter [H]
Popular pub en route to Mersea Island. Basic public bar; saloon has carpet and comfortable seats, with a no-smoking bar at the back. Bar snacks available. Regular guest beers.
⌂ ♿ ≷ (St Botolphs) ♣ ⌓

Try also: Royal (Greene King)

Colne Engaine

Five Bells
Mill Lane ☎ (0787) 224166
11–11
Adnams Extra; Greene King IPA, Abbot Ale; Ridleys IPA [H]
Large spacious one-bar pub in traditional timbered wall and ceiling design. Function room and restaurant. Families welcome; a very popular local. Guest beers include Mauldons and Nethergate.
⌂ ❀ ⊨ ◐ ◑ ♣ P

Coxtie Green

White Horse
173 Coxtie Green Road
☎ (0277) 372410
11–2.30; 6–11
Adnams Bitter; Greene King IPA; Tetley Bitter [H]
Small, cosy and friendly country pub. Good for families in summer, with large garden and car park. No food Sun. Occasional guest beers.
❀ ◐ ◑ ⊞ ♣ P

Debden (Saffron Walden)

Plough
High Street OS558333
☎ (0799) 40396
12–3; 6 (5 in football season)–11
Greene King IPA, Rayments

BBA, Abbot Ale [H]
Cosily refurbished rural local. Super garden for children. Good bar food; fish Wed and barbecue in summer.
⌂ Q ❀ ◐ ◑ ⊞ ♣ P

Dedham

Anchor
Heath Road ☎ (0206) 323131
11–3; 6–11 (may extend afternoons)
Adnams Bitter; Greene King IPA [G]
Recently decorated pub in peaceful location. One spacious bar area and large beer garden. Fine food. ⌂ ❀ ◐ ◑ ♣ P

Lamb Inn
Lamb Corner, Birchwood Road
☎ (0206) 322216
11–3; 5–11 (may vary, 11–11 Sat)
Camerons Strongarm Premium; Courage Directors; Tolly Cobbold Bitter [G]
14th-century grade I listed building with restaurant separate from main pub. Stone-floored public bar with original mechanical darts scorer. Beware sloping floor in public bar! Children welcome.
⌂ Q ❀ ◐ ◑ ⊞ ♿ ♣ P

Dovercourt

Devonshire Arms
1 Ramsey Road
☎ (0255) 506525
11–11 (closed Thu afternoon)
Courage Directors; Tolly Cobbold Mild, Bitter [H]
Imposing 1932 roadhouse. Ask to see the performing dog! Live music Sun. No eve meals Sun.
Q ❀ ⛼ ◐ ◑ ⊞ ♿ ♣ P

Try also: Cliff Hotel (Shades Bar), Marine Parade

Duton Hill

Rising Sun
½ mile W off B184 (old A130) OS604269 ☎ (037 184) 204
11–3; 6–11
Adnams Extra; Ridleys IPA [H]
Timber-framed local in rural setting with large garden and children's play area. Mainly fried bar food at reasonable prices. ⌂ ❀ ◐ ◑ ⛺ ♣ ⌔ P

Earls Colne

Castle
77 High Street (A604)
☎ (0787) 222694
11–3; 5–11 (11–11 Thu–Sat)
Greene King XX Dark, IPA, Abbot Ale [H]
12th-century building with 16th-century murals in the dining area. Unusually quiet public bar with pool table. Eve meals Wed–Sat; no food Sun.
⌂ ❀ ⛼ ◐ ◑ ⊞ ♣ P

Drum Inn
21 High Street (A604)
☎ (0787) 222368
12–3; 6–11 (12–11 Fri & Sat)
Greene King IPA, Abbot Ale; Younger Scotch [H]
Exposed woodwork is adorned with brasswork, pots and bottles from ceiling to carpet in main bar. Separate games room. Wooden bar on old brickwork. Soft background music. Guest beers. ⌂ ❀ ⛼ ◐ ♣ P

East Donyland

Walnut Tree
Fingeringhoe Road OS021216
☎ (0206) 869309
11.30–2.30; 6–11 (11.30–11 Sat)
Felinfoel Double Dragon; Greene King IPA; Wadworth 6X [H]
Landlord and landlady are real ale enthusiasts. Wide range of hot and cold food. Good summertime trade. Guest beers.
♞ ❀ ◐ ◑ ⊞ ♿ ♣ P

Elsenham

Crown
High Street (B1051)
☎ (0279) 812827
11–2.30; 6–11
Benskins Best Bitter [H]
Deservedly-popular village pub with reputation for good food (not Mon eve or Sun) and friendly atmosphere. Devil Amongst the Tailors played. Always a guest beer.
⌂ Q ❀ ◐ ◑ ⊞ ≉ ♣ P

Epping

Forest Gate Inn
Bell Common (off B1393)
☎ (0378) 72312
11–3; 5.30–11
Adnams Bitter [H]**; Greene King Abbot Ale** [G]**; Ridleys IPA** [H]**; Theakston Best Bitter; Wadworth 6X** [G]
Traditional pub with no jukebox or machines. Guest beers.
⌂ Q ❀ ◐ ◑ ♣ ⌔ P

Finchingfield

Red Lion
Church Hill (B1053)
☎ (0371) 810400
10.30–3; 6–11
Adnams Extra; Ridleys Traditional Mild [G]**; IPA** [H]
Well worth a stop during any visit to this much photographed village. Live music Sat eves. Wide range of meals at reasonable prices. Traditional Mild not always available.
⌂ Q ♞ ❀ ⛼ ◐ ◑ ♣ P

Fobbing

White Lion
Lion Hill (off B1420)
OS716839 ☎ (0375) 673281
11–2.30; 6–11
Ind Coope Burton Ale; Tetley Bitter [H]
300 year-old pub in village that hatched the Peasants' Revolt. Petanque played. No food Sun.
Q ◐ ⊞ ♣ P

Fuller Street

Square & Compasses
OS747161 ☎ (0245) 361477
12–3; 6–11
Ridleys IPA [H]
Friendly, isolated local, popular with cyclists and walkers. Unusual pitch penny stool in public bar. Well known as a folk pub: live folk music first Fri eve in month. No food Sun/Mon eve. ⌂ Q ❀ ◐ ◑ ⊞ ♿ ⛺ ♣ P

Gestingthorpe

Pheasant
1 mile off B1058
☎ (0787) 61196
11–3; 6–11 (11–11 summer)
Adnams Bitter; Bateman XXXB; Greene King IPA; Mauldon Squires; Nethergate Bitter, Old Growler [H]
Multi-room village pub with tiled and carpeted areas. Generally busy, acting as a social centre with folk singing, quiz nights, shooting outings, skittles, etc. Restaurant includes veg specialities cooked on the premises. No chips!
⌂ ♞ ❀ ◐ ◑ ♣ P

Grays

Bricklayers Arms
48 Bridge Road (near A126)
☎ (0375) 372265
11–2.30 (3 Sat); 5.30 (7 Sat)–11
Charrington IPA; Fuller's ESB (winter) [H]
Friendly two-bar pub with pool table in public bar. ❀ ◐ ⊞ ♣ P

Wharf
Wharf Road (off London Road)
☎ (0375) 372418
11–2.30; 6–11
Taylor Walker Best Bitter; Tetley Bitter [H]
Quaint, listed inn on the Thames, in an area which recently changed from industrial to new housing. ⌂ ❀ ◐ ⊞ ≉

Great Chesterford

Plough
High Street (near B1383, and M11 jct 9) ☎ (0799) 30283
11–3; 6–11
Greene King IPA; Abbot Ale [G] & [H]
Superb 18th-century village local. Small, intimate and very friendly. There must be few pubs left where you can choose beer from the handpumps, or have it drawn from casks in the

cellar below and carefully carried up to the bar! No food Sun. ⌂ Q ▣ ◐ ≢ ♣ P

Great Clacton

Robin Hood
211 London Road
☎ (0255) 421519
11–2.30 (3.30 summer); 6–11
Draught Bass; Charrington IPA [H]
Several medieval cottages merged to form a large multi-roomed pub with exposed beams. Emphasis on food, including vegetarian.
⌂ ▣ ◐ ◑ ♿ ⛺ P

Great Dunmow

Cricketers
22 Beaumont Hill (B184)
☎ (0371) 873359
11–2.30; 6–11
Ridleys IPA [H]
Friendly pub opposite duck pond on village green. Beer only licence until 1976, when extended into bakery next door. Ovens still in family room. Simple but varied menu (cold food only Wed eve and Sun lunch). Q ▣ ◐ ◑ ♿ ♣ P

Great Saling

White Hart
2 miles N of A120 OS701254
☎ (0371) 850341
11–3; 6–11
Adnams Extra; Ridleys IPA [H]
Popular, comfortably refurbished, Tudor village pub with wonderful gallery in saloon. They claim to have invented the 'huffer' (a very large, filled bap, popular in NW Essex) and sell a wide range. Near first USAAF airfield, now used for private flying.
⌂ ▣ ◐ ◑ ♿ ♣ P

Great Sampford

Red Lion Inn
Finchingfield Road (B1053)
☎ (079986) 325
11.30–2.30; 6–11
Ridleys Traditional Mild [G] **&** [H], **IPA** [H]
Fine village pub, rebuilt after burning down in 1980. Varied menu from bar and separate restaurant (set menu Sun lunchtimes).
⌂ Q ▣ ◐ ◑ ♣ P

Great Wakering

Anchor
23 High Street
☎ (0702) 219265
10–11
Charrington IPA [H]
Two-bar local with plenty of atmosphere. Pianist and sing-along Fri and Sat nights with jellied eels! Many items of interest decorate the walls and ceiling. The last pub before Foulness Island. No food Sun.
⌂ ▣ ◐ ♿ ♣ P

Halstead

Dog Inn
Hedingham Road (A604)
☎ (0787) 477774
11–2.30; 6–11 (12–2.30; 7.30–10.30 Sun)
Adnams Bitter; Nethergate Bitter, Old Growler [H]
Unpretentious roadhouse with electronic games in public bar. Larger lounge has original beams. Good, value-for-money food. ⌂ ▣ ◐ ◑ ♿ ♣ P

Harlow

Willow Beauty
Hodings Road
☎ (0279) 37328
11–3; 6–11
Greene King Rayments BBA, Abbot Ale [H]
Pleasant new town pub close to town centre, shops and sports centre. Splendid view over cricket pitch. Regular quiz nights. ▣ ◐ ♿ ≢ (Harlow Town) ♣ P

Try also: Cock, Great Parndon

Harwich

Alma Inn
25 Kings Head Street (off the quay) ☎ (0255) 503474
10.30–2.30; 6.30–11 (may extend Sat)
Tolly Cobbold Mild, Original [H]
Elizabethan timber-framed, Georgian-refronted town pub with a nautical flavour, used by professional fishermen lunchtimes. Mild is the mainstay of this friendly pub. Sandwiches from the bar at lunchtimes or there is an *à la carte* restaurant (no eve meals Sun).
⌂ ▣ ◐ ◑ ♿ ≢ (Harwich Town) ♣

Hatfield Heath

White Horse Inn
The Heath (A1060)
☎ (0279) 730351
11–2.30 (3 Fri & Sat); 5.30 (5 Fri & Sat)–11
Greene King IPA, Abbot Ale [H]
Friendly public bar and recently refurbished lounge bar, very popular at weekends.
Q ▣ ◐ ◑ ♣ P

Hazeleigh

Royal Oak
Fambridge Road (1 mile S of Maldon) OS849047
☎ (0621) 853249
11–3; 6–11
Greene King IPA, Abbot Ale [G]
Very friendly pub, just out of town. ⌂ ▣ ♿ ⛺ ♣ ⌓ P

Henny Street

Swan
Off A131, on country back-road from Sudbury to Bures OS879384 ☎ (078729) 238
11–3; 6–11
Greene King IPA, Abbot Ale [H]
Riverbank inn with separate restaurant (booking required). Decor is fairly plush, with overstuffed sofas as well as more usual pub seating. Many pictures on wall, some of which may be for sale. Outside a large strip of grass borders river and offers views of Stour Valley. No eve meals Sun. ▣ ◐ ◑ P

Heybridge

Maltsters Arms
Hall Road (100 yds off B1022)
☎ (0621) 853880
11–3; 6–11
Greene King IPA, Abbot Ale [G]
Comfortable locals' pub. Unusual stillage.

High Beach

Duke of Wellington
Wellington Hill (off A104)
☎ (081) 508 1566
11–3; 7 (6 Sat)–11
Ind Coope Burton Ale; Taylor Walker Best Bitter; Tetley Bitter [H]
Friendly and extremely well-kept pub close to Epping Forest beauty spot. Barbecues summer evenings (no food Sun lunch). Mini-zoo in the large garden includes goats.
⌂ Q ▣ ◐ ◑ ⛺ ♣ P

High Easter

Cock & Bell
Off B1060, 2 miles from Leaden Roding
☎ (024531) 296
12–2.30; 7–11
Mauldons Squires; Shepherd Neame Master Brew Bitter, Bishops Finger [H]
Circa 14th-century, Tudor-style listed building with an interesting history and good architectural features. Military collection, including armoured personnel carrier in car park. Rolls Royce service available.
⌂ Q ▣ ◐ ◑ ♿ ⛺ ⌓ P

Ingatestone

Star
High Street ☎ (0277) 353618
11–3; 6–11
Greene King IPA, Abbot Ale [G]

Cosy well-worn interior offers a friendly welcome. Folk and country music live two or three nights per week. Converted bakehouse at rear suitable for family use in summer.
♔ Q ♨ ❀ ≠ ♣ P

Lamarsh

Red Lion
1½ miles from Bures, on country back road to Sudbury
OS892355
☎ (0787) 227918
11–3; 6–11
Adnams Bitter; Greene King IPA; Webster's Yorkshire Bitter Ⓗ
Carpeted lounge-type bar with many apparently genuine beams and an obligatory range of 'rural' bric-a-brac. An emphasis on food and a well-used pool table. Petanque.
♔ Q ❀ ◐ ◑ ♿ Ⓐ ♣ P

Leigh-on-Sea

Crooked Billet
51 High Street
10.30–3; 6–11
Ind Coope Burton Ale; Taylor Walker Best Bitter Ⓗ
16th-century listed building with two bars and view across the Thames. Adorned with pictures of old Leigh. Small cosy public bar with timbered walls, big fireplace and cast-iron, wooden-top tables. Wooden armchairs and stools, plus bay window seats and settles. Handy for cockle sheds. Very limited parking. ♔ Q ❀ ⊟ ≠ P

Little Braxted

Green Man
Kelvedon Road (1½ miles SE of village) OS849130
☎ (0621) 891659
11–3; 6–11
Ridleys IPA Ⓗ
Country pub in pretty village. Comfortable lounge and traditional public bar. Good value food. 'Conkers' played when in season. ♔ ⊨ ◐ ⊟ ♣ P

Little End

White Bear
149 London Road (by A113)
☎ (0277) 362185
11–3 (4 Sat); 7–11
Benskins Best Bitter; Ind Coope Burton Ale Ⓗ
Excellent country pub off main road. Summer barbecues in large garden overlooking fields. Regular boot sales, vintage car rallies, motorbike meets, etc. Restaurant open Wed–Sat 7–9.30, Sun 12–4. No food Mon eve. Guest beers.
♔ ❀ ◐ ◑ ⊟ ♣ P

Littley Green

Compasses
OS699172 ☎ (0245) 362308
11–3; 6–11 (11–11 Sat)
Ridleys Traditional Mild, IPA Ⓖ
Ridleys brewery tap (one mile from brewery). Simple, friendly country pub with growing folk music following. Food speciality is the Essex 'Huffer'.
♔ Q ❀ ⊟ ♣ P

Loughton

Wheatsheaf
15 York Hill ☎ (081) 508 9656
10–2.30; 5.30–11
Draught Bass; Charrington IPA; Fuller's ESB (winter) Ⓗ
This friendly town-centre local has a display of fishing tackle decorating the saloon bar wall. Popular with local cricket teams.
♔ Q ❀ ◐ ⊖ ♣ P

Try also: Victoria, Smarts Lane

Magdalen Laver

Green Man
Green Man Road
☎ (0279) 411752
11–2.30; 6–11
Courage Directors; Greene King IPA, Abbot Ale; Nethergate Bitter Ⓗ
Hard to find, but well worth the effort. Comfortable bar and relaxing atmosphere. Circular pool table. ♔ ❀ ♣ P

Maldon

Blue Boar Hotel
Silver Street ☎ (0621) 852681
11–3; 6–11
Adnams Bitter, Old Ⓖ
Superb oak-beamed coaching inn attracting good mix of customers. Newcomers made welcome. ♔ Q ❀ ⊨ ◐ ◑ ⊟ ♿ P

Queen's Head
The Hythe ☎ (0621) 854112
10.30–11 (10.30–3.30; 5–11 Tue & Thu)
Greene King IPA, Abbot Ale Ⓗ
Three-bar pub with nautical atmosphere; overlooks the estuary. ♔ Q ❀ ⊟ ♣ P

Manningtree

Station Buffet
The Station ☎ (0206) 391114
12–2; 6–11
Adnams Bitter Ⓗ
Tiny, rough and ready pub with pleasant, local staff – a rail buff's dream. Busy at commuter time and lunchtime; quiet evenings. Varied selection of guest beers from far and wide. Access from the platform. ♔ ♨ ◐ ◑ ♿ ≠ P

Mashbury

Fox
Fox Road OS650127
☎ (0245) 31573
12–3; 6.30–11
Ridleys Traditional Mild, IPA Ⓖ
Difficult-to-find old pub, with simple country bar. New emphasis on food, with varied menu and separate dining area; children and vegetarians catered for. Large garden.
♔ ❀ ◐ ◑ ♿ ♣ P

Matching Tye

Fox Inn
2 miles off B183 at Newmans End/Matching Green road jct
OS516113 ☎ (0279) 731203
12–3; 6–11
Friary Meux Best Bitter; Ind Coope Burton Ale; Tetley Bitter Ⓗ
Traditional Essex village pub with open log fire. Boules terrain in rear garden.
♔ ❀ ◐ ♿ ♣ P

Try also: Hare & Hounds

Mill Green

Viper
Highwood Road OS641019
☎ (0277) 352010
11–2.30 (3 Sat); 6–11
Ruddles Best Bitter, County Ⓗ
Unspoilt country pub in quiet woodland setting. Fine traditional public bar with wooden wall seats and floor. Award-winning garden. Hub of local footpath routes – sylvan gem! ♔ Q ❀ ◐ ⊟ ♣ P

Moreton

White Hart Inn
Off A414 ☎ (027783) 228
10.30–2.30; 6–11 (may vary)
Adnams Bitter; Courage Best Bitter; Greene King Abbot Ale; Marston's Pedigree Bitter Ⓗ
Friendly traditional pub in small village, serving farming community. Good restaurant open Mon to Sun lunch. (Courage Best is sold as 'Websters Wonderful Wallop').
♔ ❀ ◐ ◑ ⊟ ♿ ♣ ○ P

Try also: Moreton Massey

Mountnessing

Prince of Wales
Roman Road (B1002)
☎ (0277) 353445
11–3; 6–11
Adnams Extra; Ridleys Traditional Mild, IPA Ⓗ
Pleasant one-bar pub facing common. ♔ ❀ ◐ ◑ ♣ P

Orsett

Foxhound

High Road ☎ (0375) 891295
11–3.30 (4 Sat); 6–11
Courage Best Bitter, Directors Ⓗ
Friendly village inn with photographs of the pub's history and building around the saloon bar, which uses a tree trunk for a pillar in the centre. Good food (not Sun, or Mon, Tue, Wed eves). ♣ P

Panfield

Bell Inn

Kynaston Road OS735252
☎ (0376) 24641
11–3; 6–11
Adnams Extra; Ridleys IPA Ⓗ
Pretty, 400 year-old multi-beamed village local. Strong on sports, with two football teams (pitch in garden), three darts teams and a golf society. Occasional barbecue. Mind your head in the lounge! No food Sun lunch. ♣ P

Paslow Wood Common

Black Horse

Stondon Road
☎ (0277) 821915
12–3; 6–11
Adnams Bitter; Bateman XB; Fuller's ESB; Greene King Abbot Ale; Hook Norton Old Hookey; Marston's Pedigree Bitter Ⓗ
Always buzzing, this 1742-built pub, full of beams and brasses, is known for its monster beer menu, which changes each week. Extensive food menu also. Occasional draught cider. ♣ P

Prittlewell

Spread Eagle

267 Victoria Avenue
☎ (0702) 348383
11–2.30; 5 (6 Sat)–11
Charrington IPA Ⓗ
Friendly traditional two-bar local near football ground. Good family atmosphere. ♣ P

Purleigh

Bell

The Street ☎ (0621) 828348
11–2.30; 6–11
Adnams Bitter; Benskins Best Bitter Ⓗ
Attractive 16th-century pub; friendly and comfortable, with superb views over Blackwater Estuary. Good value food. Q ♣ P

Radley Green

Thatchers Arms

Off A414 OS622054
11–2.30; 6–11
Adnams Extra; Ridleys IPA Ⓗ
Secluded and friendly one-bar country local. Q ♣ P

Rayleigh

Paul Pry Tavern

14 High Road
☎ (0268) 742859
10–3; 6–11
Ruddles Best Bitter, County; Webster's Yorkshire Bitter Ⓗ
Popular pub with very large outside drinking area with a playground for children. ⇌ P

Rickling Green

Cricketers Arms

½ mile off B1383 (old A11)
☎ (079988) 322
11–3; 6–11
Camerons Strongarm; Tolly Cobbold Bitter Ⓖ
A perfect setting: Victorian village local on boundary of cricket green; the highest score in English cricket was made here in 1882! A good mix of typical public bar, comfortable saloon, family room and restaurant. Good food in bars and restaurant. Guest beer. ♣ P

Rochford

Golden Lion

35 North Street
☎ (0702) 545487
11.45–3; 5–11 (11–11 Sat)
Crouch Vale Best Bitter; Fuller's London Pride; Greene King Abbot Ale Ⓗ
Traditional unspoilt, friendly, weatherboarded, one-bar pub in old market town. Local CAMRA branch Pub of the Year two years running. Guest beers and cider. No food Sun. ⇌ ♣

Old Ship

12 North Street
☎ (0702) 544210
11–3; 6–11
Ind Coope Burton Ale; Tetley Bitter; Young's Bitter Ⓗ
Friendly former coaching inn with comfortable period interior. Soon to expand outside area for extra parking and larger garden for children's play area. An enclosed area for families is also planned. ⇌ ♣ P

Saffron Walden

Axe

60 Ashdon Road
☎ (0799) 22235
11–2.30; 6–11
Greene King IPA, Abbot Ale Ⓗ
Comfortable local. Bar snacks and *à la carte* restaurant (not Sun/Mon eve); veg option. Q ♣ P

Try also: Sun (Ridleys)

St Osyth

White Hart

71 Mill Street
☎ (0255) 820138
11–3; 7–11
Adnams Bitter; Whitbread Flowers Original Ⓗ
Friendly village pub with old photographs of Essex life displayed. Don't miss the ancient ceramic loos. Games room and guest beers. Q ♣ P

Salcott-cum-Virley

Sun

The Street ☎ (0621) 860461
11–2.30 (3 Sat); 6–11
Adnams Bitter Ⓗ; **Greene King Abbot Ale** Ⓖ; **Tolly Cobbold Bitter** Ⓗ
Quiet village local near Essex Marshes and bird sanctuary. Bar snacks. ♣ P

Shalford

Fox

Church End OS721279
☎ (0371) 850140
11–11
Ridleys IPA Ⓗ
Remote, cosy, beamed old pub. Folk music on last Mon of month; live music some Sats. Children welcome. Home-cooked food at reasonable prices; veg and children's choices included. Q ♣ P

Shoeburyness

Parsons' Barn

Frobisher Way
☎ (0702) 297373
11–2.30 (3 Fri, 3.30 Sat); 6–11
Adnams Bitter Ⓖ, **Broadside** Ⓗ; **Greene King IPA, Abbot Ale; Ruddles Best Bitter; Webster's Yorkshire Bitter** Ⓗ
17th-century barn, converted 1983 to spacious pub with children's room and garden. Alcoves for meals. P

Southend-on-Sea

Liberty Belle

10 Marine Parade
☎ (0702) 66936
10–11
Courage Best Bitter, Directors; John Smith's Bitter Ⓗ
A gimmick-free seafront pub catering for serious drinkers, not disco-seekers. Much nautical memorabilia adorns walls and ceiling. Particularly suitable for disabled – ramped throughout. Meals and accommodation

summer only.
(Central)

Railway Hotel
Clifftown Road
☎ (0702) 343194
11–11
Draught Bass; Charrington IPA Ⓗ
Fine example of Victorian pub architecture with etched and stained windows.
(Central)

South Fambridge

Anchor Hotel
Fambridge Road
☎ (0702) 203535
10–2.30; 7 (6 Fri & Sat)–11
Adnams Bitter; Greene King Abbot Ale; Marston's Pedigree Bitter Ⓗ
Olde worlde pub, with beams, near River Crouch and river towpaths and walks. Log-effect gas fires in bar. Special evening events arranged. Good food available in bar; also separate restaurant. Children allowed if quiet and well-behaved. Guest beers. P

Southminster

Rose Inn
Burnham Road (B1021)
☎ (0621) 772915
11.30–3; 5 (6 Sat)–11
Greene King IPA, Abbot Ale, Winter Ale; Ridleys Traditional Mild (occasionally) Ⓖ
Friendly roadside inn with real public bar. Varied menu (no food Sun, or Wed eve).
Q P

South Weald

Tower Arms
Weald Road
☎ (0277) 210266
11–2.30; 6–11
Adnams Bitter; Greene King IPA, Abbot Ale; Ruddles Best Bitter; Young's Special Ⓗ
16th-century listed building and former shooting lodge. Set in an attractive village opposite a delightful 11th-century church; a cosy, friendly local with a good atmosphere, if a little on the expensive side. Large garden with petanque pitches.
P

Stanford-le-Hope

Rising Sun
Church Hill ☎ (0375) 671911
11–2.30 (3.30 Fri & Sat); 5.30 (6 Sat)–11
Courage Best Bitter, Directors; John Smith's Bitter Ⓗ
Cosy local in shadow of 900 year-old village church.
Children's play area. No food Sun. P

Stansted Mountfitchet

Dog & Duck
Lower Street (off B1351)
OS516251 ☎ (0279) 812047
10.30–2.30; 5.30–11
Greene King Rayments BBA, Abbot Ale Ⓗ
Charming, weatherboarded, timber-framed old local with wonderful pub sign. Near Norman castle. Rear patio and small raised garden. Take care! – very low beam in lounge. Public bar is popular with senior citizens in morning. Good lunchtime snacks (not Sun).
Q P

Stapleford Abbotts

Rabbits
Stapleford Road (B175)
☎ (04028) 203
11–2.30; 6–11
Benskins Best Bitter; Ind Coope Burton Ale Ⓗ
Nice country pub with children's play area in garden. Good value meals.
Q P

Stisted

Dolphin
Coggeshall Road (A120)
☎ (0376) 21143
10.30–3; 6–11
Adnams Extra; Ridleys Traditional Mild, IPA Ⓖ
Unspoilt, much-beamed pub with log fires. Good garden for children. Q P

Onley Arms
The Street (off A120)
☎ (0376) 25204
11–3; 7–11
Adnams Extra; Ridleys IPA Ⓗ
Built in 1853 by the Onley family for their estate workers, and still popular in this rural village. Separate restaurant. Petanque. Q P

Thaxted

Star
Mill End ☎ (0371) 830368
11–2.30; 5 (6 Sat)–11
Benskins Best Bitter; Ind Coope Burton Ale Ⓗ
Not to be missed; a friendly pub set in a magnificent village with a cathedral-size church and a superb medieval guildhall. Vast fireplaces and exposed beams. 'Happy hour' 5–6, Mon–Fri. P

Try also: Swan Hotel (Free)

Tillingham

Cap & Feathers
8 South Street
☎ (062187) 212
11–3; 6–11
Crouch Vale Woodham IPA, Best Bitter, SAS, Willie Warmer Ⓗ
Splendid 15th-century village pub. Good value beer and food (home-smoked fish a speciality). Folk music first Sun each month. Bar billiards a shilling a game. CAMRA Pub of the Year national winner 1990.
Q P

Tolleshunt D'Arcy

Queen's Head
15 North Steet OS930120
☎ (0621) 860262
11–2.30 (3 Fri, 3.30 Sat); 6 (7 Sat)–11
Greene King IPA, Abbot Ale Ⓗ
Very popular village pub with comfortable saloon and beautiful (quiet) public bar. Eve meals Thu, Fri, Sat only.
Q P

Toppesfield

Green Man
3 Church Lane OS739374
☎ (0787) 237418
11–2.30; 7–11
Greene King IPA, Abbot Ale Ⓗ
Comfortable welcoming pub in remote village. Petanque played on summer Thu eves, and quizzes on Sun. Sun lunches by prior arrangement.
Q P

Waltham Abbey

Old English Gentleman
85 Highbridge Street
☎ (0992) 712714
11–11
McMullen Original AK, Country Best Bitter Ⓗ
Pleasant riverside pub on the Herts–Essex border. Q (Waltham Cross) P

Walton-on-the-Naze

Royal Marine
3 Old Pier Street
☎ (0255) 674000
10–3; 6–11
Marston's Pedigree Bitter; Whitbread Flowers IPA, Wethered Bitter Ⓗ
Two-bar locals' pub; haunt of morrismen and lifeboatmen. Live folk music every other Thu and occasional jazz. Wonderfully shabby decor.
Q

Westcliff-on-Sea

Cricketers Inn
228 London Road

☎ (0702) 343168
10.30–11
Greene King IPA, Abbot Ale [H]
Very large town pub split into three bars – the Tudor bar, saloon bar and Sportsman bar. The last is fitted with large screen TV and three dartboards. Saloon bar has comfortable bar stools with backs. ◖ ⊟ ♿ ♣ P

Palace Theatre Centre
430 London Road (A13)
☎ (0702) 347816
12–2.30 (incl. Sun); 6–11
Crouch Vale Best Bitter, SAS; Greene King IPA, Abbot Ale [H]
Functional and sociable, friendly theatre bar. Foyer bar offers regular good quality guest beers. Live music Sun lunch and eve. Courtyard patio. Quiet children welcome. No parking but regular bus service passes theatre. No food Sun eve.
Q ❀ ◖ ◗ ♿ ⇌

White Notley

Cross Keys
1 The Street ☎ (0376) 83297
11–3; 6.30–11
Ridleys Traditional Mild, IPA [H]
Fine village local built in the 14th century, formerly Chappells brewery.
♨ ☺ ❀ ◖ ◗ ⊟ ♿ ⇌ ♣ P

White Roding

Black Horse
High Street ☎ (027976) 322
11–2.30; 6.30–11
Adnams Extra; Ridleys IPA [H]
Large friendly local, decorated with horse brasses and other equine artefacts. Good-priced food in lounge bar. Watch out for wobbly floorboards in public bar. ♨ Q ❀ ◖ ◗ ⊟ ♿ ♣ P

Wicken Bonhunt

Coach & Horses
Wicken Road (B1038)
☎ (0799) 40516
11–2.30; 6–11
Greene King IPA, Rayments BBA, Abbot Ale [H]
Cosy, thatched, timber-framed rural local, with good, low-cost pub food. ♨ Q ❀ ◖ ◗ ⊟ ♣ P

Wickham Bishops

Mitre
2 The Street
☎ (0621) 891378
11.30–3; 5.30–11
Adnams Extra; Ridleys IPA [H]
Homely, welcoming 400 year-old beamed pub with inscribed beam in public bar dated 1771. Look out for other interesting curiosities.
♨ Q ❀ ◖ ◗ ⊟ ♣ ○ P

Witham

George
36 Newland Street
☎ (0376) 511098
10–2.30 (3 Fri, 4 Sat); 5.30–11
Adnams Extra; Ridleys Traditional Mild, IPA [H]
Welcoming town-centre pub with public bar. Separate games room/music room. Quiet 16th-century timber-framed saloon bar. Lunches Mon-Fri only.
Q ☺ ◖ ⊟ ♿ ⇌ ♣ P

Victoria
Powers Hall End OS807152
☎ (0376) 511809
11–2.30 (3 Fri, 12–2 Sun); 6 (7 Fri)–11
Ridleys Traditional Mild, IPA [G]
Spacious, tastefully renovated old country house on the edge of town. Large public bar and comfortable lounge. No food Mon, Tue, Wed eve, or all day Sun. ♨ ☺ ❀ ◖ ◗ ⊟ ♣ P

Wivenhoe

Rose & Crown
The Quay (B1028)
☎ (020622) 3663
11–2.30; 6–11 (11–11 summer)
Friary Meux Best Bitter; Ind Coope Burton Ale; Tetley Bitter [H]
Fairly basic quayside bar, popular with yachtsmen and fishermen. Parking difficult. Pricey! ♨ ◖ ⇌ ♣ P

Woodham Mortimer

Hurdlemakers Arms
Post Office Road (off A414)
OS813045 ☎ (024541) 5169
11–3; 6–11
Greene King IPA, Abbot Ale [H]
Splendid, friendly, traditional pub with stone-flagged saloon and fine public bar.
♨ Q ☺ ❀ ◖ ⊟ ♿ ♣ P

Wormingford

Crown Inn
Main Road (B1508)
☎ (0787) 227405
11.30–3; 6–11
Greene King IPA, Abbot Ale [H]
Lovely 17th-century half-timbered inn with open fires. Large garden with seven tables and huge barbecue. Garden safe for children, with goat, geese and a collection of ornamental pheasants. No food Sun eve; must book for Sun lunch.
♨ Q ☺ ❀ ◖ ◗ ⊟ ♣ P

Writtle

Wheatsheaf
70 The Green
☎ (0245) 420695
11–2.30 (3 Sat); 5.30–11
Greene King IPA, Abbot Ale, Winter Ale [H]
Small and friendly two-bar local in pleasant village. ❀ ⊟ ♣

Young's End

Green Dragon
Upper London Road (A131)
☎ (0245) 361030
11–3; 6–11
Greene King IPA, Abbot Ale [H]
Modernised lounge, and original public bar which is a pleasure to see. Large outside play area with giant toy dragon for children. Q ❀ ◖ ◗ ⊟ ♣ P

THE SYMBOLS

- ♨ real fire
- Q quiet pub – in at least one bar
- ☺ indoor room for children
- ❀ garden or other outdoor drinking area
- ⌸ accommodation
- ◖ lunchtime meals
- ◗ evening meals
- ⊟ public bar
- ♿ easy disabled access
- ▲ camping facilities at the pub or nearby
- ⇌ near British Rail station
- ⊖ near Underground station
- ♣ pub games
- ○ real cider
- P pub car park

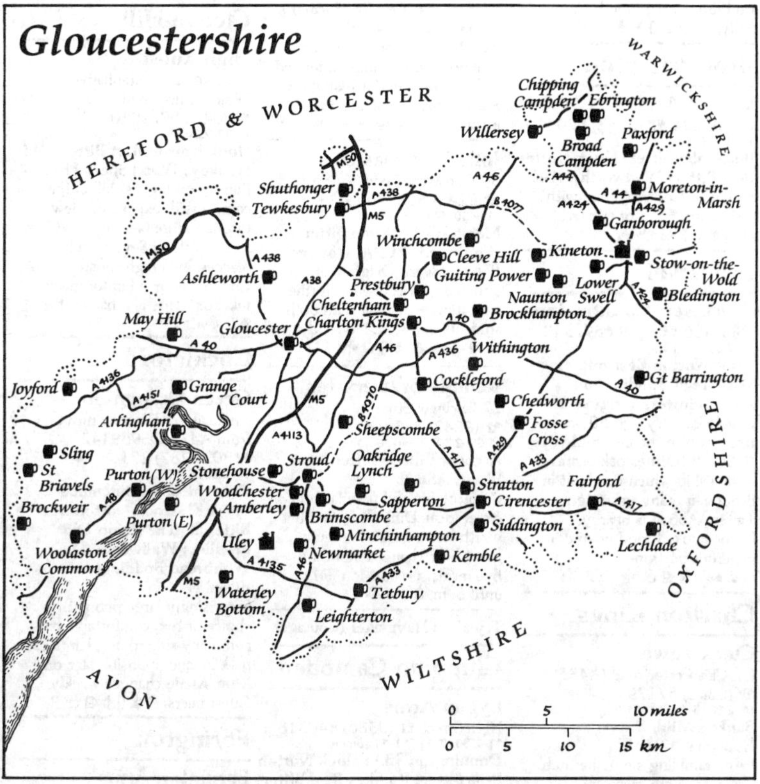

Donnington, *Stow-on-the-Wold*; **Uley**, *Uley, Dursley*

Amberley

Black Horse

OS850016 ☎ (0453) 872556
11.30–3; 6–11
Fuller's London Pride, ESB; Greenalls Davenports Traditional Bitter; Taylor Landlord; Tetley Bitter; Wadworth 6X
Lively local in village set in the middle of a common. Guest beers. Children welcome in summer. Q

Arlingham

Red Lion

The Cross OS708109
☎ (0452) 740269
11–2.30; 6.30–11
Draught Bass; Marston's Pedigree Bitter; Smiles Best Bitter; Theakston Best Bitter
Simple, well-run pub in village centre. Piano in lounge. Guest beers. Shove-ha'penny.
Q P

Ashleworth

Arkle

The Village OS812255
☎ (045 270) 395
11.30–2.30; 7–11
Donnington XXX (winter), **BB, SBA**
Good, honest village local with single large bar – not too plush, with pool table. Popular skittle alley. Q P

Try also: Boat Inn (Free)

Bledington

Kings Head

On B4450 OS245228
☎ (060 871) 365
11–2.30; 6–11
Hook Norton Best Bitter; Tetley Bitter; Wadworth 6X
Comfortable, very popular pub by the village green. Specialises in food (not Sun); booking essential at weekends. Children welcome at lunchtime. Cider available in summer.
P

Brimscombe

Kings Arms

Bourne Lane (off A419)
OS874023 ☎ (0453) 882552
11.30–2.30; 6.30–11
Ind Coope Burton Ale; Ruddles Best Bitter, County; Wadworth 6X; Webster's Yorkshire Bitter
The public bar is the lower section of a split-level layout, with pool table and jukebox. Upper saloon is quiet and comfortable. Q

Broad Campden

Bakers Arms

☎ (0386) 840515
11.30–2.30; 6.30–11 (11–11 winter)
Wadworth 6X; Whitbread Flowers IPA, Flowers Original
Fine old country pub boasting exposed Cotswold stone walls and oak beams. Framed hand-woven rug depicting the inn hangs on wall in bar. Folk music

on third Tue of month. Aunt Sally. ⌂ Q ❀ ◖ ◗ ♣ ⌓ P

Brockhampton

Craven Arms
OS035224 ☎ (0242) 820410
11–3; 6–11
Butcombe Bitter; Hook Norton Best Bitter; Wadworth 6X [H]
Extended Cotswold pub with restaurant. Food-orientated.
⌂ Q ❀ ◖ ◗ ⊟ ♣ P

Brockweir

Brockweir Country Inn
Off A466 ☎ (029 689) 548
11–2.30; 7–11
Hook Norton Best Bitter; Whitbread Boddingtons Bitter, Flowers Original [H]
Lovely country pub 50 yards from river in the beautiful Wye Valley. It features oak beams from a ship which was built in Brockweir many years ago. Tintern Abbey is nearby. Home-cooked food offered in generous portions.
⌂ ❀ ⛟ ◖ ◗ ⊟ ♿ ♣ ⌓ P

Charlton Kings

Clock Tower
On Cirencester road (A435)
☎ (0242) 571794
11–2.30; 5–11 (11–11 Sat)
Banks's Mild, Bitter; Hanson's Bitter [E]
Large rambling single-bar pub decorated with memorabilia from the age of the horse and cart. ❀ ◖ ◗ P

Chedworth

Seven Tuns
OS053122 ☎ (0285) 720242
12–3 (not winter Mon); 6.30–11
Courage Best Bitter, Directors [H]
Stone-built pub in attractive village. Old water wheel in garden where stream flows noisily. Cochin chickens roam pub yard. Skittles played.
⌂ ❀ ◖ ◗ ⊟ ♣ P

Cheltenham

Bayshill Inn
85 St Georges Place
☎ (0242) 524388
11–3; 5–11
Hall & Woodhouse Tanglefoot; Wadworth IPA, 6X [H], **Old Timer** [G]
Very popular town-centre pub without frills. Good value lunches – hot snacks only in evening. No hot food Sun. Cribbage is popular. ❀ ⛟ ◖ ◗ ♣

Beaufort Arms
184 London Road (A40, 1 mile E of centre) ☎ (0242) 526038
10.30–2.30; 6–11
Hall & Woodhouse Tanglefoot; Wadworth IPA, 6X, Farmer's Glory, Old Timer [H]
Excellent local on main road. The beers are lovingly attended to by a conscientious landlord. Racing theme in decor and menu. ❀ ⛟ ◖ ◗ ⊟ ♣ P

Jolly Brewmaster
39 Painswick Road
☎(0242) 512176
11–2.30; 6–11
Marston's Pedigree Bitter; Whitbread WCPA, Flowers IPA, Flowers Original [H]
Situated near college of further education – popular with both students and staff. No food at weekends. ⌂ ❀ ◖ ⊟ ♣

Kemble Brewery Inn
27 Fairview Street
☎ (0242) 243446
11.30–2.30 (3 Sat); 6–11
Archers Village Bitter, Best Bitter, ASB [H]
Comfortable and popular back-street local. Difficult to find but worth seeking out. Premium guest beer changes monthly. Eve meals served Mon–Fri until 8pm. ❀ ◖ ◗ ♣

Try also: Haymaker (Courage)

Chipping Campden

Lygon Arms
High Street ☎ (0386) 840318
11–2.30; 6–11 (11–11 summer)
Donnington SBA; Hook Norton Best Bitter; Ruddles Best Bitter; Wadworth 6X [H]
Comfortable and friendly free house in one of the loveliest towns in the country. Tables in sheltered courtyard. Piano in bar.
♘ ❀ ⛟ ◖ ◗ ⊟ ♿ ⌓

Try also: Volunteer (Free)

Cirencester

Brewers Arms
70 Cricklade Street
☎ (0285) 653763
11–3; 7 (6 Mon & Fri)–11
Arkell's 2B Bitter, 3B Best Bitter, Kingsdown Ale [H]
Unpretentious busy drinking establishment. Wide range of curries. Upstairs family/dining/function room.
No food Tue eve. ♘ ❀ ◖ ◗ ♣

Kings Head Hotel
Market Place ☎ (0285) 653322
10–2.30; 6–10.30 (11 F & S)
Ushers Best Bitter; Whitbread Flowers Original [H]
Relaxing panelled two-room pub, tucked away in an alley beneath an historic hotel. Real ale also available in hotel wine bar. Guest beers. ♘ ⛟ ◖ ♿

Try also: Corinium Court (Free)

Cleeve Hill

High Roost
On B4632 Cheltenham–Winchcombe road
☎ (024 267) 2010
11.30–2.30; 7–11
Hook Norton Best Bitter, Old Hookey; Wood Special [H]
Pub set on highest hill in the county with expansive views through large bay windows across Vale of Severn. Pub is reached by a flight of steps. Children allowed in for meals. Jukebox, darts and bar skittles.
❀ ◖ ♣ ⌓ P

Cockleford

Green Dragon Inn
½ mile along Elkstone turn off from A435 OS969142
☎ (024 287) 271
11–2.30; 6–11
Draught Bass; Butcombe Bitter [G]; **Hook Norton Best Bitter** [H]; **Theakston Old Peculier; Wadworth 6X; Whitbread Boddingtons Bitter** [G]
Surprisingly large pub with a choice of two comfortable bars and many side rooms. Large car park in lane opposite. Jazz on Mon. Menu changes weekly. Guest beers. ⌂ ❀ ◖ ◗ ⊟ ⌓ P

Ebrington

Ebrington Arms
Off B4035 OS186399
☎ (038 678) 223
11–2.30; 6–11
Donnington SBA; Hook Norton Best Bitter; Theakston XB [H]
Quiet, friendly stone-built pub in the centre of the village. Organ in bar.
⌂ Q ❀ ⛟ ◖ ◗ ♣ ⌓ P

Fairford

Bull Hotel
Market Place ☎ (0285) 712535
11–3; 6–11
Arkell's 2B Bitter, 3B Best Bitter [H]
Attractive stone-built hotel in main square. Good bar meals.
⌂ ♘ ⛟ ◖ ◗ ♿ P

Fosse Cross

Hare & Hounds
On A429 Northleach to Cirencester road OS068095
☎ (0285) 720288
11–3; 6–11 (may vary)
Hook Norton Best Bitter; Wadworth 6X [H]
Comfortable stone-built pub with L-shaped bar. Snacks, children's and veg meals in bar and separate restaurant. Adjacent caravan site. Guest beers. ⌂ ♘ ❀ ◖ ◗ ♿ ⛺ ♣ P

Ganborough

Coach & Horses
On A424 3 miles N of Stow OS172292 ☎ (0451) 30208
11–2.30 (3 Sat); 6.30–11
Donnington XXX, BB, SBA [H]
A pleasant country pub on main road, popular for its beer and food. Nearest pub to the picturesque brewery. Occasional live entertainment. Pub games include bottle walking (not for the faint-hearted)! ⌂ ☺ ❀ ◖ ◗ ▲ ♣ P

Gloucester

County Tavern
44 Southgate Street
☎ (0452) 307000
11–2.30; 5.30–11
Marston's Burton Best Bitter, Pedigree Bitter [H]
Comfortable single-bar town pub, adjoining the New County Hotel, near the Cross. Good food until 9.30pm. Disabled access is through hotel.
☺ ⊨ ◖ ◗ ♿ ≢

Linden Tree
73–75 Bristol Road (A38, S of centre) ☎ (0452) 27869
11–2.30; 5.30–11 (11–11 Sat)
Hook Norton Best Bitter; Smiles Best Bitter; Wadworth 6X [H]
An excellent well-kept 'country pub' in town. Well worth a visit. Occasional guest beers. Car parking for four vehicles only. ⌂ ❀ ⊨ ◖ ◗ P

Tailor's House
43 Westgate Street (100 yds from the Cross)
☎ (0452) 21750
11–11
Marston's Pedigree Bitter; Whitbread WCPA, Flowers IPA, Flowers Original [H]
Friendly city-centre pub near cathedral. Refurbished and enlarged in 1989. Eve meals served 5–7.30pm. ◖ ◗ ♿ ≢

Try also: Tall Ship (Wadworth)

Grange Court

Junction Inn
1½ miles N of A48 OS725160
☎ (045 276) 307
11–3; 7 (6 summer)–11 (11–11 Sat)
Hook Norton Best Bitter; Theakston Best Bitter; Whitbread WCPA [H]
Pub with railway connections, as name implies; railway memorabilia in bars. Outside patio area is safe for children. Skittle alley and separate function room. May open longer in summer. Guest beers.
⌂ ☺ ❀ ◖ ◗ ⊡ ♣ P

Great Barrington

Fox Inn
1 mile from A40 OS204131
☎ (045 14) 385
11.30–2.30; 6.30–11
Donnington XXX, BB, SBA [H]
Excellent stone-built pub in beautiful position by the River Windrush. Popular with walkers and locals. One of the only two pubs in the county that have been in every edition of the *Good Beer Guide*. No food Sun; cider sold in summer only.
⌂ Q ❀ ⊨ ◖ ◗ ♣ ȯ P

Guiting Power

Olde Inn
At NW end of village OS093249 ☎ (045 15) 392
11–2.30; 6–11
Hook Norton Best Bitter; Wadworth 6X [H]
An excellent Cotswold free house, popular with locals and tourists alike. Has a wide range of interesting Danish food. Guest beers. ⌂ Q ◖ ◗ ⊡ ♣ P

Try also: Farmers Arms (Donnington)

Joyford

Dog & Muffler
Off B4432 and B4228 OS579132 ☎ (0594) 832444
11–2.30; 6–11
Samuel Smith OBB [H]
Lovely but hard-to-find olde worlde pub with lots of character. Recently extended into previous living quarters. Sizzling platter a speciality; no food Sun eve or Mon.
Q ❀ ◖ ◗ ⊡ ♿ ▲ P

Kemble

Thames Head Inn
Tetbury Road (A433) OS981986 ☎ (0285) 770259
11–3; 7 (6.30 Fri & Sat)–11
Arkell's 2B Bitter, 3B Best Bitter, Kingsdown Ale [H]
Friendly pub, half a mile from the disputed source of the Thames. Previously a free house, it was acquired by Arkell's in 1989. Q ❀ ◖ ◗ ≢ P

Kineton

Halfway House
Between B4077 and B4068 OS097266 ☎ (045 15) 344
12–3; 6.30–11
Donnington BB, SBA [H]
Lovely country pub with welcoming atmosphere, situated halfway between the two Guitings. ⌂ ❀ ⊨ ◖ ◗ ♣ P

Lechlade

Crown Inn
High Street ☎ (0367) 52198
11.30–2.30; 6–11 (11–11 Sat)
Hook Norton Best Bitter; Morland Original Bitter [H]; Wadworth 6X [H]
Friendly pub with good selection of ales, including guest beers. ❀ ◖ ◗ ♣

Leighterton

Royal Oak
Near A46 OS823912
☎ (066 689) 250
11–2.30; 7 (6.30 summer)–11
Butcombe Bitter; Hook Norton Best Bitter; Uley Old Spot Ale; Wadworth 6X [H]
Bright but tastefully modernised pub with a friendly atmosphere. Children only admitted summer lunchtimes.
⌂ Q ☺ ❀ ◖ ◗ ♣ ȯ P

Lower Swell

Golden Ball
On B4068 OS175255
☎ (0451) 30247
11–2.30; 6.30–11
Donnington XXX, BB, SBA [H]
Simple, but friendly two-room pub in centre of village. Good food (not Sun eve).
⌂ ❀ ⊨ ◖ ◗ ♣ ȯ P

May Hill

Glasshouse Inn
Off A40 OS709213
☎ (0452) 830529
11–2.30; 6–11
Butcombe Bitter; Whitbread WCPA [G]
Isolated old country pub with stone-flagged floor. Quoits played. Guest beers. Limited menu on Sun. ⌂ Q ❀ ◖ ◗ ♣ P

Minchinhampton

Old Lodge Inn
OS854008 ☎ (0453) 832047
12–3; 6–11 (11–11 Sat)
Tetley Bitter; Theakston Best Bitter; Wadworth 6X [H]
Former golf clubhouse in the middle of common. Good food (restaurant). Children's play area in garden. ☺ ❀ ◖ ◗ ⊡ ♣ P

Moreton-in-Marsh

Black Bear
High Street (A429)
☎ (0608) 50705
11–3 (4 Tue); 6–11
Donnington XXX, BB, SBA [H]
Thriving town local. Recently-added second bar serves as dining area. May remain open summer afternoons. Games include Aunt Sally.
⌂ ❀ ⊨ ◖ ◗ ⊡ ♿ ≢ ♣ P

Gloucestershire

Try also: Wellington (Hook Norton)

Naunton

Black Horse
Off B4068 OS119234
☎ (045 15) 378
11–2.30; 6–11
Donnington BB, SBA Ⓗ
Traditional pub in unspoilt Cotswold village. Disabled access via side door. Close to Cotswold Farm Park (rare breeds). ⌂ 🛏 ◐ ◑ ⊟ ♿ ♣ P

Newmarket

George
OS840996 ☎(045 383) 2530
11–2.30; 6–11
Archers Best Bitter; Hook Norton Best Bitter; Theakston Best Bitter Ⓗ
Friendly well-run local with views over the valley. Bar skittles. Guest beers.
Q ⌂ ◐ ◑ ♣ P

Oakridge Lynch

Butchers Arms
OS915038 ☎ (028 576) 371
12–2.30; 6–11
Archers Best Bitter; Butcombe Bitter; Marston's Pedigree Bitter; Ruddles Best Bitter, County; Tetley Bitter Ⓗ
A lively gem of a village pub well worth seeking out; its lights are visible from the Bisley-Oakridge road. Accommodation in adjacent cottage. Eve meals Wed-Sat only. 🔥 Q ⌂ 🛏 ◐ ◑ ♣ P

Paxford

Churchill Inn
On B4479 OS184379
☎ (038 678) 203
11–2.30; 7–11
Hook Norton Best Bitter, Old Hookey Ⓗ
Pleasant country local with keen darts following. Aunt Sally in garden. No meals Sun.
🔥 Q ⌂ 🛏 ◐ ◑ ⛺ ♣ ⚬

Prestbury

Plough
Mill Street ☎ (0242) 244175
10.30–2.30; 6–11
Whitbread WCPA, Flowers IPA, Flowers Original Ⓖ
Half-timbered thatched pub with attractive garden (quoits played). Near village church.
🔥 Q ⌂ ⊟ ♣

Purton (East)

Berkeley Hunt
At side of canal
☎ (0453) 811217
11.30–2.30 (not Mon–Fri winter); 7–11
Marston's Pedigree Bitter; Wadworth 6X Ⓖ
17th-century ex-farmhouse. Previously bargees' ale and cider house. Good old-fashioned pub offering good beer and hospitality. Snacks available both sessions.
🔥 Q ☺ ⌂ ⊟ ♿ ♣ ⚬

Purton (West)

Old Severn Bridge Hotel
Old Severn Bridge (Off A48) OS670046 ☎ (0594) 842454
12–2.30; 7–11
Burton Bridge Festival Ale; Marston's Pedigree Bitter; Wadworth 6X Ⓗ
Excellent views across the river. Named after now-demolished railway bridge. Children's play equipment in the garden. Good value home-made food. Guest beers. 🔥 Q ⌂ 🛏 ◐ ◑ P

Saint Briavels

George
High Street (Off A4228)
☎ (0594) 530228
11–3; 6–11 (may open 11–11)
Hall & Woodhouse Tanglefoot; Marston's Pedigree Bitter; Wadworth 6X Ⓗ
One-bar pub near the castle, with beams and plenty of character. Very popular with all ages. Landlord's speciality dish is 'Oriental Steamboat'. High-quality bed and breakfast accommodation.
🔥 Q ⌂ 🛏 ◐ ◑ ⛺ ♣ P

Sapperton

Daneway Inn
N of A419, 4 miles W of Cirencester OS939034
☎ (028 576) 297
11–2.30; 6.30–11
Archers Best Bitter; Wadworth IPA Ⓗ, **6X** Ⓖ
Superb old canal workers' inn set in idyllic position near the western end of Sapperton canal tunnel. Games include Ringing the Horn and quoits. Guest beers plus house beer Daneway Bitter (not brewed here).
🔥 Q ☺ ⌂ ◐ ◑ ⊟ ♣ ⚬ P

Sheepscombe

Butchers Arms
Between A46 and B4070 OS892104 ☎(0452) 812113
11–2.30; 6–11
Marston's Pedigree Bitter; Whitbread WCPA, Pompey Royal, Flowers Original Ⓗ
Excellent pub with views and hanging baskets. Eve meals in summer only.
🔥 ⌂ 🛏 ◐ ◑ ♿ ♣ ⚬ P

Shuthonger

Crown
On A38, N of Tewkesbury
☎ (0684) 293714
11–2.30; 6–11
Banks's Bitter; Draught Bass Ⓗ
Excellent roadside pub with own restaurant and good food (eve meals Tue–Sat). Guest beers. ◐ ◑ P

Siddington

Greyhound
Ashton Road ☎ (0285) 653573
11.30–2.30; 6.30 (7 Mon & Sat)–11
Hall & Woodhouse Tanglefoot; Wadworth IPA, 6X Ⓗ
Excellent 17th-century village pub, sensitively extended with interesting furniture and artefacts. Quiet lounge.
🔥 Q ⌂ ◐ ◑ ⊟ ♣ P

Sling

Orepool Inn
On B4228 ☎ (0594) 833277
11–11
Draught Bass; Wadworth 6X Ⓗ
Recently extended to provide family room. Separate games room. Live entertainment; lounge is quiet.
Q ☺ ⌂ 🛏 ◐ ◑ ⊟ ♿ ⛺ ♣ ⚬ P

Stonehouse

Spa Inn
Old Ends Lane OS798059
☎ (045 382) 2327
11–3; 6–11
Whitbread WCPA, Flowers Original Ⓗ
Cosy and welcoming pub adjoining factory estate. Popular at lunchtimes. Eve meals Sat only. Guest beers.
⌂ ◐ ◑ ⊟ ≈ ♣ ⚬ P

Stow-on-the-Wold

Queens Head
The Square ☎ (0451) 30563
11–2.30 (3 Sat); 6 (6.30 Sat)–11
Donnington BB, SBA Ⓗ
Fine old Cotswold pub, popular with tourists and locals alike. One of only two pubs in the county to be in every *Good Beer Guide* to date. Lunchtime snacks; no food Sun.
⌂ ◑ ⊟ ♣ ⚬

Stratton

Drillmans Arms
34 Gloucester Road (A417, near A435 jct) ☎ (0285) 653892
11–3; 6–11
Archers Best Bitter, ASB; Wadworth IPA Ⓗ
An 18th-century pub, this was Archers' first tied house. Good value home-made dishes supplement standard pub fare.

Guest beers. Limited parking.
♣ P

Stroud

Clothiers Arms
1 Bath Road (A46)
☎ (0453) 763801
11–2.30 (3.30 Sat); 4.30 (6.30 Sat)–11
Archers Village Bitter; Ind Coope Burton Ale; Ruddles Best Bitter; Smiles Best Bitter; Tetley Bitter; Wadworth 6X [H]
Comfortable and welcoming free house displaying memorabilia of the old Stroud Brewery Company. Evening meals finish at 9pm.
♣ P

Duke of York
22 Nelson Street
☎ (0453) 758715
12(11.30 Sat)–2.30; 6(7 Sat)–11
Butcombe Bitter; Marston's Pedigree Bitter; Smiles Best Bitter; Uley Old Spot Ale [H]
Cosy one-bar town free house. Evening meals served until 7.30pm. Guest beers.

Tetbury

Trouble House
On A433, 1 mile E of town
☎ (0666) 502206
11–2.30; 6–11
Wadworth 6X [H]
Old pub on main road outside the town, with a long and colourful history. Bar billiards.
Q ♣ P

Tewkesbury

Berkeley Arms
Church Street ☎ (0684) 293034
10.30–2.30 (3 Sat); 6.30–11
Wadworth 6X, Farmer's Glory, Old Timer [H]
Ancient pub of character near the abbey. Access to lounge is through an unusual alleyway.
Q ♣

Britannia
High Street ☎ (0684) 294208
11–3; 7–11
Greenalls Davenports Traditional Bitter [H]
Busy town-centre pub, with single, awkwardly laid-out bar
♣

Try also: Albion (Halls)

Waterley Bottom

New Inn
E of N Nibley along 1½ miles of narrow lanes OS758964
☎ (0453) 543659
12–2.30 (3 Sat); 7–11
Cotleigh WB Bitter, Tawny Bitter; Greene King Abbot Ale; Smiles Best Bitter [H], **Exhibition; Theakston Old Peculier** [G]
Large friendly free house in beautiful setting surrounded by steep hills. Two golf courses nearby. Large scale map useful for first-time visitors! Shove-ha'penny played. Cotleigh WB is a specially produced variation of Harrier SPA. Guest beers.
Q ♣ P

Willersey

New Inn
Main Street (B4632, old A46) ☎ (0386) 853226
11–2.30; 6.30–11
Donnington BB, SBA [H]
Good village pub serving the needs of the local community. Overnight accommodation includes a family room. Skittle alley. ♣ P

Winchcombe

White Hart
High Street ☎ (0242) 602359
10.30–3; 5.30–11 (11–11 Sat)
Whitbread WCPA, Flowers Original [H]
Busy town pub catering for most tastes and age groups. Guest beers. ♣ P

Withington

Mill Inn
OS032154 ☎ (024 289) 204
11–2.30; 6–11
Samuel Smith OBB, Museum Ale [H]
This is the place to bring your American friends! Ancient stone-built inn of great character with many rooms and grand fireplaces. Lovely garden overlooking a stream.
P

Woodchester

Ram
South Woodchester (off A46)
OS840022 ☎ (0453) 873329
11–3; 6–11 (11–11 Sat)
Archers Village Bitter; Holden's Bitter; Hook Norton Old Hookey; Uley Bitter, Old Spot Ale; Whitbread Boddingtons Bitter [H]
Comfortable stone-built free house looking across valley. Good food. Guest beers.
Q ♣ P

Try also: Royal Oak (Free)

Woolaston Common

Rising Sun
1 mile off A48 through village of Netherend OS590009
☎ (059452) 282
12–2.30 (not Wed); 6.30–11
Hook Norton Best Bitter; Marston's Pedigree Bitter; Theakston Best Bitter [H]
Lovely country pub with excellent views and friendly landlord. Authentic Indian curries prepared to eat in or take away (no food Wed). Beautiful floral display in summer.
Q ♣ P

DISPENSE METHODS

[G] by gravity straight from the cask
[H] by handpump
[E] by electric pump
[A] by air pressure (including electric air compressor in Scotland)

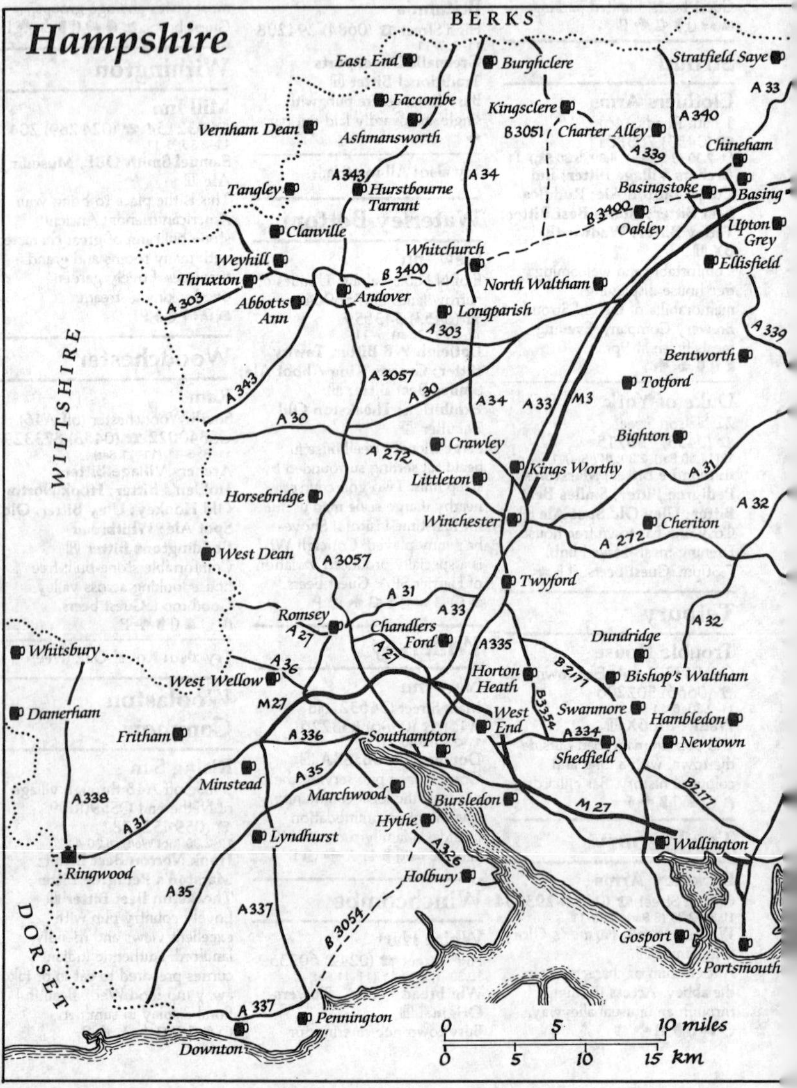

Gale's, Horndean; **Ringwood**, Ringwood

Abbotts Ann

Eagle

Off A343 ☎ (0264) 710339
11–2.30 (3 Fri, 3.30 Sat, 12–2.30 Sun); 6–11

Courage Best Bitter, Directors Ⓗ

Popular pub run by a friendly landlord in an attractive thatched village. Live music every Thu. Skittle alley. Take-away menu (no food Mon).
Q P

Aldershot

Albion

28 Waterloo Road (off A323)
☎ (0252) 319286
12–3; 5.30–11 (11–11 Fri & Sat)

Gale's XXXD, BBB, Best Bitter, XXXXX, HSB Ⓗ

Head and shoulders above the standards of other Aldershot pubs. A unique two-bar experience with most of the activity concentrated in the public. All of this and mild too!
A must. No food Sun.

Garden Gate

Church Lane East (¼ mile S of town by railway and five arch bridge) ☎ (0252) 21051
11.30–2.30 (3 Sat); 6–11.

Friary Meux Best Bitter; Ind Coope Burton Ale Ⓗ

Good, old-fashioned boozer. No-frills, just value for money. When busy, the jukebox can be obtrusive; otherwise, an intimate atmosphere. No food

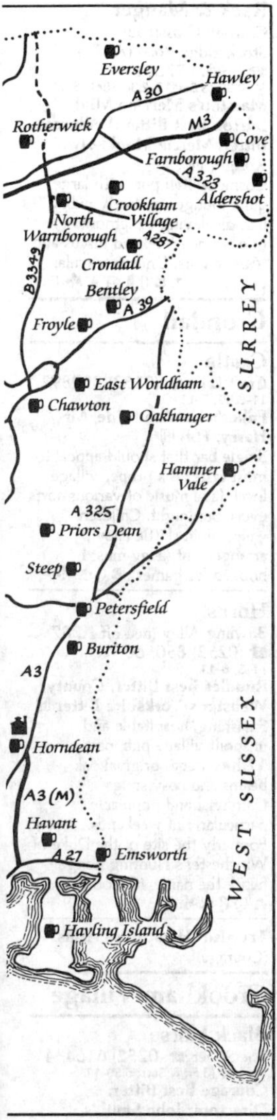

Sun. Beers due to change to Greene King. ♨ ◖ ⇌ P

Andover

Lardicake
Adelaide Road (200 yds from centre) ☎ (0264) 23447
11–11
Brakspear Special; Fuller's Chiswick Bitter, London Pride; Ringwood Best Bitter; Robinson's Best Bitter [H]
Lively and unpretentious pub close to pedestrian centre. Widest beer range in Andover. Good value bar food (not Sun); regular guest beers (range varies). Note the GWR notice in the bar. ♨ ◖ ◗ ♣ ⌓

Merrie Monk
New Street ☎ (0264) 52675
11–2.30; 5–11 (11–11 Fri & Sat)
Marston's Burton Best Bitter, Pedigree Bitter [H]
Friendly local near church and Iron Age Museum. Unspoilt by town development: a basic public bar and a comfortable lounge, depicting the Merrie Monk. Good value in a Whitbread-dominated area. Adventure playground in garden. Small dining/function room. Fish suppers Fri.
❀ ◖ ◗ ⊟ ♣ P

Ashmansworth

Plough
1 mile W of A343
☎ (0635) 253047
12–2.30 (3 Sat, not Mon, except bank hols); 6–11
Archers Village Bitter, Best Bitter; Greene King Abbot Ale [G]
Remote, two-bar country free house with regular guest beers. Beer on stillage behind bar but always cool even on the warmest of days. Village Bitter is sold as 'Plough Bitter'.
Q ❀ ♣

Basing

Millstone
Bartons Lane (½ mile from Daneshill Ind. Est.)
☎ (0256) 473560
11.30–2.30 (12–2.30 Sun); 5.30 (6 Sat)–11
Fuller's London Pride [H], ESB [E]; Gale's HSB; Gibbs Mew Bishop's Tipple; Wadworth IPA, 6X [H]
Converted farm building next to river, a popular lunchtime watering hole (no food Sun). Garden well-used in summer. Helpful and friendly staff. Close to historic tithe barn and Basing House ruins. Q ❀ ◖ ♿ P

Basingstoke

George (Hole in the Wall)
London Street (in market square)
☎ (0256) 465168
11–3; 6–11
Courage Best Bitter, Directors [H]
Small, friendly traditional pub in the older part of town with basic Victorian decor. Stands opposite the Willis Museum in the pedestrian zone. Parking nearby. Recently saved from closure by local CAMRA branch and regulars. No food Sun. ❀ ◖ ⊟ ♣ ⌓ P

Bentley

Star
London Road (A31, ¾ mile from station) ☎ (0420) 23184
11–3; 6–11
Courage Best Bitter, Directors [H]
Single, cosy bar with traditional wood-panelling. Pleasant and welcoming. Excellent home-cooking; sandwiches with real bread. Q ◖ ◗ P

Bentworth

Sun
Sun Hill (Alton Road)
☎ (0420) 62338
11.30–3; 6–11
Draught Bass; Bunces Best Bitter; Gale's HSB; Marston's Pedigree Bitter [H]
Unspoilt country pub with low beams and part quarry-tiled floor, built in 1635. Old prints and farming implements cram the walls. Wood-burning stoves in two splendid fireplaces. Regular guest beers. ♨ Q ◖ ◗ P

Bighton

Three Horseshoes
Off A31/B3047
☎ (0962) 732859
11–2.30 (12–2 Sun); 6–11
Gale's XXXD, BBB, HSB [H]
Delightful rural local, well off the beaten track. Country crafts collection in locals' bustling bar; relaxing atmosphere in quiet lounge. The sea angling club welcomes visitors. Handy for Mid-Hants steam railway (Ropley station two miles). No food Mon. ♨ Q ❀ ◖ ⊟ ♿ ♣ P

Bishop's Waltham

Bunch of Grapes
St Peters Street
☎ (0489) 892935
10–2 (2.30 Sat, 12–2 Sun); 6 (5 Sat) –11
Courage Best Bitter [H]
Excellent, unspoilt alehouse with a warm welcome, situated in a narrow medieval street. In same family for over 70 years.
Q ❀ ♣

Burghclere

Queen
Harts Lane (2 miles W of A339, just off A34) ☎ (0635) 27350
11–3 (12–2.30 Sun); 6–11
Adnams Bitter; Arkell's 3B Best Bitter; Theakston XB [H]
Friendly open-plan bar with quiet corners offering good value beer and lunches. Enthusiastic games-playing locals. Good family garden with play fort. Try to steer clear of horse racing discussions!
❀ ◖ ♣ P

Buriton

Five Bells
48 High Street

☎ (0730) 63584
11–2.30 (3 Fri & Sat); 5.30–11
Friary Meux Best Bitter; Ind Coope Burton Ale [H]
400 year-old village pub built from local stone. Village set at beginning (or end!) of South Downs way. Has a good local trade and offers an imaginative menu (including game; also veg option). Separate restaurant.
⛫ ❀ ◑ ◐ ⛟ ▲ ♣ P

Bursledon

Linden Tree
School Road (400 yds from A27/A3025)
☎ (042 121) 2356
11–2.30; 6–11
Wadworth IPA, 6X, Farmer's Glory [H], **Old Timer** [G]
Comfortable one-bar pub with no obtrusive gaming machines, just light piped music. A pergola and children's play area make this pub ideal in summer. High-quality, home-cooked food (not Sun). ⛫ ❀ ◑ P

Chandlers Ford

Cleveland Bay
1 Pilgrims Close, Valley Park (off Knightwood Road)
☎ (0703) 269814
11–11
Hall & Woodhouse Tanglefoot; Wadworth IPA, 6X, Farmer's Glory, Old Timer [H]
Situated on the edge of a housing development, this is a typical new pub. One large bar, with flagstoned floor, bare red brick and marble/carved-wood bar. Provides a variety of drinking areas. Menu includes veg option. Regular guest beers.
⛫ ✿ ❀ ◑ ◐ ♿ P

Charter Alley

White Hart
White Hart Lane (off A339, ½ mile E of Ramsdell)
☎ (0256) 850048
12–2.30 (3 Sat); 7–11
Bunces Best Bitter; Eldridge Pope Royal Oak; Palmers IPA; Taylor Landlord [H]
Locals' pub tucked down a narrow lane. The small rustic front bar has a wood burner. The very large back bar is used by diners and for games, with a skittle alley in one corner. Imaginative guest beers. Disabled access is via car park door. ⛫ ❀ 🛏 ◑ ◐ ♿ ♣

Chawton

Greyfriar
Winchester Road (¼ mile from A31/A32 jct)
☎ (0420) 83841
11–3; 6–11
Whitbread Strong Country Bitter, Flowers Original [H]
Excellent, friendly village pub opposite Jane Austen's house. Extensive pub menu with veg option; good value for area and good quality. Camping at nearby Graces Farm.
Q ❀ ◑ ◐ ♿ ▲ P

Cheriton

Flower Pots
Off A272 ☎ (0962) 771318
11–2.30; 6–11
Whitbread Strong Country Bitter, Flowers Original [G]
Fine, unspoilt local where everyone is made welcome. Ideal stop for visitors to the Watercress Line Steam Railway at Alresford (three miles). Bar snacks. Guest beers.
⛫ Q ❀ 🛏 ⛟ ▲ ♣ P

Chineham

Chineham Arms
Hanmore Road (W of A33)
☎ (0256) 56404
11.30–3; 5–11 (11.30–11 Fri & Sat)
Fuller's Chiswick Bitter, London Pride, ESB [H]
Newly-built outpost for Fuller's; considerably more attractive than most modern town pubs. Situated on the north-eastern outskirts of the Basingstoke sprawl. ⛫ ✿ ❀ ◑ ◐ ♿ ♣ P

Clanville

Red Lion
1 Mile N of Weyhill
☎ (0264) 772729
11–2.30; 6–11
Whitbread Strong Country Bitter, Flowers Original [G]
Charming, original country inn, basic but cosy. Beer served straight from the cellar. No gimmicks, just an old-style pub. Enthusiastic following for darts, dominoes and bar skittles. No food Tue eve.
⛫ Q ✿ ❀ ◑ ◐ ▲ ♣ P

Cove

Plough & Horses
90 Fleet Road
☎ (0252) 545199
11–3 (4 Sat); 5.30–11 (6 Sat)
Friary Meux Best Bitter; Gale's HSB; Ind Coope Burton Ale; Tetley Bitter [H]
Newly-designated a 'Hampshire Treasure' (by the brewery), this well-furnished pub has a fascinating collection of local Victoriana. Very well-run and almost invariably packed! Good value pub fare (not Sun). Landlord is one of the Grandmaster Burton Cellarmen. ❀ ◑ ♣ P

Crawley

Rack & Manger
Crawley Crossroads, Stockbridge Road (A272)
☎ (0962) 72281
11–2.30 (3 Sat, 12–2.30 Sun); 6–11
Marston's Mercian Mild, Burton Best Bitter, Pedigree Bitter, Merrie Monk, Owd Rodger [H]
Cosmopolitan pub with large quiet lounge and lively public bar, displaying a plethora of bric-a-brac. Weekend discos and '60s' nights. Unusual circular pool table. ⛫ ❀ ◑ ◐ ⛟ ▲ ♣ P

Crondall

Castle
Croft Lane ☎ (0252) 850892
11–3.30; 7–11
Fuller's London Pride, Mr Harry, ESB [H]
Single bar that should appeal to most tastes – a proper village local. Live music of various sorts every Sun night. Children welcome in skittle alley by arrangement (alley must be booked for games). ❀ ◑ ♿ ♣

Horns
Bowling Alley (just off A287)
☎ (0252) 850560
11–3; 6–11
Ruddles Best Bitter, County; Webster's Yorkshire Bitter [H]
Smashing, hospitable and unspoilt village pub, partly 17th-century; original oak beams and cosy snugs. Convivial and popular, particularly at weekends. Formerly the site of the Duke of Winchester's Hunting Lodge – hence the name. No food Sun.
⛫ Q ◑ ♿ ♣ P

Try also: Hampshire Arms (Courage)

Crookham Village

Black Horse
The Street ☎ (0252) 616434
11–2.30 (3 Fri & Sat); 5.30–11
Courage Best Bitter, Directors; John Smith's Bitter [H]
Excellent, atmospheric, beamed village pub serving good value food – try the 'Dustbin Omelette' (no food Sun). Busy at weekends. Near picturesque Basingstoke Canal – good for walks. Garden with aviary; excellent for children.
Q ❀ ◑ ▲ ♣ P

Damerham

Compasses
On B3078, W of Fordingbridge
☎ (07253) 231
10.30–2.30; 6–11
Ind Coope Burton Ale; Wadworth 6X [H]
Village pub with quiet lounge and lively public bars. Large

beer garden with children's play area. Excellent food includes some veg dishes. Large restaurant/function room. Jazz night Fri. Shut the Box played.
⌂ Q ❀ ⊨ ◖ ◗ ⊞ ♿ ⛺ ♣ P

Downton

Royal Oak
On A337 ☎ (0590) 642297
11–2.30; 6–11 (10.30 Mon-Thu in winter)
Whitbread Strong Country Bitter, Pompey Royal, Flowers Original [H]
18th-century pub with three real fires, in same family for 130 years. Gleaming decor and no-smoking area. Covered patio and children's garden but no dogs or children in bar. No jukebox or fruit machines. Fine, home-cooked, good value food (not Mon eve in winter). Weekend cream teas in summer.
⌂ Q ❀ ◖ ◗ ♿ P

Dundridge

Hampshire Bowman
Dundridge Lane (1 mile off B3035) OS579185
☎ (0489) 892940
11–2.30 (may vary); 6–11
Archers Village Bitter (summer); **Courage Directors; Gale's BBB, XXXXX, HSB** [G]
Pleasantly-situated, off the beaten track. One traditional brick-floored bar, once an abattoir, now HQ of the Portuguese Racing Sardine Club! Meals include veg option. Table skittles.
⌂ Q ❀ ◖ ◗ ♿ ⛺ ♣ P

East End

Axe & Compasses
1 mile W of A343, Penwood crossroads ☎ (0635) 253403
11–3; 6–11
Draught Bass [G]; **Charrington IPA; Wadworth 6X** [H]
Open-plan country pub with bar, games and dining areas. Rustic implements adorn the walls. Darts and bar billiards played. Worth seeking out. No food Sun, or Mon eve.
⌂ Q ❀ ◖ ◗ ♣ P

East Worldham

Three Horseshoes
Cakers Lane (B3004)
☎ (0420) 83211
11–2.30; 6–11
Gale's BBB, Best Bitter, XXXXX, HSB [H]
Leave the disaster zone of Alton for this pleasant country pub, originally located on a gypsy horse-trading site. One bar, with small adjoining restaurant and excellent garden. Eve meals Tue–Sat. ❀ ◖ ◗ ♿ ♣ P

Ellisfield

Fox
Green Lane (off A339)
☎ (0256) 83210
11.30–2.30; 6.30–11
Bunces Best Bitter; Hall & Woodhouse Badger Best Bitter, Tanglefoot; Marston's Pedigree Bitter; Wadworth 6X [H]
Excellent village pub, well worth the drive; in fact surprisingly close by car to Basingstoke's beer desert. Occasional guest beers. No eve meals Mon. ⌂ Q ❀ ◖ ◗ ⊞ P

Emsworth

Coal Exchange
21 South Street
☎ (0243) 375866
10.30–3; 5.30–11 (10.30–11 Sat)
Gale's XXXD, BBB, XXXXX, HSB [H]
One L-shaped bar with eating area caters for winter local trade and summer tourists. Popular landlord. Eve meals Thu–Sat. Shove-ha'penny and Shut the Box played. Disabled access is via the garden. Free council car park adjacent. ⌂ ❀ ◖ ◗ ♿ ⇌ ♣

Milkmans Arms
55 North Street
☎ (0243) 373356
10.30–3; 5 (6 winter)–11
Gale's XXXL, BBB [H], **XXXXX** [G], **HSB** [H]
Popular, newly-decorated and well-furnished pub. Personal attention ensures a good local trade. Rare outlet for light mild.
Q ❀ ◖ ◗ ⇌ ♣

Eversley

White Hart
The Street (A327)
☎ (0734) 732817
11–2.30 (3 Fri & Sat); 5.30–11
Courage Best Bitter, Directors [H]
Classic village pub with real fires and beams. Lunchtime snacks. ⌂ Q ❀ ◖ ⊞ P

Faccombe

Jack Russell
Off A343, signed from Hurstbourne Tarrant
☎ (026487) 315
12–2.30; 6–11
Palmers IPA [H]
One-bar rural inn with new conservatory dining area, but still a country atmosphere. Seafood and fresh fish feature on the menu. Regular guest beers – normally a choice of three. ⌂ ❀ ⊨ ◖ ◗ P

Farnborough

Prince of Wales
184 Rectory Road (off A325, near station)
☎ (0252) 545578
11.30–2.30; 6–11
Brakspear Bitter; Eldridge Pope Royal Oak; Fuller's London Pride; Hall & Woodhouse Badger Best Bitter, Tanglefoot; Wadworth 6X [H]
This excellent free house has the finest selection of ales for miles. A terrific atmosphere, free from electronic games; relaxed and informal with a lively buzz of conversation. Crowded most of the time but well worth the occasional crush. Good value lunches (not Sun). Guest beers.
Q ◖ ⇌ (North) P

Fritham

Royal Oak
Off B3078 OS242141
☎ (0703) 812606
11–3 (may extend in summer); 6–11
Whitbread Strong Country Bitter, Flowers Original [G]
Unspoilt, rustic, thatched pub deep in the New Forest. The large open hearth is still used for smoking hams. With its unique family atmosphere, this pub is a real gem and well worth seeking out. Roadside parking. ⌂ Q ❀ ⊞ ♣

Froyle

Hen & Chicken
Upper Froyle (A31)
☎ (0420) 22115
11–2.30; 6–11
Adnams Broadside; Brakspear Special; Courage Best Bitter, Directors; Wadworth 6X [H]
Handsome old coaching inn, where beams and brass abound. Now a food-oriented pub with a separate buttery and restaurant. Upmarket, good value food but beer is expensive. A welcome and worthwhile stop. Regular guest beers. ⌂ Q ❀ ◖ ◗ P

Prince of Wales
Lower Froyle (off A31)
OS759443 ☎ (0420) 23102
11–2.30; 6–11
Courage Best Bitter; Theakston Best Bitter; Younger No. 3 [H]
Edwardian country pub in scenic village. Convivial, but can get very busy and noisy. Home-cooked food with organically-grown local vegetables; menu includes veg option. Up to three guest beers available. ❀ ◖ ◗ ♿ P

Try also: Anchor (Free)

Gosport

Queens Hotel
143 Queens Road (off Stoke Road/St Andrews Road)
☎ (0705) 525518

11.30–3; 7–11 (11–11 Fri & Sat)
Greene King Abbot Ale [H]
Four other beers from across the country always available. Friendly pub with large, segmented single bar. Limited food menu.

Hambledon

New Inn
West Street (off B2150)
☎ (070 132) 466
12–2.30; 7–11
Eldridge Pope Thomas Hardy Country Bitter; Gale's BBB, HSB; Ringwood Old Thumper [H]
Pleasant old village local with two bars and a friendly atmosphere. Uncomplicated bar with no food – just good, old-fashioned drinking and socialising; the best value beer in the district.

Vine Inn
West Street (off B2150)
☎ (070 132) 419
11.30–2.30 (3 Sat); 6–11
Courage Directors; Gale's BBB, HSB; Morland Original Bitter; Wadworth 6X [H]
An old village local whose two separate bars provide a pleasant drinking atmosphere. Near the old Hartridges Brewery. Occasional guest beers.
Q

Hammer Vale

Prince of Wales
Hammer Lane (off A3, signed Bulmer Hill, right at T-junction) OS867326 ☎ (0428) 52600
11–2.30; 6–11
Gale's XXXD, BBB, Best Bitter, HSB [G]
Red-brick and stained glass country pub, bordering three counties. Good food and bags of atmosphere. Live music Sun eve. Excellent walking country. No food Sun eve.
Q P

Havant

Robin Hood
6 Homewell ☎ (0705) 482779
11–11
Gale's XXXD, BBB, XXXXX, HSB [G]
Single-bar, comfortably furnished pub with busy lunch trade. Recently enlarged, but the original part of the pub has not lost its character.

Hawley

New Inn
5 Hawley Road
☎ (0276) 32012
10.30–3; 5.30–11
Morland Original Bitter, Old Masters [H]
One of the few remaining village locals in the area. The original building was destroyed by fire in 1910, but parts of the pub are 200 years-old. Excellent, friendly public bar. Lounge is more sedate and slightly insular. Thriving golf team (landlord runs Southwood Golf Club). No food Sun.
Q P

Hayling Island

Maypole
9 Havant Road (A3023)
☎ (0705) 463670
11–11
Gale's XXXD [G], BBB, Best Bitter [H], XXXXX [G], HSB [H]
Friendly 30s-style pub with good bar food (not Mon eve). Popular with locals and visitors. Circular pool table in public bar.
P

Holbury

Old Mill Inn
Limekiln Lane (Hardley Ind. Est. turn off A326)
☎ (0703) 891137
11–3; 6–11 (11–11 June–Sept)
Courage Directors; Ringwood Fortyniner, Old Thumper; Ruddles County; Webster's Yorkshire Bitter [H]
14th-century barn and adjoining cottage, converted to a large, multi-roomed pub. Popular for its varied home-made lunches. Well-equipped children's play garden is much-used. Guest beers.
Q P

Horndean

Ship & Bell
6 London Road (A3)
☎ (0705) 598641
11–2.30 (3 Sat); 5.30–11
Gale's XXXD, BBB, Best Bitter, XXXXX, HSB [H]
Traditional pub, a former coaching inn dating from the 12th century. On the site of the original Gale's Brewery, and still the brewery tap. Original well in public bar. Modernised bars; good range of games, including bar billiards. No food Sun eve.
P

Horsebridge

John O'Gaunt
½ mile off A3057
☎ (0794) 388394
11.30–2.30 (3 Sat); 6–11
Palmers IPA [H]
Friendly village free house with shove-ha'penny board on bar. Two guest beers normally available. Car park nearby. No meals Tue eve.

Horton Heath

Lapstone
Botley Road (B3354, formerly A3051) ☎ (0703) 692377
11–3; 6–11
Marston's Pedigree Bitter; Whitbread Strong Country Bitter, Flowers Original [H]
Friendly pub with a homely feel and fresh flowers on the bar. Excellent home-cooked food, including veg dishes (not Sun eve). Pub has a charity book stall and a children's play cabin in the garden. Occasional guest beers.
P

Hurstbourne Tarrant

George & Dragon
The Square (A343)
☎ (026 476) 272
10–2.30; 5–11
Courage Best Bitter, Directors; Wadworth 6X [H]
Much-photographed historic posting inn. Built in 16th century or earlier and enlarged in Georgian era. Original oak mail rack still above the fireplace. Featured in William Cobbett's *Uphusband*. Home-made food (not Sun eve).
P

Hythe

Lord Nelson
High Street (near ferry)
☎ (0703) 842169
11–2.30; 6–11
Marston's Pedigree Bitter; Whitbread Strong Country Bitter, Flowers Original [H]
Waterfront pub with quaint bars. Garden overlooks Southampton Water and yacht marina. Lunchtime snacks.

Travellers Rest
Hart Hill (off Frost Lane)
☎ (0703) 842356
11–2.30 (3 Sat); 6–11
Whitbread Strong Country Bitter, Flowers Original [H]
Friendly, two-bar pub, off the beaten track; on the Pilgrim Way between Hythe and Bucklers Hard. Also handy for walkers on the Solent Way.
Q P

Kingsclere

Crown Hotel
Market Place (B339)
☎ (0635) 298956
11–2.30 (3 Sat); 6 (7 Sat) –11
Courage Best Bitter, Directors; John Smith's Bitter [H]
Ancient, unspoilt pub; famous for the killings of three people in 1944 by American soldiers. Plenty of old photographs.

Note weather vane on church opposite.
⛫ Q ❀ ⇆ ◖ ⊞ ♿ ♣ ◌ P

Kings Worthy

Cart & Horses
London Road (A33/A333 jct; near M3 jct 9)
☎ (0962) 882360
11–3; 5.30–11 (11–11 bank hols)
Marston's Burton Best Bitter, Pedigree Bitter, Owd Rodger Ⓗ
Large, rambling, busy, smart roadhouse with a good selection of food at all times. Restaurant, children's playground and large garden. Converted 300 year-old barn acts as skittle alley/family room. The public bar provides a quiet retreat.
⛫ ♿ ❀ ◖ ◗ ⊞ ♿ ♣ ◌ P

Littleton

Running Horse
88 Main Road
☎ (0962) 880218
11–2.30; 6–11 (11–11 Sat in summer)
Gibbs Mew Wiltshire Traditional Bitter, Salisbury Best, Bishop's Tipple Ⓗ
Small pub knocked through into one bar but still retaining 'public' and 'lounge' ends. Large garden for families has animals, birds and play equipment. No meals Wed eve.
⛫ ❀ ◖ ◗ ♣ P

Longparish

Cricketers Inn
On B3048 ☎ (0264) 72335
11–2.30; 6–11
Marston's Burton Best Bitter, Pedigree Bitter Ⓗ
Games-oriented local with numerous cricketing pictures in the bars which are split into three distinct areas. The focal point of the village.
⛫ ❀ ◖ ◗ ⊞ ♿ ♣ P

Lyndhurst

Mailmans Arms
71 High Street
☎ (0703) 282257
11–2.30; 6–11
Marston's Burton Best Bitter, Pedigree Bitter Ⓗ
Popular, friendly and comfortable pub. Occasional live entertainment; barbecues in garden. Large free public car park nearby. Family room at lunchtimes only.
⛫ Q ♿ ❀ ◖ ♿ ♣

Marchwood

Pilgrim Inn
Hythe Road (off A326)
☎ (0703) 867752
11–2.30; 6–11
Draught Bass; Charrington IPA; Courage Best Bitter, Directors Ⓗ
Beautiful thatched inn with immaculate gardens; hanging baskets are a speciality – home-cooking, with veg option and children's menu. ⛫ Q ❀ ◖ ♿ P

Minstead

Trusty Servant
Off A337, Cadnam-Lyndhurst Road OS281110
☎ (0703) 812137
11–2.30 (4 Sat); 6–11
Whitbread Strong Country Bitter, Flowers Original Ⓗ
Friendly, unspoilt New Forest village local. Ideal base for touring the forest. Sir Arthur Conan Doyle is buried at the village church. The village green opposite is the outside drinking area. ⛫ ❀ ⇆ ◖ ⊞ ♣ P

Newtown

Travellers Rest
Church Road (off B2177 Southwick–Wickham road) OS609133 ☎ (0329) 833263
11–3; 6–11
Gibbs Mew Wiltshire Traditional Bitter, Salisbury Best, Bishop's Tipple Ⓗ
1750-built, picturesque, cottage-style inn with two bars (lounge is quiet) and pleasant garden. Real home-cooking (blackboard menu). Occasional impromptu folk, Irish folk music or piano evenings. Morris dancers May Day and Boxing Day. ⛫ Q ❀ ◖ ◗ ⊞ ♿ ⛺ ♣ P

North Waltham

Fox
Fox Road (off A30)
☎ (0256) 397288
11–2.30; 5.30–11
Courage Best Bitter, Directors Ⓗ
Cottage-style pub, recently-extended to incorporate restaurant, but retaining character in the bar. No food Sun eve. Bar billiards.
⛫ ❀ ◖ ◗ ⊞ ♣ P

North Warnborough

Anchor
The Street (off A287)
☎ (0256) 702740
11–2.30; 6–11
Courage Best Bitter, Directors Ⓗ
Cheerful, homely two-bar local, specialising in pub games and HQ of the local soccer team. Famous for its charity contributions. Near King John's Castle and Basingstoke Canal. No food Sun. ⛫ Q ❀ ◖ ◗ ⊞ ♣ P

Oakhanger

Red Lion
Off B3004 ☎ (04203) 2230
11–3; 6–11
Courage Best Bitter, Directors Ⓗ
Excellent public bar dominated by a 32-pound pike (stuffed) and lively locals. Saloon is more refined and food-based but not without atmosphere. Often crowded.
⛫ Q ❀ ◖ ◗ ⊞ ♿ ⛺ ♣ P

Oakley

Barley Mow
Oakley Lane ($1\frac{1}{4}$ miles along Fox Lane, which becomes Oakley Lane, from B3400)
☎ (0256) 781234
11–2.30; 5.30–11 (11–11 Sat)
Courage Best Bitter, Directors Ⓗ
Clean, friendly, two-bar local, modernised in 1987 but retaining 'village' feel. Public bar puts many other lounges to shame. Quiet and convivial at lunchtimes, 'bubbly' in evening. Good range of pub games; swings and slides for children.
❀ ◖ ◗ ⊞ ♣ P

Pennington

Musketeer
North Street
☎ (0590) 676527
11.30–3; 5.30–11
Brakspear Special; Butcombe Bitter; Felinfoel Double Dragon; Hook Norton Old Hookey; Ringwood Best Bitter Ⓗ
Attractive, one-bar pub in village centre, originally a coaching inn. A real free house with an interesting choice of beers, including occasional guests. No food Sun.
⛫ Q ❀ ◖ ◗ P

Petersfield

Good Intent
40 College Street (A3 north-bound) ☎ (0730) 63838
11.30 (11 Sat)–2.30 (12–2.30 Sun); 6–11 (closed Mon)
Ballard's Best Bitter; Draught Bass; Eldridge Pope Royal Oak; Hall & Woodhouse Tanglefoot; Marston's Pedigree Bitter; Wadworth 6X Ⓖ
16th-century free house with real beams in the single bar. The handpumps are not used as the beers come straight from the cellar. Very good restaurant (no food Sun eve). Guest beers.
⛫ ◖ ◗ ⇌ P

Old Drum
16 Chapel Street

Hampshire

☎ (0730) 64159
11–2.30; 5.15–11 (10–4; 7–11 Sat)
Friary Meux Best Bitter; Ind Coope Burton Ale Ⓗ
Low building just off town square, dating from the 17th century. Busy at lunchtime (good food – not Sun). Quieter in the evening with unobtrusive piped jazz music. Collection of old garden sprays on lounge ceiling! Large garden.
❀ 🛏 ◖ ⇌ ♣ P

Portsmouth

Alexandra
Wingfield Street, Landport
☎ (0705) 823876
11–2.30 (3 Sat); 6–11
Draught Bass Ⓗ
Friendly, well-run, single-bar estate pub. A short distance from Charles Dickens' birthplace. No food Sun. ❀ ◖ ♿ ♣ P

Bold Forrester
177 Albert Road, Southsea
☎ (0705) 823609
11–11
Marston's Pedigree Bitter; Whitbread Wethered Bitter, Boddingtons Bitter, Flowers Original, Wethered Winter Royal Ⓗ
A very busy pub, aimed mainly at the student market. Not quiet, but worth a visit for the good atmosphere. Very 'wooden' decor, but better than usual Whitbread identikit renovations. Single bar. Guest beers.
⌂ ❀ ◖ ♿ ⊕

Eldon Arms
Eldon Street, Southsea (near law courts) ☎ (0705) 851778
11–2.30 (3.30 Sat); 5.30–11
Eldridge Pope Thomas Hardy Country Bitter, Royal Oak; Wadworth Old Timer Ⓗ
A locals' pub. Interesting glazed exterior; inside a single bar is adjoined by a lounge and a restaurant. Near seafront and commercial centre. Children always welcome in lounge (no bar). ◖ ◗ ⇌ (Portsmouth & Southsea) ♣

Farmhouse Hotel
Burrfields Road (off A2030, Eastern Road, next to golf course) ☎ (0705) 671111
11–11
Courage Best Bitter; Ringwood Old Thumper; Ruddles Best Bitter; John Smith's Bitter; Younger IPA Ⓗ
A large free house in a formerly dry area. Very large bar provides comfortable seating for enjoying a good selection of reasonably-priced beers and excellent food. Golf driving range next door. Occasional guest beers. Definitely a drive-in pub – no houses or services nearby.
👶 ❀ ◖ ◗ ♿ ⊕ P

George Hotel
84 Queen Street, Portsea
☎ (0705) 821040
11–11
Gale's HSB; Marston's Pedigree Bitter, Merrie Monk, Owd Rodger; Whitbread Flowers Original Ⓗ
A classic town pub: a comfortable, one-bar, 18th-century inn with a relaxed 'wardroom' atmosphere. Handy for the Naval Heritage Centre with its museums and historic ships. Guest beers.
Q 🛏 ◖ ◗ ♿ ⇌ (Harbour)

Mermaid
222 New Road, Copnor
☎ (0705) 824397
11–3 (3.30 Sat); 6.30 (7 Sat) –11
Marston's Pedigree Bitter; Whitbread Best Bitter, Pompey Royal, Wethered Winter Royal Ⓗ
Superlative local with rare Victorian wrought-iron canopy outside and figures above the bar. Guest beer. Bar billiards. No food Sun. ❀ ◖ ⊟ ♣

Old Oyster House
291 Lockway Road, Milton (off A288) ☎ (0705) 827456
11–3; 6–11 (11–11 Sat & summer)
Marston's Pedigree Bitter; Whitbread Pompey Royal Ⓗ
Large 1930s-style pub, a former Portsmouth United Breweries house. Stands near old Milton Locks, once part of Portsmouth-London Canal. Lively public bar (table football) with quieter lounge. Meals served April-September. Q ❀ ◖ ⊟ ♣ P

Parade
31 Clarence Parade, Southsea
☎ (0705) 824838
11–11
Marston's Pedigree Bitter; Whitbread Flowers Original Ⓗ
Large L-shaped room; tiled exterior faces Southsea Common. Handy for Palmerston Road shops, Southsea Castle and D-Day Museum. ❀ ◖ ♿ ♣

Railway
119 High Street, Cosham (50 yds from station)
☎ (0705) 375606
11–11
Marston's Pedigree Bitter; Whitbread Pompey Royal, Flowers Original Ⓗ
Busy High Street local, now back to its original name after being the 'Rocket' for some time. Menu caters for children and vegetarians; eve meals until 8pm. ❀ ◖ ◗ ⇌ (Cosham) ♣ P

Royal Marines Artillery Arms
58 Cromwell Road, Eastney, Southsea (opp. Royal Marines Barracks) ☎ (0705) 820896
10.30–3; 6.30–11 (11–11 Sat)
Gale's XXXD (summer), **BBB, XXXXX, HSB** Ⓗ
Surprisingly large, street-corner local with two contrasting bars (saloon is quiet). Handy for the Royal Marines Museum. Friendly landlord. Within walking distance of Eastney Beach. Eve meals Fri and Sat. Q 👶 ❀ ◖ ◗ ⊟ ♣ ⊕

Scotts Bar
51 King Street, Southsea
☎ (0705) 826018
11–2.30; 5.30–11 (12–3.30; 7–11 Sat)
Courage Best Bitter, Directors; Gale's HSB; Ringwood Fortyniner, Old Thumper; Wadworth 6X Ⓗ
Warm, friendly, very busy back-street pub. Live music Tue night. Originally the Elm Tavern – the brewery tap for the Portsmouth and Brighton United Brewery. Unusual cash register eight-handled beer engines. No food at weekends. Children welcome.
◖ ⇌ (Portsmouth & Southsea)

Tap
17 London Road, North End
☎ (0705) 699943
11–11
Banks's Mild, Bitter; Courage Directors; Fuller's London Pride; Greene King Abbot Ale; Hall & Woodhouse Tanglefoot Ⓗ
Deservedly-popular free house in North End shopping area. Handy for Odeon cinema and continental ferry port. The beer range may vary. A rare outlet for real mild in the city.
❀ ◖ ◗ ♿ ⊕

Wellington
62 High Street, Old Portsmouth
☎ (0705) 818965
11–3; 6–11 (11–11 Sat)
Friary Meux Best Bitter; Ind Coope Burton Ale Ⓗ
One-bar pub in historic part of city, close to cathedral and Square Tower Museum that commemorates the settlement of Australia. Comfortably-furnished; water jugs and whisky miniatures displayed. Has keen cricket team.
❀ ◖ ◗ ⇌ (Harbour) ♣

Wig & Pen
1 Landport Terrace, Southsea
☎ (0705) 820696
11.30–3; 6.30–11
Marston's Pedigree Bitter; Whitbread Boddingtons Bitter, Pompey Royal Ⓗ
One-bar pub with wooden floor and a separate lounge area. A

locals' pub with a relaxed atmosphere and a friendly welcome. Popular at lunchtime with office workers. Good value meals. Guest beers. ◖ ⇌ ♣

Wine Vaults
43 Albert Road, Southsea (opp. Kings Theatre)
☎ (0705) 864712
11.30–3; 5.30–11 (11–11 Fri & Sat)
Felinfoel Double Dragon; Fuller's London Pride; Gale's Best Bitter; Morland Old Masters; Ringwood Old Thumper; Whitbread Boddingtons Bitter Ⓗ
Wood-panelled and pewed, this genuine free house now has a second, quieter 'snug' bar. Wide range of beers from 18 handpumps; beer often sold in four-pint jugs. One beer sold at a discount Mon eve. New 'attic' restaurant specialises in veg and wholefood cookery.
◖ ◗ ♿

Yorkshire Grey
25 Guildhall Walk
☎ (0705) 822010
11–11 (may close Sat afternoon, closed Sun)
Draught Bass; Charrington IPA; Gale's HSB Ⓗ
Imposing and unspoilt, late Victorian pub opposite the Theatre Royal. Traditional single bar with tiled murals and a no-smoking area. Upstairs grill room restaurant. Bar meals lunch only.
◖ ◗ ⇌ (Portsmouth & Southsea)

Priors Dean

White Horse (Pub With No Name)
OS714290
☎ (042058) 387
11–2.30 (3 Sat); 6–11
Ballard's Best Bitter; Eldridge Pope Royal Oak; King & Barnes Mild, Sussex Bitter, Festive; Ringwood Fortyniner Ⓖ
Famous old pub, winner of many awards. Difficult to find as it is set in a field without a pub sign; nevertheless it can get very busy, especially in summer. Caravan space (no tents). Guest beers. No food Sun, nor eve meals Mon/Tue.
♨ Q ❀ ◖ ◗ ▲ P

Romsey

Tudor Rose
3 The Cornmarket
☎ (0794) 512126
10–2.30 (4 Sat); 5.30 (6 Sat)–11
Courage Best Bitter, Directors Ⓗ
Small, 15th-century alehouse in town centre with friendly atmosphere. Live folk music Sun eve. Tables in cobbled court-yard in summer.
♨ Q ❀ ◖ ♿ ♣

Rotherwick

Coach & Horses
The Street ☎ (025 676) 2542
11–2.30; 5–11
Arkell's Kingsdown Ale; Bunces Best Bitter; Eldridge Pope Royal Oak; Palmers IPA; Ringwood Old Thumper; Theakston Old Peculier Ⓗ
18th-century inn with basic front bar and rear dining room. Good choice of beers, but pricey. Monthly guest beers.
♨ Q ❀ ◖ ◗ P

Shedfield

Sams Hotel
Upper Church Road (off B2177, was A333) ☎ (0329) 832213
4.30–11 (12–11 Fri & Sat)
Marston's Mercian Mild, Burton Best Bitter, Pedigree Bitter Ⓗ, **Owd Rodger** (winter) Ⓖ
Traditional roadside country inn with three bars. Impromptu folk music Sat nights. HQ of Shedfield cricket club (pitch opposite) and reputedly the birthplace of British petanque (boules). Bar billiards.
♨ ❀ ⊕ ▲ ♣ P

Southampton

Bald Faced Stag
36 Edward Road, Freemantle (off Foundry Lane)
☎ (0703) 778571
11–4; 7–11
Marston's Mercian Mild, Burton Best Bitter, Pedigree Bitter Ⓗ
Imposing street-corner local in former Victorian manor house, with two large, lively bars. The only pub in this part of the city to retain its original snug. Hard to find. ⚇ ❀ ⊕ ♣ P

Bay Tree
10 New Road (opp. Southampton Institute of Higher Education)
☎ (0703) 333187
12–3; 5 (7.30 Sat) –11
Draught Bass; Charrington IPA Ⓗ
Unpretentious, city-centre, two-bar boozer with a truly 'local' atmosphere. The public bar is lively but friendly; the lounge is more peaceful. Busy office trade at lunchtime. Upstairs family room (Sun lunch only).
Q ⚇ ◖ ⊕ ⇌ (Central) ♣

Crown & Sceptre
30 Bevois Valley Road (A335)
☎ (0703) 227081
12–2.30 (3 Sat); 6.30 (7 Sat)–11
Gibbs Mew Local Line, Salisbury Best, Bishop's Tipple Ⓗ
Ex-Watney pub, bought by Gibbs and transformed into an overnight success by its new landlord. Two bars, each with its own character, very popular with students. Can be a little noisy weekend evenings.
❀ ◖ ◗ ⊕ ♣ P

Crown & Sceptre
168 Burgess Road, Bassett (A35) ☎ (0703) 768414
11–2.30 (3 Fri & Sat); 6–11
Marston's Pedigree Bitter; Whitbread Strong Country Bitter, Pompey Royal, Flowers Original, Ⓗ
Subtly-lit, wood-panelled lounge, popular with university staff; more basic public, the haunt of locals. Brisk lunchtime food trade (good menu).
❀ ◖ ◗ ⊕

Freemantle Arms
33 Albany Road, Freemantle (off Firgrove Road, near A3057) ☎ (0703) 772092
10.30–3; 6 (7 Sat)–11
Marston's Mercian Mild, Burton Best Bitter, Pedigree Bitter Ⓗ
Friendly local in quiet cul-de-sac. Lively public bar; quieter lounge with plenty of plant life. Popular, colourful garden with large patio. ❀ ⊕ ♣

Junction Inn
21 Priory Road, St Denys
☎ (0703) 584486
11.30–3; 5 (6.30 Sat)–11
Marston's Border Mild, Burton Best Bitter, Pedigree Bitter, Merrie Monk Ⓗ, **Owd Rodger** (winter) Ⓖ
Truly evokes the Victorian local; national winner of CAMRA's Best Restored Pub Award for 1990. Hard to visit without getting into conversation with someone. No food Sun.
Q ❀ ◖ ⊕ ♿ ⇌ (St Denys) ♣

Marsh
42 Canute Road (under A3025 Itchen Bridge)
☎ (0703) 635540
11–11 (11–5; 8–11 Sat)
Marston's Mercian Mild, Burton Best Bitter Ⓗ
One of the last remaining unspoilt dockland pubs, with bars in a semi-circle around the bottom half of an old lighthouse. TV in public bar. Opposite Ocean Village. Meals served until 7pm (not Sat/Sun).
❀ ◖ ⊕ ♣

New Inn
16 Bevois Valley Road (A335)
☎ (0703) 228437
11.30–3; 6.45–11
Gale's XXXD (summer), **BBB, XXXXX, HSB,** Ⓗ **Prize Old Ale** Ⓖ

Intimate, dimly-lit ale drinkers' pub, where rudimentary but comfortable service is courteous. Very much *à la mode* in student circles—busy during term-time. Home-cooked food with veg option. ◖ ♿ ♣

Park Inn
37 Carlisle Road, Shirley (down Park Road, off Shirley High Street, A3057)
☎ (0703) 787835
11–3 (4 Sat, 12–2.30 Sun); 5 (6 Sat)–11
Hall & Woodhouse Tanglefoot; Wadworth IPA, 6X, Old Timer Ⓗ
Popular, friendly side-street local close to shopping centre. Unobtrusive background music. A bit more classy than other pubs in the area. ⛀ ♣

Richmond Inn
108 Portswood Road, Portswood (A335)
☎ (0703) 554523
11–11
Marston's Mercian Mild, Burton Best Bitter, Pedigree Bitter Ⓗ
Friendly local with uncomplicated public bar and plusher lounge; magnificent LSD cash till. Good whisky selection.
⛀ ⊟ ≹ (St Denys) ♣ P

Salisbury Arms
126 Shirley High Street, Shirley
☎ (0703) 774624
10–3 (4 Sat); 6 (7 Sat) –11
Marston's Mercian Mild, Burton Best Bitter, Pedigree Bitter Ⓗ
Genuine working-class local. Single-bar, but with well-separated areas. Lively at weekends. Small family room. Lunchtime snacks. ⛄ ♣

Steep

Cricketers
1 Church Road (off A325 at Sheet) ☎ (0730) 61035
11.45–2.30; 5.15–11
Gale's XXXD (summer), **BBB, Best Bitter, XXXXX, HSB** Ⓗ
Set in an area of outstanding beauty, popular with walkers; situated at the foot of 'Little Switzerland'. Varied menu; two pleasant bars. ⌂ ⛀ ⛼ ◖ ◗ ⊟ ♣ P

Harrow
Off A325 at Sheet
☎ (0730) 62685
10.30–2.30 (3 Sat); 6–11
Whitbread Strong Country Bitter, Flowers Original, Ⓖ
Classic, small two-bar pub in pastoral setting, with its own country garden. Unspoilt bars feature an inglenook. Toilets are across the lane! Can get very busy. Unfortunately, due to be demolished for proposed bypass! Good value snacks include home-made soup.
⌂ Q ⛀ ◖ ◗ ⊟ ♣ P

Stratfield Saye

Four Horseshoes
West End Green (off A33)
☎ (0734) 332320
12–2.30; 5–11 (12–11 Sat & summer)
Morland Original Bitter, Old Masters Ⓗ
Classic two-bar, friendly country local. Quarry-tiled public bar where locals play dominoes and darts. Meals in summer only. ⌂ Q ⛀ ◖ ⊟ ♣ P

Swanmore

Bricklayers Arms
Church Road
☎ (0489) 892461
11–2.30 (2 Tue); 4.30 (6 Tue) –11 (11–11 Fri & Sat)
Whitbread Best Bitter, Strong Country Bitter, Pompey Royal Ⓗ
Pleasant one-bar village local near the church. Menu caters for children and vegetarians (no meals Tue or Thu eves).
⌂ ⛀ ◖ ◗ ♿ ♣ P

Tangley

Cricketers Arms
5 miles N of Andover, through Charlton and Hatherden OS326528 ☎ (026470) 283
11–2.30 (12–2.30 Sun); 7–11
Whitbread Strong Country Bitter, Pompey Royal Ⓗ
Remote country pub with a cricketing theme. Extended but retains original 17th-century, oak-beamed 'Drovers Bar'. Active games teams. No food Thu. Guest beers.
⌂ Q ⛀ ◖ ◗ ⊟ ♿ ⛺ ♣ P

Thruxton

White Horse
Beside A303
☎ (026477) 2401
11–2.30; 6–11
Bunces Best Bitter; Wadworth 6X Ⓗ
Low-beamed village pub just below main road. Shove-ha'penny board available. Small dining room for bar snacks (Tue-Sat). Children welcome. Occasional guest beers.
⌂ Q ◖ ◗ P

Totford

Woolpack
On B3046 ☎ (0962) 732101
11.30–3; 6–11
Eldridge Pope Dorchester Bitter; Gale's HSB; Palmers IPA Ⓗ
Large, open-plan, stone-floored pub in Hampshire's smallest hamlet. Occasional guest beers. No eve meals Sun/Mon.
⌂ Q ⛄ ⛀ ⛼ ◖ ◗ ♣ P

Twyford

Phoenix
High Street (B3354, old A333)
☎ (0962) 713322
11.30–2.30 (12–2 Sun); 6–11
Marston's Burton Best Bitter, Pedigree Bitter Ⓗ
Friendly village inn with good value food. Accommodation available in nearby village houses. Skittle alley/function room.
⌂ ⛀ ◖ ◗ ♿ ≹ (Shawford) ♣ P

Upton Grey

Hoddington Arms
Off B3349 ☎ (0256) 862371
11–2.30; 6–11
Courage Best Bitter, Directors Ⓗ
Very pleasant village pub with jug collection, restaurant and family room. Lovely setting close to the Basingstoke Canal.
⌂ Q ⛄ ⛀ ◖ ◗ P

Vernham Dean

George
Off A343 at Hurstbourne Tarrant ☎ (0264) 87279
11–2.30 (3 Sat); 6–11
Marston's Burton Best Bitter, Pedigree Bitter Ⓗ
16th-century, unspoilt pub with an open fire; the focal point of village life. Attractive exterior; warm welcome inside. Interesting pub sign.
⌂ Q ⛄ ◗ ♿ ○ P

Wallington

White Horse
North Wallington (off Delme Roundabout, A27/A32)
☎ (0329) 235917
11–2.30; 5(7 Sat)–11
Draught Bass; Charrington IPA; Goldfinch Flashman's Clout Strong Ale Ⓖ
Small two-bar pub in pleasant village situated opposite Wallington River. Can be reached via footbridge from Fareham. Has a new dining area (no lunches Sat/Sun). Occasional guest beers.
⌂ ⛀ ◖ ◗ ⊟

West Dean

Red Lion
Off A27/B3084, next to station ☎ (0794) 40469
11–2.30; 6(6.30 Tue)–11
Whitbread Strong Country Bitter, Flowers Original Ⓗ
Welcoming local in delightful village setting, overlooking the River Dun. Public bar with traditional games, and a quieter lounge. Part of the pub is in

Wiltshire! Guest beers. ⌂ Q ✿ ⊨ ◐ ◑ ⊟ ⛺ ≉ (Dean) ♣ P

West End

Master Builder

Swaythling Road (A27)
☎ (0703) 472426
11.30–2.30; 6 (5.30 Fri)–11
Draught Bass; Palmers IPA; Wadworth 6X [H]
Large, comfortable, roadside pub. One bar, but many drinking areas, including no-smoking. Specialises in non-local guest beers. Good food (veg option) at reasonable prices till 9pm (not Sun, or Mon eve). No fruit machines. ✿ ◐ ◑ P

West End Brewery

High Street (B3035)
☎ (0703) 474796
11–2.30; 5 (6 Mon)–11 (11–11 Sat)
Marston's Mercian Mild, Burton Best Bitter, Pedigree Bitter, Merrie Monk [H]
Welcoming pub, the only one in the village with a public bar (pool, darts and shove-ha'penny); quieter lounge. Suits all ages. Cheapest beer in village. No food Sun.
✿ ◐ ⊟ ♣ P

West Wellow

Rockingham Arms

Canada Road (½ mile from A36 roundabout) ☎ (0794) 22473
11.30–2.30; 6–11
Wadworth 6X [H]
Popular village local on the edge of the New Forest. Large, lively public bar. Three regular guest beers. New restaurant.
✿ ◐ ◑ ⊟ ♿ P

Weyhill

Weyhill Fair

On A342 just N of A303 ring road ☎ (026477) 3631
11.30–2.30 (12–2.30 Sun); 6 (7 Sat)–11
Gale's HSB; Morrells Bitter, Varsity; Marston's Pedigree Bitter [H]
Free house with an amazing list of guest beers, normally changing daily; a real mild always available as well as a traditional cider. Keen quiz teams. Local CAMRA Pub of the Year 1989. No cooking Sun eve. ⌂ Q ⛀ ✿ ◐ ◑ ⌓ P

Whitchurch

Prince Regent

104 London Road (B3400)
☎ (0256) 892179
11–11
Archers Best Bitter [H]**; Hop Back Summer Lightning** [G]**; Marston's Pedigree Bitter; Theakston Best Bitter** [H]
A friendly pub on edge of town overlooking Test Valley. Attracts a cosmopolitan crowd. Cellar bar for functions. Watch out for the cats. Snooker and pool. ♣ P

Whitsbury

Cartwheel

Whitsbury Road (3 miles NNW of Fordingbridge)
☎ (07253) 362
11–2.30; 6.11
Bunces Best Bitter; Courage Best Bitter; Gibbs Mew Wiltshire Traditional Bitter; Greene King Abbot Ale; Marston's Pedigree Bitter; Wiltshire Old Grumble [H]
Comfortable free house in remote village just outside New Forest. Has previously served as a barn, bakery and wheelwright's – hence the name. Constantly-changing beer range and imaginative menu (veg and children's choices). ⌂ ✿ ◐ ◑ ♣ P

Winchester

Bell

83 St Cross Road (A333 at S edge of city) ☎ (0962) 65284
11–2.30; 5–11 (11–11 Sat)
Marston's Mercian Mild, Burton Best Bitter, Pedigree Bitter [H]
Splendid old inn adjoining the 12th-century 'Hospital of St Cross' (England's oldest charity). Quiet, friendly lounge, good for conversation, and down-to-earth public bar.
⌂ ✿ ◐ ⊟ ♿ ♣ P

County Arms

85 Romsey Road (A3090)
☎ (0962) 51950
10.30–11 (10.30–3; 5.30–11 Sat)
Marston's Mercian *or* **Border Mild, Burton Best Bitter, Pedigree Bitter** [H]
Friendly, busy, out-of-town local, near hospital and prison, with active sports teams. Originally one bar, but extended into adjoining house to create a lounge. Efficient and courteous service. Sun roast lunches. Daily 'Happy Hour' 6.30–8pm. ⌂ ✿ ⊨ ◐ ◑ ⊟ ♣ P

Exchange

9 Southgate Street
☎ (0962) 54718
10–11
Courage Best Bitter, Directors; John Smith's Bitter [H]
Busy city-centre pub. One bar with a discreet dartboard area. The outdoor drinking area – a small patio – is unusual for the city centre. Food available all day. ✿ ◐ ◑ ♿ ≉ ♣

Fulflood Arms

28 Cheriton Road (300 yds off A272) ☎ (0962) 65356
12–2.30 (incl. Sun); 6–11
Marston's Burton Best Bitter, Pedigree Bitter, Owd Rodger (winter) [H]
Traditional, friendly, back-street local. Tiled sign still proclaims Winchester Brewery.
✿ ⊟ ≉ ♣

St James Tavern

3 Romsey Road (A3090)
☎ (0962) 61288
11–11
Hall & Woodhouse Tanglefoot; Wadworth IPA, 6X, Old Timer [H]
Small, end-of-terrace pub, close to city centre but mainly a locals' pub. Odd-shaped bar with several drinking areas. Keen table football team. Guest beers. ⊨ ◐ ◑ ≉ ♣

White Swan

84 Hyde Street (A333/A272 jct) ☎ (0962) 56626
11–2.30 (3 Fri & Sat); 5–11
Marston's Burton Best Bitter, Pedigree Bitter, Owd Rodger [H]
Large pub, formerly the Winchester Brewery tap. Patio to side of pub. Sun lunches and daily specials; no eve meals Sun/Mon. ✿ ◐ ◑ ⊟ ≉ ♣

Opening Hours

The law regarding opening hours was relaxed, not before time, in 1988. Now pubs in England and Wales may open at any time during the permitted hours of 11am to 11pm (earlier opening is allowed by some local licensing districts). Sunday hours are standard: 12–3 and 7–10.30. The opening hours given for each pub description are correct at the time of going to press. However, publicans are at liberty to take advantage of the new flexibility and may stay open longer than hours shown, or indeed close during the afternoons without prior notice. Where Sunday hours differ from those given above, this is noted. The Scottish licensing laws are more generous as far as opening is concerned and pubs may stay open longer.

Hereford & Worcester

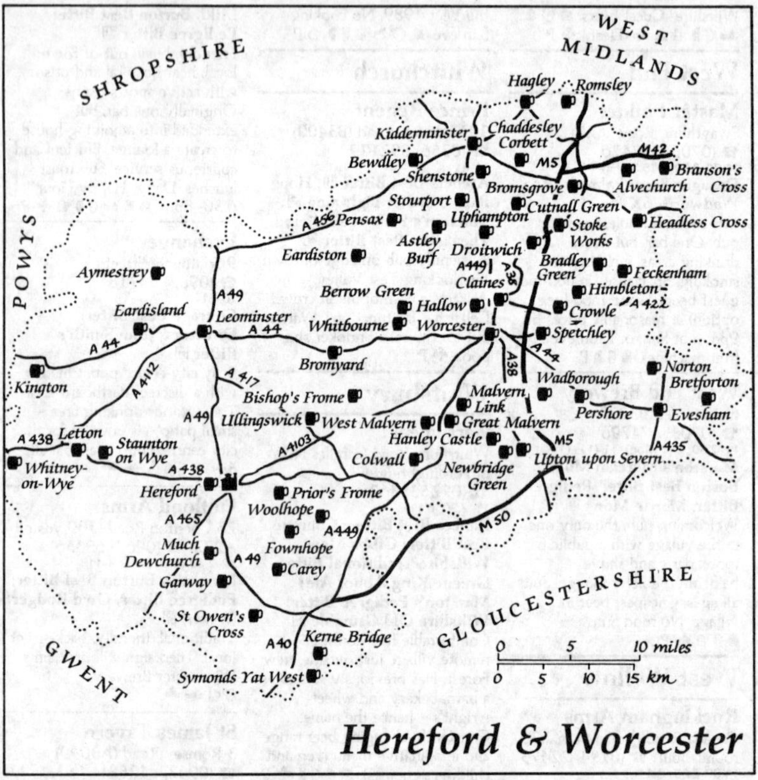

Wye Valley, Hereford

Alvechurch

Coach & Horses
Weatheroak Hill OS056741
☎ (0564) 823386
11–2.30; 5.30–11 (11–11 Fri)
Everards Old Original; Holden's Mild, Special; Hook Norton Old Hookey; Marston's Pedigree Bitter; Samuel Smith OBB; Wood Special Bitter Ⓗ
Popular pub on the old Roman road, Ryknield Street. Flagstoned bar, modern lounge and restaurant, plus large outdoor area.
♔ Q ❀ ◖ ◗ ⊞ ♣ ⊙ P

Astley Burf

Hampstall Inn
☎ (029 93) 2600
11.30–3; 6–11
Greenalls Davenports Best Mild Ale, Davenports Traditional Bitter Ⓗ
Welcoming family pub with attractive riverside setting; fishing and moorings on river.
Q ⊠ ❀ ◖ ◗ ⊞

Aymestrey

Crown Inn
☎ (0568) 81440
7–11
Marston's Pedigree Bitter; Whitbread Flowers IPA Ⓗ
Typical timber-framed village pub. Also sells Willie's Barley Bitter, produced at Lingen by part-time brewer Malcolm Williams. Lounge and bar mainly used by locals. Sun is the only lunchtime session. Eve meals Sat only. ♔ ❀ ◖ ◗ ⊞ ♣ P

Berrow Green

Admiral Rodney
On B4197 ☎ (0886) 21375
12–2.30; 6.30–11 (11–11 summer)
Banks's Mild; Ruddles County; Webster's Yorkshire Bitter Ⓗ
Large, rambling country pub with separate lounge, bar and games room. Nautical theme in bar. ♔ Q ⊠ ❀ ⊨ ◖ ◗ ⊞ ♿ ⅄ P

Bewdley

Black Boy
Wyre Hill (off A456 at Welchgate)
11–3; 6–11
Banks's Mild, Bitter Ⓔ
Several small rooms make up this friendly locals' pub near the top of a steep hill. The quality of beer makes the half mile walk from the river worthwhile.
Q ❀ ◖ ⊞ ♣

Cock & Magpie
1 Severnside North
☎ (0299) 403748
11–3; 6–11 (11–11 Sat & summer)
Banks's Mild, Bitter Ⓔ
Riverside local on former quayside in town centre. Snacks generally available. Lounge is quiet. Q ⊞ ♣

Hop Pole
Cleobury Road (A456)
☎ (0299) 402127
11–2.30 (may vary in summer); 6–11
Marston's Burton Best Bitter, Pedigree Bitter Ⓗ
Pleasant, two-roomed hostelry about a mile's drive from the town. Friendly local clientele and good value meals in the

comfortable lounge. Boules played throughout the summer.
Q ❀ ◗ ◖ ⊞ ♣ P

Horn & Trumpet
Welchgate (A456/B4194)
11–2.30; 6–11
Courage Directors; John Smith's Bitter 🄷
Lively hostelry, just a short stroll from the river. Jazz and folk evenings; pool table in separate games room.
♛ ◗ ⊞ ♣ P

Little Pack Horse
High Street ☎ (0299) 403762
11–2.30; 6–11
Ansells Bitter; Ind Coope Burton Ale; Lumphammer 🄷
The original outlet and flagship of the Little Pub Co. chain. A classic traditional pub, with low black beams and small rooms bedecked with old photos and artefacts. Renowned for its food, especially the Desperate Dan pies. ♛ Q ◗ ◖ ♣

Bishop's Frome

Green Dragon
100 yds off B4214
☎ (088 53) 647
12–3; 5–11 (12–11 Sat)
Courage Directors; Hook Norton Best Bitter, Old Hookey; Taylor Golden Best Mild, Landlord, Ram Tam; Wood Special Bitter 🄷 & 🄶
Classic village local with stone flags and oak beams. Still has much charm, despite the modern games room extension which is popular with the young. Up to 12 cask beers often available, some by gravity dispense. Good food.
♛ ❀ ◗ ◖ ⊞ ♣ P

Bradley Green

Mad O'Rourkes Kipper House
Feckenham Road OS987618
☎ (052784) 376
11–3; 6–11
Ansells Mild; Ind Coope Burton Ale; Lumphammer 🄷
A fine example of Mad O'Rourke style: trawler in the car park, diesel engine in the bar! Good food until 10pm.
❀ ◗ ◖ P

Branson's Cross

Cross & Bowling Green
Alcester Road (A435)
☎ (056 44) 2472
11–11 (11–3; 7–11 Sat)
Ansells Mild, Bitter; Tetley Bitter 🄷
Site of a pub for 500 years and a gibbet before that. Small lounge, larger restaurant/lounge; playground in large garden. No meals Sun.
♛ ❀ ◗ ◖ ⊞ ♣ P

Bretforton

Fleece
The Cross (50 yds S of B4035)
☎ (0386) 831173
10–3 (extends in summer); 6–11
Hook Norton Best Bitter; M&B Brew XI 🄷
Famous old inn owned by the National Trust. Interior has remained untouched for many years: inglenook and antiques; world-famous pewter collection. Guest beers often include one from Uley brewery. Beer festival first full weekend in July. Adventure playground in garden. ♛ Q ♉ ❀ ◗ ◖ ⊞ ♿ ♣ ♁

Bromsgrove

Red Lion Hotel
73 High Street
☎ (0527) 35387
10.30–11
Banks's Mild, Bitter 🄴
Busy one-roomed, town-centre pub. A mild drinker's retreat. No food Sun. ❀ ◗ ⇌ ♣ P

Try also: Boars Head, Charford (Banks's)

Bromyard

Crown & Sceptre
7 Sherford Street
☎ (0885) 482441
11–2.30 (3.30 Sat); 6.30–11
Banks's Bitter; Hook Norton Best Bitter; Whitbread Flowers IPA; Wood Wonderful Bitter 🄷
Deservedly-popular and the only free house in Bromyard. Plain, but comfortable bar area; large inglenook; old maps and adverts. Friendly service and good pub grub (not Wed or Sun eves). Occasional guest beer.
♛ ❀ ⊨ ◗ ◖ ♣ P

Carey

Cottage of Content
1½ miles NE of Hoarwithy
OS563310 ☎ (043 270) 242
12–2.30 (not Mon/Tue in winter); 7 (6 summer)–11
Hook Norton Mild (summer), **Best Bitter, Old Hookey; Marston's Pedigree Bitter** 🄷
Aptly-named, characterful inn in idyllic setting. 500 years old, it has a warren of oak-beamed rooms and simple furnishings. Restaurant offers an imaginative menu. ♛ ❀ ⊨ ◗ ◖ ♣ ♁ P

Chaddesley Corbett

Swan
High Street ☎ (056 283) 302
11–3.30; 7–11
Batham Mild Ale, Best Bitter 🄷
Spacious country pub with bowling green and garden. Lively bar, unusual lounge, children's room and restaurant. Jazz Thu.
♛ Q ♉ ❀ ◗ ◖ ⊞ ♣ ♁ P

Try also: Talbot Inn (Banks's)

Claines

Mug House
Claines Lane (off A449)
OS851588 ☎ (0905) 52073
11–11
Banks's Mild, Bitter 🄴
Ancient pub in churchyard setting. Unspoilt, three-roomed interior. Reputedly haunted. No food Sun. ♛ Q ♉ ❀ ◗ ⊞ ⛺

Colwall

Chase Inn
Chase Road, Upper Colwall (200 yds off Wyche road, B4218, down lane signed 'British Camp')
☎ (0684) 40276
12–2.30 (not Tue; 12–2 Sun) 6–11
Donnington BB, SBA; Wye Valley Hereford Bitter, HPA 🄷
Straightforward free house tucked away in a backwater of the Malvern Hills. Strict 'no kids/fruit machine policy'. Limited, but wholesome menu (until 8.30; not Sun eve). Bar billiards. Q ❀ ◗ ◖ ⊞ ♣

Crowle

Old Chequers
Crowle Green
☎ (090 560) 275
11–2.30 (3 Sat); 7–11
Ansells Bitter; Hook Norton Best Bitter; Theakston XB 🄷
400 year-old village inn in a country setting. The interior is spacious and smart. Comprehensive menu and wine list. ❀ ◗ ◖ ⊞ ♁ P

Cutnall Green

New Inn
On A442 ☎ (029 923) 202
11.30–3; 5.30–11
Marston's Burton Best Bitter, Pedigree Bitter 🄷
Small country pub with a welcoming atmosphere. Good quality food is served every day in the bar and in the popular dining room. ♛ ❀ ◗ ◖ ♣ P

Droitwich

Railway Inn
Kidderminster Road
☎ (0905) 770056
11.30–3; 5.30–11 (11–4; 6–11 Sat)
Marston's Burton Best Bitter, Pedigree Bitter, Merrie Monk 🄷
200 year-old coach house, now a canalside pub close to the recently-restored basin. A lively

atmosphere amongst railway memorabilia. ❁ 🛏 ◖ ≢ ♣ 🍎 P

Riflemans Arms
Station Street
☎ (0905) 770327
11–2.30; 5–11 (11–11 Sat)
Banks's Mild, Bitter [E]
Banks's premier 'Pint & Platter' pub. Friendly local with customers of all ages. Excellent food. ❁ 🛏 ◖ ◗ ⊟ ♿ ≢ P

Eardisland

White Swan
Main Road (old A44)
12–2.30; 6–11
Marston's Burton Best Bitter, Pedigree Bitter [H]
Old country pub in famous picturesque village. Nice lounge with low beams contrasts with the more basic public. Tends to get very food-oriented at weekends, so arrive early to beat the rush! Meals served until 9pm. ♨ ❁ ◖ ◗ ⊟ ♣ P

Eardiston

Nags Head
On A443, 1 mile W of village
OS058470 ☎ (054 47) 234
11–2.30; 7–11
Marston's Border Mild [E], **Burton Best Bitter, Pedigree Bitter** [H]
Friendly and comfortable locals' pub overlooking hop fields and the River Teme. Occasional quiz nights held in the hop-decorated bar. Good home-cooking in lounge. ♨ Q ❁ ◗ ⊟ ♣ P

Evesham

Trumpet Inn
Merstow Green (near Almonry Museum) ☎ (0386) 446227
11–2.30; 5 (7 Sat)–11
Draught Bass; M&B Brew XI [H]
Pleasant town pub just off the main street. Single bar, though not cavernous. No Sun lunches in winter. ❁ ◖ ♿ ≢ ♣ P

Feckenham

Rose & Crown
High Street ☎ (052 789) 2188
11–2.30; 6–11
Banks's Mild, Bitter [E]; **Everards Beacon Bitter, Tiger Best Bitter** [H]
Welcoming village pub with a varied range of guest beers (often Adnams). Lounge features unusual high-backed settles. Large, enclosed garden welcomes children.
♨ Q ❁ ◖ ◗ ⊟ ♿

Fownhope

Forge & Ferry
Ferry Lane ☎ (043 277) 391
11 (11.30 winter)–3; 6 (6.30 winter)–11
Greenalls Davenports Traditional Bitter; Wye Valley Hereford Supreme [H]
Derives its name from the old ferry across the Wye. Very traditional public and simple lounge with separate children's room. Frequented by local villagers. ♨ 🐎 ❁ 🛏 ◖ ◗ ⊟ ♣ P

Green Man Inn
Main Road (B4224)
☎ (043 277) 243
11–2.30; 6–11
Hook Norton Best Bitter; Marston's Pedigree Bitter; Samuel Smith OBB [H]
Attractive, 500 year-old coaching inn of much character with links to the Civil War. Pub residents can enjoy fishing rights on the Wye. Good value food and beer. Separate restaurant. ♨ Q ❁ 🛏 ◖ ◗ 🍎 P

Garway

Garway Moon
OS465227 ☎ (060 084) 270
12–2.30 (may vary); 6–11
Adnams Broadside; Gale's BBB [H]
Enthusiastically-run pub near the Welsh border, overlooking village green. Handy for local cricket teams. Odd selection of beers for the locale (may vary week by week).
🐎 ❁ 🛏 ◖ ◗ ⛺ ♣ P

Great Malvern

Royal Malvern Hotel
Graham Road
☎ (0684) 563411
10.30–2.30; 6–11
Wood Special Bitter [H]
Town-centre hotel bar, handy for the Winter Gardens. Has a fading Bavarian air!
Q 🐎 🛏 ◖ ◗ ≢

Try also: Retired Soldier (Marston's)

Hagley

Spencers Arms
Kidderminster Road (A456)
☎ (0562) 886448
11–2.30; 6–11
Banks's Mild, Bitter [E]
Relaxing, modern roadside inn, offering a varied lunch menu. Two comfortable lounges.
♨ ❁ ◖ P

Station
Worcester Road (200 yds from A456 jct) ☎ (0562) 882549
11–11
Banks's Mild, Bitter [E]
Very smart pub in centre of a busy village. Railway theme and old photos of the village; leaded glass above the bar and a fine wood fireplace. ❁ ◖ ≢ P

Hallow

Crown Inn
Tenbury Road (A443)
OS826584 ☎ (0905) 640408
11–2.30; 6–11
Younger Scotch, IPA, No. 3 [H]
Large pub with carvery-restaurant and extensive garden.
♨ ❁ ◖ ◗ P

Hanley Castle

Three Kings
Off B4211 ☎ (068 46) 2686
11–2.30; 7–11
Butcombe Bitter; Theakston Best Bitter; Wadworth 6X [H]
Traditional, multi-roomed, village pub, next to church. A real gem; not to be missed. No eve meals Sun.
♨ Q 🐎 ❁ 🛏 ◖ ◗ ⊟

Headless Cross

Gate Hangs Well
Evesham Road
☎ (0527) 401293
12–3; 5.30–11 (12–11 Sat)
Ansells Mild, Bitter [H]
One-roomed, traditional local. Good atmosphere; gets crowded. ♨ ❁ ◖ ♣

Seven Stars
75 Birchfield Road
☎ (0527) 402138
12–11
Ruddles Best Bitter, County; Webster's Yorkshire Bitter [H]
Locals' pub with public bar, lounge and adjoining games room. Excellent value lunches.
Q ◖ ⊟ 🍎

Hereford

Barrels
69 St Owen's Street
☎ (0432) 274968
11–2.30 (4 Wed & Thu); 5–11 (11–11 Fri & Sat)
Wye Valley Hereford Bitter, HPA, Hereford Supreme, Brew 69 [H]
Brash and lively pub, popular with the locals, on edge of city centre. Home of the Wye Valley Brewery and venue for the annual Hereford Beer Festival (August). Loud live music Sat night. Bar football. ⊟ ≢ ♣ 🍎

Lichfield Vaults
Church Street
☎ (0432) 267994
11–2.30; 6–11 (11–11 Sat, closed Sun)
Ind Coope Burton Ale; Tetley Bitter [H]
Located in an historic thoroughfare, 200 yards from the cathedral. Pleasant, wood-panelled front bar and livelier back bar. Popular with tourists and shoppers by day, and with the younger crowd at night. Outdoor drinking in back yard.
❁ ◖ ♿ ≢ ♣

Oxford Arms Hotel
111 Widemarsh Street (400 yds N of ring road)
☎ (0432) 265892
11–2.30; 6.30–11 (11–11 Fri & Sat)
Marston's Pedigree Bitter; Whitbread WCPA, Flowers Original [H]
Bright and lively public bar; sedate, flock-wallpapered lounge. Convenient for the football ground. Q ⊛ ◖ ⊞ ≠ ♣

Vaga Tavern
Vaga Street, Hunderton
☎ (0432) 273601
11.30–3; 5.30–11 (11–11 Sat)
Banks's Mild, Bitter [E]
Estate pub that predates the estate by a few decades. Club-type, 'plush' lounge and straightforward public. One of only four Banks's pubs in Whitbread-dominated Hereford.
⊞ ♣ P

Himbleton

Galton Arms
OS943586 ☎ (090 569) 672
12–2.30; 6–11
Banks's Mild, Bitter [H]
Cosy and welcoming village pub in beautiful surroundings. No lunches Mon.
⌂ Q ♘ ⊛ ◖ ◗ ⊞ ♿

Kerne Bridge

Kerne Bridge Inn
On B4228 at B4229 jct
☎ (0600) 890495
12–2.30; 7–11 (11–3; 6.30–11 (11–11 Sat) in summer)
Theakston Best Bitter; Wye Valley Hereford Bitter [H]
Value-for-money free house on bank of the River Wye. The stone facade conceals a friendly and straightforward pub. Guest beers. ⊛ 🛏 ◖ ◗ ⊞ ♣ ○ P

Kidderminster

Little Tumbling Sailors
Mill Lane (off ring road, A442)
☎ (0562) 747527
11–3; 5.30–11
Ansells Bitter; Ind Coope Burton Ale; Lumphammer [H]
Nautical-themed hostelry of the Little Pub Co., complete with land-locked lighthouse and wave machine! Noted for its seafood pies. Children's menu available. Q ⊛ ◖ ◗ ♣

Railway Train
Offmore Road (off A448)
☎ (0562) 740465
11–2.30; 6–11
M&B Highgate Mild, Brew XI [E]
A locals' pub where one can feel at ease in the games-oriented bar or small cosy snug. Beware – the Springfield is keg!
⌂ ⊛ ⊞ ≠ ♣

Station
Farfield (off A448)
☎ (0562) 822764
11–2.30; 6–11
Greenalls Davenports Traditional Bitter [H]
Excellent local near the station and Severn Valley Railway. Family room at rear also offers games facilities.
Q ♘ ⊛ ◖ ◗ ≠ ♣ ○ P

Yew Tree
Chester Road North (A449)
☎ (0562) 751786
11–3; 5.30–11
Banks's Mild, Bitter [E]
Friendly local opposite the Rose Theatre, with a lively bar and cosy, smart lounge. Large garden; barbecues in summer.
Q ⊛ ⊞ ♣ P

Kington

Royal Oak Hotel
Church Street
☎ (0544) 230484
11–3; 5.30–11
Marston's Burton Best Bitter; Pedigree Bitter [H]
First and last pub in England. Popular with pub game enthusiasts. Good, plain cooking. ⌂ ⊛ 🛏 ◖ ◗ ⊞ ▲ ♣ P

Swan Hotel
Church Street (A44)
☎ (0544) 230510
11–2.30; 6.30–11
Ansells Best Bitter; Ind Coope Burton Ale [H]
Large, single lounge bar, punctuated by original stone fireplace. Reasonably-priced food with good vegetarian selection. Splendid 17th-century restaurant predates the pub. No Sun eve meals in winter.
⌂ 🛏 ◖ ◗

Leominster

Black Horse
74 South Street (old A49)
☎ (0568) 611946
11–2.30; 6–11 (11–11 Sat)
Theakston Best Bitter; Wadworth 6X [H]
Traditional, two-bar local with dining area at rear. Live music Sun nights. Two guest beers per week. ⊛ ◖ ◗ ⊞ ♿ ≠ ♣ P

Grapes Vaults
Broad Street
☎ (0568) 611404
11–2.30; 6–11
Marston's Burton Best Bitter, Pedigree Bitter, Merrie Monk [H]
Well-run, superbly-restored town free house with real character. On-street parking outside. Meals until 9pm.
⌂ Q ◖ ◗ ≠

Greyhound
Rainbow Street
☎ (0568) 2901
12–3; 7–11 (may vary Sat)
Brains SA; Theakston Best Bitter; Younger Scotch [H]
Busy, town-centre free house with two bars. Guest beers.
⊛ ◖ ◗ ⊞ ♿ ≠ ♣ P

Letton

Swan Inn
On A438 ☎ (054 46) 304
11–3; 6–11 (11–11 Wed–Sat)
Draught Bass; Butcombe Bitter [H]
Rejuvenated roadside free house with a basic, but cosy public and a lounge, making a successful recovery from attempted brewery destruction! Food always available. Camping in pub grounds.
⌂ ⊛ ◖ ◗ ⊞ ♿ ▲ ♣ P

Malvern Link

Bakery Inn
Worcester Road
☎ (0684) 572201
11–2.30; 5.30–11
Marston's Burton Best Bitter, Pedigree Bitter [H]
Large, busy, two-bar town pub, popular with the younger set.
◖ ⊞ ≠ P

Much Dewchurch

Black Swan
On B4348 ☎ (0981) 540295
11–2.30; 6–11
Banks's Bitter [E]**; Buckley's Best Bitter** [H]
14th-century inn that claims to be one of the oldest in the county. Unusual bar layout serves a comfortable lounge and a spartan public. Shove-ha'penny played. Campsite is a mile away. Regular guest beers.
⌂ ⊛ ◖ ◗ ▲ ♣ P

Newbridge Green

Drum & Monkey
Newbridge Green (B4211)
☎ (0684) 62238
11–2.30; 5–11
Banks's Mild, Bitter; Donnington BB, SBA; Wadworth 6X [H]
Busy country pub; separate restaurant in barn.
Q ♘ ⊛ ◖ ◗ ♿ P

Try also: Plough, Longdon (Free)

Norton

Norton Grange Hotel
At A435/A439 jct
☎ (0386) 870215
11–3; 6 (7 winter)–11
Marston's Burton Best Bitter, Pedigree Bitter [H]
A family-run hotel, conveniently situated on the

main road. Pleasant garden is set back. Restaurant caters for children. ⌂ ❀ ⊨ ◖ ◗ ⛺ ♣ P

Pensax

Bell
On B4202 ☎ (0299) 896677
11–2.30; 7–11 (may vary in summer)
Hook Norton Best Bitter; Taylor Landlord; Wood Parish Bitter 🄷
Traditional snug and coal stove-heated bar. Cosy dining room serves recommended food (Sun lunch is a speciality); vegetarians and children catered for. Guest beers.
⌂ Q ❀ ◖ ◗ ⊟ ♣ P

Pershore

Millers Arms
Bridge Street
☎ (0386) 553864
12–3; 7–11
Adnams Broadside; Wadworth 6X 🄷
Comfortable and relaxed market town pub with an unspoilt, traditional appearance. Eve meals in summer only.
⌂ ❀ ◖ ◗ ⊟ ⛺

Prior's Frome

Yew Tree Inn
Off A438 OS576390
☎ (0432) 850467
12–2.30 (4 Sat); 5.30 (6.30 Sat)–11
Courage Directors; Marston's Pedigree Bitter; Ruddles Best Bitter; John Smith's Bitter 🄷
Village local, recently enhanced by traditional-style restoration. Stunning views over river valley from patio/garden. Restaurant downstairs.
⌂ ❀ ◖ ◗ ⊟ ♿ ♣ P

Romsley

Manchester Inn
Bromsgrove Road OS964779
☎ (0562) 710242
11–3; 5.30–11
M&B Highgate Mild, Brew XI 🄴
Roadside pub next to the North Worcestershire Path, with a homely public bar and a larger, comfortable lounge. A good summertime pub with a sizeable garden. No eve meals Sun.
⌂ ❀ ◖ ◗ ⊟ ♿ ♣ P

St Owen's Cross

New Inn
At A4137/B4521 jct
☎ (098 987) 274
12–2.30; 5.30–11
Draught Bass; Courage Directors; Smiles Best Bitter 🄷
Isolated 16th-century free house, complete with settles, benches and grand fireplaces. The unusual pewter beer engines originally came from a bar in Ross-on-Wye. Accommodation comprises four-poster beds, plus a caravan site. Separate restaurant/bar. Occasional guest beers.
⌂ ❀ ⊨ ◖ ◗ ⛺ P

Shenstone

Plough Inn
Off A450/A448 OS863735
☎ (056 283) 340
11–3; 7–10.30 (11 Fri & Sat)
Batham Best Bitter 🄷
Large public bar and two small snugs. This country pub is hard to find, but worth the effort.
⌂ Q ❀ ⊟ ♣ ○ P

Spetchley

Berkeley Arms
Evesham Road, Egdon (B4084) ☎ (090 565) 269
11–2.30; 6–11
Ind Coope Burton Ale; Tetley Bitter 🄷
Large roadside inn; very popular. Serves excellent food.
⌂ ❀ ◖ ◗ ♿ P

Staunton on Wye

New Inn
Off A438 ☎ (098 17) 346
12–2 (not Mon in winter); 7–11 (11.30–3; 6.30–11 summer)
Theakston Best Bitter; Younger IPA 🄷
Friendly free house, with youth hostel nearby. Comfortable lounge and public bar with separate dining area.
⌂ Q ❀ ⊟ ♿ ♣ P

Stoke Works

Boat & Railway
Shaw Lane ☎ (0527) 31065
11–2.30; 5.30–11
Banks's Bitter; Hanson's Mild Ale 🄴
Busy, canalside village local with patio drinking area and skittle alley with a bar. A good place to go after the Tardebigge Flight of locks. ⌂ ❀ ◖ ♣

Stourport

Hope & Anchor
18 New Street
☎ (029 93) 4684
11.30–3; 6–11 (may extend in summer)
Ansells Mild, Bitter 🄷
Basic bar with pool table and darts. Wooden bench furniture in traditional lounge/dining room (ask landlord to allow children in here). A short stroll from the river. ⌂ ◖ ◗ ♣

Rising Sun
50 Lombard Street
☎ (029 93) 2530
10.30–11
Banks's Mild Ale, Bitter 🄷
Refurbished friendly local. Good range of meals served (Tue–Sat). Tiny traditional bar; pleasant, canalside patio. Free parking two minutes' walk away.
Q ❀ ◖ ◗ ⊟ ♣

Rock Tavern
Wilden Lane (off Hartlebury Road) ☎ (029 93) 2962
11–2.30; 5.30–11
Banks's Mild, Bitter 🄴**; Batham Best Bitter** 🄷
Friendly, beamed local, offering an occasional guest beer. ⌂ ♣ P

Symonds Yat West

Olde Ferrie Inne
Down narrow lane at end of B4164 ☎ (0600) 890232
11–3; 6–11 (11–11 Sat & summer)
Courage Directors; John Smith's Bitter 🄷
Overlooking the scenic River Wye, a pub popular with tourists in summer (parking can be a problem). Large lounge, basic games room and separate restaurant. At least one guest beer. ⌂ ❀ ⊨ ◖ ◗ ⛺ ♣ P

Ullingswick

Three Crowns
1 mile off A417 (½ mile E of village) OS605497
☎ (0432) 820279
12–2.30 (3.30 Sat); 7–11
Ansells Bitter; Ind Coope Burton Ale; Tetley Bitter 🄷
Remote, but popular free house that has a very traditional atmosphere. A central, hop-garlanded bar divides two drinking areas. Tiled floor; dark, scrubbed-wood furniture.
⌂ Q ❀ ◖ ◗ ⛺ P

Uphampton

Fruiterers Arms
Off A449
OS839649 ☎ (0905) 820462
12–2.30; 7–11
Donnington BB 🄷
Rural pub to the north of Ombersley. Worth seeking out.
⌂ ❀ ◖ ⊟ P

Upton upon Severn

Little Upton Muggery
58 Old Street
☎ (068 46) 3620
11–3; 6–11
Ind Coope Burton Ale; Lumphammer 🄷
Friendly pub in small riverside town. Part of the Little Pub Co. chain, decorated on the theme of mugs! Good menu.
⌂ ❀ ◖ ◗ ⊟ ♿ ⛺

Wadborough

Masons Arms
Station Road (off A44)

OS899475 ☎ (0905) 840524
11.30–2.30; 6–11
Banks's Mild, Bitter [E]
Warm, cosy and well-kept village pub with consistently good beer. Only pub for miles with a separate public bar. No eve meals Sun. Q ❀ ( ) ⊞ P

West Malvern

Brewers Arms
On B4232 (then footpath)
11–3; 6–11
Marston's Burton Best Bitter, Pedigree Bitter, Merrie Monk, Owd Rodger (winter) [H]
Small, friendly, homely pub, half a mile from Worcester Beacon (the highest point of the Malvern Hills). Ideally situated for a lunchtime break. Many folk evenings. ♨ Q ❀ ( ) ⊞

Whitbourne

Live & Let Live
OS719366 ☎ (0886) 21016
11–2.30; 6–11
Marston's Burton Best Bitter [H]
Friendly, 16th-century, half-timbered house, just off the main road. ♨ Q ❀ ( ) ⊞ ♣ P

Whitney-on-Wye

Rhydspence Inn
On A438, $1\frac{1}{2}$ miles W of village
☎ (049 73) 262
11–2.30; 7–11
Marston's Pedigree Bitter; Robinson's Best Bitter [H]
The Welsh border cuts through this 14th-century drovers' inn. Splendid main entrance and many intriguing, original features. Very much a pub for the connoisseur – perhaps prices reflect this. *À la carte* restaurant. Quoits. ♨ Q ❀ ⊨ ( ) ⌂ P

Woolhope

Butchers Arms
$\frac{1}{3}$ mile W of village on Putley road OS618358
☎ (0432) 820281
11.30–2.30; 7 (6 summer)–11
Hook Norton Best Bitter, Old Hookey; Marston's Pedigree Bitter [H]
Ancient, isolated free house that almost achieves the impossible – a mix of food and drink, but still surroundings of superb character: real fires, latch doors and very low beams. Good value food (restaurant).
♨ Q ❀ ( ) ♿ P

Try also: Crown Inn (Free)

Worcester

Bridge Inn
Lowesmoor Terrace
☎ (0905) 23980
11–2.30; 5.30–11
Draught Bass; M&B Mild, Brew XI [H]
Down-to-earth, basic local near canal and Lowesmoor Wharf.
(⊞ ⇌ (Shrub Hill)

Crown & Anchor
233 Hylton Road, St Johns
☎ (0905) 421481
11–2.30; 5.30–11
Marston's Burton Best Bitter, Pedigree Bitter, Merrie Monk [H]
Busy, riverside pub, recently extended. Locals in public bar; students in the other. Skittle alley has its own bar. ⛀ ❀ ⊞ ⌂

Dragon
The Tything ☎ (0905) 25845
11–11
Hook Norton Best Bitter [H]
Lively, one-roomed pub near the city centre. Winner of local CAMRA's first Pub of the Year award in 1989. Up to four guest beers.
❀ (⊞ ⇌ (Foregate St) ⌂

Farriers Arms
9 Fish Street ☎ (0905) 27569
11–11
Courage Best Bitter, Directors [H]
Popular hostelry in quiet side-street off pedestrianised high street, near the cathedral. Quiet, olde-worlde lounge; large, basic bar which can get crowded in evenings, mainly with students. Good selection of food.
Q ❀ ( ) ⊞ ⇌ (Foregate St) P

Jolly Roger Brewery & Tap
50 Lowesmoor
☎ (0905) 21540
11–11
Jolly Roger Quaff Ale, Severn Bore Special, Old Lowesmoor [H], **Winter Wobbler** [H] & [G]
Worcester's only brewery, with the brewing visible from the bar. Lively pub with a wide range of customers. Frequent live R & B bands. Range of guest beers, plus various special brews. No food Sun. (⇌ (Foregate St/Shrub Hill) ⌂ P

Little Sauce Factory
55 London Road
☎ (0905) 350159
11–3; 6–11
Ind Coope Burton Ale; Lumphammer [H]
Unique decor as befits a member of the Little Pub Co. chain. Entire pub decorated with sauce bottles and impressive tiling (note the ceiling!). Excellent food. Limited parking. ( ) ⊞ P

Severn View Hotel
Newport Street
☎ (0905) 27600
11–2.30; 7–11
Home Mild, Bitter; Theakston XB; Younger IPA, No. 3 [H]
Spacious, riverside hotel next to bus station. 'Pay and display' car park next door.
❀ ⊨ ( ) ⊞ ⇌ (Foregate St)

Swan Inn
81 St Johns ☎ (0905) 421241
11–2.30; 5.30–11
Ansells Mild, Bitter [H]; **Banks's Bitter** [E]
Basic, L-shaped pub amongst shops in a mainly residential area of Worcester. Pool table and darts. ❀ (⊞ ♣

Hertfordshire

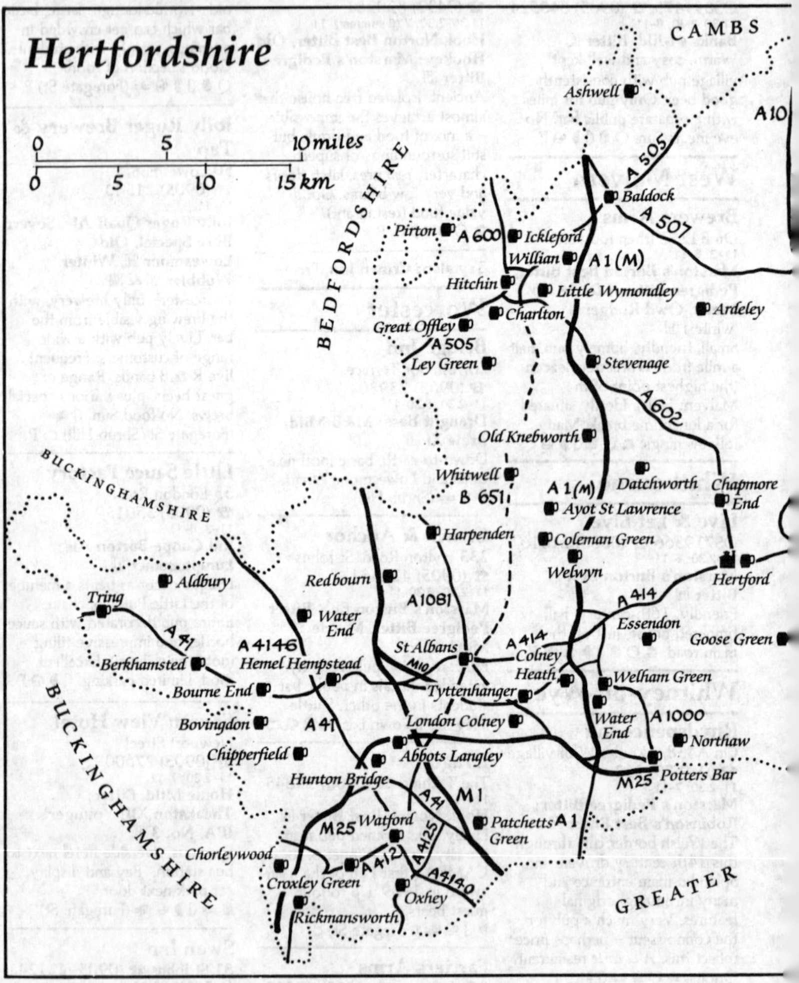

McMullen, Hertford

Abbots Langley

Swan
College Road (next to Leavesden Hospital)
☎ (0923) 672539
11–11
Greene King XX Dark, IPA, Abbot Ale H
Friendly two-bar pub. Basic games public bar and comfortable lounge. P

Aldbury

Greyhound
19 Stocks Road OS966125
☎ (044 285) 228
10.30–2.30; 5.30–11 (10–11 Sat)
Benskins Best Bitter H
Attractive pub in centre of picturesque village. Recent renovation has not spoilt it. Restaurant at rear (no eve meals Sun/Mon). Two guest beers.
Q

Ardeley

Jolly Waggoner
1 mile off B1037 OS310272
☎ (0438) 86350
11.30–3; 6–11
Greene King IPA, Abbot Ale G
Picturesque, pink-washed former cottages in charming village setting. Two small intimate bars.
Q P

Ashwell

Rose & Crown
69 High Street OS268396
☎ (046 274) 2420
10.30–2.30 (12–2 Sun); 6–11
Greene King IPA, Abbot Ale H
Unspoilt late 15th-century timber-framed village pub. Excellent variety of good, wholesome food includes children's dishes.
Q P

Ayot St Lawrence

Brocket Arms
Shaws Corner OS196168
☎ (0438) 820250
11–2.30; 7–11
Greene King IPA, Abbot Ale; Marston's Pedigree Bitter; Wadworth 6X H
14th-century building with

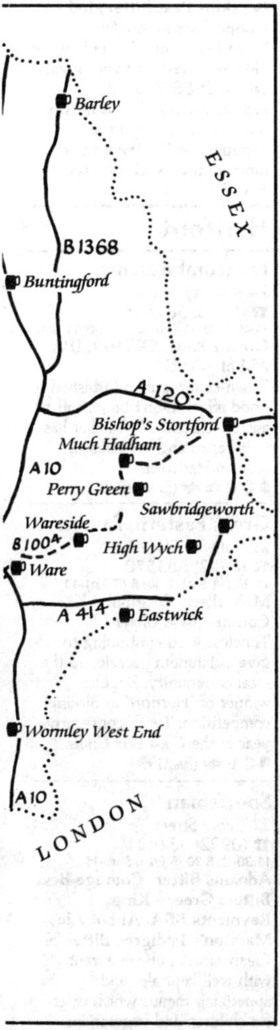

inglenooks and a walled garden. Near GB Shaw's house. Can be very busy in summer and bank holidays; best visited off peak. ⌂ ❀ ⌂ ◐ ◑ ◌

Baldock

Engine
Station Road (A507)
11–2.30; 6–11
Greene King XX Dark, IPA, Abbot Ale H
Basic bar, comfortable lounge. ◐ ⊟ ≠ P

Try also: White Hart (Greene King)

Barley

Fox & Hounds
High Street, (B1368)
☎ (076384) 459
12–2.30; 6–11
Barley Old Dragon, Flamethrower; Brakspear Bitter; Marston's Pedigree Bitter; Wadworth 6X; Whitbread Flowers IPA H
Lively and seemingly chaotic village local with informal restaurant. Extended 17th-century building with rare gallows sign spanning side road and own brewery. Ale selection on eight pumps varies constantly. ⌂ ❀ ◐ ◑ ♣ ◌ P

Berkhamsted

Boat
Gravel Path, Ravens Lane (off A41) ☎ (0442) 877152
11–3; 5.30–11
Fuller's Chiswick Bitter, London Pride, ESB H
Completely rebuilt after years of closure, this pub offers a warm welcome and shows that new pubs can be attractive. Large canalside patio. Summer barbecues Fri/Sat eve and Sun lunch. ❀ ◐ ≠ ♣ P

Rising Sun
George Street (next to lock 55 on Grand Union Canal)
☎ (0442) 864913
11–3; 6–11
Benskins Best Bitter H
Quiet canalside local which is hard to find because it has no road frontage. Pub faces a lock on the Grand Union Canal so could be perilous for the over-indulgent. ❀ ◐ ◑ ≠ ♣

Bishop's Stortford

Fox
74 Rye Street (B184)
☎ (0279) 651623
11–2.30 (4 Sat); 5.30 (6 Sat)–11
Courage Best Bitter, Directors; Greene King IPA, Rayments BBA, Abbot Ale; Mauldons Squires H
Old village-type pub dating from circa 1730. No carpets; old block floor in saloon. No music, jukebox or bandits. Bar meals include ploughmans, curries, pasta and kebabs. ⌂ Q ❀ ◐ ◑ ⊟ ≠ ♣ P

Try also: Wheatsheaf, Rye Street (Greene King)

Bourne End

Anchor
London Road (A41)
☎ (0442) 866220
11–2.30; 6.30–11
Benskins Best Bitter; Ind Coope Burton Ale H
Old roadside inn which remains unspoilt. Large collection of sewing machine treadles in bar. Shut the Box played. ⌂ ❀ ◐ ◑ ♿ ♣ P

Bovingdon

Bull
1 Chipperfield Road (off B4505) ☎ (0442) 832173
11–2.30 (4 Sat); 6–11
Benskins Best Bitter; Ind Coope Burton Ale H
Two-bar village pub which holds an annual darts match with a pub in Scotland. Wide-ranging clientele – not a youngsters' pub. Guest beer. Q ❀ ◐ ♿ ♣ P

Buntingford

Crown
17 High Street (off A10)
☎ (0763) 71422
11–2.30 (4 Mon); 5.30–11
Banks & Taylor Shefford Bitter; Draught Bass; Greene King IPA; Mauldons Squires H
Splendid, one-bar, small town pub. Weekly guest beer. ⌂ ❀ ◐

Chapmore End

Woodman
30 Chapmore End (off B158) OS328163 ☎ (0920) 463143
12–3; 6–11
Greene King IPA, Abbot Ale G
Unspoilt pub in agricultural hamlet. Back garden soon to feature activity centre and organic vegetables! XX Dark often available. ⌂ Q ❀ ⊟ ♣

Charlton

Windmill
Charlton Road (1 mile from Hitchin town centre)
☎ (0462) 32016
11–2.30; 6–11
Adnams Broadside; Charles Wells Eagle Bitter H
Village pub with pleasant atmosphere. Peacock in residence and a large number of ducks on the stream adjoining the lawn. No food Sun. Q ❀ ◐ ◑ P

Chipperfield

Royal Oak
1 The Street
12–3 (2.30 Sat); 6 (6.30 Sat)–11
Benskins Best Bitter; Friary Meux Best Bitter H**; Ind Coope Burton Ale** G
Smart, friendly pub in attractive village. Good home-made lunches (not Sun). Shut the Box played. ⌂ Q ❀ ◐ ♿ ♣ P

Chorleywood

Old Shepherd
Chorleywood Bottom (corner of common) OS029958
☎ (09278) 2740
11–3; 5.30–11
Benskins Best Bitter; Ind Coope Burton Ale; Tetley

Hertfordshire

Bitter Ⓗ
Small and friendly. Thomas the Tank Engine fans will like it, as will cat lovers. No meals Wed eve. ☋ ❀ ◖ ◗ ⇌ ⊖ ♣ P

Coleman Green

John Bunyan
1 mile off B6129/B651 near Wheathampstead OS189128
☎ (058 283) 2037
11–2.30 (3 Sat); 6–11
McMullen Original AK, Country Best Bitter Ⓗ
Isolated pub well worth pilgrims progressing to. Good, reasonably-priced fast food. Large beer garden with plenty of room for children to play. John Bunyan did *not* hide in the well in front of the pub.
⌂ Q ❀ ◖ ◗ ♿ P

Colney Heath

Crooked Billet
88 High Street (400 yds off A414) ☎ (0727) 22128
11–11
Fuller's ESB; Greene King Abbot Ale; Whitbread Wethered Bitter Ⓗ
Cottage-style pub with two bars. Doubles up as a book exchange. Mini-zoo in garden. Barbecue summer eves. At least two guest beers.
❀ ◖ ⊞ ♿ ▲ ♣ ○ P

Croxley Green

Sportsman
2 Scot's Hill (A412)
☎ (0923) 773021
11–3; 5.30–11
Benskins Best Bitter; Ind Coope Burton Ale; Tetley Bitter Ⓗ
Welcoming and comfortable local next to village green. Sporting connections include four darts teams, bar billiards and occasional parachute jumping. No food at weekends.
❀ ◖ ♿ ⊖ (Croxley) ♣ P

Datchworth

Plough
5 Datchworth Green (off A602, 2 miles from Watton) OS269182 ☎ (0438) 813000
11.30–2.30 (3 Sat); 6–11
Greene King XX Dark, IPA, Abbot Ale Ⓗ
Small village local with one cosy bar. ⌂ Q ❀ ◖ P

Eastwick

Lion
Off A414, 1 mile from Harlow
☎ (0279) 23213
10.30–4 (12–2.30 Sun); 5.30–11
McMullen Original AK, Country Best Bitter Ⓗ & Ⓔ
Friendly village local of character; worth a trip. Live music Sun eve. Good value, home-cooked food.
⌂ Q ❀ ◖ ⊞ ♣ P

Essendon

Candlestick
West End (off B158)
OS262083 ☎ (0707) 261322
11–2.30; 5.30–11
McMullen Original AK, Country Best Bitter Ⓗ
Friendly pub near Hatfield House estate. Comfortable lounge bar, plus darts and doms public bar. Pub name derived from its nickname when the landlord used to leave his customers in the dark, taking the single candlestick into the cellar – there are now over 200 of them in the lounge bar. Book eve meals (Tue–Fri).
⌂ Q ❀ ◖ ◗ ⊞ ♣ P

Goose Green

Huntsman
Lord Street ($1\frac{1}{2}$ miles from Hoddesdon) ☎ (0992) 443294
11–2.30; 6–11
Courage Directors; Greene King Abbot Ale; Mauldons Squires, Suffolk Punch; Tetley Bitter Ⓗ
Off the beaten track and worth seeking out; transformed over the past two years and now rightly popular. One and a half acres of gardens where you can share a pint with pigs, a goat, a pony and ducks. ◖ ◗ P

Great Offley

Bull
High Street (off A505)
11–2.30; 6–11
Fuller's Chiswick Bitter, London Pride, ESB Ⓗ
Straightforward village local, surrounded by eating places. King Offa of Mercia died at Great Offley. Q ⊞ ♣ P

Harpenden

Silver Cup
St Albans Road (A1081)
☎ (0582) 713094/764694
11–2.30; 5.30–11
Charles Wells Eagle Bitter, Bombardier Ⓗ
Old pub named after a horse-race run on the nearby common. Boisterous public but more sedate saloon. Outside tables overlook the common. Home-made lunches (not Sun).
❀ ◖ ⊞ ⇌ ♣ P

Hemel Hempstead

Old Bell
51 High Street
☎ (0442) 52867
10.30–2.30; 6 (7 Sat)–11
Benskins Best Bitter; Ind Coope Burton Ale Ⓗ
Immaculate multi-bar pub in the old town. Restored with great care in 1988. Food at lunchtimes (not Sun) is mostly home-made. Many local societies meet in the upstairs function rooms. Guest beer.
☋ ◖ P

Hertford

Duncombe Arms
24 Railway Street
☎ (0992) 581445
11–3; 5.30–11 (10.30–4; 6.30–11 Sat)
Greene King XX Dark, IPA, Abbot Ale Ⓔ
Town-centre pub, refurbished to good effect. Don't be put off by austere exterior. Public bar has only remaining bar billiards table in Hertford.
❀ ◖ ⊞ ♿ ⇌ (East) ♣ P

Great Eastern Tavern
29 Railway Place
☎ (0992) 583570
11.30 (11 Sat)–2.30; 6 (7 Sat)–11
McMullens Original AK, Country Best Bitter Ⓗ
Timeless local continuing to give outstanding service to the local community. Regular winner of 'Hertford in Bloom' competition. Tenth consecutive year in the *Good Beer Guide.*
❀ ◖ ⊞ ⇌ (East) ♣

Sportsman
117 Fore Street
☎ (0992) 551621
11.30–3; 5.30 (5 Fri, 6 Sat)–11
Adnams Bitter; Courage Best Bitter; Greene King Rayments BBA, Abbot Ale; Marston's Pedigree Bitter Ⓗ
Clean, smart pub-restaurant with well-kept ales and appetizing menus which cater for children and vegetarians.
◖ ◗ ⇌ (East)

White Horse
33 Castle Street
☎ (0992) 550127
12–2 (3 Sat); 5.30 (7 Sat)–11
Greene King IPA; Marston's Pedigree Bitter Ⓗ
A rare genuine free house, welcoming in every way. Ever-changing range of guest ales direct from the cask. Continues to attract locals and other connoisseurs from far and wide. Full range of country wines available. Meals Mon-Fri.
⌂ Q ❀ ◖ ⊞ ⇌ (North) ○

Try also: Millstream

High Wych

Rising Sun
1 mile W of A1184 and Sawbridgeworth
☎ (0279) 724099
12 (11 Sat)–3; 5 (5.30 Mon–Thu)–11

Courage Best Bitter, Directors [G]
Unspoilt traditional pub, run by same family for over 60 years known locally as 'Sid's'. Beer served straight from cask. Guest beers planned. ⌂ Q ⚭ ♣ P

Hitchin

Cock Hotel
High Street ☎ (0462) 434673
11–3; 6–11 (closed Sun)
Greene King IPA, Abbot Ale [H]
16th-century inn, still retaining much of its original character. There has been an inn on the site since medieval times. A pleasant quiet pub, with a divided drinking area.
⌓ ☾ ♿ ♣ P

Hunton Bridge

Kings Head
Bridge Road (off A41, S of M25 jct 20)
☎ (0923) 262307
11–3; 5.30–11 (11–11 summer)
Benskins Best Bitter; Ind Coope Burton Ale; Tetley Bitter [H]
Comfortable one-bar pub with gallery. Large garden backs on to Grand Union Canal. Old canal stables are due to be converted into children's facilities. ⚘ ☾ ◗ P

Ickleford

Cricketers
107 Arlesey Road (off A600)
☎ (0462) 432629
11–3 (4 Thu & Fri); 6–11 (11–11 Sat)
Adnams Bitter; Banks & Taylor Shefford Bitter, SOD; Tetley Bitter [H]
Lively village alehouse. Very independent – specialises in guest beers, often at least eight available, some on gravity. Shut the Box played. No food Sun.
⚘ ⌓ ☾ ♣ ⊖ P

Old George
Arlesey Road (off A600)
☎ (0462) 432269
11–3; 5.30–11 (11–11 Sat)
Greene King IPA, Abbot Ale [H]
Old country pub with a warm and friendly lounge and an extremely basic bar.
⌂ Q ⚘ ☾ ⊞ ♣ P

Ley Green

Plough
Plough Lane, Kings Walden (2 miles S of Great Offley off A505) OS162243
11–11 (11–2.30 Mon)
Greene King IPA, Abbot Ale [H]
Quiet friendly pub with set of wildlife prints. Collection of animals traps and fox heads on walls. No food Sun. ⚘ ☾ ◗ ⊞ P

Little Wymondley

Bucks Head
Stevenage Road (A602)
☎ (0438) 353320
10.30–11
Marston's Pedigree Bitter; Whitbread Boddingtons Bitter, Flowers IPA, Flowers Original [H]
400 year-old pub with many old wooden beams and two fireplaces. Petanque played in beer garden. Good home cooking (not Sun).
⌂ Q ⚭ ⚘ ☾ ♿ ♣ P

London Colney

Bull
Barnet Road (½ mile from M25 jct 22) ☎ (0727) 23160
11–2.30 (3 Fri); 5.30–11 (11–11 Sat)
Ind Coope Burton Ale; Tetley Bitter [H]
16th-century hostelry with contrasting bars: quiet and comfortable lounge; busy public bar with accent on games. Garden includes children's farmyard with real animals. No food Sun. ⌂ Q ⚘ ☾ ⊞ ♣ P

Much Hadham

Bull Inn
High Street (2 miles S of A120)
☎ (027 984) 2668
11.30–2.30; 6–11
Benskins Best Bitter; Greene King IPA; Ind Coope Burton Ale [H]
Large, friendly old village pub with garden. Good food always available, including veg and children's meals.
⌂ Q ⚘ ☾ ◗ ⊞ ♣ ⊖ P

Northaw

Sun
Judges Hill (1 mile NE of Potters Bar) OS279022
☎ (0707) 52727
11–11
Benskins Best Bitter; Ind Coope Burton Ale [H]
Opposite village green and church. Snob screen on split-level bar. ⚘ ☾ ◗ ♣ P

Try also: Two Brewers (Benskins)

Old Knebworth

Lytton Arms
Park Lane (off B197, 1½ miles past station) OS229202
☎ (0438) 812312
11–2.30 (3 Fri & Sat); 5 (6 Sat)–11
Adnams Bitter; Banks & Taylor Shefford Bitter, SOS; Draught Bass; Charrington IPA [H]
Very popular, large country pub near Knebworth Park. Dining area. Range of beers varies and includes Banks & Taylor house ale. ⌂ ⚘ ☾ ◗ ♿ P

Oxhey

Haydon Arms
76 Upper Paddock Road (off A4008) ☎ (0923) 34834
11–11 (11–3; 5.30–11 Mon & Tue)
Benskins Best Bitter; Ind Coope Burton Ale [H]
Cosy, two-bar local in villagey area; friendly locals. Good bar food. Ideal finishing place for an Oxhey pub crawl.
⚘ ☾ ⊞ ⇌ (Bushey) ♣

Rifle Volunteer
36 Villiers Road (off A411)
☎ (0923) 221814
11–3; 5.30–11
Courage Best Bitter, Directors; John Smith's Bitter [H]
Large corner local. Food-oriented at lunchtimes, but very much a locals' drinking place in evenings. ☾ ⇌ (Bushey)

Patchetts Green

Three Compasses
Near A41 ☎ (0923) 856197
11–2.30; 7–11 (11–11 Fri & Sat)
Benskins Best Bitter; Ind Coope Burton Ale; Tetley Bitter; Young's Special [H]
Deceptively large pub in rural surroundings. Conservatory doubles as restaurant. Excellent children's facilities. Display of carpenters' tools. Young's Special alternates with Adnams Bitter and Greene King IPA. No food Sun eve. ⚭ ⚘ ☾ ◗ P

Perry Green

Hoops Inn
4 miles S of A120 from Little Hadham OS439173
☎ (027 984) 3568
11.30–3; 6.30–11
Greene King IPA; McMullen Original AK [H]
Olde worlde country pub with a wealth of oak beams, very comfortable bars and pleasant gardens. Meals are good value for money. ⌂ Q ⚘ ☾ ◗ ⊖ P

Pirton

Cat & Fiddle
Great Green (3 miles NW of Hitchin) ☎ (0462) 712245
11.30–3; 5.30–11
Adnams Broadside; Charles Wells Eagle Bitter, Bombardier [H]
Friendly, beamed, village pub on village green. Interior features wrought ironwork. No food Sun. ⌂ ⚘ ☾ ◗

Hertfordshire

Potters Bar

Chequers
Coopers Lane
☎ (0707) 56469
11–11
Courage Best Bitter, Directors ⊞
Comfortable local. Caution needed on leaving the car park. Eve meals finish early.
Q ❀ ◖ ◗ ♣ P

Redbourn

Cricketers
East Common
☎ (058 285) 2410
11–2.30; 5.30–11
Benskins Best Bitter; Tetley Bitter ⊞
Village pub by the common. Lounge bar presided over by an African Grey parrot. Food available most open hours except Sun (veg option).
◖ ◗ ⊟ ♿ ♣ P

Rickmansworth

Halfway House
91 Uxbridge Road (A412 SW of centre) ☎ (0923) 772534
11–3; 5.30–11
Courage Best Bitter, Directors ⊞
Comfortable pub with improved garden and children's play area fronting River Colne. Extension planned not to interfere with existing character of bar. No food Sun. ⌂ ❀ ◖ ⇌ ⊖ ♣ P

St Albans

Farriers Arms
Lower Dagnall Street
☎ (0727) 51025
11–2.30; 5.30 (7 Sat)–11
McMullen Original AK, Country Best Bitter ⊞
A proper no-frills drinking establishment. Parking can be difficult. Shove-ha'penny and bridge played. Q ⊟ ♣

Goat
37 Sopwell Lane (off A5183 opp. abbey) ☎ (0727) 833934
11–3; 5.30–11
Greene King IPA, Abbot Ale; Hook Norton Best Bitter, Old Hookey; Marston's Pedigree Bitter; Wadworth 6X ⊞
500 year-old pub with central bar and separate seating areas. Children welcome in dining area (own menu). Jazz band on Sun lunchtimes. Very busy at weekends. Two real fire places.
⌂ ❀ ◖ ◗ ⇌ (Abbey)

Rose & Crown
St Michaels Street (opp. Verulamium Park entrance)
11.15–2.30; 5.30–11
Benskins Best Bitter; Ind Coope Burton Ale; Tetley Bitter ⊞
Fine old oak-beamed pub with inglenook, nice old furniture and bric-a-brac. Recommended lunches, with excellent veg choice. Ciders and country wines. Limited parking.
⌂ ❀ ◖ ♣ ⇔ P

White Lion
Sopwell Lane (off A5183 opp. abbey) ☎ (0727) 50540
11–3; 6 (5.30 Fri)–11 (11–11 Sat)
Adnams Bitter; Friary Meux Best Bitter; Ind Coope Burton Ale; Tetley Bitter ⊞
Historic, friendly, two-bar pub; boule pitch and backgammon. Good food; guest beers.
Q ❀ ◖ ◗ ⇌ (Abbey) ♣

Try also: Blue Anchor (McMullen)

Sawbridgeworth

King William IV
2 Vantorts Road
☎ (0279) 722322
11–11
Courage Best Bitter, Directors ⊞
Old-worlde coaching inn – the oldest in town. Set back from main road in quiet back-street by church. Full of beams and pictures. ⌂ Q ❀ ◖ ◗ ⊟ ⇌ ♣ ⇔

Market House Hotel
42 Knight Street (off Bell Street)
☎ (0279) 722807
11–3; 5.30–11
Adnams Bitter, Old; Greene King Abbot Ale; Wadworth 6X ⊞
16th-century inn with beamed inglenook. No fruit machines. Good food always available (including veg and children's meals). Guest beers planned.
⌂ Q ⊶ ◖ ◗ ⇌ P

Stevenage

Marquis of Lorne
132 High Street, Old Town
☎ (0438) 729154
11–2.30; 5–11 (11–11 Sat)
Greene King XX Dark, IPA, Abbot Ale ⊞
The first decent pub after leaving the 'New Town'. Part-vine covered frontage hides a surprisingly large interior. Traditional public bar, with a good, easy-going atmosphere; comfortable saloon. Meals 12–2 Mon–Sat. ❀ ◖ ⊟ ⇌ ♣

Red Lion
80 High Street, Old Town
☎ (0438) 351034
11–3; 6–11 (11–11 Sat)
Greene King IPA, Abbot Ale ⊞
Former coaching inn (stables still at rear). Much improved front bar enjoys a boisterous atmosphere. Rear bar is quiet during the day, but very popular and noisy in the evenings, especially weekends. Shove-ha'penny and Shut the Box played. Snacks only weekends. ❀ ◖ ⊟ ♣ P

Try also: White Horse (Greene King)

Tring

Kings Arms
King Street ☎ (044 282) 3318
11.30–2.30; 7–11
Wadworth 6X; Charles Wells Eagle Bitter ⊞
Excellent back-street local with an ever-changing range of beers. Home-cooked food always available, including veg option. Handy for Natural History Museum.
⌂ Q ❀ ◖ ◗ ♿ ♣

Tyttenhanger

Plough
Tyttenhanger Green (off A414 via Highfield Lane) OS182059
☎ (0727) 57777
11.30–2.30 (3 Sat); 6–11
Brakspear Bitter; Fuller's London Pride; Greene King Abbot Ale; Hook Norton Best Bitter; Marston's Pedigree Bitter; Theakston Best Bitter ⊞
Thriving free house with ten real ales and 1200 different beer bottles on display. Good value food from a cryptic menu (lunchtimes only). Real plough in garden. A pub well worth seeking out. ⌂ ❀ ◖ ♣ P

Ware

New Rose & Crown
35 Watton Road
☎ (0920) 462572
11.30–2.30; 5–11 (11–11 Sat)
Greene King XX Dark, IPA, Abbot Ale ⊞
Former two-bar pub, none the worse for its opening-out. Has a relaxed, airy atmosphere. ◖ ♣

Old Bulls Head
26 Baldock Street
☎ (0920) 462307
11.30–2.30; 5.30–11 (11.30–11 Fri & Sat)
Benskins Best Bitter; Ind Coope Burton Ale; Tetley Bitter ⊞
One-bar, 16th-century pub with some original timber and inglenook. The well-known Parliament Clock has been restored and put on display. Large beer garden with small play area for children. No food Sun eve. Brewery-supplied guest beer. ⌂ Q ❀ ◖ ◗ ⇌ ♣ P

Station Hotel
Station Road ☎ (0920) 463604

11–2.30; 5.30–11
McMullen Original AK 🄷
Good basic public bar and secluded saloon. Striking exterior easily upstages British Rail's attempts across the road. Very handy for missing the next train. ⊞ ≹ ♣

Try also: Victoria (McMullen)

Wareside

White Horse
On B1004 3 miles from Ware
☎ (0920) 462582
11–2.30; 6–11
Greene King Rayments BBA, Abbot Ale 🄷
16th-century village pub with large garden and *à la carte* restaurant.
⌂ Q ⚭ ⊛ ( ) ⊞ ♿ ⅄ ⌓ P

Water End

Red Lion
Water End (A4146, 2 miles from Hemel Hempstead)
☎ (0442) 3594
11–3; 6–11
Benskins Best Bitter; Ind Coope Burton Ale; Tetley Bitter 🄷
Large roadside pub which has won many awards for its fine garden. 12 guide dogs have been paid for by the charitable efforts of the pub's customers. No food Sun, except weekend summer barbecues.
⌂ ⊛ (⊞ ♣ P

Water End

Woodman
Warrengate Road (off B197)
☎ (0707) 54157
11–2.30; 6–11
Adnams Bitter; Courage Directors; Marston's Pedigree Bitter 🄷
Quiet convivial pub near North Mymms Park. Q ⊛ (P

Try also: Maypole (Benskins)

Watford

Bedford Arms
26 Langley Road (200 yds W of station) ☎ (0923) 226205
11–3; 6–11 (12–3; 8–10.30 Sun)
Benskins Best Bitter 🄷
Small town pub, the sort of place some bright spark could ruin overnight. No food weekends. Very small outdoor drinking area.
⌂ ⊛ (≹ (Watford Jct) ♣

Nascot Arms
11 Stamford Road (off Langley Road) ☎ (0923) 31336
11–3; 5.30 (6 Sat)–11
Greene King XX Dark, IPA, Abbot Ale 🄷
Two-bar pub; Dark handpump in one bar only. Can get very crowded. Covered area for children usually available. No food at weekends.
⊛ (≹ (Watford Jct)

Welham Green

Hope & Anchor
Station Road (1 mile W of A1000) OS232053
☎ (0707) 262935
11–2.30; 5.30–11
Courage Best Bitter, Directors; John Smith's Bitter 🄷
Mid 19th-century pub with sporty public bar and lounge bar bedecked with horse brasses. Prize-winning gardens. Show-piece pub for local Elders' training centre. ⊛ (⊞ ≹ ♣ P

Welwyn

Rose & Crown
14 Church Street
☎ (0438) 714190
11–2.30; 5.30–11 (12–3; 6.30–11 Sat)
Adnams Bitter; Benskins Best Bitter; Tetley Bitter 🄷
Unspoilt 16th-century pub; open-plan with separate dining and games areas. Eve meals to order only. Q ⊛ ( ) ♿ ♣ P

Whitwell

Maidens Head
67 High Street (B651)
OS185211
11.30–2.30; 6–11
McMullen Original AK, Country Best Bitter 🄷
Timbered pub of character in heart of village. ⌂ Q (⊞ P

Willian

Three Horseshoes
Baldock Lane (off A614)
OS224307
11–2.30; 6–11
Greene King IPA, Abbot Ale 🄷
Small but comfortable single-room pub. Q (

Wormley West End

Woodman
20 Wormley West End (1 mile W of A10, SW of Broxbourne)
OS339059 ☎ (0992) 463719
11–2.30; 5.30–11
McMullen Original AK 🄷
Attractive pub on edge of Wormley Woods.
⌂ Q ⊛ ( ) ⊞ ♿ P

The modern brewhouse at McMullen which complements the old traditional brewing centre

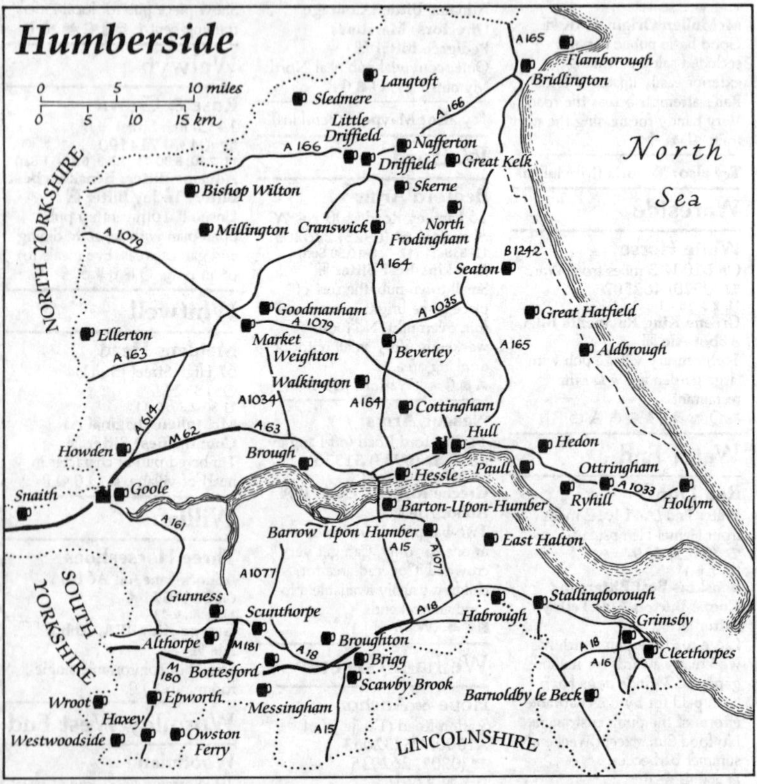

Hull, Hull; ***Old Mill***, Goole

Aldbrough

George & Dragon
1 High Street (B1242)
☎ (0964) 527230
12–3; 7–11
Younger Scotch, IPA Ⓗ
Modernised old country inn dating back 480 years. Quality food; accommodation in adjoining cottages.
◖◗ ♣ P

Althorpe

Dolphin
Trunk Road (A18)
☎ (0724) 783469
11–3; 6–11
John Smith's Bitter Ⓗ
Cosy one-bar roadside inn with emphasis on catering. Separate dining and family rooms. Meal bookings required Sat eve and Sun lunch. Q ◖◗ P

Barnoldby le Beck

Ship Inn
Main Road (off A18)
☎ (0472) 822308
11–3; 5.30 (6.30 Sat)–11
Whitbread Trophy, Castle Eden Ale Ⓗ
Comfortable village local with separate restaurant specialising in fish dishes. No food Mon.
◖◗ ♣ P

Barrow upon Humber

Royal Oak
High Street (off A1077)
☎ (0469) 30318
11–11
Bass Mild XXXX, Draught Bass; Stones Best Bitter Ⓗ
Smart village pub. No meals Sun lunchtime. ◖ ♣ P

Barton-Upon-Humber

Volunteer Arms
13 Whitecross Street (off A1077) ☎ (0652) 32309
11–3; 7–11
Burtonwood Dark Mild, Best Bitter Ⓗ
Small two-roomed pub with rather plain exterior, but very pleasant inside. Street parking opposite. Bookings needed for Sun lunch. ◖◗ ≠

Wheatsheaf
Holydyke (A1077/B1218 jct)
☎ (0652) 33175
11–3; 6.45–11
Wards Mild, Sheffield Best Bitter, Kirby Strong Ⓗ
Old pub with lounge bar and separate snug. No food at weekends. ◖ ≠ P

Beverley

Rose & Crown
North Bar Without (A164 York Road jct) ☎ (0482) 862532
11–3; 6–11
Wards Mild, Thorne Best Bitter, Sheffield Best Bitter, Kirby Strong Ⓗ
Prominently-situated next to North Bar and the nearest pub to Beverley Racecourse. Also handy for Beverley Westwood (large area of common land to the north-west of town). Comfortable, friendly atmosphere. Regular guest beers. ◖◗ ♣ P

Royal Standard
30 North Bar Within
☎ (0482) 882434
11–3 (4.30 Fri, 5 Sat); 7–11
Wards Mild, Thorne Best Bitter Ⓗ
Excellent small pub with a gem of a front bar. Maintains a very traditional atmosphere. Sport-oriented, particularly horse racing, the racecourse being nearby. Q ❀ ⊞ ♣

Sun Inn
Eastgate ☎ (0482) 881547
11–3; 6–11 (11–11 Sat)
Camerons Traditional Bitter, Strongarm Ⓗ
Old local in shadow of the magnificent Beverley Minster and handy for the Army Transport Museum. New additional drinking areas include a conservatory. Eve meals till 8pm (not Sun); veg and children's dishes. ❀ ◐ ◑ ⊞ ≈ ♣

Woolpack
37 Westwood Road
☎ (0482) 867095
11.30–2.30; 7–11
Burtonwood Dark Mild, Best Bitter Ⓗ
Small local on residential street. Close to the Westwood Hospital, with secluded beer garden to the rear and low ceilings inside. Maintains a traditional atmosphere. Local CAMRA Pub of the Year 1990. ❀ ◐

Bishop Wilton

Fleece Inn
☎ (075 96) 251
12–3; 6.30 (5.30 summer)–11 (12–11 Sat)
John Smith's Bitter; Tetley Bitter Ⓗ
Welcoming village free house catering for all tastes. Live country and western music on Fri. Pub games include bar skittles. Very good range of bar meals including veg. Supper licence till 12.30am.
Q ⊨ ◐ ◑ ♿ ⅄ ♣ P

Bottesford

Black Beauty
Keddington Road (100 yds E of A159, Messingham Road)
☎ (0724) 867628
11.30–3.30; 6 (5 Fri)–11 (11–11 Sat)
Mansfield Riding Dark Mild, Riding Traditional Bitter, Old Baily Ⓗ
Large and lively modern pub with live music Thu and Sun.
⊞ ♣ P

Bridlington

Hilderthorpe Hotel
Hilderthorpe Road
☎ (0262) 672205
11–11
Bass Mild XXXX, Draught Bass; Stones Best Bitter Ⓗ
Basic local, popular with fishermen. A dominoes pub. Straightforward good meals in summer. ♛ ◐ ◑ ⊞ ≈ ♣

Old Ship Inn
90 St John's Street, Old Town
☎ (0262) 670466
11–4; 7–11
Wards Mild, Thorne Best Bitter Ⓗ
Thriving local by the old town, with a good traditional atmosphere. Facilities for children include a covered play area. Dominoes. ♛ ⚘ ❀ ◐ ⊞ ♣

Old Star Inn
17 Westgate, Old Town
☎ (0262) 676039
11–11
Theakston Best Bitter; Younger Scotch, IPA, No. 3 Ⓗ
An old pub still retaining some of its original labyrinthine interior. Now food-oriented. Rooms for functions and meetings. Live music. ♛ ❀ ◐ ◑ P

Ridings Hotel
Hilderthorpe Road
☎ (0262) 672900
11–3; 6–11
Bass Mild XXXX, Draught Bass; Theakston Best Bitter; Younger Scotch, No. 3 Ⓗ
Bright local by the railway station with a fine room for functions. Good basic lunches.
◐ ≈ ♣

Brigg

Britannia
Wrawby Street (A15/A18)
☎ (0652) 52342
11–3; 6.30–11
Burtonwood Dark Mild, Best Bitter Ⓗ
Small, unpretentious two-room pub. Darts and dominoes popular with the regulars. Street parking to the front and rear.
♛ ❀ ◐ ⊞ ≈ ♣

Queens Arms
Wrawby Street (A15/A18)
☎ (0652) 53174
11–3; 6.30–11
Bass Mild XXXX, Draught Bass Ⓗ
A pleasant, open-plan lounge bar. Good value meals (not Mon or Tue/Sun eves). Quizzes alternate with jazz on Tue. Street parking at front.
◐ ◑ ≈ ♣

White Horse
Wrawby Street (A15/A18)
☎ (0652) 52242
11–2.30; 5–11
Wards Mild, Sheffield Best Bitter Ⓗ
Welcoming old inn popular for its meals as well as its beer. The landlord's home-made pork pie recently won a national award.
❀ ◐ ◑ ⊞ ≈ ♣ P

Try also: White Hart (Mansfield)

Brough

Buccaneer
Station Road
☎ (0482) 667435
11–3, 6 (6.30 Sat)–11 (11–11 Fri)
Tetley Mild, Bitter Ⓗ
Town-style pub with lively games-oriented bar and comfortable traditional lounge. Aviation decorations and pub's name derived from local British Aerospace factory. ❀ ◐ ⊞ ≈ ♣

Broughton

Red Lion
High Street ☎ (0652) 52560
11–11
Mansfield Riding Traditional Bitter Ⓗ
Extensively altered pub offering good value, unusual food.
♛ Q ⚘ ❀ ◐ ⊞ ♿ ⅄ ♣ P

Cleethorpes

Fishermans Arms
25 Wardle Street (corner of Seaview Street)
☎ (0472) 691811
11–11
Bass Mild XXXX Ⓔ, **Draught Bass** Ⓗ
Basic two-bar pub close to sea front. Due for sympathetic refurbishment. No meals Sun. Friendly staff. ◐ ⊞ ≈ ♣

Submarine
Sea Road (opp. pier)
☎ (0472) 691435
11–11
Ind Coope Burton Ale; Tetley Mild, Bitter Ⓗ
Formerly the Pier Hotel, now sailing officially under its traditional nickname. Recent refurbishment has left the main bar smarter and more comfortable. Music room, now called 'Waves', has video jukebox and flashing lights.
❀ ◐ ⊞ ≈

Willys
17 High Cliff Road (sea front)
☎ (0472) 602145
11–11
Bateman Dark Mild, XB; Willys Original, Old Groyne Ⓗ
Young persons' pub with quieter, traditionally-styled upstairs room. Very busy at weekends. Always a minimum of two guest beers and an excellently-kept, growing range of beers from Willys' own house brewery. ❀ ◐ ♿ ≈

Try also: Smugglers

Cottingham

Tiger Inn
King Street ☎ (0482) 845066
11–11
Bass Mild XXXX, Draught Bass; Stones Best Bitter ⊞
Very busy village centre local, extended into a large single-room pub with bar and darts areas. Good quality food.
◖ ♿ ♣

Try also: Cross Keys (Tetley)

Cranswick

Pack Horse
Main Street (½ mile off A164)
☎ (0377) 70298
12–3 (not Mon–Fri); 7–11
Old Mill Traditional Bitter; Tetley Bitter ⊞
Small village local with a pleasantly decorated long, single through-room which is both cosy and comfortable. Close to railway station. ⛫ ▦ ♿ ⇌ (Hutton Cranswick) ♣ P

Driffield

Rose & Crown
North Street (A166)
☎ (0377) 43041
12–11 (11–11 Sat)
John Smith's Bitter ⊞
Small, friendly and comfortable local on the northern edge of the town, oak-beamed in the traditional style. Collection of coins. ▦ ◖ ♣ P

East Halton

Black Bull
Townside ☎ (0469) 40207
11.30–3; 5–11 (11–11 Fri, Sat & summer)
Bass Mild XXXX; Stones Best Bitter ⊞
Well-kept village local with friendly bar and comfortable lounge. Weekly quiz nights and usual pub games.
Q ▦ ◖ ◗ ⊕ ♿ ▲ ♣ P

Ellerton

Boot & Shoe
Off B1228 halfway between York and Goole
☎ (0757) 288346
12–3 (not Mon or winter); 7–11
Old Mill Traditional Bitter; Tetley Bitter ⊞
Charming, multi-roomed single-storey pub in attractive, off-the-beaten-track setting. Cosy bars with low beams and a friendly atmosphere. Well worth seeking out. No meals Mon eve.
⛫ Q ◖ ◗ P

Epworth

Queen's Head
Queen's Street (off A161)
☎ (0427) 872306
11–3.30; 7–11
John Smith's Bitter ⊞
Built in 1664 as a farmhouse, now a bustling open-plan local in the centre of Wesley's home town. No meals Sun or Mon.
◖ P

Flamborough

Royal Dog & Duck
☎ (0262) 850206
11–4; 6.30–11
Draught Bass; Stones Best Bitter ⊞
Old village-centre pub with beams, bric-a-brac and a comfortable atmosphere. Good meals include local specialities. Separate dining room.
⛫ ⛾ ▦ ◖ ◗ ⊕ ▲ ♣ P

Goodmanham

Goodmanham Arms
Main Street ☎ (0430) 872329
11–3; 7–11
Old Mill Traditional Mild, Traditional Bitter; Theakston Best Bitter ⊞
Quaint village local opposite a Norman church on the Wolds Way long-distance footpath. Front room bar frequented by local rural community.
⛫ Q ⛾ ▦ ♣ P

Goole

Old George
Market Place (next to clock tower) ☎ (0405) 763147
11–3; 7–11
Bass Light 5 Star, Draught Bass; Stones Best Bitter ⊞
Lively town-centre pub with emphasis on food at lunchtimes (except Sun). Local history memorabilia adorns the walls.
▦ ◖ ⇌ ♣ P

Try also: Woodlands (John Smith's)

Great Hatfield

Wrygarth Inn
Between B1242/B1243
☎ (0964) 532155
12–3; 7–11
Camerons Traditional Bitter; Hull Mild; Tetley Bitter ⊞
Prominent building on old Hull to Hornsea road which offers good value beer and food in a variety of drinking areas. No food Mon.
⛫ ⛾ ▦ ◖ ◗ ♿ ▲ ♣ P

Great Kelk

Chestnut Horse
Between A165/B1249/A166
OS105583 ☎ (026 288) 263
11–11
Bass Mild XXXX; Stones Best Bitter; John Smith's Bitter ⊞
Delightfully friendly and unspoilt cottage-style inn serving small rural community. Excellent, good value meals.
⛫ Q ⛾ ▦ ◖ ◗ ⊕ ♿ ▲ ♣ P

Grimsby

Angel
175 Freeman Street
☎ (0472) 42402
11–11
Matthew Brown Mild; Younger IPA, No. 3 ⊞
Recently-refurbished local, retaining a haven of peace and quiet in the form of a small hatch-served back room which links bar and lounge.
Q ⊕ ⇌ (Docks) ♣ P

Corporation
88 Freeman Street
11–11
Bass Mild XXXX, Draught Bass ⊞
The finest surviving example of the type of pub once found on virtually every street corner in this part of town. Recent and extensive renovation has actually enhanced the appeal of this classic local.
◖ ⊕ ⇌ (Docks) ♣

Hope & Anchor
148 Victoria Street
☎ (0472) 342565
11–3; 5.30–11 (11–11 Fri & Sat)
Ind Coope Burton Ale; Tetley Mild, Bitter ⊞
Town drinking house close to bus station. Beer policy is attracting regular clientele from all parts of the town. Guest beers. No meals Sun.
▦ ◖ ⊕ ⇌ (Town) ♣

Palace Buffet
Victoria Street
☎ (0472) 342837
11–11
Bass Mild XXXX, Draught Bass; Stones Best Bitter ⊞
A Victorian house which was once the bar of the now demolished Palace Theatre. Although little-changed externally, the interior has been comfortably modernised over the years, making the pub popular with all age groups. Close to National Heritage Fishing Museum. ▦ ◖ ⊕ ♣ P

Rutland Arms
26–30 Rutland Street (off Cleethorpe Road)
☎ (0472) 241345
11–11
Old Mill Traditional Mild, Traditional Bitter, Bullion Bitter ⊞
A real success story: a blend of social club and locals' pub rolled into one, with strangers treated as part of the family. Both ale and food are good value (no meals Sun). Live entertainment.
▦ ◖ ⇌ (New Clee) ♣ P

Try also: Oak Tree (John Smith's)

Gunness

Jolly Sailor
Doncaster Road (A18)
☎ (0724) 782423
12–3; 5–11
Bass Special Bitter, Draught Bass 🄷
Renovated 1930s pub with growing emphasis on catering. Ring the Bull game.
⌂ Q ◐ ◗ ⊟ ⇌ (Althorpe) ♣ P

Habrough

Horse & Hounds
Station Road (A180/A160 jct 1½ miles towards Immingham)
☎ (0469) 576940
11–11 (closes 3–7 if no demand)
Theakston XB, Old Peculier; Younger IPA, No. 3 🄷
Part of the Habrough Hotel. A tastefully-converted former farmhouse and rectory, part dating from 15th century.
⌂ Q ❀ ⛿ ◐ ◗ ⊟ ♿ P

Haxey

Loco
31–33 Church Street (B1396)
☎ (0427) 752879
7 (6 Fri)–11 (open Sun lunch)
John Smith's Bitter, Magnet 🄷
Former village Co-op, fish shop and cottage, thoughtfully converted into a pub with a railway theme. The bar was constructed from a church pulpit whilst the stone floor came from the roof of a manor. Varied memorabilia includes an engine smokebox which opens to reveal the television. Lunches on Sun. ⛑ ◗ ⊟ ♿ ♣

Hedon

Shakespeare Inn
9 Baxtergate (near B1239/B1362 jct)
☎ (0482) 898371
11–11
Vaux Bitter; Wards Mild, Thorne Best Bitter, Sheffield Best Bitter, Kirby Strong 🄷
One-roomed, cosy and friendly old inn. Joint winner of local CAMRA Pub of the Year 1988. Over 3,000 beer mats adorn the ceiling and much breweriana covers the walls. Eve food till 7, Mon–Fri only. ⌂ ❀ ◐ ◗ ♣ P

Hessle

George Inn (Top House)
40 Prestongate (in pedestrianised street off square)
☎ (0482) 648698
11–11
Bass Mild XXXX; Stones Best Bitter 🄷
Separate rooms and a good local atmosphere survive intact after a chintzy redecoration. Very much a real, not designer, pub. No lunches Sun. ❀ ◐ ⊟ ♣

Hollym

Plough Inn
Northside Road (100 yds off A1033) ☎ (0964) 612049
12–3; 7–11
Tetley Mild, Bitter 🄷
200 year-old village pub of wattle and daub construction. Three rooms, one a games room. Food includes veg option; special culinary requests usually indulged.
⌂ ⛑ ❀ ◐ ◗ ⊟ ♿ Ʌ ♣ P

Howden

Barnes Wallis
Station Road (1 mile N of town on B1228, next to station)
☎ (0430) 430639
12–3; 7–11
Old Mill Traditional Bitter; Tetley Bitter 🄷
Comfortable and friendly pub dedicated to the traditional beer drinker. Barnes Wallis memorabilia. Large range of British and foreign bottled beers and always at least two guest beers. ⌂ ❀ ⇌ ♣ P

Hull

Bay Horse
113 Wincolmlee (400 yds from North Bridge on W side of river) ☎ (0482) 29227
11–3; 6.30–11
Bateman Dark Mild, XB, XXXB 🄷
Extensively altered and extended in 1990, this is Bateman's only tied house north of the Humber and should not be missed by any discerning drinker in this area of limited choice. ◐ ♿ ♣

Duke of Edinburgh
1 De La Pole Street (1st left off A63 E of river)
☎ (0482) 225382
11–3; 6–11 (11–11 Sat)
Camerons Traditional Bitter 🄷
Small, boisterous local with very informal atmosphere. Popular with all ages. Features live music, discos and piano sing-alongs. Good value meals. Opposite extensive new Victoria Dock housing development. ⌂ ❀ ◐ ♣

Duke of Wellington
104 Peel Street (between Spring Bank and Beverley Road)
☎ (0482) 29603
11–4 (5 Sat); 6–11
Taylor Landlord; Tetley Mild, Bitter 🄷
Often crowded, back-street, restyled Victorian local. Still the nearest thing to a free house in Hull, it features regular guest beers and seafood snacks.
❀ ♣ P

East Riding
37 Cannon Street (½ mile N of city centre) ☎ (0482) 29134
11–3.30; 6.30–11
Tetley Mild, Bitter 🄷
Small, old-fashioned industrial pub, located on street corner. A no-nonsense bar features rugby league memorabilia; the comfortable wood-panelled lounge offers 'freebies'– snacks, nuts, saveloys, mussels, etc.
⊟ ♣

Gardeners Arms
Cottingham Road (B1233, 100 yds from A1079 jct)
☎ (0482) 42396
11–11
Tetley Mild, Bitter 🄷
The large video jukebox lounge at the rear for the younger drinker is balanced by a friendly locals' bar with a darts-oriented, mixed clientele. Eve meals till 7.30pm, except Fri and Sat.
❀ ◐ ◗ ♣ P

Halfway House
595 Spring Bank West (1½ miles from city centre, near fairground) ☎ (0482) 53227
12–3; 6.30–11
Bass Mild XXXX, Draught Bass; Stones Best Bitter 🄷
Well-patronised suburban pub on dual carriageway. Large U-shaped bar with lots of wood and no plastic. Cosy, plush back lounge. Basic, good value lunches. ❀ ◐ ⊟ ♿ ♣ P

Minerva
Nelson Street (opp. Corporation Pier) ☎ (0482) 26909
11–11
Minerva Pilot's Pride; Tetley Mild, Bitter 🄷
Famous riverside pub with its own brewery and four contrasting rooms. Built in 1830 and restored with great care, leaving the central wood-panelled bar surrounded by inter-linking rooms. Handy for Hull Marina. Food served till 8pm Mon–Sat. ⌂ ◐ ◗ ⊟ ♣

Oberon
Queen Street (near Corporation Pier) ☎ (0482) 24886
11–3; 5.30–11
Bass Mild XXXX, Draught Bass 🄷
A good weekend bet to avoid the Old Town crowds. This is a perennial favourite with Hull's discerning drinkers: a fairly plain two-roomer with a friendly, relaxed atmosphere. Frequented by Humber pilots. Q ⊟ ♣

Old Blue Bell
Market Place (in alleyway next to Market Hall and Holy Trinity Church ☎ (0482) 24382
11–2.30; 7–11
Samuel Smith OBB, Museum Ale [H]
Famous pub in Old Town. Its layout includes a small snug and an upstairs room used by a folk club on Sun eves. Unusual bell collection in bar. Excellent value food. ◐ ♣

Olde White Harte
25 Silver Street
☎ (0482) 26363
11–11
Theakston XB; Younger IPA, No. 3 [H]
Largely 16th-century courtyard pub in commercial area. Two large sit-in fireplaces, original timber and stained glass windows. Important in the Civil War: its Plotters' Room hosted the meeting which refused King Charles entry to the city. Good food. ◐

Station Inn
202 Beverley Road (A1079, ½ mile from city centre)
☎ (0482) 41482
11–11
Tetley Mild, Bitter [H]
Mock-Tudor, street-corner pub next to site of former Hull to Hornsea and Withernsea Railway. Traditional Tetley bar and cosy, warm back room. Reputation for quiz nights. Extensive choice of good value meals. Q ◐ ♣

Langtoft

Ship Inn
Front Street ☎ (0377) 87243
12–3; 7–11
Camerons Traditional Bitter, Strongarm [H]
Cosy, friendly village local with a reputation for good food. Supper licence till 12pm. Children welcome in pool room or restaurant. ◐ ◑ ♣ P

Little Driffield

Downe Arms
By-passed by A166
☎ (0377) 42243
12–2.30; 7–11
Camerons Traditional Bitter [H]
Thoroughly renovated in a pleasant and neat style, this 17th-century inn retains much comfort and charm.
Q ◐ ◑

Market Weighton

Half Moon
High Street (A1079)
☎ (0430) 873446
11–3; 6–11 (11–11 Thu–Sat)
Burtonwood Dark Mild, Best Bitter [H]
Friendly local in centre of market town. One very long drinking area which is like a public bar at one end, and a comfortable, well-appointed lounge at the other. No meals Wed. ◐ ♣ P

Messingham

Green Tree
33 High Street (A159)
☎ (0724) 762395
11.30–3; 5–11 (11.30–11 Fri & Sat)
Bass Mild XXXX, Special Bitter, Draught Bass [H]
Single-roomed old village pub, refitted in the 'cottage' lounge fashion. Occasional barbecues in summer. ◐ ♣ P

Try also: Horn (John Smith's)

Millington

Gate Inn
2 miles NE of Pocklington
☎ (0759) 302045
12–2.30 (not Mon–Fri); 7.30–11
Draught Bass [H], **Malton Owd Bob** [G]; **Tetley Bitter** [H]
Splendid traditional village pub with one bar serving three linked areas. Only open Mon–Fri lunchtimes by prior arrangement. Occasional guest beers. No eve meals Thu.
Q ◐ ◑ ♣ P

Nafferton

Cross Keys
North Street (200 yds off A166) ☎ (0377) 44261
12–2.30 (4 Sat); 7–11
Old Mill Traditional Bitter; John Smith's Bitter, Magnet; Younger Scotch [H]
Friendly, spacious and cosy local at northern end of village with an array of rooms catering for all tastes. No meals Mon and Tue eves. ◐ ◑ ♣

North Frodingham

Star
Main Street (B1249)
☎ (026 288) 365
7–11 (open Sun lunch)
Camerons Traditional Bitter, Strongarm [H]
A relaxed and friendly atmosphere and excellent food from an imaginative menu (not Thu eve). Separate games area in newly-constructed part of the pub. Old BP sign instructs 'Buy from the pumP'! ◑ ♣ P

Ottringham

White Horse
Main Road (A1033)
☎ (0964) 622385
11–3; 6–11
John Smith's Bitter; Tetley Mild, Bitter [H]
Former posting house dating from 17th century. A busy food pub and deservedly popular. Open-plan bar retains its intimate corners. ◐ ◑ ♣ P

Owston Ferry

Crooked Billet
Silver Street ☎ (042 772) 264
11–3 (not Mon); 7–11
Wards Mild, Thorne Best Bitter [H]
Trent-side village pub with pool, darts and boxing! Occasional live music. No meals Sat and Sun eves.
◐ ◑ ♣ P

Paull

Crown Inn
Main Street (2 miles off A1033)
☎ (0482) 898383
11–3; 7–11 (11–11 Fri & Sat)
Bass Mild XXXX, Draught Bass; Stones Best Bitter [H]
Formerly a row of Georgian cottages, this is now a tastefully furbished pub with superb views of the Humber Estuary. Excellent family room. Eve meals Fri and Sat only.
◐ ♣ P

Humber Tavern
Main Street (2 miles off A1033)
☎ (0482) 899347
11–11
Tetley Bitter; Wilson's Original Mild, Wilson's Original Bitter, Webster's Yorkshire Bitter [H]
Victorian building by the Humber Estuary, with fine views. Eve meals till 7pm.
◐ ◑ ♣

Ryhill

Crooked Billet
Pitt Lane (400 yds off A1033)
☎ (0964) 622303
11–3 (5 Sat); 7–11
Tetley Mild, Bitter [H]
Picturesque, 17th-century cottage-style inn with pleasant, old-world interior. Formerly a smugglers' haunt. Part of the lounge was once a slaughter house. ◐ ◑ ♣ P

Scawby Brook

King William IV
On A15 ☎ (0652) 53147
11–3 (3.30 Sat); 6.30–11
Vaux Samson; Wards Mild, Sheffield Best Bitter [H]
Attractive, white two-roomed pub with a wood-panelled snug and a recently extended lounge. Very busy weekend lunchtimes. Quiz night on Wed.
◐ ♣ P

Scunthorpe

Bridge House Hotel
Station Road
☎ (0724) 847590
11–3; 5–11 (11–11 Fri & Sat)
Ind Coope Burton Ale; Marston's Pedigree Bitter; Tetley Bitter Ⓗ
Town-centre hotel next to Scunthorpe railway station with bar meals (ask) and a restaurant. Mr Smith's Bar is plush and quiet but more expensive.
Q ⌂ ◖ ◗ ⇌ P

Old Mill
High Street East
☎ (0724) 849911
11–3; 5 (6 Sat)–11
Tetley Bitter Ⓗ
Conversion from the old Scunthorpe town windmill, still retaining the restored tower which provides a highly visible local landmark. Single bar/lounge with upstairs lounge suitable for children. ☺ ❀ ◖ ⇌ P

Riveter
50 Henderson Avenue
☎ (0724) 862701
11.30–11
Old Mill Traditional Mild, Traditional Bitter, Bullion Bitter Ⓗ
New pub converted from a former social club in the Old Mill Brewery style. The first of Old Mill's growing estate. No meals Sat or Sun. Small car park.
♨ ◖ ⊞ ♿ ♣ P

Seaton

Swan Inn
On B1244 ☎ (0964) 533582
11–3; 7–11
John Smith's Bitter Ⓗ
Friendly, welcoming village atmosphere in a comfortably decorated imposing building adorned by a 1950s AA enamel sign. Good garden for children. Handy for Hornsea Mere.
♨ ☺ ⊞ ♣ P

Skerne

Eagle Inn
Wandsford Road
☎ (0377) 42178
11–3; 7–11
Camerons Traditional Bitter Ⓗ
Extremely welcoming and unpretentious. Beer is served from mezzanine cellar using a Victorian cash register beer engine. No food. Unspoilt; a rare find. ♨ Q ❀ ♣ P

Sledmere

Triton Inn
On B1252/B1253
☎ (0377) 86644
12–3; 7–11 (12–11 summer)
Tetley Bitter; Younger Scotch Ⓗ
Splendid pub next to Sledmere House and surrounded by typical Wolds countryside. Children welcome in restaurant and front hall.
♨ ☺ ❀ ⌂ ◖ ◗ ⊞ ♣ P

Snaith

Brewers Arms
10 Pontefract Road
☎ (0405) 862404
11–2.30; 6–11
Old Mill Traditional Bitter, Bullion Bitter Ⓗ
Excellent conversion of an impressive country lodge dating from 1720. Original well in centre of lounge; secret tunnel reputedly runs to local stately home. Separate restaurant and live music every Sun eve.
❀ ⌂ ◖ ◗ P

Stallingborough

Green Man
110 Station Road
☎ (0472) 883464
11–11
Bass Mild XXXX, Draught Bass; Stones Best Bitter Ⓗ
Old village pub near to Humber Bank. A recent addition is the large, pleasant lounge with a raised dining area. No meals Sun–Tue eves. ❀ ◖ ◗ ⊞ ⇌ ♣ P

Walkington

Barrel Inn
35 West End (B1230)
☎ (0482) 868494
11.30–2; 6.30–11 (11.30–11 Sat)
Hull Mild; Tetley Bitter; Wilson's Original Bitter Ⓗ
Comfortable one-roomer with a good mix of customers in an attractive village which claims to be right at the centre of the county. ♨ ❀

Westwoodside, Isle of Axholme

Park Drain Hotel
Park Drain (400 yds off B1396) OS726988 ☎ (0427) 752255
10.30–4; 6–11
Bass Mild XXXX; Stones Best Bitter Ⓗ
Unusual, remote Victorian pub built for (supposed) mining community. Large bar, comfortable lounge and excellent restaurant. Straw-fired central heating; water wells in car park. No meals Mon eve.
♨ ❀ ◖ ◗ ⊞ ▲ ♣ P

Wroot, Isle of Axholme

Cross Keys Inn
High Street (4 miles off B1396) OS715032 ☎ (0302) 770231
12–3 (not Tue–Thu); 7–11
Theakston XB; Younger Scotch Ⓗ
Focal point of this remote village community, catering for all ages and tastes in its various rooms. ♨ ❀ ◖ ◗ ⊞ ♣ P

THE SYMBOLS

♨ real fire	⌂ accommodation	⇌ near British Rail station
Q quiet pub – in at least one bar	◖ lunchtime meals	⊖ near Underground station
☺ indoor room for children	◗ evening meals	♣ pub games
❀ garden or other outdoor drinking area	⊞ public bar	○ real cider
	♿ easy disabled access	P pub car park
	▲ camping facilities at the pub or nearby	

Isle of Wight

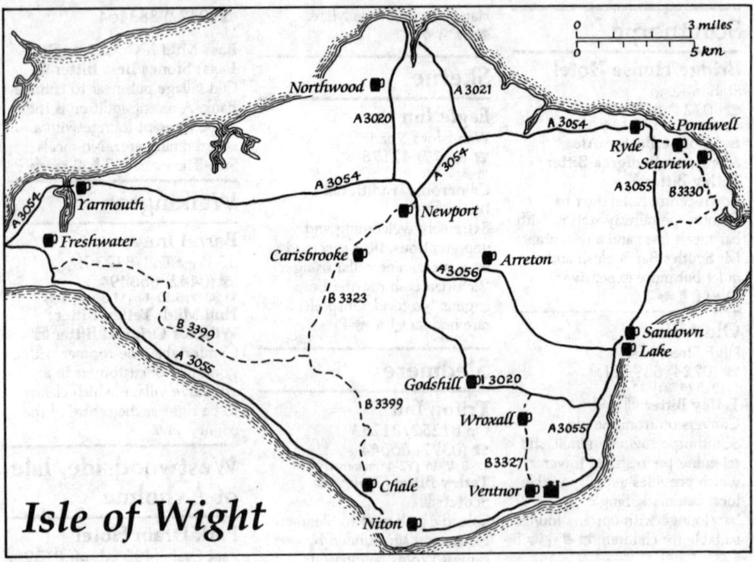

Burts, *Ventnor*

Arreton

Hare & Hounds
Downend (A3056)
☎ (0983) 528159
11–3; 6–11 (11–11 summer)
Burts VPA, Tanner
Splendid, historic thatched pub in pleasant position on downs, above Arreton Valley. Also adjacent to Robin Hill Country Park and near Arreton Manor. Skull of last man hanged on island adorns bar! P

Try also: White Lion (Whitbread)

Carisbrooke

Shute Inn
Clatterford Shute (off B3323)
☎ (0983) 523393
11–3; 7–11
Draught Bass; Burts VPA; John Smith's Bitter
Pleasant Georgian hotel in delightful setting beneath Carisbrooke Castle. No food Sun eve. Guest bitter.
P

Chale

Wight Mouse
Clarendon Hotel (B3399, 100 yds from A3099 jct)
☎ (0983) 730431
11–11
Burts VPA; Gale's HSB; Marston's Pedigree Bitter; Whitbread Strong Country Bitter
Busy, superb old stone pub, extensively improved. Accent on food and families. Massive garden with pets and play area. Only island pub with sheep in the garden. Nearby is Blackgang Chine theme park. Two car parks. P

Freshwater

Royal Standard
School Green Road
☎ (0983) 753227
11–11
Burts Mild, VPA, Tanner
Homely town pub in village hotel. Excellent public bar and good value food.
♣ P

Godshill

Griffin
Newport Road
☎ (0983) 840226
10.30–3; 6–11
Whitbread Strong Country Bitter, Flowers Original
Excellent country local which has avoided over-commercialisation despite crass surroundings. Fine views from garden. Q ♣ P

Try also: Chequers (Courage)

Lake

Manor House
Sandown Road (A3055)
☎ (0983) 403558
11–3 (4 Sat); 5.30 (6 Sat)–11
Draught Bass; Burts VPA
Large village pub with many rooms. P

Newport

Castle
91 High Street
☎ (0983) 522528
10.30–3; 6–11
Marston's Pedigree Bitter; Whitbread Fremlins Bitter, Best Bitter
Very ancient, stone-floored, beamed pub. Bulmer cider available.

Niton

Buddle Inn
St Catherine's Road
☎ (0983) 730243
11–11
Marston's Pedigree Bitter; Whitbread Fremlins Bitter, Strong Country Bitter, Flowers Original
Excellent ancient pub with enthusiastic landlord. Near picturesque St Catherine's Bay and lighthouse (open to public). Range of beers likely to change.
P

Northwood

Travellers Joy
85 Pallance Road (off A3020)
☎ (0983) 298024
10.30–3; 5–11
Burts VPA; Courage Directors; Gibbs Mew Bishop's Tipple; Ruddles County; Theakston Old Peculier; Wadworth 6X

Excellent beer exhibition pub, unique to the island and well worth seeking out. Guest beers. P

Try also: Horseshoe (Whitbread)

Pondwell

Wishing Well
On B3330 ☎ (0983) 613222
11–3 (4.30 summer); 6.30 (6 summer)–11
Burts VPA; Courage Directors; John Smith's Bitter [H]
Large popular free house with self-catering chalets and campsite adjacent. Near Flamingo Park waterfowl and water gardens. P

Ryde

Castle
164 High Street
☎ (0983) 811138
10.30–11
Gale's BBB, XXXXX, HSB [H]
Split-level, one-bar town pub, with notable etched windows. Recently saved from redevelopment and re-opened after a one-year closure. Shove-ha'penny played.

Try also: Esplanade Bars (Free)

Sandown

Commercial
15 St Johns Road
☎ (0983) 403848
11–3; 6–11
Gale's XXXL, BBB, XXXXX, HSB [H]
Fine, comfortable town pub with good, basic public bar and a friendly welcome from Gale's' longest serving licensee (25 years).

Seaview

Seaview Hotel
High Street ☎ (0983) 612711
11–3; 6–11
Burts VPA, Tanner [H]
An imposing and elegant late-Victorian seafront hotel in a pleasant yachting village. Views of sea from front lounge and restaurant, while locals frequent the excellent public bar at the rear. No meals Sun eve. P

Try also: Old Fort (Free)

Ventnor

Mill Bay
Esplanade ☎ (0983) 852892
10.30–3; 6–11 (11–11 summer)
Burts Mild, VPA, Tanner [H]
Seafront town pub with two basic rooms. Situated near foot of the 'Cascade'.

Spyglass Inn
Undercliffe House (W of Esplanade) ☎ (0983) 855338
10.30–3; 7–11 (11–11 summer)
Ind Coope Burton Ale [H]
Superb free house on seafront, with terrace overlooking sea. Enormous children's room (no-smoking) and one other no-smoking bar. Landlord staged mini beer festival in 1989. House beer (Spyglass Ale) brewed by Gibbs Mew. Tiny car park. P

Wroxall

Star
Clarence Road (B3327)
☎ (0983) 854701
11–3; 7 (6 summer)–11
Burts Mild, VPA, 4X, Tanner [H]
Smart, comfortable, two-bar village pub in pleasant country setting. Completely and tastefully refurbished after a major fire. P

Yarmouth

Kings Head
Quay Street ☎ (0983) 760351
11–3; 6.30–11 (11–11 summer)
Gale's HSB; Marston's Pedigree Bitter; Whitbread Pompey Royal, Flowers Original [H]
Splendid busy pub near yacht harbour and car ferry terminal. Plenty of character.

All Yarmouth pubs serve real ale

Fuller's: clearly pleased at winning the Champion Beer of Britain award!

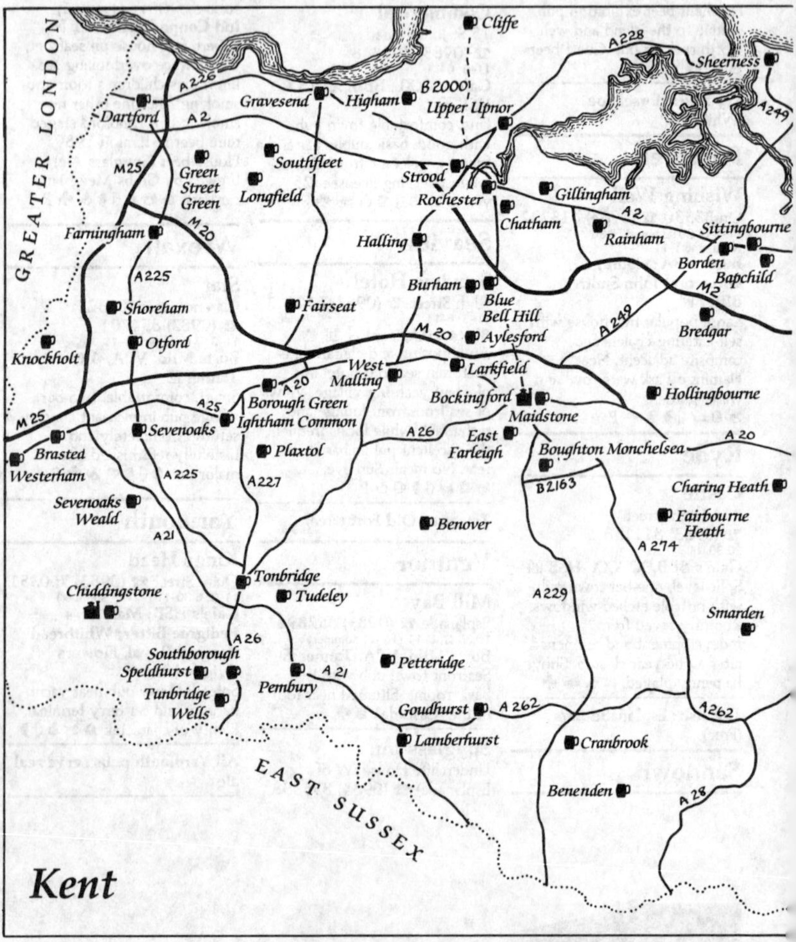

Goacher's, *Bockingford*; **Larkins**, *Chiddingstone*; **Shepherd Neame**, *Faversham*

Ashford

Beaver Inn

Beaver Road (A2070, ¾ mile S of station) OS005414
☎ (0233) 620264
11–2.30 (12–2 Sun); 7–11
Shepherd Neame Master Brew Bitter Ⓗ
Two-bar pub with local trade. Note mistakes in smoking room window. This is its 11th year in the *Guide*, but due for refurbishment. Q ⊞ ≠ P

Hare & Hounds

Maidstone Road, Potters Corner (A20, 2½ miles from town)
☎ (0233) 621760
11–2.30; 6–11
Courage Best Bitter, Directors; John Smith's Bitter Ⓗ
Friendly and busy pub just out of town. Popular for its steaks; also fresh fish and home-cooked specials (no food Sun lunch or Tue eve). ❀ (◗

Try also: Prince Albert (Free)

Aylesford

Bush

17 Rochester Road
☎ (0622) 717446
11–2.30 (12–2.30 Sun); 6 (7 Sat)–11
Courage Best Bitter, Directors Ⓗ
Comfortable pub with an amazing collection of ties. Situated in an historic village surrounded by warehouses. Bill Tidy would like the barman! No food Sun, or Mon eve. ❀ (◗ P

Bapchild

Fox & Goose

2 Fox Hill (A2)
☎ (0795) 472095
11–3; 6–11
Courage Best Bitter Ⓗ
Popular village local with aviary in garden. ⛺ ❀ (⊞ ♣ P

Benenden

King William IV

The Street (B2086)
☎ (0580) 240636
11.30–2.30; 6–11
Shepherd Neame Master Brew Bitter Ⓗ
Excellent village local. Basic public bar with jukebox, one-armed bandit, etc.; saloon bar relaxed, quieter and a bit more

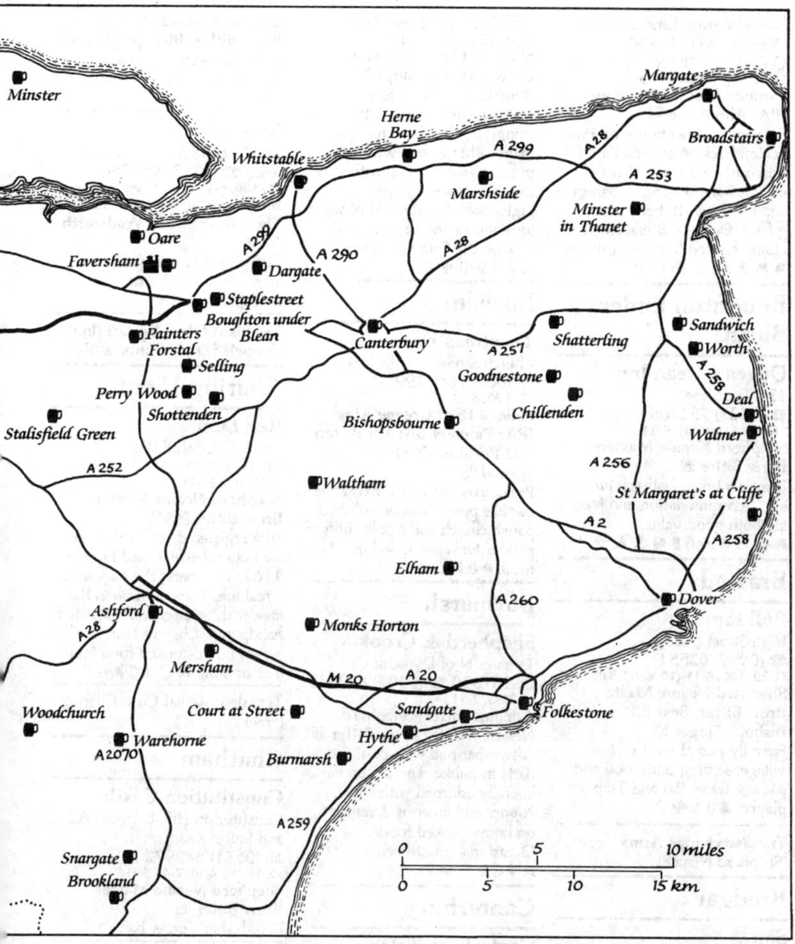

'OK-Ya'. No food Sun, or Mon eve. ♣ P

Benover

Woolpack Inn

Benover Road (B2162, 1 mile S of Yalding) ☎ (089 273) 356
11–2.30 (3.30 Sat); 6–11
Shepherd Neame Master Brew Bitter, Bishops Finger H
Attractive, 17th-century country pub with a good family room and a skeleton in the cupboard! Excellent value-for-money food but ploughmans only Sun lunch (no food Sun eve). P

Bishopsbourne

Mermaid

Bishopsbourne (½ mile off A2)
☎ (0227) 830581
11–2.30; 6–11
Shepherd Neame Master Brew Bitter H
Attractive little pub in a typically Kentish village, well worth a detour from A2. Unusual electronic heads and tails tosser by dartboard. ♣

Blue Bell Hill

Robin Hood

364 Common Road, Chatham (1 mile W of A229) OS734628
☎ (0634) 861500
11–3; 6–11
Courage Best Bitter, Directors H
A rural setting; three bars and an inglenook. Live music and barbecues in the garden. This 17th-century pub caters for all tastes with always a friendly welcome. No food Sun. Clay pigeon shooting.
♣ P

Borden

Plough & Harrow

Oad Street (near A249/M2 jct 5) ☎ (0795) 843351
11–3; 6–11
Shepherd Neame Master Brew Bitter H
Pleasant free house with restaurant. Guest beers.

Borough Green

Fox & Hounds

Maidstone Road (A25)
☎ (0732) 882334
11–2.30; 6.30–11
Everards Tiger Best Bitter; Harveys Best Bitter H
Friendly village pub: many pictures of foxes but the only hound is live. Guest beers.
P

Try also: Railway (Free)

Boughton Monchelsea

Red House

Hermitage Lane (from Marlpit

down Wierton Lane, left fork Wierton Place, 1 mile) OS783489 ☎ (0622) 743986
11–3; 7–11 (11.30–11 Sat)
Exmoor Ale; Greene King IPA, Abbot Ale [H]
Enterprising free house off the beaten track. Worth finding if you can! Beer range always includes one of King & Barnes' and a Wadworth beer, plus guests. Occasional real cider. Home-cooked fare (veg option).
⌂ ♉ ❀ ◐ ◑ ⅄ ♣ ♁ P

Boughton under Blean

Queen's Head Inn
111 The Street
☎ (0227) 751369
11–3 (may extend); 6–11
Shepherd Neame Master Brew Bitter [H]
Unpretentious, 16th-century inn. Accommodation and food are both good value.
⌂ Q ♉ ❀ ⛟ ◐ ◑ ⊞ ♿ ⅄ ♣ P

Brasted

Bull Inn
High Street (A25)
☎ (0959) 62551
10.30–2.30; 6–11 (10.30–11 Sat)
Shepherd Neame Master Brew Bitter, Best Bitter, Bishops Finger [H]
Friendly pub at west end of village, serving both local and passing trade. Bat and Trap played. ❀ ◐ ◑ ♣ P

Try also: Kings Arms (Shepherd Neame)

Bredgar

Sun
The Street (B2163)
☎ (062 784) 221
11–3; 6–11
Courage Best Bitter, Directors; John Smith's Bitter [H]
Spacious country inn with a good selection of food.
⌂ ❀ ◐ ◑ P

Broadstairs

Neptunes Hall
1 Harbour Street
☎ (0843) 61400
11–2.30; 6–11 (11–11 summer)
Shepherd Neame Master Brew Bitter, Bishops Finger [H]
Large Victorian pub with three contrasting bars. Often packed with discerning tourists and locals. ❀ ◐ ◑ ≢ ♣

Brookland

Woolpack
1 mile S of Brookland on A259, by sharp bends OS978245
☎ (06794) 321; (0679) 344321 mid 1991.
11–3 (12.30–3 Sun); 6–11
Shepherd Neame Master Brew Bitter, Bishops Finger [H]
Remote 'beacon keeper's' cottage, circa 1410, with smuggling connections, like many other Romney Marsh pubs. A two-bar pub with very low beams and a huge inglenook. A collection of water jugs adorns the bar. Try your luck on the Spinning Jenny.
⌂ ❀ ◐ ◑ ⊞ ♣ P

Burham

Toastmasters
Church Street
☎ (0634) 861299
12–3.30; 6–11
Fuller's ESB; Greene King IPA; Palmers BB; Theakston Old Peculier; Young's Special [H]
Previously the Royal Exchange. Bar has pews from demolished parish church and a collection of pewter tankards. Good quality food. ❀ ◐ ◑ ♁ P

Burmarsh

Shepherd & Crook
$1\frac{1}{2}$ miles N of Dymchurch OS101320 ☎ (0303) 872336
11.30–3; 7–11
Adnams Bitter; Shepherd Neame Master Brew Bitter [H]
A two-bar pub with pool and darts in public. The saloon bar is liberally adorned with china, copper and firearms. Emphasis on home-cooked food. Occasional guest beer.
⌂ ❀ ◐ ◑ ⊞ ♣ P

Canterbury

Canterbury Tales
12 The Friars (off High Street, opp. Marlowe Theatre)
☎ (0227) 768594
11–2.30; 5.30–11
Goacher's Maidstone Light, Maidstone Dark; Shepherd Neame Master Brew Bitter [H]
Attractive old pub, recently redecorated in elegant 1920s pastels. Theatrical memorabilia. Guest beers.
◐ ◑ ♿ ≢

Gentil Knyght
Shipman Avenue (400 yds off ring road in London Road estate) ☎ (0227) 765891
11–3 (4 Sat); 7–11
Shepherd Neame Master Brew Bitter [H]
Housing estate pub with cosy saloon and large games room (pool, and Bat and Trap played).
♉ ❀ ◐ ◑ ⊞ ♿ ♣ P

Kentish Cricketers
14 St Peter's Street (near Westgate) ☎ (0227) 464227
10–3; 5.30–11
Shepherd Neame Master Brew Bitter, Bishops Finger [H]
Cosy, lace-curtained oasis for shoppers, visitors and locals.
◐ ♿ ≢

New Inn
19 Havelock Street (off ring road) ☎ (0227) 464584
11–3.30; 6–11 (11–11 Sat)
Brakspear Special; Everards Tiger Best Bitter; Wadworth 6X [H]
Tiny free house, popular with students. Guest beers.
❀ ≢ (East)

Try also: Olive Branch (Ind Coope); **Simple Simon's** (Free)

Charing Heath

Red Lion
Off A20 OS928493
☎ (023 371) 2418
11–2.30; 6.30–11
Shepherd Neame Master Brew Bitter [H]&[E]
First registered in 1709 as an ale house; became Red Lion in 1762. Two bars: the saloon has a real fire. The only pub in the area with an electrically assisted handpump. Cosy restaurant serves home-cooked food (not Tue or Sun). ⌂ Q ❀ ◐ ◑ ⊞ P

Try also: Royal Oak, Charing (Free)

Chatham

Constitution Castle
Constitution Hill (between A2 and Luton Road)
☎ (0634) 843972
12–11 (12–4.30; 7–11 Sat)
Shepherd Neame Master Brew Bitter [H]
Refurbished corner bar. ♣

Ropemakers Arms
70 New Road (A2)
☎ (0634) 402121
11–3; 7–11 (12–3; 7.30–10.30 Sun)
Burton Bridge XL Bitter; Goacher's Maidstone Light; Greene King Abbot Ale; Marston's Pedigree Bitter [H]
Friendly free house with display of knots and splices. No food Sun. ◐ ≢ ♣

Try also: Shipwrights Arms, Richard St

Chiddingstone

Castle Inn
S off B2027 Leigh-Penshurst road, following signs.
☎ (0892) 870247
11–3; 6–11
King & Barnes Sussex Bitter; Larkins Sovereign Bitter, Porter Ale; Shepherd Neame Master Brew Bitter [H]
Historic inn with attractive tile-hung frontage in National Trust village. Pub dates back to 1420

and is totally unspoilt. Small, traditional public bar, plus larger, comfortable saloon. Pretty garden at rear. Separate restaurant with extensive wine list. ⌂ Q ❀ ◐ ◑ ⊞

Chillenden

Griffins Head
OS271535 ☎ (0304) 840325
10–2.30; 6–11
Shepherd Neame Master Brew Bitter Ⓗ, **Stock Ale** Ⓖ, **Bishops Finger** Ⓗ
Friendly, rambling, rural village pub – very busy and popular. Good range of reading material! Outdoor barbecue area. ❀ ◐ ◑ P

Cliffe

Black Bull
Church Street (off B2000)
☎ (0634) 220893
12–3; 7–11 (11–11 Sat)
Bateman XXXB; Goacher's Maidstone Dark; Young's Special Ⓗ
Large, cosy, three-bar pub in old village. Specialises in SE Asian cuisine in its unusual cellar restaurant. ⌂ ❀ ◐ ◑ ⊞ ♣ P

Court at Street

Welcome Stranger
On B2067, 1 mile W of Port Lympne Wildlife Park
OS090354 ☎ (0233) 720400
12–2.30; 6–11
Shepherd Neame Master Brew Bitter Ⓗ
A friendly house where beer (not lager) drinkers are made very welcome. A small, quiet, one-bar pub, ideal for a chat and a pint or two. Regular guest beer. Q

Cranbrook

Prince of Wales
High Street ☎ (0580) 713058
11.30–2.30; 6.30–11
Harveys Best Bitter Ⓗ
Renowned and lively town-centre free house. Both bars can get very busy, especially at weekends. Home of Mad Dogs rugby team. Guest beers.
⌂ ♉ ❀ ◐ ◑ ⊞ ♣

Dargate

Dove Inn
Plum Pudding Lane (off A299)
☎ (0227) 751360
11–3; 6–11
Shepherd Neame Master Brew Bitter Ⓗ
Attractive, mellow, wood-panelled inn. Lovely garden with dovecote. Children welcome at lunchtime. Veg meals served; no food Sun eve.
⌂ ♉ ❀ ◐ P

Dartford

Fulwich
St Vincents Road
☎ (0322) 223683
11–2.30; 6.30–11; (11–3.30; 7–11 Sat)
Ind Coope Burton Ale; Tetley Bitter Ⓗ
Thriving locals' pub with a large public bar. Publican displays a number of deserved awards for good cellar-keeping. Darts and pool. ◐ ⊞ ⇌ ♣

Malt Shovel
3 Darenth Road
☎ (0322) 224381
10.30–2.30; 5–11 (10.30–11 Fri & Sat)
Young's Bitter, Special, Winter Warmer Ⓗ
Pub of great character with quiet, unspoilt public bar. Eve meals 7–8.45pm (not Sun/Mon); veg option.
⌂ Q ❀ ◐ ◑ ⊞ ⇌ ♣ P

Royal Oak
57 Spital Street
☎ (0322) 71703
10–3; 6–11
Courage Best Bitter, Directors
Pleasant, historic town-centre pub with easy-going atmosphere. ◐ ⇌ ♣ P

Deal

Admiral Keppel
Manor Road (off A258)
10–11
Draught Bass; Charrington IPA Ⓗ
Three linked bars. Live music. Tricky car park. ◐ P

Clarendon Hotel
Beach Street (on seafront)
☎ (0304) 374748
10.30–3; 6–11
Shepherd Neame Master Brew Bitter Ⓗ
Recently-refurbished, smart (no jeans!), multi-bar seafront hotel. Live music. ◐ ◑ ⇌

Deal Hoy
16 Duke Street (off High Street)
☎ (0304) 363972
10–2.30; 6.30–11
Shepherd Neame Master Brew Bitter, Bishops Finger Ⓗ
Noisy and friendly back-street local, recently-refurbished as one open bar. ⇌

Dover

Eagle Hotel
London Road (near Sainsburys)
☎ (0304) 201543
11–2.30 (12–2 Sun); 6–11
Courage Best Bitter, Directors; John Smith's Bitter Ⓗ
Impressive two-bar corner pub. Bar snacks (not Sun). ⊞

Gordon House Hotel
32 East Cliff (opp. Eastern Docks) ☎ (0304) 204459
11–11
Draught Bass; Harveys Best Bitter Ⓗ
Friendly, lively hotel, popular with tourists, travellers and dock workers. ⛟ ◐ ◑

Old Endeavour
124 London Road
☎ (0304) 204417
11–11
Shepherd Neame Master Brew Bitter Ⓗ
Busy town pub, large but cosy. Despite refurbishment is still popular with bikers. ♣

Royal Oak
Lower Road, River (off A256 by the 'river')
☎ (0304) 822073
11–3; 6–11
Shepherd Neame Master Brew Bitter Ⓗ
Open-plan lounge pub in expanding residential area.
◐ ⇌ (Kearsney) P

White Lion
35 Tower Street, Tower Hamlets ☎ (0304) 204754
11–3.30; 7–11
Shepherd Neame Master Brew Bitter Ⓗ
Welcoming, cosy local in residential area. ❀ ⇌ (Priory)

East Farleigh

Walnut Tree
Forge Lane, Dean Street
OS743530 ☎ (0622) 726368
12–3; 6–11
Shepherd Neame Master Brew Bitter Ⓗ
Busy, traditional, low-beamed country pub with interesting memorabilia. Large beer garden, ideal for children. Shut the Box played. Good range of home-cooked food (veg option).
⌂ ❀ ◐ ◑ ⇌ ♣ P

Elham

New Inn
High Street OS177349
☎ (0303) 840288
11–3; 7–11
Shepherd Neame Master Brew Bitter Ⓗ
A very welcoming two-bar village pub. Separate family room with table skittles and other traditional games and a childproof garden with toys behind the pub. Other pubs in the village sell real ale.
⌂ ♉ ❀ ⛟ ◐ ◑ ⊞ ♣ P

Fairbourne Heath

Pepperbox
2 miles S of A20 at Harrietsham
OS859501 ☎ (0622) 842558
11–3; 6–11
Shepherd Neame Master Brew Bitter, Bishops Finger Ⓖ
Centuries-old quiet, comfortable

pub overlooking farmland. Good food with veg option (not Sun). ⌂ Q ▩ ◖ ◗ P

Fairseat

Vigo Inn
Gravesend Road (A227, 1 mile N of A20 jct)
☎ (0732) 822547
12–2.30 (not Mon); 6–11
Goacher's Maidstone Light; Harveys XX Mild Ale, Best Bitter; Young's Bitter, Special Ⓗ
Ancient travellers' pub; basic structure is a medieval wooden barn. Name comes from a survivor of the famous battle who ran the pub; the new village is now named after it. Regular haunt of mild drinkers. No keg here! Rare Daddlums table. Guest beers and a Goacher's house beer.
⌂ Q ♣ ⌽ P

Farningham

Chequers
High Street ☎ (0322) 865222
11–11
Bateman XB; Greene King IPA; Fuller's London Pride, ESB Ⓗ
Enterprising free house in pleasant village just off A20. Serves various guest beers. No food Sun eve. ▩ ◖ ◗

Faversham

Anchor
52 Abbey Street
☎ (0795) 536471
10.30–3; 6–11
Shepherd Neame Master Brew Bitter, Best Bitter, Bishops Finger Ⓗ
A pub full of character at the end of an historic street. Good value food. ⌂ ♞ ▩ ◖ ⊞ ♣

Mechanics Arms
44 West Street
☎ (0795) 532693
11–3; 7–11
Shepherd Neame Master Brew Bitter Ⓗ
Small but splendid side-street local. Q ◖ ⊞ ≠ ♣

Folkestone

Clifton Hotel
The Leas (near Leas Cliff Hall)
☎ (0303) 851231
10–3; 6–11
Draught Bass Ⓗ
A relaxing and comfortable bar in a three star hotel overlooking the sea. Guest beer.
⌂ Q ♞ ▩ ⊨ ◖ ◗ ≠ (Central) ♣

Richmond Tavern
1 Margaret Street
☎ (0303) 54857
11–2.30 (4 Sat); 6 (7 Sat)–11
Shepherd Neame Master Brew Bitter Ⓗ
Small but lively locals' pub, off the beaten track. Serious fund-raising for guide dogs (12 dogs in the last six years).
≠ (Central)

Try also: Honest Lawyer (Shepherd Neame)

Gillingham

Roseneath
79 Arden Street (200 yds off High Street) ☎ (0634) 52553
11–4; 7–11
Goacher's Maidstone Light; Greene King Rayments BBA Ⓗ
Thriving back-street local with a selection of good value food (not Sun) and guest beers. ◖ ◗ ≠

Try also: Monarch (Shepherd Neame)

Goodnestone

Fitzwalter Arms
The Street (follow the walls of the Fitzwalter Estate!)
OS255546 ☎ (0304) 840303
12–3; 7–11
Shepherd Neame Master Brew Best Bitter Ⓗ
Old gate lodge of the Fitzwalter Estate. Friendly multi-bar pub. Bar billiards. ⌂ Q ⊞ ♣

Goudhurst

Green Cross Inn
Station Road (1 mile W of village on A262) ☎ (0580) 211200
11–2.30; 6–11
Exmoor Ale; Harveys BB Ⓗ
Friendly country pub with open-plan front bar. Emphasis on traditional English food (veg option). Simple use of wood and light colours adds to the atmosphere.
⌂ Q ▩ ⊨ ◖ ◗ ♣ ⌽ P

Gravesend

Bat & Ball
113 Wrotham Road (A227, just off town centre)
☎ (0474) 352097
11–3.30; 6–11 (11–11 Sat)
Ruddles Best Bitter, County; Webster's Yorkshire Bitter Ⓗ
Large, friendly pub with a balcony overlooking the cricket ground. No food Sun. Shove-ha'penny played.
▩ ◖ ◗ ⊞ ♿ ≠ ♣ P

Darnley Arms
9 Trafalgar Road
☎ (0474) 334051
11–3; 5.30–11
Bateman XB; Greene King IPA, Abbot Ale Ⓗ
Friendly street-corner local serving a range of unusual beers – a welcome change from the run-of-the-mill pubs found in the area. ≠

Jolly Drayman
1 Love Lane (near town centre)
☎ (0474) 352355
11.30–2.30 (12–2.30 Sun); 5–11 (11.30–3; 7–11 Sat)
Draught Bass; Charrington IPA; Fuller's ESB Ⓗ
Old pub, recently renovated inside. Once formed part of the Wellington Brewery. No food at weekend. ▩ ◖ ≠ ♣ P

Peacock
78 Peacock Street (off A226)
☎ (0474) 324563
12–3; 7–11
Courage Best Bitter, Directors; John Smith's Bitter Ⓗ
Undergoing internal renovations. Landlord also plans live music. ≠

Green Street Green

Ship
Green Street Green Road (B260, 4 miles S of Dartford)
☎ (04747) 2279
11 (12 Sat)–2.30; 6–11
Courage Best Bitter, Directors; Young's Bitter Ⓗ
Deservedly-popular, two-bar pub, part of which dates from the 17th century. Excellent value lunches – especially the bacon doorsteps! Regular gourmet nights, but usually snacks only in evening.
⌂ ♞ ▩ ◖ ◗ ♣ P

Halling

Plough
High Street (A228)
☎ (0634) 240200
11–3; 6–11
Courage Best Bitter; John Smith's Bitter Ⓗ
Friendly village local. No food Sun. ⌂ ▩ ◖ ◗ ⊞ ≠ ♣ P

Try also: Homeward Bound

Herne Bay

Heron
Station Road
☎ (0227) 372990
11–2.30 (4 Fri); 5.30–11 (11–11 Sat)
Shepherd Neame Master Brew Bitter Ⓗ
Local house, next to station, whose exterior belies its traditional interior. Bar snacks.
♞ ▩ ⊞ ≠ ♣ P

Prince of Wales
Mortimer Street
10–3; 6–11
Shepherd Neame Master Brew Bitter Ⓗ
Traditional interior with atmosphere to match. Q ⊞ ♣

Rose Inn
111 Mortimer Street

☎ (0227) 375081
10–11
Everards Tiger Best Bitter; Shepherd Neame Master Brew Bitter Ⓗ
Smart, friendly and comfortable town-centre house. Normally two guest beers, one sometimes replacing Tiger. Good value snacks (not Sun). Q ⊕

Higham

Chequers Inn
Church Street (over bridge at station) ☎ (047 482) 2794
11–3; 6–11
Courage Best Bitter Ⓗ
Two-bar local with a relaxed, warm and friendly atmosphere. Occasional special theme nights. Sells Russian Stout. Wholesome food, with veg option (not Sun lunch). ❀ ◖ ◗ ⊕ ≥ ♣ P

Hollingbourne

Pilgrim's Rest
Upper Street (5½ miles from Maidstone on B2163)
☎ (0622) 880210
11–2.30; 7–11
Adnams Bitter; Shepherd Neame Master Brew Bitter; Wadworth 6X Ⓗ
500 year-old village pub. Live music on Wed. Guest beers.
❀ ◖ ◗ ♿ ≥ ♣ P

Hythe

Kings Head
117 High Street
☎ (0303) 266283
10.30–2.30; 6.30–11
Shepherd Neame Master Brew Bitter, Bishops Finger Ⓗ
A pleasant 'no gimmicks', high street pub. Separate room with hatch to main bar used mainly as restaurant; children welcome if dining. Lots of plastic flowers. Real food (not Sun), from sandwiches to steak pies; home-cooked specials in winter. ◖

Ightham Common

Harrow
Common Road (¼ mile S of A25, 1 mile W of Ightham village) OS588557
☎ (0732) 885912
12–3; 6–11
King & Barnes Sussex Bitter Ⓗ
The ultimate small pub with everything: stone floors, open fires and a cosy atmosphere. Worth finding. No food Mon lunch. ♨ Q ⇔ ◖ ◗ P

Knockholt

Harrow
Harrow Road, Knockholt Pound (300 yds from Pound in direction of Sevenoaks)
☎ (0959) 32168
11–2.30 (3 Sat); 6–11
Friary Meux Best Bitter; Gale's HSB; Ind Coope Burton Ale; King & Barnes Sussex Bitter Ⓗ
Parts of building date from 14th century. Sympathetically-extended to include old stable, giving split-level drinking and a food area (eve meals Thu–Sat). Pub has all the elements of the village local; set on its outskirts in wonderful walking country. Guest beers. ♨ ❀ ◖ ◗ ♣ P

Lamberhurst

Horse & Groom
High Street (B2100)
☎ (0892) 890302
10.30–2.30; 6–11
Shepherd Neame Master Brew Bitter, Bishops Finger Ⓗ
Attractive pub in pleasant village location. Lively public bar with framed Page & Overton sign (Croydon Brewery) above fireplace; relaxed and comfortable saloon. A friendly welcome assured to strangers and regulars alike. Good food. ♨ ❀ ⇔ ◖ ◗ ⊕ ♣

Larkfield

Bricklayers Arms
440 New Hythe Lane (off A20)
☎ (0622) 718151
11–2.30 (Sun 12–2); 6–11
Courage Best Bitter, Directors; John Smith's Bitter Ⓗ
Very clean, well-run pub which uses smoke extractors. Comfortable saloon bar. No food Sun. Fishing in nearby lakes. Petanque played.
♨ ❀ ◖ ◗ ⊕ ≥ (New Hythe) ♣ P

Try also: Monks Head

Longfield

Railway
Station Road (corner of B260)
☎ (047 47) 2217
11–2.30 (3 Sat); 5.30 (7 Sat)–11
Ruddles Best Bitter, County; Webster's Yorkshire Bitter Ⓗ
Good value village local which until recently stocked the entire range of Truman cask beers. Worthington White Shield is available. Bar snacks Mon–Fri.
♨ ❀ ⊕ ♿ ⛺ ≥ ♣ ◌ P

Maidstone

Admiral Gordon
1 Milton Street (A26, 1 mile from centre)
☎ (0622) 726803
11–2.30; 6–11 (11–11 Sat)
Courage Best Bitter, Directors Ⓗ
Small, friendly, street-corner local with two bars. Saloon bar has a distinct nautical theme. Popular with students from the nearby college at lunchtime. Good value food (not Sun).
🐂 ❀ ◖ ◗ ⊕ ≥ (West)

Dragoon
40 Sandling Road (A229, N of centre) ☎ (0622) 752620
10–2.30; 5 (6 Sat)–11
Shepherd Neame Master Brew Bitter Ⓗ
Friendly street-corner local with emphasis on traditional games – two bar billiards tables and darts. Split-level drinking areas surround bar. ◖ ⊕ ≥ (East) ♣ P

Flowerpot
96 Sandling Road (A229, N of centre) ☎ (0622) 752956
11–3; 6–11
Benskins Best Bitter; Ind Coope Burton Ale Ⓗ
Pleasant, cosy local with many pub games and good value food. Note the fine pargetting.
◖ ≥ (East) ♣

Greyhound
77 Wheeler Street
☎ (0622) 754032
11–3; 6–11
Shepherd Neame Master Brew Bitter Ⓗ
Popular, two-bar pub. Local home guard attends first Mon in the month! Good value food menu caters for children.
Q ❀ ◖ ◗ ⊕ ♣ P

Wheelers Arms
1 Perry Street (off Sandling Road – A229 – N of centre)
☎ (0622) 752229
11–2.30; 6 (5.30 summer)–11
Shepherd Neame Master Brew Bitter, Best Bitter Ⓗ
Popular street-corner pub with hop-festooned bar and beer garden. Folk club Sat eve.
❀ ◖ ⊕ ≥ (East) ♣

Margate

Orb
243 Ramsgate Road
☎ (0843) 220663
11–11
Shepherd Neame Master Brew Bitter, Stock Ale, Bishops Finger Ⓗ
Long-established favourite of the beer-lovers of East Kent. All you could ask of a town pub. No food Sun. Q ❀ ◖ ⊕ ♣ P

Spread Eagle
25 Victoria Road
☎ (0843) 293396
11–3; 5.30–11 (11–11 Sat)
Adnams Bitter; Bateman Dark Mild, XB; Burton Bridge Porter; Marston's Pedigree Bitter; Young's Special Ⓗ
Small back-street establishment with ever-changing range of top quality independent ales. Well

worth the short walk from the beach. Guest beers. No food Sun. ❀ ◐ ♣

Marshside

Gate Inn
1½ miles up Chislet turning on A28 ☎ (022 786) 498
11–2.30 (3 Sat); 6–11
Shepherd Neame Master Brew Bitter, Stock Ale, Bishops Finger Ⓖ
Lively country pub: excellent value, with something for everyone. Duck-infested garden. Voted best pub in South East by CAMRA in 1989. Does not serve keg lager during Lent. Excellent value food; famous doorsteps; veg option.
⌂ Q ☺ ❀ ◐ ◑ ♿ ▲ ♣ P

Try also: Prince of Wales, Hoath (Shepherd Neame)

Mersham

Royal Oak
The Street (½ mile from A20 jct) OS052398 ☎ (0233) 624218
11–2.30; 6–11
Shepherd Neame Master Brew Bitter Ⓗ
A very popular locals' pub with three bars (particularly unspoilt public bar). Tie collection in the saloon bar; separate family area off saloon. Traditional village pub with traditional food.
⌂ Q ☺ ❀ ◐ ◑ ⊟ P

Minster (Sheppey)

Prince of Waterloo
428 Minster Road (B2008)
☎ (0795) 872458
11–3; 6–11
Ind Coope Burton Ale Ⓗ
Popular village local.
⌂ ☺ ❀ ◐ ◑ ⊟ ♣

Minster in Thanet

Saddler
7–9 Monkton Road (B2047)
☎ (0843) 821331
11–2.30; 6–11
Shepherd Neame Master Brew Bitter Ⓗ
Simple and friendly, old-style country inn. Good value bar snacks. Q ⊟ ⇌ ♣

Monks Horton

Black Horse
Fiddling Lane OS113405
☎ (0303) 812182
11.30–2.30; 7–11 (closed Mon)
Shepherd Neame Master Brew Bitter; Ruddles County; Webster's Yorkshire Bitter Ⓗ
17th-century, with many additions over the years. Timber and brick bar. Emphasis on food in dining area where young families are welcome (lunchtime only as it can get very busy in the eve). Barbecue every Sun eve in summer; children welcome. Black Horse house beer. Cider in summer.
⌂ ☺ ❀ ◐ ◑ ⌽ P

Try also: Tiger, Stowting (Free)

Oare

Three Mariners
Church Road
☎ (0795) 533633
11–3; 6–11
Shepherd Neame Master Brew Bitter Ⓗ
Rambling inn in centre of village, with a nautical theme. Bat and Trap played.
⌂ ❀ ◐ ◑ ♣ P

Otford

Horns
66 High Street (near River Darent) ☎ (095 92) 2604
11–2.30; 6–11
Charrington IPA; Harveys BB; King & Barnes Sussex Bitter Ⓗ
Friendly 15th-century inn with two comfortable bars and good food. Village has some fine old houses and a ruined 16th-century archbishop's palace.
⌂ Q ❀ ◐ ◑ ⇌ P

Painters Forstal

Alma Inn
Painters Forstal Road (1½ miles off A2 at Ospringe)
☎ (0795) 533835
11–3; 6–11
Shepherd Neame Master Brew Bitter Ⓗ
Kentish weatherboarded inn, surrounded by hopfields.
Q ❀ ◐ ⊟ ▲ ♣ P

Pembury

Black Horse
12 High Street (old A21)
☎ (089 282) 2012
11–11
Adnams Bitter; Harveys BB, XXXX (Old); Larkins Best Bitter; Young's Special Ⓗ
In the centre of Pembury, this pub acts as a real community local. Bar divided into several drinking areas, with old church pews for seating. Restaurant offers good home-cooked fare.
⌂ Q ❀ ◐ ◑

Perry Wood

Rose & Crown
OS042552 ☎ (0227) 752214
11–3; 7–11 (closed Mon)
Shepherd Neame Master Brew Bitter; Wadworth 6X Ⓗ
16th-century free house set amongst splendid woodland, with restaurant and attractive garden (Bat and Trap played). Guest beers. ⌂ Q ❀ ◐ ◑ ♣ P

Petteridge

Hopbine Inn
Petteridge Lane (off A21, ½ mile S of Brenchley) OS667413
☎ (0892) 722561
11–2.30; 6–11
King & Barnes Mild, Sussex Bitter, Broadwood, Old, Festive Ⓗ
Attractive, part-weatherboarded and tile-hung, country pub, built into side of a hill. The idyllic setting, friendly welcome, plus full range of King & Barnes beers, make it well worth seeking out. No food Wed.
⌂ ❀ ◐ ◑ ♣ P

Plaxtol

Rorty Crankle Inn
The Street (off A227)
☎ (0732) 810254
11–2.30; 7–11
Bateman XB, XXXB Ⓗ
Comfortable pub in centre of picturesque village. Landlord is from Lincolnshire and pub has a long association with Bateman's beers. 'Rorty Crankle' means 'Happy Corner' in Anglo-Saxon. No-smoking area to left of main bar. ❀ P

Try also: Golding Hop (Free)

Rainham

Rose Inn
249 High Street (A2)
☎ (0634) 31047
11–11
Shepherd Neame Master Brew Bitter Ⓗ
Friendly locals' pub with a collection of cribbage score boards. Small car park. No food Sun. ◐ ◑ ⊟ P

Rochester

Britannia
376 High Street
☎ (0634) 461514
11–3; 6–11
Goacher's Maidstone Light; Greene King IPA, Abbot Ale; King & Barnes Festive; Ruddles County Ⓗ
Pleasant town lounge, accessible from both Rochester and Chatham stations. No food Sun.
◐ ⇌ ♣

Coopers Arms
10 St Margarets Street (200 yds S of A2, near castle)
☎ (0634) 404298
11–2.30 (3.30 Sat); 5 (6.30 Sat)–11
Courage Best Bitter, Directors; John Smith's Bitter Ⓗ
This ancient hostelry, mentioned in the *Domesday Book*, has two cosy bars and a

warm, welcoming atmosphere. Ideally situated for visitors to the city's main tourist attractions. Barbecue on summer Fri eves. No food Sun.
⌂ Q ✿ ◐ ≷ P

Greyhound
68 Rochester Avenue (between B2097 and Delce Road)
☎ (0634) 844120
10–3 (may be 5 Sat); 6–11
Shepherd Neame Master Brew Bitter 🄷
This cosy, two-bar, Victorian terraced local has chaises longues and a range in the saloon. The public is basic. Try the tasty home-made pie of the day. No food Sun. ⌂ ✿ ◐ ⊞ ≷

Two Brewers
113 High Street
☎ (0634) 812448
11–2.30; 7–11
Friary Meux Best Bitter; Ind Coope Burton Ale 🄷
Friendly, one-bar pub. Bar snacks (not Sun). ≷ ♣

Who'd Ha Tho't It
9 Baker Street (100 yds off B2097) ☎ (0634) 841131
11–11
Brains Dark; Greene King Abbot Ale; Woodhams XXX Bitter 🄷
This lively back-street boozer has a good, mixed clientele. The second bar can be booked. The three guest beers rotate from a list of 36. (Woodhams is brewed by Goachers). Good cottage pie. No food Sat or Sun.
⌂ ✿ ◐

Try also: Roebuck (Courage); **Under the Clock** (Free)

St Margaret's at Cliffe

Cliffe Tavern Hotel
High Street ☎ (0304) 852749
11–2.30; 6–11
Harveys Best Bitter; Shepherd Neame Master Brew Bitter; Ruddles County 🄷
Large weatherboarded hotel in popular holiday resort. Secluded suntrap garden, two bars and a restaurant serving imaginative food (with veg option).
Q ✿ ⛼ ◐ ◑ ▲ P

Sandgate

Ship
65 High Street (A259)
☎ (0303) 48525
11–2.30; 6–11
Friary Meux Best Bitter 🄷; **Ind Coope Burton Ale; Gale's HSB** 🄶
Highly energetic landlord claims to sell more Burton Ale than Gatwick Airport! A busy and pleasant seafront pub. Excellent blackboard menu. HQ of 'Sandgate Clog Morris'. Public bar features caricatures of locals.
✿ ◐ ◑ ⊞

Sandwich

Crispin
2 High Street
☎ (0304) 617365
10–2.30; 6–11
Draught Bass; Charrington IPA 🄷
Large corner pub that gives the impression of having separate bars. Cosy and welcoming. Note: all pubs in town serve real ale. ⌂ ◐ ◑ ≷

Market Inn
7 Cattle Market (opp. Guildhall)
☎ (0304) 612033
10–2.30; 6–11
Shepherd Neame Master Brew Bitter 🄷
One-bar terraced pub, small and popular. Generous servings of good food. ◐ ◑ ≷

Selling

White Lion
The Street ☎ (0227) 752211
11–3; 6–11
Shepherd Neame Master Brew Bitter 🄷
Very well-appointed country inn with separate restaurant.
⌂ Q ✿ ◐ ◑ ≷ P

Sevenoaks

Royal Oak Tap
High Street (opp. Sevenoaks School) ☎ (0732) 458783
11–3; 6–11
Bateman XXXB; Ruddles County; Webster's Yorkshire Bitter 🄷
Pleasant, comfortable pub in old part of town. Guest beers. Handy for Knole Park. Eve meals Mon–Thu.
⌂ ✿ ◐ ◑ ♿ ♣ P

Vine Tavern
Pound Lane (off A225)
☎ (0732) 454641
11–3; 6–11
Friary Meux Best Bitter; Gale's HSB; Ind Coope Burton Ale; Tetley Bitter 🄷
Popular, multi-level pub, close to Ancient Vine cricket ground. Contains suitable mementoes. Bat and Trap. No food Sun.
⌂ ✿ ◐ ♣ P

Sevenoaks Weald

Chequer Tree
Scabharbour Road
☎ (0732) 463386
11.30–2.30; 6–11
Ruddles Best Bitter, County; Webster's Yorkshire Bitter 🄷
Records date from 1839; believed to be on site of one of Henry VIII's hunting lodges. Bat and Trap played.
⌂ Q ✿ ◐ ◑ ▲ ♣ P

Try also: Prince of Wales

Shatterling

Green Man
Pedding Hill (A257 Ash-Wingham Road)
☎ (0304) 812525
12–3; 6.30–11
Adnams Bitter; Young's Bitter, Special 🄷
Isolated roadhouse. Welcoming visitors and catering for a variety of tastes. Bat and Trap.
✿ ⛼ ◐ ◑ ▲ ♣ P

Sheerness

Red Lion
High Street, Bluetown
☎ (0795) 663165
12–3; 6–11
Draught Bass; Greene King Abbot Ale 🄷
Welcoming real ale mecca in old docks area. Guest beers.
◐ ⊞ ≷ ♣

Seaview Hotel
Broadway ☎ (0795) 662003
11–3; 6–11
Shepherd Neame Master Brew Bitter 🄷
Thriving inn with remains of windmill in car park.
♉ ✿ ⛼ ◐ ◑ ≷ ♣ P

Shoreham

Royal Oak
2 The High Street
☎ (095 92) 2319
10.30–2.30 (3 Sat); 6–11
Marston's Pedigree Bitter; Wadworth 6X 🄷
Walls well-covered with paintings by local artists (for sale), and large cartoons of local drinkers. Try the pub games: Toad in the Hole, darts and table skittles. Ask about the unique old game called Tripletell, not on show.
⌂ ✿ ◐ ◑ ⊞ ≷ ♣ ⌽

Shottenden

Plough
Shottenden Road (off A252 near Chilham)
☎ (0227) 730244
11–3; 6–11
Courage Best Bitter; Shepherd Neame Master Brew Bitter 🄷
Comfortable country free house with summer barbecues at weekends. Occasional live jazz. Guest beers. ⌂ ✿ ◐ ◑ ♣ P

Sittingbourne

Park Tavern
86 Park Road (off A2)
☎ (0795) 72486
11–3; 7–11

Shepherd Neame Master Brew Bitter [H]
Increasingly-rare example of a comfortable street-corner local. Bar billiards. Q ◖ ⊞ ≠ ♣

Smarden

Bell
Bell Lane (1 mile from village) OS8970430 ☎ (023 377) 283
11–2.30; 6–11
Brakspear Special; Fuller's London Pride; Goacher's Maidstone Light; Harveys BB; Shepherd Neame Master Brew Bitter [H]
Low-beamed ceilings and stone floors characterise this very popular 16th-century inn, set in open countryside. Three bars with a large family room off main bar. Good, but limited bar food range.
⌂ Q ♨ ❀ ⊨ ◖ ◗ ⊞ ♣ ⍥ P

Chequers
High Street (B2077)
☎ (023 377) 217/623
10–2.30; 6–11
Courage Best Bitter, Directors; John Smith's Bitter [H]
Medieval pub in centre of picturesque Kentish village. Good food; book restaurant.
⌂ Q ❀ ⊨ ◖ ◗ ⊞ ♣ P

Snargate

Red Lion
On B2080, Brenzett–Appledore road OS990286
☎ (067 94) 648; (0679) 344648 mid 1991
11–3; 7–11
Adnams Bitter; Bateman XB [G]
A wonderfully unspoilt small, rural pub with real fires, timber and stone floors. Marble counter top. Piano and Toad in the Hole played. Large garden. Occasional guest beers and ciders. A must if you are in the area. ⌂ Q ❀ ⊞ ♣ P

Southborough

Bat & Ball
141 London Road (A26)
☎ (0892) 28448
10–3; 6–11
Harveys BB; Wadworth 6X; Charles Wells Bombardier [H]
Comfortable and popular one-bar pub offering a good range of beers and a friendly welcome. Good value and well-presented bar meals (not Sun lunch). Guest beers. ⌂ ◖ ◗

Southfleet

Black Lion
Red Street ☎ (047 483) 2386
11–2.30; 6–11
Ruddles Best Bitter, County; Webster's Yorkshire Bitter [H]
Thatched country pub with restaurant attached. Its history dates back to the Great Plague. Serves excellent bar meals, with veg option. ⌂ ❀ ◖ ◗ P

Speldhurst

George & Dragon
Speldhurst Hill (2 miles W of A26) OS554414
☎ (0892) 863125
11–2.30; 6–11
Harveys Pale Ale, Best Bitter, XXXX (Old); King & Barnes Sussex Bitter; Larkins Best Bitter; Marston's Pedigree Bitter [H]
One of the least spoilt pubs in the country, with large, stone-flagged public and cosy saloon bars. Restaurant upstairs. Pub dates back to 1212 and is a real classic, with ancient beams and sandstone walls.
⌂ Q ❀ ◖ ◗ ⊞ ⍥

Stalisfield Green

Plough
Stalisfield Road (on downs 2 miles N of Charing) OS954529
☎ (0795) 89256
10.30–3; 6–11
Adnams Extra; Ind Coope Burton Ale [H]
Old and impressive pub set in lovely countryside. Q ❀ ◖ P

Staplestreet

Three Horseshoes
☎ (0227) 750842
11–3 (4.30 Sat); 6–11 (11–11 Thu & Fri)
Shepherd Neame Master Brew Bitter [G]
Typically Kentish pub with list of landlords going back to 1690. Collection of stone bottles; many tabletop games. Bar snacks lunchtime and early eve. ⌂ Q ❀ ♿ ⛺ ♣ P

Strood

Horseshoe
51 Cuxton Road (A228 one-way system)
☎ (0634) 718414
11–3; 6–11 (11–11 Sat)
Ind Coope Burton Ale [H]
Friendly and vibrant local. Good value bar meals (not Sun).
❀ ◖ ◗ ≠ ♣ P

Three Crutches
Old Watling Street (near A2/M2 jct)
☎ (0634) 717473
11–2.30; 6–11
Friary Meux Best Bitter; Ind Coope Burton Ale; Tetley Bitter [H]
Recently-renovated lounge but unspoilt public bar. ❀ ◖ ◗ ⊞ P

Tonbridge

George & Dragon
17 Shipbourne Road (just past A227/B245 jct)
☎ (0732) 358924
11–3; 6–11
Courage Directors; Harveys Best Bitter [H]
Large, one-bar pub consisting of original part of building (dating from 1478), plus more recent extension. Popular with office workers at lunchtime and young people in evenings. Generous portions of home-cooked fare (children's and veg dishes).
❀ ◖ P

Rose & Crown
125 High Street (A26)
☎ (0732) 357966
11–3; 6–11 (11–11 Sat)
Draught Bass [H]
Small, comfortable bar in an imposing historic hotel. A good place for meeting friends, conducting business or simply sitting and watching the world go by. Guest beers. Q ⊨ ◖ ◗ P

Uncle Tom's Cabin
54 Lavender Hill (off Pembury Road)
11–2.30; 6–11 (may vary)
Greene King XX Dark, IPA [H]
Small, friendly free house in terraced street. Offers the best selection of beers in Tonbridge; always two guest beers on offer, usually from small independents. ❀ ≠ ♣

Tudeley

George & Dragon
Five Oak Green Road (B2017, Tonbridge-Paddock Wood road) ☎ (0892) 832521
11–2.30 (3.30 Fri & Sat); 6–11
Courage Best Bitter, Directors [H]
Attractive, part-weatherboarded pub, dating back to 16th century. Cosy, low-ceilinged saloon with dining area, plus games-oriented public bar. Pub overlooks hop gardens and sells the best pint of Courage for miles. Bat and Trap.
⌂ ❀ ◖ ◗ ⊞ ♿ ♣ P

Tunbridge Wells

Beau Nash Tavern
61 Mount Ephraim (A264, overlooking common)
☎ (0892) 39350
11.30–2.30; 5.30–11 (11–11 Sat)
King & Barnes Sussex Bitter, Broadwood; Ruddles Best Bitter, County; Webster's Yorkshire Bitter [H]
Small, friendly pub frequented by all ages. Known for its fine food (veg and children's dishes). It is the ideal place for a quiet drink. ⌂ Q ❀ ◖ ◗ ♣

Broker's Arms

5 Langton Road
☎ (0892) 41000
11–3 (4 Sat); 6–11
Brakspear Special; Greene King Abbot Ale; Harveys Pale Ale, Best Bitter; Larkins Porter Ale; Marston's Pedigree Bitter Ⓗ
Attractive and friendly free house on edge of common. Split-level interior with bare brick floor, beamed ceiling and inglenook. Restaurant upstairs. Good food. ♨ ◖ ◗

Crystal Palace
69 Camden Road
☎ (0892) 22815
11–3.30 (4.30 Sat); 7–11
Harveys XX Mild Ale, Pale Ale, Best Bitter, XXXX (Old) Ⓗ
Busy, two-bar pub, with comfortable saloon and down-to-earth public bar. Provides a welcome refuge from the hustle and bustle of the nearby Calverly Road shopping precinct. ◖ ⊞ ♣

High Brooms Hotel
102 High Brooms Road (150 yds from station)
☎ (0892) 28543
11–3; 6–11
Harveys Best Bitter Ⓗ
Authentic workers' local, unspoilt by recent decoration. ❀ ⊞ ♿ ⇌ (High Brooms) ♣ P

Upper Upnor

Tudor Rose
29 High Street
☎ (0634) 715305
12–3; 7–11
Young's Bitter, Special, Winter Warmer Ⓗ
Friendly pub with quiet rooms, inglenook and separate games area. Near castle and river. Guest beers. No food Sun. ♨ ♉ ❀ ◖ ◗ ♣

Walmer

Lifeboat
The Strand (on seafront opp. lifeboat station)
☎ (0304) 375948
10–2.30; 6–11
Draught Bass; Charrington IPA Ⓗ
Two separate bars: one noisy, one quiet. ⊞

Try also: Lord Clyde (Shepherd Neame)

Waltham

Lord Nelson
☎ (0227) 70628
11.30–2.30; 7–11 (closed Tue)
Adnams Bitter; Hall & Woodhouse Tanglefoot; Shepherd Neame Master Brew Bitter; Charles Wells Bombardier Ⓗ
Attractive, elegant, Georgian pub with collection of blacksmith's implements. Reasonably-priced, home-made food (veg option). Bar billiards and Bat and Trap played. ♨ ❀ ◖ ◗ ⊞ ♿ ⛺ ♣ ⌓ P

Try also: Compasses, Crundale (Free)

Warehorne

Woolpack
Off B2067, $1\frac{1}{2}$ miles from Hamstreet OS989326
☎ (023 373) 2022
11–2.30; 7–11
Larkins Best Bitter Ⓗ
A 15th-century pub on the northern edge of Romney Marsh. A smuggler's tunnel runs from the cellar to the church opposite. Occasional guest beers. ♉ ❀ ◖ ◗ ♣ P

Westerham

General Wolfe
High Street (A25)
☎ (0959) 62104
11–3; 6–11
Friary Meux Best Bitter; Gale's HSB; Ind Coope Burton Ale Ⓗ
Small, weatherboarded pub with real character. The best bet in this popular tourist town. No food at weekend. Small car park. ♨ ◖ ♣ P

West Malling

Bull
1 High Street
☎ (0732) 842753
11 (12.30 Sun)–2.30; 6–11
Draught Bass; Charrington IPA; Everards Old Original Ⓗ
Unspoilt town pub with horseshoe bar. Watch the blackboard for forthcoming guest beers. ❀ ⇌ ♣

Lobster Pot
47 Swan Street (400 yds from station) ☎ (0732) 843265
12–2.30 (incl. Sun); 6–11
Beer range varies Ⓗ
Pleasant, multi-bar pub on two levels, with wood panelling and flock wallpaper. All beers are guest beers (usually four on at a time). The range includes Archers, Bateman, Everards, Felinfoel, Fuller's and Goacher's. Food very much to the fore – all tables set with candles and condiments. Snooker room upstairs. One bar is quiet. Q ◖ ◗ ⊞ ⇌ ♣

Swan Hotel
Swan Street (400 yds from station) ☎ (0732) 843000
10–2.30; 6–11
Draught Bass; Charrington IPA Ⓗ
Traditional, wood-beamed original pub/hotel. Real fire in lounge. Children's room is upstairs. ♨ Q ♉ ⛟ ◖ ◗ ⊞ ♿ ⇌ P

Whitstable

Coach & Horses
Oxford Street (A290)
☎ (0227) 264732
10–3; 7–11
Shepherd Neame Master Brew Bitter Ⓗ
Popular local in High Street. Bar snacks: salt beef rolls recommended. Q ❀ ♣

Noah's Ark
83 Canterbury Road
☎ (0227) 272332
11–3; 6–11
Friary Meux Best Bitter Ⓗ
Basic, friendly, two-bar local on main road. ⊞ ⇌ ♣

Woodchurch

Bonny Cravat
OS943349 ☎ (0233) 860345
11–3; 6–11
Shepherd Neame Master Brew Bitter, Bishops Finger Ⓗ
Large, busy village local, opposite church. Separate saloon and public bars with separate prices. Good value food: daily home-made specials and veg option. ❀ ◖ ◗ ⊞ ⛺ ♣ P

Worth

St Crispin
Off A258, near Deal
☎ (0304) 612081
10.30–3; 6–11
Adnams Broadside Ⓖ; **Gale's HSB; Marston's Pedigree Bitter** Ⓗ, **Merrie Monk** Ⓖ; **Shepherd Neame Master Brew Bitter** Ⓗ
Old pub, tastefully refurbished and extended and popular locally for food. Beer range liable to change. Read the old sign near the door (inside)! ♨ Q ❀ ⛟ ◖ ◗ ⛺ ♣ ⌓ P

Help keep real ale alive by joining CAMRA. Your voice helps encourage brewers big and small to brew cask beer and offer all beer drinkers a better choice. For membership details see page 504.

TIME CALLED FOR FREMLINS

After closing a brewery every year throughout the decade, Whitbread drew breath and closed no brewery in 1989. It was not to last. As the year ended, Whitbread announced the closure of their newly-acquired Higsons brewery in Liverpool and the Fremlins brewery, in Faversham, Kent. Whitbread's record of a closure a year had to be maintained somehow.

FREMLINS

TRADITIONAL BREWERS

The logic behind the Fremlins closure is limited even by Whitbread's standards – the brewery had been modernised and was in a prime position to export beer to the Continent come 1992. However, Fremlins has closed to suit Whitbread's accountants, and the beers will be brewed in Cheltenham, that home of dull beers which are promoted under the names of dead breweries. Fremlins will become another name like Wethered of Marlow, or Strong's of Romsey, beers ruined by Whitbread brewery closures.

Kent branches had no option but to not submit any Fremlins pubs for this year's *Good Beer Guide*. In part this is because we have no idea what the substitute 'Fremlins' will be like. But is also in clear recognition of the damage Whitbread has done, and is doing, to the British brewing industry.

The Fremlins brewery, closed by Whitbread in 1990

Lancashire

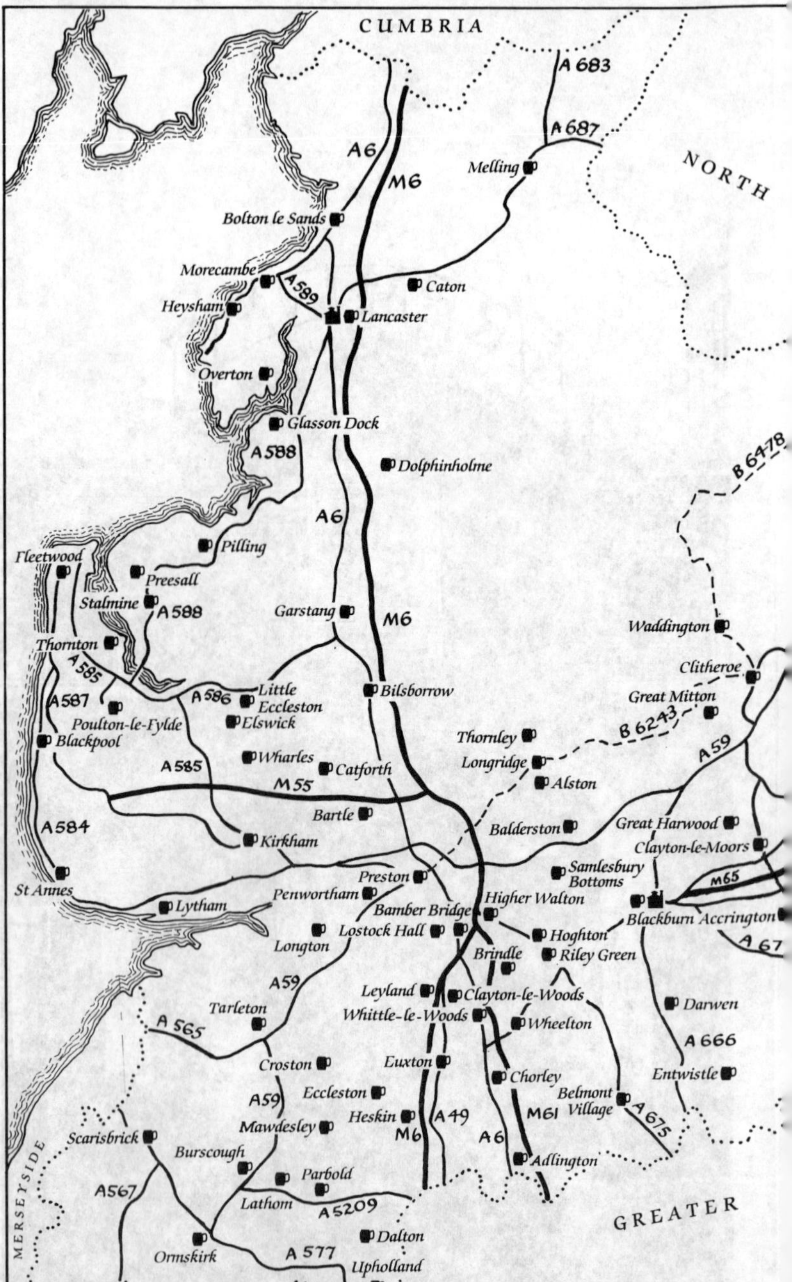

Matthew Brown, Thwaites, *Blackburn;* **Mitchell's,** *Lancaster;* **Moorhouse's,** *Burnley*

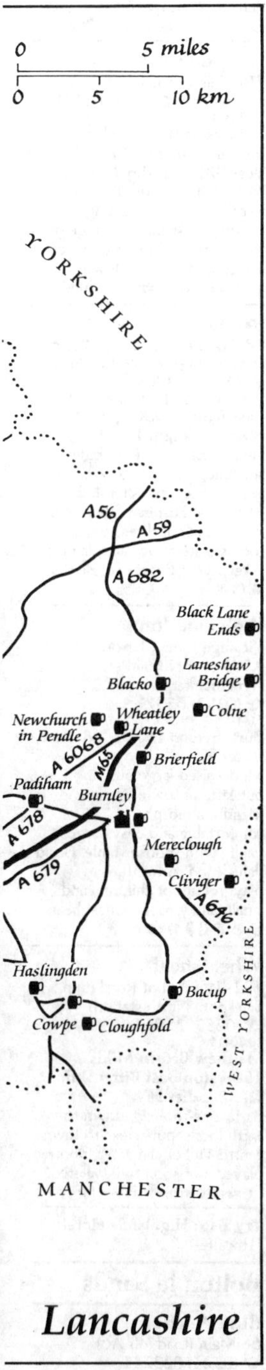

Lancashire

Accrington

Great Eastern
Arnold Street (off A679)
☎ (0254) 34483
12–5; 7–11 (11–11 Sat)
Thwaites Mild, Bitter [H]
Friendly, traditional local in improved part of town.
⊟ ⇌ ♣ P

Nags Head
78 Blackburn Road
☎ (0254) 33965
11–11
Thwaites Best Mild, Bitter [H]
Three-roomed, street-corner local close to town centre and bus and rail stations. ⇌ ♣

Adlington

White Bear Inn
5a Market Street (A6)
☎ (0257) 482357
11–11
Matthew Brown Mild; Theakston Best Bitter, XB, Old Peculier [H]
Large, three-room stone pub. Medium-sized bar area with separate room for diners and small pool room. Good value meals. Open all day Sun for food. ♛ ⛟ ❀ ◖ ◗ ⊟ ⇌ ♣

Alston

White Bull
Preston Road (B6243, between Grimsargh and Longridge)
☎ (0774) 784151
11–3; 6–11
Thwaites Best Mild, Bitter [H]
Spacious pub, recently-refurbished and popular with the young crowd. ♛ ❀ ◖ ♣ P

Aughton

Dog & Gun
223 Long Lane (¾ mile from A59) ☎ (0695) 423303
11–3; 5.30–11
Burtonwood Dark Mild, Best Bitter [H]
Rural pub, with bowling green, on edge of town.
♛ Q ❀ ⊟ ⇌ (Aughton Pk) ♣

Bacup

British Queen
10 Union Street
☎ (0706) 873008
11.30–3 (4 Fri & Sat); 7.30–11
Banks's Mild, Bitter [H]
Three-roomed local with friendly atmosphere, handy for market. Cellar cooled by River Irwell. Sing-alongs on Thu, Sat and Sun.

New Inn
11 Rochdale Road
☎ (0706) 873130
11–11
Thwaites Mild, Bitter [H]
200 year-old pub with four rooms served by central bar. Original wood-panelled ceiling has been retained, as well as 19th-century wall paintings.
♛ ⛟ ♣

Balderston

Myerscough
Whalley Road (A59)
☎ (0254) 812222
11.30–3; 5.30–11
Robinson's Best Mild, Best Bitter, Old Tom (winter) [H]
Large, wood-panelled lounge and separate quiet room with real fire. Popular with locals; strangers made very welcome. Children admitted until 9.30. Relaxed 'country pub' atmosphere. Quiz nights most Weds. ♛ Q ⛟ ❀ ◖ ◗ P

Bamber Bridge

Old Hob Inn
8–9 Church Road (off A6/B6258) ☎ (0772) 36863
11–3; 5.30–11 (11–11 Sat)
Matthew Brown Mild, Bitter; Theakston Best Bitter, Old Peculier [H]
Family-run, 17th-century, thatched pub with small restaurant and a friendly, welcoming atmosphere. No food Mon eve; many dishes cooked in beer. ⛟ ❀ ◖ ◗ ⇌ P

Bartle

Sitting Goose
Sidgreaves Lane (A5085)
OS486329 ☎ (0772) 690344
11.30–3; 6–11
Thwaites Best Mild, Bitter [E]
Comfortable pub in wooded Fylde countryside. Large garden for children's play. Q ❀ ◖ ◗ P

Belmont Village

Black Dog Inn
2 Church Street
☎ (020 481) 218
12–4; 6.30–11
Holt Mild, Bitter [H]
Popular moorland village pub where the landlord whistles the classics. Occasional live orchestras; no jukebox. No food Mon. ♛ Q ⛟ ❀ ⛍ ◖ ◗

Bilsborrow

Owd Nell's
St Michaels Road (off A6)
☎ (0995) 40010
11–11
Whitbread Chester's Best Mild, Fremlins Bitter, Boddingtons Bitter, Castle Eden Ale [H]
Canalside tavern with thatched roof and flagged floor. Good outside facilities for children. Popular with canal users. Informal restaurant next door. Owd Nell's house bitter is brewed by Whitbread.
❀ ⛍ ◖ ◗ ♿ P

White Bull
On A6, by canal

☎ (0995) 40324
12–3; 7–11
Matthew Brown Mild; Theakston Best Bitter; Younger No.3 [H]
Modernised but unspoilt, friendly, canalside pub.
⌂ Q ❀ ♣ P

Blackburn

Imperial
25 Davenport Road
☎ (0254) 54460
11–3; 6–11
Thwaites Mild, Bitter [H]
Classic, small-roomed, terraced local spared the open-plan treatment. Wedge yourself round the tiny bar and join in.
⊕

Moorgate Arms
Livesey Branch Road (A6062, ¼ mile from football ground)
☎ (0254) 51408
12–11 (11–11 Fri & Sat)
Thwaites Mild, Bitter [H]
Old corner pub with etched windows situated near Leeds–Liverpool Canal. Separate games room. Children allowed in small beer garden. Unusual snacks. ❀ ♿ ⇌ (Mill Hill) ♣

Park Hotel
85 Montague Street
☎ (0254) 676524
11–11
Matthew Brown Mild, Bitter [H]
Open-plan local with original Matties windows, near new technical college.

Quarrymans
Dukes Brow ☎ (0254) 51691
12–3; 7–11 (11–11 Sat)
Thwaites Mild, Bitter; Whitbread Boddingtons Bitter [H]
Open-plan local; low beams hung with assorted plates.

Uncle Toms Cabin
42 Larkhill Street
☎ (0254) 54345
11–4.30 (3 Tue); 7–11 (11–11 Fri & Sat)
Thwaites Mild, Bitter [H]
Lively local lurking behind Thwaites brewhouse. Handy for the markets. ◖ ⊕ ⇌

Woodlands Hotel (Pecker's Bar)
Preston New Road (A677, 1 mile W of centre)
☎ (0254) 691122
11–11
Courage Directors; John Smith's Bitter [H]
Bar on ground floor of main road hotel. Nightly disco after 8.30. Close to Billinge Hill Country Park. ❀ ⛟ P

Try also: Borough Arms (Bass)

Black Lane Ends

Hare & Hounds
Skipton Old Road (3 miles from Colne centre on old Colne–Skipton road)
OS928433 ☎ (0282) 863070
12–3 (not Tue & Thu); 6.30–11
Taylor Bitter Ale, Golden Best Mild [H]
Cosy, friendly pub situated high in the Pennines. Live music Fri and Sat nights. Good value home-cooked meals.
⌂ ◖ ◗ ⊕ ♣ P

Blacko

Cross Gaits
Beverley Road (off A682, Barnoldswick Road)
☎ (0282) 66312
11.30–3; 6.30–11
Burtonwood Dark Mild, Best Bitter [H]
Friendly old pub in pleasant countryside. Home-cooked food. ⌂ ❀ ◖ ◗ ▲ ♣ P

Blackpool

Bispham Hotel
Red Bank Road (off A584)
☎ (0253) 51752
11–3; 6–11
Samuel Smith OBB [H]
Large, friendly pub near Promenade. Live music some eves. Games room with pool table. Sun meals only in season.
◖ ⊕ ♿ ♣ P

Empress Hotel
59 Exchange Street, North Shore (400 yds from rail and bus stations) ☎ (0253) 20413
11–11 (1 am Fri & Sat, Easter–Nov)
Thwaites Best Mild, Bitter [H]
Large, friendly Victorian hotel close to seafront. Entertainment and late extensions some nights. Good value food served in season. Well-appointed family room. ⛄ ⛟ ◖ ◗ ⊕ ⇌ (North) ♣

Mount Pleasant
103 High Street, North Shore
☎ (0253) 293335
11–11
Matthew Brown Mild, Bitter; Theakston Best Bitter, Old Peculier [H]
Small, friendly corner local close to rail and bus stations and Promenade. Pool and darts.
⊕ ⇌ (North) ♣

Raikes Hotel
Liverpool Road (off Church Street) ☎ (0253) 294372
11–11
Draught Bass; Stones Best Bitter [H]
Recently-modernised, large suburban pub with bowling green. Barbecues during summer and safe children's play area. Comfortable restaurant (no food Sun; children welcome).
Q ❀ ◖ ⊕ ♿ ⇌ (North) ♣ P

Ramsden Arms Hotel
204 Talbot Road (by bus and rail stations) ☎ (0253) 23215
10.30–11
Ind Coope Burton Ale; Jennings Bitter; Mitchell's Best Bitter; Tetley Dark Mild, Mild, Bitter [H]
Excellent, award-winning, country-style pub on fringe of town centre. Good economical accommodation. Well worth a visit. ⛟ ◖ ⊕ ♿ ⇌ (North) ♣ P

Saddle
286 Whitegate Drive, Marton (A583/Preston Old Road jct)
☎ (0253) 63065
11.30–3; 5.30–11 (11.30–11 Fri & Sat)
Bass Mild XXXX, Special Bitter, Draught Bass [H]
Unimpressive exterior hides a splendid, locally-renowned pub which oozes character and friendly atmosphere. Real coal fires in each of three cosy rooms. Alterations are planned – keep your fingers crossed!
⌂ Q ❀ P

Welcome Inn
Vicarage Lane, Marton (off A583 near Normid Hypermarket)
☎ (0253) 65372
11–11
Burtonwood Dark Mild, Best Bitter [H]
Modernised large pub on outskirts of town. Warm and friendly atmosphere; comfortable and cosy, large vaults with snooker table. Good value food. Adventure playground for children, and small family room. Guest beer.
Q ⛄ ❀ ◖ ◗ ⊕ ♿ ▲ ♣ P

Wheatsheaf
192–194 Talbot Road (opp. Blackpool North station)
☎ (0253) 25062
10.30–11
Matthew Brown Mild; Theakston Best Bitter, XB, Old Peculier [H]
Basic, one-roomed, down-to-earth locals' pub, close to town centre. Full of character; pool played, but soon to be altered.
Q ⇌ (North) ♣ P

Try also: Highlands Hotel (Thwaites)

Bolton le Sands

Blue Anchor
68 Main Road (off A6)
☎ (0524) 823241
11–11
Mitchell's Dark Mild, Best Bitter [H]
Robust, friendly local in heart of large village. Separate games room and snug. Garden has a

pets corner. Parking difficult. ♔ ❀ ◖ ◗ ♣

Brierfield

Wagon & Horses
Colne Road ☎ (0282) 63962
11.30–2.30; 5–11 (11–11 Fri & Sat)
Thwaites Best Mild, Bitter H
A former winner of Best Refurbished Pub award from CAMRA. Friendly bar staff. Four separate rooms – one is gas lit. ♔ Q ❀ ◖ ⇌ ♣ P

Brindle

Cavendish Arms
Sandy Lane (B5256 Leyland–Blackburn Road)
☎ (025 485) 2912
11–3; 5.30–11 (11–11 Sat)
Burtonwood Dark Mild, Best Bitter H
Traditional village pub with lots of stained glasswork and wood carvings. Public bar and dining room. Originally named the Gerrard Arms after the family who lived at nearby Hoghton Towers. Within easy reach of M6 and M61 motorways.
♔ Q ♉ ❀ ◖ ◗ ⊕ ♣ P

Burnley

Commercial Inn
Briercliffe Road, Harle Syke
☎ (0282) 28823
11.30–3; 6–11
Bass Mild XXXX, Special Bitter H
Comfortable local. Retains two separate tap rooms to cater for darts. Handy for Queen Street Mill (heritage museum). ♔ ⊕ ♣

General Scarlett
243–245 Accrington Road (A679, 400 yds from M65 jct 10) ☎ (0282) 831054
11.30–3; 7–11
Moorhouse's Premier Bitter, Pendle Witches Brew H
Lively, one-roomed locals' pub, opposite the brewery, named after General Scarlett, of the Charge of the Light Brigade.
⇌ (Rose Grove) ♣ P

Lanehead
Hillingdon Road
☎ (0282) 59491
11–3; 5.30–11 (11–11 Fri & Sat)
Thwaites Bitter H
Friendly landlord and landlady at this popular locals' pub with a busy games room. Good, inexpensive lunches. ❀ ◖ ⊕ P

Mechanics (Shuttle Bar)
Manchester Road (next to Town Hall) ☎ (0282) 30055
11–3; 5.30–11
Moorhouse's Pendle Witches Brew; John Smith's Bitter; Thwaites Mild, Bitter H
Part of a local authority refurbishment to create an arts/theatre complex. Very busy with younger people at weekend. Jazz Sun lunch; popular national blues festival at Easter. Guest beers. ♉ ◖ ♿ ⇌

Try also: Manor Barn (Burtonwood)

Burscough

Martin Inn
Martin Lane (off A570/B5242 OS414127 ☎ (0704) 892302
11–3; 5.30–11
Courage Directors; John Smith's Bitter H
Remote, welcoming hotel in the heart of the country. Part stone-floored with comfy furnishings and friendly atmosphere. Bar meals until 10pm and separate restaurant. Close to Martin Mere Wildfowl Trust reserve.
♔ ❀ ⛟ ◖ ◗ ♣ P

Catforth

Running Pump
Catforth Road (off B5269)
☎ (0772) 690265
11–3; 6–11
Robinson's Best Mild, Best Bitter H, **Old Tom** (winter) G
Cosy, rural Fylde pub with warm, friendly atmosphere. Family dining room offers children's menu. Look out for the original village pump at front of pub. ♔ Q ♉ ◖ ♿ ♣ P

Caton

Station
2 Hornby Road (A683)
☎ (0524) 770323
11–3; 6–11 (11–11 Sat)
Mitchell's Dark Mild, Best Bitter H
Dated 1830 (pre-railway!). Several comfortable rooms are set around a small bar. Bowling green. ♔ ❀ ◖ ◗ ♣ P

Chorley

Crown
46 Chapel Street
☎ (025 72) 75644
11–11
Matthew Brown Mild; Theakston Best Bitter, XB H
Town-centre pub opposite church. Handy for shopping centre and station. ◖ ♿ ⇌

Malt n' Hops
Friday Street
11–2; 5–11 (11–11 Fri & Sat)
Hydes' Anvil Bitter; Wilson's Original Mild, Webster's Yorkshire Bitter; Whitbread Boddingtons Bitter H
Small comfortable pub, formerly a shop, just north of the town centre. Ideal for train-spotters; public car park opposite. Regular guest beers. No food Sun. ♔ ◖ ⇌

Market Tavern
21 Cleveland Street
☎ (025 72) 77991
11–4; 7–11
Ind Coope Burton Ale; Walker Mild, Best Bitter, Winter Warmer H
Small, busy town-centre pub with four small rooms full of character. Local black puddings a speciality. Voted Lancashire CAMRA Pub of the Year in 1989. ♔ Q ◖ ⊕ ⇌

Queens Tavern
6 Preston Road (A6 N of centre) ☎ (025 72) 75902
11.30–3; 6.30–11 (11.30–11 Fri & Sat)
Hartleys XB; Marston's Pedigree Bitter; Whitbread Chester's Best Mild, Trophy, Castle Eden Ale H
Large local with imposing frontage on main road.
Q ◖ ⇌ ♣

Shepherds Arms
38 Eaves Lane (opp. bus garage, near Leeds–Liverpool Canal bridge 66) ☎ (025 72) 75659
11–11
Matthew Brown Mild, Bitter; Younger No.3 H
A locals' pub on north side of town centre. Small, comfortable rooms, with public bar at rear. Friendly welcome assured. Cheap beer for senior citizens.
⊕ ⇌ ♣

Clayton-le-Moors

Old England for Ever
13 Church Street (off A680, near canal) ☎ (0254) 33435
11–3; 7–11
Matthew Brown Mild, Bitter H
Friendly, unspoilt local, boasting original tiled hallway. Handy for Leeds–Liverpool Canal. ⊕ ♣

Clayton-le-Woods

Halfway House
470 Preston Road (A6)
☎ (0772) 34477
11–3.30; 5–11 (11–11 Fri & Sat)
Banks's Mild, Bitter E
Spacious roadhouse where wood panelling abounds. Reputedly half-way from London to Glasgow. Separate restaurant in the greenhouse. Open fire in family room; children welcome until 9pm.
♔ ♉ ❀ ◖ ◗ P

Clitheroe

Cross Keys
Lowergate ☎ (0200) 28877
12–3 (5 Fri & Sat); 7–11
Vaux Lorimers Best Scotch; Wards Sheffield Best Bitter H
Locals' pub, popular with young people. Interesting toilets!

Guest beers. Food summer only.
❀ ◖ ⊟ ♿ ⅄ ♣

Try also: Station (Thwaites)

Cliviger

Queens Hotel
414 Burnley Road (A646)
☎ (0282) 36712
12–3 (Sat & Sun only); 7–11
Burtonwood Dark Mild, Best Bitter 🄷
Unaltered, cosy village local. Children welcome. Bar snacks; hikers may eat own food on premises. ⌂ Q ⊟ ♣

Cloughfold

Ashworth Arms
325 Bacup Road, Rawtenstall
☎ (0706) 215397
11.30–3; 7–11
Bass Mild XXXX, Special Bitter 🄴
Traditional local with two lounges, pool room and games room. ♣ P

Colne

Spinners Arms
12 Primet Hill (A56, 50 yds from station)
☎ (0282) 863495
12–11
Tetley Mild, Bitter 🄷
Small, homely local, tastefully furnished. Lunchtime bar snacks. A local CAMRA Pub of the Month winner. ◖ ⇌ ♣ P

Cowpe

Buck
Cowpe Road (½ mile from A681 jct) ☎ (0706) 213612
12–2 (not Mon, 4 Sat); 7–11
Taylor Golden Best Mild, Best Bitter; Thwaites Best Mild, Bitter; Whitbread Boddingtons Bitter 🄷
Comfortable, two-roomed, terraced local in quiet village, nestling in the valley of the River Irwell. Good value lunches Fri–Sun. ⌂ ❀ ◖ ♣ P

Croston

Black Horse
West Head Road
☎ (0772) 600338
11–11 (12 restaurant)
Banks's Mild; Draught Bass 🄷
Excellent, large village pub with small restaurant and family room. Children's play area and bowling green at rear. Regular guest beers always available.
⌂ ⚇ ❀ ◖ ◗ ⊟ ♿ ⇌ ♣ ⌽ P

Dalton

Prince William
Beacon Lane (Parbold to Upholland road)
☎ (0695) 623989
11–11 (open till 5 Sun for food)
Burtonwood Dark Mild, Best Bitter 🄷
Popular pub in attractive hilly countryside. Photographs of the present Prince William adorn the walls. Menu caters for children and vegetarians. Crazy golf course in garden.
⌂ ❀ ◖ ◗ ⅄ ♣ P

Darwen

Entwistle Arms
15 Entwistle Street
☎ (0254) 70575
12.30–3; 6.15–11 (12.30–11 Sat)
Thwaites Best Mild, Bitter 🄷
Comfortable locals' pub just off the town centre, behind St Peter's church. Emphasis on pub games. ⇌ ♣

Greenfield Inn
Lower Barn Street (25 yds off Cranberry Lane)
☎ (0254) 703945
12–3; 5.30–11
Matthew Brown Mild, Bitter; Moorhouse's Pendle Witches Brew; Taylor Landlord; Theakston XB 🄷
Small, one-roomed pub, off the beaten track, next to Blackburn–Bolton railway line. Nice friendly local, with good value food. Guest beers.
❀ ◖ ◗ ♣

Sunnyhurst Hotel
Tockholes Road
☎ (0254) 873035
11–3; 7–11 (11–11 Sat)
Thwaites Mild, Bitter 🄷
Small, clean, tidy two-roomed pub, with a homely atmosphere. Situated close to Darwen Moors and Tower; ideal for walkers and ramblers. ❀ ◖

Try also: George Inn; Golden Cup (Thwaites)

Dolphinholme

Fleece
½ mile W of village OS509532
☎ (0524) 791233
12–3; 6–11 (12–11 Easter–Oct)
Mitchell's Dark Mild, Best Bitter, ESB 🄷
Former farmhouse on lonely crossroads. Cosy lounge, original little tap room and dining/family room (cold snacks only). ⌂ ❀ ⊟ ♿ ♣ P

Eccleston

Farmers Arms
Town Gate
(B5250) ☎ (0257) 451594
11.30–11
Hartleys XB; Whitbread Chester's Best Bitter, Boddingtons Bitter, Castle Eden Ale 🄷
Old village pub with extensive menu (open all day Sun for meals). Long split-level bar and separate games room.
⌂ Q ❀ ⊭ ◖ ◗ ⊟ ♿ P

Elswick

Boot & Shoe
Beech Road ☎ (0995) 70206
12–3; 6–11 (11–11 Sat)
Thwaites Best Mild, Bitter 🄷
Large, attractive, modern village local offering a friendly welcome and a good selection of food. A large family room is complemented by a spacious outdoor play area. Barbecues every Fri eve in summer.
⌂ Q ⚇ ❀ ⊭ ◖ ◗ ⊟ ♿ ⅄ ♣ P

Entwistle

Strawberry Duck Hotel
Overshaws Road OS727178
☎ (0204) 852013
12–3 (not Mon in winter); 7–11 (12–11 Sat, 11–11 summer)
Marston's Pedigree Bitter; Taylor Golden Best, Best Bitter, Landlord 🄷
Old, isolated but busy country pub next to railway station. Good base for walks in hill country, woods and around reservoirs.
⌂ ⚇ ❀ ⊭ ◖ ◗ ⊟ ⇌ ♣ P

Euxton

Euxton Mills Hotel
Wigan Road (A49/A581 jct)
☎ (02572) 64002
11–3; 5.30–11
Burtonwood Dark Mild, Best Bitter 🄴
Very cosy, comfortable pub serving excellent meals, including veg and children's choices (not Mon eve).
Q ◖ ◗ ⊟ ♿ ♣ P

Fleetwood

North Euston
Esplanade ☎ (03917) 6525
11–3.30; 6–11
Ruddles Best Bitter, County; Webster's Yorkshire Bitter, Wilson's Original Bitter 🄷
Large Victorian edifice near the sea; large, elegantly-appointed public rooms and family room. Meals range from bar snacks to à la carte restaurant menu. This three star hotel is famous for its fish and chips. ⚇ ❀ ⊭ ◖ ◗ ♿ P

Queens
Poulton Road (Beach Road jct)
☎ (03917) 6740
11–11
Thwaites Best Mild, Bitter 🄷
Busy pub in residential area at junction of two major roads.
❀ ◖ ♿ P

Wyre Lounge
Marine Hall, Esplanade
☎ (03917) 71141

11–3 (not winter); 7–11
Everards Tiger Best Bitter; Moorhouse's Premier Bitter; Taylor Landlord Ⓗ
Popular amenity at the Marine Hall complex. Voted 1989 Pub of the Year by the local CAMRA branch. Good selection of real ales served in comfortable surroundings. Guest beers. ❀ ◐ ♿ P

Garstang

Royal Oak
Market Place ☎ (09952) 3318
11–3.30; 7–11 (11–11 Thu–Sat)
Hartleys XB; Robinson's Best Mild, Best Bitter, Old Tom Ⓗ
Interesting old coaching inn; modern furniture in the three lounges detracts little from its old-fashioned feel. ❀ 🛏 ♿ ♣ P

Glasson Dock

Caribou
Victoria Terrace
☎ (0524) 751356
11.30–3; 7–11
Thwaites Best Mild, Bitter Ⓗ
Old pub named after ship skippered by former owner. Public car park by basin. Family room in summer. ⌂ ♘ 🛏 ◐ ◑ ♣

Try also: Dalton Arms

Great Harwood

Merrie England
St Huberts Road (off Blackburn Road) ☎ (0254) 888358
11–11
Whitbread Flowers IPA, Castle Eden Ale Ⓗ
Substantial, stone-built corner pub with friendly atmosphere. ⊟ ♣

Victoria
St Johns Street
☎ (0254) 884810
11.30–4; 6–11
Matthew Brown Mild, Bitter Ⓗ
Superbly-renovated, turn-of-the-century pub, with original tiled walls. Floodlit bowling green. Ceilidh nights first Fri of month; summer barbecues. Children welcome and well catered for. ⌂ Q ♘ ❀ ◐ ♿ ▲ ♣

Great Mitton

Owd Ned's River View Tavern
Mitton Hall (B6246, 2 miles from Whalley) OS718385
☎ (025486) 544
11–11
Marston's Pedigree Bitter; Whitbread Chester's Best Mild Ⓗ
Overlooking the River Ribble in picturesque countryside, this pub places an emphasis on food and provides good facilities for children. Owd Nell's house beer and other guests make six draught beers in total. ♘ ❀ 🛏 ◐ ◑ P

Haslingden

Woolpack
488 Manchester Road
☎ (0706) 214195
12–3; 5.30 (7 Sat)–11 (12–11 Thu & Fri)
Ruddles Best Bitter; Wilson's Original Mild, Webster's Yorkshire Bitter, Wilson's Original Bitter Ⓗ
Smart and comfortable roadside inn with large lounge and separate dining room. Handy for the cricket club. ❀ ◐ ◑ P

Try also: Crown (Tetley)

Heskin

Farmers Arms
Wood Lane (B5250)
OS532154 ☎ (0257) 451276
12–3; 5–11 (opens 5 Sun eve for food)
Hartleys XB; Marston's Pedigree Bitter; Whitbread Chester's Best Bitter, Castle Eden Ale Ⓗ
Country-style pub with attractive exterior. Public bar is popular with locals. The split-level lounge features horsey artefacts and stuffed animals: try to spot the squirrel! Eve meals until 8pm. ♘ ❀ ◐ ◑ ⊟ ♣ P

Heysham

Royal
7 Main Street
☎ (0524) 859928
11–11 (closed 3–6 Mon & Tue)
Mitchell's Dark Mild, Best Bitter Ⓗ
Old, rambling, low-beamed building. Good local trade but also packed with holidaymakers in the season. Children admitted to games room.
⌂ ♘ ❀ ◐ ⊟ ♿ ♣ P

Higher Walton

Mill Tavern
15 Cann Bridge Street (A675)
☎ (0772) 38462
11–3; 5.30–11
Burtonwood Best Bitter Ⓗ
Large, tastefully-modernised local: pleasant, open-plan lounge with small games area. Landlord sponsors a motor-cycle racing team. No food Sun.
◐ P

Hoghton

Black Horse Hotel
Gregson Lane (off Preston–Blackburn old road)
☎ (025 485) 2541
11.30–11
Matthew Brown Mild, Bitter; Theakston Best Bitter, XB Ⓗ
Large, friendly, open-plan pub with plush seating; separate games area. Traditional English home-cooked fare is good value (veg option). ◐ ♿ ♣ P

Kirkham

Queens Arms
7 Poulton Street (A585)
☎ (0772) 686705
11–11
Theakston Best Bitter, XB, Old Peculier Ⓗ
Excellent, well-run, lively town-centre local. A former Matthew Brown house, this recent convert to real ale is full of character. ❀ ◐ ♿ ▲ ≢ ♣ ⟲

Lancaster

Howe Ghyll Arms
Green Lane (just off Halton Road) ☎ (0524) 32011
11–3; 6–11
Mitchell's Dark Mild, Best Bitter Ⓗ
An old private house, converted and extended in 1982 to form a large pub. Howgill (*sic*) Brook runs between mature trees in the garden. Dining/family room. ⌂ ❀ ◐ ⊟ ♿ ♣ P

John O'Gaunt
55 Market Street
☎ (0524) 65356
11.30–3 (11–5 Sat); 7–11 (11.30–11 Fri)
Ind Coope Burton Ale; Jennings Bitter; Tetley Mild, Bitter Ⓗ
Pub with handsome original frontage. Usually busy, it is popular with both students and older customers. Frequent live music. Varied menu of home-cooked food, lunch and early eve (not Sat eve); hotpot for Sun lunch. Newspapers provided. ◐ ◑ ≢

Lord Ashton
36 North Road
☎ (0524) 841185
11–3; 7–11
Thwaites Bitter; Whitbread Boddingtons Bitter Ⓗ
Small town-centre pub, quiet and comfortable, operating by an interesting partial tie arrangement (may sell other beers alongside Thwaites). Disabled access via side door. Chess and backgammon played. No food Sun. Public car park nearby. ◐ ♿ ≢ ♣

Moorlands
Quarry Road (behind Town Hall)
12–3 (not Mon); 7–11
Mitchell's Dark Mild, Best Bitter Ⓗ
Lively, turn-of-the-century local. The decor of its many rooms makes some concessions to the

90s but also includes original stained glass. ⊟ ♿ ♣

Post House
Waterside Park, Caton Road (by M6 jct 34) ☎ (0524) 65999
11–11 (supper licence)
Mitchell's ESB Ⓗ
Expense-account hotel, built 1983. Real ale in lobby bar with comfortable seats, soft music and plastic plants. The excellent ESB is a local rarity. Cold snacks all day.
☋ ❀ ⛫ ◖ ♿ P

Three Mariners
Bridge Lane (off Damside Street) ☎ (0524) 64877
11–11
Mitchell's Dark Mild, Best Bitter, ESB Ⓗ
Alleged to be Lancaster's oldest pub. Bridge Lane, once the main road to Scotland, is the strip of cobbles in front of the pub! Dark, antique decor and generally young clientele. Upstairs cellar where beer is pumped to produce head.
⌂ ❀ ◖ ◗ ≠ ♣ P

Try also: Park; Fox & Goose

Laneshaw Bridge

Alma Inn
Emmott Lane (½ mile from village, off A6068)
☎ (0282) 863447
11.30–3; 6.30–11 (all day Sun for meals)
Ind Coope Burton Ale; Tetley Mild, Bitter Ⓗ
Comfortable country inn set in scenic location. Known locally for good food and ale. Separate public bar with pool table and jukebox. ⌂ ❀ ◖ ◗ ⊟ ♣ P

Try also: Hargreaves Arms (John Smith's)

Lathom

Railway Tavern
Station Road, Hoscar Moss (¾ mile from A5209) OS469116
11–3; 5.30–11
Jennings Bitter Ⓗ**; Tetley Mild, Bitter** Ⓔ
Unpretentious and unspoilt pub by rural railway station.
⌂ Q ❀ ◖ ◗ ⊟ ≠ (Hoscar) ♣

Ship Inn
Wheat Lane (300 yds from A5209, over canal swing bridge) OS452115
☎ (0704) 893117
11–3; 6–11
Taylor Landlord; Tetley Bitter; Whitbread Chester's Best Bitter Ⓗ
Known locally as 'the Blood Tub', this authentic free house has recently expanded into the cottage next door. Frequent guest beers. No food Sun.
Q ☋ ❀ ◖ ♣

Leyland

Crofters Arms
373 Leyland Lane (1 mile W of centre) ☎ (0772) 422420
11–3; 6–11
Matthew Brown Mild, Bitter; Theakston Best Bitter; Younger No.3 Ⓗ
A real locals' pub where darts and pool teams gather in the games room. Landlord likes to keep ale on stillage for two weeks to mature. ❀ ◖ ⊟ ♣ P

Dunkirk Hall
Dunkirk Lane (B5248/B5253 jct) ☎ (0772) 422102
11.30–3; 5–11 (11–11 Fri & Sat)
Courage Directors; John Smith's Bitter Ⓗ
Converted 17th-century farmhouse. Now a listed building, it features flag floors, oak beams and panelling. Veg and children's meals on request.
❀ ◖ ◗ P

Original Ship
95 Towngate
☎ (0772) 456674
11–11
Matthew Brown Mild, Bitter; Theakston Best Bitter, XB, Younger No.3 Ⓗ
Pine-panelled, comfortable, town-centre pub with spacious games area. One large bar. No food Sun. ❀ ◖ ≠ ♣ P

Little Eccleston

Cartford Country Inn & Hotel
Cartford Lane (½ mile off A586, through village, by toll bridge) ☎ (0995) 70166
12–3; 7–11 (11.30–3; 6.30–11 summer)
Marston's Pedigree Bitter; Moorhouse's Pendle Witches Brew; Taylor Landlord; Whitbread Boddingtons Bitter Ⓗ
Delightfully-situated free house by River Wyre, full of character and comfort. Extensive range of home-made dishes, plus children's menu. Pool table; large outdoor play area; comfortable accommodation; 1½ miles of fishing rights. Guest beers. Meet George, the ghost of a sheep rustler!
⌂ Q ☋ ❀ ⛫ ◖ ◗ ⊟ ♿ ♣ P

Longridge

Alston Arms
Inglewhite Road
☎ (0774) 783331
11–3; 6–11
Matthew Brown Mild, Bitter; Theakston Best Bitter; Younger No.3 Ⓗ
Small, friendly pub on outskirts of town, on road to Chipping. Large beer garden and children's play area. Houses a tractor and double decker bus. ⌂ Q ❀ ◖ ◗ P

Old Oak
111 Preston Road (B6243)
☎ (0774) 783648
11–11
Matthew Brown Mild, Bitter; Theakston Best Bitter, XB; Younger No.3 Ⓗ
Stone-built pub on road from Preston. Oak settles around the fire; public bar is used for games. ⌂ ❀ ◖ ⊟ ♣ P

Towneley Arms
41 Berry Lane
☎ (0774) 782219
11–3.30; 6–11
Tetley Mild, Bitter Ⓗ
Town-centre pub next to closed railway station, with wood-panelled rooms off main bar area. Large roaring fire is especially welcoming in winter.
⌂ Q ⊟ P

Longton

Dolphin (Flying Fish)
Marsh Lane OS459254
☎ (0772) 612032
12–3 (Sat & Sun only); 7–11
Thwaites Best Mild, Bitter Ⓗ
Remote farmhouse pub on the edge of Longton Marsh, haunt of wildfowlers and clay pigeon shooters. Small, old-fashioned tap room, and lounge in new extension. ⌂ Q ❀ ⊟ ♿ ♣ P

Longton Arms
2 Liverpool Old Road, Walmer Bridge (just off A59)
☎ (0772) 612335
2 (1 Fri, 12 Sat)–11
Greenalls Mild, Bitter Ⓔ
Small, terraced locals' pub with tiny vault. ⌂ ⊟ ♣ P

Lostock Hall

Victoria
Watkin Lane (A582)
☎ (0772) 35338
11–3; 6–11
John Smith's Bitter, Magnet Ⓗ
Popular pub with large vault where a friendly welcome is assured. Home of local Pigeon Club. Bus stop outside.
❀ ◖ ⊟ ♿ ≠ ♣ P

Lytham

County Hotel
Church Road (B5261)
☎ (0253) 739995
11–11
Whitbread Boddingtons Bitter Ⓗ
Smart, busy town-centre pub with one large room and a separate restaurant. Accommodation is a recent addition. ⌂ ❀ ⛫ ◖ ◗ ≠ P

Hole in One

Forest Drive (off B5261, by Fairhaven Golf Course)
☎ (0253) 739968
11–3.30; 6–11 (11–11 Fri & Sat)
Thwaites Bitter [H]
Pleasant, modern pub serving new housing development. Good home-made food.
Q ◖ ♿ P

Try also: Captain's Cabin

Mawdesley

Black Bull
Hall Lane OS500152
☎ (0704) 82202
12–3; 5.30–11 (12–11 Sat)
Greenalls Mild, Bitter [H]
400 year-old, rambling country pub, once known as 'Hell's Hob'; old fireplace has giant poker. Disabled access is via back door. No food Mon.
⌂ Q ⊗ ◖ ◗ ♿ ♣ P

Melling

Melling Hall
Wennington Road
☎ (05242) 21298
12–2.30 (closed Wed in winter); 6–11
Hartleys XB; Taylor Landlord; Whitbread Boddingtons Bitter [H]
17th-century manor house, converted in the 1940s to a well-appointed (two star) hotel. Friendly locals' bar via left-hand door. Garden play area.
⌂ ⊗ ◖ ◗ ⊟ ♿ ♣ P

Mereclough

Kettledrum Inn
302 Red Lees Road
☎ (0282) 24591
11–3; 5.30–11
Courage Directors; John Smith's Bitter, Magnet; Theakston Best Bitter, XB, Old Peculier [H]
Attractive roadside pub on the outskirts of Burnley, with gaslit restaurant upstairs serving a wide variety of meals (booking advisable). Regular guest beers.
⌂ Q ⊗ ◖ ◗ ♣ P

Morecambe

Davy Jones' Locker
76 Marine Road West
11–6; 7–11
Mitchell's Best Bitter, ESB [E]
Cellar bar beneath Clarendon Hotel (keg-only) which will send food down to order (own bar food summer lunchtimes only). Liable to flooding during storms. Nautical theme and large open fire.
⌂ ◖ ≠

George
Lancaster Road
☎ (0524) 418477
11–11
Thwaites Best Mild, Bitter [H]
Large, 1936 'Brewer's Jacobean' suburban local in Torrisholme Village. Panelled lounge; games room and dining room (children welcome).
⊗ ◖ ⊟ ♿ ♣ P

Pier Hotel
285 Marine Road Central
☎ (0524) 417928
11–4; 7–11 (may vary)
Matthew Brown Mild, Bitter; Theakston Best Bitter, XB, Old Peculier [H]
A seafront bar but, in essence, a friendly, traditional local. Outdoor seating on pavement. Lunches in the holiday season only. ⌂ ◖ ⊟ ♣

Try also: Joiners (Thwaites)

Newchurch in Pendle

Lamb Inn
OS823394 ☎ (0282) 698812
12–4; 7–11
Moorhouse's Premier Bitter, Pendle Witches Brew [H]
Small, comfortable pub with good value meals, situated in a village associated with the Pendle Witches.
⌂ ☋ ◖ ◗ ⊟ ♣ P

Ormskirk

Buck i' th' Vine
35 Burscough Street
☎ (0695) 72647
11.30–3; 5.30–11 (11–11 Thu–Sat)
Walker Mild, Bitter, Best Bitter [H]
Historic pub on pedestrian street, with unique sweetshop window bar counter. No food Sun/Mon. ⌂ Q ☋ ⊗ ◖ ⊟ ≠ ♣

Golden Lion
41 Moor Street (A570)
11–3; 5.30–11 (11–11 Thu-Sat)
Tetley Dark Mild, Mild, Bitter [H]
Tudorish exterior, housing a pleasantly-refurbished town-centre pub. Handsome bar and comfortable, split-level lounge.
⊗ ◖ ⊟ ≠ ♣

Horse Shoe
24 Southport Road (A570)
☎ (0695) 72956
11–11
Tetley Mild; Walker Best Bitter [H]
Friendly alehouse in terrace opposite Civic Hall and famous tower-and-steeple parish church.
⌂ ⊟ ≠ ♣

Queen Inn
81 Aughton Street (300 yds from A59 roundabout)
☎ (0695) 72114
11.30–11
Vaux Bitter [H]
Handsome town pub, comprising pleasant hall bar and several small rooms.
⌂ Q ⊶ ⊟ ≠ ♣

Overton

Ship
9 Main Street
☎ (052471) 231
11.30–3 (4 Fri & Sat); 7–11 (extends in summer)
Thwaites Best Mild, Bitter [H]
Genuine late Victorian village pub which has been remarkably well-preserved. Notable features include stuffed birds and birds' eggs. Small quiet rooms (children admitted); thick sandwiches always available, but no meals Tue. ⌂ Q ⊗ ◖ ♣ P

Try also: Globe (Mitchell's)

Padiham

Hand & Shuttle
1 Eccles Hill Street
☎ (0282) 71795
11–3.30; 6–11
Thwaites Best Mild, Bitter, Daniel's Hammer [H]
Two-roomed local, unspoilt by modern pub trends. A former local CAMRA Pub of the Month winner. Q ◖ ⊟ ♣ P

Parbold

Railway Hotel
1 Station Road
☎ (02576) 2917
11–3; 5.30–11 (11–11 Sat & bank hols)
Burtonwood Dark Mild, Best Bitter [H]
Popular village pub, full of railway 'numerasignia'! A must for railway enthusiasts. Daily newspapers provided. Children welcome until 8pm. ☋ ≠ P

Penwortham

Kingsfold Tavern
Kingsfold Drive
☎ (0772) 742297
12–3; 6–11 (12–11 Fri & Sat)
Younger Scotch, IPA [H]
New pub in centre of a large housing area. Large public bar and split-level lounge; separate food bar and children's room. Live music every Fri and Sat.
☋ ⊗ ◖ ◗ ⊟ ♿ ♣ P

Pilling

Golden Ball
School Lane (off A588)
☎ (0253) 790212
11–3; 7–11 (11–11 Sat)
Thwaites Mild, Bitter [H]
Large, traditionally furnished pub, popular with the locals. Good family facilities include children's garden play area. Two bowling greens, one floodlit.
⌂ Q ☋ ⊗ ◖ ◗ ⊟ ♣ P

Poulton-le-Fylde

Old Town Hall
Church Street
☎ (0253) 892257
11–11
Ruddles County; Webster's Yorkshire Bitter, Choice Ⓗ
Village-centre pub, until recently the village hall, sporting a painted ceiling. Easy access from Blackpool; next to large shopping centre and public car park. Quiz games and pool. ◖ ♿ ⇌ ♣

Queens
Higher Green
☎ (0253) 883471
11–11
Bass Special Bitter, Draught Bass Ⓗ
Large, pleasant, Victorian pub opposite park and near the town square. ⊞ ♿ ⇌ ♣ P

Try also: Thatched House

Preesall

Saracens Head
Park Lane (off A588)
☎ (0253) 810346
12–2; 5–11 (11.30–5; 7–11 Sat)
Thwaites Best Mild, Bitter Ⓗ
Excellent, well-furnished and friendly village local. Real fires in both bar and lounge, which also has piano. Bar snacks at both sessions. ♨ ⊛ ⊞ ▲ ♣ P

Preston

Black Horse
166 Friargate
☎ (0772) 52093
10.30–11
Hartley's Fellrunners; Robinson's Best Mild, Best Bitter, Old Tom Ⓗ
Excellent, grade II listed, town-centre pub with side rooms and upstairs bar. Wonderful curved, tiled bar; varnished wood walls; screens with stained glass windows and an ornate mosaic floor. Q ⇌

George Hotel
89 Church Street (near bus station) ☎ (0772) 51529
11–3; 7–11
Thwaites Mild, Best Mild, Bitter, Daniel's Hammer Ⓔ
Old-fashioned town-centre boozer with several drinking areas off a small bar. Unusually, both Thwaites' milds are on offer. ⊞ ♣

Lamb & Packet
91a Friargate
11.30–11 (11.30–3; 6.30–11 Sat; closed Sun lunch)
Thwaites Best Mild, Bitter, Daniel's Hammer Ⓗ
Small pub near polytechnic; often crowded during term-time. Eve meals 4.30–6.30, Mon–Fri. ◖ ◗ ⊞ ⇌ ♣

Mitre Tavern
90 Moor Lane
☎ (0772) 51918
11.30–3; 6.30–11 (11–11 Sat)
Vaux Lorimers Best Scotch, Samson; Wards Sheffield Best Bitter Ⓗ
Friendly, 60s-built roadside local. Good value food.
◖ ⊞ ♿ ♣ P

New Britannia
6 Heatley Street (off Friargate)
☎ (0772) 53424
11–3 (4 Fri & Sat); 6–11 (closed Sun lunch)
Hartleys XB; Marston's Pedigree Bitter; Whitbread Trophy, Castle Eden Ale Ⓗ
Small, side-street pub near the polytechnic, popular with bikers and the heavy metal creed. Often crowded weekend eves. No food Sat. ◖ ♿ ⇌ ⌽

New Inn
27 Queen Street
☎ (0772) 51602
12–11
Thwaites Best Mild, Bitter Ⓗ
Comfortable, two-bar suburban pub. ⊞ ♣ P

Old Blue Bell
114 Church Street
☎ (0772) 51280
11–2.30 (4 Sat); 5.30 (7 Sat)–11
Samuel Smith OBB Ⓗ
Very old, comfortable town-centre pub with one large room and two small snugs. No food Sun. ♨ ◖ ♿ ⇌ P

Sun
112 Friargate
☎ (0772) 52335
11–4; 7–11
Thwaites Mild, Bitter Ⓗ
Comfortable town-centre pub comprising small games room and large lounge. A quiet haven. No food Sun. ◖ ⇌ ♣

Unicorn
378 North Road
☎ (0772) 57870
12–2; 6–11 (12–11 Sat)
Matthew Brown Mild; Theakston Best Bitter, XB, Old Peculier Ⓗ
Comfortable pub on main road in good drinking area. Regular live music and quiz nights. Home of Preston Folk Club. No food at weekends. ⊛ ◖ ♣

Riley Green

Royal Oak
At A675/A6061 jct
☎ (0254) 21445
11–11
Thwaites Mild, Bitter Ⓗ
Old, low-ceilinged pub, formed from a row of cottages. Several separate, cosy drinking areas and a large collection of model steam engines. Near Leeds–Liverpool Canal and historic Hoghton Towers (open to the public in summer). Eve meals Wed–Sun. ♨ Q ◖ ◗ P

St Annes

St Annes Tavern
The Square, St Annes Road West (opp. station)
☎ (0253) 727327
11–11
Whitbread Trophy, Castle Eden Ale Ⓗ
Modern pub, built on the site of the former St Annes Hotel, with a typical Whitbread interior.
◖ ♿ ⇌

Samlesbury Bottoms

Nabs Head
Nabs Head Lane (1 mile S of A677) OS622292
☎ (025 485) 2455
11.30–3; 7–11
Thwaites Mild, Bitter Ⓗ
Comfortable, remote pub where everyone is made welcome. Formerly a mill manager's house. You can see Blackpool Tower on a clear day! Good-value, home-cooked food (not Mon or Tue eves). Q ◖ ◗ ▲ P

Scarisbrick

Heaton Bridge Inn
2 Heatons Bridge (B5242)
☎ (0704) 840549
11–11
Tetley Mild, Bitter Ⓗ
Old, canalside pub, recently refurbished without spoiling the original interior. An abundance of bric-a-brac adorns the walls. Lunchtime snacks. ♨ Q ⊛ ♣ P

Stalmine

Seven Stars
Hallgate Lane (A588, Hambleton–Preesall Road)
☎ (0253) 700207
11.30–3; 6.30–11
Thomas Greenall's Original Bitter Ⓗ
Popular inn in an attractive Wyre village, a recent convert to real ale. A 400 year-old building with brasses and pews, reputedly haunted by a 'grey lady'. Good value accommodation within easy reach of Blackpool, Trough of Bowland and Lake District. No Food Tue.
♨ Q ⊛ 🛏 ◖ ◗ ♿ ▲ ♣ P

Tarleton

Cock & Bottle
Church Road (off A59)
☎ (0772) 812258
11–3; 6–11
Thwaites Best Mild, Bitter Ⓗ
Modernised village pub split into a basic vault and a plush lounge with restaurant

aspirations. Children's playground in garden.
♣ P

Thornley

Derby Arms
Chipping Lane
☎ (0772) 782623
11–3; 6–11
Greenalls Mild, Bitter, Thomas Greenall's Original Bitter [H]
Stone-built, old-fashioned, comfortable country pub, boasting views of Longridge Fell. Excellent food in bar or dining area. Q P

Thornton

Burn Naze Hotel
1 Gamble Road (off B5268)
☎ (0253) 852954
11–11 (11–3; 6–11 Wed)
Tetley Mild, Bitter [H]
Late Victorian-style pub, built by the United Alkali Company for its chemical workers. Still a pub of much local character. Stands next to the ICI complex.
♣ P

Upholland

Hare & Hounds
242 Ormskirk Road (near M58 jct 5) ☎ (0695) 21803
12–11 (12–4; 7–11 bank hols)
Greenalls Mild, Bitter, Thomas Greenall's Original Bitter [H]
Olde-worlde, 17th-century inn, (reputedly haunted), with its own bowling green. Beware Scrumpy Jack Cider on handpump — it's keg.
♣ P

White Lion
Church Street (off A577)
☎ (0695) 622727
12–3; 7–11
Ind Coope Burton Ale; Jennings Bitter; Tetley Mild, Bitter [H]
Picturesque village pub opposite the parish church. Limited parking. P

Try also: Old Dog (Greenalls)

Waddington

Lower Buck Inn
Church Road ☎ (0200) 28705
11–11
Taylor Best Bitter; Tetley Bitter [H]
Unaltered Dickens pub in a grade I listed building. Good village local with facilities for families. Two guest beers always available. Small car park.
Q ♿ ♣ P

Wharles

Eagle & Child
Church Road (2 miles off B5269 Kirkham Road, near radar station) OS448356
☎ (0772) 690312
12–3 (not Mon–Fri in winter); 7–11
Wards Sheffield Best Bitter; Wadworth 6X [H]
Country free house with thatched roof and beamed ceilings. A very popular pub with ever-changing guest beers.
Q ♿ P

Wheatley Lane

White Swan Hotel
300 Wheatley Lane Road (off A6068 Padiham bypass, ½ mile from M65 jct 13) OS837382
☎ (0282) 66971
12–2 (closed some lunchtimes); 8–11
Marston's Pedigree Bitter, Merrie Monk; Moorhouse's Pendle Witches Brew; Ruddles Best Bitter, County; Taylor Landlord [H]
A nice quiet pub that gets busy at weekends. Sports a racing theme and unusual tables. A total of 13 beers (including guests) available. Q P

Wheelton

Dressers
Briers Brow (off A674)
☎ (0254) 830041
11–3; 5.30–11
Marston's Pedigree Bitter; Whitbread Boddingtons Bitter [H]
Popular, low-beamed free house in a row of cottages, half a mile from the Leeds-Liverpool Canal. Children welcome at lunchtime.
♣ P

Whittle-le-Woods

Royal Oak
216 Chorley Old Road
☎ (0254) 76485
2.30–11
Matthew Brown Mild, Bitter [H]
Small, terraced pub, full of atmosphere and offering a friendly welcome. Home-made pickles available. Q ♣

Try also: Dog (Thwaites)

Truman celebrating the days when they offered a range of cask beers *(see page 14)*

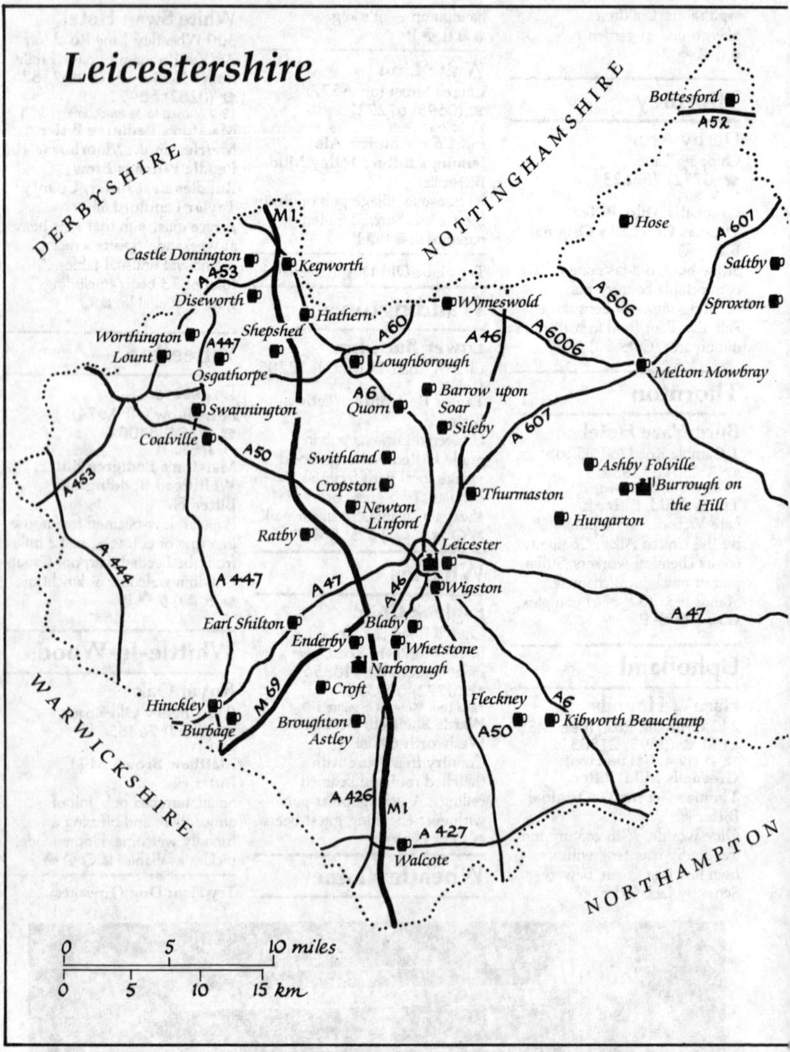

Everards, Narborough; **Hoskins**, Leicester; **Hoskins & Oldfield**, Leicester; **Parish**, Burrough on the Hill

Ashby Folville

Carington Arms

Folville Street
☎ (0664) 840228
12–2.30; 7–11 (11–2; 6–11 summer)
Adnams Bitter; Everards Mild, Beacon Bitter, Tiger Best Bitter, Old Original [H]
Old village pub with open bar and separate dining area. Long-alley skittles and petanque court. Pleasant garden area.
⌂ ❀ ◖ ◗ ♣ P

Barrow upon Soar

Navigation Inn

87 Mill Lane (bottom of lane)
☎ (0509) 412842
11–2.30; 6–11
Courage Directors; Greenalls Shipstone's Mild, Shipstone's Bitter; Marston's Pedigree Bitter [H]
Very welcoming canalside pub, particularly popular in the summer but busy all year round. Large L-shaped lounge and snug which doubles as a family room. Beware: Scrumpy Jack cider on handpump is *not* traditional. Skittles alley. ⛵ ❀ ◖ ♿ ♟ ♣ P

Blaby

Black Horse

Sycamore Street (off Leicester Road) ☎ (0533) 771209
11–3; 5.30 (6 Sat)–11
Greenalls Shipstone's Mild, Shipstone's Bitter [H]
Bustling pub with games-dominated bar and larger,

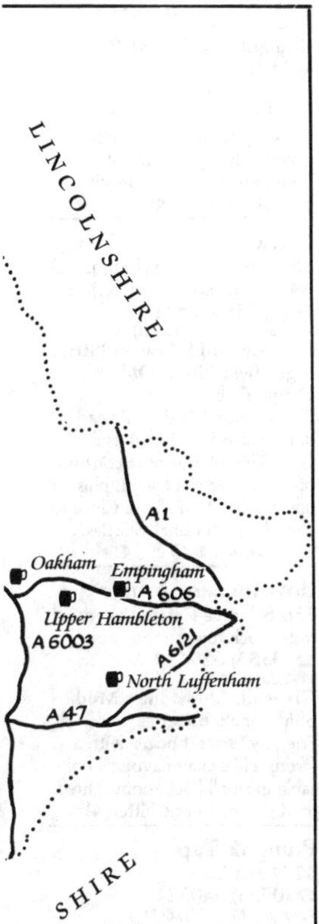

comfortable lounge. The high volume of mild sales reflects the true price differential still apparent here, despite the modern trend. ⊟ ♣ P

Bottesford

Rutland Arms
2 High Street ☎ (0949) 43031
11–2.30; 6–11
Greenalls Shipstone's Bitter [H]
Basically a U-shaped room with bar and lounge areas. A good range of food is available. An attractive large fireplace is surrounded by hanging brass plates. ⌂ ♨ ❀ ◐ ◗ ⊟ ♿ ⇌ P

Broughton Astley

George & Dragon
Green Road (off Main Street)
☎ (0455) 282256
11–2.30; 7–11 (11–11 Sat)
Marston's Border Mild, Burton Best Bitter, Pedigree Bitter [H]
Friendly village inn with darts, dominoes and table skittles teams. Open-plan, but with separate drinking and games areas. The walking stick collection has become something of a tradition. Piano-led sing-alongs. ♣ P

Burbage

Sycamores Inn
Windsor Street
☎ (0455) 39268
11.30–2.30 (12–2.30 Sun); 6 (6.30 Sat)–11
Marston's Mercian Mild, Burton Best Bitter, Pedigree Bitter [H]
The Sycamores' unusual name comes from the two trees that stood in the grounds when it was built in 1925. It is essentially still a pub: no meals, only sandwiches. Large garden with children's play area.
⌂ Q ❀ ⊟ ♿ ♣ P

Burrough on the Hill

Stag & Hounds
Main Street ☎ (066477) 375
12–2.30 (not Sept–Easter, except Sat); 7–11
Parish Mild, Bitter, Poachers Ale, Baz's Bonce Blower [H]
The Parish Brewery tap. Bonce Blower is the strongest, regularly-available real ale in the country. Home-cooked food, including Sun lunches, available in the separate restaurant. Inclusive brewery tour/beer/food package available by reservation. ⌂ ❀ ◐ ◗ P

Castle Donington

Cross Keys
Bondgate ☎ (0332) 812214
11–3; 5.30 (6 Sat)–11
Draught Bass; Vaux Samson; Wards Thorne Best Bitter, Sheffield Best Bitter [H]
Popular free house with large C-shaped bar and low ceilings. A big log fire provides atmosphere in winter. Opens all day when events are on at the nearby Donington circuit and concert arena. Guest beers. No food Sun. ⌂ ❀ ◐ ⊟ ⛺ P

Moira Arms
Bondgate ☎ (0332) 810480
12–3; 6–11 (12–11 Fri & Sat)
Ansells Mild; Ind Coope Burton Ale; Tetley Bitter [H]
Friendly, open-plan local with wood-panelled lounge and busier bar. The jazz/rock guitarist John McLaughlin played his first live concert in the yard. ⌂ ❀ ⊟ ♣ P

Coalville

Snibstone New Inn
2 Belvoir Road (opp. clock tower) ☎ (0530) 33976
10.30–3; 5.30–11
Marston's Border Mild, Burton Best Bitter, Pedigree Bitter, Owd Rodger (winter) [H]
Large bar, popular with locals. Home-made food; Indian meals a speciality. Comfortable lounge with pictorial history of Coalville. ⌂ ❀ ◐ ◗ ⊟ ♿ ♣

Croft

Heathcote Arms
Hill Street ☎ (0455) 282439
11–2.30; 5.30–11 (11–11 Sat)
Adnams Bitter; Everards Mild, Beacon Bitter, Tiger Best Bitter, Old Original; Mole's Brew 97 [H]
Unspoilt old pub on top of hill overlooking river. Relaxed and friendly atmosphere. Good, traditional home-cooked food. Skittles (alley and table). Guest beer. ⌂ ♨ ❀ ◐ ◗ ⊟ ♣ ⌽ P

Cropston

Bradgate Arms
Station Road (75 yds from B5328/B5330 jct)
☎ (0533) 362120
11–2.30; 6 (5.30 Fri, Sat & summer)–11
Hoskins Beaumanor Bitter, Penn's Ale, Premium, Old Nigel; M&B Mild; Tolly Cobbold Mild [H]
Situated near Bradgate Park, a pub extensively-changed since its free house days. It has, however, retained a cosy snug, but the main part of the pub is somewhat dominated by a lower-level restaurant. The milds alternate. Guest beers.
♨ ❀ ◐ ◗ ♿ ♣ P

Diseworth

Plough Inn
33 Hallgate ☎ (0332) 810333
11–2.30; 4.45 (6 Sat)–11
Draught Bass [E]
A rambling village inn with many rooms, beams and quiet corners. Very skilfully enlarged without losing its 'small pub' character. Close to East Midlands Airport. Restaurant/function room. ⌂ ❀ ◐ P

Earl Shilton

Red Lion
168 High Street (A47)
☎ (0455) 843356
11–2.30; 5.30–11
Draught Bass; M&B Mild [H]
Busy three-roomed local. All

beer is served from a central bar. ♿ ▲ ♣ P

Empingham

White Horse
2 Main Street (A606)
☎ (078086) 221
11–11
Courage Directors; John Smith's Bitter, Magnet [H]
Stone-built pub close to Rutland Water. A very popular eating house, retaining a quiet bar away from the food. Open from 8am for coffee.
☾ ☽ ♿ ▲ P

Enderby

Plough
Mill Hill ☎ (0533) 863307
11–2.30; 5 (6 Sat)–11
Marston's Burton Best Bitter, Pedigree Bitter [H], **Owd Rodger** (winter) [G]
Spacious hilltop pub due for refurbishment. Popular with the local business community on weekday lunchtimes. ☾ ☽ P

Fleckney

Old Crown Inn
High Street ☎ (0533) 402223
12–2.30 (incl. Sun, 11.30–3.30 Sat); 5–11
Adnams Bitter; Everards Mild, Beacon Bitter, Tiger Best Bitter, Old Original [H]
Very welcoming and comfortable 200 year-old 'clean air' pub. Large lounge; small quiet snug. Excellent home-made food includes veg dishes. Guest beers. ☾ ☽ P

Hathern

Dew Drop
49 Loughborough Road
☎ (0509) 842438
12–2; 7–11
Hardys & Hansons Best Mild, Best Bitter [H]
Pleasant and welcoming two-roomed village pub. Large bar with beams and an open fireplace; smaller lounge, both bustling with village life. Very small car park. Q ♣ P

Hinckley

Greyhound Inn
New Buildings
☎ (0455) 615235
11–2.30 (12–2 Sun); 5 (5.30 Sat)–11
Marston's Mercian Mild, Burton Best Bitter, Pedigree Bitter [H]
Lively, traditional four-roomed pub just off the town's pedestrianised area. Live jazz Wed and Thu. Q ☾ ☽ ♿ ♣

Hose

Black Horse
Bolton Lane ☎ (0949) 60336
11–2.30 (12–2 Sun); 7–11
Home Mild, Bitter [H]
Authentic, unaltered village alehouse with busy bar, cosy lounge and skittle alley. Recently sold by Home to Paragon Inns – a new pub-owning chain. As yet, thankfully, no plans exist to change anything.
Q ☾ ♿ ♣ P

Rose & Crown
Bolton Lane ☎ (0949) 60424
11.30–2.30; 7–11
Beer range varies [H]
Comfortable country inn with bustling bar, relaxed lounge and separate dining area. Constantly-changing range of real ales: usually five brews available. Beware: Bateman (always available) is under gas pressure. ☾ ☽ ♿ ♣ P

Hungarton

Black Boy
Main Street ☎ (053 750) 601
11–2.30; 6–11 (may extend in summer)
M&B Mild, Brew XI [H]
Friendly village pub with small, comfortable lounge and larger, more basic bar. Excellent, filling home-cooked food and snacks (not Sun). Also sells local and home-made produce. Large car park; rural aspect.
Q ☾ ☽ ▲ ♣ P

Kegworth

Cap & Stocking
20 Borough Street (off A6)
☎ (0509) 674814
11.30–3; 6–11
Draught Bass; M&B Mild [G]
Wonderful, old-fashioned back-street pub, with beer served in jugs straight from the cellar. Stuffed animals in profusion and an antique Wurlitzer contribute to the illusion of stepping back in time. Eve meals to 7.45pm. Petanque. ☾ ☽ ♿ ♣

Kibworth Beauchamp

Coach & Horses
2 Leicester Road (A6)
☎ (0533) 792247
11.30–3; 5–11 (11–11 Fri & Sat)
Ansells Bitter; Ind Coope Burton Ale; Tetley Bitter [H]
Friendly old coaching inn, popular with locals and passing trade. Home-made food available: bar snacks and restaurant meals. Original coin filled beams. ☾ ☽ ♣ P

Leicester

Black Boy
35 Albion Street (200 yds behind Grand Hotel)
☎ (0533) 540422
11–11 (11–2.30; 7–11 Sat, 12–2; 7.30–10.30 Sun)
Draught Bass [H]; **M&B Mild** [E]
Excellent town pub, very popular with business people weekday lunchtimes. Wood-panelled lounge with restored Victorian ceiling. Eve meals on request. Q ☾ ♿ ♣

Black Horse
65 Narrow Lane, Aylestone (off A426 & Middleton Street)
☎ (0533) 832811
11–2.30; 6–11 (11–11 Sat)
Everards Mild, Beacon Bitter, Tiger Best Bitter, Old Original [H]
A pub since 1790; in its early days it also functioned as a farm. The interior now consists of bar, lounge and snug, plus an upstairs function room. Close to Grand Union Canal. Skittles. Guest beers. Q ☾ ♣

Bowlturners Arms
156 Belgrave Gate (400 yds from clock tower)
☎ (0533) 625419
11–3.30; 5–11
Greenalls Shipstone's Mild, Shipstone's Bitter [H]
Friendly locals' boozer with a strong Hibernian flavour. Pool table in small back room. Three mild pumps to one bitter.

Pump & Tap
42 Dunns Lane
☎ (0533) 540324
12–3 (not Mon-Fri); 6–11
ABC Best Bitter; Ind Coope Burton Ale; Tetley Bitter [H]
Two basic bars with sawdust on the floors and old church furniture. Handpump sets and taps on the walls. Popular with students. Q

Salmon Inn
19 Butts Close Lane (behind St Margaret's bus station)
☎ (0533) 532301
10.30–11 (10.30–3; 5.30–11 Tue & Wed)
Banks's Mild, Bitter [E]
Friendly locals' pub with cosy lounge and basic bar, close to new shopping centre. Still has an off-sales hatch. ♿ ♣

Shakespeare's Head
Southgates (opp. Holiday Inn)
☎ (0533) 624378
11–2.30; 6 (5.30 Sat)–11
Greenalls Shipstone's Mild, Shipstone's Bitter [H]
Typical, early 60s, two-roomed pub by the underpass. Drinks also served in the foyer. Q ♣

Ship Inn
13 Soar Lane (near old Central Station) ☎ (0533) 624415
11–3 (12–2.30 Sun); 5.30–11
Greenalls Shipstone's Mild, Shipstone's Bitter [H]
Small, friendly, two-roomed, basic locals' pub with a strong

darts following. Close to Grand Union Canal. ❀ ⊟ ♣ P

Sir Charles Napier
Glenfield Road
☎ (0533) 621022
11–11 (11–3; 6.30–11 Sat)
Courage Directors; John Smith's Magnet [H]
Deceptively spacious 1930s pub, one of only two so-named in the country. Situated at the end of a row of terraced houses, it still retains the original three-room layout (including smoke room). No food Sun.
Q ◐ ◑ ⊟ ♿ ♣

Tom Hoskins
131 Beaumanor Road (off Abbey Lane, near Wade Street)
☎ (0533) 681160
11.30–3; 5.30 (6 Sat)–11
Hoskins Beaumanor Bitter, Penn's Ale, Premium, Old Nigel; Tolly Cobbold Mild [H]
The brewery tap: a lively bar and a comfortable lounge. Brewery tours can be arranged – ring for details. Carry kegs filled. Varied guest beers. No food Sun. ❀ ◐ ⊟ ♣ P

Tudor
100 Tudor Road
☎ (0533) 620087
11–2.30 (3 Sat, 12–2.30 Sun); 6–11
Everards Mild, Beacon Bitter, Tiger Best Bitter, Old Original [H]
Popular Victorian corner pub in terraced residential area. Cosy lounge; lively bar. Games room. Guest beers. 🐎 ❀ ⊟

Union Inn
27 Middleton Street, Aylestone (off A426, 300 yds E of canal bridge 106 ☎ (0533) 831796
11–11 (11–3; 4.30–11 Tue–Thu)
Marston's Burton Best Bitter, Pedigree Bitter [H]
Popular and busy pub, mainly used by locals, near canal. Table skittles. Q ❀ ◐ ⊟ ♣ P

Victory
Aylestone Road (opp. Granby Halls) ☎ (0533) 544105
11–11 (11–3; 6–11 Sat)
Everards Mild, Beacon Bitter, Tiger Best Bitter, Old Original [H]
Large lounge, smaller ale bar, pool room and upstairs function room. Formerly the Bedford, it was renamed in 1979 to honour Leicester Tigers RFC's success in the John Player Cup. Guest beers. Parking is limited.
❀ ◐ ♣ P

Westcotes
48 Latimer Street (off Hinckley Road – A47 W – 100 yds W of A46 jct) ☎ (0533) 541056
12–3; 5.30–11
Banks's Mild, Bitter [E]
Former Everards pub, built into terraced housing, with a mainly local clientele. Pleasant lounge with subdued lighting; well-lit bar at rear. Access to car park is from Ridley Street. ❀ ⊟ ♣ P

Loughborough

Duke of York
126 Nottingham Road (Ratcliffe Road jct) ☎ (0509) 216234
11.30–3; 6 (7 Sat)–11
Draught Bass; M&B Mild [E]
Cosmopolitan pub on main road with a large, basic bar and neat lounge. Popular with both office and factory workers at lunchtimes. No meals Sun.
◐ ⊟ ≢ ♣ P

Peacock
26 Factory Street (off A6, S side of town) ☎ (0509) 214215
11.30–2.30; 7–11
Draught Bass; M&B Mild [H]
Traditional back-street local with three drinking areas. Friendly relaxed atmosphere; thriving pub games.
♨ ❀ ⊟ ≢ ♣ P

Swan in the Rushes
The Rushes ☎ (0509) 217014
11–2.30 (3.30 Sat); 5 (6.30 Sat)–11
Bateman XXXB; Marston's Pedigree Bitter; Tetley Bitter [H]
Large, two-roomed pub, always bustling with a good cross-section of the community. Home-cooked food a speciality. Guest mild in rotation and always at least six ales available. Interesting selection of bottled beers. ♨ 🛏 ◐ ◑ ⊟ ♿ P

Lount

Ferrers Arms
Nottingham Road, Ashby
☎ (0530) 412982
11.30–2.30 (12–2.30 Sun); 7–11
Marston's Pedigree Bitter [H]
One-room bar with two distinct drinking areas. Sadly due for modernisation. ♨ ❀ ◐ ♣ P

Melton Mowbray

Cherry Tree
Edendale Road (800 yds from A607 roundabout)
☎ (0664) 60856
11–11 (11–4; 6–11 Sat)
Draught Bass; M&B Mild; Stones Best Bitter [H]
Large, recently-modernised locals' pub in housing estate. Friendly, thriving bar; relaxing lounge. ❀ ◐ ⊟ ♣ P

Crafty Fox
Leicester Road (A607 1 mile W of town) ☎ (0664) 410363
11–11
Courage Directors; John Smith's Bitter [H]
Busy, spacious modern pub furnished in colonial style, with a central bar and a restaurant to one side. Children welcome until 8.30pm. ❀ ◐ ◑ ♿ P

Newtown Linford

Bradgate
Main Street ☎ (0503) 242239
11–2.30; 5.30–11 (11–11 Sat)
Everards Mild, Beacon Bitter, Tiger Best Bitter, Old Original, Old Bill Winter Warmer [H]
Recently-modernised, large and spacious pub-restaurant, close to Bradgate Park. Monthly change of guest beers. Q 🐎 ❀ ◐ ◑ ♣ P

North Luffenham

Horse & Panniers
12 Church Street
☎ (0780) 720091
11–2 (4 Sat); 6–11
Adnams Bitter; Everards Mild, Beacon Bitter, Tiger Best Bitter [H]
Excellent two-room village pub known locally as the 'Nag and Bag'. A Grade II listed building dating back to 1640. Winner of the Everards Best-Kept Cellar competition. Guest beers.
♨ ❀ ⊟ ♿ ♣ P

Oakham

Wheatsheaf
Northgate ☎ (0572) 723458
11–2.30 (3 Fri & Sat); 6–11
Adnams Bitter; Everards Beacon Bitter, Tiger Best Bitter [H]
17th-century, two-roomed pub; popular with locals. Friendly atmosphere. ♨ Q ❀ ◐ ≢

Osgathorpe

Oak
Main Street ☎ (0530) 222443
12–2.30 (2 Sun, not Mon–Fri, except bank hols); 6.30–11
M&B Mild; Marston's Pedigree Bitter [H]
Cosy, olde-worlde pub in village centre. Two drinking areas. Popular with locals and friendly to visitors. ♨ ❀ ♿ ♣ P

Quorn

Royal Oak
High Street ☎ (0509) 413502
11.30–2.30; 6.30–11
Draught Bass; M&B Mild [H]
Basic three-roomed pub on the main road. Welcoming and spacious with a strong darts following. Pool table upstairs.
❀ ⊟ ♿ ♣

Ratby

Plough Inn
Burroughs Road
☎ (0533) 392103
11–3; 5.30 (6 Sat)–11

Marston's Burton Best Bitter, Pedigree Bitter [H]
Friendly village local with restaurant. P

Saltby

Nags Head
1 Back Street OS850262
☎ (0476) 860491
12–2.30; 7–11
Greene King Abbot Ale; Ruddles Best Bitter [H]
200 year-old stone-built pub with a beamed and wood-panelled bar. Interesting bar billiards room. Home cooking and four-poster accommodation.
Q P

Shepshed

Railway
160 Charnwood Road
☎ (0509) 503283
11–11
Marston's Mercian Mild, Pedigree Bitter [H]
Busy two-roomed local on the industrial edge of the town. A large bar and a comfortable lounge, with much railway memorabilia, make up this unpretentious and deservedly-popular pub. Known as the 'Bottom Railway'. P

Richmond Arms
48 Forrest Street (off B5330)
☎ (0509) 503309
11–2; 7–11
Draught Bass; M&B Mild [H]
A fine two-roomed alehouse, with a sporting emphasis: darts and dominoes are played and the pub doubles as the HQ of the local rugby club.

Sileby

Free Trade Inn
27 Cossington Road
☎ (050981) 4494
11.30–2 (2.30 Fri); 5.30 (6.30 Sat)–11
Everards Mild, Beacon Bitter, Tiger Best Bitter, Old Original [H]
Large, smart pub with two well-kept lounge bars. The BMW and gin and tonic brigade mix well with the Sileby locals! Regular guest beers. Book for Sun lunch. P

Railway Inn
36 King Street
☎ (050981) 2447
11–2.30 (3.30 Sat); 5.30–11
Draught Bass; M&B Mild [E]
A real no-frills pub with a basic lounge and an even more basic bar, serving the cheapest beer for miles around. Licensee's wife produces wonderful pen and ink local scenes which are for sale.
P

Sproxton

Crown at Sproxton
Coston Road
☎ (0476) 860035
11–2.30 (not Mon); 7–11
Adnams Bitter; Everards Mild; Marston's Pedigree Bitter [H]
An imposing stone farmhouse, converted into a cosy bar and restaurant. The 16th-century stables and slaughterhouse form a function room. No food Mon. Guest beers.
Q P

Swannington

Robin Hood
2 Spring Lane (off A447)
☎ (0530) 34398
11–3 (12–2.30 Sun); 7–11
Draught Bass; M&B Mild [E]
Recently-modernised pub comprised of a comfortable lounge and an unspoilt bar with an attractive fireplace. Popular with locals. P

Swithland

Griffin
Main Street ☎ (0509) 890535
11–2.30; 6–11
Adnams Bitter; Everards Mild, Beacon Bitter, Tiger Best Bitter, Old Original [H]
Large, friendly, well-run inn with distinctive drinking areas. Situated in Charnwood Forest. Good quality lunches. Guest beer. P

Thurmaston

Harrow Inn
635 Melton Road
☎ (0533) 696279
11–2.30 (3 Fri & Sat); 5.15 (6 Sat)–11
Greenalls Shipstone's Mild, Shipstone's Bitter [H]
Friendly, two-roomed locals' pub. Entertainment on Sat nights. A centre for pub games. No meals Sun. P

Unicorn & Star
796 Melton Road
☎ (0533) 692849
10.30–3 (2.30 Tue–Thu); 6 (5.30 Tue–Thu)–11
Greenalls Shipstone's Mild, Shipstone's Bitter [H]
Friendly pub known to the villagers as the 'Top House'. Popular with pub games players. P

Upper Hambleton

Finch's Arms
Oakham Road
☎ (0572) 756575
11–3.30; 6–11 (11–11 summer)
Greene King IPA, Abbot Ale; Marston's Pedigree Bitter; Ruddles Best Bitter, County [H]
Upmarket pub on peninsula in Rutland Water. Very popular with tourists. Features lounge bar and restaurant with exposed stone walls. Q P

Walcote

Black Horse
Main Street ☎ (0455) 552684
12–2.30 (incl. Sun); 5.30–11
Hook Norton Best Bitter, Old Hookey; Hoskins & Oldfield HOB Bitter; Taylor Landlord [H]
Busy and comfortable, old roadside pub, renowned for its authentic oriental bar meals. Parties catered for in separate dining area by prior appointment. No food Tue. Guest beers. P

Whetstone

Wheatsheaf Inn
High Street ☎ (0533) 864891
11–2.30 (12–2.30 Sun); 6 (5 Fri & Sat)–11
Ansells Mild; Ind Coope Burton Ale; Tetley Bitter [H]
Pub dating back to 1846, with separate lounge and bar rooms. Pub games include table and long-alley skittles.
P

Wigston

Meadowbank
Kelmarsh Avenue (200 yds off A50) ☎ (0533) 811926
11–2.30; 6–11 (11–11 Sat)
Banks's Mild, Bitter [E]
Newish estate pub in the Banks's style; friendly, comfortable and functional with good use of wood and brick. Food and beer both excellent value (no food Sun). TV in bar; table skittles. P

Worthington

Malt Shovel
Main Street ☎ (0530) 222343
12–2 (2.30 Fri, not Mon); 7 (6.30 summer)–11
Marston's Pedigree Bitter [H]
240 year-old pub with a comfortable lounge and a lively bar. Garden has a variety of animals. Excellent meals (not Mon eve). P

Wymeswold

White Horse
Far Street ☎ (0509) 880490
11.30–2.30 (3 Sat); 6.30 (6 Sat)–11
Home Mild, Bitter [H]
Bustling village local with busy, basic bar and comfortable lounge. Electronic games thankfully kept out of the way of drinkers. A real, traditional, no-frills pub. No meals Sun.
P

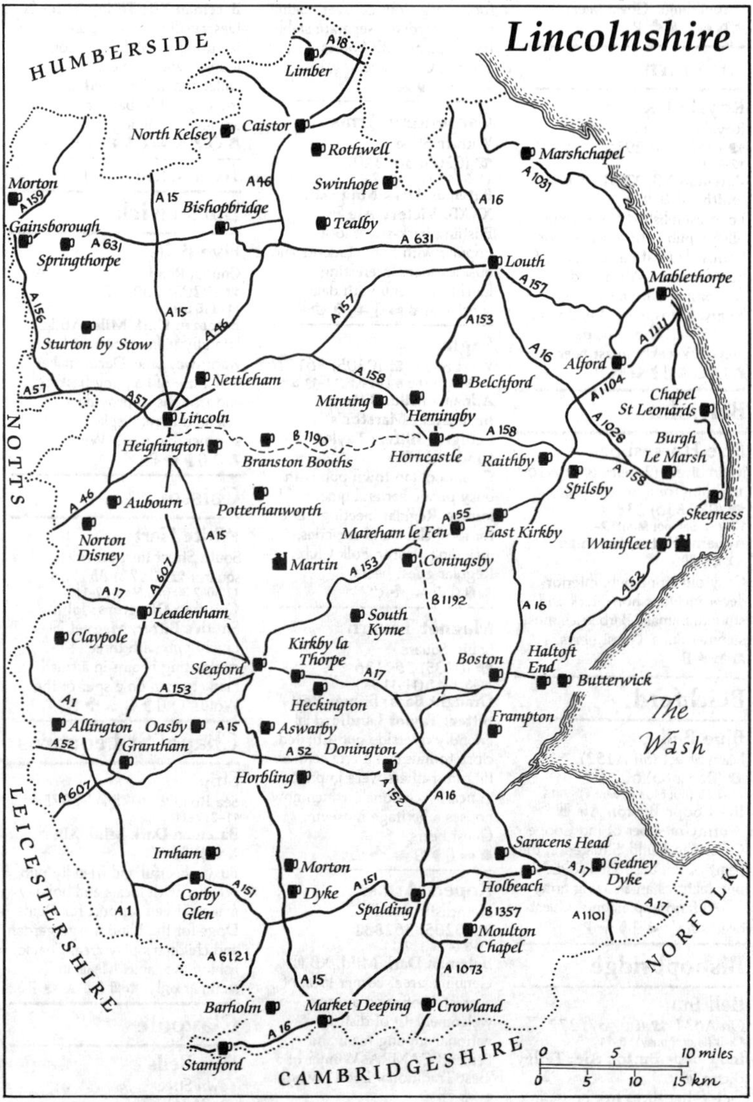

Bateman, *Wainfleet*; **Martin**, *Martin*

Alford

Half Moon

25–26 West Street
☎ (0507) 463477
10–3.30; 6–11
Bass Mild XXXX, Draught Bass; Bateman XB; Wards Sheffield Best Bitter, Kirby Strong [H]
Lively and popular town pub with a reputation for good food (separate restaurant). Host to many clubs and societies and handy for Alford's renowned craft markets. Open all day if sufficient trade. ❁ ◐ ◑ ⊞ ♣ P

Allington

Welby Arms

The Green ☎ (0400) 81361
12–2.30 (3 Sat); 5.30–11
Courage Directors; John Smith's Bitter [H]
Friendly village pub, with separate bar and lounge areas. Good selection of home-cooked meals on offer. No meals Sun eve in winter.
⌂ Q ❁ ◐ ◑ ⊞ ♿ ♣ P

Aswarby

Tally Ho

Main Road (A15)
☎ (052 95) 205
12–2.30; 6–11
Adnams Bitter; Bateman XB [H]
Comfortable, welcoming roadside inn, deservedly popular for its food. Accommodation is provided in converted

outbuildings. Guest beers.
♨ ⚘ 🛏 ◖ ◗ ♣ P

Aubourn

Royal Oak
Royal Oak Lane
☎ (052285) 291
12–2.30; 7–11
Bateman XB, XXXB; Samuel Smith OBB [H]
Long established (19th-century) village pub with mock-Tudor beams clad with a selection of horse brasses. Warm and welcoming with a cosy and happy atmosphere. Mind your head if tall! Shove-ha'penny played. Weekly guest beer.
♨ Q ⚲ ⚘ ◖ ◗ ⊟ ♣ P

Barholm

Five Horseshoes
Main Street (2 miles N of A16 at Tallington)
☎ (077836) 238
12–2 (3 Sat, not Mon); 7–11
Adnams Bitter; Bateman XXXB [H]
Cosy old stone pub. Interior decor includes horse tack and stuffed animals. Barbecues most summer Suns. Guest beers.
♨ ⚲ ⚘ P

Belchford

Blue Bell
Main Street (off A153)
☎ (065 883) 602
11–2.30 (not Mon or winter); 7–11
Ind Coope Burton Ale [H]
Worthy member of Ind Coope Cellarman Guild. Situated in the heart of the unspoilt Wolds, the pub features an amazing array of old farm implements. Guest beers. ♨ Q 🛏 ◖ ◗ ♣ P

Bishopbridge

Bell Inn
On A631 ☎ (06737) 272
11–3 (later if busy); 6–11
Ind Coope Burton Ale; Tetley Bitter [H]
Out-in-the-sticks free house in a tiny hamlet at the head of the New River Ancholme. Unpretentious games room/bar, comfortable but unfussy lounge and a pleasant dining room. On the traditional route to the Lincolnshire coast.
⚘ 🛏 ◖ ◗ ⊟ ♣ P

Boston

Burton House Hotel
Wainfleet Road (100 yds from Burton Corner)
☎ (0205) 362307
10.30–3; 6–11
Bass Special Bitter; Bateman XB; Stones Best Bitter [H]
Busy and comfortable two-star hotel with emphasis on good food. Large lounge overlooking mature gardens; separate stable bar. Popular with boules players. Guest beers.
♨ ⚘ 🛏 ◖ ◗ ⛺ P

Carpenters Arms
Witham Street
☎ (0205) 362840
11–3 (4 Fri & Sat); 7–11
Bateman Dark Mild, XB, XXXB, Victory Ale [H]
Bustling back-street local, popular with both students and businessmen. Interesting lunchtime menu with daily special. ♨ ⚘ 🛏 ◖ ⥱ ♣ ⌓

Eagle
West Street ☎ (0205) 361116
11–3; 6 (5 Thu & Fri)–11 (11–11 Sat)
Adnams Mild, Bitter, Broadside; Marston's Pedigree Bitter; Taylor Landlord [H]
Cosmopolitan town pub with busy public bar and quieter lounge. Regular meeting place for local clubs and societies, including Boston Folk Club. Regular guest beers.
♨ ⚘ ◖ ⊟ ⥱ ♣ ⌓

Magnet Tavern
South Square
☎ (0205) 369186
11–3; 6–11 (11–11 Sat)
Draught Bass; Stones Best Bitter; Taylor Landlord [H]
Friendly riverside pub situated close to music and arts centres. Pilgrim Fathers were imprisoned in nearby Guildhall, which now houses a heritage museum. Guest beers.
♨ 🛏 ◖ ◗ ⊟ ⥱ ♣ ⌓

Ropers Arms
Horncastle Road
☎ (0205) 362881
11–3 (4 Sat); 7–11
Bateman Dark Mild, XB [H]
Genuine street-corner local of character, offering a warm welcome. HQ of district national angling team and Fenland CAMRA. Winner of a 'Best Traditional Local' award.
⊟ ♣ ⌓

Branston Booths

Green Tree
Bardney Road
☎ (0522) 791208
11–3; 5.30–11
Draught Bass; Stones Best Bitter; Wards Mild, Sheffield Best Bitter [H]
Cosy and welcoming rural local. Go steady along the straight or you'll miss it. Guest beers.
♨ ⚘ ◖ ◗ ⊟ ♣ P

Burgh Le Marsh

White Hart
High Street ☎ (0754) 810321
11–3; 6–11
Bateman XB; Tetley Bitter [H]
Deservedly popular pub featuring a tastefully decorated lounge, with fine china collection and a cheerful, friendly public bar. Restaurant in adjoining building.
♨ Q ⚲ ⚘ 🛏 ◖ ◗ ⊟ ♣ P

Try also: Red Lion (Free)

Butterwick

Five Bells
Church Road
☎ (0205) 760282
11–3 (5 Sat); 7–11
Bateman Dark Mild, XB [H]
Friendly village local with a warm welcome. Decor makes much use of hanging baskets and troughs to provide a splendid floral display in summer. No meals Wed.
♨ ⚘ ◖ ◗ ♣ P

Caistor

White Hart
South Street (just off town square) ☎ (0472) 851734
11.30–2.30 (not Mon); 7–11
Courage Directors; John Smith's Bitter, Magnet [H]
Lively pub with three contrasting rooms in a small market town on a spur of the Wolds. Q ◖ ◗ ⊟ ♿ ♣ P

Chapel St Leonards

Ship
Sea Road ☎ (0754) 72975
11–3; 7–11
Bateman Dark Mild, XB, XXXB [H]
Busy, cheerful and friendly pub, popular with locals and holiday-makers. Keen support for Guide Dogs for the Blind. Large garden and children's play area. Coarse fishing available. Meals in summer only. ♨ ⚘ ◖ ◗ ⛺ ♣ P

Claypole

Five Bells
Town Street
☎ (0636) 626561
12–3; 6.30 (7 winter)–11
Vaux Samson; Wards Sheffield Best Bitter [H]
Revitalised village local catering for a variety of customers. First pub in this expanding village to go 'real' after being sold off by John Smith's. No food Tue. Guest beers. ⚘ ◖ ◗ ⊟ P

Coningsby

Leagate Inn
Leagate Road (B1192)
☎ (0526) 42370
11.30–2.30; 6.30–11
Marston's Pedigree Bitter; Taylor Landlord; Whitbread Castle Eden Ale [H]
16th-century coaching inn close

to the site of a former gibbet. Roaring fires; popular for food. Large gardens and fish ponds. Jaguar Car Club and Koi (tropical fish) Keepers Society meet here. P

Corby Glen

Woodhouse Arms
Bourne Road ☎ (047684) 316
12–2.30; 7–11 (12–11 Sat)
Bateman XB, XXXB; Marston's Pedigree Bitter Ⓗ
Pleasant, open-plan pub with separate restaurant. Prominently situated on the edge of the village (a conservation area). No meals Sun eve. P

Try also: Glaziers Arms (Free)

Crowland

George & Angel
2 North Street
☎ (0733) 210550
10.30–3; 6–11 (10.30–11 Sat)
Ruddles Best Bitter, County; Webster's Yorkshire Bitter Ⓗ
Popular, small town pub with basic bar and comfortable lounge. Grade II listed building near to Trinity Bridge and Crowland Abbey. Eve meals by arrangement. Q P

Donington

Queen Inn
49 Station Street (off A52)
☎ (0775) 820281
11–3; 6.30–11
Ansells Bitter; Ind Coope Burton Ale Ⓗ
Basic roadside local offering a friendly welcome. Snacks available. P

Dyke

Wishing Well
Main Street (½ mile E of A15)
☎ (0778) 423626
10.30–3; 7–11
Adnams Broadside Ⓖ**; Greene King IPA, Abbot Ale** Ⓗ**; Marston's Pedigree Bitter** Ⓖ
Friendly, well-appointed village local with large lounge and smaller bar. Very popular for its food; often used for parties. No meals Sun eve.
P

East Kirkby

Red Lion
Main Road ☎ (079 03) 406
11–3; 7–11
Bateman XB; Wards Sheffield Best Bitter, Kirby Strong Ⓗ
Friendly village local, with fine horological display. The Lincolnshire Air Museum with its Lancaster Bomber is nearby. Guest beers. P

Frampton

Moores Arms
Church End OS328392
☎ (0205) 722408
10.30–3; 6.30–11
Draught Bass; Stones Best Bitter Ⓗ
Smart and busy. Good garden and excellent restaurant. P

Gainsborough

Drovers Call
Lea Road (A156)
☎ (0427) 612044
11–3; 5.30–11 (11–11 Sat)
Bass Mild XXXX, Special Bitter, Draught Bass; Stones Best Bitter Ⓗ
Large, cheerful pub on the outskirts of town with bowling greens at the rear. Very busy at weekends. Popular with locals and passing trade alike.
(Lea Rd) P

Try also: Vestry Bar (Bateman)

Gedney Dyke

Chequers
☎ (0406) 362666
11–3; 7–11
Adnams Bitter; Draught Bass; Bateman XB; Greene King Abbot Ale Ⓗ
Comfortable country pub; well worth seeking out, especially if hungry as well as thirsty. Bridge played – beginners welcomed.
P

Grantham

Angel & Royal
High Street ☎ (0476) 65816
11–3 (4 Sat); 6–11
Draught Bass; Courage Directors Ⓗ
Historic coaching inn, associated with Richard III, with fine masonry and timbered ceilings. A huge real fire is set in a large stone-arched fireplace. Three-star hotel accommodation. Guest beers.
Q P

Beehive
10–11 Castlegate
☎ (0476) 67794
11–3 (4 Fri & Sat); 5 (7 Sat)–11
Mansfield Riding Dark Mild, Riding Traditional Bitter, Old Baily Ⓗ
Recently renovated town pub. An L-shaped room is lined with sofa-type benches, with old-fashioned wooden tables and chairs in the middle. Popular with the younger generation. Friendly and cosy atmosphere. Serves fine home-cooked meals (not Sat/Sun eves).

Chequers
25 Market Place
☎ (0476) 76383
12–3 (11–5 Sat); 7 (5 Thu)–11 (11–11 Fri)
Home Bitter; Theakston XB, Old Peculier; Younger IPA, No. 3 Ⓗ
Lively town-centre ale house. The fine collection of pump clips behind the bar indicates the range of guest beers available. The pictures for sale in the back room art gallery are painted by locals.

Five Bells
79 Brook Street (opp. Kings School) ☎ (0476) 67152
11–2.30; 5–11
Greenalls Shipstone's Mild, Shipstone's Bitter; Marston's Pedigree Bitter Ⓗ
Warm and friendly pub, recently refurbished to include accommodation. Excellent selection of home-made food, including veg options.

Shirley Croft Hotel
Harrowby Road (off A52)
☎ (0476) 63260
11–2.30; 6.30–11
Bateman XB, XXXB Ⓗ
Splendid and interesting Victorian-style hotel. A centre for such diverse activities as chess, power lifting and archery. Recently extended. Live music Sat. P

Haltoft End

Castle
On A52 ☎ (0205) 760393
11 (12 winter)–3; 6 (7 winter)–11 (11–11 Sat in summer)
Bateman Dark Mild, XB, XXXB Ⓗ
Friendly local on main tourist route. Good adventure playground. No meals Sun-Tue eves. Q P

Heckington

Nags Head
34 High Street
☎ (0529) 60218
11–2.30; 7 (6.30 summer)–11
Ruddles Best Bitter, County; Webster's Yorkshire Bitter Ⓗ
300 year-old, oak-beamed pub with a friendly welcome. Emphasis on catering, with many home-made dishes.
Q P

Heighington

Butcher & Beast
Fen Road ☎ (0522) 790386
11–3; 7–11
Bateman Dark Mild, XB Ⓗ
Modernised, friendly, 19th-century village pub. P

Lincolnshire

Hemingby

Coach & Horses
☎ (065 887) 280
12–2 (not Mon-Fri, except bank hols); 7–11
Bateman Dark Mild, XB Ⓗ
Pleasant village pub. Modernised and carpeted throughout but retaining original oak-panelling and low beams. ♔ Q ✿ ♿ ♣ P

Holbeach

Bell
21 High Street (B1105)
☎ (0406) 23223
10.30–3; 6–11
Elgood's Bitter Ⓗ
Friendly pub with good conversation. Extensive collection of malt whiskies.
⊷ ◖ ◗ ⊞ ♿ ♣

Crown Hotel
5 West End ☎ (0406) 23941
11–3; 6.30–11
Adnams Bitter; Draught Bass; Stones Best Bitter Ⓗ
Town-centre pub with mixed clientele. Emphasis on food from an extensive menu.
⊷ ◖ ◗ ♿ ♣ P

Horbling

Plough
4 Spring Lane (off B1177)
☎ (0529) 240263
11–2; 7–11
Greene King IPA, Abbot Ale Ⓗ
Small village local. Tiny snug; pool in back bar; quiet lounge. Good value food. One of few pubs owned by a Parish Council. Guest beers.
♔ Q ⛀ ⊷ ◖ ◗ ⊞ ♿ ♣ P

Horncastle

Bull Hotel
Bull Ring ☎ (065 82) 3331
11–3; 7–11
Draught Bass; Stones Best Bitter Ⓗ
Comfortable and busy wood-panelled hotel, renowned for its medieval banquets.
♔ ✿ ⊷ ◖ ◗ ♣ ⚲ P

Red Lion
Bull Ring ☎ (065 82) 3338
11–3; 7–11
Greenalls Shipstone's Bitter, Davenports Traditional Bitter Ⓗ
Cosmopolitan meeting place in a market town, now trading in antiques rather than horses. Local theatre flourishes in the hotel's converted stables. Book for eve meals. ♔ ⊷ ◖ ◗ ♿ P

Try also: Black Swan (Bateman)

Irnham

Griffin Inn
Main Road ☎ (047 684) 201
11.30–2.30; 7–11 (closed Mon)
Greene King IPA Ⓗ
Wonderful ancient inn in estate village where time has stood still. Surrounded by attractive rolling countryside. Guest beers.
Q ⊷ ◖ ◗ ⊞ P

Kirkby la Thorpe

Queens Head
Church Lane (A17/A1121 jct)
☎ (0529) 305743
11.30–2.30; 6–11
Draught Bass Ⓗ
Comfortable, well-converted village pub offering a friendly welcome and good food.
✿ ◖ ◗ P

Leadenham

George Hotel
(200 yds from A17/A607 jct)
☎ (0400) 72251
10–2.30; 6–11
Ruddles County; Theakston Old Peculier; Whitbread Castle Eden Ale Ⓗ
Large but interesting bar with Tudor-style walls and a beamed ceiling. Up to 500 different types of whisky on surrounding shelves. Stone fireplace with basket fire at one end of the room. ♔ ⛀ ✿ ⊷ ◖ ◗ P

Try also: Hare & Hounds, Fulbeck (Bateman)

Limber

New Inn
High Street ☎ (0469) 60257
11–2.30 (3 Sat); 7–11
Bateman XXXB; Tetley Bitter; Wards Sheffield Best Bitter; Younger No. 3 Ⓗ
Substantial pub owned by the Earl of Yarborough (a name used to describe a poor bridge hand and which adorns many pubs in the area not owned by him). A magnificent mausoleum is close by. Guest beer replaces XXXB. No meals Sat/Sun.
♔ Q ✿ ⊷ ◖ ⊞ ♿ ♣ P

Lincoln

City Vaults
2 Alfred Street (off High Street)
☎ (0522) 521035
11.30–3 (12–2 Sun); 5.30 (6 Thu–Sat)–11
Wards Mild, Sheffield Best Bitter Ⓗ
Friendly traditional ale house, popular with pub games players.
Q ◖ ⊞ ⇌ ♣

Harvest Moon
Wolsey Way, Glebe Park (off A158) ☎ (0522) 536684
11–3; 6–11
Theakston XB; Younger Scotch, No. 3 Ⓗ
A former farmhouse, converted into a one-roomed pub on a modern estate. Restaurant at rear. ♿ ♣ P

Jolly Brewer
27 Broadgate
☎ (0522) 28583
11–11
Draught Bass; Everards Tiger Best Bitter; Hardys & Hansons Best Bitter; Younger IPA, No. 3 Ⓗ
Art Deco-style free house within easy reach of city centre. Varied clientele. Guest beers.
✿ ⇌ ♣ ⚲ P

Monks Abbey
85 Monks Road
☎ (0522) 544416
11–11
Courage Directors; John Smith's Bitter Ⓗ
Friendly local pub – comfortably furnished, with one side for games, the other for sitting and drinking. ⊷ ◖ ◗ ♣

Queen in the West
Moor Street, Carholme Road, (off A57) ☎ (0522) 526169
11–3; 6–11
Bateman XB; Marston's Pedigree Bitter; Taylor Landlord; Theakston XB; Wards Sheffield Best Bitter; Younger No. 3 Ⓗ
Busy town pub with smart comfortable lounge, full of bric-a-brac, contrasting with a basic public bar. Guest beers. No meals weekends. Q ◖ ⊞ ♣

Small Beer (off-licence)
91 Newland Street West (off A57) ☎ (0522) 528628
10.30–10.30
Bateman XXXB; Martin Stanley Bitter; Taylor Landlord; Wards Sheffield Best Bitter Ⓗ
Popular, well-established real ale off-licence. Regular outlet for Martin Brewery. Wide range of British and foreign bottled beers and ever-changing variety of guest beers. ⚲

Strugglers
83 Westgate (behind castle)
☎ (0522) 524702
11–3; 5.30–11 (11–11 Fri & Sat)
Bass Mild XXXX, Draught Bass Ⓗ
Basic and, at times, bursting with people. A real gem; small but cosy and evocative of a Lincoln somehow lost in other pubs. Strong on tradition. Shove-ha'penny played.
Q ✿ ⊞ ♣

Victoria
6 Union Road (behind castle)
☎ (0522) 536048
11–11

Bateman XB; Everards Old Original; Taylor Landlord; Theakston Old Peculier Ⓗ
Very popular pub with a varied clientele. No fruit machines or jukebox; a true pub atmosphere. Constantly-changing range of guest beers, but at least one mild, one bitter and one premium bitter always included. Special eves highlight particular regions/breweries. A must for visitors. Q ❀ ◖ ⊟ ♿ ⛀

Louth

Wheatsheaf
62 Westgate
☎ (0507) 606262
11–3; 5–11
Draught Bass; Stones Best Bitter Ⓗ
Situated in a quiet Georgian terrace, this inn, dating from 1625, is equally attractive inside and out. No meals Sat/Sun. ⌂ Q ❀ ◖ ♣ P

Woolpack
Riverhead Road
☎ (0507) 606568
11–3; 7–11
Bateman Dark Mild, XB, XXXB Ⓗ
A former 19th-century wool merchant's house, now a traditional, friendly inn with three rooms to suit all tastes. The short walk from the town centre is well rewarded.
⌂ Q ❀ ⊟ ♣ P

Try also: Boars Head (Bateman)

Mablethorpe

Montalt Arms
George Street (off High Street)
☎ (0521) 72794
11–3; 7–11
Draught Bass; Bateman XXXB; Stones Best Bitter Ⓗ
A comfortable, L-shaped, wood-panelled lounge bar with a well-appointed restaurant. Photographs of old Mablethorpe adorn the walls. Not a typical seaside tripper's pub! Occasional guest beers. Parking is very limited.
⌂ ❀ ◖ ◗ P

Mareham le Fen

Royal Oak
Main Street ☎ (065 886) 357
11–3; 7–11 (11–11 Sat)
Bateman XB, XXXB Ⓗ
500 year-old thatched pub, formerly Sir Richard Mint's blacksmith's shop. Attractive garden with stocks for unruly customers. Excellent home-made food includes XXXB sausages.
⌂ ❀ ◖ ◗ ⛀ P

Market Deeping

Old Coach House
Bridge Foot ☎ (0778) 341460
11–3; 6.30 (5.30 Wed–Sat)–11
Bateman XXXB; Greene King IPA, Abbot Ale; Marston's Pedigree Bitter Ⓗ
1870s coach house, converted to a pub in 1988. Consists of a restaurant and bar with a stone-flagged floor, and, up a spiral staircase, a bar with jukebox and pool. No meals Sun eve in winter. ❀ ◖ ◗ ⊟ ♿

Vine
19 Church Street
☎ (0778) 342387
11–2.30 (3 Sat); 5.30–11
Charles Wells Eagle Bitter, Bombardier Ⓗ
Popular local; formerly 1870s prep school. Large busy bar with smaller lounge. The many social activities include quiz nights and an annual barn dance. ⌂ ◖ ⊟ ♿ ♣ P

Marshchapel

Greyhound
Seadyke Way (A1031)
☎ (047 286) 267
11–3.30 (4 Sat); 6.30–11
Bateman Dark Mild, XB, XXXB Ⓗ
Comfortable local with small lounge-cum-snug, plus dining area and large public bar. No food Mon eve. ⌂ Q ◖ ◗ ⊟ ♣ P

Minting

Sebastopol Inn
Main Street (off A158)
☎ (065 887) 688
12–2; 7–11
Adnams Mild, Bitter, Broadside; Bateman XB; Wards Sheffield Best Bitter Ⓗ
Comfortable 16th-century village local. Home-made food with a veg option. Pleasant garden. ⌂ Q ❀ ◖ ◗ ⊟ ♣ P

Morton (Bourne)

Five Bells
Haconby Lane
☎ (077 837) 332
12–2; 7–11
Greene King Abbot Ale; Tetley Bitter; Wards Mild, Sheffield Best Bitter Ⓗ
Comfortable and welcoming village pub. Popular with younger people. ⌂ ❀ ◖ ♣ P

Morton (Gainsborough)

Crooked Billet
Crooked Billet Street
☎ (0427) 612584
11–3; 6.30–11
Bass Mild XXXX, Special Bitter Ⓗ
Traditional pub with three bars and a collection of naval hats. Part of the pub served as a WW1 mortuary. Q ⊟ ♣

Moulton Chapel

Wheatsheaf
4 Fengate (B1357)
☎ (0406) 380525
12–3 (not Wed, 11.30–4 Sat); 7–11
Adnams Mild; Elgood's Bitter; Everards Old Original; Greene King IPA Ⓗ
Friendly two-room pub in out-of-the-way Fenland village. Collection of pottery pigs. Eve meals by arrangement.
⌂ ❀ ◖ ◗ ⊟ ♿ ⛺ ♣ P

Nettleham

Plough
The Green ☎ (0522) 750275
11–3 (4 Sat); 7–11 (11–11 Fri)
Bateman Dark Mild, XB Ⓗ
Comfortable and welcoming. A low-beamed village pub with character. Landlord well-known for his rabbit pies and geniality. Excellent facilities for meetings or special occasions. ⛟ ❀ ◖ ♣

Try also: White Hart (Bateman)

North Kelsey

Royal Oak
High Street ☎ (065 27) 544
12–3; 7–11
Stones Best Bitter; Wards Sheffield Best Bitter Ⓗ
Friendly and popular free house with open-plan bar, separate games room, and small snug at rear. Quiz nights on Tue.
⌂ ❀ ◖ ◗ ⊟ ♣ P

Norton Disney

St Vincent Arms
Main Street ☎ (052 285) 478
12–3; 7–11
Adnams Bitter; Bateman XXXB; Marston's Pedigree Bitter Ⓗ
Lively, well-appointed local. The village has connections with Walt Disney's family origins, and pictures of his visits adorn the pub walls.
⌂ ❀ ◖ ◗ ⊟ ♣ P

Oasby

Houblon Arms
Main Street (off B6043)
☎ (05295) 215
11–2.30 (12–2.30 Sun); 7–11
Bateman XB, XXXB; Taylor Landlord Ⓗ
One large room with low-beamed ceiling, stone walls and inglenook fireplaces. Popular eating place for local townsfolk.
⌂ Q ❀ ◖ ◗ P

Potterhanworth

Chequers
Cross Street (off B1178)

Lincolnshire

☎ (0522) 790189
11–3 (not Mon–Thu in winter); 6–11
Mansfield Riding Dark Mild, Riding Traditional Bitter, Old Baily [H]
Friendly village local with popular host. A single room with an emphasis on food. Doubles dartboard.
Q ❀ ◗ ⊟ ♣ P

Plough
Plough Hill (B1190/B1202 jct)
☎ (0522) 791448
11–3; 7–11 (11–11 Sat in summer)
Draught Bass; Tetley Bitter [H]
Large, comfortable roadside pub with an ever-changing guest beer range. Good garden for children.
♨ Q ❀ ◖ ◗ ⊟ ♿ ⛺ ♣ ⌽ P

Raithby

Red Lion
Main Road ☎ (0790) 53727
11–3 (not Mon-Fri); 7–11
Home Bitter; Theakston XB; Younger IPA [H]
Attractive pub in a picturesque Wolds village. Excellent food from an interesting menu to suit all tastes (lunches weekends only; eve meals Tue–Sat). Separate restaurant. Guest beers. Bar billiards. ♨ ◖ ◗ ♣ ⌽ P

Rothwell

Nickerson Arms
Hillrise (off A46)
☎ (047 289) 300
12–2.30; 7–11
Bateman XB; Marston's Pedigree Bitter; Taylor Landlord [H]
Deservedly popular Wolds pub with restaurant and excellent outdoor children's facilities. House beer, Rothwell Village Bitter, is brewed by Hoskins & Oldfield. No food Thu or Sun eve. Regular guest beers.
♨ Q ❀ ◖ ◗ ⊟ ♿ ♣ P

Saracens Head

Saracens Head
Washway Road (A17)
☎ (0406) 22708
10.30–3; 6–11
Greene King IPA, Abbot Ale [G]
An unspoilt, hospitable pub, situated on a sharp bend.
♨ Q ♘ ❀ ⊏ ⊟ ♣ ⌽ P

Skegness

Vine Hotel
Vine Road (off Drummond Road, 1 mile S of town centre)
☎ (0754) 610611
10–3; 6–11
Bateman Dark Mild, XB, XXXB [H]
Attractive building in secluded setting, reputedly the haunt of smugglers in former times, and visited by Alfred, Lord Tennyson. A sanctuary from the hurly-burly of the resort in summer and a biting east wind in winter! ♨ ❀ ⊏ ◖ ◗ ⊟ ♿ ♣ P

Try also: County Hotel, North Parade (Bateman)

Sleaford

Marquis of Granby
65 Westgate
☎ (0529) 303223
11–3; 6.30–11
Ind Coope Burton Ale; Tetley Bitter [H]
Small, cosy one-room pub with welcoming fire in winter. Popular in the evening with locals and often crowded. Good-value, regularly-changed menu, comprising home-cooked specials with veg dishes (till 8 pm). ♨ ❀ ◖ ◗ ♿ ⇌ ♣

Nags Head
64 Southgate (opp. Boston Road/Southgate jct, by monument) ☎ (0529) 413916
11–3; 7–11 (11–11 Sat)
Bateman XB, XXXB, Victory Ale [H]
Family-run, no-frills pub with one large bar. Often crowded at weekends. Good value pub food. Large function room.
♨ ❀ ◖ ◗ ⇌ P

Try also: Rose & Crown (John Smith's)

South Kyme

Hume Arms
High Street (B1395)
☎ (0526) 861004
11–2.30; 7–11
Ansells Bitter; Tetley Bitter; Wards Sheffield Best Bitter [H]
Quiet village pub opposite river, with separate bar, lounge and restaurant. No meals Mon/Tue eves.
Q ❀ ◖ ◗ ⊟ ♿ ⛺ ♣ P

Spalding

Red Lion Hotel
Market Place
☎ (0775) 722869
11–4; 5–11
Adnams Bitter; Draught Bass; Marston's Pedigree Bitter [H]
Pleasant, small, family-run hotel with a friendly atmosphere.
⊏ ◖ ◗

Ship Albion
37 Albion Street
☎ (0775) 769644
10.30–3; 7–11
Bateman Dark Mild, XB, XXXB [H]
A small, comfortable pub, recently acquired by Bateman and tastefully redecorated. Good cheap bar food. Usually a quiet pub but can be hectic at weekends. ❀ ⊏ ◖ ◗ ⊟ P

White Horse
Church Gate
☎ (0775) 766740
11–3 (4 Sat); 6–11
Samuel Smith OBB, Museum Ale [H]
A large, recently and extensively refurbished pub just off the town centre. Very pleasant conservatory and patio for summer. A pub with good character, but can get very crowded at weekends.
♨ ❀ ◖ ◗ ⊟ ♿ P

Spilsby

George Hotel
Boston Road ☎ (0790) 52528
11–11
Home Bitter [E]
Comfortable hotel with large bar in historic market town. Spilsby is noted for its theatre, housed in the old courtrooms.
♘ ❀ ⊏ ◖ ◗ ♣ P

Try also: Red Lion (Bateman)

Springthorpe

New Inn
Hill Road (off A631)
☎ (042 783) 254
11–2.30; 6.30–11
Bateman XXXB [H]
Small country pub in picturesque village. Food a speciality. Expect a song from the genial host!
♨ Q ❀ ◖ ◗ ⊟ ♣ P

Stamford

Dolphin
60 East Street
☎ (0780) 55494
11–2.30; 6–11
Charles Wells Eagle Bitter, Bombardier; Mansfield Riding Traditional Bitter [H]
18th-century building, divided into several small rooms. Friendly local atmosphere. Good value lunches. Stamford's unique game, Push-penny, is played here. Q ❀ ◖ ◗ ♿ ⇌ ♣

Green Man
29 Scotgate ☎ (0780) 53598
11–2.30; 5–11 (11–11 Fri & Sat)
Greene King IPA; Ruddles Best Bitter, County; Wards Sheffield Best Bitter [H]
Beer drinkers' and sports enthusiasts' pub. Oak-beamed interior, dating from 1796, divided into two areas. Guest beer. No meals Sun or bank hols. ♨ Q ❀ ⊏ ◖ ⇌ ♣

White Swan
21 Scotgate ☎ (0780) 52834
11–3; 6–11
Bateman Dark Mild, XB,

XXXB, Victory Ale Ⓗ
Refurbished and re-opened by Bateman in 1988. Push-penny played. ⛫ ♣

Sturton by Stow

Plough Inn
Till Bridge Lane (A1500)
☎ (0427) 788268
11–2.30; 6–11
Adnams Bitter; Bateman XB; Marston's Pedigree Bitter Ⓗ
Country pub with a traditional bar and food-oriented lounge. Guest beers. ⛫ ❀ ◖ ◗ ⊕ P

Swinhope

Clickem Inn
On B1203, 3 miles from Binbrook ☎ (047 283) 253
11–2.30 (not Mon, 3 Sat); 7–11
Bateman Dark Mild, XB, XXXB; Taylor Landlord; Younger No. 3 Ⓗ
Isolated but popular Wolds pub. Name is derived from the click of the gate to the field opposite, into which farmers drove flocks before drinking in the pub. Guest beer replaces one of the range. ⛫ ♘ ❀ ◖ ◗ ♿ ♣ P

Tealby

Kings Head
Kingsway (off B1203)
☎ (067 388) 347
10.30–3; 7 (6 summer)–11
Courage Directors; John Smith's Bitter Ⓗ
Beautiful thatched pub in delightful village on the edge of the Wolds. Viking Way nearby. Large garden for eating outside on sunny days. ❀ ◖ ◗ ⊕ ♿ ♣ P

Wainfleet

Red Lion
33 High Street
☎ (0754) 880301
11–3; 7–11 (11–11 Sat)
Bateman Dark Mild, XB, XXXB Ⓗ
Large pub just off market place and nearest Bateman outlet to the brewery. Spacious bar and cosy lounge with imposing fireplace.
⛫ ❀ ⛟ ◖ ◗ ⊕ ⛺ ≹ ♣ P

Try also: Jolly Sailor (Free)

THE GBG QUIZ

Round Two: Getting Tougher

16. Why was Directors Bitter so called?
17. Which brewery takes its name from a Roman emperor?
18. At which Southwark inn did Chaucer's Canterbury pilgrims commence their journey?
19. What does LVA stand for?
20. Which brewery has a ram for a mascot?
21. Which musical duo advertised Courage Best on TV?
22. By what name is the Old Swan at Netherton, Dudley better known?
23. Which beer campaigning society predated CAMRA by eight years?
24. Which is the world's largest brewing company?
25. What nickname did CAMRA give to Watneys in the 1970s campaign against keg beer and pub closures?
26. In cider making, what is a cheese?
27. Why are Scottish beers called 60/-, 70/- and 80/-?
28. Which country boasts the largest number of commercial breweries?
29. Which order of monks brews beer in Belgium and the Netherlands?
30. Which mineral makes Burton upon Trent water so suitable for pale ales?

Greater London

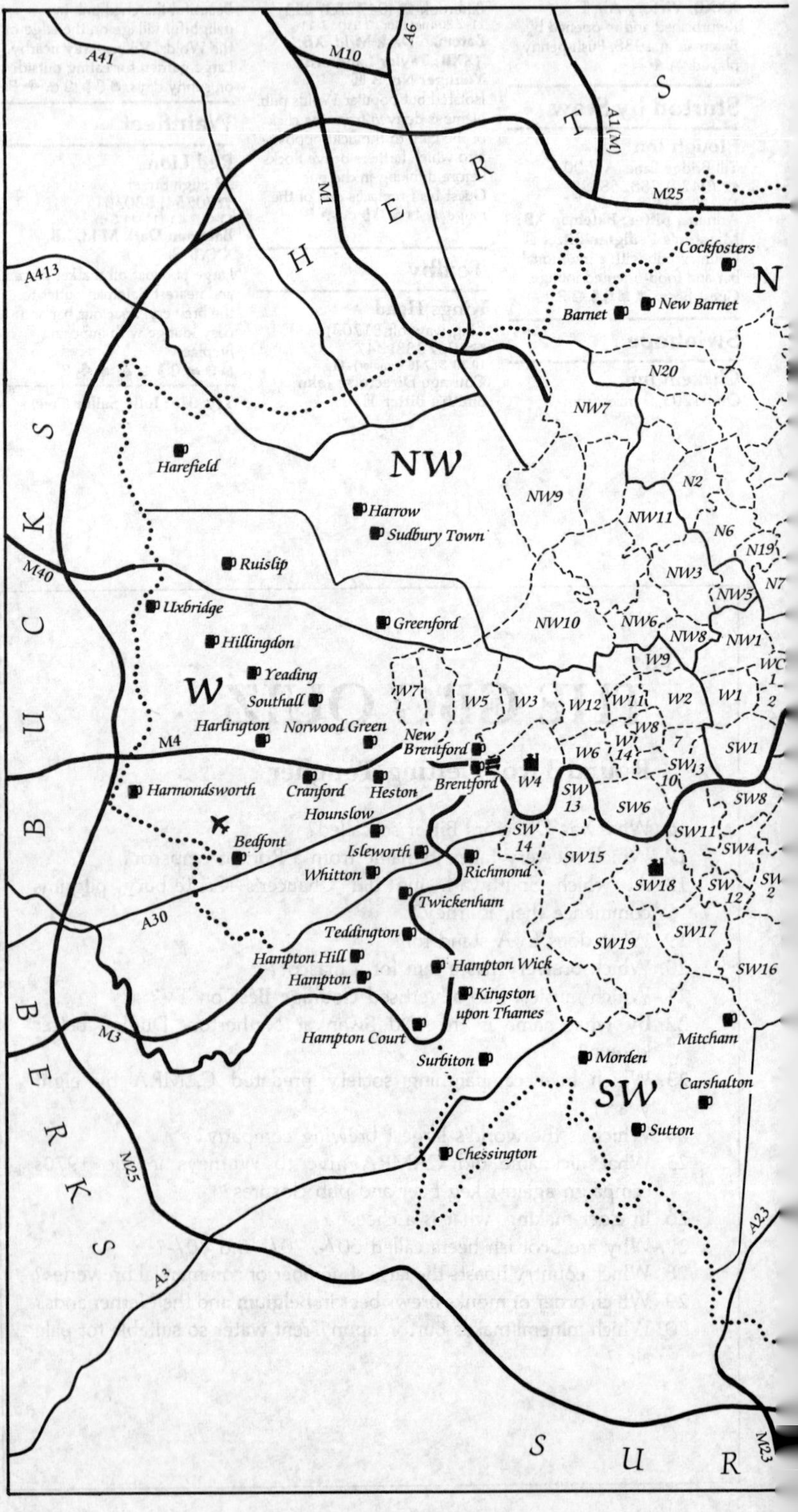

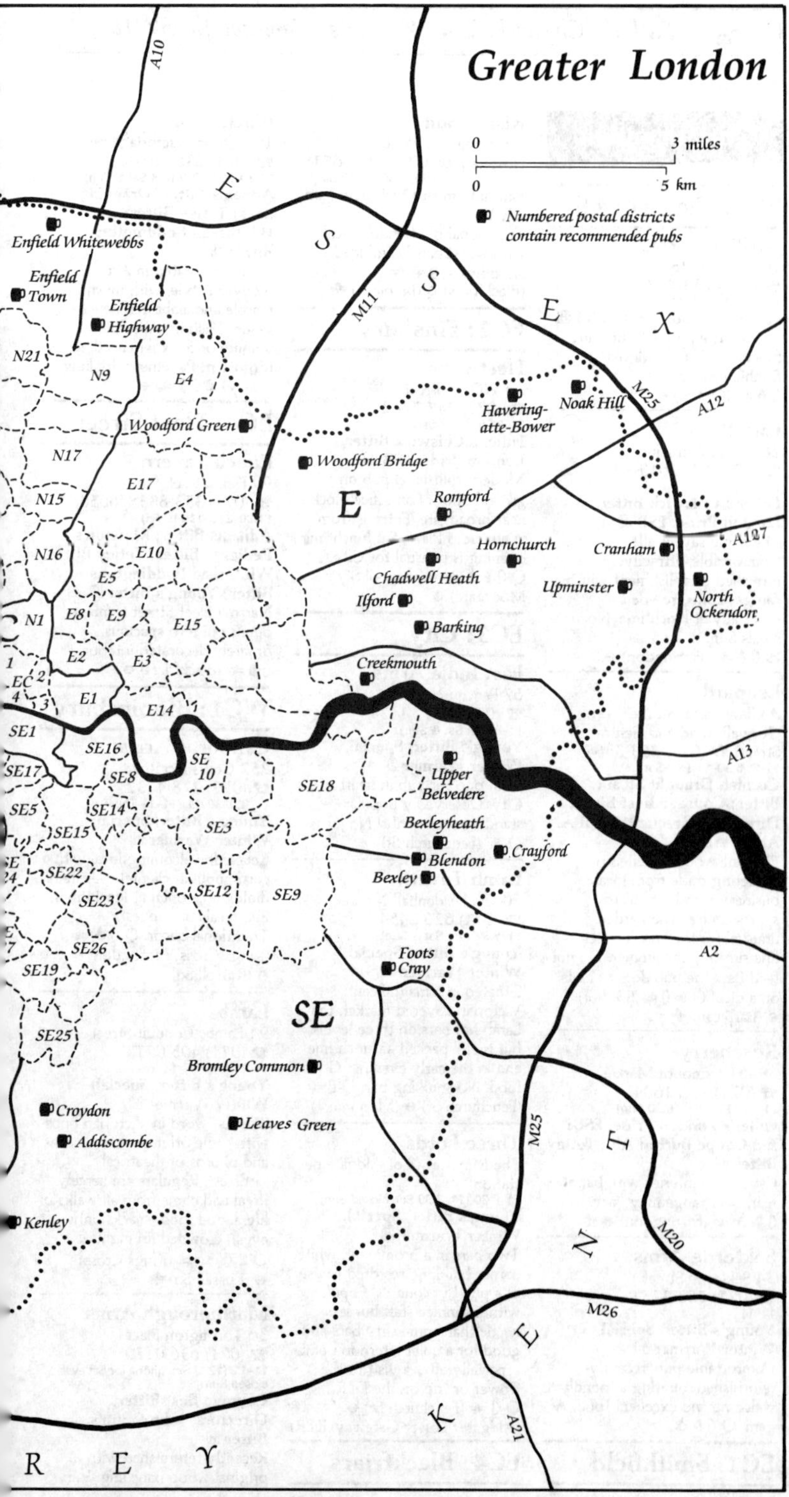
Greater London
0
3 miles
0
5 km
Numbered postal districts contain recommended pubs
E
S
S
E
X
A10
M11
M25
A12
A127
A13
A2
M20
M26
A21
Enfield Whitewebbs
Enfield Town
Enfield Highway
N21
N9
E4
Woodford Green
N17
E17
N15
N16
E10
E5
N1
E8
E9
E15
E2
E3
EC
1
2
4
3
E1
E14
SE1
SE16
SE17
SE8
SE 10
SE18
SE5
SE14
SE15
SE3
SE22
SE23
SE12
SE9
SE26
SE19
SE25
SE
Woodford Bridge
Havering-atte-Bower
Noak Hill
Romford
Hornchurch
Cranham
Chadwell Heath
Upminster
North Ockendon
Ilford
Barking
Creekmouth
Upper Belvedere
Bexleyheath
Crayford
Blendon
Bexley
Foots Cray
Bromley Common
Croydon
Leaves Green
Addiscombe
Kenley
K
E
N
T
R
E
Y

Greater London

Fuller's Chiswick, W4; Young's Wandsworth, SW18

Central London

EC1: Clerkenwell

Artillery Arms
102 Bunhill Row
☎ (071) 253 4683
11–3; 5–11 (11–11 Fri)
Fuller's London Pride, ESB Ⓗ
Lively little pub with upstairs function room overlooking Bunhill cemetery.
(Old St)

City Pride
28 Farringdon Lane
☎ (071) 608 0615
11–11
Fuller's Chiswick Bitter, London Pride, ESB Ⓗ
The name says it all! Comfortable, attractively-furnished establishment which can get quite crowded, especially at lunchtime. No meals Sun.
(Farringdon)

Leopard
33 Seward Street (between Goswell Road and Central Street) ☎ (071) 253 3587
11–3; 5.30–11 (not Sat)
Cornish Draught Steam Bitter; Courage Best Bitter, Directors; Greene King IPA, Abbot Ale Ⓗ
Pleasant wood-panelled pub, attracting trade from local businesses and the nearby sports centre. The garden, unusual for the area, creates a fine sun-trap in summer. Do not feed Ben, the pub dog, as he is on a diet! Q (Old St) (Barbican)

Roseberry
59–61 Exmouth Market
☎ (071) 278 1604
11–11 (12–4; 7–10.30 Sun)
Fuller's London Pride, ESB; Ind Coope Burton Ale; Tetley Bitter Ⓗ
Cavernous interior with bar at rear. Beer range may vary.
(Farringdon)

Sekforde Arms
34 Sekforde Street
☎ (071) 253 3251
11–11
Young's Bitter, Special, Winter Warmer Ⓗ
Comfortable pub, recently-refurbished, offering a friendly welcome and excellent food. A gem. Q

EC1: Smithfield

Rising Sun
Cloth Fair (near St Barts Hospital) ☎ (071) 726 6671
11–11 (11.30–3.30; 5.30–11.30 Sat)
Samuel Smith OBB, Museum Ale Ⓗ
Traditional old London local with wood panels and leaded windows.
(Blackfriars) (Barbican)

EC2: Finsbury

Fleetwood
36 Wilson Street
☎ (071) 247 2242
11–9.30 (11–3 Sat)
Fuller's Chiswick Bitter, London Pride, ESB Ⓗ
Modern split-level pub on ground floor of an office block near Broadgate. Entry is from Whitecross Place. Sat lunchtime opening is unusual for City.
Q (Liverpool St/ Moorgate)

EC3: City

East India Arms
67 Fenchurch Street
☎ (071) 702 4442
11–9 (not Sat & Sun)
Young's Bitter, Special, Winter Warmer Ⓗ
Plain one-bar pub in heart of City. Deservedly popular — standing room only! No jeans.
Q (Fenchurch St)

Lamb Tavern
10–12 Leadenhall Market
☎ (071) 626 2454
11–9.30 (not Sat & Sun)
Young's Bitter, Special, Winter Warmer Ⓗ
Situated in a magnificent Victorian covered market, the Lamb has bars on three levels but is still packed at lunchtime and in the early evening. Good food. No-smoking bar. Q (Fenchurch St) (Monument)

Three Lords
The Minories (S of Aldgate bus station)
11–8.30 (11–2.30 Sat, closed Sun)
Young's Bitter, Special, Winter Warmer Ⓗ
Two bars in a prominent, white corner building, restored to use as a pub by Young's. Popular with insurance staff but less hectic than some City bars and good for a quiet afternoon pint, especially after a visit to the Tower or trip on the DLR.
Q (Fenchurch St) (Aldgate/Tower Gateway, DLR)

EC4: Blackfriars

Black Friar
174 Queen Victoria Street
☎ (071) 236 5650
11.30–3; 4.30–9 (not Sat & Sun)
Adnams Bitter; Draught Bass; Tetley Bitter; Whitbread Boddingtons Bitter Ⓗ
Richly decorated in Art Nouveau style, with much marble and alabaster, hence its grade II listing. Absolutely unique: once experienced, never forgotten! Pavement drinking area. Q

EC4: Fleet Street

Punch Tavern
99 Fleet Street
☎ (071) 353 8338/6658
11.30–3; 5–11 (10 Fri)
Adnams Bitter; Marston's Pedigree Bitter; Tetley Bitter; Whitbread Boddingtons Bitter; Young's Bitter Ⓗ
Narrow Fleet Street frontage opens out into spacious, ornately decorated interior.
(Blackfriars)

WC1: Bloomsbury

Calthorpe Arms
252 Grays Inn Road
☎ (071) 278 4732
11–3; 5.30–11 (11–11 Thu–Sat)
Young's Bitter, Special, Winter Warmer Ⓗ
Relaxed, welcoming local with a cosmopolitan clientele. Upstairs dining area open at lunchtimes. Eve meals on request. Traditional decor. Q (Kings Cross/Farringdon) (Russell Sq)

Lamb
94 Lambs Conduit Street
☎ (071) 405 0713
11–11
Young's Bitter, Special, Winter Warmer Ⓗ
The last word in Victorian pubs with some original snob screens and photos of theatrical 'artistes'. Regulars are fiercely loyal and come from all walks of life. Good food (snacks only eves); crowded Fri nights.
Q (Kings Cross) (Russell Sq)

Marlborough Arms
36 Torrington Place
☎ (071) 636 0120
11–11 (12–3 Sat, phone for Sat eves, closed Sun)
Courage Best Bitter, Directors; John Smith's Bitter Ⓗ
Recently refurbished with original wood panelling. Very

popular with students from nearby universities. Pool table in separate room. Friendly and efficient bar staff. Not too far from Oxford Street.
◐ ⇌ (Euston) ⊖ (Warren St) ♣

WC1: Holborn

Cittie of Yorke
22–23 High Holborn
☎ (071) 242 7670
11–11 (11–3; 5.30–11 Sat, closed Sun)
Samuel Smith OBB, Museum Ale Ⓗ
1890s gothic building on site of a 15th-century pub and 17th-century coffee house. Large 'baronial hall' at rear with period screens and vats; Georgian iron stove. Chintzy front bar and maze of vaulted cellars have piped music.
⌂ Q ◐ ♿ ⇌ (Farringdon) ⊖ (Chancery Lane)

Rugby Tavern
19 Great James Street (200 yds from Theobalds Road)
☎ (071) 405 1384
11 (12 Sat)–3 (11–11 Fri, closed Sat eve, 12–3; 8–10.30 Sun)
Fuller's Chiswick Bitter, London Pride, ESB Ⓗ
Very comfortable medium-sized pub. Clientele mainly from offices. *Tom Brown's Schooldays* theme pervades.
◐ ◑ ♣

WC1: Kings Cross

Hansler Arms
133 Kings Cross Road
☎ (071) 837 4445
11–11
Brakspear Bitter; Marston's Pedigree Bitter; Whitbread Castle Eden Ale Ⓗ
Comfortable, cosy atmosphere, music level subdued. Guest beer. ◐ ⇌ ♣

Skinners Arms
114 Judd Street
☎ (071) 837 6521
11–11 (12–3; 7–11 Sat)
Greene King IPA, Rayments BBA, Abbot Ale Ⓗ
Two-bar pub with varied clientele. The lounge has been recently refurbished and has a real fire. Pool and darts in the public bar. No food Sun.
◐ ◑ ⊞ ⇌ (St Pancras) ⊖ ♣

WC2: Covent Garden

Freemasons Arms
81 Long Acre
11–11
Greene King IPA, Rayments BBA, Abbot Ale Ⓗ
Large busy pub just off Covent Garden. Lounge bar with food service upstairs.
◐ ◑ ⇌ (Charing Cross) ⊖ ♣

Marquess of Anglesey
39 Bow Street
11–11
Young's Bitter, Special, Winter Warmer Ⓗ
Busy corner pub near market hall and London Transport and Theatre museums. Upstairs bar and restaurant.
◐ ◑ ⇌ (Charing Cross) ⊖

WC2: Holborn

Newton Arms
31 Newton Street
11–11 (11–3; 5.30–11 Sat, closed Sun)
Ind Coope Burton Ale; Taylor Walker Best Bitter; Young's Bitter Ⓗ
Modern pub set in base of office block. ◐ ◑ ⊖

WC2: Lincoln's Inn Field

Seven Stars
53 Carey Street (behind Law Courts, off Strand/Fleet Street)
☎ (071) 242 8521
11–11 (closed Sat & Sun)
Courage Best Bitter, Directors Ⓗ
Traditional old-world pub, founded 1602. Popular with legal profession from nearby law courts. Q ◐ ◑ ⊖ (Temple)

WC2: St Giles

Angel
61 St Giles High Street
☎ (071) 240 2876
12–11 (12–3; 7–11 Sat, closed Sun)
Courage Best Bitter, Directors, John Smith's Bitter Ⓗ
Historic pub, with reputedly haunted cellar, in the shadow of Centrepoint. Note attractive tiling in side passage.
Q ◐ ⊖ (Tottenham Ct Rd) ♣

WC2: Trafalgar Square

Chandos
29 St Martins Lane
11–11
Samuel Smith OBB, Museum Ale Ⓗ
Large, popular, wood-panelled pub with upstairs bar and restaurant. Floodlit figure of cooper on roof.
◐ ◑ ⇌ (Charing Cross) ⊖ ♣

E1: Spitalfields

Pride of Spitalfields
3 Heneage Street
☎ (071) 247 8933
11–11
Fuller's London Pride, ESB; Young's Bitter Ⓗ
Single-bar pub appealing to visitors and locals alike. Good value for this part of London: handy for Brick Lane's famous curry houses. Guest beers. Pavement drinking area. ❀

E1: Stepney

Fish & Ring
141a White Horse Road
☎ (071) 790 2688
11–11 (11–5; 7–11 Sat)
Fuller's London Pride, ESB Ⓗ
Friendly, cosmopolitan pub with reasonably-priced beer. Live music at weekends. Guest beers.
◐ ⊞ ⇌ (Limehouse) ⊖ ♣

Ship on the Green
60 Stepney Green
11–3.30; 6–11
Camerons Strongarm; Tolly Cobbold Original Ⓗ
East End local with a maritime theme. At one time known as the 'Ace of Hearts' but has now reverted to its original name.
⊖ (Stepney Green) ♣

N1: Barnsbury

Crown
116 Cloudesley Road (800 yds NW of the Angel – A1/A502 jct) ☎ (071) 837 7107
11–3; 5–11 (11–11 Sat)
Fuller's Chiswick Bitter, London Pride, Mr Harry, ESB Ⓗ
19th-century pub retaining original features. Long U-shaped bar with snob-screens. Etched glass partitions divide separate drinking areas. Caters for locals and trendy Islington crowd. Patio out front; food bar at rear.
⌂ ❀ ◐ ◑ ⊖ (Angel) ♣

N1: Canonbury

Marquess Tavern
32 Canonbury Street (off A104)
11–11
Young's Bitter, Special, Winter Warmer Ⓗ
Elegant Georgian building in well-heeled suburb. The large single bar is divided into a comfortable 'lounge' with food bar, and a plainer public area. Two real fires with fine brass surrounds; small patio.
⌂ Q ❀ ◐ ◑ ⇌ (Essex Rd) ⊖ (Highbury & Islington) ♣

N1: Highbury

Compton Arms
4 Compton Avenue
☎ (071) 359 6883
11–11
Greene King IPA, Rayments BBA, Abbot Ale Ⓗ
Small but characterful pub hidden behind Highbury roundabout. An unexpected haven from the traffic and modern life. Q ❀ ◐ ⇌ (Highbury & Islington) ⊖ ♣

Greater London

N1: Hoxton

George & Vulture
63 Pitfield Street
☎ (071) 253 3988
11–3 (4 Sat); 5 (7 Sat)–11
Fuller's Chiswick Bitter, London Pride, ESB 🄷
Unspoilt back-street local with impressive exterior. Comfortable lounge; pool and darts in the public bar. Pavement drinking area.
❀ ◖ ⊟ ⇌ (Old St) ⊖

Prince Arthur
49 Brunswick Place
☎ (071) 253 3187
11–11 (11–5; 8–11 Sat)
Shepherd Neame Master Brew Bitter 🄷
Popular little side-street local. Sandwiches, rolls and pies lunchtimes.
⇌ (Liverpool St) ⊖ (Old St)

N1: Islington

Kings Head
59 Essex Road
☎ (071) 226 1825
11–11
Marston's Pedigree Bitter; Whitbread Flowers IPA, Boddingtons Bitter 🄷
Single-bar pub that serves excellent lunchtime food. Quiet piped music and a good local atmosphere.
❀ ◖ ◗ ⇌ (Essex Rd) ⊖ (Angel)

Prince Albert
16 Elia Street
☎ (071) 837 5040
11–3.30; 5.15–11 (11.30–4.30; 7–11 Sat)
Charrington IPA 🄷
Pleasant, small, two-bar pub with bar billiards in public bar. Tenant has been here for 23 years. Toasted sandwiches only in eve. Q ❀ ◖ ⊟ ⊖ (Angel) ♣

NW1: Camden

Edinboro Castle
57 Mornington Terrace
☎ (071) 387 8916
11–11
Draught Bass; Charrington IPA 🄷
One-bar pub refurbished a couple of years ago after an extensive fire. Mystery surrounds the new spelling of the pub name, but inside there are many prints of Edinburgh. Some Bass and Charrington mirrors have survived. Two pool tables. ❀ ◖ ⇌ (Camden Rd) ⊖ (Camden Town)

NW1: Marylebone

Perseverance
11 Shroton Street
☎ (071) 723 7469
11–3; 4.45–11 (11–11 Fri & Sat)
Draught Bass; Charrington IPA; Fuller's ESB (winter) 🄷
Friendly pub, recently converted to a single horseshoe-shaped bar. Near a famous fish and chip restaurant on Lisson Grove. Pianist and singer on Sat and Sun eves. No meals weekends.
◖ ⇌ ⊖

NW1: Primrose Hill

Prince Albert
11 Princess Road
☎ (071) 722 1886
11–11
Draught Bass; Charrington IPA 🄷
Well-preserved pub close to London Zoo (children welcome in the small but comfortable conservatory). Good selection of food and a happy hour early in the evening. Guest beer.
Q ♨ ◖ ◗ ⇌ ⊖ (CamdenTown)

NW1: Regent's Park

Gloucester Arms
5 Ivor Place
11–11 (11–3; 7–11 Sat)
Ind Coope Burton Ale; Taylor Walker Best Bitter; Tetley Bitter; Young's Bitter, Special 🄷
Hospitable, one-bar pub with dartboard in small back room. Some Victorian etched glass. Jukebox has 1960s records and is not too loud. Pavement drinking area. No disabled access to ladies WC. The Addlestones cider is not traditional. ❀ ◖ ♿ ⇌ (Marylebone) ⊖ (Baker St) ♣

SE1: Borough

Ship
68 Borough Road
☎ (071) 403 7059
11–11
Fuller's Chiswick Bitter, London Pride, ESB 🄷
Cosy pub with jovial licensee – a rarity in this busy area. Cold buffet in evening. ❀ ◖ ◗ ♿ ⇌ (London Bridge) ⊖ ♣

SE1: Southwark

Founders Arms
52 Hopton Street (near Blackfriars Bridge)
☎ (071) 928 1899
11–11
Young's Bitter, Special, Winter Warmer 🄷
Modern riverside pub overlooking Thames. Friendly bar staff. Ramp to house for disabled access; WCs more of a problem.
❀ ◖ ◗ ⇌ (Blackfriars) ⊖

Horseshoe
26 Melior Street (off Weston Street) ☎ (071) 403 6364
11–3; 5.30–11
Draught Bass; Courage Best Bitter, Directors; Felinfoel Bitter, Double Dragon; Fuller's London Pride 🄷
Friendly pub around the back of Guy's Hospital. Relaxed atmosphere, but busy most times. Boules played.
❀ ◖ ⇌ (London Bridge) ⊖ ♣ ⍉

Wheatsheaf
6 Stoney Street
☎ (071) 407 1514
11–11 (11–3; 7–11 Sat)
Courage Best Bitter, Directors; John Smith's Bitter 🄷
Small Victorian treasure located in the heart of Borough fruit market. Traditional glass and wooden partition between saloon and public bars.
◖ ⊟ ⇌ (London Bridge) ⊖ ♣

SE1: Tower Bridge

Anchor Tap
20a Horselydown Lane
☎ (071) 403 4637
12–3; 5.30–11 (12–11 Fri)
Samuel Smith OBB, Museum Ale 🄷
A classic, with five rooms on the ground floor (only open lunchtimes), and three more on the first floor. A no-smoking room on each floor. Full meals to 10pm seven nights a week. Reputedly John Courage's first pub, it was the Courage brewery tap. ⌂ ♨ ❀ ◖ ◗ ⇌ (London Bridge) ⊖ (Tower Hill) ♣

SE1: Waterloo

Kings Arms
25 Roupell Street (rear of station) ☎ (071) 928 5745
11–3 (11–3.30; 8–11 Sat, 12–2.30; 7–10.30 Sun)
Ind Coope Burton Ale; Taylor Walker Best Bitter; Tetley Bitter 🄷
An absolute gem of a pub used by city people and locals. Two excellent bars, with a huge collection of miniatures. Guest beer. Q ❀ ◖ ⊟ ⇌ ⊖ ♣

SW1: Belgravia

Antelope
22 Eaton Terrace
☎ (071) 730 7781
11–11
Adnams Bitter; Benskins Best Bitter; Ind Coope Burton Ale; Tetley Bitter; Wadworth 6X 🄷
Originally a Benskins house now part of the Nicholson chain; large rugby following.
◖ ⊖ (Sloane Sq)

Grouse & Claret

14–15 Little Chester Street
☎ (071) 235 3438
11–11 (11.30–3; 6.30–11 Sat)
Brakspear Bitter; Marston's Pedigree Bitter; Thwaites Bitter; Whitbread Boddingtons Bitter Ⓗ
Split-level, two-bar, wood-panelled pub with separate wine bar and restaurant.
◖ ◗ ⇌ (Victoria) ⊖

Star
6 Belgrave Mews West
☎ (071) 234 2806
11.30–3 (11.30–11 Fri, 11.30–3; 6.30–11 Sat)
Fuller's Chiswick Bitter, London Pride, ESB Ⓗ
Busy, unspoilt mews pub, with two real fires. Has featured in every edition of the *Good Beer Guide*. No meals Sun.
♨ Q ◖ ◗ ⊖ (Hyde Pk Crnr)

Turks Head
10 Motcomb Street
11–11
Draught Bass; Charrington IPA Ⓗ
Comfortable Georgian pub with raised section at rear, surrounded by bookshelves. No food Sun. ◖ ◗ ⊖ (Hyde Pk Crnr)

SW1: Pimlico

Rising Sun
44 Ebury Bridge Road
11–11
Young's Bitter, Special Ⓗ
Popular locals' pub near coach station. Forecourt drinking area.
Q ❀ ◖ ◗ ⇌ (Victoria) ⊖

SW1: St James

Red Lion
2 Duke of York Street
11–11 (closed Sun)
Arkell's 3B Best Bitter; Ind Coope Burton Ale; Tetley Bitter; Whitbread Boddingtons Bitter Ⓗ
Magnificent miniature gin palace, with engraved glass, mirrors and a mahogany island bar. Interior dates from 1871.
◖ ⊖ (Piccadilly Circus)

SW1: Sloane Square

Fox & Hounds
29 Passmore Street
11–3 (12–2 Sun); 5.30–11
Draught Bass; Charrington IPA Ⓗ
Small, cosy pub holding one of the last beer and wine only licences in the country. Snacks lunchtime (not Sun). Q ⊖

SW1: Trafalgar Square

Old Shades
37 Whitehall
11–11 (11–3; 7–11 Sat, closed Sun eve)
Draught Bass; Charrington IPA; Young's Bitter Ⓗ
Long, wood-panelled bar with lounge at rear. Good value beer for area. Obtains licence from Buckingham Palace.
♨ ◖ ◗ ⇌ (Charing Cross) ⊖

SW1: Westminster

Barley Mow
104 Horseferry Road
☎ (071) 222 2330
11–11 (11–4; 7–11 Sat)
Ruddles Best Bitter, County; Webster's Yorkshire Bitter Ⓗ
Large, comfortable pub with a fine collection of Hogarth prints. Grand piano in bar; live music.
◖ ◗ ⇌ (Victoria) ⊖ (St James's Pk)

Buckingham Arms
62 Petty France
☎ (071) 222 3386
11–11 (11–3; 7–11 Sat, 12–2 Sun)
Young's Bitter, Special, Winter Warmer Ⓗ
Excellent pub near passport office. ◖ ◗ ⇌ (Victoria) ⊖ (St James's Pk)

Morpeth Arms
58 Millbank
11–11
Young's Bitter, Special, Winter Warmer Ⓗ
Comfortable pub facing river near Tate Gallery. Remains open on Sun afternoons for food service only.
◖ ◗ ⇌ (Vauxhall) ⊖ (Pimlico)

Paviours Arms
Page Street
☎ (071) 834 2150
11–11 (11–4; 8–11 Sat)
Fuller's Chiswick Bitter, London Pride, ESB Ⓗ
Large, comfortable, two-bar pub in Art-Deco style. ◖ ◗ ⊞ ♣

Westminster Arms
9 Storeys Gate
☎ (071) 222 8520
12–3; 5–11 (closed Sun eve)
Adnams Bitter; Arkell's 3B Best Bitter; Brakspear Bitter; King & Barnes Sussex Bitter; Marston's Pedigree Bitter; Whitbread Boddingtons Bitter Ⓗ
Small, panelled pub near Parliament Square, Westminster Abbey and Central Hall. Wine bar downstairs; food bar upstairs. Guest beers. ◖ ◗ ⊖

W1: Fitzrovia

Bricklayers Arms
31 Gresse Street
11–11 (11–3; 5.30–11 Sat)
Samuel Smith OBB, Museum Ale Ⓗ
Small, wood-panelled pub with upstairs bar where food is served.
◖ ◗ ⊖ (Tottenham Ct Rd) ♣

George & Dragon
151 Cleveland Street
12–11 (7–11 Sat)
Draught Bass; Charrington IPA; Fuller's ESB (winter) Ⓗ
Small corner local. Recently, very tastefully refitted.
◖ ⊖ (Gt Portland St)

King & Queen
1 Foley Street
11–11 (11–3; 7–11 Sat)
Ruddles Best Bitter, County; Webster's Yorkshire Bitter Ⓗ
Impressive, red brick, Gothic pub with friendly service. No food weekends. ◖ ⊖ (Goodge St)

W1: Marylebone

Barley Mow
8 Dorset Street
11–11 (closed Sun)
Adnams Bitter; Tetley Bitter; Wadworth 6X Ⓗ
Possibly the oldest pub in Marylebone. There are two private 'boxes' fronting the bar which were used by a previous owner in his pawnbroking activities. ◖ ⊖ (Baker St)

Beehive
7 Homer Street
11–3; 5.30–11
Whitbread Wethered Bitter, Flowers Original Ⓗ
Small, cosy, side-street pub with much local trade. No lunches on Sun. Q ◖ ⇌ ⊖

Dover Castle
43 Weymouth Mews (off Weymouth Street)
11–11 (11–3.30; 7–11 Sat)
Adnams Bitter; Marston's Pedigree Bitter; Ruddles County; Whitbread Boddingtons Bitter Ⓗ
Cosy panelled pub in mews. An ex-coaching inn dating from 1777. Mirrors under beam enabled coachmen in public bar to see when passengers were ready to leave.
Q ◖ ◗ ⊖ (Regent's Pk)

Turners Arms
26 Crawford Street
11–11
Shepherd Neame Master Brew Bitter, Best Bitter Ⓗ
Small, ex-Younger house which has much improved the local choice of beers since its acquisition by Shepherd Neame. Snacks only eves. ◖ ◗ ⇌ ⊖ ♣

Windsor Castle
29 Crawford Place
11–11
Draught Bass; Charrington IPA Ⓗ
Comfortable pub decorated with a British Royalty theme.
Q ◖ ⊖ (Edgware Rd)

Worcester Arms
89 George Street
11–11 (12–4; 7–11 Sat)
Brakspear XXX Mild, Bitter;

Greater London

Greene King Abbot Ale; Marston's Pedigree Bitter; Thwaites Bitter 🄷
Busy free house with some attractive woodwork and a nice Courage Alton mirror.
◖ ⊖ (Baker St) ♣

W1: Mayfair

Guinea
30 Bruton Street (off NE corner of Berkeley Sq)
11–11 (11–3; 6.30–11 Sat, closed Sun)
Young's Bitter, Special 🄷
Small, intimate mews pub. There has been a pub on this site since 1423. High-class restaurant at rear (no lunches Sat). Originally known as 'One Pound One'.
Q ◖ ◗ ⊖ (Green Pk)

Windmill
6–8 Mill Street (off Conduit Street)
11–11 (closed Sun)
Charrington IPA; Greene King IPA, Abbot Ale; Whitbread Boddingtons Bitter 🄷
A new pub with a split-level bar and a first-floor restaurant. Choose your new Bentley while enjoying your pint!
◖ ◗ ⊖ (Oxford Circus)

W1: Soho

Dog & Duck
18 Bateman Street
12–11 (11–3; 5.30–11 Sat)
Adnams Bitter; Ind Coope Burton Ale; Marston's Pedigree Bitter; Tetley Bitter 🄷
Small, corner pub with decorative tiles, incorporating a dog and duck motif, and large mirrors. Upstairs bar open 7–11 Tue-Sat. Snacks at lunchtime.
⊖ (Oxford Circus)

East London

E2: Bethnal Green

Approach Tavern
47 Approach Road
☎ (081) 980 2321
11–11
Courage Directors; King & Barnes Sussex Bitter; Premier Pitfield Bitter 🄷
Easy-going, two-bar pub which attracts people from all walks of life.
⊟ ♿ ⇌ (Cambridge Heath) ⊖ ♣

Nelson's Head
32 Horatio Street
☎ (071) 739 6054
11.30–3; 5–11 (12–4; 7–11 Sat)
Bateman Dark Mild, XB, XXXB 🄷
Bateman's only London pub and a rare outlet for cask-conditioned mild in the capital. Tucked away, but well worth seeking out. Door to gents marked 'members only'!

E3: Bow

Earl of Ellesmere
19 Chisenhale Road
☎ (081) 980 5830
11–2.30; 5.30–11
Ind Coope Burton Ale; Tetley Bitter; Young's Bitter 🄷
Plushly-decorated, East End pub which gets crowded at weekends.

Lord Tredegar
50 Lichfield Road
☎ (081) 980 5155
11.30–11
Ind Coope Burton Ale; Tetley Bitter; Young's Bitter, Special 🄷
Friendly back-street pub with 'Brewer's Tudor' interior.
⛫ ❀ ◖ ⊖ (Mile End)

E3: Bromley-by-Bow

Beehive
104–6 Empson Street
☎ (071) 987 3745
11–3; 5–11
Brain's SA; Whitbread Flowers Original 🄷
Back-street local offering an imaginative choice of guest beers. Not cheap, but the variety is welcome. No food Sun lunchtime or weekend eves.
⛫ ◖ ◗ ♿ ⊖ (Devons Rd, DLR) ♣

E4: Chingford

Royal Oak
219 Kings Mead Hill
☎ (081) 529 1492
11–3; 5.30–11 (11–11 Sat – public only in afternoon)
McMullen Original AK, Country Best Bitter, Stronghart 🄷
Suburban pub, well-regarded for its food. Award-winning floral displays outside in summer. One of the last genuine public bars in the area. Bar billiards.
❀ ◖ ◗ ⊟ ♿ ♣ P

E5: Clapton

Anchor & Hope
15 High Hill Ferry (on River Lea, 800 yds N of Lea Bridge Road) ☎ (081) 806 1730
11–3; 5.30 (6 Sat)–11
Fuller's London Pride, ESB 🄷
Incredibly tiny riverside pub without frills and seemingly unchanging. Wall-to-wall bodies, especially in summer when the crowds spill out onto the riverbank. ❀ ⇌ ♣

E8: Hackney

Lady Diana
95 Forest Road
11.30–3; 5.30–11
Adnams Bitter; Fuller's London Pride; Greene King Abbot Ale; Wadworth 6X 🄷
Friendly, comfortable pub, decorated with photographs of old Hackney. Guest beers. Try the pizzas. ❀ ◖ ◗ ♿
⇌ (Hackney Central) ♣

E9: Homerton

Royal Standard
84 Victoria Park Road
☎ (081) 985 3224
11–3 (Sat); 5.30 (7 Sat)–11
Courage Best Bitter, Directors 🄷
Unpretentious, two-bar pub close to Victoria Park. Pavement drinking area. No food weekends. ❀ ◖ ⊟ ♿ ♣

E10: Leyton

Drum
559 Lea Bridge Road
11–11
Greene King IPA, Abbot Ale; Marston's Pedigree Bitter; Theakston XB; Younger IPA 🄷
Friendly pub with spacious split-level interior. Lack of piped music makes for a relaxing atmosphere. Lunches (incl. Sun).
Q ◖ ♁

Holly Bush
32 Grange Road
☎ (081) 539 3709
11.30–3; 7–11
Greene King IPA, Abbot Ale 🄷
Lively local; easily the best pub in the area.
❀ ⊟ ⇌ (Midland Rd) ♣

E14: Stepney

Queen's Head
8 Flamborough Street
☎ (071) 790 6481
11–2.30; 5 (7.30 Sat)–11
Young's Bitter, Special, Winter Warmer 🄷
Listed pub with royal connections (see plaque in saloon bar), on the corner of a Georgian square. All are made welcome, whether locals or newcomers. No food weekends.
◖ ⊟ ⇌ (Limehouse) ⊖ ♣

E15: Stratford

Essex Arms
82 Leytonstone Road
☎ (081) 534 3487
11–11
Draught Bass; Charrington IPA 🄷
Popular two-bar pub with traffic light in lounge.
⊟ ⇌ (Maryland)

Try also: Princess of Wales (Taylor Walker)

E17: Walthamstow

College Arms
807 Forest Road (near Shernall Street jct) ☎ (081) 531 8001
11–11
Greene King IPA, Abbot Ale; Marston's Pedigree Bitter; Theakston XB; Younger Scotch 🄷
Former shop premises, now a drinking house adorned with school paraphernalia. Guest beer and/or special offer often available. Gets busy some evenings, when invaded *en masse* by the nearby polytechnic. Q ◖ ⇶ (Wood St)

Coppermill
205 Coppermill Lane
☎ (081) 520 3709
11–11
Fuller's London Pride, ESB; Greene King Abbot Ale; Tetley Bitter 🄷
Small, back-street free house on the western edge of Walthamstow close to a vast expanse of waterworks, reservoirs and marshes. Excellent value. Two guest beers. ♿ ⇶ (St James St) ♣

Barking

Britannia
1 Church Road
☎ (081) 594 1305
11–3; 5–11 (11–11 Sat)
Young's Bitter, Special, Winter Warmer 🄷
Large, friendly pub, recently very well refurbished. Now very comfortable without being over the top. No food Sun.
❀ ◖ ⊟ ♿ ⇶ ⊖ ♣ P

Chadwell Heath

White Horse
118 High Road (A118)
☎ (081) 597 0229
11–11
Benskins Best Bitter; Ind Coope Burton Ale; Tetley Bitter 🄷
A White Horse inn has been on this site, on the Roman road to Colchester (AD 43), since Elizabethan days. Present pub is around 100 years old, with a comfortable interior. The large garden has outside bar in summer. ❀ ◖ ⇶ P

Cranham

Thatched House
348 St Marys Lane (B187)
☎ (040 22) 28080
12 (11 summer)–3 (3.30 Fri); 5.30–11 (11–11 Sat)
Draught Bass; Charrington IPA; Fuller's ESB (winter) 🄷
Friendly, locals' pub on edge of countryside with garden, family room and large car park. Frequent event nights, eg Burns or Cockney, with food supplied at a nominal charge. No lunches Sun. ♘ ❀ ◖ P

Creekmouth (Barking)

Crooked Billet
113 River Road
☎ (081) 594 2623
11–3.30; 5 (6 Sat)–11
Charrington IPA; Fuller's ESB (winter) 🄷
Friendly, family pub in the Creekmouth industrial area. Sing-alongs Fri and Sat in the saloon with the old piano. Bar billiards in public. Good value meals (till 9pm; not Sun lunch).
♨ ❀ ◖ ◗ ⊟ ♣ P

Havering-atte-Bower

Orange Tree
Orange Tree Hill
☎ (0708) 40471
11–3; 5.30 (6 Sat)–11
Ind Coope Burton Ale; Taylor Walker Best Bitter 🄷
Friendly two-bar pub with frequent darts and quiz tournaments, etc. About to undergo alteration with restaurant planned. ❀ ◖ ⊟ ♣ P

Hornchurch

Bull Inn
109 High Street (A124, next to Sainsburys) ☎ (040 24) 42125
11–11 (11–4; 6–11 Sat)
Friary Meux Best Bitter; Ind Coope Burton Ale; Tetley Bitter 🄷
Traditional, neat, town-centre pub with separate dining area off bar (no food Sun). Music at background level.
❀ ◖ ⇶ (Emerson Pk) ⊖ ♣ P

Chequers
North Street (next to station)
☎ (040 24) 42094
11–3 (4 Sat); 5.30 (6 Sat)–11
Friary Meux Best Bitter; Young's Special 🄷
Friendly town pub with good turnover of ale. Old off-licence has been altered into a games room. Music played at background level. Guest beer. No meals weekends.
◖ ⇶ (Emerson Pk) ♣ P

Ilford

Rose & Crown
16 Ilford Hill (near A406/A118 jct) ☎ (081) 478 7104
11–3; 5–11 (11–11 Thu–Sat)
Adnams Bitter; Benskins Best Bitter; Ind Coope Burton Ale; Tetley Bitter 🄷
Large, one-bar, Victorian-style pub close to new North Circular Road flyover. ❀ ◖ ⇶

Noak Hill

Bear Inn
Noak Hill Road
11–3.30 (4 Sat); 5.30 (6 Sat)–11
Draught Bass; Charrington IPA; Tolly Cobbold Original 🄷
Large pub, recently-rebuilt and comfortably-furnished, with large garden and car park. Barbecues, etc. in summer. Quizzes. No food Sun.
♘ ❀ ◖ ◗ ♿ ♣ P

North Ockendon

Old White Horse
Ockendon Road (B186)
☎ (0708) 853111
11–2.30; 6–11
Taylor Walker Best Bitter 🄷
Popular village inn with brass blowlamp collection. Traditional public bar. No food Sun.
❀ ◖ ◗ ⊟ ♣ P

Romford

Durham Arms
101 Brentwood Road
☎ (0708) 748601
11–3.30; 5 (6 Sat)–11
Ind Coope Burton Ale; Tetley Bitter 🄷
Pub just outside town centre. The large garden has swings and slide and is safe for children. Barbecues in summer.
❀ ◖ ♿ ⇶ P

Upminster

Huntsman & Hounds
Ockendon Road (B1421)
☎ (040 22) 20429
11–3; 5–11 (11–11 Fri & Sat)
Friary Meux Best Bitter; Taylor Walker Best Bitter; Tetley Bitter 🄷
Friendly pub near countryside with family room and well-equipped playground for children. No food Sun.
♘ ❀ ◖ ⊟ ⛺ P

Woodford Bridge

Crown & Crooked Billet
13 Cross Road
☎ (081) 504 0362
11–3.30; 5.30–11 (11–11 Fri & Sat)
Draught Bass; Charrington IPA 🄷
Popular pub next to the village green. Eve meals till 8pm. No food Sun. ❀ ◖ ◗ P

Woodford Green

Cricketers
299–301 High Road, Salway Hill ☎ (081) 504 2734
11–3 (4 Sat); 5.30–11
McMullen Original AK, Country Best Bitter 🄷

Excellent value, cosy, traditional local. ⊛ ◖ ⊞ P

Travellers Friend
496–498 High Road (A104)
☎ (081) 504 2435
11–11
Courage Best Bitter, Directors; Greene King Abbot Ale; Marston's Pedigree Bitter; Ridleys IPA Ⓗ
Small, friendly, wood-panelled pub with original snob screens. Very pleasant function room on first floor. Courage Best is disguised as 'Webster's Wonderful Wallop'! Q ◖ P

North London

N2: East Finchley

Old White Lion
Great North Road (A1000)
11–11
Draught Bass; Charrington IPA Ⓗ
Spacious and comfortable, two-bar pub, featuring a wood-panelled interior. A fine example of 1930s 'Brewer's Tudor' architecture. Handy for local commuters and cinema-goers.
⊛ ◖ ◗ ⊞ ♿ ⊖ ♣ P

Welch's Ale House
130 High Road (A1000)
11–3; 5.30–11 (11–11 Sat)
Felinfoel Double Dragon; Fuller's London Pride; Greene King Abbot Ale; Marston's Pedigree Bitter; Ruddles County; Webster's Yorkshire Bitter Ⓗ
Former ice cream parlour with a wide range of flavours still available, albeit of a completely different type! Often crowded. Guest beers always available. No food weekends. ◖ ⊖ ⌓

Windsor Castle
The Walks (off A1000)
11–11
Greene King Abbot Ale; McMullen Country Best Bitter; Marston's Pedigree Bitter; Whitbread Boddingtons Bitter Ⓗ
Single-bar pub with eclectic style of decor. Numerous theatre programmes and posters from a bygone era adorn the walls. No meals Sun lunch.
⊛ ◖ ◗ ♿ ♣

Try also: Grogblossom Beershop

N6: Highgate

Victoria
28 North Hill
11–3 (4 Sat); 5.30–11 (11–11 summer)
Marston's Pedigree Bitter; Whitbread Wethered Bitter, Flowers Original Ⓗ
Convivial pub featuring trad jazz on Sun eves. Guest beers.
⊛ ◖ ◗ ⊖

N7: Holloway

Admiral Mann
7 Hargrave Place
☎ (071) 485 4739
11–3 (4 Sat); 5.30 (7 Sat)–11
McMullen Original AK, Country Best Bitter Ⓗ
Traditional pub with wood-panelled walls; separate public bar. Hidden in a side-street, totally at odds with its surroundings.
◖ ◗ ⊞ ♿ ⇌ (Kentish Town) ⊖

N9: Lower Edmonton

Beehive
Little Bury Street
11–3; 5.30–11
Ind Coope Burton Ale; Tetley Bitter; Young's Bitter Ⓗ
Pleasant suburban hostelry, attracting loyal custom from a wide section of the local community. Eve meals till 9pm; no food Sat or Sun. ⊛ ◖ ◗ ♣

Jolly Farmer
17 Church Street (200 yds W of Edmonton Green)
☎ (081) 807 3696
11.30–3; 5.30–11 (11.30–11 Fri & Sat)
Ind Coope Burton Ale; Taylor Walker Best Bitter; Tetley Bitter Ⓗ
Former two-bar locals' pub recently transformed into a neo-Victorian drinking emporium.
⊛ ◖ ◗ ♿ ⇌ ♣

N15: Turnpike Lane

K K McCool's
265 West Green Road (A504)
☎ (081) 889 2071
11.30–11
Bateman XXXB; Marston's Pedigree Bitter; Tolly Cobbold Bitter; Whitbread Boddingtons Bitter Ⓗ
Well-presented, single-bar conversion with much imported panelling and 'library'. Beer range subject to change. ◖ ⊖

N16: Stoke Newington

Prince of Wales
59 Kynaston Road
☎ (071) 254 5088
12–11
Draught Bass; Charrington IPA Ⓗ
One-bar family pub with darts, pool, crib, etc. Guest beer.
⛫ ⊛ ◖

N17: Tottenham

Chequers
841–843 High Road
☎ (081) 808 3841
11–11 (11–4; 7–11 Sat)
Draught Bass; Charrington IPA Ⓗ
Well-run, quiet pub with strong darts following (four teams). Q ⊛ ◖ ◗ ♿ ⇌ (White Hart Lane) ♣

N19: Holloway

J J Moon's
37 Lanseer Road (off Holloway Road) ☎ (071) 263 4658
11–11
Greene King IPA, Abbot Ale; Marston's Pedigree Bitter; Theakston XB; Younger Scotch Ⓗ
Pleasant, corner-house local with central bar. Food available at all times (veg menu). Full roast lunches on Sun. Guest beers. ⊛ ◖ ◗ ⊖ (Archway) ⌓

N20: Whetstone

Bull & Butcher
1277 High Road (A1000)
11–11
Ind Coope Burton Ale; Tetley Bitter; Young's Bitter Ⓗ
Comfortable three-bar pub with separate games area. Live music in back room occasionally. No food Sun.
⛫ ◖ ⊞ ⊖ (Totteridge) ♣

N21: Winchmore Hill

Dog & Duck
74 Hoppers Road (off A111)
11–11
McMullen Country Best Bitter; Marston's Pedigree Bitter Ⓗ
Small, single-bar pub, attracting diverse clientele. Individual without being eccentric; homely without being parochial. Also sells Whitbread beers. ⛫ ⊛ ♿

Green Dragon
889 Green Lanes (A105)
11–11
Courage Best Bitter, Directors Ⓗ
Fine pub which continues to achieve the high standards it sets itself. Excellent in all respects. London CAMRA's Pub of the Year 1989.
⊛ ◖ ⊞ ⇌ ♣ P

Barnet

Albion
74 Union Street (off A1000)
☎ (081) 441 2841
11–3 (12–2.30 Sun); 5.30 (7 Sat)–11
Benskins Best Bitter; Ind Coope Burton Ale Ⓗ
Homely, split-level pub just off High Street, with large garden and outdoor gents' loos. No lunches Sun. ⊛ ◖ ♣ P

Olde Mitre Inn
58 High Street (A1000)
☎ (081) 449 6582
11–11
Benskins Best Bitter; Ind Coope Burton Ale; Tetley Bitter Ⓗ
Oldest pub in Barnet (1630), grade II listed. Single bar with three individual drinking areas. Noted by Samuel Pepys in 1660 as serving rotten mutton, but since much improved! Recently-renovated but untarnished. No food Sun.
⊖ (High Barnet) P

Olde Monken Holt
193 High Street (A1000)
☎ (081) 449 4280
11–11
Courage Best Bitter, Directors Ⓗ
Excellent wood-panelled pub run to consistently high standards. Eve meals till 9pm.
Q ♣

Weaver
Greenhill Parade, Great North Road (A1000)
☎ (081) 449 8002
11–3; 5.30 (7 Sat)–11 (11–11 Fri)
Adnams Bitter; Fuller's London Pride, ESB; Theakston Best Bitter Ⓗ
Small, one-roomed bar in former shop. Well laid-out in an unusual style. Range of ales liable to change. No food Sun.
≈ (New Barnet) ⊖ (High Barnet) ♣

Cockfosters

Trent Tavern
Cockfosters Road (A111)
11–3; 5.30–11
Courage Best Bitter, Directors; John Smith's Bitter Ⓗ
Modern pub on busy main road with unusual pale wood panelling. Popular with students from nearby college.
⊖ ♣ P

Enfield Highway

Red Lion
371 Hertford Road (A1010)
11–3; 5.30–11
Draught Bass; Charrington IPA Ⓗ
Fine Edwardian, two-bar pub. Saloon comfortable but not luxurious; public bar functional but not spartan. No food Sun.
♣

Enfield Town

Kings Head
Market Place (off A110)
☎ (081) 363 0123
11–11
Ind Coope Burton Ale; Taylor Walker Best Bitter; Tetley Bitter Ⓗ
Classic Victorian town pub overlooking ancient market square. Single island bar serves several distinctive drinking areas. Town centre site ensures it is always busy. Good mix of clientele. No food Sun. ≈

Old Wheatsheaf
3 Windmill Hill (A110)
☎ (081) 363 0516
11–3; 5.15 (7 Sat)–11
Ind Coope Burton Ale; Taylor Walker Best Bitter; Tetley Bitter Ⓗ
Comfortable, two-bar pub in traditional style, retaining its olde-worlde charm. Lots of character and architectural interest. Not to be missed. Good value lunches (not Sun).
≈ (Enfield Chase) ♣ P

Enfield Whitewebbs

King & Tinker
Whitewebbs Lane (1¼ miles W of M25/A10 jct) OS331998
11–3; 5.30–11
Benskins Best Bitter; Ind Coope Burton Ale; Taylor Walker Best Bitter; Tetley Bitter Ⓗ
Award-winning, 17th-century rural gem with high standard of service. Winner of national Burton cellarmanship award for 1989. Large garden with enclosed playground. No food Sun. Bulmer cider.
♣ P

New Barnet

Duke of Lancaster
Lancaster Road (off Approach Road) ☎ (081) 449 0465
11–11
Courage Best Bitter, Directors Ⓗ
Tucked-away beneath a railway embankment. Functional public bar; comfortable saloon adorned with agricultural implements. Raised area to the rear has snooker table and dartboard. No food Sun. ≈ ♣

North West London

NW3: Belsize Park

Sir Richard Steele
97 Haverstock Hill
☎ (071) 483 1261
11–3; 5.30–11 (11–11 Sat)
Draught Bass; Charrington IPA Ⓗ
Popular, with a varied clientele and unusual artefacts. Food available lunch and eves (not Sun). ⊖ ♣ P

NW3: Hampstead

Flask
14 Flask Walk
☎ (071) 435 3240
11–3; 5.30–11
Young's Bitter, Special, Winter Warmer Ⓗ
Friendly and characterful pub with the only public bar for miles. No food Sun.
Q ⊖

Holly Bush
22 Holly Mount
☎ (071) 435 2892
11–3 (4 Sat); 5.30 (6 Sat)–11
Benskins Best Bitter; Ind Coope Burton Ale; Tetley Bitter; Young's Special Ⓗ
Traditional local with real gas lights in front bar and post-war-style lounge at rear (live jazz Thu eves). Anyone who appreciates an unspoilt bar should visit this pub, converted in the 18th century from stables. Family room till 8pm. Pavement drinking area. Lunches Tue–Sun; eve meals Tue–Sat. Q ⊖ ♣

Spaniards Inn
Spaniards Road
☎ (071) 455 3276
11–11
Draught Bass; Charrington IPA; Greene King IPA; M&B Highgate Mild; Young's Bitter Ⓗ
Attractive old building with low ceilings and two small rooms for intimate drinking. Enterprising food with vegetarian dishes available.
Q P

NW5: Dartmouth Park

Lord Palmerston
33 Dartmouth Park Hill
☎ (071) 485 1578
11–11
Courage Best Bitter, Directors Ⓗ
Popular, well-appointed pub with comfortable interior. Good 'doorstep' sandwiches and casseroles available lunchtimes. Snacks only eves. Conservatory doubles as a family room.
Q ⊖ (Tufnell Pk)

NW5: Kentish Town

Bull & Last
168 Highgate Road
☎ (071) 267 3641
11–11
Draught Bass; Charrington IPA; Fuller's ESB Ⓗ
Comfortably-furnished local opposite Parliament Hill Fields. Interesting prints of local landmarks from days past. Food

until 9pm.
◐ ◑ ♿ ⇌ (Gospel Oak)

Pineapple
51 Leverton Street
☎ (071) 485 6422
11–11
Friary Meux Best Bitter; Ind Coope Burton Ale; Marston's Pedigree Bitter Ⓗ
A small, Victorian back-street hides this cosy, true free house of the same period. Regular local trade and excellent Bass mirrors. Snacks lunchtimes.
Q ♿ ⇌ ⊖ ♣

NW6: Kilburn

Queens Arms
1 Kilburn High Road
☎ (071) 624 5735
11–11 (11–4; 6.30–11 Sat)
Young's Bitter, Special, Winter Warmer Ⓗ
Large 1950s wood-panelled pub. Has enormous collection of old photographs. Roof garden. Limited parking. No meals Sun.
⌂ ❀ ◐ ◑ ⊟ ⇌ (Kilburn High Rd) ⊖ (Kilburn Pk) ♣ P

NW7: Mill Hill

Rising Sun
Highwood Hill (at A5109/B552 jct)
12–3; 5.30 (6 Sat)–11
Ind Coope Burton Ale; Taylor Walker Best Bitter Ⓗ
Traditional inn in rural setting with lots of character. Outdoor loos. Food till 9pm. ❀ ◐ ◑ ♣ P

NW8: Maida Vale

Crockers
24 Aberdeen Place
☎ (071) 286 6608
11–11
Arkell's Kingsdown Ale; Brakspear Special; Vaux Samson; Wards Sheffield Best Bitter; Young's Special Ⓗ
A genuine folly built by the owner who believed Marylebone station would be built next door. Extensive pub with large spacious lounge featuring refurbished Victorian interior. Bar billiards. House beer.
♉ ❀ ◐ ◑ ⊟ ⊖ (Edgware Rd) ♣

NW8: St John's Wood

Blenheim
21 Loudon Road (corner of Carlton Hill)
☎ (071) 328 5884
11–3; 5.30 (6.30 Sat)–11
Greene King XX Dark, IPA, Abbot Ale Ⓗ
Attractive pub in well-off residential area. Comfortably-furnished, with pictures relating to Blenheim. Popular with cricket fans. No food Sun.
Q ◐ ⇌ (S Hampstead) ⊖

Knights of St John
7 Queen's Terrace
☎ (071) 586 5239
11–3; 5.30–11
Charles Wells Eagle Bitter, Bombardier Ⓗ
Three-storey building with a listed frontage. The pub does not reflect the more upmarket conditions prevailing in the area, having a distinct village-style, locals' appeal. No food Sun. ♉ ◐ ⊖ ♣

Rosetti
23 Queens Grove
☎ (071) 722 7141
11–3; 5.30–11 (11–11 Fri & Sat)
Fuller's London Pride, ESB Ⓗ
Tiled floor, marble-topped tables and hanging plants bring an air of Italy to NW London. Cómplemented by a quality Italian restaurant on the third floor, the split-level lounge bar is a cool and relaxing haven from everyday bustle.
Q ❀ ◐ ◑ ⊖ P

NW9: Kingsbury

J J Moon's
553 Kingsbury Road
11–11
Greene King Abbot Ale; Marston's Pedigree Bitter; Theakston XB; Younger Scotch Ⓗ
Converted shop, creating an oasis in the area. Good lunchtime food, including roast meat dishes and several veg meals. Can get crowded weekend eves. Guest beers.
Q ◐ ◑ ⊖

NW10: Harlesden

Fishermans Arms
Old Oak Lane
☎ (081) 965 6819
11–11 (11–3; 7–11 Sat)
Benskins Best Bitter; Ind Coope Burton Ale; Tetley Bitter Ⓗ
No-frills, two-bar local, built around railway community near Grand Union Canal. Lunches Mon–Fri.
◐ ⊟ ⇌ (Willesden Jct) ⊖

Grand Junction Arms
Acton Lane ☎ (081) 965 5670
11–11
Young's Bitter, Special, Winter Warmer Ⓗ
Large pub with good moorings on the Paddington arm of the GUC. Great garden for kids in summer. Public bar prices are cheaper than saloon. No food Sun. Q ❀ ◐ ◑ ⊟ ♿ ⇌ ⊖ ♣ P

NW11: Golders Green

Royal Oak
1117 Finchley Road (A598 ½ mile S of North Circular)
11–11
Benskins Best Bitter; Ind Coope Burton Ale; Tetley Bitter Ⓗ
Fine two-bar pub with large comfortable saloon and rear public bar which is a mecca for pool players. Eve meals till 8.30pm, Mon–Sat. ❀ ◐ ◑ ♣ P

Harefield

Plough
Hill End Road
☎ (0895) 822129
11–3; 5.30–11
Brakspear Bitter; Fuller's London Pride; Greene King Abbot Ale; Marston's Burton Best Bitter, Pedigree Bitter; Wadworth 6X Ⓗ
Excellent one-bar free house near the hospital. Good value food (not Sun) and barbecues. Very friendly; busy in summer. Stocks an additional three ales.
⌂ ❀ ◐ P

White Horse
Church Hill ☎ (0895) 822144
11–3; 6–11
Benskins Best Bitter; Ind Coope Burton Ale; Tetley Bitter Ⓗ
Nice, old pub in very pleasant area. Cosy and friendly with beer garden at rear. Food can be provided for DIY barbecue by arrangement. A guest beer (Adnams, Greene King or Young's) is also available. The Addlestones cider is not traditional. ⌂ Q ❀ ◐ ◑ ⊟ ♣ P

Harrow

Castle
30 West Street
☎ (081) 422 3155
11.30–11 (11–11 Fri & Sat)
Fuller's London Pride, ESB Ⓗ
Little-changed, traditional and well-run pub in a conservation area. Contains two bars, both very popular and lively. Parking can sometimes take a little time.
Q ❀ ◐ ⊟ ⇌ (Harrow-on-the-Hill) ⊖ ♣

Kingsfield Arms
111 Bessborough Road
☎ (081) 422 2727
11–3 (5 Sat); 5.30 (7 Sat)–11
Courage Best Bitter, Directors Ⓗ
Pleasant, one-bar pub on the outskirts of town. Darts room at rear and a no-smoking area. Popular with both regular and passing trade. ❀ ◐ ⇌ (Harrow-on-the-Hill) ⊖ ♣

Sudbury Town

Sudbury Arms
Sudbury Heights Avenue

☎ (081) 902 5026
11–3; 7–11 (11–11 Thu–Sat)
Courage Best Bitter, Directors [H]
Fine 1930s pub which boasts three separate bars, largely unspoilt by time. Q ◖ ◗ ⊕ ⊖

South East London

SE3: Blackheath

Bitter Experience
129 Lee Road (off A20, near Lee Gate shopping precinct)
☎ (081) 852 8819
11–9.30 (10–2; 3–9.30 Sat, 12–2; 7–9 Sun)
Fuller's London Pride; Shepherd Neame Master Brew Bitter [G]
A popular off-licence, with a vast range of real ales and ciders stored in a temperature-controlled room at the rear of the shop. A wide selection of English and foreign bottled beers also on offer.

British Oak
109 Old Dover Road
☎ (081) 858 1082
11–3 (4 Sat); 5 (6 Sat)–11 (11–11 Fri)
Courage Best Bitter, Directors; John Smith's Bitter [H]
Lively, two-bar local with genuine pub atmosphere. Quiz nights every other Tue. No food weekends. ❀ ◖ ⊕ ♣

SE5: Camberwell

Cambria
40 Kemerton Road
☎ (071) 733 9001
11–3; 5.30–11
Draught Bass [H]
Imposing Victorian exterior despite being a back-street local. Two spacious bars and a quiet snug within. Upstairs snooker table available at landlord's discretion. Family sing-alongs at weekends. No food Sun.
Q ❀ ◖ ⊕ ⇌ (Loughborough Jct) ⊖ (Brixton) ♣

Station Tavern
18 John Ruskin Street
☎ (071) 703 3256
11–4; 5.30–11
Charrington IPA [H]
Locals' pub; very cheap, with an unassuming private bar complete with real coal fire. Pianist Sat and Sun eves.
⌂ Q ⊕ ⇌ (Elephant & Castle) ⊖ ♣

Wickwood Tavern
58 Flaxman Road
11–11
Young's Bitter, Special, Winter Warmer [H]
Friendly and very popular pub hidden in the back streets. Pleasantly-decorated. Piano in the saloon; darts in the public. Jovial atmosphere. ⌂ Q ♉ ◖ ⊕ ⇌ (Loughborough Jct) ⊖ (Brixton) ♣

SE8: Deptford

Dog & Bell
116 Prince Street (off A200)
☎ (081) 692 5664
11–11
Fuller's London Pride, ESB [H]
Small and isolated back-street free house which is worth searching for. One bar with separate private room. Decorated with Beryl Cook pictures. Different guest beers every week. No food Sun. Good variety of games.
⌂ Q ♉ ❀ ◖ ⇌ ♣

Royal George
85a Tanners Hill
☎ (081) 692 2594
11–3; 5.30–11 (11–11 Sat)
Samuel Smith OBB, Museum Ale [H]
Busy locals' pub with games room upstairs. Quiz nights Wed. ❀ ◖ ⇌ (New Cross) ⊖ ♣

SE9: Eltham

Royal Eltham
1 Kingsley Wood Drive, New Eltham ☎ (081) 857 1232
11–3 (4 Fri & Sat, 12–2 Sun); 5.30–11
Courage Best Bitter, Directors; John Smith's Bitter [H]
Wood-panelled saloon is in the style of a gentlemen's club, with RAF and other military memorabilia. Genuine public bar (cheaper beer) is more basic, with a wide range of games – chess, backgammon, shove-ha'penny, etc. ❀ ⊕ ♣ P

White Hart
2 Eltham High Street
☎ (081) 850 1562
11–3; 5.30–11
Courage Best Bitter, Directors [H]
Large mock-Tudor pub, in traditional Courage wooden panelling, with collection of copper pots. Family conservatory. No meals Sun.
♉ ❀ ◖ ⇌ ♣

SE10: Greenwich

Cricketers
22 King William Walk
☎ (081) 858 3630
11–11 (11–4; 6–11 Sat)
Charrington IPA [H]
Two-bar pub in centre of Greenwich. Convenient for Cutty Sark, Royal Maritime Museum and Greenwich Hospital. Collection of banknotes and Toby jugs.
◖ Ʌ ⇌ ♣

Mitre
291 Greenwich High Road
11–3; 6–11 (11–11 Sat, 12–3; 7.30–10.30 Sun)
Draught Bass; Charrington IPA [H]
Unspoilt locals' pub next to St Alfeg's church and near the weekend antiques market. Lunches Tue–Sat. Q ◖ ⊕ ⇌

Try also: Richard I (Young's)

SE12: Lee

Crown
117 Burnt Ash Hill (off South Circular towards Mottingham)
☎ (081) 857 6607
11–11
Young's Bitter, Special, Winter Warmer [H]
Excellent local with an affable and friendly atmosphere. By far the best beer in this desert; an oasis well worth finding.
Q ❀ ◖ ◗ ♿ ⇌ ♣ P

SE14: New Cross

Rose
272 New Cross Road, New Cross Gate (opp. station)
☎ (081) 692 3193
11–3.30; 5.30–11 (11–11 Sat)
Courage Best Bitter, Directors [H]
Comfortable pub with celtic influence. Limited parking. ❀ ◖ P

SE15: Peckham

Beehive
122 Meeting House Lane (400 yds from police station)
☎ (071) 639 6283
11–4; 7–11
Shepherd Neame Master Brew Bitter, Best Bitter [H]
Locals' back-street pub, although not basic. ❀ ◖ ◗ ⇌ (Queens Rd/Peckham Rye)

Old Nuns Head
15 Nunhead Green, Nunhead (off Linden Grove)
☎ (071) 639 1745
11–11
Draught Bass; Charrington IPA; Fuller's ESB [H]
Well-built, turn-of-the century, suburban boozer. Excellent panelled rooms. Top class dart players often perform.
◖ ◗ ⇌ (Nunhead) ♣

SE16: Bermondsey

Manor Tavern
78 Galleywall Road, Rotherhithe
☎ (071) 237 3396
11–3 (4.30 Sat); 4.45 (7 Sat)–11 (11–11 Fri)
Charrington IPA [H]
Unspoilt, unchanging, friendly community local with strong darts following. Small and isolated but worth finding for its very reasonably-priced lunches (not weekends). ❀ ◖ ⊕

⇌ (S Bermondsey) ⊖ (Surrey Quays) ♣

SE17: Walworth

Crown
115 Brandon Street
☎ (071) 703 3580
11–11 (11–4; 7–11 Sat)
Draught Bass; Charrington IPA Ⓗ
Traditional, street-corner local near East Street market. Once a Wenlock ale house: see photographs on the walls.
⊛ ⇌ (Elephant & Castle) ⊖

Globe
20 Darwin Street
☎ (071) 703 1916
11–4; 7–11
Courage Best Bitter; John Smith's Bitter Ⓗ
Two-bar pub with fine, modern mirrored surround. Close to the Old and New Kent Roads junction. Eve meals 8–10pm (no food Sat or Sun). ◑ ◗ ⊞ ⇌ (Elephant & Castle) ⊖ ♣

SE18: Woolwich

Anglesey Arms
91 Woolwich New Road
☎ (081) 317 0834
11–11 (11–3; 6–11 Wed)
Shepherd Neame Master Brew Bitter Ⓗ
Spartan, basic local pub in the town centre with friendly management. Many games played: Trivial Pursuit, chess, backgammon, crib, etc.
◑ ◗ ⇌ (Arsenal) ♣

Bull
151 Shooters Hill
☎ (081) 856 0691
11–3; 5.15–11
Courage Best Bitter, Directors Ⓗ
Two-bar local sited at the top of Shooters Hill – the opening setting of *A Tale of Two Cities*. No food Sun. Note the rare outside gents' loo. ⊛ ◑ ⊞ ♣

Red Lion
6 Red Lion Place, Shooters Hill
☎ (081) 856 0333
11–11 (11–4.30; 7–11 Sat)
Courage Best Bitter, Directors Ⓗ
Large pub with highwayman connections. Once a Beasley's pub. ⊛ ♣ P

SE19: Crystal Palace

Railway Bell
14 Cawnpore Street (off Gipsy Hill) ☎ (081) 761 4521
11–3.30; 5.50–11 (11–11 Fri & Sat)
Young's Bitter, Special, Winter Warmer Ⓗ
Very popular pub keen on charity events, including special barbecues. A stiff walk uphill from Gipsy Hill station. Hard to find but well worth it; very friendly.
⛫ ⊛ ◑ ◗ ⇌ (Gipsy Hill) ♣

Royal Albert
42 Westow Hill (A214 near A212 jct) ☎ (081) 670 1208
11–3; 5.30–11 (11–11 Sat)
Draught Bass; Charrington IPA Ⓗ
Front public bar, with side entrance to lounge at rear. A large jug collection hangs from the beams in the lounge. Close to Crystal Palace park and National Sports Centre. Lunches Mon-Fri. Q ⊛ ◑ ⊞ ⛺ ⇌ (Gipsy Hill/Crystal Palace) ♣

SE22: East Dulwich

Clockhouse
196a Peckham Rye (opp. the common) ☎ (081) 693 2901
11–11
Young's Bitter, Special, Winter Warmer Ⓗ
Nice, little friendly house. Clocks adorn the walls, with antique clocks in a case at the rear. Note the superb collection of framed bottle labels from defunct breweries, donated by a former bar manager.
Q ⊛ ◑ ◗ ♿ ⇌ ♣

Crystal Palace Tavern
193 Crystal Palace Road
☎ (081) 693 4968
12–11
Ind Coope Burton Ale; Taylor Walker Best Bitter Ⓗ
Friendly, back-street local which has retained a lot of its original Victorian character. Extension to the saloon bar planned. Pianist weekends. Landlord trains Taylor Walker managers and staff. Take-away curries weekday lunchtimes. Q ⊛ ◑ ⊞ ♣

SE23: Forest Hill

Dartmouth Arms
7 Dartmouth Road (off South Circular)
11–3 (4 Fri & Sat); 5.30 (7.30 Sat)–11 (12–3; 7.30–10.30 Sun)
Courage Best Bitter, Directors Ⓗ
Unspoilt 1950s interior decor. Lounge at rear. Large car park.
Q ⊞ ⇌ P

Prince of Wales
52 Perry Rise
☎ (081) 699 7591
11–11
Draught Bass; Charrington IPA; Fuller's ESB (winter) Ⓗ
Quiet and friendly, one-bar pub, mainly serving local residential trade. Very busy at weekends but conversation is still a feature. No food Sat.
Q ⊛ ◑ ⇌ ♣

Railway Telegraph
112 Stanstead Road
☎ (081) 699 6644
11–3; 5.30–11 (11–11 Fri & Sat)
Shepherd Neame Master Brew Bitter, Best Bitter Ⓗ
Basic, two-bar, locals' boozer on the South Circular road. Garden has excellent facilities for children. Old-time pianist at weekends. No food Sun.
⊛ ◑ ⊞ ⇌ ♣

Try also: Malt Shovel (Free)

SE24: Herne Hill

Commercial
212 Railton Road
☎ (071) 274 3924
11–11
Draught Bass; Charrington IPA; Fuller's ESB; Greene King IPA Ⓗ
Excellent two-bar, Victorian pub opposite Herne Hill station. Very friendly; cheap beer for area. Dominoes played. Wood panelling in both bars; TV in Railway Bar. ⊞ ♿ ⇌ ♣

SE25: South Norwood

Prince of Denmark
152 Portland Road (A215, next to swimming baths)
☎ (081) 654 1769
11–11
Courage Best Bitter, Directors Ⓗ
Large, friendly and traditional old pub. Spacious wood-panelled saloon at rear (side entrance) and public bar at front. Live music Sun eves.
⊛ ⊞ ♿ ⇌ (Norwood Jct) ♣

Try also: Albion (Courage)

SE26: Sydenham

Bricklayers Arms
189 Dartmouth Road
☎ (081) 699 1260
11–11
Young's Bitter, Special, Ⓗ, **Winter Warmer** Ⓖ
Extensively and pleasantly refurbished local which has retained its thriving public bar. Fields a rugby (union) team. A very cosy and welcoming children's room is another feature. No food Sun.
♨ ⊛ ◑ ⊞ ⇌ (Forest Hill) ♣

Dulwich Wood House
39 Sydenham Hill
☎ (081) 693 5666
11–3; 5.30–11 (11–11 Fri & Sat)
Young's Bitter, Special, Winter Warmer Ⓗ & Ⓔ
Deservedly-busy, two-bar pub with a country atmosphere. The garden bar uses electric pumps; the large garden boasts a petanque piste (adults only), a climbing frame for children and

a barbecue in summer. Real fires in both bars. No meals Sun.
⛫ Q ❀ ◖ Ⓐ (Crystal Palace) ≷ (Sydenham Hill) ♣ P

SE27: West Norwood

Hope
49 Norwood High Street
☎ (081) 670 2035
11–11
Young's Bitter, Special, Winter Warmer Ⓗ
Excellent local at rear of West Norwood station which can be very busy at weekends. Friendly, with a very warm welcome, decorated in typical Young's style. Ask about meals.
Q ❀ ◖ ≷ ♣

Kings Head
62 Norwood High Street
☎ (081) 670 4056
11–11
Draught Bass Ⓗ
Splendid, comfortable, two-bar local. Excellent beer at very keen prices; friendly and very warm welcome. Games room also serves as children's room when not busy. Old-fashioned tills still in use.
♉ ◖ ◗ ⊟ ♿ ≷ ♣

Addiscombe

Claret Wine Bar
5a Bingham Corner, Lower Addiscombe Road (A222)
☎ (081) 656 7452
11.30–11
Eldridge Pope Royal Oak; King & Barnes Broadwood; Palmers IPA Ⓗ
Don't be put off by the name and location (in a parade of shops) – this is a comfortable pub with the emphasis on ale. Good value food at lunchtime (not weekends). ❀ ◖ ≷

Cricketers
47 Shirley Road (A212, just off A222) ☎ (081) 654 3833
11.30–2.30; 5–11 (11–3; 5–11 Fri, 11–3; 6–11 Sat)
Courage Best Bitter, Directors Ⓗ
Faded 'Brewer's Tudor' pub, popular with all ages. Fake beams and an odd collection of artefacts manage to provide a good atmosphere. Food weekday lunchtimes.
❀ ◖ ≷ (Woodside) ♣ P

Bexley

Black Horse
62 Albert Road (off A223)
☎ (0322) 52337
11–3; 5.30–11
Courage Best Bitter, Directors Ⓗ
Small, bustling, back-street local, in contrast with the disco haunts of the village centre. No food Sun. ❀ ◖ ≷ ♣

Bexleyheath

Bitter Experience
216 Broadway
☎ (081) 304 2039
11–2; 6–9 (10.30–9.30 Thu–Sat, 12–2; 7–9 Sun)
Adnams Bitter; Greene King Abbot Ale; King & Barnes Sussex Bitter; Moorhouse's Premier Bitter; Shepherd Neame Master Brew Bitter Ⓖ
Off-licence whose services are now needed more than ever. Now simply the only reliable outlet for independent real ale in Bexley Borough. Guest beers and ciders. ≷

Royal Oak (Polly Clean Stairs)
Mount Road/Alers Road (off A227) ☎ (081) 303 4454
11.30–2.30; 7–11
Courage Best Bitter, Directors; John Smith's Bitter Ⓗ
The former Upton village stores, now a village-style local in the centre of a residential area. The only sound to be heard is that of contented drinkers enjoying a rare local gem. Cold food only served (not Sun). Q ❀ ◖ P

Try also: Kings Head (Courage)

Blendon

Three Blackbirds
Blendon Road (near Danson interchange on A2)
☎ (081) 303 4260
11–11
Draught Bass; Charrington IPA; Fuller's ESB (winter) Ⓗ
Fine old inn with unusual decor in contrasting bars. An extensive range of good value lunches is offered, including veg option. Petanque.
❀ ◖ ⊟ ♣ P

Bromley Common

Bitter End
139 Masons Hill (A21, ½ mile S of centre) ☎ (081) 466 6083
12–3; 5–10 (5–9 Mon, 11–10 Sat, 12–2; 7–9 Sun)
Beer range varies Ⓖ
Still as good as ever. Quality beer at reasonable prices for the take-home connoisseur.
≷ (Bromley S)

Bricklayers Arms
143 Masons Hill (A21, ½ mile S of centre) ☎ (081) 460 4552
11–2.30 (12–2.30 Sun); 5.30–11
Shepherd Neame Master Brew Bitter Ⓖ
George celebrates 20 years as licensee of this friendly family local this year. He believes in tradition; the Master Brew spends five days in the cellar before sale and new opening hours have passed this pub by. May offer Bishops Finger on occasions. No food Sun.
◖ ≷ (Bromley S) ♣

Crayford

One Bell
Old Road ☎ (0322) 523495
11–11
Ind Coope Burton Ale; Tetley Bitter; Young's Bitter Ⓗ
Attractive old inn with four small bars and a prize-winning garden. ❀ ◖ ≷ P

Croydon

Builders Arms
65 Leslie Park Road (off A222)
☎ (081) 654 1803
11.30–3; 5 (6.30 Sat)–11 (11–11 Fri)
Fuller's Chiswick Bitter, London Pride, ESB Ⓗ
Very popular, small, country-style pub in back-street. Two rather over-decorated saloon-standard bars are lined with bookcases and artefacts vaguely connected with building. Excellent food all sessions (till 9pm), except Sat and Sun eves.
❀ ◖ ◗ ≷ (E Croydon/ Addiscombe)

Crown
90 Stanley Road (off A235, near Mayday Hospital)
☎ (081) 684 4952
11–11
Ruddles Best Bitter; Webster's Yorkshire Bitter Ⓗ
Excellent street-corner local. Large bar with collection of plates on walls and full range of traditional pub games (ask). Good value home-cooked food (to 8pm, Mon–Fri). Live music Sat and Sun nights. ◖ ◗ ♣

Dog & Bull
24 Surrey Street (off High Street) ☎ (081) 667 0877
11–11
Young's Bitter, Special, Winter Warmer Ⓗ
Plain one-bar pub in Croydon street market; a local 'institution'. Pub name depicted in stained glass windows. No food Sun.
Q ◖ ⊟ ≷ (E/W Croydon)

Golden Lion
144 Stanley Road (off A235)
☎ (081) 684 1395
11–11
Courage Best Bitter, Directors; John Smith's Bitter Ⓗ
Warm, friendly street-corner local with keen darts teams and regular fund-raising activities.
❀ ⊟ ♣

Lion
182 Pawsons Road (off A212)
☎ (081) 684 2978
11–11
Draught Bass; Everards Tiger Best Bitter; Greene King Abbot Ale; King & Barnes Sussex Bitter, Festive; Young's Special Ⓗ
Quiet front bar with food counter (no food Sun); contrasting noisy back bar with games area. Guest beers.
Q ❁ ◖ ⇌ (Thornton Heath/ Selhurst) ♣

Pitlake Arms
73a Waddon New Road (off ring road) ☎ (081) 688 0428
11–3; 5.30 (7 Sat)–11
Fuller's London Pride; Greene King IPA, Abbot Ale; Ruddles Best Bitter Ⓗ
Former Allied street-corner pub now a successful free house. Decor includes railway memorabilia and collections of model cars, brass taps and old cameras. CD music system can be rather loud. No food weekends.
❁ ◖ ♿ ⇌ (W Croydon) ♣

Porter & Sorter
Station Road (unmarked road between station and post office)
☎ (081) 688 4296
11–3; 5 (7 Sat)–11 (closed Sun eve)
Courage Best Bitter, Directors Ⓗ
Refurbished local, popular with commuters and post office workers, providing a welcome refuge from the anonymous concrete jungle outside. Pavement drinking area. No food Sat or Sun.
❁ ◖ ⇌ (E Croydon) P

Star
101 Southbridge Road (A236 near A235 jct)
☎ (081) 688 6285
11–2.30; 6–11
Charrington IPA Ⓗ
Family-run, small, friendly pub with welcoming staff. Frequent charity events.
❁ ♿ ⇌ (S Croydon) ♣ P

Try also: Gloucester (Young's)

Foots Cray

Seven Stars
40 High Street (A211)
☎ (081) 300 2059
11–11
Draught Bass; Charrington IPA; Fuller's ESB (winter) Ⓗ
16th-century pub retaining many nooks and crannies. Good value for the area. Attractive and popular. No food Sun.
◖ ⊟ ♣ P

Kenley

Wattenden Arms
Old Lodge Lane ($1\frac{3}{4}$ miles off A22 at Kenley Station)
☎ (081) 660 8638
11–11
Draught Bass; Charrington IPA Ⓗ
Justifiably-acclaimed, upmarket local, run by the current licensee for the last 25 years. The interior has a patriotic theme. Excellent pub food. Lunches Mon-Sat; eve meals Tue–Thu till 9pm. Happy hour 5.30–7pm (Mon–Fri). Q ❁ ◖ ◗ P

Leaves Green

Crown Inn
Leaves Green Road
☎ (0959) 72920
11–2.30 (3 Sat); 5–11
Shepherd Neame Master Brew Bitter, Best Bitter, Bishops Finger Ⓗ
Pleasant and spacious road-house with a separate and excellent restaurant (book weekends), which allows the drinking area to retain a pub atmosphere. Large children's room becomes crowded at weekends. No eve meals Sun/Mon. ⛫ ❁ ◖ ◗ ♿ P

Upper Belvedere

Royal Standard
39 Nuxley Road (off A206)
☎ (03224) 33737
11–3; 6–11 (11–11 Fri & Sat)
Draught Bass; Charrington IPA Ⓗ
Old-style family establishment with a warm welcome. No food at weekends. ❁ ◖ ⊟ ♣ P

Try also: Queens Head (Courage)

South West London

SW2: Brixton

Hope & Anchor
123 Acre Lane (A2217)
☎ (071) 274 1787
11–11
Young's Bitter, Special, Winter Warmer Ⓗ
Large one-bar pub, comfortably appointed. Friendly local with garden; children welcome. Bar skittles played.
⌂ Q ❁ ◖ ◗ ♿ ⇌ ⊖ ♣

SW3: Chelsea

Princess of Wales
145 Dovehouse Street
☎ (071) 351 5502
11–11 (11–4; 8–11 Sat)
Courage Best Bitter, Directors Ⓗ
Small pub tucked behind the Royal Marsden Hospital.
Q ◖ ⊖ (S Kensington)

Rose
86 Fulham Road
☎ (071) 589 6672
11–3; 5 (7 Sat)–11 (11–11 Fri)
Fuller's Chiswick Bitter, London Pride, ESB Ⓗ
Ornate pub with much elaborate wood and tile work. Theatre upstairs. ◖ ◗ ⊖ (S Kensington)

Surprise
61 Christchurch Terrace
11–11
Draught Bass; Charrington IPA Ⓗ
Locals' pub with interesting frieze. Upmarket Chelsea prices.
◖ ♣

SW4: Clapham

Railway Tavern
18 Clapham High Street
☎ (071) 622 1696
11–11
Draught Bass; Charrington IPA; Exmoor Gold; Fuller's ESB Ⓗ
Modern-looking High Street pub with friendly atmosphere. Very good lunches. All home-cooked: speciality gammon on the bone. Live music — folk/ blues/jazz — and disco on Fri nights. Children's club in function room Sun lunchtime, with magicians, etc.
◖ ⇌ (High Street)
⊖ (Clapham N)

Rose & Crown
2 The Polygon, Old Town
11–11
Courage Best Bitter, Directors Ⓗ
New vibrant landlady has put this pub back on the real ale map. Now a firm favourite with locals and visitors. Anything can happen and usually does. The pub has an unusual Simonds ceramic sign. Pavement drinking area. ❁ ◖ ⊖ (Clapham Common)

SW6: Fulham

Jolly Brewer
308 North End Road
11–11
Ruddles County; Webster's Yorkshire Bitter Ⓗ
Busy local in lively street market. ⊖ (Fulham Bdwy) ♣

SW6: Parsons Green

White Horse
1 Parsons Green
☎ (071) 736 2115
11.30 (11 Sat)–3; 5 (7 Sat)–11
Draught Bass; Charrington IPA; M&B Highgate Mild; Traquair House Ale Ⓗ
Large, popular, upmarket pub facing the green, with a terrace for outside drinking. Hearty breakfasts served at weekends

(from 11 Sun). Hosts an annual Old Ale festival. ◖ ◗

SW6: West Brompton

Atlas
16 Seagrave Road
11–11
Ruddles Best Bitter, County; Webster's Yorkshire Bitter 🄷
Built in 1868; a popular back-street local near Earls Court exhibition hall. ❀ ◖ ⊖

SW7: South Kensington

Anglesea Arms
15 Selwood Terrace
11–3; 5.50 (7 Sat)–11
Adnams Bitter; Brakspear Special; Eldridge Pope Thomas Hardy Country Bitter; Greene King Abbot Ale; Whitbread Boddingtons Bitter; Young's Bitter 🄷
One bar, comfortably-furnished and very busy at most times. No music machines. ◖ ◗ ⊖

SW8: South Lambeth

Surprise
16 Southville (off Wandsworth Road) ☎ (071) 622 4623
11–11
Young's Bitter, Special, Winter Warmer 🄷
Excellently-run, one-bar pub with good home-made food (veg options). ⌂ Q ❀ ◖ ◗ ⊞ ⇌ (Wandsworth Rd) ♣

SW8: Vauxhall

Roebuck
84 Ashmole Street (off Clapham Road) ☎ (071) 820 9793
11–11
Draught Bass; Charrington IPA 🄷
Warm, comfortable new pub. Guest beer changes frequently. Ideal for Oval cricket.
⚇ ❀ ◖ ♿ ⇌ ⊖ (Oval) P

SW10: West Brompton

Fox & Pheasant
1 Billing Road (off Fulham Road)
Draught Bass; Charrington IPA 🄷
Tiny, two-bar pub much-used by locals. Near Chelsea football ground. ◖ ⊞ ⊖ (Fulham Bdwy)

SW10: West Chelsea

Chelsea Ram
22 Burnaby Street
☎ (071) 351 4008
11–3; 5.30–11 (11–11 Fri & Sat)
Young's Bitter, Special, Winter Warmer 🄷
Quiet, comfortable local, built as a pub in the 1880s but not licensed until 1984. No jukebox or piped music. Q ◖

SW11: Battersea

Woodman
60 Battersea High Street
☎ (071) 228 2968
11–3.30; 5.30 (6.30 Sat)–11
Adnams Bitter; Gale's HSB; Hall & Woodhouse Badger Best Bitter, Tanglefoot; Wadworth 6X 🄷
Large, one-bar pub with extensive garden which features a barbecue in summer. Bar billiards. ❀ ◖ ◗ ♿ ♣ ⌀

SW11: Clapham Junction

Beehive
197 St John's Hill
11–3 (12–2 Sun); 5.30 (6.30 Sat)–11 (may vary)
Fuller's Chiswick Bitter, London Pride, ESB 🄷
Small, welcoming, award-winning local, with few equals. Reasonably-priced lunches (no food Sun). ◖ ♿ ⇌

Windsor Castle
36 St John's Hill
11–11
Courage Best Bitter, Directors 🄷
Large, two-bar pub, very popular with local business clientele. Friendly service. Good value food (veg option).
❀ ◖ ⊞ ⇌ ♣

SW12: Balham

Nightingale
97 Nightingale Lane (between Clapham and Wandsworth Commons) ☎ (081) 673 1637
11–3; 5.30–11 (11–11 Fri & Sat)
Young's Bitter, Special, Winter Warmer 🄷
A firm favourite of those who recognise a good pint. Often packed; a true local in every sense, run by a team of professionals. Crib played.
Q ⚇ ❀ ◖ ⇌ (Wandsworth Common) ⊖ (Clapham S) ♣

Prince of Wales
270 Cavendish Road
☎ (081) 673 5864
11–3.30 (5 Sat); 5 (7 Sat)–11
Courage Best Bitter, Directors; Hop Back GFB; John Smith's Bitter 🄷
A long-standing favourite where good beer is the norm and service to the community is legendary. Very good value roasts and keen beer prices. Quiet oasis of a saloon and a noisy, boisterous public bar. No food weekends.
Q ❀ ◖ ⊞ ⇌ ⊖ ♣ P

SW13: Barnes

Bulls Head
373 Lonsdale Road (A3003)
☎ (081) 876 5241
11–11
Young's Bitter, Special, Winter Warmer 🄷
World-famous modern jazz venue fronting river. Music every night. Over 100 whiskies and fine wines. Restaurant to rear; beer at pub prices.
❀ ◖ ◗ ⇌ (Barnes Bridge) ♣

Coach & Horses
27 Barnes High Street (A3003)
11–3; 5.30–11 (11–11 Fri & Sat)
Young's Bitter, Special, Winter Warmer 🄷
Homely, wood-panelled single-bar pub with a glorious fireplace. Nice watering-hole after a stroll along the river-banks. Respectable drinking area to the rear.
⌂ ❀ ⇌ (Barnes Bridge)

Red Lion
2 Castlenau (between Hammersmith bridge and Barnes station)
☎ (081) 748 2984
11.30–11
Fuller's Chiswick Bitter, London Pride, ESB 🄷
Excellent two-bar period pub with ornate dining area to rear.
⌂ Q ❀ ◖ ◗ ♿ ⇌ P

SW14: Sheen

Hare & Hounds
216 Upper Richmond Road (200 yds E of Sheen Lane)
☎ (081) 876 4304
11–11
Young's Bitter, Special, Winter Warmer 🄷
Spacious wood-panelled saloon and two other large, open rooms: a snooker room (with full-size table) and a smaller, comfortable public bar. Very good food.
⌂ Q ❀ ◖ ⊞ ⇌ (Mortlake) ♣

SW15: Putney

Fox & Hounds
167 Upper Richmond Road (near station)
☎ (081) 788 1912
11–11
Marston's Pedigree Bitter; Whitbread Flowers IPA, Wethered Bitter 🄷
Busy and enterprising pub with spacious back room. Real ales well-promoted and well-kept. Guest beers. No food Sun.
❀ ◖ ⇌ ⊖ (E Putney) ♣

Jolly Gardeners
61 Lacy Road (300 yds from

Putney High Street)
☎ (081) 788 7508
11–11
Fuller's Chiswick Bitter, London Pride, ESB Ⓗ
Excellent back-street pub with popular jazz in saloon bar Sun lunch. No food Sun. Always a friendly welcome. Q ⌂ ◖ ⊟ ⇌ ⊖ (Putney Bridge) ♣

SW16: Streatham

Pied Bull
498 Streatham High Road (opp. common) ☎ (081) 764 4003
11–11
Young's Bitter, Special, Winter Warmer Ⓗ
Pub which has regained much of its past glory, thanks to sensitive refurbishment and enlightened management. Attracts a wide cross-section of the community, including shoppers. Public bar always crowded. ♨ Q ⌂ ◖ ⊟ ⇌ (Streatham Common) ♣ P

SW17: Earlsfield

Leather Bottle
538 Garratt Lane (A217)
☎ (081) 946 2309
11–11
Young's Bitter, Special, Winter Warmer Ⓗ
Large, pleasant, two-bar pub with spacious outside drinking area. ♨ ⌂ ◖ ⊟ ♿ ⇌ ♣ P

SW17: Tooting

Castle
38 High Street (opp. tube station) ☎ (081) 672 7018
11–11
Young's Bitter, Special, Winter Warmer Ⓗ
Large, three-bar pub near Tooting Broadway. Good lunches (incl. veg dishes). No smoking in dining area. 🐴 ⌂ ◖ ⊟ ♿ ⊖ (Tooting Bdwy) ♣ P

SW18: Earlsfield

Country House
2 Groton Road
☎ (081) 874 2715
11–3; 5.30–11 (11–11 Sat)
Courage Best Bitter, Directors Ⓗ
Excellent, well-run, two-bar local, hidden-away. Copper-topped tables in lounge. A rare find in London. Lunchtime snacks. Q ⊟ ♿ ⇌ ♣

SW18: Southfields

Gardeners Arms
268 Merton Road
☎ (081) 874 7624
11–11
Young's Bitter, Special Ⓗ
Recently-refurbished and extended comfortable ale house on busy road. Three specials on menu (no food Sun).
♨ ⌂ ◖ ♿ ⊖ ♣

SW18: Wandsworth

Grapes
39 Fairfield Street (off A3/A265 one-way system)
Young's Bitter, Special, Winter Warmer Ⓗ
Immaculate pub which belies its main road image. Highly-polished interior makes this a peaceful stop for the weary traveller. Sun lunchtimes recommended. Lunches Mon-Fri. ♨ Q ⌂ ◖ ⇌ (Wandsworth Town)

Spread Eagle
71 Wandsworth High Street (opp. brewery)
☎ (081) 874 1326
11–11
Young's Bitter, Special, Winter Warmer Ⓗ
Pub which has mellowed well since refurbishments. Always a good bet for ale. Q ◖ ⊟ ⇌ (Wandsworth Town) P

SW19: Merton

King's Head
18 High Street (old A24)
☎ (081) 540 7992
11–11
Young's Bitter, Special, Winter Warmer Ⓗ
Large, comfortable pub opposite pedestrian access to Savacentre. Large saloon with no-smoking room at back. Public bar leads to separate pool room. No food Sun.
⌂ ◖ ◗ ⊟ ⊖ (Colliers Wood) ♣ P

Princess Royal
25 Abbey Road (150 yds from Merton High Street jct)
☎ (081) 542 3273
11–3; 5 (6.30 Sat in winter)–11
Courage Best Bitter, Directors Ⓗ
Locals' corner pub with friendly atmosphere. Comfortable saloon bar; small public where you look down on main bar. No food Sun.
⌂ ◖ ⊟ ⊖ (S Wimbledon) ♣

SW19: Wimbledon

Rose & Crown
55 The High Street (A219)
☎ (081) 947 4713
11–11
Young's Bitter, Special, Winter Warmer Ⓗ
Large village pub; parts date from 17th century. Usually very busy. Q ⌂ ◖ ◗ P

Carshalton

Racehorse
17 West Street (off A232)
☎ (081) 647 1296
11–11
Courage Best Bitter, Directors Ⓗ
Modest Edwardian building with two bars. The larger has a restaurant area at the rear and a raised drinking area at the front window. No food Sun.
⌂ ◖ ◗ ⊟ ♿ ⇌ ♣ P

Try also: Railway (Fuller's)

Chessington

North Star
271 Hook Road (A243)
☎ (081) 397 4227
11–11 (11–3; 5.30–11 Sat)
Draught Bass; Charrington IPA; M&B Highgate Mild Ⓗ
One of few pubs in London serving Highgate Mild. Popular with locals and passing trade. Lunch menu offers choice for vegetarians and children. No food Sun. Q 🐴 ⌂ ◖ ♣ P

Kingston upon Thames

Boaters Inn
Canbury Gardens, Lower Ham Road (off A307)
☎ (081) 541 4672
11–3; 5–11 (11–11 summer)
Greene King Abbot Ale; Marston's Pedigree Bitter; Wadworth 6X; Whitbread Boddingtons Bitter Ⓗ
Modern pub, popular with all types, in middle of riverside gardens, with its own moorings. Range of beers varies every few weeks. No meals Sun eve. ⌂ ◖ ◗

Cardinal
174 Tudor Drive (off A307)
☎ (081) 546 3885
10.30–3; 5–11 (10.30–11 Fri & Sat)
Courage Best Bitter, Directors; John Smith's Bitter Ⓗ
Good-sized estate pub which has a strong following with both local residents and businesses. Large garden at rear used for barbecues most Fri & Sat eves, weather permitting. No lunches Sun. ⌂ ◖ ♿ ♣ P

Cocoanut
16 Mill Street (off Fairfield South)
11–3; 5.30–11 (11–11 Sat)
Fuller's Chiswick Bitter, London Pride, ESB Ⓗ
More a community than a pub. A warm welcome and good food (not Sun; veg option).
Q ⌂ ◖ ⇌ ♣

Druids Head
3 Market Place
☎ (081) 546 0723
11–11 (12–2; 7–10.30 Sun)
Whitbread Wethered Bitter, Flowers Original Ⓗ
Only pub left in market place.

Staircase to function room dates from 1680. Q ⇌ ♣

Lamb
16 Acre Road (off A307)
☎ (081) 549 5584
11–2.30; 5–11 (11–11 Fri & Sat)
Courage Best Bitter, Directors Ⓗ
Small, comfortable local, the venue for seven darts teams. The licensee and regulars are strongly involved in charity work. No food Sun. ◍ ◖ ⇌ ♣

Wych Elm
93 Elm Road (off Acre Road)
☎ (081) 546 3271
11–3; 5–11 (11–11 Fri & Sat)
Fuller's Chiswick Bitter, London Pride, ESB Ⓗ
Winner of several prizes for floral displays. Not easy to find but well worth the effort. No meals Sun. ◍ ◖ ⊞ ♣

Mitcham

Kings Arms
268 London Road
☎ (081) 648 0890
11–11 (11–3; 5.30–11 Tue, 11–3.30; 7–11 Sat)
Young's Bitter, Special, Winter Warmer Ⓗ
A haven from the traffic bedlam of the Fairgreen. The landlady of many years' standing ensures a relaxed and trouble-free atmosphere. ♔ ◍ ◖ ⊞ ♣ P

Morden

Beverley Tavern
Lower Morden Lane (B279)
☎ (081) 337 3071
11–3; 5.30–11 (11–11 Fri & Sat)
Ruddles Best Bitter, County; Webster's Yorkshire Bitter Ⓗ
Large, welcome sight in the Lower Morden pub desert. Named after the Beverley Brook, which eventually runs into the Thames at Putney. Large, airy family room/conservatory is complemented by an outside play area. Eve meals are in the carvery restaurant. Limited parking. ⚇ ◍ ◖ ◗ ⊞ ♣ P

Richmond

Orange Tree
45 Kew Road
☎ (081) 940 0944
11–11
Young's Bitter, Special, Winter Warmer Ⓗ
Extremely popular pub in a large Victorian building with fringe theatre upstairs. Excellent bar and restaurant meals, catering for children and vegetarians (no eve meals Sun). ♔ Q ◍ ◖ ◗ ♿ ⇌ ⊖

Princes Head
28 The Green
☎ (081) 940 1572
11–3; 5.30–11 (11–11 Fri, Sat & summer)
Fuller's Chiswick Bitter, London Pride, ESB Ⓗ
Attractive pub, established around 1740 on a site facing a picturesque green. Lounge bar is in traditional style, enhanced with interesting old prints and photographs of Richmond's bygone days. Good home-cooked bar food. ◍ ◖ ◗ ♿ ⇌ ⊖

Red Cow
59 Sheen Road (A305)
☎ (081) 940 2511
11–11
Young's Bitter, Special, Winter Warmer Ⓗ
A fine pub with many original Victorian features. A simply-furnished, compact, but comfortable, lounge bar, and real fire in the winter, create a friendly and welcoming atmosphere. Occasional live music nights. Good value food. ♔ ◖ ◗ ⊞ ⇌ ⊖ ♣

White Cross Hotel
Water Lane ☎ (081) 940 0909
11–11
Young's Bitter, Special, Winter Warmer Ⓗ
Fine old Thames-side pub with a lot of character, in a splendid picturesque setting. Good bar food and restaurant (children admitted). Riverside terrace bar and barbecue (summer). No food Sun eve. ♔ Q ◍ ◖ ◗

Try also: Mitre (Young's)

Surbiton

Bun Shop
22–26 Berrylands Road (off A240, near crown court)
☎ (081) 399 3124
11–11
Adnams Bitter; Draught Bass; Charrington IPA; Greene King IPA; Young's Bitter, Special Ⓗ
Long established free house, purchased 1988 by partnership of regulars. Live music and skittle alley in separate function room. Lunches Mon-Fri.
Q ⚇ ◖ ⇌ ♣

Victoria
28 Victoria Road
☎ (081) 399 3007
11–11
Young's Bitter, Special, Winter Warmer Ⓗ
Large pub on main road near station. One bar, but separate drinking areas. No food Sun.
Q ⚇ ◍ ◖ ⇌ ♣

Waggon & Horses
1 Surbiton Hill Road (A240)
11–2.30; 7–11 (11–11 Fri & Sat)
Young's Bitter, Special, Winter Warmer Ⓗ
Opposite Assembly Rooms. Landlord has been here over 21 years. Frequent charity collections. Family room on Sun lunchtime only. No food Sun.
Q ⚇ ◍ ◖ ⊞ ♣

Sutton

Jenny Lind
53 Carshalton Road (A232 600 yds E of centre)
☎ (081) 642 6741
12–2.30 (4 Sat); 5.30 (6 Sat)–11
Friary Meux Best Bitter; Tetley Bitter Ⓗ
Well-decorated, one-bar pub with games area. Named after the opera-singing 'Swedish Nightingale' who once visited the area. Galleried exterior. No food Sun. ◍ ◖ ⇌ ♣

Lord Nelson
32 Lower Road
☎ (081) 642 4120
11–11
Young's Bitter, Special, Winter Warmer Ⓗ
Former two-bar pub with still identifiable public and saloon areas at either end of the bar face. Lunches Mon–Sat. ◖ ♣

New Town
7 Lind Road (off A232 600 yds E of centre) ☎ (081) 642 0567
11–2.30 (12–2 Sun); 5.30–11
Young's Bitter, Special, Winter Warmer Ⓗ
Small, plain public bar with adjoining games room and contrasting large three-level lounge. Bar billiards. No lunches Sat or Sun. Q ◍ ◖ ⊞ ⇌ ♣

Try also: Windsor Castle (Fuller's)

West London

W2: Bayswater

Heron
The Watergardens, Norfolk Crescent
11–3; 5 (7 Sat)–11
Ind Coope Burton Ale; Marston's Pedigree Bitter; Tetley Bitter; Whitbread Boddingtons Bitter; Young's Bitter Ⓗ
Pleasant free house in upmarket residential area. ◖ ◗ ⇌ (Paddington) ⊖ (Edgware Rd)

W2: Paddington

Marquis of Clanricarde
36 Southwick Street
11–11
Courage Best Bitter, Directors Ⓗ
Large, comfortable, basic pub.
◖ ◗ ⇌ ⊖

White Hart
31 Brook Mews North (off B410)

12–11
Courage Best Bitter, Directors Ⓗ
Pleasant, well-hidden mews pub, formerly-owned by Reefers Bexley brewery. ◐ ◗ ⇌ ⊖

W3: Acton

Castle Hotel
140 Victoria Road
☎ (081) 992 2027
11–11 (11–3; 7–11 Sat)
Fuller's London Pride, ESB Ⓗ
Comfortable local. Can be very busy at lunchtimes when you may spot a famous face or two from the nearby BBC rehearsal studios. Ideal for a quiet evening pint. No lunches weekends.
❀ ◐ ⊟ ⊖ (N Acton) ♣ P

Kings Head
214 High Street
☎ (081) 992 0282
11–11
Fuller's Chiswick Bitter, London Pride, ESB Ⓗ
Comfortable horseshoe bar; many prints, including some of 19th-century Acton. Jasper the parrot is still dangerous! Name refers to Henry VIII.
⌂ ❀ ◐ ⊖ (Acton Town) ♣

W4: Chiswick

Bell & Crown
72 Strand-on-the-Green
☎ (081) 994 4164
11–11
Fuller's Chiswick Bitter, London Pride, ESB Ⓗ
Busy riverside pub with conservatory overlooking the Thames. Now greatly-extended into next-door premises, with better view of river. No lunches weekends.
Q ◐ ◗ ⇌ (Kew Bridge)

City Barge
27 Strand-on-the-Green
11–3; 5.30–11 (11–11 summer)
Courage Best Bitter, Directors Ⓗ
Riverside pub with two contrasting bars: one old, one modern. Has now added an *à la carte* restaurant. No lunches Sun.
❀ ◐ ⇌ (Gunnersbury) ⊖

Windmill
214 Chiswick High Road
11–11
Fuller's Chiswick Bitter, London Pride, ESB Ⓗ
Excellent modern pub, its interior decorated in 'Swiss chalet' style. Often very busy. No eve meals Sun.
❀ ◐ ◗ ⊖ (Turnham Green) ♣

W5: Ealing

Duffy's Free House
124 Pitshanger Lane
☎ (081) 998 6810
11–3 (4 Fri & Sat); 5.30–11
Draught Bass; Fuller's London Pride; Greene King IPA; McMullen Country Best Bitter Ⓗ
Friendly free house in under-pubbed North Ealing. Converted from a dairy in 1985 after a period as a wine bar. No keg beers, and all draught ales at the same price. ❀ ◐ ◗

Fox & Goose
Hanger Lane
☎ (081) 997 2441
11–11
Fuller's London Pride, ESB Ⓗ
Small public bar and large saloon in a welcome refuge from the infamous Hanger Lane gyratory system. Very busy weekday lunchtimes.
❀ ◐ ◗ ⊟ ⊖ (Hanger Lane) P

Plough
297 Northfield Avenue (B452)
☎ (081) 577 1416
11–11
Fuller's Chiswick Bitter, London Pride, ESB Ⓗ
Very popular two-bar pub with attractive alcoves in saloon for a quieter drink. New conservatory backs onto garden. Good food at all times.
⌂ ❀ ◐ ◗ ⊟ ⊖ (Northfields) ♣ P

W6: Hammersmith

Black Lion
2 South Black Lion Lane
☎ (081) 748 2639
12–3; 5.30–11
Ruddles Best Bitter, County; Webster's Yorkshire Bitter Ⓗ
Charming 17th-century inn with 300 year-old chestnut tree in beer garden. Bar billiards.
❀ ◐ ◗ ⊖ (Stamford Brook) ♣

Blue Anchor
13 Lower Mall
☎ (081) 748 5774
11.30–3.30; 5.30–11 (11–11 Fri, Sat & summer)
Courage Best Bitter, Directors; John Smith's Bitter Ⓗ
Busy Thames-side pub with pewter bar top and an impressive set of handpulls (not all in use). ◐ ◗ ⊖

Cross Keys
57 Black Lion Lane
11–3; 5–11 (11–11 Sat)
Fuller's Chiswick Bitter, London Pride, ESB Ⓗ
Very popular pub midway between King Street and River Thames.
❀ ◐ ⊖ (Stamford Brook) ♣

Dove
19 Upper Mall
☎ (081) 748 5405
11–11
Fuller's London Pride, ESB Ⓗ
Historic, 17th-century riverside inn; connections with Charles II and Nell Gwyn. *Rule Britannia* was composed in an upstairs room! ◐ ◗ ⇌ ⊖

Thatched House
115 Dalling Road
☎ (081) 748 6147
11–11
Young's Bitter, Special Ⓗ
Popular local with great atmosphere.
❀ ◐ ◗ ⊖ (Ravenscourt Pk) ♣

Try also: Builders Arms (Young's)

W7: Hanwell

Fox
Green Lane (off A3002)
☎ (081) 567 3912
11–3; 5.30–11
Courage Best Bitter, Directors Ⓗ
A quiet pub, tucked away by the Grand Union Canal. Gets busy in the summer months with boat people. Very good food with generous portions; however, the drinks are not cheap. Sun lunch is served until 4pm. Q ❀ ◐ ◗ ♣

Viaduct
221 Uxbridge Road (A4020, where it crosses the River Brent)
☎ (081) 567 1362
11.30–3.30; 5–11 (11–11 Fri & Sat)
Fuller's London Pride, ESB Ⓗ
The locals were over the moon when this former 'fizz' pub converted to the 'real thing' in 1989. Careful renovations and the retention of the excellent public bar have improved matters even more. The pub name alludes to the famous Wharncliffe GWR viaduct.
❀ ◐ ⊟ ⇌ ♣ P

White Hart
324 Greenford Avenue (off B455) ☎ (081) 578 1708
11–3 (3.30 Sat); 5.30 (6 Sat)–11
Fuller's London Pride, ESB Ⓗ
Large three-bar pub on the northern outskirts of Hanwell. Boisterous saloon, cosy private, and locals' public. There is also a jug and bottle (off-sales section) – a rarity in London nowadays. Winner of Fuller's Best-Kept Cellar award 1990.
Q ◐ ⊟ ⇌ (Castle Bar Park) ♣

W8: Kensington

Britannia
1 Allen Street (off High Street)
11–11 (11–3; 5.30–11 Sat)
Young's Bitter, Special, Winter Warmer Ⓗ
Very busy, wood-panelled pub, retaining public bar. Split-level lounge has two bars. The long-defunct Britannia brewery stood next door. Conservatory can be reserved for functions.
◐ ⊟ ⊖ (High Street Kensington)

Windsor Castle
114 Campden Hill Road
☎ (071) 927 8491
11–11
Draught Bass; Charrington IPA Ⓗ
Three-bar pub, built in 1835. Unspoilt, with much wooden panelling and a cosy atmosphere. Vine in garden; no machines. No eve meals Sun.
Q ⛲ ◐ ◑ ⊖ (Notting Hill Gate)

W9: Little Venice

Warwick Castle
6 Warwick Place
11–11
Draught Bass; Charrington IPA; Fuller's ESB; Morrells Varsity Ⓗ
Excellent traditional pub near canal basin. Morrells is a rare beer for the area.
⌂ Q ◐ ◑ ⊖ (Warwick Ave)

W9: Maida Vale

Truscott Arms
55 Shirland Road
11–11
Draught Bass; Brakspear Special; Greene King Abbot Ale; Whitbread Flowers IPA, Boddingtons Bitter, Castle Eden Ale Ⓗ
Large free house with ten handpumps and an ever-changing range of beers. No food Sun.
◐ ◑ ⊖ (Warwick Ave) ♣

Warrington
93 Warrington Crescent
11–11
Brakspear Special; Fuller's London Pride, ESB; Young's Special Ⓗ
Enormous, ornate Victorian 'gin palace', with fantastic decor and a semi-circular, marble-topped bar. ◐ ◑ ⊖ (Warwick Ave) ♣

W11: Holland Park

Prince of Wales
14 Princedale Road
11–3; 5–11 (11–11 Sat)
Draught Bass; Charrington IPA Ⓗ
Victorian pub with nice etched windows. Right of way runs through one bar. ⛲ ◐ ⊟ ⊖ ♣

W12: Shepherds Bush

Crown & Sceptre
57 Melina Road
11–11 (7–11 Sat if football at QPR)
Fuller's Chiswick Bitter, London Pride, ESB Ⓗ
Popular back-street local. No food weekends.
◐ ⊖ (Goldhawk Rd) ♣

W14: West Kensington

Britannia Tap
150 Warwick Road (A3220)
☎ (071) 602 1649
11–11 (11–3; 5.30–11 Sat)
Young's Bitter, Special, Winter Warmer Ⓗ
Was one of London's smallest pubs, but extended some years ago. Retains a certain charm.
◐ ◑ ⇌ (Kensington, Olympia) ⊖

Radnor Arms
247 Warwick Road
☎ (071) 602 7708
11–11 (11–3; 6.30–11 Tue, Wed & Sat)
Adnams Bitter; Everards Mild, Beacon Bitter, Tiger Best Bitter, Old Original Ⓗ
Basic one-bar pub with wooden trim. Regular guest beers. Busy lunchtimes. ◐ ◑ ⇌ (Kensington, Olympia) ⊖ ♣

Seven Stars
253 North End Road
☎ (071) 385 6273
11–11
Fuller's Chiswick Bitter, London Pride, ESB Ⓗ
Wood-panelled, two-bar pub in 1930s Art-Deco style. Friendly atmosphere. ◐ ⊟ ⊖

Bedfont

Beehive
333 Staines Road, Feltham (A315) ☎ (081) 890 8086
12–4; 5.30–11
Fuller's London Pride, ESB Ⓗ
Excellent pub with friendly, lively atmosphere. Attractive lounge; well-kept garden with children's play area. Good value home-cooked food (not Sun). Barbecues summer months.
⛲ ◐ ⊟ P

Brentford

Brewery Tap
47 Catherine Wheel Road
☎ (081) 560 5200
11–11
Fuller's London Pride, ESB Ⓗ
Friendly and comfortable local on canal bank. Live music Thu/Fri/Sun; lunches Mon-Fri (incl. veg dishes).
Q ⛲ ◐ ⊟ ⇌ ♣

O'Riordans Tavern
3 High Street
☎ (081) 560 5543
11–11
Adnams Bitter; Draught Bass; Bateman XXXB; Felinfoel Double Dragon; Wadworth 6X Ⓗ
Well-patronised free house with direct access to Thames-side walk and opposite the Kew Bridge Engine Museum. Lunches Mon–Fri. Guest beers.
⌂ Q ◐ ♣

White Horse
24 Market Place
☎ (081) 560 0188
11–3; 5.30–11 (11–11 Thu–Sat)
Draught Bass; Charrington IPA; Fuller's ESB (winter) Ⓗ
Tastefully-refurbished and extended old pub on River Brent. Attractive riverside garden; modern large conservatory. Garden bar in summer. Q ⛲ ◐ ◑ ⇌ ♣

Cranford

Queens Head
123 High Street (off A312)
☎ (081) 897 0722
11–11
Fuller's Chiswick Bitter, London Pride, ESB Ⓗ
Lovely Tudor-style pub. One bar but two distinct drinking areas. A separate lounge to the side is used for food and drink but does not have a bar. No eve meals Sat or Sun. ⌂ ⛲ ◐ ◑ ♣ P

Greenford

Black Horse
425 Oldfield Lane
☎ (081) 578 1384
11–11
Fuller's London Pride, ESB Ⓗ
Popular, friendly pub with mooring facilities on the Paddington arm of the Grand Union Canal. Large garden with children's play area. Watch out for the parrot. Weekday lunches. Q ⛲ ◐ ⊟ ⇌ ⊖ ♣ P

Hampton

White Hart
70 High Street (A304)
☎ (081) 979 5352
11–3; 5.30–11 (11–11 Fri & Sat)
Greene King Abbot Ale; Moorhouse's Pendle Witches Brew; Ringwood XXXX Porter; Taylor Landlord Ⓗ
Comfortable, tasteful, mock-Tudor free house with a relaxed atmosphere and a large welcoming fire. No food weekends. Guest beers.
⌂ Q ⛲ ◐ ♿ ⇌ P

Hampton Court

Kings Arms
Lion Gate, Hampton Court Road ☎ (081) 977 1337
11–11
Adnams Mild, Broadside; Gale's HSB; Hall & Woodhouse Badger Best Bitter, Tanglefoot; Wadworth 6X Ⓗ
Imposing, historic building backing on to palace grounds and facing Bushy Park gates. Sawdust on floor in public and mosaic in saloon. Upstairs restaurant (closed Sun eve and

Mon). Guest beers.
♣

Hampton Hill

Windmill
80 Windmill Road (off A312)
☎ (081) 979 6398
11–3 (3.30 Sat); 5.30–11
Draught Bass; Charrington IPA H
Small, friendly pub with ornate terracotta front and Charrington's green and clear windows. Darts area decorated with presentation cheques to local Mencap branch. No food Sun. ♣ P

Hampton Wick

White Hart
1 High Street (on Kingston Bridge roundabout)
☎ (081) 977 1786
11–3; 5–11 (11–11 Thu–Sat & summer)
Fuller's Chiswick Bitter, London Pride, ESB H
Impressive pub with spacious, tasteful, oak-panelled lounge. Attractive beer garden/patio and barbecue, with adjoining function room. Good home-cooked food. Bushy and Hampton Court parks nearby.
♣ P

Harlington

Crown
49 Bath Road, Heathrow (A4)
☎ (081) 759 9581
11–3; 5.30–11
Courage Best Bitter, Directors H
A 'shrine' to Concorde: a fine two-bar house on the northern perimeter of Heathrow Airport. Popular with air crews (off duty!), the odd tourist and beer drinkers. Gents: hats off in the saloon, or else! Good value food. Q ♣ P

Harmondsworth

Crown
High Street ☎ (081) 759 1007
11–3; 5–11 (11–11 Fri & Sat)
Courage Best Bitter, Directors H
Delightful village pub in one of the last remaining genuine Middlesex villages. Recent alterations have actually enhanced the atmosphere. Good interesting food available most sessions. Two real fires.
Q ♣

Heston

Master Robert Hotel (Robert Inn)
366 Great West Road (Sutton Lane/A4 jct)
☎ (081) 570 6261
11–3; 5–11 (11–11 Fri & Sat)
Fuller's Chiswick Bitter, London Pride, ESB H
A smart bar in a three-star hotel. Was originally a motel, claimed to be the first in the country. *A la carte* menu in the restaurant. The cocktail bar has no real ale.
P

Hillingdon

Star
Blenheim Parade, Uxbridge Road ☎ (081) 573 1096
11–11
Draught Bass; Charrington IPA H
Friendly and comfortable local with basic bar. No food Sun.
♣

Hounslow

Chariot
34 High Street (A315)
☎ (081) 572 8044
11.30–11
Fuller's Chiswick Bitter, London Pride, ESB H
Friendly and very busy main street pub on two levels. Excellent home-made lunches every day; steaks and grills in evenings (not Sun). Caters for vegetarians. On site of former Kings Arms.
⊖ (Hounslow E) P

Earl Russell
274 Hanworth Road (A314) ☎ (081) 570 1560
11–11
Fuller's London Pride, ESB H
Traditional Victorian local with friendly atmosphere. Good value lunches (not Sun).
(Hounslow Central) ♣ P

Jolly Farmer
177 Lampton Road (off A4)
☎ (081) 570 1276
11–3; 5.30–11 (11–11 Fri & Sat)
Courage Best Bitter, Directors H
Popular, cosy, family local, 100 yards south of junction with Great West Road. Friendly licensees. Very good home-cooked lunches and bar snacks (Mon-Fri). ⊖ (Hounslow Central) P

Try also: White Bear (Fuller's)

Isleworth

Castle
18 Upper Square
☎ (081) 560 3615
11–11
Young's Bitter, Special, Winter Warmer H
Roomy two-bar pub in Old Isleworth conservation area. Spacious conservatory away from bar is ideal for families. Situated near river and Syon Park. No food Sun.
Q ♣ P

Town Wharf
Swan Street
☎ (081) 847 2287
11.30–3; 5.30–11 (may vary, 11–11 summer)
Samuel Smith OBB, Museum Ale H
Splendid two-bar pub built on site of disused wharf. Well-planned, comfortable upstairs lounge with balcony. Riverside terrace provides ideal outdoor drinking area with fine Thames views. Family room in downstairs bar. Quizzes Mon eves. ♣ P

Try also: Swan (Fuller's)

New Brentford

Lord Nelson
9 Enfield Road (off B452)
☎ (081) 560 8932
12–11 (12–4; 7–11 Sat)
Fuller's Chiswick Bitter, London Pride, ESB H
Apart from the beer, people seek out this little two-bar, back-street local for its international menu. Caribbean food is the speciality at weekends.
(Brentford Central) ♣

Norwood Green

Plough
Tentelow Lane (off A3005)
☎ (081) 574 1945
11–11
Fuller's Chiswick Bitter, London Pride, ESB H
Oldest pub in the area. The current timber-framed building dates back to the 17th century and brings a touch of the country to what is now an urban area. Q ♣

Wolf
176 Norwood Road (set back from A3005, between canal bridge and green)
☎ (081) 574 2038
11–11
Taylor Walker Best Bitter; Tetley Bitter H
A new conservatory due to open during 1991 will no doubt provide an excuse for another collection to join the chamber pots on the ceiling and mangles in the garden! ♣ P

Ruislip

Six Bells
Ducks Hill Road, Ruislip Common (A4180)
☎ (0895) 639466
11–11 (11–3; 5.30–11 Jan–Mar)
Benskins Best Bitter; Ind Coope Burton Ale; Taylor Walker Best Bitter; Tetley Bitter; Young's Bitter H
Lovely little local with stone-flagged floor and low ceiling. Plentiful outside seating, partly-

protected. Convenient for ramblers and visitors to the Lido. Skittle alley. Barbecues Fri–Sun eves and Sun lunchtime.
♔ Q ❀ ◐ ◑ ♣ P

Southall

Beaconsfield Arms
63–67 West End Road (off A4020) ☎ (081) 843 1581
11–4; 6–11 (11–11 Sat)
Greene King IPA, Abbot Ale Ⓗ
A veritable cornucopia of real ale awaits anyone venturing here (three guests usually include a mild). Now consists of one bar, following extensive redecoration. Various clubs and societies meet in the upstairs room. Lunches Mon–Fri.
❀ ◐ ⇌ ♣ P

Old Oak Tree
The Common (corner of Regina Road) ☎ (081) 574 1714
11–11
Courage Best Bitter, Directors Ⓗ
Out-of-the-way, canalside pub with moorings. Easier to find by boat or on foot along the towpath than by road. Bar billiards. ❀ ◐ ⊕ ♣ P

Scotsman
96 Scotts Road
☎ (081) 574 1506
11–3; 5.15–11
Fuller's Chiswick Bitter, London Pride, Mr Harry, ESB Ⓗ
Street-corner local with two highly-contrasting bars. Very lively public, popular with young pool and darts players; quiet comfy saloon. ♔ Q ◐ ⊕ ♣

Teddington

Queen Dowager
49 North Lane (off A313)
☎ (081) 977 2583
11–3 (4 Sat); 5.30 (7 Sat)–11 (11–11 Fri)
Young's Bitter, Special, Winter Warmer Ⓗ
Comfortable, often quiet pub close to shops and main car parks. Comfortable and peaceful garden to the side and rear. Named after the widow of William IV who returned to Teddington after his death.
Q ❀ ◐ ⊕ ⇌ ♣

Twickenham

Eel Pie
9–11 Church Street (off A305)
☎ (081) 891 1717
11–3; 5.30–11 (11–11 Wed–Fri)
Adnams Mild; Everards Tiger Best Bitter; Gale's HSB; Hall & Woodhouse Badger Best Bitter, Tanglefoot; Wadworth 6X Ⓗ
Popular ex-wine bar near riverside in Twickenham's oldest shopping street. Guest beers always available; traditional and continental lunches (not Sun). ❀ ◐ ♿ ⇌ ♣

Pope's Grotto
Cross Deep (A310)
☎ (081) 892 3050
11–3; 5.30–11 (11–11 Sat)
Young's Bitter, Special, Winter Warmer Ⓗ
Large, attractive pub overlooking Radnor Gardens and River Thames. Popular with all age groups, accommodated in a split-level drinking area with a comfortable atmosphere.
❀ ◐ ◑ ⊕ ⇌ (Strawberry Hill) ♣ P

Prince Albert
30 Hampton Road (A311)
☎ (081) 894 3963
11–11
Fuller's Chiswick Bitter, London Pride, ESB Ⓗ
Small Victorian local. Recent expansion of the bar area has not changed the pub's character. Caters for all ages, but often gets crowded in the evening.
Q ❀ ◐ ⇌ (Strawberry Hill) ♣ P

Try also: Old Anchor (Young's)

Uxbridge

Crown & Sceptre
135 High Street
☎ (0895) 36308
11–3; 5.30 (5 Sat)–11
Courage Best Bitter, Directors Ⓗ
Good traditional pub, offering an extensive menu of home-cooked specials, including fish dishes, at reasonable prices. The landlady is a very accomplished cook and her steak and kidney pie has won numerous awards. Ideal for a bite and pint whilst shopping. No food Sun.
♔ ❀ ◐ ⊖ ♣

General Eliott
St Johns Road, Uxbridge Moor
☎ (0895) 37385
12–3; 5–11 (11–4; 7–11 Sat)
Benskins Best Bitter; Ind Coope Burton Ale; Tetley Bitter Ⓗ
Comfortable, modernised canalside (Grand Union) pub, with moorings close by. Friendly atmosphere and a good mix of clientele. No food Sun.
❀ ◐ ◑ ⊖ ♣ P

Three Tuns
24 High Street
☎ (0895) 33960
11–3; 5–11 (11–11 Thu–Sat)
Ind Coope Burton Ale; Tetley Bitter; Young's Bitter, Special Ⓗ
An attractive, modernised old coaching inn with a conservatory to the side. Large patio drinking area to the rear. Busy evenings. No food Sun; eve meals in summer only.
♔ ❀ ◐ ◑ ⊖

Whitton

Admiral Nelson
123 Nelson Road (½ mile W of Twickenham RFU stadium)
☎ (081) 894 9998
11.30–11
Fuller's Chiswick Bitter, London Pride, ESB Ⓗ
Busy high street pub, popular with Harlequins RFC. Very successful tug-of-war team. Varied menu with food available at all times, Mon–Sat.
♔ ❀ ◐ ◑ ⇌

Yeading

Walnut Tree
115 Willow Tree Lane (off A312) ☎ (081) 845 0849
11.30–3; 5.30–11
Fuller's London Pride, ESB Ⓗ
A very lively locals' pub. Boasts a golf society and a soccer team.
❀ ◐ ◑ ⊕ ♣

Allied Breweries' Houses

Since the compilation of this guide, a number of Allied houses in the South East have been sold. Readers may therefore find that beer ranges have changed in these pubs. The counties affected extend from Kent to Oxfordshire.

Greater Manchester

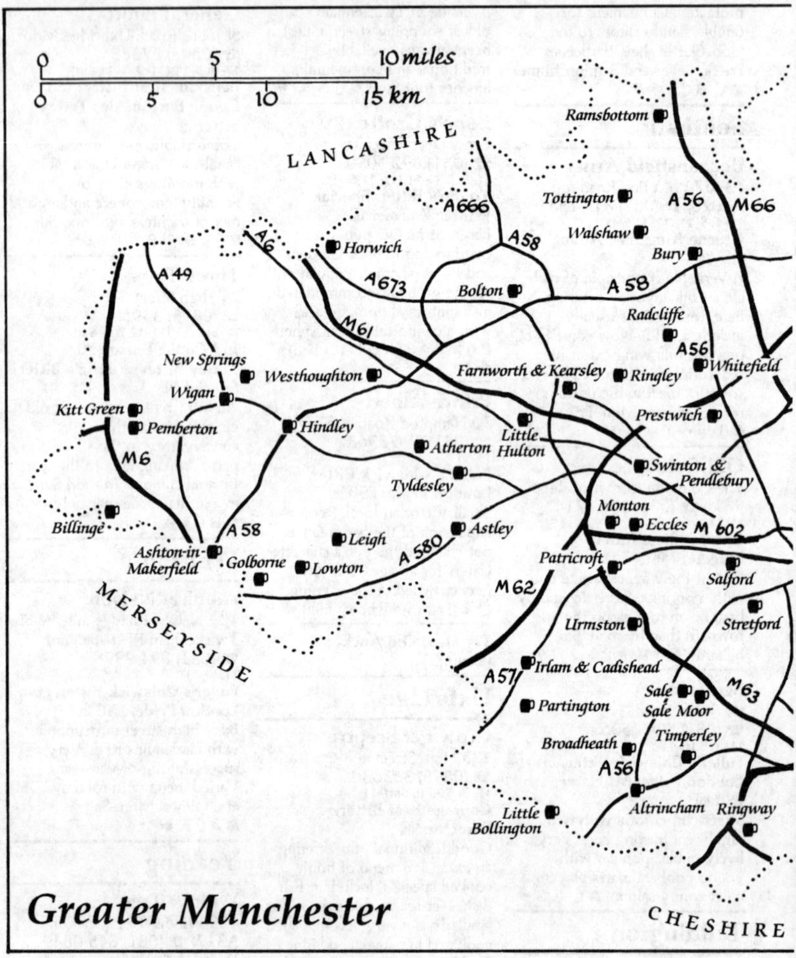

***Hydes' Anvil**, Manchester; **Holt**, Cheetham; **Lees**, Middleton Junction; **Oak**, Heywood; **Robinson's**, Stockport; **West Coast**, Chorlton-on-Medlock*

Altrincham

Bakers Arms
Pownall Road (next to Sainsburys) ☎ (061) 928 1411
11.30–3; 5–11 (11.30–11 Mon, Fri & Sat)
Hydes' Anvil Mild, Bitter Ⓔ
Lively vault. The only Hydes' in Altrincham. Worth finding.
◐ ⊟ ≹ ♣ P

Try also: Tatton Arms (Boddingtons)

Ancoats

Jolly Angler
47 Ducie Street (between London Road and Great Ancoats Street)
☎ (061) 236 5307
11.30–4.30; 7–11 (11–11 Fri & Sat)
Hydes' Anvil Mild, Bitter Ⓗ, **Strong Ale** Ⓖ
Basic, one-roomed pub featuring folk music and sing-alongs.
🏠 ≹ (Piccadilly) ♣

White House
122 Great Ancoats Street
☎ (061) 228 3231
12–3; 5–11
Caledonian 80/- Ale, Merman XXX; Holt Bitter; Thwaites Bitter Ⓗ
Comfortable and friendly pub close to Ashton and Rochdale canals, yet convenient for city centre. Early eve meals to order only.
⊛ ◐ ◑ ⊟ ♿ ≹ (Piccadilly) ♣

Ashton-in-Makerfield

Eagle & Child
233 Heath Road (off A49)
☎ (0942) 726421
12–3.30; 7–11
Greenalls Mild, Bitter, Thomas Greenall's Original Bitter Ⓗ
Pleasantly-extended and

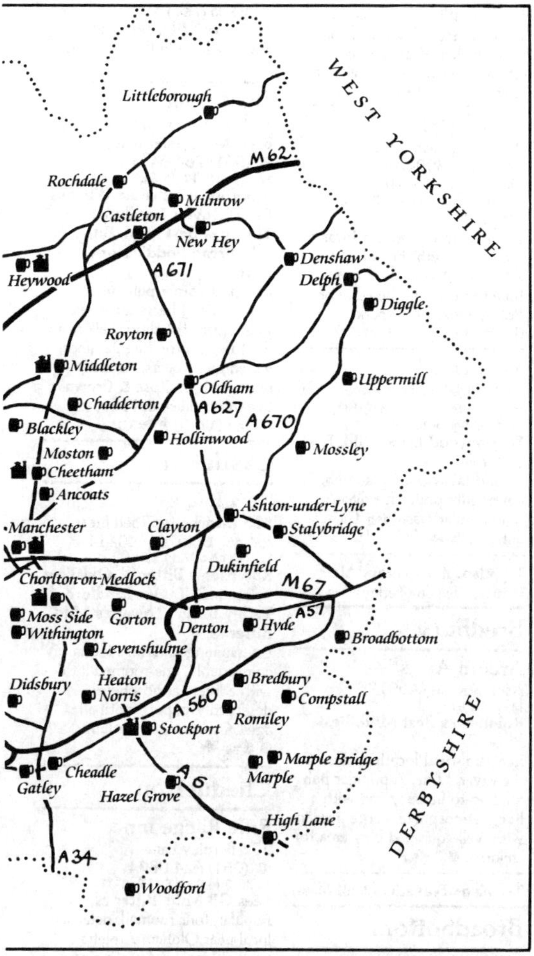

upgraded. Features a large collection of commemorative plates on a mining theme.
⌂ ◖ ◗ ⊟ ♿

Ashton-under-Lyne

Oddfellows

Kings Road, Hurst
☎ (061) 330 6356
12–11
Robinson's Best Mild, Best Bitter Ⓗ **&** Ⓔ
Formerly at the end of a terrace, this comfortable pub, with lounge, tap, snug and original stained glass bar, has been in the same family since 1914. Reputed birthplace of the NUM. Snug known locally as the 'Vestry'. Lunches Fri and Sat only. ⌂ ◖

Station

2 Warrington Street
☎ (061) 330 6776
11.30–11 (11.30–4; 7–11 Sat)
Marston's Border Mild, Pedigree Bitter; Whitbread Boddingtons Bitter Ⓗ
Recently-extended by the addition of a conservatory (busy in summer, as is the well-laid-out garden). Comfortable bar with three distinct areas will interest railway enthusiasts. Folk club Sat. Guest beers. ⌂ ◖

Witchwood

152 Old Street
☎ (061) 344 0321
11.30–3 (4 Sat); 5 (7 Sat)–11 (11.30–11 Fri)
Banks's Bitter; Holt Bitter; Marston's Pedigree Bitter; Old Mill Bullion Bitter; Theakston XB Ⓗ
Two-roomed pub which caters for the beer drinker and live music fan: bands most eves and Sun lunch. Entertainment gets regular mentions in the evening newspaper and has a good local reputation. Guest beers. ◖ ♣

Astley

Cart & Horses

221 Manchester Road
☎ (0942) 882680
12–11
Holt Mild, Bitter Ⓗ
Holt's new wave Laura Ashley-style lounge; comfortable and cosy with separate no-smoking room and traditional tap room. Eve meals served 5–8pm.
◖ ◗ ⊟ ♣ P

Atherton

Atherton Arms

6 Tyldesley Road (A577)
☎ (0942) 882885
11.30–11
Holt Mild, Bitter Ⓗ
Ex-Labour Club. Very large lounge with several seating areas. Well-lit tap room with full-size snooker table and pool table. ⊟ ♿ ≹ ♣ P

Letters Inn

2 Wigan Road
☎ (0942) 883289
12–11
Tetley Dark Mild, Bitter Ⓗ
Pleasant, town-centre, two-roomed pub: tap room and L-shaped, lamp-lit lounge, which has a low ceiling. ◖ ⊟ ♣ P

Try also: Bay Horse (Tetley)

Billinge

Hare & Hounds

142 Upholland Road
☎ (0744) 892843
12–3.30; 7–11
Tetley Mild, Bitter Ⓗ
Large, comfortable pub; red brickwork at its best. ⊟ ♿ P

Holts Arms (Foot o' Causeway)

Crank Road (lane opp. hospital)
☎ (0744) 622705
2–11
Burtonwood Dark Mild, Best Bitter Ⓗ
Unspoilt country inn, still under threat of modernisation. Vault and thriving bowling section (crown green, of course!).
⌂ Q ⌂ ⊟ ♣ P

Blackley

Old House at Home

52 Bottomley Side (path between Slack Road and Crumpsall Vale)
☎ (061) 740 7185
12–4 (5 Sat); 7–11
Wilson's Original Mild, Wilson's Original Bitter, Webster's Choice Ⓗ
Three-roomed, cottage-style local in an isolated setting, best approached on foot. Good, simple value-for-money food

(not Sun). Extensive vault with games areas. ⚘ ◖ ⊞ ♿ ♣ P

Pleasant
390 Chapel Lane (corner of Crab Lane) ☎ (061) 740 3391
1 (12 Sat)–11
Robinson's Best Mild, Best Bitter [H], Old Tom [G]
Small community pub with vault, lounge and golf society club room, on the fringe of the 18th-century Crab village.
Q ⚘ ⊞ ♣

Bolton

Ainsworth Arms
606 Halliwell Road (A6099/A58 jct)
☎ (0204) 40671
11.30–3; 5.30–11 (11.30–11 Sat)
Ind Coope Burton Ale; Walker Mild, Best Bitter [H]
Popular, comfortable local with a friendly welcome. ⌂ ◖ ♣

Clifton Arms
94 Newport Street
☎ (0204) 392738
11–11
Jennings Bitter; Tetley Mild, Bitter [H]
Comfortable, homely, town-centre 'local' which has kept its character despite refurbishments.
◖ ⊞ ⇌ ♣

Howcroft Inn
36 Pool Street (via Vernon Street off St George's Road, A673) ☎ (0204) 26814
12–4; 6.30 (5.30 summer)–11
Walker Mild, Best Bitter [H]
Excellent local just outside town centre. A former CAMRA Pub Preservation Group award-winner. Bowling green is crowded in summer. Small car park. ⌂ ⚘ ◖ ⌀ P

Lodge Bank Tavern
264 Bridgeman Street
☎ (0204) 31946
1–5; 7–11
Lees GB Mild, Bitter [H]
Cheerful, recently-enlarged locals' pub. Winner of unusual awards from obscure groups!
⚘ ♿ ⇌ ♣ P

Maxims
28 Bradshawgate
☎ (0204) 23486
11.30–4; 7.30–11
Vaux Samson [H]
Large, modernised, town-centre pub with upstairs function room which doubles as a disco. Crowded – and noisy – at weekends. Cellar visits available when quiet. Occasional guest beers. ◖ ⇌

Oddfellows Arms
140 St Helens Road (A579, Daubhill) ☎ (0204) 62164
11.45 (11.30 Sat)–11
Greenalls Mild, Bitter [E]
Large, bustling Victorian pub with fine etched windows and notable stained glass over stairway showing Oddfellows coat of arms. ⊞ ♣

Park Hotel
259 Bridgeman Street
☎ (0204) 399486
12–5; 7–11 (12–11 Sat)
Tetley Dark Mild, Mild, Bitter [H]
Sociable, three-roomed local awaiting refurbishment and offering entertainment from time to time. On the edge of Bobby Heywood's park.
◖ ⊞ ⇌ ♣

York Hotel
112–114 Newport Street (opp. station) ☎ (0204) 383892
11–11 (11–4; 7–11 Sat)
Burtonwood Dark Mild, Best Bitter [H]
Comfortable, open-plan pub, deservedly popular. Bolton's only regular *Good Beer Guide* entry. ◖ ♿ ⇌ ♣

Try also: Arkwrights Ale House, Nelson (Tetley)

Bredbury

Ardern Arms
Ashton Road (A6017)
11–3; 5.30–11
Robinson's Best Mild, Best Bitter [E]
In a semi-rural location, close to the River Tame. A popular pub tending to be busy and with a lively atmosphere. Large garden with well-equipped play area for children. ⚘ ◖ ♣ P

Try also: Travellers Call (Lees)

Broadbottom

Shoulder of Mutton
138 Lower Market Street (1 mile from A57)
11–3; 5.30–11
Thwaites Mild, Bitter [H]
Unpretentious, popular pub in a village which clings to the hillside, in the foothills of the Pennines. ◖ ⊞ ⇌ ♣

Try also: Cheshire Cheese (Free)

Broadheath

Railway Inn
153 Manchester Road
☎ (061) 941 3383
11–11 (11–3; 7–11 Sat)
Whitbread Boddingtons Bitter [H]
Basic, former ale-only terraced pub next to disused railway station. ◖ ⊞ ♣

Bury

Help Me Thro'
141 Crostons Road
12–3; 5.30 (7 Sat)–11
Thwaites Mild, Bitter [H]
Friendly local in the middle of a terrace. ⌂ ⚘ ♣ P

Tap & Spile
36 Manchester Old Road (off Bury–Manchester road)
☎ (061) 764 6461
12–3; 5–11 (12–11 Sat)
Moorhouse's Pendle Witches Brew; Taylor Landlord; Thwaites Best Mild, Bitter; Whitbread Boddingtons Bitter [H]
Compact corner pub with the best range of beers for miles. Well worth the short walk from the town centre. Regular and varied guest beers. Recently-renamed from Rose & Crown. Eve meals finish at 7pm (not served Sun). ◖ ◗ ⇌ ⌀

Castleton

New Inn
818 Manchester Road (near station) ☎ (0706) 40414
12–11 (12–5; 7–11 Sat)
Robinson's Bitter [H], Old Tom (winter) [G]; Taylor Landlord; Tetley Bitter; Thwaites Mild, Bitter [H]
Unassuming exterior hides a comfortable, one-roomed local with a lively atmosphere; deservedly-popular with all ages. Games room upstairs.
⌂ ⚘ ⇌ ♣

Chadderton

Rifle Range Inn
372 Burnley Lane
☎ (061) 624 0874
11.30–3 (4 Sat); 5 (7 Sat)–11
Lees GB Mild, Bitter [H]
Popular, four-roomed, detached local near Oldham Athletic football ground. Sporting and musical interests dominate. Handy for A627(M) and M62. No food Sun. ◖ ♣ P

Cheadle

Queens Arms
177 Stockport Road (200 yds from M63 jct 11 roundabout on A560) ☎ (061) 428 3081
12–11
Robinson's Best Mild, Bitter [H]
Multi-roomed, traditional pub; a rare outlet for Robinson's ordinary bitter. Garden has children's play area. Can be busy at lunchtime because of new office complex nearby. Children welcome until 7.30pm. No food at weekend.
⌂ Q ♞ ⚘ ◖ ♣ P

Cheetham

Derby Brewery Arms
95 Cheetham Hill Road

☎ (061) 832 9362
11–11
Holt Mild, Bitter 🄷
Holt's brewery tap. A large, two-roomed pub, rescued from Whitbread theme treatment. No food at weekend.
◖ ⊟ ♿ ≋ (Victoria) ♣

Queen's Arms
6 Honey Street
☎ (061) 834 4239
12–4; 7 (6 Wed & Thu)–11 (12–11 Fri)
Taylor Landlord; Theakston Best Bitter, XB, Old Peculier 🄷
Cosy free house offering an excellent view of Irk Valley and city from an extensive beer garden. Belgian bottled beers; British guest beers. Eve meals to order only (early).
✿ ◖ ◗ ♿ ≋ (Victoria) ♣

Chorlton-on-Medlock

King's Arms
4a Helmshaw Walk (A6 – 192 bus – to Ardwick Green, then Kale Street and Skerry Close)
☎ (061) 273 1053
12–11
Dobbin's Dark Mild, North County Mild, Dobbin's County Best Bitter, Dobbin's Extra Special Bitter 🄷
Brewer-owner Brendan Dobbin's single-minded approach to brewing brings, as well as the ales listed, a fine stout and many 'one-off' brews (look out for Sierra Nevada!). The two-bar inner-city pub often has music sessions, but main bar is quiet. No food at weekend.
Q ♉ ◖ ⊟ ≋ (Piccadilly) ♣ P

Mawson
Brunswick Street (off Upper Brook Street, A34)
☎ (061) 273 2157
11–11
Ind Coope Burton Ale; Tetley Mild, Bitter 🄷
A superb example of a multi-roomed local: good oak panelling and leaded glass abound. Library in quiet lounge. A good place to relax. Close to university, but set back from road, so can be difficult to spot.
Q ⊟ ♣ P

Clayton

Strawberry Duck
74 Crabtree Lane (off Ashton New Road) ☎ (061) 223 4415
11.30–11 (11.30–5; 7–11 Sat)
Holt Bitter; Webster's Green Label; Whitbread Boddingtons Bitter 🄷
Enterprisingly-run and thriving free house which caters for all age groups. Guest beers are an added attraction. Located beside Ashton Canal – part of the Cheshire Ring. Good-value, home-cooked fare (not Sat or Sun). ◖ ♣ P

Compstall

Andrew Arms
George Street
☎ (061) 427 2281
11–3; 5.30–11
Robinson's Best Mild, Best Bitter 🄷
Popular pub near Etherow Nature Reserve. Busy in summer and on public holidays, when the small outside drinking area is crowded. Q ⊟ ♣

Delph

Horse & Jockey
Huddersfield Road (A62)
OS014094 ☎ (0457) 874283
1–2.30 (Sat only); 8–11
Marston's Mercian Mild, Owd Rodger; Moorhouse's Pendle Witches Brew 🄷
Isolated pub on road into high Pennines; can be very windy. Good atmosphere, enhanced by real fires in each bar. Guest beers. ♨ ⊟ ⛺ P

Denshaw

Rams Head (Owd Tupps)
Ripponden Road (A640, 1 mile N of village) OS977119
12–2 (Sun only); 7–11
Taylor Landlord 🄷**; Theakston Best Bitter** 🄶**, XB** 🄷**, Old Peculier** 🄶
Isolated, wind-swept, moortop pub with roaring fires. Children not permitted. Guest beers.
♨ Q

Denton

Dog & Partridge
148 Ashton Road
☎ (061) 236 3954
12.30 (12 Sat)–11
Robinson's Best Mild, Bitter 🄷
Small, friendly terraced local. An outlet for the increasingly rare Robinson's ordinary bitter. ♨

Red Lion
Crown Point (A57/A6017 jct)
11–3; 5.30–11
Hydes' Anvil Mild, Light, Bitter 🄴
Spacious, red-brick, Victorian-style pub with a prominent corner location at the centre of Denton. Q ⊟ ♣ P

Didsbury

Station
682 Wilmslow Road
☎ (061) 445 3152
11–3; 5.30–11 (11–11 Sat)
Marston's Mercian Mild, Burton Best Bitter, Pedigree Bitter 🄷
Traditional, family-run village pub in increasingly busy (and fashionable) area. Although tiny, has active games teams and a loyal local following.
Q ✿ ⊟ ♣

Diggle

Diggle Hotel
Station Road (off A670, via Huddersfield Road) OS011081
☎ (0457) 872741
12–3; 7–11 (11–11 Sat)
Taylor Golden Best, Landlord; Whitbread OB Mild, Boddingtons Bitter, OB Bitter 🄷
Quaint village pub comprising a bar area and two rooms. Excellent menu caters for children and vegetarians. Often visited by morris men in summer. Q ♉ ✿ 🛏 ◖ ◗ P

Dukinfield

Lamb Inn
103 Crescent Road (B6170)
☎ (061) 330 4944
11–11
Whitbread Boddingtons Bitter 🄷
Well-cared for and popular pub with good vault and comfortable lounge. Handsome red brick exterior with Dutch gables. ✿ ◖ ⊟ ♣ P

Try also: Newborough (Hydes' Anvil)

Eccles

Crown & Volunteer
171 Church Street (A57)
☎ (061) 789 4809
12–4; 7–11
Holt Mild, Bitter 🄷
Well-run, two-roomed, community pub with 1930s-style interior. Live music at weekends. Q ⊟ ≋ ♣

Lamb
33 Regent Street (A57 near M602 jct) ☎ (061) 789 3882
11–11 (11–5; 7–11 Sat)
Holt Mild, Bitter 🄷
A classic, four-roomed, Edwardian pub with etched glass windows, a beautiful mahogany bar and Art Nouveau tiles. Games room has a full-size snooker table. ⊟ ≋ ♣ P

Farnworth & Kearsley

Church Hotel
61 Church Road, Kearsley (off A5082) ☎ (0204) 71696
12–3; 7–11
Thwaites Mild, Bitter 🄷
Deceptively-large pub, tucked away next to town centre.
✿ ⊟ ≋ (Farnworth) ♣

Greater Manchester

Clock Face
65 Old Hall Street, Kearsley (off A5082) ☎ (0204) 71912
11–3.30; 5.15 (7 Sat)–11
Tetley Mild, Bitter [H]
A superb example of a traditional pub.
⊕ ♿ ≈ (Farnworth) ♣

Try also: Britannia (Whitbread)

Gatley

Horse & Farrier
Gatley Road (A560)
☎ (061) 428 2080
11–3; 5.30–11 (11–11 Sat)
Hydes' Anvil Light, Bitter [E], **Strong Ale** [G]
A multi-roomed old coaching house with attractive stained glass windows and wood panelling. Handy for the cinema. No food at weekend.
▲ Q ⊛ ◐ ≈ P

Prince of Wales
Gatley Green (off A560)
11.30–3 (4 Sat); 5.30–11
Hydes' Anvil Mild, Bitter [E]
Ex-country pub swallowed up in Manchester expansion. Main bar and darts room. A popular, well-managed local with a relaxed atmosphere. Good value lunches (not Sun). Photos of the pub's history on wall – see it in full flood. Q ◐ ≈ ♣

Golborne

Millstone
52 Harvey Lane (near Haydock Park racecourse)
☎ (0942) 728031
12–4.30 (6 Sat); 7–11
Greenalls Mild, Bitter [H]
Popular, friendly, locals' pub. Central bar has an L-shaped tap room with a small, lobby-style, lounge-side drinking area. Away from the bar are two comfortable, bright lounges housing the landlady's vast collection of ornamental brass.
⊛ ◐ ◑ ⊕ ♿ ♣ P

Try also: Horns Inn (Greenalls)

Gorton

Railway
61 Pottery Lane (opp. station)
☎ (061) 220 8549
11–11
Holt Bitter; Theakston XB; Thwaites Best Mild, Bitter; Younger Scotch, IPA [H]
Openshaw Brewery's former tap, reborn to serve the best range of beers and cider in East Manchester. Local CAMRA's Pub of the Year for 1989. Simple, but pleasant surroundings; a fine local. Guest beers and ciders. Sun lunch only by arrangement.
◐ ≈ (Ashburys) ♣ ⌽

Waggon & Horses
736 Hyde Road (A57)
☎ (061) 223 3019
11–11
Holt Mild, Bitter [H]
Large, popular pub with local atmosphere. Local CAMRA Pub of the Year in 1988. Beer prices notably low for area.
≈ (Ryder Brow) ♣ P

Hazel Grove

Grapes
196 London Road (A6)
☎ (061) 483 4479
11.30–3; 5.30–11
Robinson's Best Mild, Best Bitter [E]
A good, friendly, multi-roomed pub with nice oak panelling. Snacks weekday lunchtime.
⊕ ≈ ♣ P

Heaton Norris

Nursery
Green Lane (off A6)
☎ (061) 432 2044
11.30–3; 5.30–11 (11.30–11 Sat & bank hols)
Hydes' Anvil Mild, Bitter [E]
Large, comfortable 1930s pub, well hidden away in a pleasant suburban area. Traditional layout: vault, smoke room, lobby and lounge, with fine wood panelling. Immaculate bowling green. Good home-made lunches. Limited menu on Sat; no food Sun. Q ⊛ ◐ ⊕ ♣ P

Heywood

Engineers Arms
Aspinall Street (off A58)
☎ (0706) 68365
11–3.30; 6–11 (11–11 Fri & Sat)
Samuel Smith OBB [H]
Warm and friendly local.
⊛ ⊕ ♣ P

Wishing Well
89 York Street (A58)
☎ (0706) 65673
11.30–11
Taylor Golden Best, Landlord; Theakston Best Bitter, Old Peculier; Younger Scotch [H]
Modernised, town-centre local with a variety of rooms catering for all tastes. ◐

High Lane

Royal Oak
Boxton Road (A6)
☎ (06632) 2380
11–3; 5.30–11
Burtonwood Dark Mild, Best Bitter [H]
Comfortable roadside inn with occasional live music.
⊛ ⊷ ◐ ≈ (Middlewood) ♣ P

Hindley

Ellesmere
32 Lancaster Road
☎ (0942) 56922
11.30–4; 7–11
Burtonwood Dark Mild, Best Bitter [H]
A once-basic pub now very pleasantly refurbished. However, it still remains an earthy, locals' boozer. ⊕ ♿ ♣

Hollinwood

Old Post Office
439 Manchester Road (A62/A6104 jct)
☎ (061) 681 6277
11.30–11
Whitbread OB Mild, Boddingtons Bitter, OB Bitter [H]
Boisterous local with loyal following. Faces demolition for road-widening scheme. Lunchtime snacks. ⊕ ≈ ♣

Woodman Inn
684 Manchester Road (A62, near A6104 jct)
☎ (061) 682 4005
11–6; 7.30–11
Lees GB Mild, Bitter [H]
Pleasant, busy roadside inn. Menu includes home-made pies. ⊛ ◐ ≈

Horwich

Toll Bar
2 Chorley New Road (A673/B5238 jct)
☎ (0204) 696320
12–3 (4 Fri, 5 Sat); 7–11
Thwaites Mild, Bitter [H]
Home of Horwich Morris Men. Folk club Mon. Handy for walks to Rivington and Winter Hill. Interesting external *trompe l'oeil*. ▲ Q ♉ ◐ ⊕ ♣ P

Try also: Bowling Green (Tetley)

Hyde

Bush
278 Market Street
☎ (061) 368 2494
11.30 (10.30 Fri)–3 (4 Fri & Sat); 5.30 (7.30 Sat)–11
Robinson's Best Mild, Best Bitter [H]
Popular, two-roomed local frequented by all ages. Large, comfortable lounge gets busy at weekends; small former vault now accommodates an increasingly popular pool table. A thriving social centre. ◐ ♣ P

Crown
173 Market Street
☎ (061) 368 2993
11–11
Robinson's Best Mild, Best Bitter [H], **Old Tom** [G]
Four-roomed local with a narrow vault at the front. Mixed clientele of all ages. Fish tanks in lounge; 'log-end' dartboard.
◐ ⊕ ≈ ♣

Irlam & Cadishead

Coach & Horses
Liverpool Road
☎ (061) 776 1626
11–11
Whitbread Boddingtons Mild, Boddingtons Bitter ⊞
Comfortable, open-plan, L-shaped lounge. A central bar separates the lounge from the unspoilt vault. Thriving social and fishing club, bowling teams and quiz nights. Lunches served Mon–Fri. ⊛ ◖ ⊟ ♿ ♣ P

Try also: Railway (Boddingtons)

Kitt Green

Old Springs
Springs Road (near Heinz factory) ☎ (0942) 211209
11.30–3.30; 6.30–11
Burtonwood Dark Mild, Best Bitter ⊞
Homely pub, named after local wells (one remains near bowling green). Good value meals until 9pm. Q ⊛ ◖ ⊟ ♣ P

Leigh

Brewery Inn
Brewery Lane (off A572 opp. St Joseph's Hall)
☎ (0942) 672974
12–5; 7.30 (7 Sat)–11
Tetley Mild, Bitter ⊞
Street-corner local. Separate tap room is served by a central bar. The lounge houses pool table and dartboard. There is another small, cosy lounge away from the bar. A good traditional pub next to the former George Shaw brewery. ⊛ ⊟ ♣ P

Railway Hotel
160 Twist Lane (A578)
☎ (0942) 673916
11–11
Ind Coope Burton Ale; Tetley Dark Mild, Mild; Walker Bitter ⊞
Serves local and passing trade in small tap room and large lounge. Has an alcove drinking area and plenty of standing room. Mirror-finished bar with hidden door. Meals finish at 7pm. ◖ ◗ ♣

Try also: Boars Head (Tetley)

Levenshulme

Sidings
Broom Lane (off A6)
☎ (061) 257 2084
11–11
Holt Mild, Bitter ⊞
Recently-established, friendly and comfortable pub. Has built up a considerable local following and hosts numerous community and charity events. Highly commended in CAMRA's Pub Design awards.
⊛ ◖ ⊟ ♿ ⇌ ♣ P

Little Bollington

Old No. 3
Lymm Road (A56)
☎ (0925) 756115
11.30–3; 5.30–11 (11.30–11 summer, may vary)
Courage Directors; John Smith's Bitter ⊞
Former stagecoach stop, reputedly haunted. Excellent food selection (and portions); 'grizzly bear steaks' a speciality, but veg option and children's meals also available.
⌂ Q ⊛ ◖ ◗ ♿ ⛺ P

Swan with Two Nicks
Park Lane (off A56)
☎ (061) 928 2914
11.30–3; 5.30–11
Whitbread Chester's Best Mild, Chester's Best Bitter, Castle Eden Ale ⊞
Typical country pub at back of Dunham Park, adjacent to Bridgewater Canal. ⌂ Q ⊛ ◖ ♿ P

Try also: Wheatsheaf

Littleborough

Queens
57 Church Street (A58)
☎ (0706) 79394
12–3; 6 (6.30 Sat)–11 (12–11 Fri)
Thwaites Best Mild, Bitter ⊞
Small, friendly town-centre pub.
⇌ ♣

Little Hulton

Dukes Gate
Cleggs Lane
☎ (061) 790 1893
11.30–11 (11.30–4; 7–11 Sat)
Holt Mild, Bitter ⊞
1980s pub with large vault and lounge. Deservedly-busy, despite a somewhat remote location. ◖ ⊟ ♿ ♣ P

Try also: Pied Piper (Robinson's)

Lowton

Red Lion
324 Newton Road
☎ (0942) 671429
11.30–3.30; 5.30–11 (11.30–11 Sat)
Greenalls Mild, Bitter, Thomas Greenall's Original Bitter ⊞
Large, open-plan pub with pleasant lounge and pool room with bar. A smaller lounge away from the bar leads to bowling green and garden. Meals in bar or dining area (children and vegetarians catered for).
♨ ⊛ ◗ ⊟ ♿ ♣ P

Manchester City Centre

Castle Hotel
66 Oldham Street
☎ (061) 236 2945
11.30–5.30; 7.30–11
Robinson's Best Mild, Best Bitter, Old Tom ⊞
Listed building. Public bar opens onto street; two further rooms behind the bar. A well-run establishment in a difficult area of the city.
♨ ⊟ ♿ ⇌ (Victoria/Piccadilly)

Circus
86 Portland Street
☎ (061) 236 5818
12–3; 5.30 (later Sat)–11 (may vary)
Tetley Bitter ⊞
Very small, basic, unspoilt two-room pub with tiny quadrant bar. An amazing survivor in the city centre. Front door may be closed at busy times (especially Fri/Sat nights), but there is a back door on Reyner Street.
Q ⇌ (Piccadilly/Oxford Rd)

Marble Arch
73 Rochdale Road, Collyhurst (A664, ½ mile from centre)
☎ (061) 832 5914
12–11
Beer range varies ⊞
Popular free house with some striking architectural features (listed building). There are two rooms, each with its own bar and altogether 14 beer pumps. People come for the food, too.
◖ ◗ ⊟ ⇌ (Victoria)

Mr Thomas's Chop House
52 Cross Street
☎ (061) 832 2245
11–11 (11–3; 7–11 Sat, closed Sun)
Marston's Pedigree Bitter; Whitbread Boddingtons Bitter ⊞
Dutch-style, terracotta listed building. Interior has Italian mosaic floor, carved oak panelling and tiled walls. In CAMRA's *Good Pub Food*, this traditional gentleman's chop house was established 1867; present building dates from 1920. Eve meals finish at 7pm. Q ◖ ◗ ⇌ (Oxford Rd/Deansgate)

Peveril of the Peak
127 Great Bridgewater Street
12–3 (not Sun); 5.30 (7 Sat)–11
Wilson's Original Mild, Wilson's Original Bitter, Webster's Choice ⊞
A classic town pub; 10 years in the *Good Beer Guide*. Note the original tiles outside and the stained glass within. The yuppies are almost here! Table football. ⌂ ⊟ ♣

Sir Ralph Abercrombie
Bootle Street (off Deansgate)
☎ (061) 834 1807
11–11
Marston's Pedigree Bitter;

Whitbread Chester's Best Mild, Chester's Best Bitter, Boddingtons Bitter, Castle Eden Ale [H]
Popular and comfortable pub with large trade from adjacent police HQ.
☸ ◖ ⇌ (Oxford Rd/Deansgate)

Vine
38 Kennedy Street
☎ (061) 236 3943
11–11 (11.30–4.30 Sat)
Courage Directors; John Smith's Bitter [H]
Busy city-centre pub with listed exterior. ◖ ⇌ (Oxford Rd)

Wheatsheaf
30 Oak Street
☎ (061) 834 4077
11–4; 7–11 (11–11 Sat)
Jennings Bitter; Tetley Mild, Bitter [H]
An old market pub tucked away in a new housing development. A vault and some original features have survived internal alterations. Snacks available.
♨ ☸ ⊟ ♿ ⇌ (Victoria/Piccadilly)

White Lion
43 Liverpool Road
☎ (061) 832 7373
11.30–3; 5 (8 Sat & Sun)–11
Whitbread Chester's Best Mild, Chester's Best Bitter [H]
In the Castlefield conservation area; well-placed for the museums, canal and Roman remains. No food at weekend.
Q ◖ ⇌ (Deansgate)

Try also: Britons Protection (Tetley); **City Arms** (Courage); **Crown** (Wilson's)

Marple

Bowling Green
161 Stockport Road
☎ (061) 427 7918
11.30–11
Ruddles Best Bitter; Wilson's Original Mild, Wilson's Original Bitter, Webster's Choice [H]
Lively pub which lost its original layout in refurbishment but retains several separate drinking areas, including a good vault. Not for shrinking violets!
☸ ⊟ ⇌ (Rosehill) ♣ P

Crown
Hawk Green
☎ (061) 449 8533
11–3; 5.30–11
Robinson's Best Mild, Best Bitter [H]
Smart, restaurant-style pub in attractive building; formerly a farmers' pub. Overlooks pleasant green. ☸ ◖ ◗ P

Marple Bridge

Travellers Call
134 Glossop Road
☎ (061) 427 4169
11–2.30; 4.30–11 (11–11 Sat)
Robinson's Best Mild, Best Bitter [H]
Extensively-altered, pleasant stone pub. Bar in L-shaped lounge. Separate games room.
☸ ◖ ◗ ♣ P

Try also: Lane Ends (Tetley)

Middleton

Joiners Arms
37 Cross Street (off Archer Park, behind Arndale Centre)
☎ (061) 643 6982
12–3; 7–11
Whitbread OB Mild, OB Bitter [H]
Excellent, two-roomed pub with comfortable lounge and basic tap room. No jukebox, just friendly conversation. Etched windows of former Phoenix (Heywood) brewery still feature. Good value lunchtime snacks (not Sun). Q ☸ ⊟ ♣

Tandle Hill Tavern
14 Thornham Lane, Slattocks
OS898091 ☎ (0706) 345297
12.30 (12 Sat)–3; 6–11 (12–3 (weekends only); 7.30–11 winter)
Lees Bitter [H], **Moonraker** (winter) [E]
Welcoming, isolated pub near Tandle Hill Country Park, approached by footpath or bumpy road. Customers include farmers, horse riders and joggers. Family room at lunchtime and until 9pm; meals always available. Local CAMRA branch 10K run held each October. ⌂ Q ♨ ☸ ◖ ◗ ♣

Milnrow

Waggon Inn
Butterworth Hall (off Newhey Road, B6225)
☎ (0706) 48313
11–11
Burtonwood Dark Mild, Best Bitter [H]
Busy village local built in 18th century. Separate family room; warm welcome guaranteed. Tables outside. ⌂ ♨ ☸ ⇌ (Milnrow/Newhey) ♣ P

Monton

Drop Inn
204–206 Monton Road
☎ (061) 789 5068
11.30–4 (4.30 Sat); 5.30 (7 Sat)–11
Courage Directors; John Smith's Bitter, Magnet [H]
Unusual H-shaped pub that was originally two shops. Comfortable interior with two bars. Lunchtime food (not Sun) is very reasonably priced. 'Log-end' dartboard. ◖ ♣

Park Hotel
142 Monton Road
☎ (061) 788 9045
11–11 (11–4; 7–11 Sat)
Holt Mild, Bitter [H]
Popular 50s pub in posher part of Eccles. Large vault and lounge, and a pleasant snug, unusual for pubs of this era. Quiet, except for Sun lunch.
Q ⊟ ♿ ⇌ (Patricroft) ♣ P

Mossley

Tollemache
Manchester Road
☎ (045 75) 2354
11–3; 5–11
Robinson's Best Mild, Best Bitter [H]
Popular, cosy local alongside the Huddersfield Narrow Canal. Much oak panelling; a tidy original bar. Q ☸ ◖ ⊟ P

Moss Side

Claremont
124 Claremont Road (150 yds from A5103 jct)
☎ (061) 226 1741
11–11 (11–3; 7–11 Sat)
Holt Mild, Bitter [H]
Vast, inter-wars pub, one of Holt's biggest sellers. Sadly now shares this inner-city area's general decline, but reliable for a good pint in lively surroundings. A raw, uncompromising Manchester drinking shop and none the worse for that! Generous snacks. Q ⊟

Moston

Blue Bell
Moston Lane (1 mile from Rochdale road)
11–11 (11–5; 7–11 Sat)
Holt Mild, Bitter [H]
Large Edwardian pub with a modified, semi-open-plan layout. Caters for all ages. The busiest pub in an area dominated by Bass and Wilson's. ♨ ⊟ ♿

Dean Brook Inn
St Marys Road (100 yds from station) ☎ (061) 682 4730
11–11
Marston's Mercian Mild, Burton Best Bitter [H]
Comfortable community pub occupying a long terrace. Caters for an older clientele. Menu provides for children and vegetarians, plus daily specials.
♨ ☸ ◖ ◗ ♿ ⇌ (Newton Heath) ♣

Newhey

Bird in the Hand (Top Bird)
113 Huddersfield Road (A640)
☎ (0706) 847978
11–3; 5–11 (11.30–11 Sat)
Samuel Smith OBB [H]
Friendly locals' pub, with lounge and busy vault.
Q ⇌

Try also: Bottom Bird (Samuel Smith)

New Springs

Colliers Arms
Wigan Road (near Leeds–Liverpool Canal on B5238)
☎ (0942) 831171
12.30–5.30; 7.30–11
Burtonwood Dark Mild, Best Bitter [H]
18th-century pub: everything a local pub should be, a journey into the past. Not to be missed. Computer for rugby coupon. Limited parking. ⌂ Q ⊞ ♣

Oldham

Dog & Partridge
49 Constantine Street,
☎ (061) 665 2264
12–3 (4 Sat); 7–11
Matthew Brown Mild, Bitter; Theakston Best Bitter [H]
Welcoming, four-roomed pub, formerly with own brewhouse. No food at weekend.
⌂ ✿ ◖ ⊞ ♣ P

Gardeners Arms
Dunham Street, Waterhead (off A62) ☎ (061) 624 0242
11.30–11 (11.30–5; 7–11 Sat)
Robinson's Best Mild, Best Bitter [H]
Four-roomed local with a fine combination of tiles and brasses in the public bar. Bar snacks weekday lunchtimes.
♞ ✿ ⊞ ♿ ♣ P

Robin Hood Inn
119 Lees Road (opp. main fire station) ☎ (061) 624 1494
11.30–11
Whitbread OB Mild, OB Bitter [H]
Three-roomed pub where the vestibule is the serving and main drinking area. Comfortable and welcoming. Meals are a new feature.
♞ ◖ ◗ ⊞ ≢ (Mumps) ♣ P

Rose of Lancaster
315 Manchester Street, Werneth (A62)
☎ (061) 627 1047
11.30–11
Whitbread OB Mild, Boddingtons Bitter, OB Bitter [H]
Busy, four-roomed, traditional pub (built 1900 for former Oldham Brewery Company Ltd.), in notable drinking area. Impressive ornate terracotta and tiled exterior. May be demolished for highway scheme. Visit it soon!
✿ ◖ ≢ (Werneth) ♣

White Swan Hotel
185 Huddersfield Road (A62)
☎ (061) 624 5454
11–11
Robinson's Best Mild, Bitter, Old Tom [H]
Cosy town local with four rooms, including a snug. Rare outlet for Robinson's Bitter. Lunchtime snacks.
⊞ ≢ (Mumps) ♣

Try also: Auld Lang Syne (Free)

Partington

King William IV
Manchester Road (A6144)
☎ (061) 775 2840
11.30–3; 5 (7 Sat)–11
Marston's Mercian Mild, Burton Best Bitter [E]
Low-beamed village pub with separate 'cocktail lounge'. Cooked food Fri lunch only.
⌂ ⊞ ♿ ♣ P

Patricroft

Grapes
431 Liverpool Road (just E of M63 jct 2) ☎ (061) 789 6971
11–11 (11–4.30; 7–11 Sat)
Holt Mild, Bitter [H]
Impressive, multi-roomed Edwardian pub, full of mahogany and etched glass, with a magnificent staircase. 'Log-end' dartboard. ⊞ ≢ ♣ P

Pemberton

Dog & Partridge (Jem Lowe's)
30 Charel Street (just off A577)
12–4; 6–11
Greenalls Mild, Bitter [E]
Unspoilt old boozer, worth seeking out. ⊞ ♣

Prestwich

Commercial Inn
271 Bury Old Road, Heaton Park (A665)
☎ (061) 773 3661
12–11
Tetley Mild, Bitter [H]
Well-run, friendly local with a good social mix. Popular with sportsmen: pub has its own football and cricket teams. Comfortable lounge and snug; well-used vault. Home-cooked food, including children's menu.
Q ✿ ◖ ⊞ ≢ (Heaton Park) ♣ P

Royal Oak
23 Whittaker Lane (100 yds off A665, near station)
11–11
Hydes' Anvil Light, Bitter [E]
Tucked-away, friendly local with a good mix of clientele. Pleasant decor in comfortable lounge and newsroom. Basic vault.
Q ⊞ ≢ (Heaton Park) ♣ P

Try also: Red Lion (Holt); **Turf Tavern** (Free)

Radcliffe

Masons Arms
190 Sion Street
12–3; 7–11 (11–11 Sat)
Thwaites Mild, Bitter [H]
Although close to the town centre, a village atmosphere is enhanced by a rural outlook and a sparkling social scene, including ancient Bull Ring game. ⌂ ✿ ◖ ≢ ♣ P

Papermakers
21 Church Street East
☎ (061) 723 3415
12–11
Holt Mild, Bitter [H]
A typical Holt's back-street pub, hidden from main road and overshadowed by old paper mills. A friendly atmosphere awaits the local or stranger who 'stumbles' upon this pub. Quiz nights every Tue. Benches on street for summer drinking.
Q ✿ ⊞ ≢ ♣ P

Try also: Old Cross (Holt)

Ramsbottom

Royal Oak
39 Bridge Street
☎ (0706) 822786
12–4; 7–11 (12–11 Fri & Sat)
Thwaites Best Mild, Bitter [H]
Friendly, village-centre pub near East Lancs light railway, a growing tourist attraction. The lounge features brassware, paintings and plates. Traditional games room; cosy snug with dartboard. Bar meals at lunchtime (children's menu).
♞ ◖ ♣

Ringley

Horseshoe
395 Fold Road, Stoneclough (off A667) ☎ (0204) 71714
11–3; 7–11
Thwaites Mild, Bitter [H]
Comfortable friendly pub with an emphasis on food at lunchtime. ⌂ ✿ ◖ ≢ (Kearsley)

Try also: Lord Nelson (Thwaites)

Ringway

Romper
Pinfold Lane (off A538, 500 yds from M56 jct 6)
☎ (061) 980 6806
11–11 (11–3; 5.30–11 Sat)
Whitbread Boddingtons Mild, Boddingtons Bitter [H]
A multi-roomed, stone-floored country pub by the airport. Genuine beams and a real fire complete the traditional atmosphere; lunches (Mon–Fri) are good value for the area.
⌂ Q ✿ ◖ ⊞ ♣ P

Greater Manchester

Rochdale

Healey Hotel
172 Shawclough Road (B6377)
☎ (0706) 45453
11.30–2; 4–11 (11.30–11 Fri & Sat)
Robinson's Best Mild, Best Bitter Ⓗ, **Old Tom** (winter) Ⓖ
Unspoilt, stone-built, terraced 1930s pub with original wood and tiled bar area. Games room with open-topped table football. Convenient for Healey Dell nature reserve. Q ♣

Merry Monk
234 College Road (300 yds from A6060/B6222 jct)
☎ (0706) 46919
11.30–11
Marston's Border Mild, Burton Best Bitter, Pedigree Bitter Ⓗ
Friendly and unpretentious back-street local with unusual Ring the Bull game in lounge. Guest beers. ♣ P

Navigation
116 Drake Street (A640 near station) ☎ (0706) 523566
11–11 (11–4; 7–11 Sat)
Holt Mild, Bitter Ⓗ
Two-room local on a main road: attractive lounge with active games room. Good lunchtime menu includes veg option.
❀ (⊟ ≹ ♣

Try also: Cemetery (Free)

Romiley

Duke of York
Stockport Road (B6104)
☎ (061) 430 2806
11–3; 5.30–11
Courage Directors; John Smith's Bitter Ⓗ
Attractive, comfortable pub with long history. Excellent vault. Q ❀ ( ) ⊟ ≹ ♣ P

Spread Eagle
Hatherlow ☎ (061) 430 2846
11.30–11
Whitbread Boddingtons Bitter Ⓗ
This attractive three-storey pub dates from 1722. The low-ceilinged lounge has much panelling and original beams (along with new additions) and is alive with pictures, etc. The large vault is stark by contrast and often busy. ❀ (⊟ ≹ ♣ P

Royton

Greyhound Inn
1 Elly Clough, Holden Fold (off A663) ☎ (061) 624 4504
11.30–3; 7–11
Lees GB Mild, Bitter Ⓔ
A friendly local, slightly off the beaten track but well worth a visit. Q ❀ (♣ P

Halfway House
613 Rochdale Road (A671)
☎ (061) 624 0166
11–3 (4 Fri & Sat); 6–11
Lees GB Mild, Bitter Ⓗ
Public house which serves the local community. Numerous sports and social activities and outings. Strong sports teams, including Royton Town ladies darts team, motto: 'win or lose, have a booze'! ☺ ❀ (♣ P

Try also: Puckersley Inn (Lees)

Sale

Railway Inn
35 Chapel Road (behind town hall)
11.30–3; 5.30–11
Robinson's Best Mild, Best Bitter, Old Tom (winter) Ⓔ
Rendered unimaginatively open-plan in the mid 70s but avoided attracting the young lager drinkers and retained its regulars. Access to the Bridgewater Canal across the road. ❀ (⊟ ≹ ♣ P

Sale Moor

Legh Arms
178 Northenden Road (A6144/B5166 jct)
11–11
Holt Mild, Bitter Ⓔ
Large, refurbished, multi-roomed local, acquired from Taylor's Eagle Brewery in 1924. Retains many original features. Island bar serves large vault, lounge, snug, lobby and smoke room. Bowling green. Live music in lounge Tue, Fri, Sat and Sun nights. Q ❀ ⊟ ♣ P

Try also: Railway (Robinson's)

Salford

Beehive
74 Holland Street, Pendleton (by railway footbridge, off Langley Road, S off Cromwell Road, A567)
☎ (061) 745 7623
11.30–11
Greenalls Mild, Bitter, Thomas Greenall's Original Bitter Ⓗ
Unspoilt hidden local. Windows display original 'Groves & Whitnall' legend. Pub name in unusual 'oeil de boeuf' corner window. No food at weekends.
☺ ❀ (⊟ ≹ (Pendleton) ♣

Blackfriar
13 King Street (Trinity Way/A6041 jct)
☎ (061) 834 7407
11–11
Whitbread Higsons Mild, Boddingtons Bitter Ⓗ
Recent refurbishment has left this well-run pub with a traditional interior layout. Children may be accommodated.
⌂ Q (⊟ ♿ ≹ (Victoria) ♣

Crescent
18–21 Crescent (A6, near university ☎ (061) 736 5600
12–2.30 (not Sat); 5 (7.30 Sat)–11 (12–11 Fri)
Holt Mild, Bitter Ⓗ
Sprawling, listed Georgian terraced building. Busy with students during term. A pub of interesting, if idiosyncratic character. No food at weekend. Guest beers.
⌂ (≹ (Crescent) ♣ ⊙ P

Peel Park Inn
270 Chapel Street (A6, between hospital and cathedral)
☎ (061) 832 2654
11–11
Courage Directors; John Smith's Bitter, Magnet Ⓗ
Small, one-roomed pub. ⛟ (≹

Star
Back Hope Street
1–5 (12.15–6 Sat); 8–11
Robinson's Best Mild, Best Bitter Ⓗ
Small pub with only one bar (in the vault). Haunt of students on term-time evenings. Regulars only at lunchtime. ❀ ⊟

Union Tavern
105 Liverpool Street
☎ (061) 736 2885
11–4.30; 7–11
Holt Mild, Bitter Ⓗ
Honest, basic boozer in desolate area on fringe of enterprise zone. ⊟ ≹ ♣ P

Waggon & Horses
Bolton Road (old A6), Irlams o' th'Height
11–11 (11–5; 7–11 Sat)
Holt Mild, Bitter Ⓗ
Popular, large, modern pub with lounge and vault. ⊟ P

Try also: Braziers (Boddingtons)

Stalybridge

Station Buffet
Buffet bar, platform one, Stalybridge station
☎ (061) 338 2020
12–3 (not Sun, Mon & Tue); 5 (7 Sat)–11
Moorhouse's Premier Bitter Ⓗ
Recently-expanded to two rooms, but still retaining its unique atmosphere. Wide selection of foreign bottled beers and three guests which change frequently; new brews appear amazingly quickly. Worth missing a train for!
⌂ ( ) ≹ ⊙ P

White House
1 Water Street (opp. bus station)

11-3; 5.30-11
Matthew Brown Mild; Theakston Best Bitter, XB Ⓗ
No-frills, former Cunninghams of Warrington pub. Good selection of malt whiskies. ≹ ♣

Stockport

Arden Arms
23 Millgate (near market place)
☎ (061) 480 2185
11.30-3; 5.30-11 (11.30-11 Fri & Sat)
Robinson's Mild, Best Bitter, Old Tom Ⓗ
Multi-roomed, listed building. Alterations have enhanced the character of Stockport's famous time capsule. Well worth a visit. Collection of grandfather clocks; delightful snug hidden behind bar. No food Sun; limited parking.
Q ♨ ⊛ ◖ ♿ ≹ ♣ P

Blossoms
2 Buxton Road, Heavily (A6)
☎ (061) 480 2246
11.30-3.30; 5.30-11
Robinson's Best Mild, Best Bitter, Old Tom Ⓗ
A bustling, multi-roomed pub. Its street-corner location gives it an unusual shape. The lounge oozes character, and features an old Bells poster. Popular meeting spot for local lacrosse stars. Lunchtime snacks (not Sun). ⌂ ♣ P

Boar's Head
Market Place
☎ (061) 480 3978
11.30-4 (3 Wed, 3.30 Mon & Thu); 7 (6 Fri)-11 (closed Sun)
Samuel Smith OBB, Museum Ale Ⓗ
Vibrant market local appealing to all tastes. Live music six nights a week, with late licence (midnight) in music room. Excellent set menu. Plus veg option. ◖ ≹

Grapes
1 Castle Street, Edgeley
☎ (061) 480 3027
11-11 (11-4; 7-11 Sat)
Robinson's Best Mild, Best Bitter, Old Tom (winter) Ⓗ
Lively, down-to-earth boozer on shopping precinct; handy for football ground. Free public car park at rear. ⊕ ≹ ♣

Greyhound
27 Bowden Street, Edgeley
11-11
Whitbread Boddingtons Mild, Boddingtons Bitter Ⓔ
An uninspiring modern exterior hides a classic, bustling local, full of character and artefacts. Easy to overlook, but should not be. ⊕ ≹ ♣ P

Midway
263 Newbridge Lane (400 yds off ring road, A626)
☎ (061) 480 2068
11.30-3; 5 (7 Sat)-11
Courage Directors; John Smith's Bitter, Magnet Ⓗ
Comfortable, welcoming, one-bar pub decorated in country style with beams and brasses. Terrace at rear overlooks River Goyt. Families welcome here and in restaurant. Good bar lunches; eve meals Tue-Sat.
⊛ ◖ ◗ P

Red Bull
14 Middle Hillgate
☎ (061) 480 2087
11-3; 5-11 (11-11 Fri & Sat)
Robinson's Best Mild, Best Bitter Ⓗ
Large, two-roomed country-style pub in the heart of town. Friendly and busy, sporting brass decorations and stone-flagged floor. Excellent lunches – short but imaginative menu; veg option (not Sun).
⌂ Q ◖ ≹ P

Stretford

Melville Hotel
Barton Road
☎ (061) 865 8006
11-11 (11-3.45; 7-11 Sat)
Holt Mild, Bitter Ⓔ
Large pub with function room and evening barbecue in summer.
⊛ ⊕ ≹ (Humphrey Park) ♣ P

Swinton & Pendlebury

Cricketers Arms
227 Manchester Road (A6 near A572 jct) ☎ (061) 794 2008
11.45 (12 Sat)-3.30; 7-11
Holt Mild, Bitter Ⓔ
Small, friendly old local with thriving public bar. ⊕

Park Inn
137 Worsley Road, Swinton (A572) ☎ (061) 794 4296
11-11
Holt Mild, Bitter Ⓗ
Smart old local with tiny snug at rear and triangular public bar.
◖ ◗ ⊕ ♣ P

Timperley

Quarrybank Inn
151 Bloomsbury Lane
☎ (061) 980 4345
11.30-3; 5.30-11 (11.30-11 Fri & Sat)
Hydes' Anvil Mild, Bitter Ⓔ, **Strong Ale** Ⓖ
Thriving village local due for refurbishment; lively vault, bowling green. Menu caters for children and vegetarians (no food Sun eve). ♨ ⊛ ◖ ◗ ⊕ ♣ P

Tottington

Dungeon Inn
9 Turton Road
☎ (020488) 3346
12-3; 7-11 (11-11 Sat)
Thwaites Mild, Bitter Ⓗ
Derives its name from ancient lock up at rear. Frieze, depicting many local scenes, and excellent tilework are a feature. Busy and lively. ⊕ ♣

Tyldesley

Half Moon
115 Elliot Street
☎ (0942) 873206
11-4 (5 Sat); 7-11
Holt Mild, Bitter Ⓗ
Large lounge with bar and pool room; lounge has alcove drinking areas. Coin collection. It has been licensed since 1871 but only been a pub since 1984. Regular guest beers. ⊛ ♣

Mort Arms
235 Elliot Street
☎ (0942) 883481
12-11
Holt Mild, Bitter Ⓗ
Two-roomed friendly town-centre local. A traditional Holt's bar with dark wood wall panelling displaying local poetry. Standard tap room and a large comfortable lounge. ⊕ ♣

Welcome Traveller (Skennin Bob's)
166 Elliot Street
☎ (0942) 891832
7-11 (12-11 Fri & Sat)
Ruddles Best Bitter; Wilson's Original Mild, Original Bitter Ⓗ
Large, town-centre pub, with separate tap room; 'best' side has lower games area. Large standing area around the bar; the lounge is away from the bar. Nickname comes from a previous landlord. ⊕ ♣

Uppermill

Cross Keys Inn
1 mile up Running Hill Gate, off A670 ☎ (0457) 874626
11-3; 6.30-11 (11-11 summer)
Lees GB Mild, Bitter Ⓗ
Attractive, 18th-century stone building, popular with locals and the focus of many activities. Menu caters for children and vegetarians.
⌂ Q ♨ ⊛ ◖ ⊕ ⛺ ♣ P

Urmston

Manor Hey
130 Stretford Road
☎ (061) 748 3896
11.30-3; 7-11
Theakston Best Bitter; Younger Scotch, No. 3 Ⓗ
Hotel bar serving home-made food, including Sun roast lunch. Children's and veg options.
Q ⛫ ◖ ◗ ≹ P

Try also: Lord Nelson (Holt)

Greater Manchester

Walshaw

White Horse
18 Hall Street
☎ (020488) 3243
12–3; 7–11
Thwaites Mild, Bitter Ⓗ
Typical, friendly local on the edge of the countryside.
Q ◖ ◗ ⊕ ♣ P

Westhoughton

Brinsop Arms
584–592 Chorley Road (A6, off M61 jct 6)
☎ (0942) 815011
11–11
Marston's Pedigree Bitter; Tetley Bitter; Walker Best Bitter; Whitbread Flowers IPA, Boddingtons Bitter, Castle Eden Ale Ⓗ
Former rural pub transformed into a hotel/restaurant complex. Regular guest beers.

Hartcommon
490 Wigan Road (A58, on Hindley/Hartcommon border)
☎ (0942) 813356
12–3 (4 Sat); 7–11
Matthew Brown Mild; Theakston Best Bitter, XB, Old Peculier Ⓗ
Small, three-roomed pub, half a mile from town centre. A true local of character where a warm welcome is assured. ⊕ ♣ P

White Lion
2 Market Street (A58)
☎ (0942) 813120
11–11
Holt Mild, Bitter Ⓗ
Excellent, unspoilt local with thriving tap room. ♞ ⊕ ≋ ♣ P

Try also: Rose Hill Tavern (Holt)

Whitefield

Coach & Horses
71 Bury Old Road (A665)
☎ (061) 798 8897
11–11 (11–5; 7–11 Sat)
Holt Mild, Bitter Ⓗ
Built in 1830 and virtually unchanged. Once a staging post for the Burnley to Manchester mail coach. A friendly haunt of CAMRA members. 13th year in this guide. Waiter service.
Q ⊛ ⊕ ≋ (Besses o'th Barn) ♣ P

Eagle & Child
Higher Lane (A667)
☎ (061) 766 3024
12–11
Holt Mild, Bitter Ⓗ
Large, 1930s, Holt-built pub, with imposing mock-Tudor exterior and genuine Holt interior. Comfortable and friendly, with one of the few remaining bowling greens in the area.
♨ Q ◖ ≋ (Besses o'th Barn) ♣ P

Try also: New Grove; Welcome Inn (Holt)

Wigan

Bird i' th' Hand (Hen Ole)
Gidlow Lane (W of centre)
11–11
Tetley Dark Mild, Mild, Bitter Ⓗ
Bustling locals' pub with a pleasant atmosphere. ⊕ ♣

Bold Hotel
161 Poolstock Lane, Worsley Mesnes (near A49/B5238 jct)
☎ (0942) 41095
11–11
Burtonwood Dark Mild, Best Bitter Ⓗ
Small local serving excellent beers; well worth a visit. ⊕ ♣

Brickmakers
Woodhouse Lane
☎ (0942) 42618
12–3.30; 7–11
Greenalls Mild, Bitter Ⓔ
Imposing, but friendly local with a surprisingly small interior. Handy for soccer ground. ◖ ◗ ♣

Market Tavern
Market Street
11–11
Younger Scotch, IPA Ⓗ
Large, open-plan town pub, deservedly-popular. ◖ ≋

Millstone
Wigan Lane (old A49, N of centre, near rugby ground)
12–3.30; 7–11
Thwaites Best Mild, Bitter Ⓗ
Drastically-refurbished, with no public bar and modern trimmings. ◖

Old Pear Tree
Frog Lane (near bus station)
☎ (0942) 43677
12–3.30; 5.30–11
Burtonwood Dark Mild, Best Bitter Ⓗ
15 years in the *Good Beer Guide*: a warm welcome and excellent lunches. ♨ Q ⊛ ◖ ⊕ ≋ ♣ P

Seven Stars
Wallgate (near Wigan Pier on A49) ☎ (0942) 43126
12–3.30; 6–11
Thwaites Best Mild, Bitter Ⓗ
Splendid ex-Magee's pub; handy for canal and Wigan Pier; very comfortable and friendly.
◖ ⊕ ≋ ♣ P

Silverwell
Darlington Street (½ mile from centre on Hindley Road)
11.30–3.30; 7–11
Walker Mild, Best Bitter Ⓗ
Large roadside pub, basic but lively. ♨ ◖ ♿ ≋ ♣

Springfield
Springfield Road (near football ground)
11.30–3.30; 5.30–11
Walker Mild, Bitter, Best Bitter Ⓗ
Large, multi-roomed pub, very popular for live music. Impressive glasswork. ⊕ ♿ ♣ P

Swan & Railway
Wallgate (opp. station)
☎ (0942) 495032
11–3.30; 5.30–11
Bass Mild XXXX, Special Bitter, Draught Bass; Courage Directors; John Smith's Bitter; Stones Best Bitter Ⓗ
Excellent, traditional town-centre pub with railway memorabilia. Handy for the Pier. Q 🛏 ◖ ⊕ ≋

Tudor House Hotel
New Market Street (next to bus station) ☎ (0942) 42190
11–11
Bass Mild XXXX, Draught Bass; Stones Best Bitter Ⓗ
Very friendly and comfortable family hotel. Jazz on Fri eve. Cat is said to be 22 years old. Guest beers from small brewers.
♨ ⊛ 🛏 ◖ ◗ ≋

Withington

Victoria
438 Wilmslow Road (B5093)
11.30–11
Hydes' Anvil Mild, Bitter Ⓗ
Lively pub in cosmopolitan centre of Withington. One bar, but choice of three distinct drinking areas. ⊛ ♣

Woodford

Davenport Arms (Thief's Neck)
550 Chester Road (A5102)
☎ (061)) 439 2435
11–3.30; 5.15–11
Robinson's Best Mild, Best Bitter, Old Tom (winter) Ⓗ
Classic country pub: multi-roomed and unspoilt, on edge of prosperous suburbs. Licence in same family for 60 years. Near aerodrome, so much flying memorabilia. Mild outsells all lagers put together. Good home-made lunches: ploughman's with choice of up to 12 cheeses. ♨ Q ⊛ ◖ ♣ P

Join CAMRA — see page 504!

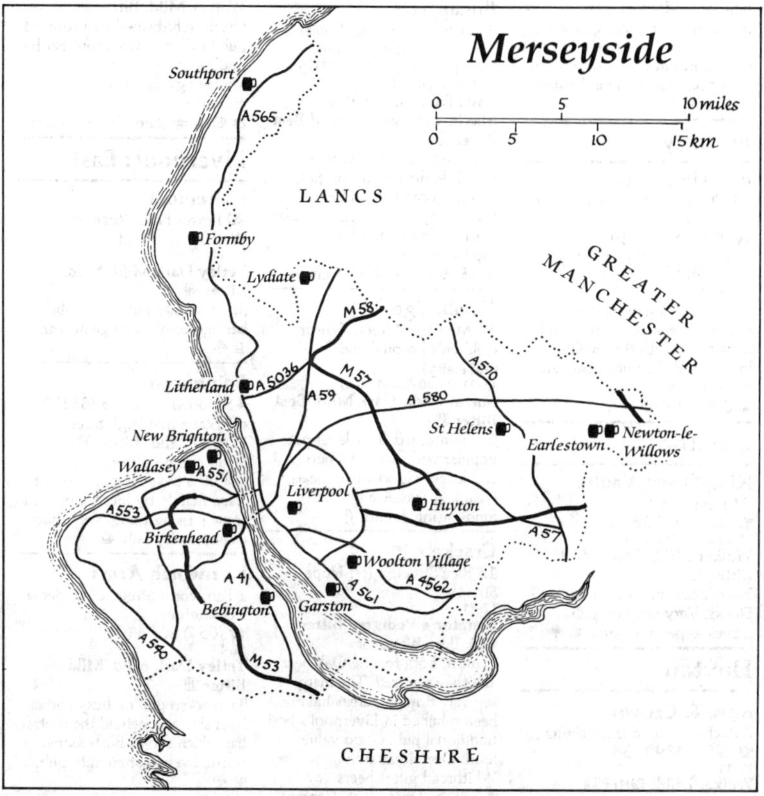

Bebington

Cleveland Arms
31 Bebington Road (near New Chester Road)
☎ (051) 645 2847
11–11 (12–3; 7.30–10.30 Sun)
Thwaites Best Mild, Bitter Ⓗ
Ever-popular, friendly local in pedestrian area. Regulars of all ages. Open-plan, with pool room and darts. Pies and pasties lunchtime. ≠ ♣

Great Eastern
New Ferry Road (towards River Mersey from New Ferry)
☎ (051) 645 3282
11–11
Banks's Mild, Bitter Ⓔ
Spacious, two-room pub with new beer garden (second in Banks's Beer Garden of the Year competition). Lounge quiet during the week. Country music on Fri. Plenty of Great Eastern memorabilia: the ship was broken up on nearby bank of Mersey. No meals Sun.
❀ ◐ ⊞ ♿ ≠ ♣

Rose & Crown
57 The Village
☎ (051) 645 5024
11.30–3; 5.30–11
Thwaites Best Mild, Bitter Ⓗ
Excellent, bustling, friendly old local, popular with office workers at lunchtime and local residents at night. No food Sun.
Q ◐ ⊞ ≠ ♣ P

Birkenhead

Copperfield
Market Street (near Town Hall)
☎ (051) 647 9837
11–11 (11–3; 5.30–11 Sat, 7–11 Sun)
John Smith's Bitter Ⓗ
Fast, friendly service in a bustling, vibrant local. Popular with office workers during the day and the younger set at night. Open-plan, with video jukebox. ◐ ≠ (Hamilton Sq)

Firemans Arms
36 Oliver Street (behind Ladbrokes bingo hall)
☎ (051) 647 8226
11–11
Wilson's Original Bitter Ⓗ
Hectic shoppers' pub by day and equally hectic pre-club pub by night. Comfortable, one-roomer, served by a single bar. Snacks lunchtimes. ≠ (Central)

George & Dragon
82 Grange Road (opp. main post office, 200 yds from Central Station)
☎ (051) 647 4513
11–11
Walker Mild, Bitter Ⓗ
Busy shopping area pub with cosy lounge, real fires and a darts-oriented bar.
♨ ◐ ⊞ ♿ ≠ (Central) ♣

Old House at Home
30 Queen Street (uphill from Green Lane station)
☎ (051) 666 1578
11–11
Banks's Mild, Bitter Ⓔ
Recently-refurbished local which has retained a public bar. Warm and friendly welcome; local pensioners well looked after.
❀ ⊞ ≠ (Green Lane) ♣

Earlestown

Houghton Arms
Houghton Close (off A572, in centre of new estate)
☎ (09252) 22338
12–4.30 (5 Sat); 6–11
Burtonwood Dark Mild, Best Bitter Ⓗ
A once end-terrace pub which has been extended into neighbouring premises, the rest of the houses having been demolished and new houses

built around. Open-plan, featuring a long lounge bar with a raised section at one end and a games area at the other, served by a small bar. Parking limited.
☾ ⊞ ≢ ♣ P

Formby

Bay Horse Inn
13 Church Road (B5424, near police station)
☎ (07048) 74229
11.30–3; 5.30–11 (11.30–11 Fri & Sat)
Bass Mild XXXX, Draught Bass 🄷
Warm, inviting stone-floored pub with separate 'Toby Grill' restaurant. Both the small lounge and the public bar can be crowded.
⛫ Q ❀ ☾ ◗ ⊞ ♿ ♣ P

Garston

King Street Vaults
74 King Street
☎ (051) 427 5850
11–3; 6–11 (11.30–11 Sat)
Walker Mild, Bitter, Best Bitter 🄷
Basic locals' pub near Garston Docks. Very keen on pub games, especially darts. ⊞ ♣

Huyton

Rose & Crown
2 Archway Road (near church)
☎ (051) 489 1735
11–11
Walker Mild, Bitter 🄷
Large pub with multi-roomed layout. Lunchtime food is good and inexpensive. ⛀ ❀ ☾ ⊞ ≢ ♣

Litherland

Priory
64 Sefton Road (off A5036)
☎ (051) 928 1110
11.30–11
Ind Coope Burton Ale; Walker Mild, Bitter 🄷
Large, modernised, two-roomed pub. Public bar and well-appointed, split-level lounge. Beer garden and security camera car park. Good food, including Sun lunch. ❀ ☾ ⊞

Liverpool: City Centre

Augustus John
Brownlow Hill (university campus, opp. E side of RC cathedral)
11–11
Oak Old Oak Ale, Double Dagger; Tetley Mild, Bitter 🄷
Modern pub, part of university campus, but very much a proper pub used by non-university people as well as students and lecturers. Good value lunches.
❀ ☾ ♿ ≢ (Lime St) ♣

Bonapartes
21a Clarence Street, 3 (near university and off Mount Pleasant) ☎ (051) 709 5089
11.30 (12 Sat)–12.30
Vaux Samson, Double Maxim; Wards Sheffield Best Bitter 🄷
A two-roomed pub with a wood-dominated decor. Side lounge is candlelit in bistro-style. Busy after 11pm. Popular with students and others. No food weekends.
❀ ☾ ◗ ≢ (Lime St) ⊖ (Central)

Cambridge
51 Mulberry Street, 7 (near children's hospital and university)
11–11 (11.30–3; 7–11 Sat)
Burtonwood Dark Mild, Best Bitter 🄷
Single-roomed, split-level pub, popular with students, nurses and locals. Good value meals, including Sun. Many charity fund-raising events. ☾

Cracke
13 Rice Street, 1 (off Hope Street)
12–11
Marston's Pedigree Bitter; Oak Best Bitter 🄷
A must, both for the Oak beer and the pub itself. The many separate drinking areas have been retained in Liverpool's best traditional pub. Good value food. Occasional non-Whitbread guest beers.
❀ ☾ ⊞ ≢ (Lime St) ⊖ (Central)

Lion
67 Moorfields (opp. facade of former Exchange station)
11.30–11 (closed Sun)
Walker Mild, Bitter, Winter Warmer 🄷
Friendly pub with mixture of business and local clienteles. A feast of good wood, glass and tiles, plus a fine dome. Bargain lunches. Ind Coope Burton Ale served when Winter Warmer is out of season.
☾ ⊞ ⊖ (Moorfields)

Roscoe Head
24 Roscoe Street, 1 (off Leece Street, opp. bombed church)
11–11 (12–11 Sat)
Ind Coope Burton Ale; Jennings Bitter; Tetley Mild, Bitter 🄷
Customers come first in this small, unspoilt, traditional local. Has a front snug as well as two lounges off the bar area. Winner of many awards—an excellent pub.
Q ☾ ⊞ ≢ (Lime St) ⊖ (Central)

White House
185 Duke Street (corner of Berry Street)
☎ (051) 709 9094
11–11
Walker Mild, Bitter 🄷
Nicely-refurbished two-roomed pub in Chinatown. Front bar has pool; lounge has comfy furnishings and its own entrance.
⛀ ⊞ ♿ ≢ (Lime St) ⊖ (Central)

Liverpool: East

Claremont
70 Lower Breck Road, 6 (off West Derby Road)
12–11
Tetley Dark Mild, Mild, Bitter 🄷
Street-corner pub with public bar and comfy lounge at rear.
⊞ ♣

Edinburgh
4 Sandown Lane, 15 (B5178, off Wavertree High Street)
Walker Mild, Bitter 🄷
Small pub on a street corner, just off a busy shopping street. Used mainly by locals, but with some passing trade. Very much a community pub. ⊞

Farnworth Arms
1 Farnworth Street, 6 (corner of Kensington)
☎ (051) 260 4190
12–11
Tetley Dark Mild, Mild, Bitter 🄷
Two-room pub on busy corner. Irish artefacts behind the central bar which serves both rooms. A warm, lively, community pub.
⊞ ♣

Royal Hotel
213 Smithdown Road, 15 (A562 near Toxteth cemetery)
☎ (051) 733 6408
12–11
Ind Coope Burton Ale; Tetley Mild, Bitter 🄷
Wonderfully ornate exterior (mosaics); gaslit lounge, with nice panelling and stuffed animals. Try the Sun lunches (children welcome). Quizzes Tue eves. ⛀ ⊞ ♿ ♣

Royal Standard
1 Walker Street, 6 (off West Derby Road)
☎ (051) 263 2294
11–11
Draught Bass 🄷
Lively local, now in need of external and internal redecoration. The Bass survives as a result of the deceased landlord's persistence in securing the terms of his tenancy. ⊞ ♣

Waldeck
113 Lawrence Road, 15 (between Smithdown Road (A562) and Picton Road)
☎ (051) 733 7703
12–3.30; 5–11 (12–11 Thu-Sat)
Walker Mild, Bitter 🄷
Locals' pub with small bar (note waterfront mural); also has an

alcove for pool and a large lounge. Some nice old Walker stained glass windows survive. Live music Sun eve; quizzes Thu eve. ⛲ ⊟ ♿ ♣

Willowbank
329 Smithdown Road, 15 (A562 opp. Sefton General Hospital) ☎ (051) 733 5782
12–11
Ind Coope Burton Ale; Walker Mild, Bitter Ⓗ
Imposing pub just set back from the main road. Public bar at the front; lounge to the rear, adorned with old tramway pictures. No food Sun. Quizzes Wed eve. ⛲ ✿ ◖ ⊟ ♿ ♣

Liverpool: North

Abbey
153 Walton Lane, 4 (opp. Stanley Park)
☎ (051) 207 0036
11–11
Walker Mild, Bitter Ⓗ
Three-storey building with half-timbering and maroon tile work. Interior has been tastefully opened out. Busy most times but particularly on match days (close to Everton FC). ⊟ ♣

Breckside (Flat Iron)
377 Walton Breck Road, 7 (corner of Anfield Road)
☎ (051) 263 4694
12–11
Tetley Dark Mild, Mild, Bitter Ⓗ
Impressive three-roomed local, close to Liverpool FC. Its nickname reflects its shape.
⛲ ⊟ ♿ ♣

Bull
2 Dublin Street (corner of A565, Great Howard Street)
☎ (051) 207 1422
11.30–11
Tetley Mild, Bitter Ⓗ
Blue collars and suited clientele share enjoyment of the lively Irish atmosphere in this friendly one-bar corner pub. Eve meals if requested. Quiz night Mon.
◖ ⇌ (Sandhills) ♣

Clock
167 Walton Road, 4 (A59)
☎ (051) 207 3594
11–11
Walker Mild, Bitter Ⓗ
Small, two-roomed, street-corner local, with bustling bar and cosy parlour. Close to Everton FC. ⊟ ⇌ (Kirkdale) ♣

Crown Vaults
25 Kirkdale Road, 5 (Stanley Road jct)
12–11
Tetley Dark Mild, Mild, Bitter Ⓗ
Pub with tiled exterior, which looks smaller than it is. Open-plan interior but with well-defined areas. Live music; discos and quiz nights provide the entertainment. Good lively atmosphere. ⇌ (Sandhills) ♣

Melrose Abbey
331 Westminster Road (corner of Melrose Road, opp. Kirkdale station) ☎ (051) 922 3637
11.30–11
Tetley Dark Mild, Mild, Bitter Ⓗ
Three-room local. Popular with darts players, off-duty railmen, and well-behaved football supporters.
⌂ ◖ ⊟ ⇌ (Kirkdale) ♣

Prince Arthur
93 Rice Lane, 4 (A59, close to Walton Hospital)
12–11
Walker Mild, Bitter Ⓗ
Former winner of CAMRA Pub Preservation award. A visual feast outside and in. Much of the original woodwork, etched glass and tiles have been restored and enhanced. Bar and lounge plus lots of standing area in passageway (well-used). A fully appreciated pub – not just a showpiece.
⊟ ⇌ (Rice Lane/Walton) ♣

Selwyn
106 Selwyn Street, 4 (corner of Delamore Street)
☎ (051) 525 0747
11–11
Tetley Mild, Bitter Ⓗ
Three-room pub: bar with darts; lounge with pool and music, and small quiet snug. Hot snacks at all times.
◖ ◗ ⊟ ⇌ (Kirkdale) ♣

Stanley Bar
99 Stanley Road, 5 (A567, by the 'Rotunda')
☎ (051) 207 0868
12–11
Tetley Mild, Bitter Ⓗ
Pleasant three-storey building with coat of arms over the door. The multi-room interior caters for most tastes. Families welcome early in the day.
⛲ ⊟ ⇌ (Sandhills) ♣

Liverpool: South

Anglesea Arms
36 Beresford Road, 8 (opp. High Park Street market)
☎ (051) 727 4784
11.30–11 (11–11 Sat)
Tetley Mild, Bitter Ⓗ
Homely, well-kept local. Handy for market and shopping area. Lunchtime meals on request.
⛲ ⊟ ♿

Croxteth
145 Lodge Lane
11–11
Tetley Mild, Bitter Ⓗ
Large imposing exterior with island bar. Live music at weekends. Coat of arms above the door. ⛲ ♿ ⇌ (Edgehill) ♣

Mosley Arms
156 Mill Street, 8
☎ (051) 709 2721
11–11
Tetley Mild, Bitter Ⓗ
Ornate two-roomed local. Caters mainly for older clientele. The external livery is Walker's but the pub is firmly Tetley. ⊟

Poet's Corner
27 Park Hill Road, 6 (off Dingle End of Park Road)
☎ (051) 727 3240
11–11
Tetley Mild, Bitter Ⓗ
Genial two-roomed corner local known as 'Tom Masons'. Sign shows Mersey poets McGough, Henri and Patten. ⛲ ⊟

Lydiate

Running Horses
25 Bells Lane (off A567)
12–11
Ind Coope Burton Ale; Walker Mild, Best Bitter, Winter Warmer Ⓗ
Canalside pub of character, with public bar, lounge and good family room. Beer garden, play area, mini-farmyard and boules pitch. Popular with anglers.
⛲ ✿ ◖ ⊟ ♣

New Brighton

Albion Hotel
104 Albion Street (rear of Hotel Victoria) ☎ (051) 639 1832
11.30–3; 5–11 (11.30–11 Thu–Sat)
Courage Directors; John Smith's Bitter Ⓗ
Lively hotel with homely atmosphere. Regular and varied entertainment eves. Families welcome lunchtimes and before 8pm in function room. Popular for food. ⛲ ✿ 🛏 ◖ ◗ ♿ ⇌ P

Commercial
19 Hope Street (off A554, Victoria Road)
☎ (051) 639 2105
11.30–11
Walker Mild, Bitter, Best Bitter Ⓗ
Traditional street-corner local in weekend resort. Very popular with day-trippers as well as locals. Basic bar and cosy lounge with pictures of Victorian New Brighton. Table service suits the older age groups. Q ⊟ ⇌ ♣

Newton-le-Willows

Old Crow
248 Crow Lane East (A572 1 mile from centre)
☎ (09252) 5337
12–3.30 (5 Fri & Sat); 7–11
Tetley Mild, Bitter Ⓗ

Large roadside pub. The well-lit comfortable lounge is divided into two drinking areas; the popular tap room is also divided. ❀ ◐ ⊟ ♿ ♣ P

St Helens

Duke of Cambridge

Duke Street (A570)
12–4 (not Mon–Thu); 7–11
Vaux Samson; Wards Sheffield Best Bitter Ⓗ
Small local just on the edge of town centre. ⊟ ♣

Hope & Anchor

194 City Road
11.30–3.30 (5 Fri & Sat); 6.30–11
Tetley Mild, Bitter Ⓗ
Deceptively spacious pub opposite Victoria Park. Large bar and larger lounge. Disco certain nights (very loud!). ⊟ ♣

Turks Head

Cooper Street
11–11
Tetley Dark Mild, Bitter Ⓗ
Small pub, once surrounded by terraced housing, now somewhat exposed after demolitions. Re-building is underway and the pub will serve a new community. Keen darts and quiz teams.
⊟ ≈ (Central) ♣

Wheatsheaf

Westfield Street (A58)
12–11
Tetley Dark Mild, Bitter Ⓗ
Town-centre pub. Small interior subjected to 'seamless' alterations in 1989.
◐ ≈ (Central)

Southport

Bold Arms Hotel

59–61 Botanic Road, Churchtown
☎ (0704) 28192
11–11
Hydes' Anvil Bitter; Ind Coope Burton Ale; Jennings Bitter; Tetley Dark Mild, Mild, Bitter Ⓗ
Tastefully-refurbished old coaching inn in the picturesque village of Churchtown. Quizzes Mon nights. Winner of several CAMRA awards (regional Pub of the Year). Very popular.
♨ ❀ ◐ ⊟ ♿ ♣ P

Wallasey

Stanleys Cask

212 Rake Lane (B5143)
☎ (051) 691 1093
11–11
Theakston Old Peculier; Younger Scotch, IPA, No. 3 Ⓗ
Unusual pub, sold by Whitbread without a licence. Owner's fight (backed by CAMRA) succeeded on grounds that only real ale would be sold. Children welcome lunchtime and before 8pm. Varied clientele.
◐ ♿ ≈ (New Brighton) ♣

Woolton Village

Cobden Vaults

89 Quarry Street (off A562)
☎ (051) 428 2978
11–11
John Smith's Bitter Ⓗ
Friendly 'olde-worlde'-style pub in conservation-conscious village. Beer served in oversized glasses. Much bric-a-brac. ⊟

HIGSONS

'The Beer from the Heart of the City'

Higsons has been brewed in Liverpool for 209 years, fine beers brewed to suit local tastes; part of the Liverpool landscape. In recent years, Liverpool's last independent brewery was bought by Boddingtons, but still we hoped it had a future. It was therefore despicable that, when Whitbread bought Higsons, within months it had announced its closure. 'Why buy a brewery you don't want, that others might keep open?', we asked. We never got an answer.

CAMRA knew Higsons was in danger the moment it was announced that Boddingtons had sold it and the Boddingtons breweries to Whitbread. After all, a company like Whitbread which has closed ten breweries in ten years has obviously got no time for local tastes. So we were not surprised when Whitbread announced that Higsons would be closed and the beers brewed in Sheffield.

You would think that Whitbread would have learned from the closure of Wethered of Marlow, to give just one instance, that a fine beer can be ruined if moved from its home. Wethered beers, once loved, are just a pale shadow of their former self, now they are brewed in Cheltenham. The same fate awaits Higsons beers, with their strong local following, even if they are not a household name like Boddingtons. Indeed, Higsons Bitter won a Beer of the Year award in last year's *Good Beer Guide*, as one of Britain's lesser-known, but classic beers. Now the name is being used for an imposter beer: brewed elsewhere and shipped over the Pennines – a fraud.

Mersey branches have launched a vigorous campaign in support of Higsons which has made Whitbread tremble. 15,000 drinkers pledged to boycott Whitbread if the closure went ahead. At the time of writing there was talk of a new owner for the brewing plant, although everything was crowded in secrecy. But with Whitbread hanging onto the Higsons name, and the Boddingtons Pub Company still owning the pubs, the brewing heart of the city has been ripped out.

You won't find any pubs serving 'Higsons' beers in the Merseyside section of the *Guide*. That is partly because we cannot guarantee the taste of the beers from Sheffield. It is also in strong condemnation of the damage that Whitbread has done, and is doing, to the British brewing industry.

It is not just Higsons; the whole Boddingtons sell-out shows that your favourite beers may be bought tomorrow, by a national giant who wants to pad out its beer portfolio. Brewers like this don't understand what makes a beer great. What they buy today they may close tomorrow, believing we are too stupid to tell the difference.

Please think of that the next time you consider buying a pint of Whitbread.

Norfolk

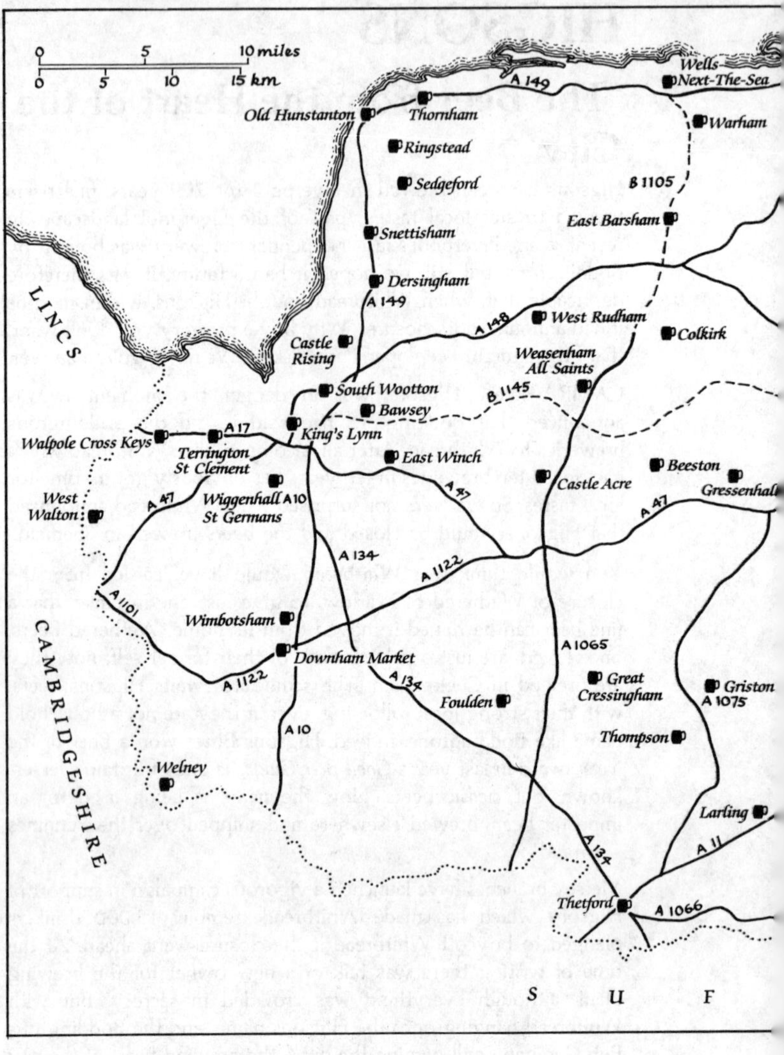

Reepham, *Reepham*; **Woodforde's**, *Woodbastwick*

Acle

Reba's Riverside Inn
Old Road (A1064, off New Acle bypass)
☎ (0493) 750310
11–3 (3.30 Sat); 6.30 (7 Sat)–11
John Smith's Bitter; Woodforde's Wherry Best Bitter Ⓗ
Small, friendly pub with restaurant, close to River Bure; moorings in nearby boat dyke.
⌂ Q ❀ ◐ P

Attleborough

Griffin
Church Street
☎ (0953) 452149
10.30–2.30; 5.30–11 (10.30–11 Thu–Sat)
Greene King Abbot Ale; Marston's Pedigree Bitter; Whitbread Wethered Bitter Ⓗ
There's a comfortable atmosphere in this 16th-century coaching inn at the centre of this market town. Fresh local produce served in bar and restaurant – also veg dishes. Guest beer.
⌂ ❀ ⇔ ◐ ≑ ♣ ⌀ P

Bawsey

Sandboy
Gayton Road (B1145, 1 mile E of King's Lynn bypass)
☎ (055 383) 557
11–2.30; 7–11
Courage Directors; Greene King IPA, Abbot Ale Ⓗ

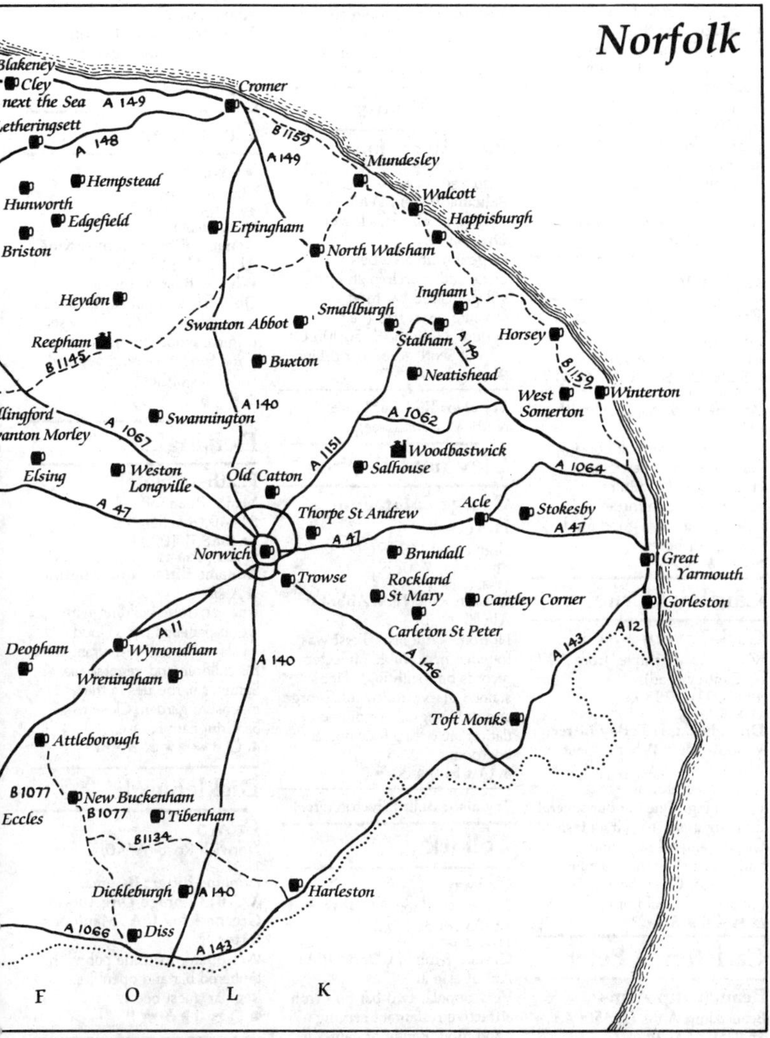

Isolated two-bar pub near Leziate Leisure Park. Family room and interesting food (children and vegetarians catered for). Guest beers.
ꝏ ▦ ◖◗ ⛺ ♣ P

Beeston

Ploughshare
The Street (off A47)
☎ (0328) 701845
11–2.30; 6.30–11
Adnams Bitter; Greene King Abbot Ale Ⓗ
Smartened up old village pub with large garden and restaurant. Guest beers and a Woodforde's house beer.
♔ Q ▦ ◖◗ ⛺ P

Billingford

Forge
Bintree Road (200 yds off B1145) ☎ (036 281) 8980
12–3; 7–11
Adnams Bitter; Greene King IPA, Abbot Ale Ⓗ
Converted old village forge with original beams. A friendly local, good for families. Guest beer. ♔ ꝏ ▦ ◗ ♣ P

Blakeney

Manor Hotel
The Quay ☎ (0263) 740376
11–2.30; 6.30–11
Adnams Bitter; Ruddles County Ⓗ
Comfortable hotel bar overlooking salt marshes. Very good, reasonably-priced food, served in bar and lounge; also a separate dining room.
Q ꝏ ▦ ⟷ ◖◗ P

Try also: Blakeney Hotel

Briston

Green Man
Hall Street (off B1354)
☎ (0263) 860993
11–3; 6–11
Greene King Abbot Ale; Woodforde's Wherry Best Bitter Ⓗ
Popular village pub, recently extended to include restaurant. Superb log fire and beams.
♔ ꝏ ▦ ◖◗ ♣ P

Brundall

Yare
Station Road
☎ (0603) 713786

Norfolk

10–2.30; 5–11 (10–11 Sat in summer)
Courage Directors; John Smith's Bitter; Woodforde's Wherry Best Bitter, Phoenix XXX Ⓗ
Comfortable and quite spacious; Broads photos and curios provide atmosphere. Liable to summer crowding as close to boatyard. Good for families. Food very good quality and value. Guest beers Fri and Sat.
⌂ ♘ ▦ ◖ ◗ ⇌ ♣ P

Buxton

Buxton Mill Tavern
Just off B1354
Coltishall–Aylsham road
OS239228 ☎ (060546) 8194
11–5; 6.30–11
Bateman XB; Samuel Smith OBB Ⓗ
Attractive watermill, housing bar, restaurant, tearoom, craftshop and furniture showroom! Comfortable, modern bar area; good food. Two guest beers.
♘ ▦ ◖ ◗ ♿ ⛺

Cantley Corner

Cock Tavern
Manor Road (3 miles from A47 on Cantley road)
☎ (0493) 700895
11–3; 6–11
Draught Bass; Tetley Bitter; Woodforde's Wherry Best Bitter Ⓗ
Popular, comfortable and welcoming. One bar but several drinking areas, to suit all tastes. Good standard pub food; barbecue in summer, families welcomed. Guest beer (occasionally mild or dark).
⌂ ♘ ▦ ◖ ◗ ⛺ ♣ P

Carleton St Peter

Beauchamp Arms
Beauchamp Arms OS350043
☎ (050843) 247
11–3; 6–11 (11–11 summer)
Woodforde's Wherry Best Bitter, Phoenix XXX Ⓗ
Popular Broadland riverside pub, much frequented by holidaying families.
♘ ◖ ◗ ⊟ ⛺ P

Try also: Rockland New Inn (Brent-Walker)

Castle Acre

Ostrich Inn
Stocks Green (off B1065)
☎ (0760) 755398
12–3; 7 (6 summer)–11
Greene King XX Dark, IPA, Rayments BBA, Abbot Ale Ⓗ
Attractive, 16th-century coaching inn on Peddars Way. Caters for locals and tourists with good meals (featured in CAMRA's *Good Pub Food*). Historic village, complete with ruined priory and castle. Camping in pub's grounds.
⌂ Q ♘ ▦ ⛟ ◖ ◗ ♿ ⛺ P

Castle Rising

Black Horse Inn
Off A149 ☎ (055 387) 225
11.30–2.30 (3 summer); 6.30–11
Adnams Bitter; Whitbread Wethered Bitter, Flowers Original Ⓗ
Large inn situated between castle and church in an historic village. Good bar food and a separate restaurant (veg option). Note the 1:50000 OS map of Scotland on bar ceiling!
⌂ Q ▦ ◖ ◗ ⛺ ⏲ P

Try also: Red Cat Hotel, North Wooton (Free)

Cley next the Sea

George & Dragon Hotel
High Street (A149)
☎ (0263) 740652
11–3; 6.30–11
Greene King IPA, Abbot Ale Ⓗ
Norfolk Naturalists Trust was founded here; Bible on lectern records bird sightings. Fine stained glass window of George and the Dragon. Accommodation includes a four-poster bedroom.
⌂ Q ▦ ⛟ ◖ ◗ ♿ ♣ P

Try also: Bell, Wiveton (Free)

Colkirk

Crown
Crown Road (off B1146)
☎ (0328) 862172
10.30–3; 6–11
Greene King XX Dark, IPA, Abbot Ale Ⓗ
Very popular two-bar pub with attractive restaurant serving good food. Range of games in public bar. Bowling green.
⌂ Q ▦ ◖ ◗ ♿ P

Cromer

Bath House
The Promenade
☎ (0263) 514260
10–3; 5.30–11 (11–11 summer, closed mid Jan–mid March)
Bateman XXXB; Greene King Abbot Ale, Rayments BBA; Samuel Smith OBB Ⓗ
Very pleasant bar on lower promenade by pier and beach. Single bar which has split levels. Friendly landlord. Regular guest beers. Q ▦ ⛟ ◖ ◗ P

Wellington
Garden Street
☎ (0263) 513750
10.30–11
Adnams Bitter; Greene King Abbot Ale Ⓗ
Two-bar pub, popular with locals and always busy. Eve meals in summer only.
⌂ ▦ ◖ ◗ ⇌ ♣

Deopham

Victoria
Church Road
☎ (0953) 850783
12–2.30 (not Tue); 7–11
Adnams Bitter; Greene King Abbot Ale; Woodforde's Wherry Best Bitter Ⓗ
Quiet friendly pub with pleasant atmosphere. Single bar boasts original wood beams. Very good food, including veg and children's dishes.
⌂ ▦ ◖ ◗ ⛺ ♣ ⏲ P

Dersingham

Feathers Hotel
Manor Road (off A149, on B1440 to Hillington)
☎ (0485) 40207
11–2.30; 5.30–11
Adnams Bitter; Charrington IPA Ⓗ
Fine carrstone building with wood-panelled bars. Good meals in bar and restaurant cater for children and vegetarians. Summer barbecues in the extensive garden. Close to Sandringham House.
⌂ Q ▦ ⛟ ◖ ◗ ♿ ⛺ ♣ P

Dickleburgh

Crown
Norwich Road (A140)
11–11
Adnams Bitter; Bateman XXXB; Courage Directors; Greene King IPA; Mauldons Bitter Ⓗ
Welcoming roadside pub with timbered bar and open fire. Regular guest beers.
⌂ Q ♘ ◖ ◗ ♿ ♣ P

Diss

White Elephant
Stuston Road (B1118 off A1066) ☎ (0379) 651904
10–2.30; 6–11 (10–11 Sat)
Adnams Bitter; Greene King Abbot Ale Ⓖ
Cosy locals' pub with separate restaurant area serving reasonably-priced food. Two brick fireplaces and brick bar. Games area. ⛟ ◖ ◗ ♣ ⏲ P

Downham Market

Cock Tavern
Lynn Road ☎ (0366) 385047
11–2.30; 7–11
John Smith's Bitter; Whitbread Castle Eden Ale Ⓗ
Comfortable and friendly pub with award-winning healthy

food; veg option. No food Sun lunch or Tue eve. ⌂ Q ❀ ◖ ◗ P

Crown Hotel
Bridge Street (opp. Town Hall)
☎ (0366) 382322
11–2.30; 6–11 (11–11 Fri & Sat)
Bateman XXXB; Greene King Abbot Ale; Woodforde's Wherry Best Bitter [H]
Totally unrenovated bar in old coaching inn displaying memorabilia from local wartime RAF base. Regular guest beers.
⌂ Q ❀ ⛟ ◖ ◗ ⇌ P

East Barsham

White Horse Inn
Fakenham Road (B1105)
☎ (0328) 820645
11.30–2.30; 6 (7 winter)–11
Adnams Bitter; Greene King Abbot Ale; Tolly Cobbold Original; Woodforde's Wherry Best Bitter [H]
Traditional country pub in a lovely 16th-century beamed building, now one single bar with a separate restaurant. Splendid large fireplace.
⌂ Q ⛟ ◖ ◗ ♿ ♣ P

East Winch

Carpenters Arms
Lynn Road (A47)
☎ (0553) 841228
11–2.30; 6 (6.30 Sat)–11
Greene King IPA, Abbot Ale [H]
Welcome pub on dry part of A47. Closed by Watneys and reopened as a free house after a local campaign. Relaxed and friendly atmosphere. Features guest beers not normally available locally.
Q ❀ ◖ ◗ ♿ ♣ P

Eccles

Old Railway Tavern
Station Road (next to station)
☎ (095 387) 788
12–2.30; 5.30–11
Adnams Bitter; Greene King IPA, Abbot Ale [H]
Known locally as the 'Tap'. Mind your head on entering! Family room doubles as pool room. Good value food (not Sun lunchtime).
⌂ Q ⛵ ❀ ◖ ◗ ⇌ (Eccles Road) ♣ ⌓ P

Edgefield

Three Pigs
3 miles S of Holt on B1149
OS098344 ☎ (0263) 87634
11–2.30; 6 (7 winter)–11
Adnams Bitter; Woodforde's Wherry Best Bitter [H]
Unspoilt pub, over 200 years-old, with single brick fronted bar. Thought to have had smuggling connections. Small site for five caravans (CC approved). Guest beer in summer. Home-cooked food (not Mon eve). Q ❀ ◖ ◗ P

Elsing

Mermaid Inn
Church Street (from A47 and A1067 follow sign to Lyng)
☎ (036 283) 640
12–2.30; 7–11 (varies weekends)
Adnams Bitter [H], Old, Tally-Ho [G]; Charles Wells Bombardier [H]; Woodforde's Norfolk Nog (Xmas) [G]; Young's Special [H]
Last pub in village, set opposite the church which contains a famous brass. Now one single bar, with plain decor. Separate restaurant (caters for children and vegetarians); no food Mon. Unusual guest beers.
⌂ ❀ ◖ ◗ ♣ P

Erpingham

Spread Eagle
☎ (0263) 761591
11–2.30; 6.30–11
Woodforde's Wherry Best Bitter, Porter, Phoenix XXX, Norfolk Nog, Baldric [H]
Situated on the Weavers Way. Formerly Woodforde's brewery tap – the old brewhouse stands alongside. Very popular with both locals and tourists, particularly walkers. Woodforde's house beer on draught. ⌂ Q ❀ ◖ ◗ ♿ ▲ ⌓ P

Try also: Saracens Head, Wolterton (Free)

Foulden

White Hart Inn
White Hart Street (3 miles from A134 nr. Mundford)
☎ (036621) 638
12–3; 6–11
Greene King IPA, Abbot Ale [H]
Typical country pub with a nice atmosphere and a nicely appointed, spacious restaurant. Guest beers.
⌂ Q ❀ ◖ ◗ ♣ ⌓ P

Try also: Great Danes Head, Beechamwell (Free)

Gorleston

New Entertainer
80 Pier Plain
☎ (0493) 653218
11.30–4; 7–11 (11.30–11 Sat)
Adnams Extra, Broadside; Draught Bass; Greene King XX Dark, Abbot Ale; Wadworth 6X [H]
Formerly a Lacons house, this Victorian building has an unusual rounded end. Sympathetic modernisation included new window to match Lacons' model. A good range of beers and friendly service. Q ♣

Short Blue
47 High Street
☎ (0493) 602192
11–11
Everards Old Original; Greene King IPA; Scotties Hopleaf Best Bitter, William French [H]
A cosy, wood-panelled interior in a pub named after the world's largest fishing fleet. Stained glass windows in bar; the rear garden overlooks the river. Now sells own brewery (Scotties) beers, with regular guests. Q ❀ ◖ ◗

Great Cressingham

Windmill Inn
Water End (off A1065)
☎ (07606) 232
11–2.30; 6.30–11
Adnams Bitter, Old, Broadside; Draught Bass; Bateman XXXB; Samuel Smith OBB [H]
Original oak-beamed pub with three bars and four other areas, including a conservatory. Large garden and full caravanning facilities in grounds; safe for children. Ask for board games. Two guest beers.
⌂ Q ⛵ ❀ ◖ ◗ ⊞ ♣ P

Try also: Swan, Hillborough (Free)

Great Yarmouth

Albert Tavern
20–21 Southgates Road (facing South Quay)
☎ (0493) 855016
10.30–3; 5 (7 Sat)–11
Greene King IPA [H]
Large, one room pub with circular bar and separate games area. Good value food. Guest beers (total of six real ales available). Close to South Denes campsite. ⌂ ⛵ ◖ ▲ ♣

Clipper Schooner
Friars Way (off South Quay)
☎ (0493) 854926
11–3; 7–11
Adnams Mild, Bitter, Broadside [H]
Modernised, two-roomed 1930s pub. A popular local close to the old town wall, Blackfriars Tower and docks. Piano in bar. No food at weekend. ⛵ ❀ ◖ ♿ P

Red Herring
24–25 Havelock Road (near old town wall)
11–3.30; 6–11
Adnams Mild, Bitter; Courage Directors [H]
One-bar pub; pool played in separate room. Popular with

locals. Paperback library service. Home-cooked food. Four guest beers in summer; twice-yearly beer festivals. ♉ ◖◗ ♣ ⌽

Talbot
Howard Street North (by police station) ☎ (0493) 843175
11–11
Greene King Abbot Ale; Scotties Hopleaf Best Bitter; Younger No. 3 🄷
Popular with the young leather brigade. A one-room pub close to the market place. Good guest beer range. Euchre played. ≹ ♣

Gressenhall

Swan
The Green (off B1146)
☎ (0362) 860340
11.30–3; 7–11
Greene King IPA 🄷**, Abbot Ale** 🄶
Friendly locals' pub, handy for Norfolk Rural Life Museum. No food Wed eve; book for Sun lunch. ♔ Q ♉ ❀ ◖◗ ⊞ ♿ ♣

Try also: Beetley New Inn

Griston

Waggon & Horses
Church Road (3 miles S of Watton on B1075) OS944994
☎ (0953) 883847
11–3; 6.30–11
Greene King XX Dark, IPA, Rayments BBA, Abbot Ale 🄷
Large, comfortable village pub, generally quiet and friendly. Good quality food (veg option). Rare outlet for XX Dark in this area. Q ❀ ◖◗ ♣ P

Happisburgh

Hill House
The Hill (100 yds off B1159)
☎ (0692) 650004
11–3 (2.30 winter); 6 (7 winter)–11
Adnams Bitter; Greene King Abbot Ale; Woodforde's Wherry Best Bitter 🄷
16th-century pub with beamed ceiling and inglenook. Restaurant offers daily home-cooked specials (veg and children's dishes, too). Plenty of toys in family room, situated in adjoining outbuilding.
♔ Q ♉ ❀ ◖◗ ♣ P

Try also: Victoria, Happisburgh Common (Free)

Harleston

Cherry Tree
74 London Road (½ mile out of town on A1143)
☎ (0379) 852345
11–2.30; 5.30–11
Adnams Mild, Bitter, Old, Extra 🄷
Unspoilt village pub with two bars. Lounge heated by cooking range. Outside loos.
♔ Q ❀ ◖ ♣ P

Hempstead

Hare & Hounds
Baconsthorpe Road (actually in Baconsthorpe) OS117372
☎ (0263) 713285
11–3; 6.30–11
Adnams Bitter; Draught Bass; Bateman XXXB 🄷
Only a mole disturbs the quiet of this lovely village pub, but it's worth finding. Separate children's room. Self-catering accommodation. Goats in the garden. House beer.
♔ ♉ ❀ ◖◗ ⊞ P

Heydon

Earle Arms
Near B1149 OS114275
☎ (026 387) 376
11–2.30; 6.30–11
Adnams Bitter, Old, Tally-Ho; Greene King Abbot Ale 🄶
Unspoilt pub in delightful old village setting, sometimes used for period TV dramas. Space for tents behind pub.
Q ♉ ❀ ⛺ ◖◗ ♿ P

Horsey

Nelson Head
The Street (just off B1159)
☎ (0493) 393378
11(10.30 summer)–2.30 (12–2 Sun); 7(6 summer)–11
Adnams Bitter, Broadside 🄷
Friendly, one-bar country pub with nautical artefacts and a separate dining room. Popular with visitors to marshes and Horsey Mill. Walking distance from Broads and beach.
♔ ♉ ❀ ◖◗ ♣ P

Hunworth

Bluebell
The Green OS070352
☎ (0263) 712300
11–3; 6–11
Adnams Bitter; Greene King Abbot Ale; Woodforde's Wherry Best Bitter 🄷
Welcoming pub on village green. Real log fire and good food. Pleasant secluded garden.
♔ Q ♉ ❀ ◖◗ ⊞ P

Ingham

Swan Inn
Swan Corner (B1151 Stalham – Sea Palling road)
☎ (0692) 81099
11–3; 7–11 (11–11 summer)
Adnams Bitter; Ruddles County; Woodforde's Wherry Best Bitter 🄷
Heavily-restored, thatched country pub with such a quantity of exposed beams and brickwork that it must be genuine (built in 14th century). Good local trade. Strong emphasis on food. Guest beers.
♔ ♉ ❀ ⛺ ◖◗ ⊞ P

King's Lynn

Lattice House
Chapel Street (off Tuesday Market Place)
☎ (0553) 777292
11–2.30; 7–11 (11–11 Fri & Sat)
Courage Best Bitter, Directors; Greene King IPA 🄷
Lively town-centre pub in an historic 15th-century building. Regular guest beers. Lunchtime snacks. ❀ ⊞ ♿ ≹ P

London Porterhouse
78 London Road (near South Gates) ☎ (0553) 766842
11.30–2.30 (3 Fri, 4.30 Sat); 5.30 (7 Sat)–11
Greene King IPA, Abbot Ale 🄶
Tiny, welcoming pub with a mixed clientele. Regular events range from conkers to quizzes. Only gravity dispense in the area. Q ❀ ◖ ≹ ♣

Tudor Rose
St Nicholas Street (off Tuesday Market Place)
☎ (0553) 762824
11–3; 5 (5.30 Sat)–11
Adnams Bitter, Broadside; Draught Bass 🄷
15th-century timbered pub with oak-beamed bars and restaurant. Excellent food in both, all freshly-made. One quiet bar and one noisy. Guest beers.
Q ❀ ⛺ ◖◗ ⊞ ≹

Try also: Bankhouse (Free); **Crossways** (Greene King); **Wildfowler** (Ansells)

Larling

Angel
Beside A11 ☎ (0953) 717963
11–11 (if busy)
Ruddles Best Bitter, County; Webster's Yorkshire Bitter 🄷
Busy pub both with holiday traffic and locals, especially from the farming community. Genuine public bar. Eve meals Fri and Sat only.
♔ Q ❀ ⛺ ◖◗ ⊞ ≹ (Harling Rd) ♣ P

Letheringsett

Kings Head
Holt Road (A148, just W of Holt) ☎ (0263) 712691
11–3; 6–11
Adnams Bitter; Draught Bass; Greene King IPA, Abbot Ale 🄷
Lovely old beamed pub in delightful garden setting. Old brewery buildings stand

adjacent to the pub. A quiet walk to River Glaven and mill nearby. Good, reasonably-priced food. Guest beer. Pool room. Children welcome.
Q ♿ ♣ P

Mundesley

Royal Hotel
Paston Road (B1159)
☎ (0263) 720096
11–2.30; 5.30–11
Adnams Bitter; Charrington IPA; Greene King Abbot Ale [H]
Old beamed bar in hotel with Nelson connections. Excellent food at reasonable prices in a comfortable dining room which caters for vegetarians. Guest beers. Lots of charm and character. Q P

Neatishead

White Horse
The Street ($1\frac{1}{2}$ miles E of A1151) ☎ (0692) 630828
11–3; 6 (7 winter)–11
Courage Directors; Greene King IPA; Whitbread Wethered Bitter [H]
Classic, traditional, rural Norfolk pub, featuring a good display of antique farming implements. Much-favoured by both locals and Broadland holiday-makers from nearby Neatishead Staithe. Separate dining room. Guest beers. Q ♣ P

Try also: Barton Angler

New Buckenham

George
Chapel Street (B1113)
☎ (0953) 860043
11–3; 6–11
Camerons Strongarm; Courage Directors; Greene King IPA; Whitbread Flowers IPA [H]
Large village pub with original sash windows.
P

North Walsham

Scarborough Hill House Hotel
Old Yarmouth Road
☎ (0692) 402151
11–3; 7–11
Bateman XB [G]
Hotel with bar and dining area, set in large grounds, in rural surroundings on the outskirts of the town. Occasional guest beers. Q P

Norwich

Black Horse
Earlham Road
☎ (0603) 624682
10.30–11
Adnams Extra; Marston's Pedigree Bitter; Whitbread Flowers IPA, Boddingtons Bitter, Flowers Original; Woodforde's Wherry Best Bitter [H]
Busy yet comfortable pub with friendly atmosphere and excellent carvery restaurant.
Q ♣

Bread & Cheese
111 Adelade Street (500 yds from A47, off Old Palace Road)
☎ (0603) 615603
11–3; 5.30–11 (11–11 Sat)
Adnams Bitter; Draught Bass [H]
Friendly corner local with regular guest beers. Note the original Bullards stained glass windows. ♿ P

Coach & Horses
Bethel Street
☎ (0603) 631337
11–11
Greene King IPA, Rayments BBA, Abbot Ale [H]
City-centre pub near the fire station. High standard of decor and good food (not Sun). Q

Freemasons
27 Hall Road
☎ (0603) 623768
11–3 (5.30 Sat); 6 (7.30 Sat)–11
Courage Best Bitter, Directors [H]
Busy, single bar with friendly licensee. Situated in a good drinking area and very popular at lunchtimes. Good for pub games. ♿ ♣

Gardeners Arms
2–4 Timber Hill
☎ (0603) 621447
11–11
Adnams Bitter; Draught Bass; Ind Coope Burton Ale; Tetley Bitter; Woodforde's Wherry Best Bitter [H]
Very old free house, popular with the younger pub-goer. Bottled beers from around the world. Unusual sign as both sides are different: Gardeners Arms one side; The Murderers the other.

Golden Star
Duke Street ☎ (0603) 632447
11–11 (11–4; 5.30–11 Sat)
Greene King XX Dark, IPA, Rayments BBA, Abbot Ale [H]
Popular and friendly pub close to city centre, with newly-refurbished back bar. The former home of the Star Brewery. Traditional home-cooking (veg option), not Sun. Q

Horse & Dray
137 Ber Street
☎ (0603) 624741
11–11
Adnams Mild, Bitter, Old, Extra, Broadside, Tally-Ho [H]
Busy, large, city Adnams house with plush decor. Real fire in main bar area, a warm welcome and good food. ♿ ♣

Jubilee
26 St Leonards Road
☎ (0603) 618734
11–11
Greene King Abbot Ale; Marston's Pedigree Bitter; Whitbread Boddingtons Bitter [H]
Victorian corner pub with two bars plus outdoor drinking area. Games room upstairs. Guest beers and Woodforde's house beer. ♣

Micawbers
92 Pottergate (up Grapes Hill, turn left and left again)
☎ (0603) 626627
11–3; 5–11 (11–11 Sat)
Adnams Bitter; Draught Bass; Hall & Woodhouse Tanglefoot; Samuel Smith OBB; Wadworth 6X [H]
City-centre pub with typical local trade. Split-level bars. Different beers at each end of pub. Popular with students. Guest beers.

Mill Tavern
2 Millers Lane (off Angel Road)
11–3; 6 (4.30 summer)–11
Adnams Mild, Bitter, Old, Broadside [H]
Long, one-roomed bar aimed at drinkers and conversationalists. Old, familiar, cosy and plain, with no gimmicks. Darts and crib are popular. Close to Waterloo Park and used by bowls players. Guest beer.
Q ♿ ♣ P

Plough
58 St Benedicts Street
☎ (0603) 626333
11–2.30; 4.30–11 (11–11 Fri & Sat)
Courage Best Bitter, Directors [H]
A very old and unspoilt city institution. Popular with a cosmopolitan crowd. ♣

Pottergate Tavern
23 Pottergate (200 yds N of City Hall) ☎ (0603) 614589
11–11 (closed Sun lunch)
Greene King XX Dark, IPA, Rayments BBA, Abbot Ale; Woodforde's Wherry Best Bitter [H]
Distinctive, 1930s corner pub with two rooms on different levels. Reasonably-priced home-cooked food (not Sun eve). Guest beers always available.
♣

Queens Arms
102 Magdalen Street
☎ (0603) 627667
10.30–11
Adnams Bitter; Benskins Best Bitter; Ind Coope Burton Ale [H]

Norfolk

Popular oak-panelled local near TV studios and 'Anglia Square' shopping precinct. Good value food (until 7.30). ◐ ♣

Reindeer

10 Dereham Road
☎ (0603) 66682
11–3; 5.30–11 (11–11 Sat)
Bateman XXXB; Elgood's Bitter; Wadworth 6X; Whitbread Boddingtons Bitter Ⓗ
Guest beers are numerous and varied in this popular city real ale-drinkers' pub with its own brewery. Bare boards; occasional folk music. House beers kept under blanket pressure. Q ❀ ◐ ◑ ♣ ⌽ P

Ribs of Beef

24 Wensum Street
☎ (0603) 619517
10.30–11
Adnams Bitter; Bateman Dark Mild; Reepham Rapier Pale Ale; Theakston Best Bitter; Whitbread Flowers IPA; Woodforde's Wherry Best Bitter Ⓗ
Up to 11 real beers (plus real cider) in this attractive and busy city-centre, riverside pub. Moorings available.
Q ♉ ◐ ♣ ⌽

Rosary Tavern

95 Rosary Road (from station, turn right along Thorpe Road then first left)
☎ (0603) 666287
11–3; 5.30–11
Adnams Bitter; Bateman XXXB; Marston's Pedigree Bitter; Phoenix XXX Ⓗ
Small, friendly free house, close to yacht station. Guest beers served from rear cellar. Woodforde's house beer available (Rosary Bitter). Limited parking. ❀ ◐ ◑ ⇌ ♣ ⌽ P

Rose

Queens Road
☎ (0603) 620159
11–2.30; 5.30–11
Adnams Mild, Bitter, Old, Broadside Ⓗ
Well-run, friendly corner pub on main route into city from Ipswich, in an area good for real ale. Live music often featured.
⌂ ❀ ◐ ♿ ♣

St Andrews Tavern

4 St Andrews Street
☎ (0603) 614858
11–11 (closed Sun)
Adnams Bitter, Broadside, Tally-Ho; Brains Dark Ⓗ
Seven handpumps in this cosmopolitan city-centre bar with conservatory. Cellar bar available for functions. Close to multi-storey car park. Good range of guest beers. ♉ ❀ ◐ ♿

Spread Eagle

Sussex Street
☎ (0603) 629760
11–3; 5–11 (11–11 Fri & Sat)
Courage Best Bitter, Directors; Greene King IPA, Abbot Ale; Whitbread Wethered Bitter Ⓗ
Traditional, one-roomed, locals' pub with pool area. Phat also played. Barbecue in garden.
❀ ♣

Try also: Coach & Horses (Greene King)

Old Catton

Woodman

11 North Walsham Road (B1150, 2 miles N of Norwich city centre) ☎ (0603) 426655
11–3; 5.30–11
Marston's Pedigree Bitter; Whitbread Flowers IPA, Wethered Bitter, Flowers Original Ⓔ
Small public bar; larger lounge. Heavy lunchtime food trade. Pleasant garden. One of the nicer pubs in this suburban area.
Q ❀ ◐ ◑ ⊟ ♿ ♣

Try also: Duke of Norfolk, Sprowston (Courage)

Old Hunstanton

Ancient Mariner

Le Strange Arms Hotel, Golf Course Road (off A149)
☎ (0485) 534411
11–3; 6–11
Adnams Bitter, Broadside; Draught Bass; Charrington IPA Ⓗ
Large bar, part of Le Strange Arms Hotel, nevertheless retaining a pub-like atmosphere. Low beams, nautical decor and intimate drinking areas for the adults, plus a room and garden for the children. Guest beers.
⌂ ♉ ❀ ⊨ ◐ ◑ ♿ ♣ P

Neptune Inn

Cromer Road (A149)
☎ (0485) 532122
12–3; 6–11
Adnams Bitter; Greene King Abbot Ale Ⓗ
Former coaching inn with a much-travelled landlord. A traditional pub in a town where few are to be found. Guest beers. Q ⊨ ◐ ◑ ♣ P

Ringstead

Gin Trap Inn

High Street ☎ (048525) 264
11.30–2.30 (3 summer); 7 (6 summer)–11
Adnams Bitter; Greene King Abbot Ale; Ruddles Best Bitter; Woodforde's Phoenix XXX Ⓗ
Petanque is played at this country village pub which boasts a collection of animal traps. A split-level bar and a pleasant garden make it ideal for idyllic summer evenings. Guest beers and a Woodforde's house beer. ⌂ ❀ ◐ ◑ ♣ P

Rockland St Mary

New Inn

12 New Inn Hill (take A146 from Norwich, fork left at Crown Point) ☎ (05088) 395
11–2.30; 6.30–11 (12–2; 7.30–11 winter)
Courage Directors; John Smith's Bitter Ⓗ
Comfortable, friendly local on edge of village. Moorings for boats opposite. Games include shove-ha'penny and Shut the Box. Excellent home-cooked food. Guest beers.
⌂ ♉ ❀ ◐ ◑ ♣ P

Salhouse

Lodge

Rectory Road (just off Wroxham Road)
☎ (0603) 782828
11–2.30; 6–11
Greene King IPA, Abbot Ale; Theakston XB; Woodforde's Wherry Best Bitter Ⓗ
Opened in 1976 in former Georgian rectory. Beautiful gardens and grounds. Nearest pub to Woodforde's brewery. Excellent food (children and vegetarians catered for).
⌂ ❀ ◐ ◑ ♿ P

Try also: Hotel Wroxham, Hoveton (Free)

Sedgeford

King William IV

Heacham Road (B1454)
☎ (0485) 71765
11–3; 6.30–11
Draught Bass; Charrington IPA; Greene King Abbot Ale Ⓗ
Lively landlord provides gossip, entertainment and music *à la carte*. Lounge, public bar and snug; good value meals (including veg option). Make a detour from the coast road to beat the traffic and find an excellent pub. Guest beers.
⌂ ❀ ◐ ◑ ⛺ ♣ ⌽ P

Smallburgh

Crown

North Walsham Road (A149, Stalham Road)
☎ (069 260) 314
11.30–2.30 (4 Sat); 5.30 (6.30 Sat)–11
Greene King IPA; John Smith's Bitter; Whitbread Flowers IPA Ⓗ
Thatched and beamed building which dates from 15th century. Large open fire; tables and chairs made from wooden barrels and firkins. A friendly locals' pub. Good food in attractive restaurant (not

Sun/Mon eves). Guest beers.
♨ ⊛ ◖ ◗ ⊡ ♣ P

Snettisham

Rose & Crown
Old Church Road (off A149)
☎ (0485) 41382
11–3; 5.30–11
Adnams Bitter; Greene King IPA, Abbot Ale; Woodforde's Wherry Best Bitter Ⓗ
14th-century inn with a separate restaurant and indoor barbecue. Penny Seat played. Children's room and newly-built play area in garden.
♨ Q ⚯ ◖ ◗ ♿ ⛺ ♣ P

South Wootton

Farmers Arms
Knights Hill Village (just off A149) ☎ (0553) 675566
11–11
Adnams Bitter, Broadside; Draught Bass; Charrington IPA; Ruddles County; Samuel Smith OBB Ⓗ
Beautiful barn conversion on old farm site still under development. Good food and regular attractions at conference centre. Motel and sports complex at hand.
♨ Q ⚯ ⊛ 🛏 ◖ ◗ ♿ ⛺ ♣ P

Try also: Ffolkes Arms, Hillington (Free)

Stalham

Kingfisher Hotel
High Street
☎ (0692) 81974/80012
11–2.30; 6.30–11
Adnams Bitter; Woodforde's Wherry Best Bitter Ⓗ
Large, modern hotel and restaurant complex.
⚯ ⊛ 🛏 ◖ ◗ P

Stokesby

Ferry Inn
Ferry Lane ☎ (0493) 751096
11–3; 6.30–11
Adnams Extra; Whitbread Flowers IPA, Wethered Bitter Ⓗ
Popular in summer, a large, single-roomed, riverside pub with a converted barn for functions. ♨ ⚯ ⊛ ◖ ◗ P

Swannington

Swannington Hall
Church Lane OS139194
☎ (0603) 868412
12–3; 6–11
Adnams Bitter; Greene King IPA, Rayments BBA Ⓗ
Large, 16th-century, moated manor house set in over five acres. Great for families with barbecue in summer. Robert Kett was caught in Swannington and held at Hall awaiting transit to Norwich where he was later sentenced to death. Guest beers.
♨ ⚯ ⊛ 🛏 ◖ ◗ ♣ P

Swanton Abbot

Weavers Arms
Aylsham Road
☎ (069 269) 655
11–2.30; 7–11
Marston's Pedigree Bitter; Whitbread Wethered Bitter, Castle Eden Ale, Flowers Original Ⓗ
Busy and popular, two-bar village locals' pub. Occasional beer festivals. Games room.
♨ ⊛ ◖ ◗ ♣ P

Try also: Jolly Farmers (Free)

Swanton Morley

Darby's
Elsing Road (B1147 jct)
☎ (036 283) 647
11–3; 6–11
Adnams Bitter, Broadside; Hall & Woodhouse Tanglefoot; Taylor Landlord; Theakston Old Peculier; Woodforde's Wherry Best Bitter Ⓗ
New pub constructed from two derelict cottages in response to Watney's threat to close one of the village pubs. Has a genuine local feel, a warm welcome and great quality (and value) food. An outstanding achievement.
♨ Q ⚯ ⊛ ◖ ◗ ♿ P

Terrington St Clement

County Arms
Marshland Street (off A17)
☎ (0553) 828511
12–11
Adnams Bitter; Greene King IPA, Abbot Ale Ⓗ
Olde-worlde charm; oak beams, open fires and a warm friendly atmosphere. Close to a renowned African Violet centre.
Q ⊛ ◖ ♿ P

Thetford

Albion
Castle Street (opp. Castle Hill ancient monument)
☎ (0842) 752796
11–2.30; 6–11
Greene King IPA, Abbot Ale Ⓗ
Small, comfortable and friendly, flint-faced pub in older part of town. By far the cheapest IPA in the area. Small garden and car park. Q ⊛ ◖ ♣ P

Bell Hotel
Bridge Street
☎ (0842) 754455
11–2.30; 6–11
Adnams Bitter, Broadside; Greene King IPA Ⓗ
Large hotel but only one public bar, comfortable and with some character. Originally a 16th-century coaching inn with exposed beams. Spirits and wines are expensive.
Q 🛏 ◖ ◗ ⇶ P

Try also: Old Mill (Free)

Thompson

Chequers Inn
Griston Road (4 miles S of Watton) OS923969
☎ (095 383) 360
11–3; 6–11
Adnams Bitter; Draught Bass; Charrington IPA Ⓗ
Unspoilt, 16th-century, thatched pub, well off the beaten track. Has well-deserved reputation amongst locals. Three bars, two of which feature very low beams and ceilings. Very small family room; excellent value food. Extremely busy all year. Guest beers.
Q ⚯ ⊛ ◖ ◗ P

Thornham

Lifeboat Inn
Ship Lane (off A149)
☎ (048 526) 236
11–3; 6–11 (11–11 summer)
Adnams Bitter; Greene King IPA, Abbot Ale Ⓗ
Overlooking the sea marshes, a 16th-century smugglers' inn, lit by oil lamps. Good value accommodation; garden play area and family room. Regular guest beers. Penny in the Hole played.
♨ Q ⚯ ⊛ 🛏 ◖ ◗ ⊡ ⛺ ♣ ◯ P

Thorpe St Andrew

Gordon
88 Gordon Avenue
☎ (0603) 34658
11–2.30; 7–11
Greene King IPA, Abbot Ale; John Smith's Bitter Ⓗ
Popular estate pub with a friendly atmosphere. Guest beer.
♨ ⊛ ◖ ♣ P

Tibenham

Greyhound
The Street (2 miles E of B1113) OS136895 ☎ (037 977) 676
12–2; 6.30–11
Beer varies Ⓗ
Popular local with two bars and selection of traditional wooden bar games, together with a small library. Woodforde's K9 house beer accompanies the guest. Menu caters for vegetarians (no food Tue).
♨ Q ⚯ ⊛ 🛏 ◖ ◗ ⊡ ♿ ⛺ ♣ P

Try also: Fox & Hounds, Great Moulton (Whitbread)

Norfolk

Toft Monks

Lion
Yarmouth Road (A143 Beccles-Haddiscoe road) OS430947
☎ (050 277) 702
11.30–2.30; 6.30–11
Adnams Bitter, Old; Woodforde's Wherry Best Bitter Ⓗ
Friendly local pub, modernised and comfortable. Formerly a Morgans house. No food Tue eve. ⌂ ♞ ☗ ⛟ ◖ ◗ ♿ ⛺ ♁ P

Trowse

Crown Point
☎ (0603) 625689
11–3; 5.30 (6.30 Sat)–11
Marston's Pedigree Bitter; Whitbread Wethered Bitter, Flowers Original Ⓗ
Solid and friendly pub featuring traditional Norfolk half-panelled walls and settles in both bars.
☗ ◖ ◗ ⊟ ♣ P

Try also: White Horse (Brent-Walker)

Walcott

Lighthouse
On B1159, coast road
☎ (0692) 650371
11–2.30; 7–11
Ind Coope Burton Ale; Tetley Bitter Ⓗ
Friendly and well-used locals' pub on remote part of Norfolk coast, close to Bacton North Sea Gas terminal. ⌂ ♞ ◖ ◗ P

Walpole Cross Keys

Woolpack Inn
On old A17 ☎ (0553) 828327
12–3; 7–11
Adnams Bitter, Broadside Ⓗ
A pleasant country pub with a friendly atmosphere, situated in a quiet position.
⌂ Q ♞ ☗ ◖ ◗ ♿ ♣ P

Warham

Horseshoes
Bridge Street
☎ (0328) 710547
11–2.30 (12–2.30 Sun); 7–11
Greene King IPA Ⓗ**, Abbot Ale; Woodforde's Wherry Best Bitter** Ⓖ
Old, unspoilt, gas-lit pub with a 1921 electric pianola and an old gramophone (Sat nights). Pub games. Pool in family room. Norfolk wheel game on bar ceiling. Eve meals Thu–Sat.
⌂ ♞ ☗ ⛟ ◖ ◗ ♣ P

Weasenham All Saints

Ostrich
Beside A1065
☎ (032 874) 221
11–3; 7–11
Adnams Extra; Greene King IPA Ⓗ
Tiny, friendly village pub beside main road. Basic furnishings and fittings, but a warm fire and a warm welcome. You can also buy your fresh vegetables here! Children welcome if eating.
⌂ Q ☗ ◖ ◗ ⛺ ♣ P

Wells-Next-The-Sea

Crown
Buttlands (near A149)
☎ (0328) 710209
11–2.30; 6–11
Adnams Bitter; Marston's Pedigree Bitter; Tetley Bitter Ⓗ
Fine hotel facing the tree-lined green. A Tudor building with a Georgian facade, formerly a school and town manor. Good food in the bar or restaurant. Guest beer.
⌂ ♞ ☗ ⛟ ◖ ◗ ♿ ♣ P

Golden Fleece
The Quay
☎ (0328) 710650
11–11
Camerons Strongarm; Whitbread Castle Eden Ale, Flowers Original, Wethered Winter Royal Ⓗ
Friendly, two-bar, locals' pub, overlooking the quay. Upstairs room for families and functions; adults only in bars. Bar snacks include tasty shellfish.
♞ ☗ ⊟ ⛺ ♣ P

Try also: Edinburgh (Free)

Welney

Three Tuns
Bedford Bank East
☎ (035 471) 254
11–2.30; 7–11
Elgood's Bitter Ⓗ
Simple, unchanged Fenland local with a long-standing, friendly landlord. Popular with fishermen and handy for the Welney Wildlife Centre.
⌂ Q ☗ ⊟ ♿ ⛺ ♣ P

Try also: Red Lion, Outwell (Elgood's)

Weston Longville

Parson Woodforde
Elsing Road (9 miles NW of Norwich, just off A1067) OS113159 ☎ (0603) 880106
12–3; 6–11
Adnams Bitter; Draught Bass; Hall & Woodhouse Tanglefoot; Marston's Pedigree Bitter; Woodforde's Wherry Best Bitter Ⓗ
Ex-Watney house, refurbished a few years ago. A three-room, rural pub with great atmosphere, fire, welcome and food.
⌂ ☗ ◖ ◗ P

West Rudham

Dukes Head
Lynn Road (A148)
☎ (048 522) 540
11–3; 5.30 (6.30 winter)–11
Adnams Bitter; Greene King Abbot Ale; Woodforde's Wherry Best Bitter Ⓗ
Flint and carrstone pub beside main road. Popular with locals and busy with summer tourists. Good selection of games and a wide variety of reference books (eg *Wisden*). ⌂ ◖ ◗ ♣ P

West Somerton

Lion
On Yarmouth–Cromer coast route, B1152/B1159 jct.
☎ (0493) 393289
11–3; 6–11
Greene King XX Dark, IPA, Abbot Ale Ⓗ
Friendly, two-bar village local, well-used by tourists in summer. Darts popular. Half-portions of meals served for children.
Q ♞ ☗ ◖ ◗ ⊟ ♿ ⛺ ♣ P

West Walton

King of Hearts
School Road (off A47)
OS472132 ☎ (0945) 584785
11–2.30; 6.30–11
Elgood's Bitter Ⓗ
Plush lounge bar and separate restaurant. Excellent beer; renowned throughout Fenland country for its food (children and vegetarians catered for).
⌂ Q ☗ ◖ ◗ ♿ P

Wiggenhall St Germans

Crown & Anchor
Lynn Road OS595140
☎ (0553) 85340
11–2.30; 7–11
Greene King IPA, Abbot Ale Ⓗ
Friendly local pub on the riverbank and near the village church. If asking directions, note that locals call the village 'St Germans'.
⌂ Q ☗ ◖ ◗ ♿ ♣ P

Wimbotsham

Chequers
7 Church Road (off old A10)
OS622050 ☎ (0366) 387704
11.45–2.30; 7–11
Greene King IPA, Abbot Ale Ⓗ
Pleasant, friendly, long, low, one-bar pub; off the usual tourist track. The resident dog likes the beer. Q ☗ ◖ ◗ ♣ P

Try also: Hare Arms, Stow Bardolph, (Greene King); **Heron**, Stowbridge (Free)

Winterton

Fishermans Return

The Lane (off B1159)
☎ (0493) 393305
11–2.30; 7–11 (11–11 summer)
Adnams Bitter; Ruddles Best Bitter; Webster's Yorkshire Bitter Ⓗ
300 year-old building with genuine beams and wood-faced interior. The large main bar offers games and music; the adjoining lounge (real fire) is quiet. Popular with both locals and holiday-makers. Food recommended (veg and children's dishes available).
Q P

Wreningham

Bird in Hand

Church Road (B1113)
☎ (050 841) 438
11–2.30; 5.30–11
Adnams Bitter, Old; Marston's Pedigree Bitter; Woodforde's Wherry Best Bitter Ⓗ
Well-designed interior with a quarry tiled floor and wooden-raftered roof, brickwork bar and room dividers. Some nice mirrors and pictures enhance the walls. Two restaurants serve well-prepared food. Woodforde's JT's Tipple is a house beer. P

Wymondham

Feathers

Town Green
☎ (0953) 605675
11–2.30 (12–2.30 Sun); 7 (6 Fri)–11
Adnams Bitter; Greene King Abbot Ale; Hall & Woodhouse Tanglefoot; Mauldons Black Adder; Wadworth 6X; Woodforde's Baldric Ⓗ
Friendly and busy pub with always a good selection of beers, including guests. Single bar gets very busy at weekend. Real cider always available.
P

Green Dragon

Church Street
☎ (0953) 607907
11–2.30; 6–11
Courage Best Bitter, Directors; Greene King IPA, Abbot Ale; John Smith's Bitter; Whitbread Flowers IPA Ⓖ
Small, friendly pub featuring panelling dating back to 13th century. Good food and good ale. Real fire creates cosy atmosphere.
Q P

Try also: Queen's Head

FRINGE BENEFITS: Bottle collecting

Bottle collecting is a heavy business, particularly if you insist on keeping the contents intact. The issue once became such a weighty matter that it was mentioned in an obsessed collector's divorce petition.

A full half-pint bottle weighs 1.25 lb, and that soon adds up when your collection runs from shelf to shelf. When the chairman of the Association of Bottled Beer Collectors, Bob Heath, moved home, he discovered that his beloved bottles weighed almost a ton and he would need a four-bedroom house just to keep his mass of glass. And he is a specialist! He only saves commemorative British issues.

The Association was formed by a meeting of collectors at the Burton Bridge Brewery in Burton upon Trent in 1983, one of the small breweries known for its range of bottled beers. But the catalyst for collecting came six years earlier – from Buckingham Palace, when almost every brewery in the land produced a special bottle to commemorate The Queen's Silver Jubilee.

Patriotic landlords began to round up the royalty brews to display in their bars, and the Silver Jubilee ales were soon followed by Royal Wedding beers as Prince Charles and then Prince Andrew got hitched. These tempting tipples, of course, swiftly gave birth to Royal Baby ales. No other hobby can claim such a noble warrant of approval.

Anyone wishing to join these clinking collectors, should send £3 (payable to ABBC) to John Minty, 53 Ridge Road, Kempston, Bedford. Members receive a quarterly newsletter, *What's Bottling.*

Northamptonshire

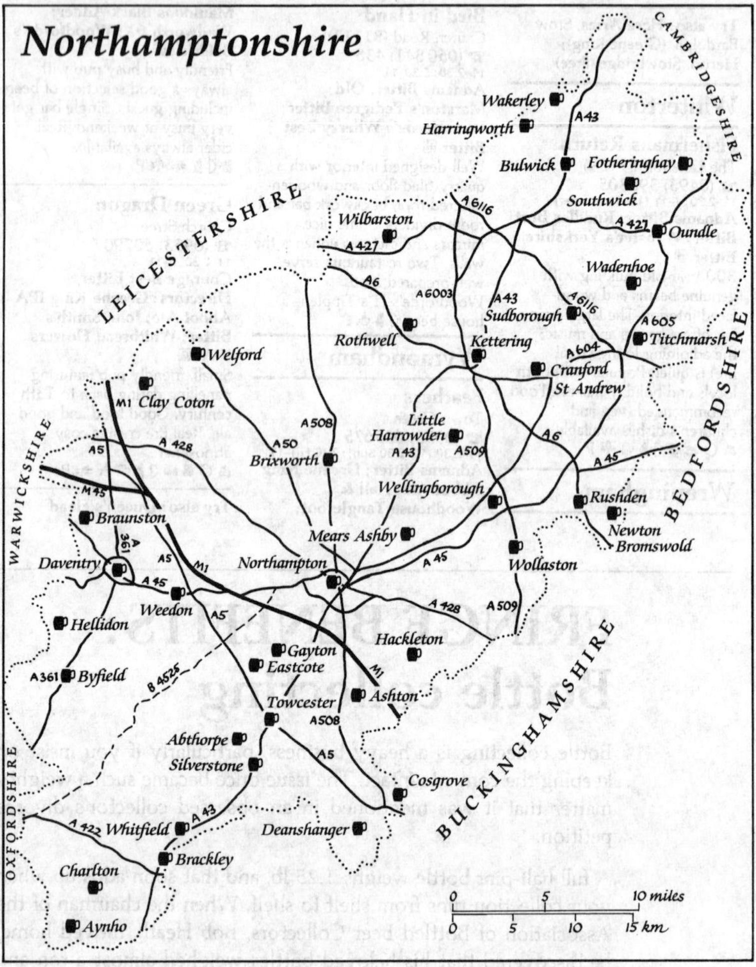

Abthorpe

New Inn
Silver Street ☎ (0327) 857306
12–3; 6–11
Hook Norton Best Bitter; Old Hookey [H]
Typical village pub where you can enjoy a game of Northants skittles in a friendly environment. The pub is hard to find but well worth the effort. No food Sun. ⌂ ❀ ◐ ◑ ♣ ○ P

Ashton

Old Crown
1 Stoke Road (1 mile from A508) ☎ (0604) 862268
12–2.30; 7–11
Charles Wells Eagle Bitter, Bombardier [H]
17th-century village local with emphasis on good food. Full *à la carte* menu offered in lounge. Large garden with children's play area. Barbecue most summer weekends. Separate bar with pool table. ❀ ◐ ◑ ⊟ ♣ P

Aynho

Great Western Arms
Aynho Station (1 mile W of Aynho on B4031)
☎ (0869) 38288
11–2; 6–11
Hook Norton Best Bitter [H], **Old Hookey** (summer) [G]
A large pub situated between the former GWR line and the Oxford Canal. Ample parking for cars and narrow boats alike. A good-sized lounge and a pleasant family room; generous garden. ⌂ Q ⛵ ❀ ◐ ◑ ♣ P

Brackley

Plumbers Arms
Manor Road ☎ (0280) 702495
11–11
Draught Bass; Hook Norton Best Bitter [H]
Good Irish atmosphere and a warm welcome guaranteed. Good home-cooking, served in a separate room.
⌂ ⛵ ⛟ ◐ ◑ ⊟ ♣ P

Braunston

Old Plough
High Street ☎ (0788) 890000
11–2.30 (12–2 Sun); 6.15–11
Ansells Mild, Bitter; Ind Coope Burton Ale [H]
Smart, semi-timbered bar with real fire and darts. Lounge has what appears to be a tree trunk in the middle. Plenty of leather seating. A pub since 1672, and in this guide for the past 11 years. ⌂ ❀ ◐ ◑ ⊟ ♣ P

Brixworth

George
Northampton Road (A508)
☎ (0604) 881439

11–3 (2.30 Wed); 5.30–11
Adnams Broadside; Mansfield Riding Traditional Bitter; Charles Wells Eagle Bitter, Bombardier [H]
Modern, two-roomed pub; rebuilt in 1979 behind the facade of the original building. No food Sun. ♣ P

Bulwick

Queen's Head

Main Street ☎ (078085) 272
11–2.30; 6–11
Adnams Bitter; Bateman XXXB [H]
Grade II listed building in quiet village. Good food in bar and restaurant (book for Sun lunch). Guest beers. Horseshoes played.
Q ♣ P

Byfield

Cross Tree

2 Banbury Road (A361)
☎ (0327) 60391
11.30–3; 7–11 (11.30–11 Sat)
Banks's Bitter [E]
Friendly village pub, in roadhouse style. Large well-equipped games room and comfortable lounge with teapot collection. Northants skittles.
♣ P

Charlton

Rose & Crown

Main Street ☎ (0295) 811317
12–3; 5–11
Marston's Burton Best Bitter, Pedigree Bitter; Morland Old Masters; Wadworth 6X [H]
The one large room of this 17th-century building copes well with the mixture of diners and drinkers. Guest beer. Food (incl. veg option) in bar or restaurant. Q ♣ P

Clay Coton

Fox & Hounds

☎ (0788) 860363
12–2.30; 7–11
Bateman XXXB; Hook Norton Best Bitter; Jennings Bitter; Wadworth 6X [H]
Situated in a tiny hamlet, this lovely, one-room pub has a nice stone-flagged bar area and a comfortable lounge area. Very much a country pub with hunting associations. Good meals. Separate skittles area. Guest beer. Q ♣

Try also: Royal Oak, Crick (Free)

Cosgrove

Navigation

Thrupp Wharf, Castlethorpe Road (off A508)
☎ (0908) 543156
12–2.30 (3 Sat); 6–11
Hook Norton Best Bitter [H]
Pleasant pub situated on the Grand Union Canal. A good stop for families, with a large family room and extensive gardens. Five guest beers. No food Sun. ♣ P

Cranford St Andrew

Woolpack

St Andrews Lane
☎ (053678) 256
11–2.30; 6–11
Camerons Traditional Bitter; Courage Best Bitter; John Smith's Bitter [H]
Classic country pub; all wood beams, brass and open fires. Has undergone a renaissance since being transferred from Manns' ownership. Traditional games in separate room. Find the village and ask. Q ♣ P

Daventry

Coach & Horses

Warwick Street
☎ (0327) 76692
11–2.30; 5 (6.30 Sat)–11
Ind Coope Burton Ale; Tetley Bitter [H]
Old coaching inn just off the High Street. An inglenook; two open real fires; busy games room and traditional function room make up this gem. Live jazz in converted stables. No food at weekend. ♣

Dun Cow

6 Brook Street (off High Street)
☎ (0327) 71545
10.30–2.30 (3 Thu–Sat); 5.30–11
Greenalls Davenports Traditional Bitter, Thomas Greenall's Original Bitter [H]
Rambling old coaching inn, with a gem of a snug bar, entered from under the coaching arch. Monthly folk club in galleried function room. Licensee is only the third this century. Children welcome at lunchtime. No food Sun. Q ♣ P

Deanshanger

Fox & Hounds

High Street ☎ (0908) 563485
12–3; 6–11
ABC Best Bitter [H]**; Draught Bass** [G]**; Wadworth 6X** [H]
Popular local with old wood-working tools in the public bar. The lounge is very homely; small restaurant. No food Sun eve. ♣ P

Eastcote

Eastcote Arms

Off A5 at Fosters Booth
☎ (0327) 830731
12–2.30 (not Mon, 12–2 Sun); 6–10.30 (11 Fri & Sat)
Banks & Taylor Eastcote Ale; Fuller's ESB; Marston's Pedigree Bitter; Samuel Smith OBB [H]
Smart village pub with two small cosy bars decorated with a wealth of prints and trophies. Very pleasant garden with views over valley. Guest beers. Ring the Bull played. Food Tue–Sat. Q ♣ P

Fotheringhay

Falcon

Main Street ☎ (08326) 254
11.30–2.30; 6 (7 Mon)–11
Adnams Bitter; Elgood's EB, GSB; Greene King IPA, Abbot Ale [H]
18th-century pub near site of Fotheringhay Castle. Small public bar and comfortable lounge. Good food (veg option) in restaurant (not Mon eve).
Q ♣ P

Gayton

Eykyn Arms

High Street ☎ (0604) 858361
11–2.30 (not Tue, 12–2.30 Sun); 7–11
Charles Wells Eagle Bitter [H]
Two-roomed village local. Long bar has skittles and darts at one end; cosy lounge has a large collection of coins and banknotes. The listed building is stone-built with an award-winning garden. Q ♣ P

Hackleton

White Hart

80 High Street (B526)
☎ (0604) 870271
11–2.30 (3 Fri & Sat); 6–11
Ruddles Best Bitter, County; Webster's Yorkshire Bitter [H]
Impressive, stone local which has records dating back to 1739. Lounge bar incorporates a 40ft glass-topped well. Two-part bar with Northants skittles.
♣ P

Harringworth

White Swan

Seaton Road ☎ (057287) 543
11.30–3; 6.30–11
Greene King IPA, Abbot Ale; Ruddles Best Bitter [H]
16th-century stone coaching inn where Walter De La Mare carved his name in the chimney breast. Stairs up to accommodation have a 'trip step', an early burglar alarm. Two bars and restaurant.
Q ♣ P

Hellidon

Red Lion

On edge of village towards Catesby OS519581
☎ (0327) 61200

12–3; 7–11
Courage Best Bitter, Directors; Greenalls Davenports Traditional Bitter [H]
Smart and chintzy country pub with a hunting theme. Real fires in both bars. Try the unusual sausages. Northants skittles played. ⌂ Q ■ ◖ ◗ ⊞ ♣ P

Kettering

Cordwainer
Bath Road ☎ (0536) 518578
11–3; 6–11 (11–11 Fri & Sat)
Home Bitter [E]
Friendly estate pub with large bar and smart lounge. Named after (now almost defunct) local leather trade. ■ ⊞ ♣ P

Try also: Bakers Arms (Banks's)

Little Harrowden

Lamb
Orlingbury Road
☎ (0933) 673300
11–2.30; 5.30–11
Charles Wells Eagle Bitter, Bombardier [H]
Pleasant village pub with cosy lounge and good games bar (Northants skittles). Traditional pub – no jukebox – unspoilt by modern trends. No food Sun lunch. ⌂ Q ■ ◖ ⊞ ♣ P

Mears Ashby

Griffin's Head
Wilby Road ☎ (0604) 812945
12–3; 7–11
Adnams Bitter; Bateman XXXB ; Whitbread Flowers IPA [H]
Mid 19th-century, brick-built local in Victorian style, hiding behind the village bus shelter! No food Sun lunch.
⌂ ■ ◖ ◗ ⊞ ♣ P

Newton Bromswold

Swan
Church Lane ☎ (0933) 314323
12–2.30; 7–11
Greene King IPA [H]**; Abbot Ale** [G]
Friendly village local with three small, interconnected rooms around a central servery. Separate games room with darts and Northants skittles. Well worth seeking out. Q ■ ⊞ ♣ P

Northampton

Barn Owl
Olden Road, Rectory Farm (estate just N of A4500, 4 miles E of centre)
☎ (0604) 416483
11–3; 6–11
Greene King IPA, Abbot Ale [H]
Excellent modern estate pub with barn owl sculpture on walls. Winner of CAMRA Best New Pub award in 1986. One room only. No food Sun.
■ ◖ ◗ ♿ ♣ P

Mailcoach
6 Derngate ☎ (0604) 36982
11–3; 5–11
Courage Best Bitter, Directors [H]
Expansive, U-shaped, lounge-pub just off town centre, catering for cosmopolitan clientele. Busy most lunchtimes with office workers; quieter at night. Handy for cultural events at the Derngate Centre or Royal Theatre. No food Sun. ◖ ≋

Queen Adelaide
50 Manor Road, Kingsthorpe (turn S 300 yds W of A50/A508 jct) ☎ (0604) 714524
11–2.30; 5.30–11
Ruddles Best Bitter, County; Webster's Yorkshire Bitter [H]
Popular local with old photos and original ceiling panelling in bar and a nostalgic games room.
Q ■ ⊞ ♣ P

Road to Morocco
Bridgewater Drive (E of Abington Park)
☎ (0604) 32899
11.30–3 (12–2.30 Sun); 6–11
Courage Best Bitter, Directors [H]
Small bar, taken up mostly by the pool table, and smart quiet lounge, done up in mock casbah style. Skeleton can be seen resting in the cellar, but we hope you won't be crossed by the Moor! ■ ⊞ ♣ P

Spread Eagle
147 Wellingborough Road (A4500) ☎ (0604) 24386
11–2.30 (3 Fri, 3.30 Sat); 5.30 (6.30 Sat)–11
Charles Wells Eagle Bitter, Bombardier [H]
Small, friendly locals' pub half a mile from town centre. U-shaped bar plus lounge and games areas. Disco Thu. ♣ P

Oundle

Ship
West Street ☎ (0832) 273918
11–3; 6–11 (11–11 Sat)
Draught Bass; Greene King IPA; Marston's Pedigree Bitter; Theakston XB [H]
Large three-roomed pub in attractive small town. Live music some Fri nights. Guest beers. Good value home-cooked fare (veg and children's dishes).
⌂ Q ☺ ■ ⊨ ◖ ◗ ⊞ ♿ ⛺ ♣ P

Try also: Rose & Crown (John Smith's)

Rothwell

Red Lion Hotel
Market Hill ☎ (0536) 710409
11–2.30; 5.30–11
Charles Wells Eagle Bitter, Bombardier [H]
Impressive ironstone building, claiming to be the last purpose-built coaching inn in England (built 1903). Four different drinking areas; some accommodation in adjacent cottages. Live music Sat.
⊨ ◖ ◗ ⊞ ♣

Rushden

Feathers
High Street ☎ (0933) 50251
11–2.30; 6–11
Charles Wells Eagle Bitter, Bombardier [H]
Town-centre local with large lounge at rear leading to patio, terraced drinking area and enclosed children's play area beyond. Cosy saloon bar at front. Separate dining area (no food Sun). ■ ◖ ⊞ ♣ P

King Edward VII
Queen Street ☎ (0933) 53478
10.30–11
Adnams Broadside [G]**; Charles Wells Eagle Bitter** [H]**, Bombardier** [G]
Busy, traditional, street-corner local, popular with all ages. Large bar with games and piano; cosy lounge. Excellent meals. A real pub. ⌂ ◖ ◗ ⊞ ♣

Silverstone

Royal Oak
7 Brackley Road (A43)
☎ (0327) 857187
12–2.30; 5–11 (12–11 Fri & Sat, 11–11 Mon–Sat in summer)
Marston's Border Bitter, Pedigree Bitter; Morland Original Bitter [H]
A vibrant town pub with a large open fireplace adding to the cosy atmosphere. Nearest pub to the racing circuit and apt to become very busy during the big race weekends. Veg option on menu (no food winter Sun eve). ⌂ ■ ◖ ◗ P

Southwick

Shuckburgh Arms
☎ (0832) 274007
11–2.30; 6–11
Adnams Bitter, Broadside; Hook Norton Best Bitter, Old Hookey; Taylor Landlord [H]
Friendly 16th-century thatched pub, adjoining village cricket pitch. Basic bar, small lounge and bar billiards area. Guest beers. Bar snacks. ⌂ Q ⊞ ♣ P

Sudborough

Vane Arms
Main Street ☎ (080 12) 3223
11–3 (not Mon); 5.30–11 (11–11 Sat)
Greene King IPA; Moorhouse's Pendle Witches Brew 🄷
Popular old thatched village pub. Exposed stone-work abounds. Good public bar and excellent lounge. No food Sun eve or Mon. Up to six guest beers.
Q ◖ ◗ ♿ ♣ P

Titchmarsh

Dog & Partridge
High Street ☎ (080 12) 2546
12–3; 6–11
Adnams Broadside; Charles Wells Eagle Bitter 🄷
18th-century village pub much improved by recent addition of a public bar. Two real fires to keep the local quiz fanatics warm. ♣ P

Towcester

Plough
Market Square (A5)
☎ (0327) 50738
10.30–11
Adnams Broadside; Charles Wells Eagle Bitter 🄷
Two-roomed pub with a pleasant lounge overlooking the market place, plus a rather dark public bar to the rear. The landlord's home-made hamburgers are a must!
Q ◖ ◗ ♣ P

White Bear
1 London Road (A5 S of town)
☎ (0327) 51486
11–2.30 (3.30 Fri); 6–11 (11–11 Sat)
ABC Best Bitter; Wadworth 6X 🄷
Street-corner local with large basic bar and cosy lounge. Separate skittles room. Due for alterations. Q ♣ P

Wadenhoe

King's Head
Church Street ☎ (080 15) 222
11–2.30; 7 (6 summer)–11
Bateman XXXB; Marston's Pedigree Bitter 🄷
16th-century building of outstanding character. Flagstoned bar with cheese skittles; comfortable lounge. Large garden down to River Nene with boat moorings. Local CAMRA Pub of the Year 1989. Summer guest beers. Lunchtime snacks. Q ♿ ♣ P

Wakerley

Exeter Arms
☎ (057 287) 817
12–2.30 (not Mon, 3 Sat); 6–11
Bateman XB; Younger IPA 🄷
Reputedly haunted, 300 year-old pub near Wakerley Woods. Public bar has bar billiards; lounge includes dining area and a wood burning stove. No food Mon. ◖ ◗ ♣ P

Weedon

Globe Hotel
On A5/A45 crossroads
☎ (0327) 40336
10.30–11
Bateman XB; Marston's Pedigree Bitter; Ruddles County 🄷
Modernised old hotel at meeting point of two major roads. Large lounge with central fireplace; separate restaurant. A traveller's rest. Guest beers.
Q ◖ ◗ ♿ ♣ P

Narrowboat
Stow Hill (A5, 1 mile S of A45 jct) ☎ (0327) 40536
11–2.30; 5.30–11 (11–11 Sat)
Charles Wells Eagle Bitter, Bombardier 🄷
Busy one-bar pub next to Grand Union Canal. Highly-rated Cantonese restaurant; traditional home-made bar food always available. Popular with families in summer. Motel accommodation. ◖ ◗ P

Wheatsheaf
34 High Street (A45)
☎ (0327) 40670
11–2.30 (3 Sat); 5.30–11
Banks's Mild, Bitter 🄷
Homely local with large collection of brassware. Open fire, wood-beamed ceiling and wheatsheaf mirror. Games room to rear. ◖ ♣ P

Welford

Shoulder of Mutton
High Street ☎ (0858) 575375
12–2.30; 7–11
Ruddles Best Bitter; Webster's Yorkshire Bitter 🄷
Welcoming 17th-century pub, tastefully renovated into a single room split by arches. Large garden with plenty of play equipment. Skittle room provides shelter in inclement weather. Menu caters for children and vegetarians (no food Thu). ◖ ◗ ♿ ♣ P

Wellingborough

Cannon
Cannon Street
☎ (0933) 79629
11–3.30; 5.30–11
Banks & Taylor SOS; Taylor Landlord; Tetley Bitter; Wadworth 6X; Charles Wells Eagle Bitter 🄷
A genuine free house with a good choice of real ales always available. Popular and friendly. Guest beers. ♣ P

Horseshoe
Sheep Street
☎ (0933) 222015
11–4.30; 7–11
Draught Bass 🄷
Lively town-centre pub with bar billiards. ◖ ♿ P

Vivian Arms
Knox Road (off Commercial Way) ☎ (0933) 223660
11–2.30 (12–2.30 Sun); 6–11
Adnams Broadside; Charles Wells Eagle Bitter 🄷
Excellent, friendly, back-street local with small lounge, wood-panelled bar, separate games room and petanque piste. Occasional live music.
Q ♿ ♣ P

Whitfield

Sun Inn
Farrier Close ☎ (028 05) 232
12–2.30; 6.30–11
Bateman XXXB; Hook Norton Best Bitter 🄷
Small country hotel with a pleasant L-shaped lounge. No real garden but useful outside tables with benches. No food Sun eve or Mon.
◖ ◗ ♣ P

Wilbarston

Fox Inn
Church Street (off A427)
☎ (0536) 771270
12–2.30 (3 Sat); 6.30–11
Marston's Burton Best Bitter, Pedigree Bitter 🄷
Cosy and friendly 400 year-old ironstone pub. Pleasant lounge and large basic bar. Small restaurant has good reputation. Petanque and Northants skittles played. ◖ ◗ ♣

Wollaston

Boot
High Street ☎ (0933) 664270
11–2.30 (12–2.30 Sun); 6–11
Camerons Traditional Bitter, Strongarm; Tolly Cobbold Original 🄷
Thatched-roofed, stone-built local with a cosy bar and a lounge untouched by progress. Games room has Northants skittles; double-nine dominoes also played. Q ♣ P

Help keep real ale alive by joining CAMRA. Your voice helps encourage brewers big and small to brew cask beer and offer all beer drinkers a better choice.

Northumberland

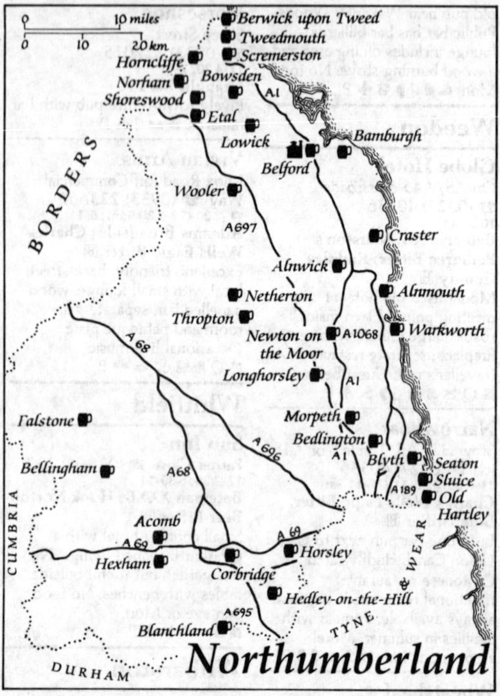

***Darling's**, Belford*

Acomb

Miners Arms Inn
Main Street
11–3; 5.30–11 (11–11 summer)
Federation Best Bitter, Special Ale; Miners Arms Own Ale; Morrells Varsity Ⓗ
Very popular village pub serving excellent ales and food (incl. veg option). Guest beers.
⌂ Q ◐ ◑ ⊕ ⛺

Alnmouth

Red Lion Inn
Northumberland Street
☎ (0665) 830584
12–2.30; 7–11 (extends in summer)
McEwan 80/-; Tetley Bitter Ⓗ
Cosy, welcoming pub on main street of picturesque estuary village. Excellent home-cooked food and seafood specialities. Accommodation includes self-catering flat.
⌂ Q ◐ ◑ ♿ ⇌ ♣ P

Schooner Inn
Northumberland Street
☎ (0665) 830216
11–11
Theakston XB; Vaux Samson Ⓗ
Comfortable hotel in main street, popular with the golfing fraternity. Guest beers.
⌂ Q ◐ ◑ ⊕ ♣ P

Try also: Sun Inn (Tetley)

Alnwick

Queens Head
Market Street
☎ (0665) 6902442
11–11
Vaux Samson, Double Maxim Ⓗ
Lively, well-run hotel in town centre where a warm welcome is assured. Rare chance to sample Double Maxim on draught in this area. Excellent menu caters for children and vegetarians.
Q ◐ ◑ ♿ ⛺ P

Tanners Arms
Hotspur Street
☎ (0665) 602553
12–3 (not Mon & Tue); 7–11
Belhaven 70/-, 80/- Ⓗ
Small pub just outside town walls, popular with younger clientele. Warm welcome assured. Guest beers.

Try also: Fleece (Vaux)

Bamburgh

Castle
7 Front Street ☎ (06684) 351
12–3; 6–11
Vaux Lorimers Best Scotch, Samson Ⓗ
Popular village pub. Menu offers veg and children's dishes.
⌂ ◐ ◑ ♿ ⛺ ♣ P

Victoria Hotel
The Grove ☎ (06684) 431
11–11
Halls Harvest Bitter; Marston's Pedigree Bitter; Tetley Bitter Ⓗ
Imposing hotel with compact bar which has retained its inglenook. Situated close to magnificent castle and unspoilt beaches. Real ale also available in cocktail bar. Guest beers.
⌂ Q ◐ ◑ ⊕ ♿ ⛺ ♣

Bedlington

Northumberland Arms
Front Street East
☎ (0670) 822754
11–3; 6–11
Thomas Greenall's Original Bitter Ⓗ
Well-established real ale pub in town centre. Numerous guest beers. ◐

Belford

Salmon
Main Street ☎ (0668) 213245
11–3; 6–11 (11–11 Sat)
Vaux Lorimers Best Scotch Ⓗ
A warm welcome is assured, at the Salmon, which is a long-standing entry in this guide. Well worth the short detour off A1. Attractive hanging baskets and window box displays in summer. Q ⊕ ⛺ ♣ P

Bellingham

Cheviot
Main Street
11–3; 6–11 (11–11 Sat)
McEwan 80/- Ⓗ
Comfortable village local. No Sun lunch in winter.

Berwick upon Tweed

Free Trade
Castle Gate ☎ (0289) 806498
12–3; 7–11 (winter hours vary)
Vaux Lorimers Best Scotch Ⓗ
Magnificent unspoilt interior where fine woodwork, glasswork and partitioning are matched in their appeal by lively local banter and good beer. Berwick's bonniest boozer!
⇌ ♣

Meadow House
North Road (A1)
☎ (0289) 304173
11–3; 6–11
Vaux Lorimers Best Scotch Ⓗ
England's northernmost pub, offering a friendly hail or farewell. Popular for bar meals

(including veg and children's options). Photographs of Berwick dating back to 1863.
Q ⊛ ◐ ◑ ⊟ ♿ ♣ P

Pilot Inn
Low Greens ☎ (0289) 304214
11–3; 7–11
Broughton Greenmantle Ale 🄷
Cosy, nautical inn on quiet residential street. Bar snacks.
Q ⊟ ⅄ ≹ ♣

Blanchland

Lord Crewe Arms Hotel
☎ (0434) 75251
11–3; 6–11
Vaux Samson 🄷
Monks, Jacobites and ghosts have all shared the pleasure of a pint in Northumberland's southernmost real ale outlet.
♜ Q ♉ ⊛ ⛟ ◐ ◑ ♣

Blyth

Kitty Brewster
549 Cowpen Road (off A189 near trading estate)
☎ (0670) 352732
11–3 (2.30 Mon & Tue); 5 (6 Fri & Sat)–11
Courage Directors; John Smith's Bitter, Magnet 🄷
Large, stone pub with warm atmosphere. Handy for new heliport! Good value meals in bar and restaurant (eve meals finish early). ⛟ ◐ ◑ ♣ P

Top House
Marlow Street (off A193)
☎ (0670) 356731
11–11
Theakston Best Bitter, XB, Old Peculier 🄷
Back-street local close to town centre. ♜ ◐

Bowsden

Black Bull
Off B6525 OS991418
☎ (0289) 88661
12–3; 7–11 (11–11 summer)
McEwan 70/- 🄷
Cosy, friendly village pub in a quiet corner of Northumberland. Worth a detour. Good value food (vegetarians and children catered for).
♜ Q ⊛ ◐ ◑ ⊟ ♿ ⅄ ♣ P

Corbridge

Wheatsheaf Hotel
St Helens Street
☎ (0434) 632020
11–11
Vaux Bitter, Double Maxim 🄷
Friendly, village-centre pub with family room and garden play area for children. Veg option on menu.
♜ Q ♉ ⊛ ⛟ ◐ ◑ ⊟ ♿ ≹ P

Craster

Jolly Fisherman
☎ (066376) 218
11–3; 6–11 (extends in summer)
Wards Sheffield Best Bitter 🄷
Well-run, split-level pub by the sea. Bar snacks include excellent crab sandwiches. In beautiful village famous for its kippers.
♜ ⊛ ♿ ⅄ ♣ P

Etal

Black Bull
☎ (089082) 200
12–3; 6–11
Vaux Lorimers Best Scotch 🄷
Thatched pub in picturesque village with castle and working watermill nearby. Q ◐ ◑ ♿ ♣ P

Falstone

Blackcock
☎ (0660) 40200
11–3; 6–11 (11–11 Sat)
Thomas Greenall's Original Bitter 🄷
Attractive stone pub on edge of Europe's largest man-made forest, not far from Kielder Water (Europe's largest man-made lake). ♉ ⊛ ⛟ ◐ ◑ ♿ ♁

Hedley-on-the-Hill

Feathers
OS078592 ☎ (0661) 843268
6–11 (12–3.30; 6–11 Sat)
Marston's Pedigree Bitter; Ruddles Best Bitter 🄷
Friendly pub in lovely hilltop village. Food at weekends only. Guest beers. ♜ Q ♉ ◐ ◑ ⊟ ♣ P

Hexham

Globe
Battle Hill ☎ (0434) 603742
11–3.30; 6–11 (11–11 Fri & Sat)
McEwan 80/-; Younger No. 3 🄷
Pleasant, traditional locals' bar.
♜ ♿ ≹ ♣

Tap & Spile
Battle Hill (70 yds from bus station) ☎ (0434) 602039
11–11
Camerons Traditional Bitter; Hadrian Gladiator Bitter; Taylor Landlord 🄷
Small, bustling pub in traditional style. Guest beers. Q ⊟ ≹ ♣

Horncliffe

Fishers Arms
Main Street (off A698)
☎ (0289) 86223
11–3; 7–11
Vaux Lorimers Best Scotch 🄷
Friendly and welcoming village pub near Britain's oldest suspension bridge. Unspoilt village with pleasant riverside walks nearby. Veg meals available. ♜ ⛟ ◐ ◑ ♣

Horsley

Crown & Anchor
On A69 ☎ (0661) 853105
11–3; 6.30–11
Vaux Lorimers Best Scotch, Samson 🄷
A good summer pub, with fine views over the Tyne Valley.
♜ ⊛ ◐ ◑ ♣ P

Longhorsley

Linden Pub
Linden Hall Hotel (on A697, off A1) ☎ (0670) 51166
11–3; 6–11
Marston's Pedigree Bitter; Theakston Best Bitter 🄷
Converted granary in magnificent country estate; popular for food (including veg and children's meals). Guest beers. ⛟ ◐ ◑ ♿ ⅄ ♣ P

Shoulder of Mutton
East Road (A697, Wooler road) ☎ (0670) 88236
11–3; 5.30–11 (11–11 Wed–Sat)
McEwan 80/-; Theakston Best Bitter 🄷
Recently-refurbished comfortable pub. Popular for good value food (including veg option). ♜ ⊛ ◐ ◑ ♿ ⅄ ♣ P

Lowick

Black Bull
2–4 Main Street (B6353)
☎ (0289) 88228
12–3; 7–11
McEwan 70/- 🄷
Renowned inn with good food and good service. Guest beers. Self-catering holiday flat to let.
♜ ⛟ ◐ ◑ ♣ P

White Swan
5 Main Street (B6353)
☎ (0289) 88249
11–2; 7–11
McEwan 70/- 🄷
Popular village local; friendly landlord and customers.
♜ Q ⊛ ◐ ◑ ⊟ ♣ P

Morpeth

Joiners Arms
Wansbeck Street
☎ (0670) 513340
11–3 (4 Fri); 5.30–11 (11–11 Sat)
Draught Bass; Taylor Landlord; Theakston XB 🄷
Typical two-roomed, traditional pub, undergoing refurbishment. Friendly staff and clientele intend to remain loyal. Busy at weekends. ⊟

Tap & Spile
Manchester Street (near bus station) ☎ (0670) 513894
11–3; 5.30–11 (11–11 Fri & Sat)
Camerons Traditional Bitter; Hadrian Gladiator Bitter; Taylor Landlord 🄷

Small but comfy pub with bar and separate lounge served via lobby hatch. Guest beers. ⊟ ♣

Wansbeck
Abbey Meadows
☎ (0670) 512575
12 (11 Fri & Sat)–11
Bass Light 5 Star; Stones Best Bitter Ⓗ
Modern Bass local on housing estate. Very comfortable. ◐ ◑ ⊟

Netherton

Star Inn
11–2; 7–11
Whitbread Castle Eden Ale Ⓗ
Remote but marvellous pub, located in the heart of some of England's most pleasant countryside. Only public transport to Netherton is the morning school bus from Thropton. Beer served on gravity from a hatch. ♨ Q ⊟

Newton on the Moor

Cook & Barker
½ mile off A1, S of Alnwick
☎ (0665) 75234
11–3; 6–11
Theakston Best Bitter Ⓗ
Recently-extended warm inviting local with separate dining room (bar snacks only at lunchtime). Worth the detour. Guest beers. ♨ ❀ ◐ ◑ ♿ ▲ ♣ P

Norham

Masons Arms
16 West Street (B6470, off A698) ☎ (0289) 823326
11–3; 6–11
Vaux Lorimers Best Scotch Ⓗ
Excellent traditional bar which has fishing rights on the River Tweed. Children's menu.
♨ Q 🛏 ◐ ⊟ ▲ ♣

Victoria Hotel
Castle Street (off B6470)
☎ (0289) 82237
11–3; 7–11
Vaux Lorimers Best Scotch Ⓗ
Lively pub near village green and impressive castle. Menu caters for children.
♨ ◐ ♿ ▲ ♣ P

Old Hartley

Delaval Arms
On A193
12 (11 Sat)–3; 6–10.30 (11 Thu–Sat)
McEwan 80/-; Theakston XB Ⓗ
Large, multi-roomed, listed building overlooking bay and lighthouse. Famous 'Blue Stone' by entrance. ⊟

Scremerston

Miners Arms
Off A1 ☎ (0289) 308821
11–11
Whitbread Castle Eden Ale Ⓗ
Small, friendly wayside pub, popular with younger locals. Food available summer only in bar and restaurant (veg and children's options).
♨ ❀ ◐ ◑ ⊟ ♿ ▲ ♣

Seaton Sluice

Waterford Arms
☎ (091) 237 0450
11–3; 6–11
Vaux Samson Ⓗ
Large pub overlooking tiny harbour. Locally-caught fish a speciality. Paintings by local artists in lounge. 🛏 ◐ ◑ ⊟ P

Shoreswood

Salutation Inn
On A698 OS924466
☎ (0289) 82291
11–3.30; 6.30–11 (extends in summer)
McEwan 70/- Ⓗ
Remote but welcoming pub offering magnificent view of Cheviots from bar. Camping on site; children's meals available.
♨ Q ❀ ◐ ◑ ♿ ▲ ♣ P

Thropton

Cross Keys
☎ (0669) 20362
11–11
Draught Bass Ⓗ
Lovely two-roomed pub on crossroads, two miles from Rothbury. Fine selection of food. ♨ Q ❀ ◐ ◑ P

Tweedmouth

Harrow
Main Street (by old bridge over River Tweed)
☎ (0289) 305451
11–3 (4 Sat); 6.30–11
Vaux Lorimers Best Scotch Ⓗ
Highly-convivial, classic pub used by truckers, seafarers and locals alike. Warm welcome guaranteed. One of the county's few entries in the first *Good Beer Guide*. Well worth a visit.
♨ ❀ 🛏 ⊟ ♿ ♣

Warkworth

Masons Arms
3 Dial Place (A1068)
☎ (0665) 711398
11–3; 6–11
Younger No. 3 Ⓗ
Welcoming, well-run village pub with a good local atmosphere. 600 years old, it was associated with the 1715 uprising. Good value home-cooked food in bar and restaurant (children catered for).
Q ❀ ◐ ◑ ⊟ ♿ ▲ ♣

Try also: Hermitage (Free)

Wooler

Anchor
2 Cheviot Street (off Market Place) ☎ (0668) 81412
11–4.30; 6–11
Vaux Lorimers Best Scotch, Samson Ⓗ
Friendly local on the road to the Cheviots. ☺ 🛏 ◐ ◑ ⊟ ▲ ♣

Ryecroft Hotel
Ryecroft Way (A697)
☎ (0668) 81459
11–11
Marston's Pedigree Bitter; Tetley Bitter; Yates Bitter Ⓗ
Well-run family hotel with a reputation for good food (veg option) and ale. Popular with locals and guests alike. Lounge has conservatory extension. Guest beers.
♨ Q ❀ 🛏 ◐ ◑ ♿ ▲ ♣ P

THE SYMBOLS

- ♨ real fire
- Q quiet pub – in at least one bar
- ☺ indoor room for children
- ❀ garden or other outdoor drinking area
- 🛏 accommodation
- ◐ lunchtime meals
- ◑ evening meals
- ⊟ public bar
- ♿ easy disabled access
- ▲ camping facilities at the pub or nearby
- ⇌ near British Rail station
- ⊖ near Underground station
- ♣ pub games
- ♁ real cider
- P pub car park

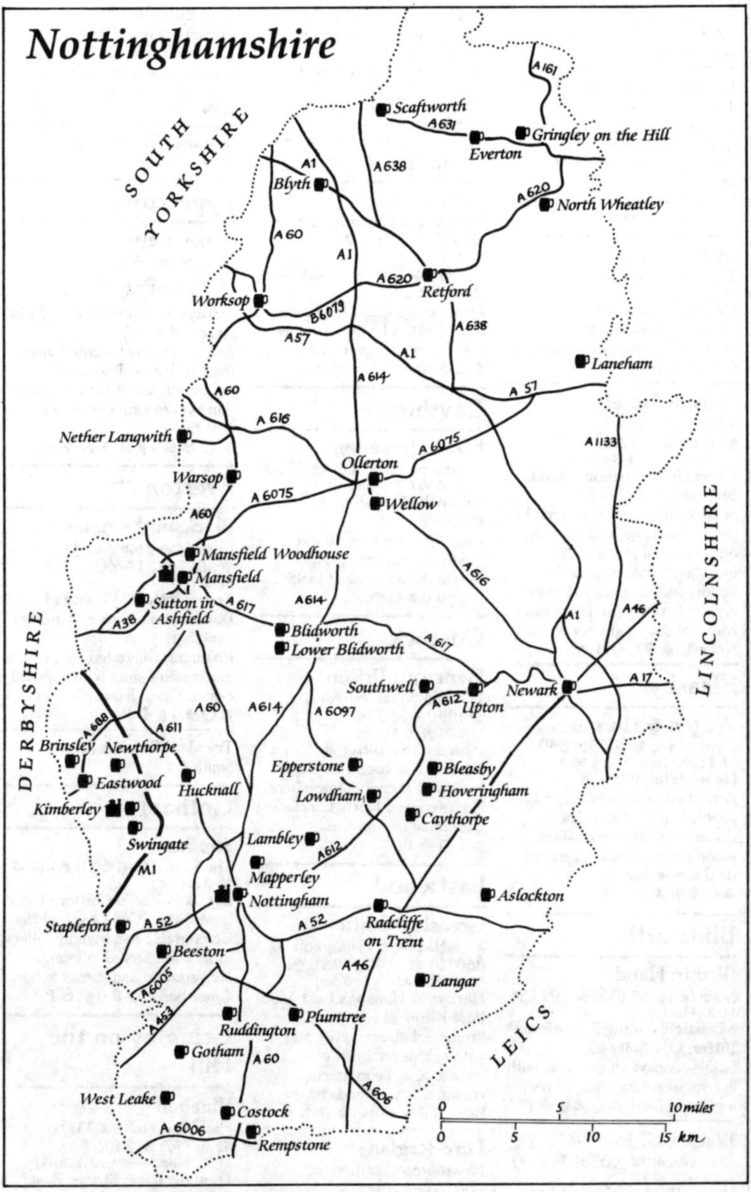

Greenalls (Shipstone's), *Nottingham*; **Hardys & Hansons**, *Kimberley*; **Mansfield**, *Mansfield*

Aslockton

Cranmer Arms

Main Street ☎ (0949) 50362
11–3; 6–11 (11–11 Sat)
Home Mild, Bitter 🄷
Friendly local pub named after Thomas Cranmer who was a native of the village. Children's play area in garden. Long-alley skittles. No meals Mon/Tue.
Q ⚘ (⇌ ♣ P

Old Greyhound

Main Street ☎ (0949) 50957
11–3; 6–11
Home Bitter 🄷 **&** 🄴
Olde-worlde pub with small rooms served by a single bar. Large indoor skittle alley which also doubles as children's room. Pool table. Q ⚘ ⇌ ♣ P

Beeston

Boat & Horses Inn

Trent Road ☎ (0602) 258589
11–3 (4 Sat); 7–11
Home Mild, Bitter 🄴

Busy two-roomed local close to canal and nature reserve.
⌂ ▣ ◐ ⊟ ≋ ♣ P

Commercial Inn
19 Wollaton Road
☎ (0602) 254480
11–2.30; 5.30–11 (11–11 Sat)
Hardys & Hansons Best Mild, Best Bitter [H]
Comfortable local, just off town centre. ▣ ◐ ⊟ ♣ P

Malt Shovel
1 Union Street
11–3; 7–11
Greenalls Shipstone's Mild, Shipstone's Bitter [E]
Friendly two-roomed town pub.
◐ ⊟ ≋ ♣ P

Queens Hotel
189 Queens Road
☎ (0602) 225262
10.30–3 (3.30 Fri & Sat); 6–11
Greenalls Shipstone's Mild, Shipstone's Bitter [E]
Solid Victorian local. Central bar serves three pub areas. Strong on traditional pub games, including Devil Among the Tailors and long-alley skittles. Aviary in rear yard. Lunches Mon-Sat (Sun and eves on request). ⌂ ▣ ◐ ⊟ ≋ ♣

Bleasby

Wagon & Horses
Gypsy Lane ☎ (0636) 830283
12–2 (2.30 Sat & Sun); 6.30–11
Home Mild, Bitter [E]
Attractive, whitewashed and pantiled country inn. The characterful interior has fine wood panelling and a genuine, rural atmosphere.
⌂ Q ▣ ⊟ ⛺ ♣ P

Blidworth

Bird in Hand
Main Street ☎ (0623) 792356
11–3 (4 Sat); 6–11
Mansfield Riding Traditional Bitter, Old Baily [H]
Single-roomed village local with central island bar. Fine views and good food. ⌂ Q ▣ ◐ ♣ P

Black Bull Inn
Main Street ☎ (0623) 792291
11.30–3; 6.30–11
Greenalls Shipstone's Mild, Shipstone's Bitter [H] & [E]
Mock-Tudor village inn with skittles. Eve meals Thu-Sat only, till 8.30. Q ◐ ◑ ⊟ ♿ ♣

Blyth

Angel
Bawtry Road (Off A1)
☎ (0909) 591213
11–3; 6–11
Hardys & Hansons Best Mild (summer); **Best Bitter** [E]
Old coaching inn with large garden in picturesque village. Good food and real fires in winter. Attracts trade from the village and off the A1.
⌂ Q ⊕ ▣ 🛏 ◐ ◑ ⊟ ♿ ♣ P

Try also: White Swan (Whitbread)

Brinsley

Durham Ox
High Street, New Brinsley
☎ (0773) 712659
12–4; 7–11
Hardys & Hansons Best Mild, Best Bitter [E]
Quiet, unassuming local dating from 1836. Old beer-cooling well lies below gents toilet.
▣ ⊟ ♿ ♣ P

Caythorpe

Black Horse Inn
Caythorpe ☎ (0602) 663520
11.45–2.30 (12–2 Sun); 6–11
Greenalls Shipstone's Bitter [H]
Unspoilt 18th-century inn, reputedly a haunt of Dick Turpin. Home-cooked food.
⌂ Q ▣ ◐ ◑ ⊟ ♣ P

Costock

Generous Briton
14 Main Street (off A60)
☎ (0509) 852347
11–2.30; 6.30–11
John Smith's Bitter [H]
Homely two-roomed village local with friendly atmosphere. Home-cooked lunches, including traditional fare on Sun.
⌂ ◐ ⊟ ♣ P

Eastwood

Greasley Castle
1 Castle Street, Hilltop (off B6010) ☎ (0773) 761080
11–4; 6–11 (11–11 Fri & Sat)
Hardys & Hansons Best Mild, Best Bitter [E]
Prominent street-corner pub with split-level, open-plan interior. Can be extremely crowded at weekends when there is live music. ▣ ⊟ ♿ ♣

Lord Raglan
Newthorpe Common (off B6010/A610)
☎ (0773) 712683
11.30–3; 5.30–11
Hardys & Hansons Best Mild, Best Bitter [E]
Genuine and popular estate pub with a very friendly atmosphere. Swings in the beer garden for children.
⌂ ▣ ◐ ⊟ ♿ ♣ P

Miners Arms
9 Mansfield Road (A608, 60 yds from B6010 jct)
☎ (0773) 712988
10.45–3; 6.30–11
Hardys & Hansons Best Mild, Best Bitter [E]
Friendly pub with bar, snug, pool room and upstairs meeting room. Close to birthplace of DH Lawrence and craft centre.
▣ ♣

Try also: Three Tuns (Greenalls)

Epperstone

Cross Keys
Main Street (off A6097)
☎ (0602) 663033
11–2.30 (12–2.30 Sun); 6–11
Hardys & Hansons Best Mild, Best Bitter [H]
Delightful white-painted village local with a well-deserved reputation for its bar meals (not Sun eves/Mon). Disabled access is at the rear.
⌂ Q ⊕ ▣ ◐ ◑ ⊟ ♿ ⛺ ♣ P

Everton

Blacksmiths Arms
Chapel Lane (off A631)
☎ (0777) 817260
12–3; 7–11
Tetley Bitter; Whitbread Boddingtons Bitter; Younger Scotch [H]
Charming converted blacksmith's shop with exposed beams. Guest beers.
⌂ Q ▣ ◐ ◑ ♣ P

Try also: Sun Inn (John Smith's)

Gotham

Sun Inn
The Square ☎ (0602) 830484
11–2.30; 6–11
Everards Beacon Bitter, Tiger Best Bitter, Old Original [H]
Comfortable and friendly village local. Food served in lounge; conversation and games in bar. Guest beers. Q ▣ ◐ ⊟ ♿ P

Gringley on the Hill

Bluebell
High Street (off A631)
☎ (0777) 817406
11.30–3 (not Mon–Wed); 6.30–11
Draught Bass; Stones Best Bitter [H]
Small beamed village pub. Recently renovated but without losing any of its atmosphere. Well-presented pub fare (book Sun lunch). ⌂ Q ◐ ◑ ♣

Hoveringham

Marquis of Granby
Main Street (1 mile off A612)
☎ (0602) 663080
12–2.30 (incl. Sun); 6.30–11
Marston's Pedigree Bitter [H]
Traditional, family-run free house in an unspoilt village,

once famous for its gravel pits. A short walk from the River Trent, the pub is popular both with locals and tourists. Good reputation for bar meals (not Sun). Guest beers.
⌂ Q ❀ ◖ ◗ ♣ P

Reindeer
Main Street ☎ (0602) 663629
11.30–3; 5.30–11
Marston's Burton Best Bitter, Pedigree Bitter Ⓗ
Old and proper pub run by a good landlord and landlady. Two rooms, beautifully furnished, with beamed ceilings and warming, real open fires. Food is a highlight with a good range of dishes. Guest beers.
⌂ Q ❀ ◖ ◗ ⊞ ♣ ⌓ P

Hucknall

Red Lion
High Street
11–3; 6–11
Home Mild, Bitter Ⓔ
Traditional town local. Very crowded at weekends. ⊞ ♿ ♣ P

Kimberley

Lord Clyde
Main Street ☎ (0602) 384907
10.30–11
Hardys & Hansons Best Mild, Best Bitter Ⓗ
Well-established, open-plan local. Extremely busy at weekends, especially with young people. Occasional disco nights. ❀ ◖ ♣

Nelson & Railway
Station Road (off B6010)
☎ (0602) 382177
10.30–3; 5–11 (10.30–11 Fri, Sat & bank hols)
Hardys & Hansons Best Mild, Best Bitter Ⓗ & Ⓔ
Delightful, cottage-style pub with wood-panelled bar and attractively restored beamed lounge with adjoining dining area. Excellent quality food (not Sun eve); cheap B&B. Sun eve quizzes. Cheap beer 5–7.30 Mon-Fri. Garden has children's swings. A pub of real character.
❀ ⛟ ◖ ◗ ⊞ ♣ P

Stag Inn
67 Nottingham Road (B6010)
☎ (0602) 383151
11–3 (3.30 Fri & Sat); 6–11
Greenalls Shipstone's Mild, Shipstone's Bitter Ⓔ
Excellent low-beamed village inn dating from 1537. Fine back garden with children's play area. Table skittles. ❀ ⊞ ♿ ♣ P

Lambley

Robin Hood
Main Street ☎ (0602) 312531
11–3; 6–11
Home Bitter Ⓔ

Originally cottages, a village local which dates back over 100 years and still retains some original beams. Used to be a Hutchinson & Sons pub. Well-known for beer and skittles parties. ◖ ⊞ ⛺ ♣ P

Laneham

Butchers Arms
Main Street ☎ (077 785) 255
12–3; 7–11
Ind Coope Burton Ale; Marston's Pedigree Bitter Ⓗ
Village local featuring a popular, old lounge with beams and inglenook. Separate games room. Home-cooking.
⌂ ❀ ◖ ◗ ⊞ ♿ ⛺ ♣ P

Langar

Unicorns Head
Main Street (near Bingham-Harby/Cropwell Bishop Road jct) ☎ (0949) 60460
11–3 (12–2.30 Sun); 6–11
Home Mild, Bitter Ⓔ
Immaculate village local well-known for its games and entertainment. Regular darts, pool and skittles team events; Sat eve sing-alongs; guest artistes Sun eve. ⌂ ❀ ◖ ⊞ ♣ P

Lowdham

Worlds End Inn
Plough Lane (100 yds off A6097) ☎ (0602) 663857
11.30–3; 5.30–11
Marston's Burton Best Bitter, Pedigree Bitter Ⓗ
Originally known as the Plough Inn, this popular country pub serves the community well. Smart but unpretentious; a welcome find out of town. Easily located – look for the flagpole in the garden.
⌂ ❀ ⊞ ⛺ ⇌ ♣ P

Lower Blidworth

Fox & Hounds
Calverton Road OS590548
☎ (0623) 792383
11–3; 6–11
Hardys & Hansons Best Mild, Best Bitter Ⓗ & Ⓔ
Multi-roomed country inn. Occasional garden entertainment in summer. Eve meals Fri-Sun only.
⌂ Q ⛴ ❀ ◖ ◗ ⊞ ⛺ ♣ P

Mansfield

Eagle Tavern
1 Woodhouse Road (near cinema) ☎ (0623) 24196
11–3; 7–11 (may vary)
Tetley Bitter Ⓗ
Small pub with popular tap room and lounge with real fire.
⌂ ◖ ◗ ⊞ ♣ P

William IV
Stockwell Gate (opp. Victoria Hospital) ☎ (0623) 21283
11–11
Mansfield Riding Dark Mild, Old Baily Ⓗ
Recently refurbished pub just off town centre. Large tap room with two pool tables and comfortable lounge.
⛴ ❀ ◖ ⊞ ♿ ♣ P

Yew Tree Inn
Woodhouse Road
☎ (0623) 23729
11–3; 7–11
Camerons Traditional Bitter, Strongarm Premium; Everards Old Original Ⓗ
Single well-decorated room with separate pool area. ♿ ♣ P

Mansfield Woodhouse

Portland Arms
2 High Street
☎ (0623) 422903
11–3; 6–11
John Smith's Bitter, Magnet Ⓗ
Popular, refurbished local. Landlord plays the organ for the Sun night sing-along.
◖ ◗ ⊞ ♿ ♣ P

Star Inn
Warsop Road (off Main Street)
☎ (0623) 24145
11–3; 6–11 (flexible in summer)
Ind Coope Burton Ale; Tetley Bitter Ⓗ
Low-beamed, three-roomed old pub, tastefully decorated. A popular local. ❀ ◖ ◗ P

Mapperley

Travellers Rest
Mapperley Plains
☎ (0602) 264412
11–11
Home Bitter Ⓔ; **Younger IPA or No. 3** Ⓗ
Popular roadhouse with award-winning food and well-geared to the needs of families (family room 5–10.30 and 12–3 weekends). Probably the highest pub in the county.
⌂ ⛴ ❀ ◖ ♿ ♣ P

Nether Langwith

Jug & Glass
Queens Walk (off A632)
☎ (0623) 742283
11.30–4; 7–11
Hardys & Hansons Best Mild, Best Bitter Ⓔ
16th-century pub set on village green alongside River Poulter. Separate restaurant.
⌂ Q ❀ ◖ ◗ ⊞ ♿ ♣ P

Newark

Nottinghamshire

Castle & Falcon
London Road
☎ (0636) 703513
11–3; 7–11
Courage Directors; John Smith's Bitter, Magnet Ⓗ
Pub on edge of the town. Lounge full of Royal Navy memorabilia; pool table in bar. Separate reception room. No food Sun eve. Q ❀ ◖ ⊟ ⇌ (Castle/Northgate) ♣ P

Crown & Mitre
53 Castlegate (50 yds from Castle/Market)
☎ (0636) 703131
11.30–3.30; 6–11
John Smith's Bitter; Vaux Double Maxim; Wards Sheffield Best Bitter, Kirby Strong Ⓗ
Smart and comfortable pub in town centre. Pool table in separate room away from the bar area. ⌂ ♉ ❀ ◖ ♣ ⊙ P

Old Kings Arms
19 Kirkgate (near church)
☎ (0636) 703416
10.30–3; 5.30–11
Marston's Border Exhibition, Burton Best Bitter, Merrie Monk, Pedigree Bitter Ⓗ
Lively and friendly pub with a good selection of food on offer. Serves morning coffee 9.30–12 and afternoon tea 3–5! Meals Tue–Sat. ◖ ◗ ⇌ (Castle)

Old Malt Shovel
25 Northgate
☎ (0636) 702036
11.30–2.30; 7 (5 Fri)–11
Taylor Landlord; Wards Sheffield Best Bitter Ⓗ
Single-room town pub which is justly popular. Well-decorated throughout. The imaginative menu is changed daily. Guest beers.
⌂ ❀ ◖ ⇌ (Castle/Northgate)

Newthorpe

Ram Inn
Beauvale (B6010)
☎ (0773) 713312
11–4; 6–11 (11–11 Sat)
Hardys & Hansons Best Mild, Best Bitter Ⓔ
Justly popular roadside pub. Warm and cosy, with excellent food. ❀ ◖ ◗ ⊟ ♿ ♣ P

North Wheatley

Sun Inn
Low Street (off A620)
☎ (0427) 880210
11.30–3; 6.30–11 (11.30–11 Sat)
Bass Special Bitter Ⓗ
Popular with all ages. Comfortable lounge and bar, plus separate pool room. Live rock music Thu eve. Large garden with children's play area. Guest beers.
⌂ ❀ ◖ ◗ ⊟ ♿ ▲ ♣ P

Nottingham

Blue Bell
50 Upper Parliament Street (between Victoria Centre and Royal Concert Hall)
☎ (0602) 470945
10.30–2.30 (12–2 Sun); 5.30–11
Home Mild, Bitter Ⓔ
Welcoming city-centre pub with efficient service. Hot and cold lunches (to order only Sun). Linked by passage to Press Bar on Forman Street (opposite Evening Post office). Q ◖

Boat Inn
Priory Street, Dunkirk, (off Abbey Street, A6005; city side of Dunkirk flyover)
☎ (0602) 786482
11–2.30 (3 Sat); 6 (6.30 Sat)–11
Home Mild, Bitter Ⓔ
A nice little one-roomed traditional back-street pub, with a friendly, welcoming atmosphere. Attractive wood-panelled walls with inlaid mirrors. ◖ ♿ ♣

Castle
Lower Parliament Street (next to ice stadium) ☎ (0602) 504601
11.30–2.30 (12–2.30 Sun); 6–11
Ansells Bitter; Ind Coope Burton Ale; Tetley Bitter Ⓗ
Lacking in exterior elegance but more than makes up for it by being smart and comfortable inside. Pool table. ❀ ◖ ◗ ♿ ♣

Coopers Arms
3 Porchester Road, Thorneywood (20 yds from Carlton Road)
☎ (0602) 502433
11–4; 6–11
Home Mild, Bitter Ⓔ
A friendly welcome is assured at this 1850s pub. ⊟ ♣ P

Crown Inn
Crocus Street, The Meadows
☎ (0602) 866152
11–3; 5.30–11 (11–11 Mon, Fri & Sat)
Home Mild, Bitter Ⓔ
Traditional street-corner local with comfortable lounge. Irish music played on tape. Disco every Fri eve. ⊟ ⇌ ♣

Lincolnshire Poacher
161–163 Mansfield Road (400 yds from Victoria Centre)
☎ (0602) 411584
11–3; 5 (6 Sat)–11
Bateman Dark Mild, XB XXXB, Victory Ale; Marston's Pedigree Bitter Ⓗ
Beer drinkers' paradise. Superbly renovated city pub with quiet room and conservatory. Famous as the first pub twinned with an Amsterdam bar! Formerly a Shipstone's house; now always serving a good range of guest beers. No meals Sat/Sun eves.
Q ❀ ◖ ◗ ♿ ♣

Lord Roberts
24 Broad Street
☎ (0602) 414886
11–2.30; 7–11
Greenalls Shipstone's Mild, Shipstone's Bitter Ⓔ
On the edge of the city centre. A traditional, welcoming local, 1990 holder of Shipstone's 'Order of the Bar'! Pool table and skittle alley. ◖ ⊟ ♣

Magpies
Meadow Lane (500 yds from Notts County FC)
☎ (0602) 863851
11–3; 5 (7 Sat)–11
Home Mild, Bitter Ⓔ
Friendly town pub on eastern edge of city. Handy for Trent Bridge cricket and Nottingham racecourse, as well as football. A haunt of sports enthusiasts, with pool particularly popular. No meals Sat/Sun eve.
❀ ◖ ◗ ⊟ ♣ P

March Hare
248 Carlton Road
☎ (0602) 504328
10.30–2.30; 6–11
Courage Directors; John Smith's Bitter Ⓗ
Longest-serving landlord in Nottingham. Locals' pub with comfortable lounge and pool table in functional bar. ◖ ⊟ ♣ P

New Market Hotel
38 Parliament Street (500 yds from Victoria Centre)
☎ (0602) 411532
11–3; 5.30–11 (11–11 Fri & Sat)
Home Mild, Bitter; Younger Scotch, IPA, No. 3 Ⓗ
Nondescript exterior hides remarkable interior. Front bar is unashamedly practical and a find for railway buffs. Comfortably furnished back lounge. Excellent home-cooked food (to order only Sun and eves). Guest ales.
Q ♉ ◖ ◗ ⊟ ♣ P

Norfolk Hotel
68 London Road
☎ (0602) 863003
11–3.30; 6.30–11
Home Mild, Bitter Ⓔ
Friendly pub on the edge of the city. Lively bar with pool table and indoor skittle alley. Separate lounge; function room upstairs. Eve meals till 7.30.
◖ ◗ ⊟ ⇌ ♣ P

Old Castle Inn
1 Castle Road (opp. Robin Hood statue) ☎ (0602) 413311
11–2.30; 5.30–11 (11–11 summer)
Ansells Bitter; Ind Coope Burton Ale; Tetley Bitter Ⓗ
Comfortable and smart mock-traditional pub. Appealing decor with wood panelling, floor and furniture. Split-level, with L-shaped bar below and two cosy drinking rooms above. ⌂ ❀ ◖

Pheasant Inn
35 Prospect Street, Radford
☎ (0602) 781940
11–2.30; 6–11
Greenalls Shipstone's Mild, Shipstone's Bitter Ⓔ
Three-roomed traditional local on the edge of town. ❀ ◖ ⊕ ♣

Queens Hotel
2 Arkwright Street
☎ (0602) 864685
11–2.30 (3 Sat); 5.30–11 (11–11 Fri)
Greenalls Shipstone's Bitter Ⓗ
Impressive street-corner hotel opposite railway station. Basic bar with pool table and Sky TV, comfortable lounge and small snug. ⚇ 🛏 ◖ ⊕ ⇌ ♣ P

Thurland Hall
Pelham Street (behind Council House) ☎ (0602) 417062
10.30–4; 5–11 (10.30 Sat)
Draught Bass Ⓗ
A solid Victorian edifice of mahogany and cut glass. Always full of friendly locals. The bar snacks (lunchtime only) are of excellent quality.

Vine
Handel Street, Sneinton
☎ (0602) 504233
11–3; 6–11
Home Mild, Bitter; Younger Scotch, IPA Ⓗ
Splendid example of corner-door pub. Real locals' bar and small, quiet, comfortable lounge. An excellent example of how to renovate a pub and retain its authentic ambience. No meals Sat/Sun. Guest beer. ◖ ⊕ ♣

Ollerton

White Hart
Station Road (signed Old Village) ☎ (0623) 822410
11–4; 7–11
Samuel Smith OBB Ⓗ
Well-kept pub in the Old Village. Cosy lounge and separate public bar.
Q ◖ ◗ ⊕ ♣ P

Plumtree

Griffin Inn
Main Road (½ mile off A606)
☎ (06077) 5745
11–2.30 (12–2 Sun); 5.30–11
Hardys & Hansons Best Mild, Best Bitter Ⓔ
150 year-old listed building with oak beams. Hosts weekly folkclub upstairs, but no jukebox or fruit machines. Single L-shaped bar/lounge. ❀ ◖ ♿ ♣ P

Radcliffe on Trent

Black Lion
Main Road (¼ mile off A52)
☎ (0602) 332138
11–2.30; 6–11
Home Mild, Bitter Ⓔ
Large mock-Tudor pub at centre of village, with friendly bar and plush lounge. Charity steam fair held first Sat in Oct. No meals Sat/Sun. ❀ ◖ ⊕ ⇌ ♣ P

Rempstone

White Lion
Main Street (A6006)
☎ (0509) 880669
11–2.30; 5.30–11
Greenalls Shipstone's Bitter Ⓗ
Small whitewashed village inn with beamed ceiling, quarry-tiled floor and much brassware.
♨ ❀

Retford

Albert Hotel
Albert Road (off London Road)
☎ (0777) 708694
11–3 (4 Thu & Sat); 7–11
Webster's Yorkshire Bitter; Whitbread Castle Eden Ale Ⓗ
A splendid, cosy pub which has become increasingly popular over the years thanks to the consistency of the beer. Competitively-priced, good food available. Occasional guest beers. ❀ 🛏 ◖ ◗ ♣ P

Market Hotel
West Carr Road, Ordsall (off A620, W of railway line)
☎ (0777) 703278
11–3.30; 6–11 (11–11 Sat)
Adnams Bitter, Broadside; Bateman XXXB; Exmoor Gold; Hall & Woodhouse Tanglefoot; Taylor Landlord Ⓗ
13 real ales in all, plus a warm and relaxing atmosphere. Resembles a mini beer festival.
Q ❀ ◖ ◗ ⇌ P

Turks Head
Grove Street
☎ (0777) 702742
11–4; 7–11
Wards Sheffield Best Bitter Ⓔ
Probably the most appealing pub in town, with attractive oak panelling. Handy for the town centre. Landlord is a sports enthusiast. Business lunches popular. ♨ 🛏 ◖ P

Try also: Hop Pole (Bass)

Ruddington

Red Lion
1 Easthorpe Street
☎ (0602) 844654
11.30–2.30 (3.30 Sat); 5.30 (6 Sat)–11
Home Mild, Bitter; Theakston XB; Younger Scotch Ⓗ
A fine, traditional, white-painted, street-corner locals' pub with two rooms. Two guest beers each week. Q ❀ ⊕ ♿ ♣ P

Three Crowns
Easthorpe Street
☎ (0602) 213226
12–3; 6–11
Greenalls Shipstone's Mild, Shipstone's Bitter Ⓔ
Tucked away in a back street and easily overlooked as it resembles a large, bay windowed house. Pleasant and comfortable. ♨ Q ⚇ ⊕ ♣

Scaftworth

King William
Off A631 ☎ (0302) 710292
12–2.30 (not Mon-Wed); 7–11
Marston's Pedigree Bitter; Tetley Bitter; Whitbread Castle Eden Ale Ⓗ
Several small rooms and a continually improved garden (now including a river garden). Various 'special' eves during the year. Good home-cooked food (not Sun/Mon eves).
♨ Q ❀ ◖ ◗ ♣ P

Southwell

Newcastle Arms
Station Road
☎ (0636) 813094
11–3; 6–11
Greenalls Shipstone's Mild, Shipstone's Bitter Ⓔ
Bustling and friendly local on the edge of historic cathedral town. Sedate lounge has interesting photographs of bygone days in Southwell; the bar is a lively centre for pub games. Separate pool room.
❀ ⊕ ♣ P

Stapleford

Old Cross
26 Church Street
☎ (0602) 394927
11–11 (11–4; 6.30–11 Sat)
Greenalls Shipstone's Mild, Shipstone's Bitter Ⓔ
Lively town-centre local with friendly atmosphere. Island bar divides large room into separate drinking areas. Covered skittle alley at rear. ♨ ❀ ♣ P

Swingate

Queen Adelaide
21 Babbington Lane (off Main Street, Kimberley)
☎ (0602) 383184
10.30–2.30; 7–11
Hardys & Hansons Best Mild, Best Bitter Ⓔ
Popular village local with a social club-like atmosphere. Upstairs pool room. Close to an ancient water tower. Well worth seeking out. ❀ ♿ ♣ P

White Lion
The Swingate (off Main Street, Kimberley) ☎ (0602) 383687
11–3; 7–11
Greenalls Shipstone's Mild, Shipstone's Bitter Ⓔ
Well-run village inn. Small and

friendly, with a fine collection of prints and plates devoted to horses. ❀ ⊞ ♿ ♣ P

Sutton in Ashfield

Railway Inn
High Pavement (off A615/B6018/A38)
☎ (0623) 555476
11.30–3; 7–11 (may extend Fri & Sat in summer)
John Smith's Bitter 🅗
Friendly local with small, unusually-shaped interior. Good food at all times. ❀ ◖ ◗ ♿ ♣

Upton

Cross Keys
Main Street ☎ (0636) 813269
11.30–2.30; 6–11
Bateman XXXB; Marston's Pedigree Bitter; Whitbread Boddingtons Bitter, Castle Eden Ale 🅗
Old, friendly pub in conservation area. Extension work is in keeping with rest of building. Upstairs restaurant open Thu-Sat eves and Sun lunch. Meals in bar/lounge at other times. Live music Sun eves. Guest beers. ⌂ ❀ ◖ ◗ P

Warsop

Hare & Hounds
Church Street
☎ (0623) 842440
11–11
Hardys & Hansons Best Mild, Best Bitter 🅗
Tudor-style town-centre pub with busy tap room and traditional lounge.
⌂ ♨ ❀ ◖ ◗ ⊞ ♿ ♣ P

Wellow

Olde Red Lion
☎ (0623) 861000
11.30–3; 5.30–11
Marston's Pedigree Bitter; Ruddles County; Whitbread Castle Eden Ale 🅗
Old beamed pub with several cosy bars. Good selection of food lunchtime and eves. Regular guest beers. Q ❀ ◖ ◗ P

West Leake

Star Inn
Melton Lane (700 yds from village on Sutton Bonington Road) OS523261
☎ (0509) 852233
12–2.30; 6–11
Draught Bass; M&B Springfield Bitter 🅗
Unspoilt, fine old coaching inn with fascinating small bar. Home of Nottingham's Pub Cat of the Year – (no less than seven feline residents)! Recommended salad bar; cold food only (no meals Sat/Sun).
⌂ Q ❀ ◖ ⊞ ♣ P

Worksop

Greendale Oak
Norfolk Street (off A60)
☎ (0909) 481373
11–3; 7–11 (may vary)
Stones Best Bitter 🅔
Small pub in terraced street. Very active sports teams.
Q ❀ ♿ ♣

Newcastle Arms
Carlton Road (A60)
☎ (0909) 485384
11–3; 5.30–11
Marston's Burton Best Bitter, Pedigree Bitter; Whitbread Trophy 🅗
Just off the town centre; a pub popular with all ages. Reasonably-priced food and guest beers. ◖ ◗ ⇌ ♣

White Lion
Park Street (B6005)
☎ (0909) 478125
11–2.30; 6–11
Marston's Pedigree Bitter; Whitbread Flowers IPA, Castle Eden Ale 🅗
Popular free house just out of town centre. Conservatory extension ideal for children.
♨ ❀ ◖ ◗ ⊞ ♿ P

Try also: French Horn (Stones)

PUB JARGON

Brew pub: one which brews its own beer.

Free house: a pub free from any brewery tie and, therefore, able to sell any beer it chooses. This is often not the case as a large proportion of 'free' houses take beer from a brewery which has given them financial assistance (the 'loan tie').

Guest beer: a beer served in addition to a pub's usual or restricted range.

Loan tie: control of a free house by a brewery through the conditions of a financial package agreed between the pub and the brewery. A brewery may offer an attractive loan arrangement in return for the pub selling its beers.

Tenant: Licensee who pays a rent and takes beer from the brewery which owns the pub. More independent than a manager.

Tied house: a pub owned by a brewery and restricted to selling its beer.

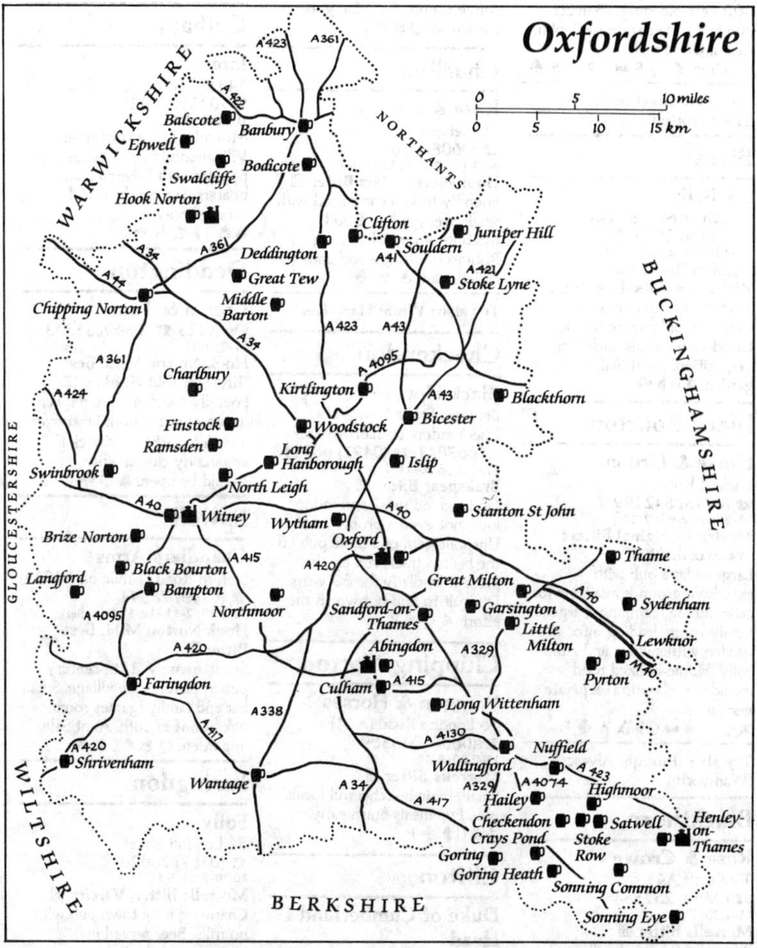

Brakspear, *Henley-on-Thames*; **Glenny**, *Witney*; **Hook Norton**, *Hook Norton*; **Morland**, *Abingdon*; **Morrells**, *Oxford*

Abingdon

Kings Head & Bell
East St Helen Street
☎ (0235) 20157
11–11
Theakston Best Bitter; Wadworth 6X; Younger No. 3 [H]
16th-century inn where Handel wrote his *Water Music* and Charles I was a frequent visitor.

Balscote

Butchers Arms
Off A422, 2 miles W of Banbury ☎ (0295) 73750
11–3; 6–11
Hook Norton Mild [G], **Best Bitter** [H]
Classic one-roomed village pub. No food, but lots of conversation. Q P

Bampton

Romany
Bridge Street
☎ (0993) 850237
11–3 (4 Sat); 6–11
Archers Best Bitter; Hook Norton Best Bitter [H]
Pleasant and friendly, small town inn offering regular and varied guest beers. Extensive menu includes veg and children's options. Q

Banbury

Britannia Inn
Windsor Street (near station)
☎ (0295) 256917
11–3; 6–11
Marston's Burton Best Bitter, Pedigree Bitter [H]
Rejuvenated, but still basic pub at the back of the town. Friendly atmosphere. Menu caters for children and vegetarians. P

Woolpack
28 Horsefair
☎ (0295) 262915
10.30–11 (10.30–3; 5–11 winter)
Ruddles Best Bitter, County; Webster's Yorkshire Bitter [H]

400 year-old snug, compact pub and restaurant near Banbury Cross. Good malt whisky selection. ⌂ Q ❀ ⛟ ◖ ◗ ⊞ ♿ ♣

Try also: Coach & Horses (Hook Norton)

Bicester

Six Bells
Church Street (off A43)
☎ (0869) 253578
12–2.30 (11–4 Sat); 7–11
Ruddles Best Bitter; Webster's Yorkshire Bitter [H]
17th-century pub next to church in old part of town. Good value meals, including veg option. Aunt Sally in garden. ❀ ◖ ◗ ♣

Black Bourton

Horse & Groom
Burford Road
☎ (0993) 842199
12–3 (not Mon); 7–11
Morland Original Bitter; Wadworth 6X [H]
Large village pub with extensive grounds available for caravanning/camping. Large family room, leading into garden with swings and Aunt Sally. Home-cooked food includes veg option; separate restaurant.
⌂ Q ☗ ❀ ⛟ ◖ ◗ ♿ ⛺ ♣ P

Try also: Plough, Alvescot (Wadworth)

Blackthorn

Rose & Crown
1 mile off A41
☎ (0869) 252534
11–2.30; 7–11
Morrells Bitter [H]
Basic Victorian pub with a friendly parlour atmosphere and an interesting jukebox. Wholesome lunchtime snacks.
⌂ ❀ ♣ P

Try also: Royal Oak (Free)

Bodicote

Plough
High Street (off A41)
☎ (0295) 62327
11–2.30; 7–11
Draught Bass; Bodicote Bitter, No. 9, Boiler Maker, Old English Porter [H]
Friendly brew pub and restaurant. Lively bar. ❀ ◖ ⊞ ♣

Brize Norton

Carpenters Arms
Station Road
☎ (0993) 842568
11–2.30; 6–11
Morland Original Bitter [H]
Good, old-fashioned, basic and vibrant village local; plenty of conversation. Aunt Sally in garden. ⌂ Q ❀ ♣ P

Charlbury

Rose & Crown
Market Street
☎ (0608) 810103
6–11 (11–11 Sat, 12–3; 7–10.30 Sun)
Hook Norton Best Bitter [H]
Friendly town-centre local with small beer garden. Good rotation of guest beers, eg Robinson's, Ringwood and Fuller's. ❀ ◖ ♿ ≉ ♣

Try also: White Hart (Free)

Checkendon

Black Horse
Between Stoke Row and Checkendon, up narrow track OS667841 ☎ (0491) 680418
11–2.30; 6.30–11
Brakspear Bitter [G]
No food, no music, no indoor loos, not even a proper address! Unspoilt gem of a basic pub off the beaten track, run by the present landlady for 60 years. Difficult to find but worth the effort. ⌂ Q ❀ P

Chipping Norton

Waggon & Horses
16 London Road (A44)
☎ (0608) 643369
11–2.30; 6–11
Morrells Bitter [H]
Small, basic but cheerful locals' pub. Eve meals finish early.
⌂ ❀ ◖ ◗ ♣ P

Clifton

Duke of Cumberland's Head
On B4031 ☎ (0869) 38534
11–2.30; 6–11
Brakspear Bitter; Donnington BB; Jennings Bitter; Wadworth 6X [H]
Thatched, 17th-century Hornton-stone building; beams, inglenook and intimate restaurant. Vibrant atmosphere. Live jazz first Tue of month.
⌂ Q ❀ ⛟ ◖ ◗ ♿ P

Crays Pond

White Lion
Goring Road 1 mile E of Goring at B471/B4526 jct
☎ (0491) 680471
11–2.30; 6–11
Courage Best Bitter, Directors [H]
Comfortable, traditional pub. Large garden with children's play area. Lounge bar has conservatory-style extension. Sun menu restricted to ploughman's lunches.
⌂ ❀ ◖ ◗ ♣ P

Culham

Lion
44 High Street (off A415)
☎ (0235) 20327
10.30–3; 6–11
Morrells Light, Bitter [H]
Village local near Thames lock; popular with fishermen and boaters. Sun lunch served summer only.
⌂ ❀ ◖ ◗ ⊞ ♿ ♣ P

Deddington

Crown & Tuns
On A423 ☎ (0869) 38343
11–3; 7–11
Hook Norton Mild, Best Bitter [H], **Old Hookey** [G]
Friendly coaching inn. Bar is a haven of peace from jukeboxes and slot machines. Knock if apparently closed when it should be open. ⌂ Q ♣

Epwell

Chandlers Arms
Sibford Road (1 mile off B4035)
☎ (0295) 78344
12–2.30; 7–11 (12–11 Fri & Sat)
Hook Norton Mild, Best Bitter [H]
Small, friendly, 17th-century pub in picturesque village. Small bar and family/games room, oak beams in both. Aunt Sally in garden. Q ☗ ❀ ◖ ◗ ♣ ⌽ P

Faringdon

Folly
54 London Street
☎ (0367) 20620
10.30–2.30; 5.45–11
Morrells Bitter, Varsity [H]
Charming little town pub with no frills. Beer served in lovingly-polished glasses.
⌂ Q ❀ ⊞ ♣

Finstock

Plough Inn
The Bottom (off B4022 Witney-Charlbury Road)
OS362162 ☎ (099386) 333
12–3; 6–11 (12–11 Sat)
Adnams Bitter, Broadside; Hook Norton Best Bitter, Old Hookey [H]
A traditional, thatched pub, built in 1772, offering a warm welcome, fine fare and guest beers. Real cider available in summer.
⌂ Q ❀ ◖ ◗ ⊞ ♿ ≉ ♣ ⌽ P

Garsington

Plough Inn
1 Oxford Road
☎ (086736) 395
11–3; 6 (5 Sat, 6.30 winter)–11
Courage Best Bitter, Directors [H]
Well-run village pub, popular

with locals and visitors. Parents can relax in the large, enclosed, prize-winning garden whilst their offspring enjoy the well-equipped play area and Aunt Sally alley. Snacks only served eves and Sun. ⌂ ◙ ◐ ⊟ ♣ P

Goring

John Barleycorn
Manor Road (off B4009)
☎ (0491) 872509
10–2.30; 6–11
Brakspear Bitter, Special [H]
Attractive, 16th-century, low-beamed inn with cosy saloon and good food. Close to River Thames and Ridgeway long distance footpath.
Q ◙ ⊨ ◐ ◗ ⊟ ♿ ⇌ ♣

Try also: Catherine Wheel (Brakspear)

Goring Heath

King Charles' Head
Reading Road (B4526)
☎ (0491) 680268
11.15–2.45; 6–11
Adnams Bitter; Brakspear XXX Mild, Bitter; Glenny Wychwood Best, Hobgoblin; Hook Norton Best Bitter [H]
Comfortable, four-roomed pub with large garden. Varied menu of good value meals including veg (eve meals 7–9.30). Attractive walks from the pub to the Thames. ⌂ ◙ ◐ ◗ ⊟ ♣ P

Great Milton

Bell Inn
The Green (off A329)
☎ (0844) 269270
12–2; 7–11
Brakspear Bitter; Donnington SBA; Marston's Pedigree Bitter; Uley Old Spot [H]
Welcoming country pub with good home-made food and regular guest beers. Bar billiards.
⌂ Q ◙ ◐ ◗ ⊟ ♿ ▲ ♣

Great Tew

Falkland Arms
OS397293 ☎ (060 883) 653
11.30–2.30 (not Mon); 6–11
Donnington BB; Hall & Woodhouse Tanglefoot; Hook Norton Best Bitter; Wadworth 6X [H]
Outstanding, 16th-century, classic pub in preserved village. Oak panels, settles, flagstones, oil lamps, clay pipes, snuff, thatched roof – a gem! Guest beers; home-made food. Four bedrooms, one with a four-poster bed.
⌂ Q ◙ ⊨ ◐ ♿ ▲ ♣ ⌓

Hailey

King William IV
Off A4074, towards Ipsden at White House pub OS641859
☎ (0491) 680675
11–2.30; 6–11
Brakspear XXX Mild, Bitter, Special, Old Ale [G]
Friendly country pub with a collection of agricultural memorabilia. Popular with walkers due to the proximity of the Ridgeway long distance footpath. Snacks available.
⌂ Q ◙ ⌓ P

Henley-on-Thames

Three Tuns
5 Market Place
☎ (0491) 573260
10–11 (12–10.30 Sun by special dispensation)
Brakspear XXX Mild [G], **Bitter, Special** [H], **Old Ale** [G]
Excellent, old town-centre pub. Small public bar; oak-beamed lounge with large fireplace (and restaurant licence). Good food, including veg options. Camping outside the town.
Q ◙ ◐ ◗ ⊟ ▲ ⇌ ♣

Highmoor

Dog & Duck
On B481, S of Nettlebed
☎ (0491) 641261
11–3; 6–11
Brakspear XXX Mild, (summer), **Bitter, Special, Old Ale** (winter) [H]
Cosy, two-bar, roadside pub in Chiltern woodland. No-smoking dining room, serving good value, wholesome, home-made food, including veg option (not Mon). Large, enclosed garden with barbecues on summer weekends. Shut the Box played.
⌂ Q ◙ ◐ ◗ ♿ ♣ P

Hook Norton

Bell
High Street (off A361)
☎ (0608) 737432
11–2.30 (3 Sat); 6–11
Hook Norton Best Bitter; Theakston XB [H]
Comfortable village-centre pub, catering for all tastes: good food; guest beers.
⌂ ⚘ ◙ ◐ ◗ ⊟ ♿ ♣ P

Pear Tree
Scotland End (off A361)
☎ (0608) 737482
11–3; 7–11
Hook Norton Best Bitter, Old Hookey [H]
Small, cheerful, welcoming pub, close to brewery. No food Sun.
⌂ Q ◙ ⊨ ◐ ⊟ ♣ P

Try also: Sun (Hook Norton)

Islip

Swan
Lower Street (B4027)
☎ (08675) 2590
11–3; 6–11
Morrells Bitter, Graduate [H]
Comfortable, one-bar village local overlooking River Ray. Eve meals Tue–Sat. Q ⚘ ◐ ◗ P

Juniper Hill

Fox
OS579325 ☎ (0869) 810616
11–2.30; 6.30–11
Hook Norton Best Bitter [H], **Old Hookey** [G]
Friendly pub in centre of hamlet described in *Lark Rise to Candleford*. ⌂ Q ◙ ♣ P

Kirtlington

Dashwood Arms
On A4095 ☎ (0869) 50225
11–2.30; 6–11 (11–11 Sat)
Halls Harvest Bitter; Ind Coope Burton Ale [H]
Comfortable, 18th-century, former coaching inn, popular with Oxfordshire Way walkers. The picturesque village is noted for polo and annual 'Lamb Ale' Morris Festival. Freshly-cooked food (not Wed).
⌂ Q ◙ ◐ ◗ ⊟ ♣ P

Langford

Bell
Off A361, through Filkins, then 1st right ☎ (036 786) 281
11–2.30; 6.30–11
Archers Village Bitter; Morland Original Bitter; Wadworth 6X [H]
Quiet, 17th-century inn and village local, difficult to find but worth the effort. Unpretentious, conventional, home-cooked pub menu (not Sun). Aunt Sally played. ⌂ Q ◙ ◐ ◗ ⊟ ♣ P

Lewknor

Olde Leathern Bottel
1 High Street (off B4009/M40)
☎ (0844) 51482
11–2.30; 6–11
Brakspear Bitter, Special, Old Ale [H]
Homely and welcoming, low-beamed pub with Cromwellian connections and various spellings! Good food, especially the steaks and curries.
⌂ ⚘ ◙ ◐ ◗ ⊟ ♣ P

Little Milton

Plough
Thame Road (A329)
☎ (0844) 278180
11–3; 5–11 (11–11 summer)
Morrells Dark, Best Bitter, Varsity, Graduate [H]
17th-century, stone-walled and timber-beamed pub with a village atmosphere. Good value food, including veg option; barbecues and pig roasts in

summer. Large, enclosed play area, and garden with pets corner. 🔥 Q 🚸 🍞 ◐ ◑ ♣ P

Long Hanborough

Swan

Millwood End (400 yds off A4095, Combe Road)
OS417144 ☎ (0993) 881347
11–2.30; 6–11
Morrells Light, Bitter, Graduate [H]
Popular, old village pub with inglenook. Garden has pets and children's play area. Barbecues at weekends in fine weather.
🍞 ◐ ◑ ♿ ⇌ ♣ P

Long Wittenham

Machine Man

Off High Street (A415)
☎ (086730) 7835
11–2.30; 6–11
Buckley's Best Bitter; Eldridge Pope Royal Oak; Marston's Pedigree Bitter [H]
Genuine village locals' pub. Good value home-made food – try the game hot pot (not Sun eve). Aunt Sally on Wed in summer. Two guest beers always available. ETB-approved accommodation.
🔥 Q 🚸 🍞 🛏 ◐ ◑ ♿ ♣

Middle Barton

Carpenters Arms

122 North Street (B4030)
☎ (0869) 40378
11–2.30 (3 Sat); 6–11
Halls Harvest Bitter [H]
Comfortable, thatched pub, popular with walkers. Good home-cooked food (not Sun eve). Q 🍞 🛏 ◐ ◑ ⊟ ♣ P

Northmoor

Dun Cow

Off A415 ☎ (086731) 295
11–2.30 (3 Sat); 6.30–11
Morland Original Bitter [G]
Delightful, unspoilt, traditional village local with no serving counter. 🔥 Q 🍞 ⊟ ♣ P

North Leigh

Woodman Inn

New Yatt Road (off A4095)
OS384132 ☎ (0993) 881790
11.30–3; 7 (may be earlier summer)–11
Glenny Witney Bitter, Hobgoblin; Hook Norton Best Bitter; Wadworth 6X [H]
Small village pub. Large garden with Aunt Sally, safe for children. Guest beers, jazz, home-made food.
🔥 Q 🍞 🛏 ◐ ◑ ♿ ♣ P

Nuffield

Crown

On A423, 2 miles W of Nettlebed ☎ (0491) 641335
11–3; 6–11
Brakspear Bitter, Special, Old Ale [H]
17th-century, beamed coaching inn with large inglenook. Excellent home-made meals. Pub is conveniently situated on Ridgeway long distance footpath. Camping for tents only. Children welcome at lunchtime.
🔥 Q 🚸 🍞 ◐ ◑ ♿ ⛺ ♣ P

Oxford

Black Boy

91 Old High Street, Headington ☎ (0865) 63234
11–3; 6–11
Morrells Light, Bitter, Varsity, Graduate [H], College [G]
Large local with bars, beers, spirits and snuffs to appeal to all. No food at weekend.
Q ◐ ⊟ ♣ P

Cricketers Arms

43 Iffley Road
☎ (0865) 726264
11–2.30; 6–11
Morland Original Bitter, Old Masters [H]
Traditional locals' pub with lively bar and a more relaxed lounge. Public bar used as family room Sun lunchtime when alcohol is served only in lounge. Outdoor seating on pavement. Q 🚸 🍞 ⊟ ♣

Dewdrop Inn

258 Banbury Road
☎ (0865) 59372
11–3; 5.30–11
Courage Best Bitter, Directors [H]
Two 1820s cottages, much-rebuilt and enlarged over the years into a comfortable pub, serving the needs of the local business people and residents. No food Sun lunch. 🍞 ◐ ⊟ ♣

Eagle & Child

49 St Giles
☎ (0865) 58085
11–2.30; 5.30–11
Ind Coope Burton Ale; Tetley Bitter; Wadworth 6X [H]
A multi-alcoved pub with connections with Tolkein and CS Lewis. Recently lovingly-restored to a condition that Tolkein knew and enjoyed. No food Sun eve. Q 🍞 ◐ ◑ ⇌

Fir Tree Tavern

163 Iffley Road
☎ (0865) 247373
12–3; 5 (6 Sat)–11
Morrells Bitter, Varsity, Graduate [H]
Small split-level pub, popular with both locals and students. Home-made pizzas a speciality. Seating outside on pavement.
🍞 ◐ ◑

Gardeners Arms

Plantation Road
☎ (0865) 59814
10.30–3; 6–11
Morrells Bitter, Graduate [H]
Friendly, one-bar pub, named after former local market gardening area. Meals served in new garden room at rear. Attracts students and locals.
🍞 ◐ ◑ ♣

Globe

59–60 Cranham Street, Jericho
☎ (0865) 57759
10.30–3; 6.30–11
Morrells Bitter, Varsity [H]
Neat and tidy side-street pub: a quiet home from home for locals and visitors. Eve meals finish at 8pm. Workingmen's accommodation (four beds to a room!). 🍞 🛏 ◐ ◑ 🍎

Hollybush

106 Bridge Street, Osney (off Botley Road)
☎ (0865) 723454
10.30–2.30; 5.30 (6 Sat)–11
Courage Best Bitter, Directors [H]
Bustling town local on Osney Island. The pub tends to ignore the fact that Osney is becoming a 'yuppy' area. Home-cooked food (not Mon eve).
Q 🍞 ◐ ◑ ⊟ ⇌ ♣ P

Marlborough House

60 Western Road (off A4144)
☎ (0865) 243617
11.30–2.30; 6–11 (11.30–11 Sat)
Halls Harvest Bitter; Ind Coope Burton Ale; Tetley Bitter [H]
Back-street locals' pub, popular with students. Folk music every other Mon; pianist every other Wed. Pool room upstairs.
🚸 ◐ ⊟ ♣

Old Tom

101 St Aldates
☎ (0865) 243034
10.30–3; 5–11
Morrells Bitter, Varsity [H]
Small, comfortable city-centre pub with a friendly atmosphere; universally popular. Good value home-cooking (no chips); eve meals finish early. Q 🍞 ◐ ◑ ⇌

Prince of Wales

80 Cowley Road
☎ (0865) 243069
10.30–2.30 (3 Mon & Fri, 4 Sat); 7–11
Morrells Light, Dark, Varsity [H]
Pleasant, homely, split-level, street-corner local, open for breakfast weekday mornings (9–10.30). Aunt Sally played.
◐ ♣ P

Temple Bar

21 Temple Street (off B480)
☎ (0865) 243251
12–2.30; 7–11
Hall & Woodhouse

Tanglefoot; Wadworth 6X, Farmer's Glory, Old Timer [H]
Popular two-bar local. Folk music sessions every Sun — bring an instrument! Parking and disabled entrance on Stockmore Street. Bar billiards. ⚘ ⊟ ♿ ♣ P

Three Goats Heads
3–5 St Michael's Street
☎ (0865) 721523
11–11
Samuel Smith OBB, Museum Ale [H]
Welcome conversion of a city-centre building into a tasteful new pub. Situated next to the Oxford Union, location of Oxford CAMRA's Beerex. Opens 9am for breakfast.
◖◗ ⇌

Turf Tavern
4 Bath Place (off Holywell Street) ☎ (0865) 243235
11–11
Archers Headbanger; Glenny Witney Bitter, Hobgoblin; Whitbread Flowers Original [H]
Famous 13th-century tavern, set in idyllic seclusion amongst the colleges and old city walls. Popular with students and tourists and consequently expensive. Guest beers.
Q ⚘ ◖◗ ♿ ♁

Victoria Arms
Mill Lane, Marston Ferry
☎ (0865) 241382
11.30–2.30; 6–11
Hall & Woodhouse Tanglefoot; Wadworth IPA, 6X, Farmer's Glory, Old Timer [H]
Riverside pub approached either by punt or down a long drive (beware the sleeping policemen!). Has been internally well-restored, retaining some character. Guest beers. ⚘ ◖◗ P

Victoria Arms
90 Walton Street, Jericho
☎ (0865) 57676
11–11
Banks's Mild, Bitter [E]
Friendly, unpretentious pub with two bars: a large, lively main bar and a snug — now a pool room. Families welcome in upstairs room. Some of the lowest beer prices in Oxford. Meals served 12–2 and 7–9.
♘ ⚘ ◖◗

Try also: Kings Arms (Free)

Pyrton

Plough
Off B4009, N of Watlington
OS687961 ☎ (049 161) 2003
11.30–2.30; 6–11 (closed Mon eve)
Adnams Bitter; Brakspear Bitter; Fuller's ESB [H]
Attractive, 17th-century, thatched pub in quiet country village. Popular for its home-made food in the bar or restaurant (not Sun eves). Campsite at Watlington (1 mile). ⌂ ⚘ ◖◗ ♿ ⛺ ♣ P

Try also: Chequers, Watlington (Brakspear)

Ramsden

Royal Oak
High Street (1 mile off B4022)
☎ (0993) 86213
11–3; 6–11
Adnams Bitter; Hook Norton Best Bitter, Old Hookey [H]
Friendly, refurbished, 17th-century coaching inn. One room, but a separate restaurant (veg option). Guest beers.
⌂ Q ⚘ ⛟ ◖◗ ♿ P

Sandford-on-Thames

Fox
29 Henley Road
☎ (0865) 777803
11–2.30; 6.30–11
Morrells Light, Bitter [G]
Straightforward roadside local, where the beer is among the cheapest in the area. Aunt Sally and dominoes played.
⌂ Q ⚘ ⊟ ♿ P

Satwell

Lamb Inn
Off B481 between Sonning Common and Nettlebed
☎ (049 17) 482
11–3; 6–11
Brakspear Bitter, Special, Old Ale [G]
Classic, old, cottage-style pub, with low beams and a huge inglenook. Excellent value home-cooked food; spit-roast Sun lunches are very popular. Children and vegetarians also catered for (no food Sun eve). Shove-ha'penny and crib played.
⌂ Q ⚘ ◖◗ ♿ ♣ P

Shrivenham

Prince of Wales
High Street ☎ (0793) 782268
11–2.30; 6–11
Hall & Woodhouse Tanglefoot; Wadworth IPA, 6X [H]
Warm and cosy country pub with a split-level, comfortable lounge and a basic bar. Good food: selection of home-cooked pizzas and decent bread (not Sun eve). Limited parking.
⌂ Q ♘ ⚘ ◖◗ ⊟ P

Sonning Common

Bird in Hand
Reading Road (B481)
☎ (0734) 723230
11–2.30; 6–11
Courage Best Bitter, Directors [H]
Low-beamed pub with large inglenook and traditional pub furnishings. Very popular restaurant (standard pub menu), but meals also available in bar (not Sun eve). Attractive, enclosed garden backs on to woodland, close to many popular walks; ideal for children. Q ⚘ ◖◗ ♿ P

Sonning Eye

Flowing Spring
Henley Road (A4155, 2 miles E of Caversham)
☎ (0734) 693207
12–2.30 (3 Fri & Sat); 5.30 (6 Sat)–11
Fuller's Chiswick Bitter, London Pride, Mr Harry, ESB [H]
Comfortable roadside pub with cosy atmosphere. Wrought-iron staircase leads to huge garden. Occasional events include steam engine rally early July and Guy Fawkes' night party. Barbecues Fri/Sat in summer. No food Sun or Mon/Tue eves. ⌂ ⚘ ◖◗ P

Souldern

Fox
Off A41, 2 miles S of Aynho
☎ (0869) 345284
11.30–3; 6–11
Draught Bass; Hook Norton Best Bitter, Old Hookey [H]
Friendly, Cotswold-stone pub in village centre.
⌂ ⚘ ⛟ ◖◗ ♿ ♣ P

Stanton St John

Star
Off B4027 ☎ (086 735) 277
11–2.30 (12–2.30 Sun); 6.30–11
Hall & Woodhouse Tanglefoot; Wadworth IPA, 6X, Farmer's Glory, Old Timer [H]
A country inn restored to an excellent standard, with further improvements this year to provide a better dining area and bar. Home-cooking a speciality (veg option) at reasonable prices. Brewery tie collection on view. ⌂ ⚘ ◖◗ ⊟ ♣ P

Stoke Lyne

Peyton Arms
500 yds off A41
☎ (086 96) 285
10–2.30 (not Mon); 6–11
Hook Norton Best Bitter, Old Hookey (winter) [G]
Small, basic village local, unchanged by time — a real rural gem. Aunt Sally played.
⌂ Q ♘ ⚘ ⊟ ♿ ♣ P

Stoke Row

Cherry Tree

Off B481, NW of Sonning Common ☎ (0491) 680430
10–2.30; 6–11
Brakspear XXX Mild, Bitter, Special, Old Ale [G]
Picturesque, low-beamed village pub. Games room with pool and shove-ha'penny; swings and slide in garden. Lunchtime snacks. ♔ Q ♨ ⌂ ♿ ♣ P

Swalcliff

Stags Head
On Shipston Road (B4035)
☎ (029578) 232
12–2.30 (not Tue, 11.30–3 Sat); 6.30–11
Hook Norton Best Bitter; Wadworth 6X [H]
Thatched, 16th-century pub with oak settles and stools; large garden. Good home-cooked food, with veg option.
♔ Q ⌂ ⛟ ◑ ◗ ♣

Swinbrook

Swan
Off A40 ☎ (099382) 2165
11.30–2.30; 6–11
Morland Original Bitter; Wadworth 6X [H]
Characterful, riverside country inn, a former watermill. Good home-cooked food. Darts, dominoes and shove-ha'penny in old tap room. ♔ Q ◑ ◗ P

Sydenham

Plough & Harrow
Emmington (on B4445, Chinnor-Thame road)
☎ (0844) 51967
12–2.30 (3 Sat); 6–11
Brakspear Bitter; Hook Norton Old Hookey; Wadworth 6X [H]
250 year-old drovers' pub now a modern eating and drinking house in typical Oxfordshire countryside, with views of the Chilterns. Excellent walking and riding country within easy reach of Oxford. Guest beers.
♔ Q ⌂ ⛟ ◑ ◗ ♣ ⛀ P

Try also: Crown (Morrells)

Thame

Rising Sun
26 High Street
☎ (084421) 4206
11–2.30; 6–11
Hook Norton Best Bitter; Marston's Pedigree Bitter; Wadworth 6X [H]
Attractive, 16th-century, oak-beamed building with an overhanging first floor. Cosy atmosphere enhanced by low ceilings. Guest beers. No food Sun eve. ♔ ⌂ ◑ ◗ ♣

Swan Hotel
8 Upper High Street
☎ (0844) 261211
11–11
Brakspear Bitter; Hook Norton Best Bitter; Whitbread Flowers Original [H]
Very popular inn re-opened in 1987 after a complete re-design. Many unusual fittings and furniture. Constantly-changing selection of guest beers from around the country. Fine restaurant and bar meals (veg and children's choices).
♔ Q ♨ ⌂ ⛟ ◑ ◗ ♣ P

Wallingford

Cross Keys
48 High Street (A4130)
☎ (0491) 37173
11–3; 6–11
Brakspear XXX Mild, Bitter, Special, Old Ale [H]
Unspoilt, three-room, 17th-century town pub. Small, comfortable lounge; public bar with separate darts room. Children's play area in garden. Reputedly haunted — ask the locals about 'Charlie'. No food Sun; eve meals until 8.30pm.
⌂ ◑ ◗ ⊕ ♣ P

Wantage

Royal Oak
Newbury Street
☎ (02357) 3129
12–2.30 (not Mon–Thu); 5.30 (7 Sat)–11
Fuller's London Pride; Glenny Hobgoblin; Hall & Woodhouse Badger Best Bitter, Tanglefoot; John Smith's Bitter; Wadworth Farmer's Glory [H]
Busy, often noisy town pub. A meeting place for the younger set (but not exclusively).
⛟ ◑ ⊕ ♣

Shoulder of Mutton
38 Wallingford Street
☎ (02357) 2835
10.30–2.30; 5.30–11
Morland Original Bitter [H]
Plain, unspoilt town local. Intimate snug attracts the younger set who enjoy a *real* pub. Not a place to take your mother-in-law! ♔ Q ⊕ ♣

Witney

Royal Oak
17 High Street
☎ (0993) 702576
10.30–2.30 (4 Thu & Fri); 5–11 (10–4; 6.30–11 Sat)
Wadworth 6X [G]; **Hook Norton Best Bitter; Morland Original Bitter** [H]; **Morrells Dark** [G]
Two-bar town pub parts of which date back to the 16th century. Courtyard eminently suitable for summer drinking. Small bar area sandwiched between public and lounge bars has cat/dog flap cut into it! No food Sun. ⌂ ◑ ⊕ ⛀

Woodstock

Queens Own
59 Oxford Street (A34)
☎ (0993) 812414
11–2.30; 6–11
Hook Norton Mild, Best Bitter, Old Hookey [H]
Compact, one-bar pub, very much for locals in a town aimed at the tourist trade. A friendly welcome for all nonetheless.
♔ ⌂ ◑ ◗ ♣

Wytham

White Hart
Off A34 ☎ (0865) 244372
11–2.30; 6–11
Ind Coope Burton Ale; Tetley Bitter; Wadworth 6X [H]
Popular 300 year-old pub in a picture-postcard village on the edge of Oxford. There is a 16th-century dovecote in the garden. Children permitted in dining room and conservatory. Excellent cold table menu.
♔ Q ♨ ⌂ ◑ ◗ P

DISPENSE METHODS

[G] by gravity straight from the cask
[H] by handpump
[E] by electric pump
[A] by air pressure (including electric air compressor in Scotland)

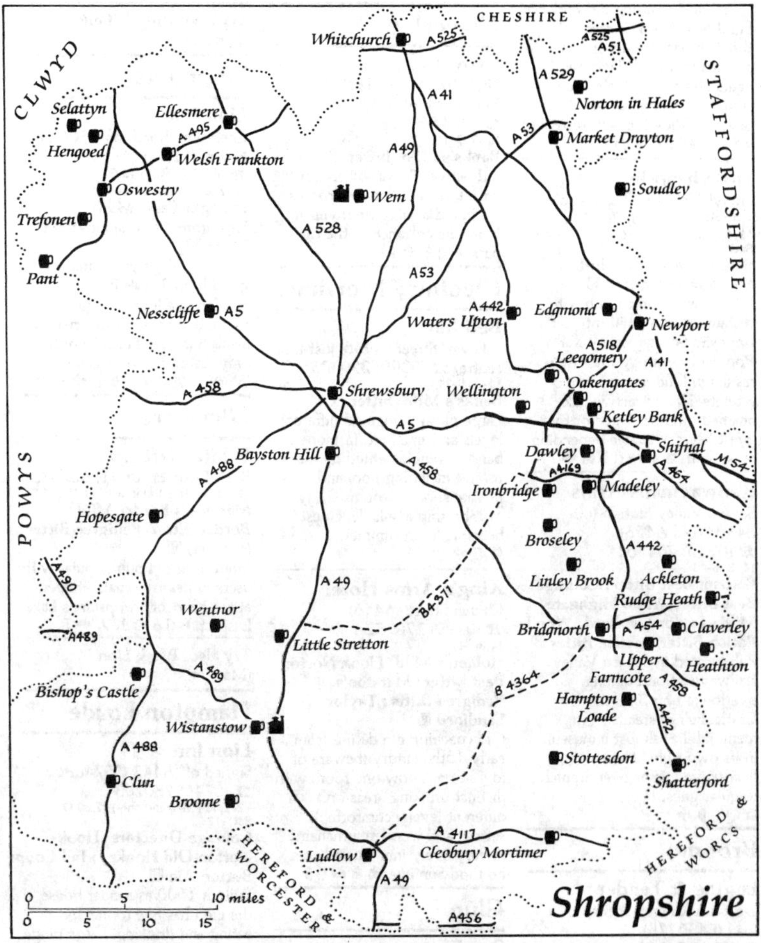

Hanby, Wem; **Wood,** Wistanstow

Ackleton

Folley Inn

On B4176, 6 miles S of Telford
☎ (07465) 225
11–2.30; 6 (7 Sat)–11
Banks's Mild, Bitter E
Open-plan lounge/bar with small, intimate ante-room. Large feature fireplace adorned with copper and brass. P

Bayston Hill

Compasses Inn

Hereford Road (A49)
☎ (0743) 722921
12–2.30 (3 Fri); 5–11 (11–11 Sat)
Draught Bass; M&B Highgate Mild, Brew XI H
Friendly main road local with lounge and separate public bar whose decor reflects a nautical connection. Note fascinating collection of carved wooden elephants. Disabled access via rear door. P

Bishop's Castle

Crown & Anchor Vaults

High Street ☎ (0588) 638203
11–11
Courage Best Bitter, Directors; John Smith's Magnet H
This Victorian-style drinking house is a recent, welcome addition to the town. Occasional live music. Regular guest beers (incl. Hanby).
Q

Three Tuns

Salop Street ☎ (0588) 638797
11.30–2.30; 6.30–11
Three Tuns Mild, XXX, Castle Steamer, Old Scrooge H
One of the four home-brew pubs still existing in the early 70s and the only one with a tower brewery. After a change of ownership the beers are establishing a distinctive character of their own. Vegetarian cooking.
Q P

Try also: Castle Hotel (Free)

Bridgnorth

Bell & Talbot

2 Salop Street (B4364/old A458) ☎ (0746) 763233
11.30–3 (4 Sat); 7 (6 summer)–11
Batham Best Bitter; Younger IPA H
Grade II listed free house with two character-laden rooms.

Courtyard, housing old brewery buildings at rear, is reached through passage decorated with a 'real ale' mural. Two guest beers always available; cider in summer. Bridgnorth has a Severn Valley Railway restricted service. ⌂ ❁ ◖ ⊞ ⊙

Hollyhead Inn
Hollybush Road (B4364/old A458) ☎ (0746) 762162
12–2.30 (3 summer); 5.30–11 (11–11 Sat)
Banks's Mild [E]; Whitbread Boddingtons Bitter [H]
Large, two-roomed pub with restaurant area, built into cliff opposite Severn Valley Railway. Popularity with young often results in loud music from satellite TV. Attractive oak-beamed interior. Three or four guest beers available depending on season. ⌂ ❁ ⛟ ◖ ◗ ⊞ ♣ P

Railwaymans Arms
Severn Valley Station (off B4364/old A458)
☎ (0746) 764361
11–3; 6–11
Batham Best Bitter; Courage Best Bitter; M&B Highgate Mild; Taylor Landlord; Wood Parish Bitter, Jubilee Bitter [H]
Pub located in Severn Valley Railway station building, overlooked by Bridgnorth Castle. Full of steam memorabilia; almost a museum in its own right! Huge decorative mirror over fireplace. Regular guest beers.
⌂ Q ◖ ◗ ♣ ⊙ P

Broome

Engine & Tender
Off Clun–Craven Arms road (B4367/8)
☎ (05887) 275
12–3; 7–11
Marston's Pedigree Bitter; Wood Parish Bitter [H]
Extended from original building, with interlinking rooms and mementoes reflecting its name. Broome Halt itself has small railway display provided by locals. Train only stops by request! Own camp site.
Q ◖ ◗ ♿ ▲ ⇌ (Halt) ♣ P

Broseley

Cumberland Hotel
Queen Street (off B4373)
☎ (0952) 882301
10–11
Banks's Bitter; M&B Highgate Mild; Ruddles Best Bitter, County [H]
Spacious, lively, friendly hotel with a serious interest in good beer and food. Low-beamed dining room where food is served on Coalport china. Menu caters for children and vegetarians. ⌂ ☺ ❁ ⛟ ◖ ◗ ⊞ P

Claverley

Crown Inn
High Street (5 miles E of Bridgnorth off A454)
☎ (07466) 228
12–3; 7–11
Banks's Mild, Bitter [E]
Attractive, Tudor-styled inn with three comfortable rooms, set in a charming rural village. Note the entrance to the car park. ❁ ◖ ◗ ♣ P

Cleobury Mortimer

Bell Inn
8 Lower Street (A456, just E of centre) ☎ (0299) 270305
11–3; 6–11
Banks's Mild, Bitter [E]
Large plush lounge on different levels and small old-fashioned bar are complemented by many rooms, including pool and private snooker rooms – day membership available. Guest beers; cider in summer.
⌂ ⊞ ♣ ⊙

King's Arms Hotel
Church Street (A456)
☎ (0299) 270252
11.30–11
Holden's Mild; Hook Norton Best Bitter; Marston's Pedigree Bitter; Taylor Landlord [H]
Old coaching inn dating from early 16th century (beware of low beams), now one room with distinct drinking areas on different levels; comfortable settees and wooden armchairs. A very lively inn. Guest beers – no food Sun eve. ⌂ ❁ ⛟ ◖ ◗

Clun

Sun Inn
High Street (A488)
☎ (05884) 277
11–3; 6–11
Banks's Mild, Bitter; Wood Special Bitter [H]
In a timeless village, in a remote area, this 15th-century listed cruck-built pub has all the ingredients to help you get away from it all. Stone-flagged public bar and a cash register set of handpumps.
⌂ Q ❁ ⛟ ◖ ◗ ⊞ ♿ ▲ ♣ P

Dawley

Three Crowns Inn
Hinkshay Road (off B4373)
☎ (0952) 590868
11–3 (4 Sat); 6.30–11
Marston's Burton Best Bitter, Pedigree Bitter [H]
Small town pub with U-shaped lounge, part of which is given over to darts and pool, so as not to interfere with other customers' drinking.
❁ ◖ ♿ ▲ ♣ P

Try also: Ring O'Bells (Marston's)

Edgmond

Lion Inn
Chetwynd Road (off B5062 at Newport Road jct)
☎ (0952) 810346
12–2.30 (3 Sat); 7–11
Draught Bass; M&B Highgate Mild, Springfield Bitter [E]
Popular village pub noted for good food. Meals in comfortable lounge dining room. Barbecues in summer. No meals Sun eve; lunch to order only. Large bar with games. Worth a visit. ❁ ◖ ◗ ⊞ ♣ P

Ellesmere

White Hart Inn
Birch Road ☎ (0691) 622333
11.30 (12 Thu–Sat in winter)–3; 7–11
Marston's Border Mild, Border Bitter, Pedigree Bitter (summer) [H]
Interesting old pub popular with users of nearby canal. Situated at the heart of Shropshire's Lake District. ❁ ◖ ◗ ⊞ ♿ ▲ ♣ P

Try also: Black Lion (Marston's)

Hampton Loade

Lion Inn
Signed off A442 OS748862
☎ (0746) 780263
12–2.30 (weekend only); 7.30 (7 Sat)–11
Courage Directors; Hook Norton Old Hookey; Ind Coope Burton Ale [H]
Built in 1600 as a cider house, the Lion has five rooms for eating and drinking. Large range of home-made country wines. Note the butter cross dating from the Great Plague behind the pub. Chain ferry crossing to SVR station (restricted service). Guest beers in summer.
⌂ Q ❁ ◖ ◗ ⊞ ▲ ♣ P

Heathton

Old Gate Inn
1 mile off B4176, 8 miles W of Dudley ☎ (07466) 431
12–3; 6–11
Holts (HP&D) Bitter, Entire [H]
Splendid rural setting for a traditional Holts' pub in a restored 16th-century building. Note the photos of the pub 90 years ago, complete with the work of a drunken signwriter. Good food (including veg option) in a relaxed atmosphere. Barbecue and sandpit in garden. Guest beers. ⌂ Q ❁ ◖ ◗ ▲ P

Hengoed

Last Inn
3 miles N of Oswestry off B4579 ☎ (0691) 659747
12–3 (Sun only); 7–11
Marston's Border Bitter, Pedigree Bitter; Wood Special Bitter Ⓗ
Country pub with separate games and family rooms. Occasional guest beers. Eve meals Mon–Wed only.
⌂ ☺ ◐ ◑ ⊞ ♿ ⌂ P

Try also: Butchers Arms, Wern

Hopesgate

Stables Inn
S of Minsterley, off A488 at Hope OS343019
☎ (074383) 344
11–2.30 (not Mon); 7–11
Ind Coope Burton Ale; Marston's Pedigree Bitter; Wood Special Bitter Ⓗ
Small remote pub on high ground. It forgoes the distractions of jukebox, pool or fruit machine in favour of quoits and sometimes boules. Massive open fire in winter. Lunches served Fri–Sun. ⌂ Q ❀ ◐ ◑ ♣ P

Ironbridge

Robin Hood Inn
Waterloo Street (B4373)
☎ (095 245) 3100
12–2.30; 7–11
Draught Bass; M&B Springfield Bitter Ⓗ
Family-run, 17th-century free house overlooking the River Severn. Comfortable surroundings and a pleasant atmosphere. Good food served daily, lunch and eves.
Q ❀ ⛟ ◐ ◑ ♿ P

Try also: Bird in Hand (Banks's)

Ketley Bank

Lord Hill Inn
Main Road (B5061, off A442 at Greyhound interchange)
☎ (0952) 613070
12–2.30 (not Tue–Thu); 7–11
M&B Highgate Mild, Springfield Bitter; Younger IPA Ⓗ
Popular two-room free house offering a wide selection of guest beers. Cellar once contained the village bakery and mortuary; former brewery next door. Twice winner of local CAMRA Pub of the Year.
⌂ ☺ ❀ ◐ ◑ ⊞ ♣ P

Leegomery

Malt Shovel
Hadley Park Road (A442)
☎ (0952) 242963
12–2.30 (incl. Sun); 5–11
Marston's Pedigree Bitter Ⓗ
Plain, compact bar and a comfortable, pleasant lounge with brasses. Traditional pub favoured by more mature imbibers. ⌂ Q ❀ ◐ ⊞ ♣ P

Linley Brook

Pheasant Inn
¼ mile off B4373 OS680978
☎ (0746) 762260
12–2.30 (incl. Sun); 7 (6.30 summer)–11
Banks's Mild Ⓗ
Unspoilt, traditional free house, run by traditional landlord with traditional values, set in attractive rural location. Well worth finding. Generally a 'no children in pub' rule. Two guest beers always available.
⌂ Q ❀ ◐ ◑ ⊞ ♣ P

Little Stretton

Green Dragon
On B4370, off A49
☎ (0694) 722925
11.30–3; 6–11
Ruddles Best Bitter, County; Wood Parish Bitter Ⓗ
Extremely well-appointed lounge bar in idyllic surroundings at foot of Long Mynd. Popular with walkers. Full range of meals, usually with vegetarian option.
⌂ Q ❀ ◐ ◑ ♿ P

Ludlow

George Hotel
Castle Square ☎ (0584) 872055
11–5; 7–11
Ansells Mild, Bitter Ⓗ
Genuine town-centre drinkers' pub, reputedly haunted. Across the square the castle is one of the earliest built of stone and a major venue for the annual Ludlow Festival. ⛟ ◐ ◑ ⊞ ⇌ ♣

Try also: Church Inn (Free)

Madeley

All Nations
Coalport Road (off Legges Way) ☎ (0952) 585747
12–3; 7–11
All Nations Pale Ale Ⓗ
Long-established brew pub. A listed building, it overlooks the award-winning Blists Hill Museum. Q ❀ ⊞ ♣ P

Market Drayton

Kings Arms
Shropshire Street
☎ (0630) 652417
Marston's Mercian Mild, Burton Best Bitter, Pedigree Bitter Ⓗ
Ancient former coaching inn, built 1674. Friendly, two-roomed locals' pub with L-shaped bar and smaller snug, catering for all ages. Good selection of malt and Irish whiskies. ⊞ ♣ P

Sandbrook Vaults
Shropshire Street
☎ (0630) 5281
11–4; 7–11
Younger Scotch, IPA Ⓗ
An interesting, half-timbered 17th-century building. A large L-shaped lounge bar caters for locals and shoppers at lunchtime; popular with young people in evening. ❀ ◐ ♣

Nesscliffe

Nesscliffe Hotel
On A5 ☎ (0743) 81253
11–3; 6–11
Banks's Mild, Bitter Ⓔ
Large, 18th-century hotel, conveniently placed for exploring Welsh border country.
⌂ Q ❀ ⛟ ◐ ◑ ⊞ ♿ ⛺ ♣ P

Newport

King's Head Inn
Chetwynd End (A519, Chetwynd Road/Forton Road jct) ☎ (0952) 812860
11.30–3; 6.30–11 (11–11 Fri & Sat)
Marston's Burton Best Bitter, Pedigree Bitter Ⓗ
Friendly pub at north end of town. Three rooms, lounge bar and dining room. All home-cooked, fresh food with barbecues and pig roasts in summer. No meals Sun eve.
⌂ Q ❀ ◐ ◑ ⊞ ⛺ ♣ P

Norton in Hales

Hinds Head
Main Road ☎ (0630) 43014
12–3; 6–11
Draught Bass; M&B Mild, Springfield Bitter, Brew XI Ⓔ
Welcoming village local, off the beaten track but well worth a visit. Large comfortable lounge bar, smaller bar and a restaurant. Choice of 30 malt whiskies. Etched window with hind's head logo advertises 'Joules Fine Stone Ales'.
⌂ ❀ ◐ ◑ ⊞ ♣ P

Oakengates

Rose & Crown
Holyhead Road (B5061)
☎ (0952) 614348
11–2.30; 6–11
Ansells Mild, Bitter; Ind Coope Burton Ale Ⓗ
Popular roadside inn with spacious beamed bar and comfortable lounge. Good lunches are very popular with office staff, so get there early. Guest beers. ❀ ◐ ⊞ ♣ P

Try also: Albion Inn (Marston's)

Shropshire

Oswestry

Black Lion
59 Salop Road
☎ (0691) 652745
12–11
Marston's Border Exhibition, Pedigree Bitter [H]
Popular, if modest, traditional local a few minutes from the town centre. ⊟ ♣

Golden Lion
Upper Church Street
☎ (0691) 653747
12 (flexible closing); 7–11
Marston's Border Bitter, Pedigree Bitter, Merrie Monk [H]
Popular locals' pub close to parish church. No food Sun.
Q ⊛ ◐ ⊟ ♣ P

Sun Inn
Church Street
☎ (0691) 653433
12–3; 7–11
Banks's Mild; Ind Coope Burton Ale; Tetley Bitter [H]
Street-corner pub. Sympathetically renovated as a genuine free house. Dining area serves home-cooked food. Clog Iron Bitter, the house beer, is available, plus occasional guest beers. Original Walkers windows. Q ◐ ⊟ ♿ ♣

Try also: Oak Inn (M&B)

Pant

Cross Guns
On A483 ☎ (0691) 830316
11.30–3.30; 7–11
Marston's Border Exhibition, Burton Best Bitter, Pedigree Bitter [H]
Pleasantly-situated, Welsh border pub with small stone-flagged bar.
♨ Q ⊛ ◐ ◑ ⊟ ♿ ⛺ ♣ P

Try also: Powis Arms (Marston's)

Rudge Heath

Royal Oak
Bridgnorth Road (at A454/B4176 crossroads)
☎ (07466) 248
11.30–2.30; 6–11
Banks's Mild, Bitter [E]
Large, three-roomed pub with open fires, offering a wide range of malt whiskies. Live music at weekends (pianist).
♨ Q ⊛ ⊟ ♿ ○ P

Selattyn

Cross Keys
On B4579 Oswestry–Glyn Ceiriog road
☎ (0691) 650247
11–11 (flexible closing afternoons)
Banks's Mild, Bitter [H]
17th-century gem of a village local, just off Offa's Dyke footpath. ♨ Q ⊛ ♿ ♣ P

Shatterford

Red Lion
Bridgnorth Road (A442)
☎ (02997) 221
11.30–2.30; 6.30–11
Banks's Mild, Bitter [E]**; Draught Bass; Batham Best Bitter; Hook Norton Old Hookey; Ruddles County** [H]
Small bar on two levels and large dining room (great food includes veg and children's choices). Two car parks – one in Shropshire, one in Hereford and Worcester! Four guest beers at all times. ♨ Q ⊛ ◐ ◑ ⛺ P

Shifnal

Plough Inn
Broadway (B4379)
☎ (0952) 460678
7–11 (11–11 Thu–Sat, closed Mon)
Draught Bass; Hook Norton Old Hookey [H]
Oak-beamed pub divided into four separate areas, with long, narrow bar split into two. Cosy atmosphere. Large garden with barbecue facilities. Guest beers. ♨ ⊛ ⊟ ⇌

Star Hotel (Oddfellows)
Market Place (A464)
☎ (0952) 461517
12–3; 5.30–11
Greene King Abbot Ale [H]
Stylish and comfortable, single-bar pub,with tiered dining area. Highly imaginative menu includes daily specials and veg option. Guest beers. Live music Sun. No food Sun eve.
♨ 🛏 ◐ ◑ ⇌ P

White Hart
4 High Street (B4379)
☎ (0952) 461161
11–3 (not Mon); 6–11
Ansells Mild, Bitter; Holden's Stout; Ind Coope Burton Ale [H]
16th-century coaching inn with exposed beams taken from old ships. Good food (Tue–Sat); German dishes a speciality. Two guest beers taken from all over the country; house beer brewed by Holden's available (called 'Poty'). ⊛ ◐ ⊟ ⇌ P

Shrewsbury

Castle Vaults
Castle Gates ☎ (0743) 58807
11–3; 6–11 (closed Sun eve)
Marston's Border Mild, Pedigree Bitter; Ruddles Best Bitter [H]
Free house in the shadow of the castle. Landlord exercises discretion over customers admitted. Mexican food a speciality. No-smoking area. Occasional guest beers.
♨ ⊛ 🛏 ◐ ◑ ⇌

Dog & Pheasant
Severn Street ☎ (0743) 52835
12–3 (5 Fri & Sat); 7–11
Ansells Mild, Bitter; Ind Coope Burton Ale [H]
Tidy, two-roomed terraced pub, behind the prison in the Castlefields area of town. A stone's throw from the River Severn. Q ⊟ ⇌ ♣

Dolphin
St Michaels Street
☎ (0743) 50419
11–3; 6–11 (11–11 Fri & Sat)
Cornish Draught Steam Bitter; Greene King Abbot Ale; Mitchell's ESB; Oakhill Yeoman Ale; Smiles Best Bitter; Taylor Landlord [H]
Late-Georgian pub with a porticoed porch. No keg beers or lager – the only gas in this pub is in the lamps. Beer range changes regularly. Q ⊟ ♣

Loggerheads
Church Street (just off Dogpole)
☎ (0743) 55457
10.30–11
Draught Bass; M&B Mild [E]
Cosy side-street pub with four rooms; one has a shove-ha'penny board and strong sporting links. Don't miss the room on the left with its scrubbed top tables and high-backed settles. Q ◐ ◑ ⊟ ♿ ⇌ ♣

Old Bell
115 Abbey Foregate
☎ (0743) 56041
11–3; 6–11
Ansells Mild, Bitter; Ind Coope Burton Ale [H]
On road up to Lord Hill's Column (highest Doric example in Britain). Public bar, snug and pool/bar billiards/jukebox room in an 18th-century house. Over 100 years in same family, 40 with present landlord. Yard for outdoor drinking at rear gives access for disabled.
Q ⊛ ⊟ ♿ ♣ ○

Try also: Station Hotel (Bass); **Proud Salopian** (Free)

Soudley

Wheatsheaf Inn
Off A41, 1 mile SE of Cheswardine ☎ (063 086) 311
12–3; 7 (7.30 winter)–11
Marston's Border Mild, Burton Best Bitter, Pedigree Bitter, Owd Rodger (winter) [H]
Friendly, remote village pub (dating back to 1784), on the Staffordshire border. Frequented by users of the Shropshire Union Canal (1 mile south of pub). Games include bar skittles.
♨ ⊛ ◐ ◑ ⊟ ♿ ♣ P

Stottesdon

Fox & Hounds
High Street (3 miles off B4363 at Billingsley)
☎ (074632) 222
11–11 (6–11 winter)
Fox's Mild, Woody's Bitter, Dasher's Draught, Hound's Bitter, Winter Ale [H]
Brew pub in small village in the heart of the Shropshire countryside. Skittle alley at rear of pub is for hire. Brewery can be viewed through window at back. Occasional guest beers.
Q ♣ P

Trefonen

Efel Inn
☎ (0691) 659840
12 (flexible closing); 7–11
Marston's Border Bitter, Border Exhibition, Pedigree Bitter [H]
Small country pub in Welsh border village, adjacent to Offa's Dyke footpath.
Q ♣ P

Try also: Barley Mow (Free)

Upper Farmcote

Red Lion o'Morfe
Off A458, 3 miles E of Bridgnorth OS919770
☎ (07466) 678
11.30–3 (3.30 Sat); 7–11
Banks's Mild, Bitter [E]; **Wood Special Bitter** [H]
Excellent, three-roomed country pub with large lounge, small bar and games room. Families welcome in the conservatory. Eve meals Mon–Thu until 9pm.
Q ♿ ♣ P

Waters Upton

Lion Inn
On A442, Telford–Hodnet road ☎ (0952) 83317
12–3; 6–11
M&B Highgate Mild [E]
Multi-level pub with three separate drinking areas. Front room is used as a post office and general store. Many pictures of the Lion steam engine. Guest beer changes fortnightly.
♣ P

Wellington

Plough Inn
King Street (ring road)
☎ (0952) 255981
12–2.30; 7–11
Ansells Mild, Bitter; Ind Coope Burton Ale; Tetley Bitter [H]
Comfortable, traditional local pub, popular for its lunches. Eve meals Thu–Sat only. Basic, uncarpeted bar is dominated by pool table. Warm welcome; the sedate atmosphere primarily appeals to an older clientele. Holder of Master Cellarman award for Burton Ale. Outdoor drinking on main road benches.
♣ P

Welsh Frankton

Narrowboat Inn
Ellesmere Road (A495)
☎ (0691) 661051
11.30–3 (extends summer & weekends); 7–11
Draught Bass; Ind Coope Burton Ale; Ruddles County; Wadworth 6X [H]
Modern pub on edge of Shropshire Union (Llangollen) Canal. Boats for hire. Guest beers. ♿ ♣ P

Wem

Dickin Arms
Noble Street ☎ (0939) 33085
11.30–3; 6–11 (11–11 Thu–Sat)
Marston's Mercian Mild, Burton Best Bitter, Pedigree Bitter [H]
A two-roomed, side-street pub, close to defunct brewery. An oasis in Greenalls land.
♣

Try also: Railway, Yorton (Wood)

Wentnor

Crown Inn
Off A488/A489, near Bishop's Castle OS385928
☎ (058861) 613
12–2.30; 7–11
Whitbread Best Bitter, Flowers Original [H]
In a little village nestling below the south west lip of the Long Mynd; a haven for visitors to the South Shropshire hills. Guest beers. ♣ P

Try also: Horseshoes, Bridges (Free)

Whitchurch

Star Hotel
Watergate Street
11–3; 7–11 (11–11 Fri & Sat)
Marston's Mercian Mild, Burton Best Bitter, Pedigree Bitter [H]
Small, friendly local in the home town of Joyce, the famous clock-making family whose firm has celebrated its 300th anniversary. Q ♣

Wistanstow

Plough
W of A49, off A489
☎ (0588) 672523
12–2.30; 7–11
Wood Parish Bitter, Special Bitter, Wonderful Bitter, Christmas Cracker [H]
Village local and the Wood brewery tap. Home-cooked food using local produce. Large lounge with bottle collection. Down steps to the bar, which is in the original part of the building.
♿ P

One of these Hall & Woodhouse ales is a Lost Beer (see page 14)

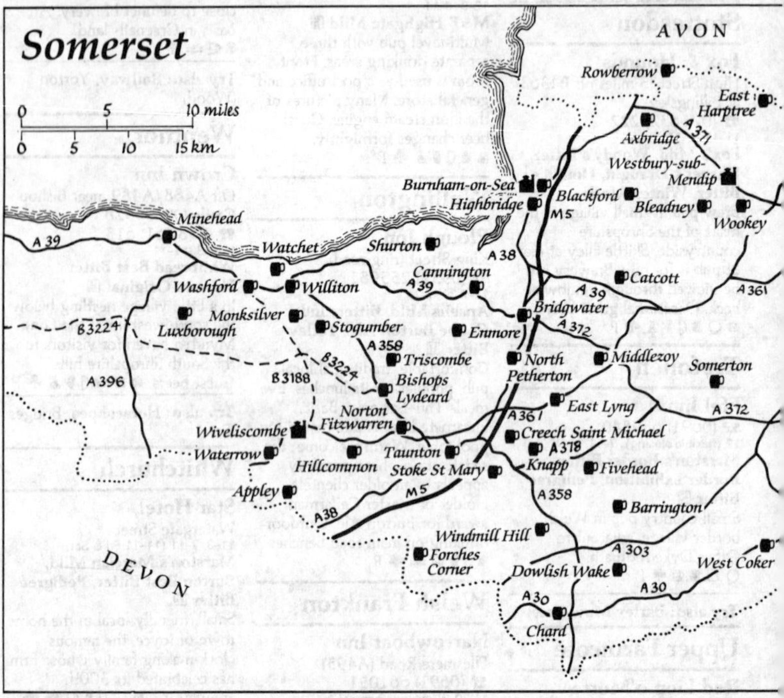

Ash Vine, *Trudoxhill*; **Berrow**, *Burnham-on-Sea*; **Cotleigh**, **Exmoor Ales**, *Wiveliscombe*; **Miners Arms**, *Westbury-sub-Mendip*; **Oakhill**, *Oakhill*

Appley

Globe Inn
Off A38 through Greenham
☎ (0823) 672327
11–2.30; 6.30–11
Cotleigh Tawny Bitter 🄷
Thriving country pub with traditional corridor serving area and a variety of rooms. Guest beer. Q ♣ P

Axbridge

Lamb Inn
The Square ☎ (0934) 732253
11–2.30 (3 Sat); 6.30–11
Butcombe Bitter; Wadworth 6X 🄷
Rambling pub in The Square opposite King John's hunting lodge, now owned by Butcombe Brewery. Large terraced garden. Unusual bar made out of bottles. No food winter Sun eves. Guest beer.
Q

Barrington

Royal Oak
☎ (0460) 53455
12–2.30; 6.30–11 (12–11 Sat)
Cotleigh Tawny Bitter; Exmoor Ale 🄷
Pleasant old stone pub in pretty village with two bars, comfortable lounge and good public; skittle alley and function room. Good range of beers with at least two guest ales always on. Q ♣ P

Bishops Lydeard

Bell Inn
West Street (off A358)
☎ (0823) 432968
10.30–2.30; 6–11
Exmoor Ale; Wadworth 6X; Webster's Yorkshire Bitter 🄷
Village pub, popular with all ages. Large public bar with tiled floor and adjoining games/children's room. Carpeted lounge and conservatory dining area with wide menu choice. Ten minutes from West Somerset railway by foot. Two skittle alleys. Guest beers.
♣ P

Blackford

Sexeys Arms
On B3139 W of Wedmore
☎ (0934) 712487
11–2.30; 6.30 (or 7)–11
Courage Bitter Ale, Best Bitter 🄷
13th-century village inn with cosy oak-beamed lounge warmed by a real fire. Basic bar has a dartboard and an unusual roof. Meals in bar or restaurant, except Tue & Wed eve. Book restaurant meals – especially weekends. ♣ P

Bleadney

Stradlings Inn
On B3139, between Wells and Wedmore ☎ (0749) 73576
11–3; 5.30–11
Theakston Best Bitter, XB, Old Peculier (winter) 🄷
Converted 19th-century cider mill, reputedly haunted. Two bars, one intimate with inglenook, the other larger and close to stream at front. Downstairs games room. The restaurant retains many original features. Large patio. Occasional guest beer. Q ♣ P

Bridgwater

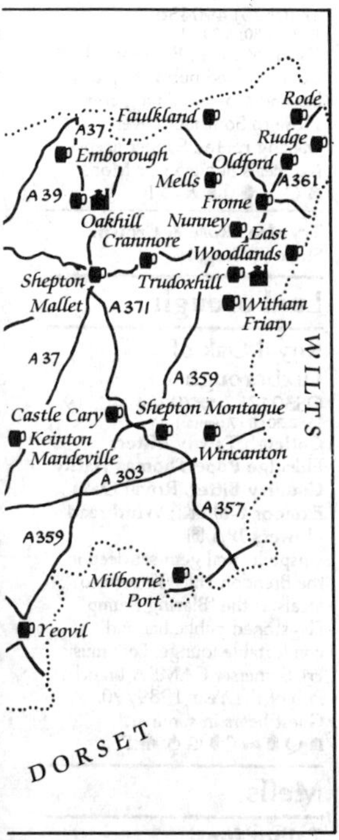

Fountain Inn
1 West Quay
☎ (0278) 424115
11–2.30 (12–2.30 Sun); 7–11
Butcombe Bitter; Cotleigh Harrier SPA; Exmoor Ale Ⓗ
Enlarged town pub near river. Long bar with dartboard at one end. Enamel signs on wall. Guest beers. Lunchtime snacks.
Q ⇌ ♣

Try also: Cross Rifles (Ushers)

Burnham-on-Sea

Royal Clarence Hotel
The Esplanade
☎ (0278) 783138
11–11
Butcombe Bitter; Royal Clarence Clarence Pride; Wadworth 6X Ⓗ
Seafront pub with large main hotel bar and small lounge bar. Own brewery in old skittle alley. Always three guest beers on offer.
♨ ⛬ 🛏 ◐ ◗ ⊞ ♿ ▲ ♣ P

Cannington

Malt Shovel Inn
Blackmoor Lane (off A39 just before village from either direction) ☎ (0278) 653432
11.30–3; 6.30–11 (7–11 winter)
Butcombe Bitter; Wadworth 6X Ⓗ
Thatched country pub on secluded road at back of village. Multi-roomed, with separate restaurant and large children's room. Guest beer and real ciders. Worth searching out.
⌂ Q ♨ ⛬ 🛏 ◐ ◗ ♿ ▲ ⍥ P

Castle Cary

White Hart
Fore Street ☎ (0963) 50255
11–3; 5.30–11 (11–11 Sat)
Courage Best Bitter; John Smith's Bitter Ⓗ
Popular, well-run, modernised pub with mixed clientele, though predominantly young. Taunton cider.
⌂ ♨ ⛬ 🛏 ◐ ◗ ⊞ ♿ ♣ ⍥ P

Catcott

King William
Off A39 ☎ (0278) 722374
11.30–3; 6–11
Draught Bass; Eldridge Pope Dorchester Bitter, Royal Oak; Palmers IPA Ⓗ
Village pub with modern restaurant extension. Small public bar with dartboard; traditional lounge bar. Food bar has an old well, discovered when extension was added. Family room has skittle alley.
Q ♨ ⛬ ◐ ◗ ⊞ ♿ ♣ ⍥ P

Chard

Old Ship Inn
Furnham Road (A358)
☎ (0460) 65485
11–3; 5.30–11
Eldridge Pope Royal Oak; Exmoor Ale; Hall & Woodhouse Tanglefoot Ⓗ
One-bar pub with exposed stonework. Good local trade. Guest beer usually available. No meals Sun. ⌂ ♨ ⛬ ◐ ◗ ♣ P

Cranmore

Strode Arms
Off A361 ☎ (074 988) 450
11.30–2.30; 6.30–11
Wadworth IPA, 6X Ⓗ
Attractive country inn, part-dating back to the 14th century. Opposite village duckpond and close to East Somerset Railway. Two guest beers and real cider. Wide-ranging menu but no meals Sun eve in winter. Shove-ha'penny played.
⌂ Q ⛬ ◐ ◗ ♣ ⍥ P

Creech Saint Michael

Bell Inn
1 mile off A38
☎ (0823) 442881
11–3; 6.30–11
Ruddles County; Ushers Best Bitter Ⓗ
Active village pub with games area/skittle alley and separate eating area on higher level.
♨ ⛬ ◐ ◗ ♣ P

Dowlish Wake

New Inn
1 Mile S of Ilminster
OS365164 ☎ (0460) 52413
11–2.30; 6–11
Butcombe Bitter; Theakston Old Peculier; Wadworth 6X Ⓗ
Well-kept, stone-built and wood-beamed convivial village pub. Traditional public bar and comfortable lounge with inglenook; three real fires, good range of games. Home-cooked fare includes veg option (book on Sun). Perry's cider farm is within staggering distance.
⌂ Q ♨ ⛬ ◐ ◗ ⊞ ♿ ♣ ⍥ P

East Harptree

Castle of Comfort
On B3134 OS544532
☎ (0761) 221321
11.30–2.30; 7–11
Draught Bass; Butcombe Bitter; Ruddles Best Bitter Ⓗ
Remote, stone-built former coaching inn on site of Roman road. A real ale ghost in residence: ask landlord! Live music Fri. Guest beers.
Q ⛬ ◐ ◗ ⊞ ♣ P

East Lyng

Rose & Crown
On A361 ☎ (082 369) 235
11–2.30; 6.30–11
Butcombe Bitter; Eldridge Pope Royal Oak; Palmers IPA Ⓗ
Comfortable village pub with stone fireplace and wooden beams. The well-tended garden offers fine views across Sedgemoor. Disabled access at rear. Skittle alley. Accommodation must be booked. ⌂ ⛬ 🛏 ◐ ◗ ♿ ♣ P

East Woodlands

Horse & Groom
1 mile E of A361/B3092 jct
OS792445 ☎ (0373) 62802
12–2.30 (3 Sat); 6–11
Butcombe Bitter; Exmoor Ale; Fuller's London Pride; Oakhill Bitter; Wadworth 6X Ⓖ
Well worth finding, 17th-century inn on western edge of Longleat estate. Two small bars, one with a serving hatch and the other with a fine open fireplace and flagstone floor. 12 single malts always available. Guest beer and Wilkins cider on gravity.
⌂ Q ♨ ⛬ ◐ ◗ ⊞ ▲ ⍥ P

Emborough

Somerset

Old Down Inn

On A37/B3139 crossroads
☎ (0761) 232398
12–3; 7–11
Draught Bass [G] & [H]
Atmospheric coaching inn circa 1640, with a diversity of rooms and old furniture. Rebuilt after burning down in 1886. Guest beers in summer. No meals Sun lunch or winter eve.
⌂ Q ♘ ⊨ ◖ ◗ ⊟ ▲ ♣ P

Enmore

Enmore Inn

$1\frac{1}{2}$ miles from Bridgwater on Durleigh Road
☎ (0278) 422052
11–3; 7–11
Butcombe Bitter; Oakhill Bitter; Whitbread Flowers Original [H]
Modernised country pub with separate restaurant. Large beer garden. Guest beers.
Q ♘ ❀ ◖ ◗ ▲ ♣ P

Faulkland

Tuckers Grave Inn

On A366, $\frac{1}{2}$ mile N of village
☎ (037 387) 230
11–2.30; 6–11
Draught Bass; Butcombe Bitter [G]
The burial place of a 1747 suicide, this former farm cottage has doubled as an inn for over 200 years. The story of Tucker can be found above the parlour fire. Cheddar Valley cider.
⌂ Q ❀ ◖ ⊟ ▲ ♣ ♁ P

Fivehead

Crown Inn

400 yds off A378
☎ (046 08) 312
11–2.30; 7–11 (may vary)
Courage Best Bitter; Whitbread Boddingtons Bitter [H]
Stone 16th-century pub, with later extensions, which retains the original fireplace and wattle ceiling. Comfortable lounge with partitioned-off restaurant area. Children welcome in skittle alley. Guest beers.
⌂ ❀ ◖ ◗ ⊟ ♣ P

Forches Corner

Merry Harriers

OS183171 ☎ (082 342) 270
12–2.30; 6.30–11
Cotleigh Tawny Bitter; Exmoor Ale [H]
15th-century inn on Blackdown Hills. Friendly atmosphere with good meals in bar or dining room. Live music Thu and Sun eves. Good camping. Regular guest beers.
⌂ ♘ ❀ ◖ ◗ ♿ ▲ ♣ P

Frome

Sun

6 Catherine Street
☎ (0373) 73123
11–3; 6–11 (11–11 Sat)
Felinfoel Double Dragon; Hall & Woodhouse Tanglefoot; Marston's Pedigree Bitter; Wadworth 6X; Whitbread Flowers Original [H]
Lively former coaching inn in historic part of town. An impressive oasis. Well worth finding. Thatcher cider and guest beers. No meals Sun lunch. ⌂ ⊨ ◖ ♣ ♁

Highbridge

Coopers Arms

Market Street (next to station)
☎ (0278) 783562
11–3; 5.30–11
Greene King Abbot Ale; Palmers IPA; Smiles Exhibition [E]
Modernised pub with two lounge bars, a public and a skittle alley/darts bar. Beers in cellar listed on blackboard. Ask which guest beer is on.
Q ❀ ⊟ ♿ ⇶ ♣ P

Hillcommon

Royal Oak

On B3227 (old A39)
☎ (0823) 400295
11–3; 7–11
Draught Bass; Exmoor Ale [H]
Friendly roadside local. Comfortable lounge overlooks large garden with fine views of the Blackdown Hills and Wellington Monument. Good down-to-earth public bar. Children welcome in skittle alley lunchtimes.
Q ❀ ◖ ◗ ⊟ ♣ P

Keinton Mandeville

Quarry Inn

High Street (B3153, 7 miles W of Castle Cary)
☎ (045 822) 3367
12–2.30; 6 (7 Sat)–11
Oakhill Bitter; Wadworth 6X [H]
This popular, welcoming pub was once the quarrymaster's house. 160 years-old, local stone-built, with old photos and maps in the bar. Separate dining area. Skittle alley.
⌂ ❀ ◖ ◗ ▲ ♣ P

Try also: Three Old Castles (Free)

Knapp

Rising Sun

Off A361 OS301254
☎ (0823) 490436
11.30–2.30; 6.30–11
Draught Bass; Exmoor Ale [H]
Country food pub with plush bar and separate dining area. Close to Somerset Levels walking routes. Supper licence. No meals Sun eves or Mon.
⌂ Q ♘ ❀ ◖ ◗ ▲ ♁ P

Try also: Rose & Crown, Stoke St Gregory

Luxborough

Royal Oak of Luxborough

OS304257 ☎ (0984) 40319
11–2.30; 6 (7 winter)–11
Cotleigh Tawny Bitter; Eldridge Pope Thomas Hardy Country Bitter, Royal Oak; Exmoor Gold [G]; Whitbread Flowers IPA [H]
Unspoilt rural gem set deep in the Brendon Hills. Known to locals as the 'Blazing Stump'. Flagstoned public bar and comfortable lounge. Folk music Fri. Somerset CAMRA branch Pub of the Year 1989/90. Guest beers in summer.
⌂ Q ❀ ⊨ ◖ ◗ ⊟ ♿ ♣ P

Mells

Talbot Inn

High Street (between A361/A362, 3 miles W of Frome) OS727493
☎ (0373) 812254
11–3; 6 (4.30 Sat)–11
Butcombe Bitter; Wadworth 6X [G]
15th-century coaching inn with three bars leading off central cobblestoned courtyard. Guest beers and Wilkins cider.
⌂ Q ❀ ⊨ ◖ ◗ ⊟ ♣ ♁ P

Middlezoy

George Inn

Main Road (off A372)
☎ (0823) 69215
12–2.30 (not Mon); 7–11
Cotleigh Tawny Bitter; Oakhill Bitter [H]
17th-century pub near site of Battle of Sedgemoor. Ever-changing range of guest beers from near and far. Twice-yearly beer festivals held by licensee. Flagstone floor in bar; exposed beams. Lounge mainly used for food or quiet drinking. No meals Mon.
⌂ Q ❀ ⊨ ◖ ◗ ⊟ ▲ ♣ ♁ P

Milborne Port

Queens Head

High Street ☎ (0963) 250314
10.30–2.30 (12–2.30 Sun); 6–11
Draught Bass; Butcombe Bitter; Hook Norton Best Bitter; Wadworth 6X [H]
Genuine village pub with large

courtyard, separate restaurant and skittle alley. Excellent food. Piano. Guest beers. Two real ciders.
Q ♣ P

Minehead

Old Ship Aground
Quay Street ☎ (0643) 702087
11–2.30; 7–11 (may stay open summer afternoons)
Ruddles County; Ushers Best Bitter [H]
Large inn overlooking harbour with cosy public bar and comfortable lounge bar/patio area for families (summer only). Excellent base for exploring coastline and near to preserved West Somerset Railway.
Q ♣

Wellington Hotel
☎ (0643) 704371
10.30–11
Draught Bass; Exmoor Ale [H]
Large hotel in town centre. Public bar extensively updated with satellite TV, loud music and gaming machines. Quiet and more refined lounge bar. Expensive for area.
♣

Try also: Kildare Lodge

Monksilver

Notley Arms
☎ (0984) 56217
11–2.30 (12–2.30 Sun); 6–11
Ruddles County; Ushers Best Bitter [H]
Old village pub with well-deserved reputation for food: all freshly-prepared and home-cooked. Good family room.
P

North Petherton

Lamb Inn (Carvey's Freehouse)
Fore Street (A38)
☎ (0278) 662336
11–3 (12.30–2.30 Sun); 7–11
Cotleigh Tawny Bitter [H]
Friendly pub on busy road, with a larger interior than it promises from outside. Cosy split-level lounge and dining area. Skittle alley. Guest beers.
Q ♣

Norton Fitzwarren

Ring of Bells
On A361 near Taunton Cider
☎ (0823) 275995
11–3.30; 6–11
Cotleigh Tawny Bitter, Old Buzzard [H]
Lively pub, with two carpeted bars and a good skittle alley in which children are welcome at lunchtime. Good value food. Three guest beers usually available. ♣ P

Nunney

George Inn
Church Street (½ mile N of A359/A361 jct)
☎ (037 384) 458
11–11
Draught Bass; Bunces Benchmark; Butcombe Bitter [H]
Comfortable former courthouse and coaching inn opposite remains of Nunney Castle which was badly damaged during the Civil War. Q ♣ P

Oakhill

Oakhill Inn
Fosse Road (A367)
☎ (0749) 840442
11–3 (4 summer); 6.30–11
Draught Bass; Oakhill Bitter [H]
Renovated roadside inn, a short distance from Oakhill Brewery. No meals Sun eve. Guest beer.
Q ♣ P

Oldford

Ship
On B3090, ½ mile S of A361
☎ (0373) 62043
11–3.30; 6–11 (11–11 Sat)
Ruddles Best Bitter; Ushers Best Bitter; Webster's Yorkshire Bitter [H]
A warm welcome is enjoyed in this pleasantly modernised pub with three areas leading off a central bar. Good garden for children and reasonably-priced food. ♣ P

Rode

Cross Keys
20 High Street (next to Bass depot) ☎ (0373) 830354
11–2.30; 6–11
Draught Bass; Charrington IPA [H]
Traditional two-bar pub. Former Fussells' brewery tap. Q ♣ P

Rowberrow

Swan Inn
Off A38 at Churchill
OS451583 ☎ (0934) 85237
12–2.30; 6–11
Draught Bass; Butcombe Bitter; Wadworth 6X [H]
Large converted farmhouse with character. Q ♣ P

Try also: Miners Arms (Free)

Rudge

Full Moon
Lower Rudge (1 mile N of A36 at Standerwick) OS829518
☎ (0373) 830936
12–2.30 (not Mon); 6–11
Draught Bass; Butcombe Bitter; Wadworth 6X [H]
In a time warp, this pub has flagged floors and small rooms. New owners plan to expand facilities while retaining traditional character. Lunch on Sun. Q ♣ P

Shepton Mallet

Horseshoe Inn
Bowlish (¾ mile from centre on A371 to Wells)
☎ (0749) 342209
11.30–3; 6–11
Wiltshire Old Swan Mild, Stonehenge Best Bitter, Old Grumble, Old Devil, Exhibition Ale [H]
Warm welcome and good company in a two-bar local on the western outskirts of town. No meals Sun eve or Mon.
♣

Kings Arms
Leg Square ☎ (0749) 343781
11–2.30; 6–11
Halls Harvest Bitter; Ind Coope Burton Ale; Tetley Bitter; Wadworth 6X [H]
17th-century pub of character in northern part of town known locally as the Dustbowl. Beware the Addlestones cider dispensed through a fake handpump. No meals Sun eve.
Q ♣ P

Shepton Montague

Montague Inn
Off A359 ☎ (074 981) 3213
12–2; 6.30 (6 winter)–11
Butcombe Bitter; Marston's Pedigree Bitter [G]
Remote but convivial country pub. Guest beer and Sandford Dry cider on gravity. Lunchtime meals Sat and Sun only in winter. Q ♣ P

Shurton

Shurton Inn
Off A39 ☎ (0278) 732695
11–3; 6–11
Exmoor Ale; Hall & Woodhouse Badger Best Bitter [H]
Comfortable village pub close to Hinckley Point power station. Extensive menu of bar meals and a restaurant. Regular live music. Has been known to celebrate Xmas on Midsummer Day! Guest beers and real cider. Skittles. Q ♣ P

Somerton

Unicorn at Somerton
West Street ☎ (0458) 72101
11–4 (sometimes 2); 5.30–11
Draught Bass; Oakhill Bitter [H]
16th-century coaching inn with original fireplace. Comfortable and relaxing bar with four real

ales (including guest beers). Cider in summer. Boules and skittles.
⌂ Q ♉ ▦ ⛐ ◐ ◑ ♿ ♣ ⊙ P

Stogumber

White Horse Inn

2½ miles off A385 S of Williton
☎ (0984) 56277
11–2.30; 6–11
Cotleigh Tawny Bitter; Exmoor Ale Ⓗ
Traditional old English family-run pub, situated in a quaint village between the Quantocks and the Brendons. Extensive bar menu. Cider in summer only.
⌂ ▦ ⛐ ◐ ◑ ⊟ ♣ ⊙ P

Stoke St Mary

Half Moon

Off A358 at Henlade
☎ (0823) 442271
11–2.30; 6–11
Marston's Pedigree Bitter; Whitbread Flowers IPA Ⓗ
Popular renovated country pub with stone-flagged bar and separate dining areas.
▦ ◐ ◑ ♿ ⛺ P

Taunton

Black Horse

36 Bridge Street (100 yds from Cannon cinema)
☎ (0823) 272151
11–3; 7–11
Marston's Pedigree Bitter; Whitbread Boddingtons Bitter, Flowers IPA Ⓗ
Busy town pub popular with all ages. Live music every Sun and Wed. Guest beers.
▦ ◐ ◑ ♿ ⇌ ♣

County Hotel

East Street ☎ (0823) 337651
10.30–2.30; 5.30–11
Exmoor Ale; John Smith's Bitter; Ushers Best Bitter Ⓗ
Plush bar with cricketing theme in historic town-centre hotel. Good bar snacks.
⌂ Q ♉ ⛐ ◐ ◑ ♿

Harp Inn

Shoreditch Road (B3170, S of town centre)
☎ (0823) 272367
11.30–2.30; 6.30–11
Courage Best Bitter; Directors Ⓗ
Cosy old pub on road to racecourse. Quiet traditional public bar with pool and darts. Pleasant lounge. ⌂ ▦ ◐ ◑ ⊟ ♣ P

Mason's Arms

Magdalene Street (next to St Mary's Church)
☎ (0823) 288916
10.30–2.30; 5–11
Draught Bass; Exmoor Ale; Wadworth 6X Ⓗ
Comfortable side-street pub in town centre with a single through bar. The only free house in Taunton offering a choice of beers from independent brewers. Guest beers. Q ◐ ◑

Minstrels (Castle Hotel)

Castle Bow ☎ (0823) 272671
11–3; 6–11
Draught Bass; Eldridge Pope Thomas Hardy Country Bitter Ⓗ
Long L-shaped bar in town-centre hotel; comfortable and friendly with lots of old wood panelling. Occasional live music. Guest beer. ⛐ ◐ ◑

Wood Street Inn

Wood Street (off Bridge Street)
☎ (0823) 333011
11–2.30 (4.30 Thu–Sat); 6–11
Ruddles County; Ushers Best Bitter Ⓗ
Popular back-street local of real character with the best jukebox in town. Regular live rock music. The darts team is still bottom of the league, although the quiz team is usually top! Children welcome in pool room. Veg meals. ▦ ⛐ ◐ ♿ ⇌ ♣

Try also: Denmark Inn (Courage)

Triscombe

Blue Ball

1 mile off A358
☎ (09848) 242
11–2.30; 6–11
Cotleigh Old Buzzard; Exmoor Ale Ⓗ
17th-century thatched pub at the foot of the Quantock Hills; ideal for walkers. Extensive, picturesque garden. Dominoes and skittles played. Good food. Generally busy at weekends, especially in summer.
♉ ▦ ◐ ◑ ⛺ ♣ P

Trudoxhill

White Hart

½ mile S of A361 at Nunney Catch ☎ (0373) 84324
12 (11.30 Sat)–2.30; 7 (6.30 Fri & Sat)–11
Ash Vine Bitter, Tanker; Butcombe Bitter Ⓗ
Comfortable atmosphere in a village pub with a purpose-built brewery at the rear. Thatchers cider. ⌂ ▦ ◐ ◑ ♣ ⊙ P

Washford

White Horse

S of A39 at Washford
☎ (0984) 40415
11–2.30; 6–11
Ruddles Best Bitter *or* **County; Ushers Best Bitter; Webster's Yorkshire Bitter** Ⓗ
Country pub with extensive garden and livestock. Occasional live music.
⌂ ♉ ▦ ◐ ◑ ⛺ ♣ ⊙ P

Watchet

West Somerset Hotel

Swain Street ☎ (0984) 34434
11–11
Ruddles County; Ushers Best Bitter Ⓗ
A friendly family-run establishment, concentrating on good beer, good food and a sporting atmosphere. The building is an old coaching inn and an ancient smugglers' tunnel still runs from the cellar to the harbour. ▦ ⛐ ◐ ◑ ⊟ ♿ ♣

Try also: Bell Inn

Waterrow

Rock Inn

On B3227 ☎ (0984) 23293
11–2.30; 6–11
Cotleigh Tawny Bitter; Exmoor Gold; Ushers Best Bitter Ⓗ
Old pub built against a rock face in a pretty little hamlet, the natural rock forming part of the fireplace. One end of the bar is public-style; the other end is a cosy lounge with a restaurant off it. Cider in summer only.
⌂ Q ⛐ ◐ ◑ ♿ ⛺ ♣ ⊙ P

West Coker

Royal George

11 High Street
☎ (093586) 2334
11–2.30 (12–2 Sun); 6–11
Draught Bass; Charrington IPA; Hall & Woodhouse Tanglefoot Ⓗ
Historic pub with oak-beamed ceilings and friendly atmosphere. Separate games room with bar billiards. Excellent refurbishment with black oak-raftered skittle alley and compatible stonework.
⌂ Q ▦ ◐ ◑ ♿ ♣ ⊙ P

Williton

Foresters Arms Hotel

55 Long Street (A39 at eastern approach of town)
☎ (0984) 32508
11–2.30; 5–11 (11–11 Sat & summer)
Cotleigh Tawny Bitter; Hall & Woodhouse Tanglefoot; Hook Norton Best Bitter Ⓗ
17th-century coaching hotel with skittle alley, beer garden, lounge and public bars, family room and cosy restaurant. Guest beers.
⌂ Q ♉ ▦ ⛐ ◐ ◑ ⊟ ♿ ⛺ ♣ ⊙ P

Try also: Egremont Hotel

Wincanton

Bear

12 Market Place
☎ (0963) 32581
11–2.30; 5.30–11 (11–11 Sat)
Draught Bass; Marston's Pedigree Bitter; Smiles Best Bitter Ⓗ
Comfortable oak-beamed hotel with collection of Toby jugs. Guest beer.
⛫ Q 🛏 ◖ ◗ ♿ ⛺ ♣ P

Dolphin Hotel
High Street ☎ (0963) 32215
11–2.30; 6–11
Courage Best Bitter; Marston's Pedigree Bitter; Oakhill Bitter Ⓗ
Lively, convivial high street hotel bar. Guest beer.
⛫ ❀ 🛏 ◖ ◗ ⊞ ♿ ♣ P

Windmill Hill

Square & Compass
Off A358 at Stewley Cross Garage OS310165
☎ (0823) 480467
12–2.30; 7–11
Draught Bass; Exmoor Ale, Gold Ⓗ
Homely pub off the beaten track. Garden offers magnificent view and children's playground. Reasonably-priced varied menu, catering for vegetarians. Separate restaurant welcomes children lunchtimes.
⛫ ❀ ◖ ◗ ⛺ ♣ P

Witham Friary

Seymour Arms
OS745409
11–3; 6–11
Ushers Best Bitter Ⓗ
Old village local, unspoilt by progress. Central serving hatch and fine garden. Taunton and Bulmer's cider on gravity dispense. Bar billiards table.
⛫ Q ♉ ❀ ⊞ ⛺ ♣ ⊖ P

Wookey

Burcott Inn
On B3139 W of Wells
☎ (0749) 73874
11–2.30 (3 Sat); 6–11
Butcombe Bitter Ⓗ
Deservedly-popular roadside pub with friendly atmosphere. Over 40 different guest beers per year and always two available (mid- and high-gravity). L-shaped bar with copper serving top; small games room. Dining room welcomes children. No meals Sun eve. Garden has an old cider press.
⛫ Q ❀ ◖ ◗ ♿ ⛺ P

Try also: Ring O'Bells (Free)

Yeovil

Alexandra
South Western Terrace (next to old station car park)
☎ (0935) 23723
11–11
Gale's XXXD, Best Bitter, HSB Ⓗ
Traditional town pub offering the Gale's range of country wines in addition to excellent beer. Taunton cider. ◖ ⊞ ⊖

Armoury
1 The Park (A30, opp. hospital)
☎ (0935) 71047
11–2.30 (3 Fri & Sat); 6.30 (6 Fri & Sat)–11
Butcombe Bitter; Hall & Woodhouse Tanglefoot (summer); **Wadworth 6X, Farmer's Glory, Old Timer** Ⓗ
Very busy town pub, simply furnished and reputedly converted from an old armoury.
❀ ◖ ♿ P

THE GBG QUIZ

Round 3: The Halfway Point

31. In which part of the British Isles can beer only be brewed by law from malt, hops, yeast, water and minute amounts of sugar?
32. Name three varieties of hop.
33. By what name is Plzensky Prazdroj better known?
34. Which famous comedian was born within the smell of Hartleys brewery?
35. Which breweries use the following logos:
    a spotted pig?
    a thistle?
    a running wild boar?
    a leaping hart?
    a unicorn?
36. What is the name of Keg Buster's dog?
37. How did Old Peculier get its name?
38. Who brews Black Adder; who brews Baldric?
39. Who was the first Editor of this publication?
40. Which brewing family produced the only English pope? (And it wasn't Eldridge Pope!)
41. What is a gyle?
42. What type of yeast is used in cider making?
43. Which star of a cult TV comedy series once owned a brewery?
44. Which beer is named after the man who beat the gong at the start of Rank films?
45. What is the correct temperature for serving draught ale?

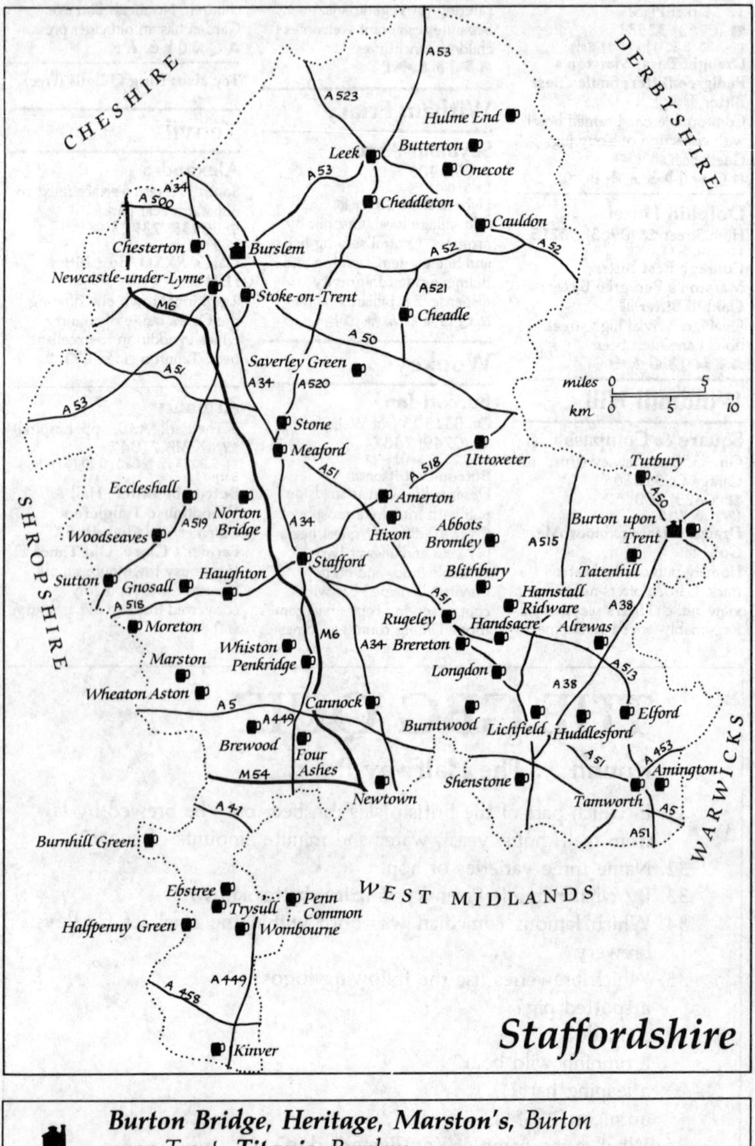

Burton Bridge, Heritage, Marston's, Burton upon Trent; **Titanic,** Burslem

Abbots Bromley

Bagot Arms

Bagot Street
☎ (0283) 840371
11–2.30; 5–11
Marston's Pedigree Bitter H
18th-century coaching inn, a meeting place for Blithfield traditionalists. P

Coach & Horses

Main Street ☎ (0283) 840256
11.30–2.30; 6.30–11
Ansells Bitter; Ind Coope Burton Ale H
Friendly and comfortable; a former 18th-century coaching inn. Bar billiards. ♣ P

Alrewas

George & Dragon

Main Street ☎ (0283) 790202
11–2.30 (3 Sat, 12–2.30 Sun); 6–11
Marston's Pedigree Bitter H
Busy village-centre pub and classy restaurant which caters for children and vegetarians. ♣ P

Try also: William IV

Amerton

Plough Inn

Uttoxeter Road (A518, 1 mile E of A51) ☎ (0889) 270308
11.30–2.30 (extends summer & bank hols); 6–11
Courage Best Bitter, Directors H
Smartly-decorated main road pub; strong on value-for-money food. Within easy reach of Chartley Castle and Uttoxeter

racecourse. Families welcome at all times. ♨ ⊕ ◐ ◑ ⊟ ⛺ ♣ P

Amington

Pretty Pigs
Shuttington Road
☎ (0827) 63129
11–3; 5–11
Draught Bass; M&B Mild, Brew XI 🄴
Large, friendly pub renowned for good value food. Situated between the railway line and a small lake for which the pub holds the fishing rights. Carvery restaurant upstairs. ⊕ ◐ ◑ ⊟ ♣ P

Try also: Good Companions (Free)

Blithbury

Bull & Spectacles
Uttoxeter Road (B5014)
☎ (088922) 201
12–3; 6–11
Ind Coope Burton Ale; Marston's Pedigree Bitter 🄷
15th-century country pub, close to Blithfield Reservoir. Guest beers. ♔ ⊕ ◐ ◑ ⊟ ♣ P

Brereton

Talbot
Main Road ☎ (0889) 582748
11.30–3.30; 6–11
Draught Bass 🄷
Old-style pub, offering a friendly atmosphere and good-value meals. ⊕ ◐ ◑ P

Brewood

Three Stirrups
Engleton Lane/Shop Lane
☎ (0902) 850243
11.30–3 (4 Sat); 5.30 (6 Sat)–11
Draught Bass; M&B Highgate Mild, Springfield Bitter 🄷
Basic bar and upmarket lounge. ♔ ♨ ⊟ ♣ P

Burnhill Green

Dartmouth Arms
Snowden Road OS787006
☎ (07465) 268
11–2 (2.30 Sat); 6–11 (12–2 (2.30 Sat); 7–11 winter)
Ansells Mild, Bitter; Ind Coope Burton Ale 🄷
Popular village pub with small restaurant area; no eve meals Sun. ♔ Q ⊕ ◐ ◑ P

Burntwood

Trident
116 Chase Road (off A5190)
☎ (05436) 2790
12–2.30 (4 Sat); 7–11
Marston's Pedigree Bitter 🄷
Genial two-roomed local. See the aviator landlord's collection of pictures and models in lounge. Pool table. Q ⊟ ♿ ♣ P

Burton upon Trent

Anglesey Arms
Bearwood Hill Road, Winshill (off A50) ☎ (0283) 64791
10.30–2.30 (3 Sat); 5.30–11
Marston's Burton Best Bitter, Pedigree Bitter, Owd Rodger 🄷
Popular local pub with a traditionally-renovated lounge, altered to include family room in conservatory. Has the oldest bowling green in Burton. Good value snacks. ♨ ⊕ ⊟ ♣ P

Burton Bridge Brewery
23 Bridge Street (A50, 25 yds W of river) ☎ (0283) 36596
11.30–3; 5.30–11
Burton Bridge XL Bitter, Bridge Bitter, Porter, Top Dog Stout, Festival Ale, Old Expensive 🄷
Brewery tap; very friendly and well worth visiting. It boasts a unique skittle alley upstairs. Upstairs lounge open Fri and Sat; jazz Thu; guest beer on Sun. NCP car park at rear is free eves. ♔ Q ◐ ⊟ ♣ ⌚

Coopers Tavern
Cross Street (off Station Street)
☎ (0283) 32551
11.30–2.30; 5.30–11
Draught Bass 🄶
Victorian side-street pub, formerly a Bass brewery annexe. Still retains its old tap room, with high wooden benches, disused barrels for tables and a unique atmosphere. The only outlet for Bass straight from the cask in Burton. ♔ Q ◐ ♿ ⇌ ♣

Elms Inn
Stapenhill Road (near Trent bridge) ☎ (0283) 62272
11–3; 6–11
Draught Bass 🄷
Popular three-room local with small bar and snug. Q ⊕ ⊟ ♣ P

Prince Alfred
Derby Street ☎ (0283) 62178
11–3; 5–11
Courage Directors; John Smith's Bitter 🄷
Burton's longest serving landlord at one pub – 31 years. Smart lounge with CD jukebox; basic bar with dartboard and pool table area. Sun lunches only by arrangement.
⛟ ◐ ⊟ ♿ ⇌ ♣ P

Roebuck Hotel
Station Street ☎ (0283) 68660
11–11
Ansells Mild, Bitter; Ind Coope Burton Ale; Tetley Bitter 🄷
One-room pub opposite the Ind Coope brewery, modernised in Victorian style. Guest beers. No food Sun. ◐ ⇌ ♣

Butterton

Black Lion
Opp. church OS075565
☎ (05388) 232
12–3 (not Wed); 7–11
McEwan 70/-, 80/- (summer); **Theakston Best Bitter; Younger No. 3** 🄷
An absolute gem in a picturesque village setting, near Manifold Valley. Four contrasting rooms serve a mixed age group. Good, varied menu and excellent accommodation. Ideally situated for walking. ♔ ♨ ⛟ ◐ ◑ ⊟ ♣ P

Cannock

Unicorn
62 Church Street (Hednesford road) ☎ (0543) 504331
12–2.30 (3.30 summer); 7–11
Ansells Mild, Bitter 🄷
Small, basic town pub with busy bar and quiet lounge.
♔ ⊕ ◐ ⊟ ♿ ⇌ ♣ P

Cauldon

Yew Tree
Off A52/A523
☎ (0538) 308348
11–3; 6–11
Draught Bass; Burton Bridge XL Bitter; M&B Mild 🄷
One of the finest pubs in the country, dating back to the 17th century. Superb collection of assorted bric-a-brac, including working polyphonia, pianola, grandfather clocks and sundry Victoriana. Old yew tree in car park. Q ♨ ⊕ ♿ ⛺ ♣ P

Cheadle

Queens Arms
47 Queen Street
☎ (0538) 752373
11–3; 6.30–11
Draught Bass 🄷
Small, unspoilt, multi-roomed pub on road to Alton Towers. Camping at Hales Hall (½ mile).
Q ⊕ ⊟ ⛺ ♣

Cheddleton

Black Lion
Hollow Lane (off A520)
☎ (0538) 360355
11–3; 7–11
Marston's Burton Best Bitter, Pedigree Bitter 🄷
Pleasant village local, next to church. Once owned by Walkers brewery of Leek.
♔ Q ⊕ ♣ P

Chesterton

Black Horse
Castle Street (2½ miles N of Newcastle) ☎ (0782) 561313
12–3 (4 Sat); 7–11
Ansells Bitter; Ind Coope

Burton Ale; Tetley Bitter [H]
Recently-modernised locals' pub, sporting a traditional bar and a comfortable, Edwardian-theme lounge. Outdoor patio area is part-covered. Former Alton's Derby Ales house.
❀ ◐ ⊞ ♿ ♣ P

Ebstree

Holly Bush
Ebstree Road
OS854959 ☎ (0902) 895587
11–2.30 (11.30–3 Sat); 6–11
Ansells Mild, Bitter; Ind Coope Burton Ale; Tetley Bitter [H]
Pleasant country pub, half a mile west of Staffs and Worcester Canal. No food Sun eve.
♔ ❀ ◐ ◑ ⊞ ♣ P

Eccleshall

Crown
High Street ☎ (0785) 850437
11–3 (4 Fri); 7–11
Draught Bass [E]
Straightforward pub in town centre. ♘ ❀ ⊞ ♣ P

Royal Oak
High Street ☎ (0785) 850230
11–3; 6.30–11
Burtonwood Best Bitter [H]
Large town-centre pub and restaurant, serving good value food (veg option). ❀ ◐ ◑ ♿ ♣ P

Elford

Crown Inn
The Square ☎ (0827) 85602
12–2.30 (12–2 Sun); 7–11
Draught Bass [H]
Nice village pub: good beer; friendly atmosphere; helpful landlord. A good place to go for a quiet evening's drinking in the country. No meals Sun lunch.
♔ Q ♘ ❀ ◐ ◑ ⊞ ♿ ⛺ ♣ P

Four Ashes

Four Ashes
Station Drive (A449)
11–3 (12–2.30 Sun); 5–11 (11–11 Sat)
Banks's Mild, Bitter [E]
Large, busy, roadside pub. Oak-beamed ceiling is mostly original timber. Industrial view in middle of rural Staffordshire. Children's playground. No food Sun. ♔ ❀ ◐ ⊞ ♣ P

Gnosall

Boat Inn
Wharf Road (200 yds off A518)
OS822202 ☎ (0785) 822208
11–3; 6–11
Marston's Burton Best Bitter, Pedigree Bitter [H], **Owd Rodger** (winter) [G]
Canalside pub with table skittles, 'Sound Hound' and bar billiards. Menu caters for children and vegetarians.
♔ ❀ ◐ ◑ ⛺ ♣ P

Horns
High Street ☎ (0785) 822441
11–3 (3.30 Sat); 6–11
Draught Bass; M&B Springfield Bitter [E]
Well-patronised, friendly village-centre pub. Ask the landlord about the 'carved' bar-front. Home-cooked food (not Sun eve). ◐ ◑ ⊞ ♣ P

Halfpenny Green

Royal Oak
OS825920 ☎ (0384) 88318
11.30–2.30 (3 Sat); 6–11
Banks's Mild, Bitter [E]
Popular, old country local on the crossroads near Bobbington aerodrome. Good value food.
♔ ❀ ◐ ◑ ⊞ ♣ P

Hamstall Ridware

Shoulder of Mutton
Yoxall Road ☎ (088922) 389
11–3; 6 (7 winter)–11
Draught Bass; Wards Sheffield Best Bitter [H]
An oasis of real ale in the Staffordshire countryside, close to Ridware Arts centre. Regular guest beers. Meals for children and vegetarians. ♔ ❀ ◐ ◑ ♣ P

Handsacre

Crown Inn
The Green ☎ (0543) 490239
11–3; 6–11
Draught Bass; M&B Highgate Mild [H]
Friendly, picturesque, canalside pub. Lunchtime bar snacks.
Q ❀ ⊞ ♣ P

Haughton

Bell
Newport Road (A518)
☎ (0785) 780301
11–3; 6–11
Courage Best Bitter, Directors [H]
Modernised, main road, village pub: one room with two distinct areas. Unusual collection of book matches. Regular guest beers. ♔ ❀ ◐ ◑ ♿ ♣ P

Hixon

Green Man
Lea Road OS005262
☎ (0889) 270931
12–3 (11.30–4 Sat); 6–11
Draught Bass [H]
Village pub, north of High Street. Keen fundraisers, with varied events all year. Home-cooked food (veg and children's dishes); eve meals Tue–Sat.
♔ ❀ ◐ ◑ ⊞ ♿ ⛺ ♣ P

Huddlesford

Plough
Huddlesford Lane (off A38)
☎ (0543) 432389
11–2.30; 6–11
Ansells Mild, Bitter; Ind Coope Burton Ale [H]
Rural pub alongside canal featuring an L-shaped lounge with bar area. No meals Sun, or Mon eve. ❀ ◐ ◑

Hulme End

Manifold Hotel
10 miles E of Leek on B5054
☎ (02884) 537
11–3; 6.30–11
Wards Mild, Thorne Best Bitter, Sheffield Best Bitter [H]
Formerly known as the 'Light Railway', this impressive stone-built hotel is set in open countryside by the River Manifold. Friendly welcome, excellent accommodation and food. Occasional live folk or jazz. Guest beers in summer.
♔ Q ❀ ⛿ ◐ ◑ ♿ ⛺ ♣ P

Kinver

Cross
Church Hill (off High Street)
☎ (0384) 872435
12–3 (4 Sat); 7–11
Banks's Bitter; Hanson's Mild Ale [E]
Popular pub with plain bar and smart lounge near Staffs and Worcester Canal. Same licensee for over 30 years. Award-winning, restored Tudor house next door. ♔ ⊞ ♣ ⚲ P

Plough & Harrow (The Steps)
High Street ☎ (0384) 872659
12–2.30 (3.30 Sat); 7–11
Batham Best Bitter, XXX [H]
Three-roomed pub; the basic bar offers Devil-Among-the-Tailors and shove-ha'penny. Bar snacks Tue–Sat. Q ♘ ⊞ ♣ P

Try also: George & Dragon (Allied); **Old Plough** (Greenalls)

Leek

Dyers Arms
On A523, Macclesfield Road
☎ (0538) 382321
11–3; 6.30–11
Draught Bass [H]
Refurbished inn on edge of town, opposite Brindley watermill. ♣ P

Flying Horse
Ashbourne Road (A523, 1 mile out of centre)
☎ (0538) 382766
11–3; 7–11
Marston's Mercian Mild, Burton Best Bitter, Pedigree Bitter, Merrie Monk [H]
L-shaped bar/lounge with good atmosphere. ♣ P

Sea Lion
36–40 Russell Street
11–11
Banks's Mild, Bitter [H]
Refurbished street-corner local.
⊕ ♣

Swan
St Edwards Street
☎ (0538) 382081
11–3; 6–11
Draught Bass [E]
Imposing timbered building on street corner, although exterior is mainly 19th century. Old photographs of Leek adorn the lounge walls. Lunchtime snacks.
Q ⛴ ❀ ⊕ ♣ P

Wellington
104 Strangman Street
☎ (0538) 382639
11–3; 7–11
Marston's Mercian Mild, Burton Best Bitter, Pedigree Bitter [H]
Popular, good old-fashioned street-corner local of two rooms. All beer is served from lounge; note the unusual pump sleeves. ⊕ ♣

Lichfield

Carpenters Arms
Christchurch Lane (off A461)
☎ (0543) 262098
12–3 (4 Fri & Sat); 7–11
Banks's Mild, Bitter [E]
Friendly local in residential area of city. ♣ P

City Frog
Frog Lane (opp. police station)
☎ (0543) 254103
11–3 (12–2 Sun); 5.30–11 (11–11 Fri & Sat)
Draught Bass [H]
Lively city pub, convenient for Chinese and Indian eating houses. ◖ ⇌ (City) ♣

Earl of Lichfield
Conduit Street
☎ (0543) 251020
11–11
Marston's Burton Best Bitter, Merrie Monk, Pedigree Bitter, Owd Rodger [H]
Single-room city-centre pub boasting a fine collection of water jugs. Lunchtime snacks.
⇌ (City)

Queens Head
Queens Street (150 yds off western bypass)
☎ (0543) 262529
11–3; 7–11
Marston's Pedigree Bitter [H]
No-frills, traditional pub – good company. ⊕ ♣

Try also: Horse & Jockey

Longdon

Swan with Two Necks
40 Brook End (off A51)
☎ (0543) 490251
12–2.30; 7–11
ABC Best Bitter; Ansells Mild, Bitter; Ind Coope Burton Ale [H]
400 years old, with authentic heavy beams, low ceiling and original slab floor; smart restaurant run by Belgian landlord/chef. ▲ Q ❀ ◖ ◗ P

Marston

Fox
1 mile NW of Wheaton Aston
OS835140 ☎ (0785) 840729
12–4; 6 (7 winter)–11
Hall & Woodhouse Tanglefoot; Lloyds Derby Bitter; Marston's Pedigree Bitter, Owd Rodger; Wadworth 6X; Wood Special Bitter [H]
Enterprising country free house, popular with cyclists. Guest beers. ▲ Q ❀ ◖ ◗ ⊕ ♿ ♣ ⍥ P

Meaford

Darlaston Inn
On A34/A51 jct
☎ (0785) 813267
12–3; 6–11
Ansells Bitter; Ind Coope Burton Ale; Tetley Bitter [H]
Large, open-plan pub in centre of traffic island! Many mementoes of local interest displayed, including old telephone box. Big on food, especially steaks. ❀ ◖ ◗ P

Moreton

Rising Sun
2 miles E of A41 OS799168
☎ (0952) 70251
12 (11 Sat)–3; 7–11
Marston's Burton Best Bitter, Pedigree Bitter, Owd Rodger (winter) [H]
Friendly, somewhat isolated, country pub. Bar billiards in snug, which also serves as a family room. Snacks available.
▲ ⛴ ❀ ♣ P

Newcastle-under-Lyme

Castle Mona
Victoria Street (off A34)
☎ (0782) 612849
12–3.30 (may vary); 7–11
Greenalls Wem Best Bitter, Davenports Traditional Bitter, Thomas Greenall's Original Bitter [H]
Two-roomed pub in quiet corner of town, ten minutes' walk from the centre. Attracts a thriving sports and social fraternity. ⊕ ♿ ♣

Victoria
62 King Street (A53)
☎ (0782) 615569
11–3 (4 Sat); 5 (7 Sat)–11
Draught Bass; Stones Best Bitter [H]
Two-roomed corner pub, a few minutes' walk from town centre. Strong games and quiz following. Handy for New Victoria Theatre. Hot beef baps are a Fri lunchtime speciality. Easy parking. Q ❀ ⊕ ♣

Newtown

Ivy House
Stafford Road (A34)
☎ (0922) 476607
12–2.30 (2 Sun); 7–11
Draught Bass; M&B Highgate Mild, Springfield Bitter [E]
Old low-ceilinged pub on busy main road, opposite Hardys nightclub. Split-level lounge with a friendly atmosphere. A very popular pub. Q ❀ ⊕ ♣ P

Norton Bridge

Railway
Station Road (off A520)
☎ (0785) 760289
11–3; 7–11
Draught Bass [H]
Tastefully-renovated pub a few yards from West Coast main line railway junction.
▲ ❀ ⊕ ♿ ⇌ ♣ P

Onecote

Jervis Arms
On B5063 ☎ (0538) 206
12–2.30; 7–11
Draught Bass; Ruddles County; Stones Best Bitter; Theakston XB, Old Peculier [H]
Free house in a lovely country setting on the banks of the River Hamps. Strong emphasis on excellent-value food, including veg dishes. A family-oriented pub. Q ⛴ ❀ ⛟ ◖ ◗ P

Penkridge

Cross Keys
Filance Lane (by Staffs & Worcs Canal bridge 86) OS925134
☎ (0785) 712826
11–3 (4 Sat); 6.30–11
Draught Bass [H]; **M&B Highgate Mild, Springfield Bitter** [E]
Modernised pub, attracting much canal trade in summer. Barbecue in garden. No food Sun eve. ❀ ◖ ◗ ♣ P

White Hart
Stone Cross (A449, 20 yds from B5012 jct)
☎ (0785) 712242
11.30–4; 6–11
Draught Bass; M&B Highgate Mild, Springfield Bitter, Brew XI [E]
Excellent village-centre hostelry with a brook running through the beer garden. Eve meals till 9pm. ▲ ❀ ◖ ◗ ⊕ ♿ ⇌ ♣ P

Staffordshire

Penn Common

Barley Mow
Pennwood Lane (off Wakeley Hill) OS949902
☎ (0902) 333510
12–3; 6.30–11 (11–11 Sat)
Ansells Mild, Bitter; Ind Coope Burton Ale [H]
Tucked away on the edge of Penn Common, this early 17th-century pub has recently been knocked into a single room. No food Sun. ♜ Q ⊛ ◐ ◗ P

Rugeley

Albion
Albion Street
11–4; 5.30–11 (11–11 Fri & Sat)
Banks's Mild, Bitter [H]
Lively town-centre local catering for all tastes. ⊛ ♣

Try also: Red Lion

Saverley Green

Hunter
Sandon Road (1 mile S of A50) OS970385 ☎ (0782) 392067
11–4; 7–11
ABC Best Bitter; Ind Coope Burton Ale; Tetley Bitter [H]
Cosy, friendly pub with family room. Occasional beer festivals; guest beers. ♜ ⊛ ◐ ◗ ▲ P

Shenstone

Railway
Main Street ☎ (0543) 480503
11.30–2.30 (3 Fri & Sat); 5.30–11
Marston's Pedigree Bitter, Merrie Monk [H]
Village pub with a good atmosphere; locals tend to use bar, but there is also a split-level lounge. ⊛ ◐ ⊟ ⇌ ♣ P

Stafford

Bird in Hand
Mill Street ☎ (0785) 213074
11–11 (11–4; 7–11 Sat)
Courage Best Bitter, Directors [H]
Popular and enterprising pub with bar, snug, lounge and games room. ⊛ ◐ ⊟ ⇌ ♣

Coach & Horses
4 Mill Bank ☎ (0785) 223376
11–3.30 (4.30 Sat); 7–11 (11–11 Fri)
Draught Bass; M&B Springfield Bitter [H]
Straightforward town-centre pub near main post office and Victoria Park. Lunchtime snacks. ⊟ ⇌ ♣

Cottage By The Brook
Peel Terrace (B5066, opp. shoe factory) ☎ (0785) 223563
12–2.30; 7–11 (12–11 Fri & Sat)
ABC Best Bitter; Ind Coope Burton Ale; Tetley Bitter [H]
Large, lively, four-roomed pub. Bar snacks. Real fires in lounge and club room – children welcome in latter.
♜ ⛟ ⊛ ⊟ ♿ ♣

Holmcroft
Holmcroft Road (100 yds off A5013) ☎ (0785) 52634
11–3; 6–11 (11–11 Sat)
Banks's Mild, Bitter [E]
Popular estate pub with long-established landlord. No food Sun. ⊛ ◐ ⊟ ♣ P

Railway Inn
23 Castle Street, Castletown
☎ (0785) 42890
12–2.30 (not Sat); 6 (7 Sat)–11
Ansells Bitter; Ind Coope Burton Ale [H]
Victorian, street-corner local with large whisky selection. Guest beers. Menu caters for children and vegetarians.
♜ Q ◐ ◗ ⊟ ⇌ ♣

Stafford Arms
Railway Street
☎ (0785) 53313
11.30–2.30 (not Sat); 7.30–11
Titanic Premium Bitter [H]
Fine, one-roomed pub whose beers have attracted a strong following. At least five guest beers available at all times. No food Sun. ◐ ⇌ P

Sun Inn
7 Lichfield Road (opp. Apollo Cinema) ☎ (0785) 42208
11–3; 6–11
Draught Bass [H]
Pleasant, multi-roomed pub with its own 'olde-worlde' restaurant. Reference library for crossword and quiz-loving customers. ⛟ ⊛ ◐ ◗ ⊟ ⇌ ♣ P

Try also: Kings Head (M&B)

Stoke-on-Trent
Fenton:

Malt n' Hops
295 King Street (A50, ½ mile from Longton)
☎ (0782) 313406
12–3; 5.30–11
Burtonwood Dark Mild [H]
Main road free house in an area dominated by the big brewers. Single room with an ever-changing range of guest beers – usually at least five at any one time. House beer is brewed by Burtonwood. ⇌ (Longton) ♣

Hanley:

Coachmakers
Lichfield Street (next to bus station)
12–3; 7.30–11
Draught Bass [H]
Good old-fashioned, traditional local: three rooms, including a tiny public bar and a drinking corridor. ♜ Q ⊟ ♣

Highland Laddie
69 Wellington Road
12–3; 7–11
Ansells Mild, Bitter; Ind Coope Burton Ale [H]
Friendly, back-street local, recently refurbished. Live music Sat night. ♜ ⊟ ♣

Rose & Crown
Etruria Road (opp. Festival Park)
☎ (0782) 280503
12–3 (not Sun); 7–11
Ansells Mild, Bitter; Gibbs Mew Wiltshire Traditional Bitter; Ind Coope Burton Ale [H]
Former Parkers brewery showpiece, with traditional bar and comfortable, homely lounge; now essentially a restaurant. Friendly welcome and high standards of service. Booking advised Sat eve (no meals Sun). Guest beers.
♜ ⊛ ◐ ◗ ⊟ ♿ ⇌ (Etruria) P

Hartshill:

Jolly Potters
296 Hartshill Road (A52)
☎ (0782) 45254
11–3; 6 (7 Sat)–11
Draught Bass; M&B Mild [H]
Unspoilt, small pub of character, with four rooms and a drinking corridor. A rare outlet for M&B Mild. Bar snacks. Q ⊟ ♣

Longport:

Packhorse
Station Street
12–3; 7–11
ABC Best Bitter; Ansells Mild, Bitter; Ind Coope Burton Ale [H]
Canalside pub, popular with wide range of ages. Moorings available nearby. No meals Sun eve. Guest beers. ⊛ ◐ ◗ ⇌

Longton:

Gardeners Rest
30 Trentham Road
☎ (0782) 317617
11–3 (4 Sat); 6 (7.30 Sat)–11
Draught Bass [E]
Corner local; L-shaped lounge bar with a lively atmosphere.
⇌ ♣

Northwood:

Cross Guns
Vincent Street (off B5049)
☎ (0782) 268520
1 (12 Sat)–3.30; 7.30–11
Draught Bass; M&B Mild; Stones Best Bitter [H]
Friendly, two-roomed local in side-street near Northwood Stadium. Lunchtime snacks.
Q ⊛ ⊟ ♣

Northwood Inn
55 Botany Bay Road
☎ (0782) 271020
12–3; 7–11
Ansells Mild; Ind Coope Burton Ale [H]

Friendly locals' pub. Single bar has a smaller room leading off. Note old Parkers pub sign preserved inside.

Penkhull:

Greyhound
Manor Court Street
☎ (0782) 48978
12–3; 6.30–11
Ansells Bitter; Ind Coope Burton Ale; Tetley Bitter H
Built in the 16th century as the local manor courthouse, the pub's cellars used to hold prisoners. Rebuilt in 1936, but some original materials were retained. Smart bar and quiet lounge. Q P

Stoke:

Blacks Head
16 North Street
12–3 (4 Sat); 5.30 (7 Sat)–11
Draught Bass H
200 year-old traditional Potteries local on the edge of Stoke town centre. A continually changing range of guest beers on offer.

Glebe Hotel
35 Glebe Street
11–11
Banks's Mild, Bitter E
Two-roomed pub: the public bar has a pool table while the lounge is popular with locals and students. Good home-cooked food. Now Grade I listed building, but plans for development are in hand.

Tunstall:

White Hart
43 Roundwell Street
☎ (0782) 835817
12–3.30 (5 Fri & Sat); 7–11 (10.30 Sat)
Marston's Border Bitter, Pedigree Bitter H
Friendly, local corner pub at the edge of town centre.

White Horse
143 Brownhills Road (next to tile factory) ☎ (0782) 835587
11–3; 7–11
Bass Worthington BB, Draught Bass; M&B Springfield Bitter H
Traditional, basic locals' pub of a type becoming harder to find. Drinking corridor, outdoor gents and bags of Potteries character. Do not miss this bastion of pub culture – enjoy it while you can! Q

Stone

Pheasant
Old Road (N of centre)
☎ (0782) 814603
11–3 (12–2 Sun); 6–11
Draught Bass; M&B Springfield Bitter H
Friendly local, still retaining the characteristics of a former Joules brewery house.

Sutton

Red Lion
Newport Road (A519)
☎ (0952) 811048
11–3; 6–11 (11–11 Sat)
Banks's Mild, Bitter E
Lively, main road, country pub. Children's adventure play-ground, but family room not available Sun lunch.
P

Tamworth

Albert Hotel
Albert Road ☎ (0827) 64694
11–2.30; 7–11
Holden's Mild; Hoskins Beaumanor Bitter, Penn's Ale, Premium, Old Nigel H
A treat in Tamworth – a comfortable and friendly alternative to M&B and Ansells.
P

Tamworth Arms
71 Lichfield Street
☎ (0827) 67056
11.30–2.30; 5.30 (4.30 Thu)–11 (11–11 Fri, 11–3; 7–11 Sat)
Draught Bass; M&B Mild H
Locals' pub; comfortable and friendly.

Tatenhill

Horseshoe Inn
Main Street ☎ (0283) 64913
11.30–3; 5.30–11 (11.30–11 Sat in summer)
Marston's Pedigree Bitter H, **Owd Rodger** (winter) G
Popular, 18th-century, village inn with unspoilt beamed lounge and excellent food. Pleasant, well-tended garden.
Q P

Try also: Bridge Inn, Branston (Marston's)

Trysull

Plough
School Road (150 yds from the green) ☎ (0902) 892254
11.30–2.30; 6–11 (11–11 Sat)
Banks's Mild, Bitter E
15th-century, half-timbered village pub. Barbecues on summer eves – Fri, Sat and Sun, but otherwise no food Sun.
P

Tutbury

Cross Keys
Burton Street (A50)
☎ (0283) 813677
11–3 (incl. Sun); 7–11
Ansells Bitter; Ind Coope Burton Ale H
Small, two-roomed village local overlooking the Dove Valley.
Q P

Uttoxeter

Vaults
22 Market Place
☎ (0889) 562997
11–2.30 (3 Sat); 5.30 (7 Sat)–11
Draught Bass H
Friendly, unspoilt hostelry, full of local character. A true gem. Check before taking children in eve. Q

Wheaton Aston

Hartley Arms
56 Long Street (by Shropshire Union Canal bridge 19)
☎ (0785) 840232
12–3; 6.30–11 (11–5; 7–11 Sat)
Banks's Mild, Bitter E
Popular canalside house at end of village. Plush lounge and comfortable bar with piano. Menu offers veg and children's options. No food Sun.
P

Whiston

Swan
2 miles W of A449 OS895144
☎ (0785) 712460
11–3 (not Tue); 7–11
Ansells Bitter; Ind Coope Burton Ale H
Reputable country pub with a comfortable lounge and a small popular bar. P

Wombourne

Red Lion
Old Stourbridge Road (off A449) ☎ (0902) 892270
11–11
Draught Bass H; **M&B Springfield Bitter** E
17th-century coaching inn on original main road, now bypassed. Varied menu offers veg and children's choices, and pensioners' special meals. No food Sun; eve meals Thu–Sat only. P

Try also: Old Bush (Banks's)

Woodseaves

Cock
Newport Road (A519)
☎ (078574) 270
12 (11.30 Sat)–11
Banks's Mild, Bitter E
Lively, friendly village local.
P

Join CAMRA — see page 504!

Suffolk

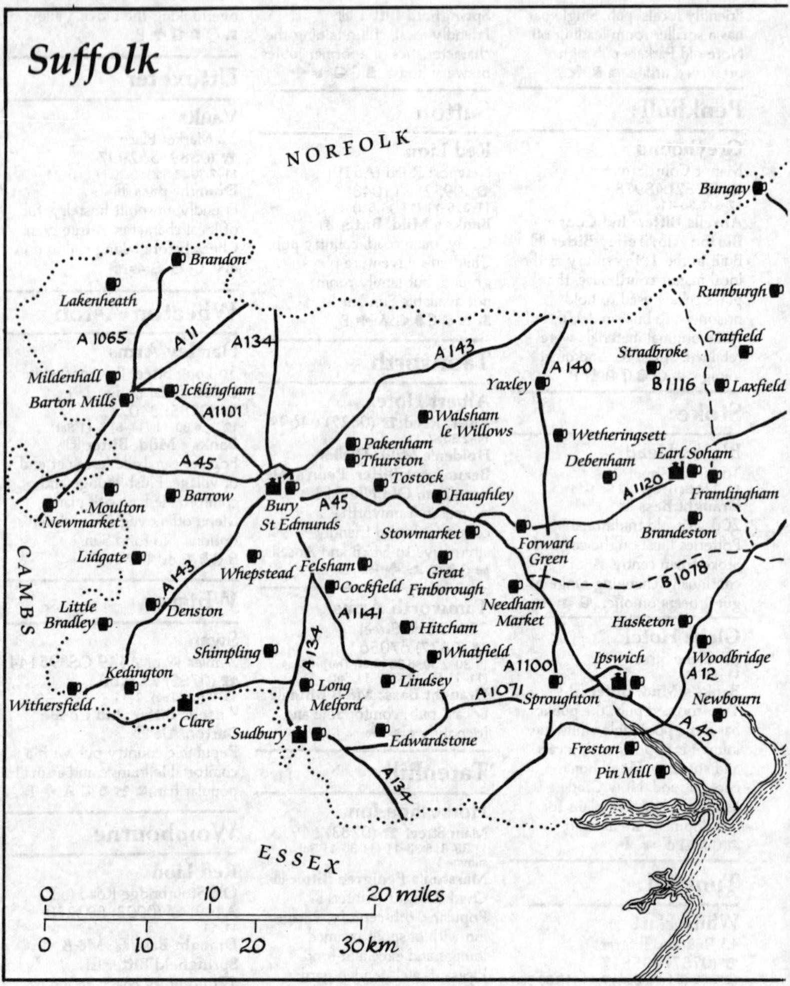

Adnams, Southwold; **Greene King**, Bury St Edmunds; **Mauldons**, Sudbury; **Nethergate**, Clare; **Forbes**, **Scotties**, Lowestoft; **Tolly Cobbold**, Ipswich

Aldeburgh

Mill Inn

Market Cross (opp. Moot Hall)
☎ (0728) 452563
11–2.30; 6–11
Adnams Bitter 🄷
Once in the centre of town, this old timber-beamed inn is now just a few yards from the sea. Several little inter-connected seating areas and a separate dining room. Book for eve meals (not Sun). Cheap beer and food, both of good quality.

White Hart

High Street ☎ (0728) 453205
11–2.30; 6–11
Adnams Bitter, Old, Broadside 🄷
One room with wood panelling and a nautical atmosphere.

Try also: Railway Hotel (Adnams)

Barrow

Weeping Willow

Bury Road ☎ (0284) 810492
11.30–3; 5–11
Greene King XX Dark, IPA, Abbot Ale 🄷
Large beamed village pub with friendly hosts and lively company. Menu offers veg choice. Q P

Try also: Three Horseshoes (Greene King)

Barton Mills

Bull Inn

The Street (off A11)
☎ (0638) 713230

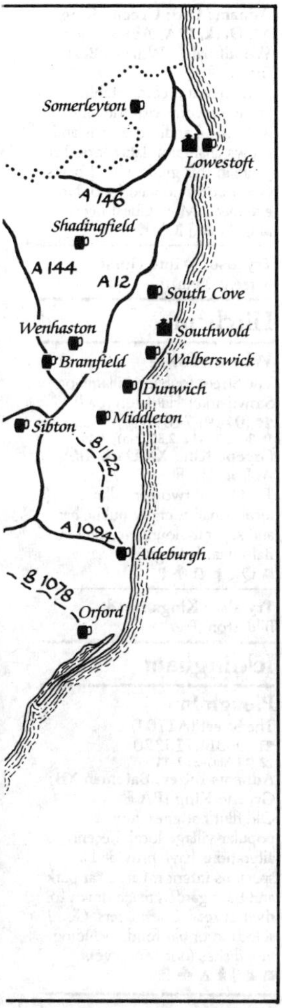

11–11
Adnams Bitter; Draught Bass; Charrington IPA H
Excellent classic-style coaching inn. Family-run, with comfortable accommodation. Good food and lively bar. Guest beers. P

Try also: Bell (Greene King)

Bramfield

Bell
The Street (by A144)
☎ (096 279) 395
11–2.30; 6.30–11
Adnams Mild, Bitter G
Down-to-earth local with Ringing the Bull game. Nearby is the only thatched church with a detached round tower in the whole county. Opposite church gate is a crinkle-crankle wall.
♣ P

Brandeston

Queens Head
☎ (072 882) 307
11.30–2.30; 5.30 (6 Mon)–11
Adnams Mild, Bitter, Old, Broadside H
Excellent country pub which recently won an award for the best garden in the Adnams estate. Playthings are provided for the children (welcome until early evening), while for adults there is a quiet drinks-only back bar.
Q ♣ P

Brandon

Duke of Wellington
Thetford Road
☎ (0842) 810219
11–2.30; 7–11
Greene King XX Dark, IPA, Abbot Ale H
Busy local, just out of town centre. No parking on the premises or in the street but public car park nearby. Q ♣

Try also: Five Bells (Greene King)

Bungay

Chequers
23 Bridge Street (just off town centre) ☎ (0986) 893579
12–3; 5.30–11 (12–11 Sat)
Adnams Bitter; Greene King IPA, Abbot Ale H
400 year-old traditional drinkers' pub with covered patio and barbecue. Always four guest beers available. ♣ P

Bury St Edmunds

Dog & Partridge
29 Crown Street
☎ (0284) 764792
11–2.30; 5 (7 Sat)–11
Greene King XX Dark, IPA, Abbot Ale H
Ancient, well-appointed pub, next to brewery and handy for theatre, abbey gardens and town. Pleasant intimate atmosphere. Very popular for lunches. ♣ P

Elephant & Castle
2 Hospital Road (by Westgate St/A143 roundabout on Parkway) ☎ (0284) 755570
11–2.30; 5–11
Greene King XX Dark, IPA, Abbot Ale H
Homely two-bar pub. Good value meals prepared by landlady. Car park entrance on Parkway South. No eve meals on Sun. Petanque played.
♣ P

Flying Fortress
Mount Road, Great Barton (off A143, 2 miles along Mount Road towards Thurston)
☎ (028 487) 665
12–3; 5–11
Adnams Bitter; Draught Bass; Greene King IPA; Mauldons Bitter E
Friendly free house on old aerodrome with many photos and artefacts connected with the Flying Fortress. Good choice of home-cooked food. Petanque played in garden which is safe for children. ♣ P

Try also: Rising Sun (Greene King)

Cockfield

Three Horseshoes
Stows Hill (A1141, Lavenham Road) ☎ (0284) 828177
12–3; 6–11
Greene King XX Dark, IPA, Abbot Ale H
15th-century former thatched hall-house and court. Striking lounge bar with exposed crown post and tie beam circa 1350. Games-oriented public bar. Excellent selection of home-cooked food (not Tue or Sun eves). ♣ P

Cratfield

Poacher
Bell Green OS312751
☎ (098 683) 206
11–11 (variable in winter)
Adnams Bitter; Greene King IPA, Abbot Ale H
A drinking house with food as a sideline. Bottle collection contains over 1300 miniatures. Taxidermy specimens in glass cases. Guest beers.
♣ P

Debenham

Cherry Tree
Cherry Tree Green
☎ (0728) 860275
11–2.30; 5.45–11
Tolly Cobbold Mild, Bitter H
Large, friendly village pub with bowling green, at the edge of a picturesque former market town which boasts many half-timbered buildings and a fine church with pre-Norman stone work in the tower. Pub has good home-cooked food and a play area for children.
Q ♣ P

Denston

Plumbers Arms
Wickham Street
☎ (0440) 820350
11–2.30; 5–11
Greene King XX Dark, IPA, Abbot Ale H
Large, friendly country pub dating back to 1700s. Original stopping point for horse traffic

between Bury and Haverhill. Fine beers and good selection of wines. Book for eve meals after 7. ⌂ Q ☺ ⊛ ◖ ⊟ ♣ P

Try also: Compasses, Stansfield (Greene King)

Dunwich

Ship Inn

St James Street
☎ (072873) 219
11–3.30; 7 (6 Summer)–11
Adnams Bitter, Old, Broadside (summer); **Greene King Abbot Ale** [H]
An old smugglers' inn with a nautical air, oak beams and tiled floors. Some of the handpumps are at the back of the bar. Sketches of the old churches of Dunwich (washed away by the sea) are on display. A food-oriented pub. Cider in summer only.
⌂ Q ☺ ⊛ ⊨ ◖ ◗ ⛺ ♣ ⊖ P

Earl Soham

Victoria

On A1120 ☎ (0728) 82758
11–2.30; 5.30–11
Earl Soham Gannet Mild, Victoria Bitter, Albert Ale, Jolabrugg (Xmas) [H]
Old country pub serving beer and food which are both made on the premises. Very popular and can get crowded, especially when local musicians arrive to entertain. ⌂ Q ⊛ ◖ ◗ ♣ ⊖ P

Edwardstone

White Horse

Mill Green (1 mile N of Boxford off A1071)
☎ (0787) 211211
11.30–2 (3 Sat); 6.30–11
Greene King XX Dark, IPA [H], **Abbot Ale** [G]
Traditional Suffolk pub with a good selection of games, including steel quoits. Excellent value bar food all week and a full menu Thu–Sun (book for Sun lunch). Large collection of enamel advertising signs.
⌂ Q ⊛ ◖ ◗ ⊟ ♣ ⊖ P

Try also: Fox, Groton (Greene King)

Felsham

Six Bells

Opposite church
☎ (04493) 268
11–2.30; 6 (7 Sat)–11
Greene King XX Dark, IPA, Abbot Ale [H]
Basic but comfortable village local in an interesting building which dates back to 16th century. Still displays the rules to the Felsham Jolly Boys' Society circa 1930. Original beer engines fitted unusually at rear of bar. ⌂ Q ⊛ ⊟ ♣ P

Forward Green

Shepherd & Dog

By A1120 ☎ (0449) 711361
10.30–2.30; 5.30–11
Greene King IPA, Abbot Ale [H]
A good honest ale house.
⌂ ☺ ⊛ ⊟ ♣ P

Framlingham

Railway Inn

Station Road (B1116)
☎ (0728) 723693
11–3; 5.30–11
Adnams Bitter, Old [H]
Two-bar pub in keeping with the historic and solidly traditional atmosphere of this old town. A few minutes' walk from the 13th-century castle. The lounge walls are covered with old prints. ⌂ Q ⊛ ◖ ⊟ ♣ P

Freston

Boot

Shotley Road
☎ (047384) 277
11.30–3; 5.30–11
Tolly Cobbold Bitter, Original [H]
Charming olde-worlde pub, home of Freston Mummers who perform medieval plays. All home-cooked food; Fri is fresh fish day. Camping at village hall nearby. Guest beers.
⌂ ⊛ ◖ ◗ ⊟ ⛺ ♣ P

Great Finborough

Chestnut Horse

High Road (B1115)
☎ (0449) 612298
11–3; 6–11
Greene King XX Dark, IPA, Abbot Ale [H]
Good friendly village local with mixed clientele. No eve meals Tue or Sun. Ask landlord about garden bathroom facilities.
⌂ ⊛ ◖ ◗ ⊟ ♿ ⛺ ♣ P

Hasketon

Turks Head

Low Road (sign to Hasketon from A12) ☎ (03943) 2584
11 (11.30 winter)–2.30; 6 (7 winter)–11
Tolly Cobbold Bitter [H]
Listed 16th-century country pub, with putting green and large children's play area. Children also welcome in lounge. Specialises in value-for-money bar meals (limited winter menu). ⌂ ⊛ ◖ ◗ ⊟ ⛺ ♣ P

Haughley

Railway Tavern

Old Street (off A45 by old station) ☎ (0449) 673577
11–2.30; 5.30 (6.30 Sat)–11
Adnams Old; Greene King XX Dark, IPA, Abbot Ale; Woodforde's Wherry Best Bitter [H]
19th-century, comfortable railside tavern with friendly welcome. Landlord breeds and shows champion labradors. Ten years in this guide. Guest beers. Good home-cooked food. No eve meals Mon. Guest beers.
⌂ Q ☺ ⊛ ◖ ◗ ♿ ♣ P

Try also: White Horse (Greene King)

Hitcham

White Horse

The Street (outside village, on Stowmarket-Hadleigh road)
☎ (0449) 740981
11.30–2.30 (12–2.30 Sun); 7–11
Greene King XX Dark, IPA, Abbot Ale [H]
Traditional two-bar village local: small friendly public bar and separate lounge-restaurant. Bar billiards league.
⌂ Q ◖ ◗ ⊟ ♣ P

Try also: Kings Head, Bildeston (Free)

Icklingham

Plough Inn

The Street (A1101)
☎ (0638) 713370
12 (11 Sat)–3; 7–11
Adnams Bitter; Bateman XB; Greene King IPA [H]
Old flint cottages, now a popular village local. Recent alterations have provided a spacious interior. Large car park and beer garden reach down to river at rear. Guest beers. Good selection of bar food, including veg dishes (not Mon eve).
⌂ ⊛ ◖ ◗ ⛺ ♣ P

Ipswich

Duke of York

212 Woodbridge Road
☎ (0473) 257115
11–2; 7–11
Adnams Mild, Bitter, Old, Broadside [H]
Friendly local, a short distance from the town centre. Pleasant lounge and public bar with dartboard. ⊟ ♣ P

John Bull

482 Woodbridge Road
☎ (0473) 727675
11–2.30; 6.30 (7 Sat)–11
Greene King XX Dark, IPA, Abbot Ale [H]
Homely, out-of-town pub, with four distinct bars, catering for all tastes. Q ⊟ ♿ P

Lions Head

213–215 Cauldwell Hall Road
☎ (0473) 727418
11–2.30; 5–11

Tolly Cobbold Mild, Bitter, Old Strong [H]
Plethora of plates and pleasant pub atmosphere. Large garden has a play area. Value for money lunches with meals served till 9.30 (not Sun).
♣ P

Lord Nelson
Fore Street ☎ (0473) 254072
11–4; 6–11 (11–11 Fri & Sat)
Adnams Mild, Bitter, Old, Broadside [H]
Dating back to 1663, this town pub has a lively public bar and a quiet lounge with a well-stocked aquarium. Pub games include shove-ha'penny. ♣

Thrasher
Nacton Road (opp. Ipswich airport, off A45)
11–2.30; 5.30–11
Greene King XX Dark, IPA, Abbot Ale [H]
Active pub with a good mix of local and passing trade. Comfortable lounge and public bar – do not be put off by the exterior! Games include steel quoits in the garden.
♿ ▲ ♣ P

Trafalgar
168 Spring Road
☎ (0473) 725276
11–2.30 (3 Fri & Sat); 5.30–11
Mauldons Bitter; Tetley Bitter; Theakston Best Bitter [H]
Popular free house, a short walk from the town centre. Superb selection of guest ales served in a friendly atmosphere. Shove-ha'penny is played here, but beware — the landlord plays Pass the Pigs for pints!
♿ ♣ P

Water Lily
100 St Helens Street
☎ (0473) 257035
11.30–2.30; 7.30–11
Tolly Cobbold Mild, Bitter, Old Strong [G]
Only Ipswich pub with beer served straight from the barrel. Comfortable snug and spacious back garden. No food Sun.
Q ♿ ♣

Woolpack
1 Tuddenham Road
☎ (0473) 253059
11–2.30; 5.30 (7 Sat)–11
Courage Directors; John Smith's Bitter; Tolly Cobbold Bitter [H]
Oldest brick-built pub in town, with the smallest bar; spacious lounge featuring an open fire, plus games room and smoke room. Pub is fronted by patio drinking area. A country pub in the town. Q ♣ P

Try also: County Hotel (Adnams); **Malt Kiln** (Free)

Kedington

White Horse
Sturmer Road
☎ (0440) 63564
11–3; 5–11
Greene King XX Dark, IPA, Abbot Ale [H]
Very popular village pub near a much-visited Saxon church. Large garden for summer barbecues. Excellent bar food, including veg dishes (must book Sun lunch).
Q ♣ ⛀ P

Lakenheath

Half Moon
4 High Street
☎ (0842) 861484
11–2.30; 6–11
Greene King XX Dark, IPA [H]
Popular local on outskirts of village. A fine flint building retaining the classic Victorian layout of two bars and centre servery for off-sales. Inexpensive, good quality food.
Q ♿ ♣ P

Plough
Mill Road (off B1112)
☎ (0842) 860285
11–2.30 (3 Sat); 6–11
Greene King IPA, Abbot Ale [H]
Fine Victorian flint building in centre of busy village. Two bars: public is used as pool room. No food Sun. ♣ P

Laxfield

Kings Head (Low House)
Gorams Mill Lane (off B1117 by side of church)
☎ (098683) 395
11–3; 6–11
Adnams Bitter, Old, Broadside; Mauldons Low House Bitter, Black Adder [G]
15th-century alehouse full of old wooden beams and settles. No bar: beer is brought in from the back room. Separate dining area with à la carte menu. An unspoilt rural gem where bowls is played. The village has an interesting museum.
Q ♣ ⛀ P

Lidgate

Star
The Street (B1063)
☎ (063 879) 275
11–2.30; 7–11
Greene King IPA, Abbot Ale [H]
The centre of activity in a pleasant village. Spit-roast beef a speciality. Barbecues every summer weekend (no food Tue eve). Beware of ducks crossing road near village pond.
Q P

Lindsey

Red Rose
☎ (0449) 741424
11–2.30; 6–11
Adnams Bitter; Greene King IPA, Abbot Ale; Mauldons Lindsey Bitter [H]
300 year-old beamed village pub near Kersey. Comfortable public bar and separate restaurant. Beer garden, complete with mini zoo, housing animals and birds, from goats to peacocks.
♣

Try also: Kersey White Horse (Free)

Little Bradley

Royal Oak
Bury Road (A143)
☎ (044083) 229
11.30–3; 6–11
Greene King IPA, Abbot Ale; Mauldons Bitter; Nethergate Bitter [H]
Main road pub, recently enlarged. Landlord is very friendly and regards keg as unworthy to be called beer.
♿ ♣ P

Long Melford

George & Dragon
Hall Street (A134)
☎ (0787) 71285
11–2.30; 5–11 (11–11 Fri & Sat, 12–2.45; 7–10.30 Sun)
Greene King IPA, Abbot Ale [H]
Traditional inn with large, lively public bar and good food. Regular live music in public bar.
♣ P

Swan
Hall Street (A134)
☎ (0787) 78740
11–2.30 (3.30 Fri & Sat); 5–11
Greene King XX Dark, IPA, Abbot Ale [H]
Popular local with keen darts and quiz league players. Traditional two-bar pub, with food served in separate eating area. Q ♣

Middleton

Bell
The Street (off B1122)
☎ (072873) 286
11–11 (may vary)
Adnams Mild (summer), **Bitter, Old, Broadside** [G]
Attractive, old listed building on edge of marshes. Handy for Minsmere RSPB Reserve and Suffolk Heritage Coast.
Q ♣ P

Mildenhall

Queens Arms
42 Queensway
☎ (0638) 713657
11–2.30; 7–11
Greene King IPA, Abbot Ale ⊞
Homely pub on outskirts of small town serving a local trade of all ages. Small range of food, all home-made. Q ❀ ⛺ ◐ ◑ ♣ P

Moulton

Kings Head
Bridge Street
☎ (0630) 750156
11–3; 5–11
Greene King IPA, Abbot Ale ⊞
Lively and welcoming local facing the village green. Near ancient packhorse bridge in a village close to England's horse racing capital, Newmarket. Lunches Wed–Sun; eve meals Mon–Sat. ♨ ❀ ◐ ◑ ⊟ ♣ P

Needham Market

Swan Hotel
9 High Street
☎ (0449) 720280
11–11
Greene King XX Dark, IPA, Abbot Ale ⊞
Old town inn with beamed bar and restaurant. Snacks available all day. A former Tolly pub which was sold by Brent-Walker to Greene King in 1989.
❀ ⛺ ◐ ◑ ⇌ P

Try also: Lion (Tolly Cobbold)

Newbourn

Fox Inn
The Street ☎ (047 366) 307
11–2.30; 6 (7 winter)–11
Tolly Cobbold Bitter ⊡
14th-century inn, with original beams throughout. Bar and lounge now one, featuring a tiled floor and traditional furniture. Popular in the summer for its outside drinking area: garden skittles.
♨ Q ☕ ❀ ◐ ▲ ♣ P

Newmarket

Five Bells
16 St Marys Square
☎ (0638) 664961
11–2.30; 6.15–11
Greene King XX Dark, IPA, Abbot Ale ⊞
Traditional one-bar pub with good local trade and enthusiastic games teams. Petanque played in garden.
♨ ❀ ♣ P

Orford

Jolly Sailor
Quay Street ☎ (0394) 450243
11–2.30 (12–2.30 Sun); 6–11
Adnams Bitter, Old ⊞
16th-century quayside inn, long since deserted by the sea. Unusual collection of stuffed miniature dogs! Live music most Sat nights. Family room suitable for older children. Good home-cooked food, including fresh Orford cod when available. Eve meals finish at 8.45. ♨ Q ☕ ❀ ⛺ ◐ ◑ ⊟ ♣ P

Pakenham

Fox
The Street (S of B1088 near A134) ☎ (0359) 30347
11.30–2.30; 7–11
Greene King XX Dark, IPA, Abbot Ale ⊞
Traditional small village pub with log fires. Collection of model/toy vehicles and Greene King dray photographs. Patio and large riverside garden with sheep and ducks. The restaurant is in the old village reading room. ♨ Q ❀ ◐ ◑ ♿ ♣ P

Pin Mill

Butt & Oyster
Turn off Shotley Road at Chelmondiston
☎ (047 384) 224
11–2.30 (4 Sat); 7–11 (11–11 summer)
Camerons Bitter, Strongarm; Tolly Cobbold Mild, Bitter ⊡
Internationally-known riverside inn. Unchanged and unchanging.
♨ Q ☕ ❀ ◐ ◑ ⊟ ♣ P

Rumburgh

Buck
Mill Road (4 miles NW of Halesworth) OS345815
☎ (098 685) 257
11–11
Adnams Mild, Bitter, Old; Greene King IPA; Mauldons Bitter (summer); **Webster's Yorkshire Bitter** ⊞
A real pub, which has retained its individual small rooms, flag floors and boarded walls and ceilings. New dining area and games room where children are admitted. The building is thought to have been the guest house for the priory. Cider summer only.
♨ ❀ ◐ ◑ ⊟ ▲ ♣ ⌽ P

Shadingfield

Fox
London Road (S of Beccles on A145) ☎ (0502) 79610
11.30–2.30; 7–11
Adnams Bitter, Old, Broadside ⊞
Cosy roadside country pub with no-smoking room. Note the unusual inn sign, and coins set into the bar. Has a two-acre caravan meadow. Good value food is served in jumbo portions and includes veg dishes (not Sun or Wed eves).
♨ Q ☕ ❀ ◐ ◑ ▲ ♣ P

Shimpling

Bush
Signed off A134
☎ (0284) 828287
11–2.30; 5.30–11
Greene King XX Dark, IPA, Abbot Ale ⊞
16th-century timbered building with a good, friendly public bar and separate restaurant. Photographic display of village history. ♨ ❀ ◐ ◑ ⊟ ▲ P

Sibton

White Horse
Halesworth Road (leave A1120 by garage in Peasenhall) OS357703 ☎ (072 879) 337
11.30–2.30 (not Mon, except bank hols); 7–11
Adnams Bitter ⊞
16th-century free house with a very pleasant separate dining room and immaculate lavatory facilities. An additional hand-pulled beer available in summer. Well-behaved children welcome. Camping for CC members only. No food Sun eve.
♨ Q ☕ ❀ ⛺ ◐ ◑ ▲ ♣ P

Somerleyton

Dukes Head
Sluggs Lane (off B1074)
☎ (0502) 730281
11–2.30 (3 summer); 6–11
Marston's Pedigree Bitter; Whitbread Wethered Bitter ⊞; **Flowers Original, Wethered Winter Royal** ⊡
Broadland family pub in scenic village near River Waveney. Good family room with interesting views from picture windows.
♨ Q ☕ ❀ ◐ ◑ ⊟ ▲ ♣ ⌽ P

South Cove

Five Bells
Southwold Road (S of Wrentham on B1127)
☎ (050 275) 249
11–2.30; 7 (6.30 summer)–11 (11–11 bank hols)
Adnams Bitter, Old, Broadside (summer) ⊞
Set back off the road. Pub with a long bar covered by a thatched canopy, collections of stuffed animals and birds, and rural artefacts. Caravan site in grounds. ♨ Q ❀ ◐ ◑ ⊟ ▲ ♣ P

Southwold

Red Lion
South Green (near seafront)
☎ (0502) 722385

11–11 (11–3; 7–11 winter)
Adnams Bitter, Broadside Ⓗ
Wood-panelled pub with various artefacts (mainly maritime and weaponry) on walls. Back room with real fire and comfortable seating.
♨ ✿ ⌸ ◖ ◗ ▲ P

Sole Bay
East Green ☎ (0502) 723736
11–11
Adnams Mild (summer), **Bitter, Old, Broadside** Ⓗ, **Tally–Ho** Ⓖ
Brewery tap with one L–shaped room, faded decor and model ships. Sporting trophies adorn bar. Covered corridor outside back door has seating and caged birds. No Sun lunches in winter. ◖ ▲ ♣

Try also: Any Adnams pub

Sproughton

Beagle
Old Hadleigh Road
☎ (047 386) 455
11–2.40; 5–11
Adnams Mild, Bitter, Broadside; Greene King IPA, Abbot Ale; Theakston Best Bitter Ⓗ
Large free house, converted from a row of whitewashed cottages. Comfortable lounge and friendly bar, beamed throughout. Varied menu of good home-cooked food (not Sun). Worth seeking out.
♨ Q ✿ ◖ ⊞ ♿ ♣ P

Stowmarket

Royal William
53 Union Street (near station)
☎ (0449) 674553
12–2.30; 5–11
Greene King XX Dark, IPA, Abbot Ale Ⓖ
Fine old pub, still serving beer by gravity dispense. Background music and a good friendly atmosphere. Close to East Anglian Museum. No meals Sun eve. Q ✿ ◖ ◗ ≹ ♣

Stradbroke

Queens Head
Queens Street
☎ (037 984) 384
11–3 (varies); 6.30–11
Adnams Bitter, Old, Tally–Ho; Greene King IPA, Abbot Ale Ⓗ
15th-century coaching inn hidden behind a Victorian brick facade. A locals' pub with bar meals and a cook-your-own barbecue in summer. Recently-opened pergola beer garden. Occasional jazz nights.
♨ ✿ ⌸ ◖ ◗ ♿ ▲ ♣ P

Sudbury

Waggon & Horses
Acton Square, Church Walk (off one-way system, right after fire station) ☎ (0787) 312147
11–3; 6.30–11
Greene King XX Dark, IPA, Abbot Ale Ⓗ
Revitalised back-street pub with public bar, games room, restaurant and snug. Interesting architecture incorporates different styles and ages. Entrance through courtyard area. Next to site of old Phoenix Brewery.
♨ Q ◖ ◗ ⊞ ≹ ♣ P

Thurston

Black Fox
Barrels Road OS938653
☎ (0359) 30636
12–2.30; 7–11
Adnams Bitter; Greene King IPA; Mauldons Bitter Ⓖ
Basic village ale house. All beer has to be fetched from a back room and is well worth the wait. Three separate public rooms — games, social and lounge (one bar only). Difficult to find but definitely worth it. Guest beers in summer.
♨ Q ✿ ⊞

Tostock

Gardeners Arms
Church Road (2 miles from A45/A1088 roundabout)
☎ (0359) 70460
11–2.30; 7–11
Greene King IPA, Abbot Ale Ⓗ
Original beamed building on the village green. Restaurant offers veg dishes. Quoits played. Basic bar, but fine comfortable lounge with large open fire. ♨ ✿ ◖ ◗ ⊞ ♿ ♣ P

Walberswick

Bell Hotel
Ferry Road ☎ (0502) 723109
11–3; 6–11
Adnams Bitter, Extra, Old, Broadside Ⓗ
Around 600 years-old, with stone floors and oak beams. A collection of small rooms caters for diners, drinkers and local fishermen. Mon eve meals served Easter-October only. No food Sun. Snacks only lunchtimes.
♨ Q ⊗ ✿ ⌸ ◗ ♿ ♣ P

Walsham le Willows

Six Bells
High Street ☎ (0359) 259726
11.30–2.30; 5.30 (6.30 Sat)–11 (12–2; 7–10.30 Sun)
Greene King XX Dark, IPA, Abbot Ale Ⓗ
Fine old beamed pub in a pleasant village. No food at weekends. ♨ Q ✿ ◖ ⊞ ♣ P

Wenhaston

Star
(off A12 Halesworth to Blyburgh Road) OS427750
☎ (050 270) 240
11–3; 6–11
Adnams Mild (summer), **Bitter, Old** Ⓖ
Traditional, basic village pub, with the now-rare cask-cooling cupboards behind the bar.
♨ Q ✿ ◖ ◗ ♣ P

Wetheringsett

Cat & Mouse Inn
Pages Green OS145652
☎ (0728) 860765
11–3; 5–11
Adnams Mild, Bitter; Brakspear Bitter; Marston's Pedigree Bitter; Mauldons Special; Nethergate Bitter Ⓗ & Ⓖ
Hard-to-find traditional rural pub. Cottage-like interior, with low-beamed ceilings. Home-made food with veg option. Eve meals require 24 hours' notice. Ales often change but there is always a selection of 12 beers. Highly commended in Pub of the Year (CAMRA's East Anglia Region). ♨ Q ✿ ◖ ⊞ ▲ ♣ ○ P

Whatfield

Four Horseshoes
The Street ☎ (0473) 827971
11.30–2.30 (not Mon); 7–11
Adnams Bitter, Broadside; Greene King IPA Ⓗ
Friendly, cosy and traditional village inn, with church pew seats. Haven for war game players. Caravan for hire in pub grounds. The lounge is quiet.
♨ Q ✿ ◖ ◗ ⊞ ▲ ♣ P

Whepstead

White Horse
Rede Road (use B1066 off A143, Whepstead is 4 miles S of Bury) OS825585
☎ (0284) 488542
11.30–3; 6.30–11
Greene King IPA, Abbot Ale Ⓗ
Difficult to find (Rede Road is one mile north of Whepstead church) but worthwhile. Interesting dishes include Chinese and Indian, home-cooked by landlady who comes from Mauritius.
♨ Q ✿ ◖ ◗ ⊞ ♿ ♣ ○ P

Withersfield

White Horse
Hollow Hill ☎ (0440) 706081
12–2.30; 5–11
Greene King IPA; Nethergate

Bitter 🄷
17th-century thatched country inn, popular for business lunches. More local trade evenings and weekends; summer brings tourists. Oak beams and log fire feature in the bar. A la carte menu in restaurant (no food Sun lunch).

Woodbridge

Anchor
19 Quay Street (opp. station)
☎ (03943) 2649
11.30–3; 6–11 (11–11 Sat)
Greene King XX Dark, IPA, Abbot Ale 🄷
Friendly pub near quayside, popular in the summer and at weekends. Original beams in quiet back room date from 17th century. Good value bar food.
♜ Q ♞ ⛃ ⇔ ◐ ◑ ⇌ ♣

Olde Bell & Steelyard
103 New Street
☎ (03943) 2933
11–3; 6–11
Greene King IPA, Rayments BBA, Abbot Ale 🄷
Traditional Grade I listed building, with unusual weighbridge over road. Generally smoke-free atmosphere, with no-smoking family room. Vast range of pub games. Pizzas only on the menu. Limited parking.
♜ Q ♞ ⛃ ◐ ◑ ⊟ ⇌ ♣ P

Seckford Arms
Seckford Street
☎ (03943) 4446
11–11
Adnams Bitter, Broadside; Draught Bass; Felinfoel Double Dragon 🄷
Genuine family-run free house, with regular rotation of real ales. Superb Mayan wood carvings feature throughout; exposed beams in the lounge; heated footrail in the bar. Extended to cater for families in no-smoking area. ♞ ⇔ ◐ ◑ ⊟ ♣

Yaxley

Bull
Ipswich Road (on crossroads, off A140/B1117)
☎ (037983) 604
11–3; 5.30–11 (11–11 Sat)
Adnams Bitter, Broadside; Woodforde's Wherry Best Bitter 🄷
Genuine free house – a 16th-century high-beamed pub with large garden and children's play area. On a busy main road but near Thornham Estate, a thatched church and public walks. Pub games include bar billiards. Summer guest beers; Mauldons house beer.
♜ Q ⛃ ◐ ◑ ⛺ ♣ ◯ P

MEANWHILE, back at the lab …

Ever had one of those arguments over the best beer ever? Or a full and frank debate with barstaff about why the cloudy pint of acetic beer you have just received is still on sale? Sadly, no absolute reference is available to decide between beers for quality or superiority. However, a little knowledge can greatly improve the discussion and, in cases of altercation, save wounded pride or worse.

Many drinkers appreciate a beer for its overall impression and find vivisection irrelevant and distracting. Pubs have many other activities after all. Other drinkers may wish to identify and list components and judge accordingly. Each to their preference. Not everyone is worried about the original gravity of beers or ingredient labels on food, but that's no excuse to remove the information.

As many drinkers are aware, beer is, as yet, unlabelled for its contents and, despite strenuous requests, not all brewers are willing to declare ingredients. Moreover, official descriptions of beers are often simple, banal or just advertising hype. Obtaining an objective impression is left to the consumer, individually or collectively.

An important CAMRA aim is to provide the consumer with criteria for judging beer quality. Developing beer appreciation and challenging substandard products is difficult and requires some basic guidelines as well as constant practice. Some of these guidelines have been developed in conjunction with Brewlab, an independent laboratory service which provides training and analysis for the small brewing industry. Simple flavour profiling has been undertaken to outline the typical features of beers so that styles and brands may be considered in detail. Identification of common faults is stressed so that poor pints may be rejected with confidence and their quality assured. No brewer wishes his product to be served in poor condition and an informed consumer is vital in helping maintain the highest standards.

To help with full assessment, Brewlab also provides a simple flavour kit, containing a range of flavour components to reinforce recognition abilities and for comparison with beer characteristics. It is against this background that our 'tasting notes' in this guide have been carried out.

Although overdrinking carries well known dangers, beer is a safe food and grows no harmful bacteria. The brewing industry has developed strict criteria for many aspects of beer quality and these protect the consumer from the common dangers of adulteration and outright poisoning. Brewlab helps the smaller brewery without laboratory facilities by providing basic analyses and by yeast culturing and infection analysis. A variety of training courses and workshops, to introduce and develop the skills needed to establish and run a brewery, is also available, and beer tastings for brewers and consumers are also held, at a variety of venues, to illustrate beer quality. These provide participants with the opportunity to develop skills in flavour recognition and to taste beers selected for quality and for faults. With such support breweries can provide quality products with assurance and meet the strict quality demands of informed and aware consumers.

For more information, contact Dr Keith Thomas at Brewlab, c/o Dept. of Biology, City of London Polytechnic, Old Castle Street, London, E1 7NT. Tel. (071) 283 1030 Ext. 413.

BREWLAB

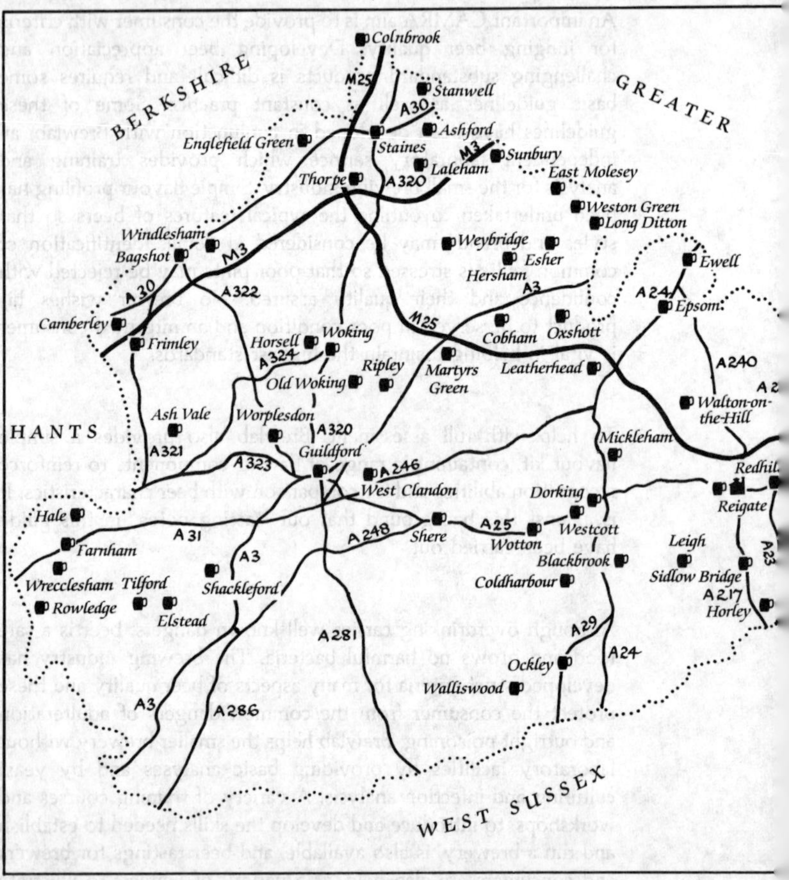

***Pilgrim**, Reigate*

Ashford

Black Dog

337 Staines Road West
☎ (0784) 254348
10.30–3 (4 Sat); 5.30 (6 Sat)–11
Charrington IPA H

Small two-bar pub which dates back to 1854 and extends a friendly welcome to all. Collections of old pipes, brasswork and fire extinguishers. Lunchtime snacks. Q ♣ P

Ash Vale

Admiral Napier

72 Vale Road (A321)
☎ (0252) 25535
11–2.30 (3 Sat); 6–11
Friary Meux Best Bitter; Taylor Walker Best Bitter H

A fine pub by the Basingstoke canal, with traditional wood panelling and bench seats in its compact interior. P

Try also: Old Ford (Courage)

Bagshot

Foresters Arms

173 London Road (A30)
☎ (0276) 72038
11–2.30 (3 Sat); 5.30–11
Courage Best Bitter, Directors H

Comfortable and deceptively roomy locals' pub with warm atmosphere and exceptionally friendly hosts. Shut the Box and skittle alley available. Garden ideal for children. No food Sun.
Q ♣ P

Three Mariners

56 High Street (off A30)
☎ (0276) 73768
11–3 (5 Sat); 5.30 (7 Sat)–11 (11–11 Fri)
Courage Best Bitter, Directors; John Smith's Bitter H

A fine example of a classic village pub. Artefacts, unearthed during renovations and dating back to the 15th century, are on display. Excellent bustling public bar and cosy no-smoking alcove in lounge bar. A well-run and deservedly-popular pub. Good value Sunday roasts.
≠ ♣ P

Blackbrook

Plough

Blackbrook Road (off A24 Beare Green-Dorking road)
OS181467 ☎ (0306) 886603
11–2.30 (12–2.30 Sun); 6–11 (10.30 Mon–Thu in winter)
King & Barnes Sussex Bitter, Broadwood, Old, Festive H

A rural two-bar pub with an excellent menu, including veg option (eve meals Tue–Sun). Old sewing machine tables in public bar, which also houses a collection of nearly 500 ties –

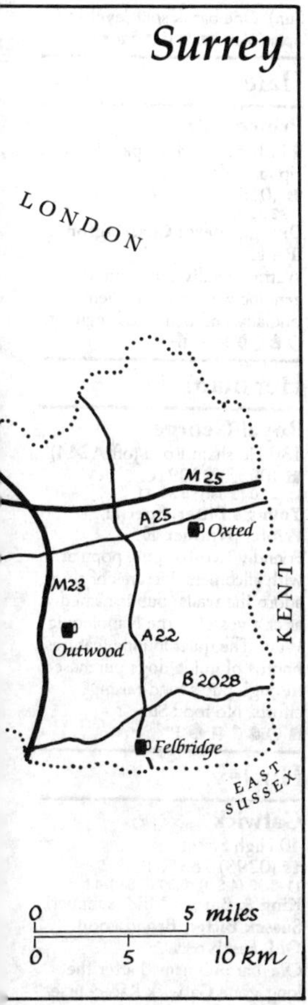

contributions welcome. A regular in this guide. ❀ ◐ ◑ ⊞ P

Camberley

Ancient Foresters
23 Park Street
☎ (0276) 64830
11–3 (4 Sat, 12–2.30 Sun); 5.30–11
Draught Bass; Fuller's ESB [H]
Basic town-centre pub – a haven for footsore shoppers. Quiet during the week but bustling and sometimes boisterous at the weekends. No food Sun. ◐ ♿ ⇌ ♣

Lamb
593 London Road, Blackwater (A30) ☎ (0276) 33832
11–3; 5.30 (5 Fri, 6.30 Sat)–11
Morland Original Bitter, Old Masters [H]
Fresh and airy atmosphere. A modern stone-paved floor, liberal use of wood, and profuse plant life, which helps to segregate the restaurant section from the bar.
❀ ◐ ◑ ⇌ (Blackwater) P

Try also: William IV (Bass)

Cobham

Silvermere Tavern
Silvermere Golf Club, Redhill Road (B366) ☎ (0932) 64988
11–11
Wadworth 6X; Whitbread Boddingtons Bitter [H]
Large, single-storey, modern bar, part of golf and leisure complex open to all. Patio overlooks man-made lake; barbecues held on summer eves. Breakfast is served most mornings; sustenance after that early round of golf! Q ❀ ◐ ◑ P

Coldharbour

Plough Inn
Coldharbour Lane OS152441
☎ (0306) 711793
11.30–3; 6.30 (7 winter)–11
Adnams Broadside; Bateman XXXB; Gibbs Mew Bishop's Tipple; Hall & Woodhouse Badger Best Bitter; Ringwood Old Thumper; Theakston Old Peculier [H]
Family-run, 350 year-old pub near Leith Hill, in good walking country. 850 feet above sea level, it is the highest pub in SE England. Children welcome lunchtime at weekends only. No eve meals Sun/Mon.
⌂ ⚇ ❀ ◐ ◑ ♿ ♣ ⌽

Colnbrook

Star & Garter
Park Street ☎ (0753) 682157
11–3; 5.30–11
Courage Best Bitter, Directors [H]
An honest locals' pub with a garden by the River Colne. Eve meals finish early. ❀ ◐ ◑ ♿ ♣ P

Dorking

Cricketers
81 South Street (A25, one-way system) ☎ (0306) 889938
11–2.30 (3 Fri & Sat); 5.30 (6 Sat)–11
Fuller's Chiswick Bitter, London Pride, ESB [H]
Town-centre pub which can become crowded in the evening. Pleasant, sheltered patio garden. Chess and backgammon played. Lunches (including veg option) are good value and quality (Mon–Fri). ❀ ◐ ♣

Old House at Home
24 West Street (A25, one-way system) ☎ (0306) 889664
11–3 (3.30 Sat); 5.30 (6 Sat)–11
Young's Bitter, Special [H], **Winter Warmer** [G]
Revitalised since becoming a Young's house, this one-bar pub attracts good conversationalists. Interesting old building with much bric-a-brac. Restaurant menu eves until 9pm.
⌂ ❀ ◐ ◑ ♿ ⇌ (West)

Try also: Bush, Horsham Road (Free)

East Molesey

Bell Inn
4 Bell Road (off B369)
☎ (081) 941 0400
11–3; 5 (6 Sat)–11
Courage Best Bitter, Directors; John Smith's Bitter [H]
A listed building, an historic coaching inn, complete with stables. Known as the 'Crooked House', because of irregular angles of gables and windows. Structure dates from 1460 and was frequented by Claude Duvalier, the 18th-century highwayman. Limited parking. No food Sun. Q ❀ ◐ ♿ ♣ P

Europa
171 Walton Road (B369)
☎ (081) 979 8838
11–2.30; 5–11 (11–11 Sat)
Courage Best Bitter, Directors [H]
Friendly local with three distinctive bars, including a no-nonsense public with pool table and dartboard. Skittle alley planned. No food Sun.
Q ❀ ◐ ⊞ ♣

Prince of Wales
23 Bridge Road (off A3050 & B369) ☎ (081) 979 1925
11–11
Courage Best Bitter, Directors [H]
Excellent local, only a stone's throw from Hampton Court Palace. Pub has two shove-ha'penny boards. A curious 'snug' area just off main bar accommodates about a dozen people.
❀ ◐ ⇌ (Hampton Court) ♣ P

Elstead

Star
Milford Road (B3001)
☎ (0252) 703305
11–2.30 (3 Fri, 4 Sat); 5.30 (7 Sat)–11
Courage Best Bitter, Directors [H]
A proper village pub: plenty of 'local' atmosphere in the public; cosy and comfy saloon with a big open fire. Convenient for visits to Thursley Common nature reserve. No food Sun.
⌂ ❀ ◐ ⊞ ♿ ♣ P

Woolpack
Milford Road (B3001)
☎ (0252) 703106
11–3; 6–11
Friary Meux Best Bitter; Ind Coope Burton Ale [G]
Attractive pub with large, open-plan bar. Accent is on meals (children's menu available).
Q ⚇ ❀ ◐ ◑

Surrey

Englefield Green

Sun
Wick Lane (follow signs to Savill Gardens)
☎ (0784) 432515
11–11
Courage Best Bitter, Directors; John Smith's Bitter [H]
Single-bar pub near Windsor Great Park.
⌂ Q ♘ ▦ ◖ ◗ ♿ ♣ P

Epsom

Barley Mow
12 Pikes Hill (off A2022)
☎ (0372) 721044
11–3; 5.30–11
Fuller's London Pride, ESB [H]
Back-street local full of nooks and crannies. Conservatory at rear houses a piano. Varied lunch menu (also for children who are welcome in the conservatory). Good service even when busy. No food Sun.
Q ♘ ▦ ◖ ♿ ♣

Try also: Kings Arms, East Street (Young's)

Esher

Claremont
2 Church Street (A244 westbound) ☎ (0372) 64083
10.30–11
Courage Best Bitter, Directors [H]
Friendly, side-street local which once had its own brewery. Walls adorned with pictures of racehorses – Sandown Racecourse is just down the road. No food Sun. ◖ ⊟ ♣

Ewell

King William IV
17 High Street (off A24)
☎ (081) 393 2063
11–2.30 (3 Sat); 5.30 (6.30 Sat)–11
Friary Meux Best Bitter; Ind Coope Burton Ale; Tetley Bitter [H]
Friendly local, liberally adorned with mementoes of the Sailor King. Note original etched windows. Live music Sat eves in back bar.
⌂ ▦ ◖ ⊟ ♿ ≠ (East/West) ♣ P

Farnham

Lamb
43 Abbey Street (near Maltings) ☎ (0252) 714133
11–2.30 (may extend); 6–11
Shepherd Neame Master Brew Bitter, Best Bitter, Bishops Finger [H]
Homely bar, haunt of thriving darts teams and pool enthusiasts. Try the excellent 'doorstep' sandwiches. Use town-centre car parks.
⌂ ▦ ◖ ◗ ≠ ♣

Try also: Queens Head (Gale's)

Felbridge

Woodcock
Woodcock Hill (A22)
☎ (0342) 325859
11–2.30; 6–11
Harveys Best Bitter; King & Barnes Sussex Bitter; Ruddles County [H]
A small beamed bar with leaded windows, attached to an up-market restaurant, from which the bar food takes its cue. Children's and vegetarian choices available.
⌂ ♘ ▦ ⇹ ◖ ◗ ♿ P

Frimley

Railway Arms
78 High Street
☎ (0276) 23544
11–2.30 (12–2 Sun); 6–11
Ind Coope Burton Ale; Taylor Walker Best Bitter; Tetley Bitter [H]
A pub with a structure unchanged this century, now sensitively renovated to offer a compact, tidy saloon and a proper public bar. ◖ ⊟ ♿ ≠ ♣

Guildford

Live & Let Live
57 Haydon Place
☎ (0483) 64372
11–2.30 (3 Sat); 5.30–11
Courage Best Bitter, Directors [H]
Haven of retreat from city-centre bustle, retaining local back-street atmosphere despite surrounding development. Cosy wood-panelled saloon leads into more basic games area. ◖ ≠ ♣

Royal
132 Worplesdon Road, Stoughton (A322, ½ mile N of A3, Guildford bypass)
☎ (0483) 575173
11–11
Courage Best Bitter, Directors [H]
Worth seeking out, on the outskirts of town, for a warm and friendly welcome. Large saloon dominates in size only, with hyperactivity in the public! No food at weekend.
▦ ⇹ ◖ ⊟ ♿ ♣ P

Spread Eagle
46 Chertsey Street (A320)
☎ (0483) 35018
10.30–2.30 (3 Fri, 3.30 Sat); 5–11
Courage Best Bitter, Directors; John Smith's Bitter [H]
Close to town centre and usually crowded, especially with lunchtime food trade (no meals Sun). One bar is split-level and open-plan. ♘ ▦ ◖ ♿ ≠ ♣ P

Hale

Prince Alfred
9 Bishops Road, Upper Hale (off Upper Hale Road)
☎ (0252) 712546
11–2.30; 6–11
Draught Bass; Charrington IPA [H]
Warm, friendly pub with a genuine welcome; ebullient landlady and dedicated regulars.
Q ▦ ◖ ◗ ⊟ ♿ ♣ P

Hersham

Royal George
130 Hersham Road (off A244)
☎ (0932) 220910
11–2.30 (3 Sat); 5.30–11
Young's Bitter, Special, Winter Warmer [H]
Friendly two-bar pub, popular with allcomers. Pictures of ships adorn the walls: pub is named after a vessel in the Napoleonic Wars. The quiet lounge features photos of guide dogs purchased through pub's fund-raising efforts. No food Sun.
⌂ Q ▦ ◖ ⊟ ♣ P

Horley

Gatwick
40 High Street
☎ (0293) 783801
11–3.30 (4 Sat); 5.30 (7 Sat)–11
King & Barnes Mild (summer), **Sussex Bitter, Broadwood, Old, Festive** [H]
One-bar pub named after the long-gone Gatwick Racecourse, which explains the collection of horse racing memorabilia.
▦ ◖ ◗ ≠ ♣

Try also: Foresters Arms (Charrington)

Horsell

Plough
Cheapside (off South Road)
☎ (0483) 741050
11–2.30 (3 Sat); 5.30 (6 Sat)–11
Benskins Best Bitter; Friary Meux Best Bitter; Gale's HSB; King & Barnes Sussex Bitter; Tetley Bitter [H]
Although a suburban pub, agricultural implements lend it a rural air, accentuated by its slightly isolated position, by commonland away from the village centre. Good food and outdoor drinking facilities.
▦ ◖ ◗ ♣ P

Laleham

Three Horseshoes
25 Shepperton Road
☎ (0784) 452617
11–11
Ruddles Best Bitter, County;

Webster's Yorkshire Bitter [H]
Popular pub near the Thames. Children welcome in the conservatory. ⌂ ⛝ ❀ ◖ ◗ P

Leatherhead

Running Horse
38 Bridge Street (off A2012)
☎ (0372) 372081
11–3 (3.30 Fri & Sat); 5.30–11
Friary Meux Best Bitter; Gale's HSB; Tetley Bitter [H]
A listed building with lounge bar, dating from 1520. John Skelton, Poet Laureate to Henry VII, wrote of Elinour Rumming brewing 'Nappy Ale' here. Good value food (not Sun).
Q ❀ ◖ ⊟ ≠ ♣ P

Leigh

Plough
Church Road OS224468
☎ (030678) 348
11–2.30 (12–2.30 Sun); 6–11
King & Barnes Sussex Bitter, Broadwood, Old, Festive [H]
Traditional country inn with a public bar for games, and a lounge with attached restaurant area for good food (not Sun, or Mon eve). This 15th-century inn enjoys an attractive setting by the village green.
⌂ Q ❀ ◖ ◗ ⊟ ♣ P

Long Ditton

New Inn
Rushett Road, (opp. recreation ground) ☎ (081) 398 1893
11–2.30; 5.30 (5 Fri)–11 (11–11 Sat)
Marston's Pedigree Bitter; Whitbread Wethered Bitter [H]
A lively, sporting pub with a loyal, local following; reputedly haunted. Whitbread guest beers are rotated regularly. Amusements in garden for children. No food at weekend.
❀ ◖ ♣

Martyrs Green

Black Swan
Old Lane (off A3, just S of M25 jct) OS089573
☎ (0932) 62364
11–11
Fuller's London Pride, ESB; Hall & Woodhouse Badger Best Bitter, Tanglefoot; Ringwood Old Thumper; Theakston Old Peculier [H]
Small, ivy-clad, 18th-century free house on country crossroads, serving 13 different real ales (including guests). Close to Wisley Gardens. Lots of small areas: games area doubles as family room. Regular live entertainment. Restaurant offers veg and children's options (not Sun or Mon eves).
⌂ ⛝ ❀ ◖ ◗ ♣ P

Mickleham

King William IV
Byttom Hill (off A24 southbound) OS174538
☎ (0372) 372590
12–2.30; 7–10.30 (11–2.30; 6–11 summer)
Adnams Bitter, Old; Hall & Woodhouse Badger Best Bitter; Marston's Pedigree Bitter [H]
Charming pub perched on a rocky hillside. Cosy old-fashioned public bar and tiny lounge. Splendid garden can be a real suntrap. Beer range extended in summer. Specialises in veg cooking; children's menu in summer (no food Sun).
⌂ Q ❀ ◖ ⊟ ♣

Ockley

Cricketers
Stane Street (A29)
☎ (0306) 79205
11–3; 6–11
Fuller's London Pride; Gale's HSB; Hall & Woodhouse Badger Best Bitter; King & Barnes Sussex Bitter [H]
Attractive pub dating from 1542 with Horsham flagstones on the floor and, unusually, the roof. Large inglenook. The cheapest pint in the area.
⌂ ◖ ◗ ♣ P

Old Woking

White Hart
150 High Street
☎ (0483) 763202
11–3 (3.30 Sat); 5 (6 Sat)–11
Courage Best Bitter, Directors; John Smith's Bitter [H]
Close enough to Woking to be a suburban pub but retaining its local village atmosphere. Good contrasting bars: public is small and lively; saloon more spacious and quiet. No meals Sun. ❀ ◖ ◗ ⊟ ♣

Outwood

Dog & Duck
Prince of Wales Road
OS313460
☎ (034 284) 2964
11–11
Adnams Bitter, Broadside; Everards Tiger Best Bitter; Hall & Woodhouse Badger Best Bitter, Tanglefoot; Wadworth 6X [H]
Friendly rural pub serving good food (veg option and children's menu). It has an impressive range of traditional games, including Ringing the Bull.
⌂ ❀ ◖ ◗ ♿ ♣ P

Oxshott

Bear
Leatherhead Road (just outside village, on A244)
☎ (0372) 842747
11–3; 5.30–11
Young's Bitter, Special [H], **Winter Warmer** [H]&[G]
A former Courage house, set back from main road, with small restaurant area, offering good-value meals. Comfortably-appointed. ⌂ Q ❀ ◗ ♣ P

Oxted

Crown
High Street, Old Oxted (off A25) ☎ (0883) 717853
12–2.30; 6–11
Adnams Bitter; Pilgrim Surrey Bitter; Ruddles Best Bitter; Young's Bitter [H]
Ancient inn with bars on two levels; the upper one (used as a family room at weekends) features some fine Victorian pine panelling and 'Play School' windows! Good quality home-cooked food. ⛝ ❀ ◖ ◗ ≠ ♣

Redhill

Home Cottage
3 Redstone Hill (A25)
☎ (0737) 762771
11–3; 5.30–11 (11–11 Thu–Sat)
Young's Bitter, Special, Winter Warmer [H]
Excellent pub behind the station. One bar, with distinct lounge and public areas. Fine etched glass and unusual banks of handpumps. No food Sun.
⌂ Q ❀ ◖ ◗ ♿ ≠ ♣ P

Plough
11 Church Road, St Johns (off A23) ☎ (0737) 766686
11–3; 6 (6.30 Sat)–11
Friary Meux Best Bitter; Gale's HSB; Ind Coope Burton Ale; Tetley Bitter [H]
Well-run 17th-century pub in St Johns conservation area, next to Earlswood Common. Well-known locally for its food served in bar and restaurant (veg option); no meals Sun.
Q ❀ ◖ ◗ ♿ ♣ P

Reigate

Nutley Hall
Nutley Lane (off A25, behind main car park)
☎ (0737) 241741
11–3; 5.30–11 (11–11 Fri & Sat)
King & Barnes Sussex Bitter, Broadwood, Old, Festive [H]
Basic local with separate dining room at the rear (no meals Sun). The pub can get busy in the evenings. Active cricket team.
◖ ♿ ≠ ♣ P

Yew Tree
99 Reigate Hill (A217, off M25 jct 8) ☎ (0737) 244944
11–11
Courage Best Bitter,

Directors; John Smith's Bitter [H]
Comfortable wood-panelled pub, halfway up Reigate Hill. The best Courage beer for miles. Food available all day until 10pm. ⌂ ❀ ◖ ◗ P

Ripley

Seven Stars
Newark Lane (B367, ½ mile W of village) ☎ (0483) 225128
11–3.30; 5.30–11
Benskins Best Bitter; Friary Meux Best Bitter; Gale's HSB; Ind Coope Burton Ale; Tetley Bitter [H]
Imposing 30s-style building on edge of village and adjoining countryside. Can be quiet but in summer proximity to the Wey Navigation might bring in the crowds. Good garden. Shut the Box played. ⌂ ❀ ◖ ◗ ♿ ♣ P

Talbot
High Street (old A3)
☎ (0483) 225188
11–3; 5.30–11
Friary Meux Best Bitter; Ind Coope Burton Ale; King & Barnes Sussex Bitter [H]
15th-century coaching inn with two irregular-shaped bars. Exposed beams and low ceilings create a dark atmosphere; easy to imagine Nelson *en route* to Portsmouth entertaining Mrs Hamilton. Good to be able to drink and still hear the clock tick. ⌂ Q ❀ ⊭ ◖ ◗ ⊟ ♿ P

Rowledge

Hare & Hounds
The Square
☎ (025 125) 2287
11–3; 6–11
Courage Best Bitter [H]
Comfortable, relaxed and friendly pub on village crossroads; the centre of village life. High standards provided and also expected of customers. Cheap bar billiards. Excellent garden for children.
❀ ◖ ◗ ♿ ♣ P

Shackleford

Cyder House
Pepperharrow (off A3)
OS935453 ☎ (0483) 810360
11–2.30; 5.30–11
Gale's HSB; Greene King IPA; Hook Norton Best Bitter; Ringwood Fortyniner, Old Thumper; Wadworth 6X [H]
Off the beaten track and worth finding. This free house is deservedly popular, with drivers and walkers alike and caters well for children. Likely to be crowded on Sun and in summer. Can be food oriented: best to go early or late if sole intention is to drink. Guest beers.
⊗ ❀ ◖ ◗ ⌓ P

Shere

Prince of Wales
☎ (048 641) 2313
11–2.30; 6–11
Young's Bitter, Special, Winter Warmer [H]
Situated in a delightful village near a pretty stream. Ideal for a Sunday afternoon stroll or as stop-over for more serious walking. Small public bar, dominated by pool table, contrasts with more sedate lounge often given over to diners. Excellent children's facilities. ⌂ Q ⊗ ❀ ◖ ◗ ⊟ ♿ ⅄ (Farley Green) ♣ P

Sidlow Bridge

Three Horseshoes
Ironsbottom (off A217)
OS249463 ☎ (0293) 862315
12–2.30 (3 Sat); 7 (6 Fri)–11
Brakspear Bitter; Fuller's London Pride, ESB; Greene King IPA [H]
Small, rural, 17th-century beer house, a former coaching stop on the London to Brighton run. Helicopters welcome (phone in advance), but no motorbikes! Summer barbecues. Guest beers.
Q ❀ ◖ ♣ P

Staines

Beehive
35 Edgell Road
☎ (0784) 452663
11–11
Courage Best Bitter, Directors; John Smith's Bitter [H]
A splendid three-roomed, back-street local with a friendly welcome. As yet unspoilt by the brewery. ⌂ Q ❀ ◖ ⊟ ♿ ⇌

Bells
124 Church Street
☎ (0784) 454247
11–3; 5.30–11
Courage Best Bitter, Directors; John Smith's Bitter [H]
An excellent pub on the edge of town and close to the river. Good choice of food (eves until 6.30). Q ❀ ◖ ◗

Blue Anchor Inn
High Street ☎ (0784) 452622
11–11
Ruddles Best Bitter; Webster's Yorkshire Bitter [H]
A 'landmark' pub in the town. The building dates back to the 15th century and is as vibrant now as it must have been then. Note the 'window tax' frontage. Live music is a regular feature. Outdoor drinking on front patio. Games include Nine Men's Morris.
⌂ Q ❀ ⊭ ◖ ♿ ⇌ ♣ P

Stanwell

Wheatsheaf
Town Lane ☎ (0784) 253512
10.30–11
Courage Best Bitter, Directors [H]
Friendly roadside pub. Menu caters for children and vegetarians. ❀ ◖ ♣ P

Sunbury

Hare & Hounds
132 Vicarage Road
☎ (0932) 782242
11–3; 5.30–11 (11–11 Fri & Sat)
Fuller's Chiswick Bitter, London Pride, ESB
Originally a two-bar pub with off-licence. Now refurbished to include a separate food servery and eating area. No meals Sun eve. ❀ ◖ ◗ ♿ ⇌ P

Thorpe

Rose & Crown
Green Road ☎ (09904) 2338
11–3; 5.30–11 (11–11 summer)
Courage Best Bitter, Directors; John Smith's Bitter [H]
Superb example of a village-green pub, best visited in the summer months to enjoy the outside drinking facilities, but convivial throughout the year.
⌂ Q ❀ ◖ ◗ ♿ ⅄ ⇌ (Virginia Water) P

Tilford

Barley Mow
Tilford Green
☎ (025 125) 2205
11–2.30 (3.30 Sat); 6 (5.30 Sat in summer)–11
Courage Best Bitter, Directors; John Smith's Bitter [H]
Idyllic setting adjoining cricket green and outdoor drinking area with nearby river crossing. Pub dates from 1730 and was the home of early cricket hero, William 'Silver Billy' Beldham. Apparently his spirit is still in evidence, but in the nicest possible way!
⌂ Q ❀ ◖ ◗ ♿ ⅄ ♣

Virginia Water

Stag & Hounds
Wellington Avenue
☎ (09904) 2353
11–2.30; 5 (6 Sat)–11
Courage Best Bitter [H]
Warm welcome to occasional visitors and locals alike.
⌂ Q ❀ ◖ ♿ ♣ P

Walliswood

Scarlett Arms
Walliswood Green Road
OS120381 ☎ (030679) 243
11–2.30; 5.30–11
King & Barnes Mild, Sussex Bitter, Broadwood, Old, Festive Ⓗ
Classic country pub dating from 1620, featuring a stone-flagged floor and large inglenook. Note mis-spelt name on the inn sign.
⌂ Q ❀ ◖ ◗ ♣ P

Try also: Punchbowl, Oakwood Hill (Free)

Walton-on-the-Hill

Chequers
Chequers Lane (B2220)
☎ (0737) 812634
11–2.30; 5.30–11 (11–11 Fri & Sat)
Young's Bitter, Special, Winter Warmer Ⓗ
A large pub with parts dating back 200 years, although it has been much extended. There is only one bar, but several distinct areas. Restaurant has a French flavour (must book); no eve meals Sun. ⌂ Q ❀ ◖ ◗ ♣ P

Fox & Hounds
Walton Street (B2220)
☎ (0737) 812090
11–11
Draught Bass; Charrington IPA; Fuller's ESB (winter); **M&B Highgate Mild** Ⓗ
Large and comfortable village pub serving excellent beer and food (all day). Smart, efficient service. No music. ⌂ Q ❀ ◖ ◗ P

West Clandon

Onslow Arms
The Street (A247)
☎ (0483) 222447
11–2.30 (3 Sat); 5.30–11
Courage Best Bitter, Directors; King & Barnes Sussex Bitter, Broadwood; Young's Bitter, Special Ⓗ
Attractive inn with leaded windows, dating from 1623. Takes its name from a local family. The rambling, warren-like interior includes a restaurant (no food Sun eve). The beer range varies and up to eight interesting real ales are on at any one time.
Q ❀ ◖ ◗ ♿ ≠ (Clandon) P

Westcott

Cricketers
Guildford Road (A25)
☎ (0306) 883520
11–3; 5.30–11
Adnams Bitter; Fuller's London Pride; Hall & Woodhouse Badger Best Bitter, Tanglefoot; Pilgrim Surrey Bitter Ⓗ
Reasonably-priced friendly free house. The single bar is on three levels, catering for pool players, dogs walking their owners and, on the top level, diners (no eve meals Mon or Wed). Tiny garden. ❀ ◖ ◗ ♣

Weston Green

Alma Arms
Alma Road (off A309)
☎ (081) 398 4444
11–3 (2.30 Mon–Fri in winter); 6–11 (closes 2.30 Sun lunchtime in winter)
Courage Best Bitter, Directors Ⓗ
Cosy pub off the beaten track, with friendly atmosphere. Built as a hunting lodge it overlooks the green and pond. Children's play area. No food Sun.
Q ❀ ◖ ≠ (Esher) ♣ P

Weybridge

Old Crown
83 Thames Street (off A317)
☎ (0932) 842844
10.30–3 (3.30 Sat); 5–11
Courage Best Bitter, Directors Ⓗ
16th-century riverside pub with weatherboarded facade. Several rooms; each has a different atmosphere. Food available at all times; home-cooked specials and fresh fish (Thu/Fri).
Q ❀ ◖ ◗ ⊕ ♣ P

Prince of Wales
Anderson Road, Oatlands Park (off A3050) ☎ (0932) 852082
11–11
Adnams Bitter; Fuller's London Pride; Ind Coope Burton Ale; Tetley Bitter; Whitbread Boddingtons Bitter Ⓗ
A cosy pub with traditional decor. No fruit machines or noisy games to spoil the atmosphere. Good value restaurant (not Sun eve). Look for painting of famous characters drinking in the pub.
Q ❀ ◖ ◗

Windlesham

Bee
School Road (B386, 50 yds from A30) ☎ (0276) 73359
11–11
Courage Best Bitter, Directors Ⓗ
Pleasant, well-run village local with a mixed clientele and a growing reputation for food (not Sun). Eve meals finish early when the Bee becomes a haunt of village regulars. The only 'Bee' in the country. Summer Punch and Judy shows in garden. ❀ ◖ ◗ ♿ ♣ P

Half Moon
Church Road (off B386)
☎ (0276) 73329
11–2.30 (3 Fri & Sat); 5.30–11
Fuller's London Pride; Greene King IPA, Abbot Ale; Ruddles Best Bitter, County; Taylor Landlord Ⓗ
A pleasant, characterful pub in an attractive village, with a welcoming log fire. Boasts an enterprising range of guest beers (four usually). Large garden with children's play area. No food Sun. ⌂ Q ❀ ◖ ⌓ P

Woking

Old Stillage
12 Chertsey Road (off A320)
☎ (0483) 725625
11–3; 5.30–11 (11–11 Fri & Sat)
Greene King Abbot Ale; Marston's Pedigree Bitter; Ruddles Best Bitter; Wadworth 6X; Webster's Yorkshire Bitter Ⓗ
Ex-wine bar, recently refurbished with mirrors to create an impression of space. Always crowded, however: at lunchtimes with shoppers and office workers and in the evenings with army types. Loud disco Tue–Sun. Guest beers.
◖ ◗ ≠

Star
Wych Hill, Hookheath
☎ (0483) 760526
11–2.30 (3 Sat); 5.30 (6 Sat)–11
Benskins Best Bitter; Friary Meux Best Bitter; Gale's HSB; King & Barnes Sussex Bitter; Tetley Bitter Ⓗ
Generally busy pub on outskirts of town which attracts a happy mix of ages. One large single bar with adjoining restaurant and showbiz theme. Difficult to find without local knowledge and hard on cyclists!
⛀ ❀ ⛟ ◖ ◗ P

Worplesdon

Fox
Fox Corner (B380, 200 yds from A322 jct)
☎ (0483) 232520
11–2.30 (3 Sat); 5–11
Courage Best Bitter, Directors Ⓗ
Rural atmosphere survives despite proximity to urban developments. Centre of activity is the public bar whilst the saloon is tranquil. Gents toilet is a building in itself! No food Sun. Q ❀ ◖ ⊕ ♣ P

Wotton

Wotton Hatch
Guildford Road (A25)
☎ (0306) 885665
11–2.30 (3 Sat); 5.30–11
Fuller's Chiswick Bitter, London Pride, ESB Ⓗ
A former Surrey Trust house, this 300 year-old inn was acquired by Fuller's in 1964. A pub of contrasts – from an old-fashioned public bar to a high-class restaurant. Award-winning garden. ⌂ Q ❀ ◖ ◗ ⊕ ♣ P

Wrecclesham

Sandrock
Sandrock Hill Road (off B3384)
☎ (0252) 715865
11–2.30; 5.30–11 (11–11 Sat)

Batham Mild Ale, Best Bitter; Brakspear Bitter, Holden's Bitter; Theakston Bitter; Young's Bitter, Special 🄷
If you live within 50 miles and have never been – why? A must for any serious real ale drinker: eight handpumped beers, including mild and old regular guests. Recently-extended without loss of atmosphere. Limited parking. Bar billiards. ⛫ Q ❀ ◖ ♣ ⌂ P

TECHNICAL TERMS

ABV:	alcohol by volume. The percentage of alcohol in the beer.
Blanket pressure:	a light covering of carbon dioxide added to cask beer to prevent air reaching the beer and so deteriorating it. Too much gas can make the beer fizzy, like keg beer.
Bottle-conditioned:	a beer which is allowed to continue its fermentation in the bottle and which has to be poured carefully because of its light sediment. The best-known examples are Worthington White Shield and Guinness Original.
Brewery-conditioned:	a beer which is chilled, filtered and usually pasteurised at the brewery to stop any further fermentation. As seen in keg and bright beers and lagers.
Cask-breather:	device which allows carbon dioxide (rather than air) into the cask to replace drawn off beer. Its purpose is to keep beer fresh if it has to remain in the cask longer than a few days, but it is criticised for spoiling the natural maturing process of the beer.
Cask-conditioned:	a beer which, not having been filtered, chilled or pasteurised, still contains sugars and yeast and is allowed to continue its fermentation in the cask after leaving the brewery.
Dry hopping:	putting fresh hops into the beer in the cask. This adds aroma and a new bitterness to the beer.
Finings:	a substance made from the swim bladder of the sturgeon and used for clearing the beer. Also known as isinglass. Synthetic alternatives have become available, popular for producing 'vegetarian' beers.
Full mash:	mash traditionally produced from grist, not malt extract.
High gravity brewing:	producing very strong beer which is watered down in the cask.
Original gravity:	system for discerning the amount of duty payable on a beer, which also provides a rough indication of the beer's alcoholic strength. It is a reading taken by hydrometer of the amount of fermentable material there is in the wort prior to fermentation. Water has a gravity of 1000 degrees, so a beer with an OG of 1040 would have 40 parts of fermentable material in its volume before fermentation. As a rough guide, a beer with an OG of 1040 is about 4 per cent alcohol, 1045 4.5 per cent alcohol, etc. Most beers display their gravities as a range, e.g. 1038–1042, to allow for the slight variation from brew to brew.
Secondary fermentation:	fermentation which is allowed to take place in the cask or bottle.

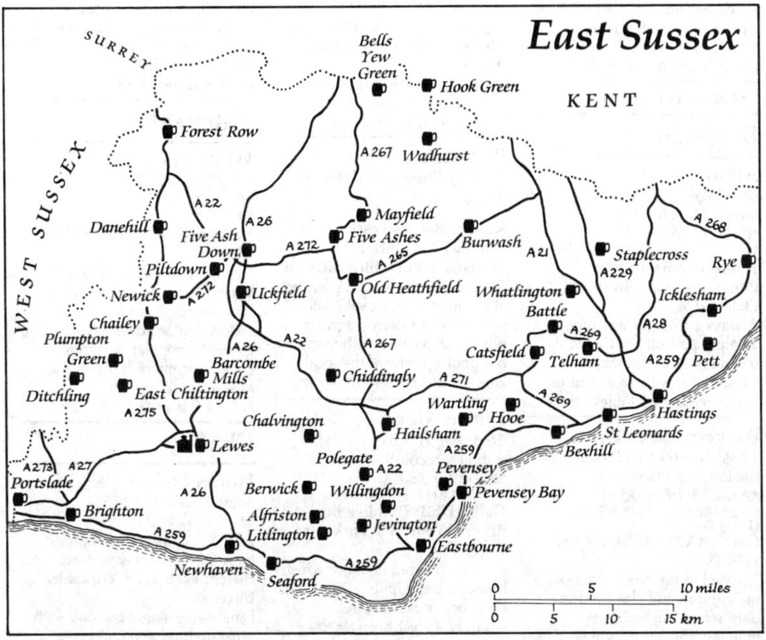

Harveys, Lewes

Alfriston

Market Cross/ Smugglers

Waterloo Square
☎ (0323) 870241
11–2.30 (3 Sat); 6.30–11
Courage Best Bitter, Directors Ⓗ
A two-ghost pub and a pub with two names, dating from 1358. Lots of beams; cosy, intimate atmosphere. Attractive conservatory and new outdoor drinking area. Note collection of early kitchen aids. Q ◖◗ ⛺

Try also: Star

Barcombe Mills

Anglers Rest

1 mile W of A26 OS428150
☎ (0273) 400270
Hours vary
Harveys Best Bitter, XXXX (Old); Marston's Pedigree Bitter; Wadworth 6X Ⓗ
Single-bar pub in rural location by disused railway station and not far from River Ouse. Beer range changes. Popular but extensive menu specialises in fish. Children's games in garden. ◖◗ ⛺ ♣ P

Battle

Chequers

Lower Lake (just S of town on Hastings Road)
☎ (04246) 2088
10–3; 6–11
Marston's Pedigree Bitter; Whitbread Flowers Original Ⓗ
Smart, well-kept pub on site of Battle of Hastings; handy for the Abbey. Dates from the 15th century and boasts oak beams and a ghost. Busy food trade. Note the copper bar top and the unusual wooden signs. Boules team. ◖◗ ⛺ ≈ P

Try also: Kings Head (Courage)

Bells Yew Green

Brecknock Arms

☎ (089275) 237
11.30–2.30; 6–11
Harveys XX Mild Ale, Pale Ale, Best Bitter, XXXX (Old) Ⓗ
Small village pub in a Victorian building of character; unpretentious but with a clean and comfortable saloon. Lunchtime bar snacks.
Q ♿ ≈ (Front) ♣ P

Berwick

Cricketers Arms

300 yds W of Alfriston roundabout on A27
☎ (0323) 870469
11–3; 6–11
Harveys Best Bitter, XXXX (Old) Ⓖ
Timeless country pub with tiled floor and rustic furniture giving true rural atmosphere. Attractive gardens; good pub grub. All beer on gravity from kitchen-type area behind bar, so don't look for handles. Ideal base for walks.
Q ◖◗ ⛺ ≈ ♣ P

Bexhill

Bell Hotel

1 Church Street
☎ (0424) 219654
10.30–11 (12–2; 7–10.30 Sun)
Courage Best Bitter, Directors Ⓗ
Large, rambling hotel in heart of old town, next to parish church and old manor barn. Various drinking areas to choose from, some of which are dedicated to aquatic life (including the largest goldfish in town!).
◖◗ ≈ ♣

Sportsman

15 Sackville Road
☎ (0424) 214214
10.30–3; 5–11 (10.30–11 Fri & Sat)
King & Barnes Sussex Bitter, Festive; Webster's Yorkshire Bitter Ⓗ
Welcoming, friendly, town-centre pub; jovial atmosphere created by terrific bunch of

locals. Secluded and sunny beer garden. Frequent evening functions throughout year. Guest beers. ♣

Try also: Traffers (Free)

Brighton

Albion
28 Albion Hill (steep hill behind former Tamplins brewery)
(0273) 604439
11–11
Whitbread Best Bitter, Pompey Royal, Flowers Original [H]
Always a friendly welcome; 10p per pint off for CAMRA members. A traditional-style, corner local with an accent on bar billiards (two tables). ♣

Basketmakers Arms
12 Gloucester Road (corner of Cheltenham Place)
(0273) 689006
11–3 (3.30 Fri); 5.30 (5 Fri)–11 (11–11 Sat)
Gale's XXXD, BBB, XXXXX, HSB [H]
Situated in the North Laine area of Brighton and close to the only remaining maltings building, this busy local is adorned with many old tins.

Hand in Hand
33 Upper St James's Street, Kemptown (100 yds from seafront) (0273) 602521
11–11
Adnams Broadside; Hall & Woodhouse Badger Best Bitter, Tanglefoot; Kemptown Bitter, Celebrated Strong Ale [H]
Small pub with its own brewery. Decor defies description! Meals include veg option.

Lamb & Flag
9 Cranbourne Street (next to Churchill Square shopping centre) (0273) 26415
11–11
Charrington IPA [H]
Popular lunchtime local with good passing trade. Close to all the shops. Bar snacks. Q

Leconfield Arms
116 Edward Street (440 yds E of Royal Pavilion)
(0273) 687515
11–11
Courage Best Bitter; John Smith's Bitter [H]
Small, multi-bar local with wood panelling and leaded glass windows. Music can occasionally be overpowering. No keg bitter sold. Take care when visiting toilets! ♣

Lord Nelson
36 Trafalgar Street (200 yds E of station) (0273) 682150
10–3; 5.30–11
Harveys XX Mild Ale (summer), **Pale Ale, Best Bitter, XXXX (Old), Armada Ale** [H]
Two-bar town local; often crowded, particularly at lunchtime. ♣

Pedestrian Arms
Foundry Street (SE of station)
(0273) 697014
11–11
King & Barnes Festive; Ruddles Best Bitter; Webster's Yorkshire Bitter [H]
Small, back-street local popular at all times with Royal Mail workers from nearby sorting offices. Decorated with many old photographs of the local area. Lunchtime snacks. ♣

Prince Albert
48 Trafalgar Street (below station forecourt)
(0273) 28400
11–3; 6–11 (11–11 Fri & Sat)
Gale's HSB; Ruddles Best Bitter; Webster's Yorkshire Bitter [H]
A grade II listed building which houses a basic 'public'-type bar. Live rock music features strongly. Guest beer. ♣

Royal Standard
59 Queens Road
(0273) 29813
10.30–11
Draught Bass; Greene King Abbot Ale; Harveys Best Bitter; Whitbread Boddingtons Bitter, Higsons Bitter [H]
Small, one-bar pub with friendly, club-like atmosphere. Numerous guest beers served by gravity from alcove next to bar. Restaurant downstairs caters for children and vegetarians. Q

Sir Charles Napier
50 Southover Street (between the 'Level' and Queens Park)
(0273) 601413
11–3; 6–11
Gale's XXXD, BBB, XXXXX, HSB [H]
An enlarged corner local in the heart of a good area for pubs; can be crowded in the evening. No food Sun; eve meals till 9pm. ♣

Burwash

Bell
High Street (A265)
(0435) 882304
11–2.30; 6–11
Hall & Woodhouse Tanglefoot; Harveys Best Bitter, XXXX (Old) [H]
A classic, superbly-kept pub, reputed to date from 1609. Was mentioned in *Puck of Pooks Hill*. Has collections of barometers and mulling irons. A pub with a warm atmosphere and something for everyone. Games include Toad in the Hole and Ring the Bull.
Q ♣ P

Catsfield

White Hart
On A261 OS723137
(0424) 892650
10–3; 6–11
Draught Bass; Charrington IPA [H]
Village local with a surprisingly large interior dominated by a long, sturdy bar. Good, welcoming atmosphere. Small garden is popular in summer. Handy for many footpaths and near good fishing.
♣ P

Chailey

Horns Lodge
South Chailey (A275)
(0273) 400422
Hall & Woodhouse Badger Best Bitter; Harveys Best Bitter; Webster's Yorkshire Bitter [H]
Family-run, single bar pub with separate food and children's areas. Winner of many pub games trophies. ♣ P

Try also: Kings Head

Chalvington

Yew Tree Inn
Off A22 at Golden Cross OS525099 (032 183) 326
11–2.30; 6–11
Harveys Best Bitter [H]
Remote rural pub, well off the beaten track. Exposed oak beams and brick floors in both bars; renovated back bar has an inglenook. Pub boasts one of the oldest cricket pitches in the country, with an active team (soccer team, too). Camping in grounds. Q ♣ P

Chiddingly

Six Bells
Off A22 (0323) 872227
10.30–2.30; 6–10.30 (11 Fri & Sat, closed Mon)
Courage Best Bitter, Directors [H]; **Harveys Best Bitter** (winter) [G]
Cosy cavern of memorabilia. Innovative menu.
♣ P

Danehill

Coach & Horses
School Lane (¾ mile NE of village, off A22) OS412286
(082 574) 369
11–2.30; 6–11
Harveys Best Bitter, XXXX (Old) [H]
Beer range changes weekly in

this remote and unspoilt pub. Saloon is small and cosy; public has an adjacent eating area (menu changes fortnightly). Guest beers. Bar billiards.
⛫ Q ❀ ◐ ◗ ⊟ ♣ P

Ditchling

North Star
19 North End (400 yds N of Ditchling crossroads)
☎ (07918) 5890
12–2.30; 6–11
Adnams Broadside; Hall & Woodhouse Tanglefoot; Harveys Best Bitter, XXXX (Old); Shepherd Neame Master Brew Bitter, Bishops Finger Ⓗ
Friendly village local with a collection of jugs in the 'welcome bar'. Occasional live music; quiz night Thu. Beer range may vary. Home-cooked meals are excellent value; limited choice, but includes veg option. ◐ ◗ ⊟ ♣

Eastbourne

Black Horse
220 Seaside ☎ (0323) 23143
11–3; 5.30–11
Draught Bass; Charrington IPA Ⓗ
A friendly corner local with a large, fairly basic public bar and smarter saloon. Family atmosphere; keen fund-raising for guide dogs. Darts and bar billiards; quiz night on Sun. Good value lunches. Street-front tables. Q ❀ ◐ ⊟ ♿ ♣

Hurst Arms
76 Willingdon Road ($1\frac{1}{2}$ miles N of centre on A22)
☎ (0323) 21762
11–3; 6–11
Harveys XX Mild Ale (summer), **Best Bitter, XXXX (Old), Armada Ale** Ⓗ
Imposing, red-brick Victorian local named after nearby windmill. Busy, bustling public and quieter saloon. Sells the best Harveys in the area. Hot and cold snacks always available.
❀ ⊟ ♣

Lamb Inn
High Street (1 mile N of centre on A259) ☎ (0323) 20545
10.30–3; 5.30–11
Harveys XX Mild Ale, (summer), **Best Bitter, XXXX (Old), Armada Ale** Ⓗ
Harveys' Old Town showpiece: half-timbered exterior; full of antique furniture. Rumoured secret passage connects the 12th-century crypt with nearby church. Convenient for Towner Art Gallery and Gildredge Park. Meeting place for numerous local societies. Q ⛾ ❀ ◐ ◗ ⊟ P

Maxims
53 South Street (200 yds from Town Hall) ☎ (0323) 21713
11–2.30; 5.30–11
Harveys Best Bitter; Theakston Best Bitter; Younger IPA Ⓗ
Smart, sophisticated town café-bar with unusual beers for the area. Rebuilding has resulted in a basement Tapas bar, a ground-floor bar – all brick and polished wood – and an upstairs restaurant. Food is highly recommended (veg option).
◐ ◗ ⇌

East Chiltington

Jolly Sportsman
Chapel Lane (off B2116) OS372153 ☎ (0273) 890400
11.30–2.30 (not Mon); 6 (7 winter)–11
Harveys Best Bitter Ⓗ
A true centre of village life. Well off the beaten track, with good views of the South Downs and Sussex Weald. Popular with ramblers. Separate areas for dining (meals Wed–Sun), and pool. Guest beers in summer. ❀ ◐ ◗ ♣ P

Five Ash Down

Firemans Arms
On old A26, N of A272 crossroads OS477237
☎ (082581) 2191
Hours vary
Harveys Best Bitter; Younger IPA Ⓗ
Two-bar pub run by steam railway enthusiast. Good local trade and a welcome for visitors. Traction engine meet on New Year's Day. Three guest beers.
⛫ ⛾ ❀ ◐ ◗ ⊟ ♣ ⌽ P

Five Ashes

Five Ashes Inn
On A267 ☎ (082585) 485
11–2.30; 6–11
Courage Directors; Harveys Best Bitter; Hook Norton Old Hookey Ⓗ
Small country inn on a fairly busy road. Inglenook and oak beams; small saloon and tiny public – not recommended to the claustrophobic, but can be very entertaining. Guest beers.
⛫ ⛾ ❀ ◐ ◗ ⊟ ♣

Forest Row

Brambletye
The Square ☎ (0342) 824144
11–3; 5.30–11
Draught Bass; Harveys Best Bitter; Marston's Pedigree Bitter Ⓗ
Large, family-owned hotel. Sherlock Holmes and Dr Watson took rooms here in *The Return of Sherlock Holmes*. Good traditional food in bar and restaurant; veg option.
⛫ ❀ ⛿ ◐ ◗ P

Hailsham

Grenadier
High Street ☎ (0323) 842152
10–3; 6–11
Harveys XX Mild Ale, Best Bitter, XXXX (Old) Ⓗ
Two-bar town pub in the classic Victorian style. Genuine public bar – workers welcome – and a small, odd-shaped saloon. Look for the original gas lamp fittings. Shove-ha'penny.
❀ ⊟ ♿ ♣ P

Hastings

First In, Last Out
14–15 High Street, Old Town
☎ (0424) 425079
11–3; 7–11
St Clements Old Crofters, Cardinal Sussex Ale; Tetley Bitter; Wadworth 6X Ⓗ
Small, friendly brew pub; window in bar overlooks full mash brewery. Excellent beer – the cheapest in Hastings. Open central fireplace; alcove-style seating gives privacy. Not to be missed. Guest beers.
⛫ Q ◐ ⛺ ♣

Palace Bars [Pigs in Paradise]
White Rock (Seafront, A259)
☎ (0424) 439444
11.30–11
Draught Bass; Canterbury Ale; Charrington IPA; Whitbread Flowers Original Ⓗ
Two-bar pub with vast interior behind its small frontage. Enjoys a fantastic Bohemian atmosphere. Wide range of board games. A must for all pasta lovers. Occasional guest beers. No disabled access to gents WC. ◐ ◗ ♿ ⇌

Royal Standard
East Beach Street, Old Town (A259) ☎ (0424) 420163
12 (11 Sat)–3; 7–11 (11–11 Sat in summer)
Shepherd Neame Master Brew Bitter, Bishops Finger Ⓗ
Compact, two-bar pub just off the seafront. Collection of naval memorabilia. Warm welcome and easy atmosphere, but watch out for door-operated spider at bar! Note the wall-mounted pub sign. ⛫ ❀ ⛺ ♣

Hooe

Red Lion
Off B2095 at Hooe Common OS692106 ☎ (0424) 892371
10.30–2.30 (3 Sat); 6–11
Draught Bass; Charrington IPA Ⓗ
This village local has been a pub since 1609. Noisy, popular public bar; quieter saloon and snug, all with a good

atmosphere. Steam rally and car memorabilia on saloon walls. A village meeting place with occasional morris dancing. Meals Mon-Fri; limited Sat lunch menu. ⌂ Q ❀ ◖ ◗ ⊟ ♣ P

Hook Green

Elephants Head

On B2169, 2 miles W of Lamberhurst OS655359
☎ (0892) 890279
11–3; 6–11
Harveys XX Mild Ale (summer), **Pale Ale, Best Bitter, XXXX (Old), Armada Ale** ⊞
A fairly recent addition to Harveys' estate and unusual in offering their entire range. A beautiful old pub with lots of corners to sit in. Large south-facing garden offers views of hop gardens beyond. An idyllic spot for a pint. ⌂ Q ❀ ◖ ◗ ♣ P

Icklesham

Queens Head

Parsonage Lane (up lane opp. the church, off A259)
☎ (0424) 814552
11–3; 6–11
Greene King IPA, Abbot Ale; Harveys Best Bitter; Taylor Landlord ⊞
Very attractive, but hard-to-find, tile-hung pub in a quiet country setting. Old farm implements add to the warm, friendly atmosphere. Garden offers magnificent views. Frequent guest beers (range often changes). Good quality food. Boules. ⌂ Q ❀ ◖ ◗ ⊟ ♿ ♣ P

Jevington

Eight Bells

High Street (B2101)
☎ (032 12) 4442
11–2.30 (12–2 Sun); 6–11
Courage Best Bitter, Directors; Harveys Best Bitter; John Smith's Bitter ⊞
A 600 year-old village locals' pub, complete with wooden beams and window seats. Warm welcome assured; excellent home-cooking served. Paintings by local artists and locally-grown produce for sale. Has an attractive, safe garden.
Q ❀ ◖ ◗ ♣ P

Lewes

Black Horse Inn

55 Western Road (old A27, opp. County Hall)
☎ (0273) 473653
11–2.30; 6–11
Brakspear Special; Harveys Best Bitter, XXXX (Old) ⊞
Pictures of old Lewes pubs abound in the public bar which is traditionally furnished and often crowded. The saloon at the rear is smaller and much more sedate. Bar billiards and Toad in the Hole.
Q ⛟ ◖ ⊟ ♿ ♣

Dorset Arms

22 Malling Street (behind the brewery) ☎ (0273) 477110
12–3; 6–11
Harveys Pale Ale, Best Bitter, XXXX (Old), Armada Ale ⊞
Closed in the 60s by Watneys who inherited it from Tamplins; re-opened as a free house, closed again and redeveloped as Harveys' brewery tap: now hopefully settled. A large and comfortable pub. Beware: top pressure is used on the mild.
⌂ ⚯ ❀ ⛟ ◖ ◗ ♣

Fruiterers Arms

1 Sun Street (near police station)
☎ (0273) 475509
10.30–3 (may extend); 6–11
Shepherd Neame Master Brew Bitter, Best Bitter, Bishops Finger ⊞
Tucked away in the back streets but worth finding. Public bar is dominated by a pool table; saloon is small and cosy. Excellent value meals. Toad in the Hole played. ◖ ◗ ⊟ ♿ ♣

Litlington

Plough & Harrow

on Exceat to Alfriston road OS523018 ☎ (0323) 870632
11–2.30 (12–3 Sat); 6.30–11
Hall & Woodhouse Badger Best Bitter, Tanglefoot; Harveys Best Bitter ⊞
Always six beers available (including guests) in this smart, busy village pub. Huge food trade in restaurant area. Children's servery and aviary. Railway theme extends to models in the bar. ⌂ ❀ ◖ ◗ P

Mayfield

Rose & Crown

Fletching Street (on lane signed Tidebrook, ¼ mile E of village) OS592271 ☎ (0435) 872200
11–3.15; 6–11
Adnams Bitter; Harveys Best Bitter ⊞
Excellent, atmospheric pub with rooms at different levels and an inglenook. Rare guest beers and good food combine to make this village local well worth finding. ⌂ Q ❀ ⛟ ◖ ◗ ⊟ ♣ P

Try also: Carpenters Arms; Railway Inn

Newhaven

Bridge Inn

Bridge Street
☎ (0273) 514059
11–11
Whitbread Strong Country Bitter, Flowers Original ⊞
Old pub, still with some character despite being made into one bar. Boasts circular pool table. Menu caters for children and vegetarians.
⛟ ◖ ◗ ⥈ (Town)

Engineer

76 Railway Road (400 yds from A259) ☎ (0273) 514460
11–11
Charrington IPA ⊞
Cheerful pub near harbour used by workmen and dockers. Quiz nights popular. Menu offers children's portions and veg option. Euchre, pool and darts played.
⌂ ❀ ◖ ◗ ⥈ (Town/Harbour) ♣

Jolly Boatman

135 Lewes Road
☎ (0273) 514457
11–3; 6–11
Harveys XX Mild Ale, Best Bitter, XXXX (Old) ⊞
Friendly, edge-of-town pub: one bar with darts and Toad in the Hole. Pool room above (no bar). Good simple pub food (not Sun). ◖ ♣

Prince of Wales

49 South Road
☎ (0273) 513364
11–3; 6.30–11
Whitbread Flowers Original ⊞
A real town pub with a green tiled facade, and leaded lights of old United Brewery. Photos of ships and Old Newhaven.
◖ ◗ ⊟ ⥈ (Town) ♣

Try also: Hope; Sheffield Arms

Newick

Royal Oak

Church Road (off A272)
11–2.30; 6–11
Marston's Pedigree Bitter; Whitbread Strong Country Bitter, Pompey Royal, Flowers Original ⊞
Traditional, oak-beamed public bar in what used to be the village manor house. Comfortable saloon with food. Interesting panel shows wattle and daub wall. Small garden.
⌂ ❀ ◖ ◗ ⊟ ♣ P

Old Heathfield

Star Inn

Church Street (off B2096)
☎ (043 52) 3507
11–3; 6.30 (6 summer)–11
Gale's HSB; Ruddles Best Bitter; Webster's Yorkshire Bitter ⊞
14th-century village local actually in the churchyard. Warm, relaxing atmosphere in saloon with inglenook; small, cosy public bar. Award-winning

gardens offer good views. Cider-drinking ghost! Pub has record of serving beer for 600 years. No eve meals Sun/Mon.
⌂ Q ❀ ◖ ◗ ⊞ ♣ P

Pett

Two Sawyers
Pett Road (off A259)
☎ (0424) 812255
11–3; 6–11
King & Barnes Sussex Bitter; Marston's Pedigree Bitter; Whitbread Strong Country Bitter, Flowers Original; Young's Special H
Rambling, deceptively large 17th-century farmhouse converted to a pub; warm, friendly welcome assured. Three bars; real fires everywhere, one of which is in two bars at once! Note the unusual table in saloon. Frequent guest beers.
⌂ Q ❀ ⊨ ◖ ◗ ⊞ Å ♣ P

Pevensey

Royal Oak & Castle
High Street ☎ (0323) 762371
11–3; 5–11
Courage Best Bitter, Directors H
Victorian-style pub near castle gate. Large garden at back of pub with play area. Small, high-ceilinged bar area. ⌂ ♘ ❀ ◖ ◗ Å ⇌ (West Ham) ♣ P

Pevensey Bay

Moorings
Beach Road (off Seaville Drive)
☎ (0323) 761126
11–3; 6–11
Harveys Best Bitter; Ruddles Best Bitter, County; Theakston Best Bitter H
A small pub, practically on the beach. Brick-built bar; a new games and family room and a small dining area at one end. Very busy at weekends. Guest beers. ⌂ ♘ ❀ ◖ ◗ Å ⇌

Try also: Castle Inn (Charrington)

Piltdown

Peacock
Shortbridge (on B2102, off A272) ☎ (0825) 762463
Hours vary
Harveys Best Bitter; King & Barnes Festive H
Picturesque, oak-beamed pub with inglenook and restaurant. Pleasant garden. Near site of Piltdown Man hoax. Guest beers. ⌂ ❀ ◖ ◗ P

Plumpton Green

Fountain
Station Road
☎ (0273) 890294
10.30–2.30; 6–11
Young's Bitter, Special H, **Winter Warmer** G
Young's most southerly tied house; a *Good Beer Guide* perennial. Landlord is a well known character who had a beer bottled and named in his honour for the 21st anniversary of his taking over the pub. Large inglenook fireplace; Toad in the Hole played.
⌂ ◖ ⇌ (Plumpton) ♣ P

Polegate

Dinkum
54 High Street
☎ (032 12) 2029
10.30–11
Harveys Best Bitter, XXXX (Old), Armada Ale H
Two-bar, family-run traditional pub: plush saloon, proper public, games room and garden. Good value food. Name derived from WWII when it was frequented by Australian servicemen stationed nearby.
⌂ Q ♘ ❀ ◖ ⊞ ⇌ ♣ P

Portslade

Blue Anchor
81 Station Road (A259/A2038)
☎ (0273) 502567
11–11
Marston's Pedigree Bitter; Whitbread Pompey Royal, Flowers Original, Wethered Winter Royal H
Small, friendly pub with two separate bars catering for public and saloon bar customers in the truest sense. Not spruced up by the brewers and consequently frequented by few young drinkers. A busy lunchtime trade for good value snacks.
Q ◖ ⊞ ⇌ ♣

Rye

Ypres Castle Inn
Gun Gardens (behind castle, off A259) ☎ (0797) 223248
11–4; 6–11
Marston's Pedigree Bitter; Whitbread Pompey Royal, Wethered Winter Royal H
Family-run pub just behind castle, offering magnificent views of harbour and fishing port. Jazz/blues music Fri and Sun eves. Caters for all tastes; welcoming atmosphere; excellent safe gardens; guest beers. ⌂ Q ❀ ◖ ◗ ⇌ ♣

St Leonards

Duke
48 Duke Road, Silverhill (off A2100) ☎ (0424) 436241
11–11
Benskins Best Bitter; Friary Meux Best Bitter; Ind Coope Burton Ale; Tetley Bitter H
Traditional corner local with contrasting bars. Bustling locals' public bar and quiet 1960s lounge. Has wide excellently-kept beer range (including guests) at most reasonable prices. Successful trivia team. Always a friendly welcome.
Q ❀ ◖ ⊞ ♣ ⌀

Horse & Groom
Mercatoria (off London Road)
☎ (0424) 420612
11–3; 5.30–11
Courage Directors; Harveys Pale Ale, Best Bitter, XXXX (Old) H
Smart, comfortable pub with soft furnishings and lots of sporting photographs and prints. Very popular with locals and has a friendly, pleasant atmosphere.
Q ♘ ◖ ♿ ⇌ (Warrior Sq) ♣

Seaford

Beachcomber
Dane Road (on seafront)
☎ (0323) 892719
11–11
Draught Bass; Charrington IPA; Hall & Woodhouse Badger Best Bitter, Tanglefoot; Harveys Best Bitter, XXXX (Old) H
Clean, spacious seafront pub with large, classy restaurant and excellent facilities for families. Live entertainment Thu eve.
♘ ❀ ◖ ◗ ♿ ⇌ ♣ P

White Lion
74 Claremont Road (A259)
☎ (0323) 892473
11–2.30; 6–11
Charrington IPA (summer); **Harveys Best Bitter, XXXX (Old); Marston's Pedigree Bitter; Young's Special** H
Lively, welcoming social centre. The food is a joy; comfortable, homely atmosphere.
❀ ⊨ ◖ ◗ ⊞ ⇌ ♣ P

Staplecross

Cross Inn
From A229 at Cripps Corner onto B2165 OS782224
☎ (058 083) 217
11–2.30; 6–11
Adnams Bitter; Harveys Best Bitter; Ruddles Best Bitter H
15th-century village local: beams and low ceilings; inglenook large enough to hold a party in; and resident ghost. Relaxed atmosphere. Has connections with old wool trade – hence village name. Shove-penny played. ⌂ Q ♘ ♿ ♣ P

Telham

Black Horse
Hastings Road (A2100)
☎ (042 46) 3109
11–3; 6–11

Marston's Pedigree Bitter; Whitbread Flowers Original ⊞
Attractive, weatherboarded rural pub with friendly atmosphere. Beamed bar and separate restaurant. Unusual pool table on first floor and skittle alley on second floor. Boules played in summer.
♜ ❀ ◐ ◑ ♿ ♣ P

Uckfield

Alma Arms
Framfield Road (B2102 E of centre) ☎ (0825) 762232
Hours vary
Harveys XX Mild Ale, Pale Ale, Best Bitter, XXXX (Old) ⊞
Traditional town pub, in same family for generations. Beer is served from wall mounted handpumps in well-preserved public bar. A rare opportunity to sample the full Harveys range. Small garden. No meals Tue, Sat or Sun.
Q ❀ ◐ ⊟ ♿ ⇌ ♣ P

Try also: Brickmakers Arms (Free)

Wadhurst

Greyhound
St James Square (B2099)
☎ (08928) 3224
11–3; 6–11
Draught Bass; Charrington IPA ⊞
Built as an inn in 1502; haunt of the locally famous Hawkhurst gang in 18th century. Now a large, cosy pub recently subtly altered, but to good effect. Large garden with play area. Separate restaurant.
Q ❀ ◐ ◑ ♿ ♣ P

Wartling

Lamb in Wartling
On minor road 50 yds E of Pevensey village (A259)
OS658092 ☎ (0323) 832116
11–2.30; 6.30–11
King & Barnes Sussex Bitter, Broadwood; Marston's Pedigree Bitter ⊞
Comfy, welcoming village pub with log fires in both bars. Separate snooker room (children welcome). Excellent restaurant/carvery (not Mon); no bar meals Sun/Mon.
♜ Q ⛟ ❀ ◐ ◑ ♣ P

Whatlington

Royal Oak
On A21 ☎ (0424) 870492
11–2.30; 6–11
Harveys Best Bitter; Marston's Pedigree Bitter; Young's Special ⊞
Attractive country inn circa 1490, comfortable and welcoming; look for the 80ft well inside. Huge fireplace; resident ghost; old beams and hop festoons abound. List of landlords since 1509 displayed. Current landlord also owns a butcher's shop. ♜ ⛟ ❀ ◐ ◑ ♣ P

Willingdon

Red Lion
99 Wish Hill (just off A22)
☎ (0323) 502062
11–3; 5.30–11
King & Barnes Sussex Bitter, Broadwood, Old, Festive ⊞
Friendly local, one of the pubs which escaped the Watney grip in 1988–89. Model for the pub in Orwell's *Animal Farm*. No food Sun. ❀ ◐ ◑ ♣ P

Harvey's fine old brewery in Lewes

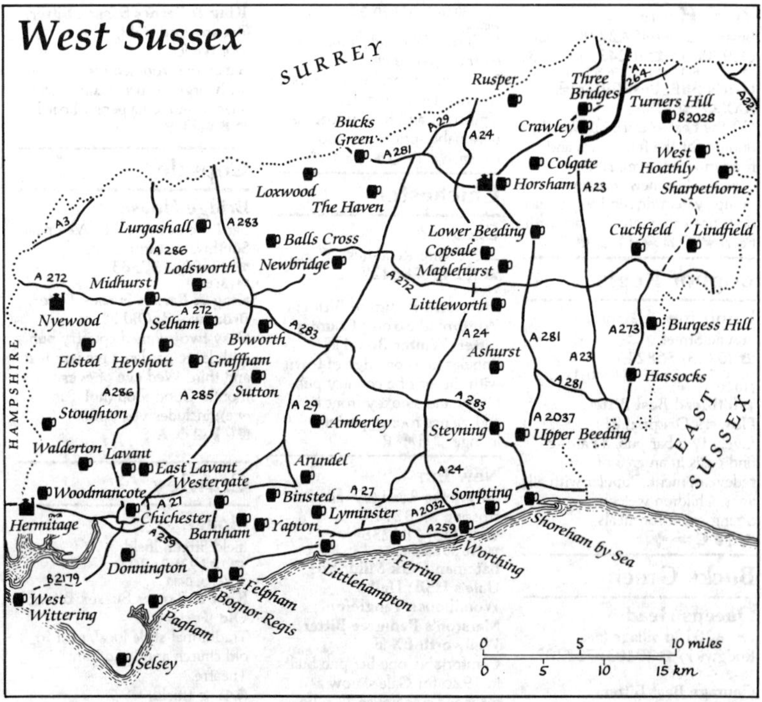

***Ballard's**, Nyewood; **King & Barnes**, Horsham; **Sussex**, Hermitage*

Amberley

Black Horse
High Street OS032133
☎ (0798) 831552
11–3; 6–11
Friary Meux Best Bitter; Ind Coope Burton Ale H
Two-bar village local with bistro. Convenient for chalk pits museum and Amberley Castle nearby. Popular with walkers and tourists; parking a problem in summer. Menu caters for children and vegetarians.

Arundel

Swan Hotel
High Street ☎ (0903) 883214
11–11
Courage Directors; Hall & Woodhouse Badger Best Bitter, Tanglefoot; Marston's Pedigree Bitter; Theakston Best Bitter H
Large pub with separate restaurant and seating area. Various live bands from jazz to heavy rock every Sun, otherwise fairly quiet. Guest beer always available.
Q

White Hart
3 Queen Street
☎ (0903) 882374
11–11
Ruddles Best Bitter, County; Webster's Yorkshire Bitter H
Popular one-bar pub, decorated with mock beams and farming artefacts; look out for tractor seat bar stools. Three guest beers always available. Food at bar or in restaurant – good, but pricey. Q

Try also: Eagle (Free)

Ashurst

Fountain
Just S of Partridge Green
☎ (0403) 710219
11–2.30; 6–11
Marston's Pedigree Bitter; Whitbread Strong Country Bitter H, **Pompey Royal, Flowers Original** G
Quaint, 16th-century, oak-beamed, stone-floored village pub with inglenook, next to the village duck pond. Beer served from stillage behind bar. Beware blind corner parking. One guest beer always available. Popular for food (veg and children's dishes). Q P

Balls Cross

Stag
Off A283 near Kirdford
☎ (0403) 77241
11–3; 6–11
King & Barnes Mild, Sussex Bitter, Broadwood, Festive H
Friendly and popular old village pub with a stone floor, low ceilings and an inglenook. Serves as a polling station. No food Sun.
Q P

Barnham

Morrell Arms
Yapton Road (under rail bridge)
☎ (0243) 553320
11–2.30; 6–11 (11–11 Sat)
Friary Meux Best Bitter; Ind Coope Burton Ale G
Three-bar local laden with drinking memorabilia. Antique auctions are held alternate Wed. Live music every Thu night, and the second last Sun in month. Ring the Bull played. Pub has its own vineyard.
Q P

Binsted

Black Horse
Binsted Lane (off A27/B2132)
OS980064 ☎ (0243) 551213
11–2.30; 6–11 (11–11 Fri & Sat)
Gale's BBB, Best Bitter [E], **XXXXX** [G], **HSB**
Off the beaten track but worth finding for the fine views and food (not Sun eve). HSB dispensed by new vacuum pump system driven by gas (gas does not come into contact with beer). ♨ Q ❀ 🛏 ◐ ◑ ♿ ♣ P

Bognor Regis

Lamb Inn
Steyne Street
☎ (0243) 868215
10.30–2.30 (6 Sat); 5 (7 Sat)–11 (10.30–11 Fri)
Whitbread Best Bitter, Flowers Original [H]
Lively two-bar pub, a hard-to-find oasis in an area of redevelopment. Popular with all ages. Children welcome in dining room for meals.
♨ ◐ ◑ ⊟ ≠ ♣

Bucks Green

Queens Head
On A281 in village (near Rudgwick) ☎ (0403) 722202
11–3; 6–11
Courage Best Bitter, Directors; John Smith's Bitter [H]
Immaculate oak-beamed pub with a comfortable family room. Good food (children's and veg meals available). Occasional guest beers. No motorcycles.
♨ Q ♉ ❀ 🛏 ◐ ◑ P

Try also: Fox (King & Barnes)

Burgess Hill

Brewers Arms
London Road (A273)
☎ (0444) 232153
11–2.30; 6–11 (11–11 Fri & Sat)
Draught Bass; Charrington IPA [H]
A comfortable locals' pub with the old Kemptown brewery logo in the brickwork. Regular live music. ❀ ◐ ⊟ ≠ ♣

Woolpack
West Street ☎ (0444) 245178
11–2.30 (3 Sat); 6–11
Benskins Best Bitter; Friary Meux Best Bitter; Ind Coope Burton Ale; Tetley Bitter [H]
The newest pub in town: a listed farmhouse! Nominated in CAMRA's pub awards. Children's play area in garden. See blackboard for special dishes in restaurant (booking advised).
❀ ◐ ◑ ♿ P

Byworth

Black Horse
OS986211 ☎ (0798) 42424
11–2.30; 6–11 (11.30–2.30; 6.30–11 winter)
Ballard's Wassail; Young's Bitter, Special [H]
Cosy village local with scrubbed wooden tables and floor. Upmarket and trendy: beer is reasonably-priced but food is expensive. ♨ Q ❀ ◐ ◑ ⊟ ♣ P

Chichester

Chequers
203 Oving Road (just off A27)
☎ (0243) 786427
11–11
Marston's Pedigree Bitter; Whitbread Strong Country Bitter, Winter Royal [H]
Popular local on edge of town, with the air of a country pub. Lively and smokey front bar and games room; quieter lounge. ❀ ◐ ♣ P

New Inn
34 Whyke Road (by railway crossing on B2145)
☎ (0243) 782238
11 (10.30 Sat)–11
Bateman Dark Mild, XB; Gale's HSB; Hall & Woodhouse Tanglefoot; Marston's Pedigree Bitter; Wadworth 6X [H]
Comfortable one-bar pub built in 1926 for Gale's, now a managed free house. Can be noisy and cramped during frequent live music evenings. Complete interior alterations planned. ❀ ◐ ⛺ ♣ P

Park Tavern
11 Priory Road (opp. Priory Park) ☎ (0243) 785057
11–2.30 (3 Fri & Sat); 5–11
Gale's BBB, Best Bitter, XXXXX, HSB [H]
Busy pub in city centre. Lunchtime meals served in bar; fresh pasta restaurant (evenings only). ◐ ◑ ♿

Rainbow
56 St Pauls Road (100 yds N of fire station) ☎ (0243) 785867
11–11
Friary Meux Best Bitter; Ind Coope Burton Ale; King & Barnes Sussex Bitter; Tetley Bitter [H]
Friendly and spacious local, worth the short walk from town. Patio garden to rear; good children's area indoors. Regular special food eves; try the beef rissoles with bubble and squeak. ♨ Q ♉ ❀ ◐ ◑ ♣ P

Try also: Chequers (Whitbread)

Colgate

Dragon
Off A264 between Horsham and Crawley OS229327
☎ (0293) 83206
11–3; 5.30–11
King & Barnes Sussex Bitter, Broadwood, Old, Festive [H]
Small, two-roomed country inn with large car park. Lunchtime snacks, shove-ha'penny board.
♨ ❀ ⊟ ♣ P

Copsale

Bridge House
Bar Lane (2 miles E of A24 near Southwater turn)
☎ (0403) 730383
11–3; 6–11
King & Barnes Sussex Bitter, Broadwood, Old [H]
Cosy two-roomed country pub with large garden. Live jazz first and third Wed eve of every month. Good food (not Tue eve); includes veg option.
❀ ◐ ◑ ⊟ ♿ ⛺ P

Crawley

Plough
Ifield Street, Ifield
☎ (0293) 24292
11–2.30; 6–11
King & Barnes Sussex Bitter, Old, Festive [H]
Traditional-style local, next to old church and Ifield Barn Theatre.
❀ ⊟ ≠ (Ifield) ♣

White Hart
High Street ☎ (0293) 520033
11–3 (may extend); 6–11
Harveys Best Bitter, XXXX (Old), Armada Ale [H]
Town-centre local near shopping centre. Very busy lunchtime trade. Always friendly. Only Harveys in area. No food at weekend. ◐ ⊟ ≠ P

Try also: Royal Oak; Gate

Cuckfield

Kings Head
South Street ☎ (0444) 454006
11–11
Harveys Best Bitter; King & Barnes Sussex Bitter, Broadwood, Festive [H]
Popular 18th-century, two-bar coaching inn. Live music in back bar on Sat. Restaurant not always open, but bar food is available. Children welcome at lunchtime. ♨ ♉ ❀ 🛏 ◐ ◑ ♣ P

White Harte
South Street ☎ (0444) 413454
11–3; 6–11
King & Barnes Mild (summer), **Sussex Bitter, Broadwood, Old, Festive** [H]
Friendly two-bar pub with olde-worlde atmosphere; genuine oak beams and inglenook in saloon bar. Children welcome in summer only. No food Sun.
♨ Q ♉ ❀ ◐ ⊟ ♣ P

Donnington

Blacksmiths Arms
Selsey Road (2 miles S of Chichester on B2201)
☎ (0243) 783999
11.30–2.30; 6–11
Draught Bass; Charrington IPA; Hall & Woodhouse Badger Best Bitter, Tanglefoot; Ringwood Best Bitter, Old Thumper Ⓗ
A fine example of potential realised on release from Watney's grip. A recent extension is most welcome in this compact pub. Busy at lunchtimes, with an enterprising menu and excellent food; weekly curry night. Guest beers. Ringwood Best is sold as 'Blacksmiths Bitter'. Good family facilities. ⌂ ♞ ❀ ◖ ◗ ♣ P

East Lavant

Royal Oak
Pook Lane (just off A286)
☎ (0243) 527434
11–2.30 (3 Fri & Sat); 6–11
Friary Meux Best Bitter; Ind Coope Burton Ale; Tetley Bitter Ⓖ
Pub at the heart of a pretty Sussex village, near Goodwood Racecourse. Popular for food (not Sun or Mon in winter). Oak-beamed and open-fired; splendid smell of woodsmoke in winter. Guest beers.
⌂ Q ❀ ◖ ◗ Δ P

Elsted

Elsted Inn
Elsted Marsh, near Midhurst (3 miles SW of A272) OS818197
☎ (0730) 813662
11.30–3; 5.30–11
Ballard's Trotton Bitter, Best Bitter, Wassail; Marston's Pedigree Bitter Ⓗ
Isolated free house which can get very busy but is worth the effort of finding. Guest beers always available. Good food; menu changes daily and includes veg and children's dishes. ⌂ Q ❀ ◖ ◗ ⊟ ♣ P

Felpham

Southdowns
133 Felpham Way (A259/B2132 jct)
☎ (0243) 583916
11–11
Friary Meux Best Bitter; Ind Coope Burton Ale; Tetley Bitter Ⓗ
Large but friendly pub on busy A259. Caters well for families. A wide variety of snacks and meals available. ♞ ❀ ◖ ◗ ⊟ ♣ P

Ferring

Henty Arms
2 Ferring Lane (440 yds off A259) ☎ (0903) 41254
10.30–3; 6–11 (10.30–11 Sat)
Friary Meux Best Bitter; Ind Coope Burton Ale Ⓗ
Two-bar village local where charcoal-grilled steaks are a speciality. Q ❀ ◖ ◗ ⊟ ♣ P

Try also: Greystoke (Free)

Graffham

White Horse
Heyshott Road (3 miles E of A286 outside village) OS921179 ☎ (07986) 331
11–3; 6.30–11
Bateman XXXB; Eldridge Pope Dorchester Bitter; Palmers IPA Ⓗ
Good-value, one-bar village pub with log fires. Restaurant area (book Sun lunch); children welcome in conservatory. Garden has splendid downland views. Guest beer.
⌂ Q ♞ ❀ ◖ ◗ Δ ♣ P

Hassocks

Hassocks
Station Approach East
☎ (07918) 2113
11–11
Marston's Pedigree Bitter; Whitbread Pompey Royal, Flowers Original Ⓗ
Former Victorian railway hotel, now one large bar. Very popular with the young. Loud disco Wed eve. Good value food. ❀ ◖ ⇌ P

The Haven

Blue Ship
Take Rudgwick road off A29 OS084306 ☎ (0403) 722709
11–3; 5.30–11
King & Barnes Sussex Bitter, Broadwood, Old Ⓖ
Lovely olde-worlde pub, circa 1400. Beer on thralls behind bar; four rooms; bar billiards. The best pub in the area.
⌂ Q ♞ ❀ ◖ ◗ ⊟ ♿ ♣ P

Heyshott

Unicorn Inn
1 mile E of A286 OS898181
☎ (0730) 813486
11.30–2.30; 7–11 (11–3.30; 6–11 summer; supper licence until 12)
Ballard's Best Bitter, Wassail; Marston's Burton Best Bitter, Pedigree Bitter Ⓗ
Pleasant, one-bar country pub; popular with locals, diners and walkers. Fine views of South Downs to rear. Good food, including three veg options (no eve meals winter Mon).
⌂ Q ❀ ◖ ◗ ♣ P

Horsham

Boars Head Tavern
Worthing Road (1 mile S of centre on old A24)
☎ (0403) 54353
11–2.30; 6–11
Eldridge Pope Dorchester Bitter, Royal Oak; Palmers IPA; Wadworth 6X Ⓗ
Horsham's only genuine free house, recently renovated. No food Sun eve. Regular guest beers. Dorchester Bitter is sold as 'Boars Head Bitter'. ❀ ◖ ◗ P

Coot
Merryfield Drive
☎ (0403) 65744
11–2.30 (3.30 Sat); 6–11
Charrington IPA Ⓗ
Comfortable pub on the west side of town popular with all ages. Ten consecutive years in this guide. No food Sun.
❀ ◖ ⊟ ♣ P

Dog & Bacon
North Parade (1 mile N of centre on B2237)
☎ (0403) 52176
11–2.30; 6–11
King & Barnes Sussex Bitter, Broadwood, Old Ⓗ
Comfortable and welcoming hostelry with two contrasting bars and extra seating in a side room off the hallway. Food highly recommended. Due for a major refurbishment.
⌂ Q ❀ ◖ ⊟ ♣ P

Stout House
29 The Carfax (opp. bandstand)
☎ (0403) 67777
10–4; 7.30–11
King & Barnes Sussex Bitter, Broadwood, Old, Festive Ⓗ
Good, town-centre pub, one of the best and cheapest of King & Barnes' houses. Old and friendly, traditional in style with low beams. Q ⊟ ⇌ ♣

Try also: Nelson; Tanners Arms (King & Barnes)

Lavant

Earl of March
Lavant Road (A286, 2 miles N of Chichester)
☎ (0243) 774751
10.30–2.30; 6–11
Ballard's Best Bitter; Courage Directors; Ringwood XXXX Porter, Old Thumper; Ruddles Best Bitter, County Ⓗ
Deceptively-large, roadside pub, specialising in home-made food (particularly game in season). Open-plan arrangement allows for quiet dining area and space for families. Dogs welcome. Consistently the best value pub in the area. Guest beers.
♞ ❀ ◖ ◗ ♿ ♣ P

Lindfield

Linden Tree
47 High Street
☎ (044 47) 2295
11–3; 6–11
Adnams Bitter; Fuller's Mr Harry; Harveys XXXX (Old); Marston's Pedigree Bitter; Ringwood Old Thumper; Wadworth 6X H
Small, upmarket free house with subdued lighting; always a friendly welcome. Can get very busy and rather smokey in winter months. Regular entry in this guide. Beer range liable to vary. No food Sun.

Littlehampton

Foresters Arms
31 Horsham Road (A259 E of centre) ☎ (0903) 716570
11–2.30; 6–11
Friary Meux Best Bitter; Tetley Bitter H
Locals' pub on main coast road. Rather sparse, with a small lounge bar. Well-represented in local sports' leagues. Live music once a week. P

Globe
Duke Street (off High Street precinct) ☎ (0903) 716557
10–11
Ruddles Best Bitter, County H
Busy shopping-centre pub with a friendly atmosphere. Two floors for games: pool, bar billiards and darts. Near the site of former Henty & Constable brewery – now a car park. Food served until 5pm. P

Littleworth

Windmill
Littleworth Lane (1 mile N of Partridge Green) OS193205
☎ (0403) 710308
11–3; 5.30 (6 Sat)–11
King & Barnes Mild, Sussex Bitter, Old, Festive H
A fine example of all that we expect of a country local: slightly difficult to find, guaranteed welcome, jovial host and a well-kept range of beers. Long may it continue.
Q P

Lodsworth

Hollist Arms
☎ (07985) 310
11–3; 6–11
Ballard's Trotton Bitter; King & Barnes Sussex Bitter, Festive H
Traditional, village centre pub with three bars and a central servery. Separate restaurant. Occasional guest beers. Shove-ha'penny played.
P

Lower Beeding

Crab Tree
On A281, near Leonardslee Gardens ☎ (0403) 891257
11–3; 5.30–11
King & Barnes Sussex Bitter, Broadwood, Old, Festive H
Roadside pub in rural area with four contrasting drinking areas off a central bar.
Q P

Plough
Leechpool Hill Road (A279)
☎ (0403) 891277
11–3; 6–11
King & Barnes Sussex Bitter, Broadwood, Old, Festive H
Friendly local. Probably the cheapest pub in the area. Good food. Q P

Loxwood

Onslow Arms
High Street (B2133)
☎ (0403) 752452
11–2.30; 4.30–11 (11–11 summer & Sat in winter)
King & Barnes Sussex Bitter; Broadwood, Old, Festive H
Two-roomed village local on banks of the Wey-Arun Canal. Lounge has low ceilings and furniture to match.
P

Lurgashall

Noahs Ark
The Green (1 mile W of A283, 5 miles N of Petworth)
☎ (042 878) 346
11–2.30; 6–11
Friary Meux Best Bitter; King & Barnes Sussex Bitter H
Slate-floored pub in idyllic village green setting. Traditional locals' bar and a small saloon. Open-air theatre in July each year. Food highly recommended (not Sun).
Q P

Lyminster

Six Bells
Lyminster Road (A284)
☎ (0903) 713639
10–3; 6–11 (10–11 summer)
Friary Meux Best Bitter; Ind Coope Burton Ale; King & Barnes Sussex Bitter H
Roadside pub with oak beams, horse brasses and inglenook; once a coaching inn. Excellent food with children's and veg dishes. P

Maplehurst

White Horse
Park Lane (between A281 & A272) ☎ (0403) 891208
12–2.30; 6–11
Adnams Broadside; Brakspear Special; King & Barnes Sussex Bitter, Broadwood H
Pleasant pub deep in the rolling Sussex Weald; its large garden offers excellent views. The widest bartop in Sussex! Children welcome in the spacious conservatory. Guest beers. P

Midhurst

Crown Inn
Edinburgh Square
☎ (0730) 813462
11–11
Gale's HSB G**; Ruddles Best Bitter, County; Webster's Yorkshire Bitter** H
17th-century building with a spit roast in its fireplace. Friendly atmosphere; often noisy. Book for restaurant.

Swan
Red Lion Street,
☎ (0730) 812853
11–11
Harveys Pale Ale, Best Bitter, XXXX (Old), Armada Ale H
Beautifully renovated town pub with split-level bars. One wall has painted mural dating back to 1450. Home-cooked food always available.

Wheatsheaf
Wool Lane ☎ (0730) 813450
11–3; 6–11
King & Barnes Mild, Sussex Bitter, Broadwood, Old, Festive H
Smart, one-roomed pub with beamed interior. Popular for lunches. Alterations due soon, to include old church next door as a family room.

Newbridge

Limeburners
On B2133, near Billingshurst
☎ (0403) 782311
11–3; 6–11
Friary Meux Best Bitter; Ind Coope Burton Ale H
Welcoming one-roomed hostelry, formed from three cottages after the closure of the Wey and Arun Canal. Named after canalside limekilns; built in 1805. Bar billiards. No food Wed eve. P

Pagham

Lion Hotel & Country Club
Nytimber Lane
☎ (0243) 262149
11–11
Courage Best Bitter, Directors; Ringwood Best Bitter, XXXX Porter, Old Thumper; Young's Special H
Very popular one-bar pub, originally a 15th-century inn with beams a-plenty. 40 malt

whiskies available. Food is very popular and good value (children's menu). ⛭ ◖ ◗ ♿ ♣ P

Rusper

Royal Oak
Friday Street OS186369
☎ (0293) 871393
11–3; 6–11
King & Barnes Sussex Bitter, Broadwood, Old, Festive [H]
Small, well-kept country pub of character with cosy bars. Difficult to find, outside the village, but worth the effort. Ring the Bull played.
♜ Q ♉ ⛭ ◖ ◗ ♣ P

Try also: Plough (Free)

Selham

Three Moles Inn
Off A272, 1 mile S of halfway bridge OS935206
☎ (07985) 303
11–2.30; 5.30–11
King & Barnes Mild, Sussex Bitter, Broadwood, Old [H]
Small, somewhat isolated, country local which really is worth finding. Impromptu folk music and pub games are often a feature of the evening sessions. Bar skittles. Ploughman's lunches served (eves too). ♜ Q ⛭ ▲ ♣ P

Selsey

Lifeboat
26 Albion Road (near lifeboat station on E beach)
☎ (0243) 603501
10.30–2.30; 6–11
Ruddles Best Bitter, County; Webster's Yorkshire Bitter [H]
Deceptively-large seaside pub, popular with locals and visitors. Separate restaurant; roast beef every Wed eve; seafood a summer speciality. No food Mon/Sun eves or Sun lunch in summer. Large garden.
Q ⛭ ◖ ◗ ⊟ ♿ ▲ ♣

Sharpethorne

Bluebell
Station Road (off High Street)
☎ (0342) 810264
12–2.30; 6–11
Courage Best Bitter, Directors; Fuller's ESB; Harveys Sussex Bitter; Marston's Pedigree Bitter; Wadworth 6X [H]
Friendly, one-roomed hostelry with central bar area. Old track of Bluebell Railway runs next to pub. Occasional guest beers. Good range of games. Menu offers veg option and children's half portions; no food Mon eve.
♜ Q ⛭ ◖ ◗ ♿ ♣ P

Shoreham by Sea

Ferry Inn
1 East Street (corner of High Street) ☎ (0273) 454125
11–3; 5–11
Courage Best Bitter, Directors [H]
Interesting, split-level pub with a quiet basement saloon bar. Takes its name from the (redundant) ferry to Shoreham beach. Q ◖ ⊟ ≋ ♣

Marlipins
High Street ☎ (0273) 463369
10–3.30; 5.30–11
Draught Bass; Charrington IPA [H]
Really popular and busy 18th-century inn: low beams and cosy bar. Next door to even older town museum. Lunchtime snacks. Q ⛭ ≋

Sompting

Gardeners Arms
West Street (¼ mile S of A27)
☎ (0903) 35618
11–2.30 (3 Sat, 12–2 Sun); 6–11
Gale's HSB; Ruddles Best Bitter; Webster's Yorkshire Bitter [H]
Unspoiled local in attractive village setting between Worthing and Lancing. Beware the ghost in the cellar who does not like alterations! Patio for summer quaffing.
♜ Q ⛭ ◖ ◗ ⊟ ♣ P

Marquis of Granby
West Street (100 yds off A27)
☎ (0903) 31102
11–11 (11–3; 6–11 Sat)
Gale's HSB; Marston's Pedigree Bitter; Whitbread Fremlins Bitter, Strong Country Bitter, Flowers Original [H]
Large, comfortable one-bar pub. Higher gravity beers may vary.
Q ⛭ ◖ ◗ ♿ P

Steyning

Star Inn
130 High Street
☎ (0903) 813078
11–3; 6–11 (11–11 Sat)
Marston's Pedigree Bitter; Whitbread Best Bitter, Pompey Royal, Flowers Original [H]
A traditional and lively local offering a warm welcome to all the family. Comfortable and warm saloon bar. Lots of genuine timber and low ceilings in public. Children's play area in gardens which are next to the village stream.
♜ Q ♉ ⛭ ◖ ◗ ⊟ ♿ ♣ P

Stoughton

Hare & Hounds
Off B2146 through Walderton OS791107 ☎ (0705) 631433
11–3; 6–11 (11–11 Fri & Sat in summer)
Ballard's Wassail; Eldridge Pope Royal Oak; Fuller's London Pride, Mr Harry; Whitbread Boddingtons Bitter [H]
A fine Sussex flint building. A warm welcome within a popular, remote pub nestling in the South Downs. Humorous posters advertise the guest beers. Local seafood often on a menu which also caters for children. ♜ Q ⛭ ◖ ◗ ⊟ ♣ P

Sutton

White Horse
The Street OS978152
☎ (07987) 221
11–2.30 (3 Sat); 6–11
Bateman XB; King & Barnes Mild, Sussex Bitter; Young's Bitter, Special [H]
Basic village local popular with walkers. Convenient for Bignor Roman villa. Beer range may vary. Eve meals summer only (not Sun/Mon).
♜ Q ⛭ ◖ ◗ ⊟ ♣ P

Three Bridges

Maid of Sussex
Gales Drive ☎ (0293) 525404
11–3 (3.30 Sat); 6–11
Courage Best Bitter, Directors [H]
Large and friendly estate pub. No food Sun. ♉ ⛭ ◖ ⊟ ≋ ♣ P

Turners Hill

Red Lion
Lion Lane ☎ (0342) 715416
11–2.30; 6–11
Harveys Best Bitter, XXXX (Old) [H]
Very popular, traditional village local. ♜ Q ⛭ ♣ P

Upper Beeding

Bridge
High Street ☎ (0903) 812773
11–2.30 (3 Sat); 5.30–11
King & Barnes Mild (summer), **Sussex Bitter, Broadwood, Old** [H]
Friendly, two-bar local in a pleasant location on the banks of the River Adur. Shove-ha'penny and table skittles played. Due to be renovated.
⛭ ◖ ⊟ ♣

Walderton

Barley Mow
250 yards E of B2146 OS789106 ☎ (0705) 631321
11–2.30 (3 summer); 6–11
Friary Meux Best Bitter; Ind Coope Burton Ale; King & Barnes Sussex Bitter [H]
Pleasant downland pub in good walking country. Four interconnecting rooms and a skittle alley (must book). Stream runs beside garden. Good

home-cooked food includes game in season and veg option.
♨ Q ❀ ◖ ◗ ♣ P

Westergate

Labour in Vain
Nyton Road (A29, 1½ miles S of A27 Fontwell roundabout)
☎ (0243) 543173
11–2.30 (3 Sat, may extend); 6–11
Ballard's Best Bitter Ⓗ, **Wassail** Ⓖ; **Harveys Best Bitter; Young's Bitter, Special** Ⓗ
Fine village local warmed by a large log fire. Extensive good value menu, including veg food option, in bar and small no-smoking restaurant. Convenient for Fontwell racecourse.
♨ Q ❀ ◖ ◗ ♣ P

West Hoathly

Cat Inn
Church Lane
☎ (0342) 810369
11–2.30 (12–2 Sun); 6–11
Harveys Best Bitter, XXXX (Old); King & Barnes Festive Ⓗ
Old pub opposite the church in a picturesque village. Wood panelling around walls is from the former Star Lane brewery in Lewes. Emphasis on food, both in the bar and restaurant (not Sun eve) – pricey. Q ❀ ◖ ◗ P

Try also: Vinols Cross (Free)

West Wittering

Lamb Inn
Chichester Road (1 mile from village centre on B2179)
☎ (0243) 511105
11–2.30; 6–11
Ballard's Best Bitter, Wassail; Bunces Benchmark, Best Bitter; Gale's HSB; Harveys Pale Ale Ⓗ
Old roadside inn with a welcoming atmosphere and an excellent range of beers.
Separate food bar.
♨ Q ❀ ◖ ◗ ♿ ▲ P

Woodmancote

Woodmancote Arms
(from A259 at Southbourne turn N and right at 2 T-junctions) OS775076
☎ (0243) 372612
11–3; 7–11
Marston's Burton Best Bitter, Pedigree Bitter, Merrie Monk Ⓗ
Rambling, one-bar village free house, with restaurant at rear featuring an extensive menu (veg option). Q ❀ ◖ ◗ ♿ ▲ ♣ P

Worthing

Chapmans Hotel
27 Railway Approach
☎ (0903) 30690
10.30–11
Gale's HSB; Hall & Woodhouse Tanglefoot; Harveys Sussex Bitter; Ruddles County; Wadworth 6X Ⓗ
Revitalised Victorian hotel striving to cater for all tastes. Guest beers. ☋ ❀ ◖ ◗ ⇌ P

Coach & Horses
Arundel Road, Clapham (A27)
☎ (0903) 64665
10.30–2.30; 6–11
Friary Meux Best Bitter; Ind Coope Burton Ale; Tetley Bitter Ⓗ
Main road house at the far west of town, whose landlord was an Olympic boxing gold medallist. Good range of meals.
♨ ❀ ◖ ⊟ P

Jolly Brewers
39–41 Clifton Road
☎ (0903) 200060
11–2.30; 5.30–11
Draught Bass; Charrington IPA Ⓗ
Cosy locals' pub on outskirts of town centre. Good value food includes daily specials, veg and children's dishes.
Q ❀ ◖ ◗ ⊟ ⇌ ♣ P

Old House at Home
77 Broadwater Street East, Broadwater ☎ (0903) 32661
10.30–2.30; 5.30–11
Draught Bass; Charrington IPA Ⓗ
Genuine, unspoilt Sussex flint-faced pub in Broadwater village. Dating from the 17th century and once a smugglers' inn, it comes complete with a ghost. Comfortable and warm saloon bar is full of curios; lively public bar. Guest beer in winter. Good selection of games.
♨ Q ❀ ◖ ⊟ ♣ P

Pawn & Castle
21 Rowlands Road (100 yds off seafront) ☎ (0903) 36232
11–2.30; 6–11 (11–11 Sat)
Harveys Best Bitter; King & Barnes Sussex Bitter; Whitbread Flowers Original; Young's Special Ⓗ
Small free house with two bars, popular with shoppers. Good range of guest beers; always a friendly welcome.
◖ ⊟ ♿ ⇌ ♣ ⌾

Yapton

Maypole Inn
Maypole Lane (off B2312) OS977042 ☎ (0243) 551417
11–2.30; 5.30–11 (11–11 Sat)
Bateman XB; Gale's XXXD; Ringwood Best Bitter, Old Thumper; Theakston Best Bitter; Whitbread Flowers IPA Ⓗ
Excellent, welcoming pub; hard to find, but worth the effort. Holder of local CAMRA Mild Trophy. Pub teams have fine collection of wooden spoons! Beer range varies. No food Sun or Tue eve.
♨ Q ❀ ◖ ◗ ⊟ ♿ ♣ P

THE SYMBOLS

- ♨ real fire
- Q quiet pub – in at least one bar
- ☋ indoor room for children
- ❀ garden or other outdoor drinking area
- ⊨ accommodation
- ◖ lunchtime meals
- ◗ evening meals
- ⊟ public bar
- ♿ easy disabled access
- ▲ camping facilities at the pub or nearby
- ⇌ near British Rail station
- ⊖ near Underground station
- ♣ pub games
- ⌾ real cider
- P pub car park

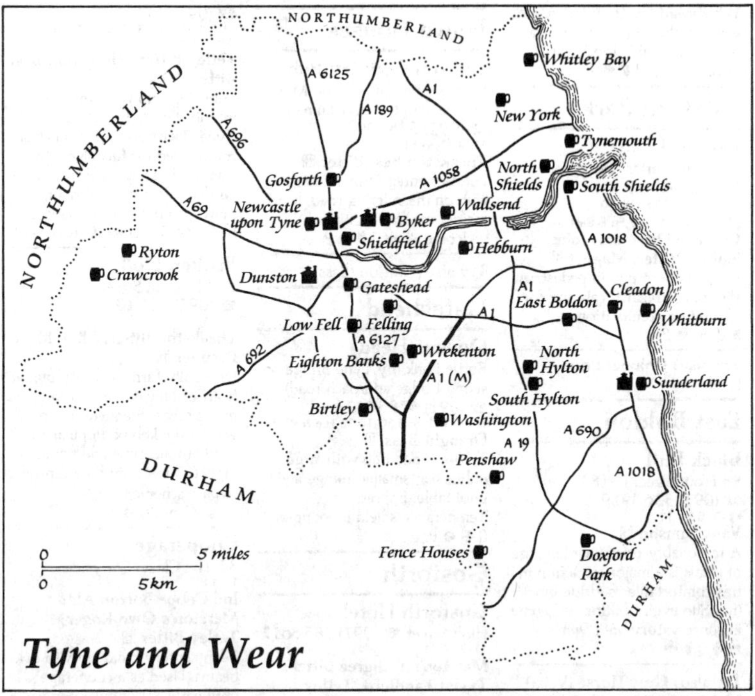

Big Lamp, *Newcastle upon Tyne*; **Federation**, *Dunston*; **Hadrian**, *Byker*; **Vaux**, *Sunderland*

Birtley

Coach & Horses

Durham Road (A6127)
☎ (091) 410 2756
11–11
Bass Light 5 Star; Stones Best Bitter H
Large roadhouse with a good quality restaurant and some of the lowest priced beer in the county. P

Byker

Cumberland Arms

Byker Buildings (off A193, Byker Bridge)
☎ (091) 265 6151
11–11
Adnams Bitter; Hadrian Gladiator Bitter H**; Hoskins Beaumanor Bitter** G
Friendly, basic two-roomed traditional pub overlooking City Farm. Upstairs music room features city's up and coming bands. Ask what beers are on – many are served by gravity from the cellar. Guest beers.
(Byker/Manors) P

Free Trade Inn

St Lawrence Road (off A186)
☎ (091) 265 5764
11–11
McEwan 80/-; Theakston XB; Younger No.3 H
Basic, split-level pub with fine view upriver. Popular with arts and music crowd; generally has live music or theatrical performances once weekly and occasional displays by local artists and photographers. Good alternative jukebox.

Glendale

Potts Street ☎ (091) 265 5174
11–11 (11–3; 6–11 Wed & Thu)
Draught Bass; Stones Best Bitter H
Cosy, friendly locals' bar, twice winner of CAMRA's local Pub of the Year award in early 80s.

Ship Inn

Stepney Bank (off A193, under Byker Bridge)
☎ (091) 232 4030
11–11
Marston's Pedigree Bitter; Whitbread Castle Eden Ale H
Friendly local, next to City Farm. Live folk music at weekends when it can be very full. Near award-winning crafts and music centre. Popular with musicians, actors and students. Good value food.
(Manors)

Tap & Spile

33 Shields Road
☎ (091) 276 1440
11–3; 5.30–11 (11–11 Fri & Sat)
Camerons Traditional Bitter; Taylor Landlord H
Two-roomed pub with much bric-a-brac. The first of the Tap & Spile chain. Much-exposed brick and wood give turn of the century appearance. Up to 11 guest beers. Q

Cleadon

Cottage Tavern

North Street (A1018)
☎ (091) 536 7883
11–11 (may vary)
Vaux Samson H
One-roomed hostelry, frequented by local business community. Can be busy early evenings. Pleasant walks on nearby hills. Lunchtime snacks.

Crawcrook

Rising Sun

Greenside Road
☎ (091) 413 3316
11.30–11
Marston's Pedigree Bitter;

Whitbread Castle Eden Ale ⊞
Comfortable and popular local pub. Good value food (not Fri or Sun eves). ◐ ◑ ♣ P

Doxford Park

Doxford Lad
President Carter Shopping Centre, Mill Hill Road
☎ (091) 528 0119
11–3; 6–11 (11–11 Fri & Sat)
Courage Directors; John Smith's Bitter, Magnet ⊞
Large modern pub in pedestrian shopping precinct, catering for expanding conurbation.
✿ ◐ ♿ ♣ P

Try also: Colonel Prior (Tetley)

East Boldon

Black Bull
98 Front Street (A184)
☎ (091) 536 3969
11–3; 5.30–11
Vaux Samson ⊞
A reasonably-priced, wide range of meals is a major attraction in this comfortable roadside inn (not Sun eve). Children welcome in conservatory until 9pm.
♘ ✿ ◐ ◑ ♣

Try also: Grey Horse (Vaux)

Eighton Banks

Lambton Arms
Rockcliff Way
☎ (091) 487 8137
11–3; 5.30 (6 Sat)–11
Whitbread Castle Eden Ale ⊞
Comfortable, one-roomed, stone pub with four distinct areas and a reputation for good quality food (including children's and veg meals). ◐ ◑ P

Ship
Off B1295, over railway crossing ☎ (091) 416 0273
11–3; 5.30–11 (11–11 Sat)
Vaux Samson, Double Maxim ⊞
Popular, comfortable, old village pub, ideally situated with scenic views. ✿ ◐ P

Felling

Old Fox
Carlisle Street
☎ (091) 438 0073
12–4; 6–11 (12–11 Fri & Sat)
Ruddles Best Bitter; Webster's Yorkshire Bitter, Webster's Choice ⊞
Friendly locals' pub south of Gateshead town centre. One room plus pool and darts areas. Licensee holds permit for local CAMRA festival and also organises his own events. Guest beers. ⌂ ⊨ ◐ ⊖

Try also: Wheatsheaf (Big Lamp)

Fence Houses

Chilton Country Pub
Black Boy Road, Chilton Moor (minor road to Great Lumley)
☎ (091) 385 2694
11.30–2; 7–11
Theakston Best Bitter ⊞
Food-oriented former country club on meandering road, hence mainly car trade. Children welcome. ✿ ⊨ ◐ ◑ ♿ P

Try also: Station (Bass)

Gateshead

Queens Head
Bottle Bank (by Tyne Bridge on swing bridge approach road)
☎ (091) 478 3749
11–11 (11–3; 5.30–10.30 Tue & Wed)
Draught Bass ⊞
Two-roomed pub with large public bar, smaller lounge and pool table. Impressive Temperance shield in lounge.
◐ ⊕ ⊖ P

Gosforth

Gosforth Hotel
High Street ☎ (091) 285 6617
11–3; 7–11
Marston's Pedigree Bitter; Taylor Landlord; Tetley Bitter ⊞
Busy corner pub, recently renovated. ◐

Hebburn

New Clock
Victoria Road East
☎ (091) 489 3556
11–3; 6–11 (11–11 Thu–Sat)
Vaux Samson ⊞
Large roadside pub favoured by the younger generation. Name stems from large ornate clock on the roof, acquiring the 'New' after refurbishment. Unusual red felt pool table! Draught Double Maxim sometimes available.
✿ ◐ ♣ P

Low Fell

Aletaster
Durham Road
☎ (091) 487 0770
11–3; 5.30–11 (11–11 Sat)
Bateman XXXB; McEwan 80/-; Marston's Pedigree Bitter; Theakston Best Bitter, XB ⊞
Old-style pub with wide selection of real ale: 13 handpumps! Guest beers. Bar snacks. Skittles and shove-ha'penny played. ♣ ⌽ P

Newcastle upon Tyne

Bridge Hotel
Castle Garth (opp. Castle Keep)
☎ (091) 232 6451
11 (11.30 Sat)–3; 5.30 (5 Fri, 6 Sat)–11
Tetley Bitter; Theakston Best Bitter, XB ⊞
Imposing pub with impressive interior beside bridge across Tyne. Two rooms and function room (used for folk club, etc). Can get busy at weekends. Beer garden offers view of river, railway and city walls. Guest beers. Q ✿ ◐ ⊕ ⇌ (Central) ⊖ P

Broken Doll
85 Blenheim Street
☎ (091) 232 1047
11–11
Theakston Bitter, XB, Old Peculier ⊞
Unusually furnished, city pub at heart of Newcastle's thriving music scene. Frequent live bands and loud jukebox. Popular for food at lunchtime and fun at night! Threatened by a central bypass scheme.
◐ ⇌ (Central) ⊖ ⌽

Cooperage
32 The Close, Quayside
11–11
Ind Coope Burton Ale; Marston's Owd Roger; Tetley Bitter ⊞
14th-century building with oak beams. Used as a cooperage until early 70s, now a popular and friendly pub with late-night club at weekends. Economiser in use on handpumps. Guest beers (eight handpumps).
Q ◐ ⇌ (Central) ⊖ ⌽

Crown Posada
31 The Side, Quayside
☎ (091) 232 1269
11–3; 5.30 (7 Sat)–11 (11–11 Fri)
Hadrian Gladiator Bitter; McEwan 80/-; Stones Best Bitter; Taylor Landlord ⊞
Favourite haunt of a cross-section of Novocastrians, united mainly by their love of fine beer in an unhurried atmosphere (can get busy weekends). Stained glass windows and Laura Ashley wallpaper. Guest beers.
⇌ (Central) ⊖

Duke of Wellington
High Bridge (between Bigg Market and Grey Street)
☎ (091) 261 8856
11–11
Alloa Arrols 80/-; Halls Harvest Bitter; Ind Coope Burton Ale; Jennings Bitter; Taylor Landlord; Tetley Bitter ⊞
Single-roomed pub near Theatre Royal and fashion shops. Once owned by CAMRA Investments, now an Allied house. Many fine prints and pictures. Popular and often full, especially at weekends. On the fringe of the trendy Bigg Market drinking area.
◐ ♿ ⇌ (Central) ⊖ (Monument)

Forth Hotel
Pink Lane (opp. Central station)
☎ (091) 2326478
11–3; 5–10.30 (closed Sun lunch)
Ind Coope Burton Ale; Jennings Bitter; Taylor Landlord; Tetley Bitter Ⓗ
Friendly, characterful pub with L-shaped bar, seating area and pinball/games/jukebox area. Pub, like locality, can be crowded in evenings and very quiet during the day. Recommended first port of call on leaving station.
⇌ (Central) ⊖

Newcastle Arms
St Andrews Street (off Newgate Street) ☎ (091) 2323567
11–11
Ind Coope Burton Ale; Tetley Bitter Ⓗ
Traditional, large basic boozer with TV and slot machines (which replaced the piano) and excellent photographs of old local pubs. Three separate areas: snug, bar and seating.
⊖ (St James's)

Olde George
Cloth Market
☎ (091) 2323956
11–11
Draught Bass; Stones Best Bitter Ⓗ
Wood-beamed old pub serving fine beer and food in city centre. Veg and children's meals available.
◐ ♿ ⇌ (Central) ⊖ (Monument)

Playhouse Theatre Bar
Barras Bridge (opp. Haymarket Metro) ☎ (091) 2327079
11–3; 5.30–11
Federation Best Bitter, Special Ale; Taylor Landlord Ⓗ
Busy bar in theatre foyer; has café atmosphere at lunchtimes – checked tablecloths, flowers on tables, etc. Varied live entertainment in evenings, including Jazz Festival and RSC Fringe. May charge entry at night. Guest beers. Eve meals till 7.30 (not weekends).
◐ ◑ ⊖ (Haymarket)

Rose & Crown
164–166 City Road (A186)
☎ (091) 2324724
11–11
Draught Bass; Hadrian Gladiator Bitter; Theakston XB Ⓗ
Large, friendly two-roomed pub near Tyne Tees TV studio; threatened by proposed quayside development. Weekly quiz. Large collection of advertising mirrors, signs and jugs. ♿ ⊖ (Manors) ♣

Rosies
St Andrews Street
11–11
Alloa Arrol's 80/-; Ansells Mild; Jennings Bitter; Tetley Bitter Ⓗ
Quintessential city-centre pub with views of urban decay and football ground; city wall and Chinatown lie beyond. Cheerful staff. Particularly busy Fri nights. ◐ ⊖ (St James's)

Strawberry
Strawberry Place
☎ (091) 2326865
12–11
McEwan 80/-; Theakston Best Bitter, XB Ⓗ
Basic three-roomed pub, near St James's Park, with mixed clientele. Under threat from bypass scheme which will run a road through the city centre! Somewhat ramshackle but intensely lovable pub – Newcastle needs it.
⊖ (St James's) P

Three Bulls Heads
Percy Street
☎ (091) 2326798
11–11
Draught Bass; Stones Best Bitter Ⓗ
Busy city-centre pub which was demolished and rebuilt five years ago. Central bar serves some of the most expensive Bass in the city but quality is consistently good.
◐ ⊖ (Haymarket)

Villa Victoria
144 Westmorland Road
☎ (091) 2322460
11–11
Draught Bass; Stones Best Bitter Ⓗ
Traditional local to west of city centre. An impressive building which stands in splendid isolation. Some students at lunchtimes, but mainly locals. Pool table.

Try also: Bacchus (Free)

New York

Shiremoor House Farm
Middle Engine Lane (off Norham Road North)
☎ (091) 2576302
11–3; 6–11
Stones Best Bitter; Taylor Landlord; Theakston Best Bitter, Old Peculier Ⓗ
Renovated and extended farm buildings, highly-commended in CAMRA's Pub Design awards. Near Stephenson Railway Museum. Guest beers. Q ◐ ◑ P

North Hylton

Shipwrights
Ferryboat Lane (off A1231)
☎ (091) 5495139
11–3; 7–11 (restaurant 12)
Vaux Samson; Wards Sheffield Best Bitter Ⓗ
Old, much-extended riverside pub next to original ferry landing between the Hyltons, now overshadowed by six-lane A19 Wear Bridge. Pleasant open-ceilinged first floor restaurant. ◐ ◑ ♣ P

North Shields

Chainlocker
New Quay (opp. ferry landing)
☎ (091) 2570147
11.30–3; 5.30–11
Ruddles Best Bitter, County; Wilson's Original Bitter, Webster's Choice Ⓗ
Friendly pub, handy for ferry. Home-cooked seafood. Guest beers. Q ◐ ◑

Magnesia Bank
1 Camden Street (off Saville Street) ☎ (091) 2574831
11–11
Greenalls Davenports Traditional Bitter, Thomas Greenall's Original Bitter; Ruddles County; Yates Bitter Ⓗ
Former club, converted into a popular, comfortable lounge. Beware keg cider on handpump. Occasional guest beers.
◐ ⊖

Porthole
New Quay ☎ (091) 2576645
11–3; 6–11
McEwan 80/-; Ruddles Best Bitter Ⓗ
Interesting pub with nautical memorabilia. Handy for North Shields ferry. Guest beers.
◐

Tap & Spile
184 Tynemouth Road
☎ (091) 2572523
11–3; 5.30–11 (11–11 Fri & Sat)
Camerons Traditional Bitter; Taylor Landlord; Yates Bitter Ⓗ
Comfy, L-shaped pub with warm atmosphere. Bar games a speciality, including bagatelle. Up to eight guest beers.
Q ◐ ⊖ ♣

Wolsington House
Burdon Main Row (opp. Smiths Dock Gates)
☎ (091) 2578487
11–3; 6–11 (11–11 Sat)
Hartleys XB; Theakston Best Bitter Ⓗ
Impressive pub. Brimming over with atmosphere; always warm and friendly. Very popular venue for live music (a band every night). Frequented by a very mixed crowd. Occasional guest beers. ◐

Penshaw

Grey Horse
Village Green (off A183)

Tyne & Wear

☎ (091) 584 4882
11–3 (4 Sat); 6 (5.30 Sat)–11
Tetley Bitter Ⓗ
Pleasant village pub in shadow of local folly made famous by Lambton Worm legend. No food Sun.

Ryton

Jolly Fellows
☎ (091) 413 2604
12–4; 7–11
Whitbread Castle Eden Ale Ⓗ
Lively pub in pleasant village.
P

Shieldfield

Globe Inn
Barker Street
☎ (091) 232 0901
11–11
Draught Bass; Stones Best Bitter Ⓗ
Friendly, basic, two-roomed pub across motorway footbridge from polytechnic. Popular with locals, students and social workers. Regulars keen on sport. Q (Manors/Jesmond) P

Queens Arms
1 Simpson Terrace (off A193)
☎ (091) 232 4101
11–11
McEwan 80/-; Theakston Best Bitter, XB, Old Peculier Ⓗ
Cosy one-roomed pub with subdued lighting in both main drinking areas. Near new cinema complex. Popular with students from nearby polytechnic and professionals. Displays work by local artists as well as fine old posters.
(Manors/Jesmond)

South Hylton

Golden Lion
Lion Place (under A19 Wear Bridge) ☎ (091) 534 2282
11–3; 5.30–11
Tetley Bitter Ⓗ
Food-oriented pub with large conservatory in quiet riverside setting. Good views of the Wear and pleasant walks.
P

South Shields

Ashley
269 Stanhope Road (B1298 opp. West Park)
☎ (091) 427 1682
11–11
Federation Special Ale Ⓗ
Large, end-of-terrace former social club on town outskirts. Relaxed atmosphere. Lunches Fri–Sun only.
(Tyne Dock)

Dolly Peel
137 Commercial Road
(B1301/B1302 jct)
☎ (091) 427 1441
11–11
Bateman XXXB; Taylor Landlord; Theakston XB; Younger No.3 Ⓗ
Excellent little pub named after a local character. Always a friendly welcome and guaranteed quality. Large whisky selection plus constantly-changing guest ales.
Q

Eureka
164 Frederick Street, Laygate (by Rekendyke Industrial Estate)
☎ (091) 455 5155
11–3 (4 Fri & Sat); 5 (5.30 Fri & Sat)–11
Theakston Best Bitter, XB, Old Peculier; Younger No.3 Ⓗ
Interesting old pub, tastefully refurbished in traditional manner. Children welcome.
Q

Railway
43–45 Mill Dam
☎ (091) 455 5227
11–11
Bateman XXXB; Federation Best Bitter, Special Ale; Fuller's London Pride, ESB; Taylor Landlord Ⓗ
Terraced pub, a recently-acquired free house, near revitalised riverside. Large public bar and dimly-lit lounge with brass beer engines. Varied guest ales. Snacks available.

Steamboat
47–49 Mill Dam
☎ (091) 454 0134
11–11
Vaux Lorimers Best Scotch, Samson; Wards Sheffield Best Bitter Ⓗ
Historic riverside pub with ornate exterior and panelled interior. Once the haunt of press gangs and smugglers as well as royalty – ask about the secret passageway. Winner of BBC Townscape Award. Lunch served Sun only.

Try also: Chichester Arms (Tetley)

Sunderland: North

Pilot Cutter
Harbour View, Roker (A183)
☎ (091) 567 1402
12–3; 7–11 (11–11 Fri, Sat & summer)
Theakston Best Bitter, XB, Old Peculier; Younger No.3 Ⓗ
Popular, one-roomed, end-of-terrace, coastal road pub overlooking docks and harbour. Near football ground, so usually packed on match days. Ever-changing guest ales.

Wolseley
40 Millum Terrace, Roker (A183) ☎ (091) 567 2798
12–3; 5.30–11 (11–11 summer)
McEwan 80/-; Theakston Best Bitter Ⓗ
Popular roadside pub overlooking harbour, near Roker Park. Locals' bar and friendly lounge always packed on match days. Shove-ha'penny played. P

Try also: Greensleeves (Free)

Sunderland: South

Chesters
Chester Road (A183)
☎ (091) 565 9952
11–11
Vaux Samson; Wards Sheffield Best Bitter Ⓗ
Large roadside pub amongst local shops, just out of town centre. Impressive frontage. Guest beers. P

Ivy House
Worcester Street (near Park Lane bus station)
☎ (091) 567 3399
11–11
Vaux Samson; Wards Sheffield Best Bitter Ⓗ
Side-street pub with eccentric decor on outskirts of town centre; a popular student haunt. Regular guest beers. Lunchtime snacks. P

Saltgrass
Hanover Place, Ayres Quay, Deptford (E of Queen Alexandra Bridge)
☎ (091) 565 7229
11.45–3; 5.30–11
Vaux Samson, Double Maxim; Wards Sheffield Best Bitter Ⓗ
Popular, low-ceilinged pub near the river. Roaring fire in winter; barbecues in summer. Children always welcome. Popular with staff from local colleges. Snacks.

Tap & Spile
Nelson Street, Hendon
☎ (091) 514 2810
12–3; 6–11 (12–11 Thu, 11–11 Fri & Sat)
Camerons Traditional Bitter, Strongarm Premium; Everards Old Original; Stocks Old Horizontal Ⓗ
Out-of-town traditional alehouse, popular with students. Originally the Salem Hotel, prior to Tap & Spile conversion. Excellent range of guest ales.

Tynemouth

Tynemouth Lodge
Correction House Bank, Tynemouth Road

☎ (091) 257 7565
11–11
Belhaven 80/-; Marston's Pedigree Bitter; Theakston Best Bitter; Wards Sheffield Best Bitter Ⓗ
Popular pub in improving area for real ale. The landlord is a CAMRA stalwart – friendly welcome assured.
🏠 Q ❀ ◐ ♿ ⊖ 🍏 P

Wallsend

Rose Inn
Rose Hill Bank, Willington Quay (A187)
☎ (091) 567 2798
11–11
Marston's Pedigree Bitter; Ruddles County; Theakston Old Peculier; Webster's Yorkshire Bitter Ⓗ
Large Victorian roadhouse with growing reputation for quality real ale and good food. Caters for children and vegetarians.
Q ◐ ◑ ⊖ (Hadrian Rd) P

Washington

Millhouse Hotel
Blackfell (B1288 at A1(M)/A69 jct)
☎ (091) 415 1216
12–11 (11–11 Sat)
McEwan 80/- Ⓗ
Large roadside pub, by peripheral road network. A handy stop for travellers.
❀ ⊞ ♿ ♣ P

Try also: Keelboat (Camerons)

Whitburn

Jolly Sailor
East Street (A183)
☎ (091) 529 3221
11–11
Bass Light 5 Star, Draught Bass Ⓗ
Coastal village pub, reputedly haunted. Huge locally-caught fish a speciality. Children welcome. 🏠 Q ❀ ◐ ⊞

Whitley Bay

Railway Hotel
Hillheads Road
☎ (091) 252 5220
12–4; 6–11 (may extend afternoons)
Camerons Traditional Bitter; Everards Old Original; Tolly Cobbold Mild, Bitter Ⓗ
Two-roomed pub near ice rink, serving a mixed clientele. Eve meals finish early. ◐ ◑ ⊞ ⊖ P

Wrekenton

Seven Stars
27 High Street
☎ (091) 487 2245
11–11
Theakston Best Bitter Ⓗ
Busy local with popular landlord in former Gateshead real ale desert. ⊞ ♿ P

The Big Lamp Brewery

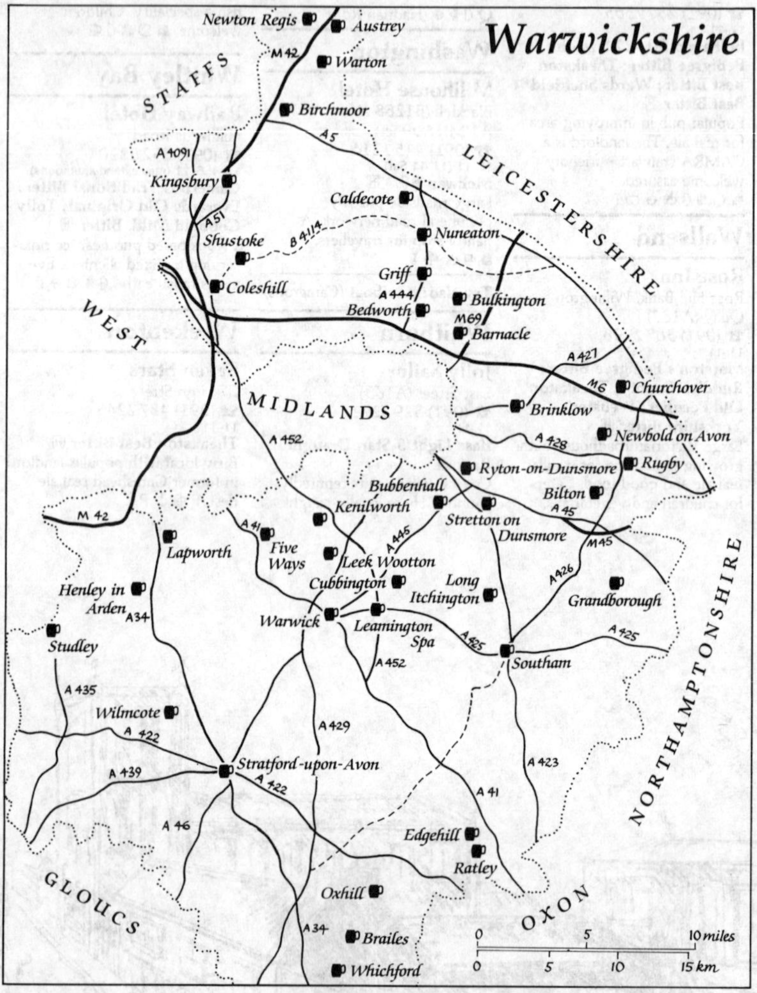

Austrey

Bird in Hand

Church Lane (off Main Street)
☎ (0827) 830260
12–2 (2.30 Sat); 7 (6 Sat)–11
Marston's Pedigree Bitter Ⓗ
Grade I listed building with thatched roof, by the village cross. Lunchtime snacks. A quiet quality pint guaranteed.
Q P

Barnacle

Red Lion

Lower Road
11–2.30; 7–11
M&B Mild, Brew XI Ⓗ
Pleasant village local with comfortable lounge and basic bar. ♣ P

Bedworth

Newdigate Arms

Newdigate Road
☎ (0203) 314867
12–2.30 (3 Fri, 3.30 Sat); 5–11
Ansells Mild, Bitter; Ind Coope Burton Ale; Tetley Bitter Ⓗ
Recently-refurbished estate pub. Bar has games area; lounge has separate dining area. New family room leads to garden with children's play area.
♣ P

Old Goose

Orchard Street, Collycroft (off B4113 N of town)
☎ (0203) 313266
12–3; 7–11
Ansells Mild, Bitter Ⓗ
Bar split into two areas – one basic, the other a comfortable lounge with pool table. Small conservatory, which acts as family room, leads to garden with children's play area.
Q ♣

Bilton

Black Horse

43 The Green (B4071)
☎ (0788) 811473
11–2.30 (3 Sat); 5.30–11
Ansells Mild, Bitter; Ind Coope Burton Ale Ⓗ
Village pub with busy, comfortable and welcoming lounge, and plain bar-cum-games room. Pleasant garden behind the pub. Electronic music is non-obtrusive. Disabled access at rear. ♣ P

Birchmoor

Gamecock Inn

Cockspur Street
☎ (0827) 895144
11–2.30; 7–11

Draught Bass [H]
Very friendly ex-mining village pub serving a mainly local clientele. Old, decorated oak bar; quiet small lounge. Folk club on Sat nights. Beware: mild on handpull is keg. ⚇ ⊛ ⊟ ♣ P

Try also: Wolferstan Arms, Shuttington (M&B)

Brailes

Gate
On B4035 in Upper Brailes
☎ (060885) 212
11.30–3; 6–11 (11.30–11 Sat)
Hook Norton Mild, Best Bitter, Old Hookey [H]
Friendly, old village local next to site of the former Brailes brewery. Children are made very welcome. Aunt Sally in garden. No eve meals Sun.
⌂ ⊛ ◐ ◑ ⊟ ▲ ♣ P

Try also: George (Hook Norton)

Brinklow

Raven
Broad Street (on the Fosse Way ½ mile from A4029)
☎ (0788) 832655
11–2.30; 7–11
Marston's Border Mild, Burton Best Bitter, Pedigree Bitter [H]
This fantastic village local has now been in this guide for 15 years. The bar is fairly basic while the lounge is very cosy, with two fires, a piano and wood panelling. Ash trays made at the village pottery. Menu has imaginative veg option.
⌂ ⚇ ⊛ ◐ ◑ ⊟ ♿ ♣ P

Bubbenhall

Malt Shovel
Lower End (off sideroad, off A445) ☎ (0203) 301141
11.30–2.30; 6–11
Ansells Mild, Bitter; Tetley Bitter [H]
Very friendly country pub exceedingly popular for meals: Italian landlord has certificates and a passion for good food (and beer). Bowling green.
⌂ Q ⊛ ◐ ◑ ⊟ ♣ P

Bulkington

Rule & Compass
Leicester Street (off B4109)
11–3; 5–11
Draught Bass; M&B Mild, Brew XI [H]
Large lounge with basic bar and upstairs restaurant in a very popular village local. Garden has children's playthings.
⊛ ◐ ◑ ⊟ ♣

Caldecote

Royal Red Gate
Watling Street (A5/A444 jct NW of Nuneaton)
11–3; 6–11
Marston's Best Bitter, Pedigree Bitter [H]
Large lounge divided into separate areas. Bar has bar billiards table. Garden seating.
Q ⊛ ◐ ⊟ ♣ P

Churchover

Haywaggon
The Green (¾ mile off A426)
☎ (0788) 832307
12–2.30; 6.30–11
Beer range varies [H]
Large white pub and restaurant at the end of the village. Inside features old oak beams, a flagstoned bar and collections of plates and jugs. No regular but three guest beers, often changed. No food Sun eve.
⊛ ◐ ◑ P

Try also: Stag & Pheasant, Newton (Banks's)

Coleshill

Green Man
High Street ☎ (0675) 463376
10.30–3; 5.30–10.30 (10.30–10.30 Fri)
Draught Bass; M&B Mild, Brew XI [H]
Unspoilt old pub with traditional, basic public bar. Very small car park.
⚇ ◐ ⊟ ♿ ♣ P

Cubbington

Queens Head
Queen Street
☎ (0926) 429949
11.30–2.30; 5.30–11 (11.30–11 Sat)
Ansells Mild, Bitter [H]
Traditional, two-bar village local, popular with all ages. Comfortable, quiet lounge; busy bar with emphasis on games. Disabled access from car park.
⌂ Q ⊛ ⊟ ♿ ♣ P

Edgehill

Castle Inn
1 mile N of A422, near Banbury ☎ (092587) 255
11.30–3 (12–2 Sun); 6–11 (11–11 Sat)
Hook Norton Mild, Best Bitter, Old Hookey [H]
17th-century folly, welcoming a good mixture of locals and tourists. Marvellous views over battlefield. Pub reputedly haunted by a Roundhead. Vast array of whiskies and fruit wines. ⌂ ⊛ ◐ ◑ ⊟ ▲ ♣ ○ P

Five Ways

Case is Altered
Rowington Road (off A41)
OS422270 ☎ (0926) 484206
11–2.30 (12–2 Sun); 6–11
Ansells Mild, Bitter; Ind Coope Burton Ale; Samuel Smith OBB; Whitbread Flowers Original [G]
Rural pub which is trapped in a time-warp even down to the sixpenny bar billiards. Rare cask pumps used to dispense beer (not really gravity at all). Lounge only open at weekends. Children welcome in games room. ⌂ Q ⚇ ⊛ ⊟ ♿ ♣ P

Grandborough

Shoulder of Mutton
Sawbridge Road (off A423, near Southam)
☎ (0788) 810306
11.30–2.30 (3 Sat); 7–11
Marston's Pedigree Bitter; Whitbread Flowers IPA, Flowers Original [H]
Wood-panelled lounge; plain bar with table skittles. Large garden. ⊛ ◐ ◑ ⊟ ♿ ♣ P

Griff

Griffin Inn
Nuneaton Road (B4113, 1 mile N of Bedworth)
☎ (0203) 312149
11–3; 5–11
Draught Bass; M&B Brew XI [H]
Old coaching inn with several rooms, unspoilt by renovations. Live music Tue nights. Large garden used by model car and shooting clubs. Well worth visiting. ⌂ Q ⚇ ⊛ ⊟ ♣ P

Henley in Arden

Three Tuns
High Street (A34)
☎ (05642) 2723
11–3; 5.30–11
Ansells Mild, Bitter; Hanson's Bitter; Marston's Pedigree Bitter; M&B Brew XI [E]
Unusual divided room, leading to a garden at back. Q ⊛ ⇌ ○

Kenilworth

Clarendon Arms
44 Castle Hill (opp. castle)
☎ (0926) 52017
11–3; 5.30–11
Courage Best Bitter, Directors [H]
Pleasingly-renovated old pub, now somewhat food-oriented, though drinkers are still made very welcome. Q ⚇ ⊛ ◐ ◑ ♿

Clarendon House Hotel
High Street (A452/A459 jct)
☎ (0926) 57668
11.30–2.30; 6–11
Hook Norton Best Bitter, Old Hookey; Whitbread Flowers IPA, Flowers Original [H]
Rather plush hotel bar, but with a welcoming atmosphere nevertheless. Jeans are OK but

not sleeveless shirts! Meals in restaurant only. Q 🛏 ◖ ◗ P

Earl Clarendon

Warwick Road
☎ (0926) 54643
11–2.30; 6–11
Marston's Burton Best Bitter, Pedigree Bitter [H]
Yet another 'Clarendon' – a friendly locals' pub with sing-songs at weekends.
Q ⊛ ◖ ⊞ ♿ ♣

Virgins & Castle

7 High Street (A452/A459 jct)
☎ (0926) 57668
11–2.30; 6–11
Greenalls Davenports Traditional Bitter [H]
Medieval pub, retaining small separate rooms. Its name celebrates a great Elizabethan party in the castle (the virgins being the Queen's handmaidens). No meals Sun eve.
♨ Q 🚼 ⊛ ◖ ◗ ⊞ ♿ ♣

Kingsbury

Royal Oak

Coventry Road
☎ (0827) 872335
12–2.30 (incl. Sun, 3.30 Sat); 6–11
Marston's Burton Best Bitter, Pedigree Bitter [H]
Enlarged and refurbished comfortable pub: split-level lounge with traditional bar area at one end. Reasonably-priced typical pub food served until 9pm (not Sun lunch).
🚼 ⊛ ◖ ◗ ♿ ♣ P

Try also: White Horse

Lapworth

Navigation

Old Warwick Road (B4439)
☎ (05643) 3337
11–3; 5.30 (6 Sat)–11
Draught Bass; M&B Mild, Brew XI [H]
Two-roomed pub alongside Grand Union Canal. Tiled floor in bar. Garden adjoins canal.
♨ Q ⊛ ◖ ◗ ⊞ ⇌ (not Sun) P

Leamington Spa

Hope & Anchor

Hill Street ☎ (0926) 423031
11–3; 5.30–11 (11–11 Sat)
Ansells Mild, Bitter [H]
Victorian street-corner local, a good example of an Ansells Heritage inn. Busy, single L-shaped drinking area. ♨ ♣

Newbold Comyn Arms

Newbold Terrace East (edge of Newbold Comyn Park)
☎ (0926) 438810
11.30–3; 7–11 (11–11 summer)
Marston's Burton Best Bitter, Pedigree Bitter, Merrie Monk [H]
New bar, tastefully-converted from former stable block. Separate family room adjoins bar. Large outdoor patio and excellent children's playground. Skittle alley and disabled toilet. Especially popular in summer and deservedly so. Regular guest beers. ♨ 🚼 ⊛ ◖ ◗ ♿ ♣ P

Red House

113 Radford Road
☎ (0926) 881725
11.30–2.30; 5–11 (11.30–11 Fri, 11–11 Sat)
Draught Bass; M&B Mild, Springfield Bitter [H]
Very popular roadside local with large, well-furnished garden at rear, away from road and safe for children. Separate bar and lounge areas. Unusual set of pink and blue-handled beer engines. Lunchtime bar snacks Mon–Fri. ♨ Q ⊛ ♣

Somerville Arms

Campion Terrace
☎ (0926) 426746
11–2.30 (3 Fri & Sat); 5.30–11
Ansells Mild, Bitter; Ind Coope Burton Ale; Tetley Bitter [H]
Excellent Victorian back-street, corner pub. Large busy front bar; very small, cosy lounge at rear. Always friendly. Q ⊞ ♣

Leek Wootton

Anchor

Warwick Road
☎ (0926) 53355
11–3; 6–11
Draught Bass; M&B Brew XI [H]
Friendly village pub with a basic locals' bar. Plusher lounge has servery for the excellent bar food (not Sun), including veg and children's options.
♨ Q ⊛ ◖ ⊞ ♿ ♣ ⌓ P

Long Itchington

Harvester

Church Lane
☎ (0926) 812698
11–3; 6–11
Hook Norton Best Bitter, Old Hookey [H]
Pleasant village pub; comfortable lounge with fish tank and excellent restaurant. Children welcome. Guest beers.
🚼 🛏 ◖ ◗ ⊞ ⌓ P

Newbold on Avon

Boat

Main Street ☎ (0788) 76995
11–2.30; 6–11
Greenalls Davenports Best Mild Ale, Davenports Traditional Bitter [H]
Long canalside pub with dining area at one end. Main room has skittles and narrow boat regalia. No eve meals Sun in winter.
⊛ ◖ ◗ P

Newton Regis

Queens Head

Main Road ☎ (0827) 830271
11–4.30; 6–11
Draught Bass [H]
Very nice, friendly pub in pretty village. Anyone interested in gardening and drinking should visit. Landlord extremely helpful. Very good choice of food. Campsite next to duck-pond. 🚼 ⊛ ◖ ◗ ⊞ ♿ ⛺ ♣ ⌓ P

Try also: Rose Inn, Baxerley (M&B)

Nuneaton

Hayrick

Meadowside (off B4114, 3 miles E of centre)
☎ (0203) 348181
11–3; 7–11
Courage Best Bitter, Directors [H]
Modern estate pub with two lounges. Well-known for its glass-walled toilets! 🚼 ⊛ ◖ ♣ P

Oxhill

Peacock Inn

1 mile S of A422
☎ (0295) 88301
11.30–2.30 (12–2.30 Sun); 6.30–11
Draught Bass [E]**; Donnington BB** [H]
Stone-built, cosy village local; friendly landlord. Large garden.
♨ ⊛ ◖ ◗ P

Ratley

Rose & Crown

Off E crest of Edge Hill
☎ (029587) 636
12–3; 6.30–11 (12–2.30, not Mon; 7.30–11 winter)
Arkell's Kingsdown Ale; Bateman XXXB; Donnington SBA; Greene King Abbot Ale; Hook Norton Best Bitter; Morland Old Masters [H]
Beautiful old building, dating back to 1098. Two resident ghosts, one a Roundhead refugee from the Battle of Edgehill. Guest beers regularly available. Home-cooked food (veg option); no Sun eve meals in winter. ♨ Q ⊛ ◖ ◗ ♿ ⛺ ♣ P

Rugby

Engine Inn

Bridget Street (behind Mobil garage on Corporation Street)
☎ (0788) 79658
10–11
M&B Mild [E]**, Brew XI** [H]
Traditional, turn-of-the-century pub still with its original four bars, panelling and engraved, frosted mirrors. Quiet, except for taped music in one bar.
Q ⊛ ◖ ⊞ ♿ ♣

Half Moon

28–30 Lawford Road (A428)

☎ (0788) 74420
11–2.30; 5.30–11 (11–11 Fri, 10–11 Sat)
Ansells Mild, Bitter; Ind Coope Burton Ale H
Wonderful terraced pub close to town centre, very friendly and welcoming to locals and outsiders. Single L-shaped room with darts in one corner. Guest beer Mon–Thu. ♣

Peacock
69 Newbold Road (A426)
☎ (0788) 67923
11.30–3 (4 Fri, 5 Sat); 7–11
Bateman Dark Mild; Hoskins Beaumanor Bitter, Penn's Ale, Premium, Old Nigel H
Large corner Victorian pub near GEC works. Small snug bar separate from lounge; games room. Folk club meets in upstairs function room every Tue. Always a warm greeting from landlord. Guest beer. No food Sun eve. ◐ ◑ ⊞ ≹ ♣

Raglan Arms
50 Dunchurch Road (A426)
☎ (0788) 544441
12–2.30 (incl. Sun, 11–3 Sat); 7–11
Marston's Burton Best Bitter, Pedigree Bitter, Merrie Monk H
Deceptively-large terraced pub very close to Rugby's famous public school. A pub simply to sit and drink in – no food or electronic games to distract. Guest beers in summer. Q ♣ P

Seven Stars
James Street
11–2.30; 6–11
M&B Brew XI H
Excellent locals' boozer in new estate. Table skittles. ❀ ⊞ ≹ ♣

Ryton-on-Dunsmore

Blacksmiths Arms
High Street ☎ (0203) 301818
12–2.30; 6–11
Draught Bass; M&B Brew XI H
Quiet lunchtime village local which becomes a busy diners' pub in the eve. Brass and copper decorate the walls and beams.
⌂ ◐ ◑ ♿ P

Shustoke

Plough Inn
The Green ☎ (0675) 81557
12–2.30; 7 (6.30 Thu–Sat)–11
Draught Bass; M&B Mild, Brew XI H
Old-world, cosy country pub of labyrinthine design. Keen prices. Landlord cooks evening meals himself (Thu–Sat). No meals Sun lunchtime. ⌂ Q ❀ ◐ ◑ ♿ ♣ P

Southam

Old Mint
Coventry Street (100 yds N of A423/425 jct)
☎ (0926) 812339
11–2.30 (3 Sat); 6.30 (6 Sat)–11
Hook Norton Best Bitter; Marston's Pedigree Bitter; Theakston XB; Wadworth 6X; Whitbread Flowers Original H
Characterful 15th-century building of local stone, reputedly a mint in the Civil War. Two cosy bars are adorned with copper, brassware and a collection of weaponry. Said to be haunted. Very busy at weekends. Guest beers.
⌂ ❀ ◐ ◑ ⊞ P

Stratford upon Avon

Shakespeare Hotel (Froth & Elbow Bar)
Chapel Street (next to Town Hall) ☎ (0789) 294771
11–2.30; 5.30–11
Courage Directors; Donnington XXX; Hook Norton Best Bitter, Old Hookey; John Smith's Bitter H
Beautiful Tudor building, popular with tourists and locals alike. Real ale in Froth & Elbow bar. Beers may vary.
⌂ Q ❀ ⛍ ◐ ⊞ ♿ ♣ ⌽

White Swan
Rother Street (opp. American fountain) ☎ (0789) 297022
11–2.30; 6–11
Adnams Bitter; Marston's Pedigree Bitter; Wadworth 6X H
Very comfortable hotel with oak beams and wood-panelled walls. Note the original 16th-century wall painting of Tobit and the Angels.
⌂ Q ✇ ⛍ ◐ ◑ ≹ P

Stretton on Dunsmore

Shoulder of Mutton
Brookside (off A45)
☎ (0203) 542601
12–2; 8–11 (12–2; 8–10.30 Sun)
M&B Mild H
Wonderfully-unspoilt, 19th-century pub with 1950s extension. Small snug and larger bar with fancy floor and grand piano. Great character.
⌂ ⊞ ♿ ♣ P

Studley

Railway Inn
Station Road
☎ (052 785) 2597
11–3; 5.30–11 (11–11 Fri & Sat)
Ansells Mild, Bitter; Ind Coope Burton Ale H
Lively one-bar pub with several distinct areas for drinking and games. Railway theme echoes the time when it served the Sambourne and Studley station (pre-Beeching). ⌂ ❀ ◐

Try also: Shakespeare (Banks's)

Warton

Fox & Dogs
Orton Road ☎ (0827) 892448
11.30–3; 6–11
Marston's Pedigree Bitter H
Really friendly pub, popular with the locals. Comfortable rooms with low-beamed ceilings. Large garden overlooks open countryside. ❀ ⊞ ♣ P

Warwick

Dun Cow
Birmingham Road (A425)
☎ (0926) 491293
11–3; 6–11 (11–11 Fri & Sat)
M&B Mild, Brew XI H
Traditional town pub close to restored canal basin. Look for the brass plaques on the wall. Thriving darts team. No food Sun. Q ✇ ◐ ◑ ♿ ♣ P

Racehorse
36 Stratford Road (A429)
☎ (0926) 491039
11.30–3; 6 (6.30 Sat)–11
Everards Mild, Beacon Bitter, Tiger Best Bitter E
Large, out-of-town roadhouse with comfortable lounge and good public bar. Good value meals – chips with everything. Regular handpulled guest beer.
❀ ◐ ◑ ⊞ P

Whichford

Norman Knight
☎ (060 884) 621
12–3; 7–11
Hook Norton Best Bitter, Old Hookey H
Undeveloped little village local facing the green. Old Hookey not always available.
⌂ ❀ ⊞ ♿ ⛺ ♣ P

Wilmcote

Swan House Hotel
Off A34 ☎ (0789) 67030
11–11
Hook Norton Best Bitter; Theakston XB H
Old-world hotel featuring 18th-century beamed ceilings and a natural well. Maria's Bar is a popular meeting place for locals. Bar snacks and home-cooked dishes. ⌂ Q ❀ ⛍ ◐ ◑ ≹ P

Join CAMRA — see page 504!

West Midlands

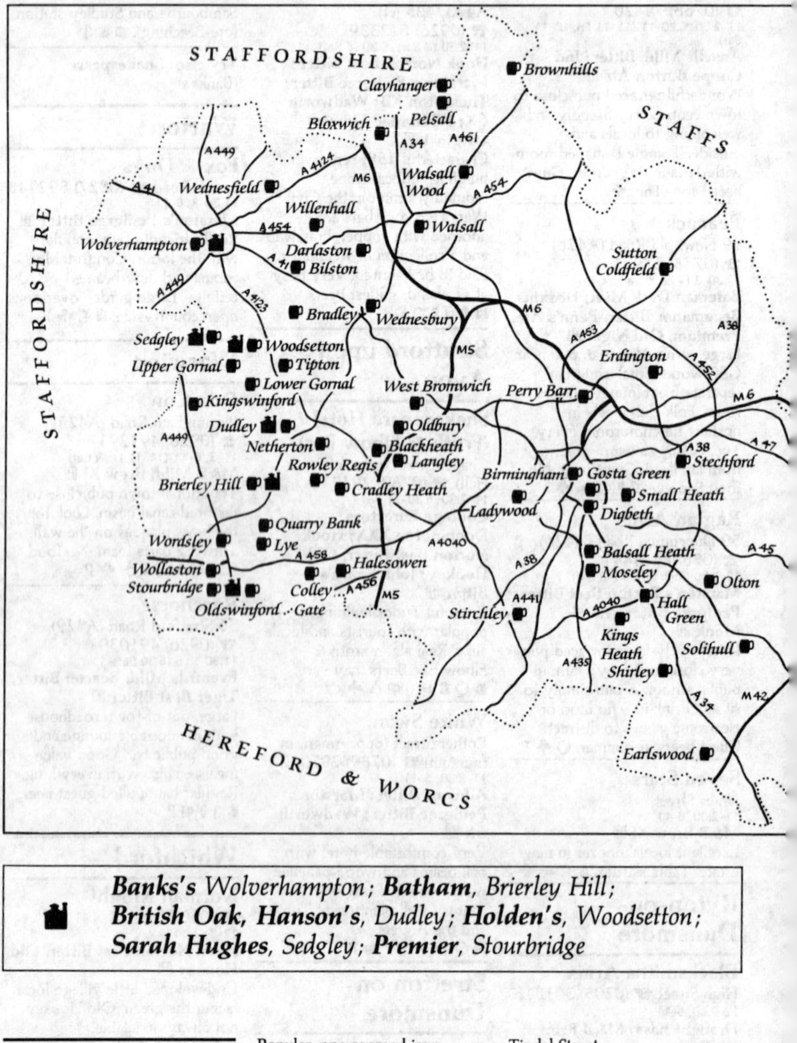

■ **Banks's** Wolverhampton; **Batham**, Brierley Hill; **British Oak, Hanson's**, Dudley; **Holden's**, Woodsetton; **Sarah Hughes**, Sedgley; **Premier**, Stourbridge

Bilston

Greyhound & Punchbowl

High Street (A4039)
☎ (0902) 404331
11–3; 7–11 (11–11 Fri & Sat)
Draught Bass; M&B Highgate Mild, Springfield Bitter Ⓔ
15th-century former manor house, with richly-carved, 16th-century hand-worked ceilings. A ghost reputedly carries a glass of whisky from the ladies to the bar! ⌂ ❀ ◐ ◑ ⊞ ♣

Trumpet

58 High Street (A4039)
☎ (0902) 493723
12–3; 8–11 (incl. Sun)
Holden's Mild, Bitter Ⓔ**, Special** Ⓗ
Popular, one-roomed jazz centre; live groups nightly and Sun lunch. Local caricatures and old film star photos on walls. Front of pub was recently replaced due to rotting timbers. No food at weekend. ❀ ◐

White Rose

20 Lichfield Street, Swan Bank (A41, opp. Town Hall)
☎ (0902) 492497
12 (11 Sat)–3; 7–11
M&B Highgate Mild, Springfield Bitter Ⓔ
Spotlessly clean and friendly. Quality of beer and pool games equally high. ⊞ ♣

Birmingham Balsall Heath:

Old Moseley Arms

Tindal Street
☎ (021) 440 1954
11–2.30; 5.30–11 (11–11 Fri & Sat)
Ansells Bitter; Ind Coope Burton Ale Ⓗ
Friendly, two-roomed Brummie pub. Worthwhile hunting out. ◐ ⊞ ♣

City Centre:

Craven Arms

Upper Gough Street
☎ (021) 643 6756
11–10.30 (11–11 Thu–Sat)
M&B Mild, Brew XI Ⓔ
Friendly Brummie pub, frequented by GPO staff. Take time to look at the original Holders Brewery glazed brick frontage. ◐ ⊞ ⇌ (New St) ♣

Gough Arms

Upper Gough Street

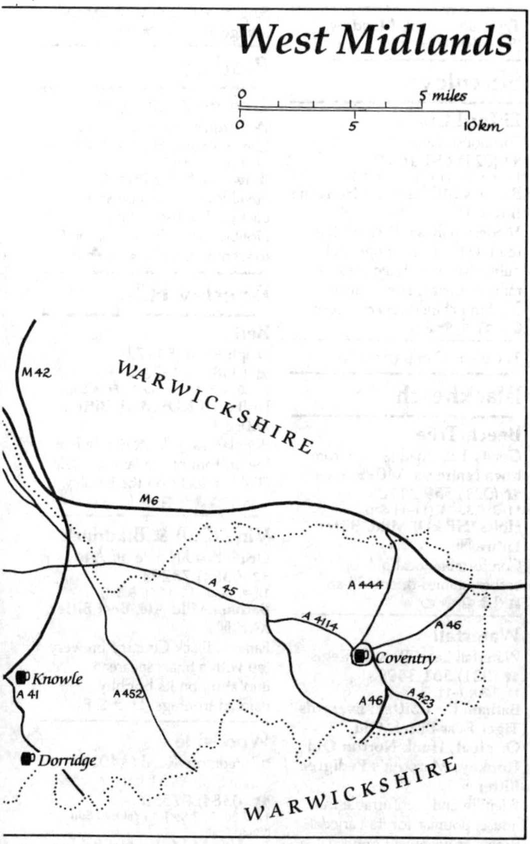

☎ (021) 643 0081
11–3; 5–11 (11–11 Thu–Sat)
Courage Best Bitter, Directors Ⓗ
Friendly, Brum back-street local, worth seeking out.
◐ ⊞ ≹ (New St) ♣

Gunmakers
Bath Street ☎ (021) 236 1201
11–3; 5–11
Draught Bass; M&B Mild, Brew XI Ⓔ
Noisy, small pub in Gun quarter. Opposite St Chad's Cathedral. ◐ ⊞ ≹ (Snow Hill) ♣

Prince of Wales
Cambridge Street
11.30–3; 5 (7 Sat)–11
Ansells Mild, Bitter; Ind Coope Burton Ale; Tetley Bitter Ⓗ
Intimate, convivial pub. A much-loved local institution, frequented by players from the nearby repertory theatre and CBSO. Only a stone's throw from the site of the International Convention Centre. ⊞ ♣

Queens Tavern
23 Essex Street (off Horsefair)
☎ (021) 622 3491
12–2.30; 5 (7 Sat)–11
Courage Best Bitter, Directors Ⓗ
Smart, popular, one-roomed city pub; located behind Hippodrome Theatre.
◐ ◑ ♿ ≹ (New St)

Woodman
106 Albert Street
☎ (021) 643 1959
11–2.30; 5 (7 Sat)–11
Ansells Mild, Bitter; Ind Coope Burton Ale; Tetley Bitter Ⓗ
Victorian pub with a great welcome from a friendly landlord. Quiz and pub games nights. Good sandwiches and pies. ⊞ ♿ ≹ (Moor St) ♣

Digbeth:

Cannonball
28 Adderley Street
☎ (021) 772 1403
10.30–2.30; 7–11 (8–10.30 Sun, closed Tue)
Holden's Bitter Ⓗ
Two-roomed pub with jazz in upstairs concert room Thu–Sun nights. Jazz session Wed lunch, too. Outside toilets.
◐ ◑ ⊞ ≹ (New St)

Market Tavern
Moseley Street
☎ (021) 622 5560
12–3; 5–11 (12–11 Fri, 11–11 Sat, closed Sun)
Ansells Mild, Bitter; Ind Coope Burton Ale; Tetley Bitter Ⓗ
Nicely-restored, traditional Victorian pub in back street near markets. Good value food.
◐ ◑ ⊞ ♿ ≹ (New St) ♣

Erdington:

Lad in the Lane
22 Bromford Lane (A4040)
☎ (021) 377 7184
11–3; 6–11
Ansells Mild, Bitter; Ind Coope Burton Ale Ⓗ
Birmingham's oldest pub (1306). Children's playground. A friendly place. ❀ ◐ ⊞ ♣ P

Gosta Green:

Sacks of Potatoes
Lister Street ☎ (021) 359 6409
11–11 (11–3; 6–11 Sat)
Draught Bass; M&B Mild, Springfield Bitter Ⓗ
Lively pub in the heart of Aston University.
❀ ◐ ◑ ⊞ ♿ ≹ (Moor St) ♣ P

Hall Green:

Baldwin
Baldwins Lane (½ mile from Robin Hood Island)
☎ (021) 744 3356
11–11 (12–2; 7–10.30 Sun)
Courage Best Bitter, Directors; John Smith's Bitter Ⓗ
Pub based on half a ship; the other half is the Three Magpies 1½ miles away. Completely refurbished, with a comfortable lounge and bar. Garden has safe children's play area: swings, slide and bouncy castle occasionally. Barbecues. No food Sun. ⛱ ❀ ◐ ◑ ⊞ ♿ ≹ (Yardley Wood/Hall Green) P

Dog & Partridge
Priory Road ☎ (021) 474 2132
11–3; 6–11
Ansells Mild, Bitter; Tetley Bitter Ⓗ
Large old pub on bank of River Cole (no better than a stream). Has a garden of sorts and a football pitch between pub and river. Large bar, lounge and snug. Q ❀ ◐ ◑ ⊞ ♿ ≹ (Yardley Wood) P

Kings Heath:

Station
7 High Street
☎ (021) 444 1257
11–11 (11–3; 6–11 Sat)

West Midlands

Ansells Mild, Bitter; Ind Coope Burton Ale; Tetley Bitter Ⓗ
Newly-renovated pub still retaining some of its original tiling. ◐ ◗ ♣

Try also: Hare & Hounds (Ansells)

Ladywood:

Vine
Rawling Street
☎ (021) 454 7943
11–3; 5.30–11
Ansells Mild, Bitter; Ind Coope Burton Ale; Tetley Bitter Ⓗ
Bustling, one-roomed public house. ◐ ≹ (Five Ways) ♣

Moseley:

Prince of Wales
Alcester Road
☎ (021) 449 4198
11–3; 5.30–11
Ansells Mild; Ind Coope Burton Ale Ⓗ
Busy high street pub with a lively public bar and two back rooms served through a hatch in the passageway. Q ❀ ◐ ◗ ⊞ ♿

Perry Barr:

Wellhead Tavern
76 Franchise Street (just off A34 on outer ring road, behind Polytechnic) ☎ (021) 331 4554
12–3 (2.30 Sun); 5 (7 college holidays)–11
Ansells Mild, Bitter; Gibbs Mew Wiltshire Traditional Bitter; Harveys Best Bitter; Ind Coope Burton Ale; Tetley Bitter Ⓗ
Local CAMRA Pub of the Year 1987 and 89. A good mix of students and regulars. Extensive lunchtime food, including veg menu. First pub in Birmingham with its own bitter.
❀ ◐ ⊞ ≹

Small Heath:

Black Horse
Green Lane (200 yds from A45) ☎ (021) 773 7271
11–11 (11–3.30; 6.30–11 Sat)
M&B Mild, Brew XI Ⓔ
Compact pub near Islamic centre. Interesting mix of clientele. ❀ ◐ ⊞ ♣

Stechford:

Colehall Farm
Colehall Lane
☎ (021) 784 0155
11–3; 5.30–11
Banks's Mild, Bitter Ⓗ
Renovated Georgian farmhouse with display of agricultural implements in the lounge; background music. Nice, friendly crowd. ❀ ◐ ⊞ ♣ ⌀ P

Try also: Brook Meadow (Banks's)

Stirchley:

Lifford Curve
Fordhouse Lane
☎ (021) 451 1634
11–3; 5.30–11 (11–11 Fri & Sat)
Banks's Mild, Bitter; Hanson's Bitter Ⓔ
Modern pub, set back off the road, with large lounge and public bar; decorated on a railway theme. Home-made food (no chips) weekdays only.
❀ ◐ ⊞ ♿ ♣ P

Try also: Camp (Ansells)

Blackheath

Beech Tree
Gorsty Hill Road (½ mile from town centre on A4099)
☎ (021) 559 2170
11–3; 6.30–11 (11–11 Sat)
Holts (HP&D) Mild, Bitter, Entire Ⓗ
Comfortable local pub on corner; games-oriented bar.
⛫ ◐ ◗ ⊞ ♣ ⌀

Waterfall
Waterfall Lane, Rowley Regis
☎ (021) 561 3499
11–2.30; 7–11
Batham Best Bitter; Everards Tiger Best Bitter, Old Original; Hook Norton Old Hookey; Marston's Pedigree Bitter Ⓗ
Friendly and comfortable free house, popular for its varied choice of beers and good value food. Has a waterfall in the garden and a photographic 'rogues gallery' in the bar. Function room hosts regular quiz nights. Guest beers.
⛫ ❀ ◐ ◗ ⊞ ♣ P

Bloxwich

Romping Cat
97 Elmore Green Road (near B4210/A4124 jct)
11–11
Banks's Mild, Bitter Ⓔ
Small, basic three-roomed pub with a round-cornered bar and tiny smoke room. ❀ ⊞ ≹ ♣

Saddlers Arms
Fishley Lane, Lower Farm Estate, Little Bloxwich
☎ (0922) 405839
11–3; 6–11 (11–11 Sat)
Banks's Mild, Bitter Ⓗ
Modern estate pub with a nice lounge and a friendly atmosphere. ☋ ❀ ⊞ ♣ P

Station Hotel
Station Street (off A34)
☎ (0922) 477074
11–3; 6–10.30 (11 Fri & Sat)
Ansells Mild, Bitter; Ind Coope Burton Ale Ⓗ
Single-room pub with bar and lounge areas. ❀ ≹ ♣

Bradley

George & Dragon
Wootton's Square (off Hall Green Street) ☎ (0902) 41538
12–3 (2.30 Sat); 7–11
Banks's Mild, Bitter Ⓔ
Small locals' pub almost in backyard of the Britannia. Doubles as barber's shop on Sun for senior citizens. ❀ ⊞ ♣ P

Brierley Hill

Bell
Delph Road (B4172)
☎ (0384) 72376
11.30–3; 5–11 (11.30–11 Fri & Sat)
Holts (HP&D) Mild, Bitter, Entire Ⓗ
Popular, early Victorian pub at the bottom of the famous Delph Flight of locks on the Dudley Canal. ⛫ ❀ ◐ ⊞ ♣ P

Vine (Bull & Bladder)
Delph Road (¾ mile off A461)
☎ (0384) 78293
12–4; 6–11 (12–11 Fri & Sat)
Batham Mild Ale, Best Bitter, XXX Ⓗ
Famous Black Country brewery tap with a Shakespearean quotation on its brightly painted frontage. ☋ ❀ ⊞ P

Woodside
67 Pedmore Road (A4036 ½ mile S of A461 jct)
☎ (0384) 77550
12–2.30; 5 (7 Sat)–11 (closed Sun lunch)
Banks's Mild; Burton Bridge Bridge Bitter; Fuller's ESB; Moorhouse's Pendle Witches Brew; Taylor Golden Best Mild, Landlord Ⓗ
Smart free house convenient for Merry Hill shoppers. Good value menu (not Sun lunch), including veg dishes. Guest beers changed monthly on a regional basis. Draught cider in summer. ⛫ Q ☋ ⛟ ◐ ◗ ⊞ ⌀ P

Brownhills

Crown
Watling Street (Rising Sun Island, A452/A5 jct)
☎ (0543) 372604
10.45–11 (12–2.30; 7–10.30 Sun)
Banks's Mild, Bitter Ⓔ
Busy, two-roomed local serving good value food. ❀ ◐ ◗ ⊞ ♣ P

Prince of Wales
98 Watling Street (A5)
☎ (0543) 372551
12–3 (Sat only); 7.30–11
Ansells Mild, Bitter Ⓗ
Small, one-roomed, main road pub.

Wheel Inn
96 Lindon Road (B4152)
☎ (0543) 378408

11.30–3; 6.30–11 (11–11 Fri & Sat)
Banks's Mild, Bitter [E]
Increasingly popular urban pub; family-run. Occasional cheap beer nights. Limited menu.
P

Clayhanger

George & Dragon
Church Street (off A4124)
☎ (0543) 372047
(12–3 (Fri & Sat only); 7–11
Ansells Mild, Bitter
Village pub with a basic bar, a pleasant lounge and a popular games room. Small car park.
P

Colley Gate

Little White Lion
Windmill Hill (A458)
☎ (0384) 635089
11–2,.30; 6–11
Ansells Mild; Ind Coope Burton Ale; Lumphammer [H]
Ever-popular Little Pub Co. hostelry, well-noted for its bear steaks, sizzlers and Desperate Dan pies. Only Lumphammer is visible on the pumps so ask for other beers. Live music Tue eve.
Q P

Why Not Inn
Whynot Street (off A458 by Cradley Labour Club)
☎ (0384) 61019
12–2.30 (3 Fri & Sat); 6–11 (supper licence till 12 Fri & Sat)
Ma Pardoe's Mild, Bitter; Wiltshire Stonehenge Best Bitter, Old Grumble, Old Devil [H]
Individual old pub on the edge of town, with a late weekend supper licence. Tables and chairs in yard. Guest beers.

Coventry

Biggin Hall Hotel
214 Binley Road, Copsewood
☎ (0203) 451056
11–3 (4 Sat); 4 (6 Sat)–11 (11–11 Fri)
Marston's Mercian Mild, Burton Best Bitter, Pedigree Bitter, Owd Rodger [H]
Not a hotel, despite the name. Smart bar; quiet lounge at rear (large centre table is popular with locals). Games rooms at rear doubles for families. The best Marston's in Coventry; good food, too.
P

Black Horse
Spon End ☎ (0203) 77360
10–3; 4.30–11
Draught Bass; M&B Mild, Brew XI [H]
Busy old pub with three small rooms (one disguised as a wide corridor); wood panelling in lounge. Threatened with demolition. Q P

Boat Inn
Black Horse Road, Exhall (off A444) ☎ (0203) 361438
11–3 (may close early); 6–11
Ansells Mild, Bitter; Ind Coope Burton Ale; Tetley Bitter [H]
A Heritage Inn; classic wood-panelled area at end is popular with locals. All one room, but not obviously so. Very friendly place and people.

Earlsdon Cottage
24 Warwick Street
☎ (0203) 75745
11–3; 5–11
Draught Bass; M&B Mild, Brew XI [E]
Large, multi-roomed pub. Very popular, with standing room only at night. Music in back room (speakeasy-cum-'talent' night) some customers' performances are legendary! This pub changes licensees, not the reverse. No food Sun.
Q

Elastic Inn
Lower Ford Street (by bus station) ☎ (0203) 227039
11–11
Ansells Mild, Bitter; Tetley Bitter [H]
Single-bar pub near bus station and leisure centre. Limited lunch menu.

Greyhound Inn
Sutton Stop, Longford (track leading to canal stop, off A444)
☎ (0203) 363046
11–3; 6–11
Draught Bass; M&B Mild, Springfield Bitter [H]
Old canalside pub in Hawkesbury conservation area. Outside drinking on canal bank. Famous for excellent pies.
P

Haven
Dillotford Avenue, Cheylesmore
☎ (0203) 419029
11–2.30; 5.30–11 (11–11 Fri & Sat)
Courage Best Bitter, Directors; John Smith's Bitter [H]
Popular estate pub in middle-class residential area. All welcome. P

Malt Shovel
Spon End ☎ (0203) 220204
11–2.30 (may extend); 7 (6 Sat)–11
Ansells Mild, Bitter; Tetley Bitter [H]
Small but deservedly-popular, one-room pub with many nooks and crannies. The original Heritage pub (spot the additions — there aren't many!).
P

Miners Arms
Aldermans Green Road
☎ (0203) 360457

11–2.30; 7–11
Ansells Mild, Bitter; Tetley Bitter [H]
Friendly, estate-style pub on main road. P

Nursery Tavern
Lord Street ☎ (0203) 674530
11.30–2 (3 Sat); 7–11
Ruddles Best Bitter, County; Webster's Yorkshire Bitter, Choice [H]
Pleasant pub in inner city residential area, once the watchmaking district — property designs in the back streets sometimes reflect this. Community spirit is much stronger than in other parts of the city. No food at weekend.
Q

Old Windmill
22 Spon Street
☎ (0203) 252183
11–2.30; 5.30 (6 Sat)–11
Ruddles Best Bitter, County; Webster's Yorkshire Bitter, Choice [H]
16th-century building, altered in recent years. At one time run by a Mrs Brown and still known as 'Ma Brown's' by many. Street is full of restored and rebuilt timber-framed buildings — a definite tourist stop.
Q

Prince William Henry
Foleshill Road
☎ (0203) 687776
11.30–11
Draught Bass; Brew XI [E]
Large, lively pub close to canal and Courtaulds main Coventry works. P

Town Wall Tavern
Bond Street (behind Belgrade Theatre) ☎ (0203) 220963
11–3; 5–11
Draught Bass; M&B Mild, Brew XI [H]
Old pub near old Town Wall and restored buildings in Spon Street. Car parks on three sides but still a local gem. Small snug is of a type known locally as 'Donkey Box' — visit it!
Q

Cradley Heath

Black Country Inn
Graingers Lane
☎ (0384) 410216
11–2.30; 7–11
Draught Bass; M&B Highgate Mild, Springfield Bitter [H]
Modern version of a period pub: several drinking areas served from one focal bar. Many interesting artefacts to be spotted. Live music weekly and a free 'n' easy on Mon eve.
P

Waggon & Horses

Reddal Hill Road (A4100)
☎ (0384) 636035
11–3; 7–11
Banks's Mild, Bitter E
Vibrant, main-street, Black Country pub. P

Darlaston

Green Dragon
55 Church Street (500 yds N of A4038/A46 jct)
☎ (021) 526 3674
11–2.30; 7–11
M&B Highgate Mild, Springfield Bitter H
Small and lively, two-roomed local with strong darts emphasis. Handpumps are a rarity in M&B pubs, so enjoy.

Dorridge

Railway Inn
Grange Road
☎ (0564) 773531
11–3; 4.30–11 (11–11 Wed, Fri & Sat)
Draught Bass; M&B Mild, Brew XI H
Tenanted by the same family for many years and has stayed traditional, unusual for the area.
Q (not Sun) P

Dudley

Lamp Tavern
Upper High Street (A459)
☎ (0384) 254129
11–3; 6–11 (11–11 Sat)
Batham Mild Ale, Best Bitter, XXX H
Busy, friendly pub at west end of town centre near Hanson's Brewery. Large children's play area with climbing equipment.
P

Old Vic
King Street ☎ (0384) 236082
11–3; 4.30–11 (11–11 Fri & Sat)
Home Mild, Bitter; Theakston XB; Younger IPA, No. 3 H
Boisterous town-centre pub; one room around an island bar. Guest beers (usually three).

Earlswood

Bulls Head
Lime Kiln Lane (off B4102)
☎ (021) 728 2335
12 (11 Sat)–2.30; 5.30 (6 Sat)–11
Ansells Mild, Bitter; Ind Coope Burton Ale; Tetley Bitter H
Rambling lounge with unusually high bar. A water pump stands outside the bar which has a tiled floor. Very popular staging point for Sunday cyclists. Garden area has swings and slides. Q P

Halesowen

Beehive
Hagley Road (B4183, 800 yds from centre)
☎ (021) 550 1782
11–11
Banks's Bitter; Hanson's Mild Ale E
Comfortable lounge and large rear function room, with a wide range of meals available in both. Bar popular with locals for the beer, pool and Sun eve sing-alongs. P

King Edward VII
Stourbridge Road (A458)
☎ (021) 550 4493
11–2.30; 5.30–11
Ansells Bitter; Banks's Mild; Ind Coope Burton Ale H
Ever-popular and comfortable pub next door to the town's football ground. Good value food and a high standard of beer: landlord was a finalist in the 1989 National Cellarmanship competition.
P

Rose & Crown
Hagley Road (B4183, 1 mile from centre)
☎ (021) 550 2757
12–2.30 (3 Sat); 5.30 (6 Sat)–11
Holts (HP&D) Mild, Bitter, Entire H
Recently taken over by Holts and refurbished with various drinking/eating areas disposed around a central bar — many interesting and unusual artefacts. Lunchtime snacks (not Sun). P

Waggon & Horses
Stourbridge Road (A458)
☎ (021) 550 4989
11–2.30; 7–11 (may vary)
Batham Mild, Best Bitter; M&B Mild; Lloyds Country Bitter H
A constant real ale festival: ten handpumps offer a merry-go-round of beers from around the country. Occasional live music, quiz nights, party nights, etc. Pool table and cosy snug.
Q

Kingswinford

Park Tavern
Barnett Lane (500 yds from A4101) ☎ (0384) 287178
☎ (0384) 287178
12–3 (4.30 Sat); 5 (6 Sat)–11
Ansells Bitter; Batham Best Bitter; Ind Coope Burton Ale H
Pleasant local near Broadfield House Glass Museum. P

Knowle

Red Lion
High Street ☎ (0564) 772461
11–3; 5.30–11
Ansells Bitter; Ind Coope Burton Ale; Tetley Bitter H
Honest, basic bar with original grate and beams. Long lounge where the seating arrangement affords some privacy. Wine bar and function room available for hire. Wrought iron sign overhangs street. P

Langley

Crosswells
High Street (just off B4182)
☎ (021) 552 2629
11–2.30; 6–11 (11–3; 7–11 Sat)
Holts (HP&D) Mild, Bitter, Entire H
Busy, two-room Victorian pub close to Holt Plant & Deakin Brewery. P

Try also: Brewery Inn (Holts)

Lower Gornal

Red Cow
84 Grosvenor Road (off B4176) ☎ (0384) 253760
12–4.30; 6 (7 Sat)–11
Banks's Bitter; Hanson's Mild Ale E
Old Black Country local of character; a pub since 1835. A traditional oasis in an area of redevelopment. Comfortable, snug lounge. P

Try also: Miner's Arms, Chapel House (Holden's)

Lye

Shovel
Pedmore Road (off Lye Cross)
☎ (0384) 423998
11.30–3; 6–11.30
Banks's Mild E**; Batham Best Bitter; Everards Tiger Best Bitter; Hook Norton Old Hookey; Ruddles County** H
Noted for its choice of beers and excellent range of food. Guest beers always available.

Netherton

Elephant & Castle
Cradley Road (B4173)
☎ (0384) 636849
12–2.30 (3 Fri); 5.30–11 (11.30–3.30; 7–11 Sat)
Holts (HP&D) Mild, Bitter, Entire H
Comfortable Black Country local where occasional impromptu piano recitals by the landlord are a feature. Summer barbecues. Q (Cradley Heath) P

Old Swan
Halesowen Road (A459)
☎ (0384) 253075
12–2.30; 6–11
Ma Pardoe's Mild, Bitter; Wiltshire Stonehenge Best Bitter, Old Grumble, Old Devil, Exhibition Ale H
Famous, extended Black Country institution. The

original old bar, complete with enamelled ceiling and cast iron artefacts, provides a quiet haven, as does the unspoilt snug beyond. Guest beers. ⌂ Q ❀ ◖◗ ⊞ ♣ P

Oldbury

Waggon & Horses

Church Street

☎ (021) 552 5467

12–2.30 (3 Fri); 5.30 (5 Fri, 6 Sat)–11

Draught Bass; Batham Best Bitter; Everards Old Original; Hanson's Mild Ale; Marston's Pedigree Bitter [H]

Popular, listed Victorian town pub with original tiled walls, a copper ceiling and Holts (of Aston) Brewery window. Now engulfed by new civic centre. Regular guest beers. ⌂ ❀ ◖◗ ⊞ ♿ ⇌ (Sandwell & Dudley)

Try also: Railway (M&B)

Oldswinford

Shrubbery Cottage

Heath Lane (200 yds from A491/B4186 jct at Oldswinford Cross)

☎ (0384) 377598

12 (11.30 Sat)–2.30; 6–11

Holden's Mild, Bitter, Special, XL Old Ale [H]

Small, friendly, one-room local near the college; still the only Holden's pub in the Stourbridge area. Evening meals finish early. Guest beers. ⌂ ❀ ◖◗ ⇌ (Stourbridge Jct) P

Olton

Lyndon

Barn Lane, Richmond Road

☎ (021) 743 2179

12–2.30; 6 (6.30 Sat)–11

Ansells Mild, Bitter; Ind Coope Burton Ale; Tetley Bitter [H]

Large, two-tier lounge; the conservatory overlooks the garden and children's adventure playground. Smoke room and bar offer alternative seating areas. ⚇ ❀ ◖◗ ⊞ ♣ P

Pelsall

Old House at Home

Walsall Road (B4154)

11–3; 5–11 (11–11 Fri & Sat)

Banks's Mild, Bitter [E]

Popular pub near the common. Bar snacks. ⊞ ♣ P

Quarry Bank

Church Tavern

High Street (A4100)

☎ (0384) 68757

10–2.30; 5 (6 winter)–11 (10–11 Sat)

Holts (HP&D) Mild, Bitter, Entire [H]

Cheerful, welcoming pub with Black Country society connections and traditional local cooking (book for Sun lunch); no eve meals Tue or Sun. Wed is quiz night. ⌂ ◖◗ ⊞ ♿ ⇌ (Cradley Heath) ♣ P

Rowley Regis

Sir Robert Peel

Rowley Village (B4171, 400 yds from Blackheath town centre) ☎ (021) 559 2835

12–4; 7–11

Ansells Mild, Bitter [H]

Welcoming remnant of the old hilltop village. The cheerfully-decorated bar and lounge are separated by a central passageway with framed cartoons and its own servery. ⌂ ❀ ⊞ ⇌ ♣

Sedgley

Beacon Hotel

Bilston Street (A463, ¼ mile E of High Street) ☎ (090 73) 3380

12–2.30; 5.30–10.30 (11.30–3; 5.30–11 Fri & Sat)

Burton Bridge Porter; Sarah Hughes Original Dark Ruby Mild; M&B Springfield Bitter [H]

Superb example of a lovingly restored Victorian hostelry. The three-tier brewery at the rear was re-opened in 1987 after 30 years' closure. Regular guest beers. ⌂ Q ⚇ ❀ ◖ ⊞ ♣ P

Try also: Mount Pleasant (Holts)

Shirley

Bernies Real Ale Off-Licence

266 Cranmore Boulevard (off A34) ☎ (021) 744 2827

12–2 (not Mon); 5.30–10

Hook Norton Best Bitter; Hoskins Old Nigel; Smiles Best Bitter; Taylor Landlord; Titanic Premium Bitter; Wadworth 6X [H] & [E]

Situated in a row of shops–miss it at your peril! A truly remarkable and variable selection of ales from small breweries. Worth a visit just to see what's available. Real cider, too. Always ask to sample. ☌

Solihull

Golden Lion

Warwick Road (A41 opp. Mell Square shopping area)

☎ (021) 704 9969

10.30–11 (10.30–3.30; 7–11 Sat)

Courage Best Bitter, Directors; John Smith's Bitter [H]

Popular, three-roomed pub boasting the only public bar in the town centre. ❀ ◖◗ ⊞ ♣ P

Harvester

Tanhouse Farm Road (500 yds from A45/B4025 jct)

☎ (021) 556 1637

12 (11 Sat)–2.30; 6–11

Courage Best Bitter, Directors [H]

Estate pub in quiet location. Large, basic bar, usually busy; even larger, sumptuous lounge, quiet lunchtimes and not opened till 7.30 in the evenings midweek. A real ale gain! ❀ ⊞ ♣ P

Stourbridge

Red Lion

Lion Street (just off ring road)

☎ (0384) 397563

12–2.30 (3 Fri, 4 Sat); 7–11

Draught Bass [H]; **M&B Brew XI** [E]

Popular, two-roomed pub with additional parlour for functions or meals. Good value food includes veg and Indian dishes. ⌂ ❀ ◖◗ ⊞ ⇌ ♣

Royal Exchange

Enville Street (A458)

☎ (0384) 396726

12–11

Batham Mild Ale, Best Bitter [H]

Two-roomed local near the town centre, now returned to former high standards. The only Batham house in Stourbridge. Upstairs restaurant. ❀ ◖◗ ⊞ ♣ ☌

Sutton Coldfield

Duke Inn

Duke Street (off Birmingham Road) ☎ (021) 355 1767

11.30–3; 5.30–11

Ansells Mild, Bitter; Ind Coope Burton Ale; Tetley Bitter [H]

Traditional side-street local, miraculously unspoilt. Lunchtime snacks. Q ❀ ⊞ ⇌ ♣

Laurel Wines

63 Westwood Road

☎ (021) 353 0399

12–2; 5.30 (5 Sat)–10.30

Batham Best Bitter; Burton Bridge Festival Ale; Marston's Pedigree Bitter [G]

Real ale off-licence which offers at least four guest beers. ☌ P

Three Tuns

19 The High Street

☎ (021) 355 2996

11–3; 7 (5 Sat)–11

Ansells Mild, Bitter; Ind Coope Burton Ale; Tetley Bitter [H]

Listed coaching inn with a haunted cellar, log fires and a friendly atmosphere. ⌂ ❀ ⊞ ⇌ P

Try also: Station

Tipton

West Midlands

Noah's Ark
Wood Street (off Owen Street, B4517) ☎ (021) 557 1421
11–3 (4 Fri); 5.30–11 (11–11 Sat)
Banks's Bitter; Hanson's Mild Ale Ⓔ
Modernised, one-roomed local, near the Birmingham-Wolverhampton Canal, decorated with photographs of old working boats. ❁ ⇌ ♣ P

Old Court House
Lower Church Lane (B4163, 400 yds off A461)
☎ (021) 520 2865
11.30–2.30 (3 Fri & Sat); 6–11
Home Mild, Bitter; Theakston XB; Younger IPA, No.3 Ⓗ
One-roomed alehouse with a varied clientele. Live rhythm and blues on Tue. No food at weekend. Guest beers.
❁ ◖ ⇌ (Dudley Port) ♣ ⌓ P

Upper Gornal

Crown
Holloway Street, Ruiton (off A459) ☎ (0902) 884035
12–3.30; 7–11
Banks's Bitter; Hanson's Mild Ale Ⓔ
Popular, friendly old local at the top of the 'Bonk'. Windows indicate it was a home-brew house at the turn of the century. The snug is quiet.
♨ Q ⊻ ⊞ ♣ ⌓ P

Old Mill
Windmill Street (off A459)
☎ (0902) 887707
12–3; 6.30–11
Holden's Stout, Mild, Bitter, Special, XL Old Ale Ⓗ
Comfortable and welcoming two-roomed hostelry with upstairs restaurant. House beer (Old Mill Bitter) is brewed by Holden's. ❁ ◖ ◗ ⊞ ♣ P

Walsall

Birchills Tavern
Birchills Street (off A454)
☎ (0922) 24474
8–11
Ansells Bitter; Holden's Bitter Ⓗ
Small, basic pub with small lounge and quiet bar.
Q ❁ ⊞ ⇌ ♣ P

Duke of Wellington
Birmingham Street (off A34)
☎ (0922) 25604
12–11
M&B Highgate Mild, Springfield Bitter, Brew XI Ⓔ
Traditional local; a bright, busy bar and a comfortable lounge. No food Sun. ❁ ◖ ⊞ ♣ P

Hamemaker's Arms
87 Blue Lane West (A454)
☎ (0922) 28083
11.30–3; 6–11 (11–11 Sat)
Banks's Mild, Bitter Ⓔ
Pleasantly-modernised 30s pub, handy for the town centre. Large, well-laid-out bar, and very comfortable farmhouse-style lounge. No food Sun; eves until 9pm. ❁ ◖ ◗ ⊞ ⇌ ♣ P

New Inns
5 John Street ☎ (0922) 27660
12–3; 5.30–11
Ansells Mild, Bitter; Ind Coope Burton Ale Ⓗ
Small-room, Victorian back-street local with cosy lounge. Traditional, warm and comfortable; a rare haven from jukebox and fruit machines. Beautifully-cooked, interesting food; sumptuous Sun roasts. No eve meals Sun or Mon.
♨ Q ❁ ◖ ◗ ⊞ ⇌ ♣

Queen Street Tavern
Queen Street ☎ (0922) 32267
12–3; 8–11
M&B Highgate Mild, Brew XI Ⓔ
Small, street-corner local in industrial area. L-shaped bar displays photographs of Old Walsall. ⊞ ♣

Walsall Arms
Bank Street (behind Royal Hotel, off A34)
☎ (0922) 26660
12–3; 5.30 (7 Sat)–11
Draught Bass Ⓗ**; Banks's Mild Ale, Bitter** Ⓔ**; Marston's Burton Best Bitter, Pedigree Bitter** Ⓗ**; M&B Highgate Mild** Ⓔ
A restrained, well-designed modernisation of a Victorian local. Small, separate rooms and a passageway drinking area make this busy pub very social and conversational. Skittle room popular for functions. No food at weekend. Q ❁ ⊞ ⇌ ♣

White Lion
Sandwell Street
☎ (0922) 28542
12–3; 7–11
Ansells Mild, Bitter; Ind Coope Burton Ale; Tetley Bitter Ⓗ
Large, popular Victorian local with separate pool room. Beware of sloping floor in bar.
❁ ◖ ⊞ ♣ P

Walsall Wood

Royal Exchange
Litchfield Road (A461, near Oak Park recreation centre)
☎ (0543) 372317
11.30–3.30; 5.30–11
Ansells Mild, Bitter; Ind Coope Burton Ale; Tetley Bitter Ⓗ
Pleasant lounge; typical working class bar. Limited choice, but good value meals (Mon–Fri). Well-located for local sports centre. ❁ ◖ ♣ P

Wednesbury

Cottage Spring
106 Franchise Street (off B4200) ☎ (021) 526 6354
12–3.30 (may vary); 7–11
Holden's Mild, Bitter Ⓔ**, Special, XL Old Ale** Ⓗ
Back-street local boozer: basic bar, comfortable lounge. Quiet early in evening. Hot and cold sandwiches at lunchtime. Open quiz night Thu – win a gallon of beer! ⊞ ♣ P

Woodman
Wood Green Road, Wood Green (500 yds from M6 jct 9)
☎ (021) 556 1637
11–11 (11–4; 6–11 Sat)
Courage Directors Ⓗ
Large roadside pub: cosy smoke room, basic bar and even more basic pool/games room, currently under threat from redevelopment.
⊻ ⊞ ⇌ (Bescot) ♣ P

Wednesfield

Broadway
Lichfield Road (A4124)
☎ (0922) 405872
11.30–2.30 (3 Sat); 5 (6 Sat)–11
Ansells Mild, Bitter; Holden's Bitter; Ind Coope Burton Ale; Tetley Bitter Ⓗ
Pleasant, multi-roomed pub with wood panelling in lounge. Back lounge has ornate plaster coving and stained glass partition. Eve meals till 8.30; no food Sun. ❁ ◖ ◗ ⊞ ♿ ♣ P

Pyle Cock
Rookery Street
☎ (0902) 732125
11–3; 5–11
Banks's Mild, Bitter Ⓔ
A gem of a pub, apart from the loss of its handpulls.
Q ⊞ ♿ ♣ P

Spread Eagle
Broad Lane South
11.30–2.30; 5–11 (11–11 Fri & Sat)
Banks's Mild, Bitter Ⓔ
Large, 1920s estate pub on edge of Wolverhampton Borough. Roomy bar and smoke room; huge lounge. A warm welcome is assured. No food at weekends. ◖ ⊞ ♣ P

West Bromwich

Merry Go Round
Garratt Street, Carters Green (off A41) ☎ (021) 553 4338
11–3; 6.30–11
Ansells Mild, Bitter; Ind Coope Burton Ale Ⓗ
Large, two-roomed estate pub: basic bar, comfortable lounge. No food Sun eve. ◖ ◗ ⊞ ♣ P

Sow & Pigs
Hilltop (A41)

☎ (021) 553 3127
12–3; 6–11 (11–5; 7–11 Fri, 11–11 Sat)
Banks's Bitter; Hanson's Mild Ale [E]
Cosy, quiet lounge; plain bar is enhanced by porcine murals.
⌂ Q ♞ ❀ ◖ ◗ ⊟ ♣ ⊖

Wheatsheaf
High Street (Old A41)
☎ (021) 553 4221
10.30–3; 5–11 (11–11 Fri, 11–3; 6–11 Sat)
Holden's Mild, Bitter, Special, XL Old Ale [H]
Bright, popular local on Carters Green, an area offering a wide choice of ales. Eve meals Thu–Sat. ❀ ◖ ◗ ⊟ ♣

Try also: Oddfellows (Premier); **Railway** (Camerons)

Willenhall

Falcon Inn
Gomer Street West
12–11
Banks's Mild, Bitter [E]; **Ruddles Best Bitter, County; Samuel Smith OBB; Wadworth 6X** [H]
Two-roomed locals' pub with a traditional bar – a darts venue most nights. Uley Pig's Ear available regularly, plus other occasional guest beers.
❀ ⊟ ♣ ⊖

Robin Hood
54 The Crescent (off A454)
☎ (0902) 608006
12–3; 7 (5.30 Fri)–11
Ansells Mild; Ind Coope Burton Ale; Tetley Bitter [H]
One-roomed pub with a warm and friendly atmosphere. Walsall CAMRA branch Pub of the Year 1989. ⌂ ❀ ♣ P

Three Tuns
8 Walsall Road
☎ (0902) 631652
11–11 (may close in afternoon)
M&B Highgate Mild [E]
Small, two-bar pub: a basic Black Country boozer. Back bar is quiet. Q ⊟ ♣

Wollaston

Bulls Head
High Street ☎ (0384) 394073
11.30–3; 6–11
Greenalls Davenports Traditional Bitter [H]
Recently-refurbished, oak-panelled lounge and comfortable bar. ⊟ ♣ P

Foresters Arms
Bridgnorth Road (A461)
☎ (0384) 394476
11 (11.30 Fri)–2.30; 6 (5.30 Fri)–11
Ansells Bitter; Ind Coope Burton Ale; Tetley Bitter [H]
Pleasant, one-roomed local overlooking rolling countryside. Good food (including veg options) and summer barbecues.
❀ ◖ ◗ ♣ P

Plough
Bridgnorth Road (A461)
☎ (0384) 393414
11–3; 7–11
Draught Bass [H]; **M&B Mild, Springfield Bitter** [E]
Popular, two-roomed roadside local with additional pool room. Large garden. ❀ ◖ ⊟ ♣ P

Wolverhampton

Brewery Tap
Dudley Road, Blakenhall
☎ (0902) 351417
11–10.30
Holts (HP&D) Mild, Bitter, Entire [H]
Typical Holt, Plant & Deakin bric-a-brac pub. Single large room with old Black Country decor. View 'entire' brewery while you sup. Eve food just snacks, but some hot. ◖ ♣ P

Clarendon
Chapel Ash (A41)
☎ (0902) 20587
11–11
Banks's Mild, Bitter [E]
Imposing, Victorian, multi-roomed brewery tap with rare corridor bar. ♞ ◖ ⊟ ♣ P

Combermere Arms
Chapel Ash (A41)
☎ (0902) 21880
11–2.30; 6–11
Draught Bass; M&B Springfield Bitter [H]
Cunningly disguised as a terraced house. Interesting tree growing in gents! Hand-pulled Springfield and Bass are both rare for the area. Eve meals finish at 8pm; occasional barbecues. ❀ ◖ ◗ ⊟ ♣ ⊖

Exchange
Exchange Street (near Civic Centre)
10.30–11
Banks's Mild, Bitter [E]
Basic town-centre local. Busy lunchtimes with trade from nearby offices. ⊟ ⇌ ♣

Great Western
Sun Street (off A4124)
☎ (0902) 351090
11–11 (11–2.30; 6.30–11 Sat)
Batham Best Bitter; Holden's Stout, Mild, Bitter, Special [H]
Revitalised pub next to old low-level station; railway memorabilia. Excellent value Black Country food. Eve meals for parties with advance notice. No food Sun. Pleasant new garden and patio. House beer (Shunters Bitter) is brewed by Holden's. ⌂ ❀ ◖ ⇌ ♣

Homestead
Lodge Road, Oxley (off A449)
☎ (0902) 787357
11.30–3; 6–11
Ansells Mild, Bitter; Holden's Bitter; Ind Coope Burton Ale; Tetley Bitter [H]
Large, pleasant, suburban pub with excellent children's playground. Plush lounge and basic bar. Selection of whiskies.
❀ ◖ ◗ ⊟ ♣ P

Lewisham Arms
Prosser Street, Park Village (off A460) ☎ (0902) 53505
11.30–3; 6–11 (11–11 Sat)
Banks's Mild, Bitter [E]
Gloriously-unspoilt Victorian alehouse. ⊟ ♣

Mitre
Lower Green, Tettenhall (off A41) ☎ (0902) 753487
12–3; 6 (7 Sat)–11
Draught Bass; M&B Highgate Mild, Springfield Bitter [E]
Pleasant old pub with varied rooms by village green. Deservedly-popular. No meals Sun and only on occasional eves. ❀ ◖ ⊟ ♿ ♣ ⊖

Newhampton Inn
Riches Street, Whitmore Reans, (off A41) ☎ (0902) 745773
11–11
Courage Best Bitter, Directors; John Smith's Bitter [H]
Surprisingly large, bustling, traditional street-corner local with cosmopolitan clientele, spread between three distinctly different rooms (smoke room is quiet). Crown green bowling and large beer garden at rear. Regular live music in bar.
⌂ Q ❀ ⊟ ♣

Old Ash Tree
Dudley Road (A459)
☎ (0902) 342218
11–11
Banks's Mild, Bitter [E]
Cosy locals' pub with a surprisingly large garden and floodlit bowling green at rear.
❀ ⊟ ♿ ♣ P

Posada
Lichfield Street
☎ (0902) 710738
11–2.30; 5–10.30 (11–10.30 Fri & Sat).
Holts (HP&D) Mild, Bitter, Entire [H]
Town-centre Victorian pub with original bar fittings and tiled front. Only Holt, Plant & Deakin outlet in town centre. Popular with students. No food at weekend. ◖ ♿ ⇌ ♣

Queens Arms
Graisley Row (off A449, Penn Road) ☎ (0902) 26589
12–3 (3.30 Sat); 5 (7 Sat)–11
Ansells Mild, Bitter; Ind Coope Burton Ale; Tetley Bitter [H]
Small, friendly pub in middle of industrial estate. Part of old

brewery visible at rear. Thriving darts and domino teams. Regular trivia quizzes. Eve meals on request. ⛯ ◖ ⊟ ♿ ♣ P

Royal Oak
School Road, Tettenhall Wood (½ mile uphill from Compton roundabout) ☎ (0902) 754396
12–3 (4 Sat); 6–11
M&B Highgate Mild, Springfield Bitter, Brew XI Ⓔ
Charming pub with large games room and beautifully-kept garden. Real Brew XI is rare for area. No meals Sun. ⚇ ⛯ ◖ ⊟ ♣

Stamford Arms
Lime Street, Penn Fields (off Lea Road)
12–2.30; 6–11
Banks's Mild, Bitter Ⓗ
Many-roomed Victorian pub. A hidden gem in the old part of town. Q ⚇ ⛯ ⊟ ♿ ♣

Swan at Tettenhall
Lower Street, Lower Green, Tettenhall (off A41)
☎ (0902) 755943
11–2.30 (3 Sat); 5.30 (7 Sat)–11
Holts (HP&D) Mild, Bitter, Entire Ⓗ
Pleasant and popular, Holts-styled, olde-worlde pub.
◖ ♿ ♣ P

Woodsetton

Park Inn
George Street (just off A457)
☎ (0902) 882843
12–3; 6 (7 Sat)–11
Holden's Mild Ⓗ**, Bitter** Ⓔ**, Special, XL Old Ale** Ⓗ
Friendly and comfortable brewery tap. Occasional summer barbecues. No meals Sun. ⛯ ◖ ♿ ⇌ (Tipton) ♣ P

Wordsley

Samson & Lion
Brierley Hill Road (B4180)
☎ (0384) 77796
12–2.30 (3 Fri & Sat); 7–11
Banks's Mild; Batham Best Bitter; Ind Coope Burton Ale; Tetley Bitter Ⓗ
Old canalside local undergoing development. Facilities for boaters provided. Meals in bar and restaurant; children and vegetarians catered for. Guest beers. ⛫ ⚇ ⛯ ◖ ◗ ⊟ ♿ ♣ ⚲ P

The Vine (Bull & Bladder) home of Batham's ales

WIN A TRIP TO MUNICH'S OKTOBERFEST

Munich's Oktoberfest is one of the world's great festivals. It was initiated in 1810 as a celebration of the engagement of Crown Prince Ludwig and Princess Theresa. Each year an enormous fair takes place on the Theresienwiese (Theresa's Meadow), a highlight of which is the series of colourful beer halls, serving the produce of Bavaria's major breweries.

Some four million litres of pure Bavarian beer are drunk in these cavernous, lively, raucous beer halls. Now the *Good Beer Guide*, in association with GTF Tours, is pleased to offer the chance for two readers to join in the fun. Simply answer the two questions given below. The first all-correct answer drawn from among the entries after the closing date will win its sender a weekend for two at the 1991 Oktoberfest. Ten runners-up prizes of specially engraved *Good Beer Guide* pewter tankards will also be awarded.

GTF, for 17 years a specialist in German, Austrian and Swiss holidays, has arranged two nights' weekend bed and breakfast accommodation at the central Germania Hotel – a short walk from the fairground, with return flights from Gatwick airport. Britain's largest tour operator which specialises in these three countries, GTF offers more than 24 charter flights a week, as well as short breaks, longer holidays, touring, fly-drive and go-as-you-please arrangements. Tailor-made, special interest trips, like beer tastings and excursions to festivals, are a speciality. For more information ring (071) 229 2474.

The questions:
1. What did the abbreviation CAMRA originally stand for?
2. What name is given to the German beer purity law?

Please send your answers on a postcard to:

GBG Competition
Campaign for Real Ale Ltd.
34 Alma Road
St Albans
Herts, AL1 3BW

Closing date: Monday, 1 July 1991

Rules: The competition is open to all readers over 18 years of age, except members of CAMRA's National Executive and employees. No purchase of this book is necessary. The prize is composed of a return flight for two people from Gatwick to Munich, leaving on Friday, returning on Sunday (dates to be confirmed), and bed and breakfast, twin-room accommodation at the Hotel Germania or a hotel of similar standard. A standard return rail ticket from the winner's home to Gatwick is also included. No cash alternative is available. Winners will be notified by the end of July 1991. Readers wishing to know the result of the competition can send an SAE to the above address for details. The Editor's decision in all matters is final and no correspondence can be entered into.

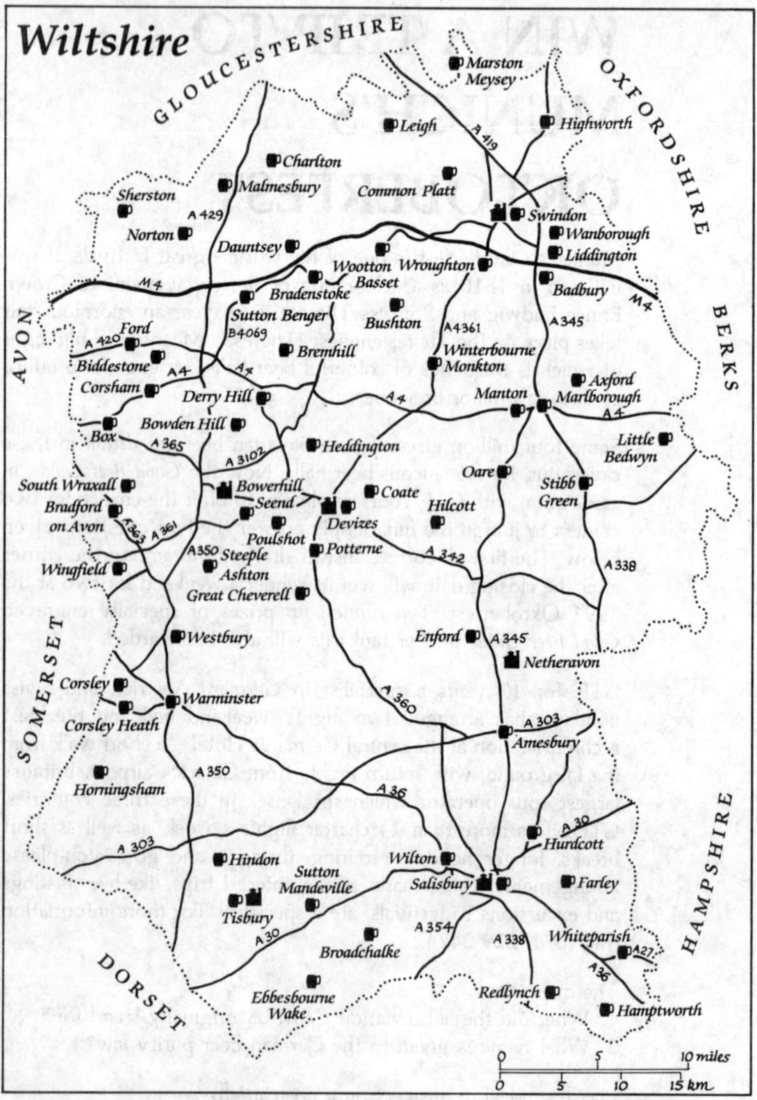

Archers, Arkell's, *Swindon*; **Bunces**, *Netheravon*; **Gibbs Mew, Hop Back** *Salisbury*; **Mole's** *Bowerhill*; **Wadworth**, *Devizes*; **Wiltshire**, *Tisbury*

Amesbury

Antrobus Arms Hotel
15 Church Street (off A345)
☎ (0980) 623163
10.30–2.30; 6–11
Draught Bass; Wadworth IPA, 6X Ⓗ
Georgian hotel with displays of coaching memorabilia. Pretty garden with cedars and fountain. Nearest pub to Stonehenge (two miles).
Q P

Axford

Red Lion
☎ (0672) 20271
11–3; 6–11
Archers Village Bitter; Marston's Pedigree Bitter; Wadworth 6X Ⓗ
Attractive riverside pub with a low-ceilinged, pine-boarded bar.
♣ P

Badbury

Bakers Arms
Off M4/A345
☎ (0793) 740313
11–3; 6–11
Arkell's 2B Bitter, 3B Best Bitter, Kingsdown Ale (winter) Ⓗ
Small neat roadside pub with

well-recommended food.
Q ♣ P

Try also: Plough (Arkell's)

Biddestone

White Horse
Village Green
☎ (0249) 713305
11–2.30; 6–11
Courage Bitter Ale, Best Bitter, Directors [H]
16th-century pub alongside green and duck pond in a picturesque village which attracts tourists all year round.
Q ♣

Bowden Hill

Rising Sun
1 mile E of Lacock
☎ (024973) 363
12–3; 7–11
Mole's IPA, Cask Bitter, Brew 97; Wadworth 6X [H]
Sympathetic improvements to the bar have doubled the size but retained the friendliness of this pub. Marvellous view from terrace garden. Good home-cooked lunchtime food; guest beer and Mole's house brew. Worth a detour. Q ♣ P

Box

Quarrymans Arms
Box Hill (off A4 into Bargates; left at Quarryhill; left at grass triangle) OS834693
☎ (0225) 743569
11–3 (4 Fri & Sat); 7–11
Butcombe Bitter; Marston's Pedigree Bitter; Wadworth 6X [H]
A pub off the beaten track but worth visiting. Breathtaking views; popular with walkers, cyclists, etc. Excellent home-cooked food.
♿ ♣ P

Bradenstoke

Cross Keys
Off B4069 ☎ (0249) 890279
12–2 (2.30 Sat); 7–11
Bunces Benchmark; Tetley Bitter; Wadworth 6X [H]
A village pub with bar food and a restaurant catering mostly for local, rather than passing, trade. Larger public bar with small lounge. Snacks only eves.
Q ♣ P

Bradford-on-Avon

Bunch of Grapes
14 Silver Street
☎ (02216) 3877
11–2.30; 6.30–11
Bunces Old Smokey; Felinfoel Double Dragon; Hook Norton Best Bitter; Smiles Best Bitter [H]
Small, friendly town pub with cosy front lounge and lively public bar. Wide variety of guest beers. Excellent pub food (not Sun). ♣

Bremhill

Dumb Post
Dumb Post Lane (off A4)
OS975727 ☎ (0249) 813192
11–3 (not Thu); 7–11
Archers Best Bitter; Draught Bass; Wadworth 6X [H], **Old Timer** [G]
Free house set in calm countryside. Warm welcome assured. Good outlook. Limited range of good value snacks at lunchtime. Q ♿ ♣ P

Broadchalke

Queens Head
Off A354 via Coombe Bisset
☎ (0722) 780344
11–3; 7–11
Exmoor Ale; Ringwood Best Bitter; Ruddles Best Bitter; Wadworth 6X [H]
15th-century part flintstone pub, formerly a bakehouse and stables, and once part of the Pembroke Estate. One good-size bar with exposed flints and large inglenook. Quiet rural setting.
Q ♣ P

Bushton

Trotting Horse
OS063778 ☎ (0793) 731338
11–2.30; 7–11
Ind Coope Burton Ale; Tetley Bitter; Wadworth 6X [H]
A pub of character, full of nooks and crannies and with a huge malt whisky collection. Guest beers. Recommended food. Worth finding.
♿ ♣ P

Charlton

Horse & Groom
On B4040 ☎ (0666) 823904
12–3; 6–11
Archers Village Bitter; Mole's Cask Bitter; Wadworth 6X [H]
A country inn in traditional Cotswold stone, set well back from the road. Small saloon; large public. Guest beers. Good quality restaurant.
Q ♿ ♣ P

Coate

New Inn
Off A361 OS040616
☎ (0380) 86644
12–2 (11.30–2.30 Fri, 11.30–3.30 Sat, not Thu in winter); 6.30–11
Wadworth IPA, 6X, Old Timer [G]
Friendly, traditional pub.
Landlord is member of the Society for Preservation of Beer from the Wood.
Q ♿ ♣ P

Common Platt

Foresters Arms
OS110868 ☎ (0793) 770615
11–2.30; 6–11
Courage Best Bitter, Directors [H]
Friendly local in a village gradually being swamped by sprawling Swindon.
Q ♿ ♣ P

Corsham

Two Pigs
38 Pickwick (A4, 80 yds NE of B3353 jct) ☎ (0249) 712515
12–2.30 (Fri & Sat only); 7–11
Draught Bass; Fuller's London Pride; Hook Norton Best Bitter; Marston's Pedigree Bitter; Wadworth 6X [H]
One-bar pub of excellent character, serving a variety of real ales (normally between four and eight on offer). Live blues/jazz Mon eves. Live folk Sun lunchtime. Bunces supplies a house beer called 'Pigswill'. Cider in summer. No dogs. No under-21s. ♿

Corsley

Cross Keys
Lyes Green (½ mile N of A362 towards Chapmanslade)
☎ (037388) 406
11.30–2.30 (3 Sat, not Mon & Tue); 6.30–11
Draught Bass; Butcombe Bitter; Mole's Cask Bitter [H]
A welcoming free house of character, this spacious pub is popular with visitors and local trade alike. Grand open fire.
♣ P

Corsley Heath

Royal Oak
On A362 ☎ (037388) 238
11–2.30; 6–11
Draught Bass; Wadworth 6X, Farmer's Glory (summer), **Old Timer** [H]
Popular country roadside pub with three bars and a restaurant in a converted barn. Close to Longleat estate and Cley Hill.
♿ ♣ P

Dauntsey

Peterborough Arms
Dauntsey Lock (B4069, was A420) ☎ (0249) 890409
11–3; 6–11 (not Mon)
Greenalls Davenports Traditional Bitter; Hook Norton Old Hookey; Mole's

Wiltshire

Cask Bitter; Tetley Bitter; Wadworth 6X [H]
Welcoming family atmosphere with meals served in both bars (including veg options). Garden play area.
⌂ Q ♉ ❀ ◖ ◗ ⊞ ♿ ▲ ♣ P

Derry Hill

Lansdowne Arms Inn
On A342, 1 mile from A4
☎ (0249) 812422
11–3; 6–11
Wadworth IPA, 6X, Farmer's Glory, Old Timer [H]
Spacious, popular country pub with good view. Large garden with children's playground. Excellent bar food of same quality as restaurant. Occasional draught ciders.
⌂ ❀ ◖ ◗ ⊞ ▲ ○ P

Devizes

Black Swan
Market Place
☎ (0380) 723259
11–2.30; 6–11
Wadworth IPA, 6X [H]
Cosy L–shaped bar in 1737 coaching inn. Popular with brewery workers and market traders, who use the separate restaurant for business lunches. Excellent accommodation.
⊨ ◖ ◗ ▲ P

Hare & Hounds
Hare & Hounds Street
☎ (0380) 723231
11–2.30; 6.30–11
Wadworth IPA, 6X [H]
Friendly, tucked-away pub with a relaxed atmosphere. Mainly used by locals. ⌂ ❀ ◖ ♿ ▲ ♣ P

Ebbesbourne Wake

Horseshoe Inn
Off A30 S of Fovant
OS242993 ☎ (0721) 780474
11–2.30; 6–11
Bunces Best Bitter; Wadworth 6X, Old Timer [G]
Remote 18th-century inn at foot of old ox drove. Formerly hatch-door service; now converted into two tiny bars displaying old country tools. Guest beer.
⌂ Q ♉ ❀ ⊨ ◖ ◗ ⊞ ▲ ♣ ○ P

Enford

Swan
Off A345 over river
☎ (0980) 70338
11.30 (12 winter)–2.30; 6.30 (7 winter)–11 (11–11 Sat)
Hop Back Special; Wadworth 6X [H]
Well-run, value-for-money free house with unusual gantry sign straddling road. Children welcome in small bar at lunchtimes. Guest beers.
⌂ ❀ ◖ ◗ ♣ P

Farley

Hook & Glove
The Street (between A30/A36, 6 miles SE of Salisbury)
☎ (0722) 72247
11–2.30; 6–11
Exmoor Ale; Wadworth 6X [H]
Family-run rural pub with small public bar. The large lounge has a dining area and the food is good. Guest beers.
⌂ Q ❀ ⊨ ◖ ◗ ⊞ ♿ ▲ ♣ P

Ford

White Hart
Off A420 ☎ (0249) 782213
11–3; 6–11 (11–11 Sat)
Draught Bass; Fuller's London Pride, ESB; Hall & Woodhouse Badger Best Bitter, Tanglefoot; Marston's Pedigree Bitter [H]
Excellent ancient inn, full of atmosphere. Ten real ales regularly available. Trout stream at bottom of garden.
⌂ Q ♉ ❀ ⊨ ◖ ◗ ⊞ ♿ ○ P

Great Cheverell

Bell Inn
57 High Street (600 yds N of B3098) ☎ (0380) 813277
12–2.30; 7–11
Archers Best Bitter [H]
Comfortable one-bar pub with separate restaurant and skittle alley. Fuller's London Pride is a frequent guest beer. Wide-ranging menu. ⌂ ❀ ◖ ◗ ♣

Hamptworth

Cuckoo
Hamptworth Road (off B3079)
OS243197 ☎ (0794) 390302
11.30–2.30; 6–11 (11.30–11 Sat)
Adnams Broadside; Bunces Best Bitter; Hall & Woodhouse Badger Best Bitter, Tanglefoot; Wadworth IPA, 6X [G]
Popular basic pub in quiet rural setting on edge of New Forest. Good garden for children. Petanque played in summer. Bar snacks. Guest beers.
⌂ Q ♉ ❀ ♿ ▲ ♣ ○ P

Heddington

Ivy
Off A3102 ☎ (0380) 850276
11–3; 7–11
Wadworth IPA, 6X, Old Timer [H]
Thatched village pub with stone-flagged bar. Warm welcome in a quiet rural setting. Garden and children's/games room. ⌂ Q ♉ ❀ ▲ ♣ P

Highworth

Saracens Head
Market Place (off A361)
☎ (0793) 762284
11–11 (11–2.30; 6–11 Sat)
Arkell's 2B Bitter, 3B Best Bitter [H]
Smart (no T-shirts), beamed, oak-panelled bar of character. Can be crowded. Q ❀ ⊨ ◖ ◗ P

Try also: Globe (Courage)

Hilcott

Prince of Wales
☎ (0672) 85394
11–3; 6.30–11
Wadworth IPA, 6X [H]
Cosy, single-bar local with separate dining and games area. Bar billiards. Guest beers.
⌂ Q ❀ ◖ ◗ ♿ ▲ ♣ P

Try also: Barge, Honey Street (Courage)

Hindon

Grosvenor Arms
High Street (B3089 off A303)
☎ (0747) 789253
11–2.30; 6–11
Draught Bass; Ushers Best Bitter; Wadworth 6X; Webster's Yorkshire Bitter [H]
18th-century coaching inn with old stables attached. Rambling bar has a part-flagstone floor, a vast open fire, an assortment of sewing machines and old bar seating. Pianist Sun. Good food. Hindon is steeped in history: agricultural riots started here in 1830. ⌂ Q ❀ ◖ ◗ ▲ P

Horningsham

Bath Arms
Off B3092, 1 mile S of Longleat House ☎ (09853) 308
11–3; 6–11
Draught Bass; Eldridge Pope Dorchester Bitter, Best Bitter; Wadworth 6X [H]
Fine country hotel in idyllic setting on edge of Longleat Park. Wilkins cider (summer) and a wide choice of malt whiskies. High class restaurant. Horningsham has won an award for Best-Kept Village in Wiltshire. Q ❀ ⊨ ◖ ◗ ⊞ ♣ ○ P

Hurdcott

Black Horse
Black Horse Lane (off A338 3 miles NE Salisbury)
☎ (0980) 611565
11–2.30 (3.30 Fri & Sat); 6–11 (11–11 Sat in summer)
Gibbs Mew Wiltshire Traditional Bitter, Salisbury Best [H]
Old building at the end of a country lane. Formerly three cottages and a forge. Wattle and daub upstairs; beamed bar below. It became a pub around the turn of the 20th century. Jovial company. Eve meals Wed–Sat. ❀ ◖ ◗ ▲ ♣ P

Leigh

Foresters Arms
Malmesbury Road (B4040)
☎ (0793) 750901
12–2.30 (not Mon–Fri); 7–11
Hall & Woodhouse Tanglefoot; Wadworth 6X, Old Timer [G]
Straightforward roadside pub with pool table in popular bar. Live country and western music Wed eves. ✿ ◖ ◗ ⊡ ♿ ⛺ ♣ P

Liddington

Village Inn
Ham Road (off B4192)
☎ (0793) 790314
11–3; 7–11
Fuller's ESB; Marston's Pedigree Bitter; Wadworth 6X; Whitbread Flowers IPA, Flowers Original [H]
Busy, smart single-bar pub.
🔥 Q ✿ 🛏 ◖ ◗ ♿ P

Little Bedwyn

Harrow
Off A4 ☎ (0672) 870871
12–2.30 (not Mon–Fri); 5.30 (6 Sat)–11
Hook Norton Best Bitter; Marston's Pedigree Bitter [H]
Modernised, but neat, snug little pub with interior subdivided into small rooms. No meals Mon eve. 🔥 Q ✿ ◖ ◗ ♣

Malmesbury

Red Bull
Sherston Road (B4040 1½ miles W of town) ☎ (0666) 822108
11–2.30 (3.30 Sat); 6–11
Archers Best Bitter; Draught Bass; Whitbread Boddingtons Bitter [H]
Popular family pub with garden play area and children's room/skittle alley.
🔥 🐎 ✿ ◖ ♿ P

Manton

Up The Garden Path
High Street (off A4)
☎ (0672) 512677
11.30–2.30; 6.30–11
Archers Best Bitter; Hook Norton Best Bitter; Wadworth 6X [H]
Cosy village inn with friendly landlord. As name implies, pub is approached by a steep path.
🔥 Q ✿ ◖ ◗ ♿ ♣ P

Marlborough

Green Dragon
High Street (A4)
☎ (0672) 512366
11–3; 6–11
Wadworth IPA, 6X, Old Timer [H]
Ancient building with busy bar on several levels. Bare brick walls and pottery. Popular with younger people eves. No food Sun eve. 🐎 ✿ 🛏 ◖ ◗

Try also: Lamb (Wadworth)

Marston Meysey

Spotted Cow Inn
2½ miles from A419/A417
☎ (0285) 810264
11–2.30; 6–11
Wadworth 6X; Whitbread Boddingtons Bitter [H]
Hospitable, Cotswold-stone country pub, once a farmhouse. Children welcome. Guest beers. Recommended food.
🔥 Q ✿ ◖ ◗ ♿ ♣ P

Norton

Vine Tree
100 yds E of ford on Foxley Road OS888846
☎ (0666) 837654
12–2.30; 6.30–11
Greene King Abbot Ale; Wadworth 6X [H]
Cosy remote pub offering a large menu. Young farmers Wed. Guest beers and house ale, Vine Tree Bitter.
🔥 ✿ ◖ ◗ ♿ ⛺ P

Oare

White Hart
On A345 ☎ (0672) 62273
11–2.30; 6.30–11
Wadworth IPA, 6X [H]
Typical old village pub, full of friendly locals. Fine choice of meals. 🔥 ✿ 🛏 ◖ ◗ ⊡ ♿ ♣ P

Potterne

George & Dragon
High Street (A360)
☎ (0380) 722139
12–2.30; 6.30–11
Wadworth IPA, 6X [H]
Coaching inn with Civil War connections, built by the Bishop of Salisbury circa 1500. Has own agricultural museum and licensed shooting gallery. Books for sale. No meals Mon.
Q ✿ 🛏 ◖ ◗ ♣

Poulshot

Raven
Poulshot Road (½ mile off A361)
☎ (0380) 828271
11–2.30; 6.15–11
Wadworth IPA, 6X, Old Timer [G]
Welcoming village pub with walled garden. A listed building from early 1700s. Wadworth's dray horses holiday home nearby! Deservedly popular.
🔥 ✿ ◖ ◗ ⊡ P

Redlynch

Apple Tree Inn
Orchard Road, Morgans Vale (off B3080) ☎ (0725) 20403
12–2.30 (3 Sat); 6–11
Draught Bass; Bunces Best Bitter; Wadworth 6X; Webster's Yorkshire Bitter [H]
16th-century thatched inn, originally a cider house. Small friendly public bar and cosy lounge, both with real fires. Small popular restaurant (no meals Sun/Mon eves). Guest beers. 🔥 Q ✿ ◖ ◗ ⊡ ⛺ ♣ P

Salisbury

Avon Brewery Inn
75 Castle Street
☎ (0722) 27280
11–2.30; 4.30–11 (11–11 Fri, Sat & summer)
Eldridge Pope Dorchester Bitter [E], **Thomas Hardy Country Bitter, Royal Oak** [H]
Former cider-house with splendid Victorian bow-front and riverside garden. Lunches (not Sun) are unusual and imaginative. Lively, eclectic clientele wins quizzes and loses rugby matches. Guest beers.
✿ ◖ ♿

George & Dragon
85 Castle Street
☎ (0722) 333942
11–11
Ruddles Best Bitter, County; Ushers Best Bitter [H]
Old town pub circa 1530, formerly a brothel. Long rear garden to river. Barbecues in summer; good food all year round. 🔥 Q ✿ ◖ ◗ ♣ 🍏

Haunch of Venison
Minster Street
☎ (0722) 22024
11–11
Courage Best Bitter, Directors [H]
Old-English chop house circa 1320. Busy city-centre pub with many historical and unusual features, including a mummified hand, pewter-topped bar and rows of taps formerly used to dispense fortified wines and spirits. No food Sun eve.
🔥 Q ◖ ◗ ⇌

Wyndham Arms
27 Estcourt Road (off Churchill Way east ring road)
☎ (0722) 28594
12–2.30 (not Mon–Thu); 4.30–11 (12–11 Sat)
Hop Back GFB, Special, Entire Stout, Summer Lightning [H]
Wiltshire's only pub-brewery. A pleasantly-refurbished Victorian corner pub with one bar and two adjoining rooms. Excellent value for money. ♣

Try also: Five Bells (Gibbs Mew); **Queens Arms** (Ushers)

Seend

Wiltshire

Bell
Bell Hill (A361 W of village)
☎ (0380) 828338
11–3; 6–11
Wadworth IPA, 6X [H]
Well-run roadside inn with former brewery at rear. Excellent, home-cooked lunches Mon–Sat (eve food planned).
⌂ ⚇ ⊛ ◖ ⊟ ▲ ♣ P

Sherston

Rattlebone Inn
Church Street (B4040)
☎ (0666) 840871
12–2.30; 7–11 (11–11 Sat)
Butcombe Bitter; Wadworth 6X [H]
Busy free house with a comfortable, foody lounge and a lively public bar with a range of pub games. Garden with boules pitch. Guest beers.
⌂ Q ⊛ ◖ ◗ ⊟ ♿ ♣ P

South Wraxall

Longs Arms
Upper South Wraxall (½ mile W of B3109) ☎ (022 16) 4450
12–2.30 (3 Sat); 5.30 (6.30 Sat)–11
Wadworth IPA, 6X, Old Timer [H]
Relaxed, friendly village pub with spacious comfortable lounge and snug locals' public bar. Good food. Occasional guest beers in summer. No meals Sun/Mon eves.
⌂ Q ⊛ ◖ ◗ ⊟ ♣ ◔ P

Steeple Ashton

Longs Arms
High Street (1 mile SE of A350)
☎ (0380) 870245
11–2.30; 6–11
Gibbs Mew Wiltshire Traditional Bitter, Salisbury Best [H]
Old coaching inn in pretty village. Bar once used as a magistrates' court. Shove-ha'penny played. Real fire in function room.
⌂ Q ⚇ ⊛ ◖ ◗ ⊟ ♣ ◔ P

Stibb Green

Three Horseshoes
On A346 ☎ (0672) 810324
11–3; 6–11
Wadworth IPA, 6X, Old Timer [H]
Pretty thatched pub with small, cosy beamed bar and tiny intimate lounge/diner. No food Sun eve. ⌂ ⊛ ◖ ◗ ⊟ ♣ P

Sutton Benger

Wellesley Arms
10 High Street (B4069)
☎ (0249) 720251
11–3; 6–11
Wadworth IPA, 6X, Old Timer [H]
All that an English pub should be: traditional log fire; good home-cooked food. Skittle alley.
⌂ Q ⊛ ◖ ◗ ⊟ ▲ ♣ P

Sutton Mandeville

Lancers Inn
On A30, 8 miles W of Salisbury ☎ (072 270) 220
11–3; 6–11
Fuller's London Pride; Wadworth 6X [H]
Large pub in quiet surroundings with good views of Fovant Badges on nearby hills. The large bar displays landlord's 'record' catch of trout. Skittle alley. Guest beers. Cider in summer.
⌂ ⚇ ⊛ ⊨ ◖ ◗ ▲ ♣ ◔ P

Swindon

Bakers Arms
Emlyn Square
☎ (0793) 535199
11–2.30; 7–11
Arkell's 2B Bitter, 3B Best Bitter [H]
Genuine, old-fashioned local in heart of the railway village. Traditional public bar and small cosy lounge. A rarity in Swindon. Q ⊛ ◖ ⊟ ♿ ≋ ♣

Beehive
55 Prospect Hill
☎ (0793) 523187
12–11
Morrells Dark, Varsity [H]
Unique, lively pub with bar on five levels. Just behind the college. Eve meals till 6.30 pm.
⌂ ◖ ◗ ♿ ≋ ♣

Glue Pot
5 Emlyn Square
☎ (0793) 523935
11–11
Archers Village Bitter, Best Bitter, ASB [H]
Imposing, listed stone building in Brunel's railway village. One carpeted and busy bar. Guest beers. ◖ ♿ ≋ ♣ P

Wheatsheaf
32 Newport Street
☎ (0793) 523188
11–3; 5.30–11
Wadworth IPA, 6X, Farmer's Glory, Old Timer [H]
Very busy two-bar inn. Bare boards in the public bar; comfortable lounge.
⊛ ⊨ ◖ ◗ ⊟ ♿ ♣

Tisbury

South Western Hotel
Station Road
☎ (0747) 870160
11–3; 6–11
Wiltshire Old Swan Mild, Stonehenge Bitter, Old Grumble, Old Devil [H]
Large old Victorian railway pub, 200 yards from the station and 400 yards from the Wiltshire Brewery. Country rambles start here. No food Thu eve.
⌂ ⊛ ⊨ ◖ ◗ ▲ ♣ P

Wanborough

Black Horse
Bishopstone Road (former B4507) ☎ (0793) 790305
11–3; 5.30–11 (11–11 Sat)
Arkell's 2B Bitter, 3B Best Bitter [H]
Cheerful, genuine village local. Garden has aviary, animals, children's games and fine views of the Vale of the White Horse. Annual British Day to coincide with Beaujolais Nouveau. Home-cooked lunches Mon–Sat.
⊛ ◖ ⊟ ▲ ♣ P

Try also: Calley Arms (Whitbread)

Warminster

Old Bell Hotel
42 Market Place
☎ (0985) 216611
10–3; 5.30–11
Draught Bass; Hall & Woodhouse Tanglefoot; Wadworth 6X [H]
Old coaching inn whose lunchtime business trade contrasts with younger evening clientele. Upstairs function room. ⊛ ⊨ ◖ ◗ ⊟ ≋ P

Westbury

Crown Inn
Market Place
☎ (0373) 822828
11–2.30; 5.30–11 (11–11 Sat)
Wadworth 6X, Farmer's Glory (summer), **Old Timer** [H]
Bustling small town local with good value food (not Sun or Mon/Tue eves).
⊛ ◖ ◗ ⊟ ♣ ◔ P

Ludlow Arms
3a Fore Street (A350)
☎ (0373) 822612
11–11
Hall & Woodhouse Badger Best Bitter, Tanglefoot [H]
Popular market place local with loud jukebox; live music most Suns. County cider; guest beers. No food Sun eve. ⚇ ⊛ ◖ ◗ ♣ ◔

Try also: Oak (Bass)

Whiteparish

Kings Head
The Street (A27)
☎ (0794) 884287
11–2.30 (3 Sat); 6–11
Whitbread Best Bitter, Strong Country Bitter [H] & [G]
Traditional, unspoilt village local with a friendly atmosphere. Good value food.
⌂ Q ⊛ ◖ ◗ ♣ ◔ P

Wilton

Bear Inn
12 West Street
☎ (0722) 742398
11–2.30; 5.30–11
Hall & Woodhouse Badger Best Bitter 🄷
Small 16th-century pub with one public bar. Quiet during week but noisy and busy at weekends. Ten minutes' walk from Wilton House and Wilton carpet factory. No food Sun.
⌂ ❀ ◖ ♣

Wingfield

Poplars
Shop Lane (400 yds S of A366/B3109 jct)
☎ (0225) 752426
11–2.30; 6 (4 Fri & Sat)–11 (11–11 summer)
Wadworth 6X, Farmer's Glory (summer), **Old Timer** 🄷
Delightful old country pub with its own cricket pitch and thriving team. No meals Sun in winter. ⌂ Q ❀ ◖ ◗ ⊟ ♿ ⛺ ♣ P

Winterbourne Monkton

New Inn
Off A4361 OS099723
☎ (067 23) 240
11–3; 6–11
Adnams Bitter; Wadworth 6X 🄷
Small, friendly village local near Avebury stone circle. Guest beers. ⌂ Q ❀ ⛟ ◖ ◗ ♿ ♣ P

Wootton Bassett

Old Nick
61 Station Road
☎ (0793) 848102
11–2.30; 6–11 (11–11 Fri & Sat)
Gibbs Mew Bishop's Tipple; Ind Coope Burton Ale; Tetley Bitter; Wadworth 6X, Old Timer 🄷
Formerly the police station, now an extensive bar with pool table. The adjoining courthouse is a disco-bar. Guest beers.
⌂ ❀ ◖ ◗ ⊟ ♿ ♣ P

Wroughton

Fox & Hounds
Markham Road
☎ (0793) 812217
11–3; 5.30–11
Arkell's 2B Bitter, 3B Best Bitter, Kingsdown Ale 🄷
Neat single-bar motel at top of the high street.
⌂ ❀ ⛟ ◖ ◗ ♿ ♣ P

Wadworth's Northgate Brewery, Devizes

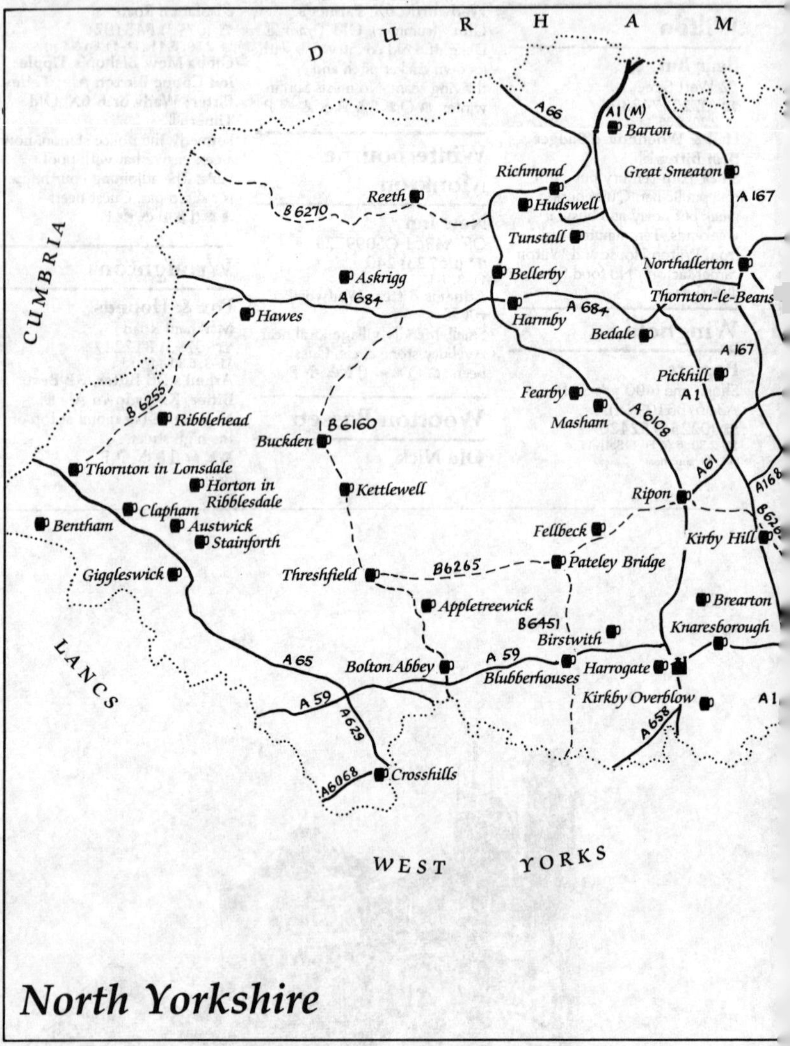

Big End, *Harrogate*; **Cropton**, *Cropton*; **Franklin's**, *Bilton*; **Malton**, *Malton*; **Marston Moor**, *Kirk Hammerton*; **North & East Riding**, *Scarborough*; **Selby**, *Selby*; **Samuel Smith**, *Tadcaster*; **Whitby's Own**, *Whitby*

Acaster Malbis

Ship Inn

Moor End ☎ (0904) 705609
11–3; 7–11 (11–11 summer)
Taylor Landlord; Tetley Mild, Bitter Ⓗ
17th-century coaching house overlooking the River Ouse at the edge of the village. Own mooring and fishing rights. Boat trips are laid on from York for bar meals. Excellent restaurant and marquee extension to cope with tourist overflow. Wed is quiz night. Children's play area in garden. 🏨 ❀ 🛏 ◐ ◑ ⛺ P

Appletreewick

Craven Arms

Main Street (white road between Barden Tower and Burnsall) ☎ (075672) 270
11.30–3; 6.30–11 (11–4; 6–11 summer)
Robinwood Old Fart; Tetley Bitter; Theakston Best Bitter, XB, Old Peculier Ⓗ
Typical Dales pub. Two rooms both have real fires, one in a

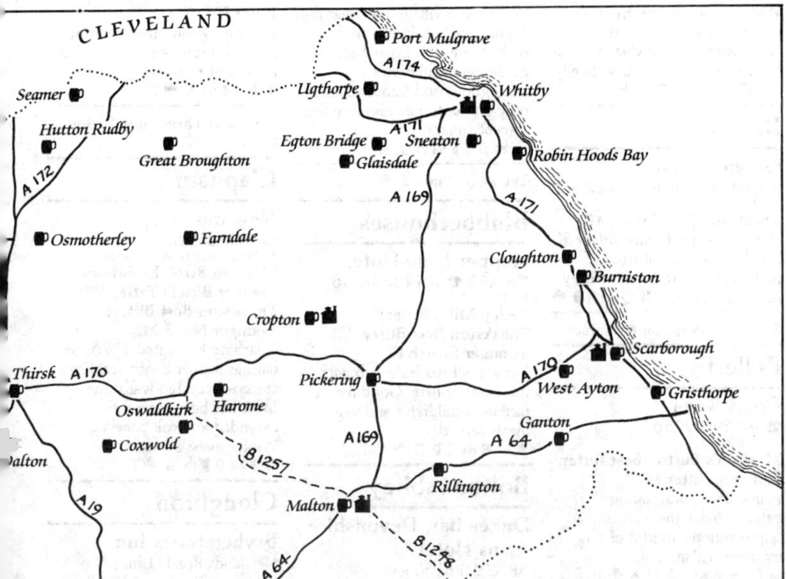

Yorkshire range. Menu caters for children and vegetarians. Camping in the village.
⌂ Q ♞ ⛫ ◐ ▭ ⛺ ♣ ◌ P

New Inn
Main Street (white road between Barden Tower and Burnsall) ☎ (075 672) 252
11.30–3; 6.30 (7 winter)–11
John Smith's Bitter; Younger Scotch Bitter, No. 3 Ⓗ
Friendly welcome in a pub comprised of an L-shaped bar and another separate room. Bottled beers include a large range of foreign brews.
⌂ Q ♞ ⛫ ⛟ ◐ ⛺ ♣ ◌ P

Askrigg

Kings Arms
Off A684 ☎ (0969) 50258
11–3; 6.30–11
McEwan 80/-; Younger No. 3 Ⓗ
A truly English blend of informality and elegance in a small country hotel.
⌂ Q ♞ ⛫ ⛟ ◐ ▭ ♣ P

Try also: Crown

Austwick

Game Cock
☎ (046 85) 226
varies lunchtime; 6–11
Thwaites Bitter Ⓗ
Old-fashioned little bar, conservatory and restaurant. No food winter Mon.
⌂ Q ⛫ ⛟ ◐ ♣ P

Barton

King William IV
1 Silver Street
☎ (032 577) 256
11.30–3 (11–4 Sat); 6.30–11
John Smith's Bitter, Magnet Ⓗ
Roadside local with one large bar and a snug just separate. Children welcome until 9pm. Quoits played. No food Tue; eve meals only in summer.
⌂ ♞ ⛫ ◐ ⛺ ♣ P

Beal

Kings Head
Main Street ☎ (0977) 673487
12–3 (Fri & Sat); 7–11
Tetley Bitter Ⓗ

With its 'time-warp' front bar and numerous rooms, this pub really is the hub of village life in the evenings. In the same family for 47 years. ♣ P

Bedale

Green Dragon
Market Place ☎ (0677) 22902
11–3; 6–11
Theakston Best Bitter, XB; Webster's Yorkshire Bitter [H]
Popular main bar at front of building now supplemented by restaurant at rear. Q ♣

Try also: Waggon & Horses

Bellerby

Cross Keys
☎ (0969) 22256
11–3; 5.30–11
Marston's Burton Best Bitter, Pedigree Bitter [H]
A deceptive, uninspiring exterior hides the warm, unpretentious interior of this excellent village pub.
Q ▲ ♣ P

Bentham

Horse & Farrier
Main Street ☎ (05242) 61381
11–11 (11–4; 6–11 Mon, Tue & Thu)
Theakston Best Bitter, XB; Whitbread Boddingtons Bitter; Younger Scotch [H]
Single large bar incorporating a games area, a cosy nook around an old cast-iron fireplace and a fish tank. ♣ P

Punch Bowl
Low Bentham (B6480, W end of village) ☎ (05242) 61344
11.30–2.30; 6–11
Mitchell's Best Bitter [H]
18th-century, old-time village inn. Extended in 1986 into barn to form restaurant (open weekends). Small neat rooms remain. No food Mon. Angling available. Q ♣ P

Try also: Sun Dial (Thwaites)

Birstwith

Station Inn
500 yds N of bridge over River Nidd ☎ (0423) 770254
11.30–3 (12–2.30 Sun); 6.30–11
Tetley Mild, Bitter [H]
Old converted railway station, with one bar serving as a large lounge, two smaller areas and a snug. Q P

Bishopthorpe

Ebor Inn
46 Main Street
☎ (0904) 706190
11–3.30; 5.30–11 (11–11 Sat)
Samuel Smith OBB, Museum Ale [H]
Welcoming village pub near the Archbishop's Palace, popular with race-goers. Large beer garden with children's play area; good food (sandwiches only on Sun); quiz night on Sun (except summer).
Q ♿ ▲ ♣ P

Try also: Marcia (Bass)

Blubberhouses

Hopper Lane Hotel
On A59 ☎ (094388) 246
11–11
Tetley Mild, Bitter; Theakston Best Bitter, XB; Younger Scotch [H]
Stone-built roadside pub with rural atmosphere. Good family facilities; children's and veg meals served.
♣ P

Bolton Abbey

Dukes Bar, Devonshire Arms Hotel
At A59/B6160 jct
☎ (075671) 441
11–3; 5.30–11 (11–11 summer)
Franklin's Bitter; Tetley Bitter; Younger Scotch [H]
Comfortable public bar, busy in summer. Handy for Bolton Abbey and riverside walks. Regular guest beers.
♿ ▲ ♣ P

Brearton

Malt Shovel
Just off B6165
☎ (0423) 862929
12–3 (not Mon); 6.30–11
Big End Piston Bitter; Old Mill Traditional Bitter; Theakston Best Bitter, XB [H]
16th-century pub with stone walls and original oak beams. Enjoys a reputation for good food (no meals Mon).
Q ♿ ♣ P

Buckden

Buck Inn
☎ (075676) 227
11–3; 6–11
Marston Moor (various); **Tetley Bitter; Theakston Old Peculier; Younger Scotch, No. 3** [H]
Imposing village hostelry in excellent walking area. Retains an unspoilt bar room. Regular Marston Moor beers in rotation. Games include bar skittles.
♿ ▲ ♣ P

Burniston

Oak Wheel Inn
Coastal Road
☎ (0723) 870230
11.30–3; 6.30–11
Camerons Traditional Bitter [H]
Friendly two-roomer, catering for both locals and visitors, with a pleasant restaurant upstairs.
▲ ♣ P

Try also: Three Jolly Sailors (Bass)

Clapham

New Inn
☎ (04685) 203
11.30–3; 7–11 (supper licence)
McEwan 80/-; Moorhouse's Premier Bitter; Tetley Bitter; Theakston Best Bitter; Younger No. 3 [H]
Coaching inn, dated 1776: one bar has leather bench seats and stucco-decorated walls: the other has been recently extended and oak-panelled. Winter guest beers.
♿ ▲ ♣ P

Cloughton

Bryherstones Inn
Newlands Road (1 mile N of village on Ravenscar Road) OS010959 ☎ (0723) 870744
11.30–3; 6.30–11 (supper licence until 12)
Camerons Traditional Bitter; Younger Scotch, No. 3 [H]
Popular country pub where families are welcome in the lower room, especially during the day. Lively in the evenings.
▲ ♣ P

Try also: Blacksmiths (Bass)

Colton

Olde Sun Inn
Main Street ☎ (0904) 84261
11–3; 7–11 (may extend in summer)
Draught Bass; Stones Best Bitter [H]
17th-century inn, set in a picturesque village: three lounges and one bar provide a cosy local atmosphere. Pleasant outdoor drinking areas.
Q ♣ P

Coxwold

Fauconberg Arms
Three miles S of A170
☎ (03476) 214
11–3; 6–11
Tetley Bitter; Theakston Best Bitter; Younger Scotch [H]
In an idyllic setting on the main street of a lovely village, this beautifully-appointed old inn and restaurant is generally busy but packed at mealtimes.
♣ P

Cropton

New Inn
Rosedale turn from A170 at Wrelton OS756890
☎ (07515) 330

12–2.30; 7–11 (11–3; 5.30–11 summer)
Cropton Two Pints Bitter, Special Strong Bitter; Tetley Mild, Bitter H
A brew pub producing distinctive beers using local malt and well water. Children are welcome in the large garden and well-equipped family room. Large lounge with separate restaurant and pool room.
P

Crosshills

Dalesway Inn
Skipton Road (A629)
(0535) 33618
11–3.30; 5–11 (11–11 Fri & Sat)
Bass Light 5 Star, Draught Bass; Stones Best Bitter H
Popular village pub on busy road between Keighley and Skipton. Spacious, cosy atmosphere in a clean and comfortable open-plan, three-room pub. Tap room offers pool, darts and dominoes. Good value food — try the Dalesway Special. P

Dalton

Jolly Farmers of Olden Times
Between A19 and A1, near Thirsk and just S of A168 OS431762 (0845) 577359
11–2.30 (4 Sat, not Thu); 7.30–11
Ruddles Best Bitter; Webster's Choice H
200 year-old beamed village pub with comfortable lounge area, quiet bar, games room and small restaurant. Book for bargain three-course Sun lunches. Regular guest beers.
P

Drax

Huntsmen
Main Street (0757) 618080
11–11
Taylor Bitter; Tetley Bitter; Theakston Best Bitter, XB, Old Peculier H
Traditionally laid-out pub, somewhat opened-out, but retaining several rooms. Occasional live music, usually country and western. Eve meals served until 8pm (not Sat/Sun).
P

Egton Bridge

Horseshoe Hotel
7½ miles W of Whitby, ½ mile from station OS801054
(0947) 85245
11–3 (varies in summer); 6.30–11
Tetley Bitter; Theakston Best Bitter, XB, Old Peculier H
Large hotel by the River Esk standing in its own grounds. Ideal for walkers and salmon fishers (reserve tickets well in advance). Famous gooseberry show in August.
Q P

Postgate
7½ miles W of Whitby OS805054 (0947) 85241
11–11 (11–3; 7–11 winter)
Camerons Traditional Bitter, Strongarm H
Attractive hotel overlooking the rustic railway station. Menu caters for children and vegetarians. Quoits played.
Q P

Farndale

Feversham Arms
Church Houses (7 miles N of Kirkbymoorside) OS669974
(075 133) 206
11–3; 5.30 (7 winter)–11
Tetley Bitter H
Inn set in a tiny hamlet in the North Yorks moors. Popular with walkers, the bar has stone-flagged floor, cast iron range and ceiling hooks once used for curing hams. Good value food.
P

Fearby

Kings Head
Fearby Cross (W of Masham off A6108) (0765) 89448
12–3 (weekends only in winter); 7 (8 winter)–11
Theakston Best Bitter, Old Peculier H
Small, unspoilt pub known locally as the 'Cross'.
Q P

Fellbeck

Half Moon
On B6265 (0423) 711568
12–3; 6.30–11
Taylor Landlord; Theakston Best Bitter; Younger Scotch H
Pleasant roadside inn, close to the local beauty spot of Brimham Rocks. Traditional bar and large sunny lounge.
Q P

Ganton

Greyhound Inn
(0944) 70116
11–3; 7–11
Tetley Bitter H
A welcome haven from the maelstrom of the A64. Close to the championship golf course and the Wolds Way. Very much a food pub. P

Giggleswick

Black Horse Hotel
Church Street
(07292) 2506
12–3; 6.30–11
Taylor Best Bitter; Tetley Bitter; Younger Scotch H
Secluded, family-run, 17th-century hotel. Q (Settle) P

Glaisdale

Anglers Rest
Off A171 OS779053
(0947) 87261
11–3; 7–11 (varies in summer)
Tetley Bitter; Theakston Best Bitter, Old Peculier H
Friendly old hilltop pub formerly called the Three Blast Furnaces. Live music.
P

Great Broughton

Jet Miners
High Street (0642) 712427
11.30–3.30; 7–11
Theakston XB; Younger IPA H
Very old pub, originally associated with the area's jet mining industry. Extensively-modernised to provide improved facilities for food, on which there is a strong emphasis (veg option). Menu offers children's dishes; the garden features a bouncy castle.
P

Great Smeaton

Bay Horse
On A167 (060981) 466
12–3 (not Mon & Tue); 6.30–11
Courage Directors; John Smith's Bitter H
Small free house in middle of a row of roadside cottages. Two linked rooms, functional bar and soft-furnished lounge. Guest beers.

Try also: Grange Arms, Hornby (Free)

Gristhorpe

Bull Inn
(0723) 512359
11.30–4; 7–11
Younger Scotch, IPA, No. 3 H
Enlarged old village local specialising in home-cooked food. Children, five years and over, welcome for meals.
P

Try also: Grapes, Filey (John Smith's)

Harmby

Pheasant
(0969) 22223
11–3; 6–11
Tetley Bitter H
Popular rural inn at gateway to Wensleydale. Q P

Harome

North Yorkshire

Star Inn
Main Street (off A170 3 miles SE of Helmsley)
☎ (0439) 70397
11.45–3; 5.45–11
Camerons Traditional Bitter; Taylor Landlord; Tetley Bitter; Theakston Best Bitter, Old Peculier 🄷
Old thatched inn with comfortable lounge bar. Restaurant offers excellent, if pricey, meals; veg option, no food Mon. Coffee lounge upstairs with backgammon, trivial pursuit, etc.
⌂ ❀ ◖ ◗ ♿ ▲ ♣ P

Harrogate

Coach & Horses
16 West Park (A61)
☎ (0423) 568371
11–11
John Smith's Bitter 🄷
A welcoming pub within easy walk of the town centre, commanding an excellent view over the 'Stray'. No lunches on Sun. ◖ ⊟ ♿ ≹ ♣

Dragon
Skipton Road (A5, 1½ miles from centre) ☎ (0423) 503405
11–11
John Smith's Bitter 🄷
Very popular, large corner local with roomy lounge and smaller, wood-panelled snug.
❀ ◖ ⊟ ♿ ♣ P

Hales Bar
1 Crescent Road
☎ (0423) 569861
11–11
Draught Bass; Stones Best Bitter 🄷
A gem in the true sense of the word. A gas-lit lounge, with unusual gas cigar lighters, adds to the excellent atmosphere.
Q ◖ ⊟ ♿

Muckles
11 West Park
☎ (0423) 504463
11–3; 5–11 (11–11 Sat)
Tetley Bitter 🄷
Busy pub within easy walking distance of the town centre, next to the 'Stray'. ◖ ⊟ ≹ ♣ P

Tap & Spile
31 Tower Street (between West Park Stray and town centre)
☎ (0423) 526785
11.30–3; 5–11 (11–11 Fri & Sat)
Camerons Strongarm 🄷
Traditionally-furnished pub: three rooms with exposed brick and stonework, wooden floors and furnishings. Up to ten constantly-changing guest beers; a mecca for real ale drinkers. Note: no disabled access to ladies WC. Next to municipal car park.
❀ ◖ ⊟ ♿ ≹ ♣

Woodlands
Wetherby Road (at major crossroads 1½ miles from centre)
☎ (0423) 883396
11.30–3; 5.30–11
Ruddles Best Bitter; Webster's Yorkshire Bitter, Choice 🄷
Spacious open-plan bar and conservatory with unusual ceiling. Handy for the Great Yorkshire Showground.
❀ ◖ ♿ ♣ P

Try also: West Park Hotel (Tetley)

Hawes

Board Hotel
Market Place ☎ (09697) 223
11–3; 6–11
Marston's Burton Best Bitter, Pedigree Bitter 🄷
Upstanding mid 19th-century stone frontage and a modernised interior which retains an unpretentious market pub atmosphere.
⌂ Q ❀ ◖ ◗ ⊟ ▲ ♣

Try also: Crown

Haxby

Tiger Inn
29 The Village
☎ (0904) 768355
11–2.30 (4 Fri & Sat); 6–11
Samuel Smith OBB 🄷
Friendly two-roomed local in one of York's commuter villages. A wide difference in character between the lounge and tap room, but always busy. No food Sat/Sun. Q ◖ ⊟ ♣ P

Heslington

Deramore Arms
Main Street ☎ (0904) 413433
11–3; 5.30–11 (11–11 Fri & Sat)
Tetley Bitter 🄷
Friendly two-roomed pub near York University. The pleasant wood-panelled lounge is popular with students; locals use public bar. ❀ ◖ ⊟ ♣ P

Horton in Ribblesdale

Golden Lion
☎ (07296) 206
11.30–3 (4 summer); 7 (6 summer)–11 (11.30–11 Sat)
Tetley Mild, Bitter; Younger Scotch, No. 3 🄷
Many-roomed village pub in ideal position for Pennine Way and Three Peaks walkers. Campsite in village.
☋ ❀ ⊨ ◖ ◗ ⊟ ▲ ≹ ♣ P

Hudswell

George & Dragon
2 miles SW of Richmond
☎ (0748) 3082
11–3; 6–11
Webster's Yorkshire Bitter, Choice 🄷
Well worth seeking out: locals' bar on right; small room on left. Fine views to rear.
⌂ Q ♞ ☋ ❀ ◖ ◗ ⊟ ▲ ♣ P

Hutton Rudby

Kings Head
36 North Side
☎ (0642) 700342
12–3; 6.30–11
Camerons Traditional Bitter, Strongarm 🄷
Warm, friendly pub with a very strong local following, but welcoming to visitors. Combined lounge/bar with small snug. All pubs in Hutton Rudby sell real ale. ⌂ Q ☋ ❀ ♣

Kettlewell

Kings Head
☎ (075 676) 242
11.30–3; 6–11 (11–11 summer)
Taylor Landlord; Tetley Mild, Bitter 🄷
Fine three-storey building tucked away in heart of village. Opened-out interior retains inglenook and bench seating. Separate room for families, or for dining, on request. Breakfast served to campers.
⌂ ☋ ❀ ⊨ ◖ ◗ ♿ ▲ ♣ P

Kirby Hill

Shoulder of Mutton
☎ (0748) 2772
12–3 (not Mon); 7–11
Ruddles County; Theakston Best Bitter; Webster's Choice 🄷
Fine country pub in a beautiful hillside setting overlooking Lower Teesdale and the ruins of Ravensworth Castle. Small, friendly front bar, pool room and restaurant (closed Sun/Mon eves). Mon eve sing-along! ⌂ Q ❀ ⊨ ◖ ◗ ⊟ ♣ P

Kirkby Overblow

Shoulder of Mutton
Main Street ☎ (0423) 871205
12–3; 6.15–11
Tetley Mild, Bitter 🄷
Pleasantly-furnished, stone-built village inn with a through lounge and bar. ⌂ ❀ ◖ ◗ ♿ ▲ P

Kirk Hammerton

Crown Inn
Station Road
☎ (0423) 330341
12–3 (not Mon–Fri, or Sat in winter); 7.30–11
Marston Moor Cromwell Bitter, Brewers Pride, Porter, Brewers Droop 🄷
Old village pub with strong angling connections — close to

River Nidd (special Sun hours for anglers 8–10; 4–6). Pleasant outlet for Marston Moor ales, brewed in outbuildings to the rear of the pub. Lunches served Sat/Sun only. ⌂ Q ⚈ ◖ ◗ ⊕ ▲ ♣ P

Knaresborough

Groves
Market Place
☎ (0423) 863022
11–11
Theakston Best Bitter Ⓗ
18th-century pub dominating the corner of an historic market place. ◖ ⊕ ▲ ≢ ♣

Marquis of Granby
31 York Place
☎ (0423) 862207
11.30–3 (4 Wed); 7–11
Samuel Smith OBB Ⓗ
Built at the turn of the century: two bars, recently sympathetically-renovated in Victorian style.
⌂ Q ⚈ ◖ ⊕ ♿ ▲ ≢ ♣ P

Mitre
Station Road
☎ (0423) 863589
11–11
Tetley Bitter; Theakston Bitter, XB Ⓗ
Large and inviting pub/hotel alongside station, with bistro bar and large comfortable lounge. Regular guest beer.
⚈ ⛟ ◖ ◗ ▲ ≢ ♣ P

Old Royal Oak
7 Market Place
☎ (0423) 863139
11–11
John Smith's Bitter Ⓗ
Prominently-situated in the market square. Live music Wed lunch and Sat eve. Eve meals summer only. ⛟ ◖ ◗ ▲ ≢ ♣ P

Wellington
23 Briggate ☎ (0423) 862582
Hours vary
Samuel Smith OBB, Museum Ale (summer) Ⓗ
Friendly locals' pub with genial atmosphere. Good value lunches. ◖ ⊕ ▲ ≢ ♣ P

Malton

Blue Ball
14 Newbiggin
☎ (0653) 692236
11–2.30; 5.30–11 (11–11 Tue, Fri & Sat)
Draught Bass; Stones Best Bitter; Tetley Bitter Ⓗ
A multi-roomed symphony in brown featuring good food (veg option) and guest beers.
Q ⚈ ◖ ◗ ≢ P

Crown Hotel (Suddaby's)
12 Wheelgate
☎ (0653) 692038
11–3 (4 Sat); 5.30 (6.30 Sat)–11 (11–11 Fri)
Malton Pale Ale, Double Chance Bitter, Pickwick's Porter, Owd Bob Ⓗ
A neat hotel offering a full range of local beers. The functional bar is complemented by a conservatory-style extension where children are welcome. Guest beers. Menu includes three veg options, but eve meals only for residents.
⌂ Q ♉ ⛟ ◖ ◗ ≢ ♣ P

Masham

Bay Horse
Silver Street ☎ (0765) 89236
11–11
John Smith's Bitter; Tetley Bitter; Theakston Best Bitter, XB, Old Peculier Ⓗ
Typical market town pub with friendly atmosphere. Popular public bar; separate comfortable lounge with raised dining area.
⌂ ⚈ ⛟ ◖ ◗ ⊕ ♣ ⊖

Northallerton

County Arms
219a High Street
☎ (0609) 70610
11–3; 7–11
John Smith's Bitter; Tetley Bitter Ⓗ
A relatively new public house which has quickly built up a strong reputation for the quality of its beer. ◖ ≢ ♣

Osbaldwick

Derwent Arms
2 miles E of York centre, off A1079, Hull Road
☎ (0904) 413498
11–11
Draught Bass; Stones Best Bitter Ⓗ
Pleasantly-situated in an old village, now a suburb of York. Large, comfortable lounge and smaller bar. Good value lunches.
⚈ ◖ ⊕ ♣ P

Osmotherley

Golden Lion
☎ (060983) 526
11–3; 6–11
John Smith's Bitter Ⓗ
Candles and fresh flowers help create an intimate atmosphere. Children welcome at lunchtime only. ⌂ ♉ ⚈ ◖ ◗ ⊕ ▲ ♣ P

Three Tuns
South End ☎ (060 983) 301
12–4; 7–11 (may open all day)
McEwan 80/-; Theakston Best Bitter, Old Peculier; Younger Scotch, No. 3 Ⓗ
Very old pub, dating back to Tudor times, with a homely atmosphere. Deservedly-popular; well placed to service the needs of long distance walkers (campsite nearby).
⌂ Q ♉ ⚈ ◖ ◗ ⊕ ▲ P

Oswaldkirk

Malt Shovel
Off B1363 ☎ (043 93) 461
11–2.30; 6.30–11
Samuel Smith OBB Ⓗ
Beautifully-restored interior with 17th-century staircase and imposing, large, open fire; warm and welcoming. No food Mon.
⌂ ♉ ⚈ ⛟ ◖ ◗

Pateley Bridge

Crown Hotel
19 High Street (B6265)
☎ (0423) 711348
11–3; 6 (7 winter)–11 (11–11 Sat)
John Smith's Bitter Ⓗ
Popular and friendly small hotel on main street of delightful village in beautiful Upper Nidderdale. Open-plan double lounge area with central servery and adjoining restaurant (veg option). ⌂ ⛟ ◖ ◗ ▲ ♣

Pickering

Black Swan Hotel
Birdgate ☎ (0751) 72286
10.30–11
John Smith's Bitter, Magnet Ⓗ
An old coaching inn, now catering for visitors and locals in the town centre. Children welcome in restaurant.
⌂ ⛟ ◖ ◗ ♣ P

Station Hotel
Park Street ☎ (0751) 72171
11–11
Younger Scotch, IPA Ⓗ
A popular two-roomed pub, opposite the station. Games-oriented bar and comfortable lounge. Complemented by a separate restaurant where children may dine.
⌂ ⚈ ⛟ ◖ ◗ ⊕ ♣ P

Pickhill

Nags Head
2 miles off A1
☎ (0845) 567391
10.30–2.30; 5.30–11
Tetley Bitter; Theakston Best Bitter, XB, Old Peculier, Younger Scotch Ⓗ
Restaurant and accommodation of a high standard. Good local following in the public bar.
⌂ Q ♉ ⚈ ⛟ ◖ ◗ ⊕ ♣ P

Port Mulgrave

Ship Inn
20 Rosedale Lane (off A174 Staithes-Hinderwell road)
OS793188 ☎ (0947) 840303
11–11
Tetley Bitter; Younger No. 3 Ⓗ

North Yorkshire

Old terraced pub, a quarter of a mile from high cliffs on Cleveland Way. Caters for children. ⛫ Q ♞ 🛏 ◖ ◗ ⛺ ♣

Try also: Ellerby Hotel

Reeth

Buck Inn

☎ (0748) 84210
11–3; 6–11
Webster's Yorkshire Bitter, Choice Ⓗ
Imposing hotel on a road junction overlooking the village green. ⛫ Q ⛁ 🛏 ◖ ◗ ♣ P

Ribblehead

Station

☎ (05242) 41274
11–3; 7–11 (11–11 Sat in summer)
Marston's Pedigree Bitter; Tetley Bitter Ⓗ
Stands next to famous and now safeguarded viaduct. Most trade is car-borne trippers. Two bars with parquet floor and beamed ceiling. Two bunkhouses provide basic accommodation. ⛫ ♞ ⛁ 🛏 ⛺ ⇌ ♣ P

Richmond

Black Lion Hotel

Finkle Street (just off market place) ☎ (0748) 3121
11–11
Camerons Strongarm; Everards Old Original Ⓗ
Warm, friendly public bar; no-smoking lounge; restaurant upstairs. ⛫ Q ♞ 🛏 ◖ ◗ ♣ P

Holly Hill Inn

Top of Sleagill OS172003
☎ (0748) 5171/2192
11–11
Theakston Best Bitter, XB, Old Peculier; Younger Scotch Ⓗ
Pub with a great enthusiasm for traditional beer. Q ⛁ ◖ ⊞ ♣ P

Try also: Turf Tavern

Rillington

Coach & Horses

Low Moorgate
☎ (09442) 373
11–3; 6–11
McEwan 80/-; Younger Scotch Ⓗ
A popular pub, situated prominently on the A64, featuring good food in the cat-bedecked, two-roomed interior. Children very welcome in restaurant and garden.
⛁ ◖ ◗ ⊞ ⛺ ♣ P

Ripon

One Eyed Rat

Allhallowgate
☎ (0765) 707704
12–3 (Fri & Sat); 5–11
Big End Piston Bitter; Taylor Landlord Ⓗ
A small terraced pub, very popular with students. Four guest beers. ⛫ ⛁ ♣

Station

North Road (A61, ¾ mile from centre) ☎ (0765) 2140
11–11
Tetley Mild, Bitter Ⓗ
Large three-roomed pub with traditional decor and a friendly atmosphere.
Q ⛁ 🛏 ◖ ◗ ⊞ ♿ ⛺ ♣ P

Water Rat

Bondgate Green (off B6265)
☎ (0765) 5521
11–3; 6.30–11
Big End Yorkshire Rose Bitter, Old Lubrication; Marston's Pedigree Bitter; Old Mill Traditional Bitter Ⓗ
A riverside pub with patio, overlooking the weir and with a splendid view of the cathedral. Wildlife abounds. Home-cooked fare includes veg option. Guest beers. Q ♞ ⛁ ◖ ◗

Wheatsheaf

Harrogate Road (A61 S of city)
☎ (0765) 2410
11–3; 6–11
Vaux Samson; Wards Sheffield Best Bitter Ⓗ
Old inn with intricate carving. Sunken garden with peacocks.
⛫ Q ♞ ⛁

Robin Hoods Bay

Laurel Inn

☎ (0947) 880400
12–3; 7.30–11 (11.30–3 (may vary); 7–11 summer)
Theakston Best Bitter, XB, Old Peculier Ⓗ
Small, friendly local in picturesque cliffside village. Guest beers available, but not usually in holiday season.
⛫ Q ♞ ⛁ 🛏 ♣

Victoria Hotel

Station Road
☎ (0947) 880205
11–3; 6.30–11
Camerons Traditional Bitter, Strongarm; Everards Old Original Ⓗ
Large hotel, built in 1897, with imposing garden views over village and bay. Family room with pool table recently added.
⛫ ♞ ⛁ 🛏 ◖ ◗ ⊞ ⛺ P

Try also: Bay Hotel

Rufforth

Tankard

Wetherby Road (B1224)
☎ (090483) 621
11–3; 6–11 (11–11 Sat)
Samuel Smith OBB Ⓗ
Popular two-room village local with large children's play area at rear. Recently-redecorated but still maintaining its original character. No meals Sun eve or Mon lunch. ⛫ ⛁ ◖ ◗ ♣ P

Saxton

Greyhound

☎ (093 781) 7202
11–3; 6–11 (11–11 Sat)
Samuel Smith OBB Ⓗ
Splendid, small village pub with unspoilt decor. Three small rooms have stone flags and beams. Casks are mounted on gantries behind the bar. Food available Mar–Oct only.
⛫ Q ♞ ⛁ ◖ ♣ P

Scarborough

Alma Inn

Alma Parade (3 mins' walk from station) ☎ (0723) 385587
11–3 (4.30 Fri & Sat); 6.30–11
Tetley Mild, Bitter; Younger Scotch, IPA, No. 3 Ⓗ
Traditional free house with eyecatching exterior. Pleasant, snug drinking alcoves around one semi-circular bar. Collection of old typewriters. Lunchtime bar snacks (not Sun). ⛫ ⛁ ⇌

Black Lion

North Street (off Westborough)
☎ (0723) 360744
11–3; 7–11
Camerons Traditional Bitter, Strongarm Premium Ⓗ
Friendly pub, just off main shopping precinct, popular with locals and shoppers alike. Family room; folk club Mon. Only outlet in town for Strongarm Premium. Eve meals in summer only; menu caters for children and vegetarians.
Q ♞ 🛏 ◖ ◗ ♿ ⇌ ♣

Highlander

15 The Esplanade (on South Cliff) ☎ (0723) 365627
11–11
Wm Clark's Thistle Mild, Bitter, EXB, 68; Tetley Bitter; Younger IPA Ⓗ
Large hotel with public bar, overlooking the South Bay. Its distinctive Scottish flavour is enhanced by a huge whisky collection. Wm Clark's beers from own (North and East Riding) brewery, situated behind the hotel. ⛫ Q ⛁ 🛏 ◖ ⇌

Hole in the Wall

26 Vernon Road
☎ (0723) 373746
11.30–2.30 (3 Sat); 7–11
Malton Double Chance Bitter; Theakston Best Bitter, XB, Old Peculier Ⓗ
Thriving ale house, just off the town centre. Guest beers always available. No food Sun (veg option). Q ◖ ⊞ ⇌ ♣

Leeds Arms

St Mary's Street (Old Town)

☎ (0723) 361699
11.30–3; 7–11
Draught Bass 🄷
Subdued old town gem with a nautical atmosphere.

New Tavern
131 Falsgrave Road (A170/A64)
☎ (0723) 366965
11–3; 5–11
Camerons Traditional Bitter, Strongarm 🄷
A popular two-roomed local away from the town centre in a busy shopping area.

Spa Hotel
Victoria Road
☎ (0723) 372907
11–3; 5.30–11
Tetley Mild, Bitter 🄷
Games-oriented, popular local: a typical 'Tetley-style' town-centre pub. Basic lunchtime bar snacks, with chips!

Trafalgar
Trafalgar Street West (5 mins from Columbus Ravine/ Northway roundabout)
☎ (0723) 372054
11–11
Camerons Traditional Bitter, Strongarm 🄷
Smart, busy, games-oriented local attracts a wide clientele, especially at weekends. Note the large picture of the famous battle in lounge.

Seamer

Kings Head
12 Hilton Road
☎ (0642) 710397
12–3 (not Mon–Fri); 7–11
McEwan 80/-; Theakston XB; Younger Scotch 🄷
Cosy and popular, traditional pub. Bar, lounge and tap room are arranged around central bar. Family room unsuitable for small children. Q P

Selby

Abbey Vaults
James Street (100 yds from Minster) ☎ (0757) 702857
10–4; 6.30–11
Mansfield Riding Dark Mild, Riding Traditional Bitter 🄷
Modern town-centre pub with separate games room.
P

New Inn
Gowthorpe ☎ (0757) 703429
11–11 (11–3; 5.30–11 Tue & Wed)
Tetley Mild, Bitter 🄷
Typical town pub in heritage listed building. The separate wood-panelled smoke room has a bowed and glazed serving hatch. Q

Shipton

Dawnay Arms
On A19 ☎ (0904) 470334
11.30–2.30; 6–11
Camerons Traditional Bitter, Strongarm 🄷
Quiet roadhouse renowned for its good food (not Wed). Plush lounge with two basic side rooms. P

Sneaton

Wilson Arms
Beacon Way
☎ (0947) 602552
12–3; 7–11 (may vary in summer)
Theakston Best Bitter, XB, Old Peculier 🄷
Background music can be turned off on request. Quoits played. Menu caters for children and vegetarians. P

Stainforth

Craven Heifer
Off B6479 ☎ (07292) 2599
11–3; 6.30 (5.30 summer)–11
Thwaites Best Mild, Bitter 🄷
Welcoming village pub with a variety of rooms. Handy for limestone country and Catrigg Force waterfall.
P

Stamford Bridge

Three Cups
York Road (A166)
☎ (0759) 71396
11–2.30; 6.30 (6 summer)–11
Draught Bass; Stones Best Bitter 🄷
The site of an inn since 1215. Open-plan interior, with a wishing well visible through glass portholes in the bar. The carvery restaurant attracts much out-of-town trade. Large outdoor drinking area to rear is safe for children.
P

Stutton

Hare & Hounds
Manor Road
☎ (0937) 833164
11.30–3.30; 6.30–11
Samuel Smith OBB 🄷
At the village centre: a large, comfortable lounge bar, popular with both locals and passing trade. Gourmet menu changes daily; children's meals and veg option. Leave room for pud!
P

Sutton upon Derwent

St Vincent Arms
7 miles E of York on B1228
☎ (090485) 349
12–3; 7–11
Courage Directors; John Smith's Bitter, Magnet 🄷
Attractive, timber-framed village inn near River Derwent. Cosy bars and separate restaurant (veg option). Regular guest beers. Q P

Tadcaster

Angel & White Horse
1 Bridge Street
☎ (0937) 835470
11–2.30; 5 (7 Sat)–11
Samuel Smith OBB, Museum Ale (winter) 🄷
The Sam Smith's brewery tap, in a former coaching inn. Large bar with fine wood panelling. Views of the brewery yard at rear. No food Sat.

Thirsk

Olde Three Tuns
15 Finkle Street (just off market place) ☎ (0845) 23291
11–3; 6–11
Tetley Bitter 🄷
A 16th-century pub which has undergone complete but sympathetic restoration. No food Sun. P

Thixendale

Cross Keys
Just off main road
☎ (0377) 88272
11.30–3.30 (not Mon in winter); 6–11
Tetley Bitter 🄷
One-roomed traditional village local with cheerful and welcoming atmosphere, on the Wolds Way. Local game features on the menu in season. There is a youth hostel in the village.

Thornton in Lonsdale

Marton Arms
Off A65/A687 jct
☎ (05242) 41281
12–11
Theakston Best Bitter; Webster's Yorkshire Bitter; Younger Scotch 🄷
Pre-turnpike coaching inn, dated 1679 but reputedly older. Large, comfortable, oak-beamed lounge; good home-cooking. Serves up to 12 guest beers.
P

Thornton-le-Beans

Crosby
Off A168 ☎ (0609) 772776
11–3 (not Tue in winter); 6–11
Webster's Yorkshire Bitter 🄷
Large, well-appointed village pub. The horseshoe-shaped partitions were installed by a former jockey owner. Ring the Bull game. Q P

Threshfield

Old Hall

On B6265 ☎ (0756) 752441
11–3; 5.30–11
Taylor Best Bitter, Landlord; Younger Scotch Ⓗ
Popular Dales pub with fine wood panelling and range. Plans in hand for accommodation and conservatory. Guest beers. Varied, high quality menu includes veg option.
⛫ ☸ ◖ ◗ ⛺ ♣ P

Tunstall

Bay Horse
2 miles off A1
☎ (0748) 818564
12–3 (Sat only); 7–11
Samuel Smith OBB Ⓗ
200 year-old pub in centre of village. Predominantly local custom, with a warm friendly atmosphere. Quoits played. Children welcome in lounge during early eve. Eve meals Wed–Sat summer only.
⛫ Q ☸ 🛏 ◗ ⧉ ⛺ ♣ P

Ugthorpe

Black Bull
Off A171 6 miles W of Whitby
☎ (0947) 840286
11–3; 7–11 (may vary in summer)
Tetley Bitter; Theakston Best Bitter, XB, Old Peculier Ⓗ
Excellent village pub set in row of cottages. Live music Sun lunch. Children welcome in pool room; quoits also played. Menu includes veg option and children's choice. Occasional guest beers. ⛫ ☸ 🛏 ◖ ◗ ⧉ ♣ P

Try also: Ellerby Hotel

Upper Poppleton

Lord Collingwood
Hodgson Lane
☎ (0904) 794388
11–3 (4 Sat); 6 (5.30 Fri, 6.30 Sat)–11
Theakston Best Bitter, XB, Old Peculier (summer); **Younger Scotch, No. 3** Ⓗ
Plush L-shaped bar with two distinct areas, one of which houses darts. Lots of charm with brasses and much Laurel and Hardy memorabilia. Set on picturesque village green, complete with maypole. Camping a mile away at Nether Poppleton. No eve meals Wed or Sun. ⛫ ☸ ◖ ◗ ⛺ ≋ ♣ P

West Ayton

Forge Valley Hotel
5 Pickering Road
☎ (0723) 862146
11–3; 6–11
Camerons Traditional Bitter Ⓗ
A lively village social centre with live music and wholesome traditional food, including veg and children's dishes. Jukebox and videos in family room.
⛫ ♘ ☸ 🛏 ◖ ◗ ⧉ ⛺ ♣ P

Wheldrake

Alice Hawthorn
31 Main Street
☎ (090 489) 89203
11–3; 7–11
Camerons Traditional Bitter Ⓗ
Named after a locally-bred horse which won 51 of its 71 races, and 16 cups. A popular pub set amid pretty cottages; pleasant bar and lounge.
⛫ Q ☸ ◖ ◗ ⧉ ♿ ♣ P

Whitby

Buck Inn
St Annes Staithe (near Fish Quay, past swing bridge, W of town) ☎ (0947) 601378
11–3; 7–11 (11–11 summer)
John Smith's Bitter, Magnet Ⓗ
Recently-refurbished quayside pub, popular with locals and visitors. Sky TV in bar and family room, which is also used for functions. Local seafood served fresh every day; eve meals summer only.
♘ 🛏 ◖ ◗ ≋ ♣

Duke of York
Church Street
☎ (0947) 600324
11–3 (may vary); 7–11 (11–11 summer)
Courage Directors; John Smith's Bitter, Magnet Ⓗ
Harbourside pub with magnificent views, situated at the foot of 199 steps which lead up to the Abbey. Serves as a folk centre in folk week (Aug).
◗ ≋ ♣

Little Angel
Flowergate ☎ (0947) 602514
10.30–11
Tetley Bitter Ⓗ
Street-corner local whose fabric contains much of historic interest. Mounting steps outside. Home-cooked steak pie recommended, but veg meals also served; Sun lunch summer only. 🛏 ⧉ ≋ ♣

Try also: Fleece; Wellington

York

Acorn Inn
9 St Martins Lane (off Micklegate) ☎ (0904) 629820
12–3; 7–11
Camerons Traditional Bitter; Everards Old Original Ⓗ
Genial back-street local, close to main thoroughfare. Quiz night Sun. ⧉ ≋

Brown Cow
36 Hope Street, Walmgate
☎ (0904) 634010
11–4; 6–11 (11–11 Fri & Sat)
Taylor Best Bitter, Landlord Ⓗ
Small two-roomed local surrounded by modern housing, tucked inside city walls. Comfortable and pleasantly decorated. ♣

Fox Inn
168 Holgate Road
☎ (0904) 798341
11–3; 5.30–11
Tetley Mild, Bitter Ⓗ
Tastefully-modernised, four-roomed Tetley Heritage inn of real character. Q ☸ ◖ ⧉ ♿ ♣ P

Golden Ball
Cromwell Road, Bishophill, (just inside Victoria Bar)
☎ (0904) 652211
11–3; 7–11
Courage Directors; John Smith's Bitter, Magnet Ⓗ
Unspoilt, traditional three-room pub within residential quarter of walled city. Appeals to all. Well-preserved original exterior.
⛫ ☸ ⧉ ≋

John Bull
Layerthorpe (off Foss Islands road)
11.30–3; 5.30–11 (11.30–11 Fri & Sat)
Franklin's Bitter; Taylor Best Bitter, Landlord; Wards Sheffield Best Bitter Ⓗ
Excellent ex-John Smith's free house boasting original 1930s decor and rare enamelled signs in bar. Regular live music; unique atmosphere. Deservedly-popular with students and locals. Guest beers usually available. Lunchtime snacks.
⛫ Q ☸ ⧉ ♿ ⌽

Red Lion
Merchantgate (off Piccadilly)
☎ (0904) 623988
11–3; 5–11
Courage Directors; John Smith's Bitter, Magnet Ⓗ
One-roomed town pub in a 14th-century building. Reputed to have been frequented by Dick Turpin. Restricted eve menu, served summer only.
☸ ◖ ◗ ♿ ♣ P

Royal Oak
19 Goodramgate (near York Minster/Monk Bar)
☎ (0904) 653856
11–11
Camerons Traditional Bitter; Everards Old Original; Tolly Cobbold Old Strong Ⓗ
Well-preserved, three-roomed pub that prides itself on home-cooking and home-made bread; eve meals until 7.30pm.
♘ ◖ ◗ ⧉

Spread Eagle
98 Walmgate
☎ (0904) 635868
11–11

Taylor Best Bitter, Landlord; Theakston XB, Old Peculier H
Sympathetic refurbishments have enhanced the popularity of this convivial, bustling free house. Smart restaurant upstairs; good value bar food downstairs. Beer a bit pricey. Guest beers.

Tap & Spile

29 Monkgate (200 yds through Monk Bar) ☎ (0904) 656158
11.30–3; 5.30–11 (11.30–11 Sat)
Camerons Traditional Bitter; Hadrian Gladiator Bitter; Old Mill Traditional Bitter; Stocks Old Horizontal H
Built in 1897 (possibly as a school) and opened as a pub in early 1900s. Traditional ale house with one large bar and raised games area. Home-cooked bar lunches. Up to six guest beers and draught cider occasionally. Annual beer festival at pub. Q P

York Arms

26 High Petergate
☎ (0904) 624508
11–11
Samuel Smith OBB, Museum Ale H
Quaint pub, overshadowed by the Minster, that attracts locals, tourists and students. Two lounges and delightfully-preserved bar. No-smoking dining area.

York Beer Shop

28 Sandringham Street, Fishergate ☎ (0904) 647136
11 (10 Sat, 4 Mon)–10 (12–2; 7–10 Sun)
Bateman XXXB; Malton Owd Bob; Old Mill Bitter; Taylor Best Bitter, Landlord H
Excellent value draught beer in any quantity; an extensive range of bottled beers, many naturally-conditioned, and a good selection of traditional, hand-made cheeses make this the ultimate off-licence. Guest beers.

One of the Oktoberfest's cavernous beer halls (see competition page 313)

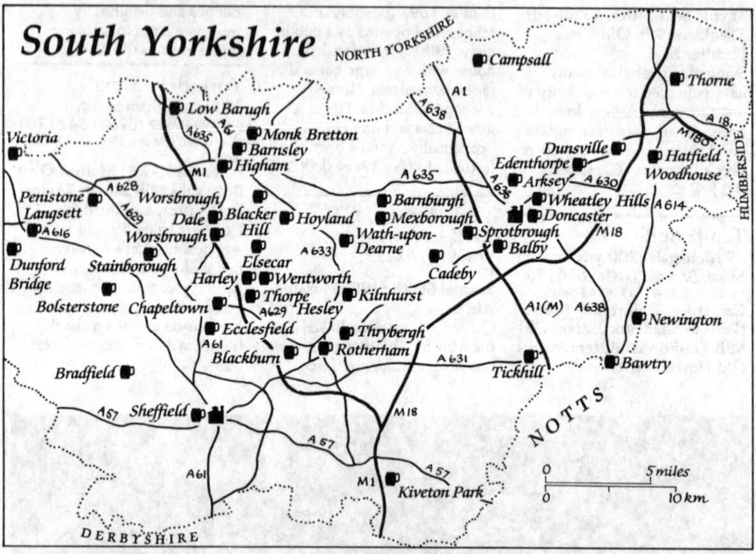

Stocks, *Doncaster*; **Wards,** *Sheffield*

Arksey

Plough
2 High Street
☎ (0302) 872472
12–3; 7–11
John Smith's Bitter [H]
Convivial locals' pub hidden away behind the village church. Traditional tap room for darts and dominoes; the larger lounge is adorned with commemorative plates. ⊞ ♣

Balby

Spinney
Forest Rise, Grenville Estate (off A630) ☎ (0302) 852033
11–3.30 (4 Fri & Sat); 6.30–11
Home Bitter; Theakston Best Bitter, XB [H]
Thriving Younger estate pub with games-oriented tap room and large comfortable lounge. Bar snacks served at both sessions. Q ⊞ ♿ ♣ P

Barnburgh

Crown
Doncaster Road (outside village on road to High Melton)
☎ (0709) 894223
11–3.30; 6.30–11
Courage Directors; John Smith's Bitter, Magnet [H]
Comfortable, modern two-roomed pub with good bar meals (veg option only in restaurant). Quiet public bar and large lounge with picture windows. Q ❀ ◐ ◑ ⊞ ♿ P

Barnsley

Manx Arms
Sheffield Road (off roundabout on A61) ☎ (0226) 293766
11–3.30; 7–11
Ind Coope Burton Ale; Marston's Pedigree Bitter; Taylor Golden Best, Landlord; Tetley Bitter; Theakston Old Peculier [H]
Popular free house catering for all ages. Comfortable and friendly atmosphere; very busy at weekends. Up to six handpulled guest beers and two ciders. An oasis in the local real ale desert. Parking is limited.
⇌ ⌽ P

Try also: **Silkstone** (Tetley)

Bawtry

Turnpike
28–30 High Street (A614/A638)
☎ (0302) 711960
11–3; 6–11
Stocks Best Bitter, Old Horizontal [H]
Tastefully converted from a wine bar to cater for all tastes, and local and passing trades. The interior is of wood, glass and brick, with a part-concrete floor – mind the step! Good value, varied menu (no eve meals Fri–Sun). Guest beers.
♨ ❀ ◐ ◑

Blackburn

Crown
Blackburn Road (near M1 jct 34) ☎ (0709) 560498
11–3; 6–11
Tetley Bitter [H]
A central bar serves several drinking areas. The garden is a real pleasure for children. ❀ ◐ ♣

Sportsman
Blackburn Road (near M1 jct 34) ☎ (0709) 551124
11–3; 6–11
Tetley Bitter [H]
Wonderfully solid stone pub, dating from 1919, where a friendly welcome is guaranteed. Several separate rooms, one with a snooker table. ♣

Blacker Hill

Royal Albert
Wentworth Road (800 yds off B6096) ☎ (0226) 742193
11–3 (4 Fri & Sat); 7–11
Wards Sheffield Best Bitter [H] & [E]
The hub of village life. Splendid small, wood-panelled snug and basic public bar. Q ⊞ ♣ P

Bolsterstone

Castle
Off old A616 at Deepcar crossroads OS271968
☎ (0742) 882145
12–3; 6 (7 Sat)–11
Stones Best Bitter [E]
Stone-built pub in small idyllic village. Lounge and public bar are well frequented by both locals and hikers. Popular quiz night on Tue. No food Sun. ◐ ⊞

Bradfield

Haychatter
Bradfield Dale (off B6077 on Strines Road) ☎ (0742) 81332
7.30–11 (Closed lunch, except Sun & bank hols)
Beer range varies Ⓗ
Remote three-roomed country inn with pleasant atmosphere. Set in beautiful countryside but only a few minutes' drive from the city. Well worth seeking out. Popular with hikers.
⌂ ☼ ▲ ♣ P

Cadeby

Cadeby Inn
Main Street ☎ (0709) 864009
11–11
Ind Coope Burton Ale; John Smith's Bitter, Magnet; Samuel Smith OBB; Tetley Bitter Ⓗ
Converted farmhouse in rural village which has retained its atmosphere and character. Large lounge and cosy public bar. Good bar meals, including a traditional Sun lunch.
⌂ Q ☼ ◖ ◗ ⊟ P

Campsall

Old Bells
High Street ☎ (0302) 700423
11–3; 7–11
Webster's Yorkshire Bitter, Webster's Choice Ⓗ
Originally a farm, now a rambling old pub: four rooms, each with its own character, and a restaurant. ⌂ ◖ ◗ ⊟ ♿ ♣ P

Chapeltown

Norfolk Arms
White Lane (A6135/ Warren Lane jct, near M1 jct 35a)
☎ (0742) 468414
12–4; 7–11
Wards Sheffield Best Bitter Ⓗ
Blades welcome in this Owls pub! Will also tolerate football players and anglers. Landlord's jokes guaranteed to kill at 30 paces. Black pud and chitterlings on bar Sun lunchtime! Family room suitable for older children.
♞ ☼ ◖ ♿ ⇌ ♣ P

Prince of Wales
80 Burncross Road (A629 near M1 jct 35) ☎ (0742) 467725
11.30–3; 5.30–11 (11–11 Fri, 11–4; 6–11 Sat)
Wards Sheffield Best Bitter, Kirby Strong Ⓗ
Traditional tap room with refurbished lounge. Clean air pub with friendly clientele.
⌂ Q ☼ ◖ ⊟ ⇌ ♣ ⍥ P

Try also: Commercial (Free)

Doncaster

Corner Pin
St Sepulchre Gate West
☎ (0302) 323142
11.30–3; 4.45–11 (11.30–11 Fri & Sat)
John Smith's Bitter, Magnet Ⓗ
Street-corner local just away from town centre and two minutes' walk from the station. Good food. ◖ ◗ ⇌ ♣

Hallcross
33–34 Hallgate (next to Odeon cinema) ☎ (0302) 328213
11–3; 6–11
Stocks Best Bitter, Select, Old Horizontal Ⓗ
A very popular town pub, the Hallcross is the home of Stocks Brewery. Interesting collection of mirrors and pictures. Hot and cold lunchtime snacks. ☼ ⍥

Masons Arms
Market Place
☎ (0302) 364391
11–4; 7.30–11 Mon, 10.30–4; 7.30–11 Tue, 11–4; 7–11 Wed & Thu, 10.30–11 Fri, 10.30–4; 7–11 Sat
Tetley Bitter Ⓗ
200 year-old Tetley Heritage Inn. Many photos of old 'Donny' and a history of the pub on display. Haunt of the local morris men. Q ☼ ⊟ ⇌

White Swan
34a Frenchgate
☎ (0302) 366573
11–4; 6–11 (11–11 Tue, Fri & Sat)
Vaux Samson; Wards Sheffield Best Bitter Ⓗ
Last of the 19 pubs that once adorned Frenchgate. A tiled passageway leads to the lounge while the front tap room boasts the highest bar in Britain – 5ft 3ins! Bar snacks available 11.30–2. ⊟ ♿ ⇌

Dunford Bridge

Stanhope Arms
Windle Edge Lane (off A628)
☎ (0226) 763104
11–3; 7–11
John Smith's Bitter, Magnet Ⓗ
Originally built as a shooting lodge: several rooms interlink with a small bar. Tiny, quiet snug and separate dining room. Excellent home-made food (breakfasts available). Sun evening snuff club. Children welcome in snug until 8. Camping in grounds.
⌂ Q ♞ ☼ ◖ ◗ ♿ ▲ ♣ P

Dunsville

Flarepath
High Street
12–4; 7–11
Courage Directors; John Smith's Bitter, Magnet Ⓗ
Modern, comfortable main road pub. John Smith's/Courage local flagship. ⊟ ♣ P

Ecclesfield

White Bear
46 Stocks Hill
☎ (0742) 467749
12–3.30; 7–11
Tetley Bitter Ⓗ
Village-centre pub with large public bar and alcoved lounge. Organizes its own long distance walk, 'the White Bear Wanderer', 29 miles from Castleton, Derbyshire, ending (gratefully) at the public bar.
Q ⊟ ♣ ⍥ P

Edenthorpe

Ridgewood
Thorne Road (A18)
☎ (0302) 882841
11–11
Samuel Smith OBB Ⓗ
Named after a famous race-horse. Comfortable, spacious lounge and more basic tap room which cater for local and passing trade. Extensive beer garden with children's playground. ☼ ◖ ◗ ⊟ ♣ P

Elsecar

Market Hotel
2 Wentworth Road (just off B6097) ☎ (0226) 742240
11–4; 7–11
Stones Best Bitter Ⓔ & Ⓗ
Traditional local in historic mining village. Unspoilt, multi-roomed interior, each room having a different character. Friendly and talkative landlord. Wed night quiz. Q ☼ ⊟ ⇌ ♣ P

Harley

Horseshoe
9 Harley Road (B6090, ¼ mile from A6135, signed Wentworth) ☎ (0226) 742204
12–3; 6.30–11
John Smith's Bitter, Magnet Ⓗ
Village local by day, with a characterful bar, the Horseshoe attracts discerning diners at night and for Sun lunch: excellent value meals with veg option. ⌂ ◖ ◗ ♣

Hatfield Woodhouse

Green Tree
Bearswood Green (A18/A614)
☎ (0302) 840305
11–3; 6–11
Vaux Bitter; Wards Thorne Best Bitter Ⓗ
Very welcoming 17th-century posting house with an emphasis on food. ⌂ ☼ 🛏 ◖ ◗ ♿ P

Robin Hood & Little John
Main Street (A614)

☎ (0302) 840213
11–4; 6–11
Stones Best Bitter Ⓗ
Friendly, comfortable village local which is very busy at weekends. ❁ ◖ ⊟ ♿ ♣ P

Higham

Engineers Inn

Higham Common Lane (off A635) ☎ (0226) 384204
11.30–3; 7–11 (11.30–4; 6.30–11 Sat)
Samuel Smith OBB Ⓗ
Village pub with superb unspoilt tap room and plush lounge. Landlord's collection of old beer bottles on display.
❁ ◖ ⊟ ♣ P

Try also: Spencer Arms (John Smith's)

Hoyland

Furnace Inn

Milton Road (500 yds from centre, off B6097)
☎ (0226) 742000
11.30–3.30; 6.30–11
Vaux Samson Ⓗ; **Wards Thorne Best Bitter, Sheffield Best Bitter** Ⓔ, **Kirby Strong** Ⓗ
Welcoming stone-built inn by old forge pond. Good value lunchtime snacks. Q ❁ P

Kilnhurst

Ship Inn

1 Hooton Road (B6090)
☎ (0709) 584322
11.30 (11 Sat)–2.30; 6–11
Marston's Pedigree Bitter Ⓗ
1752 coaching inn; oldest building in the village, perilously close to railway and canal. Collection of paper money on the beams. Varied entertainment almost every evening for all tastes. Good bar food and upstairs restaurant (not Sun eve). ❁ ◖ ◗ ♿ P

Try also: Terrace (Stones)

Kiveton Park

Forge

Wales Road (B6059)
☎ (0909) 770045
11–3; 6–11
Home Bitter; Theakston Old Peculier; Younger IPA Ⓗ
Posters in the lounge recall the Forge's former life as the Regal cinema. It was converted to a pub in 1966. Strong local trade appreciates the beer (landlord has won the Younger's Master Cellarman Award). ⊟ ≹ ♣ P

Langsett

Waggon & Horses

On A616 ☎ (0226) 763147
12–3; 7.30–11 (7–11 Sat)
Draught Bass; Stones Best Bitter Ⓗ
Mature stone pub at the side of a large reservoir. Comfortable interior, free from music, slot machines and other distractions. Good home-cooked food (not Sat lunch or Sun/Mon eves. Booking for Sun lunch advised). Known locally as 'Billy Green's'.
⌂ Q ❁ ◖ ◗ P

Low Barugh

Millers Inn

Dearne Hall Road (B6428)
☎ (0226) 382888
11.30–2.30 (not Tue); 5.30–11 (11.30–11 Fri & Sat)
Taylor Landlord; Tetley Bitter Ⓗ
Busy pub on site of old watermill. Small tap room with dartboard. Good value food served in lounge. Regular guest beers. ⌂ ❁ ◖ ◗ ⊟ ♣ P

Mexborough

Concertina Band Club

9a Dolcliffe Road (off main street) ☎ (0709) 580841
12–4; 7–11
John Smith's Bitter, Magnet; Wards Sheffield Best Bitter Ⓗ
Small, friendly private club steeped in history. Visitors welcome. Guest beers. ≹ ♣

Monk Bretton

Sun Inn

Burton Road
☎ (0226) 203361
11.30–3; 5–11
John Smith's Bitter, Magnet Ⓗ
Pleasant and popular local, catering for all ages. Large lounge with quiet areas.
Q ❁ ◖ ♿ ♣ P

Newington

Ship Inn

Newington Road (200 yds from A614) ☎ (0302) 710334
12–2.30; 7–11
Home Bitter; Theakston XB; Younger Scotch, No. 3 Ⓗ
Popular village local with a good choice of both beer and food. Doncaster CAMRA's Pub of the Season for spring 1990.
❁ ◖ ◗ ♣ P

Penistone

Cubley Hall

Mortimer Road, Cubley
☎ (0226) 766086
11–3; 6–11
Ansells Bitter; Ind Coope Burton Ale; Tetley Bitter Ⓗ
Former country house with plush multi-room interior. Fine plasterwork and mosaic tiled floors. Wide selection of excellent home-cooked food. Two children's rooms and a lawned garden. Regular Allied Breweries guest beer. ☋ ❁ ◖ ◗ P

Try also: Britannia (Stones)

Rotherham

Bridge

Greasbrough Road (opp. station) ☎ (0709) 363683
11–3; 6–11
Stones Best Bitter Ⓔ
Many-roomed pub next to the famous chapel on the bridge. A meeting place for local groups. Watch out for the phantom miner! ◖ ⊟ ≹ ♣

Effingham Arms

Effingham Street (opp. bus station) ☎ (0709) 363653
11–11
Stones Best Bitter Ⓗ
Town-centre pub with a nautical theme. The stained glass windows depict the voyage of Sir Francis Drake which was sponsored by the Duke of Effingham. ⊟ ≹ ♣

Limes

38 Broom Lane (B6410 100 yds from B6021 jct)
☎ (0709) 363431
11–11
Theakston Best Bitter, Old Peculier; Younger Scotch, IPA, No. 3 Ⓗ
Very comfortable bar lounge. Emphasis on meals (served 10.30 am–11 pm), including a very cheap special dish. Well-appointed hotel with special weekend rates. 🛏 ◖ ◗ P

Tabard

Valley Road, E. Herringthorpe (A6123/Chaucer Road jct)
☎ (0709) 364761
11–11
Courage Directors; John Smith's Bitter, Magnet Ⓗ
Large estate pub serving a varied clientele. Outdoor play area for children. Table football machine in family room. Regular oldies nights. ☋ ❁ ◖ ⊟ ♣ P

Tivoli Inn

Holmes Lane (from town centre: 1st left past Millmoor football ground) ☎ (0709) 560205
12–4; 7–11
Marston's Burton Best Bitter, Pedigree Bitter Ⓗ
Off the beaten track but well worth finding, this pub takes its name from the old cinema, finally demolished in 1989. Ideal for train spotters! Do not confuse with the Tivoli *Club* at the football ground. ◖ ≹ ♣ P

Woodman

Midland Road
☎ (0709) 561486
12–3; 7–11
Stones Best Bitter Ⓗ
Sturdy two-roomed ex-Bentley's pub in Masbrough. Strong games teams with darts

downstairs and snooker upstairs.
⛃ ⊟ ♣

Try also: Turners Arms (Wards)

Sheffield: Central

Bath Hotel
66 Victoria Street (rear of Glossop Road baths)
☎ (0742) 729017
12–3; 5 (7.30 Sat)–11 (12–2; 7.30–10.30 Sun)
Ind Coope Burton Ale; Tetley Bitter Ⓗ
A Tetley Heritage pub, converted from Victorian cottages to form a small friendly two-roomed local. The original ground lease prohibits use of the site as an alehouse or for other noxious activities!
Q ◐ ⊟ ♿ ♣

Brown Bear
109 Norfolk Street
☎ (0742) 727744
11.30–3 (not Sun); 5–11
Courage Directors; John Smith's Bitter Ⓗ
Popular city-centre meeting place with two comfortable rooms. Patronised by cast, audience (and snooker players) from nearby Crucible Theatre. Decorated with thespian memorabilia. Q ◐ ⇌ (Midland)

Fagans
69 Broad Lane (A57 between city centre and university)
☎ (0742) 728430
11.30–3; 5.30–11 (11.30–11 Fri & Sat)
Ind Coope Burton Ale; Tetley Bitter Ⓗ
Lively, popular pub with small snug. Frequent impromptu folk music sessions. Friendly atmosphere. Eve meals only by prior arrangement.
⛃ ◐ ⇌ (Midland) ♣

Fat Cat
23 Alma Street (off A61 northbound)
☎ (0742) 728195
12–3; 5.30–11
Marston's Merrie Monk, Pedigree Bitter, Owd Rodger; Taylor Landlord; Theakston Old Peculier Ⓗ
Sheffield's first real ale free house, situated in Kelham Island conservation area. Two comfortable rooms (one no-smoking), corridor drinking area and upstairs room for overspill (children at lunchtimes), when not booked for functions. Planning permission obtained for brewhouse. Eve meals Mon only. ♠ Q ☋ ⛃ ◐ ◗ ♣ ⌼

Moseleys Arms
81 West Bar (A61 near police station) ☎ (0742) 721591
11–3; 5.30 (7 Sat)–11 (11–11 Fri)
Stones Best Bitter Ⓗ
Superbly renovated pub just off city centre. Three well-appointed rooms, comfortably furnished and catering for all ages. Snooker room upstairs.
◐ ♿ ⇌ (Midland) ♣

Norfolk Arms
2 Suffolk Road (A61 near station) ☎ (0742) 727598
11–11
Courage Directors; John Smith's Bitter, Magnet Ⓗ
Popular two-roomer with pleasant lounge and spacious tap room with pool table. Busy and friendly. Well patronised by bus drivers, postmen and railway workers.
⊟ ♿ ⇌ (Midland) ♣

Red Deer
18 Pitt Street (off West Street, near Jessops Hospital)
☎ (0742) 722890
11.30–3; 5 (7.30 Sat)–11 (11.30–11 Fri)
Ind Coope Burton Ale; Tetley Mild, Bitter Ⓗ
Busy, friendly one-roomed local with active folk club. Popular with students and professionals. Excellent home-cooked meals; eve meals only by prior arrangement. ⛃ ◐

Red House
168 Solly Street
☎ (0742) 727926
11.30–3; 5–11 (11.30–4.30; 8–11 Sat, 12–2.30; 7–10.30 Sun)
Wards Thorne Best Bitter, Sheffield Best Bitter Ⓗ
Comfortably furnished local with three separate drinking areas around a central bar. Live folk music most nights; quiz Thu. Once known as the Irish Embassy, but also popular with students. Guest beers. No food Sun. Q ◐ ♿ ♣

Royal Standard
156–158 St Marys Road (inner ring road near Bramall Lane football ground)
☎ (0742) 722883
11–3.30 (12–2.30 Sun); 5.30–11
Wards Mild, Sheffield Best Bitter, Kirby Strong Ⓗ
Busy pub with large lounge, snug and tap room. Fine wood-panelled bar. Popular with the business community at lunchtime, and students in the evenings. Pool and darts in tap room.
⛃ ◐ ⊟ ♿ ⇌ (Midland) ♣ P

Rutland Arms
86 Brown Street
☎ (0742) 729003
11–3; 5.30 (7 Sat)–11
Ind Coope Burton Ale; Tetley Bitter Ⓗ
Comfortably refurbished one-roomed pub just off city centre. Unusual Gilmour's tiled frontage. Popular with business people at lunchtime; varied evening clientele.
Q ⛃ ⛟ ◐ ◗ ♿ ⇌ (Midland)

Washington
79 Fitzwilliam Street (off West Street) ☎ (0742) 754937
11.30–3 (12–2 Sun); 6.30–11
Ind Coope Burton Ale; Tetley Mild, Bitter Ⓗ
Two comfortably furnished rooms featuring an extensive display of teapots. Popular meeting place for numerous groups. Folk music Tue. Lunchtime snacks. ⛃ ⊟ ♣

Sheffield: East

Belfry
Eckington Road, Beighton
☎ (0742) 477309
11–2.30 (3 Sat); 5.30 (6 Sat)–11
Greenalls Shipstone's Bitter Ⓗ
Large, modern, open-plan pub with restaurant at rear. Pool table and other games are to the left of the main entrance; comfortable lounge area to the right. ⛃ ◐ ◗ ♿ ♣ P

Carlton
563 Attercliffe Road (opp. Staniforth Road jct)
☎ (0742) 443287
11.30–3; 5–11
Ruddles Best Bitter; Webster's Yorkshire Bitter Ⓗ
Deceptive, Tardis-like building, appearing to be larger inside than its exterior would imply. A warm and friendly watering-hole attracting custom from all over the city. Shelf above the bar is adorned with regulars' pewter tankards. Lunch served Fri only. ♠ ⇌ (Attercliffe Rd) ♣

Cocked Hat
75 Worksop Road (off Attercliffe Road)
☎ (0742) 448332
11–11 (11–4; 7–11 Sat, 12–2; 7–10.30 Sun)
Marston's Burton Best Bitter, Pedigree Bitter Ⓗ
In the Attercliffe Environmental Corridor, this gem of a Victorian-style pub offers a warm and friendly welcome. Noted for its lunchtime meals and substantial snacks. Tea and coffee are served till 10pm. Opposite new athletics stadium.
♠ ⛃ ◐ ◗ ♣

Manor Castle
239 Manor Lane
☎ (0742) 724768
12–3 (4 Mon, Fri & Sat); 5.30 (7 Sat)–11
Tetley Bitter Ⓗ
Large, traditional tap room with two small lounges, built in the grounds of the now-ruined Sheffield Manor which served as prison for both Cardinal Wolsey and Mary, Queen of Scots. One lounge is quiet. Q ☋ ⛃ ⊟ ♣

Milestone
Peaks Mount, Crystal Peaks,

Waterthorpe (next to bus station) ☎ (0742) 471614
11–11
Banks's Mild, Bitter Ⓔ
Built in 1988 to serve the new Crystal Peaks shopping centre. Tap room with pub games has viewing glass into cellar. Large, quiet lounge has conservatory extension. Popular with shoppers at lunchtime and cinema-goers in the evenings.
Q ❀ ◖ ⊡ ♿ ♣ P

Sheffield: North

Carlisle Hotel
5 Carlisle Street East (B6082)
☎ (0742) 726857
11–3; 5.30–11
Stones Best Bitter Ⓔ
Three separate and distinct rooms served from a central bar. Plenty of character with an amazing range of *objets d'art* scattered around. Unusual pub games include table football and a pinball machine. ⊡ ♣

Denison Arms
33 Watery Street
☎ (0742) 727845
11–3.45; 7–11
Stones Best Bitter Ⓔ
Splendid example of an unspoilt local; tastefully decorated bow-windowed lounge and smaller pool room. ⊡ ♣

Foundry Arms
111 Barrow Road (B6082)
☎ (0742) 426498
11–3; 6–11
Tetley Bitter Ⓗ
Much-changed in 1988 but features such as wood panelling and the tap room have been retained. Separate area for pool.
❀ ◖ ⊡ ♣

Mill Tavern
2–4 Earsham Street
☎ (0742) 756461
11–11
Old Mill Traditional Mild, Traditional Bitter, Bullion Bitter Ⓗ
A much-changed pub in recent years. The mock-Tudor front hides a single bar and plenty of rough stonework. ♣

Robin Hood
Myers Grove Lane, Little Matlock (right turn after Pine Grove Country Club)
☎ (0742) 344565
11.30–3; 7–11
Stones Best Bitter Ⓔ
Country pub on site of a failed spa development. Four interconnecting rooms. Live piano music at weekends. Stuffed animal collection in bar.
⌂ Q ❀ ◗ ⊡ ♣ P

Sheffield: South

Abbey
944 Chesterfield Road (A61)
☎ (0742) 745374
11–11 (11–4.30; 6.30–11 Sat)
Tetley Bitter Ⓗ
Large suburban local with comfortable lounge and cosy, busy smoke room. Well-used bowling green at rear.
⌂ ❀ ◖ ⊡ ♣ P

Byron House
16 Nether Edge Road (off A621) ☎ (0742) 551811
11.30–3 (4 Fri); 5.30–11 (11.30–11 Sat)
Draught Bass; Stones Best Bitter Ⓔ
Friendly, two-roomed suburban local with plush lounge and traditional tap room. Q ⊡ ♣

Fleur de Lys
Totley Hall Lane (A621 Baslow Road) ☎ (0742) 361476
11–3; 5–11 (11–11 Fri & Sat)
Draught Bass; Stones Best Bitter Ⓗ
Large suburban local on outskirts of city. Split-level lounge with separate carvery area. Quiet, cosy wood-panelled snug. Large grassed garden with children's play area.
⌂ Q ❀ ◖ ◗ ♿ ♣ P

Old Mother Redcap
Prospect Road, Bradway (near B6054) ☎ (0742) 360179
11–3; 5.30–11 (11–11 Sat)
Samuel Smith OBB Ⓗ
Modern estate pub with large comfortable lounge in farmhouse style. Mainly local trade. ❀ ◖ ♣ P

Shakespeare Inn
106 Well Road (off A61 at Heeley bridge)
☎ (0742) 553995
12–3.30; 5.30–11
Tetley Bitter Ⓗ
Open-plan pub, retaining three distinct drinking areas. Cosy and friendly. Close to Heeley City Farm; magnificent view over Heeley Valley. ❀ ♣

White Lion
615 London Road (A61 S from city centre) ☎ (0742) 551500
12–11 (12–3.30; 7–11 Sat)
Ind Coope Burton Ale; Tetley Mild, Bitter Ⓗ
Unspoilt Victorian Heritage pub, carefully restored to retain many rooms and tiled main corridor. Cosmopolitan clientele. Lunches served Thu–Sun.
⌂ ❀ ◖ ♣ ⌓

Sheffield: West

Bull's Head
396 Fulwood Road
☎ (0742) 302008
11–11
Draught Bass; Stones Best Bitter Ⓗ
One-roomed lounge with tap room atmosphere to the right. Comfortable sofas. All woodwork is in ash. Q ❀ ◖ P

Devonshire Arms
118 Ecclesall Road (opp. Wards' brewery)
☎ (0742) 722202
11–11
Vaux Double Maxim; Wards Thorne Best Bitter Ⓗ, **Sheffield Best Bitter** Ⓔ, **Kirby Strong** Ⓗ
Public house with one main bar that serves all areas. Separate conservatory used mainly for lunches, including Sun (veg option). Nice furnishings, fine bric-a-brac and old prints.
❀ ◖ ♿ ♣ P

Firwood Cottage
279 Whitehouse Lane
☎ (0742) 346057
12–3 (4 Sat); 6.30 (7 Sat)–11
Tetley Bitter Ⓗ
Small, friendly local with neat appearance in both rooms. Interesting display of WWI silk postcards. Disabled access is via rear door. Q ❀ ⊡ ♿ ♣

Fox & Duck
225–227 Fulwood Road (A57)
☎ (0742) 663422
11–11
Courage Directors; John Smith's Bitter, Magnet Ⓗ
Busy two-roomed pub in centre of Broomhill shopping area. Traditional-style furnishings with extra large tables. Tenancy held by University Students' Union.

Old Grindstone
3 Crookes ☎ (0742) 660322
11–11
Wards Sheffield Best Bitter Ⓗ & Ⓔ, **Kirby Strong** Ⓗ
Spacious Victorian-style lounge with adjoining conservatory. Oak-panelled games room modelled on a gentleman's club offers snooker, pool and darts. Regular guest beer. Quiet until 7.30, when last food orders are taken. Q ❀ ◖ ◗ ⊡ ♿ ♣

Sportsman
57 Benty Lane (A57)
☎ (0742) 660502
11.30–3; 5–11 (11.30–11 Fri & Sat)
Draught Bass; Stones Best Bitter Ⓗ
Well-furnished, large split-level lounge. Smaller games room with sporting theme. Wide selection of home-made lunchtime food.
Q ❀ ◖ ⊡ ♿ ⛺ ♣ P

Sprotbrough

Boat Inn
Nursery Lane, Lower Sprotbrough (between Sprotbrough and Warmsworth)
☎ (0302) 857188
11–3; 6–11 (11–11 Sat in summer)

Courage Directors; John Smith's Bitter, Magnet [H]
Imaginative conversion of farm buildings in an attractive riverside setting. Bar meals and separate restaurant. No bar meals Sat and Sun eves.
Q ▦ ◖ ◗ P

Try also: Ivanhoe (Samuel Smith)

Stainborough

Strafford Arms
Park Drive (off B6099)
☎ (0226) 287488
11–3; 7–11 (11–11 Sat in summer)
Courage Directors; John Smith's Bitter, Magnet [H]
Adjoining a quaint local cricket ground, the traditional country pub exterior hides a large, modern interior with an award-winning Yorkshire range.
♨ ▦ ◖ P

Thorne

Rising Sun
Hatfield Road (A614)
☎ (0405) 812688
11–3; 6–11
Wards Thorne Best Bitter [H]
Fine traditional three-roomed locals' pub situated beside canal. Eve meals by prior arrangement only. ♨ ▦ ◖ ⊟ ♿ ♣ P

Thorpe Hesley

Horse & Tiger
Brook Hill (B6086, near A629 and M1 jct 35)
☎ (0742) 468072
11–3; 6–11 (11–11 Sat)
Tetley Bitter [H]
Restored to its former glory, this 1920s pub stands on the site of an earlier one: the history and plans are displayed. Garden has children's play area. Good value lunchtime bar snacks.
♘ ▦ ♣ P

Masons Arms
Thorpe Street (off B6086)
☎ (0742) 468079
11–3; 6–11
Theakston XB, Old Peculier; Younger Scotch, IPA, No. 3 [H]
Live music Thu and Sun eves at this pub dating from 1818 but much-extended since. Two quiet rooms and two family rooms. Landlord holds Master Cellarman awards; his beer is consistently excellent.
Q ♘ ▦ ◖ P

Thrybergh

Royal Oak
Hollings Lane
☎ (0709) 853562
11.30–3.30; 6.30–11 (11–11 summer)
Tetley Bitter [H]
Upmarket roadside pub converted from former colliery manager's house. Difficult-to-find entrance via car park. Lounge and public bar, also family room. Camping in car park. ♘ ▦ ◖ ⊟ ♿ ⛺ ♣ P

Tickhill

Buttercross
Northgate ☎ (0302) 745191
12–2.30; 7–11 (11–4; 7–11 summer)
Clark's Burglar Bill, Hammerhead; Marston's Pedigree Bitter [H]
Attractive old building with comfortable lounge and lively tap room either side of central bar. Large beer garden.
♨ ▦ ◖ ◗ ⊟ ♿ ♣

Scarbrough Arms
Sunderland Street
☎ (0302) 742977
11–3; 6–11
Courage Directors; John Smith's Bitter, Magnet [H]
Named after a local landowner, this welcoming hostelry stands at the centre of an historic village. Three totally different rooms: a large lounge, a games room-cum-bar and a cosy middle room with real fire and barrel furniture. No lunches on Sun. Six of the seven pubs in the village serve real ale.
♨ ▦ ◖ ⊟ ♿ ♣ P

Victoria

Victoria Inn
Hepworth (A616)
☎ (0484) 682785
12–2; 7–11
Tetley Bitter; Younger IPA [H]
Old-fashioned, unspoilt pub comprising basic lobby bar and intimate lounge. Toasted sandwiches served from antique grill behind bar. P

Wath-upon-Dearne

New Inn
West Street (A633)
☎ (0709) 872347
11–3; 5 (7 Sat)–11 (11–11 Fri)
John Smith's Bitter, Magnet [H]
This lively two-roomed local, once the Whitworth Brewery tap, is popular with a wide cross-section of the community, from bikers to BAs! Good food, including veg meals in bar and upstairs restaurant. Guest beers.
▦ ◖ ◗ ⊟ ♿ ♣ P

Sandygate
Sandygate (A633 near A6023 jct) ☎ (0709) 877827
11–11
Theakston Best Bitter, XB, Old Peculier; Younger IPA, No. 3 [H]
Large, imposing former hospital, now a hotel, overlooking the Dearne Valley; decorated and furnished to a high standard. Excellent food, including veg option. ♨ ♘ ▦ 🛏 ◖ ◗ ⊟ ♿ ♣ P

Wentworth

George & Dragon
Main Street (B6090 1½ miles from A6135)
☎ (0226) 742440
12–3 (12–2.30 Sun); 7–11
Oak Wobbly Bob; Taylor Best Bitter, Landlord, Porter; Tetley Bitter; Theakston Old Peculier [H]
Traditional village local, full of character(s). If there ever was a traditional English country pub, it may still be here. Wide range of high-gravity guest beers: just as well it's on the Rotherham to Barnsley bus route. Children welcome for meals.
♨ Q ▦ ◖ ⊟ ◠ P

Wheatley Hills

Wheatley Hotel
Thorne Road
☎ (0302) 364092
10.30–11
Courage Directors; John Smith's Magnet [H]
Large, well-appointed hotel just out of Doncaster centre. The excellent facilities often attract coach parties on summer evenings. ♘ ▦ 🛏 ◖ ◗ ⊟ ♣ P

Worsbrough Dale

Boatmans Rest
Edmunds Road (250 yds from B6100 Station Road jct)
☎ (0226) 286620
12–3; 7–11
John Smith's Bitter; Tetley Bitter [H]
Olde-worlde-style tavern, known locally as the 'Pod'. Lunch served only on Sun.
♘ ▦ ◗ ♿ ♣ P

Try also: Ship (Tetley)

Worsbrough Village

Edmunds Arms
25 Worsbrough Village (off A61) ☎ (0226) 206865
11–3 (4 Fri & Sat); 7–11
Samuel Smith OBB [H]
Splendid village inn set opposite a picturesque church, and near an historic watermill and country park. Good value food (booking advisable for weekends). No meals Sun or Mon eves. Q ▦ ◖ ◗ ⊟ ♿ P

Join CAMRA — see page 504!

West Yorkshire

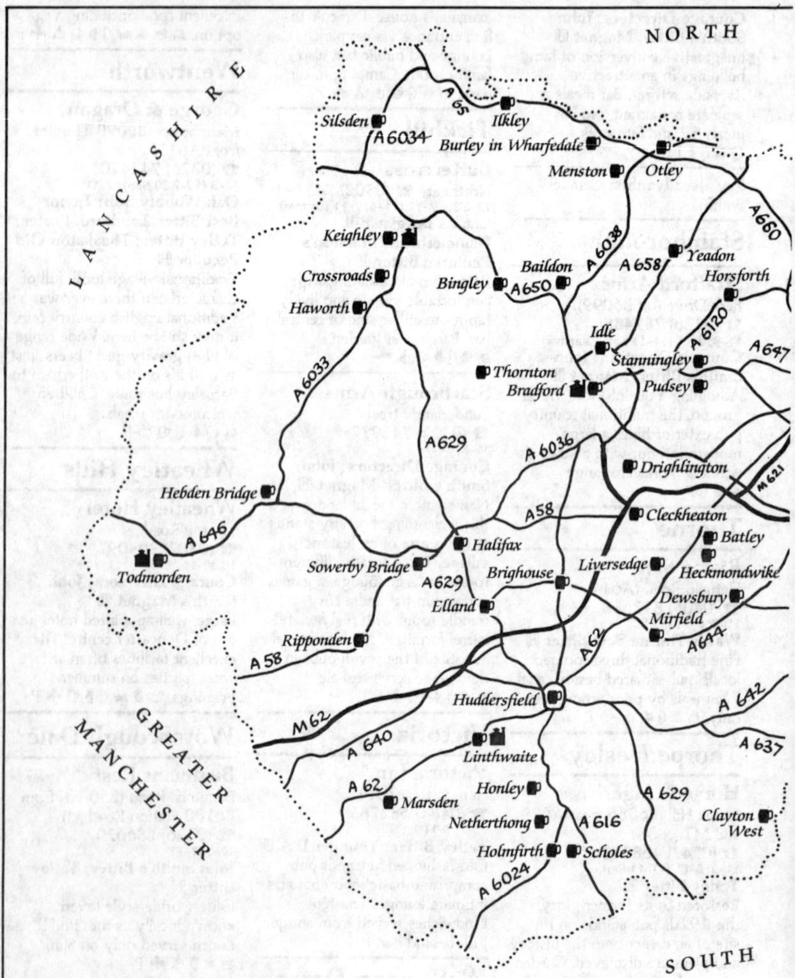

Clark's, *Wakefield*; **Linfit**, *Linthwaite*; **Taylor**, *Keighley*; **Robinwood**, *Todmorden*; **Trough**, *Bradford*

Aberford

Arabian Horse
Main Street (off A1)
☎ (0532) 813312
11–2.30; 5–11 (11–11 Sat)
Theakston Best Bitter; Younger Scotch, No.3 Ⓗ
Whitewashed pub on village green where locals and travellers off the A1 mix well. Public children's playground next to stream. No food Sun.
Q ♿ ♣ P

Altofts

Poplar Inn
Church Road (½ mile from Normanton on Castleford Road)
☎ (0977) 893416
11–11 (may vary)
John Smith's Bitter Ⓗ
Friendly pub; entertainment most Sun nights. ≋ ♣ P

Baildon

New Inn
Otley Road, Charlestown
(A6038 1 mile NE of Shipley)
☎ (0274) 586530
11–11 (11–4; 6–11 Sat)
Marston's Pedigree Bitter Ⓗ
Formerly a row of weavers' cottages, a series of discreet drinking areas, suitable for all ages. Excellent home-cooked meals (veg option) plus pizzas at all times. Steak meals Fri and Sat nights for a fiver; no eve meals Sun–Tue. Quiz night Wed.
Q ≋

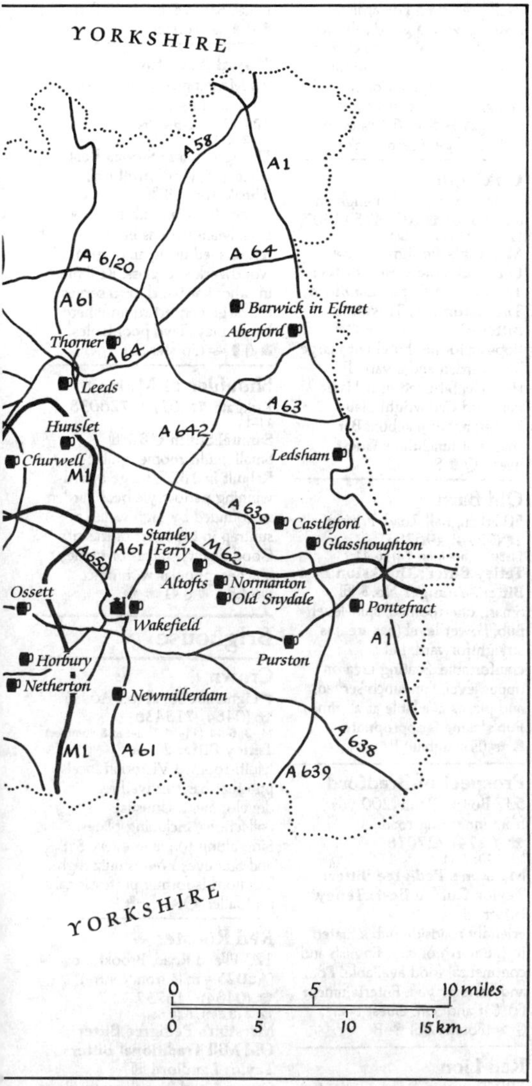

Barwick in Elmet

New Inn

Main Street ☎ (0532) 812289
11–3 (11.30–3.30 Fri & Sat); 6–11
Courage Directors; John Smith's Bitter Ⓗ
Oak-beamed roadside inn, extended into adjoining cottages dating from 1820. Beer is served from a tiny bar with a serving hatch. This must be one of the smallest bars in the Leeds area. Lunchtime bar snacks (not Sun). ❀ ⊕ ♿ ♣

Batley

Wilton Arms

4 Commercial Street (off A652)
☎ (0924) 479996
11–3; 5–11 (11–11 Mon, Fri & Sat)
Bass Mild XXXX, Light 5 Star, Draught Bass; Stones Best Bitter Ⓗ
Busy three-roomed central pub popular at all times. Pig Snout played! ⛟ ◐ ⊕ ⇌ ♣ P

Bingley

Brown Cow

Ireland Bridge (50 yds over bridge on Harden Road from A650 jct) ☎ (0274) 569482
11.45–3; 7–11
Taylor Bitter Ale, Best Bitter, Landlord, Ram Tam Ⓗ
Wood panelling, stained glass and comfortable armchairs give a cosy, rural feel to this riverside pub. Stuffed and mounted brown cow's head on wall! Lunches popular with business community. ❀ ⛟ ◐ ⇌ P

Ferrands Arms

Queens Street (off A650)
☎ (0274) 563949
11.30–11
Taylor Bitter Ale, Best Bitter, Landlord, Ram Tam Ⓗ
A popular pub, situated near arts centre. Pop music and quizzes. Traditional, home-cooked fare (not Sun). ◐ ⇌ ♣

Bradford

Albion

25 New Line, Greengates (100 yds from A658/A657 jct)
☎ (0274) 613211
11.45–3; 4.45–11 (11.45–11 Fri & Sat)
Tetley Mild, Bitter Ⓗ
Roadside pub with cosy lounge and busy tap room. ⊕ ♿ ♣

Blue Pig

Fagley Road, Fagley
OS193351 ☎ (0532) 562738
11.30–11
Tetley Bitter; Theakston Best Bitter XB; Younger No.3. Ⓗ
Popular pub yet hidden away, almost astride the Leeds/Bradford boundary on the Leeds Country Way. Flooding necessitated the building of low front wall and torturous entrance way. Regular quiz eves; can be noisy. Guest beers. ❀ ♣ P

Brown Cow

886 Little Horton Lane (1 mile from centre on ring road/Wibsey Road jct)
☎ (0274) 574040
12–3; 7–11
Samuel Smith OBB Ⓗ
Two-room local where the lounge has been extended into cottages alongside original building. Public bar-cum-games room at front. ⊕ ♿ ♣

Corn Dolly

110 Bolton Road
☎ (0274) 720219
12–11
Draught Bass; Stones Best Bitter; Taylor Best Bitter; Theakston Best Bitter, XB Ⓗ
Country-style pub near city centre. Country & Western music Wed and Sun. Regular guest beers. Try the jumbo sandwiches.
◐ ◑ ♿ ⇌ (Interchange/Forster Sq) ♣ P

Crow's Nest

Bell Dean Road (B6145 3 miles from city centre)
☎ (0274) 481311
11–11 (11–4; 7–11 Sat)
Old Mill Traditional Mild, Traditional Bitter, Bullion Bitter Ⓗ

Large, open-plan pub, part tap room, part split-level lounge. The only Old Mill tied house in the area. Cellar is above the bar! Live music Wed, Fri, Sat, Sun eves. ♣ P

Drop Kick
Huddersfield Road, Low Moor
☎ (0274) 670207
11–3 (may vary); 7–11 (11–11 Sat)
Thwaites Bitter [H]
Modern pub, opened in 1980, taking its name from rubgy league at the nearby Odsal Stadium. Large open-plan lounge where home-cooked lunches are served (try the plate pies). Games room with three pool tables, shared by nine teams. ◖ ♣

Fighting Cock
21–23 Preston Street (off Thornton Road)
☎ (0274) 726907
11.30–11
Marston's Pedigree Bitter; Old Mill Traditional Bitter; Taylor Golden Best, Landlord; Theakston Old Peculier; Wadworth 6X [H]
Basic, but recently extended, back-street alehouse in an industrial area with a wide choice of beers, real cider and foreign bottled beers. Famous, for its chilli con carne and 'Dockers' Wedges'. Guest beers. ◖ ♿ ♣

Hogshead
Haigh Hall Road, Greengates (off New Line, A657)
☎ (0274) 612670
11–11 (11–3; 6.30–11 Sat)
Trough Bitter, Wild Boar Bitter, Hogshead [H]
Former conservative club. Large games area at rear includes ten-pin bowling. Discount on drinks 11–7. Disabled access is via side door. ♿ ♣ P

Macrory's Bar
Beechfield Hotel, 4 Easby Road (400 yds from Alhambra Theatre) ☎ (0274) 729524
12–3; 5.30–11 (12–11 Thu–Sat)
Courage Directors; John Smith's Bitter, Magnet [H]
Cellar bar beneath a hotel with wooden benches and tables, and solid fuel-burning stove (Yorkshire range is disused). Interesting, good-value menu with daily specials and veg option. Popular with students. Free live bands on Sun night. ◖ ⇌ (Interchange) P

New Beehive Inn
171 Westgate
☎ (0274) 721784
11–11
Clark's Hammerhead; Old Mill Traditional Bitter; Taylor Golden Best, Landlord; Tetley Bitter [H]
Well-preserved Edwardian hostelry with a good selection of traditional ales. The only gas-lit pub in Bradford. Live trad jazz on Fri nights. Comfortable family room. Frequent guest beers. ◖ ◗ ♿ ⇌ (Interchange/Forster Sq)

Oakleigh
4 Oak Avenue, Manningham (off A650) ☎ (0274) 544307
12–3; 6–11 (12–11 Sat)
Marston's Pedigree Bitter; Old Mill Traditional Bitter; Taylor Best Bitter, Landlord; Theakston XB; Thwaites Bitter [H]
Popular former hotel with large beer garden and a varied clientele. Situated near Lister Park and Cartwright Hall Museum. No jukebox. Bar snacks at lunchtime. Guest beers. Q P

Old Barn
50 Frizinghall Road, Frizinghall
☎ (0274) 496281
11.30–4 (not Mon–Fri); 6–11
Tetley Bitter; Theakston Best Bitter; Younger No.3 [H]
Smart, one-roomed, split-level pub. Lower level (bar area) is straightforward, but comfortable. Seating area on upper level. Sun lunch served, and pizzas available at all times. Pub's name is appropriate.
⇌ (Frizinghall) P

Prospect of Bradford
537 Bolton Road (200 yds from inner ring road jct)
☎ (0274) 727018
12–4.30; 7–11
Marston's Pedigree Bitter; Taylor Golden Best; Tetley Bitter [H]
Friendly roadside pub situated to the north of city. English and continental food available. Pool and darts played. Entertainment Fri, Sat and Sun. Guest beers. ◖ ⇌ (Forster Sq) ♣ P

Red Lion
589 Thornton Road, Girlington (B6145, 2 miles from centre)
☎ (0274) 496684
11 (11.30 Thu)–3; 5.30–11 (11–11 Fri & Sat)
Samuel Smith OBB, Museum Ale [H]
Traditional local with friendly atmosphere. Home-made food (not Wed or Sun). Backgammon played. ◖ ♣ P

Ring O'Bells
18 Bolton Road
11–11 (11–4; 7–11 Sat)
Tetley Mild, Bitter [H]
Comfortable and popular city-centre pub, close to station and cathedral. Collection of toby jugs; fine glass and woodwork. Frequented by workers from Royal Mail sorting office. Live music Sat eve. No food Sun.
◖ ◗ ⇌ (Forster Sq)

Royal Standard
22 Manningham Lane (A650 off inner ring road)
☎ (0274) 394396
11–3; 5–12
Draught Bass; Stones Best Bitter; Taylor Landlord; Theakston XB [H]
Large Victorian pub with two bars. Main bar has been refurbished using all original woodwork and glass. Real fire in other bar which also serves the large concert room where bands play. Two pool tables.
◖ ◗ ⇌ (Forster Sq)

Shoulder of Mutton
Kirkgate ☎ (0274) 726038
11–11
Samuel Smith OBB [H]
Small, multi-roomed pub. Rebuilt in 1825. Large award-winning patio-style beer garden, surrounded by high walls: a suntrap in the heart of the city. Good quality value-for-money lunches, popular with office workers. ◖ ⇌ ♣

Brighouse

Crown
6 Lightcliffe Road (off A644)
☎ (0484) 715436
11–3; 5–11 (11–11 Thu–Sat & summer)
Tetley Bitter [H]
Multi-roomed Victorian locals' pub that has survived re-development. Unusual collections, including plates. Sing-along to piano every Sat and Sun eve; Wed is quiz night. Landlord is former professional footballer. Q ♿ ♣ P

Red Rooster
123 Elland Road, Brookfoot (A6025 ½ mile from centre)
☎ (0484) 713737
12–2 (3 Sat); 5 (6 Sat) –11
Marston's Pedigree Bitter; Old Mill Traditional Bitter; Taylor Landlord [H]
Compact and friendly roadside local (extension planned). Five guest beers. ♣ P

Star
29 Bridge End, Rastrick (A643)
☎ (0484) 714499
11.30–3; 5 (7 Sat)–11
Tetley Mild, Bitter [H]
Tucked-in next to railway viaduct. Large, busy taproom; comfy, unusually-shaped lounge. Limited parking. ♣ P

Burley in Wharfedale

White Horse
Main Street ☎ (0943) 863113
12–3.30; 5–11 (12–11 Mon, Fri & Sat)
Tetley Mild, Bitter [H]

Main road pub, easy to miss. One and a half rooms, full of character. Dominoes played. All four pubs in Burley serve real ale. ⛫ ≢ ♣

Castleford

Garden House Hotel
Wheldon Road
☎ (0977) 552934
11–11 (may vary)
Wards Thorne Best Bitter Ⓗ
Friendly pub just out of town-centre near River Aire. Handy for Castleford RL ground: lounge bar is full of RL photos and drawings. Good food at attractive prices – try the mixed grill. ⛫ Q ♞ ✿ ◖ ◗ ≢ ♣

Pointer (Dog)
Marchant Street, The Potteries, Whitwood Mere (off Savill Road) ☎ (0977) 553953
11–11 (may vary)
Camerons Traditional Bitter, Strongarm Ⓗ
Friendly, former Tetley pub comprising two lounges and one bar. Only Camerons pub in town. Landlord former rugby league player. Well worth a visit. ⛫ ⊟ ≢

Churwell

Commercial
Elland Road ☎ (0532) 532776
11.30–3; 5.30–11
Tetley Mild, Bitter Ⓗ
Welcoming, beautifully-restored pub, known locally as 'Top 'Ole' due to it being the highest of the three local pubs on Churwell Hill. Children welcome in one-room Sun lunchtimes. Q ♞ ✿ ◖ ⊟ ♿ P

Clayton West

Junction Inn
Wakefield Road (A636)
☎ (0484) 865117
11.30–3; 5–11
Whitbread Trophy Ⓗ
Comfortable main road village pub with friendly landlord. Close to terminus of proposed light steam railway.
⛫ Q ◖ ♣ P

Cleckheaton

Rose & Crown
12 Westgate (near A638/A643 jct)
☎ (0274) 872785
11–11
Tetley Mild, Bitter Ⓗ
Bustling, lively town pub with separate games room. ♣

Crossroads

Quarry House Inn
Bingley Road (off A629)
☎ (0535) 42239
12–3; 7–11 (11.30 if dining)
Bass Light 5 Star, Special Bitter, Draught Bass; Stones Best Bitter Ⓗ
Family-run converted farm-house set in open countryside. The bar in a small and cosy public is a former pulpit. Good quality food. Camping at Ashgrove Farm.
⛫ Q ♞ ✿ ◖ ◗ ⊟ ♿ ▲ P

Try also: Crossroads Inn

Dewsbury

John F Kennedy
Webster Hill (A644 near bus station) ☎ (0924) 461519
12–4 (Sat only); 7–11
Taylor Landlord; Tetley Bitter Ⓗ
Alternative pub with strong following. Unchanged for many years. Often spills over with bikers. Regular guest beers at weekends. ≢

Market House
Church Street (near bus station)
☎ (0924) 450555
11–3 (4 Sat); 5 (7 Sat)–11 (11–11 Fri)
Tetley Mild, Bitter Ⓗ
A Tetley Heritage pub and rightly so; basic, with character.
⛫ ⊟ ♿ ≢ ♣

Drighlington

Valley Inn
68 Whitehall Road (A58)
☎ (0532) 852483
11–3; 5.30–11
Samuel Smith OBB Ⓗ
Ideal starting place for country walks; the Leeds Country Way runs past the pub, which offers fine views across the valley. Children welcome at weekend lunchtime. No food Wed or Sun. ⛫ ♞ ✿ ◖ ♣ P

Elland

Barge & Barrel
Park Road (A6025)
☎ (0422) 373623
12–11
Marston's Pedigree Bitter, Owd Rodger; Oak Best Bitter, Tyke Bitter, Old Oak Ale; Taylor Landlord Ⓗ
Large Victorian-style pub refurbished with polished wood and leaded glass. Four drinking areas, including a well-equipped family room. The front room boasts a fine fireplace. Usually four guest beers.
⛫ ♞ ✿ ◖ ◗ ♿ ♣ P

Colliers Arms
66 Park Road (A6025)
☎ (0422) 372007
11.30–3; 5.30–11 (11–11 Sat)
Samuel Smith OBB, Museum Ale Ⓗ
Smart low-ceilinged cottage pub of two rooms and recently built conservatory. It stands next to the canal and has own moorings. Eve meals: Mon–Fri in summer; Thu–Sat in winter till 8pm. Disabled access is via conservatory.
⛫ ✿ ◖ ◗ ⊟ ♿ ♣ P

Glasshoughton

Houghton Hotel
Front Street (A656)
☎ (0977) 554437
11–11 (may vary)
John Smith's Bitter Ⓗ
Friendly locals' pub which can get very full at weekends. Home of Houghton Greyhounds RL team. ⛫ ⊟ ♣ P

Rock Inn
Rock Hill (off A656)
☎ (0977) 552985
11–11 (may vary)
Wards Mild, Thorne Best Bitter, Kirby Strong Ⓗ
Old pub with two real fires. Local CAMRA Pub of the Year 1989. Can get very full at weekends. Parking very difficult – illegal parking will cost you!
⛫ Q ⊟ ♣

Halifax

Bowling Green
55 Winding Road
☎ (0422) 352745
11.30–11
Wilson's Original Bitter Ⓗ
Comfortable two-roomed pub off town centre. Handy for bus and railway stations. 🛏 ◖ ♿ ≢

Clarence Hotel
77 Lister Lane
☎ (0422) 363266
11.30–3; 5–11 (11.30–11 Fri & Sat)
Draught Bass; Old Mill Traditional Bitter; Stones Best Bitter; Taylor Landlord; Tetley Bitter Ⓗ
Busy street-corner local. Well-used dartboard and pool table.
✿ 🛏 ◖ ♿ ≢ ♣ P

Dean Clough Inn
36 Lee Bridge
☎ (0422) 346708
11–11 (11–3; 7–11 Sat)
Draught Bass; Stones Best Bitter; Tetley Bitter Ⓗ
Smartly-refurnished Edwardian pub with single V-shaped lounge. Located beneath the concrete flyover of the A629, Keighley road. Food at all times, specializing in pizzas; veg dishes available. ◖ ◗

Sportsman Inn
Lee Lane, Shibden (off A647)
OS093272 ☎ (0422) 367000
12–3; 6–11 (11–11 Sat)
Old Mill Traditional Bitter; Ruddles County; Taylor Landlord; Tetley Bitter; Theakston Old Peculier Ⓗ
Popular hilltop freehouse with

expansive views. Squash court, solarium, sauna, and all-weather ski slope attached! Folk club Thu. Restaurant open Sun (all day); no eve meals Mon. Guest beer. ⌂ ☋ ▣ ☾ ◗ ♣ P

Travellers Inn

Tan House Hill, Hipperholme (100 yds from A58 behind camping centre)
☎ (0422) 202494
11.30–11
Ruddles Best Bitter; Webster's Green Label Ⓗ
Traditional local on old turnpike road opposite site of former railway station, two miles from town. ▣

Woodcock

213 Gibbet Street
☎ (0422) 359906
11.30–3; 5–11 (11.30–11 Fri & Sat)
Old Mill Traditional Bitter; Marston's Burton Best Bitter, Pedigree Bitter; Taylor Landlord; Theakston Best Bitter, XB Ⓗ
'No-frills' local. Live music Tue and Thu nights. 12 beers usually available from a nationwide range. ☾ ♿ ♣ ⌓

Haworth

Fleece Inn

Main Street ☎ (0535) 42172
11.30–11 (11.30–3; 7–11 winter)
Taylor Golden Best, Best Bitter, Landlord, Ram Tam Ⓗ
Ancient coaching inn, popular with 'spirits'. Village local which also makes visitors welcome. Stone-flagged bar area and a quiet room containing a spoof Brontë Museum display. ⌂ ☋ ☾ ⛺ ≢ (KWVLR) ♣

Haworth Old Hall

Sun Street
☎ (0535) 42709
12–3.30 (5.30 Sat); 5.30 (7.30 Sat) –11 (11–11 Fri & summer)
Bass Mild XXXX, Draught Bass; Stones Best Bitter, Tetley Bitter Ⓗ
17th-century Tudor building with open stonework, oak beams and mullioned window. Three rooms offering friendly welcome; large beer garden open to children. Sun lunch a speciality in the restaurant. Accommodation includes a family room. ☋ ▣ ⛟ ☾ ◗ ⊟ ♿ ⛺ ≢ (KWVLR) P

Hebden Bridge

Cross Inn

46 Towngate, Heptonstall
☎ (0422) 843833
11.30–4.30; 7–11 (may vary)
Taylor Golden Best, Best Bitter, Landlord Ⓗ
Welcoming pub in the picturesque main street of a historic hilltop village. Built in 1617, with a Victorian frontage. Parking difficult. Disabled access is via back door. ▣ ⛟ ☾ ◗ ♿ ⛺ ♣

Fox & Goose

9 Heptonstall Road (A646)
☎ (0422) 842649
11.30–3; 7–11
Ruddles Best Bitter; John Smith's Magnet; Tetley Bitter Ⓗ
Small, friendly three-roomed traditional local at foot of steep hill to Heptonstall. Parking difficult. Beer range may vary (guest beer). ☋ ▣ ☾ ◗ ≢ ♣

Nutclough House Hotel

Keighley Road (A6033)
☎ (0422) 844361
12–3 (not Mon, except bank hols); 6 (7 Mon)–11
Everards Tiger Best Bitter; Taylor Landlord; Theakston Best Bitter; Thwaites Bitter Ⓗ
Three-roomed hotel with games room and snug; very much a friendly, family pub. Beer range may increase. Half the menu choices are vegetarian. ⌂ ▣ ⛟ ☾ ◗ ♿ ≢ ♣ P

Heckmondwike

Railway Hotel

Railway Street (off B6119)
☎ (0924) 402522
11–3; 6–11 (may vary)
Stones Best Bitter Ⓗ
Ex-Springwell house near old brewery site. Unchanged local in cul-de-sac. ▣ ⊟ ♣ P

Holmfirth

Elephant & Castle

Hollowgate (off A635)
☎ (0484) 683178
11.30–4.30; 7–11
Bass Mild XXXX, Light 5 Star; Stones Best Bitter Ⓗ
A true locals' pub in a tourist area. Despite its proximity to Nora Batty's, it remains unaffected by *Summer Wine*. Separate pool room. No food weekends. ☾ ⛺ ♣ P

Farmers Arms

Liphill Bank Road, Burnlee (off A635) ☎ (0484) 683713
12–3 (not Mon); 6–11 (12–11 Sat)
Taylor Best Bitter, Landlord; Tetley Mild, Bitter Ⓗ
Popular village pub with warm atmosphere and cheerful welcome, re-establishing its former reputation. Situated on winding lane so parking can be difficult. Regular guest beers. ⌂ Q ☋ ▣ ☾ ◗ ♣ P

Rose & Crown (Nook)

7 Victoria Square
☎ (0484) 683960
11.30–11
Samuel Smith OBB; Stones Best Bitter; Taylor Best Bitter, Landlord, Ram Tam; Younger No.3 Ⓗ
Tucked out of sight, a basic boozer in surroundings to match with an interesting back court drinking area. Worth the effort of finding somewhere to park. Folk music Sun eve. Guest beers. ⌂ ☋ ▣ ⊟ ⛺ ♣

Honley

Coach & Horses

Eastgate (200 yds from A616/A6024 jct)
☎ (0484) 666135
11.30–3; 5–11 (11.30–11 Sat)
Bass Mild XXXX, Light 5 Star, Draught Bass; Stones Best Bitter Ⓗ
A bustling well-appointed pub, affectionately known as Henry's. Rare outlet for mild in the valley. Eve meals Mon only; no food weekends. Guest beers. ⌂ ☾ ⛺ ≢ P

Horbury

Shepherd Arms

Cluntergate (off A642)
☎ (0924) 274877
11–11
Theakston XB, Old Peculier; Younger Scotch, No.3 Ⓗ
Large, friendly pub on outskirts of town. An ancient inn, now well modernised in open-plan style but retaining separate bar. Guest beers occasionally. ⌂ ▣ ☾ ◗ ⊟ ♣ P

Horsforth

Fox & Hounds

Tinshill Lane, Cookridge (50 yds from station)
☎ (0532) 678415
11–11
Tetley Mild, Bitter Ⓗ
Stone-built pub with distinctive windows. Open-plan interior with partitioned snug in corner. Popular with all ages. Families welcome; children's play area outside with swings. No food Sun. ☋ ▣ ☾ ◗ ⊟ ≢ ♣ P

Try also: Fleece (John Smith's)

Huddersfield

Dusty Miller

2 Gilead Road, Longwood (1 mile SE of M62 jct 23 and off A640) OS104173
☎ (0484) 651763
12–3 (Sat/Sun only); 7–11
Marston's Burton Best Bitter, Pedigree Bitter; Oak Best Bitter; Old Mill Traditional Bitter; Taylor Golden Best, Landlord Ⓗ
Friendly multi-roomed free house, popular with all ages. Good views, low ceilings, English fittings, American plates and over 50 Scotch malt whiskies. Guest Beers.

Rat & Ratchet
Chapel Hill ☎ (0484) 516717
11–11
Marston's Pedigree Bitter; Old Mill Traditional Bitter; Taylor Landlord, Ram Tam; Thwaites Mild; Whitbread Boddingtons Bitter H
Free house, usually boasting 12 real ales. Popular with all. Occasional live music. Undergoing gradual refurbishment. P

Shoulder of Mutton
Neale Road, Lockwood (off B6108) ☎ (0484) 424835
1–4.30 (Sat only); 7–11
Taylor Landlord; Tetley Mild, Bitter; Theakston XB, Old Peculier; Thwaites Bitter H
Old-fashioned walnut-panelled pub at head of cobbled street with traditional dominoes room and legendary jukebox; pool room upstairs. 20 minutes' walk from central Huddersfield. Guest beers. ♣

Slubbers Arms
1 Halifax Old Road (off A641)
☎ (0484) 429032
11.30–4; 6.30–11
Marston's Pedigree Bitter; Old Mill Traditional Mild; Taylor Best Bitter H
Wedge-shaped pub with central bar which is undergoing gradual refurbishment without loss of character. Note the clocking-in machine and old range. The unique name is connected with the local textile trade. Guest beers. Q ♣

Yates Wine Lodge
Queensgate (ring road near polytechnic) ☎ (0484) 510974
11–11
Draught Bass; Tetley Bitter; Whitbread Boddingtons Bitter H
Spacious bar in modern Edwardiana with a high, high ceiling above the draught port, Australian wine and temperance hoardings. Well-appointed and up-market. Guest wines from around the world. Caters well for disabled visitors. ♿ ≠

Hunslet

Gardeners Arms
Beza Street ☎ (0532) 712971
11.30–11 (11–4; 7–11 Sat)
Tetley Mild, Bitter H
Classic local nestling between factories. Three small, original rooms, and a beer garden to rear. Recently redecorated but retaining an unspoilt atmosphere. Home-cooked fare with veg option. Q ♣

Garden Gate
37 Waterloo Road (pedestrian precinct) ☎ (0532) 700379
11–11 (10.30 Tue & Wed)
Tetley Mild, Bitter H
Splendid, totally unspoilt Victorian palace. A feast of glass, tiles and wood in four rooms off a central corridor. Parking nearby. Q ♿ ♣

Station Hotel
Hillidge Road
☎ (0532) 700707
11–3; 5.30–11 (11–11 Fri & Sat)
Samuel Smith OBB H
Friendly, two-roomed local, named after long-defunct Hunslet station. Pool table in tap room. ♿ ♣ P

Try also: Mulberry (S&N)

Idle

Brewery Tap
51 Albion Road
☎ (0274) 613936
11.30–3 (4 Sat); 6.30 (7 Sat)–11
Trough Bitter, Wild Boar Bitter H
One-room local with large central bar area; formerly a bakery. Part wood-panels and carpet; part stone walls and floor. Regular rock nights. Hogshead sold occasionally. ♿ ♣

Try also: Brewery Arms (Trough)

Ilkley

Midland Hotel
Station Road
☎ (0943) 607433
11–11
Courage Directors; John Smith's Bitter, Magnet H
Two-roomed pub with well-furnished lounge and unpretentious tap room. Opposite the refurbished station which gave its name to the pub. ≠ ♣ P

Wharfe Cottage
Leeds Road (A65)
☎ (0943) 607323
12 (11 Sat)–3 (not Mon); 6.30–11
Ruddles Best Bitter; Tetley Bitter; Theakston XB; Webster's Choice; Younger Scotch H
Small, but welcoming Dales-type pub on the edge of town. Extensive menu of home-cooked food, including giant Yorkshire puddings. Guest beers. ≠ ♣ P

Keighley

Albert Hotel
Bridge Street
☎ (0535) 602306
11–11 (11–3; 6–11 Mon & Tue, may vary)
Taylor Bitter Ale, Best Bitter, Ram Tam (winter) H
Spacious, popular Victorian pub in town centre. ≠ ♣

Boltmakers Arms
117 East Parade
☎ (0535) 661936
11.30–11 (11–4.30; 7–11 Sat)
Taylor Bitter Ale, Best Bitter, Landlord H
Handy town-centre local; popular with all age groups, regulars and visitors. Smallest pub in town; busy at weekends. ≠ ♣

Cricketers Arms
Coney Lane ☎ (0535) 669912
11–11 (11–4.30; 7–11 Fri & Sat)
Taylor Bitter Ale, Best Bitter, Ram Tam (winter occasionally) H
Cosy one-room local sandwiched between mills near the town centre. Lunchtime snacks. ♿ ≠ ♣

Eastwood Tavern
Bradford Road
☎ (0535) 604849
11–11
Taylor Bitter Ale, Best Bitter H
Small, homely locals' pub with three rooms: a comfy lounge, a pool room and a tap room with open fire and polished wooden seating that is a joy to behold. Sing-alongs on Sat and Sun eves, including a pop quiz. Sun lunchtime creche.
≠ ♣

Grinning Rat
2 Church Street
☎ (0535) 609747
11–11
Malton Double Chance Bitter; Old Mill Traditional Bitter; Samuel Smith Museum Ale; Taylor Landlord H
Popular, basic town-centre pub which attracts a varied clientele. Five guest beers, including a mild, usually available, along with a cider or perry. Live music Sun (jazz) and Thu. Good value snacks include pizzas.
♿ ≠ ♣

Red Pig
Church Street
☎ (0535) 605383
11.30–2.30 (4.30 Fri & Sat); 7–11
Taylor Bitter Ale, Landlord; Trough Wild Boar Bitter H
Smart, popular town-centre pub with convivial atmosphere. Many porcine artefacts. Pool played. Guest beers. ≠

Royal Hotel
Damside (off Oakworth Road)
☎ (0535) 604347
11–3; 5.30–11 (11–11 Fri & Sat)
Taylor Bitter Ale, Best Bitter H
Popular pub with a large L-shaped front room and a tap room, both with a pool table. Live entertainment Sun; disco Thu. Pizzas available at all times. ♿ ≠ ♣ P

West Yorkshire

Volunteer Arms
Lawkholme Lane
☎ (0535) 600173
11–11
Taylor Bitter Ale, Best Bitter Ⓗ
Smart two-roomed locals' pub in town centre. Difficult to find, hidden behind large Tetley pub in Cavendish Street. ⊞ ⇌ ♣

Ledsham

Chequers
Claypit Lane (off A1)
☎ (0977) 683135
11–3; 5.30–11 (11–11 Sat, closed Sun)
John Smith's Bitter; Theakston Best Bitter; Younger Scotch, No.3 Ⓗ
Delightful classic country pub in charming village. Several small and cosy rooms with beams and open fires; upstairs restaurant. ⌂ Q ♞ ⊛ ☾ ◗ ♣ P

Leeds

Adelphi
1 Hunslet Road, Leeds Bridge (lower end of Briggate)
☎ (0532) 456377
11–11 (11–3; 7.30–11 Sat)
Tetley Mild, Bitter Ⓗ
A Heritage inn: restored, multi-roomed Edwardian pub, displaying fine woodwork, tiling and glass. Live jazz Sat nights. No food at weekend. ☾ ⊞ ⇌ ♣

Albion Inn
86 Armley Road, Armley (old A647) ☎ (0532) 456729
11.30–3; 5.30–11
Tetley Bitter Ⓗ
In this guide for the 18th time! Three-room pub with brass handpumps. A Tetley Heritage inn and winner of a CAMRA Pub Preservation award. Fine part-tiled frontage advertises former owner. ⌂ Q ⊞ ♣ P

Bricklayers
St Marks Road (off A660, between university and Woodhouse)
☎ (0532) 458277
11–4; 6.30–11
Courage Directors; John Smith's Bitter, Magnet Ⓗ
Small, welcoming one-roomed bar with lots of nooks and crannies. Hidden amongst student accommodation blocks. Warm, friendly and justifiably popular. ☾ ♿ ♣ P

City of Mabgate
45 Mabgate (off A58)
☎ (0532) 457789
12–3; 5.30–11
Marston's Pedigree Bitter; Whitbread Trophy, Castle Eden Ale Ⓗ
Gem of a pub recently restored. Green tiled exterior, fine windows and an Edwardian lounge with an iron stove. No food weekends. Guest beers.
⌂ Q ⊛ ☾ ⊞ ♿ ♣

Cobourg Tavern
1 Claypit Lane (opp. Merrion shopping centre)
☎ (0532) 457886
11–11 (11–3; 7–11 Sat)
Ind Coope Burton Ale; Tetley Mild, Bitter Ⓗ
Friendly pub with mixed clientele of students and business people. ☾ ⇌

Duck & Drake
Kirkgate (between markets and parish church)
☎ (0532) 465806
11–11
Marston's Pedigree Bitter, Owd Rodger; Old Mill Traditional Mild, Traditional Bitter; Taylor Landlord; Theakston Best Bitter, XB Ⓗ
Hugely popular, no-frills beer drinkers' paradise, frequented by all from bikers to bankers. Live music Tue, Thu, Sun. Always six guest beers. No food at weekends. ⌂ ☾ ⊞ ⇌ ♣ ⌽

Eagle Tavern
North Street, Sheepscar (A61)
☎ (0532) 457146
11.30–3; 5.30–11
Taylor Golden Best, Golden Best Mild, Best Bitter, Landlord, Ram Tam Ⓗ
White-painted Georgian building with a comfortable lounge and large public bar. Regular live music. Two guest beers always available, plus real cider. Leeds CAMRA Pub of the Year 1989. 🛏 ☾ ⊞ ♣ ⌽

Florence Nightingale
Beckett Street (opp. St James Hospital) ☎ (0532) 482622
11–11 (11–4; 7–11 Sat)
Courage Directors; John Smith's Bitter, Magnet Ⓗ
Comfortable art-deco style bar, popular with patients and staff from the famous 'Jimmy's' hospital. ♿

Fox & Newt
Burley Road
☎ (0532) 432612
11–11
Fox & Newt Burley Bitter, Old Willow, Kirkstall Ruin (winter); **Marston's Pedigree Bitter; Theakston Old Peculier; Whitbread Castle Eden Ale** Ⓗ
One-roomed, bare floorboarded brew pub in period style. Popular with students from college opposite. Decor includes taxidermy, pianola and slot machines. Beers brewed with malt extract. No food at weekend. ☾

Mustard Pot
20 Stainbeck Lane, Chapel Allerton (off A61)
☎ (0532) 696284
11–11
Mansfield Riding Dark Mild, Riding Traditional Bitter, Old Baily Ⓗ
Tasteful conversion of an 18th-century house: one large room with contrasting areas. Very busy. Large beer garden with children's playground. Food served 12–8. No disabled access to ladies' WC.
⊛ ☾ ◗ ♿ ♣ P

Nags Head
20 Town Street
☎ (0532) 624938
11–3; 5.30–11 (11–11 Fri & Sat)
Samuel Smith OBB Ⓗ
Old coaching inn at the centre of Chapel Allerton village. Large L-shaped lounge has a no-smoking area; busy tap room with darts and dominoes.
Q ⊛ ☾ ⊞ ♣ P

Nelson
212 Armley Road, Armley (A647) ☎ (0532) 638505
11 (12 Sat)–3; 5.30–11
Theakston XB; Younger Scotch, No.3 Ⓗ
Two-room pub near jail which was the last home-brew pub in Leeds (ceased brewing on the death of the owner in 1952).
☾ ⊞ ♣

New Roscoe
Bristol Street (off Roseville Road) ☎ (0532) 460778
11–11
Tetley Mild, Bitter Ⓗ
Large, friendly three-roomed former club, comfortably converted. Lots of mementos from the Old Roscoe, including a replica frontage as the entrance to one of the rooms. Guest beers. Open from 8.30am for breakfast.
Q ♞ ⊛ ☾ ⊞ ♿ ♣ P

Old Unicorn
Stocks Hill, Bramley (A657, by shopping centre)
☎ (0532) 565488
11.30–3 (4 Fri & Sat, 12–2 Sun); 5.30–11
Tetley Mild, Bitter; Theakston Best Bitter; Younger No.3 Ⓗ
Comfortable, popular, 200-year-old free house, much-extended with opened-out interior. Beer garden very popular with families. Good home-cooked food with veg option. Q ⊛ ☾ ⊞ ♿ P

Pig & Whistle
East Wing, Merrion Centre
☎ (0532) 445354
11–3 (4 Sat); 4.30 (7 Sat)–11 (7.30–10.30 Sun)
Camerons Traditional Bitter; Everards Old Original Ⓗ
Modern pub in large shopping centre, under office block. Lunchtime snacks. ♿ ⇌ ♣

Queen Hotel
134 Oldfield Lane, Wortley
☎ (0532) 794597
11.30–3 (4 Mon & Fri); 5.30–11 (11–4.30; 7–11 Sat)
Tetley Mild, Bitter [H]
Attractive pub with a tiny tap room at the front and a larger lounge. A former Melbourne house which retains some fine stained glass. No food at weekends. Q P

Spring Close
Ellerby Lane (off East Street)
☎ (0532) 455668
11–11 (1–4; 7–11 Sat)
Tetley Mild, Bitter [H]
Little gem of a local, saved from redevelopment and now thriving in the care of the present landlord.

Victoria
Great George Street (behind Town Hall) ☎ (0532) 451386
11–11 (closes 2 Sun lunch)
Tetley Mild, Bitter [H]
Large three-roomed pub, refurbished in spectacular gin palace style: lots of brass and stained glass, old advertisements, etc. Q

Whitelocks
Turks Head Yard, Briggate
☎ (0532) 453950
11–11
Younger Scotch, IPA, No.3 [H]
Very popular city centre pub with unspoilt Edwardian interior, featuring a tiled bar, brewery mirrors and brass. Second bar further up the yard. Menu offers veg option.
Q

Wrens
61a Merrion Street
☎ (0532) 458888
11–3; 5–11 (11–11 Fri & Sat)
Ind Coope Burton Ale; Tetley Mild, Bitter [H]
Popular, pleasant street-corner pub near Grand Theatre. Three rooms, one of which is a no-smoking room. Guest beers.

Try also: Prince of Wales (John Smith's); **Regent, Sheepscar** (Tetley); **Town Hall Tavern** (Free)

Linthwaite

Bulls Head
Blackmoorfoot (opp. reservoir) OS097132 ☎ (0484) 842715
11–11
Stones Best Bitter; Whitbread Boddingtons Mild, Boddingtons Bitter [H]
Impressive and varied bar meals at all times, ranging from Yorkshire puds to *escargots* and special steak dinners for two. On windy hillside above the Colne Valley. P

Sair
Lane Top, Hoyle Ing (off A62) OS100143 ☎ (0484) 842370
12–4 (not Mon–Fri); 7–11
Linfit Mild, Bitter, Special, Old Eli, Leadboiler, Enoch's Hammer [H]
Uniquely atmospheric multi-roomed pub overlooking the Colne Valley. Nine home-brewed draught products usually available, including Causeway Cider. The original Enoch's Hammer was used by Luddites to smash weaving machines in the 19th century.

Liversedge

Black Bull
37 Halifax Road (A649, 400 yds from A62 jct)
☎ (0924) 403779
11.30–3.30 (4 Sat); 5.30–11
Clark's Traditional Bitter; Old Mill Traditional Bitter; Stones Best Bitter; Taylor Golden Best; Tetley Bitter [H]
No-frills locals' pub with separate front room and warm welcome for all.

Marsden

Hare & Hounds
Mount Road OS046110
☎ (0484) 844478
12–3; 7–11 (11–11 Sat)
Tetley Mild, Bitter; Theakston Best Bitter, Old Peculier [H]
Close to the Pennine Way. Tap room recently restored to former glory. Separate poolroom and horseshoe bar.
P

Menston

Fox
129 Bradford Road (A65/A6038 jct) ☎ (0943) 73025
11.30–3; 5.30–11
Taylor Best Bitter, Landlord [H]
Old coaching inn, over 300 years-old with original old wood beams and cosy corners. Outdoor tables overlook local cricket ground. P

Mirfield

Flowerpot Inn
65 Calder Road, Lower Hopton
☎ (0924) 496939
11.30–4; 7.30–11
Tetley Mild, Bitter [H]
300 year-old building, retaining some original features, including a separate tap room. Close to station and River Calder: trains, boats but no planes. P

White Gate
105 Leeds Road, Mirfield Moor (jct A62/B6119)
☎ (0924) 490471
11.30–11 (11.30–3; 7–11 Sat)
Draught Bass; Stones Best Bitter [H]
Recently-renovated in Bass Victorian-style but retaining coal fire and traditional feel. Its sign says it all: 'This gate hangs high and hinders n'one, refresh and pay and travel on'.
P

Netherthong

Cricketers Arms
Off Haigh Lane, Deanhouse (signed to Deanhouse off A6024) OS139100
☎ (0484) 682993
12–3 (not Mon–Thu); 7–11
Tetley Mild, Bitter [H]
Out-of-the-way pub but don't let that stump you: it could well bowl you over and is quite a catch! Swings and slides in the outfield. No eve meals Tue.
P

Netherton

Star Inn
211 Netherton Lane (B6117, off A642) ☎ (0924) 274496
11.30–3 (4 Fri & Sat); 6.30–11
Samuel Smith OBB [E]
Cosy and well-kept, three-roomed village local, with a friendly clientele and a lively tap room. No food Sun.
P

Newmillerdam

Pledwick Well Inn
Barnsley Road (A61, 3 miles S of Wakefield)
☎ (0924) 255088
11.30–3; 5.30 (7 Sat) –11
Camerons Traditional Bitter, Strongarm Premium [H]
Former travellers' inn, close to popular beauty spot of Newmillerdam Lake and village. Cosy front lounge with vast collection of old jugs, plates and brassware; lounge/dining room extension at side. Large sloping beer garden overlooks stream.
P

Normanton

Junction Inn
Market Place (off A655)
☎ (0924) 893021
11–5; 7–11
Wards Thorne Best Bitter [H]
Lounge with small pool room; traditional tap room. Live music Sat and Sun nights. Home-made food. Small garden.
P

Old Snydale

Cross Keys
New Road (B6133 Normanton-Featherstone Road)

☎ (0924) 892238
12–3; 7–11
Younger Scotch, No.3 🄷
Impressive whitewashed pub with notable sign, on edge of country hamlet. Two well-furnished lounge areas cater for all ages. Ask about the local ghost. Quiz night Wed; monthly clay pigeon shooting. No food weekends. ❀ ◖ ▲ ♣ P

Ossett

Boons End
Low Mill Road (off Healey Road) ☎ (0924) 273865
11–3; 5.30–11 (11–11 Sat)
Clark's Mild, Traditional Bitter, Hammerhead; Taylor Landlord; Tetley Bitter 🄷
Tucked-away, cosy old stone pub with good atmosphere and brewery artefacts. Games room is decorated with newspaper cuttings. Quiz Mon; live music every fortnight. Ossett Folk Club Thu. Guest beers. Summer barbecues. ♨ ❀ ◖ ◗ ♣ ⌓ P

Little Bull
99 Teall Street (off Queen's Drive, 1 mile from M1 jct 40) ☎ (0924) 273569
12–3; 5.30 (7 Sat)–11
Thwaites Bitter, Daniel's Hammer 🄷
Friendly, working-class local with good atmosphere. Comfortable L-shaped lounge and lively 'laugh-a-minute' tap room. ⊡ ♣ P

Otley

Bay Horse
20 Market Place
☎ (0943) 461122
11–11
Tetley Mild, Bitter 🄷
Small, unspoilt, low-ceilinged pub with tap room served from a small hatch. A series of linked areas makes up the main lounge. Pictures of old Otley and fine stained glass. Q ❀ ⊡ ♿ ♣

Junction Inn
Bondgate ☎ (0943) 463233
11–3; 5.30–11 (11–11 Thu–Sat)
Taylor Best Bitter, Landlord; Tetley Bitter; Theakston XB, Old Peculier 🄷
One-roomed, stone corner pub with many small, private areas. Lively atmosphere; popular with younger people. A Tetley 'free house'. No food Sun.
♨ ◖ ♿

Red Lion
Kirkgate ☎ (0943) 462226
11–11
Courage Directors; John Smith's Bitter, Magnet 🄷
Very well-kept pub near market place. Quite small, with three separate drinking areas served by a single bar. Menu includes veg option. Q ❀ ◖ ◗ ♿

Pontefract

Old Castle Hotel
13 Micklegate
☎ (0977) 702985
11–3; 6–11
Draught Bass; Stones Best Bitter 🄷
Large brick pub on edge of town shopping area, close to historic castle. Small but lively public bar and cosy lounge.
⊡ ⇌ (Monkhill) ♣

Try also: Yorkshire Rose (Mansfield)

Pudsey

Britannia
Swinnow Road
☎ (0532) 564885
11.30–3; 5.30 (5 Fri, 7 Sat)–11
John Smith's Bitter, Magnet 🄷
Old stone pub modernised with open-plan lounge. Wide range of home-cooked food.
Q ❀ ◖ ◗ ⊡ ⇌ (Bramley) ♣ P

George
George Richardshaw Lane (B6155) ☎ (0532) 565435
11.30–11 (11.30–4; 7–11 Sat)
Courage Directors; John Smith's Bitter, Magnet 🄷
Sturdy 19th-century stone pub with two rooms. The busy games room displays many dart and domino trophies. Pleasant, cosy best room. Good pub food lunchtime and early eve.
◖ ◗ ⊡ ⇌ (New Pudsey) ♣ P

Try also: Mason Arms (Whitbread)

Purston

White House
Pontefract Road (A645)
☎ (0977) 708659
11–4; 7–11.30
Samuel Smith OBB 🄷
Whitewashed suburban pub with pleasantly furnished L-shaped lounge. Note the collection of old photographs and adverts. Very popular with locals. ◖ ◗ ♣ P

Ripponden

Blue Ball
Blue Ball Lane, Soyland (off A58 near Baitings Dam)
☎ (0422) 823603
12–3 (not Tue); 7–11
Courage Directors; John Smith's Bitter, Magnet; Taylor Golden Best, Golden Best Mild, Landlord 🄷
Homely moorland inn dating from 1672. Fine views of surrounding moors and nearby reservoir. Folk music and sing-alongs. Guest beer. Menu has veg options and caters for children. ♨ ♘ ❀ 🛏 ◖ ◗ ♿

Bridge Inn
Priest Lane (off A58)
☎ (0422) 822595
11.30–3; 5.30–11
Ruddles County; Taylor Golden Best, Best Bitter; Younger Scotch 🄷
Ancient hostelry with splendid timber structure. Daniel Defoe is reputed to be a former patron. The beer pumps are unlabelled. Advisable to book for lunch; eve meals only in restaurant.
Q ◖ ♿ P

New Inn
Rochdale Roads, Baitings, Soyland (A58 opp. Baitings Dam) ☎ (0422) 822565
11–11
Stones Best Bitter; Thwaites Mild, Bitter 🄷
Former coaching house with several large rooms. Ideal for moorland walks. Attractive sundial on front wall. Food served all day. Guest beer.
❀ 🛏 ◖ ◗ ♣ P

Scholes (Holmfirth)

Boot & Shoe Inn
St Georges Road (follow Scholes signs from A616 at New Mill) ☎ (0484) 683626
12 (5 Tue)–11
Taylor Landlord; Tetley Mild, Bitter 🄷
Bustling village local overlooking picturesque valley. Collection of firearms on wall. Snacks always available.
♨ ❀ ♣ P

Silsden

Bridge Hotel
Keighley Road (by Leeds-Liverpool Canal bridge)
☎ (0535) 53144
11–3 (4 Sat); 7–11
John Smith's Bitter 🄷
Multi-roomed pub with interesting layout. Ideal spot for canal enthusiasts. Long descent to gents! Snacks include vegetarian pizza. Q ♘ ❀ ⊡ ▲
⇌ (Silsden & Steeton) ♣

Red Lion
47 Kirkgate ☎ (0535) 55393
11–3 (5 Sat); 7–11
John Smith's Bitter 🄷
Unpretentious, friendly local, opposite the duck pond. Impressive fireplace in main bar; separate small snug. Pool table upstairs. ♨ ◖ ⊡ ♿ ▲ ⇌ (Silsden & Steeton) ♣

Sowerby Bridge

Moorings
1 Warehouse, Canal Basin (off A58) ☎ (0422) 833940

11.30–3; 5.30 (6 Sat)–11 (12–3; 7–11 Mon)
McEwan 80/-; Moorhouse's Premier Bitter; Theakston XB; Younger Scotch 🄷
Smartly converted canal warehouse with open bar and separate eating areas. Wide range of bottled foreign beers, particularly Belgian, and extensive range of single malt whiskies. Guest beers.
Q ⛟ ❁ ◖ ◗ ≹ P

Puzzle Hall
21 Hollins Mill Lane (near A58 and river) ☎ (0422) 835547
11–11
Vaux Double Maxim; Wards Mild, Thorne Best Bitter, Sheffield Best Bitter, Kirby Strong 🄷
Old pub of character with brewery tower. A cosy local which nestles twixt canal and river. Beer range (Vaux group) may vary; draught cider in winter. ⌂ ❁ ◖ ◗ ♿ ⛺ ≹ ♣ ⌓ P

White Horse
Burnley Road (A646)
☎ (0422) 831173
12–11
Tetley Mild, Bitter 🄷
Lively main road pub with smart lounge and small tap room. Nice stained glass window frontage. Popular with sporting types. ❁ ♣ P

Stanley Ferry

Ferry Boat
Ferry Lane (A642)
☎ (0924) 290596
11–3; 7–11 (11–11 summer)
Theakston Best Bitter, XB, Old Peculier; Younger Scotch, No.3 🄷
Old canal building rebuilt in nautical style next to the marina and aqueduct dating from 1836. Pleasure craft ply the canal from the pub. Children's play area away from canal. ⛟ ❁ ◖ ◗ ♿ P

Stanningley

Old Fleece
116 Town Street (A647)
☎ (0532) 577832
12–11
Taylor Best Bitter, Landlord; Tetley Bitter; Theakston Best Bitter, XB; Whitbread Flowers Original 🄷
A busy roadside pub, recently extended into a barber's shop next door. Wide-ranging menu includes veg option. Guest beers. 🛏 ◖ ◗ ⊟ ≹ ♣

Thorner

Fox
37 Main Street
☎ (0532) 892489
11–3; 5–11
Tetley Mild, Bitter 🄷
Pleasant village inn with lounge, snug and tap room. Friendly and comfortable. Q ❁ ◖ ◗ ♣ P

Thornton

Blue Boar
Thornton Road
☎ (0274) 833298
11–11 (11–3; 5.30–11 Tue–Thu)
Taylor Best Bitter, Landlord 🄷
Open-plan bar area/lounge; separate pool and darts room. Live music Sun nights accompanied by Pablo on spoons! ♣

Todmorden

Masons Arms
1 Bacup Road, Gauxholme (under rail bridge at A6033/A681 jct)
☎ (0706) 812180
11.30–3; 7.30–11
John Smith's Bitter, Magnet; Thwaites Mild, Bitter 🄷
Well-refurbished free house with relaxed intimate atmosphere. ⌂ ◖ ◗ ≹

Staff of Life
550 Burnley Road (A646, 1½ miles N of centre)
☎ (0706) 812929
12–3; 7–11
Robinwood Best Bitter, XB, Old Fart; Taylor Best Bitter, Landlord 🄷
Atmospheric free house in wooded gorge. Overhanging crag has supernatural connections. Stone walls, flag floors. Small seafood restaurant. Guest beer. ⌂ ❁ 🛏 ◖ ◗ ⌓ P

Woodpecker
224 Rochdale Road, Shade (A6033) ☎ (0706) 816088
12–2.30; 5.30–11 (11–11 Fri & Sat)
Lees GB Mild, Bitter 🄷
Friendly local on main road. Strong games following. L-shaped interior adorned with plates, prints and mugs. ◖ ◗ ≹

Wakefield

Albion
94 Stanley Road
☎ (0924) 376206
11–3; 7–11 (11–11 Fri & Sat)
Samuel Smith OBB 🄷
Large multi-roomed, sports-oriented pub with huge coloured glass collection. Home-cooked traditional Yorkshire fare, plus veg option.
❁ ◖ ⊟ ≹ (Kirkgate) ♣ P

Beer Engine
77 Westgate End (½ mile W of centre) ☎ (0924) 375887
5 (12 Fri & Sat)–11
Old Mill Traditional Bitter; Taylor Landlord; Tetley Bitter 🄷
Popular; well-renovated, traditional ale house with stone-flagged floor, gas lighting and brewery memorabilia. No jukebox but good selection of tapes played. Two regular guest beers. ⌂ ❁ ≹ (Westgate) ♣ ⌓

Cock Inn
Batley Road, Alverthorpe
☎ (0924) 373649
12–4; 7–11
Stones Best Bitter 🄷
Cheerful 1930s pub retaining separate rooms and friendly local atmosphere. ⊟ ♣ P

Yeadon

Oddfellows
The Green ☎ (0532) 503819
11–3; 6.30–11 (11–11 Fri & Sat)
Tetley Mild, Bitter 🄷
Excellent tap room with long narrow lounge. Known locally as the 'Rag'. Try the hot meat sandwiches. ◖ ◗ ⊟ ♣ P

DISPENSE METHODS

🄶 by gravity straight from the cask
🄷 by handpump
🄴 by electric pump
🄰 by air pressure (including electric air compressor in Scotland)

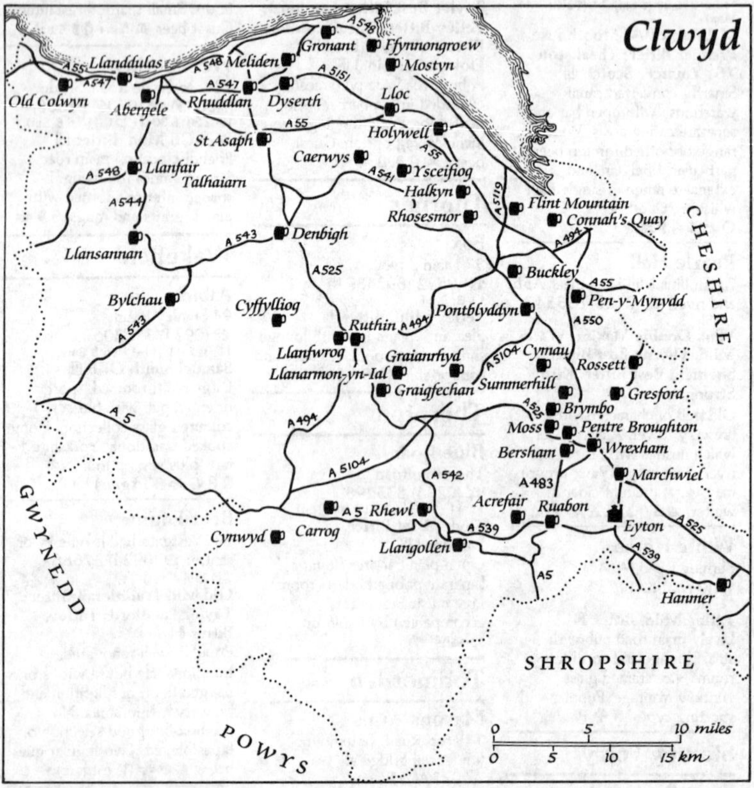

Plassey, Eyton

Abergele

Gwindy
Market Street
☎ (0745) 833485
11–11 (may vary)
Marston's Burton Best Bitter, Pedigree Bitter, Merrie Monk [H]
Old market town pub with modernised public bar and pool room. Small, comfortable lounge at rear. Lunchtime meals summer only. ♣ P

Acrefair

Duke of Wellington
Llangollen Road
☎ (0978) 820169
11–4; 6–11
Marston's Border Mild, Border Bitter, Pedigree Bitter [H]
Well-run and supported pub with tiny bar area. Attracts canal visitors in season. Watch out for the singing dog! ♣ P

Hampden Arms
Llangollen Road, Plas Madoc
☎ (0978) 821734
11–4; 7–11
Banks's Mild, Bitter [E]
Large, well-situated pub near leisure centre. Comfortable, friendly lounge; busy bar, popular with horse racing fans. ♣ P

Bersham

Black Lion
Bersham Road (B5099)
OS312492
☎ (0978) 365588
11.30–3.30 (11–5 Sat); 6.45.(6.30 Sat)-11
Hydes' Anvil Mild, Bitter [E]
Friendly, basic, two-roomed local that is worth the effort to find. Pleasant outdoor area by a stream. Handy for Bersham Heritage Centre. Q ♣ P

Brymbo

Black Lion
Railway Road
☎ (0978) 758307
12–4; 7–11
Burtonwood Dark Mild, Best Bitter [H]
Pub full of beams and brasses. Overshadowed by steelworks. ♣ P

Try also: George & Dragon (Lees)

Buckley

Red Lion
Liverpool Road
☎ (0244) 542666
11–3; 5.30–11
Burtonwood Best Bitter [H]
Roadside pub with emphasis on food. Warm lounge, decorated with brassware, and plain bar. ♣ P

Bylchau

Sportsmans Arms
Bryntrillyn, Denbigh Moors (A543) ☎ (074 570) 214
11–3; 7–11 (11–11 summer)
Lees GB Mild, Bitter [H]
The highest pub in Wales – an oasis on high moorland. Small bar, with good size comfortable lounge, maintaining a traditional atmosphere and surroundings. Q ♣ P

Caerwys

Travellers Inn
On A55 ☎ (0352) 720251
12–3; 7–11 (12–11 Sat)
Marston's Border Mild, Border Bitter, Pedigree Bitter H
Popular with locals and travellers alike, the first pub on the A55 when entering Wales. Accommodation is in a four-berth caravan.
♨ ❀ 🛏 ◖ ◗ ⊞ ▲ ♣ P

Carrog

Grouse Inn
On B5437
11–3; 6.30–11 (extends in summer)
Lees Bitter H
Simple, pleasant inn, beautifully situated alongside River Dee. Well worth a short detour from main A5 holiday route.
♨ Q ◖ ◗ P

Connah's Quay

Sir Gawain & Green Knight
Golftyn Lane
☎ (0244) 812623
11–3; 6.30–11
Samuel Smith OBB H
Converted former farmhouse with split-level interior. Frequented by college students at lunchtimes. ♨ ❀ ◖ ♿ P

Cyffylliog

Red Lion
Off B5105 4 miles W of Ruthin
☎ (08246) 664
12–3; 6.30–11
Lees Bitter H
Genuinely attractive pub in idyllic rural surroundings, with good value accommodation and food. ♨ Q 🐴 ❀ 🛏 ◖ ◗ ⊞ ♣ P

Cymau

Olde Talbot
Cymau Road (off A541)
OS297562
☎ (0978) 761410
11–4; 7–11
Hydes' Anvil Mild, Bitter E
Hilltop pub in pleasant surroundings, enjoying good views. Busy village local. Lounge is quiet and relaxing.
⊞ ♿ ♣ P

Cynwyd

Prince of Wales
On B4401
12–3; 6.30–11 (extends in summer)
Burtonwood Dark Mild H
Unspoilt, traditional village local with station clock and station-master's chair from the old Corwen station. One of two locals in a mild drinker's haven (three real milds; no real bitter). ♨ Q ⊞ P

Try also: Blue Lion (Marston's)

Denbigh

Eagle Inn
Back Row ☎ (074571) 3203
11–11
Tetley Bitter H
Popular town-centre pub with a good size bar and a separate, medium-size lounge. Live music Sat nights. ♨ ❀ ◖ ⊞ ▲ ♣ P

Plough Inn
Portland Place
☎ (074571) 2961
11–4; 7–11 (11–11 Fri & Sat in summer)
Marston's Mercian Mild, Burton Best Bitter, Pedigree Bitter H
Typical town pub and good local. Good size bar with a comfortable lounge at rear.
❀ ◖ ⊞ ♿ ▲ ♣ P

Try also: Railway Inn

Dyserth

Cross Keys
High Street ☎ (0745) 570337
11–4; 5.30–11 (11–11 Fri & Sat)
Burtonwood Best Bitter H
Basic pub in west end of village: a drinkers' den. Dyserth Waterfall is a local tourist attraction. Bar snacks only (lunchtimes). ♨ ❀ ⊞ ▲ ♣

Try also: New Inn (Marston's)

Ffynnongroew

Garth Mill
Garth Lane (off A548)
OS139816 ☎ (0745) 560141
12–3 (not Mon, except bank hols); 7–11
Younger Scotch H
Tastefully-converted, 18th-century corn mill, set in a secluded spot by a small stream.
♨ ❀ ♣ P

Flint Mountain

Coach & Horses
Northrop Road
☎ (03526) 61371
11.30–3; 5.30–11 (11–11 Sat)
Greenalls Bitter H
Good village pub; a social centre for the locals.
❀ ◖ ◗ ♿ ♣ P

Graianrhyd

Rose & Crown
1 mile off A5104
☎ (08243) 727
12 (11.30 Sat)–3; 6.30–11
Marston's Burton Best Bitter, Pedigree Bitter H
Cosy, out-of-the-way pub, popular with horse riders. Good value food with better-than-average veg choice. Occasional guest beers.
♨ Q ❀ ◖ ◗ ⊞ ▲ ♣ P

Graigfechan

Three Pigeons
On B5429, 3 miles S of Ruthin ☎ (08242) 3178
12–3 (summer only); 6.30–11
Draught Bass G
Recently-extended, out-of-the-way pub in the Vale of Clwyd. New extension is food-orientated, with generous portions, including veg option. Delightful views make it a popular stop for walkers and riders in the summer.
♨ ❀ ◖ ◗ ♿ ▲ ♣ P

Gresford

Griffin
The Green (B5373) OS345550
☎ (097883) 2231
12–3 (3.30 Fri & Sat); 7–11
Greenalls Mild, Bitter H
Pleasant well-kept inn, next to picturesque parish church. No food. ❀ ♣ P

Try also: Yew Tree (Marston's)

Gronant

Bells of St Marys
Mostyn Road (A548)
☎ (074563) 770
12–3; 6.30 (6 summer)–11
McEwan 70/-; Matthew Brown Mild; Theakston Best Bitter H
Large pub which stands alone in the countryside. Popular with drinkers and diners alike. Good vegetarian choice. Occasional guest beer. ♨ 🐴 ❀ ◖ ◗ ♿ ▲ P

Halkyn

Britannia Inn
Pentre Road (off A55)
OS211711
☎ (0352) 780272
11.30–3; 7 (5.30 summer)–11 (11–11 Sat)
Lees GB Mild, Bitter H, **Moonraker** G
500 year-old stone pub with four rooms. Popular with local farming community and tourists. Fine views over Dee to the Wirral. Meals in restaurant.
♨ Q ❀ 🛏 ◖ ◗ ⊞ ▲ ♣ P

Hanmer

Hanmer Arms
Off A539, 6 miles W of Whitchurch
11–11
Ind Coope Burton Ale; Tetley Bitter H
Family-run hotel in pretty Mereside village, set in peaceful

rolling landscape. Local produce on menu (veg option). Newly-laid bowling green.
Q P

Holywell

Beaufort Arms
Well Street ☎ (0352) 710364
11–11 (12.30 Wed, Fri & Sat)
Wilson's Original Bitter H
Large, modernised, pub popular with younger drinkers. Beer is not cheap but there's always plenty of choice. Two guest beers.

Try also: Feathers (Bass)

Llanarmon-yn-Ial

Raven
On B5431 ☎ (082 43) 787
11–11
Burtonwood Best Bitter H
Village-centre pub in pleasant location opposite church. Extensive, award-winning garden.
Q P

Llanddulas

Dulas Arms
Abergele Road
☎ (0492) 515747
12–3; 7–11 (11–4; 6–11 summer)
Lees GB Mild, Bitter, Moonraker H
Large lounge and adjoining bar, with a snug room decorated in traditional-style.
Q P

Valentine Inn
Mill Street ☎ (0492) 518189
12–3 (12–2 Sun); 5.30–11 (may vary)
Draught Bass; M&B Mild H
Tastefully-renovated, small village inn. The comfortable lounge features an inviting coal and log fire; tiny public bar. Popular spot for holiday-makers from nearby camps. Eve meals in summer only (till 8pm).
Q

Llanfair Talhaiarn

Swan Inn
Swan Square (off A548)
☎ (074584) 233
11–3 (3.30 Sat, not Thu); 5.30 (6 Sat)–11 (11–11 Sat in winter)
Marston's Mercian Mild, Burton Best Bitter, Pedigree Bitter H
Unspoilt, traditional inn with no frills and warm, welcoming atmosphere.
Q P

Llanfwrog

Cross Keys
On B5105, 1 mile from Ruthin
☎ (08242) 5281
11.30–3.30; 6.30–11
Banks's Mild, Bitter H
Cosy country pub close to two main routes to Mid Wales. Former winner of the Denbighshire Free Press Pub of the Year award. Q

Llangollen

Cambrian Hotel
Berwyn Street (A5)
☎ (0978) 860686
12–5; 7–11
Younger Scotch H
Unchanging and simply furnished, small hotel. Plenty of good-humoured character in the tiny, cosy bar; quiet front lounge, where children are welcome. Eve meals weekends only in winter.
P

Wynstay Arms Hotel
Bridge Street
☎ (0978) 860710
12–3; 7 (6 summer)–11
Ind Coope Burton Ale; Tetley Bitter H
Unspoilt 16th- and 17th-century hotel, with a number of small, intimate drinking and eating areas, each with its own character. Eve meals in summer only.
P

Llansannan

Saracens Head
Main Street ☎ (074577) 212
12–3 (not winter); 4–11
Robinson's Best Mild, Best Bitter H
Large village local with a public bar and comfortable lounge.

Lloc

Rock Inn
At A5026/A5151 jct
☎ (0352) 710049
11–11
Burtonwood Dark Mild, Best Bitter H
Excellent pub, popular with locals. Cosy lounge with teapots hanging from ceiling. Lunchtime meals in restaurant.
P

Marchwiel

Red Lion
Wrexham Road (A525/A528 jct) ☎ (0978) 262317
11.30–3; 5.30–11
Marston's Border Mild, Border Bitter, Pedigree Bitter H
Two-roomed roadside inn with popular busy bar and L-shaped quiet lounge. The garden and playground for children make for a very pleasant evening drink with the family.
Q P

Meliden

Red Lion
Ffordd Talargoch (off A547)
☎ (07456) 2565
11–3; 6–11
Draught Bass; M&B Mild; Stones Best Bitter H
Military memorabilia adorns the walls in this recently-acquired Bass pub near Prestatyn. Small public bar with medium-size lounge. Car park at front.
Q P

Try also: Star (Marston's)

Moss

Bird in Hand
Woodlands Road (off B5433)
OS303538 ☎ (0978) 755809
12–3 (not Mon); 7–11 (supper licence till 12 Tue–Sat)
Hydes' Anvil Bitter E
Well-decorated, light and airy pub, hidden at the end of a rough, narrow track. ¾-sized snooker table. No meals Mon.
P

Mostyn

Lletty Hotel
Mostyn Coast Road
☎ (0745) 560292
11.30–3.30; 7–11
Burtonwood Dark Mild, Best Bitter H
Old smugglers' inn, once known as the 'Honest Man'; now frequented by international sailors from nearby dock. P

Old Colwyn

Plough
282 Abergele Road
☎ (0492) 515387
11.30–3; 5.30–11
Greenalls Mild, Bitter, Thomas Greenall's Original Bitter H
Large village tavern, refurbished in traditional style. Disabled access is via side entrance where there is a small public bar.
Q

Try also: Sun (Marston's)

Pentre Broughton

Cross Foxes
High Street (B5433)
☎ (0978) 755973
11–11
Burtonwood Dark Mild, Best Bitter H
Recently-refurbished village local. P

Pen-y-Mynydd

White Lion Inn
On A5104
12–3 (12–2 Sun); 7.30–11
Marston's Border Bitter H
Three-roomed local full of character. Virtually untouched by the passage of time. Pickled

eggs are home-produced.
♨ Q ⊞ ♣ P

Pontblyddyn

Bridge Inn
Wrexham Road
(A5104/A54 jct)
11–11 (supper licence till 12)
Burtonwood Best Bitter; Marston's Pedigree Bitter; Plassey Farmhouse Bitter; Theakston XB [H]
Excellent old rustic pub, developing residential and catering facilities in sympathy with the building. River Alyn, to rear of pub, contains trout (fishing £3 per day for guests). Regular folk club Sun eves. Guest beers.
♨ Q 🐎 ❀ 🛏 ◖ ◗ ⊞ ♿ P

Rhewl

Sun
Off B5103 OS178448
☎ (0978) 861043
12–3; 6–11
Felinfoel Bitter [H]
Lovely old drovers' inn, set in the beautiful Dee Valley. A 14th-century pub with stone floors and real settles; a great attraction for the many hikers and hill-walkers drawn to the glorious surroundings.
♨ 🐎 ❀ ◖ ◗ ⊞ ⛺ ♣ P

Rhosesmor

Red Lion
On B5123, Mold-Holywell road OS213681
☎ (0352) 780570
12–11 (may close afternoons)
Burtonwood Dark Mild, Best Bitter [H]
Small, two-bar pub, popular with locals. Dates back some 300 years. Well worth the detour. ♨ Q ◖ ⊞ ♣ P

Rhuddlan

Castle Inn
Castle Street
☎ (0745) 590391
11.30–11 (may vary)
Marston's Burton Best Bitter, Pedigree Bitter [E]
Welcoming village local close to Rhuddlan Castle. Good size bar with separate, comfortable lounge. Lunches in summer only. Q ◖ ◗ ⛺ ♣ P

Rossett

Butchers Arms
Chester Road (A483)
☎ (0244) 570233
11.30–3; 5.30–11 (11–11 Fri & Sat)
Burtonwood Dark Mild, Best Bitter [H]
Well-run, roadside hostelry, catering for a wide range of customers. Good value Sunday lunches. ❀ ◖ ◗ ⊞ ♣ P

Ruabon

Duke of Wellington
High Street (off B5606)
☎ (0978) 820381
11–3; 7–11
Marston's Border Mild, Burton Best Bitter, Pedigree Bitter [H]
A pleasing, handsome building, enclosing a nicely-balanced pub with a cosy, comfortable lounge and a bright, busy bar. Welcoming to locals and visitors alike. Good value food served. Q ❀ ◖ ◗ ⊞ ⇌ ♣ P

Try also: Wynstay Arms (Robinson's)

Ruthin

Wine Vaults
St Peters Square
☎ (08242) 2067
12–3.30; 4.45–11
Robinson's Best Bitter [H]
Busy two-bar local just off the main town square. No food.
Q ❀ 🛏 ⊞ ⛺ ♣ P

St Asaph

Swan
The Roe (A525)
☎ (0745) 582284
1–3; 6.30–11 (12–4; 7–11 Sat)
Marston's Border Mild, Burton Best Bitter, Pedigree Bitter [H]
Good, unpretentious local with a warm welcome. A small pub with a good size bar and lounge area. Q ❀ ♿ ⛺ ♣ P

Try also: New Inn (Lees)

Summerhill

Crown Inn
Top Road (off A541) OS312535
☎ (0978) 755788
11–4; 7–11
Hydes' Anvil Mild, Bitter [E]
Pleasant village pub mostly used by locals, due to its out-of-the-way location. Good views over Cheshire Plain.
Q ❀ ⊞ ♿ ♣ P

Wrexham

Nags Head
Mount Street
11–3 (4 Mon); 5.30–11 (11–11 Sat)
Marston's Border Bitter, Merrie Monk, Pedigree Bitter [H]
Old and comfortable building that was once the showpiece of the Border Brewery estate and the brewery tap.
◖ ⊞ ⇌ (Central) ♣ P

Oak Tree Tavern
Ruabon Road (A5152)
☎ (0978) 261450
12–3; 6–11 (11–11 Sat)
Marston's Border Mild, Burton Best Bitter, Pedigree Bitter [H]
Friendly, well-kept pub. It must be a nightmare keeping all the brass and copper polished!
❀ ⊞ ⇌ (Central)

Turf
Mold Road (A541)
☎ (0978) 261484
11–3; 5–11 (11–11 Sat)
Marston's Border Exhibition, Pedigree Bitter [H]
Busy pub built into the football ground. Try some of the Stilton cheese. ❀ 🛏 ◖ ◗ ⊞ ⇌ (Central)

Try also: Golden Lion (Bass)

Ysceifiog

Fox
1 mile N of A541
OS151716 ☎ (0352) 720241
7–11 (11–11 Fri & Sat)
Banks's Mild, Bitter [H]
Unchanged by time, a real old-fashioned local. No electronic gadgets here. Welsh singing Fri eve; tiny locals' bar. ♨ Q ⊞ ♣ P

'Neighbours'
It is worth remembering that roads do not end at county borders! If you are in a strange town that is near the county boundary, then check the pages of the neighbouring county for an even bigger choice of great pubs.

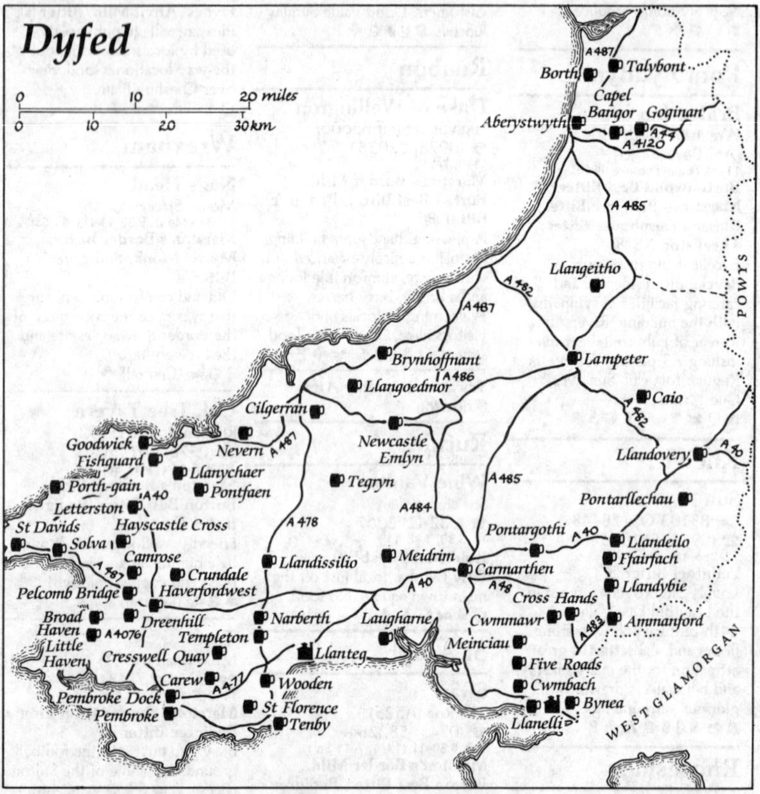

***Crown Buckley, Felinfoel**, Llanelli;*
***Pembrokeshire's Own Ales**, Llanteg*

Aberystwyth

Castle

South Road ☎ (0970) 612188
12–3; 5.30–11 (11–11 Sat)
Draught Bass; Welsh Brewers Hancock's HB [H]
Large, urban-style pub built by Roberts' brewery, only slightly altered and nearest pub to harbour and South Marine beach.

Downie's Vaults

Eastgate ☎ (0970) 624748
11–11
Banks's Mild, Bitter [E]
Impressive Masons of Dale End gantry dominates the large public bar of this pub, named after Joseph Downie, the original owner. Q

Nags Head

Bridge Street
☎ (0970) 624725
11–11 (12–2; 7.30–10.30 Sun)
Banks's Mild, Bitter [E]
As in most Banks's pubs in this area, a small, tidy lounge complements a much larger public bar. Small children's room at rear; restaurant.
P

Try also: Pier Hotel (Banks's)

Ammanford

Wernoleu Hotel

Pontamman Road (½ mile from centre off Neath Road)
☎ (0269) 592598
12–2.30 (4 Sat); 6–11
Draught Bass; Felinfoel Double Dragon; Wadworth 6X; Younger IPA [H]
Cosy and pleasant lounge in an old mansion set in attractive grounds. No meals Sun eve. Guest beers.
Q P

Borth

Friendship

On B4353 ☎ (0970) 871213
12–3; 7–11 (11–11 summer)
Burtonwood Best Bitter [H]
Welcoming seaside local, run by same family for 60 years. Now has art gallery, and children's room at rear.

Broad Haven

Royal

200 yds from coast road up Marine Road
☎ (0437) 781249
11–4; 6–11
Wadworth 6X; Welsh Brewers Worthington BB [H]
Completely renovated old pub, on coastal path close to sandy beach in sheltered, sunny position. Specialises in good food and family accommodation. Restaurant has dance floor (live music Sats).
Q P

Brynhoffnant

Brynhoffnant Inn

On A487 ☎ (0239) 654413
11–3; 5.30–11 (11–11 summer)
Draught Bass; Buckley's Best Bitter [H]
Externally, virtually unchanged since it was built in 1860. The one bar is split into three areas, with a dining area at one end and pool at the other.

Commanding sea view from car park. Hearty meals (children's portions available). Family room in summer only. Beer range may vary. ⌂ ♉ ❀ ◖ ◗ ⛺ ♣ P

Bynea

Lewis Arms
90 Yspitty Road (old A484)
☎ (0554) 772878
11–11 (may vary)
Felinfoel Bitter, Double Dragon [H]
Refurbished pub close to Loughor estuary. ❀ ◖ ⊟ ⇌ P

Caio

Brunant Arms
Off A482 ☎ (055 85) 483
11–11
Fuller's London Pride; Marston's Pedigree Bitter [H]
Comfortable and attractive bar with pool table at one end and restaurant upstairs. Close to Roman goldmines and good walking country. Landlord collects unusual pub games. One guest beer always available. Beer festivals occasionally held.
⌂ Q ❀ 🛏 ◖ ◗ ⛺ ♣ P

Try also: Drovers, Ffarmers (Free)

Camrose

Olde Inn
On B4330 ☎ (0437) 710293
6–11 (12–3; 7–10.30 Sun)
Welsh Brewers Worthington BB [H]
Pub well off the beaten track offering a friendly welcome.
⌂ ❀ ⊟

Capel Bangor

Tynllidiart Arms
On A44 ☎ (0970) 84248
11–2.30; 5.30–11
Whitbread Best Bitter, Castle Eden Ale, Flowers Original [H]
17th-century cottage inn, linked to mailcoach days. A former David Roberts pub, now a free house. Traditional settle seating round fire. A rare outlet for traditional cider in this area (Bulmers). ⌂ Q ◖ ◗ ⛺ ♣ 🍏

Carew

Carew Inn
On A4075 opp. castle
☎ (0646) 651267
11–11
Felinfoel Double Dragon; Welsh Brewers Worthington BB [H]
Situated in small village near river, ancient tidal mill and well-preserved castle, with active digs and many summer activities. Warm welcome in tiny contrasting bars adorned with cricketing photographs. Meals summer only.
⌂ Q ❀ ◖ ◗ ⊟ ♿ ⛺ ♣ P

Try also: Milton Brewery (Welsh Brewers)

Carmarthen

Drovers Arms
Lammas Street
☎ (0267) 237646
11–3.30 (11–3 Sun); 5.30–11
Felinfoel Bitter, Double Dragon [H]
An excellent replacement for some of Carmarthen's better pubs that have closed in recent years. Q ◖

Queens
Queens Street
☎ (0267) 231800
11–11 (11–3; 7–10.30 Sun)
Draught Bass; Welsh Brewers Worthington Dark [H]
Large town-centre pub with rooms to suit most tastes.
❀ ◖ ⊟ ⇌

Cilgerran

Pendre Inn
High Street ☎ (0239) 614223
11.30–3; 6–11
Draught Bass; Welsh Brewers Worthington BB [H]
Ancient stone-built pub of great character. Occasional guest beers in summer. No meals Sun lunch (snacks only).
⌂ Q ❀ ◖ ◗ ♣ P

Cresswell Quay

Cresselly Arms
OS050066 ☎ (0646) 651210
11–11 (may close winter afternoons)
Welsh Brewers Hancock's HB [H]
Old riverside pub with strong hunting and cricketing traditions. River reaches door at spring tides (dripping frogmen have been served!). Nothing has been modernised in 70 years, except the loos.
⌂ Q ❀ ♿ ⛺ ♣ P

Cross Hands

Cross Hands Hotel
Carmarthen Road (A476)
11.30–3; 6–11
Felinfoel Bitter, Double Dragon [H]
Friendly pub near A48 service area. Unassuming bar and comfortable lounge. ◖ ◗ ⊟ P

Crundale

Boot & Shoe
On B4329 ☎ (0437) 762212
11–3 (may vary, 11–11 Sat)
Welsh Brewers Worthington BB [H]
Quiet country local where the ale and food is enjoyed by all.
⌂ Q ◖ ◗ ⊟ ♣ P

Cwmbach

Farriers Arms
On B4308 ☎ (0554) 774256
12–3 (2 Sun); 7 (6 Sat)–11 (closed Mon)
Felinfoel Bitter; Marston's Pedigree Bitter [H]
Extremely attractive pub in splendid setting. Guest beer usually available. ❀ ◖ ◗ ⊟ P

Cwmmawr

Gwendraeth Arms
Gwendraeth Road (B4310)
☎ (0269) 843737
Hours vary
Felinfoel Bitter [H]**, Double Dragon** [G]
Pleasant local. ⌂ ❀ P

Dreenhill

Denant Mill
Off B4327 at Masons Arms
☎ (0437) 766569
11–3; 6–11
Beer range varies [H]
A medieval gem and a mecca for ale connoisseurs, serving a merry-go-round of different ales. ♉ ❀ 🛏 ◖ ◗ ♿ ⛺

Masons Arms
Dale Road (B4327)
☎ (0437) 760815
12–3; 6–11
Draught Bass; Welsh Brewers Worthington BB [H]
The last cottage pub in Pembrokeshire. Small homely front parlour. ⌂ Q ◖ ◗ ⛺ P

Ffairfach

Torbay
Heol Cennen (A483)
☎ (0558) 822029
11–3; 5.30–11
Draught Bass; Whitbread Flowers IPA [H]
Popular inn with a bar of strong rural character. Large and varied menu (not Sun lunch).
⌂ ❀ ◖ ◗ ⊟ ⇌ ♣ P

Fishguard

Fishguard Arms
Main Street ☎ (0348) 872763
11–3 (12–2 Sun); 6–11
Felinfoel Double Dragon (summer); Marston's Pedigree Bitter; Welsh Brewers Worthington BB [G]
Unchanged and unspoiled for many years, this real ale haven is a must. Occasional surprise live music. A friendly meeting place. Shove-ha'penny, bar skittles and chess available.
⌂ Q ⊟ ♣

Ship Inn
Newport Road, Lower

Fishguard ☎ (0348) 874033
11–3 (12–2 Sun); 7–11
Welsh Brewers Worthington Dark, BB [G]
Low-beamed pub in delightfully scenic, small harbour. Friendly and popular with locals and tourists alike. Famous as setting for films *Under Milk Wood* and *Moby Dick.* ⌂ Q ♣

Five Roads

Waunwyllt Inn

Horeb Five Roads (off B4309)
☎ (0269) 860209
12–3; 7 (6 Fri, 5.30 Sat)–11
Felinfoel Double Dragon; Theakston Best Bitter [H]
Good food and good company. Happy hour 6–7pm and supper licence. ◐ ◑

Goginan

Druid Inn

On A44 ☎ (0970) 84650
11–3; 5.30–11 (closed Sun)
Banks's Mild, Bitter; Charles Wells Bombardier [H]
Only remaining pub in village. Lead-mining associations; also sells duck eggs! Guest beer may replace one of the above.
◐ ◑ ♿ ♣ P

Goodwick

Glendower Club & Hotel

Glendower Square (off A40 at Rose & Crown)
☎ (0348) 872873
11–11
Buckley's Best Bitter [H]
Clean, popular pub with nice furnishings, a quiet lounge and family room. Clean air machine in small public bar. Friendly atmosphere. Non-members welcome. Eve meals by arrangement only.
Q ♞ ❀ 🛏 ◐ ⊞ ♿ ⇌
(Fishguard Harbour)

Try also: Rose & Crown (Free)

Haverfordwest

Bristol Trader

Quay Street ☎ (0437) 762122
11–3; 5.30–11 (11–11 Fri & Sat)
Ind Coope Burton Ale [H]
14th-century ale house of some character, situated on the banks of the river. ❀ ◐ ⇌

Georges Inn

Market Street (near St Thomas Green) ☎ (0437) 766683
11–3; 7–11 (closed Sun)
Draught Bass; Ind Coope Burton Ale; Marston's Pedigree Bitter [H]
Friendly meeting place with snob screens, good inexpensive meals and guest beers. Q ◐ ◑ ⊞

Pembroke Yeoman

Hill Street (off St Thomas Green) ☎ (0437) 762500
11–11
Ansells Bitter [H]
Quiet local serving good food.
⌂ Q ❀ ◐ ◑

Hayscastle Cross

Cross Inn

On B4330 crossroads
☎ (0348) 840216
11.30–2; 6–11 (may extend Fri, Sat & summer)
Felinfoel Double Dragon; Welsh Brewers Worthington BB [H]
Ancient pub with decor untouched. Family-owned since 1840. Good variety on menu. Village meeting place.
⌂ Q ♞ ❀ ◐ ◑ ⊞ ♿ ♣ ○ P

Lampeter

Kings Head

14 Bridge Street (A482/A485)
☎ (0570) 422598
11–3.30 (may extend); 5.30–11
Draught Bass; Buckley's Best Bitter [H]
Pleasant, unpretentious, two-bar free house in centre of university town. Menu caters for children and vegetarians. Aviary in garden. Supper licence to 12.30am.
⌂ Q ❀ 🛏 ◐ ◑ ⊞ ♿ ▲ ♣ P

Laugharne

New Three Mariners

Victoria Street (A4066)
☎ (0994) 427426
11–3; 5.30–11 (11–11 summer)
Draught Bass; Buckley's Best Bitter [H]
Former home-brew pub built around 1703. Two small, friendly locals' bars and a large, comfortable pool room. Snacks available. ⌂ Q 🛏 ⊞ ▲ ♣

Letterston

Harp

31 Haverfordwest Road (A40)
☎ (0348) 840061
11–3; 5.30–11
Ansells Bitter; Ind Coope Burton Ale [H]
Well-patronised comfortable local bar with pool table. Reasonably-priced popular meals in lounge or restaurant. Excellent value.
⌂ Q ❀ ◐ ◑ ⊞ ♿ P

Little Haven

Swan Inn

Off B4341 ☎ (0437) 781256
11–3; 6.30–11
Felinfoel Double Dragon; Welsh Brewers Worthington BB [H]
Delightful old coastal pub in rocky cove approached by footpath. Wide range of home-cooked food: specials and locally-caught seafood. Restaurant open Wed-Sat eves (book). Public car park 100 yds.
⌂ Q ❀ ◐

Llandeilo

White Horse

Rhosmaen Street (off A483)
☎ (0558) 822424
11.30–3; 6–11
Greenalls Davenports Traditional Bitter [H]; **Wadworth 6X** [G]
Cosy and attractive with a pleasant courtyard. Deservedly popular. Continuous variety of well-kept guest beers.
⌂ Q ❀ ◐ ⊞ ⇌

Llandissilio

Bush Inn

On A478 ☎ (09916) 626
11–3 (may extend); 5.30–11
Draught Bass; Pembrokeshire's Own Ales Benfro Bitter (summer) [H]
Small, low-beamed roadside inn with a cosy front bar and two dining rooms. ⌂ ❀ 🛏 ◐ ◑ ▲ P

Llandovery

Bluebell

High Street (A40)
☎ (0550) 21146
11.30–3; 6–11 (11–11 market days & some Sats)
Draught Bass; Welsh Brewers Worthington BB [H]
Small pleasant lounge and a bar of some character.
Q ◐ ◑ ⊞ ⇌ ♣

Llandybie

Red Lion

Off A483 ☎ (0269) 851202
12–3 (4 Sat); 6–11
Marston's Pedigree Bitter; Whitbread Flowers Original [H]
Interesting variety of well-appointed rooms in a listed building near historic church. Collection of old mirrors. Three rooms welcome families. No meals Sun eve. Occasional guest beers. Q ♞ ❀ 🛏 ◐ ◑ ⊞ ⇌ P

Llanelli

Bull Inn

Ann Street ☎ (0554) 756283
11.30–3; 5.30–11 (11–11 Fri & Sat)
Buckley's Best Bitter [H]
Basic pub on outskirts of town centre. Beer and food both excellent quality and value.
◐ ⊞ ♣

Clarence

42 Murray Street
11–11
Draught Bass; Welsh

Brewers Worthington Dark [H]
Busy town pub. ◖ ⊕ ⇌

Stradey Arms
Furnace (on B4308/B4309)
☎ (0554) 757968
11.30–3; 5.30 (6 Sat)–11
Buckley's Dark, Best Bitter [H]
Well-appointed pub close to Buckley's brewery. ❀ ◖ ⊕ P

Llangeitho

Three Horseshoes
On B4342 ☎ (097 423) 244
12–3; 5.30–11 (closed Sun eve)
Marston's Pedigree Bitter [H]
Traditional local in sleepy village with occasional organ sing-songs. Doubles as village fish and chip shop on Friday nights. No meals Sun. Beer range varies.
⌂ Q ❀ ◖ ◗ ⊕ ♿ ▲ ♣

Llangoedmor

Penllwyn-Du
On B4570 5 miles E of Cardigan OS241458
☎ (023 987) 533
11–11 (may not open till 5.30, 12–2.30; 7–10.30 Sun)
Felinfoel Double Dragon; Wadworth 6X; Welsh Brewers Worthington BB [H]
Ex-home-brew pub and court-house, now a comfortable, traditional country pub with fine views to the Preseli mountains. Crib and backgammon played.
⌂ ❀ ◖ ◗ ⊕ ♣ P

Llanychaer

Bridge End Inn
On A4313 2½ miles from Fishguard ☎ (0348) 872545
11–3; 5.30–11
Draught Bass; Marston's Pedigree Bitter; Wadworth 6X [G]
Rambling old pub with large, raftered family room. Landlord experiments with guest beers (50 different beers in five months). Plenty of roadside parking. ⌂ ❀ ◖ ◗ ⊕ ▲ ♁

Meidrim

Maenllwyd Inn
¾ mile W of village and B4299 OS278212
6–11 (closed Sun)
Buckley's Best Bitter [G]
A rare example of an utterly traditional country local with a whitewashed parlour and a cottage-style sitting room. Beer served by jug. No keg at all!
⌂ Q ⊕ ♿ ♣ P

Meinciau

Black Horse
On B4309
11–3; 5.30–11 (may vary)
Buckley's Dark; Felinfoel Bitter [G]
A most welcoming traditional local with always a warm fire in the winter. ⌂ Q ❀ ⊕ P

Narberth

Kirkland Arms
James Street (A478, 400 yds from centre on road to station)
☎ (0834) 860423
11–11
Felinfoel Double Dragon [H]
Pub by rugby ground, popular with fans. Interesting photographic montages, artwork by landlord, and oddly-shaped tables. Keen participation in carnivals and other local events. Fish tank in public bar.
⌂ ♘ ❀ ◖ ⊕ ♿ ▲ ⇌ ♣ P

Nevern

Trewern Arms
Off A487 N of Newport
☎ (0239) 820395
11–3; 6–11
Draught Bass [H]
A large country pub combining a traditional old public bar with large lounge and dining areas. Quiet country village setting; interesting walks nearby. Guest beers in summer.
⌂ ♘ ❀ ⊨ ◖ ◗ ⊕ ♿ ▲ ♣ P

Newcastle Emlyn

Bunch of Grapes
Bridge Street (A475)
☎ (0239) 711185
11.30–11
Courage Best Bitter, Directors [H]
17th-century building now opened out, with pine floors and furniture. Guest beers always available. Eve meals finish at 7; no food Sun. ⌂ ♘ ❀ ◖ ◗ ⊕

Red Cow
Adpar (B4333/B4571 jct, near river bridge)
☎ (0239) 710256
11–11 (may close afternoons, closed Sun eve in winter)
Draught Bass [G]
300 year-old local, notably traditional in style. Same licensee for 75 years. Table skittles. Q ♿ ♣ P

Pelcomb Bridge

Rising Sun Inn
On A478, 1 mile from Haverfordwest
☎ (0437) 765171
11.30–3; 7 (6 summer)–11
Ind Coope Burton Ale; Tetley Bitter [H]
Old country inn tastefully rebuilt, retaining original character. Family business offering a warm welcome and a friendly atmosphere. Popular with diners (daily specials).
Function room with own bar.
⌂ Q ❀ ⊨ ◖ ◗ ⊕ ♿ ▲ ♣ P

Pembroke

Old Cross Saws
109 Main Street (A4139 near brow of hill)
☎ (0646) 682475
11–11
Buckley's Best Bitter [H]
Rugby-followers' local with hand-pumped Buckley's (rare for area) and a varied menu. Larger inside than it appears from without. ❀ ⊨ ◖ ◗ ▲ ⇌ ♣ P

Try also: York Tavern (Welsh Brewers)

Pembroke Dock

Charlton Hotel
Bush Street (B4322 close to market and old dockyard)
☎ (0646) 682285
11–11
Draught Bass; Welsh Brewers Worthington Dark, BB [H]
A gem of a beer-drinker's local. Red-brick, turn-of-century corner pub with impressive bank of six handpumps and a large games room. Snacks lunchtimes. ♘ ⇌ ♣

Pontargothi

Cresselly Arms
On A40 ☎ (0267) 290221
11.30–3; 6–11
Draught Bass; Whitbread Flowers Original [H]
Pleasant pub in a scenic valley. Delightful restaurant with views of stream. ⌂ ❀ ◖ ◗ P

Salutation
On A40 ☎ (0267) 290336
11.30–3; 5.30–11
Felinfoel Double Dragon [H]
Attractive, atmospheric pub with lots of nooks and crannies. Local game and fish on menu.
⌂ Q ◖ ◗ ♣ P

Pontarllechau

Three Horseshoes
On A4069 ☎ (055 04) 210
11.30–3; 6–11
Buckley's Best Bitter [H]
Charming lounge and rustic bar set in a beautiful valley.
⌂ ❀ ◖ ◗ ⊕ ▲ ♣ P

Pontfaen

Dyffryn Arms
Off A4313
11–11
Draught Bass; Ind Coope Burton Ale [G]
Original basic, traditional, rural pub with tiled floor, log fire and friendly Welsh atmosphere. Used by locals, farmers and intellectuals. ⌂ Q ♘ ❀ ▲ ♣ P

Porth-gain

Sloop Inn
Off A487 OS815324
☎ (03483) 449
11.30–3; 6–11
Felinfoel Double Dragon; Welsh Brewers Worthington BB 🄷
Old seafarers' pub, est. 1743, in historical harbour village on national park coastal path. Original character maintained. Popular eating house with bar snacks and varied menu, including locally-caught seafood. A sun trap.
⌂ Q ❀ ◖ ◗ ♣ P

St Davids

Farmers Arms
Goat Street (off Cross Square)
☎ (0437) 720328
11–11
Welsh Brewers Worthington BB 🄷
19th-century, stone-built pub with beams, original fireplaces and flagstoned floors. Popular with local fishermen, farmers and lifeboatmen. Excellent home-cooked meals and bar snacks. The spacious terrace overlooks cathedral and surrounding hills. ⌂ Q ❀ ◖ ◗ ♣

St Florence

New Inn
High Street (200 yds down hill from church on Manorbier road) ☎ (0834) 871315
11–3; 5.30–11
Brains Bitter 🄷
Welcoming pub in heart of Floral Village of Gt Britain 1989, which has been extended without losing its essential character. Stone-flagged public bar and comfortable saloon bar (same prices). Supporter of a variety of local sports teams.
⌂ Q ❀ ◖ ◗ ⊟ ♿ ⛺ ♣ P

Solva

Cambrian Inn
Main Street (A487)
☎ (0437) 721210
11–3; 7–11
Ind Coope Burton Ale 🄷
18th-century village pub with beamed bar and restaurant. A popular and comfortable eating house (children's lunch menu) near bridge over Solva river and cliff path. ⌂ Q ◖ ◗ ⊟ ♣ P

Ship Inn
Main Street (A487)
☎ (0437) 721247
11–11
Draught Bass; Brains SA; Courage Directors; Felinfoel Double Dragon; Welsh Brewers Worthington BB 🄷
Quiet 300 year-old pub in attractive fishing and sailing village, three miles from St Davids. Free car park on quay; access to Pembrokeshire coastal path. Home-cooked full menu with daily specials (try the local crab). No meals Sun eve.
⌂ Q ⛑ ❀ ◖ ◗ ♣

Talybont

White Lion
The Square (A487)
☎ (097086) 245
11–4; 5.30–11
Banks's Mild, Bitter 🄴
Large, slate-floored public bar with everything from cribbage to bus timetables. Neat lounge.
⌂ Q ❀ 🛏 ◖ ◗ ♿ ♣

Tegryn

Butchers Arms
4 miles E of Crymych and A478 ☎ (0239) 77680
11–3; 5.30–11
Buckley's Best Bitter 🄷
Comfortable and welcoming pub in centre of small hilltop village, offering fine views of surrounding countryside. Excellent value food.
⌂ Q ⛑ ❀ 🛏 ◖ ◗ ⊟ ♿ ⛺ ♣ P

Templeton

Boars Head
On A478 ☎ (0834) 860286
11–3; 5.30–11 (11–11 Sat)
Ruddles Best Bitter; Webster's Yorkshire Bitter 🄷
Beautiful, rural, beamed, rambling pub. Hops hang in main lounge. Very good restaurant. A great experience.
Q ⛑ ❀ ◖ ◗ ⊟ ♿ ⛺ P

Tenby

Normandie Hotel
Upper Frog Street (first left after the Five Arches)
☎ (0834) 2227
11–3; 7–11
Welsh Brewers Hancock's HB 🄷
Old coaching pub with many nooks and crannies, popular with all types from local football team to those wanting special celebration dinners. CD jukebox. Children's room an integral part of pub, with range of electronic games.
⛑ 🛏 ◖ ◗ ⊟ ⇌ ♣

Three Mariners
St George Street (between the Five Arches and church)
☎ (0834) 2834
12–11 (11–11 summer)
Draught Bass; Welsh Brewers Worthington Dark, BB 🄷
Tile-floored public bar boasting a multitude of nautical photographs and popular with a large cross-section of the community. Piano and entertainment by local musicians on many nights. The pool table is in the smaller saloon bar. Meals summer lunchtimes only.
❀ ◖ ⊟ ♿ ⛺ ⇌ ♣

Try also: Coach & Horses (Allied); **Lifeboat** (Welsh Brewers)

Wooden

Woodridge Inn
Beacon View (A478, 3 miles N of Tenby) ☎ (0834) 812259
11–11
Ind Coope Burton Ale; Pembrokeshire's Own Ales Benfro Bitter; Tetley Bitter 🄷
Large roadside pub with sports and health club facilities (¾ size snooker table). Music every night in summer. Spacious and comfortable with appeal for all ages and tastes. Look out for green dinosaur slide visible from road. ⛑ ❀ ◖ ◗ ♿ ⛺ ♣ P

THE SYMBOLS

- ⌂ real fire
- Q quiet pub – in at least one bar
- ⛑ indoor room for children
- ❀ garden or other outdoor drinking area
- 🛏 accommodation
- ◖ lunchtime meals
- ◗ evening meals
- ⊟ public bar
- ♿ easy disabled access
- ⛺ camping facilities at the pub or nearby
- ⇌ near British Rail station
- ⊖ near Underground station
- ♣ pub games
- ⍥ real cider
- P pub car park

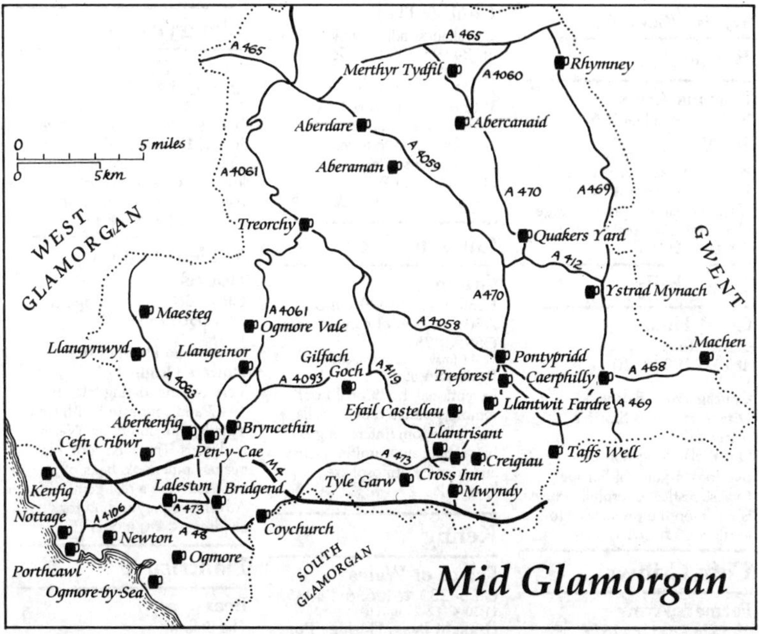

Aberaman

Temple Bar

Cardiff Road (A4224)
12–4 (12–2 Sun); 7 (6.45 Sat)–11 (may vary)
Brains SA; Bullmastiff Ebony Dark; Felinfoel Double Dragon; Samuel Smith OBB [H]
Homely local with bric-a-brac and library in bar. Separate games room. Limited parking. Guest beers. ⌂ Q ⊟ ♣ P

Try also: Rock (Free)

Abercanaid

Colliers

Nightingale Street (off A470, behind Hoover complex)
☎ (0443) 690376
11–4 (5.30 Sat); 6–11
Marston's Pedigree Bitter; Whitbread Flowers IPA [H]
Village local, comfortable and friendly. Restaurant has a mining theme. No meals Sun/Mon eves.
Q ◖ ◗ ≉ (Pentrebach) ♣

Aberdare

Conway

Cardiff Road
☎ (0685) 883666
11–11
Courage Best Bitter, Directors [H]
Comfortable single-bar pub in town centre. No lunches Sun.
◖ ≉

Glandover Arms

Gadlys Road (old road to Hirwaun) ☎ (0685) 872923
11–4 (5 Sat, 12–2 Sun); 6 (6.30 Sat)–11
Ansells Bitter; Ind Coope Burton Ale [H]
Convivial house with cellar restaurant. No meals Sun eve or Mon. ⊛ ◖ ◗ ≉ ♣

Try also: Whitcombe (Welsh Brewers)

Aberkenfig

Swan Inn

128 Bridgend Road (1 mile from M4) ☎ (0656) 725612
11.30–3.30 (12–2.30 Sun); 6–11 (may extend)
Brains Dark, Bitter, SA; Whitbread Flowers Original [H]
Pleasant, comfortable village pub serving good meals. No lunches Sun; eve meals Tue–Sat.
◖ ◗ ♿ P

Try also: Colliers Arms

Bridgend

Hunters Lodge

Church Acre, Brackla
☎ (0656) 67700
11–11 (12–3.30; 7–10.30 Sun)
Draught Bass; Welsh Brewers Hancock's HB [H]
Large friendly estate pub with pleasant decor; comfortably furnished. Restaurant in lounge is very popular at lunchtime; children and vegetarians catered for. Q ⛟ ⊛ ◖ ◗ ⊟ ♿ ♣ P

Old Castle

Nolton Street
☎ (0656) 652305
12–4; 6–11 (12–11 Fri & Sat)
Draught Bass; Brains Bitter; Welsh Brewers Worthington BB [H]
Cosy, friendly town pub without an inn sign.
⌂ Q ⊛ ◖ ≉ ♣

Pied Piper

Bridgend Industrial Estate (off A473 at Coychurch end of the estate) ☎ (0656) 669373
11.30–3; 6–11 (12 Thu, 11.30–12 Fri & Sat)
Ansells Bitter; Tetley Bitter [H]
Busy pub serving large industrial estate. Often very lively in the evening.
⊛ ◖ ◗ ⊟ ♿ ♣ P

Two Brewers

Brackla Way, Brackla (200 yds from B4181)
☎ (0656) 661788
12–4; 7–11 (11.30–11 Fri & Sat)
Brains Dark, Bitter, SA [H]
Large modern estate pub with a plush lounge and family room. No meals Sun. Backgammon available. Q ⛟ ⊛ ◖ ♿ ♣ P

Victoria

7 Adare Street
☎ (0656) 67667
11–11
Courage Best Bitter, Directors [H]
Comfortable, busy town-centre pub. No lunches Sun.
◖ ♿ ≉ ♣

Mid Glamorgan

Try also: Kings Head

Bryncethin

Masons Arms
Bridgend Road (A4061)
☎ (0656) 720253
11–11 (12–2; 7–10.30 Sun)
Brains Dark, SA; Welsh Brewers Worthington BB [H]
Unspoilt bar and plush lounge. New high-class restaurant.
◖ ◗ ♿ ♣ P

Caerphilly

Court House
Cardiff Road
☎ (0222) 888120
11–11
Courage Best Bitter, Directors; John Smith's Bitter [H]
Old Welsh long-house overlooking one of Europe's largest castles. Caerphilly cheese is made on the premises. No meals Sun. ⌂ Q ✿ ◖ ◗ ≈

Cefn Cribwr

Farmers Arms
24 Cefn Road (B4281)
☎ (0656) 743648
12–11
Draught Bass; Felinfoel Double Dragon [H]
Unspoilt village local with mining memorabilia in bar. Parking for three cars only.
⌂ Q ✿ ♿ ♣ P

Coychurch

White Horse
Main Road ☎ (0656) 652583
11.30–4; 5.30–11 (11.30–11 Fri & Sat)
Brains Dark, Bitter, SA [H]
The pub with almost everything, including a 'Champion Landlord of the Year'. Q ✿ ◖ ◗ ♿ ♣ P

Try also: Prince of Wales

Creigiau

Caesars Arms
Cardiff Road (1 mile N of village) OS078827
☎ (0222) 890486
12 (11.30 Fri, 11 Sat)–2; 7–11
Whitbread Flowers IPA [H]
Pleasant, peaceful pub in attractive rural setting. ✿ P

Cross Inn

Cross Inn
On A473 ☎ (0443) 223431
12–4.30 (12–2.30 Sun); 6.30–11
Marston's Pedigree Bitter; Whitbread Flowers IPA [H]
Bustling, small, friendly village local. Guest beer. Q P

Efail Castellau

Lamb & Flag
Castellau Road, Castellau (½ mile off B4595) OS051856
☎ (0443) 202378
12–4; 7–11 (12–11 Fri & Sat)
Whitbread Flowers IPA, Flowers Original [H]
Attractive pub in lovely countryside setting at the edge of Llantrisant Common. No meals Mon and Tue. ⌂ ✿ ◖ ◗ P

Gilfach Goch

Griffin
Hendreforgan (600 yds S of A4093 at end of narrow lane) OS988875
12–11 (may close afternoons)
Brains SA [H]
Exceptional, traditional local, remotely situated in a small valley bottom. Interesting old bric-a-brac and furniture. Cosy and friendly atmosphere.
Q ✿ P

Kenfig

Prince of Wales
Off B4283 ☎ (0656) 740356
11.30–4 (12–2 Sun); 6–11
Draught Bass; Eldridge Pope Royal Oak; Felinfoel Double Dragon; Marston's Pedigree Bitter [G]**; Wadworth 6X; Welsh Brewers Worthington BB** [H]
Old pub with exposed stone walls, a large main bar and two smaller rooms. Linked with historic Kenfig which lies buried under sand dunes. Handy for nature reserve.
⌂ Q ✿ ◖ ◗ ♿ ▲ ♣ P

Laleston

Laleston Inn
Wind Street (off A473 behind church) ☎ (0656) 652946
12–4; 7–11
Felinfoel Double Dragon; Wadworth 6X; Welsh Brewers Worthington BB [H]
15th-century free house with exposed stone walls and beams. Smart and comfortable. Live music Wed eves; jazz Sun lunchtimes. Guest beers.
⌂ ✿ ◖ ◗ P

Llangeinor

Llangeinor Arms
Off A4093 between Ogmore and Garw Valleys
☎ (0656) 870344
12–4; 7–11 (11.30–11 Sat)
Draught Bass; Welsh Brewers Worthington BB [H]
Isolated hilltop pub with superb views. Children (over 14) allowed in conservatory. Eve bar meals Mon–Fri only, but separate restaurant in old tithe barn. ⌂ ✿ ◖ ◗ P

Llangynwyd

Corner House
☎ (0656) 732393
11–3.30; 6.30–11 (11–11 Sat)
Brains Bitter; Courage Best Bitter, Directors [H]
Comfortable, welcoming village local. Good selection of reasonably-priced meals. Live music Thu. ⌂ ✿ ◖ ◗ ♣ P

Yr Hen Dy (Old House)
Off A4063 in old village centre
☎ (0656) 733310
11–11
Whitbread Flowers IPA, Flowers Original [H]
Very old inn, dating back to 1147 and connected with Cefn Ydfa legend and other Welsh traditions. Thatched roof, old beams, inglenook, bags of atmosphere – a real gem. Adventure playground for children. ⌂ ✿ ◖ ◗ ♿ ▲ P

Llantrisant

Bear
The Bullring
☎ (0443) 222271
11.30–4; 6–11
Draught Bass; Welsh Brewers Worthington BB [H]
Small, friendly local in old, hilltop market town. ♣

New Inn
Swan Street (next to hilltop church) ☎ (0443) 222232
11.30–4; 6–11
Draught Bass; Welsh Brewers Hancock's HB [H]
Village local for all age groups. Still retains traditional layout of separate rooms. A strong emphasis on food (served in a separate bar). ⌂ ◖ ◗

Try also: Pennyfarthing

Llantwit Fardre

Bush
Main Road (A473)
☎ (0443) 203958
12–4 (12–2 Sun); 6.30–11 (12–11 Fri & Sat)
Crown SBB [H]
Cosy village local, comfortably furnished. Exposed stone walls. Limited parking. Q ♣ P

Try also: Crown

Machen

White Hart
Nant y ceisiad (100 yds N of A468 under railway bridge)
☎ (0633) 441005
11–11 (may vary)
Brains Bitter [H]
Rambling pub with a cosy, windowless, wood-panelled bar. The panelling was salvaged

from a luxury liner and the small restaurant is reminiscent of a ship's cabin. Enterprising range of guest beers. Q ⊛ ◐ ◑ P

Maesteg

Beethovens
Castle Street (near town hall and bus station) ☎ (0656) 738484
11–4 (12–2 Sun); 6–11 (11–11 Fri & Sat)
Crown SBB [H]
Plush local with family room. Youngish clientele. Disco Thu; live music Tue. ⛟ ◐ ◑ ♿ ♣

Sawyers Arms
5 Commercial Street (near town hall and bus station)
☎ (0656) 734500
11–4; 6–11 (11–11 Fri & Sat)
Brains Dark, Bitter, SA [H]
Victorian exterior; comfortable interior. Live music Thu. ◐ ⊟ ♿

Merthyr Tydfil

Anchor Tavern
High Street
☎ (0685) 723840
11–11 (may close afternoons)
Draught Bass [H]
Small pub in town centre. Welcoming and full of character.
⊟ ≹ ♣

Mwyndy

Barn
100 yds off A4119
☎ (0443) 222333
11.30–11
Felinfoel Double Dragon; Welsh Brewers Hancock's HB [H]
Interesting conversion of an old barn: two bars with exposed beams and stone walls, and an upstairs restaurant. Enterprising range of guest beers, albeit expensive. Eve meals in restaurant only; no lunches Sun in bar. ♔ Q ⛟ ⊛ ◐ ◑ P

Try also: Castell Mynach (Welsh Brewers)

Newton

Globe
Bridgend Road (A4106)
☎ (065 671) 3535
11.30–3.30; 5.30–11 (11.30–11 Fri, Sat & summer)
Draught Bass [G]
Welcoming local on edge of village with excellent provision for families.
♔ ⛟ ⊛ ◐ ◑ ⊟ ⅄ ♣ P

Jolly Sailor
Church Street (off A4106)
☎ (065 671) 2403
11.30–11
Brains Dark, Bitter, SA [H]
Village green pub with a nautical flavour. ♔ ⊛ ⊟ ♿ ⅄ P

Nottage

Swan Inn
West Road ☎ (065 671) 2568
11.30–4; 6–11 (11.30–11 Sat)
Courage Best Bitter, Directors; John Smith's Bitter (occasionally) [H]
Pleasant village local. Reasonably-priced food.
⊛ ◐ ♿ ⅄ ♣ P

Ogmore

Pelican
Ewenny Road (B4524)
OS882767 ☎ (0656) 880049
11.30–4; 6.30–11 (11–11 Fri & Sat)
Courage Best Bitter, Directors; John Smith's Bitter [H]
Smart, comfortable country pub overlooking ruins of Ogmore Castle. Restaurant and bar offer excellent home cooking (including veg meals).
♔ ⊛ ◐ ◑ ⅄ ♣ P

Ogmore-by-Sea

Craig-yr-Eos
☎ (0656) 880388
12–4; 6.30–11
Buckley's Best Bitter (summer); **Crown SBB** [H]
Seaside hotel in small village on heritage coast, offering fine views of the Devon and Somerset coast.
♔ Q ⛟ ⊛ ⛿ ◐ ◑ ⊟ ⅄ P

Try also: Sealawns Hotel

Ogmore Vale

Corbetts Arms
Bridge Street (A4061)
☎ (0656) 840386
12–4; 7–11 (11–11 Fri & Sat)
Whitbread Flowers Original [H]
Comfortable valleys local with regular beer changes. ⊟ P

Pen-y-Cae

Tyr Isha
Off A4061 by Sarn motorway services; Bridgend side of M4
OS903827 ☎ (0656) 725287
12–4; 6.30–11 (11–11 Sat & summer)
Draught Bass; Welsh Brewers Hancock's HB [H]
Plush and popular converted farm house. Eve meals Thu–Sat.
♔ Q ⊛ ◐ ◑ ♣ P

Pontypridd

Bunch of Grapes
Ynysangharad Road (behind B&Q) ☎ (0443) 402934
11–11
Brains Dark, Bitter, SA; Welsh Brewers Hancock's HB [H]
Comfortable pub with sun-trap patio and a restaurant dominated by the famous vine. Regular guest beers.
⛟ ⊛ ◐ ◑ ≹ ♣ P

Greyhound
1 The Broadway (opp. railway station)
11–11
Draught Bass [H]
Small and invariably bustling pub. Q ⊛ ⊟ ≹ ♣

Market Tavern
Market Square
☎ (0443) 485331
11–11
Courage Best Bitter, Directors; John Smith's Bitter [H]
Comfortable watering hole next to market, with separate cellar bar, smart restaurant and accommodation. Q ⛿ ◐ ◑ ≹

Try also: Llanover (Free)

Porthcawl

Rock Hotel
98 John Street (opp. police station) ☎ (065 671) 2340
11.30–11
Draught Bass; Welsh Brewers Worthington BB [H]
Town pub with basic bar and comfortable lounge. Generous meal portions. ♔ ⊛ ◐ ◑ ⊟ ♿ ♣

Try also: Lifeboat

Quakers Yard

Glantaff Inn
Cardiff Road (off A470)
☎ (0443) 410822
11–11
Courage Best Bitter, Directors; John Smith's Bitter [H]
Comfortable inn with upstairs restaurant above Bargoed-Taff river. Q ⊛ ◐ ◑ ⊟ ♿ ≹ P

Rhymney

Farmers Arms
Off A469 ☎ (0685) 840257
11.30–4; 7–11
Whitbread Flowers Original [H]
Traditional local. No food Sun.
⊛ ◐ ⊟ ≹

Try also: Ffynon Glas

Taffs Well

Anchor
Cardiff Road (A4054, ½ mile N of M4/A470 jct)
☎ (0222) 810104
11–11
Whitbread Flowers Original [H]
Comfortable split-level bar with gentle nautical theme in lounge and restaurant. Outstanding bar snacks. ⊛ ◐ ◑ ≹ ♣ P

Treforest

Otley Arms

Forest Road (100 yds from station) ☎ (0443) 402033
11–11
Draught Bass; Brains SA; Crown SBB; Welsh Brewers Hancock's HB Ⓗ
Bustling suburban pub, popular with students and locals. Busy for Sun lunch. Guest beers.
◐ ◗ ⊟ ⇌ ♣ P

Treorchy

Red Cow

High Street (A4058)
☎ (0443) 773032
12–4 (5 Sat); 6.30–11
Welsh Brewers Hancock's HB Ⓗ
Smart comfortable local with four contrasting bars, including a no-smoking lounge. Eve meals Tue–Thu. Q ◗ ⊟ ⇌ ♣

Try also: Prince of Wales (Whitbread)

Tyle Garw

Boars Head

Coed Cae Lane (½ mile off A473) ☎ (0443) 225400
11.30–4; 6–11
Draught Bass; Buckley's Best Bitter Ⓗ
Small, plain, unspoilt local with friendly atmosphere. Forest walks opposite. Q ❀ ⊟ ♣

Ystrad Mynach

Olde Royal Oak

Commercial Street (A469)
☎ (0443) 814196
11–11
Draught Bass Ⓗ
Unmistakable Brewer's Tudor pub on crossroads. No meals Sun. Q ◐ ◗ ⊟ ⇌ P

THE GBG QUIZ

Round 4: Getting Very Serious

46. What was known as Goddisgoode in the Middle Ages?
47. What are the constituents of the following beer cocktails:
    Black and Tan?
    Mother-in-Law?
    Granny?
    Dog's Nose?
    Dragon's Blood?
48. Who described his local beer as being 'luminous as an autumn sunset'?
49. Where do they brew beer behind gates which never open?
50. In which country is beer thought to have originated?
51. In which TV comedy series did the heroines work in a Milwaukee brewery?
52. By what name is John Martin's Pale Ale better known?
53. Which brewery runs a pig farm to use up its waste yeast?
54. Name three varieties of malting barley.
55. Why do Morland of Abingdon claim to be 'artists in brewing'?
56. What do the initials stand for in the following beer names:
    Gale's BBB?
    Burts VPA?
    St Austell HSD?
    Lloyds VIP?
    McMullen Original AK?
57. Which brewery's family has included a famous novelist and a Director General of the BBC?
58. Which beer is named after a type of signpost?
59. Which was the first British brewery to introduce canned beer?
60. Which British brewery's beer can be seen in Manet's painting *The Bar at the Folies Bergères*?

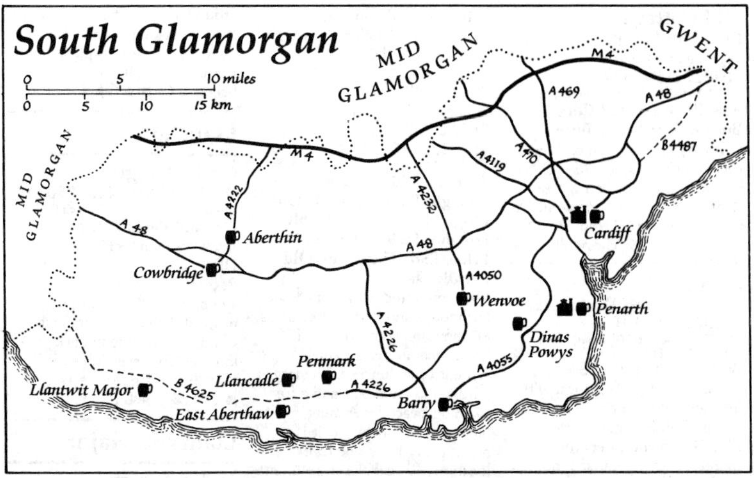

⌂ ***Brains**, Cardiff; **Bullmastiff**, Penarth*

Aberthin

Hare & Hounds

On A4222 ☎ (04463) 4892
11.30–3.30; 5.30–11 (11–11 Sat & summer)
Draught Bass [G]; Brains Dark, Bitter [E]; Welsh Brewers Hancock's HB [H], Worthington BB [G]
Excellent traditional village local, with two fine fireplaces. Recent renovation has uncovered hidden aspects of this ancient inn. Parking limited.
⌂ Q ⛀ ❀ ◐ ⊞ ♿ ⛺ ♣ P

Barry

Ship

Harbour Road
☎ (0446) 741128
11–11 (11–12 Wed–Sat)
Draught Bass; Welsh Brewers Hancock's HB [H]
Large pub/hotel on the approach to Barry Island resort. Popular with holiday-makers and families. Separate disco, good quality food and accommodation.
❀ ⛟ ◐ ◑ ⊞ ⇌ P

Try also: Bindles (Free)

Cardiff

Albert

St Mary Street
☎ (0222) 383032
11–11
Brains Dark, Bitter, SA [H] & [E]
Brains' brewery tap and the first pub that most people see after leaving the railway and bus stations. Basic downstairs bar and smarter upstairs lounge with adjoining skittle alley. No meals Sun. ◐ ⊞ ⇌ (Central) ♣

Black Lion

49 Cardiff Road, Llandaff
11–3 (12–2.40 Sun); 5–11 (11–11 Fri & Sat)
Brains Dark, Bitter, SA [H]
Typical Brains' town pub. Large, comfortable lounge and traditional bar. Very popular with locals and always busy. Children welcome in lounge at lunchtime (no meals Sun). Convenient for visitors to Llandaff Cathedral. ◐ ⊞ ♣

Canal Boat

North Road, Blackweir (A470, less than 1 mile from centre)
☎ (0222) 341410
11–3; 5.30–11 (11–11 Fri & Sat)
Brains Dark, Bitter, SA [H]
One of Brains' newest houses, built alongside the route of the Glamorganshire Canal, (very much the theme of the interior decor). Open-plan design with lounge at one end of bar and integral skittle alley at the other. Sun lunches. ❀ ◐ ◑ ♿ ♣ P

Crown

37 Bute Street
☎ (0222) 463945
11–3 (may extend); 5.30–11
Ansells Dark, Bitter; Tetley Bitter [H]
Friendly street-corner local a few yards from the city centre. Excellent easy-going atmosphere and a firm commitment to real ale. Opposite the Welsh National Opera. ◐ ◑ ♿ ⇌ (Central) ♣

Fox & Hounds

Chapel Row, St Mellons (off B4487 Newport Road)
☎ (0222) 777046
11–11
Brains Dark, Bitter, SA [H]
On the eastern outskirts of the city. Award-winning, home-cooked lunches are served in a lounge which partially converts into a dining room. Children's play area in large garden.
Q ❀ ◐ ⊞ ♣ P

Grange

136 Penarth Road, Grangetown (A4160) ☎ (0222) 230681
11–11 (11–3; 5.30–11 lounge)
Brains Dark, Bitter, SA [H]
Thriving local on main road, with large, comfortable lounge, public bar and skittle alley. Children welcome in alley till 8pm. No meals Sat or Sun.
⛀ ❀ ◐ ⊞ ⇌ (Grangetown) ♣

Grosvenor Hotel

South Park Road, Splott (E end of Splott Road, near railway bridge) ☎ (0222) 462015
12–4; 6–11 (11–11 Fri & Sat)
Brains Dark, Bitter, SA [H] & [E]
Rambling, multi-roomed locals' pub dating from the great boom of coal exports. This high barrelage house with four bars retains a few signs of the architectural mood of Tiger Bay. The cellar is prone to spring tides! Q ❀ ⊞ ♣

Old Arcade

Church Street (off High Street, near covered market)
☎ (0222) 231740
11–11 (closed Sun lunch)
Brains Dark, Bitter, SA [H]
Lively city-centre pub with emphasis on rugby union. Handy for St David's Hall.
◐ ⊞ ♿ ⇌ (Central)

South Glamorgan

Old Cottage
Cherry Orchard Road, Thornhill (1½ miles E of A469)
☎ (0222) 747582
11.30–3; 5.30–11 (11–11 Fri & Sat)
Ansells Bitter; Ind Coope Burton Ale; Tetley Bitter Ⓗ
Formerly a residential cottage, this pub opened in 1989. One bar, with upstairs dining area. Reasonably-priced, good-quality meals available till 9pm. ❀ ◖ ◗
♿ ⇌ (Lisvane & Thornhill) P

Plough
1 Merthyr Road, Whitchurch
☎ (0222) 623017
11–4.30 (4 Sat); 6.30 (7 Sat)–11 (11–11 Wed–Fri)
Brains Dark, Bitter, SA Ⓗ
Friendly village-style local with four separate rooms off a central corridor, and a large skittle alley. The menu caters for children and vegetarians (no meals Sun).
Q ❀ ◖ ⊞ ⇌ (Whitchurch) ♣

Quarry House
St Fagans Rise, Fairwater (off St Fagans Road)
☎ (0222) 565577
11–3 (12–2 Sun); 6–11 (11–11 Sat)
Courage Best Bitter, Directors Ⓗ
Converted manor house in suburban area. Good value home-cooked lunches (not Sun). Children's play area in garden.
Q ❀ ◖ ⊞ ♣ P

Radyr Arms
Station Road, Radyr (off B4262) ☎ (0222) 843121
12–2.30 (2 Sun, 11–3 Sat); 5.30–11
Brains Dark, Bitter, SA Ⓗ
A picture of this one-time mansion hangs on the wall of its large, wood-panelled lounge bar. Adjoining is a conservatory-type area, used as a children's room. Part of same building is the very popular Garth Bistro. No meals Sun.
☋ ❀ ◖ ◗ ♿ ⇌ (Radyr) P

Royal Oak
200 Broadway, Roath
☎ (0222) 473984
11–3; 5.30–11
Brains Dark, Bitter Ⓗ, **SA** Ⓖ
Large, corner local with lots of sporting memorabilia. Frequent live music. The only Brains tied house with beer on gravity dispense. Splendid stained glass windows feature several men of literary renown. ❀ ⊞ ♣

Three Horseshoes
Merthyr Road, Gabalfa (200 yds N of Gabalfa flyover, A470/A48 jct)
☎ (0222) 625703
12–11
Brains Dark, Bitter, SA Ⓗ
A 1960s pub with an unremarkable exterior but always a friendly welcome within. Award-winning ploughman's lunches. No meals Sat or Sun. ❀ ◖ ⊞ ♣ P

Ty Mawr Arms
Graig Road, Lisvane (off B4562) OS184843
☎ (0222) 754456
12–3; 6–11
Archers ASB, Golden; Draught Bass; Everards Old Original; Felinfoel Double Dragon; Fuller's London Pride, ESB; Theakston Old Peculier Ⓗ
Old, converted, stone-built farmhouse and barn. Three areas on the same level; two real fires; separate restaurant; standard pub lunches. The large garden has an aviary and a free-roaming peacock! A quiet hideaway at lunchtime, it is never really busy due to its location. 30 real ales in rotation. Family room in summer.
♨ Q ❀ ◖ ◗ ⊞ ♣ P

Try also: Eldon Arms, Ninian Park Road (Free); **Maltster's Arms,** Llandaff (Brains)

Cowbridge

Bear Hotel
63 High Street
☎ (04463) 4814
11.30–11
Brains Bitter, SA; Buckley's Best Bitter; Marston's Pedigree Bitter; Wadworth 6X; Welsh Brewers Hancock's HB Ⓗ
Large, well-appointed town-centre hotel. Q ☋ ⛟ ◖ ◗ ⊞ ♣ P

Dinas Powys

Star
Station Road (off A4055)
☎ (0222) 512176
11.30–3.30; 5.30 (5 Fri)–11 (11.30–11 Sat)
Brains Dark, Bitter, SA Ⓗ
Welcoming, spacious village pub. Live jazz Thu eve and Sun lunchtime; occasional contemporary music during university terms. The home-cooked food is highly praised, with the no-smoking bar used by diners. Children welcome if taking meals Mon–Sat lunchtime. No meals Sun.
♨ Q ❀ ◖ ⊞ ⇌ P

East Aberthaw

Blue Anchor
Off B4265 ☎ (0446) 750329
11–11
Brains Dark, SA; Buckley's Best Bitter; Marston's Pedigree Bitter Ⓗ**; Theakston Old Peculier** Ⓖ**; Wadworth 6X** Ⓗ
Well-recommended, award-winning, 14th-century thatched inn. Six inter-connecting rooms around a central bar but beware the low oak beams and narrow gangways as you explore them. Family room till 8pm. Guest beers. ♨ Q ☋ ❀ ◖ ◗ ⊞ ♣ P

Llancadle

Green Dragon
Off B4265 ☎ (0446) 750367
11–3.30; 7–11 (11–11 Fri & Sat)
Draught Bass; Welsh Brewers Hancock's HB Ⓖ & Ⓗ
Recently extended to blend sympathetically with the original thatched village pub. Children welcome in back lounge. No meals Sun eve. Usually three guest beers.
♨ Q ☋ ❀ ◖ ◗ ⊞ P

Llantwit Major

Tudor Tavern
Church Street ☎ (04465) 2297
11.30–11
Welsh Brewers Hancock's HB, Worthington BB Ⓗ
Stone-built pub next to town hall. Split-level interior with centre bar. Public quiz on Mon eves. ♣

Try also: Old White Hart (Welsh Brewers)

Penarth

Pilot
67 Queens Road (side-street near centre) ☎ (0222) 702340
12–11
Brains Dark, Bitter, SA Ⓗ
Two-bar locals' pub with a smart lounge and a traditional public bar. Situated on headland, overlooking the docks.
Q ❀ ⊞ ♿ ⇌ (Dingle Rd) ♣

Royal Hotel
Queens Road
☎ (0222) 708048
11.30–11
Brains Bitter; Bullmastiff Bitter, Son of a Bitch Ⓗ
Rare regular outlet for beers from nearby Bullmastiff brewery. A newly-acquired free house with B&B and an upstairs restaurant. Guest beers.
❀ ⛟ ◖ ⊞ ⇌ (Dingle Rd) ♣

Penmark

Six Bells Inn
Off A4226 near Cardiff (Wales) Airport. OS058687
☎ (0446) 710229
12–11
Welsh Brewers Hancock's HB Ⓗ
Friendly village pub with much Hancock's memorabilia in the bar. The landlord from 1966 to 1969 wrote a book featuring the pub. No meals Sun eve.
♨ Q ❀ ◖ ◗ ⊞ ♿ ⛺ ♣ P

Wenvoe

Horse & Jockey

Twyn-yr-odyn, St Lythans (off A4050/A48/A4232 jct)
OS117738 ☎ (0222) 593396
11.30–3.30 (4 Sat); 5.30–11
Draught Bass; Welsh Brewers Hancock's HB Ⓗ
Extremely popular pub on the outskirts of Cardiff. Main area is arranged around a central bar and leads to an adjoining room with dartboard. Panoramic views of Cardiff from outside. No meals Sun. ❀ ◐ ⅄ ♣ P

Wenvoe Arms

18 Old Port Road (off A4050)
☎ (0222) 591129
11.30–3.30; 5.30–11 (11.30–11 summer)
Brains Dark, Bitter, SA Ⓗ
Comfortable, welcoming, traditional village local. The family room leads to the garden. Camping available at local farm. Restaurant meals only eves and Sun (must book).
⌂ Q ⚭ ❀ ◐ ◗ ⊞ ♣ P

TYPES OF BEER

Ale:	these days, for the most part, another name for beer, although originally the name of an alcoholic brew of barley, long before hops were introduced into British brewing.
Barley Wine:	a strong, rich beer with a high gravity, often sold in nips ($\frac{1}{3}$ pint).
Bitter:	a British beer style deriving its name from the flavour imparted by the amount of hops used. Also known as pale ale or IPA (India Pale Ale), although increasingly used as a general term for beer.
Brown Ale:	type of sweetish, mild ale in a bottle.
India Pale Ale:	a well-hopped beer originally brewed in Burton upon Trent for export to India. The genuine product had a very high gravity, although the term is widely used for many lighter beers today.
Keg Beer:	beer which has been chilled and filtered at the brewery to stop any further fermentation. Dispensed from pressurised metal containers (Kegs) and forced to the bar by an injection of carbon dioxide gas.
Lager:	a popular beer taking its name from the German 'to store'. Lager uses different yeasts and hops from beer and should be stored at the brewery for several months.
Light Ale:	low gravity bitter in a bottle.
Mild Ale:	a low gravity beer, with fewer hops than bitter. Can be light, but is mostly dark on account of the darker roasted malt or caramel colourings.
Old Ale:	strong beer mostly brewed in winter months.
Porter:	strong, dark beer, predecessor of stout, named after the London porters who drank it.
Real Ale:	cask-conditioned, traditional draught beer.
Stout:	a dark beer which is brewed from a combination of dark, roasted malt and unmalted roasted barley. Well hopped.

West Glamorgan

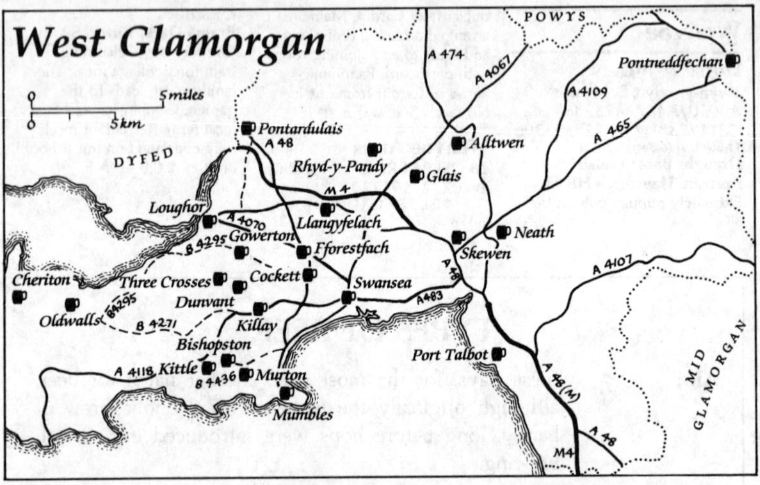

Alltwen

Butchers Arms
Alltwen Mill (off A474)
☎ (0792) 863100
12–3; 6.30–11
Everards Old Original 🄷
Comfortable free house. At least three guest beers. Restaurant overlooks Swansea Valley.
P

Bishopston

Joiners Arms
50 Bishopston Road (off B4436) ☎ (044 128) 2658
11–3.30; 5.30–11 (11–11 Thu–Sat)
Draught Bass; Welsh Brewers Worthington BB 🄷
Attractive village pub with a somewhat dark interior. Guest beer. P

Cheriton

Britannia
Llanmadoc Road, Llanrhidian
OS450930 ☎ (044 127) 624
12–3.30 (not Tue); 7–11
(11–11 Fri, Sat & summer, incl Tue)
Draught Bass (summer);
Marston's Pedigree Bitter; Welsh Brewers Hancock's HB 🄷
A necessary half-way stopping point on the annual Round-Gower cycle ride. Excellent restaurant. Guest beers in summer. P

Cockett

Cockett Inn
Waunarlwydd Road
☎ (0792) 582083
11.30–3.30 (12–2 Sun); 5.30–10.30
(11.30–11 Fri & Sat)
Buckley's Dark, Best Bitter 🄷
Large locals' bar with games; comfortable lounge. No food Sun. P

Dunvant

Found Out
☎ (0792) 203396
11.30–3; 5.30–11 (11–11 Thu–Sat)
Whitbread Flowers IPA, Best Bitter, Flowers Original, Wethered Winter Royal 🄷
Popular suburban pub. P

Fforestfach

Star Inn
1070 Carmarthen Road
☎ (0792) 586910
11.30–3.30; 5.30–11 (may vary)
Buckley's Dark, Best Bitter 🄷
Popular local serving nearby industrial estate. Lunchtime bar snacks. P

Glais

Old Glais
On B4291 ☎ (0792) 843316
12–4; 6–11 (may vary)
Ruddles Best Bitter, County; Webster's Yorkshire Bitter 🄷
Comfortable and friendly village pub. P

Gowerton

Berthlwydd
On B4295 ☎ (0792) 873454
12–3.30; 6–11
Courage Directors; Felinfoel Double Dragon 🄷
Beautifully renovated and extended free house overlooking Loughor Estuary. Excellent meals in the bar or restaurant. Guest beers. P

Commercial Hotel
Station Road ☎ (0792) 873496
11.30–3; 7–11 (11–11 Thu–Sat)
Buckley's Best Bitter 🄷
Pleasant, welcoming village pub
Ample room outside. P

Welcome to Gower
Mount Street
☎ (0792) 872611
11.30–3.30; 5.30–11 (11.30–11 summer)
Buckley's Dark, Best Bitter 🄷
Very well-appointed pub at the gateway to Gower P

Killay

Railway Inn
Gower Road
☎ (0792) 203946
11.30–3.30 (4 Sat); 5.30–11
Draught Bass; Welsh Brewers Worthington Dark, BB 🄷
Three-roomed pub next to Clyne Valley walk. Lunchtime bar snacks (not Sun). P

Kittle

Beaufort Arms
18 Pennard Road
☎ (044 128) 4521
11–3; 6–11 (11–11 summer)
Buckley's Dark, Best Bitter 🄷
A real games pub. Live jazz Wed in summer.
P

Llangyfelach

Plough & Harrow
Llangyfelach Road (B4489, off M4 jct 46) ☎ (0792) 771816
11.30–4 (12–2 Sun); 6–11
Courage Best Bitter, Directors; John Smith's Bitter 🄷
Very comfortable pub, with outdoor area overlooking Penllergaer Forest. P

Loughor

Red Lion
Glebe Road ☎ (0792) 892983
11.30–4; 6–11
Felinfoel Bitter, Double Dragon 🄷

Friendly, no-frills bar, and spacious, comfortable lounge.

Mumbles

Park Inn
Park Street ☎ (0792) 366738
11.30–3.30; 5.30–11 (11.30–11 Fri & Sat)
Ruddles Best Bitter, County Ⓗ
Small, friendly locals' pub, near the public library.

White Rose
1 Newton Road
☎ (0792) 361164
11–11
Draught Bass; Welsh Brewers Worthington Dark, Hancock's HB Ⓗ
Very popular pub with excellent service. No lunches Sun.

William Hancock
Western Lane
☎ (0792) 362133
11–11
Draught Bass; Welsh Brewers Hancock's HB Ⓗ
Formerly the Waterloo, now refurbished and hosted by a Spaniard. Unusual seafood.

Murton

Plough & Harrow
Oldway Road
☎ (044 128) 4459
11.30–3.30; 5.30–11 (11–11 Sat)
Brains SA; Ruddles Best Bitter, County; Webster's Yorkshire Bitter Ⓗ
Comfortable village pub with a piano in the bar.

Neath

King Edward VII
London Road
☎ (0639) 635708
11.30–4 (12.30–3 Sun); 5.30–11 (11.30–11 Fri & Sat)
Courage Best Bitter, Directors Ⓗ
Wood-panelled period pub.

Try also: Castle Hotel (Fuller's)

Oldwalls

Greyhound
☎ (0792) 390146
11–11
Draught Bass; Welsh Brewers Hancock's HB Ⓗ
Excellent choice of food and guest ales in a large free house.

Try also: Welcome to Town

Pontardulais

Farmers Arms
St Teilo Street
☎ (0792) 882451
11.30–4; 6 (5.30 Fri)–11 (11–11 Sat)
Draught Bass; Welsh Brewers Worthington Dark Ⓗ
Large rustic building. Weekend live entertainment.

Pontneddfechan

Angel Hotel
On B4242 ☎ (0639) 722013
11.30–4; 6–11 (may vary Sat)
Whitbread Flowers Original Ⓗ
Well-appointed pub at gateway to waterfalls. Guest beer.

Try also: Old White Horse Inn (Free)

Port Talbot

Accolade
Green Park Industrial Estate
☎ (0639) 891467
11–3.30 (may vary, 12–2 Sun); 6–11 (11–11 Fri & Sat)
Brains Dark, SA; Courage Best Bitter, Directors; Ruddles Best Bitter, County Ⓗ
Large, recently-built town pub (turn left from station).

St Oswalds
Station Road ☎ (0639) 899200
12–4; 6.30–11
Crown SBB Ⓗ
Distinctive pub with adjoining restaurant.

Rhyd-y-Pandy

Masons Arms
2 miles N of M4 jct 46
☎ (0792) 842535
11.30–4; 6–11 (may vary)
Courage Directors Ⓗ
Rural pub, popular at lunchtimes.

Skewen

Crown Hotel
216 New Road (B4291)
☎ (0792) 813309
11.30–4; 6–11 (may vary)
Brains Dark, MA, SA Ⓗ
A regulars' bar and a comfortable lounge. The only outlet for MA, a brewery mix of Dark and Bitter. Snooker table.

Swansea

Adam & Eve
High Street ☎ (0792) 655913
11–4; 5.30–11 (11–11 Thu–Sat)
Brains Dark, Bitter, SA Ⓗ
A welcome Brains outlet; a traditional three-roomed local.

Bryn-y-Mor Hotel
Bryn-y-Mor Road
☎ (0792) 466650
11–3.30; 5.30–11 (11–11 Thu–Sat)
Ansells Bitter; Buckley's Dark; Ind Coope Burton Ale; Tetley Bitter Ⓗ
Well-run suburban local. Live music at weekends (no food Sun).

Builders Arms
Oxford Street ☎ (0792) 476189
11–3.30; 7–11 (closed Sun)
Buckley's Dark, Best Bitter Ⓗ
Unusual split-level bar offering excellent cuisine: book for eve meals. Closed on Sun unless booked. Parties catered for.

Cricketers
83 King Edward Road
☎ (0792) 466524
11–11
Ansells Bitter; Ind Coope Burton Ale; Tetley Bitter Ⓗ
Energetic, young persons' pub with cricketing theme.

Duke
Wind Street ☎ (0792) 460604
11–11
Draught Bass; Welsh Brewers Worthington Dark, BB Ⓗ
Well-appointed pub, with regulars' bar, comfortable lounge and a restaurant. Food is good, so book.

Glamorgan Hotel
88 Argyle Street (near prison)
☎ (0792) 653389
11.30–3; 6–11 (11–11 Sat)
Draught Bass Ⓗ
Friendly pub, popular at lunchtimes.

Queens
Gloster Place (between the museum and the Evening Post building) ☎ (0792) 643460
11–11 (12–2.30; 4–11 Sat in winter)
Theakston Best Bitter Ⓗ
Nicely refurbished, single-bar pub on the edge of the Marina. Interesting old photographs with a nautical flavour. No TV; live music most Suns. Unusual beer for the area.

Vivian Arms
Sketty Cross, Sketty
☎ (0792) 203015
11–11
Brains Dark, Bitter, SA Ⓗ
Solidly comfortable, suburban mecca.

Westbourne Hotel
Bryn-y-Mor Road
☎ (0792) 654952
11.30–3.30; 6–11 (11.30–11 Fri & Sat)
Draught Bass; Welsh Brewers Worthington Dark, Hancock's HB Ⓗ
Popular pub with comfortable lounge. Excellent menu. Front porch for outdoor drinking.

Try also: Rhyddings (Ansells)

Three Crosses

Joiners Arms
Joiners Road ☎ (0792) 873479
12–2; 6–11 (12–11 Fri & Sat)
Ruddles Best Bitter, County; Webster's Yorkshire Bitter Ⓗ
Pleasant village local. ❀ (⊞ P

Gwent

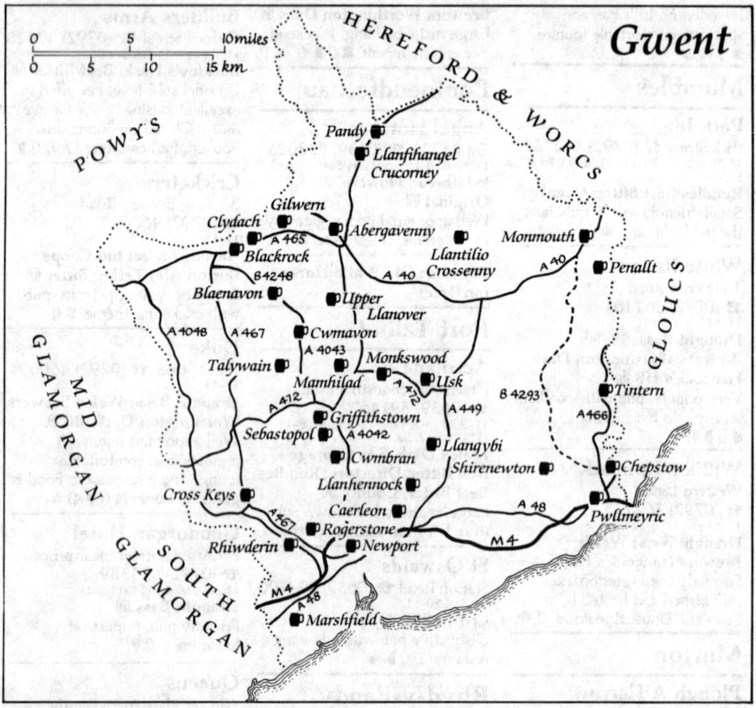

Abergavenny

Great Western Hotel
Station Road (off Monmouth Road SE of town)
☎(0873) 3593
11.30–3; 7 (6 summer)–11
Ruddles Best Bitter Ⓗ
A 150 year-old, family-run pub with lots of railway memorabilia. Comfortable bar, lounge and games room. Its proximity (30 secs) to the station makes it the best waiting room on the Marches line! Good value food. Guest beer.
🏛 ❀ ⛟ ◐ ◑ ⇌ ♣ P

Hen & Chickens Hotel
Flannel Street (off High Street)
☎ (0873) 3613
10.30–4; 7–11 (10–11 Tue, 10.30–11 Fri & Sat)
Draught Bass; Welsh Brewers Worthington BB Ⓗ
Thankfully time has stood still in this fine, unspoilt pub tucked away in a side-street near the market. Cosy bar and snug with dining room quaintly named the 'Chicks Parlour'. No meals Sun.
🏛 Q ◐ ♣

Station Hotel
37 Brecon Road (NW of centre) ☎ (0873) 4759
12–4; 6–11 (12–11 Tue, Fri & Sat)
Draught Bass; Brains SA; Greenalls Davenports Traditional Bitter Ⓗ
By popular demand this old-fashioned pub has remained unchanged. Cosy and well lived-in, the bar and lounge contain items to remind the visitor of its past railway connections (name comes from LNWR station which once stood closeby). Guest beers.
⊕ ♣ P

Blackrock

Rock & Fountain
On A465 ☎ (0873) 830393
12–3 (4 summer); 7–11
Ruddles Best Bitter, County; Webster's Yorkshire Bitter Ⓗ
Open-plan pub with separate restaurant which has a natural waterfall and is open until midnight. Nine Men's Morris and shove-ha'penny played. Guest beers in summer.
🏛 Q ⛟ ❀ ⛟ ◐ ◑ ♿ ⛺ ♣ P

Blaenavon

Cambrian Inn
Llanover Road
☎ (0495) 790327
7–11 (12–11 Sat)
Brains Bitter, SA Ⓗ
Traditional local with pool room separate from bar/lounge.
⊕ ♣

Caerleon

Kings Arms
Belmont Hill
☎ (0633) 420329
11–3; 5.30–11
Draught Bass; Welsh Brewers Worthington BB Ⓗ
Popular 17th-century inn and restaurant, formerly a flour mill. Old low beams, plenty of original stonework and wood fittings lend to the cosy atmosphere. Small public, lounge and 'Sundowner' bar with fireplace. Good reputation for food. Garden play area.
🏛 ❀ ◐ ◑ ⊕ ♣ P

White Hart Inn
High Street (on town square)
☎ (0633) 420255
11.30–3; 5–11 (11–11 Fri & Sat)
Courage Best Bitter, Directors Ⓗ
Built in 1920 on site of former hotel of same name. Comfortable, partly wood-panelled lounge adjoins public bar area. Old church pews were used in the 1987 refurbishment. Lounge contains 1960s Payramid Game (proceeds to the blind). Function/dining room. ❀ ◐ ♣ P

Try also: Old Bull Inn (Ansells)

Chepstow

Bridge Inn

Bridge Street (lower end of town by river)
☎ (029 12) 625622
11–3; 6–11
Beer range varies ⊞
300 year-old riverside pub by the iron bridge from which it took its present name in 1813. Open-plan snug, lounge and a bar which retains an original slate floor. Descriptions and origins of ales displayed in front of the four handpumps. ⌂ ◖◗ P

Coach & Horses Inn
Welsh Street (N of town arch)
☎ (029 12) 622626
11–3; 6–11
Draught Bass; Brains Bitter, SA; Ruddles Best Bitter; Ushers Best Bitter ⊞
Friendly pub near town centre with a split-level bar. Handy watering hole for walkers of Offa's Dyke. No meals Sat or Sun. Municipal car park close by. ❀ 🛏 ◖ ≹ ♣

White Lion Hotel
Bank Street (close to town arch)
☎ (029 12) 622854
11–11 (11–3; 7–11 bar, Mon–Fri)
Draught Bass; Welsh Brewers Hancock's PA, HB ⊞
Chepstow's oldest pub, part of which is formed by the town's port wall. Restored in late 80s to something like its original character. Rare outlet for Hancock's PA and the only public bar in town. Skittle alley acts as family room if not in use. No meals Sun. ❀ ◖ ⊟ ≹ ♣

Clydach

Drum & Monkey
On A465 ☎ (0873) 830542
12–5; 7–11 (12–11 Sat)
Draught Bass; Brains Bitter, SA ⊞
Open-plan pub with separate restaurant and pool room. Carvery and sing-along on Sat. ⌂ ❀ ◖◗ Ă ♣ P

Cross Keys

Eagle
High Street (400 yds off A467)
☎ (0495) 270643
12–4.30; 7–11 (11–11 Fri & Sat)
Draught Bass; Welsh Brewers Hancock's HB ⊞
Traditional valleys local in the heart of Gwent rugby-loving communities. ◖ Ă ♣

Cwmavon

Westlakes Arms
On A4043, between Pontypool and Blaenavon
☎ (0495) 772123
11–11
Draught Bass; Brains Bitter; Buckley's Dark, Best Bitter; Ruddles County; Wadworth 6X ⊞
A comfortable, small local with lots of paraphernalia. Gwent CAMRA Pub of the Year 1987 and winner of other awards. Regular guest beers. Good value food. Q ❀ ◖◗ ⊟ ♣

Cwmbran

Blinkin' Owl
Henllys Way, Coed Eva
☎ (063 33) 4749
11.30–3.30 (4.30 Sat, 12–2.30 Sun); 5.30 (6.30 Sat)–11
Brains Dark, Bitter, SA ⊞
A perennial favourite for Brains devotees in the area. A modern estate pub with a good, basic public bar, quiet lounge and adjoining dining area. No meals Sun lunchtimes.
Q ❀ ◖◗ ⊟ ♿ ♣ P

Bush Inn
Graig Road, Upper Cwmbran
☎ (063 33) 3764
11–3; 7 (6 Fri & Sat)–11
Courage Best Bitter ⊞
Charming hillside pub overlooking Cwmbran. Two adjoining drinking areas on a split-level, one of which is a cosy candlelit parlour. Very busy weekends. Locally-produced curries popular. No lunches Fri–Sun; order eve meals in advance. Sun discos. Parking limited. ⌂ ❀ ◖◗ ♣ P

Gilwern

Bridgend Inn
Main Road (off A465)
☎ (0873) 830939
12–5; 7–11 (12–11 Fri & Sat)
Draught Bass; Felinfoel Double Dragon; Greene King Abbot Ale ⊞
Olde-worlde pub with exposed beams and an open hearth. Reasonably-priced bar food. Guest beer replaces one of the above. Cider in summer. Shove-ha'penny played.
Q ❀ ◖◗ ♿ Ă ♣ ○ P

Griffithstown

Masons Arms
Station Road (near Panteg Hospital) ☎ (049 55) 763819
12–11
Courage Best Bitter, Directors ⊞
A good traditional local near Monmouthshire and Brecon Canal. Lively bar with darts and pool table; comfortable lounge. Renowned for its steaks.
❀ ◖◗ ⊟

Llanfihangel Crucorney

Skirrid Inn
Old Hereford Road (400 yds off A465)
☎ (0873) 890258
12–3; 6–11 (12–11 summer)
Courage Best Bitter, Directors; John Smith's Bitter ⊞
The oldest pub in Wales; a building dating from 1107. An excellent medieval inn with a basically furnished tap room, cosy lounge, snug and wood-panelled dining room. At the entrance to the scenic Llanthony Valley. Pamphlet on sale explains pub's history. Excellent, imaginative food.
⌂ ❀ 🛏 ◖◗ Ă ♣ P

Llangybi

White Hart
On B4596 ☎ (063 349) 258
11–3; 6–11
Marston's Pedigree Bitter; Theakston Best Bitter ⊞
This historic coaching inn, built during 12th century has known connections with Henry VIII and Oliver Cromwell. Bar, restaurant and grill room provide a good selection of meals. Book for Sun lunch. Occasional guest beer.
⌂ Q ❀ 🛏 ◖◗ P

Llanhennock

Wheatsheaf
1 mile off B4596
☎ (0633) 420468
11–3.30; 5–11 (11–11 Sat)
Draught Bass; Samuel Smith OBB; Welsh Brewers Worthington BB ⊞
Traditional old country inn.
⌂ Q ❀ ⊟ ♣ P

Llantilio Crossenny

Hostry Inn
On B4233 (Monmouth-Abergavenny Road)
☎ (060 085) 278
11–3; 6.30–11
Smiles Best Bitter, Exhibition ⊞
Friendly village pub where traditional games are played – Devil Among the Tailors, skittles and shove-ha'penny. Good food (including veg); live music fortnightly. Close to Offa's Dyke footpath.
❀ 🛏 ◖◗ ⊟ Ă ♣ P

Mamhilad

Horseshoe Inn
2 miles off A4042, near Pontypool ☎ (0873) 880542
11–3.30; 6.30–11 (11–11 summer)
Felinfoel Double Dragon; Marston's Pedigree Bitter; Whitbread Flowers Original ⊞
Former Royal Mail staging post, set in pleasant countryside near the Monmouthshire and Brecon Canal. A quiet and welcoming pub with good food. ⌂ ❀ ◖◗ P

Gwent

Marshfield

Masons Arms
10 St Mellons Road (next to village hall) ☎ (0633) 680308
12–3; 6–11
Ansells Bitter; Tetley Bitter 🄷
Comfortable lounge geared to food at lunchtime; spartan bar with TV at one end, and dartboard at the other. Variety of children's facilities in the garden. No meals Sun eve.
❀ ◖ ◗ ⊟ ♣ P

Port O'Call
Marshfield Road (2 miles S of A48) ☎ (0633) 680171
11.30–3; 5.30–11
Courage Best Bitter 🄷**, Directors** 🄶 **&** 🄷**; John Smith's Bitter** 🄷
Country pub with a split-level lounge. Excellent bar meals.
❀ ◖ ◗ ⊟ ♣ P

Monkswood

Beaufort Arms
Usk Road (A472)
☎ (049528) 215
11.30–3.30 (4.30 Fri); 6–11 (11–11 Sat)
Courage Best Bitter, Directors 🄷
Welcoming roadside pub with a separate dining area offering a varied, good value, menu. Spacious outdoor area overlooks cricket pitch. Guest beers. Q ❀ ◖ ◗ ♣ P

Monmouth

Bull Inn
Agincourt Square
☎ (0600) 2226
10.30 (10 Mon, Fri & Sat)–3 (4 Fri & Sat); 6.30–11
Draught Bass 🄷
Quiet local at top of main shopping street, next to old town hall. Eve meals summer only (not Sun). Guest beers.
◖ ◗ ♣

Punch House
Agincourt Square
☎ (0600) 3855
10.30–3; 5–11 (11–11 Fri & Sat)
Draught Bass; Wadworth 6X; Welsh Brewers Hancock's HB, Worthington BB 🄷
Historic old pub on town square. High quality meals in restaurant upstairs; bar snacks in lounge. No food Sun eve. ❀ ◖ ◗

Newport

Bailey's Real Ale Pub
Bailey Street, Baneswell (200 yds off Bridge Street in centre) ☎ (0633) 262679
11–11
Brains SA 🄷
Small, single-room bar, handy for shopping centre and nightclubs. No meals Sun. Guest beers. ◖ ⇌

Globe Inn
132 Chepstow Road, Maindee (A48) ☎ (0633) 213062
11–3 (4 Sat); 5.30–11
Courage Best Bitter 🄷
Quiet local in the heart of Maindee shopping area. ❀ ⊟ ♣

Handpost
Bassaleg Road (A467/A468 jct) ☎ (0633) 264502
11–3.30; 5.30–11 (11–11 Fri & Sat)
Ansells Bitter; Ind Coope Burton Ale; Tetley Bitter 🄷
Spacious local boasting an island bar – very rare in South Wales. No meals weekends.
⌂ ◖ ♣ P

Ivy Bush
Clarence Place (A48)
☎ (0633) 267571
11–3; 5.30–11 (11–11 Fri & Sat)
John Smith's Bitter 🄷
Lively local in the heart of Newport's eating-out area. No meals Sun. ❀ ⊨ ◖ ⊟ ⇌ ♣

Old Murenger House
High Street ☎ (0633) 63977
11–3; 5.30–11 (11–11 Sat)
Samuel Smith OBB, Museum Ale 🄷
Once the town house of the first county sheriff (1541), this is Newport's oldest pub. The split-level bar has wooden beams, high-backed wooden settles and old scenes of Sam Smith's Tadcaster Brewery. Very busy weekends. Meals till 7pm Fri and Sat (9.30 Tue–Thu). ◖ ◗ ⇌ ♣

Orange Tree
St Michaels Street, Pill (off Commercial Road)
☎ (0633) 258569
11–2.30 (12–2.30 Sun); 6.30–11 (11–11 Fri & Sat)
Brains SA 🄷
Small friendly local near docks. Difficult to track down but worth the effort. No food Sun. Guest beers. ◖ ♣

Pandy

Old Pandy Inn
Hereford Road (A465, by railway embankment)
☎ (0873) 890208
11.30–3; 6.30 (6 summer)–11
Courage Directors; Felinfoel Double Dragon; Smiles Best Bitter 🄷
A fine, stone-built country inn near the Gwent/Hereford & Worcester border. Adjacent barn has been converted into a restaurant. Small bar and snug, cosy lounge. Play area in garden
⌂ ❀ ◖ ◗ ⊟ ⅄ ♣ P

Penallt

Boat
Lone Lane (off A466 across footbridge at Redbrook)
☎ (0600) 2615
11–3; 6–11
Greene King Abbot Ale; Marston's Pedigree Bitter; Theakston Best Bitter, XB, Old Peculier; Wadworth 6X 🄶
Classic riverside pub on the Wye. Good value, home-cooked food. Live music – folk and jazz nights. The only pub in Wales with its car park in England (cross the river by footbridge). Guest beers. ⌂ ❀ ◖ ◗ P

Pwllmeyric

New Inn
On A48, W of Chepstow
☎ (0291) 622670
11–11
Draught Bass 🄴**; Ruddles Best Bitter; Whitbread Flowers IPA** 🄷
Large old coaching inn, well-run by genial host. Lounge is clad in panelling salvaged from the *Empress of France*. No meals Sun.
⌂ ❀ ◖ ◗ ⊟ ♣ P

Rhiwderin

Rhiwderin Inn
Caerphilly Road (A468)
☎ (0633) 893234
11–3; 5.30–11 (11–11 Sat)
Draught Bass; Welsh Brewers Hancock's HB 🄷
Comfortable pub with family room. Q ❀ ◖ ⊟ ♣ P

Rogerstone

Tredegar Arms
Cefn Road (B4591)
☎ (0633) 893417
11 (12 Sat & Sun)–3 (2.30 Sun); 6–11
Courage Best Bitter, Directors 🄷
Busy and comfortable pub on old main valleys road.
❀ ◖ ◗ ⊟ P

Sebastopol

Open Hearth
Wern Road (off South Street/Greenhill Road)
☎ (04955) 3752
11.30–3; 6.30–11
Draught Bass; Courage Best Bitter; Hook Norton Best Bitter; Marston's Pedigree Bitter 🄷
Nestling beside the Monmouthshire and Brecon Canal, this popular pub and restaurant is a beer mecca in the Pontypool area, offering a wide range of ales throughout the year. Good value bar meals.

Gwent CAMRA Pub of the Year 1989. Q ❀ ◐ ◑ ⊟ P

Shirenewton

Carpenters Arms

On B4235, N of village
☎ (02917) 231
11–2.30; 6–11
Courage Best Bitter; Hook Norton Best Bitter; Marston's Pedigree Bitter, Owd Rodger; Wadworth 6X [H]
Old country inn with flagstoned floors and several rooms in a variety of styles and sizes. Guest beers. ⌂ Q ❀ ◐ ◑ ⊟ ⛺ P

Tredegar Arms

☎ (02917) 274
11–3; 7–11
Smiles Best Bitter [H]
Welcoming inn in the centre of the village. Boasts large collection of malt whiskies. Guest beers. ⌂ Q ❀ ◐ ◑ ♣

Talywain

Globe Inn

Commercial Road (Main Abersychan–Varteg Road)
☎ (04955) 772053
6–11 (11–11 Sat)
Brains Bitter; Buckley's Best Bitter [H]
Lively, friendly local with separate pool room. ⌂ ❀ ◑ ⊟ ♣

Tintern

Cherry Tree Inn

Devauden Road (off A466)
☎ (0291) 689292
11–3; 6–11
Welsh Brewers Hancock's PA [G]
Small cosy pub untouched by the passage of time. Situated in a popular walking area. Bar billiards. Limited parking.
⌂ Q ❀ ♣ ⍉ P

Upper Llanover

Goose & Cuckoo

Off A4042 OS291073
☎ (0873) 880277
11.30–3; 6.30–11
Bullmastiff Best Bitter; Wadworth 6X; Welsh Brewers Worthington BB [H]
Cosy pub popular with walkers. Hard to find but definitely worth the hunt. Vegetarian menu. ⌂ Q ❀ ◐ ◑ ♣ P

Usk

Kings Head

Old Market Street (near the British Legion)
☎ (02913) 2963
11–11
Hall & Woodhouse Tanglefoot; Whitbread Flowers Original [H]
Large, traditional local. Smart oak-beamed lounge, with an impressive stone fireplace; pool table in bar. Restaurant and extensive bar menu which includes some Malaysian dishes. Guest beers. ⌂ ⛟ ◐ ◑ ⊟ P

Try also: The Inn Between

Taking back a short measure

Gwynedd

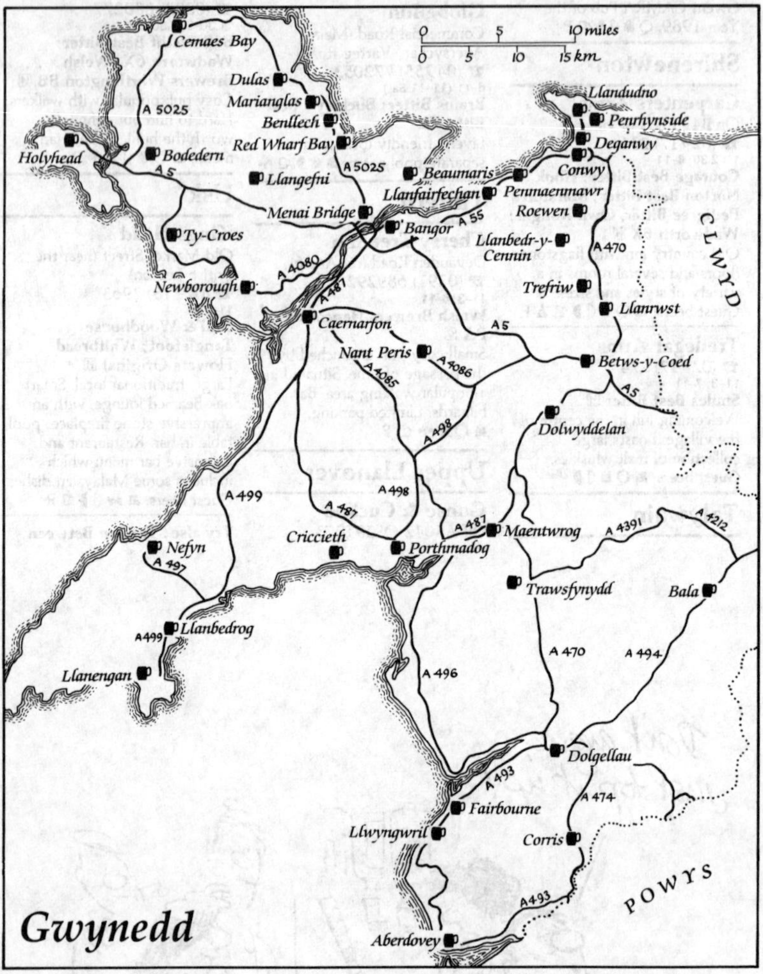

Aberdovey

Penhelig Arms
On A493 ☎ (065 472) 215
11–3; 6–11
Ind Coope Burton Ale; Marston's Pedigree Bitter [H]
Small, 19th-century, seaside town hotel with excellent restaurant. Wood-panelled fisherman's bar with central fireplace. Once visited by Charles Dickens. ⊨ ◖ ◗ ⊞

Bala

White Lion Royal
High Street ☎ (0678) 520314
11–11
Ind Coope Burton Ale; Tetley Bitter [H]
Black and white hotel, reputedly one of Wales's oldest coaching inns. Delightful lounge bar with beamed ceiling, open fireplace and high-backed settles. Smaller poachers' bar has adjacent pool room. Welsh cooking.
⌂ ⚹ ❀ ⊨ ◖ ◗ ⊞ ♿ ⌖

Bangor

Union
Garth Road ☎ (0248) 362462
11–11
Burtonwood Best Bitter [H]
One bar serving several separate rooms, packed with brass, copper, china, nautical photographs, prints and artefacts. Pub overlooks a bay near the newly refurbished Bangor pier. Q ❀ ⊨ ◖ ≉ ♣ P

White Lion
High Street ☎ (0248) 353394
11–11
Draught Bass; M&B Mild [H]
Small, friendly, one-room pub in centre. Very reasonably-priced, home-cooked bar food. Children not allowed except in tiny beer garden in summer. ❀ ◖ ≉

Beaumaris

Olde Bull's Head
Castle Street
☎ (0248) 810329
11–11
Draught Bass [H]
Historic old inn (grade II listed building) dating from 1472. Large, beamed bar full of antique weapons, brass and copperware; smaller 'china' bar. Bedrooms named after characters from the novels of Charles Dickens, who stayed here in 1859. ⌂ Q ⊨ ◖ ◗ P

Benllech

Glanrafon Hotel
Bangor Road
☎ (0248) 852687

11–3.30; 6–11 (11–11 summer)
Lees Bitter 🄷
Large, black and white-fronted hotel with comfortable, quiet lounge and a lively bar. Cheapest pint on Anglesey.
Q 🚼 ❀ 🛏 ◖ ◗ ⊞ ♣ P

Betws-y-Coed

Pont-y-Pair Hotel
☎ (06902) 407
11–11
Sam Powell Original Bitter; Tetley Bitter 🄷
Large granite building in a popular tourist town. Meeting place; centre for climbing and walking. 🛏 ◖ ◗ ▲ ≠ ♣

Bodedern

Crown Hotel
On B5109 ☎ (0407) 740734
12–3.30; 6–11 (11–11 Sat & bank hols)
Burtonwood Best Bitter 🄷
Friendly village pub with comfortable lounge, more spartan bar, and separate family room which doubles as a no-smoking lounge at night. Very reasonably-priced food and accommodation.
♨ 🚼 ❀ 🛏 ◖ ◗ ⊞ ♣ P

Caernarfon

Palace Vaults
Castle Ditch ☎ (0286) 2093
11–11
Marston's Burton Best Bitter, Pedigree Bitter, Owd Rodger (winter) 🄷
Busy pub in shadow of the massive castle, modernised in neo-Victorian style. One central bar and four distinct areas, including library and games area. Q ◖ ◗ ♿ ♣

Cemaes Bay

Stag
High Street ☎ (0407) 710281
11–3.30; 6–11 (11–11 Sat & summer)
Burtonwood Best Bitter 🄷
Friendly village pub, with an interesting collection of old photographs of the village. Most northerly pub in Wales. Families welcome in pool room. Good food. ♨ Q ❀ ◖ ◗ ⊞ ♣

Conwy

Castle Hotel
High Street ☎ (0492) 592324
11–3; 5.30–11
Draught Bass 🄷
Quiet hotel bar, popular with locals. ♨ Q 🚼 ❀ 🛏 ◖ ◗ ▲ P

Corris

Slater's Arms
Lower Corris ☎ (0654) 73324
11.30–3; 6–11 (11.30–11 Sat & bank hols)
Banks's Mild, Bitter 🄴
Old-fashioned, two-roomed pub in former slating village. Piano. YHA hostel nearby. ♨ Q ◖ ⊞

Criccieth

Castle
Station Square
☎ (076671) 2624
12 (11 summer)–11 (closed Sun)
Draught Bass 🄷
Friendly, popular town pub; cosy lounge. Meals summer only. ♨ 🚼 ❀ ◖ ◗ ⊞ ♿ ▲ ≠ ♣

Deganwy

Castle Hotel
☎ (0492) 583555
11–3; 5.30–11 (11–11 summer)
Wilson's Original Bitter, Webster's Choice 🄷
A hotel bar serving as a popular pub. The attractive gardens give spectacular views of the estuary.
♨ Q 🚼 ❀ 🛏 ◖ ◗ ♿ ▲ ≠ P

Dolgellau

Stag
Bridge Street ☎ (0341) 422533
10.30–11
Burtonwood Dark Mild, Best Bitter 🄷
Characterful, one-roomed town pub. Darts. Well-hidden patio at rear. ♨ 🚼 ❀ ◖ ⊞ ▲ ♣

Dolwyddelan

Gwydyr
Y Gwydyr ☎ (06906) 209
11–2.30 (3 summer); 7 (6 summer)–11
Banks's Bitter 🄷
Cosy village pub where Welsh is spoken as a matter of course. Visitors are made very welcome. ❀ 🛏 ◖ ◗ ⊞ ▲ ≠ ♣ P

Dulas

Pilot Boat
On A5025 ☎ (024888) 205
11.30 (11 summer)–3.30; 7 (6 summer)–11 (11–11 Sat & bank hols)
Robinson's Best Mild, Best Bitter 🄴
Interesting old country pub with low-beamed bar, stone fireplace and nautical items. Bar front is a small wooden boat. Smart lounge and separate pool room (both accommodating children). Wide range of food.
♨ ❀ ◖ ◗ ⊞ ▲ ♣ P

Fairbourne

Fairbourne Hotel
Off A493 ☎ (0341) 250203
11–3; 6–11
McEwan 70/-; Younger IPA 🄷
Large and well-appointed 300 year-old hotel in its own grounds. Excellent food in lounge bar; separate restaurant. Breathtaking views of estuary.
♨ 🚼 ❀ 🛏 ◖ ◗ ⊞ ♿ ▲ ≠ ♣

Holyhead

Boston
London Road ☎ (0407) 762449
11–3.30 (may extend); 6–11
Ansells Mild; Tetley Bitter 🄷
Busy, one-bar local on the outskirts of town, with separate areas for pool and darts, and a small lounge. Regular *Guide* entry. Handy for the station or the ferry to Ireland. ⊞ ≠ ♣

Llanbedrog

Glyn-y-Weddw
Lower Village
☎ (0758) 740212
11–3; 5.30–11 (11–11 Sat & summer, closed Sun)
Robinson's Best Mild, Best Bitter 🄴; **Old Tom** 🄶
Popular pub with pleasant outside seating area. Near sheltered beach.
♨ 🚼 ❀ ◖ ◗ ⊞ ♿ ▲

Ship
Bryn-y-Gro
☎ (0758) 740270
11–3; 5.30–11 (11–11 summer, closed Sun)
Burtonwood Dark Mild, Best Bitter 🄷
Cosy, friendly old pub, very popular with visitors. Extensive menu, two bars and a sunny garden. ♨ Q ❀ ◖ ◗ ⊞ ♿ ▲ ♣

Llanbedr-y-Cennin

Olde Bull Inn
Off B5106 ☎ (049269) 508
12–3; 6.30–11
Lees GB Mild, Bitter 🄷
Set in the beautiful Conwy Valley, with a position giving breathtaking views. Very much part of the community.
♨ Q ❀ 🛏 ◖ ◗ ▲ ♣ P

Llandudno

Cottage Loaf
Market Street
☎ (0492) 870762
11–11
Ruddles County; Webster's Yorkshire Bitter, Choice 🄷
Rebuilt bakery, hence name. Tasteful new pub with quality ale and food. ♨ ❀ ◖ ≠ P

London Hotel
Mostyn Street
☎ (0492) 76740
11.30–4; 7–11 (11–11 summer)
Burtonwood Dark Mild, Best Bitter 🄷
High standard ale, food and B&B. London theme includes red telephone box. Q 🚼 🛏 ◖ ≠

Snowdon
Tudno Street
☎ (0492) 875515
12–3 (4 Fri); 7–11 (11–11 Sat)
Draught Bass 🄷
One of the last traditional locals

in town. Comfortable lounge and always a game of darts, dominoes or cards in the public. Q ⌂ ⛟ ◖ ⊟ ⇌ ♣

Try also: Kings Head (Allied); **Sandringham Hotel** (Greenalls); **Victoria** (S&N)

Llanengan

Sun Inn
☎ (0758) 812660
11–11 (closed Sun)
Ind Coope Burton Ale; Tetley Bitter [H]
Popular pub with Hell's Mouth Beach nearby. Excellent food.
♜ Q ⌂ ◖ ◗ ⊟ ♿ ⛺ ♣ ⍉ P

Llanfairfechan

Llanfair Arms
Mill Road ☎ (0492) 680521
11–11
Draught Bass [H]
Multi-room local in the up-hill part of town. ♜ ⌂ ♿ ⛺ ⇌ ♣

Llangefni

Railway
High Street ☎ (0248) 722166
11–3.30 (5 Sat); 6.30–11 (11–11 summer)
Lees GB Mild, Bitter [H]
Friendly town pub, now partly refurbished, opening up the old back room. Larger bar counter, but retains different drinking areas, including games room. Railway pictures. Q ⌂ ♣

Llanrwst

New Inn
Denbigh Street
☎ (0492) 640476
11–11
Marston's Burton Best Bitter, Pedigree Bitter [H]
Modernised, but not spoiled; a popular local. ♜ ⌂ ◖ ♿ ⛺ ⇌ ♣

Llwyngwril

Garthangharad
On A493 ☎ (0341) 250484
12–3; 7–11
Banks's Mild, Bitter [E]
Old, three-roomed pub of character, in small coastal village. Good food and atmosphere.
Q ⛟ ⛟ ◖ ◗ ⊟ ♿ ⛺ ⇌

Maentwrog

Grapes
On A496 ☎ (076685) 208
11–11
Draught Bass; Stones Best Bitter [H]
Old inn, with parts from 13th century. Three rooms and restaurant. ♜ ⛟ ⛟ ◖ ◗ ⊟ ♣

Marianglas

Parciau Arms
On B5110 ☎ (0248) 853766
11–11
Ind Coope Burton Ale; Tetley Bitter [H]
Popular country pub with a children's play area. Comfortable lounge. Separate family dining room and public bar/games room. Food available all day. ♜ Q ⌂ ◖ ◗ ⊟ ⛺ ♣ P

Menai Bridge

Liverpool Arms
St George's Pier
☎ (0248) 712453
11–3.30; 5.30–11
Greenalls Bitter, Thomas Greenall's Original Bitter [H]
Interesting old pub with two cosy bars full of nautical prints and artefacts. Separate lounge, dining room and conservatory. Excellent food. Q ⌂ ◖ ◗ ⊟

Nant Peris

Vaynol Arms
On A4086 ☎ (0286) 870284
11–3; 6–11 (may extend in summer)
Robinson's Best Mild, Best Bitter [E]
Long, low, whitewashed inn, dominated by the foothills of Snowdon. ♜ ⌂ ◖ ◗ ⊟ ⛺

Nefyn

Sportsman
Stryd Fawr ☎ (0758) 720205
11–11 (closed Sun)
Ind Coope Burton Ale; Tetley Bitter [H]
Friendly pub to visitors and locals. Huge wood fire.
♜ Q ⌂ ◖ ◗ ⊟ ♿ ⛺ ♣

Newborough

White Lion
Malltraeth Street (A4080)
☎ (024879) 406
12–4; 6.45–11 (11–11 summer)
Marston's Burton Best Bitter, Pedigree Bitter [H]
Small, friendly village pub with small lounge and fairly spartan bar. ⌂ ◖ ⊟ ♣

Penmaenmawr

Legend
Ysyborwen, Dwygyfylchi
☎ (0492) 623231
11–11
Ansells Mild; Ind Coope Burton Ale; Tetley Bitter [H]
A very popular meeting place, recently altered and improved.
♜ ⛟ ⌂ ⛟ ◖ ◗ ⛺ ♣ P

Penrhynside

Cross Keys
Pendre Road ☎ (0492) 46415
5.30–11 (11–11 Sat)
Ansells Mild; Ind Coope Burton Ale; Tetley Bitter [H]
Traditional local and a focal point of this old quarrying village. ⌂ ⛺ ♣

Porthmadog

Ship & Castle
High Street ☎ (0766) 512217
11–11 (closed Sun)
Ansells Bitter; Tetley Bitter [H]
Friendly, comfortable, refurbished pub in late Victorian style. Pictures of Porthmadog sailing ships. Q ◖ ◗ ⛺ ⇌ ♣ ⍉

Try also: Australia (Bass)

Red Wharf Bay

Ship
Off A5025 ☎ (0248) 852568
11.30–3.30; 7–11 (11–11 summer)
Banks's Bitter; Tetley Mild, Bitter [H]
Pub of real character: a long, white building facing the sea, with low beamed ceilings, flag floors, exposed stone walls and huge fireplaces. Beer range varies. Pub food award-winner.
♜ Q ⛟ ⌂ ⛟ ◖ ◗ ⊟ ⛺ ♣ P

Roewen

Ty Gwyn
☎ (0492) 650232
12–3 (5 Fri & Sat); 6.30–11 (11–11 summer)
Lees GB Mild, Bitter [H]
Village pub in idyllic setting. Much-changed interior but has kept its atmosphere.
♜ Q ⌂ ◖ ◗ ⊟ ♿ ⛺ ♣ P

Trawsfynydd

White Lion
Main Street ☎ (076687) 277
11–3; 6–11 (11–11 summer)
Burtonwood Dark Mild, Best Bitter [H]
Traditional and unspoilt village pub in beautiful mountain area.
♜ Q ⛟ ⛟ ◖ ◗ ⊟ ⛺ ♣

Trefriw

Olde Shippe
☎ (0492) 640013
12–11
Burtonwood Best Bitter [H]
Popular village local set in an historic spa area.
♜ ⌂ ⛟ ◖ ◗ ♿ ⛺ ⇌ ♣ P

Ty-Croes

Queens Head
Bryn Du (1 mile off A4080)
OS345725 ☎ (0407) 810806
11–11
Burtonwood Best Bitter [G]
Small, largely-unspoilt country pub with wood panelled walls and timber ceilings. Several small rooms and a passage supplied from a central servery. Anglesey's only gravity dispense. Home-cooked food.
♜ Q ⌂ ◖ ◗ ⊟ ⇌ ♣ P

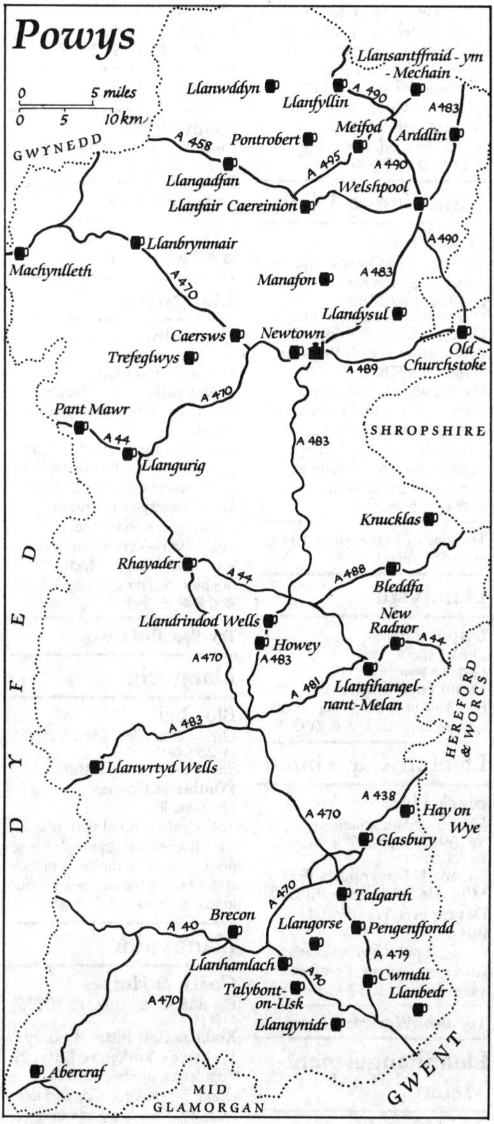

Sam Powell, *Newtown*

Abercraf

Copper Beech

Off A4067 ☎ (0639) 730269
12–4; 6–11
Courage Best Bitter; Theakston XB Ⓗ
Excellent pub in fine setting. Good food always available. Regular guest beers.
Q P

Arddlîn

Horseshoe

On A483/B4392
☎ (093875) 318
12–11 (may close afternoons)
Draught Bass; Marston's Pedigree Bitter Ⓗ
Well-restored pub on canal and Offa's Dyke. Weston's cider on draught. ♣ P

Bleddfa

Hundred House

On A488 ☎ (054781) 225
11–3; 6–11 (11–11 summer)
Marston's Pedigree Bitter; Ruddles Best Bitter; Whitbread Castle Eden Ale, Flowers Original Ⓗ
Attractive and comfortable village pub with a variety of rooms; the lounge is quiet. Supper licence to 12.30am. Food in bar and restaurant is mainly home-made. Range of beers may vary.
Q ♣ P

Brecon

Gremlin Hotel

The Watton (B4601 200 yds E of centre) ☎ (0874) 3829
12–3; 7–11
Draught Bass; Felinfoel Double Dragon Ⓖ
Welcoming pub with small, busy locals' bar, comfortable lounge and friendly hosts. Separate menus for bar and restaurant, but no food on Sun or Mon in winter.
♣ P

Try also: Olde Boar's Head

Caersws

Red Lion

Main Street (off A470)
☎ (068684) 646
11–3; 6.30–11 (12–11 Fri, 11–11 Sat)
Ind Coope Burton Ale; Tetley Bitter Ⓗ
Two-bar village local popular with tourists.

Cwmdu

Farmers Arms

On A479 6 miles S of Talgarth
☎ (0874) 730464
11–3; 6–11
Draught Bass; Brains SA; Marston's Pedigree Bitter; Welsh Brewers Hancock's HB Ⓗ
Friendly country pub. Families welcome though no separate room. Large, wholesome meals a speciality. Regular guest beers.
Q P

Glasbury

Harp Inn

☎ (04974) 373
11–3; 6–11
Robinson's Best Bitter; Whitbread Flowers IPA, Flowers Original Ⓗ
Welcoming riverside inn. No special room, but children are allowed. Q ♣ P

Maesllwch Arms Hotel

Off A438 on N side of the Wye bridge ☎ (04974) 226
11–11
Draught Bass Ⓗ
Informal hotel with a small, cosy public bar; an ideal centre

for exploring the Wye Valley and surrounding countryside. Regular guest beers.
⌂ Q ♘ ⊛ ⊨ ◖ ⊟ ▲ ♣ ◌ P

Hay on Wye

Blue Boar
Castle Street (B4348/B4350 jct) ☎ (0497) 820884
11–3; 6–11
Brains SA; Whitbread Flowers IPA, Best Bitter, Flowers Original Ⓗ
Traditional pub with an inviting locals' public bar and small, intimate lounge. A fine pub to sit and read the books you have unearthed in Hay's bookshops or to help the landlord with a crossword. Eve meals in summer only. Regular guest beers.
⌂ Q ◖ ◗ ⊟

Howey

Drovers Arms
Off A483 ☎ (0597) 822508
12 (11 summer)–3; 7 (6 summer)–11
Felinfoel Double Dragon; Marston's Pedigree Bitter Ⓗ
Late 19th-century pub on site of much earlier pub which burned down. Attractively-furnished public bar with piano; lounge bar with ornate wood carvings. Separate restaurant offers home-made dishes and speciality nights. Occasional guest beers.
⌂ ⊛ ⊨ ◖ ◗ ⊟ ▲ ♣ P

Knucklas

Castle Inn
Off B4355 ☎ (0547) 528150
12–3; 7–11 (often extends in summer)
Sam Powell Original Bitter Ⓗ
Large, baronial-style pub with high ceilings and stone-flagged floors. Self-catering accommodation available. Groups of more than six people should book meals.
⌂ ♘ ⊛ ⊨ ◖ ◗ ⊟ ▲ ≹ ♣

Llanbedr

Red Lion
☎ (0873) 810754
12–2.30; 6–11
Butcombe Bitter; Welsh Brewers Worthington BB Ⓗ
Friendly country pub at the heart of the Black Mountains. Families welcome though no separate room. Mostly home-cooked food. Regular guest beers. ⌂ Q ⊛ ◖ ◗ ▲ ♣ P

Try also: Bear, Crickhowell

Llanbrynmair

Wynnstay Arms Hotel
On A470 ☎ (06503) 431
11–2.30; 6–11
Ansells Bitter; Sam Powell Samson Ⓗ
Well-kept, comfortable, two-bar village hotel with pool room. Real fires in both bars. Food is served in the quiet lounge (children welcome) or in the restaurant. Good value accommodation. Garden is across the road. Guest beers.
⌂ Q ♘ ⊛ ⊨ ◖ ◗ ⊟ ♣ P

Llandrindod Wells

Llanerch Inn
Waterloo Road (across station footbridge from centre)
☎ (0597) 822086
11–2.30 (3.30 Fri & Sat); 6 (5 Fri)–11
Draught Bass; Robinson's Best Bitter; Welsh Brewers Hancock's HB Ⓗ
Comfortable 16th-century coaching inn with low beamed ceilings and a large stone hearth. Annual Ale Tasting Week at the end of August. Occasional guest beers.
♘ ⊛ ⊨ ◖ ◗ ≹ ♣ P

Try also: Ridgebourne Hotel, on A483 (Free)

Llandysul

Upper House
Off B4386
12–3 (not Wed); 6.30–11
Wood Special Bitter Ⓗ
Excellent unspoilt village local. Quoits in garden. ⌂ ⊛ ⊟ ♣ P

Llanfair Caereinion

Black Lion
Just off village square
☎ (0938) 810207
11–4; 5.30–11
Greenalls Davenports Best Mild Ale, Wem Best Bitter Ⓔ, **Davenports Traditional Bitter** Ⓗ
Unspoilt pub of great character with many rooms. Excellent value food. ⌂ ⊛ ◖ ◗ ⊟ ♣ P

Try also: Wynnstay Arms

Llanfihangel-nant-Melan

Red Lion
On A44 ☎ (054421) 220
12–2 (2.30 summer); 6–11
Sam Powell Original Bitter Ⓗ
Quiet pub in Radnor Forest, with a variety of comfortable rooms. Convenient for holiday-makers and hillwalkers. Quoits and table skittles played.
⌂ ♘ ⊛ ⊨ ◖ ◗ ⊟ ▲ ♣ P

Llanfyllin

Cain Valley Hotel
On A490 ☎ (069184) 366
11–3; 6–11 (11–11 summer, except Mon)
Draught Bass; Ind Coope Burton Ale; Marston's Pedigree Bitter; Sam Powell Original Bitter Ⓗ
Excellent 17th-century coaching inn. ⌂ Q ⊛ ⊨ ◖ ◗ ⊟ ♣ P

Llangadfan

Cann Office
On A458 ☎ (093888) 202
12–2.30 (11–3 summer); 6–11
Marston's Burton Best Bitter, Pedigree Bitter Ⓗ
Large, well-kept pub with fishing rights on Banwy.
⌂ ⊛ ◖ ◗ ⊟ ▲ ♣ P

Llangorse

Castle Inn
☎ (087484) 225
11–3; 6–11 (11–11 Sat)
Brains Bitter, SA; Marston's Pedigree Bitter; Wadworth 6X Ⓗ
Conveniently-situated village pub with a friendly atmosphere and comfortable surroundings. Good variety of bar meals, including a selection for vegetarians. Very clean, well-kept small lounge which doubles as dining room.
⌂ ◖ ◗ ⊟ ▲ ♣ P

Try also: Red Lion

Llangurig

Blue Bell
On A44 ☎ (05515) 254/604
11–2.30; 6–11
Sam Powell Best Bitter; Whitbread Flowers Original Ⓗ
16th-century hotel with fine slate-floored bar and inglenook; pool room, two dining rooms and a family room. Book for Sun lunch. ⌂ ♘ ⊨ ◖ ◗ ⊟ ♿ ♣ P

Llangynidr

Coach & Horses
On B4558 ☎ (0873) 730235
11–11
Ruddles Best Bitter, County; Webster's Yorkshire Bitter Ⓗ
Popular canalside pub with ample car parking. Comfortable lounge with a large adjoining dining room. Guest beers in summer. ♘ ⊛ ⊨ ◖ ◗ ⊟ ♣ P

Llanhamlach

Old Ford Inn
On A40 3 miles E of Brecon
☎ (087486) 220
11–3; 7–11
Marston's Pedigree Bitter; Whitbread Flowers IPA Ⓗ
Friendly roadside pub with a comfortable atmosphere and a magnificent view of the Brecon Beacons. Variety of reasonably-priced food, ranging from light snacks to main meals. A large collection of bottled beers on display. ⊛ ⊨ ◖ ◗ ⊟ ♣ P

Llansantffraid-ym-Mechain

Sun
On A495 ☎ (0691) 828214
12–3; 7–11 (12–11 Sat)
Marston's Border Bitter, Pedigree Bitter Ⓗ
Friendly village pub with excellent restaurant. Free site for tents and caravans at rear.
♞ ❀ 🛏 ◖ ◗ ⊞ ♣ P

Llanwddyn

Lake Fyrnwy Hotel
On B4393 ☎ (069173) 244
11–3; 6–11
Draught Bass Ⓗ
Superb view from tavern bar over Lake Fyrnwy.
♜ 🛏 ◖ ◗ ♣ P

Llanwrtyd Wells

Neuadd Arms Hotel
The Square (A483)
☎ (05913) 236
11–11
Felinfoel Double Dragon; Greene King Abbot Ale Ⓗ
Imposing hotel in centre of Britain's smallest town. Walks regularly organised in neighbouring mountains and mountain bikes hired out. Mid Wales Beer Festival held here each Nov. Guest beers.
♜ Q ♞ ❀ 🛏 ◖ ◗ ⊞ ⛺ ⇌ ♣ P

Machynlleth

Skinners Arms
Main Street (A487)
☎ (0654) 702354
11–11
Burtonwood Best Bitter Ⓗ
Wood-beamed, town-centre pub with comfortable lounge and friendly atmosphere.
♜ ◖ ◗ ⊞ ⇌

Manafon

Beehive
On B4390 ☎ (068687) 244
12–3; 7–11
Banks's Mild, Bitter Ⓗ
Pleasant, well-run, comfortable pub with unusual fireplace in public bar. Children's play area at rear. ♜ ♞ ❀ ◖ ◗ ⊞ ⛺ ♣ P

Meifod

Kings Head
On A495 ☎ (093384) 256
11–3; 6–11
Greenalls Davenports Best Mild Ale, Wem Best Bitter Ⓔ
Well-kept village pub.
♜ Q ◖ ◗ ⊞ ♿ ♣

New Radnor

Eagle Hotel
Broad Street (off A44)
☎ (054421) 208
11.30–3; 6–11 (11–11 summer)
Whitbread Flowers IPA Ⓗ
Traditional wooden-floored bar with piano; light comfortable lounge; games room; restaurant and coffee shop. Restaurant open till midnight and all day in summer. Spring Bank Holiday fundays, with music and many ales. Pub popular with paragliding enthusiasts. Regular guest beers and local farm perry.
♜ Q ♞ ❀ 🛏 ◖ ◗ ⊞ ⛺ ♣ P

Try also: Harp, Old Radnor (Free)

Newtown

Pheasant
Market Street (off A483)
☎ (0686) 625966
11–11
Burtonwood Dark Mild, Best Bitter Ⓗ
Excellent, friendly, timbered old pub with a separate games room. Public bar has a collection of unusual walking sticks.
♞ ❀ 🛏 ◖ ⊞ ⇌ ♣

Sportsman
Severn Street (off A483)
☎ (0686) 625885
11–2.30; 5–11
Ansells Mild; Ind Coope Burton Ale; Tetley Bitter Ⓗ
Comfortable, modernised town-centre local, retaining its original beams. Very popular, attracting a wide range of customers. Games room.
Q ❀ ⇌ ♣

Wheatsheaf
Pool Road (A483)
☎ (0686) 625534
11–2.30; 5.30 (5 Fri, 6 Sat)–11
Tetley Bitter Ⓗ
Comfortable edge-of-town pub with separate games room.
❀ ◖ ◗ ⇌ ♣ P

Old Churchstoke

Oak Inn
Off A489 ☎ (05885) 574
11–11
Sam Powell Original Bitter; Tetley Bitter Ⓗ
Delightful, small, stone-walled, wooden-beamed, 16th-century inn. Games room in outbuilding.
♜ ♞ ❀ ◖ ◗ ⊞ ♣ P

Pant Mawr

Glansevern Arms Hotel
On A44 ☎ (05515) 240
11–2 (not Xmas/New Year); 6.30–11
Draught Bass Ⓗ
Two impeccable, quiet, comfortable bars in hotel high up in Wye Valley. Restaurant meals only; must book eves and Sun lunchtime. No food Sun night. ♜ Q 🛏 ◖ ◗ P

Pengenffordd

Castle Inn
On A479 ☎ (0874) 711353
11–3; 6–11
Wadworth 6X; Whitbread Flowers Original Ⓗ
Friendly country local, popular with trekkers and walkers. Located high up in the Black Mountains with the highest, though unfortunately ruined, hill fort in England and Wales behind. Worth a visit.
♜ ❀ ◖ ◗ ⊞ ⛺ ♣ P

Pontrobert

Royal Oak
Off A495 ☎ (093884) 474
11.30–2.30; 6.30–11
Marston's Pedigree Bitter Ⓗ
Well-appointed village pub.
♜ ❀ 🛏 ◖ ◗ ⊞ ⛺ ♣ P

Rhayader

Cornhill Inn
West Street (B4518)
☎ (0597) 810869
11–3; 6–11 (may extend)
Ind Coope Burton Ale; Marston's Pedigree Bitter Ⓗ
Friendly, low-beamed 400 year-old pub, reputedly with a resident female poltergeist. Regular guest beers.
♜ ♞ ❀ 🛏 ◖ ◗ ⊞ ⛺ ♣ P

Triangle Inn
Cwmdauddwr (off B4518, Bridge Street)
☎ (0597) 810537
11–2.30; 6.30–11
Draught Bass; Welsh Brewers Hancock's HB Ⓗ
Beautiful little weather-boarded pub overlooking the River Wye. Ceilings so low that customers have to stand in a hole in the floor to play darts! Veg meals on request. ❀ ◖ ◗ ⛺ ♣

Try also: Royal Oak Hotel (Welsh Brewers)

Talgarth

Tower Hotel
The Square ☎ (0874) 711253
11–3; 7–11 (11–11 summer)
Whitbread Flowers IPA, Best Bitter, Flowers Original Ⓗ
Popular town-centre hotel which dominates the square of this small market town. In the shadow of the Black Mountains, it has an increasing range of well-kept ales and regular guest beers. ♜ ♞ ❀ 🛏 ◖ ◗ P

Talybont-on-Usk

Star Inn
On B4558 ¾ mile off A40
☎ (087487) 635
12–3; 6–11 (11–11 Sat & summer)
Brains SA; Bullmastiff Bitter;

Felinfoel Double Dragon; Marston's Pedigree Bitter; Smiles Exhibition; Theakston Best Bitter 🄷
CAMRA Mid and South Wales Pub of the Year 1989. At least a dozen real ales, constantly varied, in immensely popular canalside pub. Large outdoor drinking area to rear. Coach parties welcome; advance notice preferred. Veg menu. ⛪ ◑ ◐ ⌽

Trefeglwys

Red Lion

On B4569 ☎ (055 16) 255
11–2.30; 6–11
Burtonwood Best Bitter 🄷
Excellent, comfortable pub with old village photographs displayed. Good reputation for bar meals. ⛪ ♨ ❁ ◑ ◐ ⊟ ♣ P

Welshpool

Talbot

High Street ☎ (0938) 553711
11–11
Banks's Mild, Bitter 🄴
Small, well-kept, half-timbered pub. Pavement drinking area. Q ❁ ◑ ◐ ⊟ ≹ ♣ P

Try also: Raven (Banks's)

THE PEOPLE DECIDE

November 12 1989 was the wettest Sunday in Aberystwyth for 108 years. It was not so much raining as pouring. But it was not the traditional damp Welsh weather that was to blame, whipping off the sea or swirling down from the hills, but rather a drop or two of beer.

Bitter arguments had been splashed across the local newspapers for weeks about whether or not local pubs should open their doors on Sundays for the first time since 1881. The Enough is Enough campaign, prominently led by church ministers, argued that seven-day drinking would sink the Holy Day under a flood of drunkenness. They also waved the nationalist card, claiming that the traditional temperance Sunday was a part of Welsh life. The Seven Day Opening Council, supported by brewers and licensees, argued that the referendum was about freedom of choice, allowing people to decide whether or not to visit the pub on a Sunday.

Only two areas of West Wales – Ceredigion and Dwyfor – remained 'dry' on the Sabbath, the rest of Wales having gradually voted to go 'wet' under the referenda on Sunday drinking held every seven years. But they were not the only places voting in 1989. Dry supporters had also forced a poll in 12 wet areas, including Cardiff which had not voted on the issue for 20 years. In the event, after last crosses had been called on polling day, the headlines were all about Ceredigion, centred on Aberystwyth, which had narrowly splashed over onto the wet side by 828 votes out of over 21,000 cast. That Sunday, drinkers in the area celebrated. 'We had our busiest lunchtime for months,' said landlord Marco James of the Castle Hotel in Aberystwyth. Further south at Newcastle Emlyn, the vote came as a big relief to 77-year-old Nellie Griffiths, as her house, the Red Cow, had been the only dry pub in town because it was the wrong side of the boundary. Sunday drinking had obviously gone down well with the Welsh, as the biggest swings to the wet camp came in those areas which had first swung open the pub door on the Sabbath in the previous referendum. However, in Dwyfor, on the Lleyn Peninsula around Pwllheli, the dry campaigners hung on in their last stronghold, despite a two per cent move to Sunday opening.

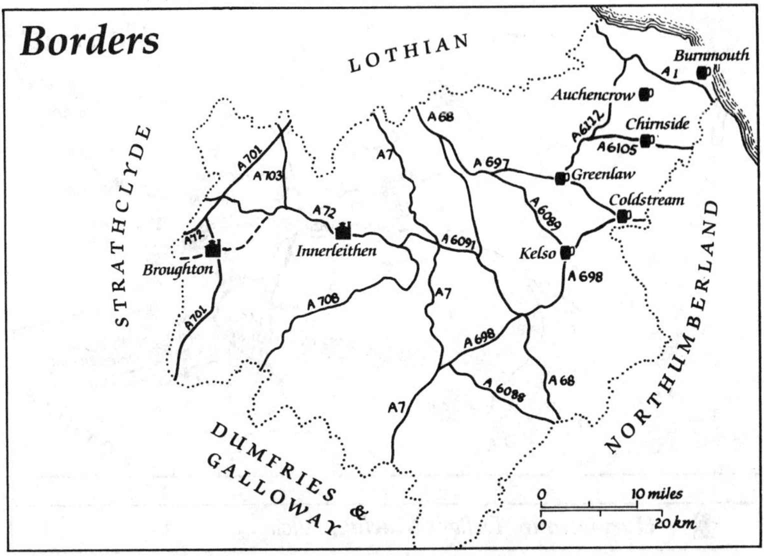

***Broughton**, Broughton; **Traquair House**, Innerleithen*

Auchencrow

Craw Inn

On B6438 ☎ (08907) 61253
11.30–3; 6–12 (11.30 Sat, 12.30–12 Sun)
Broughton Greenmantle Ale; Tennent's 80/- [H]
Atmospheric local in rather isolated village. The well-preserved interior and regular clientele make this a notable example of a Borders community pub. Opening hours not fixed. Bar billiards and putting green available. Disabled WC.
P

Burnmouth

Flemington Inn

On A1 ☎ (08907) 81277
11–11 (12 Fri, 11.30 Sat, 12.30–2.30; 6.30–11 Sun)
Alloa Arrol's 80/-; Tetley Bitter [H]
First and last pub in Scotland. Comfortable and friendly, with good local trade for drink, and passing trade for food.
P

Chirnside

Waterloo Arms Hotel

On B6437 ☎ (089081) 520
11.30–11 (12 Fri, 11.30 Sat, 12.30–11 Sun)
Belhaven 80/-; Broughton Greenmantle Ale [H]
Largish, semi-modern village pub on crossroads, displaying cross-border influences.
P

Coldstream

Newcastle Arms Hotel

50 High Street (A697)
☎ (0890) 2376
11–12 (11.30 Sat, 12.30–11.30 Sun)
Alloa Arrol's 80/-; Tetley Bitter [E]
Comfortable and friendly hotel lounge bar with a thriving trade just across the Tweed from England. Bar meals are available all day and families are made most welcome. Eve meals in restaurant only. P

Greenlaw

Cross Keys Hotel

3 The Square, Main Street (A697) ☎ (036 16) 247
11 (12.30 Sun)–11 (11–2.30; 5–11 Mon–Thu in winter)
Tetley Bitter [H]
Plain, wee, locals' bar with a well-used dartboard (sited near the door — so watch out when entering). A pool table occupies another little room off the bar. The lounge is only open eves. There is an impressive range of 60 malt whiskies.

Kelso

Red Lion Inn

Crawford Street (off the square)
☎ (0573) 24817
11–12 (1 am Fri, 12.30–2.30; 6.30–11 Sun)
Tetley Bitter [H]
Superb traditional Borders boozer with a surprisingly ornate interior. There is a splendid ceiling and a fine bar back topped with old casks. The counter is made from a single piece of mahogany and is thought to be the longest in Scotland. Not to be missed! Families welcome.

'Neighbours'

It is worth remembering that roads do not end at county borders! If you are in a strange town that is near the county boundary, then check the pages of the neighbouring county for an even bigger choice of great pubs.

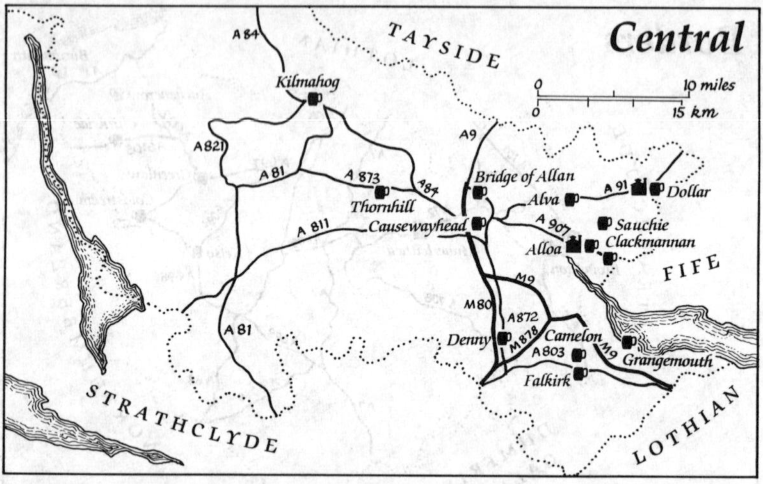

Harviestoun, *Dollar*; **Maclay**, *Alloa*

Alloa

Crams Bar
8 Candleriggs
☎ (0259) 722019
11–11 (12 Fri & Sat; 12.30–2.30, 7–11 Sun)
Maclay 80/- 🄰
Small, popular pub, opposite the site of the old Younger brewery. Lots of character. Q ⊕

Alva

No.5 Inn
Brook Street ☎ (0259) 60416
11–12 (1 am Sat, 12.30–2.30; 6.30–12 Sun)
Maclay 80/- 🄰
Attractive local, nestling at the foot of the Ochil Hills. A former local CAMRA Pub of the Year.
◐ ⊕ ▲ ♣

Bridge of Allan

Queens Hotel
24 Henderson Street
☎ (0786) 833268
11–1 am (12.30–1 am Sun)
Alloa Arrol's 80/- 🄰; **Tetley Bitter** 🄷; **Younger IPA** 🄰
Well-established lounge bar; separate TV room has satellite TV. Mexican restaurant has just opened within the hotel. Occasional guest beers. Q ◐ ⊕ ▲ ♣ P

Westerton Arms
34 Henderson Street
☎ (0786) 833659
11–11 (12 Thu–Sat, 12.30–2.30; 6.30–11 Sun)
Theakston Old Peculier; **Younger IPA** 🄰
Well-decorated lounge bar with feature fireplace; open-plan public bar. Good quality, value-for-money food.
◐ ◑ ⊕ ▲ ≋ P

Camelon

Crossbow
Union Road ☎ (0324) 24414
11–11.45 (12.45 Fri & Sat, 12.30–2.30; 6.30–11 Sun)
Harviestoun Old Manor; **Tennent's 80/-** 🄷
Uninspiring, modern exterior conceals a friendly and well-kept interior. Look for the rare Heriot 80/- mirror in the lounge. ◐ ⊕ ♣ P

Rosebank
Main Street ☎ (0324) 611842
11–2.30; 5–11 (11.30 Thu, 12 Fri & Sat, 12.30–2.30; 6.30–11.30 Sun)
Whitbread Castle Eden Ale 🄷
Part of the Beefeater chain, opened in 1988 in the former bonded warehouse of the Rosebank Distillery. Won the prestigious Times/Royal Institute of Chartered Surveyors Conservation Award in 1989. Food in bar and restaurant.
◐ ◑ ⊕ ♿ P

Causewayhead

Birds & Bees
Easter Cornton Road
☎ (0786) 73663
11–2.30; 5–1 (11–1 am summer, 12.30–2.30; 6.30–11 Sun)
Harviestoun Old Manor 🄰; **Tetley Bitter** 🄷; **Younger IPA** 🄰
Converted farm: open-plan bar with 'designer' art made from old farm bric-a-brac. Popular pub for petanque.
◐ ◑ ♿ ▲ ♣ P

Clackmannan

County Hotel
Main Street ☎ (0259) 722912
11–11 (12 Fri & Sat, 12.30–2.30; 6.30–11 Sun)
Maclay 80/- 🄰
Popular village local with historic clack at front. One of the few pubs to appear in this guide for ten consecutive years.
⊕ ♿ ♣

Denny

Royal Oak Hotel
169 Stirling Street
☎ (0324) 823768
11–2.30; 5–11 (11–11 Sat, 12.30–2.30; 6.30–11 Sun)
Younger No.3 🄰
Popular locals' pub, run by the same family since 1925. Very pleasant atmosphere. One of the few outlets for No.3 in the area.
Q ◐ P

Dollar

Kings Seat
19 Bridge Street
☎ (0259) 42515
11–2.30; 5–11 (12 Thu–Sat, 12.30–2.30; 6.30–11 Sun)
Belhaven 70/-, 80/-; **Courage Directors** 🄷
Cosy pub with a friendly atmosphere where the beer is complemented by good bar food. ◐ ◑ ▲

Strathallan Hotel
Chapel Place ☎ (0259) 42205
11–12 (1 am Fri & Sat, 11–11 Sun)
Harviestoun Ale 🄷
Friendly village hotel, Harviestoun brewery's nearest outlet. Holds an annual mini

beer exhibition.
P

Falkirk

Behind the Wall
14 Melville Street
☎ (0324) 33338
11–11.30 (12 Thu, 12.45 Fri & Sat, 12–3; 6.30–11 Sun)
Whitbread Castle Eden Ale H
Large, lively bar and bistro with a 'cops and robbers' theme. Built in old Playtex bra factory! Full range of meals includes a vegan option.
(Grahamston)

Woodside
76 High Station Road
☎ (0324) 29393
11–12 (12.30–2.30; 6.30–12 Sun)
McEwan 80/- A
Fine wood-panelled bar, with notable Campbell, Hope & King windows. Pool table.
(High)

Grangemouth

Ship Inn
102 Newhouse Road
☎ (0324) 482206
11 (11.30 Sun)–2.30; 5.30–11 (11–11 Fri & Sat)
Maclay 80/- A
Basic, friendly bar with a shipping theme; modern lounge. Friendly atmosphere throughout. P

Kilmahog

Lade Inn
1 mile outside Callander, at A84/A821 jct
☎ (0877) 30152
11–2.30; 5.30–11 (12 Fri & Sat, 12.30–11 Sun)
Ruddles County; Webster's Yorkshire Bitter, Choice H
Owned and managed by Canadians, this inn provides excellent hospitality. The landlord's son runs a mini-brewery in Canada. Good food with veg and children's choices; try the steak pie cooked in Ruddles. Courtesy bus available.
Q P

Sauchie

Mansfield Arms
7 Main Street
☎ (0259) 722020
11–12 (12.30–3; 6.30–12 Sun)
Harviestoun Ale; Tetley Bitter A
A friendly atmosphere and a warm welcome to all in this family-run pub. Good meals: large helpings, and the best prices in the district. Occasional guest beers.

Thornhill

Crown Hotel
Main Street (A873, Stirling-Aberfoyle road)
☎ (078685) 217
11–12 (may vary)
McEwan 80/- A
An old coaching inn, a wee gem of a pub. Look out for the pigeon near the gents toilet!
Q P

FRINGE BENEFITS: History

Collectors of beermats, labels and bottles gradually build up their own cardboard, paper and glass picture of British beers and breweries over the decades. But if you want to put British brewing history into sharper focus, you need to join the Brewery History Society.

Founded in 1972, the society stimulates research into brewery history and encourages the exchange of information, notably through an excellent quarterly journal which contains articles on old breweries, many with photographs. The society maintains its own photographic collection, a vital picture of the past now that so many old brewery buildings have been demolished, besides an archive of books, magazines and papers.

Members are urged to visit their local county record offices, museums and reference libraries to dig out further information about our fast disappearing malt and hops past, particularly since many of the major companies show surprisingly little interest in their history. Members are even encouraged to interview former brewery employees to liven up the dusty dates of takeovers and closures with personal recollections.

To help in this task send £6 (payable to the BHS) to their membership secretary, Jeff Sechiari, Manor Side East, Mill Lane, Byfleet, Weybridge, Surrey, KT14 7RS.

Dumfries & Galloway

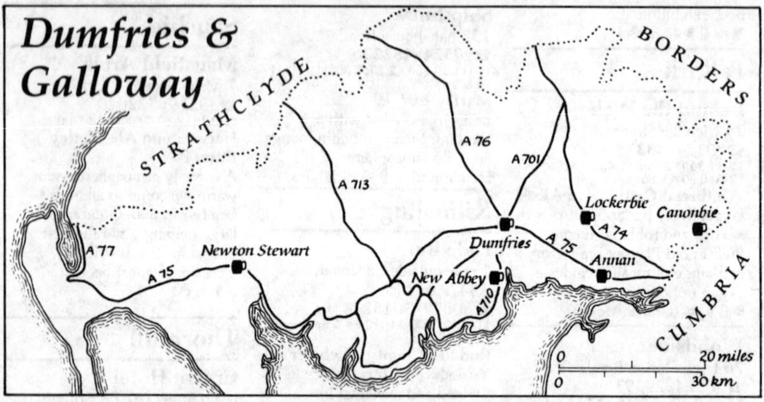

Annan

Blue Bell
High Street (A75, beside river)
☎ (046 12) 2385
11–11 (12.30–2.30; 6.30–11 Sun)
McEwan 80/-; Theakston Best Bitter [H]
Lively, ex-State brewery pub. Bar billiards. Q

Canonbie

Riverside Inn
On B6357, just off A7
☎ (03873) 71512
11–2.30 (not Sun); 6.30–11 (12 Fri & Sat, 7–11 Sun)
Yates Bitter [H]
Pleasant country inn with good food. Two guest beers.
Q P

Dumfries

Douglas Arms
75 Friars Vennel
☎ (0387) 56002
11–2.30; 5–11 (11–11 Wed & Thu, 11–12 Fri & Sat, 12.30–2.30; 6.30–11 Sun)
Broughton Greenmantle Ale, 80/- Ale; Theakston Best Bitter [A]
Down-to-earth, basic, one-roomed pub brought back to life by Broughton.

New Bazaar
39 White Sands (beside River Nith) ☎ (0387) 68776
11–11 (12 Thu–Sat, 12.30–2.30; 6.30–11 Sun)
Broughton Greenmantle Ale, Special Bitter, Greenmantle 80/-Ale, Old Jock [A]
First acquisition by the brewery in Dumfries; popular, with a loyal following. Two rooms off the bar afford some privacy. Beware the sliding door to gents toilet!

Ship Inn
97 St Michael Street
☎ (0387) 55189
11–2.30; 5–11 (12.30–2.30; 6.30–11 Sun)
McEwan 70/-; 80/- [A]
Excellent, cosy, two-roomed pub, one of the most popular places to drink in town. A varied clientele comes to enjoy good chat and atmosphere.
Q

Tam O' Shanter
117 Queensbury Street
☎ (0387) 54055
11–2.30; 5–11 (closed Sun)
Greenalls Bitter; McEwan 80/- [E]
Basic pub centred on a small one-roomed public bar with small side rooms to supplement. Popular with local council employees.

Lockerbie

Kings Arms Hotel
29 High Street
☎ (05762) 2410
11–11 (12.30–2.30; 6.30–11 Sun)
McEwan 80/- [A]
17th-century coaching inn in town centre.

New Abbey

Criffel Inn
2 The Square ☎ (038 785) 244
11–2.30; 5.30–11 (12.30–2.30; 6.30–11 Sun)
Broughton Special Bitter [A]
Small public bar with a relaxed atmosphere, in a pleasant village near Sweetheart Abbey. Owner is steam traction engine fanatic; the walls are adorned with pictures of engines.
Q

Newton Stewart

Creebridge House Hotel
Minigaff Road (B7079)
☎ (0671) 2121
12–2.30; 6–11 (12.30–2; 7–11 Sun)
McEwan 80/-; Theakston Best Bitter, Old Peculier [H]
Comfortable hotel, close to town centre. Good food.
Q

All the pubs listed in the *Good Beer Guide* are selected and inspected by volunteer CAMRA members. You can have your say, too. Suggestions for pubs to be included in (or excluded from) future editions are very welcome and will be passed on to the local CAMRA branch. Use the form on page 502

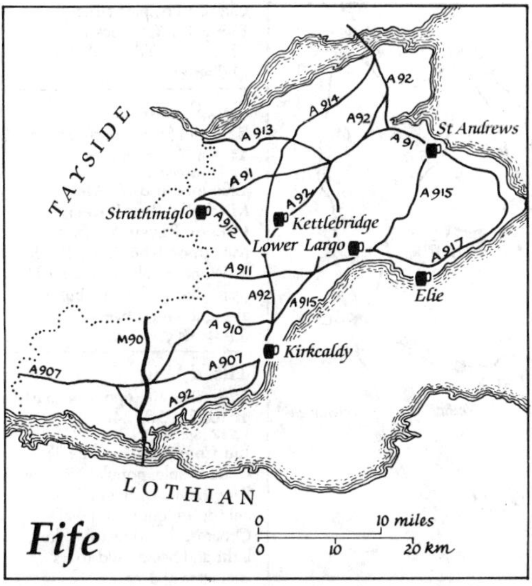

Elie

Ship Inn
The Toft (off Castle Green)
☎ (0333) 330246
11–12 (12.30–2.30; 6.30–11 Sun)
Belhaven 80/- Ⓗ
Unspoilt pub with strong nautical features, overlooking picturesque harbour.
♨ Q ♉ ❀ ⊞ ▲

Kettlebridge

Kettlebridge Inn
4 Cupar Road
☎ (0337) 30232
11–2.30; 5–11 (11–11 Sat, 12.30–11 Sun)
Ind Coope Burton Ale; Tetley Bitter Ⓗ
Pleasant and popular village local. Reasonably-priced menu caters for children and vegetarians (eve meals Thu–Sun). ♨ Q ❀ 🛏 ◖ ◗ ⊞ ♿ ▲

Kirkcaldy

Novar Bar
17 Nicol Street
☎ (0592) 260545
11–2.30; 5–11 (11–12 Thu–Sat, 12.30–2.30; 6.30–11 Sun)
Theakston Best Bitter Ⓗ
Large, vibrant 1960s pub, built on the site of the old Novar Bar. Same management for three generations. Excellent and super value meals available until 6.30. Worthington White Shield stocked. ◖ ⊞ ♿ ⇌ ♣

Lower Largo

Railway Hotel
2 Station Wynd
☎ (033 320) 239
11–11 (12.30–2.30; 6.30–11 Sun)
Maclay 80/- Ⓗ
Comfortable but basic pub in an attractive setting, close to the birthplace of Alexander Selkirk, the 'real-life' Robinson Crusoe. Lunchtime snacks. ♉ ❀ ▲ P

St Andrews

Ardgowan Hotel
2 Playfair Terrace (50 yds E of Links/Golf Place jct)
☎ (0334) 72970
12–2.30; 5–11.45 (11.35 Sat, 12.30–2.30; 6.30–11 Sun)
McEwan 80/-; Younger No.3 Ⓐ
Modern basement lounge with photos of old Fife. Very popular for bar meals. No rooms let in Jan. 🛏 ◖ ◗

Ma Bell's
The Scores (E of R&A clubhouse) ☎ (0334) 72611
12–11.30 (12.30–2.30; 6.30–11 Sun)
Ruddles County; Webster's Choice Ⓗ
Very popular basement lounge beneath St Andrews Golf Hotel. Very busy in term-time. Guest beers. 🛏 ◖ ▲

Russell Hotel
26 The Scores (E of R&A clubhouse) ☎ (0334) 73447
12–2.30; 5–11
Broughton Greenmantle Ale Ⓗ; **McEwan 80/-** Ⓐ; **Theakston Best Bitter** Ⓗ
Small, well-furnished lounge with restaurant. 🛏 ◖ ◗ ♿ ▲

Strathmiglo

Strathmiglo Inn
61 High Street
☎ (033 76) 252
11–2.30; 5–11 (12 Thu–Sat, 12.30–2.30; 6.30–12 Sun)
Belhaven 80/-; Taylor Golden Best Ⓗ
Traditional coaching inn with restaurant, public bar and lounge. Guest beers.
🛏 ◖ ◗ ⊞ ♿ ▲ ♣ P

THE SYMBOLS

- ♨ real fire
- Q quiet pub – in at least one bar
- ♉ indoor room for children
- ❀ garden or other outdoor drinking area
- 🛏 accommodation
- ◖ lunchtime meals
- ◗ evening meals
- ⊞ public bar
- ♿ easy disabled access
- ▲ camping facilities at the pub or nearby
- ⇌ near British Rail station
- ⊖ near Underground station
- ♣ pub games
- ⍥ real cider
- P pub car park

Grampian

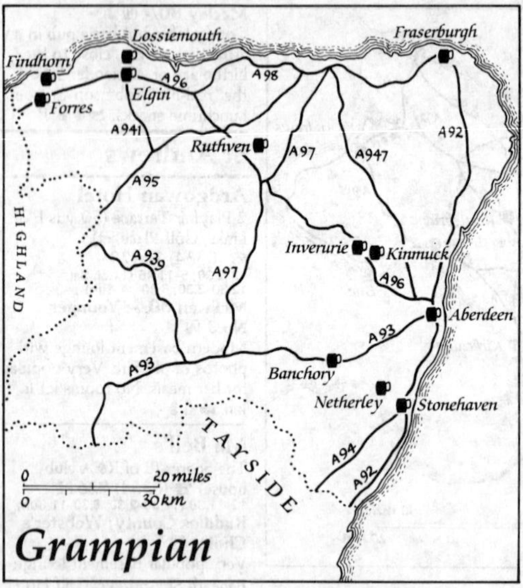

Aberdeen

Atholl Hotel

54 Kingsgate
☎ (0224) 323505
11–2.30; 5–11 (11.30 Fri & Sat, 12.30–2.30; 6.30–11 Sun)
McEwan 80/-; Tennent's 80/- [H]
Plush, upmarket hotel, but with good atmosphere and food. Tennent's 80/- is sold as 'Atholl Ale'. Q ⊨ ◖ P

Blue Lamp

121 Gallowgate
☎ (0224) 647472
11–11 (6.30–11 Sun)
McEwan 80/- [A]**; Taylor Best Bitter; Theakston Best Bitter** [H]
Now extended by the addition of an excellent stone-floored lounge with free CD player. Great 60/70s jukebox (free) and frequent live music. Friendly staff. Guest beer. ◖ ⊟ ♿ ≢ ♣

Camerons

6–8 Little Belmont Street (by graveyard) ☎ (0224) 644487
11–11.45 (closed Sun)
Belhaven 80/-; Taylor Landlord [A]
Old coaching house with modern additions. The original tiny bar and snug are retained. Meals served in the lounge.
◖ ◗ ⊟ ≢

Carriages (Brentwood Hotel)

101 Crown Street
☎ (0224) 595440
11–2.30; 5–11 (12–2.30; 6.30–11 Sun)
Taylor Landlord [H]
Comfortable lounge bar providing excellent-value food and friendly service. Bombay mix and nuts on bar are free. Good accommodation.
Q ⊨ ◖ ◗ ≢ P

Ferryhill House Hotel

Bon Accord Street
☎ (0224) 590867
11–11 (11.30 Thu–Sat, 12.30–5; 6.30–11 Sun)
Broughton Greenmantle Ale; McEwan 80/-; Taylor Landlord [A]**; Theakston Best Bitter** [H]
Comfortable lounge with large outdoor drinking area. Near city centre. Q ⛍ ❀ ⊨ ◖ ◗ ≢ P

Kirkgate

18 Upper Kirkgate (near Marischal College)
☎ (0224) 640515
11–10.45 (11.45 Thu–Sat, 12.30–2.30; 6.30–10.30 Sun)
Belhaven 80/- [H]
Basic local bar, a haunt of the KGB! Popular with students.
◖ ◗ ♿ ≢ ♣

Moorings Bar

2 Trinity Quay
☎ (0224) 587602
11–12 (12.30–2.30; 6.30–11 Sun)
Caledonian 80/- Ale [H]
Rock and real ale rendezvous. Ear protection not always necessary! Chess played. Guest beer. ◖ ◗ ♿ ≢ ♣

Prince of Wales

1 St Nicholas Lane
☎ (0224) 640597
11–10.45 (11.45 Fri, 12.30–2.30; 6.30–10.45 Sun)
Caledonian 80/- Ale; Orkney Raven Ale [H]**; Younger No. 3** [A]
Rare example of a traditional Scottish long bar. Mecca of the North; a joy not to be missed. Guest beers, plus either Broughton Old Jock or Theakston Old Peculier.
Q ◖ ≢ ♣

Tap Room

22 Guild Street (opp. station)
☎ (0224) 589411
10–11 (closed Sun)
Caledonian 80/- Ale; Mitchell's Best Bitter; Orkney Raven Ale [H]
Modernised, but the better for it. Wooden tables — a bit like a 'caff' during the day, but lively at night. Guest beers.
◖ ◗ ≢ ♣ ⌽

Tilted Wig

55 Castlegate (opp. law courts)
☎ (0224) 583248
12–12 (Sun 7–11)
Ind Coope Burton Ale [H]
Comfortable, popular town pub. Law theme, with legalistic anecdotes/quotes on walls. Ornaments and pictures, low light and beams add to its character. ◖ ◗ ≢

Under the Hammer

North Silver Street
☎ (0224) 640253
11–12 (6.30–10.30 Sun)
Belhaven 80/-; Tetley Bitter [H]
Small, compact wine bar beneath auction rooms. Close ties with local art/folk scene. Frequent live music. ◖ ◗ ≢

Banchory

Tor-na-Coille

Inchmarlo Road (A93)
☎ (03302) 2242
11–11 (12.30–2.30; 6.30–10.30 Sun)
Theakston Best Bitter [H]
Large hotel on west side of town, boasting large, open gardens. Excellent sports facilities nearby. Q ⛍ ❀ ⊨ ◖ ◗ P

Elgin

Thunderton House

Thunderton Place
☎ (0343) 548767
11–11 (11.45 Fri & Sat, 12.30–2.30; 6.30–11 Sun)
Belhaven 80/-; Broughton Greenmantle 80/- Ale; Caledonian 80/- Ale; Tennent's 80/- [H]
The third most historic building in Moray, beautifully restored to Victorian standards. Family room has western-style swing doors. Guest beer. Menu caters for children and vegetarians. ⛫ ⛍ ◖ ◗ ♿ ≢

Findhorn

Crown & Anchor

Across road from Yacht Club
☎ (0309) 30243
11–11 (11.45 Fri & Sat, 12.30–11 Sun)
Brakspear Bitter; Courage

Directors; Tennent's 80/-; Wadworth 6X Ⓗ
A beautiful setting, an excellent selection of bottled beers and two guest beers. What more could one want?
🏠 ❀ 🛏 ◖◗ 🍴 ♿ ⛺ ♣ P

Forres

Red Lion Hotel

Tolbooth Street (just off High Street) ☎ (0309) 72716
11–11 (11.45 Fri & Sat; 12.30–11 Sun)
McEwan 80/-; Younger No. 3 Ⓔ
Known as 'Red Beastie'; a welcoming and popular spot. No-frills public bar and comfortable lounge. Longest-serving real ale outlet in Grampian. 🛏 ◖ 🍴 ⇄

Fraserburgh

Crown Bar

45 Broad Street/Shore Street
☎ (0346) 28452
11–11 (12.30–2.30; 6.30–10.30 Sun)
McEwan 80/- Ⓐ
Friendly, homely bar with long, wooden bar top. An oasis in an oil desert; up the lane from the harbour. 🍴

Inverurie

Thainstone House Hotel

Off A96 on Kintore side of Inverurie ☎ (0467) 21643
11–11 (12.30–11 Sun)
Tennent's 80/- Ⓗ
Imposing country house set back from the road. Very friendly atmosphere in large upstairs bar. Barbecues on the lawn summer Sundays.
🏠 Q 🐴 ❀ 🛏 ◖◗ P

Kinmuck

Boars Head

Signed from B993 and B979
☎ (0224) 791235
11–2.30; 5–11 (12.30–2.30; 7–11 Sun)
Taylor Landlord Ⓗ
National winner of CAMRA 1989 Pub of the Year. Still serves beer from the cupboard. Guest beers. Snacks available both sessions. Q 🍴 ♣ P

Lossiemouth

Beach Bar

Commerce Street
☎ (034381) 3164
11–2.30 (extends in summer); 5–11 (11–11.45 Fri & Sat, 12.30–2.30; 6.30–11 Sun)
Marston's Pedigree Bitter *or* **Theakston Best Bitter** Ⓗ
Comfortable bar, originally the town swimming baths! One or two folk evenings a week. Large selection of malt whiskies. Eve meals summer only; veg and children's dishes available.
🏠 ❀ ◖◗ 🍴 ♿ ♣ P

Clifton

Clifton Road
☎ (034381) 2100
11–2.30; 5–11 (11–11.45 Fri & Sat, 12.30–2.30; 6.30–11 Sun)
McEwan 80/-; Younger No. 3 Ⓔ
Comfortable bar near harbour. Guest beer. 🏠 🍴 ♿ ♣ P

Netherley

Lairhillock Inn

On B979, 1 mile W of village
☎ (0569) 30001
11–11 (12.30–2.30; 6.30–10.30 Sun)
Courage Directors; McEwan 80/-; Orkney Raven Ale Ⓐ
Friendly, remote bar which is cosy and comfortable. Look for the building with 'inn' on the roof. Family room in summer. Guest beers. 🏠 Q 🐴 ❀ ◖◗ 🍴 P

Ruthven

Borve Brewhouse

Off A96, Huntly-Keith Road
☎ (046687) 343
11–11 (11.45–Fri & Sat)
Borve Ale Ⓗ
Secluded brew pub in converted schoolhouse. 🏠 Q ❀ ♿ ♣ P

Stonehaven

Marine Hotel

9–10 Shorehead
☎ (0569) 62155
11–12 (12.30–11 Sun)
McEwan 80/-; Taylor Landlord Ⓗ
Picturesque harbour pub, crowded in summer. Watch out for the 4 o'clock swim on summer Sundays.
🏠 🐴 ❀ 🛏 ◖◗ 🍴

Heriot Tennent's 80/- in danger of becoming a Lost Beer as we go to press

Highland

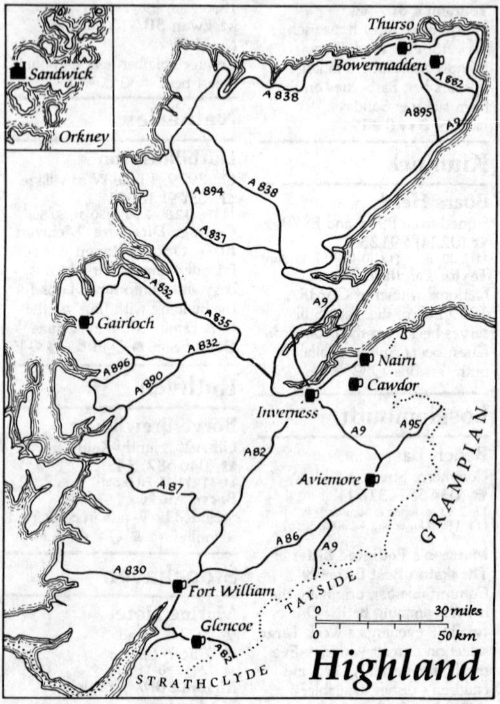

***Orkney**, Sandwick, Orkney*

Aviemore

Winking Owl
Grampian Road
☎ (0479) 810841
11–11
Alloa Arrols 80/-; Tetley Bitter [H]
Bar popular with the *après-ski* crowd and tourists. Fine restaurant.

Bowermadden

Bower Inn
From Wick take A9 N then A876 to Castletown for 11 miles ☎ (095 586) 292
11–2.30; 5–11 (12.30–2.30; 6.30–11 Sun)
Younger No. 3 [A]
Originally an old country house, recently converted to a pub and restaurant with a nautical theme, by a former submariner. Q P

Cawdor

Cawdor Tavern
The Lane ☎ (066 77) 316
11–2.30; 5–11 (11.45 Sat, 12.30–2.30; 6.30–11 Sun)
McEwan 80/- [H]
Old coaching house in a picturesque village which lies between the Culloden battlefield and magnificent Cawdor Castle.
P

Fort William

Nevis Bank Hotel
Belford Road ☎ (0397) 5721
11–2.30; 5–11 (11–1 am Fri, 11–11.45 Sat, 12.30–2.30; 6–11 Sun)
McEwan 80/-; Younger No. 3 [A]
Plain public bar at the rear of hotel on the main road north from Fort William. Situated near the entrance to Glen Nevis and so is an ideal base for anyone heading into the surrounding hills. P

Gairloch

Old Inn
The Harbour ☎ (0445) 2006
11–12 (11.30 Sat, 12.30–11 Sun)
Belhaven 80/-; Tennent's 80/- [H]
Old country coaching inn near the harbour in a quiet glen with pictureque views of loch and mountains. Warm and friendly, family-run establishment. Excellent home-made food: veg dishes and children's portions available. P

Glencoe

Clachaig
Off A82, 2 miles from village
☎ (085 52) 252
11–11 (12 Fri, 11.30 Sat, 12.30–11 Sun)
McEwan 70/-, 80/-; Younger No. 3 [A]
A classic mountaineers' pub on the old road through Glencoe with possibly the most spectacular scenery in Britain. Biggest seller of real ale in the West Highlands. Excellent beer; guest beers planned.
Q P

Inverness

Clachnaharry Inn
High Street, Clachnaharry (on outskirts of Inverness)
☎ (0463) 239806
11–11 (11.45 Thu–Sat, 12.30–2.30; 6.30–11 Sun)
McEwan 80/- [A]
Traditional coaching inn beside the sea lock of the Caledonian Canal and the single track railway line going north. The lounge bar offers a magnificent view of the Beauly Birth.

Gellions Hotel
10 Bridge Street (near main bridge over river)
☎ (0463) 233648
11–11 (1 am Wed–Fri, 11.45 Sat, 12.30–11 Sun)
Caledonian 70/- Ale; McEwan 80/-; Theakston Best Bitter [A]
Formerly an old town-centre hotel, recently converted to a modern bar complex with a traditional theme. Good beer in pleasant surroundings in the centre of Inverness. No real ale in back public bar; good value restaurant upstairs. Campsite one mile away.

Glenmhor Hotel
10 Ness Bank (E bank of river opp. cathedral)
☎ (0463) 234308
11–2.30; 5–11 (1 am Thu & Fri, 11.45 Sat, 12.30–11 Sun)
Ind Coope Burton Ale [H]
Riverside hotel with a magnificent view of the cathedral. The public bar is in the converted stable and bears the name 'Nicky Tams'. Italian bistro in hotel.
P

Heathmount Hotel
Kingsmills Road (Crown area of town, not far from centre)
☎ (0463) 235877
11–11 (12.30 Thu & Fri, 11.30 Sat, 12.30–11 Sun)
McEwan 80/-; Younger No. 3 [H]
Recently-modernised lounge bar in traditional style. Busy at

weekends. Imaginative menu.
Q ⛺ ◐ ◑ ⊕ ⇌ ♣ P

Phoenix
108–110 Academy Street
(500 yds from station)
☎ (0463) 233685
9 am–11 pm (1 am Fri, 11.45 pm Sat, 12.30–2.30; 6.30–11 Sun)
Maclay 80/- 🄷
Lively, traditional horseshoe bar with many artefacts around the walls – including an old beer engine in a glass case. Guest beer always available. Food (including veg) served in lounge – ale can be carried through.
◐ ◑ ⊕ ⇌

Nairn

Invernairne Hotel
Thurlow Road (between the links and golfcourse)
☎ (0667) 52039
11–2.30; 5–11 (12 Mon & Sat, 1 Fri, 12.30–2.30; 6.30–11 Sun)
McEwan 80/- 🄰
Spacious lounge bar in family-run hotel by the sea shore. Impressive fireplace. Live jazz Mon. Good choice of seafood.
Q ⛺ ◐ ◑ ⇌ P

Thurso

Station Bar
Princes Street (100 yds from station)
11–2.30; 5–10
McEwan 80/-; Younger No. 3 🄰
Plain and friendly, traditional Scottish bar with magnificent old brewery mirrors. Q ⇌

THE GBG QUIZ

Round 5: OK, try this!

61. Who wrote about an ideal but imaginary pub called the Moon Under Water?
62. Name three varieties of cider apple.
63. Who went for his enemy bald-headed, and set up many of his NCOs in pubs which they named after him?
64. What was the average original gravity of British ale in 1990?
65. How did Jacob Christian Jacobsen's stovepipe hat help to make brewing history in 1854?
66. Which English city had a brewery and pubs owned and run by the Government from WWI to 1973?
67. Where would you find an acrospire?
68. What is unusual about Cooper's Sparkling Ale from Australia?
69. Which inn's sign was discovered in the ruins of Pompeii?
70. Which king banned the use of hops in brewing?
71. What caused the death of eight people at Meux's Brewery in Tottenham Court Road, London in 1814?
72. A former CAMRA chairman started his own brewery in 1978. What was it called?
73. Where is George Killiam's Irish Russet Ale brewed?
74. The strength of beer is gauged from original gravity and alcohol by volume figures. What other methods are used?
75. Four brew pubs survived into the 1970s out of the many thousands which had existed previously. Name them.

Lothian

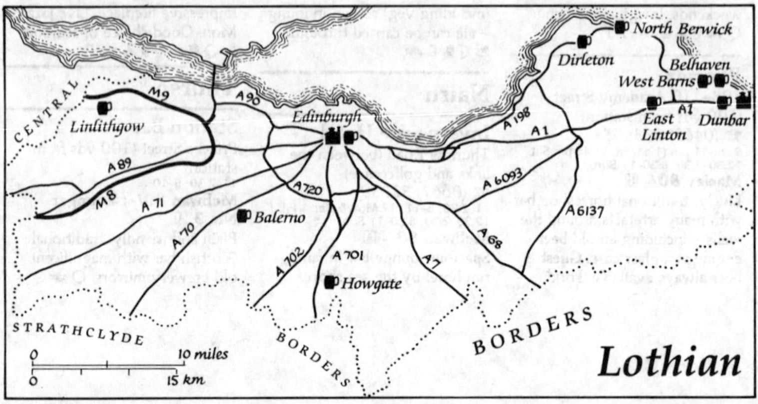

Belhaven, Dunbar; **Caledonian**, Edinburgh

Balerno

Grey Horse
22 Main Street (off A70)
☎ (031) 449 3092
11–2.30; 5–11 (closed Sun)
Belhaven 60/-, 80/- [H]
Traditionally-run, wood-panelled gem set in a village increasingly encroached upon by the city suburbs. A fine bank of four handpumps dispenses the delicious (and cheap) beer. A busy local with a number of rare brewery mirrors. ⊞ ♣

Belhaven

Mason's Arms
On A1087, off A1
☎ (0368) 63700
11–2.30; 5–11 (12.30–2.30; 6.30–11 Sun)
Belhaven 80/- [H]
Functional locals' bar at the brewery gates. Handy for the nearby beaches to the west of the historic town of Dunbar. ♠ ⊞ ≹ ♣

Dirleton

Castle Inn
Off A198 ☎ (062 085) 221
11–2.30; 5–11 (12 Fri & Sat, 12.30–2.30; 6.30–11 Sun)
Caledonian 70/- Ale [A]
Attractive local, overlooking the village green and opposite the castle ruins. The bar, with games room off, contains several fine mirrors. A handy base for the many nearby golf courses. Good tasty meals available daily in bar and lounge. ♠ Q ⊭ ◐ ⊞ ♣ P

Dunbar

Craig-en-Gelt Hotel
Marine Road (off Belhaven Road, on John Muir Clifftop Trail) ☎ (0368) 62287
12–2.30; 5.30–12 (12.30–2.30; 6.30–12 Sun)
Belhaven 80/- [H]
On a clifftop, with fine views across the bay to the ruins of Dunbar Castle. A modern, comfortable lounge bar and restaurant just a few minutes' walk from the town centre and harbour. Pool room.
Q ⊭ ◐ ◗ ≹ ♣

East Linton

Crown Hotel
27 Bridge Street (off A1)
☎ (0620) 860335
11–2.30; 5–11 (11–11 Fri & Sat, 12.30–2.30; 6.30–11 Sun)
Belhaven 80/- [A]
Cosy, wood-panelled locals' bar with a large lounge to the rear. A pair of rare Dudgeon & Co. windows are a reminder of the brewery's original name. Beware the keg 60/- and 70/-. Pool room. ♠ ⊭ ◐ ⊞ ♣

Edinburgh

Beehive Inn (Drones Bar)
18–20 Grassmarket
☎ (031) 225 7171
11–11 (6.30–11 Sun)
Theakston Best Bitter, Old Peculier [H]
Upmarket city-centre bar in shadow of castle. Friendly staff; marvellous Fowlers Brewery mirror. Regular guest beer. Eve meals summer only.
◐ ◗ ♿ ≹ (Waverley)

Bennet's Bar
1 Maxwell Street, Morningside
☎ (031) 447 1903
11–2.30; 5–11 (closed Sun)
Belhaven 70/-, 80/-; Taylor Landlord [A]
Plain, wee, old-fashioned bar tucked away under a tenement in Morningside. The atmosphere is relaxed and friendly, attracting a good mix of locals who appreciate being able to converse. Avoid the 60/- which is *not* real ale.
Q ⊞ ♿ ♣

Bow Bar
80 West Bow
☎ (031) 220 1823
11–11.30 (closed Sun)
Caledonian 70/- Ale, 80/- Ale, Merman XXX; Taylor Landlord [A]
An object lesson in how to create from scratch an atmosphere which embodies the best features of Scottish pub traditions. Six regular guest beers, Worthington White Shield and a fine range of malt whiskies are available.
Q ⊞ ≹ (Waverley)

Hampton Hotel
14 Corstorphine Road, Murrayfield (A8, opp. ice rink)
☎ (031) 337 1130
12 (11 Sat)–2.30; 5–11.30 (12.30–3; 6.30–11.30 Sun)
Draught Bass; Belhaven 80/- [A]
A welcoming, family-run hotel with a comfortable, split-level lounge bar. Good home-made food ensures a busy lunch trade. Can get crowded in the evenings, especially when rugby and ice hockey fans swell the ranks of locals. Worthington White Shield also available.
Q ⊭ ◐ P

Kay's Bar
39 Jamaica Street
☎ (031) 225 1858
11–11.45 (12.30–2.30; 6.30–11 Sun)
Belhaven 80/- [A]**; Theakston Best Bitter** [H]
Victorian wine merchant's shop, cleverly converted into New Town lounge by incorporating

shop fittings into bar furniture and decor. Extensive lunch menu. Guest beer.
🏛 Q ◐ ⇌ (Waverley)

Malt Shovel Inn
11–15 Cockburn Street
☎ (031) 225 6843
12–11.30 (12 Fri, 11.45 Sat, 12.30–2.30; 6.30–11 Sun)
Harviestoun Waverley Ale; Mitchell's Best Bitter 🄷
Large, busy but friendly pub in city centre, serving Waverley Ale, brewed exclusively for Malt Shovel Inns. Large selection of malt whiskies and bottled beers. Live music Tue and Wed. Handy for bus and rail connections. Five guest beers and Sun brunch served; eve meals till 8pm (not Sun). White Shield available.
◐ ◗ ⇌ (Waverley)

Malt Shovel Too (Coppers)
19 Cockburn Street
☎(031) 225 1441
11–11 (11.45 Thu & Sat, 12.45 Fri, closed Sun)
Harviestoun Waverley Ale; Mitchell's Best Bitter 🄷
Unassuming popular bar in the Old Town, adjacent to Malt Shovel Inn and achieving same high standards. Snacks served all day. Guest beers and White Shield always available.
⊕ ⇌ (Waverley)

Minders
114 Causewayside
12–12 (12.30–2.30; 7–11 Sun)
Caledonian 80/- Ale 🄰
Smart lounge bar on the south-side of the city, attracting young clientele in the evenings. Four regular guest beers. ◐

Robbies Bar
367 Leith Walk
☎ (031) 554 6850
11–11 (11.30 Fri & Sat, 12.30–2.30; 6.30–11 Sun)
Caledonian 70/- Ale; Taylor Landlord; Theakston Best Bitter 🄷
Fine example of a Victorian bar recreated by a young landlord. Original beer and whisky mirrors are complemented by antique wall plaques; original Aitken handpumps. Thriving local trade. 🏛 Q ♿ ⇌ (Waverley) ♣

Ryries Bar
1 Haymarket Terrace (next to station) ☎ (031) 337 7582
11–11 (12 Thu & Fri, 10–11.30 Sat, 12.30–2.30; 7–11 Sun)
Theakston Best Bitter 🄷
Rustic Edinburgh bar with beautifully preserved gantry and interesting stained glass windows. Live music Sun nights. ⊕ ⇌ (Haymarket) ♣

St James Oyster Bar
2–6 Calton Street
☎ (031) 557 2925
11–1 am (12.30–2.30; 6.30–11 Sun)
Caledonian 70/- Ale; Taylor Landlord 🄷
Underground and arty late-night joint with occasional alternative live music. Unusual range of Belgian bottled and fruit beers. Q ◐ ◗ ⇌ (Waverley)

St Vincent Bar
11 St Vincent Street
☎ (031) 225 7447
11–2.30; 5–11.45 (11–11.45 Thu–Sat, 12.30–2.30; 6.30–11 Sun)
Alloa Arrol's 80/-; Maclay 80/-; Marston's Pedigree Bitter; Tetley Bitter 🄷
A pleasing return to the pub's traditional name and decor. The bar boasts a superb gantry, pine floor and interesting old prints and mirrors. Guest beer. Q ◐

Smithie's Ale House
49–51 Eyre Place, Canonmills
☎ (031) 556 9805
11–12 (11.45 Sat, 12.30–2.30; 6.30–11 Sun)
Caledonian 70/- Ale, 80/- Ale; Taylor Landlord; Theakston Best Bitter 🄷
Edwardian-style pub (estd. 1981), attracting a varied clientele. A relaxed atmosphere is enhanced by gas lighting and an unusual display of 19 hand-painted mirrors. Guest beer. No food Sun. Q ◐

Southsider
3–5 West Richmond Street (near Surgeon's Hall, ½ mile from city centre) ☎ (031) 667 2003
11–12 (12.30–2.30; 6.30–11 Sun)
Maclay 60/-, 70/-, 80/- 🄰
Recently-rejuvenated two-bar pub with three regular guest beers. Good wholesome pub fare is augmented by Dr Kane's 'Death by Cholesterol'; no meals Sun. Worthington White Shield and Belgian bottled beers are available. Family room also used for meetings.
Q 🚼 ◐ ⊕ ⇌ (Waverley) ♣

Stockbridge Bar
48–50 St Stephen Street
☎ (031) 225 5395
11–11.30 (12.30–2.30; 6.30–11 Sun)
Caledonian 70/- Ale, 80/- Ale; Taylor Landlord 🄰
Basement bar which appeals to rugby aficionados and real ale drinkers. Serves Sun breakfast from 10am and good, home-cooked food at lunchtimes. ◐

Todd's Tap
42 Bernard Street, Leith (near the Water of Leith)
☎ (031) 554 4122
11–11 (12 summer, 1 am Thu–Sat, 12.30–2.30; 6.30–11 Sun)
Taylor Landlord; Tetley Bitter 🄷
A friendly wee pub with a front bar and back parlour warmed by a cosy log fire. Rare collection of photographs of extinct city breweries should not be missed. Six guest beers. Sun breakfast served from 11.45. 🏛 Q ◐ ⊕

Howgate

Old Howgate Inn
On A6094, near Penicuik
☎ (0968) 74244
11–2.30; 5–12 (11–12 Sat, 12.30–2.30; 6.30–11 Sun)
Belhaven 80/-; Taylor Best Bitter 🄷
Once a coaching inn, dating from 1743, this is now a finely restored cosy, wee pub and restaurant, famous for its Danish open sandwiches; more traditional Scottish fare is also provided until 10pm. Guest beer. 🏛 Q ◐ ◗ P

Linlithgow

Red Lion
50 High Street
☎ (0506) 842348
11–11 (12 Thu–Sat, 12.30–2.30; 6.30–11 Sun)
Maclay 80/-; Ind Coope Burton Ale; Tetley Bitter 🄰
Small, friendly bar, popular for pool and darts. Petanque piste in garden area. ❀ ⊕ ⇌ ♣

Four Marys
65 High Street
☎ (0506) 842171
12–2.30; 5–11 (11.30 Fri, 12–11.30 Sat, 12.30–2.30; 7–11 Sun)
Belhaven 70/-, 80/- 🄷
Attractive lounge bar with antique furniture reflecting the town's historic past. Former local CAMRA Pub of the Year. Good range of guest ales and large selection of malt whiskies. Children welcome at lunchtime only. No food Sun eve.
🚼 ◐ ◗ ⇌

North Berwick

Dalrymple Arms
Quality Street ☎ (0620) 2969
11–11 (12 Thu & Sat, 12.30 Fri, 12.30–2.30; 6.30–11 Sun)
Fuller's London Pride 🄷
Good basic boozer. Guest beer.
🏛 🚼 ❀ ♿ ⇌ ♣

West Barns

Battleblent Hotel
Off A1, on A1087, 1 mile W of Dunbar ☎ (0368) 62234
11.30–2.30; 5–11 (12 Thu & Sat, 1 am Fri, 12.30–1 am Sun)
Belhaven 80/- 🄷
Welcoming country hotel set in more than two acres, over-looking the sands of Belhaven Bay. The bar is a cosy Tudor-style lounge with an extensive range of malt whiskies. Excellent, home-made meals (until 11pm) complement the locally-brewed ale. Campsite for caravans only.
🚼 ❀ 🛏 ◐ ◗ Å P

Strathclyde

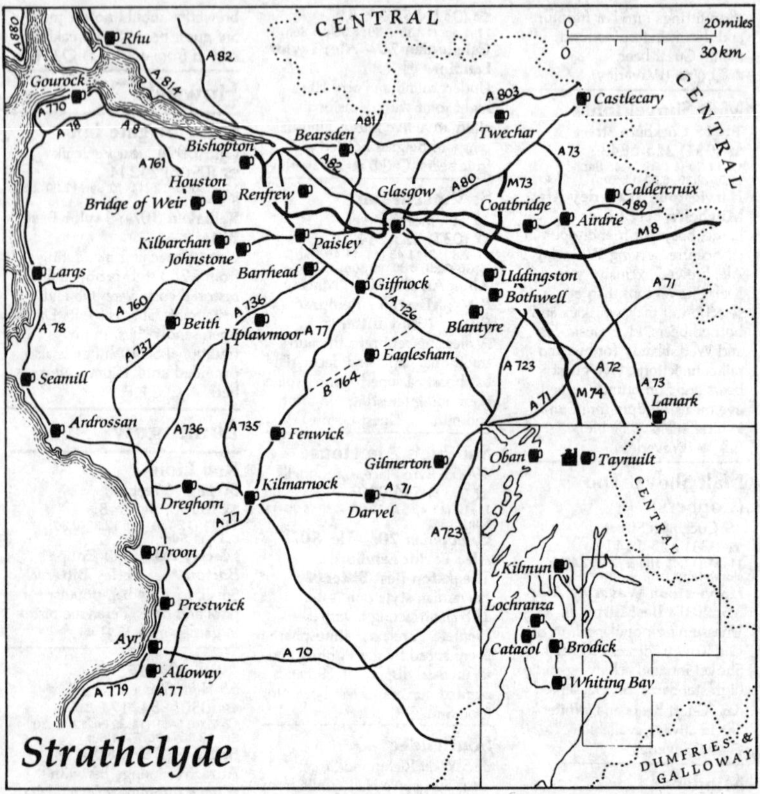

West Highland, *Taynuilt*

Airdrie

Tudor Hotel (Elizabethan Bar)

39–41 Alexander Street
☎ (0236) 64144
7–11 (12 Fri & Sat)
Ind Coope Burton Ale Ⓐ
Comfortable, wood-panelled bar in large hotel. Stained glass windows and a painting of a medieval Scottish scene on one wall. Beer may be brought through to other bars. Meals in hotel restaurant. ⚲ ⛟ ◖◗ ⇌ P

Alloway

Belleisle House Hotel (Shanter Bar)

Belleisle Park, off Doonfoot Road S of Ayr (A719)
☎ (0292) 42331
11–11 (11–6 winter)
Alloa Arrol's 80/- Ⓐ
Typical golfers' watering-hole. Pictures of golfing heroes adorn the walls. Attached to hotel located in a magnificent country park with two golf courses, gardens and a pets corner. Meals in cafeteria or hotel.
⛟ ◖◗ ♿ ♣ P

Ardrossan

High Tide Hotel

23 Parkhouse Road (A78 E of A738 jct) ☎ (0294) 61527
11–12 (1 Thu & Sat, 12.30–12 Sun)
McEwan 80/- Ⓐ
Modern hotel, half a mile from the shore. Front public bar with games; large lounge has live music and quiz nights Thu–Sun.
⚲ ⛟ ◖◗ ⊞ ⇌ (South Beach) ♣ P

Ayr

Chestnuts Hotel

52 Racecourse Road (A719)
☎ (0292) 264393
11–12 (12–12 Sun)
Broughton Special Bitter; Tennent's 80/- Ⓐ
Small lounge with vaulted ceiling, near the seafront. Over 300 water jugs hang on the walls. Excellent pub food.
⌂ Q ♞ ⚲ ⛟ ◖◗ ⇌ P

Geordies Byre

103 Main Street (old A79, N of centre and river)
☎ (0292) 264925
11–11 (12 Thu–Sat, 12.30–2.30; 6.30–11 Sun)
Broughton Special Bitter Ⓐ
Friendly public bar in the Newton end of town. Rear lounge (weekends) is full of Victorian bric-a-brac. Good selection of bottled beers from independent breweries.
Q ⊞ ♿ ⇌ (Ayr/Newton)

Old Racecourse Hotel

2 Victoria Park (near seafront)
☎ (0292) 262873
11–12 (12.30 Fri & Sat, 12–12 Sun)
McEwan 70/-; Younger No.3 Ⓗ
Tastefully-decorated lounge in impressive sandstone building. Large, central circular fireplace features prominently. Overnight accommodation on ground floor for disabled guests.
⌂ Q ⚲ ⛟ ◖◗ ♿ ⇌ P

Barrhead

Brig Inn

145 Cross Arthurlie Street

☎ (041) 881 1388
11–12 (11.45 Sat, 12.30–2.30; 6.30–11 Sun)
Belhaven 80/- [A]
Popular local, one minute from the station. Two lounges, with beer in the quieter one, as well as the public. Golf, angling and chess clubs.
⌂ Q ◖◗ ⊕ ♿ ≠ ♣ P

Bearsden

Brae Bar
Burnbrae Hotel, Milngavie Road (A81, opp. Allander sports centre) ☎ (041) 942 5951
11 (12.30 Sun)–11 (11.45 Sat)
Broughton Greenmantle 80/- Ale; McEwan 70/-, 80/- [A]; Theakston Best Bitter [H]
The bar is to the left and back of this modern hotel near the Milngavie boundary. It is well used by regulars who appreciate its friendly atmosphere and thriving social scene. Beer can be carried through to the other bars and restaurant.
⊭ ◖ ⛺ ≠ (Hillfoot) P

Beith

Eglinton Arms
48–50 Eglinton Street (B7049 S of centre) ☎ (05055) 2736
11–2.30; 5 (6.30 Sun)–11 (12 Thu & Fri, 1 Sat)
McEwan 80/- [A]
Friendly two-bar pub with lively atmosphere. Separate snug off public. Vegetarians catered for on request. Good views to rear. ❀ ◖ ⊕ P

Bishopton

Golf Inn
28–30 Greenock Road (800 yds from station)
☎ (0505) 862303
11.30–2.30; 5.30–12
Belhaven 80/-; Broughton Old Jock; Courage Directors; Harviestoun Ale, Old Manor [A]
Charming, 19th-century pub with an olde-worlde atmosphere. Q ⊕ ≠ ♣ P

Blantyre

Barnhill Tavern
113 Bardykes Road (B758 between High and Low Blantyre) ☎ (0698) 821916
11–12 (12.30–2.30; 6.30–11 Sun)
Belhaven 80/- [A]
Locals pub with splendid gantry and mirrors, reflecting Scotland's former brewing heritage: two Robert Deucher, a Lorimer & Clark and a George Younger. ⊕ ♿ P

Bothwell

Camphill Vaults
1–3 Main Street
☎ (0698) 853526
11–11.45 (12.30–2.30; 6.30–10.45 Sun)
McEwan 80/- [A]
A fine, traditional pub in a conservation area. One of the few left to retain separate alcoves and sitting rooms off the bar. Children welcome in lounge at lunchtime. Q ⛐ ⊕ ♣

Bridge of Weir

Railway Tavern
Main Street (A761)
☎ (0505) 613228
11–12 (11.45 Sat, 12.30–2.30; 6.30–11 Sun)
Belhaven 80/- [A]
Traditional village local. Real ale available in public and downstairs lounge bar. Pub has direct access from adjacent Glasgow-Kilmacolm cycle path. No food Sun. ❀ ◖ ⊕ ♿ ♣ P

Brodick

Duncans Bar (Kingsley Hotel)
Shore Road ☎ (0770) 2531
11–1 am (11–2.30; 6–12 winter, closed Sun in mid winter)
McEwan 70/- [A]; 80/- [H]
Large, comfortable bar to the side of a waterfront hotel. The hotel and beer garden in front enjoy excellent views across the bay to Goat Fell. Regular jazz and folk nights in summer.
⌂ ❀ ⊭ ◖◗ ♿ ≠ (Brodick Ferryport) P

Ormidale Hotel
☎ (0770) 2293
12–2.30; 4.30 (4 Fri in winter)–12 (11 winter, 12–12 Sat & Sun)
McEwan 70/- [A]
Attractive sandstone building overlooking golf course. The hotel has a welcoming small bar with traditional tall founts atop a bar shaped like half a boat. A large conservatory provides extra space in summer. Lunches served summer only.
⌂ Q ⛐ ❀ ⊭ ◖◗ P

Caldercruix

Railway Tavern (Taylors)
67 Main Street
☎ (0236) 842429
11–11 (12.30–2.30; 6.30–11 Sun)
Belhaven 60/- [A]
Village local across the road from a Beeching-axed railway station. ⌂ ⊕ ♿ ♣ P

Castlecary

Castlecary House Hotel
Main Street (just off A80)
☎ (0324) 840233
11–11 (12.30–3.30; 6.30–11 Sun)
Belhaven 80/-; Broughton Greenmantle 80/- Ale [A]; Harviestoun Ale [H]; Tennent's 80/- [A]; Theakston Best Bitter, Old Peculier [H]
Small, popular village hotel; a former local CAMRA Pub of the Year. Top quality accommodation and meals available. Q ⛐ ❀ ⊭ ◖◗ ⊕ ♿ P

Catacol

Catacol Bay Hotel
☎ (0770) 83231
11–1 am (may close earlier)
Tennent's 80/- [H]
Small, family-run hotel on the rocky north shore of the island, looking across to Argyll. The sometimes lively bar has food available most of the day, including pizzas from a special oven. ⌂ ⛐ ❀ ⊭ ◖◗ P

Coatbridge

Carsons
4–6 Whifflet Street
☎ (0236) 22867
11–11 (12.30–2.30; 6.30–11 Sun)
Broughton Greenmantle Ale [H], 80/- Ale [A]
Whitewashed pub with bar modernised using polished wood throughout. *Bas reliefs* on facing walls depict the pub and a brewery. Beware of low slung barrels. Meals till 6pm. ◖◗ ⊕ ♿

Darvel

Loudounhill Inn
On A71, 1 mile E of Darvel
☎ (0560) 20275
11–12
Broughton Greenmantle Ale [H]
Old coaching inn opposite Loudoun Hill (a prominent landmark and scene of a battle in 1307). ⌂ Q ⛐ ◖◗ ⊕ ♿ P

Dreghorn

Dreghorn Inn
39 Main Street (B7081, old A71, near the cross)
☎ (0294) 211557
11–11 (11.30 Thu–Sat, 12.30–2.30; 6.30–11 Sun)
Younger No.3 [A]
Very lively, friendly, one-bar village local in conservation area in Irvine new town.

Eaglesham

Eglinton Arms
Gilmour Street
☎ (03553) 2631
11–2.30; 5–11 (12 Thu–Sat, 12.30–2.30; 6.30–11 Sun)
McEwan 70/-; Younger No.3 [A]
Popular village hotel. Real ale in the lounge only. ⊭ ◖◗ P

Swan Inn
23 Poldon Street
☎ (03553) 2673
11–2.30; 5–11 (12 Fri & Sat)

McEwan 80/- Ⓐ
Busy local pub with a regular clientele.

Fenwick

Kings Arms
89 Main Road (B7061, just off A77) ☎ (05606) 276464
11–2.30; 5–12 (11–12 Fri & Sat, 12.30–2.30; 6.30–11 Sun)
Younger No.3 Ⓐ
Traditional Scottish village inn on moorland edge. White-painted exterior has half-timbered first floor projection, timber pillared porch and stained glass window. 'Olde-worlde' lounge and separate snug (children welcome). Work of local cartoonist on walls. Disabled access via rear car park. 🍼 ◐ ♿ ♣ P

Giffnock

Macdonald Hotel
Eastwood Toll
11–11 (12 Thu–Sat, 12.30–5; 6.30–11 Sun)
Younger No.3 Ⓐ
Comfortable bar in corner of large Thistle hotel. Separate pool room. ≹ (White Craigs)

Gilmerton

Bow Butts
¼ mile from A71, Darvel-Strathaven road
☎ (0357) 40333
11 (5 Tue)–12 (1 am Fri, 12.30–2.30; 6.30–11 Sun)
Belhaven 80/- Ⓗ
Small, cosy, traditional public bar with large, typical, modern lounge attached. In tiny hamlet. Attracts customers from far and wide and is well-known for food (served until 8.30).
🔥 🍼 ❀ ◐ ◑ ⊞ ♿ ♣ P

Glasgow

Allison Arms
722 Pollokshaws Road (50 yds from station)
☎ (041) 423 1661
11–11 (12.30–2.30; 6.30–11 Sun)
Belhaven 80/- Ⓐ
A fine down-to-earth 'local' with a good, mixed clientele. Quiz nights.
⊞ ≹ (Queens Park) ♣

Babbity Bowsters
16–18 Blackfriars Street (off High Street)
☎ (041) 552 5055
11–12 (12.30–2.30; 6.30–11 Sun)
Maclay 70/-, 80/-, Porter Ⓐ
Smart bar in a fashionable part of town. Recommended food.
🔥 Q ❀ 🛏 ◐ ◑ ⊞ ≹ (High St) ⊖ (Buchanan St) ♣ ⌽ P

Blackfriars
36 Bell Street (corner of Albion Street) ☎ (041) 552 5924
11–12 (12.30–2.30; 6.30–11 Sun)
Alloa Arrol's 80/-; Belhaven 60/-; Tetley Bitter Ⓐ
Wide range of guest beers available in a pub which sells several adult comics.
◐ ◑ ≹ (High St) ⊖ (St Enoch) ⌽

Boswell Hotel
27 Mansionhouse Road, Langside ☎ (041) 632 9812
11–11 (12.30–2.30; 6.30–11 Sun)
Draught Bass Ⓗ; **Belhaven 60/-** Ⓐ, **80/-; Caledonian 80/- Ale** Ⓗ
Favourite haunt of local and not-so-local ale enthusiasts. Nine ales on at all times and up to two ciders. Excellent choice of continental bottled brews.
Q 🍼 ❀ 🛏 ◐ ◑ ≹ (Langside) ⌽ P

Grove Bar
8 Kelvingrove Street (off Sauchiehall Street)
☎ (041) 221 8835
11–11 (12.30–2.30; 6.30–11 Sun)
Belhaven 80/- Ⓔ
'Keep the prices low and pack the public in' is the motto of this famous Glasgow drinking venue. A classic real pub. Snacks at all times.
♿ ≹ (Exhibition Centre) ♣

Lock 27
1100 Crow Road
☎ (041) 958 0853
11–11 (12.30–2.30; 6.30–11 Sun)
McEwan 80/- Ⓐ
Large, busy pub with additional seating on canal towpath. Island bar; interesting pictures. The only real ale in the district. Occasional live music.
❀ ◐ ◑ ♿ ≹ (Anniesland) P

Mitre Bar
12 Brunswick Street
☎ (041) 552 3764
11–11 (closed Sun)
Belhaven 60/-, 80/- Ⓗ
Simply one of the smallest and one of the best. This Victorian pub has been a staunch favourite of real ale drinkers for years. Friendly and relaxed. Good basic food until 8pm.
◐ ◑ ⊞ ≹ (Argyle St) ⊖ (St Enoch)

Quaich
52 Coustonholme Road (opp. station) ☎ (041) 632 9003
11–11 (12.30–2.30; 6.30–11 Sun)
Belhaven 80/- Ⓐ
Busy, inexpensive local on the edge of Shawland shopping area. Good food.
Q ◐ ⊞ ≹ (Pollokshaws E) P

Tennent's
191 Byres Road (Highburgh Road jct)
11–11 (12.30–2.30; 6.30–11 Sun)
Broughton Greenmantle Ale, 80/- Ale; Maclay 80/-; Theakston Best Bitter, XB, Old Peculier Ⓗ
Busy, traditional pub, popular with all sections of the community. Friendly and efficient service. A great improvement in range and quality of beers in the last three years.
◐ ◑ ⊞ ♿ ⊖ (Hillhead)

Ubiquitous Chip
12 Ashton Lane (behind underground station)
☎ (041) 334 5007
11–11 (12.30–2.30; 6.30–11 Sun)
Caledonian 70/- Ale, 80/- Ale Ⓐ
Very busy bar above famous restaurant of the same name. Popular with students and the local arts and literary fraternities. Good bar food until 1am. 🔥 Q ◐ ◑ ⊖ (Hillhead)

Victoria
157–159 Bridgegate (Stockwell Street jct) ☎ (041) 552 6040
11–12 (11.45 Sat, 12.30–2.30; 6.30–11 Sun)
Broughton Greenmantle Ale, 80/- Ale; Maclay 70/-, 80/-; Theakston Best Bitter Ⓐ
One of the most 'Glaswegian' of Glasgow's pubs with strong connections with the local folk music scene. Basic public bar and lounge; tiny toilets. Snacks.
⊞ ≹ (Argyle St) ⊖ (St Enochs)

Gourock

Spinnaker Hotel
121 Albert Road (A8 coastal route) ☎ (0475) 33107
11.30–11.45 (11–12 Sat, 12.30–11 Sun)
Belhaven 80/- Ⓐ
Small, family hotel overlooking the Firth of Clyde. 🛏 ◐ ◑

Houston

Cross Keys
Main Street ☎ (0505) 612209
11–12 (11.45 Sat, 12.30–3; 6.30–11 Sun)
McEwan 80/-; Theakston Best Bitter Ⓗ
Warm, friendly atmosphere in a cosy bar. Candlelight restaurant and downstairs poolroom.
🔥 ❀ ◐ ◑ ⊞ ♿ P

Fox & Hounds
Main Street ☎ (0505) 612248
11–12 (11.45 Sat, 12.30–2.30; 6.30–11 Sun)
Broughton Greenmantle 80/- Ale; McEwan 70/- Ⓐ
Pub with today's comfort and the atmosphere of yesterday.
🍼 ◐ ◑ ⊞ ♿ P

Houston Inn
North Street
☎ (0505) 614315
11 (12 Sun)–12 (1 am Fri, 2 am Sat)
McEwan 80/- Ⓐ; **Theakston Best Bitter** Ⓗ
Warm and cosy lounge; olde-worlde friendly, spacious bar. Food at weekends only.
🍼 ❀ 🛏 ◐ ⊞ ♿ P

Johnstone

Coanes
26 High Street
☎ (0505) 22925
11 (6.30 Sun)–11 (12 Thu & Fri, 11.45 Sat)
Broughton Greenmantle Ale; Marston's Pedigree Bitter; Tennent's 80/- Ⓐ
Cosy town-centre pub with a relaxed atmosphere. Regular rotation of three cask 80/-, plus excellent range of English guest beers. See the 'Coannection' board for details. ⧗ ⊞ ⇌ (High)

Kilbarchan

Trust Inn
8 Low Barholm (main road)
☎ (05057) 2401
11–2.30; 5–11.30 (11–12 Thu, 11–1 am Fri, 11–11.45 Sat, 12.30–2.30; 6.30–11 Sun)
Alloa Arrol's 80/-; Ind Coope Burton Ale; Tetley Bitter Ⓐ & Ⓗ
Olde-worlde pub with an atmosphere to match. Two of above beers at anytime, plus occasional Alloa guests. Handy for visitors to Weaver's Cottage. Future plans include new conservatory and family facilities. No food Sun lunch. ⧗ ◗ ⇌ (Miliken Park) ♣

Kilmarnock

Gordon's Lounge
17 Fowlds Street (ring road)
☎ (0563) 42122
11–11 (12 Fri & Sat, 12.30–2.30; 6.30–11 Sun)
Belhaven 80/- Ⓐ
Large-ish lounge at south end of town centre. A former granary attracting a good mix of customers. Generous portions of good food, including veg and children's menus. ⧗ ◗ ⇌

Kilmun

Coylet
On A815, 9 miles N of Dunoon ☎ (036984) 426
11–2.30; 5–11 (12 Fri & Sat, 12.30–2.30; 6.30–11 Sun)
McEwan 80/-; Younger No.3 Ⓐ
Welcoming lochside pub with good food. The water engine is no longer used since the water pressure from the mountain broke it! ♔ ♉ ❀ ⛟ ⧗ ◗ Å P

Lanark

Wallace Cave
11 Bloomgate (off main street)
☎ (0555) 3662
11–2 am (11.45 Sat, 12.30–2.30; 6.30–11 Sun)
Broughton Greenmantle Ale Ⓐ
200 year-old pub with some original windows. The name commemorates William Wallace's escape from the English, through the caves and tunnels beneath the pub. Snacks and pizzas. ⊞ ♿ ⇌

Largs

Clachan
14 Bath Street (B7025, just off A78) ☎ (0475) 672224
11–12 (12.30–2.30; 6.30–11 Sun)
Belhaven 70/-, 80/- Ⓐ
Cheery and popular, single-bar pub in a side-street just behind the seafront. Very busy at weekends with young people. 70/- not always available.
⧗ ♿ ⇌

Sheiling
144 Main Street (A78)
☎ (0475) 676171
11–12 (12.30–2.30; 6.30–11 Sun)
Belhaven 80/- Ⓗ
Busy pub with small lounge. Photographs of Clyde shipping adorn the walls of the public bar. ⊞ ♿ ⇌

Lochranza

Lochranza Hotel
☎ (0770) 83223
11–1 am (11–2.30; 5–12 (12.30–2.30; 6.30–12 Sun) in winter)
McEwan 80/- Ⓗ
Family hotel in attractive village with fine views across the loch. Relaxed, friendly bar with good meals. Handy for Kintyre ferry and passing yatchsmen.
♔ Q ♉ ❀ ⛟ ⧗ ◗ ⊞ Å ♣ P

Oban

Lorne Hotel
Stevenson Street
☎ (0631) 66766
11–1 am
McEwan 80/- Ⓐ**; Theakston Best Bitter** Ⓗ**; Younger No.3** Ⓐ
Large, busy, single-bar pub with a youngish clientele and efficient staff. Lunches served 12–3 (not Sun). ❀ ⧗ ♿ Å ⇌

Oban Inn
1 Stafford Street
11–12.45 am
McEwan 80/-; Younger No.3 Ⓐ
Oban's best-known beer-drinking pub, overlooking the harbour. Traditional public bar at street level. The lounge upstairs has a bit more atmosphere than most. No meals Sun. ⧗ ⊞ ⇌

Paisley

Buddies
23 Broomlands Street (½ mile W of Paisley Cross)
☎ (041) 8895314
11–11 (12 Thu & Fri, 11.45 Sat, 12.30–2.30; 6.30–11 Sun)
Belhaven 80/- Ⓗ
A friendly welcome is assured in this fine corner pub. Golf, angling and Paisley's only pub chess club. ⧗ ◗ ⊞ ♣

Bull Inn
7 New Street (off High Street)
☎ (041) 8878545
11–12 (1 am Fri, 11.45 Sat, 7–11 Sun)
Belhaven 80/- Ⓐ
Traditional, untouched pub on Paisley Heritage Trail—wood panelled walls in bar and snugs at back. Food served 12–2.30, when children are welcome. Separate lounge; satellite TV in bar. Q ⧗ ⊞ ⇌ (Gilmour St)

Lord Loundsdale
37 Loundsdale Road (from centre, follow signs for Johnstone then Foxbar)
☎ (041) 8896263
11–10.45 (11.45 Fri & Sat, 12.30–2.30; 6.30–11 Sun)
Belhaven 80/- Ⓐ
Pleasant, mock olde-worlde interior includes wooden cask tables. Lunches served in main lounge/bar area; drinks from large accessible bar. Neat patio for summer. ♔ ❀ ⧗ ◗ ♿ P

Wee Howff
53 High Street
☎ (041) 8892095
11–11 (11.30 Fri & Sat, closed Sun)
Alloa Arrol's 80/-; Ind Coope Burton Ale; Tetley Bitter Ⓗ
Traditional Scottish town-centre bar with genuinely friendly staff. Guest beers. ⇌ (Gilmour St)

Prestwick

Butlers House Hotel
132 Main Street (A79)
☎ (0292) 77566
11–12 (1 am Fri & Sat, 12.30–12.30 Sun)
Younger No.3 Ⓗ
Modern town-centre hotel. Real ale in the 'overdraught' bar but supplied to the comfortable lounge on request. Live televised English football matches Sun afternoons.
❀ ⛟ ⧗ ◗ ⊞ ♿ ⇌ P

Parkstone Hotel
Central Esplanade
☎ (0292) 77286
11–12.30 (1 am Fri & Sat)
Belhaven 80/- Ⓗ
Popular seafront hotel with modernised bar.
♔ Q ❀ ⛟ ⧗ ♿ ⇌ P

Try also: Red Lion (McEwan)

Renfrew

Ferry Inn
Ferry Road ☎ (041) 886 2104
11–11 (12 Fri, 11.45 Sat, 12.30–2.30; 6.30–11 Sun)
Belhaven 80/- Ⓗ
Next to Renfrew ferry slipway and popular with ferry crews.

Over 200 years old, the pub has fine pictures of the River Clyde in its heyday. Special feature nights and occasional mini beer festivals. ♣

Rhu

Ardencaple Hotel
Shore Road (A814)
☎ (0436) 820200
11–12 (11 Sun)
Tetley Bitter Ⓗ
Attractive, whitewashed hotel, popular with passing tourist trade. Paddle steamer pictures in public bar. Fine view of Gareloch – ideal for submarine spotting! Children welcome in conservatory. P

Rhu Inn
Gareloch Road (A814)
☎ (0436) 821048
11–12 (12.30–2.30; 6.30–11 Sun)
Broughton Greenmantle Ale Ⓐ
Small local near the village green with lounge, public bar, snug and drinking corridor. Very popular; can get extremely busy at times. Pictures of old Rhu in public bar. Children welcome in snug. P

Seamill

Glenbryde Hotel
7 Glenbryde Road (off A78 opp. Seamill hydro)
☎ (0294) 822996
12–2.30; 5–1 (12–1 Sat, 12.30–1 Sun)
McEwan 80/- Ⓗ
Cosy lounge in part of converted 19th-century flax mill. Main feature in bar is large fish tank above gantry, stocked with several tropical species. Name has reverted to original (from Glenboyd). P

Taynuilt

Station Tap
Old Station Brewery (on Glasgow-bound platform)
☎ (08662) 242
11–3; 5–11 (4.30–1 Fri, 12.30–2.30; 6.30–11 Sun, 11–1 am Sat & summer)
Alloa Arrol's 80/-; Ind Coope Burton Ale; West Highland HDL, Highland Heavy, Highland Severe Ⓗ
Converted station waiting room which serves as brewery tap for West Highland brewery. A lively public bar which opened in 1989 and has the atmosphere of a hostelry a century old. It would be handy for the trains if the timetable was improved! ♣ P

Troon

Anchorage Hotel
149 Templehill (B749)
☎ (0292) 317448
11–12 (1 am Fri & Sat)
Broughton Greenmantle Ale, 80/-; Caledonian 70/- Ale; Tetley Bitter; Theakston Best Bitter, Old Peculier Ⓗ
Ayrshire's real ale flagship, with an increased range and a new raised seating area. Appropriate nautical theme for its harbourside location. Miss at your peril! Up to three guest beers. Children welcome until 9.30pm. P

Harbour Bar
169 Templehill (B749)
☎ (0292) 312668
11–12.30 (1 Fri, 12 Sat, 11–2.30; 6.30–11 Sun)
Maclay 80/-, Porter Ⓐ
Friendly local near marina, with open views to the Firth of Clyde. Welcome return of real ale to an old favourite. ♣ P

Twechar

Quarry Inn
Main Street ☎ (0236) 821496
11–11 (1 am Fri, 11.30 Sat, 12.30–2.30; 6.30–11 Sun)
Maclay 60/-, 70/-, 80/- Ⓗ
Pot-bellied stoves, oak-panelled walls and a rare Maclay's mirror make this village local well worth seeking out. Petanque played. Q ♣ P

Uddingston

Rowan Tree
60 Old Mill Road (next to Tunnocks bakery)
☎ (0698) 812678
11–11.45 (12.30–2.30; 7–11 Sun)
Maclay 70/-, 80/-, Porter Ⓐ
Outstanding public bar with two smaller rooms off, one is a lounge, while the other is used for games, live folk music, etc. The finest pub architecture in the Maclay tied estate.

Uplawmoor

Uplawmoor Hotel
½ mile off A736
☎ (050585) 505
11–11.30 (12 Thu, 12.30 Fri & Sat, 12.30–2.30; 6.30–11 Sun)
Theakston Best Bitter Ⓗ
Country hotel in rural village. Menu caters for children and vegetarians. ♣ P

Whiting Bay

Cameronia Hotel
☎ (07707) 254
11 (12 winter)–2.30; 5 (6 winter)–11
Broughton Greenmantle Ale Ⓗ
Comfortable, small hotel with extensive views over to Holy Isle and across the Firth. Snug little bar opens onto larger lounge and dining area.
Q

Heriot Tennent's 80/-

At the time of going to press, the future of Heriot Tennent's 80/- is in considerable doubt. Draught Bass has been test marketed in Edinburgh with success and it now looks as if this national beer is to be made available throughout Scotland. If this happens, it is likely that it will displace 80/- and the Heriot brew will become another Lost Beer. Pubs listed as selling 80/- may well turn to Draught Bass during the currency of this guide.

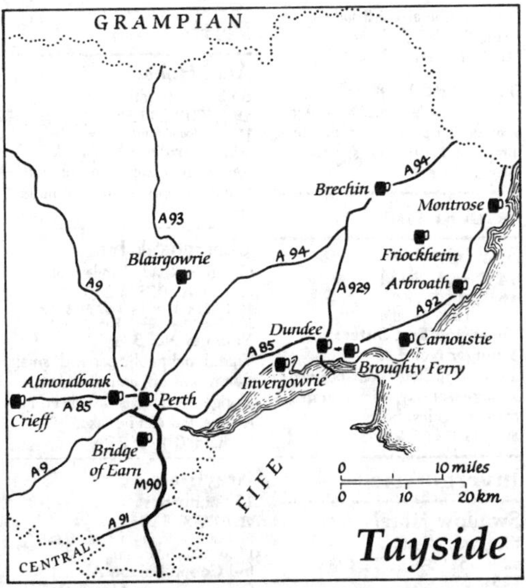

International, but friendly golfing hotel overlooking championship course. Recommended food.
Q P

Crieff

Oakbank Inn
Turret Bridge (off A85, W of town) ☎ (0764) 2420
11–11 (11.45 Fri & Sat, restricted hours off-season)
Ind Coope Burton Ale [H]
Pleasant, modern pub near Glenturret Distillery. Food till 9pm. Note the ancient oak tree in garden. ♣ P

Dundee

Breadalbane Arms
Constitution Road
11–12
Younger No. 3 [A]
Popular Dundee howff, forerunner of the modern civilized pub. No food Sun.
Q (Tay Bridge)

McGonagalls
142–146 Perth Road
☎ (0382) 22392
11–12 (12.30–2.30; 6.30–11 Sun)
Ind Coope Burton Ale; McEwan 70/- [H] **80/-** [A]**; Theakston Best Bitter** [H]
Comfortable bar with pioneering real ale landlord. Directly opposite the art college, it attracts a mixed clientele, and can get very busy during term-time. Named after Dundee's famous (bad) poet.

Mercantile
Commercial Street
11–11
McEwan 80/-; Maclay 80/-; Theakston Best Bitter [H]
Excellent reconstruction of a Victorian bar from a former warehouse. Imaginative menu in integrated no-smoking restaurant.

Mickey Coyles
Hawkhill (near West Port)
☎ (0382) 25871
11–11.30
Broughton Greenmantle Ale; Younger No. 3 [A]
Refurbished bar, named after eponymous erstwhile owner. Busy during term-time. No food Sun. (Tay Bridge)

Phoenix
105 Nethergate
☎ (0382) 200014
11–12 (12.30–2.30; 6.30–11 Sun)
Broughton Greenmantle Ale; Taylor Landlord; Theakston Old Peculier [H]
Lively town bar with salvaged Victorian back bar and screens. Run by an innovative landlord. Extensive range of bottled beers, many Belgian styles. Can get packed. Guest beers.

Almondbank

Almondbank Inn
31 Main Street (off A85)
☎ (0738) 83242
11–2.30; 5–11 (11–11.30 Fri & Sat, 12.30–2.30; 6–11 Sun)
Broughton Greenmantle Ale [A]
Modernised village pub with a reputation for good food; veg and children's options available. Children welcome in lounge.
♣

Arbroath

Corner Bar
2 Howard Street
☎ (0241) 73583
11–11 (12.30–2.30 only Sun)
McEwan 80/- [A]
Busy popular street-corner local. Lunchtime snacks.

Lochlands Bar
14 Lochlands Street (200 yds from station) ☎ (0241) 73286
11–12; (closed Sun eve in winter)
McEwan 80/-; Younger No. 3 [A]
Welcoming wood-panelled bar with Burnley FC and Orkney connections! ♣

Blairgowrie

Stormont Arms
101 Perth Road
☎ (0250) 3142
11–2.30; 5–11 (11–11.45 Fri & Sat, 12.30–2.30; 5.30–11 Sun)
Belhaven 80/- [A]
A traditional drinking man's pub, with a friendly atmosphere.
Q

Brechin

Dalhousie Bar
1 Market Street
☎ (035 62) 2096
11–12 (1 Fri, 12.30–2.30; 6.30–11 Sun)
Belhaven 80/- [H]
A basic but welcoming pub with original horseshoe bar. Exceptionally friendly owners and locals who have been instrumental in introducing cask beer to the keg wastes of the Angus area. ♣

Bridge of Earn

Cyprus Inn
Back Street (off Main Street)
☎ (0738) 812313
11–2.30; 5–11 (4.30–11.45 Fri, 11–11.45 Sat, 12.30–2.30; 6.30–11 Sun)
Belhaven 80/- [H]
200 year-old inn in quiet street, offering a warm welcome.

Broughty Ferry

Fisherman's Tavern
12 Fort Street
☎ (0382) 75941
11–12 (12.30–2.30; 7–11 Sun)
Belhaven 80/-; McEwan 80/-; Maclay 80/-; Theakston Best Bitter [H]**; Younger No. 3** [A]
Cosy, traditional, low-ceilinged pub, near lifeboat station, now offering *haute cuisine* and accommodation. Very popular. Guest beers. Eve meals 5–7pm.
Q

Carnoustie

Glencoe Hotel
Links Parade (opp. golf course)
☎ (0241) 53273
11–2.30; 5–11
Maclay 80/- [A]

Tayside

Shakespeare Bar
267 Hilltown
☎ (0382) 21454
11–12
Belhaven 80/- [A]
Plain, honest bar, handy for both Dundee Premier League football grounds. Guest beers.
⊞ ♣

Speedwell Bar (Mennies)
165 Perth Road
☎ (0382) 67783
11–2.30; 5–11 (11.30 Wed & Thu, 12 Fri, 11–12 Sat, 12.30–2.30; 7–11 Sun)
Belhaven 80/-; Ind Coope Burton Ale [H]**; McEwan 80/-; Orkney Raven Ale** [A]
Well-maintained Edwardian bar boasting fine etched glass and woodwork, L-shaped bar and two sitting rooms, one for non-smokers. Raven Ale is not always available. Q ⊞

Tally Ho
7–11 Hawkhill (West Port area)
☎ (0382) 28500
11–12
Belhaven 80/-, 90/- [H]**; Broughton Greenmantle Ale; Courage Directors; Tetley Bitter** [A]
Restyled busy, olde-worlde pub near university. Favoured by students, journos, musicos and the legal profession. No food Sun.
⌂ ♨ ❀ ◖ ◗ ♿ ⇌ (Tay Bridge) P

Willy Frew's
117 Strathmartine Road (at 'Five Roads' jct)
☎ (0382) 810975
11–11.45
Tennent's 80/- [H]
Wood-panelled corner bar with stained glass windows, ornate fireplace, gantry and sporting prints. ⊞ ♿ ♣

Friockheim

Star Inn
14 Gardyne Street
☎ (02412) 248
11–11 (12.30–11 Sun)
Theakston Best Bitter; Younger No. 3 [H]
Two-bar hostelry; oak-beamed and horsebrassy, with gourmet cooking. Guest beers.
⌂ Q ♨ ❀ ⛼ ◖ ◗ ⊞ ♿ ⍥

Invergowrie

Swallow Hotel
Kingsway West
☎ (0382) 641122
11–11
Alloa Arrol's 80/- [A]
Comfortable bar in luxury hotel with leisure facilities.
Q ⛼ ◖ ◗ ♿ P

Montrose

Salutation Inn
65 Bridge Street
☎ (0674) 72832
11–12
Younger No. 3 [A]
Busy local with good selection of whiskies. ❀ ◖ ◗ ⊞ ⇌ ♣

Perth

Auld Hoose
83 South Street
☎ (0738) 24136
11–11 (closed Sun)
Alloa Arrol's 80/- [H]
Refurbished Victorian pub with island bar and colourful ceiling.
⇌

Cherrybank Inn
Glasgow Road (1 mile S of centre) ☎ (0738) 24349
11–2.30; 4–11 (11–11.30 Fri & Sat, 12.30–2.30; 6.30–11 Sun)
Younger No. 3 [A]
Traditional public bar with small side rooms off, and a modern lounge. Real ale is dispensed in lounge, but can be taken through. ◖ ⊞ ♣ P

Greyfriars
15 South Street
☎ (0738) 33036
11–2.30; 7–11 (11–11.45 Fri & Sat, 12.30–2.30; 7–11 Sun)
Ind Coope Burton Ale; Orkney Raven Ale; Tetley Bitter [H]
Small but welcoming city pub with restaurant upstairs. Good range of foreign bottled beers. Guest ales. ◖ ◗ ⇌

Old Ship Inn
Skinnergate ☎ (0738) 24929
11–2.30; 5–11 (11–11.45 Fri & Sat, closed Sun)
Alloa Arrol's 80/-; Tetley Bitter [H]
Historic pub with ancient inn sign displayed in bar. ⊞ ⇌

Graeme Falconer, former Managing Director of Drybroughs, with two more Scottish Lost Beers

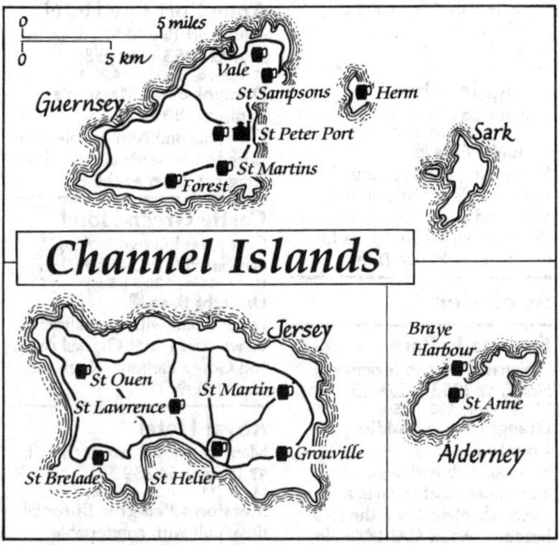

Guernsey, Randalls, St Peter Port

Alderney

Braye Harbour

Moorings Hotel
☎ (048 182) 2421
11–midnight (12–2; 8–midnight Sun)
Guernsey Real Draught Bitter [H]
Enterprising hotel with good bar snacks and separate restaurant (no food Wed eve).

St Anne

Coronation Inn
36 High Street
☎ (048 182) 2630
10 am–1 am (midnight Sat & winter, 12–2; 8–midnight Sun)
Randalls Best Bitter [G]
Unspoilt town local with a welcoming atmosphere.

Guernsey

Forest

Deerhound Inn
Le Bourg (main road, near airport) ☎ (0481) 38585
11.30–2; 6–11.45 (12–2.30; 7–10.30 Sun for meals)
Guernsey Real Draught Bitter [H]
Welcoming, cosy country inn of character; restaurant and bar meals. P

St Martins

Captains Hotel
La Fosse ☎ (0481) 38990
11–11.30 (closed Sun)
Guernsey Real Draught Bitter [H]
Attractive hotel lounge with upstairs restaurant. Handy for Moulin Huet and Saints Bays. Closed Sun, except for residents. P

Greenacres Hotel
Les Hubits ☎ (0481) 35711
12–11.45 (12–2.30; 7.30–10.30 Sun for meals)
Guernsey Real Draught Bitter [H]
Pleasant lounge bar in country hotel. Bar meals recommended. Non-residents admitted Sun only if dining. P

L'Auberge Divette
Jerbourg ☎ (0481) 38485
10.30–11 (closed Sun)
Guernsey LBA Mild, Real Draught Bitter [H]
Excellent country pub on cliff-bound peninsula. Commands panoramic views from lounge and garden. Handy for the cliff paths. P

St Peter Port

La Collinette Hotel (Bear Bar)
St Jacques ☎ (0481) 710331
12–2.30; 5–11.30 (closed Sun)
Guernsey Grizzly's Real Ale [H]
Comfortable hotel lounge bar, located on north-western edge of town. Grizzly's Real Ale is exclusive to the hotel. Closed Sun except for residents. P

Plough Inn
Vauvert ☎ (0481) 20599
10.30–2; 4.30–11 (10.30–11 Sat, closed Sun)
Guernsey LBA Mild [H]
Traditional Guernsey local, near the old quarter of town.

Salerie Inn
Salerie Corner
☎ (0481) 724484
10.30–11 (closed Sun)
Guernsey LBA Mild, Real Draught Bitter [H]
Plush lounge with strong nautical theme, recently rebuilt and enlarged. Car park opposite.

Ship & Crown
Esplanade ☎ (0481) 21368
10.30–11 (closed Sun)
Guernsey Real Draught Bitter [H]
Busy town pub, popular with the yachting fraternity. Ask for real ale.

Thomas de la Rue
The Pollet ☎ (0481) 714990
10.30–11
Guernsey Real Draught Bitter [H]
Split-level pub with public bar beneath the remodelled lounge. Lots of bric-a-brac and memorabilia of the famous banknote printer who set-up business on this very site.

Try also: Britannia; Golden Lion

St Sampsons

Pony Inn
Les Capelles ☎ (0481) 44374
10.30–11 (closed Sun)
Guernsey LBA Mild, Real Draught Bitter [H]
Large and popular pub close to Guernsey Candles and Oatlands Craft Centre. P

Vale

Hampshire Lodge
Rue Mainguy ☎ (0481) 57230
10.30–11 (12–2.30 Sun for meals, closed eve)
Guernsey LBA Mild [H]
Busy local near the island scout headquarters. Separate restaurant recently added. Open Sun lunch for diners only.
P

Herm

Mermaid Tavern
☎ (0481) 710710
10.30–11 (closed Sun)
Guernsey Real Draught Bitter [H]
Busy pub which provides a welcome relief after a walk around the island! The garden is a suntrap.

Channel Isles

Jersey

Grouville

Pembroke
Grouville coast road
☎ (0534) 55756
10–11 (11–1; 4.30–11 Sun)
Draught Bass [H]
Friendly local bar with spacious lounge, adjacent to Royal Jersey Golf Club and the beach; one mile from Mont Orgueil castle. Children's menu available (no food Sun, or Mon eve).
⛫ ♉ ⛃ ◖ ◗ ⊟ ♣ P

Seymour Inn
La Rocque (Gorey coast road)
☎ (0534) 54558
10–11 (11–1; 4.30–11 Sun)
Guernsey LBA Mild, Real Draught Bitter [H]
Recently extended to include a real ale bar; very comfortable. Excellent, good value food (not Sun). ⛫ ♉ ⛃ ◖ ◗ ⊟ ♣ P

St Brelade

La Pulente Hotel
La Pulente (extreme S end of five mile road)
☎ (0534) 41760
10–11 (11–1; 4.30–11 Sun)
Draught Bass [H]
Unspoilt local fisherman's bar and cosy lounge at southern end of St Ouen's Bay, overlooking the beach. Ideal for view with beautiful sunsets. Eve meals summer only (no food Sun). ⛫ Q ♉ ⛃ ◖ ◗ ⊟ ♣ P

Old Portelet Inn
Portelet Bay ☎ (0534) 41899
11–11 (11–1; 4.30–11 Sun)
Draught Bass; Marston's Pedigree Bitter [H]
17th-century, timber-beamed farmhouse in superb position above Portelet Bay beach. Four separate bars. Menu and large area for children.
♉ ⛃ ◖ ◗ ⊟ ♣ P

Smugglers Inn
Ouaisne Bay ☎ (0534) 41510
11–11 (11–1; 4.30–11 Sun)
Draught Bass [H]
Welcoming old inn, very close to the sands at Ouaisne Bay. Cosy and warm atmosphere. Well-known locally for its food (not Sun). ⛫ ♉ ◖ ◗ ⊟ ♣

St Helier

Esplanade Bars
Esplanade (next to Swansons Hotel) ☎ (0534) 22925
10–11 (11–1; 4.30–11 Sun)
Draught Bass; Ruddles County [H]
Spacious pub with a good atmosphere that attracts a mixed clientele. Long the local headquarters of CAMRA. No food Sun. ♉ ◖ ◗ ♣

Peirson
Royal Square ☎ (0534) 22726
10–11 (11–1; 4.30–11 Sun)
Draught Bass [H]
Historic pub opposite the seat of Government in Royal Square. Scars of the Battle of Jersey still to be seen on the walls. No food Sun. ◖ ⊟

St Lawrence

British Union Hotel
Main road (opp. parish church)
☎ (0534) 61070
10.30–11 (11–1; 4.30–11 Sun)
Guernsey LBA Mild, Real Draught Bitter [H]
A real family pub where children are positively welcomed in both lounges. Very much a locals' haunt, with excellent good value food (not Sun). ♉ ⛃ ◖ ◗ ⊟ ♣

St Martin

Anne Port Bay Hotel
Anne Port Bay (200 yds from bay) ☎ (0534) 52058
11–2.30; 5–11 (11–1; 4.30–11 Sun)
Draught Bass; Marston's Pedigree Bitter [H]
Convivial and comfortable hotel close to the beach at Anne Port. Snug bar. Q ♉ ⛟ ◖ ◗ P

Castle Green Hotel
Gorey (on hill overlooking harbour) ☎ (0534) 53103
11–11 (11–1; 4.30–11 Sun)
Draught Bass [G]
Popular pub with magnificent views over Mont Orgueil castle and Gorey harbour. No meals Sun. ◖ ⊟ ♣

Royal Hotel
Main road (opp. parish church)
☎ (0534) 56289
11–11 (11–1; 4.30–11 Sun)
Marston's Pedigree Bitter [H]
Busy pub with comfortable lounge bar. Food in bar or upstairs restaurant with pew-style seating. Children's menu.
⛃ ◖ ◗ ⊟ ♣ P

Rozel Bay Inn
Rozel Bay
☎ (0534) 63438
10–11 (11–1; 4.30–11 Sun)
Draught Bass [H]
Cosy pub situated at the bottom of a picturesque valley in an attractive fishing village. The quaint harbour of Rozel is close by. No food Sun. ⛫ ♉ ◖ ⊟ P

St Ouen

Le Moulin de Lecq
Greve de Lecq Bay
☎ (0534) 82818
11–11 (11–1; 4.30–11 Sun)
Draught Bass; Guernsey LBA Mild, Real Draught Bitter [H]
16th-century working watermill close to the beach. Popular Jersey dishes served. Large children's play area. No food Sun. ⛫ Q ♉ ⛃ ◖ ◗ P

DISPENSE METHODS

[G] by gravity straight from the cask
[H] by handpump
[E] by electric pump
[A] by air pressure (including electric air compressor in Scotland)

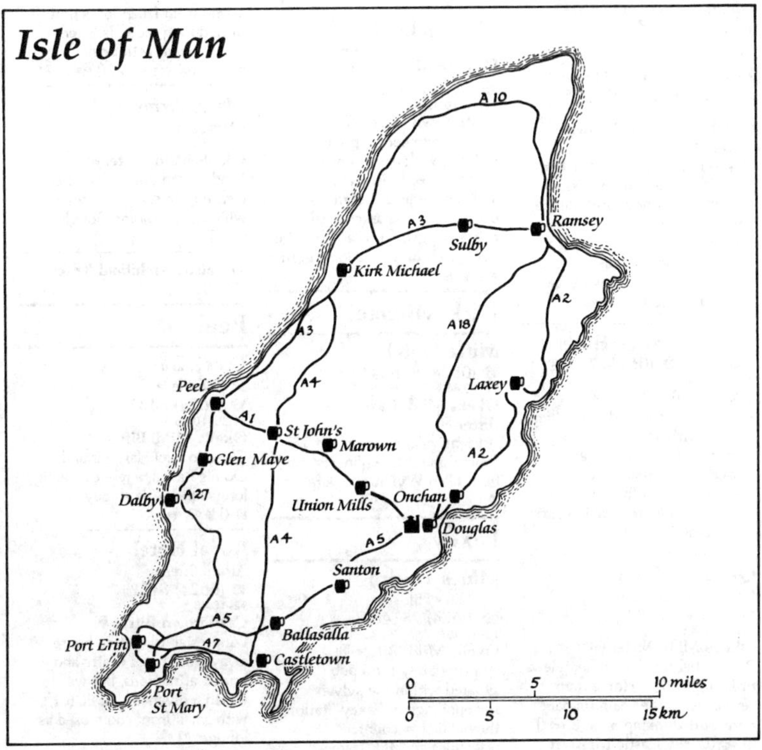

Isle of Man Breweries, Douglas

Ballasalla

Whitestone Inn
☎ (0624) 822334
12–10.45
Okells Mild, Bitter Ⓗ
The burgeoning financial and aviation circles frequent the comfortable lounges of the Whitestone, but the less upwardly-inclined individual may escape to the far-from-spartan public bar. ◖ ⊞ ♿ ♣ P

Try also: Rushen Abbey Hotel (Free)

Castletown

Castle Arms (Glue Pot)
Opp. castle entrance
☎ (0624) 824673
11.30–10.45
Okells Mild, Bitter Ⓗ
Small and comfortable one-room pub, convenient for visitors to Castle Rushen. Close to harbour. Q

Duck's Nest Hotel
Station Road
☎ (0624) 823282
11.30–10.45
Okells Mild, Bitter Ⓗ
First port of call for travellers coming to Castletown by steam train. A friendly free house (recently sold by the brewery). Busy in evening with locals. Easy street parking. ◖ ⇌

Try also: Ship Inn (Okells)

Dalby

Ballacallin Hotel
☎ (0624) 842030
12–10.45
Castletown Bitter Ⓗ
Go-ahead, well-appointed free house, with magnificent views at sunset over the Irish Sea. Quality pub catering lunchtimes and evening; Sun lunch served in dining room. ⛪ ⋈ ◖ ◗ P

Douglas

Bushy's Brew Pub
Victoria Street
☎ (0624) 75139
12–10.45
Bushy's Bitter, Old Bushy Tail Ⓗ
Increasingly popular free house in former Yates's Wine Lodge premises. Beers are brewed in the cellar. The pub has been adopted by the younger drinker and can be very busy in the evening. 'Gigs' often take place in concert room (admission charge). Parking difficult.
◖ ◗ ⊞ ♣

Foresters Arms Hotel
St George's Street
☎ (0624) 76509
11.30–10.45
Okells Mild, Bitter Ⓗ
Surrounded by re-development in the expanding Douglas financial sector, Foresters survives, untouched by modernisation. Visit while you can. Daytime parking difficult.
⛪ ⊞

Manor Hotel
Willaston (centre of large corporation housing estate)
☎ (0624) 76957
11.30–10.45
Okells Mild, Castletown Bitter Ⓗ
Former manor house manifesting its origins in its well-furnished, panelled lounge. There is also a large public bar. Customers are drawn from the local estate, and from the nearby college of further

education. Not on tourist routes. ⛫ ◐ ⊕ ♣ P

Old Market Inn
Chapel Row ☎ (0624) 75202
11.30–10.45
Okells Mild, Castletown Bitter Ⓗ
A survivor from the era when dozens of licensed premises served the harbour area. As yet totally untouched by modernisation, and offering no catering service to distract the dedicated drinker. Beware low doorway to gents! ⛫ ⊕

Quarterbridge Hotel
Peel Road ☎ (0624) 75571
11.30–10.45
Okells Mild, Bitter Ⓗ
Large, multi-roomed pub which is alive with activity during motor-cycle races, not least because it is situated at a well-known bend on the TT course. About 20 minutes' walk from town centre. ◐ ⊕ P

Queen's Hotel
Queen's Promenade
☎ (0624) 75543
11.30–10.45
Okells Mild, Bitter Ⓗ
Residential hotel with fine views of Douglas Bay. Horse-tram service from the sea terminal. Forecourt drinking area. ❀ ⛟ ◐ ⊕ ≹ (Derby Castle MER) ♣

Ridgeway Hotel
Ridgeway Street
☎ (0624) 75612
12–10.45
Okells Mild, Bitter Ⓗ
Town-centre pub with concert room for live entertainment. Parking difficult. ◐ ♣

Waterloo Hotel
Strand Street ☎ (0624) 76833
11.30–10.45
Okells Mild, Bitter Ⓗ
Close the door behind you and forget the raucous sound of amusement arcades and the pungent aroma of take-away beefburgers in the busy pedestrian street outside. ⊕

Woodbourne Hotel
Alexander Drive
☎ (0624) 76754
12–10.45
Okells Mild, Bitter Ⓗ
Imposing brick edifice in uptown Douglas with several bars (public bar has a separate side-entrance), including an unusual men-only bar. But there is ample provision for the other 50% of the population! Q ◐ ⊕ ♣

Try also: Clarendon Hotel, Old Curiosity Shop, Wheatsheaf (Okells)

Glen Maye

Waterfall Hotel
☎ (0624) 842238
11.30–10.45
Castletown Bitter Ⓗ
Attractive meeting-point for walkers, with easy rambles in several directions. Attractive and comfortable accommodation, and upmarket meals – the nearest thing to a 'Cheshire pub', according to a local guru. ❀ ◐ ◗ ⊕ P

Kirk Michael

Mitre Hotel
☎ (0624) 878244
12–10.45
Okells Mild, Castletown Bitter Ⓗ
Ancient village inn on the TT course, about five minutes' walk from Glen Wyllin campsite. ⛫ ◐ ⅄ ♣ ⌽

Laxey

Mines Tavern
Captain's Hill
☎ (0624) 781484
12–10.45
Okells Mild, Bitter Ⓗ
Appropriately for a pub situated within the sylvan surroundings of Laxey Station, the public bar counter resembles an MER tramcar. There are many railway and mining relics and pictures displayed throughout the pub. ❀ ◐ ⊕ ≹

Queen's Hotel
New Road ☎ (0624) 781195
12–10.45
Castletown Bitter Ⓗ
Recently bought from the brewery by the licensee and soon to be extended and renovated. The brewery has disposed of several pubs in this way after a change of policy. Lunchtime meals planned. ♣ P

Marown

Waggon & Horses
On main Douglas–Peel road, just W of Crosby
☎ (0624) 851291
11–10.45
Okells Mild, Bitter Ⓗ
Commodious and well-kept rural hostelry with large lounge bar; separate pool room. ◐ ♣ P

Try also: Crosby Hotel (Okells)

Onchan

Keppel Gate Hotel
Creg-ny-Baa ☎ (0624) 76548
12–10.45
Castletown Bitter Ⓗ
Famous TT vantage point, with access from Laxey direction only during races. Isolated country pub with open moorland views. ⛫ ◐ ♣ P

Manx Arms
Main Road
12–10.45
Okells Mild, Bitter Ⓗ
Modernised pub, situated at the centre of this large village, which now adjoins Douglas. ◐ ⊕ P

Try also: Archibald Knox (Okells)

Peel

Creek Inn
Station Place
☎ (0624) 842216
11.30–10.45
Okells Mild, Bitter Ⓗ
Close to Peel Harbour and Odin's Raven, a replica Viking longship. Meals all day. ⛫ ◐ ◗ ⊕ ♣

Royal Hotel
Atholl Street
☎ (0624) 842217
12–10.45
Castletown Bitter Ⓗ
Long-established free house away from town centre and tourist attractions, but well worth a diversion. Basic bar, with small front room used as lounge. ⊕ ♣

Try also: Peveril (Okells); **White House** (Okells)

Port Erin

Falcon's Nest
Station Road
12–10.45
Okells Mild, Bitter Ⓗ
Comfortable lounge which, from its elevated position, gives the customer a fine view of Port Erin Bay and Bradda Head. ⛟ ◐ ≹

Haven
Station Road ☎ (0624) 834030
11.30–10.45
Okells Mild, Castletown Bitter Ⓗ
Spacious, modern hostelry, with lounge very much in the fashionable 'café-bar' style. The public bar, however, is of high standard and is less likely to upset the more traditional imbiber. ⛫ ◐ ⊕ ♿ ≹ ♣ P

Try also: Station Hotel (Okells)

Port St Mary

Station Hotel
☎ (0624) 832249
12–10.45
Okells Mild, Castletown Bitter Ⓗ
Residential hotel outside village,

and about 10 minutes' walk from the beach. Adjacent to station, as its name informs.
⌂ ⛟ ◖ ⊟ ♣ P

Try also: Bay View Hotel (Okells)

Ramsey

Bridge Inn
Bowring Road
☎ (0624) 813248
11.30–10.45
Okells Mild, Bitter [H]
Good, basic drinker's pub, with both bars boasting interesting old photographs, enlarged to great effect. ⊟

Royal Hotel
Market Place
☎ (0624) 812146
11.30–10.45
Okells Mild, Castletown Bitter [H]
The spacious and well-furnished lounge expresses the latest 'café-bar' style, but a separate public bar is provided. ◖ ⊟

Try also: Plough (Okells)

St John's

Tynwald Hill Inn
☎ (0624) 71249
12–10.45
Okells Mild, Bitter [H]
The bar overlooks the famous Tynwald Hill, where Manx Law passed in the preceding year is read out in an historic, annual ceremony, on July 5th. Popular venue for family lunches.
◖ ⊟ ♣ P

Try also: Central Hotel (Castletown)

Santon

Lancashire Hotel
☎ (0624) 74609
12–10.45
Okells Mild, Bitter [H]
Comfortable country inn on the main road south from Douglas.
◖ ⊟ ♣ P

Sulby

Sulby Glen Hotel
TT course and Sulby Glen road jct ☎ (0624) 897240
12–10.45
Castletown Bitter [H]
Large residential pub situated on the 'Sulby Straight' – a fast section of the TT Course.
⌂ ⛟ ◖ ♣ P

Try also: Ginger Hall Hotel (Castletown)

Union Mills

Railway Inn
On main road
8–10.30 (12–1.30; 8–10 Sun, closed Sat)
Castletown Bitter [G]
Well worth visiting during its very limited opening hours; a village local which has resisted very well the approach of the 21st century. Do not expect any concession to current pub fads of food, music or low/no alcohol drinks. Very small car park. Q P

THE MANX PURE BEER ACT

The Manx Pure Beer Act permits malt, sugar and hops only as ingredients. The evidence is below!

THE BREWERS' ACT 1874

Paragraph 18: Miscellaneous.
No brewer shall use in the brewing, making, mixing with, recovering or colouring, any beer or any liquid made to resemble beer, or have in his possession any copperas, coculus Indicus, nux vomica, grains of paradise, Guinea pepper, or opium, or any article, ingredient or preparation whatever, for, or as a substitute for, malt or sugar or hops. For any offence against this section, the person offending shall incur a penalty of three hundred pounds. And all such beer, or other liquid brewed, made, or mixed as aforesaid, and also all the beer grounds and stale beer brewed, made or mixed as aforesaid and all copperas, coculus Indicus, nux vomica, grains of paradise, Guinea pepper, opium, and every other article, ingredient, or preparation as aforesaid (other than malt and sugar) in the custody or possession of such brewer, together with every copper, cooler, tun, vat or other vessel or utensil whatsoever, in which any such beer, liquid, material, article, ingredient, or preparation shall be contained, or which shall have been made use of or employed for or in the brewing, making, mixing with, recovering, or colouring such beer or liquid, shall be forfeited to Her Majesty, her heirs and successors.

Passed by Legislature: 19th June, 1874.
Obtained Royal Assent: 7th July, 1874.
Promulgated "At a Tynwald Court holden at Saint John's Chapel, the 11th day of September, 1874."

Northern Ireland

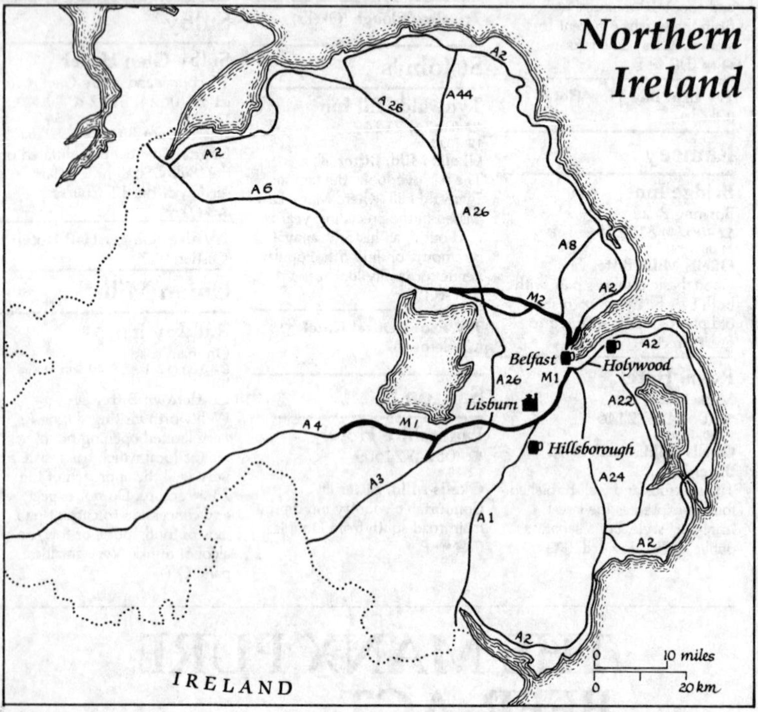

***Hilden**, Lisburn*

Belfast

Crown Liquor Saloon
Great Victoria Street (opp. Opera House)
11.30–11 (12.30–2.30; 7–10 Sun)
Worthington White Shield
A perfectly preserved celebration of high Victorian decorativism, replete with tiles, mirrors, mosaic and snug 'boxes', guarded by lions and griffins. Betjeman's favourite bar – an absolute must.
(Botanic NIR)

Kings Head
829 Lisburn Road
(0232) 667805
12–11 (7–10 Sun)
Hilden Ale
Pleasant, comfortable series of bars and lounges within a fine Victorian house. Conservatory extension and first floor restaurant. Opposite the Kings Hall.
(Balmoral NIR) P

Kitchen Bar
18 Victoria Square
(0232) 324901
11.30–11 (12.30–2.30 Sun, may close early weekday eves)
Hilden Ale
Thriving, family-run, traditional corner local in city-centre backwater. Enlivened by Friday folk fiddlers. Super service and legendary lunches. Occasional guest beers.
Q (Central NIR)

Linenhall
9 Clarence Street
(0232) 248458
12–11 (1 am Fri, closed Sun)
Hilden Ale
Compact, gregarious, triangular bar and rear sitting room with mellow brick and timber. In the shadow of the BBC; frequently bustling and busy.
(Botanic NIR)

Try also: Parlour Bar, Telfair St (Hilden)

Hillsborough

Hillside Bar
21 Main Street (off A1)
(0846) 682765
12–11 (12.30–2.30; 7–10 Sun)
Hilden Ale
Comfortable, stone-floored, multi-cornered main-street local in quaint country town. Excellent bar snacks and renowned restaurant upstairs.
Q

Holywood

Bear Tavern
62 High Street
(023 17) 6837
11.30–11 (1 am Fri & Sat, 12.30–2.30; 7–10 Sun)
Hilden Ale
Long, new (1989) narrow bar with handsome traditional interior; sloping stone floor, tiles, mahogany, cosy corners and lots of mirrors and glass. Above average food.
(Holywood NIR)

Help keep real ale alive by joining CAMRA. Your voice helps encourage brewers big and small to brew cask beer and offer all beer drinkers a better choice. For membership details see page 504.

A DESERT WITH JUST ONE OASIS

Tony Dean

CAMRA Northern Ireland and the Hilden brewery were both established in 1981, and yet, ten years on, it has to be said that the province, as far as real ale is concerned, is still an area of acute deprivation. Of course, there is a lot of good bottled Guinness about, but the number of pubs selling cask-conditioned beer barely creeps into double figures. The local Guinness/Bass trading duopoly certainly does not help, and, in addition, many discerning drinkers are distracted by an over-preoccupation with keg stout. Furthermore, there are fundamental problems of keeping and dispense, as few pubs in Northern Ireland have a cellar, and many have beer stores which are too far from the bar for reliable cask-conditioned beer.

During the eighties several varieties of real ale were available, but at the time of writing the choice in Northern Ireland has been reduced to just one – Hilden's. In the mid eighties, beer from the Herald Brewery in Coleraine was available and was deservedly popular. However, brewer Mike Herald became so frustrated at the trading restrictions generated by Guinness and Bass that he emigrated to Canada. Maiden Oak, another small brewery, in Londonderry, brewed for a short while without making any impact, and, at one time, Younger No. 3 was very popular (drinkers in the province prefer a darker beer), but S&N withdrew it when it closed down its Belfast depot in 1986. More recently, Bass Ireland test marketed Heriot 80/- from Edinburgh in a few pubs in the Belfast area. Unfortunately, this experiment was not adjudged a success, due mainly to difficulties of dispense.

It is the Hilden brewery at Hilden House near Lisburn which has been the main source of cask-conditioned beer these past ten years. The first Hilden Ale was brewed in October 1981 and has happily been available ever since, although Hilden Special Reserve is now available only occasionally.

An important breakthrough occurred in June 1990 when, after concerted pressure from the local CAMRA branch, Bass Ireland announced the welcome reintroduction of Worthington White Shield into the province. This delectable bottle-conditioned beer should find a ready market in Northern Ireland.

The prospects for draught real ale are less clear, although, happily, the existing longstanding accounts are secure enough. Because of licensing restrictions, the establishment of new pubs in Northern Ireland is notoriously difficult. Nevertheless, a slow but steady increase in the number of pubs selling cask-conditioned beer should take place over the next few years.

Tony Dean is Chairman of CAMRA Northern Ireland

THE BREWERIES

Introduction by Iain Loe

After the ructions of 1989, following the publication of the Monopolies and Mergers Commission's Report into 'The Supply of Beer', sanity at last prevailed when, after much to-ing and fro-ing, the Final Orders were published and passed by Parliament.

The main thrust was the introduction of the 'guest beer' law and restrictions on tied houses for brewers who own more than 2,000 pubs. These brewers now have to free from the tie half their houses over and above this 2,000 pub limit.

Consequently, the potential new market stemming from the guest beer clause has seen cask-conditioned beer being promoted by brewers big and small in a way that has not been witnessed for many a year.

UPS AND DOWNS

This year's brewery section sees a few changes from last year. Greenalls can now be found in the Independents listings, with the MMC rulings confirming its status as a 'regional' brewer, albeit one with expansionist tendencies. Its Midlands brewery is listed with it.

Playing it strictly by the book, Scottish & Newcastle should also now be listed as an independent, having sold off its excess pubs to take its pub holdings below the magic 2,000 limit. However, such is S&N's presence in the free trade, we have to consider it as a 'national' and, therefore, it remains in the giants' section.

Promoted to the Independents listings this year are several brew pubs which have expanded their business extensively into the free trade and should, as a result, more correctly be considered as independent brewers in their own right.

GOODBYE AND HELLO

Since the last *Guide* was published we have seen the departure of a very famous name from brewing; Boddingtons decided that it could make more money from running pubs, hotels and nursing homes than brewing and so sold its brewery, as well as that of Higsons (which it had acquired a few years earlier), to Whitbread. Whitbread subsequently closed and sold the Higsons plant, together with another of its breweries, Fremlins at Faversham in Kent, and transferred the brewing to other plants in its empire. The beers brewed using the Boddingtons and Higsons names can be found in the Nationals section under Whitbread.

Several smaller brewers have called time, at least for the present. Martin Ales of Kent has ceased brewing due to the illness of the brewer; Inn Brewing (previously known as Berkhampstead Brewery) has moved north to concentrate on producing brewing equipment for the growing band of microbrewers in the UK and overseas, and no longer brews itself. New Forest has also closed up shop.

Also missing from the Independents section this year are Beards, a pub owning company which gave up brewing many years ago, and Canterbury Ales whose beer is now brewed under contract.

But, partly as a result of the catalytic effect of the 'guest beer' clause, several new breweries have started up. It has been almost like the mini boom of micros in the late seventies. These new brewing Davids you will find in the Independents section alongside those stalwarts such as Bateman, Fuller's and, probably the oldest of them all, Shepherd Neame. New brewers such as Dent (Cumbria), Wickwar (Avon) and Old Luxters (Bucks) only started in May 1990 – we wish them and all the other new brewers the best of luck.

FUTURE THREATS

There is plenty of evidence that the appetites of the major brewers have still not been assuaged and that they are still on the lookout to acquire smaller brewers (MMC permitting), both for their tied estates and for the famous brand names of some of their beers.

It is, on the other hand, encouraging that several of the country's most famous independent brewers are still largely or wholly controlled by their founding families and, unless there is a major split within the family, these brewers would appear to be safe for some time to come. We can only hope that this is, in fact, the case, for it is these brewers by and large who, we believe, produce some of the tastiest and best value-for-money ales in the UK.

The threats are, however, not only from UK predators but also from overseas, from Europe as well as further afield: from Canada, USA, Australia and even Japan. With the single European market of 1993 approaching brewers from non-EC countries are trying to obtain a foothold in Europe before the 31 December 1992 deadline. We can therefore expect that, by the time the 1992 *Good Beer Guide* is published, several of the breweries listed in this section will have overseas owners.

THE BIG SIX?

Traditionally, CAMRA has referred to the Big Six (i.e. the six largest of the UK brewers who also own pubs). With the changes resulting from these companies' manoeuverings to avoid some of the consequences of the MMC Report, it looks like this number might be reduced to five or four. As we go to press the MMC is currently studying whether it should recommend that the proposed 'pubs-for-breweries' swap between Grand Metropolitan and Elders IXL (owners of Courage) be allowed. Scottish & Newcastle, as has already been mentioned, is, for us, still a 'national', despite selling its excess pubs to avoid the restrictions of the new legislation. Allied has adopted a waiting game and has been reluctant to show its hand. Could it be out of brewing by *GBG* 92? And then there is Whitbread, CAMRA's brewing bête-noire at present, which seems to be committed to staying in brewing, albeit with that brewing concentrated in fewer and fewer plants.

SHADES OF LIGHT AND DARK Some people say beer is beer and that's that. But beer in its taste can often be as, if not more, complex than other drinks such as malt whisky or wine. Once again CAMRA members from around the country have, with dedication above and beyond the call of duty, sampled the vast range of cask-conditioned ales available from Lands End to John O'Groats and their tasting notes have been distilled into what we believe is the best guide for steering you to the ales your tastebuds will appreciate.

Among the vast range of ales still available in the UK there are not only traditional bitters, but mild ales and, making a strong comeback, thanks mainly to the smaller brewers, dark stouts and porters, types of beer that were once very common but which have fallen in popularity since the end of WWI (Guinness being a notable exception). There is also a resurgence in lower gravity, light bitters and even a large brewer such as Courage has started to make its Bitter Ale available to landlords in the smaller nine gallon casks to ensure that the beer is in fine fettle for the customer. The brewery has also introduced a cask form of its Simonds Bitter keg beer into the South Wales market, as it realises that sometimes people want a lower gravity beer rather than the premium high gravity products that seem to be hyped so much these days.

AND FOR THE FUTURE British brewing is still very much alive and producing a very wide range of cask-conditioned ales. These ales deserve to be supported, so next time you go into a pub for a beer, don't just ask for a pint of best or bitter, study what's on offer and then try one that takes your fancy. And if there is no or only one real ale available, and the landlord is a tenant of a 'national' brewer, ask him why he doesn't stock a guest beer from one of the many independent brewers listed here.

NOTES ON THE BREWERIES SECTION The Breweries Section is your reference to all the breweries in the UK which produce real ale. It is divided into three parts: Independents, Nationals and Brew Pubs. A beers index follows to help you locate individual brews.

Each brewery is listed by the name with which its products are promoted and generally known, with the actual company trading name also given if different.

The beers are listed in increasing gravity order. Original gravities and alcohol by volume figures are provided where obtainable. As gravities can vary across a range of figures from brew to brew, we give the average figure. For a beer with a range of 1040–1044, for instance, we quote an OG of 1042.

Tasting notes are again supplied, following their success in last year's edition. Our tasting panels, each with their palates honed and tongues profiled, have managed to cover many beers not sampled last year. We are, therefore, pleased to present even more comprehensive notes than in 1990. Our aim, still, is to taste them all – but, until that is achieved, beers not tasted are marked with an asterisk.

Iain Loe is CAMRA's Research Manager.

THE INDEPENDENTS

ADNAMS

Adnams and Company PLC, Sole Bay Brewery, Southwold, Suffolk, IP18 6JW. Tel. (0502) 722424

East Anglia's famous seaside brewery, providing real ale in all its 69 pubs and 2,000–plus free trade accounts. Having expanded considerably into southern England, the brewery's attention now turns to western and northern parts. About 80% of its beer goes into the free trade, supplied from depots in Norwich, Maidstone and Heathrow, from where the Brewers Dray company distributes Wadworth, Everards and a small portfolio of other brands, as well as Adnams' own products, within the M25 London area. Looking for success in the export market.

Mild (OG 1034, ABV 3.2%) A fine mild, black with ruby tints, with a faint aroma of both malt and hops, which are more pronounced on the palate. A hint of caramel, too, and a slightly sweet finish.

Bitter (OG 1036, ABV 3.6%) A good drinking beer, its fine hoppy aroma also bearing traces of malt and fruit. The main body of the beer is hoppy and bitter, with fruit and malt undertones and a hint of bitterness. Hoppy and bitter finish.

Old (OG 1042, ABV 4.1%) Brewed for winter only, this beer is dark with red lights, full and malty, with a suggestion of roast and fruit tastes, and a fairly dry finish.

Extra (OG 1043, 4.3%) Pale in colour, but not in character. An abundance of hops in the aroma and flavour, and a pronounced dry finish. Worth drinking, but difficult to find.

Broadside (OG 1049, 4.4%) Copper-red beer with malt, fruit and a faint hoppiness in the nose. The flavour balances malt, hops and fruit well, leaving a bittersweet edge. The finish is dry with a tang of malt.

Tally-Ho (OG 1075, 6.2%) A Christmas barley wine and a definite winter warmer. Fruit and malt abound in the aroma and flavour, culminating in a delicious, bittersweet aftertaste.

ALLIED BREWERIES See page 466.

ALLOA See Allied Breweries, page 466.

ANSELLS See Allied Breweries, page 466.

ARCHERS

Archers Ales Ltd., London Street, Swindon, Wilts, SN1 5DG. Tel. (0793) 496789

Successful small brewery which was set up in 1979 and had doubled its brewing capacity by 1985. Serves 100 free trade outlets from Oxford to Bath, plus four tied houses.

Village Bitter (OG 1035, ABV 3.5%) Beer with a good aroma, a fresh, hoppy flavour and a well-balanced finish. Tasty for its class.

Best Bitter (OG 1040, ABV 4%) Well-rounded, flavoursome beer, with a good, strong, bitter finish.

Porter* (OG 1046, ABV 4.6%) An occasional brew.

ASB* (OG 1048, ABV 4.8%) A rich, fruity beer with a strong hop finish.

Golden* (OG 1053, ABV 5.3%) Another occasional beer.

Headbanger (OG 1065, ABV 6.5%) Almost a barley wine in style, enjoying a full flavour. Sweet and powerful, with a pleasant, dry finish.

ARKELL'S

Arkell's Brewery Ltd., Kingsdown, Swindon, Wilts, SN2 6RU. Tel. (0793) 823026

Family brewery established in 1843, with real ale in 61 of its 68 pubs and two of its three off-licences. Now has extensive free trade in the Thames Valley and London. The original gravity of 3B has been increased from 1038 to 1040, whilst keg 3B is now only served through special tallish founts, not the fake handpumps which caused so much confusion last year. In tied houses this is known as North Star Keg.

2B Bitter (OG 1032, ABV 3.2%) Well-balanced, if slightly thin, malty/hoppy brew. The hop flavour is strong, but not overpowering, and remains during the aftertaste. A refreshing lunchtime pint.

3B Best Bitter (OG 1040, ABV 4%) Not strong in flavour or aroma but with an interesting aftertaste. The finish is hoppy, with curious nutty and malty overtones and a hint of honey.

Mash Tun Mild* (OG 1040, ABV 4%) Has been produced on a couple of occasions and may become a full-time brew.

Kingsdown Ale (OG 1052, ABV 5%) Strong, full-bodied and tasty, with bags of hop flavour and some fruit.

Noel Ale* (OG 1055, ABV 5.5%) The Christmas offering.

ASH VINE

Ash Vine Brewery, The White Hart, Trudoxhill, Frome, Somerset, BA11 5DP. Tel. (0373) 84324

A new brewery, with mostly new equipment, set up in 1989 behind the White Hart Inn. Has extended its free trade via agencies throughout southern England and Wales. Also runs two tied houses. A new bitter, Tanker, was launched in November 1989.

Bitter (OG 1039, ABV 3.8%) A golden, straw-coloured beer with a strong hoppy aroma. The slightly chewy malt flavour is dominated by a strong hoppy bitterness and results in a long-lasting, hoppy and strong, dry, bitter finish. A light, quaffable ale.

Tanker (OG 1047, ABV 4.7%) The good hoppy/malty aroma of this golden brown beer leads on to a gently-rounded flavour of malt and hops, with an initial sweetness that gives way to a moderately bitter finish. It feels its strength but doesn't really deliver.

ASTON MANOR

Aston Manor Brewery Company Ltd., 173 Thimblemill Lane, Aston, Birmingham, B7 5HS. Tel. (021) 328 4336

Brewery which, for a while, concentrated on bottled beer but re-entered the cask beer market in early summer 1990.

JCB Bitter* (OG 1036)

AYLESBURY (ABC)

See Allied Breweries, page 468.

BALLARD'S

Ballard's Brewery Ltd., Unit C, The Old Sawmill, Nyewood, Rogate, Petersfield, Hants, GU31 5HA. Tel. (073 080) 362/301

Founded in 1980 at Cumbers Farm, Trotton, the brewery is now established in Nyewood (West Sussex, despite the confusing postal address). Supplies some 50 free trade outlets. Tends to brew Christmas ales with different names and appropriate gravities each year: Old Bounder (OG 1089) for 1989; Out to Lunch (OG 1090) for 1990, etc.

Trotton Bitter (OG 1036, ABV 3.5%) A well-flavoured drinking bitter, light copper-red in colour. The good balance of malt and hops runs through from the aroma to the finish.

Best Bitter (OG 1042, ABV 4.1%) Copper-coloured with a malty aroma. Indeed, a notably malty beer altogether, but well-hopped and with a satisfying finish.

Wassail (OG 1060, ABV 5.8%) A strong, full-bodied, fruity beer with a fruity malt aroma and a sweet finish. Dark copper-red in colour.

BANKS'S

Banks's Park Brewery, Lovatt Street, Wolverhampton, W. Midlands, WV1 4NY. Tel. (0902) 711811

1890 1990

With Hanson's makes up Wolverhampton & Dudley Breweries, the largest surviving independent 'family brewers' in the country and strong supporters of many of the original MMC recommendations. Traditional ales are served in nearly all their 850 tied houses, virtually all through electric metered dispense. Extensive club trade in cask beer and sizeable free house business. Celebrated its centenary in May 1990.

Mild (OG 1035, ABV 3.5%) The malty and hoppy aroma of this mid-brown beer leads on to a balanced, bittersweet taste of malt, roast and caramel. Malt and hops continue in the aftertaste.

Bitter (OG 1038, ABV 3.8%) Pale brown beer with a malty and hoppy aroma and a dry, bitter and malty taste.

Old Ale* (OG 1098) A very occasional brew.

BANKS & TAYLOR **Banks & Taylor, The Brewery, Shefford, Beds, SG17 5DZ. Tel. (0462) 815080**

Founded in 1981 and now serving some 50 outlets in the home counties and East Anglia, including 12 tied houses. SOD is often sold under house names.

Shefford Bitter (OG 1038, ABV 3.8%) A very drinkable, hoppy beer, with traces of malt and fruit. Hoppy aroma and a dry, hoppy finish.

Eastcote Ale or SPA (OG 1041, ABV 4%) Pleasant, suppable, well-balanced beer with a dry, hoppy aftertaste. The aroma is hoppy, too, with hints of malt and fruit.

Shefford Old Strong (SOS) (OG 1050, ABV 5%) A smooth, moreish beer, deceptively drinkable for its strength. Malt and hops extend from the aroma (where fruit is also discernible), through the flavour, to the finish.

Shefford Old Dark (SOD) (OG 1050, ABV 5%) Dark, reddish-brown ale with similar characteristics to SOS, but with an additional caramel flavour.

BARRON **Barron Brewery, Land Farm, Silverton, Exeter, Devon, EX5 4HF. Tel. (0392) 860406**

Farm brewery established in 1984 to supply outlets (currently nine) around Exeter. Beers are brewed using the farm's spring water, without the use of additives.

Exe Valley Bitter (OG 1041) Refreshing, slightly creamy, malty, pale brown bitter. Pleasant drinking.

Devon Glory (OG 1049) Mid-brown in colour, fruitily aromatic, with a sweet, fruity flavour and a pleasantly sweet aftertaste.

BASS See page 470.

BATEMAN **George Bateman & Son Ltd., Salem Bridge Brewery, Wainfleet, Skegness, Lincs, PE24 4JE. Tel. (0754) 880317**

A family brewery whose XXXB was voted CAMRA's Champion Special Bitter for the fourth year running in 1989. All 80 tied houses sell its 'Good Honest Ales' in traditional form. Serves 750 free trade outlets through much of England and has recently acquired pubs outside Lincolnshire for the first time, taking in London and Humberside as well as the Midlands.

Dark Mild (OG 1033, ABV 3%) A creamy mild tasting predominantly fruity and malty, but with some caramel and roast flavours. The finish is bitter, the aroma generally fruity and sometimes malty.

XB (OG 1036, ABV 3.8%) A distinctive, balanced bitter with a refreshing, dry, hoppy bite. Lingering hoppy finish.

XXXB (OG 1048, ABV 5%) Excellent strong bitter, its beautiful aroma and taste of hops balanced by a prominent malty presence. A worthy four-times winner of CAMRA's Special Bitter award.

Victory Ale (OG 1056, ABV 6%) A full-bodied ale with a pronounced malty aroma and a satisfying, fruity palate, which, contrasting with a moderate degree of hoppiness, makes it deceptively powerful.

BATHAM **Daniel Batham & Son Ltd., Delph Brewery, Brierley Hill, W. Midlands, DY5 2TN. Tel. (0384) 77229**

Hidden behind one of the Black Country's most famous pubs, the 'Bull & Bladder', this small family firm has managed to survive since 1877, brewing excellent beer for its eight pubs and the free trade, which now accounts for over 40% of its output. Batham also bottles its own beer.

Mild Ale (OG 1036.5, ABV 3.6%) Dark brown beer with an aroma of caramel. Caramel continues in the taste, but with balancing hop character. Sweet yet hoppy finish.

Best Bitter (OG 1043.5, ABV 4.3%) Sweet-tasting, but with bitterness and a long, dry finish. A straw-coloured beer with a flowery aroma.

XXX* (OG 1063.5, ABV 6.3%) A Christmas ale which has replaced Delph Strong Ale.

BEER ENGINE **Beer Engine, Newton St Cyres, Exeter, Devon, EX5 5AX. Tel. (0392) 851282**

Successful brew pub now serving an expanding free trade. Stands next to the Barnstaple branch railway line. Owns one other pub, the Sleeper in Seaton. Occasionally produces a bottle-conditioned beer.

Rail Ale (OG 1037, ABV 3.6%) Straw-coloured beer with a malty aroma and a hoppy/bitter flavour. Some bitterness in the aftertaste.

Piston Bitter (OG 1044, ABV 4.3%) Mid-brown in colour, a strong, malty, slightly fruity and bitter beer with a sweet aftertaste.

Sleeper Heavy (OG 1055, ABV 5.3%) Pleasant, fruity, yet sweet-tasting beer which leaves its sweetness on the palate. Mid to dark brown in colour; strong fruity aroma.

BELHAVEN **Belhaven Brewery Co. Ltd., Dunbar, Lothian, EH42 1RS. Tel. (0368) 62734**

Scotland's oldest and most renowned independent brewery, which has had a turbulent history. It is now once again in the ownership of Nazmu Virani's London-based property and leisure group, Control Securities PLC, which is planning a major expansion of its pub estate throughout the UK.

Approximately 25% of its trading accounts take real ale, which is also available in over half of Belhaven's tied houses.

60/- Light* (OG 1031, ABV 2.8%) Dark and malty.

70/- Heavy* (OG 1035, ABV 3.3%) Light and hoppy.

80/- Export* (OG 1041, ABV 3.9%) Heavy, full-bodied ale.

90/- Strong Ale* (OG 1070, ABV 7.25%) An occasional, rich brew.

BENSKINS See Allied Breweries, page 468.

BERROW **Berrow Brewery, Coast Road, Berrow, Burnham-on-Sea, Somerset, TA8 2QU. Tel. (0278) 751345**

Founded in 1982 and now supplying pubs and clubs locally, as well as the national free trade. Topsy Turvy is only brewed on demand.

BBBB or 4Bs (OG 1038, ABV 3.75%) Good pale brown drinking beer, offering a fruity aroma, a malty, fruity flavour and a good bitter finish.

Topsy Turvy (OG 1055, ABV 6.3%) Excellent straw-coloured beer. Its aroma is malty and hoppy, as is its taste, though with a hint of fruitiness and sweetness. The aftertaste combines malt with vanilla.

BIG END **Big End Brewery, 62a Otley Road, Harrogate, N. Yorks, HG2 0DP. Tel. (0423) 503299**

Established in August 1988 by CAMRA stalwart Bill Witty, with brewer Bernard Linley, and supplied its first brew to the Great British Beer Festival at Leeds. Supplies free trade outlets in Yorkshire, Lancashire and Cleveland. Brews Oliver John's Bitter (OG 1038) for the former brew pub, the Golden Lion, Leyburn, N. Yorks.

Piston Bitter or Yorkshire Rose Bitter (OG 1038) A powerful hoppiness dominates the aroma and taste, balanced by some malt and a hint of fruitiness. Malt and hops persist into a bittersweet finish.

Old Lubrication (OG 1042) Dark brown beer, with roast malt in the nose. The taste is sweetish, with malt, fruit and hops, followed by a fruity aftertaste tinged with hops.

Monkey Wrench* (OG 1056)

BIG LAMP **Big Lamp Brewery Co. Ltd., 1 Summerhill Street, Newcastle upon Tyne, Tyne & Wear, NE4 6EJ. Tel. (091) 261 4227**

Set up in 1982, now the longest-established 'new' independent real ale brewery in the North East. It supplies two tied houses and an ever-changing free trade.

Bitter (OG 1040, ABV 4.5%) Well-hopped, as evidenced in the aroma and taste, with a pleasing, dryish finish.

Prince Bishop Ale (OG 1048, ABV 5.5%) Unusually pale, almost lager-coloured, but the similarity ends there. A nicely-balanced ale with a flowery aroma and a hoppy flavour.

Old Genie (OG 1068, ABV 8%) A dark, powerful, well-balanced but sweetish, occasional brew. Very competitively-priced when available in tied trade.

Blackout (OG 1102, ABV 10.5%) A very powerful, aptly-named rare beer, mostly brewed for festivals.

BLACKAWTON **Blackawton Brewery, Washbourne, Totnes, Devon, TQ9 7UF. Tel. (080 423) 339**

One of the earliest new small breweries, dating from 1977, and now the oldest brewery in Devon. Serves 75 free trade outlets, having no pubs of its own. Prides itself on brewing from traditional ingredients with no additives.

Bitter (OG 1037.5, ABV 3.8%) A bitter which is malty in its aroma and slightly fruity and malty in its taste.

Devon Gold* (OG 1040.5, ABV 4.1%)

44 Special* (OG 1044.5, ABV 4.5%) Premium, full-flavoured bitter.

Headstrong* (OG 1051.5, ABV 5.2%) Strong and full-bodied.

BODDINGTONS See Whitbread, page 479.

BRAINS **S A Brain & Co. Ltd., Old Brewery, St Mary Street, Cardiff, S. Glamorgan, CF1 1SP. Tel. (0222) 399022**

A traditional brewery, supplying cask-conditioned beer to all its 130 tied houses and a widespread free trade. Beware of identical dispense display for keg and electrical taps. MA (OG 1036, ABV 3.6%) is only available at the Crown Hotel, Skewen.

Dark (OG 1035, ABV 3.5%) Deep brown in colour, with a full-bodied malt flavour and chocolate overtones. A rounded, bittersweet finish.

Bitter (OG 1035, ABV 3.7%) A pale, malty, distinctively bitter beer; refreshing, with an intense dry finish. Sometimes known as 'Light'.

SA Best Bitter (OG 1042, ABV 4.2%) Affectionately known as 'Skull Attack', this fine, malty, traditional premium bitter is distinctive and full-bodied, with a smooth and strong dry finish.

BRAKSPEAR **W H Brakspear & Sons PLC, The Brewery, Henley-on-Thames, Oxfordshire, RG9 2BU. Tel. (0491) 573636**

Popular country brewery with many excellent, unspoilt pubs. All 117 tied houses serve traditional ales. Also a substantial free trade. Bitter has now been added to Whitbread's 'guest' beer portfolio.

XXX Mild (OG 1030, ABV 2.8%) Dark copper-red, thin-bodied mild, with a fruity bitterness and a distinct, dry finish.

Bitter or Pale Ale (OG 1035, ABV 3.4%) A mid-brown true bitter which has little aroma but lots of hop character, with fruity undertones and a strong, bitter finish.

Special (OG 1043, ABV 4%) A bitter beer backed up with moderate maltiness and sweetness; a hint of hops gives a fine blend of flavours. The finish is pronounced and pleasantly dry.

Old Ale (OG 1043, ABV 4%) Dark brown ale, strong in caramel, which tends to mask some of the other flavours present. Lacks chocolate malt, but still has a distinct, full body and strong bitter finish.

BRENT-WALKER **Brent-Walker Breweries, PO Box 21, The Lion Brewery (Camerons), Hartlepool, Cleveland, TS24 7QS. Tel. (0429) 266666**

In 1989 the ambitious Brent-Walker group took its first steps into the brewing industry by purchasing Camerons and Tolly Cobbold from the Barclay Bros hotel group. After a cash injection of £10 million at the Camerons Hartlepool brewery, production of the Tolly Cobbold ales was insensitively transferred north from its Ipswich base. However, a management buy-out of the Tolly Cobbold plant was announced in May 1990 and plans have been put into action to brew once more at Ipswich. The initial deal involves the new company supplying Brent-Walker's East Anglian pubs with the Tolly beers listed below, then finding its way into the free trade and acquiring its own tied estate. The beers are listed without tasting notes, although the company plans to follow the traditional recipes and recreate the regional Suffolk ale taste. A working brewery museum is also in the pipeline. Meanwhile, Brent-Walker continues to expand into southern England with its Tap & Spile real ale pub chain.

Camerons Traditional Bitter (OG 1036, ABV 3.6%) A well-hopped, well-balanced beer with a bitter finish. An excellent, light and very drinkable session beer when in good condition, but not always found at its best.

Camerons Strongarm (OG 1039.5, ABV 3.9%) A pleasant and refreshing, medium-bodied ale with a lot of character. Darkish in colour, with a full, well-balanced flavour of malt and hops and a dry, bitter finish. Usually enjoys a good head, but, again, quality can vary.

Camerons Strongarm Premium (OG 1044.5, ABV 4.2%) Reputedly brewed to the 1950s Strongarm recipe. A reddish-brown, full-bodied beer with a well-rounded, malty taste and a bitter, hoppy finish. Difficult to find in its home territory.

Tolly Cobbold Mild* (OG 1033, ABV 3%)

Tolly Cobbold Bitter* (OG 1034.5, ABV 3.4%)

Tolly Cobbold Original* (OG 1037.5, ABV 3.6%)

Tolly Cobbold Old Strong* (OG 1046, ABV 4.5%) A winter ale.

BRITISH OAK

British Oak Brewery, Salop Street, Eve Hill, Dudley, W. Midlands, DY1 3AX. Tel. (0384) 236297

Brew pub set up in May 1988, now supplying 15 free trade outlets, as well as the pub. Also produces traditional cider.

Castle Ruin* (OG 1037)

Eve'ill Bitter* (OG 1042)

Col. Pickering's Porter* (OG 1046)

Dungeon Draught* (OG 1050)

Old Jones* (OG 1060)

BROUGHTON

Broughton Brewery Ltd., Broughton, Peeblesshire, Borders, ML12 6HQ. Tel. (089 94) 345

One of the most significant new breweries, set up in 1980 by former S&N executive David Younger. Broughton supplies its draught ales to some 200 outlets (including two tied houses) in Scotland, as well as pursuing an increasing bottled beer trade with the grocery sector and major off-licence chains.

Greenmantle Ale (OG 1038, ABV 4%) Beer lacking aroma. Bittersweet in taste, with a hint of fruit, and a very dry finish.

Special Bitter (OG 1038, ABV 4%) A dry-hopped version of Greenmantle.

Greenmantle 80/- Ale (OG 1042, ABV 4.25%) Formerly known as Merlin's Ale; a distinctively flavoured brew. Fruity and well-balanced, with a dry, hoppy finish.

Old Jock (OG 1069, ABV 6.7%) Strong, sweetish and fruity in the finish.

MATTHEW BROWN

See Scottish & Newcastle, page 477.

BUCKLEY

See Crown Buckley, page 417.

BULLMASTIFF

Bullmastiff, 5 Anchor Way, Penarth, S. Glamorgan, CF6 1SF. Tel. (0222) 702958

Small brewery set up in 1987 by a fanatical home-brewer. Supplies some 40 outlets locally (and others nationwide by wholesale).

Bitter (OG 1035) A pale brown beer with a distinctively bitter finish.

Ebony Dark (OG 1042) As its name suggests, a very dark brown beer, offering a clear roast malt flavour and aroma. Very drinkable, with a rich, malty aftertaste.

Best Bitter (OG 1043) A well-balanced beer, light brown in colour, with a smooth finish.

Son of a Bitch (OG 1062) A full-bodied, notably malty and well-hopped beer, mid-brown in colour. The aftertaste is bitter and distinctive; very satisfying.

BUNCES **Bunces Brewery, The Old Mill, Netheravon, Salisbury, Wilts, SP4 9QB. Tel. (0980) 70631**

Set up in 1984 on the Wiltshire Avon by Tony Bunce and his wife, this brewery continues to grow. Supplies cask-conditioned beers to around 50 free trade outlets within a radius of 50 miles. A Great Western Beer Festival award-winner in 1986, the brewery welcomes visits to its listed building by prior arrangement.

Benchmark (OG 1035, ABV 3.2%) A pleasant, bitter ale of remarkable character, which maintains one's interest for a long time. The taste is malty, the aroma subtle and the very long finish is quite dry on the palate.

Best Bitter (OG 1042, ABV 3.9%) First-rate, scrumptious beer. The piquant aroma introduces a complex malty and bitter taste with a hint of fruit. Long, fresh, bitter aftertaste.

Old Smokey (OG 1050, ABV 4.6%) A delightful, warming, dark winter ale, with a roasted malt taste and a hint of liquorice surrounding a developing bitter flavour. Very appealing to the eye.

BURTON BRIDGE **Burton Bridge Brewery, Bridge Street, Burton upon Trent, Staffs, DE14 1SY. Tel. (0283) 510573**

Established in 1982 by two former Ind Coope employees. Burton Bridge has one tied house, at the front of the brewery, and now supplies guest beers to around 300 outlets within a radius of 150 miles. Specialises in commemorative bottled beers.

Midsummer Ale (OG 1038) A summer beer.

XL Bitter (OG 1040, ABV 4%) Golden amber, malty drinking bitter, with a dry palate and finish. A faint hoppiness and fruitiness come through in the aroma and taste.

Bridge Bitter (OG 1042, ABV 4.2%) Again, golden amber in colour, robust and malty, with a hoppy and bitter palate and aftertaste. Malt and hops are both present throughout, but the dry, hoppy character dominates the finish. Some balancing fruitiness and sweetness.

Porter (OG 1045, ABV 4.5%) A dark, ruby-red, sweetish porter.

The malty, slightly fruity aroma is followed by a roast malt and fruit flavour, and a malty and fairly bitter finish. Also available in bottle-conditioned form.

Top Dog Stout* (OG 1050, ABV 5%) A new winter brew.

Festival Ale (OG 1055, ABV 5.5%) Strong, sweetish and full-bodied. The aroma is malty and slightly hoppy, and the palate has similar characteristics, with a pronounced fruitiness. Copper-coloured; a little cloying and heavy.

Old Expensive* (OG 1065, ABV 6.5%) Dark winter warmer, also known as OX.

BURTONWOOD

Burtonwood Brewery PLC, Burtonwood Village, Warrington, Cheshire, WA5 4PJ. Tel. (092 52) 25131

The tied estate of this family-run public company now totals 275 pubs, including recent acquisitions in Humberside and Chesterfield. Real ale is supplied to 210 of them, as well as to a widespread and growing free trade. A new brewhouse was completed in May 1990. A company taking full advantage of the new guest beer opportunities. Brews house beers for some free houses around Stoke-on-Trent.

Dark Mild (OG 1032, ABV 3%) Dark brown to black, nutty and malty mild, with some chocolate, caramel and a hint of bitterness. Smooth finish with some dryness.

Best Bitter (OG 1036, ABV 3.7%) Well-balanced, malty bitter, with good hoppiness and a touch of fruit. The finish is bitter and dry. A light, smooth, drinkable beer.

BURTS

Burts Brewery Ltd., High Street, Ventnor, Isle of Wight. Tel. (0983) 852153

One of Britain's most remarkable breweries which has managed to survive, serving real ale in most of its 11 pubs, despite the lowest prices in the South of England. The company's future has been secured by a family management buy-out by Alastair Phillips. Leases pubs on the island from Whitbread and serves free trade there and on the mainland (over 40 outlets).

LB* (OG 1031, ABV 3.2%) A light bitter; Mild without the added caramel. A very rare find.

Mild or BB (OG 1031, ABV 3.2%) A dark, sweet, caramel-flavoured mild, with a hint of fruit in the nose and a trace of strawberries in the aftertaste. Has developed a 'home-brew' tang.

VPA (OG 1039, ABV 3.9%) Mid-brown beer, also known as Island Ale. A delicate aroma is followed by a fruity bitterness which is spoilt by the same tang apparent in the mild.

4X* (OG 1039, ABV 3.9%) VPA with caramel.

Tanner (OG 1050, ABV 5%) A stronger version of VPA. Chestnut-coloured, with a dry, slightly malty bitterness, and a fruity and hoppy finish. Not being brewed at present.

BUTCOMBE **Butcombe Brewery Ltd., Butcombe, Bristol, Avon, BS18 6XQ. Tel. (027 587) 2240**

One of the most successful of the new wave of breweries, set up in 1978 by a former Courage Western MD. Real ale in its three houses (which are not tied) and in an extensive free trade, mostly around Avon and Somerset.

Bitter (OG 1039, ABV 4%) A golden, pale brown-coloured beer with a malt and hop aroma. The moderately bitter and malty flavour mix has a discernible fruitiness, leaving a bitter and malty aftertaste, the effect of which is often spoiled by sulphidity.

CALEDONIAN **Caledonian Brewing Company Ltd., Slateford Road, Edinburgh, Lothian, EH11 1PH. Tel. (031) 337 1286**

When Vaux closed the famous Lorimer & Clark brewery in May 1987, a management team acquired it. They now operate from the old brewery using the last three direct-fired open coppers in Britain – one of which is an original, dating back to 1869.

60/- Ale* (OG 1032, ABV 3.2%)

70/- Ale* (OG 1036, ABV 3.5%) Soft and malty in flavour.

Porter* (OG 1042, ABV 4%) Dry and nutty.

80/- Ale* (OG 1043, ABV 4.1%) Malty and flavoursome, well-balanced with hops.

Merman XXX* (OG 1052, ABV 5.1%) Dark, heavy beer.

Strong Ale* (OG 1078, 8%) Rich and deceptively strong.

CAMERONS See Brent-Walker Breweries, page 410.

CASTLE EDEN See Whitbread, page 479.

CASTLETOWN See Isle of Man Breweries, page 434.

CHARRINGTON See Bass, page 472.

CHESTER'S See Whitbread, page 480.

CHILTERN **Chiltern Brewery, Nash Lee Road, Terrick, Aylesbury, Bucks, HP17 0TQ. Tel. (0296) 613647**

Set up in 1980, now supplying 30, mainly local, outlets. Sells beer mustards, beer chutneys and beer cheeses from the brewery shop.

Chiltern Ale* (OG 1036, ABV 3.6%) Distinctive, light bitter.

Beechwood Bitter* (OG 1041, ABV 4.1%) Full-bodied and nutty.

Three Hundred Old Ale* (OG 1050, ABV 5%) A bottled beer now also available on draught.

CLARK, Wm. See North & East Riding Brewers, page 444.

CLARK'S **H B Clark & Co. Ltd., Westgate Brewery, Wakefield, W. Yorks, WF2 9SW. Tel. (0924) 373328**

Drinks wholesale company which began brewing again in 1982 and now brews Clark's Traditional Bitter and Hammerhead for 35 free trade accounts. The other beers are chiefly sold at its 'Boon' pubs (named after its founder, Henry Boon Clark), Mr Clark's Alehouse in Wakefield city centre, and the Kings Arms at Heath.

Mild (OG 1038, ABV 3.9%) Black, with a faint malty and fruity aroma. The taste is strong in caramel and roast flavours, with bitterness, and the aftertaste is malty but predominantly bitter. A beer available to the free trade but only regularly found at the Boons End in Ossett.

HB* (OG 1033, ABV 3.6%) Light, refreshing bitter.

Garthwaite Special Bitter or GSB* (OG 1035, ABV 3.7%) Another refreshing bitter with a distinctive aroma.

Traditional Bitter (OG 1038, ABV 4.1%) Pale brown beer with a disappointingly faint malty and hoppy nose. There is malt with balancing bitterness in the taste and finish. Altogether a good, smooth, clean-tasting bitter.

Burglar Bill (OG 1044, ABV 4.75%) A fuller-flavoured, well-balanced, pale brown bitter, but again with a faint aroma. Roast malt and bitterness are balanced in the taste, moving to a strong malty and bitter finish.

Winter Warmer (OG 1044, ABV 4.85%) A rich, slightly vinous, dark brown beer with a malty nose. Strong roast and malt flavours, with bitterness and underlying sweetness, and a malty and bitter aftertaste.

Hammerhead (OG 1056, ABV 5.95%) Medium brown in colour, with a malty and fruity aroma. Full-flavoured and strong, offering a mouth-filling roast malt and bitter taste, with some fruitiness. The finish is strong, combining bitterness and malt. A robust and warming beer.

CORNISH **Cornish Brewery Co., The Brewery, Redruth, Cornwall, TR15 1AT. Tel. (0209) 213591**

A wholly-owned subsidiary of JA Devenish PLC. Devenish's old Weymouth brewery closed at the end of 1985, with all production transferred to Redruth. A subsequent merger with Inn Leisure increased its tied estate by 45 houses. Cornish has also successfully developed a niche in the market with its bottled Newquay Steam Beer, available on draught as well as bottled. All 400 pubs sell real ale, many still under the name of Devenish.

JD Dry Hop Bitter (OG 1032, ABV 3.1%) There is very little aroma to this pale brown beer which has a hoppy, very bitter taste and a similarly bitter finish. A light, session beer.

Original (OG 1037, ABV 3.4%) Pale brown in colour and thin in aroma, with a bittersweet flavour which can vary. A slight bitter aftertaste. Try half and half with JD Dry Hop.

Draught Steam Bitter (OG 1037, ABV 3.4%) It is understood from sources close to the brewery that this beer is still being worked on. Samples varied from no flavour to strong and distinctive, even crunchy!

Royal Wessex Bitter (OG 1042, ABV 4.1%) A golden, straw–coloured ale with no discernible aroma. There is some hoppiness amid a mainly bittersweet flavour and bitter aftertaste. Neither unpleasant nor distinctive. Sometimes sold as Vallence's Bitter.

COTLEIGH **Cotleigh Brewery, Ford Road, Wiveliscombe, Somerset, TA4 2RE. Tel. (0984) 24086**

A brewery founded in Devon in 1979 which moved to new purpose-built premises in 1985. Serves 75 outlets, mostly in Devon and Somerset, but its beers are becoming increasingly available across the country. Owns one pub, the Prince of Wales in Holcombe Rogus, Devon.

Harrier SPA (OG 1036, ABV 3.6%) Formerly called Kingfisher Ale, a straw-coloured beer with a very hoppy aroma and flavour, and a hoppy, bitter finish. Pleasant and light, with plenty of flavour.

Tawny Bitter (OG 1040, ABV 3.8%) Mid-brown in colour, with a hoppy aroma and a hoppy, well-balanced flavour. Strong, hoppy finish. A classic beer.

Old Buzzard (OG 1048, ABV 4.8%) Ruby red beer, tasting strongly of roast malt, balanced with hops. The aroma is also of roast malt and the finish is bitter. Dangerously drinkable.

Monmouth Rebellion* (OG 1050, ABV 5%) An occasional brew.

COURAGE See page 473.

CROPTON **Cropton Brewery, New Inn, Cropton, Pickering, N. Yorks, YO18 8HH. Tel. (075 15) 330**

A former brew-pub, established in 1984 at the New Inn, this brewery was expanded in 1987 to supply its additive-free beers to the local free trade.

Two Pints* (OG 1040, ABV 4%) Full-flavoured and distinctive.

Special Strong Bitter* (OG 1060, ABV 6.3%) A powerful winter ale.

CROUCH VALE

Crouch Vale Brewery Ltd., 12 Redhills Road, South Woodham Ferrers, Chelmsford, Essex, CM3 5UP. Tel. (0245) 322744

Founded in 1981 by CAMRA enthusiasts, Crouch Vale has a single tied house – the Cap & Feathers, CAMRA's Pub of the Year 1990, as well as free trade business in Essex and Greater London (25–30 outlets). Fighting to keep its market share in the face of increasing competition from the established independents. All beers are brewed with natural ingredients.

Woodham IPA (OG 1035, ABV 3.5%) A very drinkable, pale session beer. Dry and hoppy, with a faint balancing maltiness throughout.

Essex Mild* (OG 1035) A very occasional brew.

Best Bitter (OG 1039, ABV 4%) Pleasant, copper-coloured, hoppy bitter with some balancing maltiness and fruit on the tongue. Hoppy aftertaste.

Strong Anglian Special or SAS (OG 1048, ABV 4.9%) Copper in colour and full-bodied. Malty and strong tasting, with robust bitterness.

Essex Porter (OG 1050, ABV 4.9%) A black, bittersweet porter with a slight hint of blackberries.

Santa's Revenge* (OG 1055, ABV 5.5%) A Christmas ale, also sold under house names. Despite its strength, it is dry and winey, not sweet.

Willie Warmer (OG 1060, ABV 6.1%) A fruity and well-flavoured, strong and delicious black ale.

CROWN BUCKLEY

Crown Buckley, Pontyclun, Mid Glamorgan, CF7 9YG. Tel. (0443) 225453

Buckley, the oldest brewery in Wales (estd. 1767), was taken over by Brodian in 1987. This failed to revitalise the ailing brewery which was bought out by Crown in 1989 with Harp financial backing, merging the brewing interests and creating a total tied estate of 134 pubs. Crown's excellent 1041 cask ale has subsequently been discontinued. Crown's origins are in supplying the club trade, where most of the beer is pressurised. All beer production is now at the Llanelli (Buckley) site, while kegging and bottling is done at Pontyclun, although the situation is, apparently, under review.

Buckley's Dark (OG 1034, ABV 3.4%) A mild with a roast malt aroma. Quite sweet, with traces of chocolate and a nutty, bitter finish.

Buckley's Best Bitter (OG 1036, ABV 3.8%) A well-balanced, fruity bitter which has a rather sweet, malty flavour and a pleasant bitter finish.

Crown SBB (OG 1037, ABV 3.8%) Distinctively malty beer with a pronounced bitter, hop character and a reasonably sharp finish. Not widely available.

DARLEY See Wards, page 460.

DARLING'S **Darling's Brewery, Station Road, Belford, Northumberland. Tel. (0668) 213031**

New brewery set up in the summer of 1990 by a former farmer, Peter Darling, who decided to switch from growing barley for malting to making beer himself. The bitter is named after the Longstone Lighthouse on the Farne Islands off the coast, where the father of heroine Grace Darling used to be the lighthouse keeper. They rowed out in heavy seas in 1838 to rescue five people from a wrecked steam ship.

Longstone Bitter* (OG 1040)

DAVENPORTS See Greenalls, page 425.

DENT **Dent Brewery, Hollins, Cowgill, Dent, Cumbria, LA10 5TQ. Tel. (058 75) 326**

New brewery, in operation since March 1990, using its own spring water. Supplies beer to the Sun Inn at Dent and to another five pubs (spread from Keighley to Preston) on a regular basis.

Bitter* (OG 1036)

Ramsbottom Strong Ale* (OG 1044)

DEVENISH See Cornish, page 415.

DONNINGTON **Donnington Brewery, Stow-on-the-Wold, Cheltenham, Glos, GL54 1EP. Tel. (0451) 30603**

It is a pity that Britain's most picturesque brewery, set in an old watermill alongside a lake, with water power still used for much of the machinery, is not open for visits. 15 tied houses, and a similar number of free trade outlets, all serve beer on handpumps. Look out for the mild, available only in a few of the tied houses.

XXX (OG 1036, ABV 3.5%) Thin in aroma, but flavoursome. More subtle than others in its class. Some fruit and traces of chocolate and liquorice in the taste, with a notably malty finish.

BB (OG 1036, ABV 3.5%) Again, little aroma, but a pleasing, bitter beer, with a good malt/hop balance. Not as distinctive as it used to be.

SBA (OG 1042, ABV 4%) Malt dominates over bitterness in the flavour of this premium bitter. Subtle, with just a hint of fruit and a dry, malty finish. Faintly malty aroma.

EARL SOHAM **Earl Soham Brewery, The Victoria, Earl Soham, Suffolk. Tel. (072 882) 758**

Brew pub running two tied houses and supplying other pubs.

Gannet Mild (OG 1032.5) An unusual dark mild. Maltiness and bitterness compete on the palate, with the latter more prominent at the finish. Liquorice notes, too.

Victoria Bitter (OG 1036.5) A characterful, well-hopped bitter with a pronounced maltiness. Good lingering malt and bitter finish.

Albert Ale (OG 1044.5) To your taste if you like beer both strong and hoppy. Hops are evident in both the taste and the aroma, though roast and bitter flavours achieve some balance. Very strong finish.

Jolabrugg (OG varies)

ELDRIDGE POPE

Eldridge Pope and Co. PLC, Dorchester Brewery, Dorchester, Dorset, DT1 1QT. Tel. (0305) 251251

ELDRIDGE POPE

Boasts Britain's strongest naturally-conditioned bottled beer, Thomas Hardy's Ale (OG 1125). However, the award-winning draught beers are served using a cask breather device in many of the 182 tied houses. Those houses not using the device have been designated 'Traditional Ale Houses'. Free trade covers southern England, London and the West Country. Dorset IPA has now been replaced by Thomas Hardy Country Bitter, a modification of the IPA recipe, with more hops but the same ABV. Meanwhile, the company's 'huntsman' trademark has been sold to Allied which is keen to establish its similar Tetley logo in the South.

Dorchester Bitter (OG 1033, ABV 3.3%) A light bitter with a well-balanced flavour of malt and hop and a hoppy aftertaste. A well-made session beer.

Best Bitter or EP (OG 1037, ABV 3.8%) Bland bitter with an unremarkable flavour of malt and hops in balance. Often found in keg or top pressure form.

Thomas Hardy Country Bitter* (OG 1041, ABV 4.2%)

Royal Oak (OG 1048, ABV 5%) A well-rounded brew where fruit and malt dominate in both aroma and taste. The flavour is balanced with hops and bitterness; some sweetness.

ELGOOD'S

Elgood & Sons Ltd., North Brink Brewery, Wisbech, Cambs, PE13 1LN. Tel. (0945) 583160

ELGOOD'S

Now the only brewery left in Cambridgeshire, supplying 49 of its 51 tied houses with real ale. Over 200 free trade outlets span much of East Anglia.

Bitter or EB (OG 1036, ABV 4.1%) Beer with a malty and slightly fruity aroma. There's a fine balance of malt and hops on the palate, with a fruitiness when found at its best. Satisfying bitter finish, with malt and faint hops lingering, too.

Greyhound Strong Bitter or GSB (OG 1045, ABV 5.2%) A very malty beer, with faint hops and fruit also in the flavour. Bitterness comes through in the aftertaste. Increasingly difficult to find.

Winter Warmer* (OG 1080, ABV 7.5%) Produced for Christmas 1989, but no decision has been made about its future.

EVERARDS

Everards Brewery Ltd., Castle Acres, Narborough, Leicester, LE9 5BY. Tel. (0533) 630900

A small, family-owned brewery, situated on the outskirts of Leicester, which has extended its plant and no longer licenses beers for brewing at the Heritage Brewery. 98 of its 130 tied houses sell real ale, many offering guest beers. Everards also supplies around 500 free trade outlets.

Mild (OG 1033, ABV 3.1%) Satisfying, ruby-coloured beer, with an aroma of malt and fruit. Full-bodied malt flavour, with more than a hint of cherries. Long, malty finish.

Beacon Bitter (OG 1036, ABV 3.8%) Light golden beer with an aroma of hops and honey. The flavour balances malt and hops and the finish lingers.

Tiger Best Bitter (OG 1041, ABV 4.2%) Copper-brown, with a malty, hoppy aroma and a soft, malty palate, with plenty of balancing hops and an underlying fruitiness. The finish is long, dry, hoppy and malty. A good, balanced, medium-bodied bitter.

Old Original (OG 1050, ABV 5.2%) Beer with a smooth, distinctive palate and a faint, hoppy, fruity aroma. Dry, with malt and caramel flavours and some sweetness beneath. The finish is malty and sweetish; the colour is copper brown.

Old Bill Winter Warmer* (OG 1070, ABV 7.3%) Brewed Dec–Jan.

EXMOOR

Exmoor Ales Ltd., Golden Hill Brewery, Wiveliscombe, Somerset, TA4 2NY. Tel (0984) 23798

Somerset's largest brewery, founded in 1980 and supplying over 125 pubs in the county and another 200 or so throughout the South West. Increased interest in other areas of the country has led to an expansion in production. No houses of its own.

Exmoor Ale (OG 1039, ABV 3.8%) Pale brown beer with a malty aroma and a predominantly malty taste. Bitter and malty finish. Very drinkable.

Exmoor Dark (OG 1042, ABV 4.1%) Mid-brown in colour with a malty aroma and a slight roast malt flavour. Bitter finish.

Exmoor Gold (OG 1045, ABV 4.5%) As its name suggests, a golden, straw-coloured beer with a malty aroma. The taste is sweet and malty, with a hint of hops; a sweet, malty finish, too.

FEDERATION

Northern Clubs Federation Brewery Ltd., Lancaster Road, Dunston, Tyne & Wear, NE11 9JR. Tel. (091) 460 9023

A co-operative, founded in 1919, which expanded to supply pubs and clubs through its own depots and wholesalers. This now accounts for the majority of the brewery's business, although it does have six tied houses, two of which take real ale. Only a very small proportion of the brewery's output is cask-conditioned.

Best Bitter (OG 1036, ABV 3.6%) Although variable, when on top form this has a hoppy aroma, a bitter flavour and a well-balanced aftertaste. Really an ordinary, rather than a best bitter.

Special Ale (OG 1041, ABV 4%) Can, again, be variable – if you can find it! Should be sweetish with malt and hop flavours. However, maize can be detected.

FELINFOEL **Felinfoel Brewery Co. Ltd., Farmers Row, Felinfoel, Llanelli, Dyfed, SA14 8LB. Tel. (0554) 773356/7**

The Lewis family still have the major holding in this famous Welsh brewery and they are committed to independence. Runs 86 tenanted houses and serves a direct free trade which extends from Aberystwyth to Hereford and Bristol.

Bitter (OG 1033, ABV 3.2%) A very drinkable session beer, enjoying a hoppy aroma and a bitter and slightly malty flavour. Refreshing finish. Now very difficult to find, but has recently benefitted from increased promotion.

Double Dragon (OG 1041, ABV 4.1%) Hops and malt are in the aroma of this full-bodied beer which has a balanced malt and fruit flavour and a rich, bittersweet finish.

FLOWERS See Whitbread, page 480.

FORBES **Forbes Ales, The Brewery, Harbour Road Industrial Estate, Oulton Broad, Lowestoft, Suffolk, NR32 3LZ. Tel. (0502) 587905**

Brewery set up in 1988, run by possibly the only brewer to hold a degree in sculpture. The beers, also available in bottles, are supplied to the free trade, although there is now an ale house within the brewery itself. Merrie Monarch and Black Shuck are the staple brews, with the others available as capacity permits (OGs can vary). All the beers, however, are brewed out to be stronger than even their high gravity suggests!

Light Bitter* (OG 1040) A recent, less potent addition to the range.

Best Bitter or Traditional (OG 1048) A copper-coloured, bitter beer, with a dry hoppiness dominating the palate and aftertaste, though with a moderate, balancing maltiness throughout.

India Pale Ale (OG 1048) Pale brown, with little aroma, but with a full and balanced flavour and a hoppy, bitter aftertaste.

Merrie Monarch (OG 1072) Strong, dark brown beer with hops and malt in the nose. Roast malt and fruit are prominent on the tongue, followed by a malty finish, yet not without some balancing hops and bitterness.

Black Shuck (OG 1072) As its name suggests, a very black and intense stout. Roast malt bursts onto the nose and remains throughout, but there is also a strong hop presence and a bittersweet quality. The aftertaste is dry, with roast malt and hops.

FRANKLIN'S — **Franklin's Brewery, Bilton Lane, Bilton, Harrogate, N. Yorks, HG1 4DH. Tel. (0423) 322345**

A small brewery set up in 1980 behind the Gardeners Arms. Serves three permanent and 25 guest outlets, but not the Gardeners.

Bitter — (OG 1038, ABV 4%) A tremendous, flowery, fruity nose leads into a full, balanced palate, still fruity and with hops and some malt contributing to a distinctive mix of flavours. The finish is sweet and hoppy, with some malt.

FREMLINS — See Whitbread, page 479.

FRIARY MEUX — See Allied Breweries, page 468.

FULLER'S — **Fuller, Smith and Turner PLC, Griffin Brewery, Chiswick, London, W4 2QB. Tel. (081) 994 3691**

One of the two surviving London independent brewers after the 1960s takeover spree. Pub acquisitions continue apace, with the aim of having 200 pubs by the year 2000. At present there are 156, with all but three serving real ale. Uses the CAMRA logo in advertisements for its cask beers; this is not surprising as they are regular CAMRA award-winners. An expanding free trade takes in about 500 outlets, with the brewery now having taken a majority interest in West Country Products, a London real ale distributor. Brewery redevelopments are still progressing.

Chiswick Bitter — (OG 1034, ABV 3.5%) A light but distinctive, amber beer, with strong but balanced hop and malt flavours, and some fruitiness. A refreshing, bitter finish. Champion Beer of Britain 1989.

London Pride — (OG 1040, ABV 4.1%) Fruity and well-hopped, with a strong, balancing malt presence. The finish is malty and can be either dry or sweetish. A bitter to savour.

Mr Harry* — (OG 1048, ABV 4.3%) An occasional brew.

ESB — (OG 1054, ABV 5.5%) A copper-red, strong bitter, with a rich, malty and fruity palate, saved from being cloying by a hoppy bitterness. A malty, bittersweet finish rounds off this classic beer.

FURGUSONS — See Allied Breweries, page 467.

GALE'S — **George Gale & Co. Ltd., Horndean, Portsmouth, Hants, PO8 0DA. Tel. (0705) 594050**

Hampshire's largest independent brewery with real ale in all its 95 pubs and an extensive free trade over a 40 mile radius. Unusually produces two milds and a naturally-conditioned beer sold in a corked bottle – Prize Old Ale (OG 1095, ABV 8.5 %), which is very occasionally available on draught in a select few outlets (usually at Christmas time). Best Bitter is a recent addition to the range, whilst Pompey Royal (OG 1043) is now brewed for Whitbread.

XXXL (OG 1030, ABV 2.9 %) Light brown mild ale that drinks more like a light bitter. A low aroma beer, with a malty flavour and a light bitter finish. Only available in seven of Gale's own pubs.

XXXD (OG 1031, ABV 2.9 %) A dark mild with a reddish tint. The balance is upset by a caramel sweetness and the finish is bittersweet.

BBB or Butser Brew Bitter (OG 1037, ABV 3.6 %) A mid-brown, very ordinary brew. Drinks very thinly, with meagre malt and hop characteristics. A little more flavour comes through in the finish. Also known as 'Ordinary'.

Best Bitter (OG 1040, ABV 3.8 %) A new mid-brown beer, introduced in 1989. Sweetish, with most of the flavour in the dryish finish. Not unpleasant but slightly lacking for its gravity.

XXXXX (OG 1044, ABV 4.2 %) Very dark, ruby winter brew. A malty beer with caramel sweetness and fruit dominant. Some bitterness in the finish, which is also rather sweet. The result of blending sugars, BBB and Prize Old Ale (a hint of which peeps through).

HSB (OG 1051, ABV 4.6 %) Medium brown in colour with a hoppy nose. A malty flavour lurks behind the slightly fruity sweetness. The finish is more balanced, with sweetness, malt and hoppy bitterness present.

GIBBS MEW **Gibbs Mew PLC, Anchor Brewery, Milford Street, Salisbury, Wilts, SP1 2AR. Tel. (0722) 411911**

A family brewery, established in 1856, with real ale in all but three of its 130 pubs. Extensive free trade in southern and south western England.

Wiltshire Traditional Bitter (OG 1036, ABV 3.5 %) Pleasant enough flavour of malt and hops, but frankly bland and uninspiring. Dry finish.

Local Line (OG 1036, ABV 3.5 %) A clean-tasting bitter to be savoured. Moderately-hopped and slightly fruity. An ideal lunchtime ale.

Premium Bitter (OG 1042, ABV 4.2 %) A truly bland and uninteresting beer. A small, corky taste and an overbearing sweetness are only tempered by bitterness in the aftertaste. Dwindling availability.

Salisbury Best (OG 1042, ABV 4.2 %) Rather chewy, sweet ale, decidedly lacking in bitterness. The title 'Best' is somewhat misleading, but, all the same, it's a pleasant beer.

Bishop's Tipple (OG 1066, ABV 6.5 %) Weaker than the average barley wine, but not lacking in flavour. The full-bodied taste is marvellously malty with a kick that leaves the brain rather less clear than the beer!

GLENNY — **Glenny Brewery Co., The Two Rivers Brewery, Station Lane, Witney, Oxon, OX8 6BH. Tel. (0993) 702574**

Set up in 1983 in part of the old Clinch's brewery, Glenny then moved to its own premises from which it supplies roughly 70 free trade outlets.

Witney Bitter (OG 1036, ABV 3.7%) A pleasantly hoppy and malty, light brown session beer with a roast and fruit aroma.

Wychwood Best (OG 1044, ABV 4.5%) Mid-brown, full-flavoured premium bitter. Moderately strong in hop and malt flavours, with pleasing fruity overtones which last through to the aftertaste.

Hobgoblin (OG 1058, ABV 6.2%) Powerful, full-bodied, copper-red, well-balanced brew, reminiscent of a Bavarian style. Strong in roasted malt, with a moderate, hoppy bitterness and a slight fruity character.

GOACHER'S — **P & D J Goacher, Hayle Mill Cottages, Bockingford, Maidstone, Kent, ME15 6DT. Tel. (0622) 682112**

Kent's most successful small independent brewer, producing all malt ales with Kentish hops for about 30 free trade outlets in the Maidstone area. Brewing has moved to a site in a nearby trading estate, but the company address remains the same.

Maidstone Light (OG 1036) A very hoppy but moderately malty, bitter beer, with a strong, hoppy aroma and aftertaste. Golden or pale brown in colour. An excellent session beer.

Maidstone Dark (OG 1040) Darker than most bitters, a truly bitter but also malty ale with a complex, lingering aftertaste.

Maidstone Old (OG 1066) A powerful, black old ale, known locally as 1066.

GOLDFINCH — **Goldfinch Brewery (Tom Brown's), 47 High East Street, Dorchester, Dorset, DT1 1HU. Tel. (0305) 264020**

Former free house, now a brew pub, acting out a scene from *Tom Brown's Schooldays.* Two breweries operate here, producing about 19 barrels a week, with further expansion planned. Supplies a growing free trade.

Tom Brown's Best Bitter (OG 1039, ABV 4%) A pale bitter with a fruity aroma. The taste is predominantly of malt and fruit, with some hop. Complex aftertaste. Somewhat variable in character but worth finding.

Flashman's Clout Strong Ale (OG 1043, ABV 4.5%) Malty and fruity in aroma and taste. Has a clean, bitter hop tang with some sweetness and a bittersweet aftertaste. Again, variable but worth trying.

GRAND METROPOLITAN BREWING See page 474.

GREENALLS **Greenall Whitley PLC, Wilderspool, Warrington, Cheshire, WA4 6RH. Tel. (0925) 51234**

Real ale in 517 of its 1025 tied houses, with sales of Bitter and Thomas Greenall's Original increasing in the free trade, but Mild sadly in decline. Original has been well promoted as the company's main vehicle for capturing a share of the new guest beer market and Greenalls continues to push into Yorkshire, the East Midlands and the North East. Contrary to rumours, high gravity brewing, it appears, is not being used for cask ale production. Another welcome change involves the end of sales of keg beer through fake handpumps; there are still a few examples in use, but these should soon be eradicated. The group also continues to expand into the hotel and 'upgraded' pub direction, through its De Vere hotels and Country Inns.

Mild (OG 1032, ABV 3.2%) Dark, malty mild, with a faint, malty aroma. Hints of caramel, nuttiness, fruit and bitterness in the taste and a slight malty finish. Good when on form, but let down by a tendency to be thin, sweet and bland.

Bitter (OG 1036.5, ABV 3.8%) Reasonably well-balanced beer with bitterness tending to dominate. Some fruit and sweetness, and a lingering, dry aftertaste. Can be fairly hoppy but is often thin and uninspiring.

Thomas Greenall's Original Bitter (OG 1045, ABV 4.5%) A full-bodied premium bitter with a malt and hop aroma. A bitter taste predominates, though malt, fruit, hops and a little sweetness are also apparent. Strong bitter finish, with some maltiness.

Greenalls Midlands Ltd., Star Brewery, Radford Road, New Basford, Nottingham, NG7 7FN. Tel. (0602) 785074

Following the closure of Davenports in July 1989, all beers are now brewed at the former Shipstone's brewery in Nottingham (no comprehensive tastings have been carried out on the new Davenports brews for this guide). 550 pubs are held in the tied estate, 500 serving cask ale. The past year has also seen a reduction in the number of outlets taking Davenports Mild.

Shipstone's Mild (OG 1034, ABV 3.6%) Ruby/dark brown in colour with a malty nose, but overly bitter for a mild. Resembles a bitter dosed with caramel and chocolate malt. Reliable pints are rare; in fact, any pint is rare at the rate it is fading from the scene.

Davenports Best Mild Ale* (OG 1035, ABV 3.2%)

Wem Best Bitter* (OG 1037, 3.7%) Once a distinctive bitter.

Shipstone's Bitter (OG 1037, ABV 4%) Gold in colour and almost overwhelmingly bitter in taste, with a metallic edge. Some hop in the nose, but little in the mouth. Once one of the great beers but has now lost its subtlety under Greenalls.

Davenports Traditional Bitter* (OG 1038, ABV 3.9%)

GREENE KING **Greene, King & Sons PLC, Westgate Brewery, Bury St Edmunds, Suffolk, IP33 1QT. Tel. (0284) 763222/ The Brewery, Biggleswade, Beds, SG18 0JR. Tel. (0767) 313935**

East Anglia's largest regional brewery, producing cask-conditioned beers at Bury; Biggleswade, however, is now entirely given over to lager production. Closed Rayments brewery at Furneux Pelham in 1987, but continues to brew the Rayments brand – a poor imitation of its former self. All the 750 tied houses serve cask ale (but, sadly, a great many using top pressure or cask breathers). Cask beer is also widely available in the free trade in the South East, accounting for half the production. A new distribution depot has been set up in Tunbridge Wells, to supply new trade in Kent and Sussex.

XX Dark (OG 1032, ABV 3%) A dark, russet brown mild which has quite a big taste for its strength – malty, fruity and chocolatey. The distinct, nutty finish seems to have become sweeter of late.

IPA (OG 1036, ABV 3.6%) Some landlords are able to coax a well-balanced hoppiness out of this aroma-free ale, but bland immaturity is usually the order of the day. The bitter finish is often the best feature.

Rayments BBA (OG 1036, ABV 3.6%) Undistinguished successor to the once-superb Furneux Pelham-brewed ale of this name. The inoffensive, slightly soapy flavour quickly fades into nothingness.

Abbot Ale (OG 1049, ABV 5%) Like most Greene King brews, lacks much in the way of nose but more than compensates with a veritable explosion of flavours and a strong hoppiness unusual in beers of this strength.

Winter Ale (OG 1052) A new brew which replaced Christmas Ale last year, but which, like its predecessor, is available only for a few weeks around the festive season. A fine example of the old ale style, dark, malty and warming.

GUERNSEY **Guernsey Brewery Co. (1920) Ltd., South Esplanade, St Peter Port, Guernsey, CI. Tel. (0481) 720143**

One of two breweries on this Channel Isle, serving stronger than average real ales in 15 of their 35 tied houses (excise duty is levied here on quantity not strength). Trades under the name 'Pony Ales'. Free trade covers Alderney, Herm and Jersey. Taken over by Jersey's Ann Street Brewery in

1988 and Guernsey real ale is now available in selected Ann Street houses. Grizzly's Real Ale is a brewery mix of mild and bitter, produced for just one hotel.

LBA Mild (OG 1037, ABV 3.7%) A copper-coloured mild having a complex malty and fruity aroma, with some hop character. Fruity and malty in flavour, followed by a full, dry and malty finish.

Real Draught Bitter (OG 1045, ABV 4.2%) A full-bodied bitter, pale brown in colour. The aroma is of malt and fruit, which also dominate the palate. Dry, malty finish.

GUINNESS See page 476.

HADRIAN **Hadrian Brewery Ltd., Unit 7, Foundry Lane Industrial Estate, Byker, Newcastle upon Tyne, NE6 1LH. Tel. (091) 276 5302**

Founded in 1987 by keen home-brewer Trevor Smith. Still increasing production to cope with demand – now supplying around 25 outlets, as far south as Leeds. About 30 barrels of this range of pure, adjunct-free beers are now produced each week.

Gladiator Bitter (OG 1039, ABV 4%) A smooth, well-rounded, flavoursome pint, with a nicely balanced aroma, a hoppy/bitter taste, with some underlying fruitiness, and a well-balanced, dry finish.

Centurion Best Bitter (OG 1045, ABV 4.5%) Excellently-balanced beer enjoying a strong hops and malt presence, and a pleasing, hoppy finish.

Emperor Ale* (OG 1050, ABV 5%) Strong winter warmer.

Yule Fuel* (OG 1060, ABV 6.2%) Christmas ale.

HALL & WOODHOUSE **Hall & Woodhouse Ltd., The Brewery, Blandford Forum, Dorset, DT11 9LS. Tel. (0258) 452141**

More usually known as 'Badger's', the brewery serves cask beer in all its 149 houses, although some of the pubs use a cask breather device on both the Best Bitter and the award-winning Tanglefoot. Free trade to much of southern England, including London and Bedfordshire via wholesalers.

Badger Best Bitter (OG 1041, ABV 4%) Full-flavoured, with a fruity aroma. The taste is strong in bitterness and hoppiness, with fruity undertones. Too bitter for some, but excellent drinking.

Tanglefoot (OG 1048, ABV 4.9%) Pale beer with a strong flavour of fruit and malt and some hoppiness. Bittersweet aftertaste. A strong but subtle brew.

HALLS See Allied Breweries, page 468.

HANBY **Hanby Ales, Unit C9, Wem Industrial Estate, Wem, Shropshire, SY4 5SD. Tel. (0939) 32432**

Brewery which began operations in March 1989 and moved

to new premises in February 1990. Serves about 15 outlets and the guest beer market.

Drawwell Bitter* (OG 1039, ABV 3.9%)

Treacleminer* (OG 1046, ABV 4.6%)

Nutcracker* (OG 1060, ABV 6%) The 1989 Christmas offering.

HANCOCK'S See Bass, page 472.

HANSON'S **Hanson's Brewery, High Street, Dudley, W. Midlands, DY1 1QR. Tel. (0902) 711811**

Victorian Black Country brewery with real ale in all 153 tied houses. The other half of Wolverhampton & Dudley Breweries (see Banks's). Hanson's Bitter is brewed by Banks's at Wolverhampton. Mild Ale is only available in cask-conditioned form.

Mild Ale (OG 1035, ABV 3.5%) Maltiness in the aroma and a balanced taste of malt with caramel and roast malt flavours. A dry, hoppy and malty, smooth finish.

Bitter (OG 1035, ABV 3.4%) An aroma of malt and hops precedes a rather disappointing flavour. More hops evident in the finish.

HARDYS & HANSONS **Hardys & Hansons PLC, Kimberley Brewery, Nottingham, NG16 2NS. Tel. (0602) 383611**

Nottingham's last independent brewery, arising from a merger in 1930 between two neighbouring breweries. Noted for good value beers. Sadly, a tendency to use top pressure for dispense is a feature of many managed houses.

Best Mild (OG 1035, ABV 3.1%) A dark, sweet mild, slightly malty. Can have fruity notes.

Best Bitter (OG 1039, ABV 3.9%) Golden/straw-coloured, distinctive, faintly fruity beer. Subtle in aroma; malt more prominent than hop character and balancing bitterness.

HARTLEYS **Hartleys (Ulverston) Ltd., The Old Brewery, Ulverston, Cumbria, LA12 7HX. Tel. (0229) 53269**

Brewery famous for its 'Beers from the Wood', which was taken over by Robinson's of Stockport in 1982. Supplies cask ale to all its 57 pubs. Fellrunners was introduced late in 1988, to provide a beer between the strength of the ordinary bitter and XB.

Mild (OG 1031, ABV 2.9%) Very variable in quality, but a good pint is worth finding. Malty and bitter aroma, with a not-unpleasant hint of aniseed. Smooth, drinkable and well-balanced. The aftertaste is predominantly bitter but somewhat short-lived.

Bitter (OG 1031, ABV 3%) Straw-coloured beer with little aroma. Thin and slightly bitter, with a lingering bitter aftertaste.

Drunk more by visitors than by locals, who prefer the fuller-bodied XB.

Fellrunners (OG 1035, ABV 3.3%) Very hard to find anywhere near the brewery; a little more popular in the Lake District. Darker and more malty than the bitter, with a pleasant hop character and a lasting, bitter aftertaste.

XB (OG 1040, ABV 4%) The most commonly available, but least consistent, of all the brews. Pale brown in colour, with a hoppy and fruity aroma. Strong, bitter, faintly fruity and sweet flavour, with a lingering after-bitterness.

HARVEYS **Harvey & Son (Lewes) Ltd., Bridge Wharf Brewery, Cliffe High Street, Lewes, E. Sussex, BN7 2AH. Tel. (0273) 480209**

Traditional family brewery with real ale in all 33 tied pubs and about 300 free trade outlets in Sussex and Kent. Frequently produces commemorative beers – occasionally on draught.

XX Mild Ale (OG 1030, ABV 3%) A pleasant, dark brew which is only just continuing to hold on. The aroma and taste have a malty, roast character, and the palate is fruity and sweetish. The aftertaste is similar, with lingering malt. Well worth finding.

Pale Ale (OG 1032, ABV 3.5%) A very well-hopped, refreshing brew. Hops are in the aroma and palate, with some fruit and sweetness. Hops in the finish, too, with some bitterness. A very good session beer.

Best Bitter or BB (OG 1038, ABV 4%) A fine example of a full-bodied southern bitter. Its hoppy aroma gives way to a fruity, sweetish palate. The complex aftertaste features hops, with some bitterness, yet with a lingering sweetness.

XXXX (Old) (OG 1042, ABV 4.3%) Brewed Oct–April. Rich and dark, with lively fruitiness and a caramelly flavour. Mellow and smooth when on form.

Armada Ale (OG 1046, ABV 4.5%) Well-hopped strong bitter with a powerful finish.

Elizabethan* (OG 1090) A silky-smooth barley wine, occasionally available on draught.

HARVIESTOUN **Harviestoun Brewery Ltd., Dollar, Clackmannanshire, Central, FK14 7LX. Tel. (025 94) 2141**

One of Scotland's few remaining small breweries, operating from a former dairy at the foot of the Ochil Hills, near Stirling. Now serves 20 outlets in central Scotland; beer is also available by the pint from the brewery and through real ale agencies. A new beer, Waverley Ale, is brewed exclusively for Malt Shovel Inns, Edinburgh. Changes possible in the beer range.

Waverley Ale* (OG 1036.5, ABV 3.9%)

Harviestoun Ale* (OG 1041, ABV 4.1%)

Old Manor* (OG 1050, ABV 5.1%) A dark beer with a roast malt flavour.

New Year Ale* (OG 1090, ABV 9.2%) As its name suggests, a winter brew.

HERIOT See Bass, page 473.

HERITAGE **Heritage Brewery Co., Anglesey Road, Burton upon Trent, Staffs, DE14 3PF. Tel. (0283) 63563**

The brewing company of the Heritage Museum, based in the former Everards Tiger Brewery, though it no longer brews under licence for Everards. Heritage Bitter is distributed to a small free trade by Lloyds (see page 437). Thomas Sykes Ale is mostly in corked bottles, but also on draught.

Bitter* (OG 1045, ABV 4.2%)

Thomas Sykes Ale* (OG 1100, ABV 10%)

HESKET NEWMARKET **Hesket Newmarket Brewery, Old Crown Barn, Hesket Newmarket, Cumbria, CA7 8JG. Tel. (069 98) 288**

Brewery officially opened in 1988 by telex message from a regular, Chris Bonington, from Kathmandu! From supplying the Old Crown Inn, it has expanded successfully into the free trade. Wrynose and Old Carrock are summer/winter beers respectively. A stout is planned for 1991.

Wrynose Light Bitter* (OG 1027, ABV 2.5%)

Blencathra Bitter* (OG 1035, ABV 3.5%)

Skiddaw Special Bitter* (OG 1035, ABV 3.5%)

Doris's 90th Birthday Ale* (OG 1045, ABV 4.5%)

Old Carrock Strong Ale* (OG 1060, ABV 6.25%)

HIGHGATE See Bass, page 471.

HIGSONS See Whitbread, page 479.

HILDEN **Hilden Brewery, Hilden House, Lisburn, Co. Antrim. Tel (0846) 663863**

Mini brewery in a Georgian country house, set up in 1981 to counter the local all-keg Guinness/Bass duopoly. Presently the only real ale brewery in Northern Ireland, supplying seven regular outlets and free trade which now includes England.

Hilden Ale (OG 1039) Dark and golden, with a fruity, hoppy aroma and a bitter, hoppy and fruity taste. Dry finish, with a good balance of malt and hops.

Special Reserve (OG 1042) A dry and well-balanced, deep copper-coloured beer. The aroma is of malt and fruit, and the flavour has a complex maltiness. A pronounced nutty finish.

HOLDEN'S **Holden's Brewery Ltd., George Street, Woodsetton, Dudley, W. Midlands, DY1 4LN. Tel. (0902) 880051**

One of the long-established family breweries of the Black Country, producing a good range of real ales for its 18 tied houses and over 100 free trade customers. A new brew, XB, was introduced in 1989 to fill the gap between Bitter and Special.

Stout (OG 1037, ABV 3.4%) Dark brown beer, with malt and roast in the flavour and a slight hoppy aftertaste.

Mild (OG 1037, ABV 3.6%) Well-balanced, dark brown mild of malt, roast and hop flavours and a malty and hoppy finish.

Bitter (OG 1039, ABV 3.9%) Light brown in colour. A hoppy beer, with a malty, bitter taste and a dry, hoppy finish.

XB* (OG 1041, ABV 4.1%) Often sold as a house beer, with each outlet giving it its own name.

Special (OG 1051, ABV 4.9%) A pale brown, malty bitter, with a bitter and sweet aftertaste. Strong and full-bodied.

XL Old Ale (OG 1092, ABV 8.5%) Only available in December: very fruity and sweet; a very strong and warming beer.

HOLT **Joseph Holt PLC, Derby Brewery, Empire Street, Cheetham, Manchester, M3 1JD. Tel. (061) 834 3285**

Not to be confused with Allied's Midlands company Holts (Holt, Plant & Deakin). A traditional family firm, which brews Britain's cheapest bitter. Real ale in all 96 tied houses, often delivered in hogsheads (54 gallon barrels) such is its enthusiastic following. Only one pub does not sell Mild. The fast-growing free trade to pubs and clubs currently stands at 37 outlets.

Mild (OG 1033, ABV 3.2%) Very dark beer. Good body, with a malty, fruity aroma and taste. Strong in hoppiness and bitterness for a mild, reflected in the characteristic aftertaste.

Bitter (OG 1039, ABV 4%) Pale brown in colour, with a strong hop aroma. Although balanced by malt and fruit, the uncompromising bitterness can be a shock to the unwary and extends into the aftertaste.

HOLTS (HP&D) See Allied Breweries, page 467.

HOME See Scottish & Newcastle, page 478.

HOOK NORTON **Hook Norton Brewery Co. Ltd., Hook Norton, Banbury, Oxon, OX15 5NY. Tel. (0608) 737210**

One of the most delightful traditional tower breweries in Britain, with all its 34 country pubs serving real ale. Extensive free trade.

Mild (OG 1032, ABV 2.9%) A copper-red mild with a malty aroma and a malty, hoppy taste, tinged with a little fruitiness and a sweetish balance. Hoppy and malty in the aftertaste. Splendid and highly drinkable.

Best Bitter (OG 1035, ABV 3.3%) An excellently-balanced, golden bitter. Malty and hoppy on the nose and in the mouth, with a hint of fruitiness. Dry, but with some balancing sweetness. A hoppy bitterness dominates the finish.

Old Hookey (OG 1049, ABV 4.3%) A mid-brown, unusual beer, with a strong, nutty, grainy aroma and palate, balanced by fruitiness. Sweetish and full-bodied, with a bitter, malty aftertaste.

HOP BACK **Hop Back Brewery, Wyndham Arms, 27 Estcourt Road, Salisbury, Wilts, SP1 3AS. Tel. (0722) 28594**

A brew pub, rapidly expanding into the free trade and producing some 30 barrels a week. Summer Lightning and Special are award-winners. Plans to brew Entire Stout (at present a mainly winter brew) for most of the year.

GFB (OG 1035, ABV 3.5%) Golden, with the sort of light, refreshing quality which makes an ideal session ale. Mellow and fruity in flavour, with a caramel overtone. A hint of honey in the aroma, and a long, well-balanced finish.

Special or Flintnapper (OG 1040, ABV 4%) Not that special. Hops are much in evidence but it lacks a little in flavour and body. Quite a dry palate and a slightly peppery flavour. Long start, but short finish.

Entire Stout* (OG 1044, ABV 4.6%)

Summer Lightning (OG 1050, ABV 5%) Extremely pleasurable beer with a terrific, fresh, hoppy aroma and a well-rounded, malty flavour. An excellent, long, dry finish follows. First class.

HOSKINS **Hoskins Brewery PLC, Beaumanor Brewery, Beaumanor Road, Leicester, LE4 5QE. Tel. (0533) 661122**

The smallest remaining pre-WW1 brewery. Supplies real ale to all its 11 tied houses.

Beaumanor Bitter (OG 1039, ABV 3.9%) Very drinkable and refreshing, amber-coloured beer with a thin yet satisfying texture. An aroma of hops and fruit leads on to a hoppy taste and then a long, malty finish.

Penn's Ale (OG 1045, ABV 4.3%) Full-bodied, easy-drinking beer, golden in colour and with a slightly fruity aroma. Rich, malty and well-balanced in flavour, followed by a clean, dry, crystal malt finish.

Premium (OG 1050, ABV 4.6%) Pale gold beer with fruit and toffee in the aroma, and fruit and some mustiness in the flavour. Slightly cloying, fruity finish.

Old Nigel (OG 1060, ABV 5.7%) Malt and hints of liquorice are present in the robust flavour of this winter beer. Fruity in aroma, sweet and with a lasting, pleasantly-fruity finish. Russet in colour.

HOSKINS & OLDFIELD **Hoskins & Oldfield Brewery Ltd., North Mills, Frog Island, Leicester, LE3 5DH. Tel. (0533) 532191**

Set up by two members of Leicester's famous brewing family, Philip and Stephen Hoskins, in 1984, after the sale of the old Hoskins Brewery. A wide range of beers is produced for a scattered free trade.

HOB Best Mild (OG 1035) A dark ruby mild with a chocolate and coffee aroma, and a dry, stout-like flavour. Heavy and creamy, with a lasting, dry, malty finish.

HOB Bitter (OG 1041) Golden in colour, with an aroma like peardrops. Its flavour is fruity and hoppy, with a harsh, hoppy, but sweet aftertaste. Not the beer it was.

Little Matty* (OG 1041) Darker version of HOB.

Tom Kelly's Stout (OG 1043) A satisfying stout, dark in colour, with an attractive, golden, creamy head and an aroma of malt and fruit. An exceedingly bitter but malty flavour and a dry, chocolatey finish.

EXS* (OG 1051) A bitter beer, full in body.

Old Navigation Ale (OG 1071) Ruby/black beer, with an aroma reminiscent of sherry. Sweet and fruity, with a stout-like malt flavour.

Christmas Noggin (OG 1100) Russet-coloured beer with a spicy, fruity aroma. The taste is of malt and fruit, and the finish balances malt and hops. Sweet but not cloying.

SARAH HUGHES **Sarah Hughes Brewery, Beacon Hotel, Bilston Street, Sedgley, W. Midlands, DY3 1JE. Tel. (0902) 883380**

Brewery re-opened after lying idle for 30 years, to serve the village pub and a few other outlets. Now produces for the free trade. Possibility of a bitter being added.

Original Dark Ruby Mild (OG 1058, ABV 5.5%) A full-bodied and well-balanced, strong, malty and fruity beer. The aftertaste has malt, roast and quite sweet characteristics.

HULL **Hull Brewery Co. Ltd., 144–148 English Street, Hull, Humbs, HU3 2BT. Tel. (0482) 586364/5**

Set up in 1989 by a former brewery director, Ken Platts, and publican Denis Armstrong in an old fish smokehouse. The beer is mostly sold on the Hull club scene, but also as a guest beer in a few pubs.

Mild* (OG 1032)

HYDES' ANVIL **Hydes' Anvil Brewery Ltd., 46 Moss Lane West, Manchester, M15 5PH. Tel. (061) 226 1317**

Family-controlled traditional brewery, first established in 1863 and on its present site since the turn of the century. It is the smallest of the established Manchester breweries and the only one to produce two real milds. Cask ale in all its 49 tied houses. Slowly expanding in both tied and free trade.

Mild (OG 1032, ABV 3.5%) A light, refreshing, slightly fruity drink with little aftertaste. Fruity aroma, with a hint of malt.

Light (OG 1034, ABV 3.7%) A lightly hopped session beer, complex in character, with malt dominating and a brief but dry finish. Available more in southern Manchester than Mild, and vice-versa in northern parts of the city.

Bitter (OG 1036, ABV 3.8%) Good-flavoured bitter, with a malty nose, fruity background and a malty aftertaste. A hint of bitterness throughout.

Strong Ale (OG 1080, ABV 8%) Rich and fruity in aroma and taste, rather drier than many strong ales. A fruity, yet dry finish. Brewed once a year in October, for distribution in December. Available to all outlets and the free trade in nine gallon casks. Not many landlords stock it, however.

IND COOPE See Allied Breweries, page 467.

ISLE OF MAN **Isle of Man Breweries Ltd., Falcon Brewery, Douglas, Isle of Man. Tel. (0624) 661140**

The island's only major brewery, following the merger in 1986 of the Okell and Castletown breweries. Real ale is produced under the unique Manx Brewers' Act 1874 (permitted ingredients malt, sugar and hops only). Operates from an impressive Victorian brewhouse, serving 70 tied houses, all but one selling real ale.

Okells Mild (OG 1034, ABV 3.5%) A mild, copper in colour, with a light malty and fruity aroma. The clean, crystal malt taste also has an orangey tinge. Plenty of malt in the finish.

Okells Bitter (OG 1035, ABV 3.8%) An excellent bitter, golden-coloured and aromatic of hops and fruit. Hops and malt are well matched in the flavour and the finish is dry and hoppy, becoming malty.

Castletown Bitter (OG 1035, ABV 3.9%) A refreshing, golden, dry beer, rich in hoppiness. Hops are in the aroma and finish, too, with maltose also coming through in the aftertaste.

JENNINGS **Jennings Bros PLC, Castle Brewery, Cockermouth, Cumbria, CA13 9NE. Tel. (0900) 823214**

Traditional brewery in the far North West, whose real ales are not only available in all 76 tied houses, but also in 60 free trade outlets. A new stronger beer, SL, was introduced in summer 1990.

Mild* (OG 1031, ABV 3.1%) A dark, mellow mild.

Bitter (OG 1035, ABV 3.4%) Mid-brown in colour and moderately hoppy and faintly malty in aroma. A good balance of malt and hops in the taste, with some faint caramel. The flavour is strange and flowery, but not totally unpleasant. A lingering, hoppy aftertaste.

SL* (OG 1055)

KING & BARNES

King & Barnes Ltd., The Horsham Brewery, 18 Bishopric, Horsham, W. Sussex, RH12 1QP. Tel. (0403) 69344

Independent family brewery which serves real ale in all its 60 or so country houses. Extensive free trade mostly within a radius of 40 miles. A new mid-strength best bitter, Broadwood, was introduced in September 1989. Beware of LA, a low alcohol keg beer, which although marked as such, is sometimes served on handpull.

Mild (OG 1034, ABV 3.2%) A smooth, malty, dark brown mild, with a bittersweet finish and a malty aroma. Tends to be displaced by Old Ale in winter.

Sussex Bitter (OG 1034, ABV 3.5%) A splendid, hoppy, light bitter, with good malt balance and a dry finish. Can suffer from poor cellarmanship outside the tied estate.

Broadwood (OG 1040, ABV 4%) Mid-brown with a malty aroma. A good marriage of malt and hops is present in the taste, with malt slightly dominating. Lots of flavour for its gravity.

Old (OG 1046, ABV 4.1%) A classic, dark old ale. A fruity, roast malt flavour, with some hops, leads to a sweet, malty finish. Almost like a strong mild; available from November to Easter.

Festive (OG 1050, ABV 4.8%) Copper-coloured with a malty aroma. The flavour is fruity and malty, with hop undertones. Both malt and hops are present in the finish. Good body.

LARKINS

Larkins Brewery Ltd., Larkins Farm, Chiddingstone, Edenbridge, Kent, TN8 7BB. Tel. (0892) 870328

Now operating from premises at the owner's farm at Chiddingstone, having moved from Tunbridge Wells in December 1989. Additive-free beers are brewed, partly using its own hops from the oast house next door. Supplies 60 free houses in the South East.

Traditional Bitter (OG 1035.5, ABV 3.2%) Predominantly bitter in flavour, with a dry, hoppy and bitter finish. Pale brown in colour, with a light, hoppy aroma.

Sovereign Bitter (OG 1040, ABV 4%) A moderately bitter, slightly fruity, copper red ale, with a malty/bitter finish.

Best Bitter (OG 1045.5, ABV 4.7%) Full-bodied, slightly fruity and unusually bitter for its gravity. Dangerously drinkable!

Porter Ale (OG 1053, ABV 5.5%) A black, bittersweet brew enjoying plenty of body and a pleasant bitter aftertaste. A classic.

LEES

J W Lees & Co. (Brewers) Ltd., Greengate Brewery, Middleton Junction, Manchester, M24 2AX. Tel. (061) 643 2487

One of Manchester's clutch of surviving family-owned independent breweries, serving real ale in nearly all 173 of its tied houses and clubs (mostly in northern Manchester). Free trade in the North West.

GB Mild (OG 1032, ABV 3%) Malt and roast aroma, with a malty, fruity, sweet palate. Enjoys the characteristic dry aftertaste unique to Lees beers.

Bitter (OG 1038, ABV 4%) Pale beer with a malty, hoppy aroma and a distinctive, malty, dry and slightly metallic taste. Clean, dry Lees finish. The degrees of malt, hops and bitterness can vary considerably.

Moonraker (OG 1073, ABV 7.5%) Reddish-brown in colour, having a strong, malty, fruity aroma. The flavour is rich and sweet, with some roast malt, and the finish is fruity yet dry. Only available in about a dozen outlets and where gravity dispense is employed quality can vary.

LINFIT

Linfit Brewery, Sair Inn, Lane Top, Linthwaite, Huddersfield, W. Yorks, HD7 5SG. Tel. (0484) 842370

19th-century brew pub which recommenced brewing in 1982, producing an impressive range of ales for sale at the Sair and for free trade as far away as Manchester.

Mild (OG 1032, ABV 3%) Roast malt dominates in this straightforward dark mild. Some hop aroma; slightly dry flavour. The finish is malty.

Bitter (OG 1035, ABV 3.5%) Good session beer. A dry-hopped aroma leads to a clean-tasting, hoppy bitterness, balanced with some maltiness. The finish is well-balanced, too, but sometimes has an intense bitterness.

Special (OG 1041, ABV 4%) Dry-hopping again provides the aroma for this rich and mellow bitter. Very soft profile and character; fills the mouth with texture rather than taste. Clean, rounded finish.

Stout (OG 1041, ABV 4%) A fruity, roasted aroma preludes a smooth, roasted, chocolatey flavour which is bitter but not too dry. Excellent appearance; good, bitter finish.

Old Eli (OG 1050, ABV 5%) Excellent, well-balanced premium bitter with a dry-hopped aroma and a fruity, bitter finish.

Leadboiler (OG 1063, ABV 6%) Flowery and hoppy in aroma, with a very moreish, bitter and strong flavour which provides a soft mouthfeel. Well-balanced by a prominent malt flavour. Rounded, bitter finish.

Enoch's Hammer (OG 1080, ABV 8%) Straw-coloured, vinous bitter with no pretentions about its strength or pedigree. A full, fruity aroma leads on to a smooth, alcoholic, hoppy, bitter taste, with an unexpectedly bitter finish.

Xmas Ale (OG 1082, ABV 8%) A hearty and warming ale. The flavour is strong in roasted malt, with some bitterness. Extremely vinous, with a slightly yeasty, metallic taste. Bitter finish. An adaption of Enoch's Hammer.

LLOYDS

Lloyds Country Beers, John Thompson Inn, Ingleby, Derbyshire. Tel. (0332) 863426/862469

Set up as a home-brew operation at the inn in 1977, Lloyds is now a separate business, serving five regular customers and several free trade outlets. A new session bitter is planned (OG 1034/1035). Also distributes Heritage Bitter from the Heritage Brewery Museum (see page 430).

Derby or Country Bitter* (OG 1042, ABV 4.1%) Full and fruity.

VIP (Very Important Pint)* (OG 1048, 4.3%) Heavier, darker version of the bitter.

Skullcrusher* (OG 1065, ABV 6%) A heavy Christmas beer.

Overdraft* (OG 1070, ABV 6.2%) New brew.

LORIMER & CLARK

See Vaux, page 459, and Caledonian, page 414.

McEWAN

See Scottish & Newcastle, page 477.

MACLAY

Maclay & Co. Ltd., Thistle Brewery, Alloa, Clackmannanshire, Central, FK10 1ED. Tel. (0259) 723387

One of Scotland's two remaining independent breweries after the takeover typhoon swept through the country. Supplies real ale to about half of its 28 houses and an appreciative free trade. New 30 litre beer sphere containers have been made available for the take-home/party trade.

PA 60/-* (OG 1030, ABV 3%) Flavoursome, dark session beer.

SPA 70/-* (OG 1034, ABV 3.3%) Well-hopped, quenching beer.

Export 80/-* (OG 1040, ABV 4%) Well-balanced and rich.

Porter* (OG 1040, ABV 4%) Dark and tasty.

McMULLEN

McMullen & Sons Ltd., The Hertford Brewery, Hertford, SG14 1RD. Tel. (0992) 584911

Brewers in Hertfordshire since 1827, an independent family brewery. Serves cask-conditioned beer in all its 160 pubs and in the local free trade.

Original AK (OG 1033, ABV 3.8%) Originally called AK Mild, but renamed and remarketed by the company. A pleasant, drinkable light bitter, dark in colour and presenting a malty, hoppy aroma, with slight fruit presence. Reasonably-balanced taste, and a hoppy, malty finish.

Country Best Bitter (OG 1041, ABV 4.6%) Fullish-bodied beer, with a malty, hoppy taste and a pronounced, well-balanced aftertaste. Fruit is present in both aroma and flavour. Also available in keg form.

Stronghart* (OG 1070, ABV 7%) A rich, dark winter brew.

MALTON **Malton Brewery Co. Ltd., Crown Hotel, Wheelgate, Malton, N. Yorks, YO17 0HP. Tel. (0653) 697580**

Set up in 1985 behind a pub, by an ex-Russells and Wrangham brewer, to revive Malton's proud brewing heritage. Serves about ten pubs locally and an expanding free trade in Yorkshire and the North. Prides itself on the use of malt, hops, yeast, water and finings only. Occasional special beers from time to time.

Pale Ale* (OG 1033.8, ABV 3.5%) A light session beer.

Double Chance Bitter* (OG 1037.8, ABV 3.8%) Well-hopped.

Pickwick's Porter* (OG 1041.8, ABV 4.1%) A dry stout.

Owd Bob* (OG 1054.8, ABV 5.5%) A dry, dark winter warmer.

MANNS See Grand Metropolitan, page 474.

MANSFIELD **Mansfield Brewery Company, Littleworth, Mansfield, Notts, NG18 1AB. Tel. (0623) 25691**

One of the country's major regional brewers with one or more of their real ales available in 90% of their 300-plus tied houses. Substantial free trade, especially in East Midlands clubs, and a reciprocal trading arrangement with Charles Wells. The introduction of a true cask-conditioned mild during the last year has been a most welcome development and resulted in mild sales reversing a 5% per annum decline into positive growth.

Riding Dark Mild (OG 1035, ABV 3.1%) Dark brown with a hint of red. A predominantly chocolate malt taste and finish, with a dash of fruit, follow a pleasant roast malt aroma.

Riding Traditional Bitter (OG 1035, ABV 3.5%) Pale brown, with a malty, hoppy nose. A firm malt background is overlaid with a good bitter bite and hop flavours.

Old Baily (OG 1045, ABV 4.5%) Resembles a Scotch heavy, but with a fine balance of hop, malt and fruit flavours. Dark copper-red in colour, with an aroma of malt and fruit.

MARSTON MOOR

Marston Moor Brewery, c/o Crown Inn, Kirk Hammerton, York, N. Yorks, YO5 8DD. Tel. (0423) 330341

Small brewery set up in 1984, now brewing about 600 barrels a year to supply the Crown and a scattered free trade. There is a possibility that the brewery will change its name in the next year.

Cromwell Bitter* (OG 1037.5, ABV 3.8%) A distinctive, bitter beer.

Brewers Pride* (OG 1042, ABV 4.4%) A new addition to the range.

Porter* (OG 1042, ABV 4.4%) Another new development.

Brewers Droop* (OG 1050, ABV 5.2%) Potent ale.

MARSTON'S

Marston, Thompson & Evershead PLC, The Brewery, Shobnall Road, Burton upon Trent, Staffs, DE14 2BW. Tel. (0283) 31131

One of Britain's great traditional breweries with real ale in 817 of its 885 pubs, stretching from Cumbria to Hampshire. 37% of production goes to the free trade, with Whitbread introducing Pedigree Bitter into many of its tied houses. The only brewery still using the unique Burton Union system of fermentation for its stronger ales. Four more Union sets have recently been installed. In 1984 took over Border Brewery of Wrexham; bought 49 pubs from Ansells in May 1990.

Border Mild (OG 1031, ABV 3%) Thin, almost black mild with negligible aroma before a slightly malty flavour, with hints of caramel, sulphur and bitterness. Faint, malty, sweetish finish.

Mercian Mild (OG 1032, ABV 3.2%) A copper to dark brown beer, thin, but well-balanced. Hints of roast malt and fruit in the taste, and a sweet, mild finish. A quaffing mild.

Border Bitter (OG 1034, ABV 3.4%) Thinnish, light session beer, pale brown in colour. The slight, well-balanced, malty bitter taste, with hints of fruit and hop, is echoed in the aftertaste.

Border Exhibition (OG 1034, ABV 3.4%) Originally a light mild when brewed in Wrexham, but now a thin, light, mid-brown bitter. Basically a slightly darker version of the Border Bitter, with a hint of caramel in the taste.

Burton Best Bitter (OG 1036, ABV 3.6%) A good pale brown session beer, with chameleon tendencies. Sometimes malt is the chief flavour; at other times it is bitterness, but, on the whole, the beer is well-balanced.

Pedigree Bitter (OG 1043, ABV 4.5%) Golden brown, ubiquitous beer, with hints of malt, hops and apples in the nose. The taste balances malt, hops and fruit, and the finish is good. Quality noted to be poorer in Whitbread outlets.

Merrie Monk (OG 1043, ABV 4.5%) A smooth, dark brew. Has a creamy, slightly sweet flavour, with traces of caramel, roast malt and fruit. Sweet, malty finish.

Owd Rodger (OG 1080, ABV 7.6%) Dark ruby barley wine, with a fruity nose before a deep, winey, heavy fruit flavour, with malt, hops and strawberries in the long finish. Misunderstood, moreish and strong.

MARTIN **Martin Brewery, 92 High Street, Martin, Lincoln, LN4 3QT. Tel. (052 67) 538**

New small brewery, set up in a barn at the rear of the brewer's house in 1988. Produces three barrels a week, distributed to the free trade via Small Beer of Lincoln. Only brews real ale.

Stanley Bitter (OG 1038) A copper-red bitter with a moderate to strong malty taste, balanced by a hoppy presence.

Dark Mild* (OG 1035) A new brew.

Christmas Ale* (OG 1055) Festive warmer.

MAULDONS **Mauldons Brewery, 7 Addison Road, Chilton Industrial Estate, Sudbury, Suffolk, CO10 6YW. Tel. (0787) 311055**

The head brewer at Watney's Mortlake plant revived the name of his former family brewery in 1982. Supplies over 100 free trade outlets in Suffolk, S. Norfolk, Essex, Cambridge and Hertfordshire, and provides house beers for local pubs (look out for names in pub descriptions).

FA Mild (OG 1034) 'Fine Anglian' Suffolk mild. A dark beer with a faint roast malt aroma. Its flavour is of roast malt, with a subtle hop finish.

GB* (OG 1034, ABV 3.4%) A light, golden brew.

Bitter (OG 1038, ABV 3.8%) Rich, teak-coloured bitter, somewhat lacking in aroma. However, has a very fine, predominantly malt flavour, with a beautiful hop finish. A very refreshing, quaffing ale.

Porter (OG 1042, ABV 3.8%) An excellent dark beer. The aroma is noticeably roasty and the taste is smooth and malty, with a hint of chocolate. A fine balance of hop and malt in the finish.

Squires (OG 1044, ABV 4.2%) Attractive, russet-coloured ale, with a strong fruit and hop taste and a glorious finish of malt and hops, with good balancing bitterness, which lingers in the mouth.

Special (OG 1045, ABV 4.2%) Fine copper-coloured beer with a pleasant, hoppy aroma. Hops come through strongly in the taste and linger with a balancing maltiness in the aftertaste.

Suffolk Punch* (OG 1050, ABV 4.8%) Popular, strong beer.

Black Adder (OG 1055, ABV 5.3%) Another new brew, a delicious, robust, black beer. A hint of liquorice combines with a very full-bodied, chocolate/burnt malt flavour to resemble a stout. Dangerously drinkable at this gravity.

Christmas Reserve (OG 1065, ABV 6.6%) Festive beer, distinctively copper-coloured. Its appearance belies its strength, however. Fruit is evident in the aroma and comes through strongly in the flavour. Wonderfully-balanced, with fine hop/malt notes.

MILL

Mill Brewery, Unit 18c, Bradley Lane, Newton Abbot, Devon, TQ12 4JW. Tel. (0626) 63322

Founded in 1983 on the site of an old watermill and still aiming to expand. Special brews, based on Janner's Old Original, are often sold under local pub names; 'Janner' is the local term for a Devonian. Serves nine regular outlets and the free trade in southern Devon and Torbay.

Janner's Ale (OG 1038) Pale brown-coloured, bland beer, without any discernible aroma. The flavour is bitter/hoppy and the aftertaste is also bitter, but it lacks balance.

Janner's Old Dark Ale* (OG 1040) Now only an occasional brew.

Janner's Old Original (OG 1045) A beer malty and sweet in character, with a slightly 'thick' consistency. Bitter finish.

Janner's Christmas Ale* (OG 1050) The festive beer.

MINERA

See Allied Breweries, page 470.

MINERS ARMS

Miners Arms Brewery, Westbury-sub-Mendip, Somerset, BA5 1HD. Tel. (0749) 870719

Brew pub set up in 1973 in Priddy, producing naturally-conditioned bottled beer. It later moved site and switched to brewing draught beer for the free trade, under the old pub name. Now supplies 35 outlets and two pubs of its own.

Light (OG 1035, ABV 3.2%) Thin, refreshing, straw-coloured brew, available in summer, with a blend of malt and fruit in aroma and taste, and some hoppy, bitter notes. Strong, balanced finish.

Own Ale (OG 1040, ABV 3.8%) A copper-coloured beer with a malty, fruity nose and a strong, even flavour of malt, fruit and hoppy bitterness. The finish is long, dry, hoppy and fruity.

Guvnor's Special Brew (OG 1048, ABV 4.8%) A golden, malty brew with a faint, hoppy aroma and a dry, slightly sour palate, with some citrus fruit. A dry, malty, lasting finish.

MITCHELL'S

Mitchell's of Lancaster (Brewers) Ltd., 11 Moor Lane, Lancaster, LA1 1QB. Tel. (0524) 63773/66580

Lancaster's last independent brewery, wholly owned and run by direct descendants of William Mitchell. The brewing plant is very traditional: many of the casks are still wooden and all the beers are brewed with natural spring well water. Real ale available in all but two of their 52 pubs and virtually countrywide in the free trade.

Dark Mild (OG 1033, ABV 3.6%) Malty in aroma and flavour, with a caramel sweetness and a smooth finish.

Best Bitter (OG 1035, 3.6%) Golden, light straw-coloured bitter, with a hoppy aroma, a dry, malty flavour and a delicate bitter aftertaste.

ESB (OG 1050, ABV 5.1%) Creamy in texture; malty in aroma. The flavour is also malty and fruity, with a hoppy finish.

MITCHELLS & BUTLERS (M&B) See Bass, page 470.

MOLE'S **Mole's Brewery (Wayward Ltd.), Merlin Way, Bowerhill, Melksham, Wilts, SN12 6TJ. Tel. (0225) 704734**

Established in 1982 by former Ushers brewer Roger Catte (the brewery name came from his nickname). Now serves one tied house and over 50 outlets in Wiltshire and Avon – a poor area for free trade.

IPA (OG 1035, ABV 3.5%) A pale brown beer with a trace of maltiness in the aroma. A thin, malty, dry flavour, with little aftertaste.

Cask Bitter (OG 1040, ABV 4%) A pale brown/golden-coloured beer with an aroma of malt, fruit and hops. The taste is malty, with some bitterness; the body is good, with a rounded finish of all the primary flavours. Not too bitter and a little dry.

Brew 97 (OG 1050, ABV 5%) The powerful, malty aroma precedes a strong, sweet, malty flavour, with much hoppy bitterness, and a full aftertaste of malt and dry bitterness. A high quality, creamy, easy-drinking ale, copper-brown in colour.

Landlord's Choice (OG 1050, ABV 5% but may vary) A copper-red beer with a malty aroma. The flavour, too, is malty and full-bodied, with hints of hops and banana. A strongly malty finish but with a dry bitterness which is long-lasting.

MOORHOUSE'S **Moorhouse's Brewery (Burnley) Ltd., Moorhouse Street, Burnley, Lancs, B11 5EN. Tel. (0282) 22864**

Long-established producer of hop bitters which in 1979 began brewing traditional beer. Has since had several owners: the latest, Bill Parkinson, has invested in a new brewhouse to meet increased demand. Two tied houses and about 100 free trade outlets, all with real ale.

Black Cat Mild* (OG 1034) A recent addition.

Premier Bitter (OG 1036, ABV 3.6%) Straw-coloured, clean-tasting bitter with a good balance of flavours and a distinctive, bitter finish. Refreshing.

Pendle Witches Brew (OG 1050, ABV 5%) Fruit is prominent in the aroma, leading on to a full, malty taste with some of the sweetness more commonly associated with a higher gravity brew.

Owd Ale* (OG 1065, ABV 6.4%) Only brewed four times a year.

MORLAND **Morland & Co. PLC, PO Box 5, Ock Street, Abingdon, Oxfordshire, OX14 5DD. Tel. (0235) 553377**

Traditional Thames Valley brewery with its own well. Handpumped ale is now in 191 of the 206 tied houses, but in many of these outlets a cask breather is used at the licensee's discretion. Also available in the club and free trades. Although the same brew, Morland Bitter has been renamed 'Original Bitter'.

Original Bitter (OG 1035, ABV 4%) Pale brown, medium-bodied, malty ale. Moderately-hopped but with little aroma. The dry finish is the best characteristic.

Old Masters (OG 1040, ABV 4.6%) Well-balanced, mid-brown ale offering a pleasant combination of moderate maltiness/ bitterness, with a primarily bitter aftertaste.

MORRELLS **Morrells Brewery Ltd., The Lion Brewery, St Thomas Street, Oxford, OX1 1LA. Tel. (0865) 792013**

Oxford's last surviving brewery produces one of the widest ranges of real ales in the country for all 134 of its pubs. Free trade expands as far as London, Bristol, Coventry and Northampton, and there is also a trading agreement to supply Federation outlets. A new depot should give better distribution over this wide trading area. When frighteningly low profits were announced early in 1990 it was good to hear the company stress its commitment to brewing. However, Celebration (OG 1066, ABV 6.7%) is no longer available in cask form.

Light (OG 1032, ABV 3.2%) Pale brown, thin-bodied, lightly-hopped, refreshing beer. No strong flavour.

Dark (OG 1033, ABV 3.2%) Undistinctive, thin, fruity beer. A touch of caramel masks other subtle flavours. Dark brown in colour.

Bitter (OG 1036, ABV 3.6%) Pale brown, with a fruity, hoppy aroma. A pleasant mix of malt and bitter flavours precedes a distinctly dry and sweet finish.

Varsity (OG 1041, ABV 4.1%) Malty, mid-brown, slightly sweet beer, with a fruity, hoppy aroma and a robust flavour of malt, roast and hops lasting through to the aftertaste.

Graduate (OG 1051, ABV 5.3%) A new beer, introduced in late 1989 with a gravity of 1048 which has subsequently been increased. An intense malt and roast aroma is complemented in the taste by a moderate hoppiness. Pleasant, bitter finish.

College* (OG 1073, ABV 7.6%) Normally only available in winter.

NETHERGATE **Nethergate Brewery Co. Ltd., 11–13 High Street, Clare, Suffolk, CO10 8NY. Tel. (0787) 277244**

From the time it was set up in 1986, until 1988, Nethergate only brewed one beer (winner of the Best Bitter award at the Cambridge CAMRA beer festival for three consecutive years). A second beer, Old Growler, was launched in late 1988 and is also an award-winner. These beers are now available in almost 100 outlets in Suffolk, Essex, Cambs and Herts.

Bitter (OG 1039, ABV 3.8%) Dark beer whose enticingly hoppy fragrance leads into a flavour both magnificently bitter and bitingly hoppy, with malty undertones. An extreme beer but appreciated by many.

Old Growler (OG 1054, ABV 5.1%) Dark brew based on an old porter recipe and now available all year round. A wonderfully complex beer, where the initial bitter flavour is balanced out by a peachy fruitiness. Strong hop finish, with chocolate also coming through.

NIX WINCOTT **Nix Wincott Brewery, Three Fyshes, Bridge Street, Turvey, Beds, MK43 8ER. Tel. (023 064) 264**

Pub brewery which commenced operations in 1987 and has since doubled its capacity. Now supplies eight other pubs.

Two Henrys Bitter* (OG 1040, ABV 3.75%) Amber-coloured, well-balanced beer.

Old Nix* (OG 1058, ABV 5.7%) Light in colour, but deceptively strong.

NORTH & EAST RIDING **North & East Riding Brewers Ltd., The Highlander, 15–16 Esplanade, South Cliff, Scarborough, N. Yorks. Tel. (0723) 365627**

A family-run, independent brewery, set up behind a Victorian hotel (now refurbished as a pub), to brew Scotch-style beers for the bar. These are now being supplied to a widespread free trade. The gravity of the mild has been increased from 1034, whilst 68's has been decreased from 1050.

William Clark's Thistle Mild* (OG 1038) A dark, medium mild.

William Clark's Thistle Bitter* (OG 1040) A traditional Scotch bitter.

William Clark's EXB* (OG 1040) An English-style, hoppier bitter.

William Clark's 68* (OG 1044) Stronger, premium bitter.

NORTH YORKSHIRE **North Yorkshire Brewing Company, 84 North Ormesby Road, Middlesbrough, Cleveland. Tel. (0642) 226224**

THE NORTH YORKSHIRE BREWING COMPANY

Began production in March 1990 and now supplies an expanding free trade, as well as the Tap & Barrel pub. No adjuncts in the beers. Plans to introduce a higher gravity beer (1060+) in 1991.

IPA* (OG 1040, ABV 4.2%)

Flying Herbert* (OG 1048, ABV 5.2%)

NORWICH See Grand Metropolitan, page 474.

OAK **Oak Brewing Company Ltd., Phoenix Brewery, Green Lane, Heywood, Greater Manchester, OL10 2EP.**

Brewery established in 1982, now supplying free trade from West Cheshire to West Yorkshire. Moved to its new home in Heywood, from Ellesmere Port, in early summer 1990. A stout (OG 1048) has been test-brewed and stands a good chance of becoming a regular brew. The beers have not been tasted since the brewery move.

Best Bitter* (OG 1038) A light session bitter.

Tyke Bitter* (OG 1042) Brewed for the West Riding Brewery (currently inoperative), but available throughout Oak's free trade.

Old Oak Ale* (OG 1044) A hoppy premium bitter.

Double Dagger* (OG 1050) A strong bitter.

Porter* (OG 1050) Dark winter brew.

Wobbly Bob* (OG 1060) A characterful, strong bitter.

OAKHILL **The Old Brewery, High Street, Oakhill, Bath, Avon, BA3 5AS. Tel. (0749) 840134**

Somerset brewery, despite its Avon postal address, set up by a farmer in 1984. Oakhill now produces 30–35 barrels a week, serving about 80 outlets (some of which are very occasional) in Somerset, Dorset and Wiltshire, within a 35 mile radius. Farmers Ale has been renamed Oakhill Bitter. All brewing is done in the old fermenting room of a brewery building established in 1767 but destroyed by fire in 1925.

Bitter (OG 1038, ABV 3.6%) Amber-coloured, with a malty aroma. The taste is malty and bittersweet, with a moderate, bitter finish.

Yeoman Ale (OG 1049, ABV 4.8%) Mid-brown beer with a malty aroma and a malty, sweet, fruity taste. The finish is fruity, hoppy and dry. A reasonable strong beer.

OKELL See Isle of Man Breweries, page 434.

OLDHAM See Whitbread, page 479.

OLD LUXTERS **Old Luxters Farm Brewery, Hambleden, Henley-on-Thames, Oxfordshire, RG9 6JW. Tel. (049 163) 330**

A brewery set up by David Ealand, owner and producer of Chiltern Valley Wines. The first brew was launched in May 1990 and is produced using a three and a half barrel plant from Inn Brewing. The beer is available at several local free houses in the area. Hambleden is in Buckinghamshire, despite the brewery's postal address.

Barn Ale* (OG 1042.5)

OLD MILL **Old Mill Brewery, Mill Street, Snaith, Goole, Humbs, DN14 9HS. Tel. (0405) 861813**

Brewery set up in 1983 by a former Wilson's production director. Supplies real ale to seven tied houses and 80–90 free trade customers, mostly within 40 miles.

Traditional Mild (OG 1034, ABV 3.4%) Dark brown, plain chocolate-coloured beer, with subtle roast aromas. Malt and chocolate tastes burst through in the mouth. A fine mild, deserving of a wider audience.

Traditional Bitter (OG 1037, ABV 3.75%) A fresh, hoppy beer, with a fine hop, malt and fruit aroma. The taste is multi-layered, with grain and hops, and a clean, dry finish. Everything a classic bitter ought to be.

Bullion Bitter (OG 1044, 4.5%) Faintly malty in aroma, with a bitter taste tinged with fruit and malt. Dark amber in colour, with a clear Old Mill profile and a big finish. A fine traditional premium bitter.

ORKNEY **Orkney Brewery, Quoyloo, Sandwick, Orkney, KW16 3LT. Tel. (085 684) 802**

The Orkney's first brewery in living memory – set up in 1988 by former licensee Roger White. A real ale addict, he had to brew keg 'to appease local palates', but free trade in cask beer is now increasing, although only in mainland Scotland and northern England. The new bottling plant produces bottle-conditioned as well as bright versions of Raven and Skullsplitter.

Raven Ale (OG 1038, ABV 3.8%) Still mainly keg (cask on mainland). Worth seeking out when in 'real' form. Smooth, mellow and malty, with a distinctive aroma and finish.

Skullsplitter Ale* (OG 1080, ABV 8.5%)

PAINE'S See Brent-Walker Breweries, page 410

PALMERS **J C & R H Palmer Ltd., West Bay Road, Bridport, Dorset, DT6 4JA. Tel. (0308) 22396**

The only thatched brewery in the country, in a delightful seaside setting. Cask-conditioned beer in all 66 tied houses, although a few still use pressure.

BB (OG 1030, ABV 3.2%) A light session beer, more bitter than malty. A good, hoppy taste and some aroma. Bitter aftertaste.

IPA (OG 1039, ABV 4.3%) Well-made, middle-strength bitter. The flavour is hoppy, with a good balance of malt and fruit. Again, a bitter aftertaste.

Tally Ho! (OG 1046, ABV 4.6%) Dark and complex brew with a malty aroma. The nutty taste is dominated by roast malt, but well-balanced with bitterness. Malt and bitter in the aftertaste. Not very easy to find.

PARADISE

Paradise Brewery Ltd., Paradise Park, Hayle, Cornwall, TR27 4HY. Tel. (0736) 753365

Unusual brewery in a bird park, behind its one tied house, the Bird in Hand. However, the future is uncertain, with the brewery being put on the market.

Bitter* (OG 1040) Low in aroma, lightly-hopped and with a fruity balance.

Artists Ale* (OG 1055) Smooth and full-bodied.

PARISH

Parish Brewery, Burrough-on-the-Hill, Melton Mowbray, Leics, LE14 2JQ. Tel. (066 477) 781

Brewery which started life as a brew pub, the Stag and Hounds. The pub was sold in 1988 in order to expand the capacity and concentrate on the free trade. Three more ales have been introduced since the last edition of this guide.

Mild* (OG 1033, ABV 3%)

Bitter* (OG 1036, ABV 3.5%) A copper-coloured bitter.

Porter* (OG 1048, ABV 4.5%)

Burrough Bitter* (OG 1048, ABV 4.5%)

Poachers Ale* (OG 1060, ABV 6%) Dark, sweet and malty.

Baz's Bonce Blower* (OG 1110, ABV 12%) Rich, black and treacly.

PEMBROKESHIRE'S OWN ALES

Pembrokeshire's Own Ales Ltd., Llanteglos Brewery, Llanteg, nr. Amroth, Dyfed, SA67 8PU. Tel. (083 483) 677

The only brewery in Dyfed, set up in 1985 at the Llanteglos Hamlet holiday complex. One tied house; free trade (mainly via Ansells and beer agencies) varies according to the holiday season.

Benfro Bitter* (OG 1037, ABV 3.6%) Pale, light and hoppy.

Benfro Extra (OG 1042, ABV 4%) A beer blending and balancing hops and malt. Some fruit, but prone to a nutty blandness.

Pembs Porter* (OG 1042, ABV 4%) Formerly known as Old Particular.

PHOENIX See Grand Metropolitan, page 474.

PILGRIM **Pilgrim Brewery, West Street, Reigate, Surrey, RH2 9BL. Tel. (073 72) 22651**

Surrey's only brewery, supplying real ale to London, Surrey and Sussex, as well as the Midlands and the North via wholesalers.

Surrey Bitter (OG 1038, ABV 3.7%) Mid-brown beer with a malty aroma. A good, light bitter which has a malty flavour and an underlying hoppiness which tends to come through in the finish.

XXXX Mild (OG 1042, ABV 4%) Dark, with a strong, malty flavour and pleasant fruitiness. A malty sweetness in the finish.

Best or Progress (OG 1042, ABV 4%) Light, copper-coloured beer with a malty aroma. Good balance of malt and hops in the flavour, with a dry, malty finish.

Talisman (OG 1049, ABV 4.8%) Strong ale with a dark copper colour, a fruity, malt flavour and a smooth, sweet finish. Available all year, but more common in winter.

PITFIELD See Premier Ales, page 449, and Wiltshire, page 463.

PLASSEY **Plassey Brewery, Eyton, Wrexham, Clwyd, LL13 0SP. Tel. (0978) 780277**

Founder and ex-Border brewer, Alan Beresford, has sadly died, but the brewery continues as before and is linked with tourism in an award-winning building (an old dairy on a working farm and caravan site). The site bars serve the beer, contributing to the total of four outlets.

Farmhouse Bitter (OG 1038, ABV 3.6%) Excellent, straw-coloured beer, well-hopped and bitter, with some blackcurrant fruitiness. Light and refreshing. Reminiscent of what Boddingtons Bitter used to be like!

PLYMPTON See Allied Breweries, page 467.

POOLE **Poole Brewery, The Brewhouse, High Street, Poole, Dorset. Tel. (0202) 685288**

Supplies the Brewhouse pub and free trade outlets. Beer kept under blanket pressure at the Brewhouse. Extending premises to allow for all brewing, storage and bottling to be on one site.

Bitter or Dolphin Best Bitter* (OG 1038, ABV 3.8%) Amber-coloured, balanced bitter.

Bosun Strong Bitter* (OG 1042, ABV 4.5%) Amber and rich.

SAM POWELL **Sam Powell Brewery Ltd., Mochdre Ind. Estate, Newtown, Powys, SY16 4LD. Tel. (0686) 628021**

Independent company, founded in 1880, which, after an interval of 30 years, resumed brewing in 1983, using the plant and premises of the former Powys Brewery. Real ale is supplied through wholesalers to around 60 outlets, mainly in Mid Wales and the border area.

BB (OG 1035, ABV 3%) Pale brown session beer with a subtle malt and bitter flavour and a pleasant, hoppy finish.

Original Bitter (OG 1038, ABV 3.5%) Malty, well-flavoured bitter which achieves a good balance on the tongue. Subtly bitter finish.

Samson or Old Sam (OG 1048, ABV 4.3%) A pronounced malty flavour, balanced by a distinct bitterness and a slightly sweet, fruity finish.

PREMIER **Premier Ales, Stourbridge Estate, Mill Race Lane, Stourbridge, W. Midlands, DY8 1JN. Tel. (0384) 442040**

A brewery which has seen several changes since the last edition of this guide. First it merged with London's Pitfield brewery to increase the availability of Pitfield products in the North, and Premier's in the South. Now the Pitfield name has been purchased by Wiltshire Brewery, though Premier is still the sole brewer of Pitfield ales and continues to sell them in its own estate of ten houses. Supplies about 90 free trade outlets throughout the country. No unnatural additives or preservatives are used in the beers.

Pitfield Bitter* (OG 1038, ABV 3.4%)

Old Merlin Mild* (OG 1037, ABV 3.6%)

Knightly Bitter (OG 1044, ABV 4.3%) A pale brown, malty-flavoured bitter. Quite hoppy and slightly sweet.

Pitfield Hoxton Heavy* (OG 1048, ABV 4.7%) Formerly Hoxton Best Bitter. Strong and malty.

Pitfield Dark Star (OG 1049, ABV 4.8%) Dark, with a roast malt aroma and taste, followed by a fruity and bitter aftertaste. The bottled version is pasteurised.

Black Knight Stout (OG 1050, ABV 5%) Strong, black beer with a very malty and roasty taste, and a chocolatey, dry aftertaste.

Pitfield London Porter* (OG 1058, ABV 5.6%) Dark stout.

Maiden's Ruin (OG 1075, ABV 7.4%) Very strong, fruity beer with a sweet and malty taste and a very sweet aftertaste.

RANDALLS **R W Randall Ltd., Vauxlaurens Brewery, St Julian's Avenue, Guernsey, CI. Tel. (0481) 20134**

Guernsey's smaller brewery, supplying just four of its 21 tied houses with real ales.

Best Mild (OG 1033) Copper-red, with a malty and fruity aroma and a hint of hops. The fruity character remains throughout, with a sweetish, malty undertone.

Best Bitter (OG 1046) A full, pale brown bitter, with a strong, sweetish, fruity identity, and a continuous, strong malt presence. Some bitterness in the finish.

RAYMENTS See Greene King, page 426.

REEPHAM **Reepham Brewery, 1 Collers Way, Reepham, Norfolk, NR10 4SW. Tel. (0603) 871091**

Family brewery, founded in 1983 with a purpose-built plant in a small industrial unit. Supplies real ale to 45 outlets in Norfolk, and bottled Rapier Pale Ale to supermarkets. A recent addition to the range is LA Bitter, a lower alcohol real ale.

LA Bitter* (OG 1027, ABV 2%)

Granary Bitter* (OG 1038, ABV 3.6%) Hoppy and well-balanced.

Dark* (OG 1040, ABV 3.6%) Strong mild.

Rapier Pale Ale* (OG 1044, ABV 4.2%) Award-winning dry bitter.

Gold* (OG 1044, ABV 4.2%) Pale, full-flavoured strong ale.

Stout* (OG 1045, ABV 4.2%) Strong, dry winter stout.

Brewhouse Ale* (OG 1054, ABV 5.2%) Full-bodied bitter.

RIDLEYS **T D Ridley & Sons, 88 Broomfield Road, Chelmsford, Essex, CM1 1SS. Tel. (0245) 353513/256242**

Traditional Essex brewery, selling real ale in all 65 houses and to an expanding free trade (around 300 outlets), at the lowest prices in the South East. It has reported an upsurge in sales of Mild in the last year, whilst the former PA Bitter has been relaunched as IPA (same brew). Stock Ale (1050) has been tested in cask form and may become a winter ale. All brewing takes place at the Hartford End Brewery, near Chelmsford.

Traditional Mild (OG 1034, ABV 3.5%) Formerly called XXX. Dark brown, with a powerful, hoppy and malty aroma. The palate is dry and hoppy, with underlying malt and caramel flavours, and a bitter finish. Very drinkable and all too rare.

IPA (OG 1034, ABV 3.5%) A fine, amber bitter. A hoppy, faintly fruity nose leads into a strong, lingering, hoppy bitterness, with a little balancing malt. Pleasing, dry aftertaste.

RINGWOOD **Ringwood Brewery, 138 Christchurch Road, Ringwood, Hants, BH24 3AP. Tel. (0425) 471177**

Hampshire's first new brewery, founded in 1978 in an old bakery and now housed in attractive 18th century buildings which formed part of the old Tunks' brewery in Ringwood. Famous for its award-winning Old Thumper, it has two tied houses and approximately 100 free trade accounts, from Weymouth to Chichester (plus one bar in Cherbourg!).

Best Bitter (OG 1038, ABV 3.8%) Good body for its gravity, with an aroma of malt and hops. The taste has a good technical balance, with malt, hops and some fruit present. The finish is dry. Very moreish.

Fortyniner (OG 1048, ABV 4.8%) Beer with little aroma and a taste strong in malt, which tends to mask other flavour characteristics. Some fruit in the aftertaste. Disappointing for its gravity.

XXXX Porter (OG 1048, ABV 4.8%) Brewed Oct–March, a full-bodied, ruby red porter. Its roast malt aroma leads into a bittersweet flavour, building to a lingering finish of bitter fruit.

Old Thumper (OG 1058, ABV 5.8%) Golden brown ale, initially sweet on the palate but continuing on to a bitter finish through a fruity (bananas and pears) middle period.

ROBINSON'S **Frederic Robinson Ltd., Unicorn Brewery, Stockport, Cheshire, SK1 1JJ. Tel. (061) 480 6571**

Major family brewery with all 323 tied houses selling real ale. Also owns Hartleys of Ulverston. Its own pubs are mainly concentrated in southern Manchester and Cheshire.

Best Mild (OG 1032, ABV 3.3%) A pale brown, well-balanced beer, with a sweet aftertaste. A good, refreshing drink.

Dark Best Mild (OG 1032, ABV 3.3%) Toffee/malt tasting, with a slight bitterness. Very quaffable, enjoying a fruity/malt aroma and a dry finish.

Bitter (OG 1035, ABV 3.5%) Fresh-tasting, with an aniseed tinge. Characteristic aroma and a smooth but brief finish. Only available in 20 outlets.

Best Bitter (OG 1041, ABV 4.2%) Golden beer with a good, hoppy nose. Very well-balanced taste before a slight, bitter finish.

Old Tom (OG 1080, 8.5%) Full-bodied, dark, fruity beer, similar in texture to a barley wine. The aroma is fruity and mouthwatering; the aftertaste is bittersweet. A beer to be respectfully sipped by a roaring winter fire.

ROBINWOOD **Robinwood Brewers & Vintners, Robinwood Brewery, Burnley Road, Todmorden, W. Yorks, OL14 8EX. Tel. (0706) 818160**

Small brewery founded in 1988 and continuing to expand. Now runs two tied houses to complement the growing free trade throughout the North. All draught beer is cask-conditioned, with Old Fart now available in bottle-conditioned form.

Best Bitter (OG 1036, ABV 4.1%) Beer with a faint, malty, fruity, sometimes yeasty aroma. The flavour is well-balanced, with a good, malty character which carries through to the finish (moderately bitter).

XB (OG 1046, ABV 4.7%) Both malt and hops come through in the aroma. The basic malty flavour is overtaken by bitterness and some chocolate. Good body; a malty/bitter finish, with burnt malt detectable at times.

Old Fart (OG 1060, ABV 6%) Dark brown in colour, with a fruity and slightly malty aroma. Roasted malt in the vinous, sweet and fruity taste, with some caramel and hoppy bitterness coming through. A malty, dry finish. Also available as Old XXXX Ale on request.

ROSS **Ross Brewing Company, 36 Gloucester Road, Bishopston, Bristol, Avon. Tel. (0272) 427923**

Very small Bristol brewery, producing only bottle-conditioned beers. These are available in several pubs, restaurants and wine bars in the area, as well as being distributed nationally through the wholesale trade. Plans to brew draught ales and possibly a 'super-strong' beer. Clifton and Hartcliffe are produced from organically-grown barley; Brewer's Droop, ironically, is not.

Brewer's Droop Organic Bitter* (OG 1042.5)

Clifton Dark Ale* (OG 1042.5)

Hartcliffe Bitter* (OG 1042.5)

ROYAL CLARENCE **Royal Clarence, The Esplanade, Burnham-on-Sea, Somerset, TA8 1BQ. Tel. (0278) 783138**

Seaside hotel brewery which also supplies the free trade. The beer has been renamed from Clarence Bitter.

Clarence Pride* (OG 1036)

RUDDLES See Grand Metropolitan, page 475.

ST AUSTELL **St Austell Brewery Co., 63 Trevarthian Road, St Austell, Cornwall, PL25 4BY. Tel. (0726) 74444**

Popular family-run brewery in mid Cornwall, supplying the majority of its 136 tied houses with real ale. Free trade in Cornwall and other parts of the country.

Bosun's Bitter (OG 1034, ABV 3.5%) A refreshing session beer, sweetish in aroma and bittersweet in flavour. Lingering, hoppy finish.

XXXX Mild (OG 1037, ABV 3.6%) Little aroma, but a good, lingering aftertaste. The malty, caramelly, sweet flavour is followed by a sweet, yet dryish finish. Very drinkable.

Tinners (OG 1038, ABV 3.7%) A deservedly-popular, golden beer with an appetising malt aroma and a good balance of malt and hops in the flavour. Lasting finish.

Hicks Special Draught or HSD (OG 1050, ABV 5%) An aromatic, fruity, hoppy bitter which initially gives a sweet flavour and an aftertaste of pronounced bitterness, but which has a fully-rounded palate.

Crippledick (OG 1100) A very rare brew, produced for festivals, etc., and not generally sold in pubs. One to be careful with! Very powerful, with a strong mix of flavours which are well-balanced. A wine amongst ales; very warming.

SCOTTIES **Scotties Brewery, Crown Hotel, 151 High Street, Lowestoft, Suffolk. Tel. (0502) 569592**

Brewery founded in June 1989 and now supplying beer to four outlets and the free trade.

Hopleaf Best Bitter (OG 1037) At its best, a beautifully hoppy beer with malt and fruit on the tongue and a very dry aftertaste.

William French (OG 1047) A full and beautifully balanced beer. A faint, malty aroma leads into a palate with strong malt and hop flavours, and considerable fruitiness. A full and balanced aftertaste, too.

Dark Oast* (OG 1047) A winter beer.

SCOTTISH & NEWCASTLE See page 477.

SELBY **Selby (Middlesbrough) Brewery Ltd., 131 Millgate, Selby, N. Yorks, YO8 0LL. Tel. (0757) 702826**

Old family brewery that resumed brewing in 1972 after a gap of 18 years. Real ale supplied to a few free trade outlets and the Brewery Tap off-licence in Selby, but not to the company's single tied house. Best Bitter (OG 1039) is now only brewed very occasionally.

Old Tom* (OG 1069, ABV 6.5%) Distinctive, strong ale.

SHEPHERD NEAME **Shepherd Neame Ltd., 17 Court Street, Faversham, Kent, ME13 7AX. Tel. (0795) 532206**

Fine old brewery retaining many original features, with a visitor reception centre in a restored medieval hall. Believed to be the longest continuous brewer in the land, ever since 1698. The tied estate extends to around 300 pubs, the majority selling real ale which is brewed from only East Kent hops. Free trade runs to more than 1000 outlets, principally in Kent, Essex and London, although this figure includes a sizeable proportion of keg-only business. Some outlets dispense the beers using a very low blanket pressure and the company is giving active encouragement to other pubs to convert to this method.

Master Brew Bitter (OG 1036, ABV 3.8%) A very distinctive bitter, mid-brown in colour, with a very hoppy aroma. Well-balanced with a nicely aggressive bitter taste from its hops, and leaving a hoppy/bitter finish, tinged with sweetness.

Master Brew Best Bitter (OG 1039, ABV 4%) Mid-brown, with less marked characteristics than Bitter. However, the nose is very well-balanced and the taste enjoys a malty, bitter smokiness. A malty, well-rounded finish.

Stock Ale (OG 1039, ABV 4%) A dark brown winter brew. Malt and caramel are present in the aroma, and the beer is full of different flavours: malt, caramel and hops, and all discernible. Although never strong, it lacks body and seems to have become thinner in the last few years.

Spitfire Ale* (OG 1039, ABV 4.7%) A commemorative brew (Battle of Britain) for the RAF Benevolent Fund's appeal.

Bishops Finger* (OG 1052, ABV 5.4%). Well-known bottled beer, introduced in cask-conditioned draught form in November 1989.

SHIPSTONE'S See Greenalls, page 425.

SMILES **Smiles Brewing Co. Ltd., Colston Yard, Colston Street, Bristol, Avon, BS1 5BD. Tel. (0272) 297350**

Avon's first new brewer, established in 1977 and supplying real ale to around 200 outlets, three tied houses and a new Brewery Tap next door to the city centre brewery. Due to increasing demand, beers in certain pubs have been noted as immature on occasions.

Brewery Bitter (OG 1037, ABV 3.7%) A light, golden brown beer with an aroma of hops and fruit. The good, balanced flavour has hops, nutty malt and a hint of strawberry. A good session beer, with a bitter, dry aftertaste.

Best Bitter (OG 1041, ABV 4.1%) The maltiness in the aroma, mixed with fruit and nuts, is echoed in the taste, but with occasional hints of roast malt and strawberry. A good, rounded aftertaste makes for a fine, drinking beer. Copper-brown in colour.

Exhibition (OG 1051, ABV 5.2%) This very full-bodied beer has a complex mix of hop, malt, roast and bitter flavours, and feels its strength. Dark copper-coloured with an aroma of hops, malt and fruitiness. Very moreish.

Old Vic (OG 1065, ABV 6.2%) An occasionally brewed, dark, rich, malty winter beer. Heavily vinous, fruity and sweet.

JOHN SMITH'S See Courage, page 474.

SAMUEL SMITH **Samuel Smith Old Brewery (Tadcaster), Tadcaster, N. Yorks, LS24 9SB. Tel. (0937) 832225**

Yorkshire's oldest and most traditional brewery brews its ales without the use of any adjuncts. Cask beer is fermented only in Yorkshire stone squares and racked into wooden casks. Operates the only brewery-based manufacturing cooperage in the UK. Real ale in the majority of its 250-plus tied houses, which include 26 in London, representing good value for the capital.

Old Brewery Bitter or OBB (OG 1037, ABV 3.8%) Beer with a malty predominance in the nose which follows through into both the taste and the aftertaste, although this is underscored at all stages by a gentle hoppiness. Lots of flavour and body, complemented by its attractive amber colour.

Museum Ale (OG 1048, ABV 5.2%) A fruity, amber, strong bitter. Malty, winey and sweetish in the mouth, with some bitterness in the aftertaste, though dominated throughout by fruitiness.

SPRINGFIELD See Bass, page 471.

STOCKS **Stocks Doncaster Brewery, 33–34 Hallgate, Doncaster, S. Yorks, DN1 3NL. Tel. (0302) 328213**

Originated as a brew pub and now runs three tied houses. Expanding free trade throughout the North, with Old Horizontal becoming particularly popular.

Best Bitter (OG 1037, ABV 3.6%) An ordinary session bitter, with a light aroma, hoppiness in the taste and a moderately bitter, but short, aftertaste.

Select (OG 1044, ABV 4.3%) Although having more body than Best Bitter, it is still a light beer, offering malt in the mouth and a bitter taste and finish. A bit of everything, without much of anything.

Old Horizontal (OG 1054, ABV 5%) Dark brown/black beer with red tints. A complex old, rather than strong, ale, deep and subtle, with fruit, roast and chocolate tastes. The dry and nutty finish has some liquorice notes. An enticing brew.

STONES See Bass, page 472.

SUSSEX **Sussex Brewery, Main Road, Hermitage, Emsworth, W. Sussex, PO10 8AU. Tel. (024 33) 71533**

Small, family-run brewery (formerly Hermitage Brewery), selling three brands to local free trade customers and one tied house.

Wyndham Bitter (OG 1038) Formerly Hermitage Ordinary. Malty, with some hop character and a fruity finish.

Hermitage Best Bitter (OG 1048) Subtly hoppy, with a moderately dry, hoppy finish.

Warrior Ale (OG 1060) Moderately hoppy, with a slightly hoppy, fruity finish. Generally disappointing.

TAYLOR — **Timothy Taylor & Co. Ltd., Knowle Spring Brewery, Keighley, W. Yorks, BD2 1AW. Tel. (0535) 603139**

The fame of Timothy Taylor's quality ales – which have won a barrelful of Championship medals – stretches far beyond West Yorkshire and the brewery's 29 pubs. Produces one of the widest ranges of real ales, with Landlord the pride of the pack.

Golden Best or Bitter Ale — (OG 1033, ABV 3.5%) A light, straw-coloured beer, with the Taylor nose. The soft and smooth, malty taste has a short bitter finish. Well-balanced.

Golden Best Mild — (OG 1033, ABV 3.5%) Golden Best with caramel which overwhelms the flavour. Innocuous and not unpleasant.

Best Bitter — (OG 1037, ABV 4%) A golden, well-hopped bitter, with a mildly hoppy and malty nose. The complex grain and hop taste has a distinctly bitter, dry finish. Much-underrated, a classic best bitter and very drinkable.

Landlord — (OG 1042, ABV 4.3%) A distinctive, multi-layered and complex combination of clean floral fragrance and mouth-filling grain, hop and fruit tastes. Strong finish. Epitome of the marque; a deservedly-acclaimed brew.

Porter — (OG 1043, ABV 4.4%) An occasional rich and creamy-smooth brew. Has some malt on the tongue and in the nose, but this is overwhelmed by the sweetness in the taste and finish. Too sweet for the style and not typically Taylor, but increasingly popular.

Ram Tam (XXXX) — (OG 1043, ABV 4.3%) Landlord overloaded with caramel which turns the beer black and masks the Taylor character, though the hops still come through.

TAYLOR WALKER — See Allied Breweries, page 468.

TENNENT CALEDONIAN — See Bass, page 473.

JOSHUA TETLEY — See Allied Breweries, page 468.

TETLEY WALKER — See Allied Breweries, page 469.

THEAKSTON — See Scottish & Newcastle, page 478.

THOMPSON'S — **Thompson's Brewery, 11 West Street, Ashburton, Devon, TQ13 7BD. Tel. (0364) 52478**

Began brewing in 1981 for its own pub, the London Inn, but now supplies free trade outlets around Dartmoor and southern Devon.

Mild* — (OG 1033) An occasional brew.

Best Bitter (OG 1039, ABV 4.2%) A pleasant, hoppy brew, pale brown in colour, with a hoppy aroma, a bitter, slightly yeasty taste and a strong, bitter finish.

IPA (OG 1044, ABV 4.6%) A copper-red, well-balanced beer. The hoppy aroma is followed by a strong, bitter taste and finish.

Yuletide Tipple (OG 1050, ABV 5.2%) Fruity, copper-red beer, enjoying a distinctive contrast of roast and hop flavours, and a bitter finish. Hops and fruit in the aroma.

THWAITES

Daniel Thwaites PLC, PO Box 50, Star Brewery, Blackburn, Lancs, BB1 5BU. Tel. (0254) 54431

Traditional Lancashire brewery, producing award-winning real ales, including two fine milds. Real ale supplied to 399 of its 413 houses, which include the Yates and Jackson's pubs from the brewery takeover in 1984.

Mild (OG 1031, ABV 3%) Dark brown/copper beer with a fine malty quality in both aroma and flavour. No perceptible finish.

Best Mild (OG 1034, ABV 3.2%) A rich, dark mild presenting a smooth, malty flavour and a pleasant, slightly bitter finish.

Bitter (OG 1036, ABV 3.5%) Gently-flavoured, clean-tasting bitter. Malt and hops lead into a full, lingering, bitter finish.

Daniel's Hammer* (OG 1050) A Christmas brew.

TITANIC

Titanic Brewery, 1 Dain Street, Middleport, Stoke-on-Trent, Staffs, ST6 3LE. Tel. (0782) 823447

Named in honour of the Titanic's Captain Smith, who hailed from Stoke, this brewery has gone from strength to strength since resurfacing after briefly ceasing trading in 1988. The expanding free trade includes five regular local pubs. Best Bitter has now been discontinued, with Lifeboat Ale and a new potent brew, Wreckage, a variation on their bottled Christmas Ale, introduced.

Lifeboat Ale* (OG 1040, ABV 4%)

Premium Bitter (OG 1042, ABV 4.2%) A clean, fresh aroma leads on to a dry, hoppy taste.

Captain Smith's Strong Ale (OG 1050, ABV 5%) The aroma is slightly sweet; the beer itself is dark and very drinkable.

Wreckage* (OG 1080, ABV 8%).

TOLLY COBBOLD

See Brent-Walker Breweries, page 410.

TRAQUAIR HOUSE — **Traquair House Brewery, Innerleithen, Peeblesshire, Borders, EH44 6PW. Tel. (0896) 830323**

18th-century brewhouse in the oldest inhabited house in Scotland, restored in 1965 by the 20th Laird. Traquair Ale is now produced exclusively there, in cask form as well as the bottled which is exported worldwide. More recently, another draught beer, Bear Ale, has been produced for the free trade. Despite the death of the Laird, Peter Maxwell Stuart, in early 1990, his family has vowed that brewing will continue.

Bear Ale* (OG 1050, ABV 5%) Strong draught ale.

Traquair House Ale* (OG 1075, ABV 7%) Dark and potent.

TROUGH — **Trough Brewery Ltd., Louisa Street, Idle, Bradford, W. Yorks, BD10 8NE. Tel. (0274) 613450**

Established in 1981, Trough now serves six tied houses and an increasing free and club trade. Exhibits aggressively independent management, yet does not shirk beneficial contact with larger concerns, such as the Camerons Tap & Spile chain. The range of beers has been changed over the last year and may develop further. Much improved since the introduction of full-mash brewing.

Bitter (OG 1035) A clean-tasting, refreshing bitter, pale-coloured, with a pleasing, hoppy aroma. The well-balanced taste is malty, with an identifiable hop flavour and fruit notes. Dry, piquant finish.

Wild Boar Bitter (OG 1039) A richer-textured, smooth, malty best bitter, with a pronounced hop flavour, balancing sweetness and fruitiness. The aroma is hoppy; the finish is malty/hoppy and satisfying.

Hogshead (OG 1043) Mid-brown in colour, with an inviting, fruity/malty nose. A full-flavoured, robust, strong bitter, with a strong, malty palate and a complementing hop flavour, fruit and sweetness. Rounded off by a good dry and malty finish. A welcome addition to the range in summer 1989.

TRUMAN See Grand Metropolitan, page 474.

ULEY — **Uley Brewery Ltd., Old Brewery, Uley, Dursley, Glos, GL11 5TB. Tel. (0453) 860120**

Victorian village brewery, re-opened in 1985 to serve the free trade in a wide rural area in Gloucestershire and neighbouring counties. Has no tied houses.

Bitter or Hogshead or UB40 (OG 1040, ABV 3.8%) Copper-coloured beer with a malty aroma and real bitterness in the taste. Malt and hops are present, together with a light fruitiness and a smooth finish.

Old Spot Prize Ale (OG 1050, ABV 5%) A light aroma, but a pronounced bitterness in the flavour. Chocolate malt is much in evidence and the finish is dry and bitter.

Pig's Ear IPA (OG 1050, ABV 5%) Pale-coloured, light beer, deceptively strong. Notably bitter in flavour, with a hoppy, fruity aroma and a bitter finish.

Pigor Mortis (OG 1058, ABV 5.5%) Another beer which belies its strength. No distinct aroma; sweet, smooth flavour, with hints of fruit and hops. Dry finish.

USHERS See Grand Metropolitan, page 475.

VAUX **Vaux Breweries Ltd., The Brewery, Sunderland, Tyne & Wear, SR1 3AN. Tel. (091) 567 6277**

First established in 1806 and now one of the country's largest regional brewers, Vaux remains firmly independent. Owns Wards of Sheffield, but sold off Lorimer & Clark in Edinburgh in 1987. Double Maxim has been available in cask form since 1989. Real ale in 181 out of 473 tied houses (which includes those run by Vaux Inns Ltd.); cask beer also supplied to 10% of its 700 free trade customers. Sold its four London pubs, including the Princess Louise, early in 1990.

Lorimers Best Scotch (OG 1036, ABV 3.6%) Dark, thin and with little aroma, but the roast malt flavour can shine through when the cellar temperature and pub turnover are right. Unfortunately, it is often served too cold. A replica of the original Scottish Scotch; today more of a mild?

Bitter (OG 1036, ABV 3.9%) A bitter from a brewery not used to producing bitters – and it shows. Thin and one-dimensional; a bitter taste, but nothing else. Production currently suspended due to poor sales.

Samson (OG 1041, ABV 4.1%) Has a complex flavour, with malt and hops battling it out. Sometimes dryness and bitterness are the main taste characteristics; at other times the sweet notes dominate. Like other Vaux beers, low in aroma.

Double Maxim (OG 1044, ABV 4.2%) A smooth, rich, brown ale, rarely found in draught form. Very malty throughout, with some roast. A slight, lingering fruitiness can be found in the aftertaste.

WADWORTH **Wadworth & Co. Ltd., Northgate Brewery, Northgate, Devizes, Wilts, SN10 1JW. Tel. (0380) 723361**

Delightful market town tower brewery. Its 6X is one of the South's most famous ales, widely available in the free trade and sold in canned form by British Rail. Solidly traditional, with all of the 160 houses selling real ale, although it discontinued Devizes Bitter, its light session beer, in May 1990.

Henry Wadworth IPA (OG 1034, ABV 3.8%) A golden brown-coloured beer with a gentle, malty and slightly hoppy aroma, a good balance of flavours, with maltiness eventually dominating, and then a long-lasting aftertaste to match, eventually becoming biscuity. A good session beer, more pleasing than the popular 6X.

6X (OG 1040, ABV 4.3%) Medium brown in colour, with a malty and fruity nose and some balancing hop character. The flavour is similar, with some bitterness and a lingering malty, but bitter finish. Full-bodied and distinctive.

Farmer's Glory (OG 1046, ABV 4.5%) Can be delightfully hoppy and fruity, but variable in flavour and conditioning. The aroma is of dark maltiness and it should have a dryish, hoppy aftertaste.

Old Timer (OG 1055, ABV 5.8%) A rich, copper-brown winter beer with a strong, fruity, malty aroma. The flavour is full-bodied and complete, with hints of butterscotch and peaches, beautifully balanced by a lasting, malty, dry finish. A classic beer.

PETER WALKER See Allied Breweries, page 469.

WARDS **S H Ward & Co. Ltd., Sheaf Brewery, Ecclesall Road, Sheffield, S. Yorks, S11 8HZ. Tel. (0742) 755155**

South Yorkshire subsidiary of Vaux of Sunderland which, since the closure of the neighbouring Thorne brewery in 1986, also produces Darley's beers. Over 120 of its free trade customers take real ale, which is also available in 80 of the 177 Wards/Darley tied houses.

Mild (OG 1032, ABV 3.2%) Formerly Darley Dark Mild. Malt and chocolate aromas lead onto hints of fruit, plain chocolate and hop in a predominantly grainy palate. A slowly improving mild with a smooth, dry finish.

Thorne Best Bitter (OG 1037, ABV 3.9%) Mid-brown, plain beer, short on character. Little aroma, some malt in the mouth, and a hint of bitterness in both taste and finish. Lamentably, not the Thorne of old; nor is it a best bitter.

Sheffield Best Bitter (OG 1038, ABV 4%) Notably malty aroma and taste, with slight balancing bitterness. A clean and dry, malty ale, but a new sweetness is creeping into the taste and finish. Can be variable in quality and body.

Kirby Strong Beer (OG 1045, 5%) A parody of a former brew, now a muddy brown beer with signs of Wards malt tradition all the way through. A cloying sweetness is now evident, though there is bitterness in the mouth. A beer which has lost its character.

WATNEY See Grand Metropolitan, page 474.

WEBSTER'S See Grand Metropolitan, page 475.

CHARLES WELLS

Charles Wells Ltd., Havelock Street, Bedford, Beds, MK40 4LU. Tel. (0234) 272766

Successful regional company with a tied estate stretching as far south as London. Cask beer is served in all 304 pubs plus increasingly in the free trade, but all too many tied houses use CO_2 in the dispense, sometimes with cask breathers.

Eagle Bitter (OG 1035, ABV 3.6%) A beer that is too often underrated. Pale gold in colour with a subtle, hoppy and fruity nose, with hops more prominent in the flavour. Fine bitter aftertaste.

Bombardier (OG 1042, ABV 4.2%) A beer becoming hard to find, but worth the effort. Well-balanced, with hops in the aroma and flavour, complemented by malt, fruit and a pronounced bitterness. Dry finish with some malt.

WELSH BREWERS See Bass, page 472.

WEM See Greenalls, page 425.

WEST COAST

West Coast Brewery Co. Ltd., Kings Arms Hotel, 4a Helmshaw Walk, Chorlton-on-Medlock, Manchester, M13 9TH. Tel. (061) 274 4344

Successful brewery on the premises of the Kings Arms, providing beer for this outlet and the free trade, with another pub and on-site brewery hoped for. Founded by Brendan Dobbin who ran the Hilden Brewery for some years.

Dobbin's Dark Mild (OG 1032, ABV 3%) Very full-flavoured for its gravity; much darker than North County Mild.

North County Mild (OG 1035, ABV 3.8%) Dark beer with a complex aroma. Good balance and depth of flavour, with roast malt predominant. A malty, bitter finish.

Dobbin's Best Bitter (OG 1038, ABV 4%) Pale beer with malt, hops and fruit in the aroma. Fresh, clean taste – hoppy and bitter, with some malt and a dry finish.

Dobbin's Guiltless Stout (OG 1039, ABV 4%) Very dark in colour, with roast malt strongly predominant in the smell and taste. A long, dry aftertaste.

Dobbin's Sierra Nevada Pale Ale (OG 1050, ABV 6%) Pale beer with a strong, hoppy nose. Hops are also very evident in the flavour. A well-attenuated beer, making it strong and very dry.

Dobbin's Extra Special Bitter (OG 1060, ABV 7%) A powerful, mid-brown beer with a strong, complex aroma, malt and hops on the tongue (with sweetish, fruity undertones), and a full, predominantly bitter, hoppy finish.

WEST HIGHLAND — **West Highland Brewers, Old Station Brewery, Taynuilt, Argyllshire, Strathclyde, PA35 1JB. Tel. (086 62) 246**

Brewery set up in November 1989 in listed buildings, part of an active British Rail station. Serves a regular free trade and wholesalers, as well as a brewery tap.

HDL (Highland Dark Light)* (OG 1034)

Highland Heavy* (OG 1038)

Highland Severe* (OG 1050)

WETHERED See Whitbread, page 480.

WHITBREAD See page 479.

WHITBY'S OWN — **Whitby's Own Brewery Ltd., St Hilda's, The Ropery, Whitby, YO22 4ET. Tel. (0947) 605914**

Brewery set up in 1988 in a former workhouse in this famous Yorkshire fishing port. Beers brewed solely with hops and malt – no sugar or chemicals added. Free trade (mostly as guest beers) extends from Newcastle upon Tyne to Huddersfield, and the brewery has at last finalised plans for outlets in Whitby! Other possible developments include a move to larger premises. Demon and Little Waster are new additions to the range.

Little Waster* (OG 1036)

Ammonite (OG 1038, ABV 3.8%) A light, refreshing beer, pleasant and fruity, with a hoppy aftertaste. Difficult to track down, but well worth the effort.

Woblle (OG 1045, ABV 4.5%) A copper-red, full-bodied, malty bitter, with a burnt roast flavour and a dry, hoppy finish.

Force Nine (OG 1055, ABV 5.5%) Strong and dark, with a well-balanced blend of contrasting flavours: sweet and fruity, dry and malty, with a strong, bitter finish. A beer of the winter ale type, excellent in its class.

Demon (OG 1066, ABV 6.6%) A full-bodied and well-balanced strong ale, less smooth than Force Nine, with an obvious bite and a strong finish. First brewed in 1989 to celebrate the brewery's first birthday. Not easy to find.

WICKWAR — **Wickwar Brewing Company, The Old Cider Mill, Station Road, Wickwar, Avon, GL12 8NB. Tel. (0454) 294168**

A new brewery set up by two Courage licensees, Brian Rides and Ray Penny, in an old cider mill, originally part of the site of Arnold, Perrett & Co. Ltd. brewery. The first beer was produced on 1 May 1990 and is now available in the licensees' pubs. Plans to supply other local tenants and the free trade.

Brand Oak Bitter* (OG 1039, ABV 3.9%)

Olde Merryford Ale* (OG 1049, ABV 4.9%)

WILSON'S See Grand Metropolitan, page 475.

WILTSHIRE **Wiltshire Brewery Co. PLC, Stonehenge Brewery, Church Street, Tisbury, Wilts, SP3 6NH. Tel. (0747) 870666**

Brewery set up in 1985 and now quoted on the USM. Rapidly expanding its tied estate. Bought Ma Pardoe's brew pub (Old Swan, Netherton) from Hoskins in 1989, to use as a West Midlands base to expand its trade. Now brews a cask-conditioned mild along with the bitter at the Old Swan (see Brew Pubs). Another recent acquisition has been the Pitfield name, although all Pitfield beers are still brewed by Premier Ales (see page 449). Meanwhile, Wiltshire's own Local Bitter has been discontinued.

Stonehenge Best Bitter (OG 1041, ABV 4.1%) Rather unusual, lollipop-tasting ale which will suit those with a sweet tooth. Lacks the bitterness of a more conventional beer of this gravity, but a slowly-released, subtle hop aroma adds interest.

Old Grumble* (OG 1049, ABV 5%) A good premium ale.

Old Devil (OG 1060, ABV 6%) Full-bodied ale with a multi-dimensional taste. Various flavours also follow in the aftertaste, permitting the alcohol to arrive unannounced. Beware!

Exhibition Ale* (OG 1084, ABV 8.1%) Cask-conditioned only at Christmas; otherwise bottled.

WOOD **Wood Brewery Ltd., Wistanstow, Craven Arms, Shropshire, SY7 8DG. Tel. (0588) 672523**

Village brewery which celebrated ten years of production in 1990. Just the one tied house, the adjacent Plough Inn, but an expanding free trade (52 outlets within a 50 mile radius). Recently produced a silver jubilee brew for the Severn Valley Railway.

Parish Bitter* (OG 1040, ABV 3.75%) Light, refreshing bitter.

Special Bitter* (OG 1043, ABV 4%) Full-flavoured, sweetish beer.

Wonderful Bitter* (OG 1050, ABV 4.75%) Strong and dark.

Christmas Cracker* (OG 1060, ABV 6%) Dark winter warmer.

WOODFORDE'S **Woodforde's Norfolk Ales, Broadland Brewery, Woodbastwick, Norwich, Norfolk, NR13 6SW. Tel. (0603) 720353**

Founded in 1981 in Norwich to bring much-needed choice to this Watney-dominated region, and moved in 1989 to larger premises in the picturesque Broadland village of Woodbastwick. Supplies one tied house and over 100 free trade outlets in Norfolk, Suffolk and Lincolnshire. Baldric is the most recent addition to the range.

Broadsman Bitter (OG 1036, ABV 3.7%) Light and golden, malty bitter, with a hoppy, fruity aroma and taste, and a satisfying, dry, hoppy finish. Sadly, only rarely available.

Wherry Best Bitter (OG 1039, ABV 4%) Woodforde's bread and butter brew, accounting for 75% of production. A distinctive, hoppy aroma leads into a balanced, malty, hoppy palate, with some fruitiness, and a dry, hoppy aftertaste.

John Brown's Bitter (OG 1041) A fairly full and sweetish, pale brown ale, malty throughout, with hops and some bitterness, together with a faint fruitiness, on the tongue.

Porter (OG 1041, ABV 4.3%) Dark brown, with a strong roast character dominating the aroma and taste. Well-hopped and quite dry and fruity. A good quaffing beer.

Phoenix XXX (OG 1047, ABV 4.9%) A full-bodied and fruity, strong bitter, with a complex, balanced flavour and a dry, hoppy aftertaste.

Norfolk Nog (OG 1049, ABV 5.1%) A fairly black, full-bodied brew, with roast malt dominating. Some malt and fruit in both aroma and taste. Malt lingers into a predominantly dry, roast finish.

Baldric (OG 1052, ABV 5.5%) A full, malty, mid-brown ale, with a fruity nose. Some hops and dryness are discernible in the mouth and the balanced aftertaste, which has a little of everything.

Headcracker (OG 1069, ABV 7.5%) Sweetish, strong ale, with a prominent, malt flavour throughout. Pale and powerful.

WORTHINGTON See Bass, page 470.

WYE VALLEY **Wye Valley Brewery, 69 St Owens Street, Hereford, HR1 2JQ. Tel. (0432) 274968**

Herefordshire brewery, expanding steadily into the free trade. Full range of beers available at source, the Barrels, 69 St Owens Street, Hereford.

Hereford Bitter (OG 1036) Very little nose, but a crisp, dry and truly bitter taste, with a balancing malt flavour. The initial bitter aftertaste mellows to a pleasant, lingering malt.

HPA (OG 1040) Distinctive colour of old pine and a malty nose. On the tongue the beer is malty, with some balancing bitterness and a hint of sweetness. Has a good dry finish.

Hereford Supreme (OG 1043) This rich, copper-red beer has a good malty, fruity aroma. In the complex variety of flavours, the malt, fruit and bitterness are distinctive. The finish has bitterness but can be cloyingly malty.

Brew 69 (OG 1055) A pale beer which disguises its strength. Has a well-balanced flavour and finish, without the sweetness which normally characterises beer of this strength.

YATES

Yates Brewery, Ghyll Farm, Westnewton, Cumbria, CA5 3NX. Tel. (069 73) 21081

Small, traditional brewery set up in 1986 in a converted barn by experienced brewer Peter Yates and his wife. Probably the only brewery in the country to own a herd of pedigree goats! Serves 16 free trade pubs, four clubs and other outlets through wholesalers.

Bitter (OG 1035, ABV 3.9%) Straw-coloured, with a malty and very hoppy aroma. Beautifully-balanced flavours, with a heavy bitterness and a strong, lingering aftertaste. Low original gravity, but comparatively high in alcohol. A beer becoming increasingly popular and worth looking for.

Premium (OG 1048, ABV 5.2%) Available at Christmas and a few other times of the year. Straw-coloured, with a strong aroma of malt and hops, and full-flavoured with a slight toffee taste. The malty aftertaste becomes strongly bitter.

Best Cellar* (OG 1052, ABV 5.8%) An occasional rich, smooth brew.

YOUNG'S

Young & Co.'s Brewery PLC, Ram Brewery, Wandsworth, London, SW18 4JD. Tel. (081) 870 0141

One of the most warmly regarded breweries in the country, which stood alone against the keg tide in the capital in the early seventies. Some of the award-winning beers are delivered by horse-drawn drays. All 150 houses take real ale, and the company is actively seeking to increase its tied estate. Handles 750 free trade outlets within the M25 ring, but Young's ales have appeared as far west as Devon and as far east as Suffolk. Allied Breweries are now stocking Young's Bitter and Special in roughly 160 pubs.

Bitter (OG 1036, ABV 3.7%) Known as 'Ordinary', but this golden brew is far from that. A distinctive bitterness is balanced by a malty undertone and a little fruitiness, but the finish is delightfully astringent and hoppy.

Special (OG 1046, ABV 4.8%) A full-bodied, mid-brown bitter, whose initial malty flavour gives way to a hoppy bitterness which lingers. There is a balancing sweet fruitiness to the palate, but the finish is distinctly dry.

Winter Warmer (OG 1055, ABV 5%) A dark brown ale with a malty, fruity aroma, a sweet and fruity flavour, with roast malt and some balancing bitterness, and a bittersweet finish, including some lingering malt.

YOUNGER

See Scottish & Newcastle, page 477.

THE NATIONALS

Allied Breweries

Head Office: Allied Breweries Ltd., 107 Station Street, Burton upon Trent, Staffs, DE14 1BZ. Tel. (0283) 31111

Part of the food and retailing group, Allied-Lyons, this brewing conglomerate dates from 1961 and the merger of Ansells, Tetley Walker and Ind Coope. Recent rationalisation has reduced the number of trading companies and it is likely that such restructuring will continue. The company currently controls over 6000 pubs, but it has been selling off packages to regional and local brewers, as well as to the growing number of pub chains. Allied is the only one of the 'Nationals' not to have indicated what its long term strategy is in the aftermath of the Monopolies and Mergers Commission Report.

ALLOA **Alloa Brewery Company Ltd., The Brewery, Whins Road, Alloa, Clackmannanshire, Central, FK10 3RB. Tel. (0259) 723539**

Allied's Scottish arm, established in 1810, which increased its standing north of the border early in 1987 by taking over Drybroughs from Watney, with its 155 pubs. Real ale in only 65 of its 366 tied houses, but also available in 102 free trade outlets spread throughout Scotland. Unfortunately, Arrol's 70/- was deleted in early summer 1989 and replaced by Tetley Bitter. Has an arrangement to take Maclay 70/- and 80/- as guest beers throughout Scotland, and Caledonian 70/- and 80/- in the Edinburgh area.

Arrol's 80/-* (OG 1042, ABV 4.2%) Full flavoured beer with dry hop character.

ANSELLS **Ansells Ltd., Tamebridge House, Aldridge Road, Perry Barr, Birmingham, B42 2TZ. Tel. (021) 344 4567**

Allied's Midlands and Wales company which now has responsibility for around 1600 pubs, of which about 1000 serve real ale. The company is divided into a retail company and Ansells Sales Ltd., controlling the tenanted and free trade business, which offers cask beer to some 1000 outlets. Ansells beers are brewed at Allied's main Burton brewery (see Ind Coope), as is Lumphammer (OG 1039), brewed under licence for the Little Pub Company chain.

Mild (OG 1036, ABV 3.2%) Copper-red and notably sweet throughout. Malty and slightly fruity in aroma and taste, with caramel flavour in the mouth. The finish is sweetish and malty. Also known as 'Dark' in some parts.

Bitter (OG 1037, ABV 3.5%) Mid-brown, with a faint, hoppy and sulphurous aroma. The palate is malty and bitter, with an underlying sweetness and an astringently bitter and somewhat cloying aftertaste.

FURGUSONS **Furgusons Plympton Brewery, Valley Road, Plympton, Plymouth, Devon, PL7 3LQ. Tel. (0752) 330171**

Set up in Halls' Plympton depot in 1984, this renamed brewery now offers three ales of its own for sale to all its 32 pubs and a south-western free trade (about 50 accounts). Plympton Best Bitter has now been retitled Dartmoor Best Bitter. More expansion is on the way, with new fermentation vessels planned to increase brewing capacity to 120 barrels a week.

Dartmoor Best Bitter (OG 1038, ABV 3.7%) Mid-brown, with a moderately hoppy palate and a restrained, dry, malty finish. Rather thin and a thirst-quenching session beer, but not a best bitter.

Dartmoor Strong* (OG 1044, ABV 4.5%) Light-coloured, but full-bodied bitter.

Cockleroaster (OG 1062, ABV 6.5%) A powerful, golden beer with a strong, near perfect mix of malt and hop flavours, and a fruity note which dominates the aroma. Not overpowering, but distinctive, with a good, hoppy finish.

HOLTS **Holt, Plant & Deakin Ltd., Dudley Road, Wolverhampton, W. Midlands, WV2 3AF. Tel. (0902) 50504**

Do not confuse with Manchester's Joseph Holt brewery. Black Country company set up in 1984, now running 47 traditional pubs, all serving real ale. Mild and Bitter are brewed by Tetley Walker in Warrington; Entire is brewed at the new brewery in Wolverhampton.

Mild (OG 1037, ABV 3.4%) Light and thin-bodied. A beer with faint malt and caramel in its taste.

Bitter (OG 1037, ABV 3.4%) Pale brown in colour, slightly sweet and hoppy, but lacking in character.

Entire (OG 1043, ABV 4.4%) A malty and hoppy beer, dry tasting. Seems to have lost some body in the last year.

IND COOPE **Ind Coope Ltd., Central House, 1 Ballards Lane, Finchley, London, N3 1LQ. Tel. (081) 349 3100**

Company which controls Allied's southern and south-western operations. It runs two separate tied trade companies and a free trade company, Romford Brewery (which no longer brews real ale), as well as Burton Brewery, provider of cask ales for all divisions of the Allied group.

BURTON BREWERY **Ind Coope Burton Brewery Ltd., 107 Station Street, Burton upon Trent, Staffs, DE14 1BZ. Tel. (0283) 31111**

The major brewery in the Allied group which has benefitted in recent years from a £50 million investment programme. Altogether, it now brews eight real ales for the South and the Midlands, supplying Ansells as well as the Ind Coope companies. The premium Burton Ale is now a national brand.

Burton Ale (OG 1048, ABV 4.4%) A hoppy, malty aroma, with a hint of fruit, precedes a rich, full, sweetish taste, a pleasant mixture of hops, malt and fruit. The finish is dry, hoppy and malty. Lacks body for its gravity but, when served well, it is one of the better national brews.

RETAIL **Ind Coope Retail, PO Box 105, Station Road, Watford, Herts. Tel. (0923) 228585**

This arm of Allied now controls the Halls, Friary Meux and Aylesbury (ABC) divisions, following mergers in early 1990. The total tied estate now runs to around 1700 pubs, most selling real ale, some stocking guest beers like Wadworth 6X and Draught Bass (Gale's HSB and King & Barnes Sussex in Friary pubs). Aylesbury, Halls and Friary houses maintain their own livery (but for how long?). Ind Coope Retail brews no beers of its own, all production taking place at Burton upon Trent.

ABC Best Bitter* (OG 1037, ABV 3.5%) Refreshing and well-balanced.

Benskins Best Bitter (OG 1037, ABV 3.5%) Hops dominate in the aroma, taste and finish. A slight malt presence is also detectable. Although tending to be thin, at its best it is a good, suppable pint. However, it is all too often unexceptional.

Friary Meux Best Bitter (OG 1037, ABV 3.5%) Darker than average, moderately malty, with a strange apple-like fruitiness. Thin and unremarkable.

Halls Harvest Bitter (OG 1037, ABV 3.5%) A mid-brown brew, with malt and caramel flavours dominating the sweetish palate. A fairly average bitter, lacking in aroma and hop character.

TAYLOR WALKER **Taylor Walker, 77 Muswell Hill Road, London, N10 3PH. Tel. (081) 883 6431**

Taylor Walker runs about 700 pubs (about 500 taking real ale) in Greater London, as well as the former Romford Brewery pubs in Essex. J & W Nicholson & Co. at the same address (Tel. (081) 444 9124) runs 36 in the capital, 34 of which offer ales from Adnams, Arkell's, Wadworth and others. Taylor Walker Best Bitter is now brewed at Burton upon Trent.

Best Bitter* (OG 1037, ABV 3.5%) Light, malty bitter.

JOSHUA TETLEY **Joshua Tetley & Son Ltd., PO Box 142, The Brewery, Leeds, W. Yorks, LS1 1QG. Tel. (0532) 435282**

Yorkshire's favourite brewing son, with real ale in an impressive 1000 of their 1100 pubs. Draught Tetley Bitter is now being promoted in the free trade and through Allied outlets far from its Leeds home, aided by the introduction into pubs of a new $\frac{1}{4}$ pint dispense system, with an agitator which re-creates the famous northern tight, full head. The new brewery, with its extra capacity, was opened in May 1989. Versions of Tetley Mild and Bitter are also produced at the Tetley Walker plant in Warrington.

Mild (OG 1032, ABV 3.15%) Copper-red in colour. The taste is rounded, malty and caramel-rich, with complementing bitterness. A satisfying dark mild with a short, dry finish.

Bitter (OG 1035.5, ABV 3.6%) Pale brown, with a hoppy nose. Malt and hops are balanced in the flavour, with some bitterness. A smooth, dry finish follows in this good standard bitter. Can occasionally vary in quality.

TETLEY WALKER **Tetley Walker Ltd., Dallam Lane, Warrington, Cheshire, WA2 7NU. Tel. (0925) 31231**

Of the 850 tied houses, 500 sell real ale. In addition, almost 50% of the company's production goes to the free trade. Brews Tetley Mild and Bitter, to the same specifications as the Leeds brewery, and Holts (HP&D) Mild and Bitter.

Tetley Dark Mild (OG 1032, ABV 3.15%) A smooth, dark, malty mild. Fair amount of caramel and some fruit in the taste, with hints of liquorice and bitterness. A slight, bitter finish.

Tetley Mild (OG 1032, ABV 3.15%) Again, smooth and malty, with some fruitiness and bitter notes. The aftertaste is malty, with a little dryness. A refreshing, darkish mild.

Tetley Bitter (OG 1035.5, ABV 3.6%) A hoppy, bitter beer, with a little malt. Less fruity than last year. Sharp, clean-tasting and very popular, with a lingering bitter aftertaste.

PETER WALKER **Peter Walker Ltd., 85–89 Duke Street, Liverpool, Merseyside, L69 1BZ. Tel. (051) 708 5224**

All 91 tied houses (mainly in the Merseyside, Wigan and Bolton areas, but with outposts as far afield as Chorley and Crewe) serve the Walker real ales brewed at the Tetley Walker plant in Warrington.

Mild (OG 1032, ABV 2.9%) Dark, smooth mild with fruit and caramel, which dominates hints of roast malt and bitterness. The malty aftertaste quickly gives way to a faint dryness.

Bitter (OG 1033, ABV 3.3%) A light, refreshing bitter. Maltiness and bitterness are balanced, and neither dominates. Some fruit, hop and a little sweetness, with a fairly bitter aftertaste. Drinks more like a light mild than a bitter.

Best Bitter (OG 1035, ABV 3.3%) Light, hoppy and bitter, with a dry finish. The bitterness is sometimes astringent. Significantly less fruity than a year ago. A good drinking bitter.

Winter Warmer (OG 1060, ABV 5.8%) Smooth, dark and sweet winter ale, with a strong, fruity flavour, balanced to some degree by a bitter taste and the dry character of the finish. Improves with age as sweetness declines and other flavours emerge. At its best it is dangerously drinkable.

WREXHAM LAGER **Wrexham Lager Brewery Company Ltd., 5 Central Road, Wrexham, Clwyd, LL13 7SS. Tel. (0978) 291661**

Runs about 140 pubs in North Wales, serving Allied real ales in half of them. Brews no cask beer of its own, despite having absorbed the former Lloyd & Trouncer company and closing the Minera Brewery in February 1989. Services the free trade with Allied real ales.

Bass

Head Office: Bass PLC, 66 Chiltern Street, London, W1M 1PR. Tel. (071) 486 4440

The UK's largest brewer which will remain so even if the Elders/Grand Met breweries-for-pubs deal goes through. Unique amongst the big brewers, Bass has not closed down a brewery for many years. Its 13 brewing plants include the small, mild-only Highgate brewery. At present owning almost 7000 pubs, Bass has announced that it will stay in brewing and retailing, and will, therefore, release from the tie, or sell, the 2400 pubs it is required to by November 1992. A major internal restructuring of the business is underway. 1990 saw the first major advertising campaign for Draught Bass in a long while, as the company strove to gain market share.

BASS BREWING **Bass Brewing Ltd., 137 High Street, Burton upon Trent, Staffs, DE14 1JZ. Tel. (0283) 45301**

The original home of Bass, producing national brands available throughout its estate and the free trade. Has also begun brewing Worthington BB (see Welsh Brewers).

Draught Bass (OG 1044, ABV 4.4%) A pale brown beer which can vary tremendously in character, depending on its age. A fruity, malty nose is often accompanied by a strong, sulphurous aroma. The fruity, malty palate is often sweetish, but, when at its best, a hoppy dryness is also present. The finish is bittersweet, with some lingering malt. Not an easy beer to keep and often sold too green. But, when it's good, it's a classic pint.

Worthington White Shield* (OG 1052, ABV 5.6%) A notable bottle-conditioned beer, a stand-by where draught ale is lacking. It would certainly benefit from more promotion.

MITCHELLS & BUTLERS (M&B) **Bass, Mitchells & Butlers Ltd., Cape Hill Brewery, PO Box 27, Birmingham, B16 0PQ. Tel. (021) 558 1481**

One of the largest cask beer producers in the country, although the range is limited. Bass in the Midlands has two other breweries and four trading companies. 70% of the 2230 pubs (mostly in the Walsall, Wolverhampton and Cannock area) sell real ale.

M&B Mild (OG 1036, ABV 3.4%) A dark mild, with a malty aroma and a sharp, malty flavour. Some hops in the taste and a thin, dry finish.

Brew XI (OG 1040, ABV 4.1%) Gold-coloured beer with a light, sweet flavour, balanced by some bitterness. Dryish finish; some hops in the nose. Lacks body and character.

HIGHGATE BREWERY **Highgate Brewery Ltd., Sandymount Road, Walsall, W. Midlands, WS1 3AP. Tel. (0922) 23168**

Built in 1895 and now a listed building, the Highgate Brewery is the smallest in the Bass group and has remained unchanged for many years. It is still in the unique position of brewing cask mild only.

Highgate Mild (OG 1036, ABV 3.2%) Dark brown beer, very malty in aroma and taste. Well-balanced and smooth, with roast malt and a hint of bitterness.

SPRINGFIELD BREWERY **Springfield Brewery (M&B), Grimstone Street, Wolverhampton, W. Midlands, WV10 0JR. Tel. (0902) 54551**

M&B's Wolverhampton brewery, which also brews for Charrington (IPA). There are over 600 tied houses, most of which serve real ale, and over 800 free trade accounts.

Springfield Bitter (OG 1036, ABV 3.5%) Pale-coloured brew with a slightly hoppy and bitter, yet fruity, sweet taste. Generally lacking in body.

BASS NORTH **Bass North Inns & Taverns Ltd., Headingley Office Park, 8 Victoria Road, Leeds, W. Yorks, LS6 1LG. Tel. (0532) 744444**

Responsible for 790 managed houses and 1300 tenanted pubs. Bass North is served by the breweries listed below.

BASS BREWING (TADCASTER) **Bass Brewing (Tadcaster), Tower Brewery, Tadcaster, N. Yorks, LS24 9SD. Tel. (0937) 832361**

Mild XXXX (OG 1031, ABV 3.3%) Beer with a dark brown hue and a balanced, rounded, malty/caramel and bitter palate, moving to a malty, dry finish. A pleasant, easy-drinking mild which can be difficult to find in cask-conditioned form.

Light 5 Star (OG 1031, ABV 3.3%) Pale-coloured, with a faint, hoppy nose. Smooth and lightly-flavoured, with a malt and hop balance. Short, dry finish. A session beer.

Special Bitter (OG 1035, ABV 3.7%) A misnomer. An unremarkable session bitter, pale in colour, offering a smooth balance of malt and bitterness, with sweetness also present. Slight, malty, bittersweet finish.

The Nationals

BASS BREWING (SHEFFIELD) **Bass Brewing (Sheffield), Cannon Brewery, Rutland Road, Sheffield, S. Yorks, S3 8BE. Tel. (0742) 349433**

Stones Best Bitter (OG 1038.8, ABV 4.1%) Straw-coloured, with a dry hop and faint malt aroma. Clean and refreshing, mellow taste. Tends to improve with age. Consistent quality.

WILLIAM STONES **William Stones Hope Brewery, Wadsley Bridge, Sheffield, S. Yorks, S6 1NB. Tel. (0742) 349433**

Bass's specialist bottled beer brewery.

WELSH BREWERS **Welsh Brewers Ltd., Maes-y-Coed Road, PO Box 116 NDO, Cardiff, CF4 4UN. Tel. (0222) 615831**

Part of the Bass Wales & West division until it was split up in October 1989. Covers South, Mid and West Wales and supplies these areas from the brewery below.

BASS BREWING (CARDIFF) **Bass Brewing (Cardiff) Ltd., Crawshay Street, Cardiff, S. Glamorgan, CF1 1TR. Tel. (0222) 233071**

Once the Hancock's brewery, but taken over by Bass in 1968. Supplies an extensive free trade, with real ale generally now becoming more prominent in Welsh Brewers' 400-plus pubs, most of which serve a cask beer.

Hancock's PA (OG 1033, ABV 3.3%) A mild pale ale with a faint malt flavour and a slightly bitter finish. A good session beer and lunchtime drink which has now become increasingly difficult to find.

Worthington Dark (OG 1034, ABV 3.3%) Another beer becoming hard to find. An underrated mild with a smooth finish and some maltiness, combined with a creamy sweetness, in the taste.

Hancock's HB (OG 1037, ABV 3.8%) Slightly malty, with some bitterness, although predominantly sweet. No discernible finish.

Worthington BB (OG 1037, ABV 3.8%) Light in colour, fairly malty and with some bitterness in the finish. A pleasant drinking beer.

CHARRINGTON **Charrington & Company Ltd., Anchor House, 129 Mile End Road, London, E1 4UL. Tel. (071) 790 1860**

No longer brews; Charrington IPA is produced by M&B in Wolverhampton. The estate has been extended by the addition of the West Country section of the now-defunct Bass Wales & West. Runs 589 managed and 864 tenanted houses in the South East, South West, East Anglia, Buckinghamshire and Oxfordshire, three-quarters of which sell real ale. Some houses offer guest beers.

IPA (OG 1039, ABV 3.6%) Mid-brown in colour, with an occasional fruity aroma. The palate can vary with cellar life, from very sweet to dry and bitter, when at its best. A soft, malty character lingers into the aftertaste. Bland, but not unpleasant.

TENNENT CALEDONIAN **Tennent Caledonian Breweries, 110 Bath Street, Glasgow, Strathclyde, G2 2ET. Tel. (041) 552 6552**

Bass's Scottish beer division with 180 managed houses and extensive free trade. Predominantly lager brewers – the Wellpark brewery in Glasgow no longer brews real ale.

HERIOT BREWERY **Heriot Brewery, Roseburn Terrace, Edinburgh, Lothian, EH12 5LY. Tel. (031) 337 1361**

Brews cask beer for Tennent, although the fact that it is so difficult to find in its pubs or in the free trade puts its future under a cloud. Draught Bass is poised to take over.

Tennent's 80/- (OG 1042, ABV 4.2%) Pleasant but unexceptional.

Courage

Head Office: Courage Ltd., Ashby House, Bridge Street, Staines, Middlesex, TW18 4XH. Tel. (0784) 466199

Founded in 1787, this company is at present part of the Australian Elders IXL giant. Its strategy is to remain a brewer and brand marketer, and to use its UK base to attack the rest of Europe in the post 1991 market. Courage also plans to exit from retailing by passing over control of its pub estate to Inntrepreneur Estates Ltd., a company jointly owned by Elders and Grand Met, and managed by Grand Met. Despite the massive advertising campaign for Foster's lager, the company still has a commitment to cask ale, its brewery in Bristol being the largest dedicated cask brewery in the world. But it remains to be seen how it will develop the Grand Met ale portfolio if the pubs-for-breweries deal goes through, and how many of the brands will be left once they are all owned and marketed by one company. What chance Webster's Yorkshire Bitter and John Smith's Yorkshire Bitter both surviving?

BRISTOL BREWERY **Bristol Brewery, Counterslip, Bristol, Avon, BS1 6EX. Tel. (0272) 297222**

Courage's only real ale brewery in the South, following the closure of traditional breweries in London, Reading and Plymouth. Growing demand for cask beer has resulted in expansion at this plant in recent years, with Best and Directors very well promoted nationally and Bitter Ale neglected somewhat but now being pushed more in the Bristol area. Simonds Bitter (a cask version of the bright beer named after the old Reading brewery taken over in 1960), has been tested in South Wales, whilst Best Bitter has been tried in John Smith's country.

Bitter Ale (OG 1031, ABV 3.2%) A golden/amber-coloured beer with a light aroma of hops. A light mix of malt and bitterness, plus a grainy feel, is present in the flavour and leaves a hoppy/bitter aftertaste, making a good, refreshing, light session beer.

Simonds Bitter*	(OG 1031, ABV 3.2%)
Best Bitter	(OG 1039, ABV 4%) A pale brown bitter with a malty nose, though occasionally a hop oil aroma dominates. Quite a bitter, malty taste, but rather sweet in the finish. Some brews can be very hoppy all round. A national beer, but at least this one can be enjoyable.
Directors	(OG 1046, ABV 4.8%) A full-bodied, malty bitter, with hints of fruit and a well-balanced aftertaste. Copper-brown in colour, with some aroma of hops.

JOHN SMITH'S **John Smith's Tadcaster Brewery Ltd., Tadcaster, N. Yorks, LS24 9SA. Tel. (0937) 832091**

John Smith's Bitter is now probably Courage's best known ale, thanks to extensive television advertising since its re-emergence in traditional form in 1984. Accompanied by Magnet (which was re-introduced in cask form in 1988 and which has recently been test-marketed in the South East), and very occasional brews of bottle-conditioned Imperial Russian Stout (OG 1104), it forms the real ale output of the extensively modernised Tadcaster Brewery. Runs 1418 houses, of which over 916 sell cask beer, and serves an enormous free trade.

Bitter	(OG 1036, ABV 3.8%) Copper-coloured beer with a pleasant mix of hops and malt in the nose. In the taste maltiness comes through more strongly, with the hops taking over in the finish. The brewer's quality control for this beer is excellent. Known as John Smith's Yorkshire Bitter outside the county.
Magnet	(OG 1040, ABV 4%) Copper-amber, with a fruity, malty nose, a nutty, grainy palate and balancing fruit and hops. Outstandingly long and dry finish, with lingering malt. A very palatable best bitter.

Grand Metropolitan Brewing (Watney)

Head Office: Grand Metropolitan Brewing Ltd., 91 Brick Lane, London, E1 6QN. Tel. (071) 377 0020

Formerly Watney, Mann and Truman, this company at present operates four breweries in the UK (Manns and Norwich in Northampton, and Phoenix in Brighton no longer brew). It is, however, fundamentally a retailer and sees its future in owning and running pubs, hotels and restaurants. The one jewel (now sadly tarnished) in its ale portfolio is Ruddles. If Grand Met finally leaves brewing, it will be the end of an era which began with the start of CAMRA and our early campaigns against the dreadful keg Watney's Red Barrel.

RUDDLES — **Ruddles Brewery Ltd., Langham, Oakham, Rutland, Leics, LE15 7JD. Tel. (0572) 756911**

Britain's most famous real ale brewers, taken over by Grand Met in 1986. Its beers are now national brands and widely promoted.

Best Bitter (OG 1037, ABV 3.8%) Thin and lacking in taste. A faint, fruity, malty nose leads into an astringent bitter palate, with little discernible malt or hop presence. A sulphurous quality and a sharp, metallic bitterness tend to dominate.

County (OG 1050, ABV 5%) Copper-coloured, with a fruity, malty aroma and taste; sweetish on the tongue, but with a dry, malty aftertaste. Pleasant, but nothing like the County of old. Markedly lacking in hoppiness for a bitter of this gravity.

USHERS — **Ushers Brewery Ltd., Parade House, Trowbridge, Wilts, BA14 8JY. Tel. (0225) 763171**

West Country brewery whose trading area extends from Lands End to Oxford. Its future is in considerable doubt as we await the results of the MMC enquiry into the Grand Met/Elders deal. Has over 400 pubs and brewed Truman Best Bitter for a while before it was discontinued.

Best Bitter (OG 1036, ABV 3.4%) This once very hoppy beer has little aroma and combines a grainy sweetness with a fruity, dry bitterness. Not as harsh as it has been, but often yeasty and sometimes sulphidic and metallic. Unspectacular.

Bullard's Old* (OG 1057) Dark winter ale brewed in small quantities for an East Anglian market. A relic of the Norwich brewery closed by Watney.

WATNEY TRUMAN — **Watney Truman Ltd., 14 Mortlake High Street, London, SW14 8JD. Tel. (081) 876 3434**

Grand Metropolitan's only London brewery, but brewing no real ale. Distributes Webster's and Ruddles to around 850 of its 1250 tied houses.

SAMUEL WEBSTER & WILSON'S — **Samuel Webster & Wilson's Ltd., Fountain Head Brewery, Ovenden Wood, Halifax, W. Yorks, HX2 0TL. Tel. (0422) 357188**

Now runs only 341 tied houses, 70% of which serve real ale. A new distribution depot has been opened in Manchester.

Wilson's Original Mild (OG 1031, ABV 3%) A characterless mild. A faintly malty and fruity aroma leads on to a predominantly malty/caramel flavour, with some bitterness. Thin in body. The aftertaste is slightly malty and bittersweet. Number of outlets declining.

Webster's Green Label Best (OG 1033, ABV 3.4%) A faint, hoppy aroma, with a little fruitiness at times. Some sweetness in the malty taste, and a bitter finish. A boy's bitter.

The Nationals

Webster's Yorkshire Bitter (OG 1036, ABV 3.8%) A disappointing beer with a faintly malty and fruity aroma (sometimes metallic). Often very bland in taste to offend no-one. If you are lucky it can have a good, fresh, hoppy-bitter flavour and finish (but very rare!).

Wilson's Original Bitter (OG 1036, ABV 3.8%) Fairly thin, golden beer with a good hop aroma and a strong hop flavour, which can be very bitter at times. The palate is clean and the aftertaste is very bitter. Malty overtones in taste and finish. Being nudged out by the heavily-promoted Yorkshire Bitter.

Webster's Choice (OG 1045, ABV 4.6%) A well-balanced bitter with little aroma or flavour, but with a strong hoppy/bitter finish which is sometimes intense. Not available in many outlets; drink it while you can (Ruddles County poised to take over)!

Guinness

Head Office: Guinness Brewing GB, Park Royal Brewery, London, NW10 7RR. Tel. (081) 965 7700

The brewer of the most famous of stouts has breweries around the world, with Guinness also brewed under licence in many more. Sadly, an excellent and stronger, bottle-conditioned export version, brewed in Dublin, is not available in the UK.

ARTHUR GUINNESS **Arthur Guinness, Son & Co. (Dublin) Ltd., St James's Gate, Dublin 8, Ireland. Tel. (0001) 536700**

Guinness Extra has been renamed Guinness Original. Draught Guinness (OG 1038) in Ireland is not pasteurised but is served with gas pressure.

Guinness Original* (OG 1042) Naturally-conditioned in the bottle.

GUINNESS BREWING GB **Park Royal Brewery (as above)**

Supplies British outlets, although some instances of Dublin-brewed Guinness have been noted in certain parts.

Guinness Original* (OG 1040) Again the renamed Guinness Extra which is available in bottle-conditioned form only from pubs and bars, except in Scotland where all Guinness is pasteurised. All non-returnable bottles and cans from supermarkets and off-licences throughout Britain are also pasteurised. *All Draught Guinness in the UK is keg*. Draught Guinness in a can (sic) produces the tight, creamy head by use of a small plastic sparkler at the bottom of the can.

Scottish & Newcastle

Head Office: Scottish & Newcastle Breweries PLC, Abbey Brewery, Holyrood Road, Edinburgh, Lothian. Tel. (031) 556 2591

Is it or isn't it? S&N has long been regarded as one of the UK's big brewers; it is, in fact, the fourth largest. It may never have held as many tied houses as the other 'Nationals', but its free trade has more than compensated. However, in these post-MMC days, and since its 300-plus pub sell off (to take it below the magic 2000 pub dividing line), it is now regarded by the Government as a regional brewer and thus exempt from the strictures of the MMC regulations. However, for the purposes of the *Good Beer Guide* and CAMRA, S&N is still considered to be a national brewer whose presence is felt in all corners of the kingdom, due to its great free trade. The brewery resisted the attempts of Elders to take it over in 1989, thanks to the MMC, but, if rumours are anything to go by, it could soon be under threat from US giant Anheuser Busch, or perhaps even one of Japan's big four. S&N currently operates six breweries, one of which, the Royal in Manchester, brews keg only. Some confusion exists over the origin of Theakston beers. They are, in fact, brewed both in the original brewery in Masham and at the Tyne Brewery in Newcastle.

FOUNTAIN BREWERY — **Fountain Brewery, Fountainbridge, Edinburgh, Lothian, EH3 9YY. Tel. (031) 229 9377**

Beers sold under the McEwan or Younger names, depending on the trading area.

McEwan 70/- or Younger Scotch* (OG 1037, ABV 3.7%) Well-balanced, sweetish brew, becoming increasingly rare.

McEwan 80/- or Younger IPA* (OG 1042, ABV 4.5%) Malty and sweet-flavoured, with some graininess and a dry finish.

Younger No.3* (OG 1043, ABV 4.5%) Rich and dark.

TYNE BREWERY — **Tyne Brewery, Gallowgate, Newcastle upon Tyne, Tyne & Wear, NE99 1RA. Tel. (091) 232 5091**

Produces a major proportion of all three Theakston beers, under the supervision of Masham's head brewer, Hugh Curley (see Theakston, overleaf). Has a cask-conditioned ale cellar for the training of licensees.

Theakston Best Bitter (OG 1038, ABV 3.8%)

Theakston XB (OG 1044, ABV 4.5%)

Theakston Old Peculier (OG 1057, ABV 5.6%)

MATTHEW BROWN — **Matthew Brown PLC, PO Box 5, Lion Brewery, Blackburn, Lancs, BB1 5NH. Tel. (0254) 52471**

Despite the company's new pump clips, cask ale is only available in 184 of 403 tied houses, and many pubs take Theakston and Younger ales in preference to both Matthew Brown ales. Whilst in the short term the brewery's future seems secure, its medium to long-term prospects are less rosy.

Mild (OG 1031, ABV 3.1%) Dark and reddish, with a malty, fruity nose which promises more than the taste delivers. Thin, with faint malt, hop and fruit, but very little flavour in the finish.

Bitter (OG 1035, ABV 3.5%) A pale, thin and quaffable beer with a sharpish, dry aftertaste. A soft, hoppy aroma and palate are underscored by faint maltiness and a hint of fruit.

HOME **Home Brewery PLC, Mansfield Road, Daybrook, Nottingham, NG5 6BU. Tel. (0602) 269741**

Acquired by S&N in 1986, its tied estate offers real ale in 70% of 430 pubs. Extensive free trade in the Midlands and the North. Bitter was relaunched with a £2 million campaign in late 1989, with similar repackaging for Mild underway in 1990.

Mild (OG 1036, ABV 3.6%) Notably malty, dark beer, with little aroma. Chocolate and liquorice in the flavour, whilst the finish is unusually bitter for a mild. Slightly acidic and fruity.

Bitter (OG 1038, ABV 3.8%) Again low in aroma. The flavour balances malt and hops well, with a smooth, initial taste and a lingering, dry, bitter finish. Golden/copper in colour.

THEAKSTON **T&R Theakston Ltd., Wellgarth, Masham, Ripon, N. Yorks, HG4 4DX. Tel. (0765) 89544**

Brewery which has seen extensive refurbishment over the past year, with developments not yet at an end. More than £1 million has been earmarked for the project. Runs just 10 tied houses, but enjoys a very healthy free trade. As mentioned above, Theakston's cask beers are also brewed at the Tyne Brewery, but customers are not made aware of which version they are drinking. A visitor centre is open to the public from May to October (telephone (0765) 89057, ext. 4317, for an appointment).

Best Bitter (OG 1038, ABV 3.8%) A delicate, straw-coloured beer with a hoppy and fruity nose. There is sharp, hoppy bitterness in the flavour, with some hints of malt and fruits, and the finish is dry and lasting.

XB (OG 1044, ABV 4.5%) An impressive aroma of hops and malt, with a hint of orchard fruit, precedes a well-balanced taste where the hops slightly outweigh the other elements, which include traces of vine fruits. The finish is very dry and slightly unexpected. A particularly well-made beer.

Old Peculier (OG 1057, ABV 5.6%) Not quite as black as sin, as a delicate copper-red shows through, but its impressive colour prepares the drinker for an outburst of malt and fruit on the nose. The flavours are complex, but roast malt and butterscotch stand out, with a gentle, hoppy bitterness and even forest fruit notes. The aftertaste is lasting and reveals that hops play a major part in the making of this rich, full-bodied beer.

Whitbread

Head Office: The Whitbread Beer Company, Whitbread House, Park Street West, Luton, Beds, LU1 3BG. Tel. (0582) 424200

Whitbread's appalling record of brewery closures continues. In May 1990 the Higsons brewery in Liverpool, acquired when the company bought the Boddingtons brewing capacity, was closed, along with the Fremlins plant at Faversham. Production of most of these beers was transferred to Cheltenham and Sheffield. However, Pompey Royal (OG 1043) is now being brewed by independent brewers Gale's, close to where the beer originated, but has not yet been tasted for this guide.

BODDINGTONS **Boddingtons Brewery, PO Box 331, Strangeways, Manchester, M60 3EL. Tel. (061) 831 7881**

Famous Manchester brewery, now just another Whitbread division. Boddingtons itself was responsible for a similar action when it took over and subsequently closed Oldham Brewery, transferring production to Strangeways. Expects an increase in demand for Boddingtons Bitter, these days promoted as a national brand.

OB Mild (OG 1032, ABV 3%) Copper-red in colour, with a pronounced malty aroma. A smooth caramel and fruit flavour follows, then a dry, malty aftertaste. The number of outlets is holding up at present.

Boddingtons Mild (OG 1032, ABV 3%) A sweet, dark, thin mild, with a strong caramel flavour and a sweet, fruity aftertaste. Found in a declining number of pubs and must be in danger of being phased out.

Boddingtons Bitter (OG 1035, ABV 3.8%) A pale, aromatic beer, with a sharp, refreshing first impression. The aftertaste is quite complex, with bitterness and a grainy quality dominant.

OB Bitter (OG 1037, ABV 3.8%) Pale beer with an aroma of malt. The flavour is malty and bitter, with a refreshing, slightly sourish tinge and a dry, malty finish.

CASTLE EDEN **Castle Eden, PO Box 13, Castle Eden, Hartlepool, Cleveland, TS27 4SX. Tel. (0429) 836431**

Brewery and beer which both look vulnerable to the giant's axe.

Castle Eden Ale	(OG 1040) A characteristically sweet north eastern beer, with a hoppy aroma and a nutty flavour. Possibly the most full-flavoured of the remaining Whitbread ales – probably too good to last. Sadly rare in its native territory.
CHELTENHAM	**Whitbread (Cheltenham), Monson Avenue, Cheltenham, Glos, GL50 4EL. Tel. (0242) 521401** The centre of Whitbread's cask ale production in the South, serving most of southern Britain, churning out beers which were once brewed for local palates in places as far from Cheltenham as Faversham, Romsey and Marlow.
West Country Pale Ale (WCPA)	(OG 1030) Hoppy in aroma, but not as distinctive as it used to be. Light, refreshing and hoppy, with a clean, dry finish.
Wethered Bitter	(OG 1035) When produced at the Wethered plant at Marlow this was an excellent, flowery, hoppy beer. It is now malty, with relatively little hoppy bitterness and some fruitiness. Dull and bland, lacking in the finish, and typical of the Cheltenham brews.
Fremlins Bitter*	(OG 1035) Not tasted since its move to Cheltenham.
Flowers IPA	(OG 1035) Pale brown, with little aroma, perhaps a faint maltiness. Moderately dry taste and finish, but no discernible hoppiness. Thin and uninspiring.
Best Bitter*	(OG 1036) Also available in keg form.
Strong Country Bitter	(OG 1037) Not 'strong' as in alcohol, but as in Strong's Brewery in Romsey, closed by Whitbread in 1981. A pale beer, clean-tasting, with a little maltiness and bitterness. Dry finish.
Wethered SPA*	(OG 1040) Full-bodied bitter.
Flowers Original	(OG 1044) Hoppy aroma and hops in the taste, with some malt and a hint of fruit. A notably bitter finish.
Wethered Winter Royal*	(OG 1055) Dark and warming.
SHEFFIELD	**Whitbread (Sheffield), Exchange Brewery, Bridge Street, Sheffield, S. Yorks, S3 8NL. Tel. (0742) 761101** Whitbread's remaining Yorkshire brewery, now brewing beers for sale under the Chester's and Higsons dead breweries' names. Complete refurbishment of the centre of the brewhouse is planned.
Chester's Best Mild	(OG 1032, ABV 3.4%) An almost black beer with a faint, malty, fruity nose and a palate dominated by caramel, with some malt and fruit. A sweetish, malty finish. Not the beer which once bore the name.
Higsons Mild*	(OG 1033, ABV 3.1%) Not tasted since its move to Sheffield.
Chester's Best Bitter	(OG 1033, ABV 3.4%) Pale in colour and character. Little discernible aroma; a bitter taste, but with little malt or hop

flavour, and a faint, malty, dry finish. Insipid, harsh and uninteresting.

Trophy (OG 1036, ABV 3.6%) Palish, mid-brown beer with a slight aroma and a sweetish, malty taste, with bitter notes. Often one-dimensional and bland.

Higsons Bitter* (OG 1038, ABV 3.8%) Not tasted since its move to Sheffield.

Bentley's Yorkshire Bitter* (ABV 3.8%) A resurrection of an old name to jump on the Yorkshire Bitter bandwagon.

BREW PUBS

ABINGTON PARK
Wellingborough Road, Northampton.
Tel. (0604) 31240
Cricketers Ale (OG 1032)
Cobblers Ale (OG 1037)
Lionheart Porter (OG 1046)
Extra (OG 1047)
Celebration (OG 1052)
Headspinner (OG 1060)
One of the Clifton Inns 'in-house breweries'. Uses cask breather.

ALE HOUSE
70 Raglan Road, Leeds, W. Yorks.
Tel. (0532) 455447
Meek and Mild (OG 1031)
Monster Mash (OG 1042)
XB (OG 1045)
No. 9 (OG 1046)
Simon's Super Stout (OG 1046)
Brainstormer (OG 1055)
White Rose Ale (OG 1064)
Bye Bye Bitter (OG 1079)
Housewarmer (OG 1079) is brewed at Christmas.
Real ale off-licence next to Leeds University. Started brewing in late 1987 and now offers eight handpumps, with weekly guest beers and four real ciders.

ALFORD ARMS
Frithsden, Hemel Hempstead, Herts, HP1 3DD. Tel. (0442) 864480
Cherry Pickers (ABV 3.4%)
Pickled Squirrel (ABV 4.5%)
Ivor's Brew (ABV 4.8%)
Rudolph's Revenge (ABV 5.8%)
Whitbread's first brew pub, founded in 1981. Commemorative ales also brewed. Malt extract used.

ALL NATIONS (Mrs Lewis's)
Coalport Road, Madeley, Shropshire.
Tel. (0952) 585747
Pale Ale (OG 1032)
One of four brew pubs left before the new wave arrived. The others are the Blue Anchor, Old Swan and Three Tuns. Still known as Mrs Lewis's, although she passed away in 1988.

ANCIENT DRUIDS
Napier Street, Cambridge, CB1 1HR.
Tel. (0223) 324514
Kite Bitter (OG 1040)
Druid's Special (OG 1047)
Merlin (OG 1055)
Charles Wells brew pub set up in 1984. Also produces seasonal and occasional brews. Uses malt extract.

BLACK HORSE & RAINBOW
Berry Street, Liverpool, Merseyside.
Rainbow Bitter (OG 1039)
Black Horse (OG 1045)
Full mash brew pub opened in mid summer 1990. Blanket pressure used.

BLUE ANCHOR
Coinagehall Street, Helston, Cornwall.
Tel. (0326) 562821
Medium (OG 1050)
BB (OG 1053)
Special (OG 1066)
Extra Special (OG 1070)
Historic thatched brew pub, producing powerful ales known locally as 'Spingo' beers.

BODICOTE BREWERY
Plough Inn, Bodicote, Banbury, Oxfordshire, OX15 4BZ.
Tel. (0295) 262327
Bitter (OG 1035)
Old English Porter (OG 1045) A winter brew.
No. 9 (OG 1045)
Triple XXX (OG 1050) The Christmas ale.
Brews for its pub-restaurant and some free trade. Has an ancient well. The drink listed as 'Boilermaker' is not a brew but a half-and-half mix of Bitter and Porter.

Brew Pubs

BORVE BREW HOUSE
Ruthven, by Huntly, Aberdeenshire, AB5 4SR. Tel. (046 687) 343
Borve Ale (OG 1040, ABV 3.7%)
Extra Strong (OG 1085, ABV 10%)
Moved from its original site on the Isle of Lewis in 1989 to a mainland former school, converted to a pub with brewery adjacent. Extra Strong is now matured in oak prior to racking into casks or bottling. A porter and an ordinary bitter are planned; Bishop Elphinstones Ale (OG 1053) is brewed on demand.

BUSHY'S BREWPUB
Victoria Street, Douglas, Isle of Man. Tel. (0624) 75139
Bitter (OG 1037)
Old Bushy Tail (OG 1045)
The island's only pub-brewery, with plans for brewing on another site and hopes for an extended free trade following the Isle of Man's own MMC enquiry. Produces Piston Brew (OG 1045) for the TT races.

DOG & PARROT
Clayton Street West, Newcastle upon Tyne, Tyne & Wear, NE1 4EX. Tel. (091) 261 6998
Scotswood Bitter (OG 1036)
Wallop (OG 1046, ABV 4.5%)
Whitbread malt-extract brew pub with plans to add a Scotch bitter (OG 1035) and a Christmas ale (OG 1090) to its range.

DUKE OF NORFOLK BREWERY
202–204 Westbourne Grove, London, W11. Tel. (071) 229 3551
Portobello Mild (OG 1036)
Broads Bitter (OG 1044)
Norfolk Best (OG 1048)
Dynamite (OG 1055)
Clifton Inns brew pub which began production in November 1989. Beer, brewed from whole malt with no adjuncts, is either cask-conditioned in the usual way or stored in cellar tanks fitted with a cask breather. Also provides cask ales for a couple of other London pubs.

FALCON & FIRKIN
360 Victoria Park Road, Hackney, London, E9. Tel. (081) 985 0693
Falcon (OG 1038, ABV 3.7%)
Hackney (OG 1043, ABV 4.4%)
Dogbolter (OG 1058, ABV 5.8%)
Sleighbells (OG 1077.5) is a Christmas brew.
Former Bruce brew pub providing tank beers for the Pheasant & Firkin — Pheasant Bitter (OG 1037); Barbarian Bitter (OG 1044), and cask-conditioned beer (no blanket pressure) for the Phantom & Firkin — Phantom Ale (OG 1037); Spook Ale (OG 1044), and the Flock & Firkin — Shepherd's Delight (OG 1037); Sheer Beer (OG 1044), as well as the free trade. Beers here are sold from the tank or cask-conditioned (blanket pressure). The brewery is visible from the bar.

FELLOWS, MORTON & CLAYTON
Canal Street, Nottingham, NG1 7EH. Tel. (0602) 506795
Samuel Fellows Bitter (OG 1040)
Matthew Clayton Strong Ale (OG 1048)
A Whitbread brew pub, hoping to expand its range and currently experimenting with different mashes.

FERRET & FIRKIN
114 Lots Road, Chelsea Creek, London, SW10. Tel. (071) 352 6645
Ferret Ale (OG 1044)
Golden Glory (OG 1048)
Dogbolter (OG 1059)
Full mash brew pub, with the brewery in the cellar visible from the bar. Golden Glory is a recent addition to the range. Beer is served from tanks (blanket pressure).

FLAMINGO & FIRKIN
Becket Street, Derby. Tel. (0332) 45948
Flaming Ale (OG 1037)
Al's Ale (OG 1041)
County Bitter (OG 1045)
Dogbolter (OG 1059)
The first Firkin outside of London since the Fleece in Bristol (now not brewing). The full mash brewery is on same level as the bar and can be seen through windows at the back. All beers sold through cellar tanks (blanket pressure).

FLOUNDER & FIRKIN
54 Holloway Road, London, N7. Tel. (071) 609 9574
Fish T'ale (OG 1037)
Snappy Stout (OG 1041)
Whale Ale (OG 1044)
Dogbolter (OG 1051)
Full mash brewery in the cellar is seen through floor panels. Beer is served from both cellar tanks and casks (blanket pressure). Ginger Tom (OG1051) is a hand-pulled ginger beer.

FOX & FIRKIN
316 Lewisham High Street, London, SE13. Tel. (081) 690 8925
Fox Bitter (OG 1044)
Dogbolter (OG 1059)
The second Bruce's pub, now ten years old. Visible brewery is on same level as the bar. Beers sold from cellar tanks (blanket pressure). Special brews for the Firkin chain, such as Mild (OG 1041), Porter (OG 1051) and Easter Egg Cracker (OG 1071) are produced here.

FOX & HOUNDS
Barley, Royston, Herts. Tel. (076 384) 459
Old Dragon (OG 1045)
Flamethrower (OG 1056)
Early member of the pub brewing revival which has changed its range of brews in the last year. Supplies one free house.

FOX & HOUNDS
Stottesdon, Shropshire, DY14 8TZ. Tel. (074 632) 222
Fox's Mild (OG 1036)
Woody Woodward's Wonder Water or

Woody's Bitter (OG 1037)
Dasher's Draught (OG 1040)
Hound's Bitter (OG 1044)
Millward's Mega Mild (OG 1046)
Winter Ale (OG 1070)
Supplies some other pubs in addition to itself.

FOX & NEWT
9 Burley Street, Leeds, W. Yorks, LS3 1LD. Tel. (0532) 432612
Burley Bitter (OG 1036)
Old Willow (OG 1046)
Kirkstall Ruin (OG 1066)
A Whitbread malt extract pub.

FROG & FIRKIN
41 Tavistock Crescent, London, W11. Tel. (071) 727 9250
Tavistock Bitter (OG 1037)
Bullfrog Bitter (OG 1044)
Dogbolter (OG 1059)
Visible brewery, also supplies beers for the Frigate & Firkin — Wingspan (OG 1037) and Frigate Ale (OG 1044). Beers served from cellar tanks (blanket pressure).

FROG & PARROT
Division Street, Sheffield, S. Yorks, S1 4GF. Tel. (0742) 721280
Old Croak Ale (OG 1035)
Reckless Bitter (OG 1046)
Roger's Conqueror (OG 1066)
Roger's Specials (OG 1080+)
Roger & Out (OG 1125)
Whitbread malt extract brew pub. Roger & Out listed in the *Guinness Book of Records* as the world's strongest beer in terms of alcoholic content. Four ciders are produced for the pub.

GOOSE & FIRKIN
47–48 Borough Road, London, SE1. Tel. (071) 403 3590
Goose Bitter (OG 1037)
Borough Bitter (OG 1044)
Dogbolter (OG 1059)
First of the Firkin pubs, started in 1979, still using malt extract in its cellar brewery. Beers dispensed from cellar tanks (blanket pressure).

GREYHOUND PUB & BREWERY
151–153 Greyhound Lane, Streatham Common, London, SW16 5NJ. Tel. (081) 677 9962
XXX Pedigree (OG 1036)
Special (OG 1038)
London Strong Stout (OG 1044)
Streatham Strong (OG 1048)
Streatham Dynamite (OG 1056)
A Clifton Inns brew pub. XXX Pedigree is the only real mild brewed in London. Special beers brewed for bank holidays and other occasions. Cask breathers used.

HEDGEHOG & HOGSHEAD
100 Goldstone Villas, Hove, E. Sussex, BN3 3RX. Tel. (0273) 733660
Brighton Breezy Bitter (OG 1045)
Hogbolter (OG 1060)
Prickletickler (OG 1075)
New full mash David Bruce venture which opened in July 1990. Blanket pressure used.

JOLLY ROGER BREWERY & BREWERY TAP
50 Lowesmoor, Worcester, WR1 2SG. Tel. (0905) 21540
Quaff Ale (OG 1038)
Severn Bore Special (OG 1048)
Old Lowesmoor (OG 1058)
Winter Wobbler (winter only) (OG 1091)
Now supplying three pubs, with plans for a brew pub in Hereford. Small free trade capacity. In addition to the above, brews special beers and Blazers Ale (OG 1042) for Blazers Bar at 54 Lowesmoor.

KEMPTOWN BREWERY (Hand in Hand)
33 Upper St James's Street, Kemptown, Brighton, E. Sussex, BN2 1JN. Tel. (0273) 602521
Bitter (OG 1040, ABV 3.9%)
Celebrated Strong Ale (OG 1050, ABV 5%)
Staggering in the Dark (SID) (OG 1050, ABV 5%)
Full mash brewery started in November 1989 and now brewing twice a week. Specially constructed behind the pub in the 'tower' tradition.

LAKELAND BREWERY Co.
Masons Arms, Strawberry Bank, Cartmel Fell, Grange-over-Sands, Cumbria, LA11 6NW. Tel. (044 88) 486
Bitter (OG 1038, ABV 4%)
Pub, famous for its good ale and large selection of bottled beers, which began brewing for itself in May 1990. Hopes to produce a darker, stronger beer, as well as Belgian-type fruit beer, using the pub's own orchard damsons!

LASS O'GOWRIE
Charles Street, Manchester, M1 7DB. Tel. (061) 273 6932
Bitter (OG 1035)
Strong (OG 1042)
A Whitbread malt extract brew pub.

MARISCO TAVERN
Lundy Island, Bristol Channel. Tel. (0271) 870870
Lundy Pale Ale (OG 1044)
Old Light Bitter (OG 1055)
Beers produced using Lundy water and no additives. Old Light Bitter is a new brew.

MARKET PORTER
9 Stoney Street, Borough Market, London, SE1 9AA. Tel. (071) 407 2495
Market Bitter (OG 1038)
Market Special (OG 1048)
Malt extract brew pub.

MINERVA HOTEL
Nelson Street, Hull, Humberside, HU1 1XE. Tel. (0482) 26909
Pilot's Pride (OG 1039)
Joshua Tetley brew pub, supplying other Tetley houses as guest beers. Julie's Pride

& Joy and Santa's Pleasure are occasional specials.

NORTH CORNWALL BREWERS
Tintagel Brewery, Min Pin Inn, Tintagel, Cornwall, PL34 0DX. Tel. (0840) 770241
Legend Bitter (OG 1036)
Brown Willy (OG 1055)
Converted farmhouse with possibly the only entirely female-operated brewery in the country. Malt extract used.

OLD SWAN (Ma Pardoe's)
Halesowen Road, Netherton, Dudley, W. Midlands. Tel. (0384) 253075
Ma Pardoe's Mild (OG 1034, ABV 3.2)
Ma Pardoe's Bitter (OG 1035, ABV 3.3%)
One of the great institutions of Black Country drinking which was taken over by Wiltshire Brewery in 1989. Now produces a mild in addition to a bitter.

ORANGE BREWERY
37 Pimlico Road, London, SW1W 8NE. Tel. (071) 730 5984
Pimlico Light (OG 1032)
SW1 (OG 1040)
Pimlico Porter (OG 1046)
SW2 (OG 1050)
Clifton Inns' first in-house brewery, opened in 1983. Cask breather in use.

PHOENIX & FIRKIN
Windsor Walk, London, SE5. Tel. (071) 701 8282
Rail Ale (OG 1037)
Phoenix Bitter (OG 1044)
Dogbolter (OG 1059)
Pub reconstructed from the burnt remains of Denmark Hill railway station. Full mash brewery in the cellar and beers sold from tanks (blanket pressure). Porter (OG 1051) is produced in winter.

REINDEER FREEHOUSE & BREWERY
10 Dereham Road, Norwich, Norfolk, NR2 4AY. Tel. (0603) 666821
Bill's Bevy (OG 1037)
Reindeer Bitter (OG 1047)
Old Nick Stout (OG 1050)
Red Nose (OG 1057)
Sanity Clause (OG 1067) is a winter brew, but there are no plans at present to repeat Sledgehammer (OG 1067). However, a mild which was tested may return. Blanket pressure used.

RISING SUN
Knowle Bank Road, Shraley Brook, Audley, Stoke-on-Trent, Staffordshire, ST7 8DS. Tel. (0782) 720600
Rising (OG 1040, ABV 3.9%)
Setting (OG 1044, ABV 4.4%)
Sun Stroke (OG 1055, ABV 5.6%)
Total Eclipse (OG 1072, ABV 6.5%)
New brew pub.

ROSE STREET BREWERY
Rose Street, Edinburgh, EH2. Tel. (031) 220 1227
Auld Reekie 80/- (OG 1043)
Auld Reekie 90/- (OG 1064)
Scotland's first brew pub, run by Alloa Brewery and now supplying other outlets. The gravity of 90/- has been raised from 1056. Malt extract used.

ROYAL INN
Horsebridge, Tavistock, Devon, PL19 8TJ. Tel. (082 287) 214
Tamar (OG 1039)
Horsebridge Best (OG 1045)
Heller (OG 1060)
15th-century country pub, once a nunnery, now brewing full-mash, no-additive beers. Right Royal (OG 1050) is an occasional brew (usually on sale first week of September or on special occasions).

ST CLEMENTS BREWERY
First In, Last Out, 14–15 High Street, Old Town, Hastings, E. Sussex, TN34 3EY. Tel. (0424) 425079
Old Crofters (OG 1040)
Cardinal Sussex Ale (OG 1048)
Established in 1985.

TALLY HO COUNTRY INN & BREWERY
Hatherleigh, Devon. Tel. (0837) 810306
Potboiler's Brew (OG 1036)
New brew pub whose first beer was on sale at Easter 1990. Full mash, no additives.

THREE TUNS
Bishop's Castle, Shropshire, SY9 5BW. Tel. (0588) 638797
Mild (OG 1035)
XXX (OG 1042)
Castle Steamer (OG 1045)
Old Scrooge (OG 1054)
Historic brew pub.

WILLY'S
17 High Cliff Road, Cleethorpes, Humberside, DN35 8PQ. Tel. (0472) 602145
Original (OG 1039, ABV 4%)
Festival (OG 1039, ABV 4%)
Burcom Bitter (OG 1044)
Coxswains Special Bitter (OG 1049, ABV 5%)
Old Groyne (OG 1060, ABV 6.5%)
Opened in May 1989 to supply the seafront pub and free trade. Has acquired Trotsky's in Grimsby, now renamed SWIGS (Second Willy's In Grimsby).

YORKSHIRE GREY
2 Theobalds Road, London, WC1. Tel. (071) 405 2519
City Bitter (OG 1035)
Headline Bitter (OG 1037)
Holborn Best (OG 1047)
Regiment Bitter (OG 1056)
Clifton Inns brew pub. Gravity of Regiment Bitter has been raised from 1054. Cask breather in use.

THE BEERS INDEX

The Beers Index is your easy reference to beers not always known by a brewery prefix. Thwaites Bitter will clearly be found under Thwaites in the Breweries Section, and therefore it and other such names have not been included in this index. However, if you want to find out more about Abbot Ale, for example, then this index tells you that it is brewed by Greene King and more information is available on page 426.

P

THE GBG QUIZ ANSWERS

Round One:

1. 144
2. Newton & Ridley; Ephraim Monks; Russells & Wrangham; Luxford & Copley
3. Tan Hill Inn, Stainmoor, Co. Durham
4. It was the drink of London's market porters in the 18th century
5. John; Julia; Henry; Samuel; Ben
6. To store
7. Bass
8. India Pale Ale
9. Fermented pear juice
10. No Alcohol Beer, Low Alcohol Beer
11. A straight beer glass
12. Guinness Original Stout
13. Queen Elizabeth, the Queen Mother, on a visit to a Young's pub
14. Crudgington's 6X (Keg Buster is a Bill Tidy/CAMRA cartoon creation)
15. David Bruce (the Firkin pubs)

Round Two:

16. It was originally brewed for consumption by Courage directors
17. Hadrian
18. The Tabard
19. Licensed Victuallers Association
20. Young's
21. Chas and Dave
22. Ma Pardoe's
23. Society for the Preservation of Beers from the Wood (SPBW)
24. Anheuser-Busch, USA
25. Grotneys
26. Apple pulp wrapped in cloth ready for pressing
27. The prices refer to the cost of a barrel in Victorian times which was also used for duty-calculating purposes
28. West Germany
29. Trappist
30. Gypsum

Round Three:

31. Isle of Man
32. Fuggles, Goldings, Northern Brewer, Progress, Keyworth, Mid Season, Bramling Cross, Styrian Goldings, Hallertau, Saaz, Challenger, Sunshine, Target, Yeoman, Northdown, Zenith (any others and you are showing off!)
33. Pilsner Urquell
34. Stan Laurel
35. Uley; Maclay; Ringwood; McMullen; Robinson's
36. Lampost
37. From the ecclesiastical jurisdiction (or Peculier) of Masham where it is brewed
38. Mauldons; Woodforde's
39. Michael Hardman

40. Brakspear (Nicolas Brakspear became Adrian IV, 1154–59)
41. A single brew of beer
42. Natural yeast occurring in apple skins and in the soil
43. Terry Jones (*Monty Python's Flying Circus*)
44. Charles Wells Bombardier (after Bombardier Billy Wells)
45. 54–58 ° F or 12–14 °C

Round Four:

46. Yeast
47. Stout and bitter; old and bitter; old and mild; bitter and gin; barley wine and rum
48. Thomas Hardy (in *The Trumpet Major*)
49. Traquair House (the main gates were closed after the departure of Bonnie Prince Charlie in 1745, never to be reopened until a Stuart sits on the throne of Scotland)
50. Mesopotamia (now Iraq)
51. *Laverne and Shirley*
52. Courage Bulldog
53. Adnams
54. Maris Otter; Golden Promise; Triumph; Pipkin; Halcyon; Puffin; Doublet; Natasha; Blenheim; Atem
55. The artist George Morland is said to have been related to the company's founder
56. Butser Brew Bitter; Ventnor Pale Ale; Hicks Special Draught; Very Important Pint; no-one knows!
57. Greene King (Graham Greene and Sir Hugh Greene)
58. Shepherd Neame Bishops Finger
59. Felinfoel
60. Bass

Round Five:

61. George Orwell
62. Dabinette; Yarlington Mill; Brown Snout; Michelin; Chisel Jersey; Foxwhelp; Cowarne Red; Dymock Red; Kingston Black; Joeby Crab; Skyrme's Kernel; Strawberry Norman; Knotted Kernel; Upright French; Cider Lady's Finger; Tom Putt; Eggleton Styre; Coccagee; Bloody Butcher; Tramlett's Bitter; Harry Master's Jersey; Fillbarrel; Somerset Red; Brown's Apple; Improved Dove; Porters Perfection; Sweet Coppin
63. The Marquis of Granby
64. 1038 (approx.)
65. He used it to carry two pots of Bavarian lager yeast from Munich to Copenhagen, thereby laying the basis for Carlsberg
66. Carlisle
67. In grain being germinated to make malt (it is the growing shoot)
68. It is drunk cloudy with yeast
69. The Chequers
70. Henry VIII
71. A giant vat burst and they drowned in nearly 128,000 gallons of beer
72. Bourne Valley
73. In France, by Pelforth of Lille
74. Degrees Balling; Degrees Plato; alcohol by weight
75. All Nations, Shropshire; Blue Anchor, Cornwall; Old Swan, W. Midlands; Three Tuns, Shropshire

HOW BEER IS BREWED

Ingredients: Malted barley (partially germinated barley which has been heated to produce sugars vital to the brewing process), water, hops and yeast.

Method:

1. Malted barley is ground into a coarse powder called grist which is stewed with hot water (known as 'liquor' in the trade) in a large vessel called a mash tun. Quantities are carefully measured and balanced for each individual brew and different malts and barleys are used for the various styles of beer: mild, bitter, stout, porter, etc.

2. The resulting thick liquid (wort) is left to stand so that it absorbs the sugars from the malt. It is then run off into a large kettle called a copper and the remaining grist is sparged (sprayed with hot water) to extract any last sugars, which are also added to the copper. The grist is spent and sold off to farmers for animal fodder.

3. The wort is boiled with hops for about two hours. The hops, which later act as a preservative, here add bitterness, the boiling killing off bacteria at the same time. The wort is then passed through a giant strainer, called a hop back, cooled and run into fermenting vessels, where yeast is added (pitched).

4. Yeast, fungus cells that grow by germinating with sweet liquids, converts the sugars into alcohol and carbon dioxide. The thick yeasty head which develops on the fermenting beer is skimmed off and reused or sold on to producers of products like Marmite. Fermentation is complete after about five days.

5. The next stage sees the beer run off into conditioning tanks, where the remaining yeast continues to convert the last of the sugars.

6. The beer is then put into casks (racked). Finings (normally a fish extract, but occasionally synthetic) are added to draw the yeast to the bottom and so to clear the beer. Sometimes extra sugars are introduced to encourage a strong secondary fermentation. The casks are then ready for delivery.

7. Real beer has to stand for up to 48 hours in the pub cellar while the sediment settles. A tap is knocked into the cask ready for serving the beer and a soft wooden peg is driven into the shive hole (a small hole in the top of the cask) to let out the naturally occurring carbon dioxide. Once the beer is ready to serve, the soft peg is replaced by a hard one which regulates the escape of gas. However, once a cask has been tapped and air is allowed to enter, its beer will only remain drinkable for a few days. Some landlords apply a light film of carbon dioxide to the beer in the cask to prevent the air spoiling the beer, but this (blanket pressure) stops the beer from maturing and can add extra fizz to the brew.

8. Real beer is drawn from the cask for serving by a choice of means: (a) by gravity direct from the cask into the glass (b) by a handpump (c) by an electric pump or (d) by an air pump (using air not carbon dioxide).

Keg beer: Keg beer follows the same procedure as above, up to point 5. Here, instead of conditioning and running off into casks, it is chilled, filtered, usually pasteurised and then run off into containers called kegs. These have just one opening into which carbon dioxide is introduced to force the beer to the bar when the tap is opened. Keg beer, being a dead product, does not continue to ferment or condition in the container and does not need to stand for any length of time.

Lager: Lager follows a similar procedure, too, up to point 4. But different malts provide the wort and the strain of yeast used sinks to the bottom, rather than floating on the top of the wort. Thus, lager is bottom fermented and ale is top fermented. During fermentation, the vessel is kept at a lower temperature than for ale.

After fermentation, true lagers are left to condition at the brewery for several months in cold (around 0° C), sealed containers. Very often, in Britain, this process lasts only weeks and then the lager (commonly many degrees weaker than its European namesake) follows the same schedule and serving procedure as keg beer. On the Continent many lagers are not pasteurised or filtered, and are dispensed without the addition of gas, relying instead on the pressure of their own natural CO_2 output.

CASK SIZES AND MEASURES

Butt	108 gallons (no longer used)
Puncheon	72 gallons (no longer used)
Hogshead	54 gallons (now rarely used)
Barrel	36 gallons
Kilderkin or kiln	18 gallons
Firkin	9 gallons
Pin	$4\frac{1}{2}$ gallons (now rarely used)
Yard of Ale	$2\frac{1}{4}$–$4\frac{1}{2}$ pints (not standard)
Gallon	8 pints
Quart	2 pints (a quarter gallon)
Pint	20 fluid ounces
Nip	$\frac{1}{3}$ pint (a common bottle size)
Gill	5 fluid ounces (a quarter pint, mistakenly a half pint in some areas)

CAMRA's CHAMPION BEERS

Each year at the Great British Beer Festival, a panel of experts selects Britain's top beers from nominations made by CAMRA members. The results in all categories since its inception are given below.

	Mild	Bitter	Best Bitter
1978	Thwaites Best	Ridleys	–
1979	Hanson's	Fuller's London Pride	–
1980	Thwaites Best	Exmoor Ale	–
1981	Banks's	West Riding Tyke	–
1982	Tetley	Clark's Wakefield	–
1983	Ansells	Burton Bridge	–
1984 No event	–	–	–
1985	Ansells	Gale's BBB	–
1986	Thwaites Best	Brakspear PA	–
1987	Ansells	King & Barnes Sussex	–
1988	Bateman	Tetley	Taylor Landlord
1989	Taylor Golden Best	Fuller's Chiswick	Taylor Landlord
1990	Harveys Pale Ale	Adnams	Taylor Landlord

	Special Bitter	Strong Ale	New Brewery
1978	–	Fuller's ESB	–
1979	–	Fuller's ESB	–
1980	–	Young's Special	–
1981	–	Fuller's ESB	–
1982	Taylor Landlord	Marston's Owd Rodger	–
1983	Taylor Landlord	Fuller's ESB	–
1984 No event	–	–	–
1985	Young's Special	Fuller's ESB	Old Mill
1986	Bateman XXXB	Theakston Old Peculier	Pitfield Dark Star
1987	Bateman XXXB	Fuller's ESB	Pitfield Dark Star
1988	Bateman XXXB	Ringwood Old Thumper	Banks & Taylor SOS
1989	Bateman XXXB	Theakston Old Peculier	Hop Back Summer Lightning
1990	Ind Coope Burton Ale	Robinson's Old Tom	Woodforde's Wherry Best Bitter

Beer of The Year/Champion Beer of Britain

1978	Thwaites Best Mild/Fuller's ESB (tied)
1979	Fuller's London Pride
1980	Thwaites Best Mild
1981	Fuller's ESB
1982	Taylor Landlord
1983	Taylor Landlord
1984	No event
1985	Fuller's ESB
1986	Bateman XXXB
1987	Pitfield Dark Star
1988	Ringwood Old Thumper
1989	Fuller's Chiswick Bitter
1990	Ind Coope Burton Ale

BEER FESTIVAL CALENDAR 1991

Approximate dates for 1991's major beer festivals are given below. For further details, including venues and precise dates, consult CAMRA's newspaper, *What's Brewing*, or contact CAMRA on (0727) 867201 closer to the time.

FEBRUARY
Battersea
Durham
Exeter (winter ales)

MARCH
Colchester
London Drinker (Camden)
Oldham
Wigan

APRIL
Blackpool
Ealing
Great North Western Beer Festival
Hull
Newcastle upon Tyne (University)
South Essex
Swansea

MAY
Barnsley
Cleethorpes
Darlaston (W. Midlands)
Dudley
Halifax
Merseyside
Renfrew
Stockport
Wolverhampton

JUNE
Dorking
Greenwich
Salisbury

JULY
Ashton Canals
Canterbury
Derby
Oxford
Stirling
Tynemouth

AUGUST
Great British Beer Festival
Cambridge
Durham (University)
Peterborough
Portsmouth
Truro

SEPTEMBER
Chappel (Essex)
Heart of England
Ipswich
Kirklees
Maidstone
Sheffield

OCTOBER
Bath
Bedford
Cardiff
Eastleigh
Keighley
Leeds
Loughborough
Middlesbrough
Nottingham
Stoke-on-Trent

NOVEMBER
Aberdeen
Bradford
Bury
Pig's Ear (Stratford, London)
Norwich
Taunton

Other major festivals for which dates have not yet been fixed: Bristol, Darlington, Exeter, Postling (Gloucestershire), Yeovil

BOOKS FOR BEER LOVERS

The pub-goer's essential reading list

CAMRA's publishing subsidiary, **Alma Books**, is going from strength to strength. Its list of pub guides (some regional, some specialist) is being expanded each year. Alma is able to produce the most authoritative pub guides around because it has a unique 'data base' – the 26,000 members of the Campaign. Through their untiring efforts, information in Alma guides is as thorough and up-to-date as possible; and because the work of the members is voluntary, costs, and therefore cover prices, are kept down.

The first three regional guides, **The Best Pubs in Devon and Cornwall**, **Lakeland** and **London** were joined in 1990 by three new titles: **The Best Pubs in East Anglia**, **North Wales** and **Yorkshire**. Each is the result of one man's personal, exhaustive (and exhausting) search for the best pubs – all naturally, with excellent beer – in the region. All are fascinatingly peppered with local colour, anecdotal, and, at times, down-right opinionated! They are all beautifully produced, in paperback, with witty black and white illustrations from the pen of Phil Evans.

To prove that enjoying the surroundings of a good pub and a good glass of beer is not an entirely male pursuit, Jill Adam's new guide **The Best Pubs for Families** pinpoints over 400 hostelries throughout the land where children are made just as welcome as their parents. Ideal for holidays and day trips, the descriptions include detailed information about the amenities at each pub: baby changing facilities, garden play areas and indoor amusements for children, and whether child-sized portions or menus are provided. To help plan a successful day out, details of local tourist sites of family appeal are also included.

David Kitton's **Good Cider Guide** has now been published in its third edition. In a new format, it is a worthy companion to the **Good Beer Guide**. Good traditional cider is as different a product to the cold, fizzy stuff sold in many pubs, as real ale is to keg beer. The author punctuates his exhaustive, nationwide list of producers and outlets with some fascinating insights into the history of cider, the fight to save Britain's orchards, Spanish cider and a museum dedicated to cider-making.

One of Alma's biggest sellers has been Susan Nowak's **Good Pub Food**, which is not surprising considering the huge growth that has taken place in the pub food market. However, there are many pubs whose food is as 'keg' as their beer. **Good Pub Food** is rooted in the CAMRA philosophy that if a publican cares about his beer, then everything else falls into place: food, welcome and service. The second edition of this invaluable guide is due out in the summer of 1991.

Two more new Alma titles are to be published before 1991. Barrie Pepper's **The Bedside Book of Beer** will not only appeal to insomniacs, but to anyone with an interest in the literature connected with beer and pubs, ale and inns. Barrie has spent months delving into archives and libraries to compile a fascinating anthology of poems, articles and literature, ranging from Shakespeare to James Joyce and George Orwell. Coming from CAMRA, you might expect the **Home-Brewer's Handbook** by Graham Wheeler to be the ultimate authority on the art of making your own beer – and it is! It is the definitive book for home brewers, ranging from brewing from kits to full mash, with recipes for mild, bitter, stout, barley wine and lager.

The spring and summer of 1991 will bring another clutch of publications from Alma. Former **Good Beer Guide** Editor Andrea Gillies has not been resting on her laurels, but busily writing **The Great British Pub**, Alma's first venture in hardback publishing. This glossy, full-colour production is a celebration of that finest of British institutions, the public house. The author has also selected, and gives detailed descriptions of 500 of the very best hostelries.

Two paperbacks, **The Best Waterside Pubs** and **The Best Pubs for Ramblers** will prove invaluable companions for serious (and not so serious) walkers and waterways users. No longer will you have to face a long stretch of canal not knowing when the next pub will loom over the horizon, nor tramp the country's footpaths ignorant as to whether there will be a welcoming inn at the end of it.

Finally, in anticipation of 1992, Alma has gone into Europe, and what more appropriate place to start than the home of the famous Oktoberfest? **The Best Beers and Bars in Bavaria** has been researched and written by Graham Lees, one of the founder members of CAMRA who has been living in Germany for many years. An absolute must for all real lager lovers, it also includes a section on Bohemia, another great brewing region where the much-abused Pilsner beer was developed.

CAMRA does not just support Alma publications. Three other ale books can be bought direct from the Campaign (see order form) or from good bookshops. These all come from the pen of one of CAMRA's most prolific writers, Roger Protz.

The Real Ale Drinker's Almanac, a handy pocket-sized hardback, is the essential beer drinker's *vade mecum* to all the brews and breweries in the land. Meticulously researched, it gives a brief history of every real ale brewery with detailed descriptions and tasting notes of the beers they produce. **Beer, Bed and Breakfast**, Vol. III is the new, updated listing of some of the best bed and breakfast accommodation in the land, with the additional bonus of real ale on tap. Why stay in a fancy (expensive) hotel when you can enjoy a really friendly welcome at an hospitable pub? Don't leave home without it. In his **Great British Beer Book**, Roger Protz traces the fascinating history of British beer from pre-Roman times to the present day, including the story of monastic brewing and the modern struggle between vast commercial companies and real ale devotees. The narrative is highlighted with contemporary texts, rhymes and songs. The author also tells of the history and development of inn and pub signs. An absolute must for any serious drinker.

CAMRA BOOKS AND PRODUCTS

A full list of Books, Local Guides and Products is available on request. Here is just a selection – all prices include post and packing. The blank line is left for you to order any of the books described on previous pages.

	Quantity	Price each	Amount
"The Best Pubs in . . ." Series			
Devon and Cornwall		**£3.95**	
Lakeland		**£2.95**	
London		**£3.95**	
East Anglia		**£4.95**	
North Wales		**£4.95**	
Yorkshire		**£4.95**	
National Guides			
The Best Pubs for Families		**£4.95**	
Good Cider Guide II		**£5.95**	
Beer, Bed and Breakfast III		**£6.99**	
New Editions			
CAMRA Homebrewer's Handbook		**£4.99**	
Bedside Book of Beer		**£6.99**	
CAMRA Guide to Good Pub Food (Spring 1991)		**£6.99**	
CAMRA Ties		**£5.50**	
CAMRA Sweatshirts (M, L, XL – state size and colour preference)		**£9.95**	
CAMRA Sports Shirts (M, L, XL – state size and colour preference)		**£8.95**	
CAMRA Jogging Trousers (M, L, XL – state size and colour preference)		**£9.95**	
CAMRA 'Real Ale' Wallclock		**£22.95**	
PLUS:		**£**	
		Total	**£**

Send to CAMRA Ltd, 34 Alma Road, St. Albans, Herts., AL1 3BW. (Cheques must accompany orders.) Cheques payable to CAMRA Ltd; allow 3 weeks for delivery. To place a credit card order, phone (0727) 867201

Name	
Address	
	Post Code

NEW PUB SUBMISSION

Pub Name
Address
Reason
Please supply your name and address above

INSTRUCTION TO YOUR BANK TO PAY DIRECT DEBITS

Please complete parts 1 to 4 to instruct your bank to make payments directly from your account.

Then return the form to Campaign for Real Ale Limited, 34 Alma Road, St. Albans, Herts. AL1 3BW.

To the Manager

Bank

___

___

___

1 Please write the full postal address of your bank branch in the box.

2 Name(s) of account-holder(s) ___

Address ___

___

Post Code ___

3 Account number

Banks may refuse to accept instructions to pay direct debits from some types of account

Direct Debit instructions should only be addressed to Banks in the United Kingdom.

CAMRA Computer Membership No. (for office use only)

0	0					

Originators Identification No.

9	2	6	1	2	9

4 Your instruction to the bank, and signature.

* I instruct you to pay direct debits from my account at the request of Campaign for Real Ale Limited.

* The amounts are variable and are to be debited annually.

* I understand that Campaign for Real Ale Limited may change the amount only after giving me prior notice.

* PLEASE CANCEL ALL PREVIOUS STANDING ORDER INSTRUCTIONS IN FAVOUR OF CAMPAIGN FOR REAL ALE LIMITED.

* I will inform the bank in writing if I wish to cancel this instruction.

* I understand that if any direct debit is paid which breaks the terms of this instruction, the bank will make a refund.

Signature(s) ___

___

Date ___

Join CAMRA

TRIAL MEMBERSHIP OF CAMRA FREE FOR 3 MONTHS!

The GOOD BEER GUIDE could not be produced without painstaking voluntary research by CAMRA members – thousands of them – up and down the country. Our members are even now working on more detailed local guides, or organising and serving at beer festivals, or going on organised pub crawls, or brewery visits, or trips abroad... the list is endless! You can join in.

Why not try out CAMRA membership? It's only £10.00 a year, but you can sample it *free* for 3 months before you commit yourself. Just sign the application form below, and the direct debit form overleaf, and you will become a member of CAMRA absolutely free for the next three months. You will receive:

★ the next 3 copies of What's Brewing, CAMRA's monthly newspaper;
★ an information packed Member's Handbook;
★ a Membership Card, entitling you to free or reduced rate admission to many beer festivals;
★ discounts on a range of products and publications.

If after 3 months you do not wish to continue your membership, simply write to us returning your membership card, and you will owe nothing.

If you do not wish to take advantage of this offer, but still want to join CAMRA, *just fill in the application form* (ignore the direct debit overleaf) *and send it together with your first year's subscription.* For payment by credit card phone the membership secretary on (0727) 867201.

Full membership £10; Joint husband/wife membership £12; Life membership £100/£120
Please delete as appropriate:
I/We wish to take advantage of the trial membership, and have completed the instructions overleaf.
I/We wish to become members of CAMRA.
I/We agree to abide by the memorandum and articles of association of the company.
I/We enclose a cheque/p.o. for £ (payable to CAMRA Ltd.)

Name(s)

Address

Signature(s)

CAMRA Ltd., 34 Alma Road, St. Albans, Herts., AL1 3BW.